The Palgrave Handbook of Globalization with Chinese Characteristics

Paulo Afonso B. Duarte ·
Francisco José B. S. Leandro ·
Enrique Martínez Galán
Editors

The Palgrave Handbook of Globalization with Chinese Characteristics

The Case of the Belt and Road Initiative

Editors
Paulo Afonso B. Duarte ⓘ
Universidade do Minho & Universidade Lusófona
Braga & Porto, Portugal

Francisco José B. S. Leandro ⓘ
University of Macau
Macau SAR, China

Enrique Martínez Galán ⓘ
Asian Institute of Management
Manila, Philippines

ISBN 978-981-19-6699-6   ISBN 978-981-19-6700-9 (eBook)
https://doi.org/10.1007/978-981-19-6700-9

© The Editor(s) (if applicable) and The Author(s), under exclusive license to Springer Nature Singapore Pte Ltd. 2023, corrected publication 2023
This work is subject to copyright. All rights are solely and exclusively licensed by the Publisher, whether the whole or part of the material is concerned, specifically the rights of translation, reprinting, reuse of illustrations, recitation, broadcasting, reproduction on microfilms or in any other physical way, and transmission or information storage and retrieval, electronic adaptation, computer software, or by similar or dissimilar methodology now known or hereafter developed.
The use of general descriptive names, registered names, trademarks, service marks, etc. in this publication does not imply, even in the absence of a specific statement, that such names are exempt from the relevant protective laws and regulations and therefore free for general use.
The publisher, the authors, and the editors are safe to assume that the advice and information in this book are believed to be true and accurate at the date of publication. Neither the publisher nor the authors or the editors give a warranty, expressed or implied, with respect to the material contained herein or for any errors or omissions that may have been made. The publisher remains neutral with regard to jurisdictional claims in published maps and institutional affiliations.

Cover illustration: Architect Francisco Ricarte

This Palgrave Macmillan imprint is published by the registered company Springer Nature Singapore Pte Ltd.
The registered company address is: 152 Beach Road, #21-01/04 Gateway East, Singapore 189721, Singapore

Foreword

The Belt and Road Initiative (BRI) is redefining the historical geography of contemporary capitalism. In less than a decade's time, BRI has become a global project that involves more than a hundred nations worldwide in the collective creation of transnational cooperation and development. The scale, breadth, scope, and impact of BRI are unprecedented. It is therefore not surprising that the study of BRI has mushroomed. Scholarly works have appeared across multiple disciplines and languages in staggering numbers. It is time to take stock of the findings. This Handbook offers a timely review of this intellectual endeavour.

Given the extremely broad implications of BRI, research on the topic has spanned over wide-ranging issues. They include systemic concerns at the global level such as globalization, transnational connectivity, global governance, global finance, world order and multipolar contentions, globalizing discourses, and so on; regional and international relations such as multilateralism, geopolitics and national security, geoeconomics and regionalism, debt trap and dependency, sovereign risk, and so on; and the impacts and responses at the domestic level including intervention and sovereign control, cross-border migration and exchanges, development strategy, sustainability, corruption, labour displacement, and so on. Many of these issues are perceptively explored in this Handbook.

Early research on BRI has mainly focused on the driving factors that prompted China to launch such a grandiose project. When the plan was first unveiled in 2013, it comprised highways, railroads, energy pipelines, and telecommunications ties that link China to Western Europe via Central Asian states, Iran, Turkey, Russia, the Caucasus, and the Balkans. At that time, the ostensible goals included enhancing connectivity through infrastructural networks, improving regional economic policy coordination, removing barriers to trade and investment, increasing financial cooperation, and encouraging cultural ties to build support for the project. Sceptics have underlined domestic problems in China, notably excess capacity and sluggish growth in its western hinterland, as the driving force behind the project. Others see the BRI as an eclectic collection of existing projects undertaken over the years by China and its allies, such as China and Pakistan's economic cooperation, the various economic agendas of the Shanghai Cooperation Organization,

Bangladesh–China–India–Myanmar economic cooperation, and China–Mongolia–Russia economic cooperation.

However, as time passes, the project rapidly expands in scale and scope. In addition to the land corridors in China–Mongolia–Russia, China–Pakistan, Bangladesh–China–India–Myanmar, China–Indochina Peninsula, China–Central and West Asia, and the New Eurasian Land Bridge, the maritime routes were added, connecting China with South Asia, Southeast Asia, the Middle East, Africa, and Europe through a strip of seaports via the South China Sea, the Indian Ocean, the Red Sea, and the Mediterranean Sea, eventually reaching to Australia and Latin America. It now encompasses over a hundred nations, and its significance has gone far beyond China's domestic situation. Regardless of one's analytical stand, it is undeniable that BRI has become a long-term, cross-continental, multifaceted project that is reshaping the global geo-economic landscape and world order. Research into its various dimensions, contradictions, achievements, failures, challenges, and impacts is thus imperative.

Unsurprisingly, this ambitious plan has aroused divergent views. Supporters see BRI as a new approach to promote development through multilateral cooperation and enhancement in transnational connectivity. BRI represents an alternative to the once dominated form of foreign aid and investment channelled through the World Bank and IMF, without the conditionality of market restructuring and governance reform that were often forced upon the recipient countries. Sceptics, however, caution against the economic benefits of putting heavy investments in low-return projects and high sovereign-risk countries. Critics, on the other hand, underline the huge debt burden created by large-scale infrastructural projects for host countries and warn against the potential debt trap. Many argue that BRI is in fact creating a new form of dependency. Still others believe that BRI represents China's counter strategy and challenge to the US-led international trade and financial system.

In addition to its broad empirical implications, BRI also bears major theoretical significance. Examples abound. From the outset, BRI is a state-initiated project aiming at enhancing cross-continental connectivity and resource flow, hence fostering interdependence of the world's economies, cultures, and peoples. It stands as an antithesis to neoliberalism, hitherto the main driving force of globalization. As a signifier of the free-market doctrine, neoliberalism has until now been closely associated with global capitalism. However, unlike the market-driven logic of neoliberalism, BRI exhibits a number of distinctive characteristics that set it apart from this dominant form of global capitalist expansion. The first characteristic is related to the kind of investments. Unlike conventional foreign direct investments that channel to the production of specific industrial/commercial products or components under the global value chain, transborder capital flows under BRI are mostly project-driven, especially via infrastructural projects. These investments often involve not only the construction but also the subsequent operation of infrastructural projects that are meant to improve physical connectivity. Examples include the Gwadar Port and Lahore Metro in Pakistan, the East Coast Rail Link in Malaysia, the Hambantota Port in Sri Lanka, the Mombasa–Nairobi Standard Gauge Railway in Kenya, the Piraeus Port in Greece, and the Great Stone Industrial Park in Belarus.

The second concerns the nature of actors. The state assumes a central role in BRI expansion. In contrast to neoliberal globalization that is spearheaded by multinationals and private enterprises, most of the mega-scale cooperative projects have been initiated by states or state-owned enterprises. The scale of these projects is often too big and their profit cycle too long for private investors and consortia. The states along the BRI routes not only establish bilateral economic agreements, but also directly involved in the formulation and implementation of concrete investment projects. It is therefore a state-led model of globalization, where state and interstate institutions are playing a transformative role. Such a state-led model presents an alternative path to globalization and challenges the familiar conception of a firm-based, market-led process as the sole logic driving global capitalist development.

The third characteristic underlines the nature of risks. State-led development across national boundaries faces unique uncertainties. Since investments and exchanges are governed by bilateral agreements as well as contracts, any changes in governments, laws, and state policies may lead to disputes or non-compliance with the bilateral arrangements. Some of the projects have already experienced setbacks, and many observers have highlighted the legal issues and sovereign risks in such arrangements.

In short, BRI expands our theoretical horizon about the possibilities and limitations of economic globalization which has hitherto been driven by neoliberalism. Now that such an alternative has taken shape, our next concern is whether it subverts or reproduces global domination and dependence. It brings us back to the old debate about various forms and mechanisms of dependency as well as the opportunities for autonomous development even in strongly dependent situations.

Research in this area is still embryonic but has attracted increasing attention. We already know a lot about the existing international division of labour and global value chain that sustain transnational domination under global capitalism. Such domination is achieved through a neoliberal process of accumulation, production, and distribution that is based on an intersection between city networks and global value chains. In the advanced producer service sector, interlocking networks connect major cities across the world through intra-firm flows. Multinationals and advanced producer service firms have strategically established offices in major cities, including New York, London, Frankfurt, and Tokyo. Global resource flow takes the form of inter- and intra-firm exchanges across cityscapes in the forms of capital, information, knowledge, strategy, plans, and personnel. As such, multinationals and other leading firms control global value chains through their organizational and locational power. Subsequently, global neoliberalism has created an uneven distribution of spatial power, hence reinforcing an international division of labour between the global command centres of advanced capitalist countries and those on the peripheries.

The advancement of BRI has invited conflicting responses to the question of domination and dependency. On the one hand, advocates of BRI argue that the state-orchestrated strategy promises to establish alternatives by developing new city networks in the south that will compete with those established in the north. Under BRI, new centres of resource flow have emerged, forming alternative networks linking places such Chongqing and Urumqi (China), Almaty (Kazakhstan), Cairo

(Egypt), Moscow (Russia), and Duisburg (Germany). The once peripheral areas such as Yiwu (China), Sost (Pakistan), Khorgos (Kazakhstan), Dordoi (Kyrgyzstan), and Ussuriysk (Russia) have emerged as nodal centres of long-distance resource flows. The end markets for global value chains are thus shifting and are no longer exclusively located in Europe and North America.

On the other hand, critics of BRI have highlighted the problem of debt trap experienced by host countries. This is typified by the case of the Hambantota Port project, when the Sri Lankan government was forced to lease the port to Chinese state-owned enterprise for a term of 99 years after failing to repay Chinese loans. Similar examples of leverage can be found in many projects in Africa, Central Asia, South Asia, and Southeast Asia. Critics argue that this is a new version of dependency, or even a new form of imperialism. The only difference is that the imperial centre has moved from the West to China.

In the meantime, inquiries into the question of domination have recently moved from the area of political economy to the cultural realm, where researchers have begun to analyse the discursive power of BRI. Accordingly, BRI capitalizes on the ancient idea of the silk road, and refashions it with a compelling narrative of peaceful trade, exchange of civilizations, intercultural dialogue, and harmonious co-development. It seeks to transform existing local cultures and histories with a language of shared pasts and roots linked by transnational routes and heritage. The implication of this fabricated discourse on cultural domination is now being put under close scrutiny.

All these controversies remind us of the once heated debate between modernization and dependency. And just like most previous debates, a consensus will not be easily reached. It depends not only on empirical findings but also on one's political stands as well as theoretical positions. But regardless of the outcome, a debate like this will deepen our understanding of the existing global order, capitalist logics, and developmental pathways. As such, the contribution of this Handbook to the debate is most relevant and valuable. The authors and editors should be congratulated for bringing this meaningful project to fruition.

November 2022

Tak-Wing Ngo
University of Macau, China

The original version of the book was revised: Author's name and affiliation in Chapters 42 and 46 and content changes in the Frontmatter have been updated. This correction to the book is available at https://doi.org/10.1007/978-981-19-6700-9_47

Acknowledgements

This volume is the result of an invitation made in 2020, by Palgrave to its editors, with a view to adapting what was initially a modest book proposal. The preparation of this handbook lasted from early 2020 to mid-2022, and involved senior and young scholars, international relations practitioners, members of think tanks, politicians, economists, historians, and Ph.D. students. Throughout the process, the editors had in mind four editorial avenues, to limit the possibility of a biased narrative: (1) diversity in institutional affiliations of authors; (2) encouragement of co-authorship of research, promoting multidisciplinary collaboration and involving different nationalities; (3) publication opportunity for young researchers and Ph.D. students; (4) gender balance, or at least a significant participation of women. The final outcome presented here comprises 22 single-author chapters, 24 co-authored chapters (46 chapters in total), with the participation of 80 international authors, 31 females, 49 males, and 10 junior researchers, representing 42 different academic, governmental, non-governmental, and research institutions.

The editors are particularly grateful to Professor Gershom Tse (Canada) for his editorial suggestions and English proofreading recommendations, and to Professor Tak-Wing Ngo (China) for his outstanding foreword and for having a thorough, helpful, and productive dialogue regarding the structure and rationale of this book. The editors also wish to extend their deepest gratitude to all contributors, with whom a constant academic discussion has allowed us to overcome all challenges. Likewise, the editors wish to convey sincere recognition and gratitude to Palgrave Macmillan, especially for the contractual flexibility in terms of book completion, as the challenges posed by several waves of the COVID-19 pandemic and the bleakness originating from the appalling events in Ukraine (since February 2022) have deeply affected us all. Perhaps more importantly, the editors are grateful to Palgrave for the openness shown vis-à-vis this topical issue, which is globalization with Chinese characteristics, whose impact on world affairs is already considerable and is likely to increase.

June 2022

Paulo Afonso B. Duarte
Francisco José B. S. Leandro
Enrique Martínez Galán

Contents

1 **Introduction** 1
Paulo Afonso B. Duarte, Francisco José Leandro,
and Enrique Martínez Galán

Part I Manifestations and Impacts of the BRI vis-à-vis Global Governance

2 **The BRI in Historical Perspective: PRC Economic Statecraft Since 1949** 17
Priscilla Roberts

3 **China, the BRI, and the New Vocabulary of Global Governance** ... 35
Maria Adele Carrai

4 **The Globalizing Discourse of the Belt and Road Initiative** 55
Cátia Miriam Costa

5 **The BRI in Xi's China "Grand Strategy": An Instrument to Restore Chinese Centrality in a New Era** 67
Luis Tomé

6 **People-to-People Exchanges: A Cluster of Narratives to Advance Purposeful Constructivism** 91
Yichao Li, Francisco José B. S. Leandro,
and Paulo Guilherme Figueiredo

7 **The Belt and Road Initiative in Global Governance: Impact on the International World Order** 109
Carmen Amado Mendes and Xuheng Wang

8 **Glocalization of Belt and Road Initiatives: The Importance of Local Agency** 125
Julie Yu-Wen Chen

9	The Chinese Agenda on the World Economic Forum: Assessing Political Evidence Between Rhetoric and Practice	139
	Jorge Tavares da Silva and Rui P. Pereira	
10	COVID-19 Pandemic, China, and Global Power Shifts: Understanding the Interplay and Implications	153
	Jamie P. Halsall, Ian G. Cook, Michael Snowden, and Roopinder Oberoi	
11	Enacting Inclusive Globalization in a VUCA Context While Emerging from COVID-19	167
	Tom Cockburn	
12	China's Ambition in Promoting Green Finance for Belt and Road Initiative	187
	Berna Kirkulak-Uludag	
13	Liability of Emergingness of Emerging Market Banks Internationalizing to Advanced Economies	201
	Anna Lupina-Wegener, Frank McDonald, Juan Shan, Gangfeng Zhang, and Güldem Karamustafa-Köse	
14	Chinese Health Strategy: A Tool Towards Global Governance	223
	Anabela Rodrigues Santiago	
15	Digital China: Governance, Power Politics, and the Social Game	237
	Dorothée Vandamme, Tanguy Struye de Swielande, and Kimberly Orinx	
16	The New Face of Multilateralism: The Case of "Chinese" Forums	253
	Pedro Paulo dos Santos, Yichao Li, and José Alves	
17	Secular Stagnation and World Leadership: China's Rising Path	271
	Henrique Morais	
18	Visuality and Infrastructure: The Case of the Belt and Road Initiative	285
	Dennis Zuev	
19	The Belt and Road Initiative: Can It Signalize a New Pendulum Movement?	301
	Margarida Proença	

Part II The Mutual Perceptions and the Changing Contours of Globalisation

20 The EU–China Geo-Economic Equilibrium in a World of Uncertainty 337
Enrique Feás and Federico Steinberg

21 A Shifting Current: Europe's Changing Approaches vis-à-vis China, the Belt and Road Initiative, and the COVID-19 Pandemic 353
Vassilis Ntousas and Stephen Minas

22 China in Central and Eastern Europe: New Opportunities for Small States 375
Vladimir Milić

23 China and the European Union: Inside the Economic Dynamics of a Challenging Relationship 391
Martina Basarac Sertić, Anita Čeh Časni, and Kosjenka Dumančić

24 A Review of China's Contribution to the Sustainable Development of the European Tourism Industry: A Case Study of Economic Effects and Sustainability Issues in Albania 411
Klodiana Gorica and Ermelinda Kordha

25 A Greater Eurasian Partnership? Xi and Putin's Road to Integrate and Lead 431
Ana Isabel Xavier

26 Health, Road, and Russia: Perspectives on Russian Involvement with China's Health Silk Road 447
Una Aleksandra Bērziņa-Čerenkova

27 India's Challenge to the BRI: Shaping the Global Normative Consensus 459
Harsh V. Pant and Anant Singh Mann

28 China–Pakistan Economic Corridor (CPEC): India's Conundrum and Policy Options 475
S. Y. Surendra Kumar

29 China in Latin America: To BRI or not to BRI 495
Ana Tereza L. Marra de Sousa, Giorgio Romano Schutte, Rafael Almeida F. Abrão, and Valéria Lopes Ribeiro

30 Why America Opposes the Belt and Road Initiative (BRI) 515
Robert Sutter

31 The Belt and Road Initiative's Security Challenges: The Chinese Globalization Project and Sino-American Rivalry 529
Diego Pautasso and Tiago Soares Nogara

| 32 | Sino-Iranian Cooperation in Artificial Intelligence: A Potential Countering Against the US Hegemony | 543 |

Mohammad Eslami, Nasim Sadat Mosavi, and Muhammed Can

Part III The Potential of the BRI as a Cross-Border Initiative

| 33 | China and the Wave of Globalization Focusing on the Middle East | 563 |

Flavius Caba-Maria

| 34 | China–Iran's 25-Year Deal: The Implication for the Belt and Road Initiative and Joint Comprehensive Plan of Action (JCPOA) | 575 |

Mohammad Eslami and Joel Anthony Kemie

| 35 | China's New Maritime Silk Road Cooperation: Why Malaysia, Indonesia, and the Philippines Are Clings in Disagreement? | 591 |

Muhamad Azwan Abd Rahman and Sufian Jusoh

| 36 | The Belt and Road Initiative and the Uneven Triangle of Latvia, Belarus, and China | 609 |

Māris Andžāns and Una Aleksandra Bērziņa-Čerenkova

| 37 | The Impact of Belt and Road Initiative on Asian Economies Along the Route | 623 |

Badar Alam Iqbal, Mohd Nayyer Rahman, and Nida Rahman

| 38 | The Belt and Road in the Kyrgyz Republic: Mapping Economic Risks and Risk Perceptions | 639 |

Linda Calabrese and Olena Borodyna

| 39 | Belt and Road Initiative's Economic Impact on Central Asia. The Cases of Kazakhstan and Kyrgyzstan | 657 |

Jildiz Nicharapova

| 40 | How Does BRI Affect the Degree of Globalization in Southeast Asia? | 671 |

Chien-wu Alex Hsueh

| 41 | Vietnam's Attitude Towards China's Belt and Road Initiative Amid Globalization | 689 |

Vu Quy Son

| 42 | The South Atlantic in China's Global Policy: Why It Matters? | 705 |

Laura C. Ferreira-Pereira and Paulo Afonso B. Duarte

43	**Belt and Road Initiative: Impact and Implications for Africa–China Relations**	723
	João Paulo Madeira, Ivete Silves Ferreira, and Nilton Fernandes Cardoso	
44	**The Unequal Modalities of China's Intervention in Africa**	735
	Xavier Aurégan	
45	**Africa's Thirst for Infrastructure: Contemporary Phenomenon That Makes China the Trading Partner**	753
	Paulo Elicha Tembe	
46	**Why Is China Going Polar? Understanding Engagement and Implications for the Arctic and Antarctica**	765
	Laura C. Ferreira-Pereira, Paulo Afonso B. Duarte, and Natacha Santos	

Correction to: The Palgrave Handbook of Globalization with Chinese Characteristics C1
Paulo Afonso B. Duarte, Francisco José B. S. Leandro, and Enrique Martínez Galán

Index 783

Notes on Contributors

Rafael Almeida F. Abrão is a Ph.D. Candidate at the Federal University of ABC (Brazil), financed by CAPES Foundation. He also received a Master's degree in Social Sciences from São Paulo State University, and a Bachelor of International Relations from the Federal University of São Paulo, both in Brazil. Since 2020, he is an affiliated fellow at the International Institute for Asian Studies (IIAS), Leiden University (The Netherlands).

José Alves is Full professor and Dean of the Faculty of Business at the City University of Macau, and he holds a Ph.D. in Business Administration from the University of Massachusetts Amherst. His major research interests include leadership and strategic management in China. His current research focuses on business ecosystems, innovation, and entrepreneurship in the Greater Bay Area of China. He has published and presented in international journals and conferences. He provides training to executives in China and advises companies on doing business between China and Portuguese-speaking markets.

Māris Andžāns is the Director of the Center for Geopolitical Studies Riga. He is also Assistant Professor and leads Diplomacy and Russia & Eurasia M.A. study programmes at Riga Stradins University. Previously, he has worked for the Latvian Institute of International Affairs. He was also a Visiting Fulbright Scholar at the Johns Hopkins University School of Advanced International Studies. Andžāns has ten years of experience in the public administration of Latvia. He served in positions related to the coordination of EU and NATO issues, security of transport and communications, civil–military cooperation, aviation, electronic communications, and postal issues. Among other duties, he has served as the Chairman of the National Cyber Security Council of Latvia and the Dangerous Goods Movement Consultative Council of Latvia.

Xavier Aurégan is a French geographer specialized in Geopolitics. Xavier Aurégan is Assistant Professor at the Catholic University of Lille and a research associate in three research centres: The French Institute of Geopolitics (Paris 8 University, France), French Institute for East Asian Research (INALCO, France), and the Quebec

Council for Geopolitical Studies (Laval, Quebec, Canada). Author of some fifty publications, his work focuses on African geopolitics and on both public and private actors outside the continent. This is particularly the case with China. The modalities of Chinese intervention, means, actors, and stakes are thus at the heart of his research, as are the fields of Chinese intervention in Africa (agriculture, infrastructure, health). He also analyses the relationships and power rivalries between these Chinese and African actors (rent, power, influence, networks) and the territorial impacts generated by these multiple presences.

Una Aleksandra Bērziņa-Čerenkova is a political scientist, China scholar, Head of Political Science Ph.D. programme and China Studies Centre at Riga Stradins University, Head of the Asia programme at the Latvian Institute of International Affairs, a member of the China in Europe Research Network (CHERN) and European Think Tank Network on China (ETNC). After having defended her doctoral dissertation on traditional Chinese discourse, she has held a Senior visiting research scholar position at Fudan University School of Philosophy, Shanghai, China, and a Fulbright visiting scholar position at the Center for East Asia Studies, Stanford University. Bērziņa-Čerenkova is a European China Policy Fellow at MERICS and an affiliate of the Lau Institute at King's College, London. Bērziņa-Čerenkova publishes on PRC political discourse, contemporary Chinese ideology, EU–China relations, Russia–China, and BRI. Her most recent monograph is "Perfect Imbalance: China and Russia" (World Scientific, 2022).

Olena Borodyna is a Transition Risk Analyst in the Global Risks and Resilience team at ODI with a strong understanding of political and socio-economic development dynamics and risks in emerging economies across Eurasia. She has experience in political risk analysis and an interest include energy security and transition risks, and geopolitical and economic impacts of China's growing global footprint.

Flavius Caba-Maria is the President of the Romanian Think Tank "Middle East Political and Economic Institute" (MEPEI), and director of marketing and legal consultant, offering consulting services on Middle East affairs. He is a Ph.D. Candidate at the Bucharest University of Economic Studies, focusing on international affairs—the role of the state and of the multinationals in the global economic warfare, highlighting the cases in the Middle East. B.A. in Law (BabeșBolyai University of ClujNapoca, Romania) with specialization in forensic firearms and postuniversity course in Political Science; B.A. in military science (Land Forces Academy). Also, he graduated diplomatic international courses and political adviser training programmes (Geneva Centre for Security Policy), with extended expertise on the Middle East, authoring, and coordinating articles and scientific works on Business Affairs, Defence & Security, International Relations, and Regional Development. He is a commentator on politics and security in the MENA region (Middle East and North Africa) at events around the world and in the media.

Linda Calabrese is a Research Fellow in the International Economic Development Programme at ODI and a Leverhulme Doctoral Fellow, King's College London. A development economist by training, her research interests include industrialization

Notes on Contributors   xix

and economic transformation, trade, and investment. Her work currently focuses on Chinese outward investment and the Belt and Road Initiative in Africa and Asia. Prior to joining ODI, Linda was working as a consultant on economic policy and strategy, as a country economist for the International Growth Centre in Rwanda, and as an economist for the Ministry of EAC Affairs in Uganda.

Muhammed Can is Ph.D. Candidate of Political Science and International Relations at the University of Minho, Portugal. He holds a bachelor's degree in Economics. He completed his postgraduate studies at the Swansea University (International Relations), King's College London (Espionage and Surveillance Studies), and University of St. Andrews (Terrorism Studies), UK. His current studies comparatively focus on AI strategies and policies of the US and China.

Nilton Fernandes Cardoso is Assistant Professor at the University of Cabo Verde (Uni-CV) and collaborating professor of the Master's Program in International Relations and Economic Diplomacy (RIDE) at Uni-CV. Researcher at the Brazilian Centre for African Studies (CEBRAFRICA) and at the Center for International Studies on Government (CEGOV). Ph.D. and Master's in International Strategic Studies at the Federal University of Rio Grande do Sul (UFRGS), Brazil. Bachelor's in International Relations at UFRGS.

Maria Adele Carrai is an Assistant Professor of Global China Studies at NYU Shanghai. Her research explores the history of international law in East Asia and investigates how China's rise as a global power is shaping norms and redefining the international distribution of power. Prior to joining NYU Shanghai, she was a recipient of a three-year Marie-Curie fellowship at KU Leuven. She was also a Fellow at the Italian Academy of Columbia University, Princeton-Harvard China and the World Program, Max Weber Program of the European University Institute of Florence, and New York University Law School.

Anita Čeh Časni is Associate Professor at Department of Statistics, Faculty of Economics and Business, University of Zagreb, where she obtained her Ph.D. in 2013. She is a Vice Head of Department of Statistics at Faculty of Economics and Business, University of Zagreb and a Secretary of Croatian Statistical Association. Apart from teaching at both Croatian and international EPAS accredited study programme (BDiB) she is very active in her scientific field having published numerous scientific papers in respectable international scientific journals. She has been awarded for both her scientific and teaching work. Additionally, she is a researcher on 3 COST actions, one ERASMUS+ project (Higher Education Curricula Development on the Collaborative Economy in Europe- COLECO) and scientific project financed by Croatian Scientific Foundation. She recently became a Vice director of Institute for Euro-Asian Studies thus promoting international cooperation between Faculty of Economics and Business and Euro-Asian countries. She is a reviewer for both domestic and international conferences and journals. Her research interests include applied statistical methods in tourism and macroeconomics, panel data analysis, housing economics, sustainability, and educational statistics

Tom Cockburn obtained his first degree with honours from Leicester University, England, his PGCE from University of Wolverhampton, England, his M.B.A. and Doctorate from Cardiff University, Wales. He has 8 years' experience as Head of a UK Business School, 2 years' deputy Head of School in New Zealand, 5 years Board experience on the Standing Conference of Welsh Management Education Centres, two years as Academic Learning and Teaching Fellow at UNSW, Sydney, Australia, one year as Trustee in K'aute Pasifika Trust Board, New Zealand, and was elected Associate Fellow (AFNZIM) of the New Zealand Institute of Management in 2010.

Ian G. Cook is Emeritus Professor of Human Geography at Liverpool John Moores University, UK. He is an expert on various aspects of Chinese urbanization, global ageing, social enterprise and community development. He co-founded and co-edited Contemporary Issues in Geography and Education with the late Dawn Gill in the 1980s, co-led the British Pacific Rim Seminar Series and the Community Strategies Research Team in the 1990s and has co-edited and co-authored 10 books since then. Ian has helped supervise 20 Ph.D.s and 6 M.Phil.s to completion and has published widely in a wide range of volumes and academic journals including Urban Studies, Health Policy, International Journal of Sociology and Social Policy, and Social Science and Medicine.

Cátia Miriam Costa is a researcher at the Centre for International Studies (ISCTE-IUL, Lisbon, Portugal) and invited Assistant Professor in the same university. She is Advisor to the Secretary of State of Internationalization of the 22nd Portuguese Constitutional Government and Chair of Global Iberoamerica in the European Institute of International Studies. She is a member of OceanGov, a network project support by The European Science Foundation. She also is consultant of DaST Project (Design a Sustainable Tomorrow); she is developing research in new media as well as in the digital humanities domain, and analysing the relation between technology, circulation of ideas, and international communication. Specialized in intercultural relations, she has studied deeply the non-European territories: The African, American, Asian cases both in colonial and postcolonial context and their relations with the former colonizers and within them. She has cooperated with several research centres and networks in the areas of social and political sciences. At the international level: CEIBA (centre for research on culture and development, Catalonia, Spain); "Ars, cultura Y Desarrollo" (organization for the register of orality, Valence, Spain), Kairos-Chairo (programme Ibero-american of communities, languages and sustainable development), The Human Geography Research Group (Aberdeen University), network "Appearance Matters" (supported by the European Science Foundation). At the Portuguese level: IICT (Tropical Research Institute), Center of Iberian Studies, Center of Peoples and Cultures Research (Catholic University of Lisbon), International Institute Casa de Mateus (Higher Education network), CHAM (Centre for Global History, University of Lisbon), CEsA (Centre for African and Asian Studies, University of Lisbon). She has been involved in the organization of international conferences and congresses in different scientific areas.

Julie Yu-Wen Chen received her Ph.D. in social sciences from the University of Konstanz, Germany (2009). From 2012 to 2021 she was Editor of Asian Ethnicity (Taylor & Francis). From 2018 to 2021, she was chair of Nordic Association of China Studies (NACS). She is currently Professor of Chinese Studies at the University of Helsinki, Finland. Her most recent publications are respectively: *The Chinese Model of Development: Substances and Applications in and Beyond China* (2021, Routledge Handbook); *Ethnic Conflict in Xinjiang and Its International Connections* (2021, Routledge Handbook); *Appropriate Approaches to Studying the BRI's Actual Impacts and Limits* (2020, Routledge); *The Making of the Finnish Polar Silk Road* (2020, Palgrave Macmillan). Chen is one of the Editors of the *Journal of Chinese Political Science* (Springer) and member of Advisory Scientific Board for the Project "Sinophone Borderlands: Interactions at the Edges" based at Palacky University, Czech Republic sponsored by the European Regional Development Fund (175 million CZK, around 6,8 million Euro). She also represents Finland in "COST ACTION: China in European Research Network" (European Cooperation in Science & Technology funded by EU Horizon 2020).

Jorge Tavares da Silva is a visiting Assistant Professor at the University of Aveiro, Department of Social, Political and Territorial Sciences (DCSPT) and at the Faculty of Letters, University of Coimbra. He holds a Ph.D. in International Relations from the Faculty of Economics at the University of Coimbra (Portugal), in the specific field of International Politics and Conflict Resolution. He is a Researcher at GOVCOPP - Research Unit on Governance, Competitiveness and Public Policy. He is a founding member of the Observatory of China (Portugal) and the Center for Studies and Research on Security and Defence of Trás-os-Montes and Alto Douro (CEIDSTAD). He is author of multiple articles and chapters of books in international journals, particularly on political, economic, and social issues facing contemporary China. He is coauthor of the book *Role and Impact of Tourism in Peacebuilding and Conflict Transformation* (IGI Global, 2020); Luso-Chinese Relations, from the sixteenth century to the contemporary context [in Portuguese] (IIM, 2020) and Xi Xinping—The Rise of China's New Helmsman: the Man, Politics and the World [in Portuguese] (Sílabas & Desafios, 2021).

Ana Tereza L. M. de Sousa received her Ph.D. degree in International Relations (IR) from the Universidade Estadual Paulista (UNESP). She also received a Master's degree in Social Science and a Bachelor's in IR from the same university. She is a professor and researcher at Universidade Federal do ABC (UFABC), in São Paulo, Brazil. Her current research interests are Chinese Foreign Policy and China relations with Latin America, in special Brazil. Her latest publications include Sousa, A. T. L. M. (2021). The Construction of Trade Patterns in Brazil–China Relations. *Brazilian Journal of International Relations*, v. 10, pp. 578–604; and Sousa, A. T. L. M (2020). Renminbi Internationalization: Domestic Challenges and External Implications. *Desafíos*, v. 32, pp. 1–30.

Tanguy Struye de Swielande is Professor in international relations (Ph.D.) at the UCLouvain (Belgium) and director of the Centre for International Crisis and Conflict

Studies (CECRI-UCLouvain). His research focuses on great power relations, the Indo-Pacific, power, grand strategy, and information warfare.

Pedro Paulo dos Santos is a Ph.D. candidate at the Institute for Research on Portuguese-speaking Countries, City University of Macau, China. He also received a Master's degree in Education, with specialization in Leadership and Management of Schools, from the University of Saint Joseph in Macao. His Bachelor's degree is Film and Broadcasting Production and was taken at the London Metropolitan University. He is currently a lecturer and researcher at City University of Macau. His current research interests are the People's Republic of China, Portuguese-speaking countries, international organizations, and geopolitics. He has written and appeared in several media outlets such as Teledifusão de Macau, S.A. (TDM), Hoje Macau or China Global Television Network (CGTN). He had articles presented in conferences in Macao, Hong Kong, Singapore, and Portugal. His most recent publications were *English learning of College Students in Macao*. Hu, B.; Hong, C.; Wang C.W.; Santos, P.P. (2020). Published on January 2020 on *Journal of Macao Studies*, ISSN 0872-8526 and *Geopolitical Relations between China and the South Atlantic Portuguese-speaking Countries: A Blue Evolving Partnership*. Chapter 3A pp. 269–299, in Leandro, F., Dos Santos, P. P. & Li, Y. (eds.), *China and the Portuguese-Speaking Small Island States: From sporadic bilateral exchanges to a comprehensive multilateral platform* (City University of Macau), 2021.

Paulo Afonso B. Duarte received his Ph.D. in Political Science from Catholic University of Louvain (Belgium). He is Assistant Professor at Universidade Lusófona do Porto and Invited Assistant Professor of Political Science and International Relations at the University of Minho where he teaches various courses at both graduate and postgraduate levels, and conducts research in the domains of International Relations and China studies. Paulo Duarte is the co-editor of *The Belt and Road Initiative: An Old Archetype of a New Development Model* (Palgrave, 2020). He has acted as reviewer for *Geopolitics* (Taylor & Francis), Sage journals, and Peter Lang. He conducted extensive on-the-ground research in several Central Asian countries with scholarship granted by Calouste Gulbenkian Foundation (Portugal), besides having been granted with scholarship from both the People's Republic of China and the Republic of China to carry out research both in Beijing and Taipei. He is the author of the first book on China's BRI in all Lusophone space (A Faixa e Rota Chinesa: a convergência entre terra e mar (2017) as well as of a book—Metamorfoses no Poder: Rumo à Hegemonia do Dragão? with foreword and presentation by current President of the Portuguese Republic Marcelo Rebelo de Sousa (2014)). His most recent publications include Duarte, P. (2021). "The Soft Power of China and the European Union in the context of the Belt and Road Initiative and Global Strategy." *Journal of Contemporary European Studies*, with Ferreira-Pereira; and Duarte, P. (2021) "China and the Belt and Road Initiative in Europe: The case of Portugal" In Ntousas and Minas (eds). *The European Union and China's Belt and Road Impact, Engagement and Competition*. Routledge (co-authored).

Notes on Contributors

Kosjenka Dumančić is an Associate Professor of Commercial Law and Vice Dean for international relations and projects at Faculty of economics and business University of Zagreb where she teaches Commercial Law, Law of International Trade, European Company Law, and European Market Law. She got her master's degree at "European studies" organized by Pantheon Assas, Paris II and University of Zagreb in 2003 and holds Ph.D. in European Law with thesis "Limits of the freedom to provide services in European Union." She is the director of the Institute for Euro-Asian Studies of Faculty of economics and business. Her research interests are in the fields of European company law, European internal market law, International Law and collaborative economy. She participated in different EU-founded projects. Specifically, she is the management committee member of different COST Projects and currently she is actively involved in two EU-funded Erasmus+ Projects. COLECO Project which aims to examine the impacts of the collaborative economy in Europe, focusing on peer-to-peer accommodation platforms and TERRAGOV Project. Dumančić is a coordinator of the Jean Monnet Teachers Training Project Solidary Europe for Inclusive Society (EUsolis) started in March 2022 till 2025.

Mohammad Eslami is a collaborative researcher of the Research Centre for Political Science (CICP) at the department of Political Science and International Relations at the University of Minho (Portugal). His Ph.D. thesis entitled "Strategic Culture and the Foreign Policy of the Islamic Republic of Iran: Assessing the Ballistic Missiles and Unmanned Combat Aerial Vehicles programme." He holds a B.A. Degree in Arab Studies, and a master's degree in political science and International Relations. His research interests are primarily related to Middle East Studies, Security Studies, Arms Control, and Iranian Studies. His last publication is "Iran's strategic culture: the 'revolutionary' and 'moderation' narratives on the ballistic missile programme."

Enrique Feás is Senior Analyst at the Elcano Royal Institute, Adjunct Professor at IE University and the IE School of Global and Public Affairs, and independent board member of the Instituto de Crédito Oficial (ICO). He is also member of the Advisory Board of the Asian Development Bank Institute (ADBI) and member of the Spanish Exporters and Investors Club's Committee for Reflection on Internationalization. Previously, as a State Economist and Trade Expert (currently on leave of absence), he has worked as Economic and Commercial Counsellor at the Spanish Embassies in the Philippines and in Egypt, Deputy Director for Trade Policy with Mediterranean Countries, Africa, and the Middle East, Advisor for International Affairs to the Vice President and Minister of Economy and Technical Advisor at the Deputy Directorate of Foreign Sector Studies.

Ivete Silves Ferreira is Technician at the National Institute of Territorial Management (INGT) in Cape Verde and member of the Research Group on Innovation, Technology and Territory (GRITT) at the Federal University of Pernambuco (UFPE). Received a Ph.D. in geography at the UFPE (Brazil) and his dissertation was entitled "Great Urban Project in a Small Island Country: The Chinese Project Cape Verde Integrated Resort and Casino (2014/2018)". From 2006 to 2011, she was a member of the Cape Verdean Parliament and member of the Specialized Commission of the

Economy, Environment and Land Use. Between 2012 and 2014, she coordinated the Urban Development Service in the Directorate General of Spatial Planning and Urban Development (DGOTDU).

Laura C. Ferreira-Pereira received her Ph.D. in International Relations from the University of Kent at Canterbury (UK). She is Full Professor of Political Science and International Relations of the University of Minho where she teaches various courses at both graduate and postgraduate level, and conducts research in the domains of International Relations and European Union Studies. Laura Ferreira-Pereira is the editor of *Portugal in the European Union: Assessing Twenty-Five Years of Integration Experience* (Routledge, 2014) and co-editor of *The European Union's Strategic Partnerships: Global Diplomacy in a Contested World* (Palgrave Macmillan, 2021). She has acted as the leading guest editor of Special Issues published in *European Security* (2012) and *Cambridge Review of International Affairs* (2016). She is also contributor to other leading journals such as *Journal of Common Market Studies*, *Cooperation and Conflict*, *Journal of Contemporary European Studies*, *International Politics and Journal of European Integration*, among others; and has published in several edited volumes. Her current research explores the EU's strategic partnership diplomacy and relations with the Lusophone world; Europeanization within and beyond Europe; comparative regional integration (with an emphasis on security and defence); Brexit and small states; China in global affairs and Luso-Chinese relations. Laura Ferreira-Pereira is a member of the editorial boards of the journals *Contemporary Politics and Global Society*. She is a founding member of the European International Studies Association (EISA).

Paulo Guilherme Figueiredo is a second year Ph.D. candidate at the Institute for Research on Portuguese-speaking Countries, City University of Macao (China). He has a Master's degree in Applied Management at Católica Lisbon School of Business and Economics (2017–2018). The main research area of his Master's degree is multidimensional intercultural adaptation of individuals and organizations in business contexts. His current research interests are governance and intercultural adaptation issues in the China—Portuguese-speaking countries context and business risk analysis matrixes.

Enrique Martínez Galán received a Ph.D. in economics from the University of Lisbon (Portugal) in 2018. Currently, he is assistant professor and academic program director of the Master in Development Management of the Asian Institute of Management. He was member of the Board of Directors of the Asian Development Bank and of the Asian Infrastructure Investment Bank. Previous experience also as senior advisor for multilateral affairs at the Finance Ministry in Portugal, the World Bank, the European Commission, and the Portuguese Foreign Affairs Ministry. Researcher at the Centre for African and Development Studies of ISEG-Lisbon School of Economics and Management of the University of Lisbon. Author of several books and book chapters in development finance, multilateral governance, international trade, foreign direct investment, and the Belt and Road Initiative. Co-author of several scientific articles published in the *The World Economy, Applied Econometrics and International Development, Baltic Journal of European Studies, Portuguese Review of Regional Studies, Portuguese Economic Journal and Journal for Research Administration*.

Klodiana Gorica is Full Professor at University of Tirana, Faculty of Economy Albania. From 2011 to 2016 she has been Vice Dean in Faculty of Economy, University of Tirana; member of Scientific Council 2008–2012, and after 2016 member of Council of Professors; National Expert in Higher Education Quality Assurance Albanian Agency since 2008; is involved in international initiatives, forums, and projects, not only expert but serving as Guest speaker, creating networks for Balkan and European Sustainable Tourism, monitoring, creating and managing round tables and forums; member in editorial board/research committee/keynote speaker in international journals and conferences, and international experiences in training and teaching since 1996 in universities abroad. Author and coauthor in different scientific books, 3 monographs published from Springer and IEDC, Slovenia; Springer, Germany and Switzerland; publishing articles in international scientific conferences and journals. Research activities abroad in international universities in countries such as: UK, USA, Belgium, Portugal, Norway, Slovenia, Italy, France, Israel, Portugal, Croatia, Austria, Serbia, Bosnia and Hercegovina, Montenegro, Turkey, Macedonia, Bulgaria, and Romania. She is National Contact Point for Albania in European Institute of Innovation and Technology EIT and a coordinator of BLUEWBC Project 2020–2023, for University of Tirana (Sustainable Development of BLUE Economies through higher education and innovation in Western Balkan Countries. Has been awarded "Tourism HERO" from World Tourism Network for 2021.

Jamie P. Halsall is a Reader in Social Sciences in the School of Human and Health Sciences at the University of Huddersfield, UK. His research interests include communities, globalization, higher education, public, and social policy. Currently, Jamie is a Fellow of the Royal Society of Arts and a Chartered Geographer of the Royal Geographical Society, and was awarded Senior Fellowship of the Higher Education Academy in January 2017. Jamie is the author of *Understanding Ethnic Segregation in Contemporary Britain* (Nova Publishers, 2013), and coauthor of *Sociability, Social Capital, and Community Development: An International Health Perspective* (Springer, 2015) and *Aging in Comparative Perspective: Processes and Policies* (Springer, 2012); he also co-edited *Social Enterprise in the Higher Education Sector* (Cambridge Scholars Publishing, 2021), *Mentorship, Leadership, and Research: Their Place in the Social Science Curriculum* (Springer, 2019) and *The Pedagogy of the Social Sciences Curriculum* (Springer, 2017).

Chien-wu Alex Hsueh is Associate Professor at the Graduate Institute of East Asian Studies of National Chengchi University, Taiwan. He received his Ph.D. degree from the Department of Political Science of the University of South Carolina in 2015. His specialty is in international relations, international political economy, and quantitative research design. At present he is focusing on the study of China's influences and the responses of other states. His work can be found in International Relations of the Asia-Pacific and many Taiwanese journals such as *Issues & Studies*, *Taiwanese Political Science Review*, and *Taiwan Democracy Quarterly*.

Badar Alam Iqbal (Ph.D. & DBA) had been the DAAD, Fellow at German Institute of Economic Research; Berlin, Kiel Institute of World Economics; Kiel, South Asia Institute, University of Heidelberg; Germany; Ford Foundation, American Research Center US; Fulbright Visiting Professor; US; Institute of Developing Economies; Tokyo; Former Fulbright scholar-in-Residence (SIR) 2004–2005 at School of Business; Claflin University; South Carolina, US. In 2016–2017, the Fulbright Commission Washington has again nominated for Scholar-in-residence (SIR) at School of Business; Kentucky State University; US. Currently, Iqbal is Emeritus Professor; External-Relation-Chair of Research; at Federic Bastiat Institute for African Research; Ghana. Adjunct Professor; Faculty of Economics and Finance; Monarch University; Switzerland; Visiting Professor at University of Rennes; France; University of South Africa; Pretoria; Former Extra Ordinary Professor, School of Economic Sciences; North-West University; South Africa; Visiting Professor of Research; Vaal University of Technology; South Africa; International Islamic University Malaysia. TNCR and Routledge publisher; UK has conferred on him a "Certificate of Appreciation" for his contribution to the promotion of Transnational Corporation Review. Serving Editor for special issue of Sage, Emerald; Elsevier, and Springer. Currently, he is Adjunct Professor of Economics and Finance, Monarch Business School—Zug (Switzerland).

Sufian Jusoh served as a Director and Professor at the Institute of Malaysian and International Studies (IKMAS), National University of Malaysia (UKM). Sufian is also an External Fellow of the World Trade Institute, University of Bern, Switzerland and a Distinguished Fellow at the Institute of Diplomacy and Foreign Relations, Ministry of Foreign Affairs, Malaysia. Sufian also plays a contributing role in the reform of the investment laws in Myanmar, Timor-Leste, Laos, and the Federated States of Micronesia. Sufian has been a consultant to many countries and international organizations such as the World Bank, the Asian Development Bank, ASEAN, the World Trade Organization, the World Intellectual Property Organization, the United Nations Conference on Trade and Development and the United Nations' Economic Commission for Asia and the Pacific.

Güldem Karamustafa-Köse is a researcher. She specializes in the process of learning and adaptation and examines how individuals, groups, and organizations can learn and grow through diverse experience. Her research evolves around the themes of organizational learning, cross-cultural management, M&As, internationalization, and sustainable development. Collaborating with fellow researchers on various projects, she provides guidance and support to professionals.

Joel Anthony Kemie is a collaborative researcher of the Research Centre for Political Science (CICP) at the Department of Political Science and International Relations at the University of Minho (Portugal). His research interest is on Nigeria Within China's Quest for Global Dominance: The Role of Belt and Road Initiative. He holds a B.Sc. Degree in Political Science, and M.A. in International Political Economy. Between

2016 and 2019, he worked as a project officer at the National Association for Peaceful Elections in Nigeria (NAPEN) in Abuja, Nigeria. His last publication, which is co-authored, is titled: A Neo-Marxist Contribution to International Relations Theory: A Case Study of Andre Gunder Frank on the World System Theory.

Berna Kirkulak-Uludag is a finance Professor at Dokuz Eylül University, Faculty of Business in Turkey, an adjunct faculty at Maastricht School of Management in The Netherlands, and a visiting professor at Southeast University in China. Currently, she is a Fulbright visiting scholar at Harvard University Fairbank Center for Chinese Studies. She received her Ph.D. in economics from Hokkaido University in Japan. Her research interests lie in the areas of Chinese financial markets, environmental degradation, resource economics, sharing economy, and migration. She has involved in a number of research projects including TUBITAK (Turkish Education High Council), UNESCO, ERASMUS+, and EU COST Actions. Currently, she is a Management Committee (MC) member for "China in Europe Research Network" COST Action funded by the EU. Further, she is a research associate for the "China, Law and Development" project funded by the European Research Council. Her papers have been published in top-tier journals including *Journal of Cleaner Production, Sustainability, Resources Policy, Applied Economics*, the *Pacific-Basin Finance Journal, Emerging Markets Finance and Trade*, and *PLOS One*, among others.

Ermelinda Kordha is currently Associate Professor in Department of Marketing and Tourism, University of Tirana. She received her Ph.D. degree in 20010 and M.Sc. Degree in 2006 from the Faculty of Economy, University of Tirana, Albania. Through the academic and professional career, she gained continuous qualifications especially in Tourism field focusing mainly on the fields of digital technologies in economy, marketing, and tourism, as well as in education and sustainable tourism. Scientific research work in the field of ICT, digital media, and tourism has emerged through participation in various research projects, as well over 30 papers published in conference proceedings and national and international journals. She is the first author of a monograph on ICT strategies and information society development, published by Springer in 2015. Her latest publications include Kripa D. Luci E., Gorica K., and Kordha E. 2021. New Business Education Model for Entrepreneurial HEIs: University of Tirana Social Innovation and Internationalization. AdministrativeSciences11: 122, and Kordha, E., Gorica, K., Sevrani, K. (2019). The Importance of Digitalization for Sustainable Cultural Heritage Sites in Albania. In: Stankov, U., Boemi, SN., Attia, S., Kostopoulou, S., Mohareb, N. (eds.) *Cultural Sustainable Tourism. Advances in Science, Technology & Innovation*. Springer, Cham.

S. Y. Surendra Kumar is an Associate Professor at the Department of Political Science, Bangalore University, Bengaluru, India. He holds M.Phil. and Ph.D. degrees in South Asian Studies from the School of International Studies, Jawaharlal Nehru University (JNU), New Delhi. He is a recipient of Mahbubul-Haq Research Award and Short Duration Fellowship. He has authored and co-edited books. He has contributed more than 20 chapters in various edited books and published more than 30 research articles in leading national and international journals. His main research interests are South Asian Security and Indian foreign policy with reference to US and China. He has travelled to China and South East Asian countries and is keen watcher on China in South Asia and South East Asia.

Francisco José B. S. Leandro received a Ph.D. in political science and international relations from the Catholic University of Portugal in 2010. From 2016 to 2017, he took part in a postdoctoral research program on state monopolies in China-One Belt, One Road studies. In 2014, 2017, and 2020, he was awarded the Institute of European Studies in Macau (IEEM) Academic Research Grant, which is a major component of the Asia-Europe Comparative Studies Research Project. From 2014 to 2018, he was the program coordinator at the Institute of Social and Legal Studies, Faculty of Humanities at the University of Saint Joseph in Macau, China. From 2018 to 2023 he was the associate dean of the Institute for Research on Portuguese-Speaking Countries at the City University of Macau (China). Since 2023, he is associate professor with habilitation in international relations at Faculty of Social Sciences—University of Macau (China). His most recent books are Steps of Greatness: The Geopolitics of OBOR (2018, University of Macau); The Challenges, Development and Promise of Timor-Leste (2019, City University of Macau); The Belt and Road Initiative: An Old Archetype of a New Development Model (2020, Palgrave Macmillan); Geopolitics of Iran (2021, Palgrave Macmillan); The Handbook of Special Economic Zones (2021, IGI, Global), and Disentangled Vision on Preparing the Generation Next (2023, Peter Lang Publishers). Francisco is a member of OBSERVARE (Observatory of Foreign Relations), which was founded in 1996 as a center for studies in international relations at the Autonomous University of Lisbon, Portugal.

Yichao Li (https://orcid.org/0000-0001-8588-1043) received her Ph.D. degree from the Institute for Research on Portuguese-speaking Countries, City University of Macau. She also received a Master's degree in comparative civil law (in Chinese) from the University of Macau, and a Bachelor of Laws from Nanjing University of Information Science & Technology, China. In 2020, she was awarded the Institute of European Studies in Macau (IEEM) Academic Research Grant, which is a major component of the Asia-Europe Comparative Studies Research Project. Her current research interests are the Belt and Road Initiative and Portuguese-speaking countries. Her latest publication stands as: Li, Y., & Vicente, M. (2020). Chinese partnerships and the Belt and Road Initiative: a synergetic affiliation. In Leandro, F. & Duarte, P. (eds.), *The Belt and Road Initiative: An Old Archetype of a New Development Model*. Palgrave MacMillan; and Li, Y. (2021). Chinese Partnerships with Portuguese-Speaking Small Island Developing States: Past, Present and Future Perspectives. In Leandro, F., Paulo, P., Li, Y. (eds.), *China and the Portuguese-Speaking Small Island States: From sporadic bilateral exchanges to a comprehensive multilateral platform*. City University of Macau. She is an associate researcher of the OBSERVARE—The Observatory of Foreign Relations, created in 1996 as a centre for studies in International Relations at the Autonomous University of Lisbon, Portugal.

Notes on Contributors

Anna Lupina-Wegener is a Full Professor at the IIDE within HEIG-VD and she is head of the Intercultural Management research group. She examines socio-cultural integration in cross-border mergers and acquisitions (M&As) and internationalization processes in various cultural contexts, such as Brazil, China, Mexico, Poland, and Russia. Her research was published in leading academic journals and was financed through external research grants (e.g., Interreg, SNSF, Cheque d'Innovation, Bourse d'Exellence, Leading House Asia).

João Paulo Madeira is Assistant Professor and coordinator of the programme in International Relations and Diplomacy at the University of Cabo Verde (Uni-CV, Cabo Verde). Associate Researcher at the Centre for Public Administration and Public Policies (CAPP-ISCSP-UL). Ph.D. in Social Sciences from the University of Lisbon (ISCSP-UL), having completed a mobility post-doctoral programme at FCT NOVA University with the support of the Calouste Gulbenkian Foundation as a member of the Network of Environmental Studies of the Portuguese Speaking Countries (REALP).

Anant Singh Mann holds a Master of Science in International Political Economy from the London School of Economics and political Science (LSE) and a Master of Arts (Honours) in International Relations and Modern History from the University of St Andrews. Anant has worked across several think tanks and consultancies and has written for a variety of media houses, think tanks, and academic journals, and chapters in edited volumes, including the Times of India, The Print, First Post, Money Control, News18, the Observer Research Foundation (ORF), the Nepal Institute for International Cooperation and Engagement (NIICE), and the Global Policy Journal.

Frank McDonald is a Professor of International Business at the University of Leeds Business School and a member of the Centre of International Business University of Leeds. He has pubished over 50 journal articles in for example, *Journal of World Business, Regional Studies, International Business Review, Technological Forecasting and Social Change, International Marketing Review and Management International Review*. His research focusses on the role of formal and informal institutions on the internationalisation strategies of firms, protection of intellectual property rights in internationalisation strategies, and innovation and internationalisation. He has also extensive experience of funded research on the effects of trade and FDI on regional development in host and home countries.

Carmen Amado Mendes is President of the Macau Scientific and Cultural Centre. Associate Professor of International Relations with tenure, accredited at the School of Economics of the University of Coimbra, where she established the course "China and the Portuguese-speaking Countries in World Trade." Former head of the International Relations department and coordinator of the School of Economics International Office at the same university. Holds a Ph.D. degree from the School of Oriental and African Studies—University of London, a Master's degree from the Institute of Higher European Studies—University of Strasbourg, and a Bachelor's degree from the Institute of Social and Political Sciences—University of Lisbon. She was a Post-doctorate scholar at the Institute of Political Studies of the Portuguese Catholic

University of Lisbon and visiting professor at the University of Macau, the University of Salamanca and the University of Lyon. She was a board member of the European Association for Chinese Studies, and the organizer of the 2014 EACS conference in Coimbra; and president of the International Relations Section and member of the board of the Portuguese Political Science Association. Principal Investigator at the University of Coimbra on a research project on the role of Macau in China´s relations with the Portuguese-speaking countries, funded by the Portuguese national funding agency for Science, Research and Technology; and on a project on South–South Cooperation for the Europe China Research and Advice Network, supported by the European External Action Service. Auditor of the Portuguese National Defense Institute. Co-founder of the consulting company ChinaLink, and of the Observatory for China in Portugal. Author of *China and the Macau Negotiations, 1986–1999* (HKUP) and *China's New Silk Road: An Emerging World Order* (Routledge), as well as other publications available for consultation at: www.uc.pt/feuc/carmen.

Vladimir Milić is an independent researcher based in Shanghai. He is a graduate of the Silk Road School of the Renmin University of China with a Master's degree in Contemporary China Studies. He holds a bachelor's degree in economics from Megatrend University in Belgrade, Serbia. He is a founder of the web portal savremenakina.rs which publishes analyses of Chinese economy, politics, and international relations. His research focuses on China and Central and Eastern Europe cooperation under the 16+1 mechanism and the Belt and Road Initiative. Vladimir is a frequent commentator for Serbian electronic media on issues concerning Sino-Serbian relations.

Stephen Minas is Associate Professor at the Peking University School of Transnational Law, where he directs the Sustainability Innovation and Law Center. Stephen is a senior research fellow at the Transnational Law Institute of King's College London, a member and immediate past chair of the UNFCCC Technology Executive Committee, a member of the Advisory Board of the Climate Technology Centre of Network and a member of the IUCN World Commission on Environmental Law. Stephen participates in UN climate negotiations and has consulted to or collaborated with a variety of international organizations and think tanks. Stephen holds a Ph.D. in Law from King's College London and has published widely on the law and policy of sustainable development, mainly focusing on the areas of climate change, clean energy, and ocean conservation. Stephen is co-editor of the books *EU Climate Diplomacy* (2018), *Stress-Testing the Law of the Sea* (2018) and *The European Union and China's Belt and Road* (2021).

Henrique Morais holds a Ph.D. in International Relations from Universidade Autónoma de Lisboa. He is head of unit at Banco de Portugal, and was also a member of the board and executive director of Comboios de Portugal-Cargo, chairman of the executive board of INVESFER, and a consultant at Correios de Portugal (CTT). He is Assistant Professor at Universidade Autónoma de Lisboa and member of the Obervare research centre.

Notes on Contributors

Nasim Sadat Mosavi is a collaborative researcher at Centro Algoritm—University of Minho, Portugal. Her Ph.D. thesis is entitled "Intelligent Decision Support System for Precision Medicine." Currently, she works with the Bosch Car-Multimedia Portugal on Factory of Future project; adopting Artificial Intelligence/Machine Learning techniques to propose energy demand prediction. Nasim graduated in Computer Science and pursued her master's degree in International Business from the University of Wollongong. During her 20+ years of' work experience in the field of Information System and Technology, she was involved in developing and implementing more than 100 successful projects in Dubai, Iran, K.S.A and Portugal with different industries.

Tak-Wing Ngo is Professor of Political Science at the University of Macau (China). He holds a Ph.D. from SOAS London and worked as an anti-corruption official and journalist. He taught at Leiden University and was the IIAS Professor of Asian History at Erasmus University Rotterdam and a fellow of the Netherlands Institute for Advanced Study at the Royal Netherlands Academy. Professor Ngo is currently the editor of the journal *China Information* (SSCI-indexed) and co-editor of the *Journal of Contemporary Asia* (SSCI-indexed). He also edits two book series on Governance in Asia (NIAS Press) and Global Asia (Amsterdam University Press).

Jildiz Nicharapova holds a Master's and Ph.D. degree in Political Sciences from Sciences Po Aix en Provence, University Aix-Marseille, France. Since September 2019 Jildiz is a Director for Academic Affairs of Technical School of Innovation American University of Central Asia, Bishkek, Kyrgyz Republic. Between 2015 and 2019 Jildiz was a Head of Research Office and Associate Professor at American University of Central Asia, Bishkek. Between 2012 and 2014 she worked at Academy of Public Administration under the President of Kyrgyz Republic as Associate Professor and Chair of Academic Development Council. From 2009 and 2018 Jildiz worked as Associate Professor at Kyrgyz National University School of International Relations.

Tiago Soares Nogara is a Ph.D. candidate in Global Studies at Shanghai University (上海大学) and in Political Science at the University of São Paulo (USP). He holds a M.A. in International Relations from the University of Brasília (UnB) and a B.A. in Social Sciences from the Federal University of Rio Grande do Sul (UFRGS).

Vassilis Ntousas is Head of European Operations for the Alliance for Securing Democracy programme of the German Marshall Fund of the US (GMF). His research interests lie in European foreign policy and the European Union's global engagement. Prior to joining GMF, he was the Senior International Relations Policy Advisor at the Foundation for European Progressive Studies in Brussels, where he led the foundation's global research, advocacy, and strategic convening work. In 2019–2020, he held the Stavros Niarchos Foundation Academy fellowship at Chatham House, where he remains an Academy Associate with the institute's Europe programme. He is the author of several policy papers and regularly comments on global affairs for international media outlets. He is also the co-editor of two books published by Routledge, *The European Union and China's Belt and Road: Impact, Engagement and Competition* (2021) and *EU Climate Diplomacy: Politics, Law and Negotiations*

(2018). Ntousas holds an M.Sc. in International Relations from the London School of Economics and a B.A. in International Relations and Politics from the University of Sheffield.

Roopinder Oberoi is Fellow at Institute of Eminence, Delhi School of Public Policy and Governance (DSPPG) and a Professor at the Department of Political Science, KMC, University of Delhi. She received a Ph.D. in political science from the University of Delhi. In 2012, she was awarded a postdoctoral research fellowship by the University Grant Commission of India. She has authored and edited several books: *Corporate Social Responsibility and Sustainable Development in Emerging Economies*, Lexington Publisher, USA, 2015, *Globalization Reappraised: A false Oracle or a talisman?* Vajpeyi, D and Oberoi, R, Lexington Books, USA, 2017, *Revisiting Globalization: From Borderless to Gated Globe*, Springer, UK, 2018, and *Social Enterprise in the Higher Education Sector*, Cambridge Scholars Publishing 2020, *Contestations is Global Civil Society* (Emerald Elgar, 2022). Her forthcoming book is *Disentangled vision on higher education: Preparing the generation next—* Peter Lang Publishers, Bern, Switzerland (2022). She has published more than 40 articles in peer-reviewed journals and 26 chapters in international books. She is an editor of *Social Responsibility Journal* (UK). She completed an international project on Social Enterprise and Higher Education awarded by the UK-India Education and Research Initiative UKIERI, British Council (2017–2020). She is a visiting research fellow at the University of Huddersfield UK from 2020. She is part of RC35 IPSA. She is the founder of the Centre of Innovation and Social Enterprise (CISE), KMC, University of Delhi, and the Young Leader Policy Discourse Forum (YLDPF). She is also a coordinator and convenor of the 180DC KMC chapter. Her areas of specialization include political science, public policy, public administration, global governance, CSR, social enterprise, and higher education.

Kimberly Orinx is a teaching assistant at UCLouvain (Belgium), a researcher at the Centre for International Crisis and Conflict Studies (CECRI), and a Ph.D. candidate in political sciences, specializing in international relations. Her research focuses on cognitive warfare and strategic culture.

Harsh V. Pant is a Professor of International Relations with King's India Institute. He is Vice President, Studies and Head of the Strategic Studies Programme at Observer Research Foundation, New Delhi. He is also Director (Honorary) of Delhi School of Transnational Affairs at Delhi University. Professor Pant has been a visiting professor at the Indian Institute of Management, Bangalore; a visiting fellow at the Center for the Advanced Study of India, University of Pennsylvania; a visiting scholar at the Center for International Peace and Security Studies, McGill University; a visiting professor at O.P. Jindal Global University, Sonipat; a visiting professor at Banaras Hindu University, Varanasi; and an emerging leaders fellow at the Australia-India Institute, University of Melbourne.

Diego Pautasso holds a degree in Geography from the Federal University of Rio Grande do Sul (UFRGS), a master's and doctorate in Political Science from UFRGS. He is currently Professor of Geography at the Military College of Porto Alegre. He is a contributor to the Specialization in Strategy and Contemporary International Relations at UFRGS, as well as the Study Groups on Security and International Politics, the Brazilian Center for Strategy and International Relations and the Brazilian Center for African Studies at UFRGS; the UEPB Asia-Pacific Study and Research Group; the UFSM State Capacity, Security and Defense Study Group; the PUC Minas Medium Power Research Group; and the UECE Nationality Observatory. He works in the areas of International Relations and Economic Geography research, focusing on the BRICS' development experiences, especially China and South–South relations. He is the author of the book *China and Russia in the Post-Cold War*.

Rui P. Pereira holds an M.A. in European Studies from the Portuguese Catholic University (2006–2008) and Postgraduate Degrees in Modern China (ISCSP/UTL, 2003) and International Economic Relations (ISEG/UTL, 2001–2002). He has a degree in International Relations from Lusíada University of Lisbon (1989–1994). He completed FORGEP—Training in Public Management for Middle Managers in the Public Service (National Institute of Administration, 2009) and the National Defense Auditors Course (National Defense Institute, 2008–2009). He is currently the Head of the International Relations Division at the Directorate General for Economic Activities—Ministry of Economy. He is the Focal Point of the Forum for Economic and Trade Cooperation between China and the Portuguese-Speaking Countries (Macau Forum). He is a Founding Member of the Observatory of China—Association for Multidisciplinary Investigation of Chinese Studies in Portugal, and a Member of the Association of Friends of the New Silk Road. Most recent publications: Pereira, R. (2020), "China e África: Uma Parceria de Cooperação Estratégica ou Uma (Progressiva) Relação de Dependência? A Problemática da Dívida Africana," Revista Relações Internacionais, No. 65, Instituto Português de Relações Internacionais; Pereira, R. (2020), "China and the Portuguese Atlantic: The BRI's last puzzle piece," co-authored with Tavares da Silva, J., in The Belt and Road Initiative—International Perspectives on an Old Archetype of a New Development Model (Leandro, F., Duarte, P.—editors), Palgrave Macmillan, Singapore.

Margarida Proença is a Full Professor of Economics, University of Minho (Portugal), holding a Jean Monnet Chair in European Economy. She has been the dean of the College of Business and Economics for several years, and vice-rector of the University of Minho. She is a recipient of several research grants and fellowships. Margarida Proença was also a Professor at the University of Macau (China), and as well in other universities in Portugal, Brazil, Angola, Russia, and Ukraine. Her research interests focus on new international trade and industrial economics.

Nida Rahman is a Ph.D. and M.Phil. in Economics from Department of Economics, Aligarh Muslim University, Aligarh, India. Her area of research is Foreign Direct Investment and Regional Trade arrangements. She has been associated with many projects of ICSSR (Indian Council of Social Science Research) and is currently working in the capacity of Young Professional at the ASEAN-India Centre of Research and Information System for Developing Countries (RIS), New Delhi, India. Prior to the current engagement, she has worked as a Policy Researcher in the Food and Agriculture Organization, India Office (FAIND). Additionally, she has a brief stint in the Indian Institute of Foreign Trade (IIFT) as a Research Associate. Her latest publications include "Do Trade and Poverty Cause each other? Evidence from BRICS," *Global Journal of Emerging Market Economies*, 14(1), pp. 9-31, 2022. She has also published a book review "World Trade and Development Report 2021: Trade, Technology and Institutions WTO@25: The Way Forward" in the *Journal of Asian Economic Integration*, volume 4(1).

Mohd Nayyer Rahman is working as an Assistant Professor in the Department of Commerce, Aligarh Muslim University, India. His area of research is international economics, international business, and applied econometrics. He completed his training on regional trade agreements (RTAs) in the times of pandemic from United Nations-Economic and Social Council of Asia-Pacific (UN-ESCAP), Asia-Pacific Commission, Thailand, in 2021. His research publications have covered empirical evidence on BRICS studies, causality relationship of macroeconomic variables and Latin American countries, to name a few. He became a BRICS energy author in 2020 for BRICS Youth Energy Association, Moscow and his articles are published therein. His scientific membership includes the UNCTAD Virtual Institute, United Nations, The Econometrics Society, US, Chinese Economist Society, China and European Economic Association, European Association.

Muhamad Azwan Abd Rahman is a Research Fellow at the Institute of Malaysian and International Studies (IKMAS), Universiti Kebangsaan Malaysia (UKM). He is also an Associate Fellow at the Tun Mahathir Mohamad Institute of Thought (IPDM), Universiti Utara Malaysia (UUM). He has also contributed his expertise on development studies, the particular subject matter of Malaysia, Indonesia, and China–Southeast Asia in several books impact journals, chapters in books, magazines, newsletters, keynotes, speaker, moderator, panelist, facilitator, national and international forum, and national media.

Valéria Lopes Ribeiro received her Ph.D. degree from the International Political Economy, from Federal University of Rio de Janeiro. She also received a Master's degree in economics the Federal University of Santa Catarina, and a Bachelor of Economics from Federal University of Uberlândia. She is Professor and researcher at Federal University of ABC, in São Paulo, Brazil. Her current research interests are the chinese economy and chinese relations with peripheral countries. Her latest publications include: "Chinese Expansion in Africa in the Twenty-First Century: Characteristics and Impacts." In: Paris Yelos; Sam Moyo; Praveen Jha. (Org.). *Reclaiming Africa Scramble and Resistance in the 21st Century*. 1ed.Cingapura: Springer, 2019, v., p. 33-49.; "Los cambios geoeconómicos y políticos mundiales y su impacto en la crisis brasileña reciente. " In: Fernández, V. R.; Carlos Antônio Brandão; Ordoñez, Sergio. (Org.). América Latina ante el cambio geoeconómico-político mundial: entre la crisis de hegemonía y las nuevas asimetrías del Sur global. 1ed.Ciudad del Mexico: Ediciones del Instituto de Investigaciones Económicas, 2020, v., p. 20.

Priscilla Roberts received her B.A., M.A., and Ph.D. degrees from King's College, Cambridge, where she was one of the first women admitted. She is currently an

Associate Professor of business at City University of Macau and Associate Director of the university's Asia-Pacific Business Research Centre. A recipient of numerous research grants and fellowships in the US, Great Britain, Australia, Canada, Hong Kong, and Macau, she has published 30 sole-authored, edited, and co-edited books and numerous articles, focusing upon modern international history, AngloAmerican relations, and Asian-Western relations in the twentieth and twenty-first centuries, as well as the field of American Studies. Her recent books include (with Odd Arne Westad) *China, Hong Kong, and the Long 1970s: Global Perspectives* (2017); *The Arab-Israel Conflict: A Documentary and Reference Guide* (2017); *The Cold War: Interpreting Conflict Through Primary Documents* (2018); (with Spencer C. Tucker) *Middle East Conflicts from Ancient Egypt to the 21st Century: An Encyclopedia and Document Collection* (2019); and (with Spencer C. Tucker) *The Cold War: The Definitive Encyclopedia and Document Collection* (2020).

Anabela Rodrigues Santiago is a Ph.D. student of Public Policies at University of Aveiro (Portugal) and she has received a Master's in Chinese Studies (Economy and Politics). Anabela is also a researcher in Chinese health public policies and global health governance. Currently, she is working on a project related to Chinese investments in Europe's agri-food sector—COST Action 18215/CHERN—China–Europe Relations Network. Anabela Santiago is member of European Association of Chinese Studies and the Associação Amigos da Nova Rota da Seda—Portugal.

Natacha Santos is an International Project Manager trainee working with the preparation and management of European proposals and projects. Natacha Santos has a bachelor's in History at the Faculty of Arts and Humanities of the University of Porto and a master's in International Relations at the School of Economics and Management of the University of Minho (Portugal). Her interests include the People's Republic of China, the geopolitics of the Arctic and Antarctica, Nordic countries, among others. She also is the communications assistant of the Arctic Yearbook, a repository of critical analysis on the Arctic region.

Giorgio Romano Schutte Ph.D. Associate Professor in undergraduate studies on International Relations and Economics and graduate studies on International Relations (PRI) and World Political Economy (EPM) at the Federal University ABC (UFABC). His research fields are in International Political Economy, Geopolitics of Energy, China and Brazil Foreign Policy. With work experience in trade unions, local and federal government. Author of A dinâmica dos investimentos produtivos chineses no Brasil (2020) and The challenge to US hegemony and the "Gilpin Dilemma," RBPI, 2021. He is a research fellow of the National Council of Technological and Scientific Development (CNPq) since 2018.

Martina Basarac Sertić is a senior research associate at the Economic Research Division of the Croatian Academy of Sciences and Arts. In 2020, she was elected an associate member of the Croatian Academy of Sciences and Arts. As an external associate and an assistant professor, she participated in teaching the courses Croatian Economy, Economic Policy and Economics of Education at the Department of

Macroeconomics and Economic Development and the course Statistics at the Department of Statistics (at the Faculty of Economic & Business, University of Zagreb). She currently teaches the course on Sustainable Development and Natural Resources at the Faculty of Economics at the University of Zagreb. She has published about 50 scientific and professional articles and is the editor of numerous Proceedings. Her research focuses on the macroeconomics, sectoral competitiveness, and sustainable development.

Juan Shan is Associate Professor of Marketing, Vice-Director of Department of Business Administration at School of Management, Shanghai University. She got her Ph.D. degree in Management from University Aix-Marseille III in 2011. Her research interests include brand management, luxury and counterfeited luxury consumption behaviour, and business innovation in emerging economies. She has published around 50 articles in international and Chinese refereed journals and conferences.

Michael Snowden is a senior lecturer in Mentoring Studies in the School of Human and Health Sciences at the University of Huddersfield. His research interests lie in the field of pedagogy, mentorship, social enterprise, curriculum enhancement, and learning. Michael is a regular speaker at national and international conferences concerned with the development of pedagogical strategies in various contexts. He is currently the national coordinator for the "Flexible and Innovative pedagogy" group of the Universities Association for Lifelong Learning and acts as Special Advisor to a number of agencies including the European Mentoring and Coaching Council. He is a member of the Editorial Board for the *International Journal of Coaching and Mentoring*.

Vu Quy Son (武貴山) is a research fellow at the Institute of Chinese Studies (ICS), Vietnam Academy of Social Sciences (VASS). He graduated with his Ph.D. degree from Graduate Institute of East Asia Studies, National Chengchi University, Taiwan by the support of Taiwan Scholarship. He obtained an M.A. degree in the Program of Oversea Chinese studies in Department of Chinese as a Second Language at National Taiwan Normal University. His study interests focus on China's foreign policy, China's Belt and Road initiative, the relations of China and its periphery states, especially, the relations of China and Southeast Asia countries, including Vietnam–China relations. Otherwise, he pays attention to the conflicts on the South China Sea, and the relations of China and Southeast Asia countries in respect of South China Sea issues. He is currently, a Research Fellow at Institute of China Studies—Vietnam Academy of Social Sciences.

Federico Steinberg is Senior Analyst at the Elcano Royal Institute, Lecturer in Political Economy at Madrid's Universidad Autónoma, and Special Adviser to the High Representative for Foreign and Security Policy and Vice President of the European Commission Josep Borrell. He holds a Ph.D. in Economics from the Universidad Autónoma, an M.Sc. in Politics of the World Economy from the London School of Economics and a Master's in International Affairs from Columbia University. He has been a consultant for the World Bank in Washington, DC, Ghana, and Bolivia, and has worked at the Executive Office of the Secretary-General at the United Nations headquarters in New York. He is also a frequent contributor to the Spanish and international media and has been invited to deliver speeches in more than 10 countries. He has published extensively in journals such as *Economic Systems Research, Journal of Common Market Studies, Review of International Political Economy of New Political Economy.*

Robert Sutter is Professor of Practice of International Affairs at the Elliott School of George Washington University (2011–2022). He also served as Director of the School's main undergraduate programme involving over 2000 students from 2013–2019. His earlier fulltime position was Visiting Professor of Asian Studies at Georgetown University (2001–2011). A Ph.D. graduate in History and East Asian Languages from Harvard University, Sutter has published 22 books (four with multiple editions), over 300 articles, and several hundred government reports dealing with contemporary East Asian and Pacific countries and their relations with the US. His most recent book is Chinese Foreign Relations: Power and Policy of an Emerging Global Force Fifth Edition (Rowman & Littlefield, 2021). Sutter's government career (1968–2001) saw service as senior specialist and director of the Foreign Affairs and National Defense Division of the Congressional Research Service, the National Intelligence Officer for East Asia and the Pacific at the US Government's National Intelligence Council, the China division director at the Department of State's Bureau of Intelligence and Research and professional staff member of the Senate Foreign Relations Committee.

Paulo Elicha Tembe received a Ph.D. in Economics and International Business from the Southeast University, China (2016). Since 2019, he is the head of Economics and Development Studies Department at Joaquim Chissano University, Mozambique. He is currently Professor of International Political Economy; International Trade Law; Maritime Economics and Services at Joaquim Chissano University; as well as researcher at the Center for International Strategic Studies, and Professor of Business Internationalization at Universidade Técnica de Moçambique (UDM).

Luis Tomé is Full Professor at Autónoma University of Lisbon-Portugal, where he is the Director of the International Relations Department and of its research unit OBSERVARE-Observatory of Foreign Relations. Senior Researcher at the Portuguese Institute of International Relations (IPRI). Researcher in the areas of International Relations, Geopolitics and Security Studies specialising in the Euro-Atlantic, Eurasian and Asia-Pacific regions, he is the author of more than a dozen books and numerous essays and articles published. He has also been a visiting professor at several universities in Europe, the Middle East, the United States, and Asia. He was Special Adviser for International Relations and Counter-Terrorism in the Office of the Portuguese Minister of Home Affairs; Special Advisor to the Vice-President of the European Parliament; and NATO Researcher.

Dorothée Vandamme is visiting lecturer (Ph.D.) in international relations at the UCLouvain and lecturer at the University of Mons, in Belgium. She is research fellow at the Centre for International Crisis and Conflict Studies (CECRI) and at the European Foundation for South Asian Studies (EFSAS). Her research focuses on geopolitical and sociological evolutions of Afghanistan and Pakistan, and contemporary security issues.

Xuheng Wang is a Ph.D. Candidate in International Politics and Conflict Resolution in the School of Economics (FEUC) from the University of Coimbra and the Centre for Social Studies (CES). She holds a Master's degree from the School of Economics (FEUC)—University of Coimbra (Portugal) and a Bachelor's degree from the School of business—Macao Polytechnic Institute (China). Currently, she works on the research on the role of Macao in Sino-Portuguese-speaking countries relations based on paradiplomacy in China.

Ana Isabel Xavier is Associate Professor of International Relations at Universidade Autónoma de Lisboa, lecturing also at ISCTE, Air Force Academy, and Military University Institute (Portugal). She is a full Researcher and deputy director of OBSERVARE—observatory of foreign affairs and Associate Researcher of the Centre for International Studies (CEI-IUL) and CISDI-UM—Security and Defence Research Centre of the Military University Institute. She holds a Ph.D. in International Relations from the Faculty of Economics, University of Coimbra (specializing in European Studies), a Master's in Sociology of Development and Social Transformation (2006), and a degree in International Relations (2003) from the same Faculty. She has a post-graduation degree (2005) in Human Rights and Democratization from the University of Coimbra Law School. Since 2015, she is a regular trainer at the European Security and Defence College "CSDP Training for Eastern Partnership Countries" and "CSDP Reflection Seminar." From March 2015 to February 2017, she served as Deputy Director in the Directorate of National Defence Policy (MoD) having been awarded the Cruz del Mérito Aeronáutico con Distintibo Blanco (August 2016) by the Government of Spain and the First Class National Defence Medal (December 2017). She is a regular analyst of international politics in the Portuguese public television (RTP) with a weekly insight to European affairs (Jornal 2, RTP2).

Gangfeng Zhang is an Associate Professor at the Department of Leadership and Organization Management, at the School of Management, Zhejiang University. His research focuses on cross-cultural management, international business. He has conducted applied research projects on Chinese firms' internationalization in Europe or Africa. Prof. Zhang is a coauthor of the 3rd edition of "Managing Across Cultures" textbook together with Schneider, Barsoux, and Stahl. He received his Ph.D. from University of Trento in Sociology and Social Research.

Dennis Zuev is Assistant Professor at University of Saint Joseph, China where he teaches Macau Studies and Comparative Asian Studies. He is a Senior Researcher at CIES-ISCTE, IUL, Lisbon, Portugal and an associated researcher at Instituto do Oriente, University of Lisbon, Portugal. He is also a member of the Urban Transitions Hub at University of Lisbon. Together with Gary Bratchford he is a co-editor of the Palgrave book series "Social Visualities." His book *Urban Mobility in Modern China: The case of the E-Bike* was published in 2018, and co-authored book *Visual*

Sociology: Practices and Politics in Contested Spaces in 2020. He is on editorial board of the journals *Mobilities* (Taylor & Francis) and *Visual Studies* (Taylor & Francis).

List of Figures

Chapter 6

Fig. 1 Three-level model of the interplays in people-to-people exchanges (*Source* Adapted from Leandro, 2019a, p. 41) 100

Chapter 12

Fig. 1 The green credit balance of the big five state-owned commercial banks 2011–2018 (*Source* Yin et al. [2021]. Data was compiled from CSR Report and Annual Report from ABC, BOC, BOCom, CCB, and ICBC, 2011–2018) 194

Fig. 2 The green performance of china's major banks (*Source* Author's own visualization based on the data provided by the report prepared by Choi and Escalante [2020] for Climate Policy Initiative. The original data is from Wind Data. ICBC: Industrial and Commercial Bank of China, ABC; Agriculture Bank of China, CCB; China Construction Bank, CITIC; China International Trust Investment Cooperation, CDB; China Development Bank, ADBC; Agricultural Development Bank of China) 195

Fig. 3 Financial Commitments of CDB and EXIM 2008–2019 (*Source* Global Development Policy Center [2020]) 196

Chapter 14

Fig. 1 Impact of socio-economic factors and health outcomes (*Source* County Health Ranking, 2014) 226

Chapter 16

Fig. 1 Visual model of Chinese forums (*Source* Authors) 262

Chapter 18

Fig. 1	BRI representations (*Source* Jac Depczyk [2018])	292
Fig. 2	BRI representations (*Source* Sebastien Thibault [2020])	293
Fig. 3	Common destiny. Collage of screenshots from the documentary "common destiny" (*Source* https://www.youtube.com/watch?v=YgUJX5X_xNE&t=102 s. The Belt and Road EP 1 Common Destiny CCTV [2022])	297
Fig. 4	Study the Soviet Union's advanced economy to build up our nation (*Source* Ding Hao [1953]. Landsberger Collection. Retrieved on January 2022, from www.chineseposters.net)	298

Chapter 19

Fig. 1	GDP current international dollar (PPP), China and US (*Source* WB [2021])	311
Fig. 2	GDP per capita current international dollar (PPP), China and US (*Source* WB [2021])	311
Fig. 3	Total factor productivity, constant national prices (2017 = 1) (*Source* Data from Penn World Table, version 10.0, 2021 [vd. Feenstra et al., 2015])	312
Fig. 4	Share of World Merchandise Exports—China and US 1948–2020 (%) (*Source* WTO [2021])	314
Fig. 5	Countries of the Belt and Road Initiative, 2021 (*Source* The author, based on information from Reconnecting Asia Project Database [see Annex 1])	314

Chapter 24

Fig. 1	Chinese Outbound tourism according regions in Europe (*Source* Statista.com [2021])	419
Fig. 2	Chinese arrivals in Europe (*Source* China Tourism Academy & HCG Travel Group)	420
Fig. 3	Destinations of Chinese tourists in 2019 (*Source* CTA and HCG [2019])	420

Chapter 25

Fig. 1	Countries of Eurasian Economic Union (*Source* Retrieved on December 2021, from https://www.silkroadbriefing.com/news/2019/08/22/russias-eurasian-economic-union-free-trade-area-gets-first-foothold-europe)	435
Fig. 2	Countries of the Belt and Road Initiative (*Source* Retrieved on December 2021, from https://www.cfr.org/blog/countries-chinas-belt-and-road-initiative-whos-and-whos-out)	435

Fig. 3	Belt and Road Initiative's Silk Roads (*Source* Retrieved on December 2021, from https://www.beltroad-initiative.com/belt-and-road/)	436
Fig. 4	Land and maritime routes of the Belt and Road Initiative (*Source* Bloomberg)	437
Fig. 5	China: Military Bases Abroad (*Source* Retrieved on January 2022, from https://www.bloomberg.com/graphics/2018-china-navy-bases/)	438
Fig. 6	China disputed territories (*Source* UNCLOS, CIA)	439
Fig. 7	Evolution of the military spending since 2007 (*Source* SIPRI/Statistica)	440
Fig. 8	The 10 Countries with the highest military expenditure in 2019 (*Source* Retrieved on December 2021, from https://www.sipri.org/commentary/topical-backgrounder/2020/russias-military-spending-frequently-asked-questions)	440

Chapter 27

Fig. 1	The evolution of India's connectivity initiatives (*Source* Authors)	466
Fig. 2	The concentric circles of India's policy playbook for challenging the BRI (*Source* Authors based on Fig. 1)	469

Chapter 29

Fig. 1	Latin America and the Caribbean—exports to and imports from China (1995–2019) in billions of US dollars	497

Chapter 31

Fig. 1	The siege against China (*Source* Arancón [2014] and El Orden Mundial in Pautasso, D., Nogara, T. S., & Ribeiro, E. H. Mural Internacional, Rio de Janeiro, Vol. 11, p. 8)	538

Chapter 32

Fig. 1	Major categories of AI applications in military 2020 (*Source* Klijn and Okano-Heijmans [2020])	547
Fig. 2	Examples of AI applications in military 201820192020 (*Source* Authors, based on Mori [2018]; Masuhr [2019]; and Klijn and Okano-Heijmans [2020])	548

Chapter 40

Fig. 1   Cumulative Chinese investment and the degree of globalization (Ten ASEAN States, 2005~2018) (*Note* Bars are the cumulative amount of Chinese investments since 2005. Lines are the value of the KOF Globalization index. *Source* American Enterprise Institute [2021], Dreher [2006] and Gygli et al. [2019]) 677

Fig. 2   Cumulative Chinese investment and the trade flows between the Ten ASEAN States, China, and Other Countries, 2001~2020 (*Note* Bars are the cumulative amount of Chinese investment since 2005. Solid lines are the trade volume between the country and China. Dash lines are the trade volume between the country and other countries. *Source* American Enterprise Institute [2021] and United Nations [2021]) 679

Fig. 3   Cumulative Chinese investment and net FDI inward of the ten ASEAN States, 2005~2020 (*Note* Bars are the cumulative amount of Chinese investment since 2005. Solid lines are the net FDI inward. *Source* American Enterprise Institute [2021], ASEAN [2021], and World Bank [2021]) 680

Fig. 4   Cumulative Chinese investment and the ten ASEAN states' number of material cooperation events with China and other countries, 2002~2019 (*Note* Bars are the cumulative amount of Chinese investment since 2005. Solid lines are the number of material cooperation events between the country and China. Dash lines are the number of material cooperation events between the country and other countries. 2021 *Source* American Enterprise Institute [] and ICEWS [2020]) 682

Chapter 44

Fig. 1   The diplomatic game of the two Chinas and the UNSCR 2758 (*Source* Aurégan [2016b]) 738

Fig. 2   The Chinese spatial fix in Africa (*Source* Author) 746

Chapter 45

Fig. 1   Origin of financing for Chinese-built power projects in Sub-Saharan Africa (*Source* International Energy Agency [2021]) 757

List of Graphs

Chapter 23

Graph 1	Shares in world's GDP in PPP, 2017 (*Source* Eurostat [2020]) ...	394
Graph 2	Economic growth trends for China compared to the world (*Notes* (f) forecast. *Source* International Monetary Fund [2020])	394
Graph 3	China is the world's manufacturing superpower. Top 10 countries by share of global manufacturing output in 2019*. (*Note* *Output measured on a value-added basis in current US dollars [USD]. *Source* Richter [2021])	395

Chapter 27

Graph 1	GDP for world's 6 larger economies (*Source* Data sourced from the World Bank [2021])	465

Chapter 31

Graph 1	Chinese investments and construction agreements in countries of the new silk road between 2013 and 2020 (in the US $billion) (*Source* American Enterprise Institute (AEI) [2020] Authors' elaboration)	533
Graph 2	Distribution of Chinese investments agreements on the new silk road (2013–2020) (*Source* AEI [2020] Authors' elaboration)	533

Chapter 36

Graph 1	Latvia's trade of goods with China and Belarus, 2013–2020, EUR (*Source* National Statistical System of Latvia [2021])	614
Graph 2	Latvia's foreign direct investment with China and Belarus, 2013–2020, EUR (*Source* Bank of Latvia [2021a, 2021b])	615

List of Tables

Chapter 6

Table 1	Respective expressions in Chinese and English of the concept of people-to-people exchanges in bilingual Chinese official narratives	96
Table 2	People-to-people exchanges involving China	101

Chapter 10

Table 1	The "Chinese Dream": two key economic activities	156

Chapter 11

Table 1	This Matrix shows potential locations of diverse partnership types and relationships that can be used for building scenarios for the Belt and Road project. The partnership types use axes of explicitly expressed trust and unease or anxiety concerning BRI project contract terms, conditions, and the potential level of Chinese involvement in the project host country or region. No complete and independent research and analysis have so far been published but the set of Partnership Power Relationship Asymmetry scales shown below are adapted to potentially suit some empirical testing of those relationships among the negotiators and public and private sector members of the BRI partnerships if researchers are granted access to do so by the BRI leadership	181

Chapter 12

Table 1	FDI Stocks Outward, % of GDP, 2020	190
Table 2	Milestones in China's green financing	192
Table 3	Green bond issuance by ICBC	194

Chapter 13

Table 1	Overview of the background of the interviewees	207
Table 2	Data structure	209

Chapter 16

Table 1	Comparative analysis of Chinese forums	258

Chapter 19

Table 1	Competing perspectives on hegemony and leadership	304
Table 2	Per capita income levels and growth rates across regions (BRI Countries)	316
Table 3	Impact of the Belt and Road Initiatives on GDP	317

Chapter 23

Table 1	Relative nominal growth in major indicators of China's economic strength	396
Table 2	Direct contribution of travel and tourism to GDP in leading countries worldwide—2019 (in USD billion)	399
Table 3	EU trade with China top 5- HS Sections of Imports in 2019	401
Table 4	Top 10 client and supplier countries of the EU27 in merchandise trade (value %) (2020, excluding intra-EU trade)	402

Chapter 24

Table 1	European destinations—Chinese tourism flows in 2019	422
Table 2	Assessment of yearly turnover of 1000 $ from tourism expenses	425

Chapter 29

Table 1	Chinese investments in Chile under the BRI	506

Chapter 33

Table 1	Economic figures regarding trade, imports, exports, and FDI	566

Chapter 35

Table 1	Malaysia trade according to the destination of selected countries (2001–2011) (amounts in RM million)	593
Table 2	Malaysia–China trade, 2010–2017 (amounts in US$billion)	593
Table 3	China Gross Domestic Product (US$)	594
Table 4	Chinese investment in Indonesia	597
Table 5	Majors Chinese capital projects in the Philippines	601

| Table 6 | Strong and weak relationship dimensions in the context of G2G, B2B + P2P between Malaysia and Indonesia with China | 604 |

Chapter 37

Table 1	Dynamics of the region covered by BRI (2019)	625
Table 2	BRI: Achievements in the Asian region	626
Table 3	Variables description	628
Table 4	Hausman test output	634
Table 5	Random effect panel regression output	634
Table 6	Summary of hypotheses testing	636

Chapter 40

| Table 1 | BRI investments in the 18 East and Southeast Asian countries, 2013/10–2021/6 | 674 |

Chapter 44

| Table 1 | Chinese intervention modalities in Africa (2003–2018) | 744 |

Chapter 1
Introduction

Paulo Afonso B. Duarte, Francisco José Leandro, and Enrique Martínez Galán

Every book has a story and a purpose. Every research is a collective discovery and a commitment designed to capitalize on our ability to share. It is a collective purposeful attempt to push for advancement, keeping in mind that the risk of error looms behind its conclusions.

This manuscript, *The Palgrave Handbook of Globalization with Chinese Characteristics*, is no exception. It is the result of a combination of three major factors: first, the convergence of the research agendas of its editors around the Belt and Road Initiative (BRI) and the idea of China as a re-emerging global power; second, the topicality and timeliness of the BRI itself, which is, for many, the most complete geo-economic transformational initiative since the Cold War—in terms of what it brings together, such as economics, trade, connectivity, access with consent, soft power, new material and immaterial flows, first-hand networks of agents, new perspectives of multilateralism, innovation, new financial mechanisms, new spatial development initiatives, fresh debates about the future of the international order—and is a project that has been described as "unique" in the history of mankind; and third, the fact that the BRI has been conceived to contribute substantial, decisive globalization pathways, and is, at the same time, itself, a product of globalization.

P. A. B. Duarte (✉)
Universidade do Minho & Universidade Lusófona, Braga & Porto, Portugal
e-mail: duartebrardo@gmail.com

F. J. Leandro
University of Macau, Macau SAR, China
e-mail: eurofor1152@gmail.com

E. M. Galán
Asian Institute of Management, Manila, Philippines
e-mail: EGalan@aim.edu; enriquegalan@cesa.iseg.ulisboa.pt

Center of African and Development Studies of ISEG-Lisbon School of Economics and Management, Lisboa, Portugal

© The Author(s), under exclusive license to Springer Nature Singapore Pte Ltd. 2023
P. A. B. Duarte et al. (eds.), *The Palgrave Handbook of Globalization with Chinese Characteristics*, https://doi.org/10.1007/978-981-19-6700-9_1

This volume is the result of a Palgrave's invitation in 2020 to adapt a previous, rather modest book proposal into this more comprehensive handbook of 24 single-author chapters, 23 co-authored chapters (47 Chapters in total), with the participation of 80 international authors, 31 females, 49 males, and 10 junior researchers, representing 42 different academic, governmental, non-governmental, and research institutions. The editors sincerely hope to have been able to respond not only to Palgrave's challenge (for which we are grateful), but also to the natural curiosity of a worldwide audience that wants to learn and be actively involved in developments related to the BRI and its impacts on globalization. We, therefore, dedicate this book to readers around the world, who have directly or indirectly encouraged us to contribute to the global academic debate. After all, we share the understanding that only a serious academic debate can contribute with credibility to deconstructing myths and stereotypes, and overcoming psychological barriers that often generate distorted perceptions of reality.

We understand globalization as a set of enduring multidimensional and self-generational processes that transform the global structure. These processes are caused by major technological and social advancements, and involve extensive networks of complex interdependencies across continents linked through (increasing) material, immaterial, intense, and permanent flows of interconnectedness, resulting in time compression, integration, expansion of elements of power, de-territorialization of stakeholders, and a certain individual consciousness of the world as a whole. Economic globalization plays a major role in global security, and the march towards economic globalization and a multipolar world is irreversible, as is the march towards digitalization. The current trend towards development and cooperation will likely remain unchanged, but international strategic competitions and contradictions are intensifying, global challenges are becoming more prominent, and security threats are becoming increasingly integrated, complex, and volatile.[1]

In this line of reasoning, and keeping the BRI in mind, this manuscript seeks, therefore, through a multidimensional and transversal approach to distinct complementary areas of study (e.g., economics, markets, policies, international relations, geopolitics, history, narratives, sustainability, and the COVID-19 pandemic), to deepen the debate on China vis-à-vis globalization. This book's originality lies within its hybrid and holistic approach, offering the readers a complementary, intertwined, and multi-level perspective on a multilateralism with Chinese characteristics. Based on the contribution of scholars from all continents, different walks of life, diverse genders, dissimilar educational backgrounds, and professional experiences, this volume envisages to help the readers to comprehend, recognize, identify, discuss, argue, and form their own opinions and consequently contribute to the ongoing debate about this Chinese role in the globalization process. That is the reason why the editors have made the call to forgo a concluding chapter. Nevertheless, we identify five characteristics crafting the Chinese contribution to the globalization process, namely: (1)

---

[1] Leandro, F. (2018). *Steps of greatness—The geopolitics of OBOR* (p. 193). City University of Macau.

Size—China will be the first global power with a population over 1 billion inhabitants. The continuous improvement of living standards will put the planet under pressure in relation to basic resources such as water, energy, and food—The access to resources will be a major area of concern for China and this fact will bring the consequences of the Chinese development to virtually everywhere on Earth; (2) **Political Culture**—China is a self-centric and domineering political actor, influenced by strong traces of Confucianism, which will be influencing global governance initiatives—The political culture will influence the new multi-partner networks for a global constructivism as well new ways of multilateral cooperation; (3) **Positioning and Access**—Located in the Eurasian Rimland, China dominates its offshore island (-chain) and this fact is contributing to make China a leading regional actor—Its neighbourhood and Asia will be the main concern for China in the context of global affairs; Moreover, access with consent seems to be a major driver of Chinese material and immaterial contribution to globalization, creating land and maritime economic corridors, as well as, access supporting points, and physical alternatives to the global key choke points; (4) **Human Social Capital**—On one hand, the future of human social capital emphasizes material pragmatism, quantitative approaches to science, technology and digitalization; on the other hand, it undervalues qualitative research, abstract thinking, intercultural literacy, and relational social skills—The new generations of Chinese leaders will be educated to exercise a pragmatic action, driven by economic security, encouraged by the success of lifting millions out of the poverty line between 2000 and 2022; (5) **Opposing Narratives**—The idea of a Globalization with Chinese Characteristics triggers a number critical storylines, nurturing concerns related to the cause-roots of some of the Chinese initiatives, particularly the BRI, expressing ultimate apprehensions in relation to global economic security.

This book places particular attention on the BRI's two-way, multifaceted relationship with the European Union and the US, due to their geo-economic and geopolitical relevance, as well as to their smart power and capacity to transpose their domestic standards into world standards. Furthermore, the book discusses the impact of the BRI within a shifting balance of world powers, and the displacement of the global economic centre of gravity from Europe to the Asian continent, characterized by competing views between Western and Chinese cultures, values, norms, standards, narratives, and, ultimately, power perceptions.

This book is addressed, above all, to those who are curious about China and Chinese foreign policies. The target audience is expected to already have some background and interest, and through a comprehensive and multidisciplinary approach, this new academic anthology endeavours to deepen the reader's knowledge on the BRI. The research goals of the chapters collected here have been: (1) to seek to recognize how the BRI can help China forge a less West-centric globalization, thereby reflecting the heterogeneity and active stance of the Asia–Pacific; (2) to identify opportunities and challenges pertaining to U.S.–China relations and dynamics; (3) to elucidate the impacts of Sino-European Union relations under the framework of the BRI; (4) to deepen analysis on the BRI as a global initiative capable of fostering, via multilateralism, China's momentum in world affairs; (5) to recognize the importance of digital corridors as well as the Health Silk Road as complementary tools to expand Chinese norms and global influence, especially in the post-pandemic world.

As editors we neither dictate nor impose our views; we simply let globalization reveal its own complexity, in particular how the Chinese perspective that underlies the BRI can open up new horizons for a globalization not limited to Western instances or spheres. Indeed, the BRI will likely induce a silent transformation of not only the physical and digital arteries, but also the modes of transaction in international trade. However, one should not mistakenly expect tangible results to arrive in the immediate future, as globalization with Chinese characteristics is a long-term and ongoing project. Such has long been China's stance; The Chinese project their subsistence in time and space with a perspective and rigour rather distinct from the West's immediacy and general short-term visions. Chinese re-emergence is inextricably connected to a worldview that has spanned millennia and is well expressed via the concept of *tianxia* ("everything under the heavens"), which in the era of the ancient Silk Road governed a world divided into concentric circles. Today, *tianxia* embodies the Chinese Dream and, together with the Community of Common Destiny which underlies the BRI, presupposes a return to the logistical arteries of the past that once connected China to the West. These arteries are, however, no longer only terrestrial but are also maritime, and, more recently, electronic, and they connect China to not only the West but also beyond. Indeed, this new made-in-China globalization puts China back at the centre—as China once was in the distant past—but this time with the benefits of the advanced technologies of the global village era.

To better illustrate the contours of this new globalization that China is gradually outlining, we have divided this handbook into three parts. The first part analyses the manifestations and impacts of the BRI vis-à-vis global governance. The second part addresses the mutual perceptions and the changing contours of globalization from the perspective of relations between China and major emerging powers. The third part explores the potential of the BRI as a cross-border initiative, from the perspective of how China influences the world's regional and sub-regional systems, namely, Europe, Asia, the Middle East, Africa, the South Atlantic, and the Polar regions.

* * *

1 Part I

Part I comprises 18 Chapters, organized into three groups: Chapter 2, presented by Priscilla Roberts (UK; City University of Macau, China), begins by revisiting the BRI in historical perspective, while stressing the lessons of China's economic statecraft since 1949. More precisely, Roberts seeks to highlight and explore the parallels between China's external economic policies in its first three decades and those of the

BRI era. This chapter sets the tone for all that follow, especially due to the ability of research to revisit history from today's perspective. In Chapter 3, Adele Carrai (Italy; New York University Shanghai, China) analyses Chinese endeavours to build a new vocabulary of global governance. The author aims to show how the Chinese conception of global governance has evolved, reflecting profound changes within its society and how it has continued to emphasize sovereignty, national characteristics, and the right to development. Offered by Cátia Miriam Costa (Portugal; ISCTE-UL), Chapter 4 discusses how the Chinese authorities' discourse on the Belt and Road Initiative contributes to globalizing the overall Chinese international discourse itself. In addition to its a review of literature, the chapter analyses how the Chinese political discourse has become international and has begun to go global. Chapter 5, presented by Luís Tomé (Portugal; OBSERVARE, Universidade Autónoma de Lisboa), assesses whether and how the BRI fits within (a new) Chinese grand strategy. The main argument is that the BRI can be dissociated from neither China or the Chinese Communist Party's objectives, interests, or values, nor Chinese foreign and security policies, and should be framed both in light of these broader interests and policies and in conjunction with other Chinese initiatives of recent years. Chapter 6, co-authored by Yichao Li (China; Centro de Estudos Internacionais—ISCTE-UL, Portugal), Francisco José Leandro (Portugal; City University of Macau, China), and Paulo Guilherme Figueiredo (Portugal; City University of Macau, China), puts forward a model of analysis combining international relations and constructivism to understand the Chinese concept of people-to-people exchanges (P2P). The authors further envisage to consider the function of people-to-people exchanges through the perspectives of state-to-state cooperation, corporation-to-corporation exchanges, and people-to-people interactions, especially in terms of the frames, instruments, and characteristics of exchange.

Chapter 7, co-authored by Carmen Amado Mendes (Portugal; Macau Scientific and Cultural Centre, Lisbon) and Xuheng Wang (China; University of Coimbra, Portugal), analyses if the BRI has shaken the existing world order, and whether or not it will alter global governance. According to the authors, although the initiative has succeeded in promoting Beijing's new view on global order, it has yet to produce any fundamental changes in world order. In Chapter 8, Julie Yu-Wen Chen (Chinese Taipei; University of Helsinki, Finland) explores the importance of local agency in understanding what she calls the glocalization of the BRI. Chen points out that China cannot simply push forward its BRI projects without making compromises with local/international conditionality, practices, and norms. Hence, the globalized influence of China through the BRI is not a uni-directional process. Instead, China is learning to adjust to local norms and other international (competing) standards to improve the chances of its BRI projects being accepted and realized in various foreign soils. In Chapter 9, Jorge Tavares da Silva (Portugal; University of Aveiro) and Rui Pereira (Portugal; Ministry of Economy) examine the political evidence between rhetoric and practice underlying the Chinese agenda on the World Economic Forum. In particular, the authors' aim is twofold: to explain how China and its BRI contribute to world economic wealth, and to assess China's real involvement and integration within the global economy (including the digital dimension). Chapter 10, co-authored by Jamie P. Halsall (UK; University of Huddersfield), Ian G. Cook (UK; Liverpool John Moores University), Michael Snowden (UK; University of Huddersfield), and Roopinder Roberoi (India; University of Delhi), concentrates on the interplay and implications of the COVID-19 pandemic on China and global power shifts. The authors endeavour to assess whether COVID-19 could restructure the global order. The chapter further explores how one understands the "new era," what is China's ambition in global leadership, and what response can be expected from its key competitor, the US.

In Chapter 11, Tom Cockburn (New Zealand Institute of Management; The Leadership Alliance Inc.) debates the ability of the BRI to enact an inclusive globalization in a volatile, uncertain, complex, and ambiguous (VUCA) context while emerging from COVID-19. The author concludes by recommending that scenarios are a useful means for leaders and the public to understand and to actively engage with the dynamic complexity of the VUCA environment where the former, "business-as-usual" approach is no longer a valid option. In Chapter 12, Berna Kirkulak-Uludag (Turkey; Dokuz Eylul University) discusses China's ambition in promoting green finance for the BRI. In this context, the author investigates the green credit and green bond policy of Chinese banks, and emphasizes the role of state-owned banks in greening the BRI. Chapter 13, co-authored by Anna Lupina-Wegener (Poland, University of Applied Sciences and Arts Western Switzerland), Franck McDonald (UK; CIBUL-University of Leeds), Juan Shan (China; Shanghai University), Gangfeng Zhang (China; Zhejiang University), and Güldem Karamustafa-Köse (Switzerland/Turkey; University of Lausanne), investigates the liability of emergingness pertaining to emerging market banks that are internationalizing to emulate banks of advanced economies. The study contributes to research on emerging market companies, notably by revealing the complexity related to effective embedding in host market institutional systems. The study also highlights differences between how Brazilian and Chinese banks might address this challenge. In Chapter 14, Anabela Rodrigues Santiago (Portugal; University of Aveiro—FCT-CCCM fellow) seeks to understand the Chinese's approach to health governance as a tool to achieve global governance in an evolving global order. As such, she analyses the successive health reforms undergone since 2003, as well as the contours of the Health Silk Road integrated into the BRI.

In Chapter 15, Dorothée Vandamme (France; University of Louvain, Belgium), Tanguy Struye de Swielande, and Kimberly Orinx (Belgium; University of Louvain) explain how China aims to institutionalize and ultimately impose its concept of governance in the cyber domain. The research shows that Beijing adopts an integrated vision—combining socialization through governance with power politics—and that a digital policy is at the heart of China's political objective to dominate world affairs in 2049. Chapter 16, co-authored by Pedro Paulo dos Santos (Portugal; City University of Macau, China), Yichao Li (China; Centro de Estudos Internacionais-ISCTE-UL, Portugal), and José Alves (Portugal; City University of Macau, China), sets out to understand the organizational structure of Chinese forums and how they serve the purposes of China's foreign affairs agenda, in order to draw conclusions on whether they are responsible for a new kind of multilateralism. In Chapter 17, Henrique Morais

(OBSERVARE—Universidade Autónoma de Lisboa, Portugal) evaluates the extent to which secular stagnation is leveraging China's rise to world leadership in the coming years, which has clearly been the strategic design of the BRI. The author analyses possible implications in the coming decades of secular stagnation, which is more likely to be present in the US than in China, on the economic side and on global power balances. In Chapter 18, Dennis Zuev (University of St. Joseph, Macau, China and CIES-ISCTE, IUL, Lisbon, Portugal) analyses the visual politics and spatial imaginaries of the BRI. Considering the BRI as a representational discourse, Zuev scrutinizes the immediate materiality of the BRI and the symbolism of its "spectacle." Finally, in Chapter 19, Margarida Proença (Portugal; University of Minho) discusses whether the BRI can shift the centre of gravity of economic activities (namely, industrial productions) and their dynamism from the Atlantic axis to the Pacific.

* * *

2 Part II

The second part of this handbook addresses not only the changing contours of globalization from the perspective of relations between China and major developed and emerging powers—the European Union, India, Russia, and the US—but also their mutual perceptions of each other. This second part is composed of 13 chapters.

The first group of chapters concerns the BRI's role and influence on the European Union and the wider Europe. In Chapter 20, Enrique Feás (Spain; Elcano Royal Institute) and Federico Steinberg (Spain; Universidad Autónoma de Madrid and Elcano Royal Institute) offer a novel view of European Union–China bilateral relationship from the lens of geo-economics and from the European perspective. Drawing on official documents, the chapter deconstructs the concept of European open strategic autonomy vis-á-vis China, explores areas for collaboration and conflict in the realm of economics and global economic governance, and argues that the 2020 Comprehensive Agreement on Investment represents an appropriate way to avoid economic decoupling and foster cooperation. Chapter 21, co-authored by Vassilis Ntousas (Greece; Foundation for European Progressive Studies) and Stephen Minas (China; School of Transnational Law of Peking University), assesses Europe's changing approaches vis-à-vis China in the context of the BRI and the COVID-19 pandemic. The authors provide an overview of the interlinkages between these dynamics in the pre- and post-pandemic periods, and argue that the pandemic may have strengthened the narrative for rebalancing the relationship between Brussels and national capitals on one side, and Beijing on the other, but that this shift has still not translated into meaningful changes in policy terms. In the following Chapter 22, Vladimir Milić (Serbia; Megatrend University Belgrade, Serbia) discusses whether or not China and the BRI constitute new opportunities for Central and Eastern European countries. While the role of China and the BRI in these countries has fallen short of initial predictions, the author concludes, based on case studies of two scenarios, that, on one hand, some of these countries are leveraging their newly forged connections with China to get closer to Western allies and to reaffirm their affiliation with the West; on the other hand, others use them to exert independence from Brussels. Chapter 23, co-authored by Martina Basarac Sertić (Croatia; Croatian Academy of Science and Arts), Anita Čeh Časni, and Kosjenka Dumančić (Croatia; University of Zagreb), focuses on the economic dynamics of Sino-European Union relations, and concludes that there is great untapped potential for trade, investment, and tourism flows between China and the European Union. In Chapter 24, Klodiana Gorica and Ermelinda Kordha (Albania; University of Tirana) review China's contribution to the sustainable development of the European tourism industry. Focusing on interviews with 20 tourism operators in Albania, the authors conclude that, contrary to global misperceptions, Chinese tourists prefer sustainable tourist destinations.

The second group of chapters concentrates on the role of the BRI in Russia and its neighbouring area of influence. In Chapter 25, Ana Isabel Xavier (Universidade Autónoma de Lisboa, Portugal) questions if a greater Eurasian partnership is taking place in the context of the Eurasian Economic Union (EAEU) and the BRI. Her main conclusion is affirmative: Russia and China are cooperating within the Eurasia region to compete for global leadership, as the current status quo (before 24 March 2022) in Ukraine and Chinese Taipei continues to trigger unanimous criticisms from the West. In Chapter 26, Una Aleksandra Bērziņa-Čerenkova (Latvia; Riga Stradins University) assesses the understudied facet of Sino-Russian cooperation in general and the Health Silk Road in particular. Based on a political discourse analysis, the author concludes that Russia's lack of commitment towards the Health Silk Road is consistent with its global approach towards the BRI in general.

The third group of chapters focuses on the role of the BRI in India and its neighbouring countries, particularly Pakistan. In Chapter 27, Harsh V. Pant (India; Observer Research Foundation, New Delhi, India) and Anant Singh Mann (India; Observer Research Foundation, New Delhi, India) assess how India's challenge to the BRI is shaping the global normative consensus. The authors provide a meaningful analysis on the evolution of India's China policy, its impact on Sino-Indian relationship, and how India has collaborated with other smaller nations in providing viable alternatives to the BRI. In Chapter 28, S. Y. Surendra Kumar (India; Bangalore University) discusses India's conundrum and policy options in the context of the BRI's China–Pakistan Economic Corridor (CPEC), arguably the more advanced corridor of the initiative. The author concludes that CPEC endangers India's sovereignty and strategic interests in South Asia and beyond Afghanistan, and weakens India's regional role. However, India's counter-CPEC initiatives have limited impact, as India is unable to put forth an alternative to the BRI because of limited resources. The author concludes that India and China should look at the possibility of taking a selective approach to projects linking Iran, Afghanistan, and other Central Asian countries to the CPEC, which would be a win-win situation for both countries.

The fourth group of chapters addresses the role of the BRI per opposition and rivalry with the US. In Chapter 29, Ana Tereza L. Marra de Sousa, Giorgio Romano Schutte, Rafael F. Abrão, and Valéria Lopes Ribeiro (Brazil; Federal University of ABC, São Paulo) assess the geostrategic rivalry between China and the US in Latin America. In Shakespearian fashion, the authors pose to the region the question: To BRI or not to BRI—i.e., whether or not to allow the Initiative to enter the US' backyard. Unlike most literature on the issue, this chapter uses a holistic approach to combine the political and economic dimensions as well as the interactions between a Chinese push and US pull. The authors assess four case studies (Brazil, Chile, Ecuador, and Panama) and conclude that relationships with the BRI are maturing, the degree of integration and acceptance of the BRI are not a determining factor for explaining the intensity of the relationships, and the US is rapidly elevating its attention towards increasing Chinese presence in the region. In Chapter 30, Robert Sutter (U.S.; George Washington University) discusses why the US opposes China's BRI. The author synthesizes findings of a variety of recent foreign studies on China's statecraft to offer a largely qualitative examination on how China's statecraft in the BRI works against US interests economically, strategically, and in global governance. Sutter bluntly concludes that the BRI legitimates China's predatory growth model, and fosters corruption, authoritarian rule, unsustainable lending, and dependence on China used by Beijing to leverage and control recipient countries. In the succeeding Chapter 31, Diego Pautasso (Brazil; Federal University of Rio Grande do Sul, Brazil) and Tiago Soares Nogara (Brazil; University of São Paulo) discuss the security challenges surrounding the implementation of the BRI, which are inexorably related to the Sino-American rivalry and the systemic transition of the global order. In Chapter 32, in a case study, Mohammad Eslami, Nasim Sadat Mosavi (Iran; University of Minho, Portugal), and Muhammed Can (Turkey; University of Minho, Portugal; King's College London, UK) assess Sino-Iranian cooperation in artificial intelligence as a challenge to U.S.-led globalization. Drawing on strategic documents signed by Iran and China during the last decade and focusing on military and technological agreements between the two countries, the authors find possible avenues to examine the nexus between the increasing importance of emerging technologies and China's attempt to find partners to challenge the US' hegemony.

* * *

3 Part III

The third part explores the potential of the BRI as a cross-border initiative, i.e., from the perspective of how China influences regional and sub-regional economic and political systems. In fact, as its political rationale is access with consent as well as to modify conventional patterns of structural flows connecting markets and production centres, the BRI is seeking a compromise between the notions that borders are sovereign dividers and borders represent opportunities for cooperation for mutual benefits. The third part comprises 15 chapters.

In Chapter 33, Flavius Caba-Maria (Romania; Middle East Political and Economic Institute) addresses any noteworthy implications of China's presence in the Middle East and North Africa: in the wake of the US shifting its presence from Eurasia to the Asia–Pacific, China's diplomatic engagement with developing countries in these regions has been through pursuing mutually beneficial relationships. Its focus on economic and social developments represents a diplomatic line of action with Chinese characteristics. The chapter makes a decisive conclusion: In a region where competition between states remains an issue, and regional states/blocs that often resent each other are locked in global power struggles, China is prudent to be cautious as it tries to avoid the U.S.'s mistakes, which have wreaked havoc in parts of the region and induced rejections of hegemonic power. In Chapter 34, "China–Iran's 25-Year Deal: The Implication for the Belt and Road Initiative and Joint Comprehensive Plan of Action (JCPOA)," Mohammad Eslami (Iran; University of Minho, Portugal) and Joel Anthony Kemie (Nigeria, Research Centre in Political Science (CICP)) offer an important study on China–Iran relations, arguing that for China, its comprehensive strategic partnership with Iran is considered a step for the reconstruction of the Silk Road as well as for promoting the Belt and Road Initiative. This is while Iran sees the present partnership as an alternative for the Joint Comprehensive Plan of Action, which allows the country to neutralize international sanctions and survive in the international system. The author suggests that after the US' withdrawal from the JCPOA and the imposition of new sanctions on Iran's economy, Iranian leadership has taken a step towards the East. Comprehensive Strategic Partnership is one of the most important strategic decisions of Iran during the last years, especially after the failure of the nuclear deal. The country seeks to secure its national interest under new agreements and in cooperation with new countries.

Chapter 35 addresses globalization by looking at the cases of Malaysia, Indonesia, and the Philippines. Co-authored by Muhamad Azwan Abd Rahman and Sufian Jusoh (Malaysia; Institute of Malaysian and International Studies, UKM), the chapter China's New Maritime Silk Road Cooperation: Why Malaysia, Indonesia, and the Philippines are Clings in Disagreement? uses the South China Sea as a main reference point. The authors advance that the different slant and strategies resembling Malaysia, Indonesia, and the Philippines have kept persist the Chinese claimant position in the South China Sea. Therefore, much needs to be done by Malaysia, Indonesia, and the Philippines with China to strengthen ties while competing for influence from other superpowers. In this vein of reasoning, stands the recent regional development on the Australia–UK–US pact (AUKUS). The authors conclude that each ASEAN country should have closer ties with superpowers other than China who can provide greater cooperation. The effectiveness of the BRI policy would be increased if combined with gradual improvements capable to identify cooperation insufficiencies. At the very end of the chapter, the authors make a sharp statement: The twenty-first century Maritime Silk Road can only restore the glory of Asia if it is truly collaborative. In Chapter 36, Māris Andžāns and Una Aleksandra Bērziņa-Čerenkova (Latvia; Riga Stradins University) discuss Latvian perceptions of the Belt and Road Initiative in the context of Latvian relations with China and Belarus. The chapter, entitled "The Belt and Road Initiative and the Uneven Triangle of Latvia, Belarus, and China," draws a sharp conclusion: The Latvia–Belarus–China triangle has proved to be an unstable construct largely because of the overwhelming differences between the partners that run counter to the only one commonality—interest in economic cooperation.

Chapter 37, "Impact of the Belt and Road Initiative on Asian Economies Along the Route," is co-authored by Badar Alam Iqbal (India; Monarch Business School Switzerland) Mohd Nayyer Rahman (India; Aligarh Muslim University), and Nida Rahman (India; Indian Council for Research on International Economic Relations, India). Assuming that the BRI represents a chance for increased trade, investment, and job creation for the Asian economies, the authors examine the potential influence on the growth of Asian economies that are located along the BRI corridors. The chapter reveals that there lacks empirical evidence to suggest that bilateral trade with China corresponds directly to economic growth for these Asian economies, but such lack of evidence may simply be due to the BRI's recent origin. In Chapter 38, Linda Calabrese (Italy; ODI and King's College London, UK) and Olena Borodyna (Ukraine; ODI) examine BRI-induced economic risks and risk perceptions in the Kyrgyz Republic. The main research question assumes that Chinese investment and infrastructure projects have the potential to support the transformation of the Kyrgyz economy, but these opportunities come with risks. The chapter maps these potential threats and economic risks faced by Kyrgyzstan in the context of the BRI, declaring the existence of threats to sustainable development, perceived in various ways by Kyrgyz stakeholders. The risk perceptions affect how the stakeholders react and shape the government's responses. Furthermore, it seems that Kyrgyz response to the BRI and to the Chinese presence in the country in general lacks a clear approach. While the BRI can potentially benefit the Kyrgyz economy by providing the much-needed infrastructure for economic diversification, it is unclear whether the government has a clear strategy on how to exploit these potential benefits.

In the ensuing Chapter 39, Jildiz Nicharapova (Kyrgyz Republic; Technical School of Innovation American University of Central Asia) discusses the Belt and Road Initiative's economic impact on Central Asia, particularly in Kazakhstan and Kyrgyzstan. The chapter centres its discussion on the infrastructure projects that have been implemented in the two countries and their economic impacts. In the conclusion, the author assumes a sharp and unequivocal stance by asserting that Kazakhstan is the country benefiting the most from the BRI and that China has not contributed to employment or job creation through infrastructural development, and China's investment is not welcomed by many Central Asian countries. Chapter 39, entitled "Sino-Iranian Cooperation in Artificial Intelligence: A Potential Countering Against United States Hegemony" and co-authored by Mohammad Eslami, Nasim Sadat Mosavi, and Muhammed Can (Iran; University of Minho, Portugal), offers an analysis on Sino-Iranian relations. Drawing on strategic documents signed by Iran and China during the last decade and focusing on the military and technological agreements between the two countries, this chapter seeks to find possible avenues to examine the nexus between the increasing importance of emerging technologies and Chinese-Iranian cooperation on AI. The authors argue that Iran and China, two anti-US countries, are trying to form a potential capability to oppose US hegemony by cooperating in artificial intelligence.

Chapter 40, presented by Chien-wu Alex Hsueh (Chinese Taipei; National Chengchi University), discusses how the BRI affects globalization in Southeast Asia. Hsueh analyses the correlation between Chinese investments and the different dimensions of globalization in the 10 states of the Association of Southeast Asian Nations (ASEAN), and concludes that Chinese investment projects, connected with the BRI or not, may lead to different globalization paths in different countries. In Chapter 41, Vu Quy Son (Vietnam; Institute of China Studies—Vietnam Academy of Social Sciences) presents a study on Vietnam's attitude towards the BRI amid globalization. The chapter adopts Vietnam's perspective on its historical relations with China and its understanding of Chinese history and culture. The author concludes that Vietnam is adopting a cautious policy towards China's BRI, a reticence that reflects Vietnam's expectations on developing cooperative partnerships with China. From Vietnam's perspective, the BRI creates both opportunities and challenges: the opportunities may enhance Vietnam–China cooperative relations, but the challenges cast a shadow of doubt on whether or not Vietnam should show peaceful, steady friendliness towards China.

From Asia, we move on to Africa and South Atlantic. In Chapter 42, Laura C. Ferreira-Pereira (Portugal; University of Minho) and Paulo Afonso B. Duarte (Portugal; University of Minho) attempt to answer the question: Why does the South Atlantic matter in China's global policy? The authors argue that China's stance in the South Atlantic has witnessed a critical transition. There was a shift from a traditional, exclusively economic-oriented outlook to a more security-based, geostrategic posture. This cannot be dissociated from China's proactive global foreign policy agenda and has important implications particularly for Brazil. Furthermore, both researchers assert that the South Atlantic offers a twofold advantage: On the one hand, African and Latin American shores provide China with complementary energy, food, and mineral sources. On the other hand, it might be relevant in helping China to relieve its Eastern flank from pressures from the US. Chapter 43, also jointly co-authored by João Paulo Madeira (Portugal; Uni-CV-University of Cabo Verde), Ivete Silves Ferreira (Cabo Verde; INGT-National Institute of Territorial Management), and Nilton Fernandes Cardoso (Cabo Verde; Uni-CV-University of Cabo Verde), discusses the Belt and Road Initiative's impact and implications for Africa–China relations. The authors envisage to understand how China has sought to articulate the BRI within its African policy. They acknowledge that the BRI is increasingly seen as a catalyst for regional competitiveness and economic integration. In this context, China has invested in several areas mainly in East Africa, a central region for the Maritime Silk Road. The conclusion clearly suggests that China is going through a process of establishing strategic partnerships abroad, especially with countries associated with the Economic Belt and the Maritime Silk Road.

In Chapter 44, Xavier Aurégan (France; Catholic University of Lille) discusses the unequal modalities of China's intervention in Africa. The author uses a double statistical and analytical analysis to deconstruct this relationship officially presented as "win-win." In reality, the modalities of Chinese intervention in Africa are highly concentrated, limited to a few partners, and generate (new) inequalities and extraversions. Ultimately, the New Silk Roads are the instrument of a paradigm shift in China's Africa policy. The chapter further concludes that China has created a "win-lose" rather than a "win-win" partnership by exporting its excess productive capacity and tying infrastructure financing to the signing of contracts with Chinese enterprises. In Chapter 45, Paulo Tembe (Mozambique; University Joaquim Chissano) continues the discussion on Chinese presence in Africa, arguing that Africa's thirst for infrastructure has given rise to a contemporary phenomenon that makes China a trading partner. The author argues that evidence has shown a continuous Sino-Africa cooperation, one where African resources are exchanged for infrastructure construction or Chinese capital for infrastructure in Africa. This model has its tangible and popular impact known as the Angolan model. It is a feasible model for the continent due to its weak ability to return invested capital. However, Africa can lose out on this type of model if the negotiation with China is done individually rather than jointly.

Chapter 46, jointly presented by Laura C. Ferreira-Pereira (Portugal; University of Minho), Paulo Afonso B. Duarte (Portugal; University of Minho), and Natacha Santos (Portugal, University of Minho), takes us to the extreme regions of our planet and explores the major reasons underlying China's polar initiatives. The chapter, "Understanding Engagement and Implications for the Arctic and Antarctic," offers a comparative study focusing on the interests, strategies, and implications of Chinese activities in the North and South Poles against the backdrop of geopolitical competition for natural resources and geostrategic influence. The authors argue that there are new and promising prospects for China as a "near-Arctic state." At the same time, although geographically distant, Antarctica has also become close to the heart of China's global ambitions. Here, a "nest" is being prepared with decades in advance so as to ensure the best arrangements possible after 2048. Ultimately, the North and South Poles have complemented each other in China's rising engagement in polar politics. In the final Chapter 47, Julie Yu-Wen Chen (Chinese Taipei; University of Helsinki, Finland) contemplates the importance of local agency to the glocalization of the Belt and Road Initiative. Using a qualitative analysis of the literature, the chapter contends that such glocalization or Sino-localization cannot be used as a counter-argument to globalization. The local variances are constitutive of the wider globalization forces. Given the nascent nature of most BRI projects, globalization and glocalization in the BRI context are slowly developing. Because the locals always have the power to negotiate the kind of BRI that they wish to partake in, it can be concluded that both China-led globalization and Sino-localization are forces that have yet to come. China-led globalization is still not taking shape at full scope and speed.

* * *

As we—the editors—conclude preparing this manuscript, we are deeply saddened by the horrific events taking place in the sovereign state of Ukraine, appalled by the violent scenes of an armed conflict, that impoverished all humankind. We therefore dedicate this volume to honouring the immense, tragic suffering of all human beings caught by the rage and irrationality of this unacceptable carnage. Peace is the only way forward.

June, 2022
The Editors.
Paulo Afonso B. Duarte,
Francisco José Leandro,
Enrique Martínez Galán

Part I
Manifestations and Impacts of the BRI vis-à-vis Global Governance

Chapter 2
The BRI in Historical Perspective: PRC Economic Statecraft Since 1949

Priscilla Roberts

1 Introduction

The term "economic statecraft" is increasingly employed to describe China's use of economic resources to pursue objectives spanning the political, economic, and strategic spheres. In the 1980s, it was popularized by the Princeton academic David A. Baldwin (1985), who viewed the use of assorted economic measures, whether sanctions (negative) or inducements (positive), as a less risky alternative to nuclear diplomacy and military confrontation. With the People's Republic of China (PRC) still in the early and tentative stages of paramount leader Deng Xiaoping's reform and opening up policies, the country's use of economic statecraft was then considered too limited even to feature significantly in this volume. By contrast, in a new edition published thirty-five years later (Baldwin, 2020), an afterword by Ethan B. Kapstein (2020, pp. 391, 405–428) discussed at length China's extensive and still expanding use of economic statecraft in the intervening period.

The novel prominence of Chinese economic statecraft in Baldwin's updated edition was just one example of an increasingly extensive literature focusing upon the manner in which, since the late twentieth century, China has deployed economic instruments to accomplish both diplomatic and economic objectives (e.g., Blackwill & Harris, 2016; Blanchard, 2018; Blanchard & Ripsman, 2013; CSIS, 2018; Li, 2017; Norris, 2016, 2021; Roberts, 2022; Yang with Liang, 2019). In his pathbreaking study of recent Chinese economic statecraft, William J. Norris (2016, p. 6) suggests that "China's sophisticated use of economics in its foreign policy is still a fairly recent phenomenon." Shu Guang Zhang (2002, 2014), however, discerns major elements of continuity in the manner in which, since the establishment in 1949 of the PRC, China's Communist leaders have conducted economic statecraft. Close scrutiny of how since at least the early 1900s Chinese leaders sought to use economic leverage as a foreign policy instrument suggests that, despite the change of

P. Roberts (✉)
Faculty of Business, City University of Macau, Macau, China

regime in 1949, the antecedents of contemporary Chinese economic statecraft may date back still earlier, drawing on China's experiences since the beginning of the twentieth century.

This chapter therefore seeks to set China's current deployment of economic statecraft in a broader historical perspective, framing it first within the *longue durée* of how other powers have in the past deployed economic instruments to achieve international objectives. The chapter then places China's recent use of economic statecraft within the longer history of China's own employment of such tools since around 1900, focusing on the elements of both continuity and change in China's recent economic statecraft, and seeking to discern whether such new undertakings as the Belt and Road Initiative (BRI) and Asian Infrastructure Investment Bank (AIIB) represent major alterations in both the strategy and scale of China's ambitions. Briefly, it seeks to explain why China's current economic ventures have encountered significant international pushback. The chapter concludes somewhat speculatively, offering some reflections on both the strengths and successes and the flaws and weak points of China's current international economic policies.

2 Economic Statecraft: An International Historical Perspective

The use of economic power in international affairs is a venerable and time-honoured tradition. Often, it has been employed as an adjunct to military power, to reward good service or maintain fidelity. In the fourteenth century BCE, Pharaoh Akhenaten of Egypt received letters from a vassal ruler, King Burnaburias of Kassite Babylon, professing deep loyalty and requesting lavish amounts of gold and other valuables to cover unspecified expenses (Sayce, 1890, pp. 63–67). Since at least the sixteenth century, powerful nations engaged in war have subsidized weaker allies, while seeking to deny their enemies access to valuable resources. The War of 1812 between Great Britain and the US was, indeed, prompted by British efforts to prevent the Americans from trading with Napoleonic Europe.

A century later, German submarine attacks on American shipping, intended to cut off vital war supplies shipped to the Allied powers from the US, were the proximate cause of US entry into World War I. Both Great Britain and the US assisted their wartime allies financially. What was new following this conflict was the formulation—by European and American bankers and officials—of quite a wide variety of ambitious and wide-ranging economic proposals to facilitate European recovery from wartime devastation. Most envisaged the deployment in multiple European states over a period of years of American capital from both private and governmental sources (Berghahn, 2014; Hogan, 1977; Orde, 1990; Tooze, 2014). Although these schemes proved largely abortive, at least in their original form, they were the intellectual ancestors of the post-World War II Marshall Plan. During the 1920s, proponents of these projects were more successful in designing and raising substantial loans—funded largely by private bankers, in association with international central banking institutions and the League of Nations—intended to restore currency stability and promote economic recovery and growth across Europe, financial ventures that governments of the time broadly supported and endorsed (Ahamed, 2009; Blackwill & Harris, 2016, pp. 158–159; Boyce, 2009; Cohrs, 2006; Costigliola, 1984; Frieden, 2020; Kent, 1989; Leffler, 1979; Rosenberg, 2000; Steiner, 2005; Tooze, 2014). Unfortunately, this economic architecture proved too flimsy to withstand the pressures of the Great Depression. Many held its collapse responsible for the ensuing international strife and rivalries that ultimately triggered World War II.

As the post-World War I territorial settlement unravelled during the 1930s, League of Nations member states plus the US sought to impose economic sanctions on nations designated as aggressors, in 1935 against Italy's invasion and annexation of Abyssinia, and from 1931 onwards against Japan's actions in first annexing Manchuria and then in 1937 launching a full-scale invasion of China. When World War II began in Europe in September 1939, for over two years the US remained formally neutral. America only formally joined the war in December 1941, after Japanese aircraft bombed the US Pacific Fleet in its Pearl Harbor naval base in Hawaii, whereupon Germany and Italy likewise declared war upon the US. Several months earlier, however, in spring 1941, the US introduced a massive programme of economic aid to nations—including not just Great Britain and its dominions but also China and soon the Soviet Union—that were resisting the incursions of the Axis powers, Germany, Italy, and Japan. Popularly known as Lend-Lease, and vastly extended once the US entered the war, this undertaking was effectively the forerunner of post-World War II military security programmes. Initially presented as a means of keeping the conflict at a distance from American shores by assisting other nations that were already battling US opponents, Lend-Lease continued throughout the war, as the US leveraged its position as the world's strongest economic power into military assistance for its wide array of allies (Blackwill & Harris, 2016, pp. 159–160; Dobson, 1986; Grieve, 2014; Weeks, 2004).

With victory in sight, from 1943 onwards the US took the lead in setting up international institutions—the International Monetary Fund and World Bank (International Bank for Reconstruction and Development)—that were intended to provide the investment capital for post-war recovery, while preventing any recurrence of the international economic strife and rivalries that many leading policymakers held responsible for precipitating World War II. Solid economic foundations were now perceived as fundamental to any lasting peace settlement, an essential complement to the new United Nations (UN) organization that was designed to maintain international order and stability (Frieden, 2020; Helleiner, 2014; Rauchway, 2015; Schild, 1995; Steil, 2013).

The rapidly developing Cold War between the Western powers and the Soviet Union soon brought demands for additional measures. For all its protagonists, economics were just as salient as military confrontation in waging Cold War. When the new institutions and ad hoc loans from the US to selected nations proved inadequate to prevent mounting economic difficulties in Western Europe, prompting mounting fears that the continent might succumb to communist domination, the

US launched the Marshall Plan or European Recovery Program (ERP), a multilateral government-sponsored venture intended to rebuild the economies of all non-communist European nations. This ambitious and largely successful undertaking is still considered the high point of US foreign aid programmes. Slightly later, when it became apparent that economic security alone would not suffice to reassure the nervous European governments, this was supplemented by the North Atlantic Treaty Organization (NATO) military alliance (Blackwill & Harris, 2016, pp. 161–163; Frieden, 2020; Hogan, 1987; Killick, 1997; Mackenzie, 2005; Milward, 1984; Pollard, 1985).

In addition, to assist poorer countries, President Harry S. Truman devised the Point Four programme of aid to developing or "Third World" nations. American policymakers perceived modernization, economic development, and "nation-building" as crucial to winning the loyalties of newly independent decolonizing Asian and African nations and reinforcing US hegemony in Latin America, objectives that foreign aid and the expansion of free trade were expected to promote (Eckes, 1995; Eckes & Zeiler, 2003; Ekbladh, 2010; Kunz, 1997; Latham, 2000, 2011; Shenin, 2000; Taffet, 2007; Zeiler, 1992). Cold War concerns and the commitment of American policymakers to liberal free trade norms likewise helped to facilitate both Japan's economic "miracle" of the 1950s and South Korea's emergence in the 1960s as one of Asia's most dynamic economies (Brazinsky, 2009; Forsberg, 2014). More recently, however, several retrospective works suggested that military spending was undesirably prominent as a driver of the Cold War strategy and political economy of the US (Cardwell, 2014; Oatley, 2015).

3 China's Economic Statecraft Since 1900

In a 2016 study sponsored by the Council on Foreign Relations, the leading US foreign policy think tank, two former State Department officials argued that, whereas the US had once excelled at "the systematic use of economic instruments to accomplish geopolitical objectives," the American employment of "geoeconomics" had become "a lost art," relegated to a back seat while "the United States too often reaches for the gun instead of the purse in its international conduct." Meanwhile, China, Russia, and other hostile states were deploying economic tools with great skill to promote their own global objectives while intimidating potential adversaries and effectively undercutting the international position and standing of the US (Blackwill & Harris, 2016, p. 1). The authors' apprehensions were triggered in considerable part by the increasingly assertive international economic footprint of China in the early twenty-first century, as the PRC recycled its massive profits from foreign trade into overseas aid and investments, while frequently imposing punitive sanctions and embargoes on both countries and businesses that refused to toe Beijing's line on numerous international issues.

By the second decade of the twenty-first century, China's use of economic diplomacy was attracting ever greater attention, thanks to the aggressiveness the PRC displayed in subjecting states that offended it to heavy commercial pressure; its eagerness to expand Chinese investment in and aid of various kinds to poorer states; and not least, the announcement of ambitious high-profile global schemes to remake the world's commercial and financial infrastructure on Sino-centric lines. Yet Chinese efforts to deploy such economic leverage as it possessed to its own international advantage were far from new. Shu Guang Zhang (2002, 2014) has taken the lead in exploring how from 1949 onward, Chinese Communist Party (CCP) leaders sought to use economic statecraft both to escape sanctions imposed on them by Western nations, especially the US, and to enhance the PRC's international influence and prestige.

The use of such tactics by China's rulers had still earlier antecedents. Following the 1904–1905 Russo-Japanese War, victorious Japan claimed the special strategic, political, and economic rights, including naval bases and construction and control of the Chinese Eastern Railway, that Tsarist Russia had since 1895 forcibly exercised in China's northeastern region of Manchuria. Attempting to counter Japan's demands for exclusive predominance in Manchuria, for several years Chinese officials encouraged a consortium of Western bankers to invest in railroads in the area, negotiations that were ultimately stymied by the 1911 Chinese Revolution and the difficulty of reaching terms acceptable to both the governments and the bankers involved (Hunt, 1973).

In the interwar years, largely spontaneous popular boycotts of goods produced by Britain, Japan, and other foreign nations with special quasi-colonial privileges in the country accompanied diplomatic clashes and confrontations between China and other powers. More formally, in the 1930s the Nationalist government urged the League of Nations and Western states in particular to respond to Japan's seizure of Manchuria in 1931 and the invasion of China that Japan launched in 1937 by banning both loans to and trade with Japan. Somewhat ironically, as the US gradually broadened sanctions in 1940 and 1941, intending these to deter Japan from expanding its ongoing war in China to elsewhere in Asia, the imposition in June 1941 of a total embargo on American exports of oil and petroleum to Japan proved the trigger that less than six months later impelled Japanese military leaders and politicians to attack not just the US fleet at Pearl Harbor, but all Western interests in Asia (Barnhart, 1987; Utley, 2005).

Competing political forces in China also solicited outside funding and assistance from sympathetic external allies. From the mid-1930s onward, Chiang Kai-shek's Nationalist government sought financial and ultimately military assistance from the US. Chinese officials lobbied aggressively for funds, cultivating friends and allies in the US, many linked to the missionary community, who raised money for China and put political pressure on their own government to impose sanctions on Japan. In the late 1930s, the US extended loans to China, supposedly secured by Chinese exports of tung oil and tungsten ore. From 1941 onward, China tapped into Lend-Lease funds (Blackwill & Harris, 2016, p. 159; Grieve, 2014; Xiang, 1991). At the end of World War II, the Kuomintang government won further substantial assistance from the United Nations Relief and Reconstruction Administration (UNRRA). In the later 1940s, the influence in Congress of the China lobby ensured that, in an exercise in geographic elasticity. China received funding under the Marshall Plan, and was likewise included in US legislation providing aid to Korea (Price, 1955). On the other side of the Chinese divide, from the 1920s onwards the CCP turned for fraternal assistance to the Soviet Union, leader of the international socialist camp. Soviet aid was a significant factor in the continued survival of the CCP and its ultimate victory in the Chinese Civil War, effectively counterbalancing the US funds directed to Chiang and his supporters (Westad, 1993, 2003).

In the most detailed studies to date of PRC economic statecraft during the Cold War years, Zhang (2002, 2014) describes how the Communist victory brought new challenges in this field. China had a dual role, being both a "sender" and a "target" of foreign aid. Overall, throughout this period, Chinese economic statecraft remained as earlier primarily defensive in nature, intended to mitigate the severity of the economic and political isolation to which the US in particular sought to condemn the PRC, or to boost China's ideological standing and political influence in the developing world. As a recipient, during its first decade the PRC benefited from various Soviet aid programmes, involving not just grants, loans, and technical assistance, but also the dispatch of Russian expert advisers. With amounts of Soviet funding smaller and the terms on which loans were granted often less generous than the Chinese would have wished, ill-feeling over these programmes may even have contributed to the acrimonious break in 1959, when all Soviet advisers were withdrawn.

One major objective of Chinese economic policies was to mitigate the impact of the international sanctions regime introduced at US insistence in the early 1950s, and intended to restrict both China's external trade and its access to "strategic" raw materials, manufactured goods, and foreign exchange. In response, China attempted to develop two-way trade with business interests in Western Europe, Canada, Australia, and non-communist Asia, and to persuade the governments involved to ignore the controls on dealings with China. The British-run capitalist enclave of Hong Kong, conduit for the bulk of China's scarce foreign exchange and much of its external trade, was a particularly significant loophole. So to a lesser degree was Portuguese-administered Macau, a much smaller territory whose livelihood largely depended upon its role in smuggling gold and other commodities to China, a situation American officials wryly tolerated (Garver, 2016, pp. 581–584; Zhang, 2002, 2014).

Beyond sanctions-busting, China sought to use foreign aid to developing countries both to enhance its own prestige, and also to win support and useful votes in international organizations, especially the UN. In the 1960s, following the Sino-Soviet split, China deliberately offered economic assistance to other countries as it campaigned to compete with and undercut the Soviet Union (Brazinsky, 2017; Friedman, 2015). This strategy backfired rather dramatically with the two largest recipients, Albania and Vietnam, once budgetary difficulties compelled China to cut back its largesse during the 1970s. In each case, in a virtual replay of the earlier Sino-Soviet breakdown, an ostensibly friendly and fraternal relationship rapidly degenerated into hostile recriminations and vitriolic abuse. Being too poor to be a generous donor was itself an international liability, limiting China's capacity to offer economic inducements to win over external powers (Zhang, 2014).

Zhang (2014, pp. 314–322) highlights a number of general principles dating back to the time the PRC was established, that seem to have remained consistent themes ever since. Overall: "Chinese leaders seemed to have understood and to be culturally familiar with the political instrumentality of economic power." The earliest goal of Chinese economic statecraft, one that continued throughout the 1980s and 1990s, was to "use... economic and political measures to counter and break foreign economic sanctions." Even when they sought foreign assistance, moreover, Chinese leaders "consistently tried to strike a balance between maximizing economic benefits from and minimizing political influence by the sender." The PRC habitually used "economic inducements" in its efforts "to cultivate 'friendly' relations with carefully selected countries, Communist and non-Communist alike." As it sought "economic leverage over the targets of its aid, Beijing never hesitated to employ negative economic measures when inducement proved ineffective." Lastly, as China's modernization became an overriding objective, "Beijing in the end turned development into a strategic objective of its economic statecraft." Ultimately, Zhang argues:

> China's reforms at home and its opening to the West under Deng and his associates brought to Beijing more opportunities than ever before for practising its brand of economic statecraft, and more challenges as well. While opening the Chinese market to the Western world, the PRC seized the opportunity to manipulate the expectations and realizations of business shares and gains by the industrial countries in pursuit of its foreign policy objectives.

These principles—often magnified by the massive increase in China's own economic resources—distinctly resemble those followed by Beijing until the present. Their successful implementation required a reasonably sophisticated understanding of the workings of target institutions, businesses, organizations, and governments. Norris (2016, pp. 11–14), who defines economic statecraft as "the state's intentional manipulation of economic interaction to capitalize on, reinforce, or reduce the associated strategic externalities," highlights how, since "commercial actors, rather than states per se, conduct the majority of international economic activity," in many cases such tactics involve "the intentional attempt of the state to incentivize commercial actors to act in a manner that generates security externalities that are conducive to the state's strategic interests." When dealing with Japan, Western Europe, and on occasion the US, Zhang (2014, p. 329) argues, "PRC leaders expected the anticipated economic reward for a changed foreign policy to first hook the business community, which would then put pressure on the government."

Since at least the early 1970s, for example, China's leaders had assumed that Beijing could pressure and manipulate Western governments into changing their policies by offering or withholding the economic advantages of access to the China market. In 1970, China cancelled its customary large purchases of wheat from Australia for three years, switching to Canadian and other suppliers. The underlying purpose was to motivate Australian farmers to pressure their government to accord the PRC diplomatic recognition, as Canada had already done, and also to lift existing bans on exports of nonstrategic materials to China. When these tactics proved successful, Beijing not unnaturally interpreted the outcome as evidence that such negative economic statecraft was reliable and effective (Thomas, 2017, pp. 208–212). Throughout the 1970s and 1980s, the crush of foreign businesses keen to sell to China and invest there, usually backed by governments equally eager to facilitate these deals, offered further proof positive that on the international scene, economic advantage would usually trump all other concerns.

Zhang (2014, pp. 261–270, 278–289) noted how, facing some CCP and popular scepticism over just how effectively China had previously deployed foreign aid, and indeed whether the still developing PRC could afford to spare funds for this purpose, in 1979 Deng Xiaoping decreed that, while China would continue to extend such assistance, there would be greater emphasis upon using it efficiently and on ensuring that China as well as recipient countries gained some tangible benefit from these expenditures. From then on, Beijing sought to use its limited aid resources to ensure that China received long-term advantages in some form. Likewise, foreign trade was now considered part of China's diplomatic portfolio, as were promoting Foreign Direct Investment (FDI) and transfers of advanced technology, and boosting Chinese exports of manufactured goods. Within a decade, growing Chinese prosperity meant the PRC could provide aid to additional recipient countries in Africa, Asia, and Latin America, with the number rising to 83, up from 64 in the early 1980s. China also participated in numerous UN training and technical assistance projects, contributing expert personnel.

Given that their nation had spent almost thirty years largely isolated from the liberal-capitalist West, China's leaders and cadres displayed considerable skill in learning the ropes, negotiating favourable business deals, gaining access to Western technology, and familiarizing themselves with key economic and political institutions, notably the World Bank, the International Monetary Fund, and the Asian Development Bank (ADB) (Haga, 2022; Zhang & Zheng, 2022). In doing so, they were facilitated by a level of goodwill which initially surprised many Chinese, that meant elites and even ordinary people were prepared to welcome representatives of mainland China and facilitate its integration into the prevailing global order. Until June 1989, which dramatically changed its public image, China generally enjoyed a good press. Thereafter, assisted by a range of outside businesses, institutions, and political allies, including the World Bank, ADB, leading Hong Kong-based businesses associated with the American Chamber of Commerce in Hong Kong, international oilmen, and other elites, Beijing was nonetheless able to navigate the far more difficult and turbulent international currents of the 1990s, its external clout and political influence increasing as China's economy grew at near breakneck speed (Garver, 2016, pp. 530–534; Hamilton, 2021, pp. 266–278). The tactics Chinese leaders employed when fighting the international sanctions imposed on them and battling to retain their lucrative Most-Favoured-Nation trading status in the US were excellent examples of how, in Kapstein's words (2020, p. 426), "China makes deft use of 'fifth columns' of business elites within target countries as part of its economic statecraft, creating pressure points that can act on its behalf." This was indeed a classic Marxist ploy, based on the assumption that in Western polities, capitalist big business ultimately called the shots.

In the aftermath of June 1989, external aid also attained renewed prominence in Chinese foreign policy, part of a strategy of boosting international backing for China among Third World and developing countries. From July 1989 onward, China dispatched numerous high-profile delegations on official missions to a wide range of states across Africa, Asia, and Latin America. South Korea, which had still to open diplomatic relations with China, became an important target, as were Indonesia and Singapore, both of which formally recognized China in 1990. Advantageous trade and investment deals sweetened these arrangements. Top leaders from nations that hosted Chinese officials during these difficult times made reciprocal visits to Beijing, returning home with tangible evidence of Chinese generosity and funding for projects and exchanges of all kinds. China's new-found wealth was used to good effect, allowing the PRC to deploy both commercial inducements and economic aid programmes to shore up its standing across the developing world and regionally and to win diplomatic support from the beneficiaries (Garver, 2016, pp. 490–494).

As China's economy continued to grow at breakneck speed during the 1990s and the early twenty-first century and the country amassed trillions of dollars in foreign currencies, its overtly expressed regional and global objectives became commensurately more ambitious. By the 1990s, realist theories of the primacy of the national interest, unrelenting competition among states, and the need to maintain a balance of power favourable to one's own nation, were driving much Chinese thinking on foreign relations. Chinese businesses invested heavily in Africa, Asia, the Middle East, Latin America, and some European countries, assuring access to coveted and essential raw materials needed to feed Chinese factories. Chinese external aid and humanitarian assistance programmes were likewise boosted dramatically. China sought to position itself as the leader of the developing world, to assume an ever more prominent role in existing international organizations to which it belonged, and to establish new institutions and global infrastructure networks. The Belt and Road Initiative (BRI) announced in 2013 by President Xi Jinping and incorporated in the Chinese Constitution in 2017, and the founding of the Chinese-dominated Asian Infrastructure Investment Bank (AIIB), which opened its doors in Beijing in 2016, were keystones of this architecture.

Economic strength was apparently expected to translate automatically into regional strategic predominance, with China boosting its military spending and assertiveness, claiming almost the entire South China Sea as its territorial waters and constructing artificial islands there, clashing militarily with its Southeast Asian neighbours and India, and making aggressive threats towards Taiwan. Further afield, China's acquisition of a 99-year lease on the port of Hambantota in Sri Lanka and other investments in Indian Ocean ports fueled fears that China sought to project its naval power into the region (CSIS, 2018).

4 Chinese Economic Statecraft Meets International Pushback

By the early twenty-first century, China's ever more openly expressed ambitions to establish what seemed to constitute an alternative global framework on economic and strategic fronts alike prompted growing apprehensions among influential sections of the global foreign policy-making elite, causing a major intellectual paradigm shift in thinking on China. From the 1970s until the early 2000s, Western China experts could be roughly divided into two broad camps. The first and—in policy-making terms—largely dominant outlook comprised those relatively friendly to China, who supported its integration into the existing international system, viewed it as a potential partner, supported "constructive engagement," and believed that within China itself economic progress and growth would ultimately translate into peaceful evolution towards more liberal political institutions and practices. A second, more antagonistic but overall less influential grouping consisted of individuals who regarded China with hostility, either due to a perception of China as a potential strategic rival and economic competitor of the US and a threat to Taiwan, issues Republicans tended to find particularly disturbing, or because of their distaste for China's authoritarian political system and policies, especially in such areas as human rights, legal practices, governance, and its policies on Tibet, subjects on which Democrats often felt especially strongly.

Within the elite global foreign policy community, the past decade has seen a marked shift to a far less benign view of China and its policies across a wide range of international and domestic issues. By the time Donald Trump became president in January 2017, within and beyond the US, the goodwill towards China that characterized the later twentieth century had steadily dissipated. Within the US, politicians, officials, and the intellectual community dealing with China were increasingly divided between relative moderates who, despite harbouring strong reservations over many of the PRC's actions, still believed that some degree of constructive cooperation between the two countries was attainable, and uncompromising hard-liners—the new Committee on the Present Danger: China, for example—who anticipated a future characterized by ever-intensifying Sino-American strategic, economic, and ideological antagonism (Gurtov & Selden, 2019; Nakashima, 2018; Toosi, 2019). Between 2017 and 2019, reports published by prominent American think tanks, notably the Asia Society and the Hoover Institution, and signed by leading US China specialists, some of whom had once been far less critical, recommended that the US implement a much tougher line than in the past towards China (Asia Society, 2017, 2019; Hoover Institution, 2019). Clearly, even American moderates had become far more suspicious of Chinese policies and less willing to compromise on or ignore contentious issues. In Australia, Canada, Western Europe, and much of Asia, negative views of China were reaching record highs (Zhou, 2019).

In late 2019, *Foreign Affairs*, the influential journal of the Council on Foreign Relations, a think tank whose efforts during the 1950s and 1960s had quietly helped to develop support for reopening U.S. relations with China, took the symbolic step of publishing an article with the title "The Sources of Chinese Conduct." Written by the Yale academic Odd Arne Westad (2019, pp. 88, 90), a prominent scholar of Chinese engagement with the world and of the Cold War, it was a deliberate reprise of the US diplomat George F. Kennan's famous 1947 essay "The Sources of Soviet Conduct," a seminal text that laid out the doctrine of "containment" that became the fundamental strategy underpinning Western Cold War policies. Westad, whom some critics had in the past occasionally considered too sympathetic to China, characterized Chinese nationalism as "sinister." He argued that earlier Western expectations that with prosperity China would gradually liberalize had been proven "foolish: the CCP is strengthening its rule and intends to remain in power forever." Using tactics similar to those the Soviet Union had employed in Europe in the 1940s, China was seeking "predominance" in "East Asia, a region that is as important to the United States today as Europe was at the beginning of the Cold War." Bluntly, he warned: "Unless the United States acts to countervail it, China is likely to become the undisputed master of East Asia, from Japan to Indonesia, by the late 2020s."

The think tank reports and Westad's article appeared during the Trump presidency. But several years earlier, China's use of economic power to further both economic and political objectives had already alarmed prominent foreign policy intellectuals. Blackwill and Harris (2016, pp. 93–151) devoted two chapters to how China, "the world's leading practitioner of geoeconomics," employed economic instruments—both inducements and coercion—to promote diplomatic objectives when dealing with Taiwan, North Korea, Japan, Southeast Asia, India, and Pakistan. Chinese-funded infrastructure projects in Southeast Asia and elsewhere in Asia—railways, roads, waterways, and oil and gas pipelines—were highlighted as potentially boosting China's own access to strategic mineral and agricultural resources, while enhancing Chinese influence in the recipient countries and reducing China's reliance on less secure maritime routes. Other recent studies of China's economic diplomacy, including a collection on the Maritime Silk Road Initiative (Blanchard, 2018), agree that at both national and subnational levels, it simultaneously serves assorted intertwined economic and political purposes.

As Zhang (2014, pp. 320–321, 329–330), Kapstein (2020, pp. 393–394, 419–426), Jean-Marc F. Blanchard and Norrin. F. Ripsman (2013), and several authors in the anthology edited by Mingjiang Li (2017) all note, China habitually employed a carrots-and-sticks approach; should positive economic inducements prove insufficient, Beijing showed no hesitation in switching to the use of negative pressure, sometimes exerted to intimidate individual businesses, sometimes employed to coerce entire national governments, those of Norway or Lithuania, for example, to change policies that China opposed. The effectiveness of these approaches varied greatly from case to case, according to specific circumstances. As time would show, this fundamentally zero-sum and perhaps simplistic approach to the outside world might have its limitations. Such tactics could often prove counter-productive, prompting pushback from the target countries, and indeed from international groupings such as the European Union in which they were members. In recent years, for example, China has refused to admit Australian wine and dairy products. In November 2020 bumptious Chinese diplomats compounded the offence when they rather unsubtly handed

Australian journalists a list of 14 issues, most domestic and many involving non-governmental Australian activities, on which they demanded changes. Predictably, relations between the two countries soured still further, as Australia aligned itself militarily with Japan, the US, and India, as part of the Indo-Pacific "Quad," and planned to acquire nuclear-armed submarines from Britain and the US (Buckley & Cave, 2021; Kearsley et al., 2020). Blackwill and Harris (2016, p. 120) noted how, "in some instances, even when it has achieved short-term objectives, China's economic pressure has reinforced the longer term resolve of governments, such as those in Manila and Hanoi, to act in ways far less conductive to Beijing's underlying strategic objectives."

Nowhere was this more apparent than in Asia, where Thailand and the Philippines are formal treaty allies of the US and Singapore a long-term, reliable, and effective security partner. Lee Hsien Loong (2020), Singapore's widely respected premier, writing in *Foreign Affairs* at the height of the COVID-19 pandemic, when Sino-American tensions were steadily rising, urged the US and China to "work out a modus vivendi that will be competitive in some areas without allowing rivalry to poison cooperation in others." Bluntly, he warned: "Asian countries do not want to be forced to choose between the two." Indeed: "The U.S. security presence remains vital to the Asia–Pacific region." Lee highlighted China's territorial claims in the South China Sea as one reason why other powers with competing claims there would not welcome a Chinese naval presence but found that of the US acceptable. Nor, he warned, could China expect to "displace the United States' economic role in Asia." While conciliatory in tone, Lee made it crystal clear just how misplaced was Chinese confidence that its neighbours would simply acquiesce in its efforts to win regional hegemony and eject the US from Asia.

Even before the pandemic, as an anthology edited by Yi Edward Yang and Wei Liang (2019) demonstrated, in large parts of the world, in North America, much of Europe, and among its Asian neighbours, strategic suspicions and political resentment of China and indeed of the business interests that had profited from their dealings with the PRC were rising. In developed and developing nations alike, the benefits of Chinese investment were considered questionable, with developing countries alarmed by the political and environmental impacts of China's "extractive diplomacy" and wary of growing indebtedness, and developed states fearful that China sought to control key sectors of their own economies. In all cases, China could easily find itself becoming a political football. By late 2021, in the otherwise deeply polarized US, the one issue on which both Republicans and Democrats agreed was that China represented a major strategic, economic, and ideological threat to not just their own country but many others. In Australia, Canada, much of Europe, India, and Japan, its reputation was equally problematic.

China's past experiences with Vietnam and Albania, two leading beneficiaries of its aid programmes in the 1960s and early 1970s, were proof positive that, rather than guaranteeing pliable and grateful allies, such ventures could become a poisoned chalice. Gratitude was often short-lived. In the early twenty-first century, China had spent heavily overseas, but these investments could themselves represent sources of risk, both economic and strategic, and prove hostages to fortune. In the 1950s and 1960s, even at the height of the ravages of the Great Leap Forward and Great Famine, China's leadership had prided itself on repaying its debts to the Soviet Union on or even ahead of schedule, regardless of any impact on or cost to the ordinary Chinese population (Zhang, 2014). However authoritarian many of the recipient governments involved might be, China's own debtors would not necessarily emulate this punctilious behaviour. In the aftermath of the COVID-19 pandemic, widely blamed upon China, among developing countries pressure for debt forgiveness rose rapidly. In 2020 and the first nine months of 2021, China provided at least US$12.1 billion in global debt relief to at least 23 countries (Johns Hopkins SAIS). The assumption by Chinese leaders that through adept use of its economic assets, China was on an almost effortless glide-path to attaining global predominance, with other states simply accepting this power shift as inevitable, began to appear somewhat over-optimistic.

5 Conclusion

Chinese officials often seem taken aback, dismayed, and baffled by the global cooling and international big chill Beijing has recently encountered across much of the world. While many are extremely able, their past experience has nonetheless been limited, with their understanding confined and perhaps even distorted by the very specific neoliberal mindset that was intellectually dominant in the early decades of China's reform and opening up, with economic considerations prioritized and the maximization of profits reigning supreme. In numerous respects, the international system of the 2020s is no longer that of the 1980s or even the 1990s, when China embarked on a trajectory of meteoric economic growth, with impacts that would not simply affect the PRC internally but would prompt reverberations felt globally. Since the 1990s, the Chinese government has propounded the narrative that China experienced a century of "national humiliation" at the hands of external powers, hymning its own success in allowing the country to regain its international status as perhaps the world's greatest nation (Garver, 2016, pp. 476–479). Chinese leaders seemed less attuned to the realization that elites and peoples elsewhere, including its neighbours, increasingly perceived it as a dangerous neocolonial would-be hegemon.

By no means, however, is this to argue that all China's overseas economic ventures were poorly conceived and likely to fail. The record is more fairly described as mixed (Yang with Liang, 2019). As things stand at present, it seems that the AIIB is well organized and well run (Haga, 2021), whereas the BRI is a rather sprawling and uncoordinated agglomeration of activities and projects, some effective, others ill conceived, some with a long-term pedigree and track record, others of extremely recent vintage developed hastily in response to the announcement of the BRI. Geoffrey Gunn (2021) argues that, although recently "China has worked clever strategies in both Indonesia and East Timor," each carefully tailored to the recipient, in sprawling, populous Indonesia these have met with considerably less success than in its comparatively tiny neighbour, due in considerable part to China's very different past dealings with each. Yet East Timor still balances China against other patrons, including Australia, Japan, and the US. Even when economic statecraft is effective, a range of external constraints related to specific circumstances in the target and sometimes also the sender are likely to constrict its scope.

There were indeed major success stories. Shu Guang Zhang and Ni Chen (2021), looking specifically at Brazil, hypothesize that the degree to which China's economic relationship with Latin America's largest state has weathered changes of administration—some, notably that of recent President Jair Bolsonaro, initially hostile to China—has been largely due to the "institutionalization" of the relationship through the construction of a durable administrative framework transcending political partisanship. Pedro Barbosa (2021), focusing specifically on China's economic partnership with Brazil's oil industry since the early 2000s, offers detailed insight into Chinese tactics—including countercyclical lending to and investment in that sector when credit was unavailable elsewhere—that ensured both parties found their dealings mutually beneficial, with China winning access for the indefinite future to the output of massive new oilfields Chinese investment and expertise had helped to develop.

Even the most productive partnerships may, however, ultimately prove precarious, a lesson the US learned in the late 1970s following the overthrow of the Shah of Iran. Arguably, one of the greatest inherent weaknesses of China's strategy of using economic instruments to achieve its objectives is that more often than not the targets are high-level political and business interests, as opposed to the overall population of a specific country or region, many of whom may well be at best indifferent or at worst hostile to China. Blackwill and Harris (2016) noted how China's economic dealings with many African nations brought warm relations with existing political leaders, but did little to enhance China's standing or image among the ordinary population. Blanchard and Ripsman (2013) went so far as to argue that, in any given target state, the degree to which China was able to achieve its purposes might well depend upon just how far that country's leadership was immune to domestic political pressures that opposed Chinese objectives.

From the time China's reform and opening up began, when dealing with the world beyond their borders, Chinese policymakers focused unrelentingly on groups and individuals they considered influential, in the belief that these elites would direct the national policies of their countries on a fundamentally pro-China trajectory. As developments in much of the world are demonstrating, this expectation is currently proving somewhat simplistic. As China seeks to employ the tools of economic statecraft more assertively, even aggressively, those charged with devising and implementing these policies would benefit greatly from acquiring a more sophisticated understanding of the political dynamics and social organization and functioning of other nations.

The current unsettled international situation might conceivably prove a blessing in disguise to China. The country's economic resources are great but far from inexhaustible, while among the challenges it faces are those arising from an ageing and already shrinking population, as well as the impacts of climate change and environmental degradation. A pause for reflection, reassessment, and reconceptualization, perhaps even streamlining, with the various components of the BRI reevaluated and prioritized according to both their economic and strategic feasibility and potential, might well offer an excellent opportunity to rationalize and consolidate the BRI. In the process, Chinese policymakers might also choose to contemplate the overall strengths and weaknesses of precisely how they choose to deploy the instruments of economic statecraft at their disposal. In the second half of the twentieth century, this was a field in which China, still a relatively weak power, displayed impressive skill in playing its hand. The most ironic outcome would be a scenario in which a country grown far wealthier and self-confident squandered its assets with reckless abandon beyond its borders yet won little in return.

Bibliographic References

Ahamed, L. (2009). *Lords of finance: The bankers who broke the world*. Penguin.
Asia Society, Task Force on US-China Policy. (2017). *US policy toward China: Recommendations for a new administration*. Asia Society Center on US-China Relations. https://asiasociety.org/files/US-China_Task_Force_Report_FINAL.pdf
Asia Society, Task Force on US-China Policy. (2019). *Course correction: Toward an effective and sustainable China policy*. Asia Society Center on US-China Relations. https://asiasociety.org/sites/default/files/inline-files/CourseCorrection_FINAL_2.7.19_1.pdf
Baldwin, D. A. (1985). *Economic statecraft*. Princeton University Press.
Baldwin, D. A. (2020). *Economic statecraft* (New ed.). Princeton University Press.
Barbosa, P. (2021). Chinese economic statecraft and China's oil development finance in Brazil. *Journal of Current Chinese Affairs, 20*, 366–390.
Barnhart, M. A. (1987). *Japan prepares for total war: The search for economic security, 1919–1941*. Cornell University Press.
Berghahn, V. R. (2014). *American big business in Britain and Germany: A comparative history of two "special relationships" of the twentieth century*. Princeton University Press.
Blackwill, R. D., & Harris, J. M. (2016). *War by other means: Geoeconomics and statecraft*. Belknap Press of Harvard University.
Blanchard, J.-M.F. (Ed.). (2018). *China's Maritime Silk Road Initiative and South Asia: A political economic analysis of its purposes, perils, and promises*. Palgrave Macmillan.
Blanchard, J.-M.F., & Ripsman, N. F. (2013). *Economic statecraft and foreign policy: Sanctions, incentives, and target state calculations*. Routledge.
Boyce, R. (2009). *The great interwar crisis and the collapse of globalization*. Palgrave Macmillan.
Brazinsky, G. A. (2009). *Nation building in South Korea: Koreans, Americans, and the making of a democracy*. University of North Carolina Press.
Brazinsky, G. A. (2017). *Winning the third world: Sino-American rivalry during the Cold War*. University of North Carolina Press.
Buckley, C., & Cave, D. (2021, September 27, October 6). Australia took on China. Did it get it right? *New York Times*. Retrieved on November 2021, from https://www.nytimes.com/2021/09/27/world/australia/australia-china-relations.html
Cardwell, C. (2014). *NSC 68 and the political economy of the early Cold War*. Cambridge University Press.
Center for Strategic and International Studies (CSIS). (2018). *China's Maritime Silk Road: Strategic and economic implications for the Indo-Pacific region*. CSIS. https://csis-website-prod.s3.amazonaws.com/s3fs-public/publication/180404_Szechenyi_ChinaMaritimeSilkRoad.pdf
Cohrs, P. O. (2006). *The unfinished peace after World War I: America, Britain and the stabilization of Europe 1919–1932*. Cambridge University Press.

Costigliola, F. (1984). *Awkward Dominion: American political, economic, and cultural relations with Europe, 1919–1933.* Cornell University Press.

Dobson, A. P. (1986). *U.S. wartime aid to Britain 1940–1946.* Croom Helm.

Eckes, A. E., Jr. (1995). *Opening America's market: U.S. foreign trade policy since 1776.* University of North Carolina Press.

Eckes, A. E., Jr., & Zeiler, T. (2003). *Globalization and the American century.* Cambridge University Press.

Ekbladh, D. (2010). *The great American mission: Modernization and the construction of an American world order.* Princeton University Press.

Forsberg, A. (2014). *America and the Japanese miracle: The Cold War context of Japan's economic revival, 1950–1960.* University of North Carolina Press.

Frieden, J. A. (2020). *Global capitalism: Its fall and rise in the twentieth century, and its stumbles in the twenty-first.* Norton.

Friedman, J. (2015). *Shadow Cold War: The Sino-Soviet competition for the third world.* University of North Carolina Press.

Garver, J. W. (2016). *China's quest: The history of the foreign relations of the People's Republic of China.* Oxford University Press.

Grieve, W. G. (2014). *The American military mission to China, 1941–1942: Lend-lease logistics, politics and the tangles of wartime cooperation.* McFarland.

Gunn, G. C. (2021). Chinese economic statecraft in Indonesia/East Timor: A historical and regional perspective. *Journal of Current Chinese Affairs, 50,* 317–338.

Gurtov, M., & Selden, M. (2019, August 1). The dangerous new US consensus on China and the future of US-China relations. *Asia-Pacific Journal, 17*(15), 1–11.

Haga, K. Y. A. (2021). The Asian Infrastructure Investment Bank: A qualified success for Beijing's economic statecraft. *Journal of Current Chinese Affairs, 50,* 391–421.

Haga, K. Y. A. (2022). Deng Xiaoping's use of positive economic statecraft: The importance of securing long-term partnerships with major International Financial Organizations (IFOs). In P. Roberts (Ed.), *Chinese economic statecraft from 1978 to 1989: The first decade of Deng Xiaoping's reforms* (pp. 161–208). Palgrave Macmillan. https://doi.org/10.1007/978-981-16-9217-8_6

Hamilton, P. E. (2021). *Made in Hong Kong: Transpacific networks and a new history of globalization.* Columbia University Press.

Helleiner, E. (2014). *The forgotten foundations of Bretton Woods: International development and the making of the postwar order.* Cornell University Press.

Hogan, M. J. (1977). *Informal entente: The private structure of cooperation in Anglo-American diplomacy, 1918–1928.* University of Missouri Press.

Hogan, M. J. (1987). *The Marshall Plan: America, Britain, and the reconstruction of Western Europe, 1947–1952.* Cambridge University Press.

Hoover Institution, Working Group on Chinese Influence Activities in the United States. (2019). *China's influence & American interests: Promoting constructive vigilance* (Rev. ed.). Hoover Institution Press. https://www.hoover.org/sites/default/files/research/docs/diamond-schell_chineseinfluence_oct2020rev.pdf

Hunt, M. H. (1973). *Frontier defense and the open door: Manchuria in Chinese-American relations, 1895–1911.* Yale University Press.

Johns Hopkins SAIS. China-Africa Research Initiative. Retrieved on November 2021, from http://www.sais-cari.org/debt-relief

Kapstein, E. B. (2020). Afterword: Economic statecraft: continuity and change. In D. A. Baldwin (Ed.), *Economic statecraft* (New ed., pp. 391–433). Princeton University Press.

Kearsley, J., Bagshaw, E., & Galloway, A. (2020, November 18). 'If you make China the enemy, China will be the enemy'; Beijing's fresh threat to Australia. *Sydney Morning Herald.* Retrieved on November 2021, from https://www.smh.com.au/world/asia/if-you-make-china-the-enemy-china-will-be-the-enemy-beijing-s-fresh-threat-to-australia-20201118-p56fqs.html

Kent, B. (1989). *The spoils of war: The politics, economics, and diplomacy of reparations 1918–1932*. Clarendon Press.
Killick, J. (1997). *The United States and European reconstruction, 1945–1960*. Keele University Press.
Kunz, D. B. (1997). *Butter and guns: America's Cold War economic diplomacy*. Free Press.
Latham, M. E. (2000). *Modernization as ideology: American social science and "nation building" in the Kennedy era*. University of North Carolina Press.
Latham, M. E. (2011). *The right kind of revolution: Modernization, development, and U.S. foreign policy from the Cold War to the present*. Cornell University Press.
Lee, H. L. (2020, July/August). The endangered Asian century. *Foreign Affairs, 99*(4), 52–64.
Leffler, M. P. (1979). *The elusive quest: America's pursuit of European stability and French security, 1919–1933*. University of North Carolina Press.
Li, M. (Ed.). (2017). *China's economic statecraft: Co-optation, cooperation and coercion*. World Scientific.
Mackenzie, B. A. (2005). *Remaking France: Americanization, public diplomacy, and the Marshall Plan*. Berghahn Books.
Milward, A. (1984). *The reconstruction of Western Europe, 1945–51*. University of California Press.
Nakashima, E. (2018, November 28). China specialists who long supported engagement are now warning of Beijing's efforts to influence American society. *Washington Post*. Retrieved on November 2021, from https://www.washingtonpost.com/world/national-security/china-specialists-who-long-supported-engagement-are-now-warning-of-beijings-efforts-to-influence-american-society/2018/11/28/8a5a5570-f25f-11e8-80d0-f7e1948d55f4_story.html
Norris, W. J. (2016). *Chinese economic statecraft: Commercial actors, grand strategy, and state control*. Cornell University Press.
Norris, W. J. (2021). China's post-Cold War economic statecraft: A periodisation. *Journal of Current Chinese Affairs, 50*, 294–316.
Oatley, T. H. (2015). *A political economy of American hegemony: Buildups, booms, and busts*. Cambridge University Press.
Orde, A. (1990). *British policy and European reconstruction after the First World War*. Cambridge University Press.
Pollard, R. A. (1985). *Economic security and the origin of the Cold War, 1945–1950*. Columbia University Press.
Price, H. B. (1955). *The Marshall Plan and its meaning*. Cornell University Press.
Rauchway, E. (2015). *The money makers: How Roosevelt and Keynes ended the depression, defeated fascism, and secured a prosperous peace*. Basic Books.
Roberts, P. (Ed.). (2022). *Chinese economic statecraft from 1978 to 1989: The first decade of Deng Xiaoping's reforms*. Palgrave Macmillan.
Rosenberg, E. S. (2000). *Financial missionaries to the world: The politics and culture of dollar diplomacy, 1900–1930*. Harvard University Press.
Sayce, A. H. (1890). *Records of the past: Being English translations of the ancient monuments of Egypt and Western Asia, 2nd series* (Vol. 3). Samuel Bagster.
Schild, G. (1995). *Bretton Woods and Dumbarton Oaks: American economic and political post-war planning in the summer of 1944*. St. Martin's Press.
Shenin, S. Y. (2000). *The United States and the third world: The origins of postwar relations and the point four program*. Nova Science Press.
Steil, B. (2013). *The battle of Bretton Woods: John Maynard Keynes, Harry Dexter White, and the making of a new world order*. Princeton University Press.
Steiner, Z. (2005). *The lights that failed: European international history, 1919–1933*. Oxford University Press.
Taffet, J. F. (2007). *Foreign aid as foreign policy: The alliance for progress in Latin America*. Routledge.

Thomas, N. (2017). Sino-Australian relations in the long 1970s. In P. Roberts & O. A. Westad (Eds.), *China, Hong Kong, and the long 1970s: Global perspectives* (pp. 205–232). Palgrave Macmillan. https://doi.org/10.1007/978-3-319-51250-1

Toosi, N. (2019, July 28). 'When paradigms die': China veterans fear extinction in Trump's Washington. *Politico*. Retrieved on November 2021, from https://www.politico.com/story/2019/07/28/trump-china-veterans-foreign-policy-1438389

Tooze, A. (2014). *The deluge: The Great War, America, and the remaking of the global order, 1916–1931*. Allen Lane.

Utley, J. G. (2005). *Going to war with Japan, 1937–1941* (With new introduction). Fordham University Press.

Weeks, A. L. (2004). *Russia's life-saver: Lend-lease aid to the U.S.S.R. in World War II*. Lexington Books.

Westad, O. A. (1993). *Cold War and revolution: Soviet-American rivalry and the origins of the Chinese Civil War, 1944–1946*. Columbia University Press.

Westad, O. A. (2003). *Decisive encounters: The Chinese Civil War, 1946–1950*. Stanford University Press.

Westad, O. A. (2019, September/October). The sources of Chinese conduct. *Foreign Affairs, 98*(5), 86–95.

Xiang, L. (1991). From silver agreement to tung oil loan: The origins of United States aid to China in the triangular relations between China, Japan and the United States during the 1930s. In P. Roberts (Ed.), *Sino-American relations since 1900* (pp. 238–255). University of Hong Kong, Centre of Asian Studies.

Yang, Y. E., with Liang, W. (Eds.). (2019). *Challenges to China's economic statecraft: A global perspective*. Lexington Books.

Zeiler, T. (1992). *American trade and power in the 1960s*. Columbia University Press.

Zhang, S. G. (2002). *Economic Cold War: America's embargo against China and the Sino-Soviet alliance, 1949–1963*. Johns Hopkins University Press and Woodrow Wilson Center Press.

Zhang, S. G. (2014). *Beijing's economic statecraft during the Cold War 1949–1991*. Johns Hopkins University Press and Woodrow Wilson Center Press.

Zhang, S. G., & Chen, N. (2021). Beijing's institutionalized economic statecraft toward Brazil: A case study. *Journal of Current Chinese Affairs, 50*, 339–365.

Zhang, S. G., & Zheng, H. (2022). Toward technological statecraft: Revisiting Beijing's economic statecraft in the 1980s. In P. Roberts (Ed.), *Chinese economic statecraft from 1978 to 1989: The first decade of Deng Xiaoping's reforms* (pp. 91–126). Palgrave Macmillan. https://doi.org/10.1007/978-981-16-9217-8_4

Zhou, L. (2019, October 2). Public opinion on China turns negative in Western Europe and Asia-Pacific, survey finds. *South China Morning Post*. Retrieved on November 2021, from https://www.scmp.com/news/china/diplomacy/article/3031142/public-opinion-china-turns-negative-western-europe-and-asia

Chapter 3
China, the BRI, and the New Vocabulary of Global Governance

Maria Adele Carrai

1 Introduction

China is an increasingly active member of global governance. Since the 18th National Congress of the Communist Party of China (CPC) in late 2012, and the launch of its Belt and Road Initiative (BRI) in 2013, China's global activism has prompted much debate about the nature of its impact on the mechanisms, norms, and structures of global governance. In particular, a large body of literature has been produced about the BRI (Ali, 2020; Carrai & Defraigne, 2020; Cheng, 2018; Leandro, F. J., & Duarte, 2020; Garlick, 2020; Liu, 2018, 2019a; Maçães, 2018; Wang & Zhao, 2019; Xu, 2018; Ye, 2020). The general view is that China is more and more active in revising global governance rules. This is in line with its stated objective to become a responsible global leader that participates in and helps shape major global governance institutions. China has ramped up its engagement with existing multilateral fora and contributed to creating new ones, such as the Boao Forum for Asia, the Xiangshan Forum, and the Belt and Road Forum for International Cooperation (Alden & Alves, 2017). This greater presence and assertiveness in global governance has prompted concern among many Western observers, who often paint a picture of a battle between authoritarianism and a liberal rule-based order (Doshi, 2021; Friedberg, 2012; Goldstein, 2005). While it is difficult to fully assess China's real impact, partly because global governance itself is hard to define or measure, one thing that is certain is China's attempt to shape the narrative of global governance, projecting concepts and ideas that reflect its values and priorities onto the shared international language. Very little literature (Ekman, 2017) has focused on the effect of China's rise and the BRI on the vocabulary of global governance, not just by introducing new terms, but also by attributing new meaning to words already in use.

Language is a way to assert dominance and power; it is "crucial in articulating, maintaining and subverting existing relations of power in society, both on global,

M. A. Carrai (✉)
NYU Shanghai, Shanghai, China

© The Author(s), under exclusive license to Springer Nature Singapore Pte Ltd. 2023
P. A. B. Duarte et al. (eds.), *The Palgrave Handbook of Globalization with Chinese Characteristics*, https://doi.org/10.1007/978-981-19-6700-9_3

national and institutional levels and on the local level of interpersonal communication" (Talbot et al., 2003, pp. 1–2). When entities introduce new vocabulary into international relations or reconfigure existing terms, they help reshape the structure of international society and the norms regulate it. Starting before the Opium Wars of the mid-nineteenth century, China was long dictated terms of international engagement by the West, which, for example, had the monopoly on international law; China then had to translate those terms and absorb them into its way of being in and talking about the world (Carrai, 2021). Over the past decade, as China has emerged as an assertive power and its BRI has become a ubiquitous discussion point, it has taken its own turn to shape the language of global governance.

Discussing certain apparently innocuous concepts that China has introduced to international fora, French scholar Nadège Rolland (2017, p. 122) has argued that they give important indications of how Beijing sees the Eurasian order that it seeks to produce through the BRI, in terms of both distribution of power and governing norms: "The intangible narrative that is being woven around the concrete BRI infrastructure projects is a work in progress, but it is an essential component of China's vision for itself and for the region." For Piccone (2018), China's language "hides deeper meanings in the discourse of international relations—a desire to reinforce orthodox interpretations of principles of national sovereignty and nonintervention in internal affairs, undermine the legitimacy of international mechanisms to monitor human rights, avoid 'name and shame' tactics and sanctions, and weaken protections of human rights defenders and independent media." What is clear is that, as these concepts come to be integrated within international fora, other countries must be aware of the definition differences over common terms when coming to agreements with China (Ekman, 2017).

Chinese leaders tried to infuse international global governance with new concepts well before Xi Jinping: Mao's proletarian internationalism, and more recently the notions of "harmonious society" and "peaceful rise" (on the latter, see Suettinger, 2004). The language of the BRI appears to have had the most enduring global impact, however. As part of Xi's policy to "spread China's voice," have more say in international affairs (国际话语权), and enhance its soft power, he has pushed Chinese media outlets to shape the China narrative abroad (He, 2019). Through that route, but even more through official Chinese speeches employing new terms and reinterpreting old ones in multilateral fora, China has enriched the language of global governance and a new vocabulary is being used in bilateral and multilateral official documents. What are these terms, what do they mean in China, and how have they been used in multilateral documents? What are the repercussions of their inclusion in the global governance lexicon? This chapter addresses that vocabulary through Xi's repeated use of new concepts and reinterpretation of common words and expressions. It discusses the meaning of some of these terms in Chinese, and how they have affected international discourse on global governance. It examines how existing key terms have acquired new meaning in the Chinese context. The chapter concludes by discussing the power of language and the repercussions for the practice of global governance.

2 The Belt and Road Initiative, Community of Shared Destiny, and Common Prosperity

The BRI has come to seem ubiquitous: conferences, roundtables, centres, and funds dedicated to the initiative have mushroomed in recent years. Yet the term was officially introduced only in 2013, with its official launch by Xi. The BRI serves multiple purposes for China, both domestically and in terms of foreign policy, but it is primarily a strategy for increasing China's security as an emerging global power and enabling the country to gain its rightful place in the world. Although many Chinese observers and academics have described the BRI as a highly important "strategy" rather than just an economic "initiative," and various debates have revolved around its nature, the government has officially emphasized that it should be called an initiative (倡议), in the singular, and not a strategy (战略) (CASS, 2015; Zhang & Yuan, 2017). Clearly, the government wants the BRI to appear as an open call for voluntary action for the public good, rather than as a deliberate action plan that could imply inducement, intimidation, and self-interest. The official aim is to reconnect Eurasia and the world through a network of infrastructure and trillions of dollars in investments to Asia, Europe, Africa, and Latin America. For Wang Yiwei connectivity is a key element, while "the essence of the five major goals advocated by the Belt and Road Initiative is helping developing countries achieve curve overtaking, lane-changing overtaking, and common revival as part of the inclusive globalization it aims to create" (Wang, 2017, p. 12). Investment in railways, highways, ports, energy, and telecommunications brings countries closer together and increases their trade volume. With over 14,000 projects started to date, the BRI has already increased trade in goods between China and other countries. Between 2013 and 2018, China's trade with other BRI countries surpassed US$5 trillion, and foreign direct investments exceeded US$70 billion (Xiao, 2021, p. 6).

In keeping with its ubiquity, the BRI's language is being widely taken up. The initiative has become a recurring theme of conferences, heritage sites, museum displays, expos, and film festivals across Eurasia, East Africa, and Southeast Asia. Countries aspiring to receive lucrative Chinese investments promptly adapted to rhetoric claiming ancient trade and cultural ties with China, uncovering new geographies and histories. The BRI has brought infrastructure, and the gap between developed and developing countries in particular, back to the centre of international debate. If infrastructure has historically proven a source of power in international politics, it is unsurprising that China's building of basic infrastructure all over the world has magnified concerns about its soft power and political leverage.

The BRI has propelled countries to come up with alternative visions; since its launch, many have scrambled to create their own masterplans of connectivity, development, and infrastructure. South Korea's Eurasia Initiative launched in 2013 to strengthen and expand the transregional corridor of transportation, logistics, and energy, particularly between the two Koreas, develop the "creative economy," and encourage regional actors to collaborate to secure common prosperity and international peace (Kim, 2015). Japan's Quality Infrastructure Investment Partnership was launched in 2015 by the Prime Minister Shinzo Abe (2015). Turkey's Middle Corridor project, beginning in Turkey and passing through the Caucasus and Central Asia by road and rail before reaching China, was established in 2015 as "one of the most important component[s] of the efforts to revive the ancient Silk Road" (Republic of Turkey, n.d.). The European Union's Euro-Asian Connectivity Strategy launched in 2018 with the joint communication on "Connecting Europe and Asia – Building blocks for an EU strategy," seeking to exploit existing networks and engage Asian partners through "a sustainable, comprehensive and rules-based approach to connectivity" (European Parliament, 2021). Under then-President Donald Trump, the US founded the Blue Dot Network in 2019 to try to counter China. At the 2021 G7 summit, the Biden administration launched Build Back Better World (B3W), a partnership for mobilizing infrastructure investments in low- and middle-income countries to counteract the BRI and align other countries within a liberal sphere of influence. Thus China's vision of world connectivity and its new international role, as financier and competitor, has prompted not only debate but also various counter-initiatives for infrastructure and global governance.

China sees the BRI and the infrastructure, economic, financial, and cultural integration it creates as conducive to the creation of a "community of shared destiny" (命运共同体), which is a key element of the China story it is exporting (He, 2019). The central government's first use of the term occurred at the 18th National Congress of the CPC in November 2012, which declared an intention to "promote a sense of community of shared destiny for mankind." In his report to the Congress, then-Chinese President Hu Jintao (2012) urged China to raise awareness about all people "sharing a community of common destiny." Xi then adopted the phrase to explain his ambitious foreign policy objectives, thereby shifting its meaning. While Hu was overseeing a nation on a "peaceful rise" (Zheng, 2005), Xi's China has established itself as a power wielding significant international influence. Hu used the term to describe cross-Strait ties and China's relations with its Asian neighbours, but Xi used it in an international context on his first trip abroad as president, to Moscow, as applauded by Chinese state media (Tobin, 2019, p. 40).

"Community of shared destiny" may be the most important phrase that China, particularly Xi, is using to convey its contribution to global governance. Xi highlighted the term in his report to the 19th CPC National Congress in October 2017 (Zhao, 2018) and has used it in many other speeches, including "Working Together to Forge a New Partnership of Win-Win Cooperation and Create a Community of Shared Future for Mankind," given during the general debate of the 70th Session of the UN General Assembly in September 2015, and "Work Together to Build a Community of Shared Future for Mankind" delivered at the UN Office in Geneva in January 2017. That same month, Xi became the first Chinese president to attend the World Economic Forum in Davos, where he said that "mankind has become a close-knit community of shared future" (Xi, 2017a). A few months later he described the BRI's ultimate goal as constructing a "community of shared interests" (Xi, 2017b). His report to the 19th CPC National Congress enshrined "building a community with a shared future for mankind" as a core concept and basic policy guiding Chinese diplomacy in the new era. The community of shared destiny is also codified as an integral part of Xi's thought on socialism with Chinese characteristics. Other leaders have signed on to this rhetoric, and it has been included in various bilateral and multilateral agreements, including a UN Security Council resolution (UN, 2017, p. 11).

The phrase has proliferated across official Chinese BRI documents and statements. One clause of the joint communique signed by the leaders attending the 2017 Belt and Road Forum for International Cooperation reads: "creating a prosperous and peaceful community with shared future for mankind is our common aspiration" (Belt and Road Portal, 2017). In a 2020 joint statement on the Lancang-Mekong Cooperation, which includes China, Cambodia, Laos, Myanmar, Vietnam, and Thailand, leaders committed to building "a community of shared future" for the sake of peace and prosperity (Belt and Road Portal, 2020).

As neutral and unharmful as a community of shared future seems, some scholars insist that it refers to China's aim to recreate a Sino-centric order in Eurasia and beyond (Rolland, 2017). For Rolland, "community of shared destiny" reflects Beijing's aspirations for a future world order that is different and more in line with its own interests and status. Chinese diplomat Yang Jiechi (2018) has written: "Building a community of common destiny for mankind is the overall goal of China's foreign affairs work in the new era," adding that the successful construction of this community is contingent upon first establishing a "new type of international relations," which supports—rather than seeks to contain—China's rise on the global stage and its centrality. This does indeed suggest that the phrase indicates China's long-term desire to transform the international environment to be compatible with its own governance model, and most importantly, to be making space for its new global role.

A related notion that Xi has recently emphasized is "common prosperity" (共同富裕). At the 10th meeting of the Central Committee for Financial and Economic Affairs in 2021, he said that common prosperity was crucial to improving the nation's socialist market economy, and that preventing financial risks is one of China's "three tough battles" (三大攻坚战), along with reducing poverty and pollution (Panyue, 2021). Xi frequently uses the term in speeches before domestic and international audiences. In different contexts it takes on different meanings, and a clear definition is elusive partly because of its ubiquity: in 2021, it has appeared 65 times in Xi's speeches or meetings (Bloomberg News, 2021). While the term does not suggest that everyone will enjoy equal levels of prosperity, it calls for more equality than the status quo. China's top 1% owned 30.6% of household wealth in 2020, compared with 31.4% in the US (Credit Suisse, 2021, p. 24). One distinction Xi has claimed from Western-style capitalism is that in China, "Capital serves the people" (Wei, 2021)—but he has warned that the country's wealth gap could threaten the legitimacy of the Chinese Communist Party (CCP). "Achieving common prosperity is not just an economic issue, but a significant political one that matters to the party's basis to rule," he said in a 2021 speech at the Central Party School (*The Economist*, 2021).

China has also sought to export the concept. At the 2021 World Economic Forum's Davos conference, Xi (2021) said that China will "work with other countries to build an open, inclusive, clean and beautiful world that enjoys lasting peace, universal security and common prosperity." Xi's usage of the term at regional and international institutions abroad, especially about the Chinese role in Asia, seems similarly intended to allay fears about China's rise. At a 2019 speech in Tajikistan's capital city of Dushanbe, he described Asia as heading towards "lasting peace and common prosperity" (Xi, 2019). He often uses the term in conjunction with calls for peace and multilateralism, while explicitly repudiating unilateral actions by hegemonic powers, meaning the US. At Dushanbe, Xi affirmed China's commitment to safeguarding the international order by upholding institutions like the UN and the WTO.

Xi has framed Chinese development programmes, like the BRI, through a shared goal of common prosperity, conveying the idea that China's rise serves to better both China and the world. In his 2016 speech to the G20 Business (B20) Summit, Xi (2016) said: "China's development has benefited from the international community, and we are ready to provide more public goods to the international community." This speech illustrated Xi's need to speak simultaneously to international and domestic audiences: he hailed China's progress towards achieving common prosperity by lifting over 700 million people out of poverty, a remarkable development that was "pursued by the people and its outcomes should be shared by the people."

3 Sovereignty: The Five Principle of Peaceful Coexistence and Win-Win Cooperation

One word frequently used to characterize China's foreign policy is "sovereignty." Rather than one-size-fits-all, the Chinese rhetoric around sovereignty supports the idea that each county should be allowed to choose its own development path according to its situation and national character. A 2015 document encapsulates this and much of the other language that has been used to promote the BRI so far:

> The Belt and Road Initiative is in line with the purposes and principles of the UN Charter. It upholds the Five Principles of Peaceful Coexistence: mutual respect for each other's sovereignty and territorial integrity, mutual non-aggression, mutual non-interference in each other's internal affairs, equality and mutual benefit, and peaceful coexistence… It advocates tolerance among civilizations, respects the paths and modes of development chosen by different countries, and supports dialogues among different civilizations on the principles of seeking common ground while shelving differences and drawing on each other's strengths, so that all countries can coexist in peace for common prosperity. (Belt and Road Portal, 2015)

The Five Principles of Peaceful Coexistence, elaborated in the 1950s, long since embraced as official rhetoric, and enshrined in the preamble of China's constitution in 1982, embody China's approach to global governance. They are: (1) mutual respect for sovereignty and territorial integrity, (2) mutual non-aggression, (3) mutual non-interference in internal affairs, (4) equality and mutual benefit, and (5) peaceful coexistence (*China Daily*, 2015). Premier Zhou Enlai first pronounced these tenets during his June 1954 visits to India and Burma (Ministry of Foreign Affairs, n.d.), and they accrued international attention after his address at the 1955 Bandung Conference. Subsequent Chinese leaders, including Xi, have reaffirmed the importance of the five principles for Beijing's foreign policy (Wen, 2004). Currently, China often wields them to defend activities within areas which it views as its sovereign territory but which are disputed, such as Hong Kong, Xinjiang, Tibet, or Taiwan. In a 2019 "Letter to the Editor" published in the London-based *Financial Times*, Chinese diplomat Liu Xiaoming (2019b) held up non-interference as a prerequisite for bilateral cooperation, and said China would "not tolerate interference in its own internal affairs, and will not keep silent in face of malicious slander, still less compromise its sovereignty, security and interests."

In 2017, China described the BRI as both "in line with the purposes and principles of the UN Charter" and as "uphold[ing] the Five Principles of Peaceful Coexistence" (Belt and Road Forum, 2017). A 2019 joint communique between China and Suriname agreed to "develop friendly exchanges on the basis of mutual respect" and "reaffirmed their respect for each other's independence, sovereignty and territorial integrity" (Belt and Road Portal, 2019).

Another key term related to sovereignty and the Five Principles is "win-win cooperation" ("双赢", "互利", "共赢" or as "互利共赢" or "互利双赢"), meaning something advantageous or satisfactory to all parties involved. In a speech at Moscow State Institute of International Relations, Xi (2013) first suggested constructing "a type of international relations oriented towards win-win cooperation." The government has since frequently used the phrase in its official statements, memorandums, and speeches to refer to Beijing's approach to international relations. At the Boao Forum for Asia, Xi (2015) said "win-win" eight distinct times in his keynote, spelling out its definition as the opposite of a zero-sum view of international relations. "The interests of others must be accommodated while pursuing one's own interests," he explained, "and common development must be promoted while seeking one's own development." A 2015 piece for *China US Focus* by Chinese diplomat Du Qiwen suggests the use of "win-win" in official statements is highly illustrative of China's role in the international arena (Du, 2015). Xi has used the term to emphasize China's peaceful rise within the international system and to describe the BRI. In a 2017 address at the UN Office in Geneva, he urged large countries to "treat smaller ones as equals instead of acting as a hegemon imposing their will on others" and elaborated upon China's proposition to "build a community of shared future for mankind and achieve shared and win-win development" (Xinhua News, 2017). In a keynote at a summit on the BRI, he said that the aim of the initiative was to advance win-win cooperation among countries and build a new platform for international trade (Reuters, 2019).

Many Western scholars have expressed scepticism towards China's use of "win-win." Dorsey (2019) has suggested that it is actually the case that "China wins twice," especially in countries where it has become the key source of development finance and there are large power imbalances. In 2018, John Fisher (2020), the Geneva Director at Human Rights Watch, penned a scathing piece about China's draft resolution presented at the UN Human Rights Council (HRC) entitled "Promoting the International Human Rights Cause through Win-Win Cooperation" (Permanent Mission, 2018), which he said did not acknowledge the HRC's mandate to "address situations of violations of human rights, including gross and systematic violations" or discuss any consequences if countries refused to cooperate. A recent report from US research group the Brookings Institution criticized win-win cooperation as a guise under which to eliminate "name and shame" resolutions in favour of "constructive dialogue" with states violating HRC norms and practices (Piccone, 2021).

4 Economic Globalization, Self-Reliance, and Dual Circulation

China is also transforming global governance language not only by modifying existing terms. Xi has emphasized globalization in many of his speeches; indeed, at Davos in 2017 the contrast between Xi's speech, which mentioned globalization more than 30 times, and Trump's speech, which focused on sovereignty and "America first," could have not been sharper. But when people in the West think about globalization, it is often tied to a free trade economy that opposes state intervention, such as subsidies, and promotes unhampered flows of goods and people, while for Xi it does not entail a full opening-up of the Chinese economy. Any opening up has to happen on China's terms, and the hand of the state is still heavy. Based on its own experience, China views globalization in the context of "external circulation," which invites an influx of sales in foreign markets and the technological "spillover" associated with such imports. With its reforms of 1978, China ensconced itself within the global value chain by developing labour-intensive manufacturing industries such as apparel, textiles, footwear, and toys, but the gradual upgrading of technologies and industries sparked made its exports more sophisticated, spanning electrical machinery and telecommunications (Lin & Wang, 2021, p. 10).

In 1997, the government announced two centenary goals: (1) to build a "moderately prosperous society in all respects" by 2021 and (2) to transform China into a prosperous, strong, democratic, culturally advanced, and harmonious socialist country by 2049. In a July 2021 speech celebrating the CCP's centenary, Xi said that China had achieved the goal of doubling its 2010 GDP and per capita income by 2020 (State Council, 2021). China has moved closer to the world's liberal and open-market economies since 2010 across many objective metrics. In 2020 it boasted a lower average tariff rate (9.7%) than the US (10.2%) (Lipsky, 2021). Its venture-capital investment as share of GDP currently exceeds that of every other country besides the US and the UK, and it is roughly tied with Italy on the metric of trade openness, according to the Washington, DC-based Atlantic Council. But Beijing's overall economic policy is mixed in terms of liberalization and openness. In August 2020, for example, China offered a package of tax incentives for domestic semiconductor manufacturers to reduce its overdependence on silicon imported from abroad (Myers & Bradsher, 2020). Yet it has allowed a high level of competition from foreign companies in certain industries; in 2018 the Austin-headquartered Tesla company built the first fully foreign-owned auto factory in China, and has since posted strong sale numbers (Lipsky, 2021). Thus economic globalization is not total liberalization for China, for the state controls the speed and depth of the process.

Another important aspect of China's globalization is increased self-reliance. The central government has heavily subsidized its manufacturers of semiconductors, commercial aircraft, and electric cars, among other products (Bradsher, 2021). A September 2021 report from the EU Chamber of Commerce in China expressed concern about China's recent turn inwards, stating that it is "casting considerable doubts over the country's future growth trajectory" and that Beijing's "plan to increase self-sufficiency will continue to create frictions with other major economies" (European Union, 2021). Chinese policymakers continue to debate the subject; while some argue that China should accentuate its international circulation and continue to embrace globalization, others believe that its future success lies in disentangling itself from critical sectors within the global economy that can be exploited by hostile powers like the US (Blanchette & Polk, 2020). Former central bank adviser Yu Yongding has pushed for Beijing to switch emphasis from the services economy to an industrial policy such as that reflected in "Made in China 2025," a state-led policy to ensure that China dominates global high-tech manufacturing (Sina Finance, 2020).

As tensions with the US exposed China's heavy reliance on foreign high-tech products such as semiconductors, which CCP leadership views as a significant national security risk, Xi said that China would rely mainly on "internal circulation," reducing dependence on overseas markets and technology for the sake of its long-term economic development. Certainly, he aims to boost innovation by domestic tech firms and to push such companies up the global value chain (Yao, 2020). Yet the leadership recently stressed that "dual circulation" does not signal a retreat into isolation. In an October 2020 speech, Xi said: "The new development pattern is not a closed domestic circulation, but an open domestic and international dual circulation" (China Global Television Network, 2020). Foreign companies may therefore find it easier to access China's massive consumer market in the future, although likely limited to industries like financial services and consumer goods. New regulations loosening joint venture requirements for foreign firms have already prompted investments not only from Tesla but from other US companies like JPMorgan Chase (Taplin, 2020).

Still, many Western analysts firmly believe that under dual circulation the CCP will concentrate on augmented domestic production and enhanced top-down state control (see Crabtree, 2020). A recent *New York Times* article described China's behaviour in the international trading regime as "globalization with Communist characteristics" (Myers & Bradsher, 2020). If dual circulation is an effort to shift its economy from a growth model driven by exports and infrastructure investment to a consumption-led economy, a feature of many advanced economies, this is not new to China's economic agenda. Prioritizing household consumption over reliance on investment and exports was part of its 11th Five-Year Plan (2006–2010). In 2020, consumption accounted for just 38% of China's economy (CEIC Data, n.d.), while private consumption comprised over 83% of the US economy in 2016 (Trading Economics, n.d.). As a share of GDP, China's private consumption expenditure hovers at uniquely low levels. One explanation is its high household savings rate, which nearly reached 35% in 2020, double that of the country with the second-highest average rate, India at 17% (Ernst & Young, 2021). China has a per capita GDP of $10,500, as of 2020

(Morgan Stanley, 2020), which exceeds the central value of the income range for an upper middle-income country, according to the World Bank definition (Ernst & Young, 2021), but significantly trails the US: the latter boasted an average per capita income of over $63,500 last year (World Bank, n.d.). There are signs of progress. The State Council's Development Research Center (2020) predicts that China will have at least 560 million middle-income consumers by 2024, and it is projected to attain the rank of a high-income country during its next five-year period, even using the government's conservative real economic growth prediction of 6% in 2021 (Ernst & Young, 2021).

5 Development, Rule of Law, and Human Rights

Partly due to the void created by the US under Trump, China has become an even stronger supporter of international organizations and played a much more active role in the HRC. The current global governance system and its norms are often seen as reflecting a liberal world order led by Western powers, in which human rights and rule of law play key functions. While this may be arguable, the way China uses the term "development" already reflects certain differences from general practice, where for instance, China does not impose certain liberal values or certain teleologies of development in the liberal sense. Development is at the centre of a communication and ideological competition between China and many developed countries. This is likely to intensify as China advances its model of development and governance in the world, explicitly pointing at the weaknesses of Western liberal democratic systems and positioning itself as an alternative "solution provider" according to the official term "China solution" (中国方案). This discourse has been promoted—primarily in developing countries, but also in developed countries—through training programmes for officials, politicians, engineers, technicians, and other professionals, which often include an ideological component in addition to practical training. China also creates its image as a solution provider through its international media outlets, now broadcasting in local languages in many countries and becoming media of reference, particularly where the local media landscape is weak or struggling financially.

China's discourse around the BRI emphasizes cooperation with developing nations across Eurasia to build national-level infrastructure and development projects. Chinese officials highlight the development benefits for host countries. At the first Belt and Road Forum, Xi (2017b) said that BRI implementation should focus on development, release various countries' growth potential, achieve economic integration and interconnected development, and deliver benefits to all. At the 2018 Forum, Vice Foreign Minister Le Yucheng (2018) extolled "how the BRI and Kazak Bright Road Initiative have complemented each other, how the China–Europe Railway Express has helped catalyse local growth, and how the world's biggest landlocked country has gained access to the ocean thanks to the BRI. The Kazaks hail China as 'Kazakhstan's ocean'."

Official statements summarizing high-level visits between Chinese officials and their counterparts from BRI host countries often highlight development as one aspect of the non-interference underpinning Chinese foreign policy. In 2015, Chinese Foreign Minister Wang Yi (2015) met with the press and described the BRI as not a Chinese "solo" but a "symphony" of all countries involved, in which Beijing "strives for common development and common prosperity on the basis of equality and mutual benefit." In the statement released after talks between Vice Premier Zhang Gaoli and Estonian President Kersti Kaljulaid, China explicitly reiterated its belief that "all countries should choose the development path suited to their own national conditions." A statement released after Zhang's visit to Slovenia in 2017 echoes this, stating that China–Slovenia bilateral relations set "an example of getting along well with each other among countries with different political systems, development paths, and cultural backgrounds" (Ministry of Foreign Affairs, 2017).

China has embraced ideas of human rights and rule of law, but given them new meanings, usually described as "Chinese characteristics." Rule of law (法治) has been enshrined in China's constitution since 1999: Article 5 states: "The People's Republic of China governs the country according to law and makes it a socialist country under rule of law" (National People's Congress, 2004). But many still view China as incompatible with the rule of law, observing the CCP's often blatant disregard for it. Xi has used the law to consolidate authoritarian power and control; in 2018 he amended the constitution to remove term limits on his presidency, and the laws he has passed to combat corruption have also enabled him to sideline political rivals (Carrai, 2021, p. 118). Yet the law under Xi has also expanded citizens' ability to sue the state through courts and public-interest litigation related to environmental lawsuits. China's apparently paradoxical understanding of the law is most evident in the BRI and its arbitration system, the China International Commercial Court (CICC). Most BRI projects occur on an ad hoc basis or within the framework of a bilateral investment treaty lacking precise instructions on how to resolve conflicts. It lacks (1) a multilateral treaty covering all participating nation-states; (2) a secretariat or other central body to standardize projects and provide a forum for deliberation and development; and (3) an adequate dispute resolution system (Dahlan, 2020). China has sought to improve the BRI's legal infrastructure, however, reflected in a renewed emphasis on advancing rule of law, an oft-discussed topic at the 19th Party Congress in October 2017.

The Supreme People's Court announced the CICC in 2018. Colloquially known as the "Belt and Road Court," the CICC itself contains two branches: the First International Commercial Court in Shenzhen (overseeing cases related to the sea-based Maritime Silk Road) and the Second International Commercial Court in Xi'an (reviewing cases along the land-based Silk Road Economic Belt) (Lu, 2019). The CICC has adjudicated over a dozen cases (Pham & Dai, 2021) and marks a significant step towards achieving the CCP's commitment to a "Chinese" rule of law suited to existing "national conditions" (Gu, 2019, p. 1350). Scholars have pointed to flaws within the CICC's institutional design, however. Despite its aspirations to become a "one-stop shop" dispute resolution platform for the BRI—covering litigation, arbitration, and mediation—it operates more like a domestic court. It does not enjoy broad oversight; rather, its jurisdiction is limited to international commercial and civil matters—excluding investor-state disputes and interstate trade disputes (Zhang, 2018). In addition, judges are only appointed to the court on a part-time basis and thus need to balance other responsibilities within the Supreme People's Court (Finder, 2019). The CICC's ability to adequately resolve all disputes stemming from the BRI, particularly as it continues its rapid expansion, seems questionable (Chaisse & Xu, 2021).

Some Western scholars argue that the BRI aims to promote China's development path, or "China model." US scholar Elizabeth Economy (2018) has described it as part of a strategy to "promote an alternative legal system underpinned by Chinese rules," pointing at Beijing's plans to establish special arbitration courts for BRI projects. For Andrew Batson (2019), of the French-owned investment research firm Gavekal, the BRI aims to globalize a specific aspect of China's domestic political economy: the nexus between state-owned contractors and state-owned banks. At the 19th Party Congress in October 2018, Xi defended China's unique developmental path and positioned it as an example to emulate: "the culture of socialism with Chinese characteristics has kept developing, blazing a new trail for other developing countries to achieve modernization. It offers a new option for other countries and nations who want to speed up their development while preserving their independence, and it offers Chinese wisdom and a Chinese approach to solving the problems facing mankind."

China is also using "human rights" in a different way. It has published white papers on the topic since 1991, on its overall view on human rights, its progress on human rights, and specific matters like minorities, rule of law, Tibet, or Xinjiang. While China has lifted 800 million people out of poverty to date, progress has been thin on political and civil rights, and liberal values seem not to sit well with the CCP leadership, especially after Xi eliminated presidential term limits. China sees itself as following a "unique path" of human rights. In its national report to the HRC, it argued that "[t]here is no universal road for the development of human rights in the world. As an important element in the economic and social development of each country, the cause of human rights must be promoted on the basis of the national conditions and the needs of the people of that country" (UN, 2018, p. 2).

The idea of human rights with Chinese characteristics puts the focus on national conditions, where people rather than individuals are at the centre and development rights are priority. China's almost 30-year tradition of human rights white papers demonstrates the topic's continued relevance, as well as a shift away from defensiveness—the first white paper on human rights was a response to criticisms after the Tiananmen Square protests—towards assertiveness. Recent white papers state that China can provide Chinese solutions to global human rights governance, and China has increasingly made proposals and advanced amendments at the UN General Assembly and HRC. The white paper on human rights of 2019 states that China proposes (1) subsistence and development as fundamental rights, (2) people-centred human rights, and (3) a focus on each country's historical and national conditions (State Council, 2018). This goes hand in hand with the idea of a "global community of shared destiny," which is repeated throughout the document.

6 Conclusion

This chapter has discussed part of the Chinese vocabulary that is going global, starting from the BRI. Language, never neutral and constantly evolving, shapes the way we think and act. When powers introduce new vocabulary into international relations or reconfigure existing terms, they help reshape the structure of international society and the norms that regulate it. The West has dictated the vocabulary of global governance for long time. Now that China has emerged as a great power, is taking its own turn to shape this language. Scholars have argued that even though some Chinese terms seem innocuous, they indicate Beijing's designs for a future world order aligned with its own interests, focused on national sovereignty and nonintervention in internal affairs, and undermining human rights monitoring and protection, among other things. This article showed that, whether or not these suspicions are correct, some of these terms, such as the "Belt and Road Initiative," have already become international currency. The notion of "a community of shared future for humanity," has, for instance, made its way into documents of the UN General Assembly, the Security Council, and the HRC, becoming perhaps part of a new nascent international human rights discourse. China has also started to play a much more active role in the HRC in order to block criticisms from other countries about its repression of human rights, thereby promoting a sovereigntist approach that uses the rule of law to bring civil society under state control and a vision of human rights as collective, aimed at promoting social stability and prioritizing developmental and subsistence rights. Clearly, China's assertiveness is gradually altering the meanings injected into human rights discourse over the decades. It has also been contributing more generally to global governance and its lexicon, with Chinese diplomats pushing countries to use new terms in their agreements. Some terms have already been integrated within international fora, and other countries must be aware of the definition differences when negotiating with China. The long-term impact of Chinese vocabulary on global governance is still far from being crystallized, and there are also setbacks from countries that oppose the new vocabulary. As well as being alert for possible negative ramifications, other countries should use the opportunity to engage in creating a more genuinely universal shared language for global governance.

Bibliographic References

Abe, S. (2015, May 21). *'The future of Asia: Be innovative'—Speech by Prime Minister Shinzo Abe at the Banquet of the 21st International Conference on the Future of Asia*. Prime Minister of Japan and His Cabinet. Retrieved on December 2021, from https://japan.kantei.go.jp/97_abe/statement/201505/0521foaspeech.html/

Alden, C., & Alves, A. C. (2017). China's regional forum diplomacy in the developing world: Socialisation and the 'sinosphere'. *Journal of Contemporary China, 26*(103), 151–165. https://doi.org/10.1080/10670564.2016.1206276

Ali, S. M. (2020). *China's Belt and Road vision: Geoeconomics and geopolitics*. Springer.

Batson, A. (2019, May 2). *The Belt and Road is about domestic interest groups, not development.* Andrew Batson's Blog. Retrieved on December 2021, from https://andrewbatson.com/2019/05/02/the-belt-and-road-is-about-domestic-interest-groups-not-development/

Belt and Road Forum for International Cooperation. (2017, April 10). *Full text: Vision and actions on jointly building Belt and Road (2).* Retrieved on December 2021, from http://2017.beltandroadforum.org/english/n100/2017/0410/c22-45-2.html

Belt and Road Portal. (2015, March 30). *Vision and actions on jointly building silk road economic belt and 21st-century Maritime Silk Road.* Retrieved on November 2021, from https://eng.yidaiyilu.gov.cn/qwyw/qwfb/1084.htm

Belt and Road Portal. (2017, May 16). *Joint communique of leaders roundtable of Belt and Road forum.* Retrieved on November 2021, from https://eng.yidaiyilu.gov.cn/zchj/qwfb/13694.htm

Belt and Road Portal. (2019, November 28). *Joint press communique between the People's Republic of China and the Republic of Suriname.* Retrieved on December 2021, from https://eng.yidaiyilu.gov.cn/zchj/sbwj/111197.htm

Belt and Road Portal. (2020, August 25). *Full text of Co-chairs' Statement on Cooperation of Synergizing the Mekong-Lancang Cooperation and the New International Land-Sea Trade Corridor of the Third Mekong-Lancang Cooperation (MLC) Leaders' Meeting.* Retrieved on December 2021, from https://eng.yidaiyilu.gov.cn/qwyw/rdxw/144588.htm

Blanchette, J., & Polk, A. (2020, August 4). Dual circulation and China's new hedged integration strategy. Center for Strategic and International Studies. Retrieved on November 2021, from https://www.csis.org/analysis/dual-circulation-and-chinas-new-hedged-integration-strategy

Bloomberg News. (2021, August 25). *Billionaire donations soar in China push for 'common prosperity'.* Retrieved on December 2021, from www.bloomberg.com/news/articles/2021-08-22/xi-doubles-mentions-of-common-prosperity-warning-china-s-rich

Bradsher, K. (2021, September 23). Business groups are divided as China seeks self-reliance. *The New York Times.* Retrieved on December 2021, from https://www.nytimes.com/2021/09/23/business/china-business-survey.html

Carrai, M. A. (2021). Law as an instrument of power: The Chinese socialist rule of law. In B. Faedda (Ed.), *Rule of law: Cases, strategies, and interpretations.* Ronzani/Italian Academy.

Carrai, M. A., & Defraigne, J.-C. (2020). *The Belt and Road and global governance.* Edward Elgar.

CASS. (2015). 一带一路"战略与西南边疆的开放、稳定与发展: 中国社会科学论坛(2015)暨第六届西南论坛论文集 [The Belt and Road strategy and the opening up, stability and development of the southwest frontier: Paper compilation on the CASS forum (2015) and the 6th China Southwest forum].

CEIC Data. (n.d.). *China private consumption: % of GDP.* Retrieved on December 2021, from https://www.ceicdata.com/en/indicator/china/private-consumption--of-nominal-gdp#:~:text=China's%20Private%20Consumption%20accounted%20for,an%20average%20share%20of%2049.7%20%25

Chaisse, J., & Xu, Q. (2021). Conservative innovation: The ambiguities of the China International Commercial Court. *American Journal of International Law Unbound.* Retrieved on December 2021, from https://www.cambridge.org/core/services/aop-cambridge-core/content/view/CC1670B2A6771A3115CF2628046E9B73/S2398772320000811a.pdf/conservative-innovation-the-ambiguities-of-the-china-international-commercial-court.pdf

Cheng, D. (2018). *Trade governance of the Belt and Road Initiative: Economic logic, value choices, and institutional arrangement.* Routledge.

China Daily. (2015, April 22). *Backgrounder: Five principles of peaceful coexistence.* Retrieved on December 2021, from https://www.chinadaily.com.cn/world/2015xivisitpse/2015-04/22/content_20509374.htm

China Global Television Network. (2020, October 14). *China vows to expand all-around opening-up at Shenzhen SEZ's 40th anniversary.* Retrieved on November 2021, from https://news.cgtn.com/news/2020-10-14/President-Xi-addresses-Shenzhen-SEZ-40th-anniversary-celebration-UzNg2ywG9a/index.html

Crabtree, J. (2020, December 10). *China's radical new vision of globalization*. Retrieved on November 2021, from https://www.noemamag.com/chinas-radical-new-vision-of-globalization/

Credit Suisse. (2021). *Global wealth report 2021*. Retrieved on November 2021, from https://www.credit-suisse.com/media/assets/corporate/docs/about-us/research/publications/global-wealth-report-2021-en.pdf

Dahlan, M. R. (2020). Envisioning foundations for the law of the Belt and Road Initiative: Rule of law and dispute resolution challenges. *Harvard International Law Journal*. Retrieved on November 2021, from https://harvardilj.org/wp-content/uploads/sites/15/Envisioning-Foundations-For-the-Law-of-the-Belt-and-Road-Initiative-Rule-of-Law-and-Dispute-Resolution-Challenges.pdf

Dorsey, J. M. (2019, February 5). *A China wins twice proposition: The Belt and Road Initiative* (pp. 1–13). https://doi.org/10.2139/ssrn.3329619

Doshi, R. (2021). *The long game: China's grand strategy to displace American order*. Oxford University Press.

Du, Q. (2015, May 21). *A new type of win-win international cooperation*. China US Focus. Retrieved on November 2021, from https://www.chinausfocus.com/foreign-policy/a-new-type-of-win-win-international-cooperation

Economy, E. (2018, June). China's new revolution. *Foreign Affairs*. Retrieved on November 2021, from https://www.foreignaffairs.com/articles/china/2018-04-17/chinas-new-revolution

Ekman, A. (2017, November 4). *China and the "definition gap": Shaping global governance in words*. Asan Forum. Retrieved on November 2021, from https://www.ifri.org/en/espace-media/lifri-medias/china-and-definition-gap-shaping-global-governance-words

Ernst & Young. (2021). *The seven faces of China's consumer*. Retrieved on November 2021, from https://www.ey.com/en_cn/consumer-products-retail/how-will-china-consumer-driven-economy-unfold-in-the-14th-fyp

European Parliament. (2021, April). *Prospects for EU-Asia connectivity: The 'European way to connectivity'*. Retrieved on November 2021, from https://www.europarl.europa.eu/RegData/etudes/BRIE/2021/690534/EPRS_BRI(2021)690534_EN.pdf

European Union Chamber of Commerce in China. (2021, September 23). *Position paper 2021/2022*. Retrieved on November 2021, from https://www.europeanchamber.com.cn/en/publications-annual-report

Finder, S. (2019, January 14). *China International Commercial Court starts operating*. Supreme People's Court Monitor. Retrieved on November 2021, from https://supremepeoplescourtmonitor.com/2019/01/14/china-international-commercial-court-starts-operating/

Fisher, J. (2020, October 28). *China's 'Win-Win' resolution is anything but*. Human Rights Watch. Retrieved on November 2021, from https://www.hrw.org/news/2018/03/05/chinas-win-win-resolution-anything

Friedberg, A. L. (2012). *A contest for supremacy: China, America, and the struggle for mastery in Asia*. W. W. Norton.

Garlick, J. (2020). *The impact of China's Belt and Road Initiative: From Asia to Europe*. Routledge.

Goldstein, A. (2005). *Rising to the challenge China's grand strategy and international security*. Stanford University Press.

Gu, W. (2019). China's Belt and Road development and a new international commercial arbitration initiative in Asia. *Vanderbilt Journal of Transnational Law*. Retrieved on November 2021, from https://cdn.vanderbilt.edu/vu-wp0/wp-content/uploads/sites/78/2019/01/04185731/6.-Gu-READY-FOR-PRINT.pdf

He, L. (2019). 提升新时代中国国际话语权 [Enhancing China's international discourse power in the new era]. 红旗文稿 [Red Flag Manuscript]. Retrieved on November 2021, from http://www.qstheory.cn/dukan/hqwg/2019-09/09/c_1124968280.htm

Hillman, J. E. (2017, May 12). *China's 'Belt and Road' Initiative must become a strategy*. CSIS Global Economics Monthly. Retrieved on November 2021, from https://www.csis.org/analysis/chinas-belt-road-initiative-must-become-strategy

https://data.worldbank.org/indicator/NY.GDP.PCAP.CD?locations=CN. *GDP per capita (current US$)—United States*. https://data.worldbank.org/indicator/NY.GDP.PCAP.CD?locations=US

Hu, J. (2012, November 27). *Full text of Hu Jintao's report at 18th Party Congress*. Embassy of the People's Republic of China in the United States of America. Retrieved on November 2021, from http://www.china-embassy.org/eng/zt/18th_CPC_National_Congress_Eng/t992917.htm

Kim, T. (2015, February 16). *Beyond geopolitics: South Korea's Eurasia initiative as a new Nordpolitik*. Asan Forum. Retrieved on December 2021, from https://theasanforum.org/beyond-geopolitics-south-koreas-eurasia-initiative-as-a-new-nordpolitik/

Leandro, F. J., & Duarte, P. A. B. (2020). *The Belt and Road Initiative: An old archetype of a new development model*. Springer.

Le, Y. (2018, October 15). *Remarks by Executive Vice Foreign Minister Le Yucheng at the Welcoming Dinner of the First Meeting of the Advisory Council of the Belt and Road Forum for International Cooperation (BRF)*. Ministry of Foreign Affairs of the People's Republic of China. Retrieved on December 2021, from https://www.fmprc.gov.cn/mfa_eng/wjdt_665385/zyjh_665391/t1623914.shtml

Lin, J. Y., & Wang, X. (2021). Dual circulation: A new structural economics view of development. *Journal of Chinese Economic and Business Studies*, 1–20. Retrieved on December 2021, from https://www.tandfonline.com/doi/pdf/10.1080/14765284.2021.1929793

Lipsky, J. (2021). *The 2021 economic scorecard: How China stacks up with the us and its allies*. Atlantic Council. Retrieved on December 2021, from https://www.atlanticcouncil.org/content-series/the-big-story/the-2021-economic-scorecard-how-china-stacks-up-with-the-us-and-its-allies/

Liu, W. (2018). *China's Belt and Road Initiatives: Economic geography reformation*. Springer.

Liu, W. (2019a). *The Belt and Road Initiative: A pathway towards inclusive globalization*. Routledge.

Liu, X. (2019b, October 22). Productive partnerships are never built on insults. *Financial Times*. Retrieved on December 2021, from https://www.ft.com/content/5ee8762c-effe-11e9-ad1e-4367d8281195

Lu, X. (2019, October 14). The changing perspectives of Chinese law: Socialist rule of law, emerging case law and the Belt and Road Initiative. *The Chinese Journal of Global Governance*. Retrieved on December 2021, from https://brill.com/view/journals/cjgg/5/2/article-p153_4.xml?language=en&ebody=full%20html-copy1

Mações, B. (2018). *Belt and Road: A Chinese world order*. Hurst & Company.

Ministry of Foreign Affairs of the People's Republic of China. (2017, April). *Zhang Gaoli visits Estonia*. Retrieved on December 2021, from https://www.fmprc.gov.cn/mfa_eng/wjb_663304/zzjg_663340/xos_664404/xwlb_664406/t1454471.shtml

Ministry of Foreign Affairs of the People's Republic of China. (n.d.). *China's initiation of the five principles of peaceful co-existence*. Retrieved on December 2021, from https://www.fmprc.gov.cn/mfa_eng/ziliao_665539/3602_665543/3604_665547/t18053.shtml

Morgan Stanley. (2020). https://www.morganstanley.com/ideas/china-wealth-management

Myers, S. L., & Bradsher, K. (2020, November 23). China says it remains open to the world, but wants to dictate terms. *The New York Times*. Retrieved on December 2021, from https://www.nytimes.com/2020/11/23/world/asia/china-xi-jinping-globalization.html

Panyue, H. (2021, August 17). *XI urges financial risk prevention while seeking high-quality growth*. CGTN. http://eng.mod.gov.cn/news/2021-08/17/content_4892182.htm

Permanent Mission of the People's Republic of China to the United Nations Office at Geneva and Other International Organizations in Switzerland. (2018, March 1). *Win-win cooperation for the common cause of human rights*. Retrieved on December 2021, from http://www.china-un.ch/eng/hom/t1538784.htm

Pham, H., & Dai, A. C. (2021, March 4). *The China International Commercial Court*. White & Case. Retrieved on December 2021, from https://www.whitecase.com/publications/alert/china-international-commercial-court

Piccone, T. (2018, September). *China's long game on human rights at the United Nations*. Brookings Institution. Retrieved on January 2022, from https://www.brookings.edu/wp-content/uploads/2018/09/FP_20181009_china_human_rights.pdf

Piccone, T. (2021, February 25). *UN Human Rights Council: As the US returns, it will have to deal with China and its friends*. Brookings Institution. Retrieved on December 2021, from https://www.brookings.edu/blog/order-from-chaos/2021/02/25/un-human-rights-council-as-the-us-returns-it-will-have-to-deal-with-china-and-its-friends/

Republic of Turkey Ministry of Foreign Affairs. (n.d.). *Turkey's multilateral transportation policy*. Retrieved on January 2022, from https://www.mfa.gov.tr/turkey_s-multilateral-transportation-policy.en.mfa

Reuters. (2019, April 26). *China President Xi says goal of Belt and Road is advance 'win-win cooperation'*. Retrieved on January 2022, from https://www.reuters.com/article/us-china-silkroad-xi/china-president-xi-says-goal-of-belt-and-road-is-advance-win-win-cooperation-idINKCN1S205Z

Rolland, N. (2017). *China's Eurasian century? Political and strategic implications of the Belt and Road Initiative*. National Bureau of Asian Research. Routledge.

Sina Finance. (2020, August 18). 余永定: 怎样实现从"国际大循环"到"双循环"的转变? Retrieved on January 2022, from http://finance.sina.com.cn/zl/china/2020-08-18/zl-iivhvpwy1713127.shtml

State Council. (2018). *Progress in human rights over the 40 years of reform and opening up in China*. Retrieved on December 2021, from http://english.gov.cn/archive/white_paper/2018/12/13/content_281476431737638.htm

State Council. (2020, September 1). 十四五"时期经济社会发展十大趋势 [Development Research Center of the State Council]. Retrieved on January 2022, from https://h5.drcnet.com.cn/docview.aspx?chnid=1002&leafid=26601&docid=5952322&uid=02&version=integrated

State Council Information Office of the People's Republic of China. (2021, July 1). *Xi declares China a moderately prosperous society in all respects*. Retrieved on January 2022, from http://english.scio.gov.cn/topnews/2021-07/01/content_77599525.htm

Suettinger, R. L. (2004). *The rise and descent of "peaceful rise"*. China Leadership Monitor (12). Retrieved on December 2021, from https://www.hoover.org/sites/default/files/uploads/documents/clm12_rs.pdf

Talbot, M., Atkinson, K., & Atkinson, D. (2003). *Language and power in the modern world*. Edinburgh University Press.

Taplin, N. (2020, November 3). China's risky bet on a lonely return to greatness. *The Wall Street Journal*. Retrieved on December 2021, from https://www.wsj.com/articles/chinas-risky-bet-on-a-lonely-return-to-greatness-11604398497?mod=article_inline

The Economist. (2021, August 28). Xi Jinping's talk of 'common prosperity' spooks the prosperous. Retrieved on November 2021, from https://www.economist.com/finance-and-economics/xi-jinpings-talk-of-common-prosperity-spooks-the-prosperous/21803895

The National People's Congress of the People's Republic of China. (2004, March 14). *Constitution of the People's Republic of China*. Retrieved on December 2021, from http://www.npc.gov.cn/zgrdw/englishnpc/Constitution/2007-11/15/content_1372963.htm

Thirty-First Session Geneva. (2018, November 5–16). *National report submitted in accordance with paragraph 5 of the annex to Human Rights Council resolution 16/2. China*. Retrieved on December 2021, from https://documents-dds-ny.un.org/doc/UNDOC/GEN/G18/254/62/PDF/G1825462.pdf?OpenElement

Tobin, L. (2019). Xi's vision for transforming global governance: A strategic challenge for Washington and its allies. In *China's global influence: Perspectives and recommendations*. Asia-Pacific Center for Security Studies. Retrieved on December 2021, from https://apcss.org/wp-content/uploads/2019/09/2-Xis_Vision_for_transforming_Global-Governance-Tobin.pdf

Trading Economics. (n.d.). *United States—Final consumption expenditure, etc. (% of GDP)*. Retrieved on December 2021, from https://tradingeconomics.com/united-states/final-consumption-expenditure-etc-percent-of-gdp-wb-data.html

United Nations (UN). (2017). *Resolution adopted by the Economic and Social Council on 8 June 2017*. E/RES/2017/11. Retrieved on December 2021, from https://www.undocs.org/E/RES/2017/11

United Nations (UN). (2018). *Human Rights Council working group on the universal periodic review.*

Wang, Y. (2015, February 2). *Belt and Road is 'symphony' jointly performed by all countries.* Ministry of Foreign Affairs of the People's Republic of China. Retrieved on December 2021, from https://www.fmprc.gov.cn/mfa_eng/zxxx_662805/t1234406.shtml

Wang, Y. (2017). *China connects the world. What behind the Belt and Road Initiative.* New World Press.

Wang, L., & Zhao, J. (Eds.). (2019). *The belt and road initiative in the global context* (China's Belt and Road Initiative). World Scientific.

Wei, L. (2021, September 20). Xi Jinping aims to rein in Chinese capitalism, HEW to Mao's socialist vision. *The Wall Street Journal.* Retrieved on December 2021, from www.wsj.com/articles/xi-jinping-aims-to-rein-in-chinese-capitalism-hew-to-maos-socialist-vision-11632150725

Wen, J. (2004, June 28). *Carrying forward the five principles of peaceful coexistence in the promotion of peace and development.* Embassy of the People's Republic of China in the Republic of Turkey. Retrieved on December 2021, from http://tr.china-embassy.org/eng/xwdt/t140777.htm

Xiao, G. (2021). *Financing China's Belt and Road Initiative. Investments in infrastructure.* Routledge.

Xi, J. (2013, March 23). *Follow the trend of the times and promote peace and development in the world.* Ministry of Foreign Affairs of the People's Republic of China. Retrieved on December 2021, from https://www.fmprc.gov.cn/mfa_eng/wjdt_665385/zyjh_665391/t1033246.shtml

Xi, J. (2015, March 28). *Full text of Chinese President's speech at Boao Forum for Asia.* Ministry of Foreign Affairs of the People's Republic of China. Retrieved on December 2021, from https://www.fmprc.gov.cn/mfa_eng/topics_665678/xjpcxbayzlt2015nnh/t1250690.shtml

Xi, J. (2016, September 3). *Keynote speech by H.E. Xi Jinping, President of the People's Republic of China, at the opening ceremony of the B20 Summit.* Ministry of Foreign Affairs of the People's Republic of China. Retrieved on December 2021, from https://www.fmprc.gov.cn/mfa_eng/wjdt_665385/zyjh_665391/t1396112.shtml

Xi, J. (2017a, January 17). *Full text of Xi Jinping keynote at the World Economic Forum.* China Global Television Network. Retrieved on December 2021, from https://america.cgtn.com/2017/01/17/full-text-of-xi-jinping-keynote-at-the-world-economic-forum

Xi, J. (2017b, May 14). *Full text of President Xi's speech at opening of Belt and Road forum.* Xinhua. Retrieved on December 2021, from http://www.xinhuanet.com//english/2017-05/14/c_136282982.htm

Xi, J. (2019, June 15). *Working together for new progress of security and development in Asia.* Ministry of Foreign Affairs of the People's Republic of China. Retrieved on December 2021, from https://www.fmprc.gov.cn/mfa_eng/wjdt_665385/zyjh_665391/t1672539.shtml

Xi, J. (2021, January 25). *Let the torch of multilateralism light up humanity's way forward.* Ministry of Foreign Affairs of the People's Republic of China. https://www.fmprc.gov.cn/mfa_eng/zxxx_662805/t1848323.shtml

Xie, T. (2015, December 16). Is China's 'Belt and Road' a strategy? *The Diplomat.* Retrieved on December 2021, from https://thediplomat.com/2015/12/is-chinas-belt-and-road-a-strategy

Xinhua News. (2017, January 19). *Work together to build a community of shared future for mankind.* Retrieved on December 2021, from http://www.xinhuanet.com/english/2017-01/19/c_135994707.htm

Xu, F. (2018). *The Belt and Road: The global strategy of china high-speed railway.* Springer.

Yang, J. (2018, August 1). 以习近平外交思想为指导 深入推进新时代对外工作. *Qiushi.* Retrieved on December 2021, from http://www.qstheory.cn/dukan/qs/2018-08/01/c_1123209510.htm

Yao, K. (2020, September 15). *What we know about China's 'dual circulation' economic strategy.* Reuters. Retrieved on December 2021, from https://www.reuters.com/article/china-economy-transformation-explainer/what-we-know-about-chinas-dual-circulation-economic-strategy-idUSKBN2600B5

Ye, M. (2020). *The Belt Road and beyond: State-mobilized globalization in China: 1998–2018*. Cambridge University Press.

Zhang, Y. (2018, July 2). *Zhang Yongjian: Towards a fair, efficient and convenient dispute resolution mechanism for B&R-related international commercial disputes: China's practice and innovation*. China International Commercial Court. http://cicc.court.gov.cn/html/1/219/199/203/831.html

Zhang, y., & Yuan, Z. (2017). 一带一路"与中国发展战略 [The Belt and Road and China's development strategy]. She hui ke xue wen xian chu ban she.

Zhao, X. (2018). In pursuit of a community of shared future. *China Quarterly of International Strategic Studies, 4*(1), 23–37. https://doi.org/10.1142/S2377740018500082

Zheng, B. (2005). *China's peaceful rise: Speeches of Zheng Bijian 1997–2004*. Brookings Institution. https://www.brookings.edu/wp-content/uploads/2012/04/20050616bijianlunch.pdf

Chapter 4
The Globalizing Discourse of the Belt and Road Initiative

Cátia Miriam Costa

1 Introduction

Since 1949, the People's Republic of China has developed a discourse for the international sphere. The Chinese international discourse evolved and deeply corresponded to the Chinese perspective of the International Order and simultaneously to the role China wanted to play in the international scene. Although sometimes neglected by researchers, there is a direct nexus between discourse and foreign policy, which is a relevant part of a better understanding of International Relations (Chan & Song, 2020, p. 431). However, the foreign policy discourses are still understudied and, when they become the object of study, are generally driven through a geopolitical analysis (Chan & Song, 2020, pp. 418–419). The Chinese foreign policy discourses are not an exception, giving evidence of this lack of attention to one of the most relevant elements of international relations (Mochtak & Turcsanyi, 2021, p. 744). Even the Belt & Road Initiative (B&RI) reflects this situation as an object of study. However, it is considered one of the most challenging projects having an eventual direct impact on international order.

In this chapter, we contribute to a better understanding of the Chinese discourse for foreign policy, researching how the Belt & Road Initiative discourse, the most representative Chinese international project, became global. We look at President Xi Jinping's international discourses and interpret them using discourse analyses, answering the possibility of the Belt & Road Initiative's evolution from a regional to a global project. We also focus these discourses in the channels used to spread them under an international communication perspective. Some authors highlight that without studying the discourse and the connection between language and politics, it would be impossible to fully understand how foreign policy is structured (Mochtac & Turcsanyi, 2021, p. 743). Discourse and narratives have the potential to change reality,

C. M. Costa (✉)
ISCTE, Instituto Universitário de Lisboa, Lisbon, Portugal
e-mail: catia.miriam.costa@iscte-iul.pt

and international politics is not considered an exception. Through these discourses and how they are going global, we inductively explain their contribution to the internationally created narrative by the People's Republic of China. China now has her discourses and narratives internationally projected evidence a pathway taken in the 50s of the twentieth century that evolved until now.

Some authors consider the Belt & Road Initiative as a return to the "belle epoque" of a kind of "Pax Sinica," inherited from the original Silk Road (Benabdallah, 2019, p. 93). In Chinese memory, these were times not only of peace but also of wealth, independence, and China's regional influence. The B&RI exceeded the traditional perspective of the Silk Road and became a global project, with the participation of more than fourteen dozen countries from different continents, becoming an unavoidable transcontinental initiative. Therefore, the academic forums started to interpret the B&RI as the embodiment of the Chinese answer to international order (He, 2019, pp. 181–183). Although participating in International Order and receiving its normative discourses, the B&RI represents an opportunity to spread globalization with Chinese characteristics, not frontally challenging the installed norms. Notwithstanding proposes specific characteristics for bilateral relations and stimulates particular forms of multilateral forums (some created by Chinese initiatives). The B&RI allows China to offer new shapes for international relations, attracting States for her perspective of foreign policy, expecting a similar result to one the achieved by the "exportation" of the model of Chinese Special Economic Zones (Fei, 2017, pp. 825–826; Li & Costa, 2021, p. 52). Some authors see the B&RI project as the continuity of the "March Westward" rationale, which was discussed by Chinese political circles in the 10s of the twentieth century (Leverett & Wu, 2016, pp. 124–125). Nevertheless, the B&RI brings other possible perspectives. China is getting closer to challenging the US economically and technologically, something this superpower already noticed and adapted her policy to it. To respond to this new international environment, China might have started to build the B&RI as a compliment or an alternative to the traditional international relations led by the US. The Chinese focus on items like energy, trade relations, infrastructures, and mobility contribute to this perspective (Weatherley & Bauer, 2021, pp. 2115 and 2121).

Part of China's discourse to the international community in the first decades after the 1949 Communist Revolution remains and is the base for contemporary Chinese international discourse. However, we cannot say that the Chinese discourse has only maintained the historical grounds since the 50s of the twentieth century. We note that the Chinese discourse dynamics for the international sphere resulted in China's growing role as a norm producer even more than a norm challenger, although continuing to be a norm receiver (Benabdallah, 2019, p. 92). The international community recognizes that China contributes to international organizations (mainly supporting United Nations initiatives and institutions) to be more experienced and gain a reputation. Simultaneously Chinese initiatives (Benabdallah, 2019, p. 97) create new international organizations and introduce new concepts, such as the "Five Principles of peaceful coexistence" (in a partnership with India, in 1955) or "one country, two systems." These concepts were internationally consecrated and accepted for Hong Kong and Macao Handovers (Zeng, 2011, p. 79). Consequently, a stream of scientific studies defending that China has a Chinese International Law Discourse impacting normative issues and a propositional international discourse that introduces new concepts, like the win-win concept.

Nevertheless, introducing new international concepts and normative standards sometimes results in tension observed through the discourse analyses. Sometimes the Chinese political discourse waves in-between topics that seem contradictory, like equality and hierarchy of International Order or in-between superiority and respect (Nathan & Zhang, 2022, p. 58). Often this paradox gets a solution throughout cultural relativization.

2 Chinese Discourses "Going Global"

The gradual global rise in the international scene has been analysed from different perspectives, primarily based on Western theories and approaches (Xing, 2019, pp. 3–4). Throughout her presence in the world, China is going global and able to influence. Consequently, China's discourse tends also to globality, and now China must provide a domestic and an international discourse (Mulvad, 2019, p. 454). Western politicians, intellectuals, and scientists also contributed to the global projection of Chinese discourse through their speeches, research or essays (Mayer & Balázs, 2018, p. 207). Nevertheless, Chinese intellectuals, researchers, and politicians feel the Western theory of International Relations without the contribution of Chinese philosophy and theories does not explain how China sees herself in the international community and does not understand the role China aims to play in International Order (Shih, 2013, p. 2).

China was not a dominant provider of either political or scientific discourses. The country had to conquer her space in the international sphere, reflecting the transition from a mass producer to a service provider and sophisticated producer, reflecting on the global scenario (Costa, 2020b, p. 28). China found new ways of expressing herself (Cambié & Yang-May, 2009, p. 5), athwart international communication channels (Cheng, 2018, p. 7). We can say China climbed in the economic value chain and tried to replicate the same in the international arena by climbing in the international discourse value chain. Now it is clear that China is ambitious to be one of the major discursive powers for a global audience (Chan & Song, 2020, p. 418).

The progressive notoriety of the international Chinese discourse is also remarkable, partially due to the Chinese reception of soft power theory and adaptation to Chinese characteristics (Sun, 2015, pp. 406 and 408). We also underline the diversification of Chinese media in the world, which promote the deepening and broadening of Chinese international message based on international TV and radio channels and internet sites. This new trend gets the traditional spread of Chinese international discourse out of the political forums, opening the reach of this discourse to the international sphere. The TV and radio channels and the internet pages provide open dissemination of Chinese messages to the international community without further mediation. Theoretically, the result is the easy spreading of discourses and messages to diverse audiences in the public sphere (Couldry, 2014, p. 45). Transnationalization of public spheres and strategic political communication became the axes of public diplomacy and consequently international communication and must be considered as one more instrument for the spreading of narratives. Bilateral meetings or international forums also maintains one way to boost the official message (Adolphsen, 2012, p. 92), but without the monopoly over political discourses or messages.

Some authors consider that the B&RI actions and discourse reveal China's "going global" aim but concomitantly help the political leaders to design and rebalance domestic discourses and actions with international discourses and actions, proving the building of a narrative without paradoxes (Huang & Shih, 2014, p. 23; Leverett & Wu, 2016, p. 126). Others believe the B&RI discourse is alternative to Washington Consensus (Benabdallah, 2019, pp. 99–103), can be carried outside the Washington influence (Leverett & Wu, 2016, p. 124) and based on the concepts of "shared future" and "win-win" perspective (Nathan & Zhang, 2022, p. 60). The B&RI is also highlighted as a new way for the relations within the Global South (Benabdallah, 2019, p. 97) and, therefore, an alternative to the present International Order. However, other Chinese discourses grew in the international arena. The scientific discourse is one of the most remarkable ones. Chinese authors were the ones producing more about B&RI. The seven first places for affiliation in the scientific production about the B&RI are from researchers from Chinese institutions (Costa, 2020b, p. 25). The output of a Chinese discourse combining scientific discourse and political discourse (spread through media and political forums) became predominant in the international sphere for the first time with the B&RI. This fact points out that China introduces new perspectives and concepts on it without challenging International Order. The achievement of this aim also depends on the capacity to strengthen her international discourse through the voice of her leader, President Xi Jinping.

3 Globalizing the Discourse Through the B&RI

We analyse President Xi Jinping's discourses published in the three volumes of the Governance of China, translated into English and Portuguese languages. Our primary objective is to understand how President Xi Jinping's discourse contributed to the globalization of the B&RI discourse and is promoted as an alternative to other international discourses without challenging them. We can split President Xi Jinping's discourses in speeches domestically and internationally delivered. It is interesting to underline that the international and domestic discourses were assembled, organized, and published for international and national audiences. This option might signify that Chinese political power started to give more attention to the need to attract diverse audiences, including public servants, to this international project.

It is relevant to note that the B&RI became a topic progressively to be underlined and conquered its own space in organizing Chinese political speeches. The index of the three volumes of "Xi Jinping: Governance of China" evidences the growing relevance of the B&RI, turning into an autonomous topic in the second and third volumes. By analysing these indexes, we can understand the main issues for the central power and the first figure of the Chinese state. Throughout the three books, we can find references to some pillars that are part of the Chinese foreign policy and the way China sees herself in International Order. We are referring to "Socialism with Chinese Characteristics," "Neighbouring diplomacy." Simultaneously, we also observe the evolution of some topics, from the first volume to the third: "New Model of Major Countries relations"; then, "Diplomacy of a Great Country"; and, finally, "China's Diplomacy as a Major Country."

Another significant example is the repetition of the topic "One Country, Two Systems" in the two first volumes, disappearing to give place to "Hong Kong, Macao and China's Peaceful Reunification." Here the principle itself is substituted by the experience with the two regions that completed twenty years after the Handover. Besides the B&RI, other topics conquer autonomy in the second and third volumes, such as "Moderately Prosperous Society" or "A Global Community of Shared Future."

This analysis brings into light some characteristics of the Chinese foreign policy and the self-positioning of China in International Order that are determinant to understanding the evolution of the Chinese perspective about international relations in the last decade. Significantly, the Chinese discourse becomes more globalizing and concerned with the positioning of China as a major international power, interested in peaceful development and in multiplying relations without challenging the norms. However, concurrently proposing new ways of doing international relations based on principles that are the basis for China to relate with the world (like the win-win relations, the absolute respect for sovereignty or the idea of a shared future). Instead of an ideological perspective, China purposes something alternative. Although recognizing the specificity of Chinese Socialism, China prefers to communicate and influence through the economic growth and development (like the exportation of the Special Economic Zones) than influence other states to choose the same political path as China is not simply Karl Marx's socialism. It is instead a very particular type of socialism, the Chinese one. When the index stops using "One Country, two Systems" and introduces the Macao and Hong Kong experience, China is calling attention to the fact that the "One Country, Two Systems" norm being now clearly internationally accepted and part of a political experience and not only a concept that will be wishful thinking.

Another remarkable fact is that the domestic speeches gathered in these volumes, mainly those delivered for the diplomatic staff, assemble all the principles that should be used to promote Chinese foreign policy wherein the B&RI outcomes are one of the pillars of the Chinese foreign policy. So, we will begin to analyse speeches that might help us understand domestic discourse. Notwithstanding, these discourses are recent. They are also fundamental to understanding the message given internally. The audience of these discourses formed by diplomats is also relevant, meaning the domestic and international discourses are deeply interrelated. In December 2017, President Xi Jinping delivered a speech at the Meeting for Chinese Diplomatic Envoys. He presents the latest conquers of Chinese policy, one of them reinforcing the socialism with Chinese characteristics and the refusal to return to the old path rigid close door.

President Xi Jinping stimulates Chinese diplomates to use their functions to spread successful stories involving the conquers of the last decades and the will to promote mutual understanding with every country. In June 2018, at the Central Conference of Foreign Affairs, President Xi Jinping listed the "needs" and "shoulds" of Chinese foreign policy and introduced new elements for a supposed news era of international relations. Although not referring to the B&RI specifically, the project is included in a major mindset for Chinese external relations and the concern with the basic principles of Chinese foreign policy is underlined.

The two following speeches were delivered for an international audience and are specifically dedicated to the B&RI. These speeches are not included in the separated section but in the section titled "Neighborhood Diplomacy." We refer specifically to the two speeches that established the B&RI from September and October 2013, respectively, delivered in Nazarbayev University (Kazakhstan) and the People's Representative Council of Indonesia. President Xi Jinping used a personal story to evidence the ancient relations between peoples benefiting from the Silk Road in Kazakhstan. The discourse based on the historical argument defends the aim and possibility to establish a people-to-people relationship based on friendship and good neighbouring. Both speeches are focused on each region's reality and are projected for the adjacent regions of China. So the discourses analysis indicates that there is the look for proximity characteristics with a peaceful background, pushing trade and an integrated economy as a way to promote development, growth, and peace between neighbour countries. Undoubtedly, the founding discourse of the B&RI is regionally oriented and centred in the shared opportunities to value a past that brought together those peoples and communities. The historical argument and the geographical proximity seem to be the cement for a significant project that was starting.

The following speeches were published in the second and third volumes in a separated section entitled B&RI. In the discourse titled "Dialogue About Connectivity and Cooperation in Neighbor Countries," delivered in November 2014, the regional basis of the B&RI is remembered. President Xi Jinping reinforces the fact that the project was born, and Asia should benefit this part of the world, particularly by developing together interconnectivity projects. Again, the speaker highlights the regional beginning of the project but now implicitly tells the project might be more than regional. In this speech, President Xi Jinping launches the need to have further funding and purposes of creating a financing platform autonomous from the previous ones. By mentioning this specific aspect, President Xi Jinping promotes an alternative solution for financing outside the traditional instruments available for international and national projects, without frontally challenging the International Order or major powers, giving a step to an alternative financing model.

The speech called "B&RI, reform and developed," presented at the 31st session of the Political Bureau of the Central Committee of the Chinese Communist Party, was addressed to a domestic audience. President Xi Jinping highlights the importance of the project as a way for opening up in a multidimensional way and as a significant platform to promote mutual benefit in new historical conditions. The President justifies the total Chinese involvement in the project with the benefits it will bring to all the country, namely to help develop the border regions inhabited by ethnic minorities and needing further economic growth and development. Additionally, he interconnects the implementation of the project with local enthusiasm. By doing so, President Xi Jinping is creating continuity between a project that can be easily seen as a foreign policy project into a project with a deep domestic connection regarding the growth and development of China intrinsically.

The President delivers another speech directed to a domestic audience, titled "The B&RI Benefits the People." The intervention occurred in a Symposium for the Promotion of the B&RI. First, the President enumerates all the areas in which the Chinese people should be involved: the promotion of the coordination of public policies; the connectivity of infrastructures; free trade; financial integration; the friendship between peoples; creation of win-win cooperation; the implementation of new models of cooperation; and the creation of a multilateral platform for cooperation. By enumerating and linking these topics, the President gives clues of how each Chinese political or economic structure sector can participate. Afterwards, President Xi Jinping introduced something entirely new: a New Silk Road green, sustainable, intelligent and peaceful as a way to make the project more attractive and that all the countries involved can benefit from it. Again, the President characterizes the project and brings it to the sectors China wants to lead, based on intensive knowledge: sustainability, intelligent projects, and peaceful relationships between countries.

The speech "Together Promote the B&RI," delivered in the Opening Session of the Forum B&RI in May 2017, had an audience of representatives from more than 100 countries. President Xi Jinping pronounces a speech for a global audience opening it by saying that navigating through violent seas, our ancestors created new maritime ways to link the East with the West, which used to be called Maritime Silk Road. Once more, the President uses the historical argument, now focused on an intercontinental approach. To materialize this affirmation, President Xi Jinping gives the example of Chinese voyagers like Zhang Quian and Zheng He and naming the foreign after voyagers like Marco Polo or Ibn Battutah. Significantly, the President mentions two very different regions/cultures with a long relationship with China. This perspective turns the B&RI not only in a historical project but also in a shared project as if history was built by the cooperation of these different peoples peacefully and having for base trade. The corollary is mutual learning and understanding. Again, the President enumerates all the inventions and innovations circulated among the countries that benefited from the Silk Road. Now, the topic's expansion: the Silk Road was not only a trade/economic matter. Its relevance overcame direct trade relations and included the exchange of knowledge and cultural products that connected general people but also intellectuals. Afterwards, President Xi Jinping lists all the activities developed in the last years, giving specific significance to infrastructure and financial areas. Then he uses a Chinese saying to justify that the beginnings are always hard, but the Chinese government and population still choose to keep going although there are obstacles to beginning such a project. Interestingly, there is an intention to use a traditional proverb to show the commitment of China to the project. To underline the cooperation aspect of the project and the need for mutual respect, President Xi Jinping alludes to the Five Principles of Peaceful Coexistence. At the end of the speech, he cites another Chinese proverb saying that a long journey is made step by step but completes it with an Arab proverb referring that a pyramid is built stone by stone, and a European mentioning that Rome was not built in a single day. We underline that all the proverbs have the same basis, meaning every big project has to be built step by step. The natural conclusion is that it is possible to bring together countries from such different places, but making the B&RI is an immense task that requires effort from everyone.

In the speech "Open Path to Cooperation Across the Pacific," delivered in January 2018, in the Second Ministerial Meeting of the Forum of China and the Community of Latin America and the Caribbean States, President Xi Jinping broadens the geographical scope of the B&RI, referring to China being open to work to build a platform for cooperation with other States. Then, he highlights the good international reception of the project and the involvement of some Latin American States. Again, the President tries to find a historical connection and refers to the Chinese navigators that challenged the Pacific Ocean to reach Latin America. It is interesting to point out that, although Latin American countries have significant Chinese origin communities', there are no mentions of this kind of tie.

In the speech delivered at the Eighth Ministerial Conference of China–Arab States Cooperation Forum in July 2018, President Xi Jinping starts by mentioning the close historical ties between these two cultures. These historical connections would justify that Arab States would be natural partners of China in this project. Then, the President highlights how the B&RI contributed to boosting cooperation between China and the Arab States, originating an agreement for a China–Arab future-orientated strategic cooperation and joint development, which he considered a turning point in China–Arab countries relationship. Again, the financial aspect is underlined, and this area's cooperation receives particular attention. The final paragraph of this speech announces the launch of a Sino-Arab press centre, a Sino-Arab e-library, and an Arab Festival co-hosted by the two sides. Yet, we notice the objective of involving people and culture in a project that seemed merely oriented towards economy and trade. Throughout this process, China has the opportunity to enlarge her channels of communication and connection with very different countries in order to reinforce her global soft power. Art and sports festivals and cultural projects became a relevant part of China's approach to a region or a country.

In the Fifth Anniversary of the B&RI, held on August 27, President Xi Jinping presented the speech "Ensure that Belt and Road Cooperation Delivers Solid outcomes," emphasizing the warm international welcome the project had in the past years. For the first time, it is directly connected to building a global community of shared future the B&RI project and the opportunity for China to participate in the economic governance of International Order and promote global prosperity and common development. The connection between global economic governance and the B&RI is not a minor aspect because it represents China's ambition to participate in every area of international governance. At the same time, he consolidates the convergence between the B&RI project and the Chinese worldview and completely excludes the idea of a geopolitical or military alliance. He also reinforces that any country can join the B&RI, absolutely denying the possible participation based on ideology.

The speech delivered at the Second B&RI Forum for International Cooperation, entitled "Promote High-Quality Belt and Road Cooperation," in April 2019, confirms the globalization of the B&RI discourse unequivocally. President Xi Jinping refers to a supposed synergy existing between the B&RI plans and cooperation with the principles of global and regional organizations such as the United Nations, the Association of Southeast Asian Nations, the African Union, the European Union, and the Eurasian Economic Union.[1] Then, he recalls the message of the Chinese philosopher about the need to have good roots to ensure success, comparing vigorous plants to solid projects. Again, there is the need to invoke a Chinese intellectual statement to fundament the B&RI challenge and its' overcome in the profound Chinese culture. Furthermore, the idea of cooperation in diverse formats (bilateral, trilateral, and multilateral) is reinforced to give a path to a Chinese proverb that all in nature is composed by diversity in only being like this can be successful. Consequently, B&RI discourse and project went global. At the same time, China was rethinking her position in International Order.

4 Conclusion

Unquestionably, China's foreign policy and international discourse create alternatives to the traditional International Order without opposing the previous paradigms or forcing the transformation of the ancient frame for international relations. Instead of doing that, China integrates the International Order and seeks international recognition and reputation and, simultaneously, suggests alternatives that fit better her participation in this international Order. The financial area is exciting because it reflects a former China's concern. The diversification of communication channels and the type of international discourse is another relevant finding. By using the diplomatic forums and international organizations and at the same time the radio, TV, and internet sites in other languages, China is broadening her international audience and establishing direct contact with foreign peoples and communities.

Chinese scientific discourse and law discourse also impact Chinese international discourse. Publishing in scientific journals became one of the ways scientists from the world know China and her perspective about international relations and foreign policy. The proposal of new concepts such as "one country, two systems" or "shared future" and its experimentation without its international contestation opened a way for China to introduce her perception of topics such as globalization. Going through the international discourse during the last decade, we note the trend for China's progressive auto-image as a global actor. The B&RI follows this trend. It starts as a regional discourse, founded on a supposed historical background, where China played a determinant role. This perspective justifies why the first volume of the

---

[1] We followed the order given on the speech.

President's Xi Jinping speeches does not include a separate section for the B&RI. Instead, in the first book, the B&RI is included in the section for Neighboring Diplomacy, as previously referred to. Curiously, there is a section about the New Model of Major Countries Relations, not yet mentioning China as a major country in the same volume. Only in the second and third volumes emerges a specific section for the B&RI, congregating discourses for domestic and international audiences. At the same time, this section becomes autonomous; there is the recognition of China as a major country, ready to assume more international responsibilities and further explore her capacity to suggest alternatives to the norms ruling the International Order.

This evolution side by side is not simply a coincidence. It results from how China interprets globalization and the shift of her role in the international scene. Although maintaining the historical argument to justify the B&RI project, China turns this argument into global reasoning as a subsidiary element of the ancient Silk Road. Furthermore, it uses the supposed old relations of China with different parts of the world to justify the abandonment of the regional perspective. By evoking the historical ties with Arab countries, African countries, and Latin American countries, China is globalizing her discourse and presence. The B&RI discourse was its primary contribution because it created a possibility to be a transversal project to present and debate in every forum where China participates, either from regional or global inspiration. Therefore, the B&RI discourse is a globalizing discourse and simultaneously promotes some alternative concepts and solutions China encourages for international relations.

During the period of the analysed speeches (from 2013 to 2019), the international environment somehow changed. The rise of China as a global international power in the technological and economic areas brought new concerns to other powers, particularly the US, the major superpower (Woon, 2021, p. 289). It will be exciting to analyse the discourses from 2020 to 2022, impacted by the COVID-19 pandemic and the War in Ukraine and open competition with the US in the more technologic areas of the economy. The B&RI project was not suspended but seemed to slow down under these circumstances. Concomitantly, the war in Ukraine challenged China in her foreign policy based on balance and full respect for sovereignty.

Moreover, this war challenged the states to position themselves in the International Order, which might directly impact China's bilateral and multilateral relations because now China is a very prominent actor, the more relevant one resulting from the Non-Aligned Movement. Besides the international situation, China also deals with domestic issues that might result in the tuning of the convergence between domestic and foreign policy (Costa, 2020a). Nevertheless, the B&RI globalizing discourse tends to maintain and support China's globalizing ambitions.

Bibliographic References

Adolphsen, M. (2012). *Communication strategies of governments and NGOs: Engineering global discourse at high-level international summits*. Springer.

Benabdallah, L. (2019). Contesting the international order by integrating it: The case of China's Belt and Road Initiative. *Third World Quarterly, 40*(1), 92–108. https://doi.org/10.1080/01436597.2018.1529539

Cambié, S., & Yang-May, O. (2009). *International communications strategy: Developments in cross-cultural communications, PR and social media*. Kogan Page.

Chan, S., & Song, W. (2020). Telling the China story well: A discursive approach to the analysis of Chinese foreign policy in the "Belt and Road" Initiative. *Chinese Political Science Review, 5*, 417–437. Retrieved on January 2022, from https://doi.org/10.1007/s41111-020-00146-1

Cheng, Y. (2018). Public opinions on the Belt and Road Initiative: A cross-cultural study. In Y. Cheng, L. Song, & L. Huang (Eds.), *The Belt & Road Initiative in the global arena: Chinese and European perspectives* (pp. 3–15). Palgrave Macmillan.

Costa, C. M. (2020a). China after the pandemics: How to survive international scepticism and domestic distrust? In G. L. Gardini (Ed.), *The world before and after Covid-19 intellectual reflections on politics, diplomacy and international relations* (pp. 84–87). European Institute of International Studies.

Costa, C. M. (2020b). The words of the Belt & Road Initiative: A Chinese discourse for the world? In F. Leandro & P. A. Duarte (Eds.), *The Belt and Road Initiative: An old archetype of a new development model* (pp. 23–44). Palgrave Macmillan.

Couldry, N. (2014). What and where is the transnationalized public sphere? In K. Nash (Ed.), *Transnationalizing the public sphere* (pp. 43–59). Polity.

Fei, D. (2017). Worlding developmentalism: China's economic zones within and beyond its border. *Journal of International Development, 29*(6), 825–850. https://doi.org/10.1002/jid.3277

He, B. (2019). The domestic politics of the Belt and Road Initiative and its implications. *Journal of Contemporary China, 28*(116), 180–195. https://doi.org/10.1080/10670564.2018.1511391

Huang, C., & Shih, C. (2014). *Harmoniour China's quest for relational security*. Ashgate.

Leverett, F., & Wu, B. (2016). The new Silk Road and China's evolving grand strategy. *The China Journal, 77*. https://doi.org/10.1086/689684

Li, Y., & Costa, C. (2021). International and domestic discourses of China's special economic zones: An instrument for new projects. In F. Leandro, P. Figueiredo, & Y. Li (Eds.), *Handbook of research on special economic zones as regional development enablers*. IGI Global.

Mayer, M. (2018). China's rise as Eurasian power: The revival of the Silk Road and its consequences. In M. Mayer (Ed.), *Rethinking the Silk Road: China's Belt and Road Initiative and emerging Euroasian relations* (pp. 1–42). Palgrave Macmillan.

Mayer, M., & Balázs, D. (2018). Modern Silk Road imaginaries and the co-production of space. In M. Mayer (Ed.), *Rethinking the Silk Road: China's Belt and Road Initiative and emerging Euroasian relations* (pp. 205–226). Palgrave Macmillan.

Mochtak, M., & Turcsanyi, R. Q. (2021). Studying Chinese foreign policy narratives: Introducing the Ministry of Foreign Affairs press conferences corpus. *Journal of Chinese Political Science, 26*(4), 743–761. https://doi.org/10.1007/s11366-021-09762-3

Mulvad, A. M. (2019). Xiism as a hegemonic project in the making: Sino-communist ideology and the political economy of China's rise. *Review of International Studies, 45*(3), 449–470. Retrieved on January 2022, from https://doi.org/10.1017/S0260210518000530

Nathan, J., & Zhang, B. (2022). 'A shared future for mankind': Rhetoric and reality in Chinese foreign policy under Xi Jinping. *Journal of Contemporary China, 31*(133), 57–71. https://doi.org/10.1080/10670564.2021.1926091

Shih, C. (2013). *Sinicizing international relations: Self, civilization, and intellectual politics in subaltern East Asia*. Palgrave Macmillan.

Sun, W. (2015). Slow boat from China: Public discourses behind the 'going global' media policy. *International Journal of Cultural Policy, 21*(4), 400–418. https://doi.org/10.1080/10286632.2015.1043129

Weatherley, R., & Bauer, V. (2021). A new Chinese modernity? The discourse of eco-civilisation applied to the Belt and Road Initiative. *Third World Quarterly, 42*(9), 2115–2132. https://doi.org/10.1080/01436597.2021.1905511

Woon, C. Y. (2021). 'Provincialising' the Belt and Road Initiative: Theorising with Chinese narratives of the 'Digital Silk Road'. *Asia Pacific Viewpoint, 62*(3), 286–290. https://doi.org/10.1111/apv.12320

Xing, L. (2019). China's pursuit for the "One Belt One Road" initiative: A new world order with chinese characteristics? In L. Xing (Ed.), *Mapping China's 'One Belt One Road' initiative* (pp. 1–27). Palgrave Macmillan.

Zeng, L. (2011). The contemporary construction of Chinese international law discourse. *Social Sciences in China, 32*(4), 78–91. https://doi.org/10.1080/02529203.2011.625177

Chapter 5
The BRI in Xi's China "Grand Strategy": An Instrument to Restore Chinese Centrality in a New Era

Luis Tomé

1 Introduction

Since its launch in 2013, the Belt and Road Initiative (BRI)/One Belt One Road (OBOR) has provoked multiple reactions and debates (see, e.g., Garcia, 2020; Leandro & Duarte, 2020; Maçães, 2018; Shambaugh, 2020; Summers, 2016; Tekdal, 2018; Weifeng & Esteban, 2018; Yong, 2016). Among more intermediate and neutral perspectives, the positions vary between two more extreme and opposing promoted also by governments, starting with those of China and of the US: to Beijing, the BRI "contributed to policy, infrastructure, trade, financial and people-to-people connectivity based on the needs of individual countries" (PRChina, 2021a, Chap. III); to Washington, "Countries participating in OBOR could develop economic dependence on PRC capital and be subject to predatory lending, which the PRC could leverage to pursue its geopolitical interests" (USDoD, 2021, p. 21).

At the heart of most judgements about the BRI lie perceptions and considerations concerning not only its projects, but, above all, about the impact of China's resurgence and the intentions attributed to Beijing through the BRI. Therefore, it is important to understand and analyse China's Grand Strategy in which the BRI fits, and that is the main goal and contribution of this chapter. In sum, filling a crucial gap in the existing literature related to the BRI, we attempt to answer the following central questions: of which Chinese grand strategy is the BRI part of? Has this grand strategy changed under the leadership of Xi Jinping, the BRI mentor? And how does the BRI contribute to Xi's China grand strategy?

This chapter follows a descriptive-analytical model. It draws on Chinese and other official policy papers, speeches and specialized literature on China's transformation and its impacts on Asian and world systems. It is organized into four parts. The first

L. Tomé (✉)
Autónoma University of Lisbon, Lisbon, Portugal

International Relations Department and OBSERVARE, Portuguese Institute of International Relations (IPRI-NOVA), Lisbon, Portugal

© The Author(s), under exclusive license to Springer Nature Singapore Pte Ltd. 2023
P. A. B. Duarte et al. (eds.), *The Palgrave Handbook of Globalization with Chinese Characteristics*, https://doi.org/10.1007/978-981-19-6700-9_5

presents the theoretical perspective that guides us based on an "eclectic approach" and the concept of "grand strategy." Moving on to analysis of Xi's China grand strategy, the second part explains its ambitions and goals and the third begins to frame the BRI within it, highlighting its geo-economic motivations. The fourth part analyses Xi's China international policy and the BRI's geopolitical motivations, subdividing into three topics: the connections between geo-economics and geopolitics in Asia and Eurasia; reshaping global governance and building a new Sino-centric world; and the competitive bipolarity with the US.

2 "Eclectic Approach" and the Concept of "Grand Strategy"

On a theoretical level, we follow an "eclectic approach," with the contribution of "complexity theories." From complexity theories we draw, above all, the assumption of "non-linearity," accepting that the result of behaviours and interactions is "naturally unpredictable" as also the notion of "complex adaptive systems," emphasizing the ideas of complexity, co-adaptation, and co-evolution of actors and of the system (see Erçetin & Açikalin, 2020; Tomé & Açikalin, 2019).

The "eclectic approach" assumes that none of the conventional IR theories, in isolation and by itself, can encompass and explain the entire international reality that, by nature, is complex, dynamic, unpredictable, adaptive, and co-evolutionary. This assumption is all the more relevant because of the opposing views and proposals with which liberal, realist, constructivist, systemic, critical, and other Western-based theories often struggle with respect to the behaviour and interactions of non-Western actors such as China. Thus, limiting the risk of a priori alienating aspects that may be crucial, with pragmatism and prudence, the eclectic approach goes beyond the "natural expectations" of conventional theories, combining different explanatory hypotheses and taking advantage of the potential of complementarities (Tomé, 2016; Tomé & Açikalin, 2019). At the same time, the eclectic approach facilitates and favours inclusive connections with Chinese theories of International Relations (see, e.g., Chih-yu et al., 2019; Grydehoj & Ping, 2021; Ho, 2019).

Like other notions used in International Relations and associated disciplines, the concept of "grand strategy" is used with different amplitudes and meanings (see, e.g., Balzacq & Krebs, 2021; Biscop, 2021; Brands, 2014; Freedman, 2013; Gaddis, 2019; Layton, 2018; Milevski, 2016). Interestingly, these differences and divergences show an appreciable degree of agreement on the basic definition of grand strategy. Nina Silove presents three meanings of grand strategy in which scholars subtly diverge, labelled "grand plans," "grand principles," and "grand behaviour" (Silove, 2018). Despite this distinction, the author considers that the three concepts are structurally similar in two important respects: first, as a consequence of their origins in the concept of strategy, they are each constituted by two elements—ends and means; second, each concept has three characteristics, which is what makes each of them "grand": long-term in scope, holistic, and importance (idem, pp. 45–46). Rebecca Friedman Lissner (2018) distinguishes between other three component research agendas within the grand strategy literature: the "grand strategy as variable" through which academics may study the origins of state behaviour; the "grand strategy as process," whether as a governmental strategic-planning process or as a more generic mode of decision-making; and the "grand strategy as blueprint" that proffers broad visions in hopes of influencing future governmental behaviour.

Despite the differences between the theorists, the basic conceptions of grand strategy not only complement each other but are relatively convergent in essential aspects. In operational terms, we use here grand strategy based on two definitions. The one by Hal Brands, who considers that "a grand strategy represents an integrated scheme of interests, threats, resources, and policies. It is the conceptual framework that helps nations determine where they want to go and how they ought to get there" (Brands, 2014, p. 3). And Peter Layton, who defines grand strategy as "the art of developing and applying diverse forms of power in an effective and efficient way to try to purposefully change the relationship existing between two or more intelligent and adaptive entities" (Layton, 2020; see also Layton, 2018).

3 Xi's China: Ambitions and Goals

To understand China's grand strategy, it is crucial to start by looking at its ambitions and goals. To do that, we have to examine the fusion between the interests of the state and the dominant Communist Party of China (CPC). This, incidentally, stems from Article 1 of the Constitution of PRChina: "Leadership by the Communist Party of China is the defining feature of socialism with Chinese characteristics. It is prohibited for any organization or individual to damage the socialist system" (PRChina Constitution). And according to the Communist Party of China Constitution, "The Party's highest ideal and ultimate goal is the realization of communism" (CPC Constitution, General Program).

This "ultimate goal" is pursued in what the CPC calls the "basic line," that is, "to lead all the people of China together in a self-reliant and pioneering effort, making economic development the central task, upholding the Four Cardinal Principles, and remaining committed to reform and opening up, so as to see China becomes a great modern socialist country that is prosperous, strong, democratic, culturally advanced, harmonious, and beautiful" (ibid.). First stated by Deng Xiaoping and later written into the CPC Constitution, the Four Cardinal Principles are "to keep to the path of socialism, to uphold the people's democratic dictatorship, to uphold the leadership of the Communist Party of China, and to uphold Marxism-Leninism and Mao Zedong Thought" (ibid.). From the Party's perspective, its leadership and systems are uniquely able to restore China's strength, prosperity, and prestige—in what also constitutes the Party's "original aspiration" and "mission," according to Xi (2017a, 2021a).

This is part of the logic of historical continuity that the Party also underlines when affirming that "its guides to action" are the doctrines of the five consecutive top leaders of People's China: "Mao Zedong Thought by combining the basic tenets of Marxism-Leninism with the actual practice of the Chinese revolution… Deng Xiaoping Theory… shifted the focus of the whole Party's work onto economic development and introduced reform and opening up… Jian Zemin Theory of Three Represents… Hu Jintao Scientific Outlook on Development…[and] Xi Jinping Thought on Socialism with Chinese Characteristics for a New Era" (CPC Constitution, General Program). In parallel, the Chinese leaders glorify China's history and the revolutionary tradition of the Party. Therefore, they consistently framed their efforts as seeking to restore China to a preeminent place in the world after enduring what they characterize as China's "century of humiliation" beginning in the mid-nineteenth century Opium Wars and lasting until the founding of the PRC in 1949. In essence, as stated by Xi Jinping repeatedly, echoing each of his predecessors, "only socialism can save China—and only Socialism with Chinese Characteristics can develop China" (Xi, 2012, 2021a).

On the other hand, China's grand strategy has to be framed in the light of two central notions: "comprehensive national power" and "strategic power configuration." The comprehensive national power (or the "composite national strength") is the expression that guides the modernization and increase of Chinese capabilities in all dimensions, in an articulated way, also evaluating the evolution of China and comparing it to other powers in the international system. The strategic power configuration, on the other hand, is based on the idea of "the propensity of things," and the Chinese leaders describe the end of the twentieth century and beginning of the twenty-first century as a "period of opportunity." As such, China would not need to force and even less to impose its ascension, as it would suffice to skilfully take advantage of the propensity of things and the opportunities that are offered to it, to increase, naturally and gradually, its comprehensive national power. It is, therefore, a long-term strategy that sets objectives, priorities, and milestones in virtually every aspect. China's leaders characterize their grand strategy as a major national effort that extends the scope and reach of the transformation of China, and, in turn, the world. And to Beijing, "China is still in an important period of strategic opportunity for development" (PRChina, 2019b, Chap. I).

Since the reforms launched by Deng Xiaoping, starting in 1978, and which are at the basis of China's resurgence, Beijing's goals have been encapsulated in the general ambition to build a "Moderately Prosperous Society in All Respects" by the middle of the twenty-first century. On the other hand, cultivating the idea of China's "peaceful rise" and "win-win cooperation" to favour cooperative ties and avoid anti-China containment strategies, Beijing generically pursued the so-called "24-Character Strategy": observe calmly; secure our position; cope with affairs calmly; hide our capacities and bide our time; be good at maintaining a low profile; and never claim leadership. This formula was enunciated by Deng Xiaoping, in 1990, in the aftermath of the Tiananmen tragedy, followed by Jiang Zemin and, later, by Hu Jintao who, in 2009, amended the last eight characters to "uphold keeping" a low profile and "actively achieve something" (Menon, 2016). This last part can also be translated and interpreted as "display its prowess" and "assume its responsibilities," representing an adaptation to the growing comprehensive national power of China and a response to international pressure, namely from the US, for China to assume its responsibilities as a great power and "responsible stakeholder." Globally, Xi's predecessors believed China must continue to bide its time by overseeing rapid economic growth and the steady expansion of China's influence through tactical integration into the existing global order.

This relatively low profile and essentially non-confrontational posture of PRChina changed with the rise of Xi Jinping to the leadership of the Party and the Country, in 2012. Xi is impatient with the status quo, has a high tolerance to risk, fosters a personality cult unparalleled in China since Mao, and seems to have a sense of urgency in the CPC's and China's assertion (da Silva, 2021; Markey, 2020; Shambaugh, 2021; Sutter, 2020). Jude Blachette argues that Xi's calculations are determined by his timeline, "because he sees a narrow window of ten to 15 years during which Beijing can take advantage of a set of important technological and geopolitical transformations, which will also help it overcome significant internal challenges" (Blachette, 2021, p. 10). The Chinese regime itself states that "China entered a new era after the 18th National Congress of the Communist Party of China (CPC) in 2012. President Xi Jinping has considered China's responsibilities from a global perspective, and proposed the vision of a global community of shared future and the Belt and Road Initiative" (PRChina, 2021a, Preface).

The change in the strategic posture is evident, from the outset, in the renewed ambitions expressed around key notions such as "New Era" and "Chinese Dream" or in public references to "leading" and "dominant" China's position. In a remarkable speech at the 19th Party Congress that synthesizes much of his "doctrine," Xi Jinping declared that China had assumed "a leading position in terms of economic and technological strength, defense capabilities, and composite national strength" (Xi, 2017a). Hence, "Chinese socialism's entrance into a New Era... it is of tremendous importance" (ibid.). New Era "means that scientific socialism is full of vitality in 21st century China.... blazing a new trail for other developing countries to achieve modernization. It offers a new option for other countries and nations" (ibid.). Above all, what Xi's "New Era" means is that China is at the threshold—to be crossed in the next three decades—of realizing the "Chinese Dream of national rejuvenation." And, simply, "the Chinese Dream is to make the country strong" (PRChina, 2015, Chap. II). Therefore, the central objective of the CPC and the Chinese Government, in the words of Xi (2017a), is "building a socialism that is superior to capitalism, and laying the foundation for a future where we will win the initiative and have the dominant position."

Beijing demarcates the stages of China's goals and strategy with milestones, each with objectives and priorities. As China approached an interim set of development targets for 2020 in the three-step strategic plan for modernization it has been implementing since 1987, Xi not only moved targets originally expressed for mid-century forward by fifteen years to 2035, but also expressed new mid-century goals. For its strategy in the New Era, Xi's China laid out a broad plan with a timeline linked to two symbolically important centenary milestones: "China's national strategic goal is to complete the building of a moderately prosperous society in all respects by 2021 when the CPC celebrates its centenary; and the building of a modern socialist country that is prosperous, strong, democratic, culturally advanced and harmonious by 2049 when the People's Republic of China (PRC) marks its centenary" (PRChina, 2015, Chap. II). At the ceremony marking the centenary of the CPC on 1 July 2021, General Secretary Xi declared that China had already succeeded in the First Centenary Goal (Xi, 2021a).

To bridge the lengthy gap between the two anniversaries, Xi added interim objectives for 2035 and laid out a broad "two-stage" modernization plan to reach 2049. In the first phase from 2021 to 2035, Beijing wants China to "basically" meet its initial thresholds for becoming a "great modern socialist country," continuing to prioritize economic development as "the central task" (CPC Constitution, General Program; PRChina, 2021a, 2021b; Xi, 2017a). Until 2035, China will also seek to improve its domestic rule of law and governance systems, as well as to increase its technological strength to become a "global leader in innovation" and to "basically" complete its military modernization. It also wishes to conduct a "great power diplomacy with Chinese characteristics" and "moving closer to center stage" (Xi, 2017a; see also PRChina, 2019a, 2021a). In the second phase from 2035 to 2049, Beijing aspires that China completes its development and attains "national rejuvenation," that is, by becoming "prosperous, strong, democratic, culturally advanced and harmonious." Among other objectives, China aims to have a "world-class" military (PRChina, 2015, 2019b; see also Martin, 2021; USDoD, 2021) and a position of "global leader" in a reformed international order in line with the formula "Community of Common Destiny for Mankind" or a "Global Community of Shared Future" (PRChina, 2019a, 2019b, 2021a; Xi, 2017a, 2019).

4 The Xi's China New Silk Road and Its Geo-Economic Motivations

In order to uphold and develop its goals under the banner of "socialism with Chinese characteristics in the new era," Xi's China has launched a wide range of initiatives, in the most varied fields. The most emblematic is the New Silk Road, a long-term plan for the construction of the "Silk Road Economic Belt" and the "21st-Century Maritime Silk Road" announced by Xi Jinping, respectively, in September 2013 when paying a visit to Kazakhstan, and when visiting Indonesia one month later. In November of that same year, the Central Committee of the CPC adopted a "Decision" which points the BRI as a "new pattern of allround opening" (CPC-CC, 2013). In March 2015, the National Development and Reform Commission (NDRC), the Ministry of Commerce and the Ministry of Foreign Affairs jointly published the "Vision and Actions on Jointly Building the Silk Road Economic Belt and the 21st-Century Maritime Silk Road" (NDRC, 2015). There is no official map for the BRI and its geographical scope is an open-ended network system—in addition to Europe and

Asia, the BRI is explicitly open to countries in Africa, Middle East, Oceania, and the Americas. Still, the 2015 NDRC's document identifies six land corridors (the New Eurasian Land Bridge; China–Mongolia–Russia; China–Central Asia–West Asia; the China–Indochina Peninsula Corridor; the China–Pakistan Economic Corridor; and the Bangladesh–China–India–Myanmar Economic Corridor) and two maritime routes: one running through the South China Sea and the Indian Ocean to the Mediterranean, and the other through the South China Sea to the South Pacific (ibid.). The "cooperation priorities" are now framed as policy coordination, facilities connectivity, unimpeded trade, financial integration, and people-to-people bond (see Belt and Road Portal).

Along with the BRI, China established the Silk Road Fund, in 2014, and the Asian Infrastructure Investment Bank (AIIB), in 2015, to provide financial support to the BRI projects. In May 2017 and April 2019, Beijing hosted the First and the Second *Belt and Road Forum for International Cooperation*. Meanwhile, China has multiplied platforms associated with the BRI, from the "Digital Silk Road" to the "Green Silk Road," the BRI "Space Information Corridor" and the "Healthy Silk Road." According to Xi, as he stated in the Boao Forum for Asia Annual Conference 2021, significantly titled "A World in Change: Join Hands to Strengthen Global Governance and Advance Belt and Road Cooperation": "follow the principles of extensive consultation, joint contribution and shared benefits, and champion the philosophy of open, green and clean cooperation, in a bid to make Belt and Road cooperation high-standard, people-centered and sustainable" (Xi, 2021b).

The geo-economic interests behind the BRI are relatively easy to identify. Since China set up four special economic zones in Shenzhen, Zhuhai, Shantou, and Xiamen in 1980, the country's steps towards opening up its market have never stopped. However, between the regions of Chinese territory there have always been huge developmental imbalances. This is a challenge that the BRI intends to respond to, promoting the development of China's poorest western and central regions, coordinated development accross regions, integrated urban–rural development and, ultimately, sustaining China's economic growth and social and political "harmony." Major initiatives have been implemented to support the pioneering role of the eastern region, develop the western region, revitalize the northeast, and spur the rise of the central region. In addition, new regional strategies have been launched and, since 2013, China has established 18 free trade zones (FTZs) across the country, as testing grounds to experiment new regulations and explore ways to improve the business environment that would later be replicated nationwide. According to Beijing, "These initiatives and strategies have resulted in a better configuration of China's territorial space… and reinforcing connectivity and complementarity between the regions" (PRChina, 2021b, Chap. III.3).

On the other hand, through the BRI, Beijing intends to strengthen economic ties between its regions and Central Asia, Southeast Asia and South Asia by developing infrastructure, promoting trade and enhancing interconnectivity. This not only creates huge investment opportunities for Chinese companies, but also attracts foreign investment and eases pressure from China's industrial overcapacity, spurring the development of China's western regions and reviving its economy (Belt and Road Portal, Development progress across China; PRChina, 2021a, 2021b).

Evidently, through the BRI, China intends to strengthen its ties as a country with other regional economies and markets around the world. The BRI embodies China's "going out-bringing in" and "go global" policies. From 2013 to 2018, the trade volume between China and other countries along the Belt and Road surpassed 6 trillion US$, and China's investment in those countries exceeded 90 billion US$ (Belt and Road Portal). On the other hand, in its 14th Five-Year Plan (2021–2025), Beijing announced a shift to a new "development pattern" of "dual circulation," focused on accelerating domestic consumption, shifting to higher-end manufacturing, and creating "breakthroughs" in key technologies along critical high-end global supply chains. Hence, the BRI represents also systemic benefits to the PRC's growing national industrial and technological base. In addition, the BRI helps promote the internationalization of the renminbi, reduce excessive reserves of foreign currencies (in particular, US$ and EU$), diversify energy suppliers and routes, and convert its economic power, commercial and industrial influence into political-diplomatic influence. The reality is that the BRI crosses Xi's China interests, policies and development strategies, foreign relations, and security.

5 Xi's China International Policy and the BRI

Xi's China continues to claim that its foreign policy is based on the traditional Five Principles of Peaceful Coexistence (mutual respect for each other's territorial integrity and sovereignty, mutual non-aggression, mutual non-interference in each other's internal affairs, equality and cooperation for mutual benefit, and peaceful coexistence); it follows a "peaceful development" and a "win-win cooperation"; and that China "will never seek hegemony." This is constantly reaffirmed in the most diverse official documents and speeches, including in its white paper "China and the World in the New Era" published on the occasion of the 70th anniversary of the founding of the PRChina, specifically "to respond to the world's questions about China" (PRChina, 2019a, Preface). The same ideas are repeated by Xi, including in his speech in the 76th Session of UN General Assembly in September 2021, the year that celebrates the centenary of the CPC and also the 50th anniversary of the PRChina seat in the United Nations: "we must strengthen solidarity and promote mutual respect and win–win cooperation in conducting international relations…China has never and will never invade or bully others, or seek hegemony….China will continue to bring the world new opportunities through its new development" (Xi, 2021c).

On the other hand, Beijing promotes what it calls the Community of Common Destiny for Mankind or the Global Community of Shared Future aimed "to solve the practical issues facing the world today and realize the peaceful and sustainable development of humanity. The proposal pursues the goal of universal harmony and the principles of cooperation and mutual benefit, while opposing the law of the jungle, power politics and hegemonism" (PRChina, 2019a, Chap. III.2; see also Xi, 2019).

These principles and rhetoric do not prevent Xi from expressly assuming the goal of making China a "global leader in terms of composite national strength and international influence" (Xi, 2017a). Accordingly, in addition to geo-economic interests and motivations, the BRI also serves other geopolitical and geostrategic purposes and interests. Indeed, the BRI is a crucial part of "Xiplomacy."

5.1 Connecting Geo-Economics and Geopolitics in Asia and Eurasia

Asia is China's foreign policy priority region (see PRChina, 2017, 2019a, 2019b). And towards Asia, Xi declares a kind of "Monroe doctrine with Chinese characteristics" or an "Asian co-prosperity zone with Chinese characteristics": "In the final analysis, let the people of Asia run the affairs of Asia, solve the problems of Asia and uphold the security of Asia.... The outside countries, on their part, should respect the diversity of our region and do their part to facilitate its development and stability" (Xi, 2014); "Asian countries have advanced regional economic integration and worked in union to pursue both economic and social development… As an important member of the Asian family, China has kept deepening reform and opening-up while promoting regional cooperation…the extraordinary journey of China…has exerted a significant influence in boosting development in Asia and beyond" (Xi, 2021b). In this line, there are also ideas like "New Asian Security Concept," "Asia-for-Asians," "Asia Dream," "Global Asia," or "Asian Community of Shared Destiny" that have defined, since 2013, China's Asian policy, appearing to be part of a medium- to long-term strategy to rebuild a Sino-centric Asian order. And the BRI is a powerful instrument to that end.

China's aspiration to increase its leverage in Asia implies that it provides certain "public goods," such as investment in infrastructure. And because of the enormous infrastructure demand in the region, Chinese or China-led funds (e.g., the Silk Road Fund and the AIIB) have a gap to fill. Within the scope of the BRI, Beijing has established a set of training programmes on joint discussions and planning on ways to link the BRI to regional and national initiatives, such as the Master Plan on ASEAN Connectivity 2025, Pakistan's vision of a new Pakistan, Laos' initiative to transform from a land-locked country into a land-linked country, the Philippines' massive infrastructure projects under its Build, Build, Build programme, Kazakhstan's Bright Road initiative, or Mongolia's Development Road programme. Likewise, in the context of infrastructure connectivity, to support the China–Pakistan Economic Corridor, China participated in the upgrading and expansion of the Peshawar–Karachi Motorway and the Karakoram Highway; to support the China–Indochina Peninsula Economic Corridor and the Bangladesh–China–India–Myanmar Economic Corridor, China is helping to build highways, bridges, and tunnels in Bangladesh, Myanmar,

Laos, and Cambodia, promoting connectivity between Southeast Asia and South Asia. China is also involved in the construction of sections of Kyrgyzstan's North–South highway and Tajikistan's road renovation project on the China–Central Asia–West Asia Economic Corridor. In another example, China has participated in 33 projects for the joint preservation of cultural relics with 17 Belt and Road countries—including the Angkor Wat in Cambodia, Bagan Buddhist pagodas in Myanmar, the ancient city of Khiva in Uzbekistan, the Rakhat Ancient Ruins in Kazakhstan and the Bikrampur ruins in Bangladesh (PRChina, 2021a, Chap. III). These channels of cooperation, projects, and investments contribute to further increase China's economic, commercial, and financial weight in neighbouring countries, while limiting these countries' willingness and leeway to criticize Beijing and/or, obviously, favouring their alignment with the Beijing agenda.

The same can be said of the Chinese strategy for the "great Eurasia," with the BRI helping to win friends and expand influence from East, South, and Central Asia to the Middle East and Europe. Weifeng and Esteban (2018, pp. 492–493) highlight three aspects: energy security; geopolitical influence; and maritime interests. First, since China is heavily dependent on energy imports from the Persian Gulf, the New Eurasian Land Bridge and China–Central and West Asia Economic Corridor allow it to forge stronger energy ties with Russia and Central Asian states and reduce its reliance on energy imports from the Persian Gulf. The China–Pakistan Economic Corridor and Bangladesh–China–India–Myanmar Economic Corridor facilitate China's energy imports from the Persian Gulf and Africa and reduce its dependence on the Malacca Strait.

Second, regional connectivity and multilateral cooperation enable Beijing not only to leverage its power and influence over other Eurasian partners to its interests, but also to broaden its strategic hinterland and geopolitical space. This is the case, for example, of joint programmes and discussions on the connections between the BRI and the EU's Europe–Asia connectivity strategy. Also, new rail routes for cargo trains across the New Eurasian Land Bridge have begun to operate over the last few years. There are now several Chinese–European city pairs that are linked via direct cargo trains, including Yiwu–Madrid and Suzhou–Warsaw. In addition, the connectivity between Europe and Asia promoted through the BRI allows Beijing to show itself in contexts of opportunity such as the COVID-19 pandemic crisis: "Connecting over 100 cities across more than 20 countries in Europe and Asia, the China Railway Express to Europe has made an outstanding contribution to stabilizing international industrial and supply chains during the Covid-19 pandemic" (PRChina, 2021a, Chap. III).

Third, the Maritime Silk Road helps Beijing to develop its "string of pearls" ports strategy, to expand influence in the Indian Ocean and foster its role as a maritime power from Oceania to Europe. For example, China's heavy investment in Hambantota Port (Sri Lanka), Gwadar Port (Pakistan), and Kyaukpyu port (Myanmar) allows Beijing to reinforce its naval presence in the Indian Ocean, ensuring the security of its trade and energy routes. Chinese companies, mostly state-owned/controlled ones, have either acquired the operation rights of several other internationally important ports along the BRI routes, including the Haifa New Port in Israel and the Piraeus

Container Port in Greece, and/or have invested in some others such as the Port of Rotterdam and Kumport in Turkey. China has more shipping ports at home than any other country in the world, and key investments add about another 100 ports in more than 60 countries. All of this favours China's omnipresence and its "soft power" in greater Eurasia, while inhibiting many governments from criticizing Beijing on certain sensitive issues and leading others to support Chinese policies.

The South China Sea offers a good example of the difference between Beijing's rhetoric and practice, but also of how the BRI could be a means of soft power. In July 2016, the Permanent Court of Arbitration's decision on the South China Sea ruled that "China's claims to historic rights, or other sovereign rights or jurisdiction, with respect to the maritime areas of the South China Sea encompassed by the relevant part of the 'nine-dash line' are contrary to the Convention [UNCLOS] and without lawful effect" (PCA, 2016, p. 473-X.B.2). However, despite constantly claiming to defend a "rules-based order," and being a party to the UN Convention on the Law of the Sea (UNCLOS), China not only has failed to comply with the PCA's decision (see Beijing's position in PRChina, 2016) but also continued to militarize and reinforced its positions in the South China Sea, seeming to want to impose a kind of *mare nostrum* (Tomé, 2021d).

Despite this, the European Union was slow to produce a joint statement criticizing China and, when it finally did, after tough negotiations between its members, it only issued a vague and neutral statement that recognizes the PCA's decision without direct reference to Beijing—the result of blockades caused by countries like Hungary and Greece, heavily dependent on Chinese investment and eager to play a leading role in the BRI. ASEAN's case is even more paradigmatic, as although several of its members are directly involved in disputes with China in the South China Sea, the Association cannot achieve a unified position in condemning Beijing for not complying with the PCA's binding decision. Furthermore: in August 2017, the framework for the Code of Conduct (COC) in the South China Sea was adopted between the 10 ASEAN countries and China and, in the following November, the launch of the COC negotiations was officially announced by the same 11 States, with Beijing proposing to complete these negotiations by 2022; and, in October 2018, the first China–ASEAN Maritime Exercise-2018 took place, precisely in the South China Sea.

5.2 *Reshaping Global Governance, Transforming International Order, and Building a New Sino-Centric World*

Beijing establishes a "distinction between three elements of the 'U.S.-led world order': 'the American value system', 'the U.S. military alignment system'; and 'the international institutions including the UN system'" (Fu, 2016). So, when the Chinese leaders, and Xi in particular, speak of "supporting the international order" they are only referring to the third of these elements: "there is only one international system, i.e. the international system with the United Nations at its core. There is only one international order, i.e. the international order underpinned by international law. And there is only one set of rules, i.e. the basic norms governing international relations underpinned by the purposes and principles of the UN Charter" (Xi, 2021c). At the same time, Xi's China claims "Taking a lead in reforming and developing the global governance system" (PRChina, 2019a, Chap. V.6). This means that Xi's China is willing to actively develop a strategy of embedded revisionism both in the "UN-Universe" and in the other institutions it is part of.

At the end of the "double Cold War," the PRChina was already a permanent member of the UN Security Council since 1971 and of the IMF and World Bank since 1980, when it took the place previously occupied by the Republic of China/Taiwan in these institutions. And despite the tensions caused by the Tiananmen tragedy, it was quickly integrated into the Asia–Pacific Economic Cooperation (APEC) in 1991 and, more importantly, into the World Trade Organization (WTO) in 2001. China also started to participate in multiple other multilateral mechanisms, from the Asia–Europe Meeting (ASEM) to the G20, from the ASEAN Regional Forum (ARF) to the East Asia Summit (EAS). Inevitably, in all these international institutions, China's influence increased as its comprehensive national power grew—as seen in the World Health Organization (WHO) in the context of the COVID-19 pandemic.

At the same time, Beijing has been participating and, above all, creating "parallel realities" that include organizations and numerous different mechanisms of bilateral, trilateral, and multilateral cooperation. Examples of this include the Strategic Triangle China–Russia–India and the trilateral dialogue China–Japan–South Korea; mechanisms such as BRICS (Brazil, Russia, India, China, and South Africa) or ASEAN + 3 (China, South Korea, and Japan); and institutions such as the Shanghai Cooperation Organization (SCO). The "Sino-centric system" also involves the New Development Bank (NDB) created by the BRICS in 2014 and other frameworks such as the China–Africa Summit and Forum on China–Africa Cooperation (FOCAC), China–Arab States Cooperation Forum, China–Community of Latin American and Caribbean States (CELAC) Forum, China–Pacific Island Countries Economic Development and Cooperation Forum, Boao Forum for Asia, China International Import Expo, Hongqiao International Economic Forum, China–ASEAN Expo, China–Arab States Expo, China–Africa Economic and Trade Expo, Conference on Dialogue of Asian Civilizations, World Internet Conference, Macau Forum of China with Portuguese-speaking Countries or China + 17 Central and Eastern European countries and Greece.

Adding to all this, on 15 November 2020, the 10 ASEAN countries, Japan, South Korea, Australia, and New Zealand jointly signed with China the Regional Comprehensive Economic Partnership (RCEP); on 30 December 2020, China and the EU reached an agreement in principle on the Comprehensive Agreement on Investment (CAI); and on 16 September 2021, China formally submitted a request to accede to the Comprehensive and Progressive Trans-Pacific Partnership (CPTPP or TPP11).

The BRI offers an additional bilateral and multilateral mechanism to strengthen cooperation with countries and regional multilateral groups such as the SCO,

ASEAN, EU, ASEM, Eurasian Economic Union, South Asian Association for Regional Cooperation (SAARC), BRICS, African Union or the Gulf Cooperation Council (GCC). In just a few years, the BRI has been extended from Asia and Europe to Africa, the Americas, and Oceania, and under the BRI China has signed cooperation documents with more than 160 countries and international organizations (Belt and Road Portal). The BRI is indeed the best example of China's "going out-bringing in" and "go global."

There are also the new structures developed by association with the BRI, such as the Asian Infrastructure Investment Bank (AIIB), the Silk Road Fund, and the Belt and Road Forum for International Cooperation. The list of deliverables of the First Belt and Road Forum (BRF) in May 2017 includes a total of 1,676 infrastructure projects involving highway, high-speed rail, electricity grid, port facilities, and gas and oil pipelines that have been contracted. And the list of deliverables of the second BRF, in April 2019, includes 283 concrete results (BeltandRoadForum.org).

When the AIIB started operations in January 2016, the bank had 57 founding members (37 regional and 20 nonregional), including Washington's closest allies such as the UK, Germany, France, Australia, Israel, and South Korea—and that same year Canada also joined the AIIB. Currently, the AIIB has expanded its membership to 103 members (50 regional, 41 nonregional, and 12 prospective members) (see AIIB, Members and Prospective Members). Representing approximately 79% of the global population and 65% of the global GDP, and having become the world's third-largest multilateral financial institution after the IMF and the World Bank, the AIIB is a catalyst for shaping a new global financial order, enabling Beijing to play a greater role in the global financial system. The China-led AIIB not only provides an alternative to the existing Western-dominated multilateral institutions, but it also acts as a promising instrument to shape a bargaining coalition to transform the existing global governance system and boost Beijing's global role from rule-taker to rule-maker.

The BRI also provides Beijing with great opportunities to produce common rules, promote alternative norms, and socialize ideas among countries and regions along the Silk Road and, ultimately, promote Chinese soft power (see, e.g., Duarte & Ferreira-Pereira, 2021; Voo & Xinpeng, 2020). Building platforms for the BRI to dovetail with the development strategies of participating countries, China has held over 4,000 training sessions for officials from participating countries on Belt and Road topics such as infrastructure connectivity, industrial capacity, equipment standardization, trade facilitation, and technological standardization (PRChina, 2021a, Chap. III.1). Xi Jinping himself stresses this importance: "We should seek other countries' understanding of and support for the Chinese dream…. We should increase China's soft power, give a good Chinese narrative, and better communicate China's message to the world" (Xi cit. in Xinhua News Agency, 2014).

For example, at the opening of the First BRF in Beijing, President Xi underlined that "China will enhance friendship and cooperation with all countries involved in the Belt and Road Initiative on the basis of the Five Principles of Peaceful Co-existence…. In pursuing the Belt and Road Initiative, we will not resort to outdated geopolitical maneuvering. What we hope to achieve is a new model of win–win cooperation" (Xi, 2017b). And in the cooperation principles of the final Joint Communique, the 30 participating Heads of State and of Government declared that "We uphold the spirit of peace, cooperation, openness, transparency, inclusiveness, equality, mutual learning, mutual benefit and mutual respect" (BRF Joint Communique, point 14). In line with the Five Principles, China also proposed new ideas and concepts such as Peaceful Rise, Peaceful Development, Harmonious World, and Community of Common Destiny. *Altogether*, it helps Beijing to build its soft and normative power and strengthen its role as a responsible global power.

Meanwhile, in August 2017, China established its first foreign (naval) military base in Djibouti, strategically placed at the crossroads of the BRI's trade and energy routes. According to the US Pentagon, "the PRC is pursuing additional military facilities to support naval, air, ground, cyber, and space power projection," including in Tajikistan, Cambodia, Myanmar, Thailand, Singapore, Indonesia, Pakistan, Sri Lanka, United Arab Emirates, Kenya, Seychelles, Tanzania, and Angola (USDoD, 2021, p. x).

Africa is a paradigmatic example of the intersection of China's international interests, policies, and strategies through the BRI. As of 2021, 46 African countries have signed cooperation agreements with China under the BRI, the largest number of countries on any continent in the world. And an agreement was signed between the African Union (AU) and China to align the Chinese BRI with the strategic project Agenda 2063 of the AU. In addition to other mechanisms, in 2019 the Belt & Road Africa Fund was launched, fully financed by China with US$1 billion (China–Africa Business Council, 2021). Meanwhile, Chinese investment in Africa has grown significantly, dominated by the energy and infrastructure areas, with China being the largest partner and creditor in infrastructure financing to African countries. Despite the criticisms and debates around the "debt trap" (Acker & Brautigam, 2021; Acker et al., 2020), African countries are receptive to Chinese investments and cooperation with Beijing within the scope of the BRI. And China is advancing its interests and messages in Africa. For example, the Declaration of the 2018 Beijing Summit of the Forum on China–Africa Cooperation (FOCAC) states the following: "We applaud that, under the Belt and Road Initiative, the principle of extensive consultation, joint contribution and shared benefits is observed"; "firmly uphold multilateralism and oppose all forms of unilateralism and protectionism"; and "We advocate mutual respect and equal consultation, firmly reject Cold-War mentality" (FOCAC, 2018).

At the same time, China is expanding its peace and security footprint in Africa, in a strategy "of low cost, low risk and high performance" (Kovrig, 2018; Munyi, 2020; Nantulya, 2021). On the other hand, Beijing is committed to African countries resisting US pressure, for example, over Huawei and 5G, as well as to getting African support and votes for Chinese candidates in UN agencies (Olander, 2020). And African support and votes are crucial to bolstering China's global position and its strategic interests in disputes and contentious issues. For example, in October 2020, 27 African countries were among 54 countries that signed in the UN a declaration in support of China on the introduction of the new National Security Law in Hong Kong, in response to a statement criticizing Beijing by a group from 39 countries.

5.3 The Competitive Bipolarity with the US

China has been the main beneficiary of the post "double Cold War" (US–USSR and USSR–China) world order. The "unipolar interregnum" (Gaspar, 2019, pp. 123–172) gave way to a "uni-multi-polar" world power structure and, later, to a "uni-BI-multi-polar" one, where an increasingly incomplete American supremacy coexists with several other poles of power, global and regional, from which the resurgent China came to stand out (see Tomé, 2004, 2008, 2017, 2018, 2019, 2021a). And although Xi Jinping claims that "there is no fundamental change in the trend toward a multi-polar world" (Xi, 2021b), the huge growth of its comprehensive national power makes China a veritable emerging superpower and gives the world power structure an increasingly bipolar configuration. Beijing declares that "the world is undergoing the greatest changes in a century" (PRChina, 2019a, Chap. III.1) and assumes that "the configuration of strategic power is becoming more balanced" (PRChina, 2019b, Chap. I). And the US acknowledge that "the distribution of power across the world is changing… China is the only competitor potentially capable of combining its economic, diplomatic, military, and technological power" (The White House, 2021, pp. 7–8).

On the other hand, after the end of the "double Cold War," a pattern of behaviours and interactions that we have called "congagement" (combining containment + engagement), in which the main actors compete and conflict and, at the same time, cooperate, bilaterally and multilaterally, in an environment perceived as volatile, where the course of events and the behaviour of others is uncertain (see Tomé, 2016, 2017, 2018, 2019, 2021a, 2021d). The same pattern has marked the China–US relations: at the same time that they developed economic and commercial interdependencies (becoming each other's biggest trading partner), the US–China "Constructive Strategic Partnership" and articulation in multilateral fora and cooperation on multiple regional/global issues, Chinese leaders have never ceased to denounce and criticize the "hegemonism" and "unilateralism" of the US, to demand "multipolarity" and "multilateralism," to vociferate against the "interference in China's internal affairs" and to accuse the US of promoting an "anti-China containment."

In this context, the BRI is a powerful instrument of soft balancing against the US, deterring the formation of an anti-China coalition and "anyone but China" club. The soft balancing logic lies in expanding Chinese interests without directly confronting the US, while reassuring China's partners about China's peaceful rise, drawing them to its projects and agenda. And the fact is that most of the US' formal allies and strategic partners have joined the BRI and established agreements with Beijing, including Pakistan, the Philippines, Thailand, Singapore, Australia, Portugal, Greece, Turkey, or Italy – thus including members of NATO and of the G7.

China's rise has long been seen in Washington as a challenge to American dominance in the Asia–Pacific. For example, the Obama Administration's "Pivot to Asia" strategy was designed to counterbalance China's growing role. The Trans-Pacific Partnership (TPP) and the US–EU Transatlantic Trade and Investment Partnership (TTIP) were designed to exclude China and place the US at the centre of a broad front of Asia–Pacific and Euro-Atlantic countries. In this sense, as argued by Wang Jisi "the BRI is not merely a 'Marching West' strategy to advance China's geostrategic interests in Eurasia, but also a geostrategic rebalance to the US's 'Pivot to Asia'" (cit. in Weifeng & Esteban, 2018, p. 492). The BRI then gained an additional role vis-à-vis the "American First" and protectionism of the Trump Administration, serving as a reference for Beijing to assume the defence of economic liberalism, internationalism, and multilateralism: "Economic globalization is an irreversible consequence of global economic development… Some countries have…resorted to unilateral, protectionist, and hegemonic actions…driving the world economy towards the 'recession trap'" (PRChina, 2019a, Chap. III.4).

Gradually, Xi's China's balance against the US shifted from being soft and indirect to being hard and direct (Beeson, 2020; Doshi, 2021; Markey, 2020; Medcalf, 2020; Shambaugh, 2020; Sutter, 2019, 2020; Tomé, 2019, 2021a). Confident about the growth of China's all-encompassing national power and sensing America's decline, Beijing has been reacting to Washington's policies and manoeuvres in "the same coin," from the trade war to technological boycotts and sanctions on American companies, public criticism with belligerent rhetoric, detaining alleged spies or expelling and banning American citizens and NGOs from entering Chinese territory. At the same time, Xi's China has been strengthening its ties and partnerships with countries and regimes deemed outlawed of the "American order," from North Korea to Myanmar, Venezuela or Iran, as well as with US partners and allies more estranged from Washington, such as Pakistan, Egypt, or Turkey. It was also more openly promoting partnerships and strategic alignments in a logic of counterweight to the US, from the BRICS and SCO mechanisms to the China–Russia–Pakistan triangle. In all of this, the BRI has been instrumental.

With Putin's Russia, in particular, Xi's China has developed mutual articulation, intensified since the Russian annexation of Crimea in 2014, in the context of the bilateral "comprehensive strategic partnership of coordination for a new era" (see, e.g., Gaspar, 2019; Lukin, 2018; Mações, 2018; Markey, 2020; Rolland, 2019; Shambaugh, 2020; Stent 2020; Sutter, 2019, 2020; Tomé, 2018, 2019, 2021c). Moscow is Beijing's main supplier of oil and weapons, and coordination with Russia is crucial for the BRI's development of multiple routes in Eurasia. This quasi-alliance is not because they are part of an "autocratic international." This is because China and Russia consider it to serve their respective geopolitical purposes—including containing US supremacy, dividing the West and suppressing liberal political influences in international organizations and the world order. Both share the assumption that great powers have certain "natural rights," including regional spheres of influence; they have a traditional notion of security and sovereignty, instrumentally absolutizing the principle of "non-interference in internal affairs"; and they agree on ideas like the "sovereign internet." In parallel, Moscow and Beijing have supported certain autocratic regimes through political support and waging sanctions at the UNSC, breaking international sanctions, selling them weapons and doing business.

At the same time, Beijing increased the control, surveillance and internal repression mechanisms and, in practice, diminished the autonomy of the Hong Kong Special Administrative Region and ended the "one Country, two systems" principle with the imposition of its "National Security Law." Likewise, Xi's China became increasingly assertive in its positions and demands and assumed an openly confrontational stance towards other states as well—economically and politically sanctioning its critics and certain options of other countries, militarizing the South China and East China Seas or the border with India, and threatening greater predisposition to unify Taiwan into the "mother country" by force. This posture came to be referred to as "wolf-warrior" diplomacy/strategy (see, e.g., Doshi, 2021; Koda, 2021; Martin, 2021; Zhinqun, 2020), which attests Beijing's vigorous offensive in the defence and promotion of its national interests, often in a confrontational manner, in a new "hard line" in which the Chinese state media play a prominent role.

In itself, the competition between the US and China is not new, having been fuelled for decades by many differences, disagreements, and disputes. The competition between the declining superpower and the emerging superpower can also be considered relatively normal. But in recent years, the relations between Beijing and Washington have substantially deteriorated, with the "congagement" giving way to an essentially competitive and confrontational environment. For example, China's latest defence white paper states that "International strategic competition is on the rise" and directly accuses the US of "adopted unilateral policies," "provoked and intensified competition," "undermined global strategic stability," and of seeking "absolute military superiority" (PRCHina, 2019b, Chap I). This competitive tension escalated during the Trump presidency and worsened in 2020 in the context of the pandemic crisis and the campaign for the American Presidential elections (Tomé, 2021b). Xi's assertiveness and defiant and confrontational stance contributed greatly to the bipartisan consensus that emerged in the US for a tougher approach to Beijing, and which not only continued but rose in tone during the Biden presidency (Tomé, 2021a).

It is true that China continues to be the US' biggest trading partner and the US is China's biggest. Washington and Beijing have cooperative relations within the UNSC, WTO, APEC, and the G20 and on issues as diverse as climate change, nuclear proliferation, terrorism, North Korea, or Afghanistan. China is the biggest trading partner of the vast majority of allies and partners of the US and they do not seem to want to align themselves in a pure "containment" or "decoupling" vis-à-vis China. But competition is the predominant pattern at this stage of the China–US relationship, with the Biden Administration trying to rally a front of anti-China (and anti-Russia) democracies, including the mobilization of groups like NATO, G7+, Quad or the recent AUKUS—with Beijing considering these last two as American attempts to create an "Asian NATO."

For Biden, the US is being challenged "by our most serious competitor, China" (Biden, 2021a), describing a "stiff competition with China" (Biden, 2021b), and warning that if China has hegemonic intentions "That's not going to happen on my watch" (ibid.). The American President even targeted his Chinese counterpart, stating that Xi Jinping "Doesn't have a democratic — with a small 'D' — bone in his body" (ibid.). For his part, Xi Jinping considers that "Attempts to 'erect walls' or 'decouple' run counter to the law of economics and market principles.... we must reject the cold-war and zero-sum mentality and oppose a new 'Cold War'... Bossing others around or meddling in others' internal affairs would not get one any support"

(Xi, 2021b). Biden and Xi say they do not want a "new Cold War," but just the fact that they mention it is quite significant. And, in practice, they both seem committed to promoting it.

The BRI remains crucial for Xi's China to counter Washington's containment manoeuvers, reassuring its partners, telling the "China story," deterring other virtual rivals, and undermining US power and influence. "Belt and Road cooperation pursues development, aims at mutual benefits, and conveys a message of hope," Xi insists (2021b). Aware of the instrument that the BRI represents in Xi's China grand strategy, President Biden suggests to US allies and partners that "we should have, essentially, a similar initiative, pulling from the democratic states" (cit. in Reuters Agency, 2021).

China's resurgence is huge, impressive, and impactful, reaching the category of superpower. However, there are many challenges China faces internally and externally, and its new status also entails the costs inherent to bipolarity. On the other hand, Xi's more assertive and confrontational stance is provoking increasingly adverse reactions—and some even speak of "The End of China's Rise" (Beckley & Brands, 2021). The US has abandoned "congagement" and embraced neo-containment regarding China. Taiwan has become more determined in maintaining its de facto independence. Several Southeast Asian Countries are starting to hedge against China around the South China Sea. Many economies around the world are limiting Chinese investments in strategic sectors and looking for ways to lessen dependence on production and supply chains originating in China. More and more developed countries in Europe and Asia–Pacific are walling off their telecommunications networks from Chinese influence, resisting the Chinese 5G, not wanting to share know-how and high technology with Chinese companies, intending to implement a cyber space and a digital economy separate from China and, finally, advancing in technological "decoupling" vis-à-vis China. An increasing number of countries openly and harshly criticize certain Beijing policies. The EU–China CAI agreement is frozen and several CPTPP members are demonstrating against China's accession. NATO's new strategic concept will, for the first time, include references to the "China challenge." Several Asia–Pacific countries have announced significant increases in their defence budgets and military modernization programmes to counterbalance China. European countries, India, Japan, and Australia are intensifying their articulation among themselves and with the US to counterweight China…

It is true that we could list equally adverse factors in relation to the US, but it is China we are talking about and, globally, it seems clear that the worldview of China and interactions with Beijing are no longer what they used to be. And Xi's China begins to face new dilemmas and challenges. Xi Jinping affirms that "One country's success does not have to mean another country's failure" (Xi, 2021c). It's true, although the US–China power game seems to be now more a zero-sum than one of relative gains or mutual gains. Xi also considers that "time and momentum are on China's side" (cit. in *South China Morning Post*, 2021). Well, this may not be so, we have to wait and see.

6 Final Remarks: Xi's China—Too Far and Too Fast?

Responding to the questions set out in the introduction to this chapter, we highlight three essential arguments exposed throughout it. First, China's current "grand strategy" is the result both of its "historical continuity" and impressive resurgence and of the overlapping interests and goals of China as a State and of the dominant CPC, with emphasis on the path traced by leaders such as Deng Xiaoping and Xi Jinping. Second, the strengthening of its "comprehensive national power," combined with Xi's leadership style, has made China more ambitious, confident, and assertive. Third, the BRI is part of a broader set of Xi's China policies and initiatives in his pursuit of his grand strategy and, on the other hand, in addition to geo-economic objectives, it also has associated geopolitical and geostrategic goals.

The great interests and ambitions of Xi's China can be summarized in the following list of priorities: maintaining the "dominant role" of the CPC to build "socialism with Chinese characteristics" and the "realization of communism"; preserve Chinese sovereignty against external interference in its "internal affairs"; maintain territorial integrity (including in the South and East China Seas and other territorial and border claims) and complete the unification of China (Taiwan); to promote economic and social development aiming at "a great modern socialist country"; growth of the "comprehensive national power" aiming at "the Chinese Dream of national rejuvenation"; restore China's international centrality in a "New Era"; and "reform" the international system, with China's reshaping global governance and leading the "Community of Common Destiny for Mankind" or "the Global Community of Shared Future."

For its strategy in the "New Era," Xi's China anticipated in time some of the goals set by its predecessors and laid out a broad plan with a timeline linked to two symbolically important centenary milestones reached in 2021 (the CPC's centenary) and 2049 (the PRC's centenary). According to Xi, China has already succeeded in the first centenary strategic goal of "building a moderately prosperous society in all respects," and has thus entered a new phase in which economic development remains the "central task." The continued strengthening of its comprehensive national power should lead China to complete the "dream of national rejuvenation" and become a "modern socialist country."

It wasn't just China's ambitions that Xi altered and anticipated, but also the means and the way to reach them. Taking advantage of China's growing comprehensive national power and perceiving a decline in the US and the West, China's international policy is committed to shifting the balance of power, transforming the international system in both Asia–Pacific and the world, and building a "new Sino-centric world." Thus, "Xiplomacy" changed the previous low profile stance and, essentially, the non-confrontational attitude associated with the "24-Character Strategy" enunciated by Deng to a new "Wolf Warrior Strategy," more assertive, high-profile, and confrontational.

As part of its grand strategy, Xi's China has launched a wide range of initiatives in a wide range of fields. The most emblematic is the BRI which, in addition to geo-economic interests and motivations related to the need to balance the economic development of the various regions of China and to strengthen its ties as a country with other regional economies and markets, also serves geopolitical and geostrategic purposes: energy security; increasing China's leverage in its neighbourhood and beyond; promoting the "Go Global"; building soft and normative power; increasing the legitimacy of its rising power; soft balancing against the US and deterring the formation of any anti-China coalition and "anyone but China" club; and reshaping global governance in a way that reflects its values, interests, and status.

Being the main beneficiary of the post "double Cold War" world order and the great winner of hyperglobalization, China reached the status of superpower and gives the world power structure a growing bipolar configuration. However, this status entails costs and challenges that Beijing may not have anticipated. On the other hand, Xi's China assertiveness and acceleration in defending and promoting its policies and demands is provoking increasingly adverse reactions. Has Xi's China gone too far and too fast? It is still too early to realize all the impacts of Xi's China grand strategy, but in the "second centenary" set by Xi we will certainly have the answer.

Bibliographic References

Asian Infrastructure Investment Bank (AIIB). (2021). Website. Retrieved on 18 October 2021, from https://www.aiib.org/en/index.html

Acker, K., & Brautigam, D. (2021). *Twenty years of data on China's Africa lending* (China-Africa Research Initiative Policy Brief nº 4). Johns Hopkins School of Advanced International Studies (SAIS).

Acker, K., Brautigam, D., & Yufan, H. (2020). *Debt relief with Chinese characteristics* (China-Africa Research Initiative Policy Brief nº 46). Johns Hopkins School of Advanced International Studies (SAIS).

Balzacq, T., & Krebs, R. R. (2021). *The Oxford handbook of grand strategy*. Oxford University Press.

Beckley, M., & Brands, H. (2021, October 1). The end of China's rise. Beijing is running out of time to remake the world. *Foreign Affairs*.

Beeson, M. (Ed.). (2020). *Rivalry and cooperation in the Asia-Pacific: The dynamics of a region in transition* (2 Vols.). WSPC.

Belt and Road Forum for International Cooperation. (2017, May 17). *Joint Communique of the Leaders Roundtable of the Belt and Road Forum for International Cooperation*. Beijing. Beltandroadforum.Org, Retrieved on 18 October 2021, from http://www.beltandroadforum.org/english/index.html

Belt and Road Portal—Guidance under the Office of the Leading Group for Promoting the Belt and Road Initiative, Hosted by the State Information Center. Retrieved on 18 October 2021, from https://eng.yidaiyilu.gov.cn/index.htm

Biden, J. R., Jr. (2021a, February 4). *Remarks by President Biden on America's place in the world*. U.S. Department of State Headquarters, Harry S. Truman Building, Washington, DC.

Biden, J. R., Jr. (2021b, March 25). *Remarks by President Biden in press conference*. Retrieved on 03 November 2021, from https://www.whitehouse.gov/briefing-room/speeches-remarks/2021/03/25/remarks-by-president-biden-in-press-conference/

Biscop, S. (2021). *Grand strategy in 10 words: A guide to great power politics in the 21st century*. Bristol University Press.

Blachette, J. (2021, July/August). Xi's gamble. The race to consolidate power and stave off disaster. *Foreign Affairs, 100*(4), 10–19.

Brands, H. (2014). *What good is grand strategy? Power and purpose in American statecraft from Harry S. Truman to George W. Bush*. Cornell University Press.

Chih-Yu, S., et al. (2019). *China and international theory. The balance of relationships*. Routledge.

China-Africa Business Council. (2021, August). *Market power and role of the private sector. Chinese investment in Africa*. China-Africa Business Council Report.

China Daily. (2016). Chairman Xi's 2016 new year's address (Bilingual Full Text). Retrieved on 18 October 2021, from https://chinadaily.com.cn/interface/yidian/1139302/2016-01-%2004/cd_22925566.html

CPC—Communist Party of China. (2017). *Constitution of the Communist Party of China. Revised and adopted at the 19th National Congress of the Communist Party of China on October 24, 2017*. Retrieved on 14 November 2021, from http://www.xinhuanet.com//english/download/Constitution_of_the_Communist_Party_of_China.pdf

CPC—Communist Party of China, Central Committee. (2013). *Decision on some major issues concerning comprehensively deepening the reform. Adopted at the Third Plenary Session of the 18th Central Committee of the Communist Party of China on November 12, 2013*. China.org Retrieved on 3 November 2021, from http://www.china.org.cn/china/third_plenary_session/2014-01/16/content_31212602.htm

da Silva, J. T. (2021). *XI Jinping—A Ascensão do Novo Timoneiro da China*. Sílabos e Desafios.

Doshi, R. (2021). *The long game: China's grand strategy to displace American order*. Oxford University Press.

Duarte, P. A. B., & Ferreira-Pereira, L. (2021). The soft power of China and the European Union in the context of the Belt and Road Initiative and global strategy. *Journal of Contemporary European Studies*. https://doi.org/10.1080/14782804.2021.1916740.

Erçetin, Ş. Ş., & Açikalin, Ş. N. (Eds.). (2020). *Chaos, complexity and leadership 2018. Explorations of chaotic and complexity theory*. Springer International Publishing.

FOCAC—Forum on China-Africa Cooperation. (2018, September 4). *Beijing Declaration—Toward an even stronger China-Africa community with a shared future*. Beijing.

Freedman, L. (2013). *Strategy: A history*. Oxford University Press.

Fu, Y. (2016, February 13). *Speech by the Chairwoman of the Foreign Affairs Committee of the Chinese National People's Congress at the 52nd Munich Security Conference*.

Gaddis, J. L. (2019). *On grand strategy*. Penguin Books.

Garcia, A. O. (Coord.). (2020). *China. The Belt and Road Initiative: A global transformation*. Universidad Nacional Autónoma de Mexico.

Gaspar, C. (2019). *O Regresso da Anarquia. Os Estados Unidos, a China, a Rússia e a Ordem Internacional* [The return of anarchy. The United States, China, Russia and the international order]. Alêtheia.

Grydehoj, A., & Ping, S. (2021). *China and the pursuit of harmony in world politics: Understanding Chinese international relations theory*. Routledge.

Ho, B. T. E. (2019). Chinese thinking about international relations: From theory to practice. *Asia Policy, 14*(3), 2–5.

Hun, J. K. (2016). Will IR theory with Chinese characteristics be a powerful alternative? *The Chinese Journal of International Politics, 9*(1), 59–79.

Koda, Y. (2021, September 21). China, Wolf Warrior diplomacy and Taiwan. *The Diplomat*. Retrieved on 13 November 2021, from https://thediplomat.com/2021/09/china-wolf-warrior-diplomacy-and-taiwan/

Kovrig, M. (2018, October 24). *China expands its peace and security footprint in Africa*. International Crisis Group Commentary. Retrieved on 15 October 2021, from https://www.crisisgroup.org/asia/north-east-asia/china/china-expands-its-peace-and-security-footprint-africa

Layton, P. (2018). *Grand strategy*.

Layton, P. (2020, August 17). *Defining grand strategy*. The Strategy Bridge.Org. Retrieved on 4 November 2021, from https://thestrategybridge.org/the-bridge/2020/8/17/defining-grand-strategy

Leandro, F. J., & Duarte, P. A. B. (Eds.). (2020). *The Belt and Road Initiative: An old archetype of a new development model*. Palgrave Macmillan.

Lissner, R. F. (2018). What is grand strategy? Sweeping a conceptual minefield. *TNSR-Texas National Security Review, 2*(1), 52–73.

Lukin, A. (2018). *China and Russia. A new rapprochement*. Polity.

Mações, B. (2018). *Belt and Road: A Chinese world order*. Hurst.

Markey, D. (2020). *China's western horizon: Beijing and the new geopolitics of Eurasia*. Oxford University Press.

Martin, P. (2021). *China's civilian army: The making of Wolf Warrior diplomacy*. Oxford University Press.

Medcalf, R. (2020). *Indo-Pacific empire. China, America and the contest for the World's pivotal region*. Manchester University Press.

Menon, S. (2016, January 2). What China's rise means for the world. *The Wire*. Retrieved on 12 November 2021, from https://thewire.in/external-affairs/what-chinas-rise-means-for-the-world

Milevski, L. (2016). *The evolution of modern grand strategic thought*. Oxford University Press.

Munyi, E. N. (2020). *Challenging Pax Americana: The commercial imperative in Chinese arms exports to Africa—A case study of Uganda and Kenya* (China-Africa Research Initiative Policy Brief n° 41). Johns Hopkins School of Advanced International Studies (SAIS).

Nantulya, P. (2021, September 3). *The forum on China-Africa cooperation at 21: Where to next?* AfricanCenter.org Spotlight. African Center for Strategic Studies. Retrieved on 10 November 2021, from https://africacenter.org/spotlight/focac-forum-china-africa-cooperation-21-where-to-next/

NDRC—PRChina's National Development and Reform Commission. (2015, March 28). *Vision and actions on jointly building Silk Road Economic Belt and 21st-Century Maritime Silk Road*. Retrieved on 10 November 2021, from http://en.ndrc.gov.cn/newsrelease/201503/

Nexon, D. (2021, February 15). Against great power competition. The U.S. should not confuse means for ends. *Foreign Affairs*.

Olander, E. (2020, July 6). *China's new priorities in Africa*. The China Africa Project. Retrieved on 4 November 2021, from https://chinaafricaproject.com/analysis/chinas-new-priorities-in-africa/

PCA— Permanent Court of Arbitration. (2016). *PCA Case No. 2013–19 in the matter of the South China Sea Arbitration—Award, 12 July 2016*. Retrieved on 12 November 2021, from https://pcacases.com/web/sendAttach/2086

Posen, B. R. (2014). *Restraint: A new foundation for U.S. grand strategy*. Cornell University Press.

PRChina. (2015, May). *China's military strategy*. The State Council Information Office of the People's Republic of China.

PRChina. (2016, July). *China adheres to the position of settling through negotiation the relevant disputes between China and the Philippines in the South China Sea*. The State Council Information Office of the People's Republic of China.

PRChina. (2017, January). *China's policies on Asia-Pacific security cooperation*. The State Council Information Office of the People's Republic of China.

PRChina. (2019a, September). *China and the world in the new era*. The State Council Information Office of the People's Republic of China.

PRChina. (2019b, July). *China's national defense in the new era*. The State Council Information Office of the People's Republic of China.

PRChina (2021a, January). *China's international development cooperation in the new era*. The State Council Information Office of the People's Republic of China.

PRChina. (2021b, September). *China's epic journey from poverty to prosperity*. The State Council Information Office of the People's Republic of China.

PRChina—Constitution of the People's Republic of China. (1982). Revised with all *Amendments* adopted in 1988, 1993, 1999, 2004 and 2018. Retrieved on 14 November 2021, from https://english.www.gov.cn/archive/lawsregulations/201911/20/content_WS5ed8856ec6d0b3f0e9499913.html

Reuters Agency. (2021, March 26). *Biden says he suggested to UK's Johnson a plan to rival China's Belt and Road*. Retrieved on 19 November 2021, from https://www.reuters.com/article/us-usa-britain-biden-china/biden-says-he-suggested-to-uks-johnson-a-plan-to-rival-chinas-belt-and-road-idUSKBN2BI32M

Rolland, N. (2019, February–March). A China–Russia condominium over Eurasia. *Survival: Global Politics and Strategy, 61*, 7–22.

Shambaugh, D. (Ed.). (2020). *China and the world*. Oxford University Press.

Shambaugh, D. (2021). *China's leaders: From Mao to now*. Polity Press.

Silove, N. (2018). Beyond the buzzword: The three meanings of 'grand strategy'. *Security Studies, 27*(1), 27–57.

South China Morning Post. (2021, January 12). Xi Jinping says 'time and momentum on China's side' as he sets out Communist Party vision. *SCMP*. Retrieved on 13 April 2021, from https://www.scmp.com/news/china/politics/article/3117314/xi-jinping-says-time-and-momentum-chinas-side-he-sets-out

Stent, A. (2020, February). *Russia and China: Axis of revisionists?* Brookings Institution.

Summers, T. (2016). China's 'New Silk Roads': Sub-national regions and networks of global political economy. *Third World Quarterly, 37*(9), 1628–1643.

Sutter, R. (2019, March 21). *An emerging China-Russia axis? Implications for the United States in an era of strategic competition*. Testimony before the U.S.-China Economic and Security Review Commission.

Sutter, R. (2020), *Chinese foreign relations: Power and policy of an emerging global force* (5th ed.). Rowman & Littlefield Publishers.

Tekdal, V. (2018). China's Belt and Road Initiative: At the crossroads of challenges and ambitions. *The Pacific Review, 31*(3), 373–390.

The White House. (2021, March). *U.S. interim national security strategy guidance*.

Tomé, L. (2004). *The new world's geopolitical outline* (English and Portuguese ed.). Quid Juris.

Tomé, L. (2008). Security and geopolitics in East Asia today: One region, two faces. In L. Tomé (Ed.), *East Asia today* (pp. 27–81). Prefácio Editora.

Tomé, L. (2016). Complex systems theories and eclectic approach in analysing and theorising the contemporary international security complex. In Ş. Ş. Erçetin & H. Bagci (Eds.), *Handbook of research on chaos and complexity theory in the social sciences* (pp. 19–32). IGI Global.

Tomé, L. (2017). Poder Mundial e Segurança Internacional ao Olhar o Mundo Futuro [World power and international security as it looks to the future world]. In A. P. Mateus et al., *Olhar o Mundo* [Looking at the world] (pp. 175–182). Marcador.

Tomé, L. (2018). Geopolítica da Rússia de Putin: não é a União Soviética, mas gostava de ser… [Putin's Russia geopolitics: It's not the Soviet Union, but it would like to be…]. *RI-Relações Internacionais* (60), 69–99.

Tomé, L. (2019). Região Indo-Pacífico: o factor China e motivações geopolíticas [Indo-Pacific region: The China factor and geopolitical motivations]. *Nação e Defesa nº 151-Geopolítica Aplicada*, 66–100.

Tomé, L. (2021a, March). China e Ásia-Pacífico na Política da Administração Biden: operacionalizando um 'sistema internacional estável e aberto' e um 'Indo-Pacífico livre e aberto' [China and Asia-Pacific in Biden Administration Policy: operationalizing a 'stable and open international system' and a 'free and open Indo-Pacific']. *RI-Relações Internacionais* (69), 35–68.

Tomé, L. (2021b). The impacts of the pandemic crisis on international politics. In S. Ş. Erçetin, N. Potas, & S. N. Açikalin (Eds.), *COVID-19 beyond: Effects of different fields*. Springer/World Scientific Publishing.

Tomé, L. (2021c). Construction and deconstruction of the liberal international order. *Janus.net, e-Journal of International Relations—Special Issue on Liberalism*.

Tomé, L. (2021d). Mares da China: disputas e dilemas à luz da ressurgência chinesa [China's seas: Disputes and dilemmas in light of China's resurgence]. In *Academia da Marinha—Memórias 2020*. Edições da Academia da Marinha.

Tomé, L., & Açikalin, S. N. (2019). Chapter 1. Complexity theory as a new lens in international relations: System and change. In S. Ş. Erçetin & N. Potas (Eds.), *Chaos, complexity and leadership. Explorations of chaos and complexity theory* (pp. 1–15). IGI Global/Springer.

USDoD—United States Department of Defense. (2021). *Military and security developments involving the People's Republic of China 2021. Annual report to Congress.* Washington, DC.

Voo, J. P., & Xinpeng, X. (2020). Impact of the Belt and Road Initiative on China's soft power: Preliminary evidence. *Asia-Pacific Journal of Accounting & Economics, 27*(1), 120–131.

Weifeng, Z., & Esteban, M. (2018). Beyond balancing: China's approach towards the Belt and Road Initiative. *Journal of Contemporary China, 27*(112), 487–501.

Xi Jinping. (2012, November 17). *Study, disseminate and implement the guiding principles of the 18th CPC National Congress.* Speech at the first group study session of the Political Bureau of the 18th CPC Central Committee which Xi presided over.

Xi Jinping. (2014, May 21), *New Asian security concept for new progress in security cooperation.* Remarks at the Fourth Summit of the Conference on Interaction and Confidence Building Measures in Asia by H.E. Xi Jinping President of the People's Republic of China. Shanghai Expo Center.

Xi Jinping. (2017a, October 18). *Secure a decisive victory in building a moderately prosperous society in all respects and strive for the great success of socialism with Chinese characteristics for a new era.* Speech delivered at the 19th National Congress of the Communist Party of China.

Xi Jinping. (2017b, May 14). *Work together to Build the Silk Road Economic Belt and the 21st Century Maritime Silk Road.* Speech by H.E. Xi Jinping President of the People's Republic of China at the Opening Ceremony of the Belt and Road Forum for International Cooperation.

Xi Jinping. (2019). *On building a human community with a shared future.* Central Compilation & Translation Press.

Xi Jinping. (2021a, July 1). *Speech at a ceremony marking the centenary of the Communist Party of China.*

Xi Jinping. (2021b, April 20). *Pulling together through adversity and toward a shared future for all.* Keynote Speech by H.E. Xi Jinping President of the People's Republic of China at the Boao Forum for Asia Annual Conference.

Xi Jinping. (2021c, September 21). *Bolstering confidence and jointly overcoming difficulties to build a better world.* Statement by H.E. Xi Jinping President of the People's Republic of China at the General Debate of the 76th Session of the United Nations General Assembly.

Xinhua News Agency. (2014, November 24). *Xi eyes more enabling international environment for China's peaceful development.* Retrieved on 12 November 2021, from http://news.xinhuanet.com/english/china/2014-11/30/c_133822694_4.htm

Yong, W. (2016). Offensive for defensive: The belt and road initiative and China's new grand strategy. *The Pacific Review, 29*(3), 455–463.

Zhinqun, Z. (2020, May 15). Interpreting China's 'Wolf-Warrior diplomacy'. *The Diplomat.* Retrieved on 13 November 2021, from https://thediplomat.com/2020/05/interpreting-chinas-wolf-warrior-diplomacy/

Chapter 6
People-to-People Exchanges: A Cluster of Narratives to Advance Purposeful Constructivism

Yichao Li, Francisco José B. S. Leandro, and Paulo Guilherme Figueiredo

1 Introduction

Social interactions between people form relationships, and the result of the interaction is what the world presents to us, in a sort of purposeful web of networks. As population—the total number of individuals under a singular political system—is one of the constituent elements of a state, it seems reasonable to accept that relations between states often and ultimately reflect the relations between people—in other words, a "world of our making" (Onuf, 1989), which is the typical explanation of constructivism in international relations theory. Zehfuss calls constructivism "a phenomenon [that] has become inescapable" (2004, p. 2). Societies are constructed by human beings and are created according to the kind of society that those people want to live in. The interactions of people's behaviours are closely related to how societies exist. Max Weber's sociology is one of the origins of constructivism (Brunnée & Toope, 2013, p. 122).[1] Weber (1968, p. 180) asserts that "… we are cultural human beings, endowed with the capacity and the will to take a deliberate attitude towards the world and to lend it significance."[2] Because of such capacity and will, cultures,

---

[1] In 1966, Berger and Luckmann wrote a book entitled "The social construction of reality: a treatise in the sociology of knowledge." "*Social construction*" is a term used by them in social theory and it was applied to many other fields (e.g., personal construct psychology, educational psychology, crime, communication studies, and of course the discipline of International Relations) later (Zehfuss, 2001, p. 54).

[2] Quote from M. Fuchs (2017, p. 259).

Y. Li (✉) · F. J. B. S. Leandro · P. G. Figueiredo
University of Macau, Macao, China
e-mail: A18092105144@cityu.mo

F. J. B. S. Leandro
e-mail: franciscoleandro@cityu.mo

P. G. Figueiredo
e-mail: paulo@macaulink.com.mo

norms, discourses, identities, changes, sociality, and processes of interaction, rather than power or wealth, have become core concepts that constructivists concern themselves with (Acharya & Buzan, 2019, p. 232; Checkel, 2008, p. 72; Fierke, 2010, p. 180).

The Chinese concept of *guanxi* carries, beyond the fundamental neutral connotations of grouping and networking, a certain important highlight of friendliness and familiarity that is part and parcel of the culture. Human transactions to a significant extent are based upon and facilitated by such relational qualities, and *guanxi* is a manifestation of such permeating social practice. A web of *guanxi* is a network of people we can call on for favours and introductions. In China, if you want to coax others into doing something or making something happen, exerting power or pressure alone will not take you nearly as far as complementing it with a gift on the side (Chu, 2018, pp. 11, 16, 59). But *guanxi* is a reciprocal obligation and Chinese generally expect foreigners to understand *guanxi* and behave according to its rule. *Guanxi* is a tit-for-tat arrangement between people or work units that makes the Chinese system go. It offers access to goods and services otherwise difficult to acquire. The currency of *guanxi* is normal favours, not cash (Seligman, 1999, pp. 57–65). In Chinese contexts the importance of informal groupings and networks is heightened by the elementally relationship-orientation of the culture. Human transactions are constructed and facilitated by the quality of relationships. The concept of *guanxi*, is a pervasive social practice expressing this.

In a collectivist culture, it is critical to cultivate friendly relationships and interactions in order to succeed in the workplace, as so much of the finer aspects of work and the workplace are unwritten, unprescribed by formal hierarchies, rules, or regimes (Westwood & Leung, 1999). As Qin suggests, "Culture plays a significant role in knowledge production" (2018, p. 416). It will therefore have an impact on people's world and life views across generations, in turn affecting people-to-people exchanges (P2PEs). It follows that respect for cultural diversity is the basis for enhancing mutual bilateral trust, which promotes space for creating new synergy and facilitates intercultural integration.

P2PE-related narratives have been gaining traction in both the West and the East alike, but P2PE itself is hardly a new concept: it emerged towards the beginning of the twenty-first century. Earlier still, back in the middle of the twentieth century, Terpeau already observed that "[t]he concept of 'people to people' diplomacy advanced by the Eisenhower Administration [had] received tremendous implementation [during the summer of 1959] when the Howard University Choir toured for 80 days in 18 countries from Mexico to Argentina, with three stops in the West Indies" (1960, p. 104). This event did "more to bind together in friendship the South American people and the people of the United States than years of high-level conferences can do" (p. 107). This illustrates that the arts (music in this case) can have positive effects on relations and relationships among people and peoples. P2PE via, for instance, the media, the Internet, events, publications that cover diverse fields and institutions is similar in many cases to the instruments of public diplomacy. In other words, when it is related to a state's foreign policies, P2PE inevitably plays a part in mutual facilitation. Furthermore, events held by states, organizations (e.g., corporations), and individuals can gradually influence and change the course of the narratives through which different audiences come to comprehend and interpret their actions (Edney et al., 2020, p. 10). We herein pose the question: *How do we understand people-to-people exchanges?* and attempt to answer it based on a methodology with a theoretical-inductive perspective, and a discourse analysis approached from both Chinese and English. This chapter comprises five parts: (1) an introduction; (2) a literature review; (3) a section that examines P2PE in the Chinese context; (4) a discussion on the question "How do we understand P2PE?"; and (5) a conclusion.

2 Literature Review

P2PE has yet to become a mature concept. In fact, studies that are directly related to P2PE in the literature are limited, and P2PE often appears as a second key point in topics related to diplomatic relations, for example, public diplomacy (D'Hooghe, 2005; Hartig, 2016) and soft power (Ellis, 2020; Wang, 2008). At times, scholars might even be discussing very similar ideas but under various other terms,[3] such as "people-to-people diplomacy" (Wang, 2016), and "people-to-people communication" (Payne, 2009).

P2PE also appears and is characterized differently in the literature between English and Chinese. In English, tracing back to how China discovered and developed its public diplomacy, D'Hooghe (2005, p. 102) believes that P2PE did occur within the process, and due to the necessity and freedom to opine on international issues, both the space for dialogue and participation of the Chinese people have been increasing. However, there have been limitations in China's public diplomacy resulting from decades-long domestic propagandas, which, even if not led by the government directly, were at least under government control (p. 103). In fact, the development of public diplomacy has experienced two waves so far. According to Cull (2013, pp. 3–4), the term "public diplomacy" did not appear until 1965, and carried the meaning of "the conduct of foreign policy by engagement with a foreign public." Over time, with the development of science and technology, media for public diplomacy constantly got updated, bringing in new changes to the field of public diplomacy. In 2008, public diplomacy 2.0 became the official term for public diplomacy of new online media, and with that, public diplomacy entered a new era. The main difference between the two waves lies in the fact that the former was a one-way flow of information, where participants provided limited information for the public, while the latter pays more attention to exchanges and feedback, and is geared towards further cooperation and dialogue, establishing relationships, and playing the role of non-state actors (Hartig, 2016, p. 656). Payne (2009, p. 579) thinks that the importance of people-to-people communication is "for the establishment of meaningful and sustaining relationships and the

---

[3] These other terms that exist include "citizen diplomacy," "civil diplomacy," "non-official diplomacy," and "multi-track diplomacy" (Yu, 2018, p. 81).

development of trust," while Leandro (2019a), based on the establishment of the first scientific forum of the Federación Internacional de Estudios Sobre América Latina y el Caribe (FIEALC), makes an empirical analysis which emphasizes building a new participatory model of cultural dialogue and cooperation specially designed for tripartite cooperation (Asia, Latin America, and Central and South-eastern Europe), with the Macau Special Administrative Region at the centre, and using P2PE as the leading rationale. What Leandro particularly addresses is that this trilateral cultural dialogue and cooperation platform "should be culturally inclusive, based on a self-branding effort to be recognized as a space of networking, trust, reliance, participation, facilitation, dialogue, security, multi-culturalism, identity enhancement, exchange, and multilevel partnership" (p. 45).

Given the important role that people can play in China's diplomacy, Liu (2015, pp. 243–247) believes that folk diplomacy has become indispensable. Folk diplomacy can be divided into these four stages: (1) 1949–1977, not long after the founding of the People's Republic of China—during this stage, the use of P2PE promoted intergovernmental relations and helped China seek recognition from other states; (2) 1978–1989—China began to implement the reform and opening up policy. Meanwhile, Special Economic Zones (SEZs) were established to attract foreign investment, technology, and human capital to speed up the realization of Chinese modernization, the process of which could not have been possible had it relied solely on the government. In fact, the participation of the people was particularly decisive; (3) 1990–2011—with the theme of peace and development, the Chinese government carried on with the previous ideas and began to advocate a harmonious, people-oriented society. People began to pursue their own gains more actively; (4) post-2012, topics that relate to P2PE have gained popularity, and immaterial factors have received more attention among people. People with different cultural, language, and religious backgrounds hope to understand, share, and reach consensus with one another. The process is continuous, and depends on China's priorities during different stages of its development, in which the role of the people could never be overemphasized.

In 1956, then Prime Minister Zhou Enlai defined diplomacy as a combination of three aspects, namely full diplomatic ties (officially), semi-diplomatic ties (public diplomacy), and non-diplomatic ties, but with trade and economic links (folk diplomacy) (Ministry of Foreign Affairs, n.d.). Although many scholars conceptually differentiate the three, there continues to be mixed, interchanging usage of the terms (Yu, 2017; Zhang, 2008; Zhang & Ding, 2019).[4] Further, between Chinese and English, translation (especially in terms of accuracy) has complicated the meaning of P2PE. However, mainstream views tend to converge on the point that public diplomacy and folk diplomacy (*minjian waijiao*) are different, and the distinction between the two is most easily discerned in terms of agency. For folk diplomacy (*minjian waijiao*), an agent can be an institution or individual but must not be official; for public diplomacy, the agent carries official attributes (Yao, 2019, p. 28). In 2011,

---

[4] The three examples already show the problems: these three authors expressed the same phrase "民间外交" (*minjian waijiao*) in Chinese, but the corresponding English translations are "public diplomacy," "civil diplomacy," and "people-to-people diplomacy."

former Chinese Minister of Foreign Affairs Yang Jiechi (2011) further discerned public diplomacy as usually led by the government with the ultimate purpose of safeguarding national interests. Western scholars tend to have a different understanding to this definition of public diplomacy. Snow, for example, thinks that public diplomacy "is inevitably linked to power" (2009, p. 3). Here, "power" should be noted to point towards soft power—i.e., culture, values, ideologies, in other words, aspects that emphasize the seeking and creating of mutual understanding and consensus (Hartig, 2016, p. 660). Nye in fact calls public diplomacy in the form of soft power "more important than ever" (2020, p. xix).

3 People-to-People Exchanges in Chinese Contexts

In the Chinese context, the meaning of P2PE can be decoded in multiple ways, some of which may even be misconstrued, misused, or taken out of context. Even in official documents, P2PE deviates in meaning in both literal and connotative terms between Chinese and English. To draw out the exact meaning of P2PE in the Chinese context, the authors selected, based on previous literature reviews, available, reliable Chinese official documents and their English translations, particularly those dated post-2012 (aforementioned "fourth stage" as defined by Liu, 2015) to analyze, using P2PE as a keyword to juxtapose corresponding passages in the Chinese and English versions, as presented in Table 1. We have thus come to the following two highlights:

First, the report of the 18th National Congress of the Communist Party of China (CPC) was the first time that "public diplomacy" appeared officially in a CPC report, thereby becoming a topic of the national strategic level (Yao, 2019, p. 50). In an important 2013 remark, President Xi Jinping made it very clear that, in Chinese, public diplomacy (*gonggong waijiao*), folk diplomacy (*minjian waijiao*), and cultural and people-to-people exchanges (*renwen jiaoliu*) are three different but coexisting concepts; the term "folk diplomacy" (*minjian waijiao*), however, is not observed to be used in English (only "cultural and people-to-people exchanges"). The term "public diplomacy" (*gonggong waijiao*) has also not appeared in official documents after 2013. Instead, official narratives have centred more around people, culture, and mutuality.

Second, in official narratives, *renwen jiaoliu* has always been understood as "cultural and people-to-people exchanges" and should be translated so. However, in 2017, an English document regarding China and improving people-to-people exchanges with foreign countries was released, in which *renwen jiaoliu* was referred to only as "people-to-people exchanges"; the word "cultural" was omitted. In 2021, in the white paper *China's International Development Cooperation in the New Era*, "people-to-people exchanges" encompasses both *renwen jiaoliu* and *minjian jiaoliu*.

Table 1 Respective expressions in Chinese and English of the concept of people-to-people exchanges in bilingual Chinese official narratives

Year	Text
November 2012 中国共产党第十八次全国代表大会报告 Report of 18th National Congress of the Communist Party of China	我们将扎实推进公共外交和人文交流 (**renwen jiaoliu**)，维护我国海外合法权益。We will take solid steps to promote public diplomacy as well as **people-to-people and cultural exchanges**, and protect China's legitimate rights and interests overseas
October 2013 习近平在周边外交工作座谈会上发表重要讲话 Xi Jinping Makes Important Remarks at a Conference on the Diplomatic Work with Neighbouring Countries	要着力加强对周边国家的宣传工作、公共外交 (gonggong waijiao)、民间外交 (minjian jiaoliu)、人文交流 (renwen jiaoliu)，巩固和扩大我同周边国家关系长远发展的社会和民意基础。**cultural and people-to-people exchanges** We should strive to strengthen publicity work, public diplomacy, **cultural and people-to-people exchanges** with the neighbouring countries, and consolidate and expand social and public opinion foundations of the long-term development of relations between China and its neighbouring countries
October 2017 中国共产党第十九次全国代表大会报告 Report of 19th National Congress of the Communist Party of China	加强中外人文交流 (**renwen jiaoliu**)，以我为主、兼收并蓄。推进国际传播能力建设，讲好中国故事，展现真实、立体、全面的中国，提高国家文化软实力。We will strengthen **people-to-people and cultural exchanges** with other countries, giving prominence to Chinese culture while also drawing on other cultures. We will improve our capacity for engaging in international communication so as to tell China's stories well, present a true, multidimensional, and panoramic view of China, and enhance our country's cultural soft power
December 2017 《关于加强和改进中外人文交流工作的若干意见》 China to Improve People-to-people Exchanges with Foreign Countries	《意见》指出，要丰富和拓展人文交流 (**renwen jiaoliu**) 的内涵和领域。It points out that the content of **people-to-people exchanges** should be enriched and extended

(continued)

Table 1 (continued)

Year	Text
January 2021 《新时代的中国国际发展合作》白皮书 White Book: China's International Development Cooperation in the New Era	在2015年12月中非合作论坛约翰内斯堡峰会上，习近平主席宣布3年内，同非方重点实施中非工业化、农业现代化、基础设施、金融、绿色发展、贸易和投资便利化、减贫惠民、公共卫生、人文 **(renwen)** 、和平与安全等"十大合作计划"。At the FOCAC Johannesburg Summit in December 2015, President Xi put forward ten major cooperation programmes with Africa for the following three years, covering industrialization, agricultural modernization, infrastructure, finance, green development, trade and investment facilitation, poverty reduction, public health, **cultural and people-to-people exchanges,** and peace and security 在2018年9月中非合作论坛北京峰会上，习近平主席宣布未来3年和今后一段时间重点实施产业促进、设施联通、贸易便利、绿色发展、能力建设、健康卫生、人文交流 **(renwen jiaoliu)** 、和平安全等"八大行动"。At the FOCAC Beijing Summit held in September 2018, President Xi stated that China would launch eight major initiatives in the next three years and beyond, covering industrial development, infrastructure connectivity, trade facilitation, green development, capacity building, healthcare, **people-to-people exchanges,** and peace and security 中国通过实施民生援助，加大人文交流 (renwen jiaoliu)、文化合作，形成相互欣赏、相互理解、相互尊重的人文格局，筑牢共建"一带一路"的社会基础。China promotes people-to-people exchanges and cultural cooperation with partner countries through projects designed to improve the lives of local people, thus increasing mutual appreciation, mutual understanding and mutual respect, and reinforcing the social foundation of the Belt and Road Initiative 深化民间交流 **(minjian jiaoliu)**，邀请斯里兰卡、巴基斯坦、哈萨克斯坦等共建"一带一路"国家的代表来华交流 **(jiaoliu)**，增进对中国国情和文化的认知和了解。Furthering **people-to-people exchanges.** China has invited representatives from Belt and Road countries such as Sri Lanka, Pakistan and Kazakhstan to engage in **people-to-people exchanges** in China, increasing their knowledge and understanding of China's national conditions and culture

Source Authors

On the other hand, the wordings are different in the official documents of the Forum on China–Africa Cooperation (FOCAC). Established in 2000, the FOCAC has held seven triennial ministerial conferences, and has issued a declaration and an action plan in each of those conferences. Although people-to-people exchanges are one of eight major FOCAC initiatives launched by President Xi Jinping at its Beijing Summit in 2018 (Yang, 2020, p. 33), the term P2PE has not been the first time to make an appearance in FOCAC-related official documents. According to the seven ministerial conferences' declarations and action plans, which are bilingual and are available on its official website, all documents can be seen to clearly use "cultural and people-to-people exchanges" to refer to *renwen jiaoliu*. In other words, *renwen jiaoliu* includes two dimensions—people and culture. Such inclusion is in line with the literal meaning of *renwen jiaoliu* in Chinese. "People-to-people exchanges," on the other hand, only encompass *minjian jiaoliu* or *minjian jiaowang* in the Chinese language, which should only highlight the notion of being led by people.

In fact, in the literal sense, the concept of P2PE in Chinese is a process of exchanges where definitions, connotations, and interpretations are dynamic. Zhuang (2020, p. 19) believes that P2PE refers to "extensive and daily cross-nation, non-governmental exchanges of the people, by the people, and for the people." As far as the authors are concerned, however, P2PE cannot be equated with *renwen jiaoliu*, first of all, as the latter should include both a people-to-people and a cultural dimension (but this does not mean that P2PE has no cultural aspect; all it means is that P2PE has a narrower scope, is a more concentrated expression, and has more emphasis on the role of "people"). On the other hand, P2PE is not a form of diplomacy and is different from people-to-people diplomacy. D'Hooghe (2005, p. 102) clearly distinguishes "diplomacy" as a "highly centralized and state-controlled affair—a form of modernized propaganda." Diplomacy to varying degrees is official in nature and is under official control. P2PE, on the other hand, especially when centred around individuals (and on their personal purposeful relationships), is spontaneous, informal, creative, innovative, and it sometimes even precedes official policies.

4 How Do We Understand People-to-People Exchanges?

Our understanding of P2PE is that it is a methodological instrument of constructivism that aims to establish, engage, and develop a stable and purposeful web of mutual interests, often driven by state interests. P2PE is further understood to be a set of narratives framed by state policies, designed to advance platforms for spontaneous dialogue to supplement bilateral intergovernmental relationships (IGR) between sovereigns and foster lasting bonds between different international actors. P2PE also uses thematic instruments of personal and collective dialogue to establish, promote, and reinforce multi-sectorial cooperation within a state (vertical perspective), as well as between state and non-state institutions, commercial agents and corporations, and individuals. Figure 1 shows a model that combines all of these functions of P2PE and illustrates how they relate to interculturalism in the context of constructivism. P2PEs are supposed to be developed under different frameworks, based on complementary narratives, triggering spontaneous human-binding activities that aim to strengthen human social capital through the following notions: (1) encouraging the establishment of human interaction at different levels; (2) fostering new and reciprocal relationships to promote wider dialogue mechanisms with diverse instruments; and (3) promoting mutual benefits that are reflected in deeds (Leandro, 2019a, p. 40). P2PE is based on a web of spontaneous human-binding networks, acting in different frameworks, to facilitate more than what Cantle describes as "banal interactions"[5] and promote "opportunity interactions." Therefore, P2PE broadens one's external environment, and takes place among people who share potential benefits. Networks, self-help groups, campaigns, and committees can bring people from different backgrounds together and open up new opportunities (Cantle, 2012, pp. 148–149). Furthermore, P2PE should also be able to generate *grounding interactions*, which are about consolidating one's identity and values, therefore taking place among those who share a history, helping to build individual self-confidence, sense of pride, and "growth interactions," broadening one's identity and values; this aspect takes place between people with similar curiosity. It is through growth interactions that people change the way they see themselves and others, and discover new things in common (Cantle, 2012, pp. 148–149). Thus, we believe that P2PE can be reflected in the communication between different agents, within a purposeful interplay of influences.

As shown in Fig. 1, in order for P2PE to be effective, intercultural literacy is requisite. Development of intercultural dialogue and interaction facilitates the coexistence of people from diverse backgrounds who can agree to share values and reach consensus despite their cultural differences (Barrett, 2013, p. 26). In the context of interculturalism, P2PE is a dynamic two-way process that can happen at the state-to-state, corporation-to-corporation, individual-to-individual levels. Interculturalism does not require the existence of a dominant ruling majority to establish the rules of the game. As an important dimension of interculturalism, P2PE encourages natural exchanges and connections between people in society, and accepts the result; such is what Bouchard refers to as "a capacity to reach a consensus on forms of peaceful coexistence that preserve the essential values of a society" (2013, p. 105). In this regard, interculturalism is transformative of a new consensual reality for the benefit of the whole. Interculturalism is an advanced state of multiculturalism, which stands as an initial step to construct a web of long-standing, stable, multilevel, and multi-issue relationships. As stated by Barrett, interculturalism "builds upon the foundations of multiculturalism" (2013, p. 26). Bilateralism and multilateralism, in the context of P2PE, function as an array of multidimensional frameworks capable of defusing conflicts, promoting tolerance, and above all forming a cohesive and transformative intercultural society. Without intercultural literacy, there will be no effective P2PE.

---

[5] Banal interactions are about consolidating one's external environment, and take place between people who share a community. Typically, banal interactions are fairly superficial—saying "Hello" and engaging in chit-chat. Banal interactions help to develop a sense of belonging and contribute to good community relations (Cantle, 2012, pp. 148–149).

| International Relations Theory – Constructivism |
| Core Concepts - Culture, Norms, Rules, Discourses, Identity, Change, Sociality, and Processes of Interaction |

| Interculturalism |
| Core Features - Cultural Diversity and Pluralism, Intercultural Dialogue, Interaction, Exchange, Integration, and Social Inclusion |

State-to-State Exchanges	Chinese Partnerships	Three Methods of Establishing Diplomatic Ties (Zhou Enlai, 1956)
Political Framework Flexible and Changeable	One Pillar: High-Level Dialogue on People-to-People Exchanges	(1) Full Diplomatic Ties — New Type – Cloud Diplomacy
Corporation-to-Corporation Exchanges	Economic and Trade Cooperation	(2) Semi-diplomatic Ties — Public Diplomacy
Tangible Results Intangible Effects	Entrepreneurship, Cooperate Social Responsibility, and Experience Sharing	(3) Non-diplomatic Ties but with Trade and Economic Links
Individual-to-Individual Exchanges	Human Social Capital and People-centered	Folk Diplomacy (Informal)
De-bordering Minds (Heart-to-Heart)	Internalization – Inclusiveness, Acceptance, and Appeal	People-centered Dilution of Diplomatic Intention

Fig. 1 Three-level model of the interplays in people-to-people exchanges (*Source* Adapted from Leandro, 2019a, p. 41)

At the state-to-state level, exchanges rely on the flexible political framework of Chinese partnerships, and states can reach preliminary consensus in areas where the two sides hope to strengthen cooperation in and for the future. It usually happens when the leaders of the two states meet. Under this changeable framework, considering the BRI's key areas of cooperation (HKTDC), P2PE represents a set of efforts to promote exchanges and dialogues between different cultures to form the basis for regional cooperation to develop and improve. From the Chinese perspective, the BRI is an initiative that requires P2PE to facilitate new, more advanced synergetic forms of mutually beneficial cooperation. Zhuang believes that at present, "building political trust, promoting trade and economic cooperation, and developing a people-to-people exchange have been the three major focuses of China's foreign policies" (2020, p. 10). There have been ten P2PE mechanisms between China and other countries around the world (Table 2). The earliest P2PE mechanism was established between China and Russia in 2000, and till 2020, it has already held 21 sessions (Xinhua, 2020). This dialogue is a vital part of the China–Russia comprehensive strategic partnership of coordination, which covers many fields, namely education, culture, health, sports, tourism, media, films, archives, and youth (IGCU, 2020). Along the same lines, the launch of a "people-to-people" dialogue covering education, culture, youth, research, and multilingualism between China and the European Union in 2012 can be seen as an important pillar in the relations between the two sides (European Commission, 2012). P2PE appears to be an important beacon of the PRC's foreign affairs policy and, therefore, a major rationale for any innovative form of inter-exchange and cooperation (Ministry of Foreign Affairs, 2016). However, it seems

Table 2 People-to-people exchanges involving China

2000	China–Russia People-to-People Exchange Mechanism
2010	China–US High-Level Consultation Mechanism on People-to-People Exchange
2012	China–UK High-Level People-to-People Exchange Mechanism
2012	China–EU High-Level People-to-People Exchange and Dialogue (HPPD)
2014	China–France High-level People-to-People Exchange Mechanism
2015	China–Indonesia Vice-Premier People-to-people Exchange Mechanism
2017	China–South Africa High-Level People-to-People Exchange Mechanism (PPEM)
2017	China–Germany High-Level People-to-People Exchange and Dialogue Mechanism
2018	China–India High-Level People-to-People Exchange Mechanism
2019	China–Japan High-Level People-to-People Exchange Mechanism

Source Retrieved on 15 September 2021, from http://en.igcu.pku.edu.cn/RESEARCH/P2P_Exchange_Mechanisms/China__Russia.htm

that the active process of establishing P2PE dialogue began in 2010, starting with the China–US High-level Consultation Mechanism on People-to-people Exchange. We still see this kind of dialogue as an official framework which provides the two sides with the opportunities and possibility of cooperation. Recently, due to the COVID-19 pandemic (2020–2021), a creative means of "cloud diplomacy" (Ministry of Foreign Affairs, 2021) has supplied a new platform for leaders around the world to deepen bilateral and multilateral exchanges.

At the corporation-to-corporation (C2C) level, because of the different participants, such exchanges (C2C exchanges) may be public diplomacy (when one or both companies have official status, i.e., state-owned enterprises or intergovernmental organizations), or folk diplomacy (when the companies are private). Economic and trade cooperation is an important aspect of C2C exchanges, especially in terms of intangible effects. Here, we likewise understand P2PE as an instrument of soft power. Soares (2019) asserts that people-to-people diplomacy has become a tool of China's soft power to foster relationships with and influence other countries. The Chinese government considers its overseas community as an important asset in promoting and strengthening China's presence and relationship with countries which it engages with. On the one hand, China regards culture as a soft power instrument, and culture has become an important pillar within China's strategy to secure influence internationally, as laid out in the Communique of the Fifth Plenum of the 17th Central Committee of the CPC (MOFCOM, 2010). Moreover, as stated in the 13th Five-year Plan (2016–2020) for National Economic and Social Development, P2PE is one of the dimensions of the bilateral and multilateral cooperation mechanisms of the BRI, and "overseas Chinese, returned overseas Chinese, and the relatives of overseas Chinese who live in China [can foster] bridges of communication and bonds of friendship." Additionally, the Proposal of the Central Committee of the Chinese Communist Party on Drawing Up the 14th Five-Year Plan for National Economic and Social Development and Long-Range Objectives for 2030 also emphasized "developing thriving cultural undertakings and cultural industries, and increasing the nation's cultural soft power." On the other hand, corporate social responsibility (CSR) can also be regarded as a part of the state's soft power, especially when companies go global. Going global, Chinese enterprises should prioritize not only investment interests but also a good reputation by observing the laws of the host countries and taking up more social responsibility (Li et al., 2018, pp. 3–4). This way, overseas enterprises not only create economic value and material wealth for their country (tangible results) but also directly influence the image of the country through their conduct (intangible effects). Therefore, "public diplomacy is an advanced form of CSR, making enterprise a significant power to perform public diplomacy" (Li et al., 2018, p. 4).

"Constructivism begins with deeds," and deeds are "done" (i.e., carried out as opposed to "spoken") (Onuf, 1989, p. 36). At the individual-to-individual level, our understanding of P2PE is in line with Putnam's notion (2000, p. 21) that it is a mechanism to promote social capital (bonding), as it is good for undergirding specific reciprocity and mobilizing solidarity. Likewise, P2PE is, if not an instrument of multiculturalism, at least a sort of vehicle for multicultural coexistence that advances a framework of human connectivity. P2PE is beneficial for what Putnam refers to as bridging (i.e., building relationships between heterogeneous people) and bonding (i.e., reinforcing relationships for mutual and reciprocal benefit) in the context of human social capital. Bonding social capital is, according to Briggs (1998), good for "getting by," while bridging social capital is crucial for "getting ahead." Nurturing people-to-people exchanges encompasses both ideas: establishing new human interactions and using them for mutual benefits, especially in terms of promoting social capital cooperation, policy coordination, unimpeded trade, and financial integration. All of these depend on deeds. The facts that are reflected in the deeds can then facilitate the formation of de-bordering minds, which is a process of internalization coupled with expanding inclusiveness, acceptance, and appeal.

Ultimately, the three levels are dynamic and promote one another. The authors further believe that behind political and economic diplomatic intentions, the real engine of P2PE is personal motivation, spontaneity, and mutual empathy, binding humans together by purpose. As the old Chinese saying goes, "People-to-people friendship is the cornerstone of sound state-to-state relations, and heart-to-heart communication holds the key to deeper friendship" (国之交在于民相亲, 民相亲在于心相通).

Finally, according to Leandro (2019b), P2PE reinforces high-level bilateral people-to-people bonding, driving formal relations, boosting the operation of informal mechanisms of proximity, thereby giving a closer sense of hardheaded interplay among new networks of private economic agents. P2PE should be designed for mutual advancement, based on three equally harmonizing people-to-people dimensions: (1) frames of exchange; (2) instruments of exchange; and (3) characteristics of exchange.

– Frames of exchange—Frames are the spheres where soft power—encompassing such aspects as foreign politics, domestic politics, culture, history, education, science, business, creative industries, MICE (meetings, incentives, conferences,

and exhibitions), technologies, tourism, sports, and activities that relate to environmental sustainability—is created. Among these frames are the professional and entrepreneurial sector, the education-academic and knowledge skills transfer sector, the opposition of overlapping social identities and the emotional intelligence of key leadership, the horizontal and vertical dimensions of the governmental and non-governmental relations sector, and the clear vision of the purpose of exchange. Particular emphasis is placed on continuing investment in the academic people-to-people education sector, fostering another level of interplay that conforms with international standards.
- Instruments of exchange—The function of these is to generate purposeful networks for permanent dialogue and interplay, which can be divided into two types: agents and policies. Agents are people or organizations who create and implement soft power initiatives; agents include multinational enterprises, non-governmental organizations, the private sector, individuals, think tanks, universities, hybrid ad hoc networks, and civil society. Policies are specific instruments and vehicles through which soft power is activated. Policies include laws, guidelines and policies, agreements (e.g., domestic, regional, international, MoU, FDI, FTA), programmes (e.g., foreign exchanges, cultural diplomacy, nation branding, banking, national currency), events, conferences, exhibitions, concerts, symposia, radio, filming, television, sports, digital broadcasting, and publications.
- Characteristics of exchange—it is possible to identify the dominant features of these processes of human exchange. Therefore, we have noticed the following characteristics: (1) the main goal of P2PE is clearly defined to be an instrument of mutual advancement through pragmatic and nonpartisan cooperation for entrepreneurship, innovation, and growth; (2) it has been capable of presenting a protracted, consensual, inclusive, non-confrontational, and progressive P2PE, linking ad hoc groups, with bilateral, trilateral, and multilateral involvement; (3) it has been building P2PE while being event-driven and focused on the enhancement of human social capital; (4) it has undoubtedly promoted a transformational P2PE, based on non-politicized and secular collaboration, seeking tangible rewards and mutual gratification; (5) it has been implementing people-to-people practices, which have raised the level of interculturalism and inclusion, without attempting to be merely multicultural.

5 Conclusion

With P2PE becoming increasingly important in China and the concept being used in international contexts, the variability of development, cultural diversity, and unpredictability of results in this process fully embody the characteristics of constructivism. It is in this context that the authors reiterate the main research question of this chapter: How do we understand people-to-people exchanges? Based on the reasoning presented in this chapter, P2PE can be understood as a methodological instrument of human-relational and purposeful constructivism that requires intercultural literacy to make it stable and durable. P2PE is a clutter of framework narratives, wilfully designed and framed in a vision of state policy, as an instrument of soft power (to attract), and as a mechanism to promote human social capital and to induce synergetic cooperative approaches. P2PE is ultimately designed to advance a long-lasting transformative web of human-binding spontaneous networks, which rely on human empathy and are driven by national interests.

Although the use of P2PE in the Chinese context is changeable, it is acceptable in the social context to associate P2PE with relational pillars which are designed to advance positive and transformational international relations. Compared with political consultation and economic and trade cooperation, P2PE is by and large related to soft power and to the purpose of developing it. P2PE takes people to the centre of institutional, occasional, and folk relationships, relying on culture, rules, identity, and multiple layers of human interactions, expecting that the full array of human relations will bring about transformation and advancement. In this process, China has established several people-to-people exchange mechanisms to provide a framework of fields activity, namely in education, the academia and think tanks, culture, historical conservation, health, tourism, digital connectivity, media, sports, gender, and youth. This conceptual framework is supposed to facilitate the creation of opportunities for a purposeful exchange at different levels in various arenas.

China regards culture and P2PE as instruments of soft power. When combined, P2PE and culture become an important pillar within China's strategy to secure influence internationally, as laid out in the Communique of the Fifth Plenum of the 17th Central Committee of the CPC (2010). Likewise, the establishment of people-to-people bonds as an area of BRI cooperation stands as one of the major components of a more comprehensive policy, which includes efforts to promote exchanges and dialogues between different cultures to form a basis for advancing regional cooperation. The establishment of China-related people-to-people exchange mechanisms (Table 2) precisely reflects this attempt to use P2PE and culture to promote and secure complementary methods of asserting international influence.

In relation to corporation-to-corporation exchanges, on the one hand, companies and other non-governmental organizations have achieved tangible results in economic and trade cooperation and other related fields. On the other hand, sharing experience and assuming higher levels of corporate social responsibilities has had an intangible and subtle impact on P2PE. In the case of China, the social responsibilities of Chinese corporations operating abroad have been seen as a substantial part of the transformative economic diplomacy as well as an instrument to promote a positive image and to encourage stronger P2PE.

Focusing on individuals, it seems that P2PE can be difficult to conceptualize. However, the complementary narratives on P2P are purposeful and are evaluated by the accompanying deeds. The accumulation of voluntarily offered positive prepositive narratives and the framework of opportunities thus arise will have constructive effects on people-to-people relations, in corporation-to-corporation joint ventures, and in state-to-state exchanges for mutual interest. Cognizant of the importance of intercultural literacy as a strong P2PE multiplier, the authors believe that mutual respect, reciprocity, inclusiveness, and transformative-cooperative deeds will pave the way to a higher level of intercultural development. In this vein, P2PE must also be understood as clutters of framework narratives designed to advance intercultural exchange, which occurs between people of different origins and diverse cultural backgrounds. These clutters of framework narratives represent constructive opportunities that bring people closer and bring about higher levels of understanding and acceptance of their unavoidable interdependency.

Acknowledgements This academic research was supported by the Institute of European Studies of Macau (IEEM), China – AECSRP – IEEM Academic Research Grant 2020.

Bibliographic References

13th Five-year Plan (2016–2020) for National Economic and Social Development. (2016). Retrieved on 20 May 2021, from https://www.greengrowthknowledge.org/national-documents/13th-five-year-plan-economic-and-social-development-peoples-republic-china

Acharya, A., & Buzan, B. (2019). *The making of global international relations: Origins and evolution of IR at its centenary.* Cambridge University Press.

Barrett, M. (2013). *Interculturalism and multiculturalism: Similarities and differences.* Council of Europe Publishing.

Bouchard, G. (2013). Interculturalism: What makes it distinctive? In M. Barrett (Ed.), *Interculturalism and multiculturalism: Similarities and differences.* Council of Europe Publishing.

Briggs, X. D. (1998). Doing democracy up-close: Culture, power, and communication in community building. *Journal of Planning Education and Research, 18*, 1–13. https://doi.org/10.1177/0739456X9801800101. Retrieved in October 2021, from https://journals.sagepub.com/doi/10.1177/0739456X9801800101

Brunnée, J., & Toope, S. J. (2013). Constructivism and international law. In J. L. Dunoff & M. A. Pollack (Eds.), *Interdisciplinary perspectives on international law and international relations: The state of the art.* Cambridge University Press.

Cantle, T. (2012). *Interculturalism: The new era of cohesion and diversity.* Palgrave Macmillan.

Checkel, J. T. (2008). Constructivism and foreign policy. In S. Smith, A. Hadfield, & T. Dunne (Eds.), *Foreign policy: Theories, actors, cases.* Oxford University Press.

China to improve people-to-people exchanges with foreign countries (关于加强和改进中外人文交流工作的若干意见). (2017). Retrieved on 15 May 2021, from http://www.gov.cn/zhengce/2017-12/21/content_5249241.htm (in Chinese). Retrieved on 15 May 2021, from http://english.www.gov.cn/policies/latest_releases/2017/12/22/content_281475985345802.htm (in English).

Chu, L. (2018). *Little soldiers: An American boy, a Chinese school, and the global race to achieve.* HarperCollins.

Cull, N. (2013). The long road to public diplomacy 2.0: The internet in U.S. public diplomacy. *International Studies Review, 15*(1). Retrieved on 24 May 2021, from https://ash.harvard.edu/files/cull.pdf

D'Hooghe, I. (2005). Public diplomacy in the People's Republic of China. In J. Melissen (Ed.), *The new public diplomacy: Studies in diplomacy and international relations.* Palgrave Macmillan.

Edney, K., Rosen, S., & Zhu, Y. (2020). *Soft power with Chinese characteristics: China's campaign for hearts and minds.* Routledge.

Ellis, R. V. (2020). The evolution of Chinese soft power in the Americas. In K. Edney, S. Rosen, & Y. Zhu (Eds.), *Soft power with Chinese characteristics: China's campaign for hearts and minds.* Routledge.

European Commission. (2012). *Education & culture: EU and China launch people-to-people dialogue*. Retrieved on 15 September 2021, from https://ec.europa.eu/commission/presscorner/detail/en/IP_12_381

Fierke, K. M. (2010). Constructivism. In T. Dunne, M. Kurki, & S. Smith (Eds.), *International relations theories: Discipline and diversity* (2nd ed.). Oxford University Press.

Fuchs, M. (2017). India in comparison. In T. C. Ertman (Ed.), *Max Weber's economic ethic of the world religions: An analysis*. Cambridge University Press.

Hartig, F. (2016). How China understands public diplomacy: The importance of national image for national interests. *International Studies Review, 18*, 655–680.

HKTDC. *The Belt and Road Initiative*. Retrieved on 20 May 2021, from https://research.hktdc.com/en/article/MzYzMDAyOTg5

IGCU. (2020). *Brief introduction to the China-Russia people-to-people exchange mechanism*. Retrieved on 15 September 2021, from http://en.igcu.pku.edu.cn/info/1634/1947.htm

Leandro, F. (2019a). Macau: A platform for dialogue and cooperation bridging three continents. In S. Pajović, M. Andrijević, & S. C. Prado (Eds.), *Macao (China), Europa Sudoriental, América Latina: Una mirada hacia la viabilidad de la cooperación triangular*. Universidad Megatrend y FIEALC.

Leandro, F. (2019b, December 26). People-to-people exchange helps Sino-Lusophone cultural de-bordering. *Chinese Social Sciences Today*.

Liu, Y. (2015). People-to-people exchanges in Chinese diplomacy: Evolutions, strategies, and social practice. *Stosunki Międzynarodowe—International Relations, 51*(4), 237–253.

Li, X., Lian, M., Zhong, H., & Meng, J. (2018). *Social responsibility report of Chinese enterprises in Africa*. China Social Sciences Press.

Ministry of Foreign Affairs. (2016). *China's policy paper on Latin America and the Caribbean*. Retrieved on 15 May 2021, from https://www.fmprc.gov.cn/mfa_eng/wjdt_665385/2649_665393/t1418254.shtml

Ministry of Foreign Affairs. (2021). *State Councilor and Foreign Minister Wang Yi meets the press*. Retrieved on 20 May 2021, from https://www.fmprc.gov.cn/mfa_eng/zxxx_662805/t1859138.shtml

Ministry of Foreign Affairs. (n.d.) *Zhou Enlai*. Retrieved on 24 May 2021, from https://www.fmprc.gov.cn/mfa_eng/ziliao_665539/wjrw_665549/3606_665551/t44145.shtml

MOFCOM. (2010). *Communique of the Fifth Plenum of the 17th Central Committee of the Communist Party of China*. Retrieved on 20 May 2021, from http://english.mofcom.gov.cn/aarticle/translatorsgarden/famousspeech/201011/20101107250865.html

Nye, J. (2020). Foreword. In K. Edney, S. Rosen, & Y. Zhu (Eds.), *Soft power with Chinese characteristics: China's campaign for hearts and minds*. Routledge.

Onuf, N. (1989). *World of our making: Rules and rule in social theory and international relations*. Routledge.

Payne, J. G. (2009). Reflections on public diplomacy: People-to-people communication. *American Behavioral Scientist, 53*(4), 579–606.

Putnam, R. D. (2000). *Bowling alone—The collapse and revival of American community*. Simon & Schuster.

Qin, Y. (2018). A multiverse of knowledge: Cultures and IR theories. *The Chinese Journal of International Politics, 11*(4), 415–434.

Report of 18th National Congress of the Communist Party of China. (中国共产党第十八次全国代表大会报告). (2012). Retrieved on 15 May 2021, from http://www.gov.cn/ldhd/2012-11/17/content_2268826_7.htm (in Chinese). Retrieved on 15 May 2021, from http://www.china.org.cn/china/18th_cpc_congress/2012-11/15/content_27137540_11.htm (in English).

Report of 19th National Congress of the Communist Party of China (中国共产党第十九次全国代表大会报告). (2017). Retrieved on 15 May 2021, from http://www.chinadaily.com.cn/interface/flipboard/1142846/2017-11-06/cd_34188086.html

Seligman, S. (1999). *Chinese business etiquette: A guide to protocol, manners and culture in the PRC*. Grand Central Publishing.

Snow, N. (2009). Rethinking public diplomacy. In N. Snow & P. M. Taylor (Eds.), *Routledge handbook of public diplomacy*. Routledge.
Soares, L. B. (2019). Overseas Chinese, soft power and China's people-to-people diplomacy in Timor-Leste. In A. McWilliam & M. Leach (Eds.), *Routledge handbook of contemporary Timor-Leste*. Routledge.
Terpeau, A. B. (1960). People to people diplomacy. *World Affairs, 123*(4), 104–107. Retrieved on 24 May 2021, from http://www.jstor.org/stable/20669918
Wang, S. (2016). China's people-to-people diplomacy and its importance to China-EU relations: A historical institutionalism perspective. *Journal of China and International Relations, 4*(1), 1–19.
Wang, Y. (2008). Public diplomacy and the rise of Chinese soft power. *The ANNALS of the American Academy of Political and Social Science, 616*(1), 257–273.
Westwood, R., & Leung, A. (1999). Women in management in Hong Kong and Beijing: Between pragmatism and patriarchy. In P. Fosh, A. Chan, W. Chow, E. Snape, & R. Westwood (Eds.), *Hong Kong management and labour*. Routledge.
White Book: China's international development cooperation in the new era (新时代的中国国际发展合作白皮书). (2021). Retrieved on 15 May 2021, from http://www.scio.gov.cn/zfbps/32832/Document/1696685/1696685.htm (in Chinese). Retrieved on 15 May 2021, from http://www.scio.gov.cn/zfbps/32832/Document/1696686/1696686.htm (in English).
Xi Jinping makes important remarks at a conference on the diplomatic work with neighbouring countries (习近平在周边外交工作座谈会上发表重要讲话). (2013). Retrieved on 15 May 2021, from http://cpc.people.com.cn/n/2013/1026/c64094-23333683.html (in Chinese). Retrieved on 15 May 2021, from https://www.fmprc.gov.cn/mfa_eng/wjb_663304/wjbz_663308/activities_663312/t1093870.shtml (in English).
Xinhua. (2020). *21st session of China-Russia Committee on Humanities Cooperation held via video link*. Retrieved on 15 May 2021, from http://www.xinhuanet.com/english/2020-11/26/c_139543306.htm
Yang, B. (2020). China-Africa people-to-people exchanges in the perspective of the Belt and Road Initiative ("一带一路"倡议下的中非人文交流). *West Asia and Africa, 2*, 33–40.
Yang, J. (2011). *Nuli Kaituo Zhongguotese Gonggongwaijiao Xinjumian* (努力开拓中国特色公共外交新局面). Retrieved on 24 May 2021, from http://www.gov.cn/gzdt/2011-02/16/content_1804457.htm
Yao, Y. (2019). *Xinshidai Zhongguo Gonggongwaijiao yu Minjianwaijiao: Lilun yu Shijian* (新时代中国公共外交与民间外交:理论与实践). World Affairs Press.
Yu, H. (2018). Theoretical discussion of subjects of people-to-people diplomacy (民间外交主体的理论探讨). *International Review, 5*.
Yu, X. (2017). China's People-to-people diplomacy in the new area (论新时代中国民间外交). *International Studies, 6*.
Zehfuss, M. (2001). Constructivisms in international relations: Wendt, Onuf, and Kratochwil. In K. M. Fierke & K. E. Jørgensen (Eds.), *Constructing international relations: The next generation*. Routledge.
Zehfuss, M. (2004). *Constructivism in international relations: The politics of reality*. Cambridge University Press.
Zhang, J., & Ding, Y. (2019). People's diplomacy at seventy: China's public diplomacy, sub-national diplomacy, and cultural diplomacy (中国民间外交、地方外交与人文交流70年). *Global Review, 5*.
Zhang, S. (2008). Study on China's civil diplomacy in the new century: Question, theory and significance (新世纪中国民间外交研究:问题、理论和意义). *International Review, 5*.
Zhuang, L. (2020). The gap between China's people-to-people exchange policy and its aim to promote understanding among peoples in the world. In L. T. Lee (Ed.), *Chinese people's diplomacy and developmental relations with East Asia: Trends in the Xi Jinping era*. Routledge.

Chapter 7
The Belt and Road Initiative in Global Governance: Impact on the International World Order

Carmen Amado Mendes and Xuheng Wang

1 Introduction

Whether the "Belt and Road" Initiative (BRI) has noticeably affected and can be expected, in the short term, to affect the international order has generated considerable debate. There exists a considerable literature discussing the nature of the BRI's political intent (for example, Callahan, 2016b; Carrai et al., 2020; Wang, 2016; Zhou & Esteban, 2018), and important insights have been published by Hameiri and Jones (2018), Jones (2020), and Byrnes (2020). When viewing China's path to become an emerging global power, current opinion, particularly in the west, holds that the BRI represents an immediate threat, not least because of its claimed potential to challenge the current international order, reciprocity, and the opening of international markets (Chance & Mafinezam, 2016; Ciborowski et al., 2021; Kavaliauskas, 2020).

A widely held view is that the BRI is intended to externalize China's excess capital and export its infrastructure development capacity. China's structure for internal governance appears to be systematically oriented towards supporting this objective, and the highly decentralized operating mode used, that often noticeably ignores existing governance regulations surrounding development financing, environmental and social protection, and corporate governance. This is predicted inevitably to affect existing global governance systems. Nevertheless, thus far no consensus on the impact of BRI on the international order has been reached. Where previous research often fails to scrutinize official statements and take into account the impact of the setbacks that the BRI has encountered, taking a constructivist stance, influenced by Olson and Prestowitz (2011), Rolf and Agnew (2016), and Ly (2020), this article argues that the BRI from its outset was less rigorously designed than is often predicated, and fundamentally remains a policy-in-progress.

C. A. Mendes (✉) · X. Wang
School of Economics, University of Coimbra, Coimbra, Portugal

Focusing on official statements and statistics between 2015 and 2019, and more recent articles, the body of this chapter is divided into an analysis of global governance, and a close examination of stated aims and problems experienced in BRI implementation. The research results support a conclusion that any challenge inherent in the BRI is not the result of a strategic plan to overthrow the liberal international order, but rather a consequence of vague interpretations of BRI rules, poorly managed projects, and the unexpectedly complicated requirements in initiating and sustaining viable economic cooperation.

2 Global Governance

With the proliferation of multilateral agreements, summits, and global and regional institutions, globalization has become an inevitable trend. International institutions have played an interventionist and moderating role in all aspects of global affairs, and global governance has evolved into a multifaceted network. Although this system of intergovernmental cooperation is still very limited compared to the scale of global problems, it cannot be denied that international institutions have become the main venues for political activity resulting from the nature of globalization and the world order (McGrew & Held, 2002).

The debate on global governance has predominantly focused on how political coordination between public (i.e., state and governmental organizations) and private institutions which seek to recognize common goals and solve common problems, has changed. There is no doubt that the system of global governance has transcended the classical form of multilateralism, but it cannot be called a "unified global system" supported by global laws (Cable, 1999). The system is governed by a variety of rule-making institutions, political organizations and political rights, rather than by any pre-conceived centralized global public institution that would serve to legislate for the common affairs of humanity.

Three predominant explanations of global governance have been advanced in previous studies. Under the liberal system, the state obtains realistic benefits through coordinating policy and action in an overtly interdependent world. International institutions act as relatively independent mechanisms to reconcile the contradictions between the hierarchical structure of state power and global public policy, cushioning the impact of power politics (Keohane, 2015). In the realist view, such supranational governance remains, in general, determined uniquely by the policies and interests of the most powerful states. International institutions are understood to lack independent powers and are largely used as tools to advance the interests of the most influential states and their coalitions (Krasner, 1982). Constructivists, on the other hand, bridging the liberal–realist divide, focus on the identities and norms that shape the two key elements of the international order (Klotz & Lynch, 2007). The mutually reinforcing interaction between actors, states, and institutions contributes to the creation and promotion of political identity.

The engagement of international institutions in global governance has brought about an increasing development of norms and institutions. From security issues to economic activities, individual sovereign states are absorbed into networks within different systems, to the extent that global governance involves multiple public and private players, each with their own mandated priorities and operational norms (Boughton & Bradford, 2007). For example, the International Monetary Fund (IMF) oversees the activities of the international monetary framework, the World Health Organization (WHO) monitors health issues, and *The Paris Agreement* attempts to frame unified measures for global action on climate change in the post-2020 years. This situation has resulted in, and created, a fragmentation and specificity in global governance (Ikenberry & Lim, 2017).

While acknowledging the role of state and non-state actors in affecting the current system of global governance, this theory focuses primarily on the state and governmental side of affairs. In the current global system, the traditional global governance structures established by the US and its allies lie behind the redistribution of global influence. China, which has emerged as the world's second-largest economy, supplanting Japan in that role, has been more active than its predecessor in creating multilateral institutions and adumbrating new "rules of the road." Simultaneously, and in contrast, the US has become less active, for example pulling out of *The Paris Agreement* during the Donald Trump regime, which has had an as yet undefinable impact on its power in global governance (Ly, 2021).

Much of China's institutional strength comes from its recently created economic strength and position in the global economy, rather than any pre-existing global military presence. Indeed, Beijing's growing influence and participation in international institutions largely reflects its position as an undeniably growing economic power (Olson & Prestowitz, 2011). As Glaser and Funaiole (2015) stressed, unlike other major powers, China's power comes from a confluence of economic, social, military, and geopolitical factors, and the power it possesses is inextricably linked to its economic expansion, which in turn was linked to inflows of FDI. According to a speech on global governance made by President Xi Jinping at a meeting in 2016 of the Politburo of the Communist Party of China, "The global governance structure depends on the international balance of power, and reform depends on changes in the balance of power" (Xinhua, 2016). While it is debatable whether China will challenge US dominance and create a China-centric order as its political goal for active participation in global governance, we need to be aware that, the current world order is bound to change in the context of globalization and economic interdependence among nations (Ly, 2020).

The US is predominantly viewed as the foundation of the liberal order, premised on human rights, democracy and free trade, and as such will move the world towards deeper integration, interdependence and cross-border cooperation. Whether or not the new emerging powers are seen as capable of changing the USA-led order, they are largely understood to be a throwback to pre-globalization times (Cooper & Flemes, 2013). China has been classified as a country that may be described as a "relatively obvious Westphalian sovereignty," with the consequence that its "regime is expected to be more expansionist than that of the United States," while the US has adopted a "globalist" system of sovereignty, without territorial restrictions (Rolf & Agnew, 2016).

Given this ideological climate, the BRI has largely been assimilated into the existing liberal world order of rising powers and their alleged tendency towards threatening behaviour. It is China's "grand strategy" to seek "to rebuild the Eurasian order with new ideas, norms and rules of governance" (Callahan, 2016b), making China "a normative power that sets the rules of the global governance game" (Callahan, 2016a; Zhou & Esteban, 2018). Nevertheless, in the face of this dire prediction, there are those who maintain that China is offering, or at least may be offering, some normative alternative to a solely Western-dominated global system. The Chinese government's own BRI blueprint expresses a desire for a "new model of international cooperation and global governance" (NDRC, MFA, & MOFCOM, 2015), even if the nature of any alternative model is not explicitly stated. This supports the view expressed by many scholars that the existing literature on the normative content of the BRI is extremely vague, superficial and ambiguous, and in fact reflects, in fact, the ambiguity inherent in the BRI initiative itself (Zeng, 2016a, 2016b).

3 The Belt and Road Initiative as an Imprecisely Defined Catalyst

The BRI has come to be regarded as a catalyst for China's strategic development and the global economy. The initiative was incorporated into the 13th five-year plan (2016) and the 14th five-year plan (2021–2025), and was included in the 19th session of the National Congress of the CCP in 2017 (Ohashi, 2018), becoming one of the three key policy strategies before 2020 (Huang, 2016). The BRI is claimed to have involved more than one hundred and fifty countries and organizations, accounting for about seventy per cent of the global population and fifty per cent of the global GDP (Jizhong et al., 2020). It facilitates cross-border transactions between China and participating countries, and is held to benefit them in terms of national infrastructure development, economic growth, and the well-being of their people (Tao & Zhong, 2018).

Although the BRI focuses primarily on trade, infrastructure and financial assistance, its impact extends beyond any purely trade agenda. As mentioned earlier, the BRI is widely described as a "Grand strategy" based on traditional geopolitics. Fallon (2015, p. 140) describes it as "a grand strategy for Eurasia […] no less than rewriting the current geopolitical landscape," and Arase (2019) argues that, through the BRI, China is "reshaping … the regional order of Asia to ensure its continued economic rise and eventual political leadership." The reconstruction of the ancient Silk Road through the BRI is seen as a means to reaffirm its geopolitical interests in Eurasian space, revive the so-called "Glorious moment" of Chinese civilization, and restore its great power status. In contrast, Chinese authorities play down the geostrategic significance of the BRI (ECFR, 2015), and prefer to stress that the BRI is consistent with existing principles of global governance, such as the Charter of the United Nations (Swaine, 2015). Foreign Minister Yang Jiechi notably insisted that the BRI was "by no means a tool for any country to see geopolitical advantages" (Yang Jiechi, 2015).

Based on current academic discussion, this paper will analyse the BRI from two aspects. Using official documents, an analysis is made of what we know of the intentions that lead to the BRI and the development direction for the BRI proposed by the Chinese government. At the same time, through its current achievements in economic cooperation, infrastructure, and financial assistance, the extent to which the BRI may be said to have exerted a tangible impact on the existing international order. Three key policy documents setting out China's BRI have been selected for analysis, namely:

1. *Vision and Actions on Jointly Building Silk Road Economic Belt and 21st-Century Maritime Silk Road* (here after V&A 2015), issued by the National Development and Reform Commission and Ministries of Foreign Affairs and Commerce in 2015 (NDRC, MFA, & MOFCOM, 2015);
2. *Building the Belt and Road: Concept, Practice and China's Contribution* (here after BBR 2017), issued by the Office of the Leading Group for the BRI in 2017 (BRP, 2017);
3. *The Belt and Road Initiative Progress* (here after BRIP 2019), *Contributions and Prospects*, issued by the Office of the Leading Group for the BRI in 2019 (OLGPBRI, 2019).

V&A 2015 was the first and the main document that comprehensively expounded an official Chinese vision of the BRI, and established guidelines for its implementation. BBR 2017 was launched at the first BRI Forum in an attempt to shape the international community's understanding of BRI goals and achievements. The BRIP 2019 is the latest official report from the Chinese government detailing the achievements and future development of the BRI and, as could be expected, concentrates on its successes.

China has claimed that BRI is a means towards "Maintaining a global free trade system and an open world economy" (V&A, 2015), and furthermore "Facilitates trade, investment liberalization and facilitation, and reduces transaction and business costs" (BBR, 2019). "It is also said to comply with existing market rules and international norms, to give full play to the market in the allocation of resources, and to the primacy of enterprise" (V&A, 2015, II). The documents even promise that China will "apply the laws of the market" (BBR, 2017, p. 57) when dealing with developed countries. The BRI has five well-defined goals for deepening economic integration, namely promoting "policy coordination, facilities connectivity, unrestricted trade, financial integration, and people-to-people" (V&A, 2015, IV, 5), and these five goals have come to be considered as important criteria for scholars to assess the performance of China in terms of norms compliance.

Regarding policy coordination, co-construction of the BRI and its core concepts have been written into the records of the UN, G20, Asia–Pacific Economic Cooperation (APEC), and other regional organizations. However, policy coordination itself has been rather vaguely described in BBR 2017, which principally focuses on intergovernmental negotiations to enhance cooperation in the other four areas, but not specifically on policy coordination. By the end of March 2019, the Chinese government had signed one hundred and seventy-three cooperation documents with one hundred and twenty-five countries and twenty-nine international organizations. The number of BRI co-construction member countries has extended from Asia and Europe to include nations in Africa, Latin America, the South Pacific, and other regions. The document refers to the idea of building a multilevel cooperation mechanism (BBR, 2017), which will include senior leaders to civil society organizations, and the 2019 report does not provide any more detailed description, with the result that officially announced focus of the BRI remains limited to the other four goals.

Facilities connectivity refers to the connectivity of national markets by cross-border rail, road and port, and can be considered a necessary infrastructure guarantee for urgent cooperation. This is an essential element for the formation of an economic zone and the development of regional infrastructure and networks. After several years of development, the six international economic cooperation corridors construction project (e.g., New Eurasian Land Bridge; China–Mongolia–Russia; China–Central Asia–West Asia; China–Indochina Peninsula; China–Pakistan; and Bangladesh–China–India–Myanmar) have all made progress, although at different degrees and different speeds. Railways, highways, ports, airports, pipelines, and power plants have been first considered as the key projects (Renminwang, 2017).

By the end of 2018, the China–EU train network had reached one hundred and eight cities in sixteen countries of the Eurasian continent, although it must also be noted that it has been reported that as many as 50% of goods trains returning to China did so without freight. Coordination and cooperation on Customs clearance with countries along the BRI have been expedited, and the facilitation of customs clearance has been enhanced. The average inspection rate and clearance time have decreased by 50%. In the area of road cooperation, China has signed eighteen bilateral and multilateral international transport facilitation agreements with fifteen countries along the routes, including the agreement between the governments of the Shanghai Cooperation Organization (SCO) member states on facilitation of international road transport. In port cooperation, China has signed thirty-eight bilateral and regional maritime transport agreements with forty-seven countries along BRI routes, and in air transport, China has added one thousand two hundred and thirty-nine international routes, accounting for 69.1% of the total number of newly opened international routes (OLGPBRI, 2019).

Other infrastructure developments, such as energy facilities and communication facilities, the China–Russia crude oil pipeline and the China–Central Asia gas pipeline remain in stable operation, and the eastern route of the China–Russia gas pipeline was partially ventilated in December 2019, and will achieve full ventilation by 2024. China has also signed a range of cooperation agreements with Kyrgyzstan, Tajikistan, and Afghanistan in the field of fibre-optic cables, which cumulatively represent the practical launch of the Silk Road Fibre Optic Cable project (OLGPBRI, 2019).

While Beijing's "plan" and "blueprint" are often mentioned in discussion and debate, detailed plans, with similar statistical detail, have never been clearly spelled out in official Chinese documents, leaving China's policy documents being "too broad and vague to form a operability road map" (He, 2018, p. 30). Infrastructure is still being built on the basis of specific project agreements, signed one-on-one in partnership with individual countries.

Discussion of "unrestricted trade, financial integration" has focused on cross-border trade, investment rules and liberalization of market transactions, and China has proposed maintaining a "consistency" between "integrated procedures for customs clearance, inspection and quarantine" and "standards, metrology, certification and accreditation" (BBR, 2017, pp. 25–26). Indeed, "Lower Non-tariff barriers to trade" and "Increase services, open services" (V&A, 2015, IV) have been key issues in international trade negotiations over the past two decades. Hameiri and Jones (2018) see this as the Chinese government's continued use of neoliberalist language, for example "efficiency" (BBR, 2017, p. 55), "comparative advantage" (V&A, 2015, VI), "division of labour" (V&A, 2015, IV), "value chain creation" (BBR, 2017, p. 30), as a means to articulate the goal of "Creating a high standard international business environment that attracts investors from around the world" (BBR, 2017, p. 29).

China has also engaged in further liberalization of access to foreign investment. China's average tariff level has fallen from 15.3% when it first joined the World Trade Organization (WTO) to 7.5%, and has actively worked to reduce customs clearance processes and the time needed for them. For example, according to BRIP 2019, by the end of 2018, the customs clearance time for agricultural products from China to Kazakhstan, Kyrgyzstan, and Tajikistan has been shortened by a remarkable 90%. China's total merchandise trade with the countries along the BRI exceeded US $6 trillion in 2018, with an average annual growth rate higher than that of China's foreign trade during the same period, accounting for 27.4% of China's total merchandise trade. In the same year, China's goods trade with the countries along the BRI totalled US $1.3 trillion, an increase of 16.4% year-on-year. The World Bank has analysed the trade impact brought about by the co-construction of the BRI on seventy-one potential participants, and found that the BRI would increase trade between participants by 4.1% (Baniya et al., 2020).

Another important step in the BRI is the establishment of international development financial institutions. In addition to a new development bank (formerly known as the BRICS and China Development Bank), China has established development financial institutions such as the Asian Infrastructure Investment Bank (AIIB), and the Silk Road Fund. Among these new institutions, the founding of the AIIB in January 2016, as the first international development financial institution led by China, drew significant attention. At the end of December 2017, China accounted for 29.4% of its total paid-in capital (Asian Infrastructure Investment Bank, 2017). However, some scholars have argued that the AIIB has been marginalized in BRI financing, since it has lent only $3.46 billion in 2017, of which only $1.03 billion (29.7%) was significantly related to BRI, focusing on a woefully small number of five projects, with the bank's stake being just 12%. Other Chinese participants are more involved, and in addition to the AIIB, the Export–Import Bank of China (ExIm) and the China Development Bank (CDB) are also responsible for development. In 2016, CDB and ExIm reported $101.8 billion in BRI-related loans Similarly, the China Commercial Bank provided a US $100 billion loan (Agence France-Presse, 2017) to the BRI project in 2016–2018, while CITIC Bank provided a US $102 billion loan (Li, 2017) to the BRI project in 2015. The fact that China is strengthening and strengthening its development assistance through financial functions could be interpreted as one of its challenges to the existing multilateral economic system (Hameiri & Jones, 2018).

In July 2018, the China–EU Co-Investment Fund, jointly invested by the Silk Road Fund and the European Investment Fund, began its substantive operation with an investment of five hundred million euros, which strongly facilitated the possibility for BRI joint construction to be aligned with the European Investment Plan (SRF, 2018). Multilateral financial cooperation has increased, and the People's Bank of China has carried out joint financing with the International Finance Corporation, the Pan American Development Corporation, the African Development Bank, the European Bank for Reconstruction and Development, and other multilateral development institutions under the World Bank Group, with by the end of 2018, more than one hundred projects having been supported, covering more than seventy countries and regions (OLGPBRI, 2019). Since all these funds are independent of China, it would of interest to know how big the share of Chinese investment in these ventures actually is, compared to the non-Chinese funds. If it could be shown that Chinese investment is significantly greater than non-Chinese investment this could prove that China is actually beginning to change one aspect of global financial governance. However, this information is not publicly available, and conclusions cannot be drawn.

In November 2017, the China–Central and Eastern European Interbank Association (CEE) was established, with members from fourteen countries including China, Hungary, the Czech Republic, Slovakia, and Croatia. In July and September 2018, the Banking Union of Arab States, China–Africa Financial and Financial Cooperation Bank Association was established, creating the first multilateral financial cooperation mechanism between China and the Arab States, and between African countries. While in the BRI, we may note more attention being paid to the construction of a financial market system and the formulation of a series of measures, there is no denying that the financial system that the BRI is trying to construct still lacks any clear framework. At the same time, the increase in the number of participating financial institutions has made it more difficult to avoid existing regulations being blurred. The result has been that the BRI has suffered negative impacts a result of its inadequate regulations.

It is important to note that it is not uncommon for the BRI and its partners to issue broad guidelines leaving it to others to interpret and implement them, but they have been unceremoniously criticized as "platitudes, slogans, catchphrases, and generalities" (Norris, 2016, p. 52), rather than being taken as detailed strategies that provide reliable context guidance. The result has been that some terms frequently used in BRI documents, such as "creating a new global standard" (Wang, 2015; cited in Callahan, 2016a, p. 237), or establishing "new values and norms," or "multilateralism" (Yuan, 2019, p. 110) through "multi-levels," have not been clarified.

Many interpretations have been normative, rather than descriptive, and propose what the normative content of BRI can, or should, be. These include proposals to take advantage of the Confucian culture (Bao, 2018; Dellios & Ferguson, 2017; Zhou & Zhou, 2016), or Daoism (Ling & Perrigoue, 2018; Zeng, 2016a, 2016b), or to combine ideas about the world with "global public goods" (He, 2018). The advantage of this approach is that participants can interpret expressions in a way that suits them, rather than blindly copying measures taken by other countries. The obvious disadvantage is that this may run counter to the interests of other countries, as well as the views of senior leaders, leading to large regulatory problems (Hameiri & Jones, 2018; Lampton, 2015). The Silk Road Fund (SRF), for example, also claims to comply with "internationally recognized standards," but in practice it appears that oversight of the overseas investment practices of Chinese companies remains lax and ineffective, far below the "best practices" associated with development projects (SRF, 2015).

While Chinese companies are required to comply with local laws and customs, there is substantial evidence that state-owned enterprises, at both the provincial and central levels, have violated these rules, causing a diplomatic backlash (Hess & Aidoo, 2016). While China's response to diplomatic influence, including the introduction of new rules and the dismissal of the managers of some state-owned companies, has prompted countries such as Myanmar to pay more attention to Corporate Social Responsibility (CSR) (Kirchherr et al., 2017), overall implementation and enforcement is often weak (Tan-Mullins et al., 2017). In BRI countries, 58% of the Chinese Enterprises surveyed in 2017 never issued any CSR or Sustainable Development reports (MOFCOM(CAITEC), SASAC, & UDNPC, 2017).

The lack of rules on sector-specific standards, transparency and local stakeholder consultations can lead to the financing of disruptive and controversial projects (Friends of the Earth, 2012), including oil and gas pipelines, one example being the Shwe Gas and Oil Pipeline which connects Myanmar to South-west China, and hydroelectric dams, such as those at Myitsone (Myanmar) and Cheay Arenge (Cambodia), which caused so much social opposition that they had to be suspended (Hameiri & Jones, 2018). Government data show that half of the Chinese companies operating in BRI countries fail to conduct social impact assessments before starting their projects, while more than a third ignore environmental impact assessments. Furthermore, ignorance of local regulations suggests that violations of local rules are extensive (MOFCOM (CAITEC) et al., 2017, p. 84). These failings could be taken as a systemic lack of interest in the populations that the BRI projects are intended to aid, or as a lack of experience in international aid projects.

According to official Chinese documents, the BRI was grounded on the impact of the international financial crisis on the world, in order to deal with the problems faced by the liberal order. These official documents about BRI (BBR, 2017; BRIP, 2019; V&A, 2015) do not express any intention to overturn the existing global order, but rather straightforwardly focus on concerns about the new dilemma for globalization, with one document stating:

> With the world economy slowly recovering and development diverging, profound adjustments are brewing in the pattern of international investment and trade, and in multilateral investment and trade rules. (NDRC, MFA, & MOFCOM, 2015)

Another document states,

> The global economic governance system has failed to reflect objective changes and slow progress has been made in institutional reform; developed economies have entered the post-industrial stage, but some developing countries have yet to open the door to modernization; the global trade and investment system has yet to be improved and win-win global value chains have yet to take shape; and a considerable number of countries face inadequate infrastructure and bottlenecks in their regional and sub-regional development. (BRP, 2017)

Consequently, China proposed the BRI, and stressed that it is based on the need for broader regional economic cooperation for peace, development and cooperation: "In the face of difficult challenges, only closer co-operation is the fundamental solution" (BRP, 2017).

Thus, we can see that the cooperative nature of the BRI has been emphasized repeatedly in all three government documents, and in most detail as follows,

> Belt and Road Initiative aims to build a community of shared future for mankind through consultation, joint efforts and shared benefits... Consultation is 'Everyone's business is discussed and handled by everyone', emphasizing equal participation, full consultation and on the basis of equality and voluntariness... Co-construction is that all parties are equal participants, builders and contributors, but also the responsibility and risk-sharing... Sharing is to take into account the interests and concerns of partners, to seek points of convergence of interests and maximum common denominators of cooperation. (OLGPBRI, 2019)

It is clear that economic cooperation is not the only intended aim of the BRI. Another document makes clear that China's intention is to participate actively in global governance:

> China, as the largest developing country and the second largest economy in the world, has a responsibility to promote a fair, just and equitable international economic governance system. (BRP, 2017)

Some Western politicians and critics have taken this last statement to mean that the BRI will pose a direct challenge to US leadership. The document *Belt and Road responds to a multipolar world* (BRP, 2017) does seem to suggest this possibility. But one objection to this view is that reference to "*world multipolarity*" has been documented only once, and not as a central goal of the BRI. Hameiri and Jones (2016) makes an interesting point, arguing that for years the US has been pushing China to become a "responsible power." In this sense, therefore, China can be seen as playing the role assigned to it by the current hegemonic power. Scholars have also discussed what China claims to be the BRI's unique economic model and proposed the possibility of the creation of a "Beijing Consensus" (Cooper, 2004), which would be contrary to the neoliberal Washington Consensus. However, there is no clear evidence of any statement in a BRI policy paper that the BRI has been constructed to challenge the economic model of neoliberalism.

Overall, we can assert that the rules for what the Chinese leadership wants to achieve through the BRI, what it wants to build, still remain unclear, and that although

BRI appears to have made some progress in all the five directions that it has highlighted as its goals, the BRI itself has not fundamentally had any breakthrough impact on the existing world economic order. Viewing the BRI as a project without any overall plan, or any real transparency, and which does not really fit well together with China's recent substantial military and naval development, indicates that the real nature of the BRI remains beyond our grasp.

4 Conclusion

Taking official Chinese government documents as a point of departure, the BRI does not appear to have been initiated with the intention of re-establishing the world order. However, the normative principles that China claims to adhere differ from those that motivate the US, for example, and the vision of pluralism that China advocates differs from that found in universal liberalism. The normative content of what we must understand as China's plan supports deeper international economic integration, with the aim of establishing a mixed model of bilateral and multilateral mechanisms to reduce barriers to investment by promoting infrastructure and deepening political coordination, and a strong commitment to openness and universal participation, but often in the form of what is in fact a form of bilateral cooperation. Of course, these commitments are open to question, especially in the face of the various regulatory issues facing financial institutions and the negative consequences mentioned above. Perhaps it is possible to conclude that the BRI supports bilateral cooperation, under the cloak of multilateral cooperation, that may be on the path towards becoming multilateral cooperation. What appears to be clear is that the BRI does currently not seek to undermine the existing order, but rather to complement it.

The reason for much of the ambiguity that clouds the BRI lies in the fact that its regulation and supervision are cloaked in the Chinese government's principle of "Non-interference in the governance of other countries." This may be understood as the main body of BRI's political pluralism. While the countries actively involved in the BRI have made some progress in aligning their standardization strategies and systems in the areas covered in the documents discussed in this paper, no specific document detailing the standardization framework has been forthcoming. It remains a policy-in-progress. Much of the so-called standardization has also been concentrated to bilateral cooperation. While China may have expressed a desire to establish a system of compatible standards in multilateral cooperation, any results in this direction are, thus far, not apparent. Such a lack also indicates that BRI has not yet had any significant impact on the current international order. From its practical results, the measures taken within the framework of the BRI seem to be at times at odds with one another, and deviate from global governance norms advanced by many scholars. But in contrast to the view that the BRI reflects an attempt to challenge Western dominance, the results reflect a system of governance that is internally contentious, divided, and unevenly internationalized. At the same time, relatively broad policy statements from senior leaders are interpreted by participants at different levels in different ways, resulting in inconsistent and even contradictory behaviour. Although the BRI appears to have the potential to change the international order—whether through challenges, changes, or additions—it is clear that the current US-dominated liberal economy remains firmly in place, and no major changes have occurred thus far. In conclusion, as far as the implementation of the BRI is concerned, there is no doubt that it remains in a formative stage.

Acronyms

BBR 2017	Building the Belt and Road: Concept, Practice and China's Contribution
BRIP 2019	The Belt and Road Initiative Progress, Contributions and Prospects 2019
BRP	Belt and Road Portal
CAITEC	Chinese Academy of International Trade and Economic Cooperation
ECFR	European Council on Foreign Relations
MFA	Ministry of Foreign Affairs of the People's Republic of China
MOFCOM	Ministry of Commerce of the People's Republic of China
NDRC	National Development and Reform Commission of the People's Republic of China
OLGPBRI	Office of the Leading Group for Promoting the Belt and Road Initiative
SASAC	The State-owned Assets Supervision and Administration Commission of the State Council of the People's Republic of China
SRF	Silk Road Fund
UDNPC	United Nations Development Programme China
V&A 2015	Vision and Actions on Jointly Building Silk Road Economic Belt and 21st-Century Maritime Silk Road

Bibliographic References

Agence France-Presse. (2017). China decries protectionism, but some raise concerns. *Straits Times*.
Arase, D. (2019). China's two Silk Roads Initiative: What it means for Southeast Asia. In *Turning points and transitions* (December 2018, pp. 150–165). ISEAS Publishing. https://doi.org/10.1355/9789814843089-018
Asian Infrastructure Investment Bank. (2017). *Financing Asia's future: 2017 AIIB annual report and financials*. Retrieved on November 2021, from https://www.aiib.org/en/news-events/news/2017/annual-report/common/pdf/AIIB-Annual-Report-2017.pdf
Baniya, S., Rocha, N., & Ruta, M. (2020). Trade effects of the New Silk Road: A gravity analysis. *Journal of Development Economics, 146*(January 2019), 102467. https://doi.org/10.1016/j.jdeveco.2020.102467
Bao, Y. (2018). 发挥文化"走出去"在"一带一路"建设中的引领作用 [The guiding role of Chinese culture in implementing the BRI]. *Public Diplomacy Quarterly* (1), 12–16, 142.

Boughton, J. M., & Bradford, C. I. (2007). Governance: New players, new rules. *Finance and Development, 44*(4), 10–14.

BRP. (2017). *Building the Belt and Road: Concept, practice and China's contribution.* Retrieved on November 2021, from https://eng.yidaiyilu.gov.cn/wcm.files/upload/CMSydylyw/201705/201705110537027.pdf

Byrnes, J. C. (2020). Is this belt one size fits all? China's belt and road initiative. *Penn State Journal of Law & International Affairs, 8*(2), 723–756.

Cable, V. (1999) *Globalization and global governance.* Thomson Learning.

Callahan, W. A. (2016a). China's "Asia dream": The Belt Road Initiative and the new regional order. *Asian Journal of Comparative Politics, 1*(3), 226–243. https://doi.org/10.1177/2057891116647806

Callahan, W. A. (2016b). China's Belt and Road Initiative and the new Eurasian order. *Norwegian Institute of International Affairs, 22,* 1–4. http://en.ndrc.gov.cn/newsre-.

Carrai, M. A., Defraigne, J.-C., & Wouters, J. (2020). The Belt and Road Initiative and global governance: By way of introduction. In *The Belt and Road Initiative and global governance* (pp. 1–19). Edward Elgar. https://doi.org/10.4337/9781789906226.00005

Chance, A., & Mafinezam, A. (2016). *American perspectives on the Belt and Road Initiative* (pp. 68–75). Institute for China-America Studies.

Ciborowski, R., Oziewicz, E., & Pangsy-Kania, S. (2021). The Belt and Road Initiative—Shared development or a threat for the world economy? *European Research Studies Journal, 42*(1), 364–381. https://doi.org/10.35808/ersj/1967

Cooper, A. F., & Flemes, D. (2013). Foreign policy strategies of emerging powers in a multipolar world: An introductory review. *Third World Quarterly, 34*(6), 943–962. https://doi.org/10.1080/01436597.2013.802501

Cooper, J. (2004). *The Beijing consensus: Notes on the new physics of Chinese power.* Foreign Policy Centre.

Dellios, R., & Ferguson, R. J. (2017). The human security dimension of China's Belt and Road Initiative. *Journal of Management and Sustainability, 7*(3), 48–62. https://doi.org/10.5539/jms.v7n3p48

ECFR. (2015). *'One road': China's great leap outward.* China Analysis.

Fallon, T. (2015). The New Silk Road: Xi Jinping's grand strategy for Eurasia. *American Foreign Policy Interests, 37*(3), 140–147.

Friends of the Earth. (2012). *China Development Bank's overseas investments: An assessment of environmental and social policies and practices.* Friends of the Earth.

Glaser, B. S., & Funaiole, M. (2015). *Geopolitical consequences of China's slowdown* (pp. 58–61). Retrieved on November 2021, from https://www.csis.org/analysis/geopolitical-consequences-china's-slowdown

Hameiri, S., & Jones, L. (2016). Rising powers and state transformation: The case of China. *European Journal of International Relations, 22*(1), 72–98.

Hameiri, S., & Jones, L. (2018). China challenges global governance? The case of Chinese international development finance and the Asian Infrastructure Investment Bank. *International Affairs, 94*(3), 573–593.

He, C. (2018). The Belt and Road Initiative as global public good: Implications for international law. In W. Shan, K. Nuotio, & K. Zhang (Eds.), *Normative readings of the Belt and Road Initiative: Road to new paradigms* (pp. 59–83). Springer. https://doi.org/10.1007/978-3-319-78018-4

Hess, S., & Aidoo, R. (2016). Charting the impact of subnational actors in China's foreign relations. *Asian Survey, 56*(2), 301–324.

Huang, Y. (2016). Understanding China's Belt & Road Initiative: Motivation, framework and assessment. *China Economic Review, 40,* 314–321. https://doi.org/10.1016/j.chieco.2016.07.007

Ikenberry, J. G., & Lim, D. J. (2017, April). *China's emerging institutional statecraft: The Asian Infrastructure Investment Bank and the prospects for counter-hegemony* (pp. 1–23). Project on International Order and Strategy.

Jizhong, Z., et al. (2020). *The Belt and Road Initiative 2020 Survey—A more sustainable road to growth*. Retrieved on November 2021, from https://www.centralbanking.com/central-banks/eco nomics/4737966/the-belt-and-road-initiative-2020-survey-a-more-sustainable-road-to-growth

Jones, L. (2020). Does China's belt and road initiative challenge the liberal, rules-based order? *Fudan Journal of the Humanities and Social Sciences, 13*(1), 113–133.

Kavaliauskas, J. (2020). Europe's response to the BRI. *European & Transatlantic Affairs, 4*(1), 184–190.

Keohane, R. O. (2015). After hegemony: Transatlantic economic relations in the next decade. *International Spectator, 50*(4), 80–91. https://doi.org/10.1080/03932729.2015.1074455

Kirchherr, J., Charles, K. J., & Walton, M. J. (2017). The interplay of activists and dam developers: The case of Myanmar's mega-dams. *International Journal of Water Resources Development, 33*(1), 111–131. https://doi.org/10.1080/07900627.2016.1179176

Klotz, A., & Lynch, C. M. (2007). *Strategies for research in constructivist international relations*. M.E. Sharpe.

Krasner, S. (1982). Structural causes and regime consequences: Regimes as intervening variables. *International Organization, 36*, 189–193.

Lampton, D. M. (2015). Xi Jinping and the national security commission: Policy coordination and political power. *Journal of Contemporary China, 24*(95), 759–777. https://doi.org/10.1080/106 70564.2015.1013366

Ling, L. H. M., & Perrigoue, A. C. (2018). OBOR and the Silk Road ethos: An ancient template for contemporary world politics. *Asian Journal of Comparative Politics, 3*(3), 207–218. https://doi.org/10.1177/2057891117753771

Li, X. (2017). CITIC deepens backing for B&R. *China Daily*.

Ly, B. (2020). China and global governance: Leadership through BRI. *Cogent Social Sciences, 6*(1). https://doi.org/10.1080/23311886.2020.1801371

Ly, B. (2021). China quest for global governance overhaul. *Cogent Social Sciences, 7*(1). https://doi.org/10.1080/23311886.2021.1932031

McGrew, A., & Held, D. (2002). *Governing globalization: Power, authority and global governance*. Polity Press.

MOFCOM(CAITEC), SASAC, & UDNPC. (2017). *2017 report on the sustainable development of Chinese enterprises overseas: Supporting the Belt and Road regions to achieve the 2030 agenda for sustainable development*. Retrieved on November 2021, from http://fec.mofcom.gov.cn/art icle/tzhzcj/tzhz/upload/duiwaitouzihezuofazhanbaogao2014.pdf

Naughton, B. (2010). China's distinctive system: Can it be a model for others? *Journal of Contemporary China, 19*(65), 437–460. https://doi.org/10.1080/10670561003666079

NDRC, MFA, & MOFCOM. (2015). *Vision and actions on jointly Building Silk Road Economic Belt and 21st-Century Maritime Silk Road*, China's National Development and Reform Commission.

Norris, W. J. (2016). *Chinses economic statecraft: Commercial actors, grand strategy, and state control*. Cornell Univerity Press.

Ohashi, H. (2018). The Belt and Road Initiative (BRI) in the context of China's opening-up policy. *Journal of Contemporary East Asia Studies, 7*(2), 85–103. https://doi.org/10.1080/24761028. 2018.1564615

OLGPBRI. (2019). *The Belt and Road Initiative progress, contributions and prospects 2019*. Retrieved on November 2021, from https://eng.yidaiyilu.gov.cn/zchj/qwfb/86739.htm

Olson, S., & Prestowitz, C. (2011). *The evolving role of China in international institutions*. The Economic Strategy Institute.

Renminwang. (2017). *Europe–China commerce and trade summit focuses on BRI construction*. Renminwang. Retrieved on November 2021, from http://world.people.com.cn/n1/2017/1010/c1002-29577087.html

Rolf, S., & Agnew, J. (2016). Sovereignty regimes in the South China Sea: Assessing contemporary Sino-US relations. *Eurasian Geography and Economics, 57*(2), 249–273. https://doi.org/10.1080/15387216.2016.1234403

SRF. (2015). *Social responsibility*. Retrieved on November 2021, from http://www.silkroadfund. com.cn/cnweb/19854/19878/20040/index.html

SRF. (2018). *Official launched and commencement of full operation of the China-Europe joint investment fund*. Retrieved on November 2021, from http://www.silkroadfund.com.cn/enweb/ 23809/23812/37101/index.html

Swaine, M. D. (2015). Chinese views and commentary on the One Belt, One Road Initiative. *China Leadership Monitor, 47*(2), 1–24. Retrieved on November 2021, from https://www.hoover.org/ sites/default/files/research/docs/clm47ms.pdf

Tan-Mullins, M., Urban, F., & Mang, G. (2017). Evaluating the behaviour of Chinese stakeholders engaged in large hydropower projects in Asia and Africa. *China Quarterly, 230*, 464–488. https:// doi.org/10.1017/S0305741016001041

Tao, J., & Zhong, M. (2018). The changing rules of international dispute resolution in China's Belt and Road Initiative. In *China's Belt and Road Initiative* (pp. 305–320). Springer. https://doi.org/ 10.1007/978-3-319-75435-2

Wang, Y. (2015). *"一带一路": 机遇与挑战* ['*One Belt, One Road': Opportunities and challenge*]. Renmin Press.

Wang, Y. (2016). Offensive for defensive: The Belt and Road Initiative and China's new grand strategy. *Pacific Review, 29*(3), 455–463. https://doi.org/10.1080/09512748.2016.1154690

Xinhua. (2016). *Xi calls for reforms on global governance*. Retrieved in November 2021, from https://www.chinadaily.com.cn/china/2016-09/29/content_26931697.html

Yang Jiechi. (2015). *Jointly build the 21st Century Maritime Silk Road by deepening mutual trust and enhancing connectivity*. Speech at the Session of "Jointly Building the 21st Century Maritime Silk Road" and Launching of the Year of China-ASEAN Maritime Cooperation. Retrieved on November 2021, from https://www.fmprc.gov.cn/mfa_eng/zxxx_662805/t1249761.shtml

Yuan, F. (2019). The One Belt One Road Initiative and China's multilayered multilateralism. In X. Li (Ed.), *Mapping China's "One Belt One Road" Initiative* (pp. 91–116). Springer.

Zeng, L. (2016a). Conceptual analysis of China's Belt and Road initiative: A road towards a regional community of common destiny. *Chinese Journal of International Law, 15*(3), 517–541. https:// doi.org/10.1093/chinesejil/jmw021

Zeng, X. (2016b). The geopolitical imaginations of the "One Belt, One Road" Initiative and regional cooperation. *World Economics and Politics, 1*, 46–71, 157–158.

Zhou, F., & Zhou, J. (2016). On the construction of China's cultural soft power in the background of the Belt and Road Initiative. *Journal of Tongji University (Social Science Section), 27*(5), 40–47.

Zhou, W., & Esteban, M. (2018). Beyond balancing: China's approach towards the belt and road initiative. *Journal of Contemporary China, 27*(112), 487–501. https://doi.org/10.1080/10670564. 2018.1433476

Chapter 8
Glocalization of Belt and Road Initiatives: The Importance of Local Agency

Julie Yu-Wen Chen

1 Introduction

This chapter seeks to explore the role of local agency in influencing the development of Belt and Road Initiative (BRI) projects and asks if localization plays a more pivotal role for BRI projects than forces from China or the wider international arena. China's projects within BRI can be seen as subsets of Chinese international cooperation projects. It is not always easy to single out and specify BRI projects, as China does not offer a clear and fixed list of them (Gruebler & Stehrer, 2020). A BRI project can also be an old cooperation project re-branded as BRI. For this chapter, it is crucial to recognize that there are broader and narrower definitions of BRI. A broader definition includes all China-related projects, such as Chinese foreign direct investments (FDI), Chinese-financed projects, or other kinds of international cooperation projects. Nonetheless, the narrowly defined projects are only those "derived from or included in cooperation/dialogues between China and the BRI countries," and these projects can involve "more complicated and innovative financing structures than do traditional FDI projects" (Liu et al., 2020, p. 139).

A growing body of literature and public commentaries on BRI projects have looked at these as China's strategy for intensifying regional cooperation and trade relations or from geopolitical perspectives in the context of China's rising global ambition and influence (e.g., Ambrosio et al., 2020; Flint & Zhu, 2019; Hodzi & Chen, 2018; Raymond, 2021; Yilmaz & Li, 2020; Zhang, 2018). For instance, Callahan argues that China is using the BRI and its affiliated institutions and projects to construct what Chinese President Xi Jinping calls a "community of shared destiny" whereby partnering countries are drawn into a Sino-centric sphere of relations. In a similar vein, some scholars (e.g., Chen, 2020a; Dove, 2016; Hong, 2015; Paterson, 2021) examine funding bodies for BRI projects such as the Silk Road Fund and the Asian Infrastructure Investment Bank (AIIB) and argue that these funding entities

J. Y.-W. Chen (✉)
University of Helsinki, Helsinki, Finland

are also a part of China's strategy to revise the international development order that is highly dominated by Western standards and practices.

Hodzi and Chen (2018) add that Beijing's strategy is safe and pragmatic because, as a partial global power striving to become a comprehensive global power (Shambaugh, 2013), it can use China-led institutions to delimit its sphere of influence and set the agenda and the rules of the global order without overthrowing it, without confronting the declining yet unyielding global power, the US (Hodzi & Chen, 2018; Peng, 2021). While this string of literature helps us understand different aspects of Chinese influences, motives, and strategies, it does not tell us whether the Chinese dream of creating a Sino-centric sphere of relations and influence will be accepted and realized in different parts of the world.

This chapter focuses on the power of local actors in BRI host states and scholarly efforts to conceptualize the local agency. It speaks directly to the gradual growth of empirical cases that have pointed out the discrepancy between China's ambitions and its real capacity to implement the results of BRI projects on the ground (e.g., Bitabarova, 2018; Chen, 2020b, 2020c; Pan et al., 2019). Scholars are becoming interested in local actors and their agency to translate China's proposed projects to match with the local interests. International journals such as *Political Geography* have also published special issues focusing on the BRI. One of them is guest-edited by Oliveira et al. (2020), who present views from the ground, while discussing China's role in globalization in the context of local realities.

Local actors are defined differently in various countries. They can be private or state actors, individuals, institutions, companies, or other forms of organizations. Not all local actors are supportive of their countries' cooperation in BRI projects. Opposition groups and individuals should also be considered because their positions and activism might affect the BRI projects' implementation.

With such developments in the BRI studies, this chapter offers an overview of the actual roles of local agencies, their capacities, and limits. Qualitative analysis of secondary sources from articles and books is mainly used in this chapter, while think tanks reports (e.g., Institute for International Political Studies in Italy, Hinrich Foundation in Hong Kong) and magazines on current affairs (e.g., *The Diplomat*) are also consulted to make the review more comprehensive and up-to-date.

BRI projects are complex. For their successful implementation, different models of cooperation and governance need to be considered, ranging from cooperation, governance, finance, and legal and jurisdiction models. These will pull in complex networks of actors at the local recipient level, the Chinese side, and actors in the international arena (e.g., international financial institutions and international development institutions). It is, therefore, crucial to conceptually discern to what extent local actors can exercise impact vis-à-vis the external influence of China or other stakeholders from the international arena.

The rest of the chapter is structured as follows. The next section is a review of literature that articulates the importance of local agency, showing why local proactiveness can determine the success of China's international cooperation and implementation of the BRI projects. The third section looks at how scholars have perceived the roles and actions of local agencies. The fourth section situates the discussion in measuring the power of local actors in BRI projects in the context of the wider academic debate over the relations between localization and globalization. Is localization a part of globalization or is it in opposition to globalization? The fifth session concludes this chapter. Overall, the focus of this chapter is on the question of agency, which is used to problematize our current understanding of the forces between localization and globalization.

2 Why Is Local Agency Important?

Western media have often presented BRI projects' negative impacts on local economies and societies. Terms such as "debt-trap diplomacy" and news about exploited local workers, polluted environment, among others, all portray China as pushing forward cooperative projects without regarding sustainable and long-term interests of the local people (Brautigam, 2020). Recently, more academic studies show that such negative perceptions might not be entirely accurate (e.g., Crescenzi & Limodio, 2021; Lai et al., 2020).

Scholars working on development and peace studies are among the first to elaborate on local agencies' importance. Scholars in African development studies are pioneers in this regard (e.g., Amoah, 2012; Mohan & Lampert, 2013). For instance, even before Beijing introduced the grand notion of BRI, scholars such as Giles Mohan and Ben Lampert (2013) had published a paper on reinserting African agency into China–Africa relations. The discussion continues even after the BRI concept was established in 2013, as shown in the works of Gadzala (2015), Carmody and Kragelund (2016), Alden and Large (2018), Pepa (2020), among other contributions. By considering local African agencies, scholars find out that some Chinese-prompted cooperative projects are actually more locally driven, and that Sino-African relations are not just enforced by the Chinese side upon African actors. The local agency, both state and non-state, can have the power to foster or resist cooperation with the Chinese (Alden & Large, 2018; Chiyemura et al., 2022; Mohan & Lampert, 2013; Pepa, 2020).

Concerning BRI projects, scholars have pointed out several reasons why local agency matters. First, cooperation with the local actors is, by default, how most BRI projects can be realized. As Liu et al. (2020, p. 142) note, BRI projects are often not the same as traditional FDI projects that allow Chinese firms to directly invest in host countries. Rather, BRI projects are primarily built using the Engineering, Procurement, and Construction (EPC) or Build-Operate-Transfer (BOT) contracts, and in a few cases other forms of Public Private Partnership (PPP) contracts. EPC contracts involve a deal between the local owner and the Chinese contractor, with the latter being responsible for delivering design, construction, logistics, transport, and other services, as requested by the financier. The model of "EPC plus operation" means that contractors are more deeply embedded in the host countries, as seen in the Mombasa-Nairobi railway in Kenya, as well as the Addis Ababa-Djibouti railway in Ethiopia and Djibouti (ibid.).

BOT and PPP are based on a concessional contract with the host government, as is envisioned for the Bagamoyo port project in Tanzania. Although there might be skill shortages, the degree of skill transfer in BRI projects has been criticized. For example, in the case of the Nairobi Mombasa Standard Gauge Railway, the pieces of machinery were entirely made by the Chinese, and the Chinese staff did not speak English, making skill transfer difficult. Ideally, whoever leads the project has to offer training, transfer technology, and know-how to locals in Nairobi. The Chinese contractor will run the completed project until a certain time and then hand the operation to the local operators. These contractual forms and cooperative models all involve a much deeper and long-term interaction between local actors and Chinese actors than the traditional FDI projects.

Although China might not fully appreciate the specificity of local conditions, interests, and politics, it understands the significance of local support and reactions. Beijing often openly declares the importance of third-party cooperation and respect for the host country's governance model. These elements are vital for attracting a complex network of local actors willing to help bring the idea of the BRI to their countries (Liu et al., 2020). Arguably, political and/or business elites in recipient states are likely to see the benefits that the BRI can bring to them, their communities, and societies, and thus start to mobilize and form networks to make the BRI a reality. Such processes involve negotiations among different actors in a specific BRI state. Local politics, laws, and customs will give the China-originated project a local or a "Sino-local" outlook to increase project legitimacy among the local actors.

Sometimes, local actors even use China as a card in playing their domestic games. Galen Murton et al. (2016) presented the example of the Nepali government, who used Chinese investment to further the country's state formation project. In 2018, Hong Liu and Guanie Lim revealed that the Malaysian government used the construction of the East Coast Rail Link to promote its pro-Malay policy (Liu & Lim, 2018). In this context, China is invited by the local actors to consciously or unconsciously serve certain local actors' self-interests. In the end, the final project may look different from what China originally envisioned, and can even be contradictory to China's interests.

Another important factor is that China needs local partners to navigate challenges and uncertainties (Yu, 2017, p. 367), ranging from regime change, altering of leadership through electoral cycles or coups, terrorist, or other security threats. These challenges could have significant repercussions on the implementation of BRI, as they might halt cooperation, make previously signed agreements invalid, or increase the already numerous challenges in project development.

Concerning security threats, for instance, the protracted Palestinian–Israeli conflict used to be far from China's concern. Yet, with the birth of the BRI and China's plan to construct projects across Asia, Africa, and Europe, the conflict became a "more proximal issue" (Mohamed Soliman & Zhao, 2019, p. 441). Security challenges in the Middle East and North Africa might put China's BRI projects in danger. Accordingly, China has become increasingly engaged with various regional and international actors in finding solutions to conflicts such as the one between Israel and Palestine (Alden, 2018). Another example is China's 2021 cooperation with the

Taliban that seized control of Afghanistan after the US withdrawal from the country. There are several reasons for China's cooperation with the Taliban and one of them is to hope that good relations with the Taliban would bring a secured environment for China's BRI projects in Afghanistan and neighbouring countries, such as Pakistan. In other words, Beijing's local partnerships are central to the understanding of social, political, and economic dynamics in BRI host states, thus improving the feasibility of BRI projects.

3 Defining and Discerning Local Agency

Although scholars attend to the complexity of local agency and offer empirical evidence, the knowledge is fragmented and there is a lack of systematic mapping and conceptualization. The importance of state actors in negotiating, endorsing, facilitating, legitimizing, and implementing BRI projects (Chen, 2020b, 2020c; Soulé-Kohndou, 2019; Zajontz, 2020a, 2020b) is commonly noted. Yet, scholars (such as Chiyemura, 2020) have also realized the vagueness of the concept of a state agency. It entails multi-layered institutional arrangements and frameworks, but it usually refers to a specific group of political elites, officials, bureaucrats, civil servants, technocrats, and administrators in specific policy domains with institutional and/or regulatory power to steer the development of BRI projects. Ultimately, as Mullan and Tan-Mullins alluded, it is important to determine who benefits from these projects in a certain host country. These actors would have interests in shaping the projects as they see fit for themselves and their countries.

Scholars working on African studies have the most empirical evidence and publications. Soulé-Kohndou's (2019) study of Benin suggests that bureaucrats in charge of reviewing calls for tenders and supervising the implementation of public projects exercised agency by applying procedural standards. Chiyemura (2020) revealed in her case study of Ethiopia that bureaucrats at different governance levels (e.g., central level, local level) exercised agency to design, broker, coordinate, bargain, and manage infrastructural projects in line with the Ethiopian state's beliefs and interests.

In 2018, Hong Liu and Guanie Lim were among the first to propose a conceptual framework examining three most vital variables undergirding the BRI in Malaysia: (1) the interplay involving domestic ethnopolitical goals and Chinese interests, (2) state-federal contestation, and (3) convergence of geopolitical goals (2018, p. 7). They compared three cases, the East Coast Rail, Bandar Malaysia (a development project involving residential and commercial properties in Kuala Lumpur), and Forest City. They found that the rail's partial success, Bandar Malaysia' collapse, and Forest City's arrested development suggested that BRI success or failure depended on three main conditions: fulfilment of Malaysia's long-standing pro-Malay policy, a mutual vision between state and federal authorities, and the advancement of geopolitical interests for both China and Malaysia. Overall, Liu and Lim's paper shows that China cannot just impose its will on BRI partners. Local agency and consternation of domestic institutional and power arrangements have decisive roles. This points to the fact that local actors cannot act in a vacuum. In reality, the local agency makes influence through structural or institutional arrangements. Liu and Lim (2018) reported that it is too early to say that China has created any Sino-centric community of shared destiny, although it has strategically used the BRI, in combination with diplomacy and investment to exploit the weakness of Southeast Asian countries. This speaks to the geopolitical ambition of the BRI noted at the beginning of this chapter, implying that such geopolitical perspective is limited if disregarding local agency in BRI state.

In addition to state actors, civil society or non-state actors may play a role, although the level of engagement may vary across cases. Maria Adele Carrai, for example, has compared governmental actors to civil society's involvement in BRI-related projects in Africa. Her comparative studies of Kenya's Standard Gauge Railroad and Ethiopia's Addis Ababa-Djibouti railroad point to the consternation of state and non-state forces, resulting in different levels of commitment to corporate social responsibility (CSR), which Carrai describes as China's adaptive governance on BRI (Carrai, 2021). Governments of Kenya and Ethiopia have a hands-off approach towards CSR, although certain non-state actors have become active in all cases. Kenyan civil society prompted the construction of a more environmentally friendly Standard Gauge Railroad. Ethiopia's organized labour encouraged Chinese contractors to use and train more local workers. In these two cases, Chinese actors are overwhelmingly adaptive and cooperative because they wish to avoid conflict with the host country's practices. However, Carrai (2021) cautions that such an adaptive style could either mean implementing weaker CSR, as seen in the two studied African cases, or potential stronger CSR, as seen in the cases of some European countries. This confirms the aforementioned importance of state actors: if the states could have done more for CSR, the local non-governmental agency would have even more influence.

The importance of state and non-state actors has been noted in the much wider social science community beyond the research on BRI. In several disciplines, such as political sciences, International Relations, sociology, and development studies, there are different theoretical frameworks to understand the consternation of these domestic forces in influencing politics and society in general. For example, political scientist Thomas Risse-Kappen (1999) has a domestic structure approach, highlighting the significance of winning allies in affecting the outcome of the politics of the interest groups. If we consider Chinese investors and elites in BRI host states as interest groups, then we can understand why the fundamental support of the government and various authorities in BRI host states matters. Government support can come in various ways, from endorsing the BRI by signing an MoU, changing legal regulations to facilitate cooperation, informing business companies of the opportunities available to them, to synchronizing states' policies priorities with those of the BRI.

In BRI studies, no concrete conceptual or theoretical framework has been created since 2021. Liu and Lim (2018), in their empirical studies of Malaysia, proposed a framework comparing the independent variables of "interplay involving domestic ethnopolitical goals and Chinese interests," "state-federal contestation," and "convergence of geopolitical goals" (2018, p. 7). The dependent variable is the outcome, namely whether a project is realized or not. Yu-Wen Chen (2020a) proposed a conceptual framework for understanding local agencies. She calls her framework the Sino-localized framework and includes both state and non-state, public and private, collective and individual actors in a generalized way. While Liu and Lim's framework is restricted to cases in Malaysia, Chen's framework applies to global cases.

Chen's framework is influenced by the scholarly discussion of the concept of *glocalization*, which usually accompanies discussions of globalization. Ronald Robertson (1992, 1994) brought the discussion of glocalization into social-scientific discourse. In Robertson's view, globalization has to be realized in concrete forms because the locals have to form a response towards the global influences. Chen replaced the term *global* with *Sino* to reflect the reality that the drivers of the BRI are initially from China, but she also tried to critically evaluate whether *Sino* is better than *global* when examining the development of BRIs as of 2021.

The kernel of Chen's framework is that a socially constructed arena or field(s) would emerge as a result of the interaction and dynamism triggered by local actors' reactions to the potential opportunities presented by the BRI. In some countries, the field can be more organized than in others, in the sense that actors in some countries can have clearer framings than actors in other countries of the resources and plans for carrying out BRI projects and how they can capitalize on the BRI. The roles played by local actors include (1) encoding and decoding China's intentions and initiative in the cooperation, (2) garnering supporters to advance their cause, (3) determining the level of local participation and activism, and gradually making the BRI a reality in their countries, and, lastly (4) promoting public acceptance of the BRI project (Chen, 2020b).

Chen's framework speaks also to Timur Dadabaev who publishes a lot on the situation in Central Asia, sometimes comparing the cases of Japan and Korea. Dadabaev (2018, p. 38) contends that the BRI is not a foreign policy doctrine but a "discursive strategy of engagement that largely exists in the realm of narration." In the field where interested actors engage with each other, a great deal of articulation of "self, identities, values, threats and opportunities" emerges (Dadabaev, 2018, p. 39). Chen argues that it is normal to observe frequent entries and exits of actors into the BRI field. Not all fields will be mature enough to realize BRI projects. Take the example of the Czech Republic where, although some actors have expressed interests, no concrete actions have been taken to realize BRI projects. Overall, the analytical framework in studying whether and how BRI can successfully be implemented is lacking and should be further developed.

Another often neglected dimension is the role of informal agency. This is much more covered in development studies than in the context of BRI. In African studies, for example, Isaac Odoom (2016) has argued that Giles Mohan's study of African agency hinged mostly on the elite agency. Isaac Odoom points out that non-elite agency is sui generis; ordinary people have their own agency in dealing with Chinese interests and their actions are not necessarily a result of loss of faith in African elites (Obeng-Odoom, 2019; Odoom, 2016).

Discussion of informal agency in BRI literature is not common because BRI is a much more recent phenomenon. Scholars are still grappling with what can be empirically observed and studied. For example, Elisa Gambino has written on BRI in Africa and has published in quasi-academic platforms such as *Asia Dialogue* to raise awareness of the existence of informal agency and everyday informal bargaining with Chinese employers or superiors in the BRI project's construction site. Kenyan workers use different means, such as minor defiance to bargain for their employment rights. These actions are not organized collective actions that would be formally studied by scholars. The necessity to conduct long-term ethnographic fieldwork to document these trivial daily lives of workers also makes this kind of study more difficult to realize. Anthropologist Miriam Driessen's book *Tales of Hope, Taste of Bitterness* (2019) is presented ethnographic research on Chinese road builders in Ethiopia. Nevertheless, overall academic studies on informal agency in BRI projects await further development.

4 Situating BRI Glocalization Within the Globalization Debate

While BRI projects' adaption to local interests, politics, laws, and customs might give them a local or a *Sino-Local* outlook, we still need to determine the relationship between glocalization/sino-localization and globalization. To put it simply, what is the relationship between the local and the global (in this case, the global with Chinese characteristics)? Does localization play a more pivotal role for BRI projects than forces from China or the wider international arena? This connects us to the broader social-scientific debate, especially between Roland Robertson and George Ritzer.

Outside the BRI context, Robertson (1992, 1994) argues that globalization will inevitably be transformed into glocalization because the locals will have to play their roles, and, in this vein, the local cannot be separated from the global. The global is never outside the glocal or local, but exists within them. In a different manner, Ritzer (2003, 2007) attempts to discern glocalization that is more locally controlled from *globalization* which is more *centrally* controlled by entities such as multinational organizations. This chapter does not delve into this greater debate, but rather seeks to focus on whether localization trumps the influence of China-led globalization or globalization with Chinese characteristics.

It is not that easy to answer this in the context of the BRI. As scholars such as Hoogenboom et al. (2010, p. 933) have pointed out, determining whether global forces can replace the local or whether the local can be pulled into a globally embedded structure requires a long period of empirical observation. As many BRI projects are in their early stages, we have yet to witness clear empirical evidence of China-led globalization, glocalization, or even globalization in the BRI context. Both globalization and glocalization in the BRI context are slowly evolving, but this has not yet reached the desired point. To some extent, we could even contend that these projects and their related initiatives such as the aforementioned funding bodies are still very much bound within the existing Western-led or US-led globalization.

Summers (2020, p. 149) argues that the BRI-funding body AIIB has been operating according to the international norms and standards, even in cooperation with supposed competitors such as the World Bank and other international financial institutions. Given that the AIIB was created by China, it has "Chinese characteristics," such as more emphasis on the norm of non-interference in its operations (Summers, 2020, p. 149). However, AIIB has endeavoured to capture the best practices of these organizations. This is in line with what the Chinese government has repeatedly stressed in public statements—that Beijing works closely with the existing institutions to advance the cause of the AIIB (Mitchell & Farchy, 2016).

China may want to use the BRI projects to increase its influence and change the current system, but it cannot avoid the embedded rules in running these initiatives. We may contend that, at the current stage of BRI development, China's operations are formed and limited "by the distribution and nature of structural power in the global political economy" (Summers, 2020, p. 150). The globalization that we are mainly observing is still the Western-led globalization into which China can be socialized.

However, simultaneously, we may start to observe more concrete evidence of China-led globalization or globalization with Chinese characteristics, including the results of BRI projects that foster greater connectivity between continents, countries, societies, and civilizations. Each locality will inevitably have its own path of acceptance or resistance towards these forces from above. As with previous waves of globalization, resistance from nation-states and localities is expected. State actors and local actors still have the power to navigate international influence and negotiate interests that serve their national and local interests.

5 Conclusion

This chapter highlighted the rising academic attention to local agencies in BRI host states. A local agency is vital as local actors can exercise power to influence the development and outcomes of BRI projects. This further gives BRI projects a Sino-localized or globalized outlook, if we consider globalization with Chinese characteristics as a kind of Sinolization. The main question that this chapter sought to explore is if localization plays a more pivotal role for BRI projects than forces from China or the wider international arena. As we find out, some empirical evidence has indeed suggested so. However, one cannot see localization and other global forces as mutually exclusive forces. In other words, the process of localization, glocalization, or Sino-localization cannot be seen as a counter-argument to globalization. Given the nascent nature of most BRI projects, globalization and glocalization in the BRI context are slowly developing.

To some extent, we could even argue that many BRI projects and their related initiatives (e.g., the Silk Road Fund and the AIIB) are still very much bounded within existing Western-led or US-led globalization. They have actually been operating according to existing international norms and standards, even in cooperation with supposed competitors such as the World Bank and other international financial institutions. Given that BRI and its funding bodies were founded by China, they do have "Chinese characteristics," such as more emphasis on the norm of non-interference in its operations. However, Chinese actors have endeavoured to capture the best international practices. This is in line with what the Chinese government has repeatedly stressed in public statements—that Beijing actually works closely with existing institutions to advance the cause of the BRI.

China may want to use the BRI projects to increase its influence and change the current system, but it cannot avoid following the embedded rules in running these initiatives. In this vein, we may contend that at the current stage of BRI development, China's operations are formed and limited the structure of the existing global political economic and governance system. The globalization that we are mainly observing is still the Western-led globalization into which China can be socialized. The Western-led global economy as well its entrenched and detrimental effects on developing countries, such as those in Africa, have not changed much. China's projects might deepen these entrenched problems further.

Simultaneously, however, we may start to observe more and more concrete evidence of China-led globalization, including the results of BRI projects that foster greater connectivity between continents, countries, societies, and even civilizations. Each locality will inevitably have its own path of acceptance or resistance towards these forces from *above*. As with previous waves of globalization, resistance from nation-states and localities is expected. State actors and local actors still have the power to navigate international influence and negotiate interests that serve their national and local interests.

Bibliographic References

Alden, C. (2018, September 27). *Beijing's security plans beyond Djibouti and the Horn.* Commentary for Italian Institute for International Political Studies. Retrieved on January 2022, from https://www.ispionline.it/en/pubblicazione/beijings-security-plans-beyond-djibouti-and-horn-21278

Alden, C., & Large, D. (2018). Studying Africa and China. In C. Alden & L. Daniel (Eds.), *New directions in Africa-China studies* (pp. 3–35). Routledge.

Ambrosio, T., Schram, C., & Heopfner, P. (2020). The American securitization of China and Russia: U.S. geopolitical culture and declining unipolarity. *Eurasian Geography and Economics, 61*(2), 162–194.

Amoah, L. G. A. (2012). Africa in China: Affirming African agency in Africa-China relations at the people to people level. In J. Shikwati (Ed.), *China-Africa partnership: The quest for a win-win relationship* (pp. 104–115). Inter Regional Economic Network.

Bitabarova, A. G. (2018). Unpacking Sino-Central Asian engagement along the New Silk Road: A case study of Kazakhstan. *Journal of Contemporary East Asia Studies, 7*(2), 149–173.

Brautigam, D. (2020). A critical look at Chinese debt-trap diplomacy: The rise of a meme. *Area Development and Policy, 5*(1), 1–14.

Carmody, P., & Kragelund, P. (2016). Who is in charge? State power and agency in Sino-African relations. *Cornell International Law Journal, 49*(1), 1–24.

Carrai, M. A. (2021). Adaptive governance along Chinese-financed BRI road megaprojects in East Africa. *World Development, 141*(1). https://doi.org/10.1016/j.worlddev.2020.105388

Chiyemura, F. (2020). Contextualising African agency in Ethiopia-China engagement in wind energy infrastructure financing and development. *Innovation, Knowledge and Development Working Series, 88*, 1–27.

Chiyemura, F., Gambino, E., & Zajontz, T. (2022). Infrastructure and the politics of African state agency: Shaping the Belt and Road Initiative in East Africa. *Chinese Political Science Review.* https://doi.org/10.1007/s41111-022-00214-8

Chen, I.T.-Y. (2020a). China's status deficit and the debut of the Asian Infrastructure Investment Bank. *The Pacific Review, 33*(5), 697–727.

Chen, Y.-W. (2020b). Appropriate approaches to studying the BRI's actual impacts and limits. In A. Gerstl & U. Wallenböck (Eds.), *China's Belt and Road Initiative: Strategic and economic impacts on Central Asia, Southeast Asia and Central Eastern Europe* (pp. 43–60). Routledge.

Chen, Y.-W. (2020c). The making of the Finnish Polar Silk Road: Status in Spring 2019. In H. K. Chan, F. K.-S. Chan, & D. O'Brien (Eds.), *International flows in the Belt and Road Initiative context: Business, people, history and geography* (pp. 193–216). Palgrave Macmillan.

Crescenzi, R., & Limodio, N. (2021). *The impact of Chinese FDI in Africa: Evidence from Ethiopia* (Paper in Economic Geography and Spatial Economics No. 22). LSE Geography and Environment Discussion Paper Series. Retrieved on January 2022, from http://eprints.lse.ac.uk/108455/1/Paper_22_the_impact_of_chinese_fdi_in_africa.pdf

Dadabaev, T. (2018). Silk Road as foreign policy discourse: The construction of Chinese, Japanese and Korean engagement strategies in Central Asia. *Journal of Eurasian Studies, 9*, 30–41.

Dove, J. (2016, April 26). The AIIB and the NDB: The end of multilateralism or a new beginning? *The Diplomat.* Retrieved on January 2022, from https://thediplomat.com/2016/04/the-aiib-and-the-ndb-the-end-of-multilateralism-or-a-new-beginning/

Driessen, M. (2019). *Tales of hope, tastes of bitterness.* Hong Kong University Press.

Flint, C., & Zhu, C. (2019). The geopolitics of connectivity, cooperation, and hegemonic competition: The Belt and Road Initiative. *Geoforum, 99*, 95–101.

Gadzala, A. W. (Ed.). (2015). *Africa and China: How Africans and their governments are shaping relations with China.* Rowman & Littlefield.

Gambino, E. (2020, February 26). *Job insecurity, labour contestation and everyday resistance at the Chinese-Built Lamu Port site in Kenya.* Asia Dialogue. Retrieved on January 2022, from https://bit.ly/35gqswC

Gruebler, J., & Stehrer, R. (2020). Economic (policy) implications for the Belt and Road Initiative for Central, East, and Southeast Europe. In A. Gerstl & U. Wallenböck (Eds.), *China's Belt and Road Initiative: Strategic and economic impacts on Central Asia, Southeast Asia and Central Eastern Europe* (pp. 212–228). Routledge.

Hodzi, O., & Chen, Y.-W. (2018). Follow the flow: China's strategy to global leadership. *China Quarterly of International Strategic Studies, 4*(1), 1–21.

Hoogenboom, M., Bannink, D., & Trommel, W. (2010). From local to grobal, and back. *Business History, 52*(6), 932–954.

Hong, Y. (2015. May 8). The AIIB is seen very differently in the US, Europe, and China. *The Diplomat.* Retrieved on January 2022, from https://thediplomat.com/2015/05/the-aiib-is-seen-very-differently-in-the-us-europe-and-china/

Khursheed, A., Haider, S. K., Mustafa, F., & Akhtar, A. (2019). China-Pakistan economic corridor: A harbinger of economic prosperity and regional peace. *Asian Journal of German and European Studies, 4*(7), 1–15.

Lai, K. P. Y., Lin, S., & Sidaway, J. D. (2020). Financing the Belt and Road Initiative (BRI): Research agendas beyond the "debt-trap" discourse. *Eurasian Geography and Economics, 61*(2), 109–123.

Liu, H., & Lim, G. (2018). The political economy of a rising China in Southeast Asia: Malaysia's response to the Belt and Road Initiative. *Journal of Contemporary China, 28*(116), 216–231.

Liu, W., Zhang, Y., & Xiong, W. (2020). Financing the Belt and Road Initiative. *Eurasian Geography and Economics, 61*(2), 137–145.

Mitchell, T., & Farchy, J. (2016, April 19). China's AIIB seeks to Pave New Silk Road with first projects. *Financial Times.* Retrieved on January 2022, from https://www.ft.com/content/a36af0d0-05fc-11e6-9b51-0fb5e65703ce

Mohamed Soliman, M. A. M., & Zhao, J. (2019). The multiple roles of Egypt in China's Belt and Road Initiative. *Asian Journal of Middle Eastern and Islamic Studies, 13*(3), 428–444.

Mohan, G., & Lampert, B. (2013). Negotiating China: Reinserting African agency into China-Africa relations. *African Affairs, 112*(446), 92–110.

Mohan, G., & Tan-Mullins, M. (2019). The geopolitics of south-south infrastructure development: Chinese-financed energy projects in the global south. *Urban Studies, 56*(7), 1368–1385.

Murton, G., Lord, A., & Beazley, R. (2016). A handshake across the Himalayas: Chinese investment, hydropower development, and state formation in Nepal. *Eurasian Geography and Economics, 57*(3), 403–432.

Obeng-Odoom, F. (2019). Afro-Chinese labour migration. *Forum for Social Economics, 50*(3), 276–296.

Odoom, I. (2016). *Beyond fuelling the dragon: Locating African agency in Africa-China relations* (PhD thesis). University of Alberta.

Oliveira, G. D. L. T., Galen, M., Alessandro, R., Tyler, H., & Yang, Y. (2020). China's Belt and Road Initiative: Views from the ground. *Political Geography, 82*, 1–4.

Pan, C., Clarke, M., & Loy-Wilson, S. (2019). Local agency and complex power shifts in the era of Belt and Road: Perceptions of Chinese aid in the South Pacific. *Journal of Contemporary China, 28*(117), 385–399.

Peng, B. (2021). *China and global governance: A new leader?* Palgrave Macmillan.

Pepa, M. (2020). Rethinking the political economy of Chinese-African agricultural cooperation: The Chinese agricultural technical demonstration centers. *Afrika Focus, 33*(2), 63–77.

Paterson, S. (2021. August 31). *The AIIB: Still a geo-economic tool for China?* Hinrich Foundation Paper. Retrieved on January 2022, from https://www.hinrichfoundation.com/research/article/us-china/is-aiib-a-geo-economic-tool-for-china/

Raymond, G. (2021). *Jagged sphere: China's quest for infrastructure and influence in mainland Southeast Asia.* Lowy Institute Analysis. Retrieved on January 2022, from https://www.lowyinstitute.org/sites/default/files/RAYMOND%20China%20Infrastructure%20Sphere%20of%20Influence%20COMPLETE%20PDF.pdf

Risse-Kappen, T. (Ed.). (1999). *Non-state actors, domestic structures and international institutions.* Cambridge University Press.

Ritzer, G. (2003). Rethinking globalization; Glocalization/grobaliation and something/nothing. *Sociological Theory, 21*(3), 193–209.

Ritzer, G. (2007). *The globalization of nothing 2.* Pine Forge Press.

Robertson, R. (1992). *Globalization: Social theory and global culture.* Sage.

Robertson, R. (1994). Globalization or glocalization? *The Journal of International Communication, 1*(1), 33–52.

Shambaugh, D. (2013). *China goes global: The partial power.* Oxford University Press.

Soulé-Kohndou, F. (2019). Bureaucratic agency and power asymmetry in Benin-China relations. In C. Alden & L. Daniel (Eds.), *New directions in Africa-China studies* (pp. 189–204). Routledge.

Summers, T. (2020). Structural power and the financing of the Belt and Road Initiative. *Eurasian Geography and Economics, 61*(2), 146–151.

Yilmaz, S., & Li, B. (2020). The BRI-led globalization and its implications for East Asian regionalization. *Chinese Political Science Review, 5*, 395–416.

Yu, H. (2017). Motivation behind China's 'One Belt, One Road' Initiatives and establishment of the Asian Infrastructure Investment Bank. *Journal of Contemporary China, 26*(105), 353–368.

Zajontz, T. (2020a). The Chinese infrastructural fix in Africa: A critical appraisal of the Sino-Zambian Road Bonanza. *Oxford Development Studies, 50*, 14–29.

Zajontz, T. (2020b). *The Chinese infrastructural fix in Africa: A Strategic-relational analysis of Zambia's 'Road Bonanza' and the rehabilitation of TAZARA* (PhD thesis). University of St. Andrews.

Zhang, Z. (2018). The Belt and Road Initiative: China's new geopolitical strategy. *China Quarterly of International Strategic Studies, 4*(3), 327–343.

Chapter 9
The Chinese Agenda on the World Economic Forum: Assessing Political Evidence Between Rhetoric and Practice

Jorge Tavares da Silva ⓘ and Rui P. Pereira

1 Introduction

Xi Jinping's era in the People's Republic of China (PRC) has taken an increasingly internationalist stance, engaging in dominant global issues, and by participating in large intergovernmental organizations. There is a new internationalist projection, which took shape since the process of reform and opening up initiated in 1978 (da Silva, 2021, pp. 265–283). Since the founding of the PRC until the end of the 1970s, Beijing had a marginal participation in large international organizations, mainly due to the lack of political recognition by the US and its allies. From the 1970s onwards, Beijing began to participate more in international affairs, outside the Soviet sphere, albeit cautiously, and continued to express many reservations about an international system of a liberal order dominated by Washington (the so-called "Washington Consensus"). To be sure, the Chinese economic (re)emergence brought with it a progressive participation in the post-Cold War system and in global issues, causing one of the most significant changes in international relations since the beginning of the new century (Lanteign, 2020, p. 1). In the past, the Chinese view on the functioning of the international system was influenced by the Marxist and Leninist tradition, understanding it as being modelled according to the interests of capitalism. The functioning of international organizations (IO) was interpreted sceptically, as being conditioned by the advantages of the more developed countries in facilitating their range of interests. They saw the powerful elite as someone that took advantage from the weakest states. It was from this base theory that the structuralists of international relations would flourish, conceiving the world in an imagined divide

---

J. T. da Silva (✉)
Department of Social, Political and Territorial Sciences (DCSPT), University of Aveiro, Aveiro, Portugal

Faculty of Letters, University of Coimbra, Coimbra, Portugal

R. P. Pereira
Directorate-General for Economic Activities—Ministry of Economy, Lisbon, Portugal

© The Author(s), under exclusive license to Springer Nature Singapore Pte Ltd. 2023
P. A. B. Duarte et al. (eds.), *The Palgrave Handbook of Globalization with Chinese Characteristics*, https://doi.org/10.1007/978-981-19-6700-9_9

between a dominating centre and a dominated periphery, translated into development and underdevelopment (Galtung, 1971, pp. 81–117). China participates in one of the most emblematic international initiatives, the World Economic Forum, commonly known as the Davos Forum. This chapter aims to provide a careful analysis of the participation of China in this informal gathering, the outlined objectives, and the great political messages emanating from the initiative. The main objective is to identify the discrepancies between what Beijing stands for and what happens in reality. In other words, we formulate the following question: what are the differences between the rhetoric and effective results in Xi Jinping's words at the Davos Forum? The focus of our analysis is the participation of the Chinese President on two occasions, 2017 and 2021.

In this chapter, the authors based their research on some primary sources, namely original documents such as speeches, manuscripts, interviews, and secondary sources, namely books, chapters of books, and journals. The chapter begins with an analysis of China's integration process in the international economy, linked to its growing participation in large international organizations. We then focus our approach on Beijing's participation in the World Economic Forum. Finally, we analyse the differences between the rhetoric and the practice disseminated by China in Davos Forum. We expect to conclude that, behind China's strategy as a defender of economic globalization, harmonious development, and non-confrontation, there might be a quest for a different model of economic governance with Chinese characteristics. We expect to conclude that Davos is more a channel of soft power rather than a forum for the effective definition and presentation of policy guidelines.

2 China's Participation in the International Economic Architecture

Since the beginning of the 1970s, the PRC has increased its participation in international affairs and organizations, after freeing itself from the Soviet sphere. Beijing tried to establish its legitimacy in intergovernmental organizations, after many decades without international recognition in the United Nations (Kent, 2015, pp. 139–161). The reform and opening up programme led by Deng Xiaoping, brought about a greater involvement of China in international affairs. Beijing initiated a process of adaptation to the international norms, principles, and rules. China achieved in thirty years what it took the industrialized powers 200 years to accomplish (Cunha, 2012, p. 48). In a first moment, China adopted a "role of learner in multilateral institutions" (Kent, 2015, pp. 139–161), but gradually changed its performance. There continued to be many reservations about an international system of a liberal order dominated by Washington. To be sure, there is no time in China's history where such participation has been so active in international affairs as in the era of Xi Jinping. From an economic and political point of view, we can say that China is a re-emerging country, but from the point of view of involvement in global affairs it is a novelty as in most of its millenary history it has never gone beyond the regional dimension (da Silva, 2021, pp. 265–283). As noted by Wang Yi, the Chinese foreign minister:

> Socialism with Chinese characteristics has entered a new era with its head held high, and the Chinese nation that has had a long-suffering, now takes a big leap to stand up, get richer and get stronger. Today China is close to fulfilling the dream of the great rejuvenation of the Chinese nation like never before, and approaching the centre of the world stage like never before. (Government of the PRC, 2020)

Within the scope of the United Nations (UN), for example, the Asian giant has exerted a strong influence so that the concept of "human rights" can be changed, reducing the importance of the political, civil, and cultural dimensions of minorities (Cole, 2020, p. 35). The Chinese status as a permanent member of the Security Council of the UN facilitates this role, although it counts on strong resistance from other players, particularly from the US. The greater Chinese involvement within the UN corresponds to a change in its conception of cooperation in the field of security, with the introduction of a new internationalist vision. China continues to stress that, at the regional level, strategic cooperation between partners must be established in the form of security communities, as opposed to the system of alliances that is followed in the North Atlantic Treaty Organization (NATO) (Lanteign, 2020, p. 134).

China's participation in the United Nations system, after joining the organization, in the early 1970s, within the framework of the Cold War, began to be very modest. Since 1981, however, it has given rise to a plan to finance UN peace operations, albeit without sending in any military forces. Increasing socialization and interaction with the international community were driving factors for the new stance, including Beijing's greater acceptance of international norms. Among the five members of the UN Security Council, China is the country with the largest peacekeeping operations in international theatres. Other important dynamics are humanitarian actions, cooperating with organizations such as the Association of South East Asian Nations (ASEAN), including support in the context of natural disasters. China established strong ties with this organization, in a way that it was able to control its agenda, as well as it is capable to change UN resolutions and processes according to its own interests (Kent, 2015, p. 140). The free trade agreement between China and ASEAN came about as a result of China's increasing regional influence and power (Cunha, 2012, p. 229).

China's ability to influence large international organizations is an indisputable fact in Xi Jinping's governance. More than disputing the previously established international order, Beijing seeks to participate in the established institutional architecture. For example, the UN has suffered a progressive attempt of *sinification*, including the introduction of concepts and ideas stemming from Xi Jinping's slogans, namely "win–win co-operation," "creating a community with a future for humanity," and the institutional promotion of its Belt and Road Initiative (BRI) (*The Economist*, 2019, pp. 41–42). "Common development," "common sharing," and "common prosperity" are intended to represent the virtues of the socialist system and the Party's orientations. According to the Chinese government, capitalism gives people wealth, but it does not give them prosperity and common prosperity like socialism. The UN's dependence on Chinese financial resources lends greater servility to the wishes of Beijing, which uses the tactic of economic and financial retaliation as a weapon (Angang Hu et al., 2018, pp. 98–100).

Currently, China has permanent diplomatic relations with 175 countries, it is a member of more than 150 international organizations and has signed around three hundred multilateral treaties (Shambaugh, 2013, p. 45). It is important to mention that, after the Tiananmen Crisis in 1989, China suffered marginalization from dominant powers of the international system. Even so, this involvement has particular contours, as China is also active in proposing new international and regional institutions, as if attempting to create, in parallel, an alternative international order (da Silva, 2021, pp. 265–283). These include the Asian Infrastructure Investment Bank (AIIB), the New Development Bank (NDB), located in Shanghai, also known as the "BRICS Development Bank," the Shanghai Cooperation Organisation (SCO), among others. These institutions are potentially challenging to institutions such as the World Bank, IMF, and the Asian Development Bank (ADB). China's will to reform the international financial system is implicit, gaining influence over traditional structures (Kent, 2015, p. 147). Xi Jinping's leadership has been reinforcing the country's involvement in the international stage, closely linked to domestic galvanization. The "New Helmsman" propagates the idea of the greatness of the nation—"Greater China"—promoting transnational projects, actively participating in international organizations, investing, buying, and selling in all corners of the globe. China's global projection now appears at the centre of a new world order, designed until 2049—the commemoration of the first centenary of the PRC. At this point, China must be "a modern, prosperous, strong, democratic, culturally advanced and harmonious socialist country" (Gaspar, 2020, pp. 44–45).

In this case, it fits on what is described in the literature as a "grand strategy" (*da zhanlue*). This concept arises on the initiative of Liddell Hart (1935), referred to as the highest conception of strategy, which requires the coordination and control of all the resources of a nation, with a view to achieving political objectives (Hart, 1991). One of the characteristics of China in the Xi Jinping era is the strategic shift in creating economic corridors for goods flows, strengthening connectivity with peripheral countries, developing infrastructure construction projects, and acquiring multinational companies. Among all these dynamics, the Silk Road Economic Belt together with the 21st Maritime Silk Road, sometimes referred to as the "Belt and Road Initiative" (BRI), is the most ambitious. President Xi Jinping announced this initiative in Astana, the capital of Kazakhstan, on 7 September 2013 (Xi Jinping, 2018). The project not only offers a physical manifestation of Chinese centrality through three overland and three maritime corridors that will connect China to Asia, Europe, the Middle East and Africa, but also evokes historical memories of the Silk Road and of Chinese centrality during imperial times. In the same year, Chinese President Xi made known two separate initiatives, the 21st Maritime Silk Road Initiative (MSRI) and the Silk Road Economic Belt (SREB) plan, both integrated in BRI (Blanchard, 2018, p. 1). In its original conception, the BRI was a vehicle for Chinese-led hard infrastructure development along the six corridors. Today, BRI offshoots include the so-called digital, health, and polar Silk Roads, and all countries are welcome to participate (Economy, 2022). China's strategy for technological affirmation begins in its national territory and spreads along the BRI tracks. In 2017, Xi Jinping announced the PCC's strategic vision plan, designed until 2035, to achieve leadership in the generation of mobile networks and 5G broadband; artificial intelligence; robotics; genomics; cybernetics; electronic circuits; industrial systems; green technology; facial recognition and virtual currency payment system (digital economy) (da Silva, 2021, pp. 215–216). It is "the Digital Silk Road" project, in which Beijing is gaining strategic advances in technological areas. It includes "wireless networks, surveillance cameras, subsea cables, and satellites," "from the ocean floor to outer space, and they enable AI, big data applications, and other strategic technologies" (Hillman, 2021). The new Chinese internationalist strength is built on all these dimensions, in part by the affirmation of its new technological, financial and military capacity. Among many institutions in which China is actively participating are those organized by the elite of the market economy and high finance. China uses the international arena to promote a better image, and we will refer to it specifically as regards the World Economic Forum.

3 The World Economic Forum: Origins and Evolution

The World Economic Forum (WEF) was established in 1971, as a non-profit foundation, and is headquartered in Geneva, Switzerland. It began with the idea of a German Professor of Economy, Klaus Schwab, the "multistakeholder theory," meaning that a company should serve all its stakeholders, not just its shareholders: employees, suppliers, and the community it is part to (Schwab, 2020). The vision for this "socially responsible stakeholder capitalism" became the guiding principle of the WEF (Hanley & Reyes, 2020). Davos was chosen as the home for the annual meeting for the escape from the everyday that the mountains represent in Swiss and German culture. The "spirit of Davos" is an attitude of openness and cooperation that sets the tone for the annual meeting until today.

Over the last 50 years, Davos has reflected on the key events of world history, from the fall of the Berlin Wall to the rise of economic globalization and runaway climate change. As stated in its mission, the WEF is independent, impartial, and not tied to any special interests. The Forum strives in all its efforts to demonstrate entrepreneurship in the global public interest while upholding the highest standards of governance. Moral and intellectual integrity is at the heart of everything it does (WEF, 2021). Among other milestones, the WEF has helped avert a war between Greece and Turkey, built economic bridges around the world, hosted a handshake that sealed the end of apartheid, launched an alliance that has vaccinated 700 million children, and has given a platform to leading environmentalists (Hanley & Reyes, 2020).

While working towards the Forum's mission statement of improving the state of the world, Davos has also played down criticism along the way: as a gathering of distant elites, or a futile talking shop. But its aim is to gather all those who have a stake in our common future: the leaders of global corporations are invited, but so too are academics, activists, youth, and civil society leaders (Hanley & Reyes, 2020). Traditionally, the Davos gathering takes place every year in January, but the 2022 edition, initially foreseen to be held on its traditional format between 17 and 21 January, was postponed, due to the new COVID-19 variant, Omicron. As an alternative, participants will have access to online sessions on the general theme "State of the World" (Oliveira, 2021).

4 China in the World Economic Forum: From 1979 to Early 2022

In 1979, the WEF opened the door to the People's Republic of China, when a delegation led by Qian Junrui, Director of the Institute of World Economics and Politics of the Chinese Academy of Social Sciences, participated in the Davos Symposium for the first time. Later that year, Professor Schwab paid his first visit to China, leading a Forum delegation of 20 European CEOs. The two sides signed a memorandum of understanding in Beijing and, from then on, China has never been absent from the Davos meetings. (*Global Times*, 2021).

Officially the Annual Meeting of the New Champions, more commonly known as the "Boao Forum," hosts annual meetings in the cities of Dalian and Tianjin (alternatingly every year), and it is regularly attended by the Chinese Premier (Yang, 2020). In January 2017, in the first ever appearance of a Chinese head of state at the World Economic Forum, President Xi Jinping attended the Opening Session of its Annual Meeting and delivered a keynote speech entitled "Jointly Shoulder Responsibility of Our Times, Promote Global Growth" (Xinhua, 2017). Coincidently or not, Xi's intervention at the World Economic Forum was made in the context of a newly appointed Trump administration. Following the tensions and trade war with the US, Xi has positioned China as the defender of globalization, multilateralism, sustainable and equal economic development, and growth. The key point in his speech has been to highlight the benefits of integration into the global economy, but without ignoring its problems and the doubts about globalization that China used to hold. More recently, in 2021, at a virtual Davos forum, the Chinese President has made a special address. He warned against starting a "new Cold War" and urged global unity in the face of common challenges brought by the coronavirus pandemic (Rodrigues, 2021; Xinhua, 2021a):

> Building small circles or starting a new Cold War, rejecting, threatening or intimidating others, deliberately imposing disassociation, disruption of supplies or sanctions and creating isolation or alienation, will only lead the world to division and even confrontation.

Xi's participation in the 2021 edition can also be seen as a veiled confrontation of the newly US President-elect (Joe Biden), in particular considering the US plans to revitalize global alliances to counter China's growing influence, and its criticism of

China's policy on human rights, economic and trade protectionism and the aggressive promotion of Chinese state companies as "global champions" (Öterbülbül, 2021). The Chinese president called for stronger global governance via multilateral organizations, the removal of barriers to international trade, investment, and technological exchanges, as well as stronger representation on the world stage for developing countries. From this point of view, China continues to position itself as the "champion of the weak" to preserve international law and rules, openness and multilateralism instead of supremacy ("the strong should not bully the weak") (Öterbülbül, 2021; Xinhua, 2021a). Although the 2022 edition of the WEF has been postponed until May, it was decided to hold the online Davos Agenda, which brought together leaders from governments, business, civil society, and science from around the world—and beyond—to discuss how the world will look post-COVID (WEF, 2022).

Perhaps not surprisingly, Xi Jinping has not missed the opportunity to convey, once again, China's main messages to the world, through a Special Address made in the first day (17 January). Among those, some stand out, namely: (i) to embrace cooperation and jointly defeat the pandemic; (ii) to resolve various risks and promote steady recovery of the world economy; (iii) to bridge the development divide and revitalize global development; (iv) to discard Cold War mentality and seek peaceful coexistence and win–win outcomes. Additionally, President Xi promised that: (i) China will stay committed to pursuing high-quality development; (ii) China will stay committed to reform and opening up; (iii) China will stay committed to promoting ecological conservation (Xinhua, 2022). The 2022 speech is not much different from the previous ones and reiterates the main ideas already transmitted in 2021.

In our view, the encouragement of an alternative economic and political development path is underlined, as distinct from the Western world. And it raises the question of whether China is, in fact, promoting an alternative vision for a global governance order with Chinese characteristics. Since the early days of the People's Republic of China, Beijing has sought to portray itself as a leader of the developing world and a proponent of Non-Aligned Movement principles of non-interference and anti-imperialism. In more recent years, Chinese leaders have begun to insist that they practise a "new type of international relations," eschewing traditional power politics in favour of "win-win co-operation" (Kim, 2021). The "developing country" label is also meant to signal Beijing's geopolitical alignment: even if China catches up with the West economically, the thinking goes, its loyalties will still lie firmly with the developing world—it will, as Chinese President Xi Jinping put it in a 2018 speech, "forever belong to the family of developing countries" (Ministry of Foreign Affairs of the PRC, 2018; Yan, 2021).

There is no consensus on this issue. According to Elizabeth Economy, director for Asia Studies at the US Council on Foreign Relations, many observers continue to question whether Beijing wants to shape a new international order or merely force some adjustments to the current one, advancing discrete interests and preferences without fundamentally transforming the global system (Economy, 2022). However, in Elizabeth Economy's view, Xi's vision signifies something more than ensuring that the relative weight of the country's voice or influence within the existing international system is adequately represented. It connotes a radically transformed international order, a unified and resurgent China on par with or surpassing the US. In other words, a China-centric order with its own norms and values (Economy, 2022).

The Biden administration's forays into exclusive multilateralism—that is, its attempts to form issue-based coalitions in opposition to China on technology and human rights—are bound to be a particular source of tension in the years ahead. Beijing views this as the most serious external threat to its political security and the biggest obstacle to its national rejuvenation (Yan, 2021). However, China is expected to continue to be a driver of global growth and trade, and to engage with the international economy through exports, its critical supply chains, and limited imports of capital and expertise (Economy, 2022). However, it is also increasingly clear that policies such as Made in China 2025, by enhancing government control and favouring Chinese companies over external competition, envision a largely self-sufficient China that could innovate, manufacture, and consume all within its own economy (Economy, 2022; Yan, 2021).

5 Dissonance Between Rhetoric and Practice in China's Proclaimed Ideas in Davos

Xi Jinping's statements at the Davos Forum in 2017 were widely disseminated around the world, and the Chinese leader has come to be seen as a defender of economic globalization:

> It is true that economic globalisation has created new problems. But this is no justification to write off economic globalisation altogether. Rather we should adapt to and guide globalisation, cushion its negative impact, and deliver its benefits to all countries and all nations. (The State Council Information Office, 2017)

The Chinese president supports multilateral dynamics, multilateralism and liberal economic order, free trade and investment, and international rules. This posture projects a positive image in the international public opinion that would be translated by the idea of soft power strategy. In fact, a good image usually generates trust and open windows of opportunity to cooperation between players. On the contrary, negative images provoke negative reactions and create unstable atmospheres. Beijing defends the UN system for the resolution of international conflicts, condemning openly unilateralism. In many ways, it condemned American foreign policy of interfering in the internal affairs of other states (Xinhua, 2021b).

Davos' communications demonstrate an intention of the Chinese government to promote its national image in the world and to foster diplomatic opportunities. Xi Jinping's rise to centre stage at Davos had the intention to promote China's political model, the values of socialism, and the results of its economy. China was the second biggest economy in the world in 2020, the world's number one exporter and second-largest importer of goods (Statista, 2022). Like similar meetings, this serves as a platform to convey information, shape images, and create influence in the world (Xu & Ren, 2018, pp. 398–406). The economic indicators are the main argument to its rhetoric, the superiority of its economic and political model, while the US and other democratic liberal countries are frequently under political instability. China also uses the Davos Forum to promote its vision as a green country, in Xi's words: "it is a responsibility we must assume for future generations" (CGTN, 2017). Considered a much-polluted country in Copenhagen 2009, China has become a climate diplomacy since President Trump withdrew from Paris agreement (Meidan, 2020, p. 80). However, China's president asseverations and political ideas are full of contradictions. First, in spite of Beijing's support for the advantages of free trade, in reality it is a very protectionist state. Although it is overall more open since its accession to the World Trade Organization (WTO) in 2001, China maintains many barriers to trade of goods and the free flow of capital and information (including digital content) with the rest of the World. In fact, one of the most distinctive elements of Xi's rule has been his creation of a wall of regulations designed to control the flow of ideas, culture, and even capital between China and the rest of the world (Economy, 2018). It imposes "more trade and investment barriers, discriminatory taxes, and information security restrictions than any other country by a vast margin" (Ferracane & Lee-Makiyama, 2017, p. 2). The European Commission reported in 2019 that China was the country with the highest stock of recorded barriers, with 38 obstacles hindering EU export and investment opportunities (European Commission, 2019). In relation to the environment worries, it is important to mention that China is the world's biggest public financier of coal and one of the biggest polluters. The country shows a "voracious appetite for fossil fuels," from 400 million tonnes in 1978, to 3.27 billion in 2018 (Meidan, 2020). It has struggled against the idea that it should be subject to the same constraints as rich countries that started the process of global warming at a much earlier stage. By defending its legitimacy for polluting, as it is at a late stage of development, China adds that a substantial part of its industry is destined for exports to the West (Jacques, 2009, p. 171).

In terms of its participation in the international system, China follows a kind of dual strategy. On the one hand, it strongly participates in the international architecture, but on the other hand, it creates alternative organizations. China participates in the UN system and its international agencies, but at the same time it seems that it is creating alternatives for those institutions. China takes part in organizations such as the World Bank and the IMF, but, at the same time, it creates its own development banks. This is partially justified by the aftershocks of the Asian crisis of 1997, and then the crisis of 2008. After this latest financial shock, China and the US changed substantially their relationship. Martin Jacques (2012, pp. 23–27), considered that "In a few months, the crisis served to undermine a near-universal assumption of American, and western, economic competence; in contrast, China's economic credentials have been considerably burnished."

The search for solutions for financial instability has led Beijing to find regional institutional solutions, considered by the same author as "the beginning of a new world order" (Jacques, 2012, pp. 23–27). China remains as a one-party political system with economic freedom granted in some domains, although state backing is strong in some strategic sectors. Supported by the State, companies like Huawei and ZTE Communications gain global market share from more innovative international competitors, damaging the free-market system according to the WTO principles (Atkinson, 2020). China supports a kind of "globalisation with Chinese characteristics," in which it lacks a globally competitive telecom equipment industry. A substantial part of the economic activity in China operates on the free market, according to so-called capitalist rules, but strategic sectors are subjugated to the interests of the State. The country has never had a capitalist economy, but a mixed economy instead, divided simultaneously between the market and central direction model, in the expression that Paul Samuelson and William Nordhaus defined as "Market Leninism" (1999, pp. 549–550). It is ironic that one of the loudest voices in Davos is a country that is a version of economy in state capitalism. In many ways, China develops mercantilist practices, prohibiting foreign investment and exporting in large numbers to international markets.

6 Conclusion

Ever since its creation in 1971, the WEF has been effective on its mission to discuss the themes that matter, on an independent and impartial manner, between global leaders from governments, entrepreneurs, academics, and other civil society sectors. However, according to its critics, the Davos Forum cannot avoid the perception of being a gathering of distant elites, or a futile talking shop. Certainly, one of Davos recent milestones was the participation of the President of the People's Republic of China, Xi Jinping, in the 2017 edition, followed by a second participation in the virtual 2021 edition. Nevertheless, let us not be naïve. Xi Jinping's participation at the Davos gathering, namely its advocacy of the virtues of economic globalization and multilateral governance, was, in its essence, a well-orchestrated public image operation. Xi Jinping's communications at the Davos Forum are especially an instrument of soft power, trying to show China as a responsible, environment-friendly country, an ideal location for the international globalization process and free trade dynamics. Furthermore, he intends to disseminate the success of its economic model, socialist values, when the country is one of the richest in the world, a superpower in international trade and technologically advanced, that has managed to lift millions of people out of extreme poverty. As Davos is perceived as being one of the main stages in the world for promoting the market economy, China has taken the opportunity to promote its values. However, from our point of view, there are many discrepancies between the political rhetoric and the reality of facts. Despite being regarded by a certain international public opinion as the defender of globalization, China is a country that is closed to many technological and communicational initiatives; it has high customs tariffs and practises strong economic centralism.

Additionally, Xi Jinping has not missed the opportunity to position the country itself, once again, as the "champion of the week," underlining the encouragement of the creation of an alternative economic and political development path, and a global governance order with Chinese characteristics. The coming years will help to understand whether Xi Jinping will continue to pursue a dual engagement strategy, or to follow a more aggressive posture towards a China-centric international order, with its own norms and values. In this regard, it would be important to continue to follow-up on China's highest-level participation at the World Economy Forum, as Xi Jinping has already understood its far-reaching impact and is expected to continue to use it to make his voice heard.

Bibliographic References

Angang Hu, et al. (2018). *Xi Jinpings new development philosophy* (pp. 98–100). Springer.
Atkinson, R. D. (2020). *How China's mercantilist policies have undermined global innovation in the telecom equipment industry*. ITIF—Information Technology & Innovation Foundation. Retrieved on 27 December 2021, from https://itif.org/sites/default/files/2020-china-mercantilist-telecom-equipment-industry.pdf
Blanchard, J. F. (Ed.). (2018). *China's Maritime Silk Road Initiative and South Asia—A political economic analysis of its purposes, perils, and promise*. Palgrave.
CGTN. (2017). *Full Text of Xi Jinping keynote at the World Economic Forum*. Retrieved on 14 January 2022, from https://america.cgtn.com/2017/01/17/full-text-of-xi-jinping-keynote-at-the-world-economic-forum
Clifford, P. G. (2022). *The China paradox—At the front line of economic transformation*. Walter de Gruyter.
Cole, M. J. (2020). China's strategy in the Xi era and threat to the global order. In S. Blank et al. (Eds.), *Know thy enemy*. Macdonald-Laurier Institute.
Council on Foreign Relations (CFR). (2021). *China's approach to global governance*. Retrieved on 27 December 2021, from https://www.cfr.org/china-global-governance/
Cunha, L. (2012). *A Hora do Dragão—Política Externa da China*. Zebra Publicações.
da Silva, J. T. (2021). *Xi Jinping—A Ascensão do Novo Timoneiro da China: O Homem, a Política e o Mundo* [in Portuguese]. Sílabas & Desafios.
Economy, E. C. (2018, May/June). China's new revolution: The reign of Xi Jinping. *Foreign Affairs*. Retrieved on 12 January 2022, from https://www.foreignaffairs.com/articles/china/2018-04-17/chinas-new-revolution
Economy, E. C. (2021, May 28). China's inconvenient truth. *Foreign Affairs*. Retrieved on 11 December 2021, from https://www.foreignaffairs.com/chapters/china/2021-05-28/chinas-inconvenient-truth
Economy, E. C. (2022, January–February). Can China remake the international system? *Foreign Affairs*. Retrieved on 18 December 2021, from https://www.foreignaffairs.com/chapters/china/2021-12-09/xi-jinpings-new-world-order
European Commission. (2019). *Report from Commission to the Parliament and the Council on Trade and Investment Barriers*. Retrieved on 23 December 2021, from https://trade.ec.europa.eu/doclib/docs/2020/june/tradoc_158789.pdf
Ferracane, M. F., & Lee-Makiyama, H. (2017, June 27). *China's technology protectionism and its non-negotiable rationales* (pp. 1–22). European Centre for International Political Economy (ECIPE).
Galtung, J. (1971). A structural theory of imperialism. *Journal of Peace Research, 8*(2), 81–117.
Gaspar, C. (2020). *O Mundo de Amanhã—Geopolítica Contemporânea*. Fundação Francisco Manuel dos Santos.
Global Times. (2021, August 4). Bring the World Economic Forum to China—Klaus Schwab on China's development. Retrieved on 17 December 2021, from https://www.globaltimes.cn/page/202108/1230523.shtml

Government of the PRC. 2020. 王毅: 深入学习贯彻习近平外交思想 不断开创中国特色大 [Wang Yi: In-depth study and implementation of Xi Jinping's diplomatic thoughts]. Retrieved on 24 December 2021, from http://www.gov.cn/guowuyuan/2020-08/01/content_5531832.htm

Hanley, M., & Reyes, A. (2020). *The World Economic Forum at 50: A timeline of highlights from Davos and beyond*. Retrieved on 19 December 2021, from https://www.weforum.org/agenda/2019/12/world-economic-forum-davos-at-50-history-a-timeline-of-highlights/

Hart, L. (1991). *Strategy*. Meridian.

Hillman, J. E. (2021, October). *Mapping China's Digital Silk Road*. Reconnecting Asia. Retrieved on 14 January 2022, from https://reconasia.csis.org/mapping-chinas-digital-silk-road/

Kent, A. (2015). China's changing influence on the multilateral system: From adaptation to assertion. In J. H. Chung (Ed.), *Assessing China's power* (pp. 137–161). Palgrave Macmillan.

Kim, P. (2021, November 15). China's search for allies. *Foreign Affairs*. Retrieved on 11 December 2021, from https://www.foreignaffairs.com/articles/china/2021-11-15/chinas-search-allies

Jacques, M. (2009). *When China rules the world—The rise of the Middle Kingdom and the end of the Western World*. Allen Lane.

Jacques, M. (2012, April 23). The beginning of a new world order. *New Statesman*, pp. 23–27.

Lanteign, M. (2020). *Chinese foreign policy—An introduction*. Routledge.

Lee, C. S. (2018). *Soft power made in China—The dilemmas of online and offline media and transnational audiences*. Palgrave Macmillan.

Meidan, M. (2020). China: Climate leader and villain. In M. Hafner & S. Tagliapietra (Eds.), *The geopolitics of the global energy transition* (pp. 75–90). Springer.

Ministry of Foreign Affairs of the People's Republic of China. (2018, July 26). *Xi Jinping speech Ministry of Foreign Affairs—"Turn Our Vision into a Reality"*. Retrieved on 11 January 2022, from https://www.fmprc.gov.cn/mfa_eng/wjb_663304/zzjg_663340/fzs_663828/gjlb_663832/3094_664214/3096_664218/201807/t20180727_547056.html

Nye, J. S. (2004). *Soft power—The means to success in world politics*. Public Affairs.

Oliveira, A. B. (2021, December 20). Fórum Económico Mundial adia o encontro em Davos para o verão com Ómicron a assustar. *Expresso*. Retrieved on 27 December 2021, from https://expresso.pt/economia/2021-12-20-Forum-Economico-Mundial-adia-o-encontro-em-Davos-para-o-verao-com-Omicron-a-assustar-eac3461c

Öterbülbül, S. (2021, February 20). *Rebranding China's global role: Xi Jinping at the World Economic Forum*. E-International Relations. Retrieved on 19 November 2021, from https://www.e-ir.info/2021/02/20/rebranding-chinas-global-role-xi-jinping-at-the-world-economic-forum/

Peyrefitte, A. (1976). *Quand la Chine S'Éveillera…le Monde Tremblera* [Portuguese Edition]. Parceria.

Rodrigues, J. N. (2021, January 25). Xi Jinping em Davos: "nova Guerra Fria só vai levar o mundo até ao confronto". *Expresso*. Retrieved on 19 November 2021, from https://expresso.pt/economia/2021-01-25-Xi-Jinping-em-Davos-nova-Guerra-Fria-so-vai-levar-o-mundo-ate-ao-confronto

Samuelson, P. A., & Nordhaus, W. D. (1999). *Economia*. McGraw-Hill.

Schwab, K. (2020, January 16). Capitalism must reform to survive. *Foreign Affairs*. Retrieved on 19 November 2021, from https://www.foreignaffairs.com/articles/2020-01-16/capitalism-must-reform-survive

Shambaugh, D. (2013). *China goes global: The partial power*. Oxford: Oxford University Press.

Statista. (2022). *China's share of global gross domestic product (GDP) adjusted for purchasing-power-parity (PPP) from 2010 to 2020 with forecasts until 2026*. Retrieved on 14 January 2022, from https://www.statista.com/statistics/270439/chinas-share-of-global-gross-domestic-product-gdp/

The Economist. (2019, December 7). China and United States: A new battleground, pp. 41–42.

The State Council Information Office. (2017). *Xi Jinping's keynote speech at the World Economic Forum*. Retrieved on 24 December 2021, from http://www.china.org.cn/node_7247529/content_40569136.htm

WEF—World Economic Forum. (2020a). *The World Economic Forum—A partner in shaping history, 1971–2020*. Retrieved on 27 December 2021, from https://www3.weforum.org/docs/WEF_A_Partner_in_Shaping_History.pdf

WEF—World Economic Forum. (2020b). *The World Economic Forum at 50: A timeline of highlights from Davos and beyond*. Retrieved on 19 December 2021, from https://www.weforum.org/agenda/2019/12/world-economic-forum-davos-at-50-history-a-timeline-of-highlights/

WEF—World Economic Forum. (2021). Retrieved on 27 December 2021, from https://www.weforum.org/about/world-economic-forum

WEF—World Economic Forum. (2022). Retrieved on 3 January 2022, from https://www.weforum.org/agenda/2022/01/the-davos-agenda-2022-addressing-the-state-of-the-world/

Xi Jinping. (2018). *A Governação da China—I* [in Portuguese]. Editora de Línguas Estrangeiras.

Xinhua. (2017, January 18). *Jointly shoulder responsibility of our times, promote global growth*. Retrieved on 7 January 2022, from http://www.xinhuanet.com/english/2017-01/18/c_135991184.htm

Xinhua. (2021a, January 28). *Special address by Chinese President Xi Jinping at the World Economic Forum virtual event of the Davos agenda*. Retrieved on 7 January 2022, from http://www.xinhuanet.com/english/2021-01/25/c_139696610.htm

Xinhua. (2021b). China firmly opposes U.S. interference in internal affairs under pretext of Xinjiang-related issues: Spokesperson. *China Today*. Retrieved on 14 January 2022, from http://www.chinatoday.com.cn/ctenglish/2018/zdtj/202112/t20211216_800270190.html

Xinhua. (2022, January 17). *Special address by Chinese President Xi Jinping at the World Economic Forum virtual event of the Davos agenda*. Retrieved on 25 January 2022, from http://www.xinhuanet.com/english/20220117/d3c169b45b304f6f9176969a45480784/c.html

Xu, G., & Ren, M. (2018). Comparing China's self-image and western media projected image: From the perspective of Davos forum. In *Proceedings of the 10th International Joint Conference on Knowledge Discovery, Knowledge Engineering and Knowledge Management* (IC3K 2018)—Volume 1: KDIR, pp. 398–406.

Yang, C. (2020, December 9). *WEF to host Summer Davos in Tianjin after delay*. Retrieved on 19 December 2021, from https://www.chinadaily.com.cn/a/202012/09/WS5fd0996fa31024ad0ba9adc7.html

Yan, X. (2021, July/August). Becoming strong: The new Chinese foreign policy. *Foreign Affairs*. Retrieved on 19 November 2021, from https://www.foreignaffairs.com/articles/united-states/2021-06-22/becoming-strong

Chapter 10
COVID-19 Pandemic, China, and Global Power Shifts: Understanding the Interplay and Implications

Jamie P. Halsall, Ian G. Cook, Michael Snowden, and Roopinder Oberoi

1 Introduction

China's Belt and Road Initiative (BRI) has fundamentally promoted infrastructure on land (i.e., Roads and Railways) and sea-based channels. There has been an enormous infrastructure programme driving up economic and social development, by developing and improving airports, communication technologies, electricity grids, railways, roads, and seaports. These global benefits, as Buckley (2020) notes in a recent article, have been questioned by the host countries who are involved with the BRI. From a global economic political perspective, the BRI idea is seen as a global economic connectivity project that embraces globalization and further enhances future prospects for the world as a whole. Schindler et al. have observed that "China's approach has proven attractive to many developing countries, which is evident from the number of countries that have agreed to participate in the Belt and Road Initiative" (2020, p. 4). Moreover, since the inception of the BRI strategy there has been much focus on who actually benefits and what happens in the future. Recent research by Wang (2020) demonstrates that most countries that are involved in the BRI scheme have felt a decrease in Chinese investments in the first part of 2020. The investments

J. P. Halsall (✉)
School of Human and Health Sciences, University of Huddersfield, Huddersfield, UK
e-mail: j.p.halsall@hud.ac.uk

I. G. Cook
School of Humanities and Social Science, Liverpool John Moores University, Liverpool, UK
e-mail: i.g.cook@ljmu.ac.uk

M. Snowden
University of Huddersfield, Huddersfield, UK
e-mail: m.a.snowden@hud.ac.uk

R. Oberoi
Department of Political Science, Kirori Mal College, University of Delhi, Delhi, India
e-mail: roberoi2019@gmail.com

by Chinese authorities have significantly changed, as "investments in the BRI were USD 23.4 billion in the first six months of 2020, dropping by about 50% from USD 46 billion invested during the first six months of 2019" (Wang, 2020, p. 4). This drop in investment is mainly due to the global health crisis.

The impact that COVID-19 has had on the BRI initiative is another dynamic that needs to be taken into consideration. Since the pandemic began, the global economy has been somewhat turbulent, which has had a negative impact on many economic projects across the world. According to the International Monetary Fund (IMF): "The global growth contraction for 2020 is estimated at -3.5 per cent, 0.9 percentage points higher than projected in the previous forecast" (2021). The BRI Survey of Central Banks 2021 discovered that the global pandemic has disturbed several BRI schemes, "with more than two-thirds of central banks saying it has had a negative impact on progress to some degree" (Jizhong et al., 2021). The fundamental reasons for this contraction in BRI project activities are threefold (Jizhong et al., 2021): (1) social distancing rules, (2) lockdown measures, and (3) local funding constraints.

The primary focus of this chapter is to critically examine how COVID-19 shifted economic activity away from the BRI. This chapter will firstly discuss the effects of the shifting global political order on the BRI and set the economic vision of the BRI idea that was first embraced by the Chinese government in 2013. Moving on from this, the authors will investigate the impact of COVID-19 on the BRI and the future implications of this mammoth economic infrastructure strategy.

This chapter takes an interdisciplinarity approach to the research, as the authors of this chapter come from different social science subject backgrounds, namely human geography, sociology, and politics. The authors use qualitative theorizing to blend their interdisciplinary approach, which the authors have used previously (Cook & Halsall, 2012; Cook et al., 2010, 2015; Halsall et al., 2022; Oberoi et al., 2019, 2020), and, as will be seen, the chapter has extensively engaged in peer-reviewed academic literature and documentary data sources such as social media sources and policy reports.

2 Shifting Sands of International Relations

It has been well documented that China is an economic superpower (Overholt, 1993; Schweinberger, 2014; Yueh, 2013). Since the opening up of China in the late 1970s, the country has transformed itself from a global perspective. Deng Xiaping, who introduced the "Open Door Policy," oversaw foreign business investment in the country, which set in motion China's economic modernization agenda. According to Huan (1986, p. 1), the new policy at the time changed China's economic development plan by moving away from a "self-sufficiency" strategy to "active participation" in the global world markets. From this fundamental change, China's foreign trade increased rapidly, which in turn allowed the country to be more actively involved with different international economic organizations (e.g., International Monetary Fund and the World Bank).

Historical evidence demonstrates that the open-door policy was a key turning point, as China's economic reforms have led to dramatic domestic changes. More importantly, the open-door policy has bolstered China's economy in the international market by introducing capital investment, foreign technology, and management skills (Huan, 1986). Another landmark moment was China joining the World Trade Organization (WTO) in November 2001, about which the former President of the US Bill Clinton said: "China is not simply agreeing to import more of our products, it is agreeing to import one of democracy's most cherished values, economic freedom" (in Davies, 2018). China is now the second-largest economy in the world and its economic growth has been insurmountable. For example, Lotta has pointed out that China's economic growth rate in gross domestic product (GDP) terms was "averaging close to 10% growth" while "imperialist countries' average annual growth rate was 2 to 4%" (2009, p. 30).

The dominance of China's economy can be seen clearly in the manufacturing sectors. Extensive research over the years by the economic geographer Peter Dicken (2007) observes that China is the largest producer in the clothes industry, while, in the automobile industry, China is the world's largest consumer market. For example, in the car industry, China has a number of state corporate groups and a number of factories across the country. The car manufacturer Volvo has factories in Chengdu and Daqing, whereas MG Motors has plants in Ningde, Shanghai, Nanjing, Zhengzhou, and Ford has a factory in Chongqing. The same can be said for the technology industry, as the Apple iPhone factory is based in the Chinese city of Zhengzhou. Hence, bringing these economic behaviours together, Graham et al. (2021, p. 72) conclude:

> The rise of China has been the defining feature of the twenty-first century global economy. In a globalizing marketplace, China's low-cost labor became a huge attractor of foreign direct investment. This advantage, combined with a growing domestic market, increasing technological know-how, and world-class infrastructure suitable for shipping goods anywhere in the world, made China 'the world's factory'.

The key question here is: how has China become a world leader in manufacturing and technology industries? The answer is in the way China as a country has developed a very clear strategic outlook on the way the economy will develop. Chen et al. (2020) have observed that there have been two clear strategies that have enhanced China's economic dominance: (1) the Belt and Road Initiative (BRI), and (2) Made in China 2025. Table 1 presents both visions of China delivering its economic dream.

This enhanced economic powerbase in China has caused some political frictions, with the most turbulent attitudes coming from the US. Before the election of Donald Trump, US politics was becoming increasingly concerned with China's economic dominance on the world stage (Haft, 2015). Recent predictions have suggested that China will become the largest economy by the next decade. For instance, the well-respected economist Raghuram G. Rajan has recently noted that China is "growing rapidly," stating "it is clear that the United States will not remain the largest economy in the world for much longer" (2019, p. 368). This proposed economic change has been picked up by Trump, and, when he was elected as President of the US, he went on a mission to rebalance the US' global economic advantage.

Table 1 The "Chinese Dream": two key economic activities

Vision The "Chinese Dream"	Explanation
Vision 1: *Made in China 2025*	"…specifies the goal of raising domestic sources of parts and materials to 40 percent by 2020 and 70 percent by 2025 (State Council, 2015). It reveals China's ambitions to reduce its reliance on foreign technology and make China a global powerhouse in high technology industries."
Vision 2: *Belt and Road Initiative*	"The 'Belt and Road Initiative' was introduced by Xi in 2013. It focuses on connecting China, Russia, Asia, Europe, the Middle East and Africa to further China's integration with the world, and attract investment and trade along these routes."

Source Adapted from Chen et al. (2020, p. 905)

The term used by the international press was "Trade War" with China (Zeng & Sparks, 2020). Trump's political vision was to encourage consumers to purchase American products—by making sure imported goods were more expensive to purchase. To achieve this, Trump set a new Tariff policy. It has been calculated: "The US has imposed tariffs on more than $360bn (£268bn) of Chinese goods, and China has retaliated with tariffs on more than $110bn of US products" (BBC, 2020a). A recent article by Liu and Wing (2018, p. 320) points out three fundamental reasons why the US initiated a trade war with China:

1. "The concern that China's chronically large trade surplus was depressing job creation in the US;
2. The concern that China was using illegal and unfair methods to acquire US technology at an effectively discounted price; and
3. The concern that China seeks to weaken US national security and its international standing."

Furthermore, from an economist's point of view, there has been general agreement that the Tariff arrangement between the US and China has caused a no-win situation for both parties, meaning that the economies of both the US and China have been substantially disadvantaged (Bown, 2021). For example, from an American perspective, the losers from the trade deal will be US farmers and manufacturers (BBC, 2020a), while China's losses pertain to the exporter tariffs (*The New York Times*, 2020). Therefore, in many ways, the Tariff agreement is an economic stalemate, as current political analysis suggests (Zaidi, 2021).

3 Belt and Road Initiative

As the authors have previously discussed (Halsall et al., 2022), China's Belt and Road Initiative (BRI) was launched in 2013 by President Xi Jinping as a substantial element in "China's Dream" that would aid the drive to become a developed country by 2049, one century after the founding of the People's Republic of China (PRC). BRI was to be the "project of the century," a contemporary rejuvenation of towns and cities on ancient Silk Roads across both land and sea; along what some have called "a string of pearls" emanating from China's heartland (Khan & Khalid, 2018). BRI is a global initiative, which fits neatly into China's global strategy (Clegg, 2009) that seeks to provide an alternative future to that which is dominated by Western capitalism. In large part, BRI is underpinned by the lessons learned via the extraordinary transformation of China into an urban industrial nation that is heading rapidly towards being the number one economy, supplanting the US in that position. Finance for infrastructure is a key component, leading to the inauguration of the Asian Infrastructure Investment Bank (AIIB) in 2016, with $100 billion in capital (Clark, 2017). Through such engagement, BRI promotes China's hard power via economic intervention in the economies of many countries, and its soft power via the perceived willingness to engage positively in the development trajectory of these countries, to help them out of the poverty trap. By the beginning of 2020, there were just short of 3,000 projects and signed agreements with a value of just under $4 trillion (Oxford Business Group, 2021). This was indeed incredible progress. But then, along came COVID-19. By June 2020, the Chinese Ministry of Foreign Affairs reported that 30–40% of BRI projects had been "affected by the virus" and another 20% had been "seriously affected" (ibid.). A global debt crisis developed, to which the PRC was not immune. This led to a considerable reduction in Chinese Foreign Direct Investment, as cost-cutting measures were introduced. Chinese workers working on BRI projects were repatriated, and construction supplies to such projects were reduced (ibid.). China tightened the purse strings, and this when combined with COVID-induced economic pressures led some countries to default on the loans that had been provided. Zambia became the first country to default, reaching an agreement in October 2020 to defer repayments to the China Development Bank (Dana, 2021). Djibouti soon followed, and by April 2021, the *Epoch Times* reported that the EU was refusing to pay off Montenegro's $1 billion loan from China. To respond to such issues, the PRC has encouraged private banks to replace lending via official policy banks, thus reducing State financial obligations. Garcia-Herrero (2021) reports that this substitution policy succeeded to the extent that total lending from Chinese banks actually increased by 21% in 2020, with outward investment to East Asia also increasing. However, investment in West Asia, the Middle East, and Africa declined in 2020, while that in the EU remained at the same level as previously. In sum, the Chinese bank sector is now greater than that of the EU, with assets of $45 trillion, but Garcia-Herrero suggests that the sector's "systemic risk" has increased, and Dana (2021, op. cit.) notes that Chinese banks are "over-extended" in their lending exposure.

The changes linked to COVID-19 have meant changes to BRI, about which it would seem Chinese leaders are quite sanguine because the last letter of the BRI acronym stands for "Initiative." Initiatives are not fixed, and have to respond to circumstances. In this case, BRI has become more focused on 3 sub-themes, namely support for initiatives linked to three Silk Road features: Green Silk Road, Health Silk Road, and Digital Silk Road. To this list, we can also add the Vaccine diplomacy.

Analysing these in turn, the Green Silk Road (GSR) is linked to the climate change announcements made by President Xi in September 2020, to the effect that China would limit peak emissions by 2030 and achieve carbon neutrality by 2060, although the Green Silk Road Fund was launched back in 2015. China's environmental expertise has been growing significantly in recent years as it seeks to respond to the environmental pressures that emanate from its huge scale of urbanization, forecast to reach up to 900 million people by 2050, from only 77 million urban population in 1953 (Cook, 2021). A National Model City for Environmental Protection scheme was introduced in 2008, eventually superseded by "eco-city" (*shengtai chengshi*) awards and other schemes in the 2010s. Often, international collaboration is a key element in such projects with experts from Singapore and Finland, for example, being involved in Tianjin Eco-City, the UK in Dongtan Eco-City, Germany in Qingdao Eco-Park, and Sweden in Tangshan Caofeidian New Town (ibid.). China is now leading the way in the production of electricity via wind power and is rapidly expanding solar and nuclear power, adding 72GW of wind power in 2020 alone (the US added 14GW that year), and reached 40% energy production from renewable in 2020, exporting such expertise to BRI countries such as Egypt, for instance, which like many others is seeking a "green recovery" from COVID-19 (Oxford Business Group, 2021). One attraction to such nations will be the potential economies of scale, and thus cheapness, that China can offer. There has been criticism, however, of China's export of hydrocarbon technology, but it would seem that China is now willing to reduce such exports as part of their overall "learning experience" (Dana, 2021).

The Health Silk Road (HSR) is another longer term part of the BRI that has gained momentum recently. It was in 2017 that the PRC leadership along with the WHO (World Health Organization) launched an "ambitious pledge towards universal health coverage through global health development cooperation in research and health systems, particularly among Silk Road countries" (EIAS, 2020). Chinese expertise in health areas has arisen in the context of struggling against continuing "diseases of poverty" (traditional ailments such as the snail-born disease, schistosomiasis, or tuberculosis (TB), for example, with the latter complicated by TB's growing drug resistance) and more recent "diseases of affluence" associated with growing prosperity, urbanization, and industrialization (such as hypertension, cancer, and respiratory diseases) (Cook & Dummer, 2004; Cook et al., 2013). China was seeking to position itself as a global health leader in order to expand its soft power even before the rise of COVID-19. Since then, and in part due to new expertise and products developed in its own struggle with COVID-19 which originated in Wuhan, China, the PRC leadership has taken the opportunity to directly, or indirectly via for instance the Jack Ma Foundation or via Huawei, to provide a range of products on a charitable or low-cost basis to Silk Road countries such as Nigeria, which was provided with 100,000 facemasks, 1,000 protective medical gowns, and 20,000 testing kits for COVID-19 (Oxford Business Group, 2021), and also to EU countries such as Spain or Italy, with Spain being supplied with 100,000 masks via the New Silk Road train from Yiwu in China to Madrid. Heldt (2020) reports that Chinese contributions to Italy in the early months of the pandemic were perceived to be of such importance that Italian perceptions of China became more positive than were perceptions of the EU or the US, which were felt to have abdicated their role and responsibility towards leading an effective global response to the pandemic.

A third area is the Digital Silk Road (DSR), which was also launched in 2015. This is designed to encourage digital and technological innovation, building of digital infrastructure, and is linked to what some have called the Space Silk Road (SSR) focusing on satellite launches and other Space initiatives. China in recent years has built up enormous expertise, in part linked to the huge scale of urbanization noted above, in such areas as cloud computing, smart cities, surveillance technology (including face recognition technology), and e-commerce, themes developed in the National Informatisation Strategy which ran from 2016 to 2020 (Oxford Business Group, 2021). The pandemic led to the PRC government calling for top tech firms such as Alibaba, Ten Cent, and Baidu to support the DSR via support for e-commerce and online retailing to minimize face-to-face retail contact, to assist diagnosis of COVID-19, help with digital contact tracing and with monitoring of people who should be in quarantine. On the plus side, the DSR can lead to an uptick in high value employment, while "big data analysis" systems can help tackle global challenges such as pandemics, energy use, and climate change response. On the negative side, however, are concerns about "big brother," effective monitoring, and regulation of the more intrusive aspects of big data into individual lives.

As noted above, the HSR is also linked to what has become known as "vaccine diplomacy," involving the export from China of vaccines from Sinovax or Sinopharm, for example, as well as PPE (Personal Protective Equipment) to assist in the struggle against the pandemic. Such exports tended to be cheaper and more readily available than those from the EU, UK, or US, for instance, and were welcome to many countries, rich and poor alike, who faced financial or practical difficulties in sourcing such necessary items. Apart from Spain, Italy, and Nigeria noted above, China's (and Russia's) vaccine diplomacy was particularly effective in Eastern Europe and the Balkans, and in South East Asia, with Safi (Safi, 2021) noting that China and Russia had made deals to supply more than 800 million vaccine doses to 41 countries (424 million doses from China alone to 27 countries, including 125 million doses to Indonesia). Chang has noted recently, however, (Chang, 2021) that such deals are not without problems, due to concerns in South East Asia, a big target for such vaccine diplomacy, for instance, that China is wielding too much hard and soft power in the region, an area which historically has had complex and sometimes difficult relations with China. There are also concerns that China's vaccines are less effective than those from Pfizer or other Western sources, while there may also be strong religious or cultural reasons for the rejection of vaccines more generally, regardless of where they come from.

4 COVID-19 and Implications of BRI

The COVID-19 pandemic is the single most catastrophic event of modern times, generating a social, financial, and global health threat to humanity. The impact of COVID-19 was swift, and, notwithstanding the impact on global health, triggered striking destruction of the global economy. COVID-19's effects on the global economy and financial health of nations are unparalleled (Oberoi, et al., 2021; Snowden et al., 2021) and global, with no single country untouched by the pandemic. As alluded to in the previous section, the pandemic has had a significant impact on China's capacity to invest resources into the expansive connectivity vision of the BRI. Furthermore, this is compounded by the disruption to supply chains, and the global and regional restrictions to travel caused by resolution strategies. While the tangible disruption to the BRI is challenging to determine (Mouritz, 2020), there is some evidence to suggest that the impact is significant, with Jizhong et al. (2021) suggesting that at least two-thirds of projects reported some degree of slowdown. The failure to assert an accurate assessment of the disruption leads, as Mouritz implies, to concerns of the reliability and the validity of data.

The majority of adults in Europe, Canada, and the US have received at least one dose of the COVID-19 vaccine, and many of the pandemic restrictions causing disruption to everyday life are beginning to ease. In contrast, no greater than 3% of citizens in low-income countries have received the first dose of their vaccine (Our World in Data, 2021); this inequity is reaffirmed by figures reflecting the purchase of vaccines, as more than 82% of available vaccine doses have been acquired by wealthy countries, and less than 1% by low-income countries. The World Health Organization (WHO) (2021) asserts that equitable access to safe and effective vaccines is critical to ending the COVID-19 pandemic meaning the vaccine can be described as a game-changing tool. Consequently, the notion of vaccine diplomacy, introduced in the previous section, has a resonance with the BRI. A report by Heldt (2020) illustrates that Chinese contributions to the western epicentre of the pandemic, Italy, in the early months of the pandemic were perceived to be of more positive value than those of traditional European and American partners.

The manufacture and distribution of PPE—and vaccines especially—provides nations to elevate themselves on the global stage, emphasizing the benefits and advantages of their scientific communities, political systems, markets, and ideologies. For example, as illustrated by the BBC (2020b), China allegedly asked Paraguay to change allegiance and sever diplomatic ties with Taiwan in exchange for vaccine doses from China. The extent of China's vaccine diplomacy is demonstrated by Karásková and Blablová (2021) who suggest that China has donated its vaccines in the form of "free samples" to more than 70 nations, which typically resulted in the subsequent purchase of several million doses. Furthermore, Karásková and Blablová point out that the donated vaccines were primarily those produced by Sinopharm, in preference to CoronaVac (produced by Sinovac) and Conviecia (manufactured by CanSino Biologics), the other two internationally known Chinese vaccines.

Western nations were criticized for hoarding vaccines in the early stages of the pandemic (Snowden et al., 2021); however, China diligently delayed vaccinating its nation's citizens in order to cement a lead in the global vaccine diplomacy race with resultant wide geographic dispersion of its donations, covering 70 countries worldwide, and its ability to offer supplies quickly and expeditiously to developing countries. China's ability and willingness to provide domestically produced vaccines to other nations has garnered favour with lower-income nations, without the economic cost of donating vaccines.

The WHO suggests that there are a number of key factors that influence the vaccine procurement process, which include price, supply, safety, and efficacy. However, there are uncertainties regarding the Chinese vaccines in each of these areas. As for price, state media in China reports that Sinopharm and Sinovac intend to charge the government approximately £22 per dose of their vaccines. This is in comparison to the £2 charged for a dose of the Oxford Astra Zeneca vaccine. Details about the cost of other vaccines developed in China have not been made public. Supply globally presents a challenge should china prioritize its domestic population. Vaccine safety is a key factor in the procurement process and typically approval by specific agencies is required. For example, in the US, approval by the US Food and Drug Administration is required, in the UK it is the Medicines and Healthcare products Regulatory Agency, and in the European Union the European Medicines Agency (EMA). None of the Chinese vaccine manufacturers have applied to any of the above agencies for approval. China has many COVID-19 vaccine candidates; five have received emergency use approval in China and some other countries. The first vaccine produced by Sinopharm is the front runner and has received the most emergency use approvals. Several countries have approved Sinovac's CoronaVac jab for emergency use, including Brazil, Chile, Indonesia, Laos, Mexico, and Turkey. CanSinoBIO has been granted emergency approval in Mexico and Pakistan (Barunck, 2021). Safety and efficacy are often judged synonymously, but in this area, the Chinese vaccines generate varying efficacy rates.

Most data regarding Chinese vaccines is garnered from the manufacturers and governments in countries where trials are being conducted. Sinopharm claimed that its first vaccine was 79% effective in terms of preventing symptomatic COVID-19; however, this is lower than the 86% efficacy reported by the United Arab Emirates. Sinopharm has also reported that its second vaccine, from the Wuhan institute, was found to be slightly less effective at 72.5%. The government of Turkey reported that Sinovac's CoronaVac was 91.25% efficacious at preventing symptomatic COVID-19, but researchers in Brazil announced that the CoronaVac jab was only 78% effective. Additional data suggests that the vaccine was only 50.4% effective (Barunck, 2021). Despite the continuing contradictions and lack of information available regarding the Chinese vaccines' wide and varying efficacy rates in testing (Dwyer, 2021), nations embrace what the Chinese government offers.

Chinese vaccine diplomacy, while viewed as pharma business, also embodies political incentives; the COVID-19 vaccine programme consequently reinforces and capitalizes upon developmental growth opportunities and the demands required to fulfil the notion of the Health Silk Road to position itself as a global health leader. However, it is prudent to add a cautionary note for consideration when evaluating this rapid expansion. China's speedy response in the early days of the pandemic was welcomed. But, as reported by the BBC (2020b), a number of European governments rejected Chinese-made equipment designed to combat the Coronavirus outbreak due to it being below standard or defective. This disillusionment with the PPE delivered in the first wave of the pandemic may be reflected by China's vaccines also not meeting expectations. As reported by the Reuters news in the Spring of 2021, hundreds of healthcare workers in Indonesia contracted COVID-19, despite being double vaccinated with the Sinovac vaccine. Those countries that rely on Sinovac have now chosen to give citizens a mix of vaccines in a bid to increase efficacy and curb new outbreaks, while the UAE is offering an additional third dose of the Sinopharm vaccine to boost immunity levels. Clearly, as illustrated throughout this chapter, the Belt Road Initiative remains alive, and as a result of the geopolitical and economic dynamism post-COVID-19, Chinese influence remains strong.

5 Conclusion

The authors of this chapter have been concerned with the BRI within the post-COVID-19 era. As it has been demonstrated the COVID-19 pandemic has exaggerated political and societal rigidities between China and other nations. Before the pandemic, the BRI was facing collective disparagement in host nations for its lack of accountability, transparency, dislocation of indigenous communities, adverse ecological effects, and worries of "debt-trap diplomacy" among many other problems. At the present time, the BRI is trapped by repayment, debt, and inconsistency problems. While China is looking for ways to overcome the difficulties of repayment and debt deferment, they currently appear unsurmountable in the light of the economic slump. Moreover, the global economic downturn driven by the pandemic has also augmented the probability of host nations scratching or deferring BRI ventures, particularly extensive infrastructure projects (Ying Hui, 2020).

With growing anti-Chinese sentiments in the global community post-COVID-19 these issues are not likely, even after China's economic conditions improve. Furthermore, the world is watching the mounting Chinese belligerence and expansionist strategies in the south pacific region closely, and they are not going down well with the global community. Many countries have anxieties and hesitations that joining the BRI may at some point cause serious peril of losing their sovereignty and believe that China does not shy away from breaking its treaties to change the status quo to its advantage. China has violated international guidelines and regulations in the South China Sea region, and several disputants in the South China Sea have approached global bodies like the UN to have the PCA Ruling enforced upon China. China's economic problems have increased these complications. Currently, many states are not prepared to grant leases for vital areas and seem more guarded even though China is in the course of giving concessions. But, allies are not displaying keen interest because they are uncertain about China's long-term strategy and objectives, and there is a lot of apprehension about China using its economic power for long-term political concessions. Yet, beyond global political rhetoric, Chinese government policy experts and advisors remain dedicated and realistic regarding the BRI and globalization. They view the BRI as a policy that can square against the latent "deglobalization" trend in a post-pandemic world. As the world slowly recovers from the pandemic after two years, China is expected to pursue the BRI, with more negotiation at home and more prospects overseas.

Certainly, the post-pandemic world has different priorities and challenges. It is expected that the BRI may move away from some rigid infrastructural projects to yield to softer, community developmental areas of collaboration such as, for example, technology, health, education, infrastructure, and climate change. COVID-19 showed the inadequacies in global healthcare preparedness and ICT infrastructure, particularly in emerging states, which offers a chance for China to plug these gaps through its Health Silk Road and Digital Silk Road (Ying Hui, 2020).

Moving forward, the authors of the chapter suggest that in the post-COVID-19 era, more dedicated consideration of the discourse and actions is needed by specialized policy advisors in China and other nations. In the interim, the Chinese government faces a trade-off between public spending on national financial salvage and financial grants to the BRI in response to the existing crisis. Right now, Beijing is concentrating on the prior, as new BRI projects will be a hard sell to the citizens of China. Certainly, the BRI will not be abandoned; the project will be revised in the medium- to long-run, and the choices and types of project could be diverse in a post-COVID-19 BRI. The global pandemic has created new connectivity opportunities for the BRI to modernize the global order (Zou, 2020).

Bibliographic References

Barunck, C. (2021). What do we know about China's Covid-19 vaccines? *British Medical Journal, 373*, Article 912. https://doi.org/10.1136/bmj.n912

BBC News. (2020a, January 20). *A quick guide to the US-China trade war*. Retrieved on 21st October 2021, from https://www.bbc.co.uk/news/business-45899310

BBC News. (2020b). *Coronavirus: Countries reject Chinese-made equipment*. Retrieved on 6th December 2022, from https://www.bbc.co.uk/news/world-europe-52092395

Bown, C. P. (2021). The US-China trade war and Phase One agreement. *Journal of Policy Modeling, 43*(4), 805–843.

Buckley, P. J. (2020). China's Belt and Road Initiative and the COVID-19 crisis. *Journal of International Business Policy, 3*(3), 311–314.

Chang, P. T. C. (2021, September 23). *China's vaccine diplomacy in Malaysia: Problems and prospects amid the pandemic*. SCMP. Retrieved on December 2021, from https://www.scmp.com/week-asia/opinion/article/3149793/chinas-vaccine-diplomacy-malaysia-problems-and-prospects-amid

Chen, A. W., Chen, J., & Reddy Dondeti, V. (2020). The US-China trade war: Dominance of trade or technology? *Applied Economics Letters, 27*(11), 904–909.

Clark, J. H. (2017). China's move into global investment banking, special report: Economics, *Britannica Book of the Year, 2017*. Encyclopaedia Britannica (pp. 174–175).

Clegg, J. (2009). *China's global strategy*. Pluto.

Cook, I. G. (2021). ¿ Encabezará China la lucha contra el cambio climático? [Will China lead the fight against climate change?]. *Vanguardia Dossier, 80*, 63–65.

Cook, I. G., & Dummer, T. J. B. (2004). Changing health in China: Re-evaluating the epidemiological transition model. *Health Policy, 67*, 329–343.

Cook, I. G., Gu, C., & Halsall, J. P. (2013). China's growing health inequalities: The challenges ahead. *Journal of Management and Sustainability, 3*(2), 10–18.

Cook, I. G., & Halsall, J. P. (2012). *Aging in comparative perspective: Processes and policies*. Springer.

Cook, I. G., Halsall, J. P., & Powell, J. L. (2010). Comparative aging and qualitative understanding. *Qualitative Sociology Review, VI*(1), 48–59.

Cook, I. G., Halsall, J. P., & Wankhade, P. (2015). *Sociability, social capital, and community development: An international health perspective*. Springer.

Dana, J. (2021, April 13). *Is the BRI causing a debt crisis for China?* Retrieved on December 2021, from https://asiatimes.com/2021/04/is-the-bri-causing-a-debt-crisis-for-china/

Davies, B. (2018, July 27). When the world opened the gates of China. *The Wall Street Journal*. Retrieved on December 2021, from https://www.wsj.com/articles/when-the-world-opened-the-gates-of-china-1532701482

Dicken, P. (2007). *Global shift: Mapping the changing contours of the world economy*. Sage.

Dwyer, O. (2021). Covid-19: Chinese vaccines may need changes to improve efficacy, admits official. *British Medical Journal, 373*, Article 969. https://doi.org/10.1136/bmj.n969

EIAS (2020, April 29). "The Health Silk Road": Implications for the EU under Covid-19. Retrieved on December 2021, from https://eias.org/op-ed/the-health-silk-road-implications-for-the-eu-under-covid-19/

Garcia-Herrero, A. (2021, April 12). *China's financing of the BRI during the pandemic*. ISPI, Italian Institute for International Political Studies. Retrieved on December 2021, from https://www.ispionline.it/en/pubblicazione/chinas-financing-belt-and-road-initiative-during-pandemic-29948

Graham, J. D., Belton, K. B., & Xia, S. (2021). How China beat the US in electric vehicle manufacturing. *Issues in Science and Technology, 37*(2), 72–79.

Haft, J. R. (2015). *Unmade in China: The hidden truth about China's economic miracle*. John Wiley & Sons.

Heldt, E. C. (2020). China's "Health Silk Road" offensive: How the west should respond. *Global Policy Journal*. Retrieved on December 2021, from https://www.globalpolicyjournal.com/blog/09/12/2020/chinas-health-silk-road-offensive-how-west-should-respond

Halsall, J. P., Oberoi, R., & Cook, I. G. (2022). Connecting the world: China's Belt and Road Initiative. In P. Figueiredo, F. J. Leandro, & Y. Li (Eds.) *Handbook of research on special economic zones as regional development enablers* (Chapter 1, pp. 1–21). IGI Global. ISBN13: 978179987619. https://doi.org/10.4018/978-1-7998-7619-9

Huan, G. (1986). China's open door policy 1978–1984. *Journal of International Affairs, 39*(2), 1–18.

International Monetary Fund. (2021, January 26). *World economic outlook update: Policy support and vaccines expected to lift activity*. Retrieved on December 2021, from https://www.imf.org/en/Publications/WEO/Issues/2021/01/26/2021-world-economic-outlook-update

Jizhong, Z., King, R., & Jeffery, C. (2021). *The Belt and Road Initiative 2021 survey— The impact of Covid-19 on the BRI*. Central Banking. Retrieved on December 2021, from https://www.centralbanking.com/central-banks/economics/7835241/the-belt-and-road-initiative-2021-survey-the-impact-of-covid-19-on-the-bri

Karásková, I., & Blablová, V. (2021, March 24). The logic of China's vaccine diplomacy. *The Diplomat*. Retrieved on December 2021, from https://thediplomat.com/2021/03/the-logic-of-chinas-vaccine-diplomacy/

Khan, H. U., & Khalid, I. (2018). New Delhi response to Beijing 'BRI' project: A Lucid connection with Chinese "string of pearls." *Journal of Political Studies, 25*(1), 243–254.

Liu, T., & Wing, T. W. (2018). Understanding the US-China trade war. *China Economic Journal, 11*(3), 319–340.

Lotta, R. (2009). China's rise in the world economy. *Economic and Political Weekly, 44*(8), 29–34.

Mouritz, F. (2020). Implications of the COVID-19 pandemic on China's Belt and Road Initiative. *Connections: The Quarterly Journal, 19*(2), 115–124.

Oberoi, R., Cook, I. G., Halsall, J. P., Snowden, M., & Woodcock, P. (2019). Redefining social enterprise in the global world: Study of China and India. *Social Responsibility Journal, 16*(7), 1001–1012.

Oberoi, R., Halsall, J. P., & Snowden, M. (2021). Corporate and entrepreneurial social responsibility during COVID-19: Understanding global trends and responses. *Labour & Development, 28*(1), 68–79.

Oberoi, R., Mswaka, W., Leandro, F. J., Snowden, M., & Halsall, J. P. (2020). Reimagining social innovation and social enterprise for industrial revolution 4.0: Case study of China and UK. In P. Smith & T. Cockburn (Eds.), *Global business leadership development for the fourth industrial revolution* (pp. 337–358). IGI Global. https://doi.org/10.4018/978-1-7998-4861-5

Our World in Data. (2021). *Covid-19 vaccine doses by continent*. Retrieved on December 2021, from https://ourworldindata.org/grapher/cumulative-covid-vaccinations-continent?tab=table&stackMode=relative&country=Africa~Asia~Europe~North+America~Oceania~South+America

Overholt, W. H. (1993). *China: The next economic superpower*. Weidenfeld & Nicolson.

Oxford Business Group. (2021, January 28). *Has Covid-19 prompted the Belt and Road Initiative to go green?* Oxford Business Group. https://oxfordbusinessgroup.com/news/has-covid-19-prompted-belt-and-road-initiative-go-green

Rajan, R. G. (2019). *The third pillar: How markets and the state leave the community behind*. HarperCollins.

Reuters New. (2021, June 17). Hundreds of Indonesian healthcare workers contract Covid-19 despite vaccination, dozens hospitalised. *The Straits Times*. Retrieved on December 2021, from https://www.straitstimes.com/asia/se-asia/hundreds-of-indonesian-doctors-contract-covid-19-despite-vaccination-dozens

Safi, M. (2021, February 19). Vaccine diplomacy: West falling behind in race for influence. *The Guardian*. Retrieved on December 2021, from https://www.theguardian.com/world/2021/feb/19/coronavirus-vaccine-diplomacy-west-falling-behind-russia-china-race-influence

Schindler, S., Jepson, N., & Cui, W. (2020). Covid-19, China and the future of global development. *Research in Globalization, 2*, 100020.

Schweinberger, A. (2014). State capitalism, entrepreneurship, and networks: China's rise to a superpower. *Journal of Economic Issues, 48*(1), 169–180.

Snowden, M., Oberoi, R., & Halsall, J. P. (2021). Reaffirming trust in social enterprise in the COVID-19 Era: Ways forward. *Corporate Governance and Sustainability Review, 5*(1), 120–130 (Special Issue: COVID-19).

The New York Times. (2020, January 16). Winners and losers of the trade deal. *The New York Times*. Retrieved on December 2021, from https://www.nytimes.com/2020/01/16/business/dealbook/trade-deal-us-china.html

Wang, C. N. (2020). *Brief: Investments in the Chinese Belt and Road Initiative (BRI) in the first half of 2020 during the Covid-19 pandemic*. International Institute of Green Finance, CUFE.

World Health Organization. (2021). *COVID-19 vaccines*. World Health Organization. Retrieved on December 2021, from https://www.who.int/emergencies/diseases/novel-coronavirus-2019/covid-19-vaccines

Ying Hui, L. (2020, September 28). COVID-19: The nail in the Coffin of China's Belt and Road Initiative? *The Diplomat*. Retrieved on December 2021, from https://thediplomat.com/2020/09/covid-19-the-nail-in-the-coffin-of-chinas-belt-and-road-initiative/

Yueh, L. (2013). *China's growth: The making of an economic superpower*. Oxford University Press.

Zaidi, S. M. S. (2021). American global supremacy under threat? The Chinese factor. *Politics & Policy, 49*(2), 502–528.

Zeng, W., & Sparks, C. (2020). Popular nationalism: Global times and the US–China trade war. *International Communication Gazette, 82*(1), 26–41.

Zou, R. (2020, July 30). *Assessing the impact of Covid-19 on the Belt and Road Initiative*. China US Focus. Retrieved on December 2021, from https://www.chinausfocus.com/finance-economy/assessing-the-impact-of-covid-19-on-the-belt-and-road-initiative

Chapter 11
Enacting Inclusive Globalization in a VUCA Context While Emerging from COVID-19

Tom Cockburn

1 Introduction

China's "Belt and Road Initiative" (BRI) was promoted by President Xi Jinping who used the phrase "Silk Road Economic Belt" in a speech at the Nazarbayev University in Kazakhstan on 7 September 2013 (*China Daily*, 2013). The project has a target completion date of 2049. He mentioned that the "Silk Road Economic Belt" was being built to connect the countries of Eurasia, and that it is an innovative project whose strategic objective was to enhance and develop the international mode of cooperation between the countries involved which aims to promote and develop a deeper level of cooperation and expand space for broader socio-economic focus and more equitable forms of inclusive development. It is thus presented as a model of inclusive cooperation for the benefit of people across each country (Xi, 2013). Beijing's multibillion dollar Belt and Road Initiative (BRI) has also been called a Chinese Marshall Plan, a state-backed campaign for global dominance, a stimulus package for a slowing Chinese economy, and a massive marketing campaign for something that was already happening—Chinese investment around the world (Kuo & Kommenda, 2018).

The Silk Road Economic Belt focuses on connecting China with Central Asia, Russia, and Europe (the Baltic Sea area); passing through Central Asia, West Asia to the Persian Gulf, and the Mediterranean Sea; connecting with Southeast Asia, South Asia, and the Indian Ocean (Zhao, 2015). From Southeast Asia to Eastern Europe and Africa, Belt and Road includes 71 countries that account for half the world's population and a quarter of global GDP. Along with policy coordination, facilities connectivity, unimpeded trade, and financial integration, people-to-people bonds are among the five major goals of the project. Other elements include an educational component which would involve mutual recognition of qualifications,

---

T. Cockburn (✉)
New Zealand Institute of Management, Auckland, New Zealand

academic mobility and student exchanges, coordination on education policy, life-long learning, and development of joint study programmes.

Currently, the UN and WHO have criticized rich nations for not sharing vaccines with poor countries but hoarding extra supplies for "booster doses" or to give them to younger and less vulnerable groups such as children under 18. For some time prior to the upcoming Cop26 summit in Glasgow, global collaboration between nations has been asserted by many authorities as a top priority, with reports stating that long-term global collaboration and cooperation are now even more vital to avert a climate emergency with burgeoning global issues in the over consumption of planetary resources, pollution, and rising inequality, mass migrations as well as post-pandemic economic recovery, innovation, and learning (Cockburn et al., 2015). In line with the large numbers of reports emanating from the Club of Rome, since 1972, Randers (one of the original report authors) has suggested (2013) that we may find, "40 years down the line" the Chinese have contributed majorly to solving problems of population and climate. World Economic Forum reports have been promoting long-term planning for the global environmental challenges we face for some time now.

However, in the COVID-19 pandemic period of mandatory national and local lockdowns and state control on citizens' rights to congregate freely, travel locally and nationally, as well as socializing with family and friends, distrust of government intentions and actions on public health have increasingly come in to question for many and these are seen by some as unwarranted restrictions on civil liberties as the pandemic has extended over the last 2 years which the numerous protest demonstrations in the UK, US, and EU attest. Closer to the Chinese government is the continuing Hong Kong democracy protests as citizens attempt to thwart imposition of rules made in Beijing. The rollout of the Belt and Road Initiative plan has been adversely impacted by the COVID-19 pandemic too (Kuo & Kommenda, 2018).

Nevertheless, well before the 2019 COVID-19 pandemic, concern had been expressed by various global and governmental agencies such as the UN, OECD, WEF, about the emergence of new social, citizenship, and economic challenges facing national governments or strategic unions such as the EU in the global era (Cockburn, 2020). The Groundswell report by the World Bank (2021) asserts that as many as 216 million people could move within their own countries due to slow-onset climate change impacts by 2050. Well-intentioned projects abound which espouse worthy and generally acceptable goals concerning the reduction of social exclusion and increasing national and international up-skilling for future skills and employment. For example, UK–EU papers on the Cordis project (2003) on "New Perspectives for Learning"—suggested that:

> Across Europe, there is clear evidence of declining engagement in traditional democratic processes, with governments, companies and other organisations considered to be remote, and insufficiently accountable to their stakeholders. Yet, it is also widely believed that globalisation calls for new, and more devolved kinds of political and social structure, in which individual citizens will play a more active part. This suggests that people need to be re-engaged as "active citizens", and enabled to take informed decisions about their lives, communities, and workplaces. However, many people are both disengaged and lack the skills, knowledge or understanding to do so. This is particularly true for people with little formal education and most at risk of social exclusion on other grounds. (April 2003)

Such avowed concerns have extended to other geographical areas too such as sub-Saharan Africa, where the UK government launched a five-year, public–private sector collaboration involving companies such as Cisco, Marconi, Virgin in a project entitled "Imfundo," meant to increase and improve ICT in the region (Jenkins, p. 408) as part of regional development aid efforts. The WEF asserted that governments, corporations will have to increasingly cooperate and collaborate to plan and invest so as to reduce inequality between nations and regions and avoid conflicts over resources, migrations. This chapter proposes that such collaboration must include building up social and cyber capital in technology—deficit regions (Cockburn, 2020; Smith & Cockburn, 2021). We might add, the impetus to include a greener form of cooperation and related technologies as well, which author Sha Song, in a WEF report 2021 asserts China is doing—though the WEF also distances itself from that claim by including a statement at the end of the article asserting that "The views expressed in this article are those of the author alone and not the World Economic Forum." (Sha Song, 'Green BRI' report, WEF, 2021).

This chapter rests on three major assumptions: 1. That creativity, cultural, political, and diplomatic sophistication and sensibility will be increasingly essential for successful corporate and government communications; 2. that dynamic complexity in sociopolitical, digital technologies, demographic and migration policies, economics, public health, business and environmental domains offer a huge challenge which, 3. governments, the public, and diverse professions have yet to address seriously not least of which is the leadership and public relations fields. For the third assumption or, as the start of Abrahamson, Meehan, and Samuel's book title so colloquially put it, *The Future Ain't What It Used To Be*, this chapter asserts that the term "business-as-unusual" must be expanded to include the possibility of potentially catastrophic change, in commerce, or the environment, or society, or all of the aforementioned due to the dynamic complexity of the VUCA context. Thus, the next chapter sections consider a number of international perspectives on the BRI project for comparative purposes, followed by a brief summary of complexity science concepts that can be applied and outlines key component factors in scenario-building methods and previous examples of major scenarios of note. Further, a potential survey instrument that could be used to do further research and analysis of the components parts of the ongoing construction and subsequent evolution of the BRI partnership as enacted and the core scenario components in the matrix model proposed in Table 1 is introduced. We conclude that in the global VUCA context the ambitious BRI project also has the potential to flounder or flop as much as it has to fly in political, economic, and social terms.

2 International Perspectives on the BRI Project

Despite explicit and seemingly worthy objectives about inclusivity and levelling up for deprived areas within the project's proposed boundaries, some commentators regard the project as an expression of Xi Jinping's anxiety about his own political situation at home (Blanchette, 2021), while yet others are concerned that the pandemic may never be over and the PR damage to the US and its allies in the debacle of their hurried retreat from Afghanistan has already exacerbated and accelerated a pre-existing global shift in political power eastwards (Smith & Cockburn, 2013, 2021). A 2019 study conducted by consultants CEBR forecasted that the BRI was likely to boost world GDP by $7.1 trillion per annum by 2040.

The US, Japan, and Australia, however, are also suspicious of the motives of China which has already gained millions of dollars through the new trade and investment arrangement. These states have formed a counter-initiative, the *Blue Dot Network* in 2019, followed by the G7's *Build Back Better World* initiative in 2021 (Reuters, 2021). Recently the "AUKUS" pact to share intelligence in the Pacific and build nuclear submarine capacity for Australia as a Pacific Rim country has been announced by the three leaders, Johnson (UK), Biden (US), and Morrison (AU) to replace their current diesel-powered fleet. AUKUS has prompted rebukes from Beijing spokesmen according to CNN news reports as the end of the diesel-powered submarines also means France has lost a major trade deal with Australia and has now withdrawn its diplomats from the US as a result, citing "bad faith" and breach of trust in their previous negotiations with Australia. The EU Commission has also complained publicly. However, other commentators such as Hass (2021) continue to refute the assertion of any actual or perceived loss of soft power and global influence of the US.

These have seemed to be signs portending a resurgence of a bid for global power and authority according to Cornwell: "When the Soviet Union collapsed in 1991, it seemed a foregone conclusion that the 21st, like the 20th, would be an 'American Century'. Now, for the first time in almost a millennium, a Chinese century is on the cards." (Cornwell et al., 2011, Independent.co.uk webpage). The economic growth was seen as a process that would lead to global power realignment such that it has been suggested that this is China's (or India's) century, and the US is no longer the sole remaining superpower or dominating economic force in the world (Cornwell et al., 2011; Smith & Cockburn, 2013). Fukuyama (2020) asserted due to the continuing economic downturn and related political repercussions in the Western nations, especially the US, The global distribution of power will continue to shift eastward, since East Asia has done better at managing the situation than Europe or the US. Even though the pandemic originated in Wuhan, China and Beijing initially covered it up. Other writers have suggested that it is likely to be a South Asian or polycentric century rather than a purely Chinese century (Khanna, 2011). Yet others such as Joseph Nye have refuted such contentions of power realignment entirely according to a *Financial times* article (Nye, 2010). Tim Jackson (2016) asserts one specific alternative perspective in his book "Prosperity without growth?" His view is that global economic growth has reached a tipping point: "The global economy is almost five times the size it was half a century ago. If it continues to grow at the same rate the economy will be 80 times that size by the year 2100" and demands on the planet will be unsustainable (Jackson, 2016). Jackson also believes that increased consumer indebtedness fueled growth in the last 20 years "…it is generally agreed that the unprecedented consumption growth between 1990 and 2007 was fueled by a massive expansion of credit and increasing levels of debt" (Jackson, 2016, p. 22). The collapse of the sub-prime housing lending and investment market caused a tsunami of banking defaults and financial implosion in economies in many Western countries which still causes waves of panic and uncertainty in global markets. Jackson further states that "Over the course of more than a decade consumer debt served as a deliberate mechanism for freeing personal spending from wage income and allowing consumption to drive the dynamics of growth." Next, he goes on to contrast the Western indebtedness with corresponding high levels of Eastern investment and savings, principally those in China and India, commenting that "The savings rate in China during 2008 was around 25% of disposable income, while in India it was even higher at 37%" (Jackson, 2016, p. 22). The levels of such external debt varied widely. In 2007–2008 external debt stood at 5% of GDP in China and India whereas it exceeded 900% of GDP in Ireland (pp. 22–26).

3 Emergence and Dynamic Complexity

Many commentators have suggested we have now reached the cusp of a "Green" technological phase needed to address a climate emergency set to follow the end of the current COVID-19 pandemic and related global recession allied with a reservoir of pent-up consumer demand. It is worth noting, however, that although many experts' opinions may coalesce around a set of trending points, as seen in current COVID-19 analyses, e.g., those of Johns Hopkins University and others of national government agencies, it is as well to recall that these are all interpreted patterns. That is, the points need to be viewed holistically in all dimensions unlike the typical 2-dimensional astrology star charts that neglect the depth perception. Indeed, the "observed trends" might form part of a long-term stable attractor pattern, like Schumpeter's technological waves, or Kondratieff's macroeconomic cycles of capitalism or burgeoning popular activism, bolstered and facilitated by social media, such as the current "Extinction rebellion" protests, #BlackLivesMatter, and #MeToo movements.

In the dynamics of the Volatile Uncertain Complex and ambiguous (VUCA) global environment, long-term equilibrium cyclic patterns are ultimately just as susceptible as other patterns to disruption or derailment by latent randomness. In the VUCA world of today the so-called "butterfly effect," commonly applied to climate and meteorology, is often referred to as a "surprise"-inducing factor which can derail projects. The butterfly effect is a metaphorical expression suggesting that the flapping of a butterfly's wings may eventually lead to a major storm through a series of dynamically interacting weather systems and thus complexity theory indicates that there are sensitivities which, under certain initial conditions, and in dynamically complex contexts, tiny changes in those initial conditions can generate wide variations in later outcomes.

Thus, this chapter introduces a short section, below, discussing some terms and features of dynamic complexity to preface further elaboration of the scenarios proposed. What connects these is what Bateson called the "pattern that connects" (Bateson, 1979, p. 17). That "connection" is the coherence of the situated cognition and informal, tacit, experiential, "action learning" actors engage in when conversing, projecting, and enacting their collaborative and evolving project environment, and in tandem passionately regenerating a new, or anew, the action genre, story, or script they currently perceive themselves to be occupying. The "passion" refers to their perception of their positioning within that narrative as protagonist, antagonist, or collaborator and the emotions generated or driving their actions.

4 Brief Summary on Complex Attractors and Behaviours in Context

Attractors or more correctly, basins of attractors are passive states, not goal-oriented present but spaces where a system is headed but, like drifting in a river, systems may drift into other kinds of attractors. There are 3 attractor types identified in the literature (Arrow et al, 2000; Battram, 1992; Kauffman, 1995; Lissack & Roos, 1999; Mahon, 1999). These are as described, in summary, below. They are driven by the emotional energy of the relationship binaries within the teams or between the teams. Attractors, or "centres of attraction," concern meanings, relationships, and their dynamics, including potential energy sources and "causes." Other complexity terms are included, and all are underlined in bold letters.

(1) **Point attractors** occur in a "lock in" situation. A generic example would be typical, early iterations of the prisoners' dilemma game, used in psychological research, where people invariably "cheat" and both sides lose. It is often a negatively biased or divergent, competitive binary although there could be positively biased and convergent binary relationships which also resulted in "lock in" by amplifying oppositions to a perceived common threat or third party, whereby if the participants collaborated, they could be in a "win–win" situation but instead, they engage in competitive behaviour and the outcome is not optimal. Such a point attractor is not necessarily irrevocable or permanent and might exemplify the relationship of individuals to the group in the early stages of negotiation where collaboration is seen as external and in opposition to the team brief.

(2) **Closed loop attractors** involve some co-evolution akin to predator–prey demographics, i.e., they move in synchronization. As prey increases so too does the predator species and vice versa. It is a stable, dynamic state and could be seen as symptomatic of the early stages of the internalization of the collaboration ethic. As Cornwell et al. remarked (2011, *Independent* online): "China's power shows up in three main ways: as a purchaser, mostly of raw materials; as a supplier to the rest of the world; and as an investor of its spare cash. In relation to the first, it has had a huge impact on Africa. It funds more infrastructure in Africa than all the aid of

Western nations put together, much in exchange for raw materials. As supplier to the world, it has helped hold down living costs elsewhere by producing so many cheap goods. For example, it produces two-thirds of the world's socks. As an investor, it has by and large bought financial assets – US Treasury securities in particular – rather than buying foreign firms. So, it has not exerted its power in any direct way." This is at once, both a strategic strength and a potential tactical weakness as the Chinese economy moves more upmarket, beyond mass-produced, low-cost goods and beyond the use of others' green resources, into the greener era of climate change when these exchanges noted above may then be seen as a global, as well as local threat, generating antagonism, in much the same way as has the "cheap, throwaway fashion industry" in the West or the use of child labour in mining rare earths for use in the production of computers in parts of Africa.

(3) **Strange attractors** are fundamentally unpredictable often exhibiting the so-called "butterfly effect" where small initial changes or differences can precipitate huge differences as in weather systems.

(4) **Drift** is related to the energy required to maintain "dissipative" structures. A dissipative structure, (such as an attractor) dissipates emotional or physical energy. Therefore, systems usually drift down, ceteris paribus, to the lower energy levels in any network, that is they drift down to the "basin" of an attractor. As a corollary, these structures require energy to sustain them or to break out into new situations or changes. The energy here is not solely victories in negotiation within the team brief but emotional energy supplied by participants' interaction within one or more binary relationship states. In order to prevent "lock in" to the drift, i.e., for maintaining or reaching higher energy states, some motivational energy input is required. For instance, teams see that there is "give and take" by each side rather than intransigence.

(5) **Scaling or fractals** refer to patterns of self-similarity in systems repeated "holographically," no matter the scale (Sherman & Schutz, 1998, p. 205). Famously depicted in the Mandelbrot sets; colourful pictures of the chaotic systems he investigated which demonstrated infinitely recursive, ordered, "geometric" patterns generated from disordered systems (Sanders, 1998). A concrete example is the shape of the fern which, when examined under a microscope, will be seen to have the same "toothed" pattern seen on the leaves repeated on each "tooth." Other natural fractals include the branching patterns of rivers, images of the human circulatory system, bark of old trees, the lines on our faces (Sanders, 1998, pp. 102–103). Thus, again suggesting an order found within the apparently disordered parts of the world. It is also an observable, over-arching, meta-pattern in the evolutionary structural and developmental teamwork processes observed in project teams and their brief over the term of a project. (Cockburn, 2006, 2008a, 2008b; Cockburn et al., 2007).

(6) **Freezing** is seen in negotiating networks of very limited connectivity, i.e., with only one or two connections or pairing up of members to the exclusion of other connections. An example could be so-called "Pariah states" such as Myanmar or North Korea currently. Networks of greater than 2 reduce that likelihood but won't necessarily eliminate it and those of 4, or more, exhibit dynamic complexity given the potential number of interactions.

(7) **Patching** is another metaphorical term used to describe a process by which many "…conflict laden" tasks are broken up into "patches" forming a (dynamic) "quilt" each of which, have some overlaps, but where each "patch" behaves like a coevolving species with the other patches and seeks to optimize within its own patch which can be typical of negotiations where there are multiple factions on one or either side, each with its own subset of tacit or explicit aims in the negotiation. The emerging "quilt" means that "…finding a good solution in one patch will change the problems to be solved by the parts in the other patches. These patches will themselves make adaptive moves that in turn alter the problems faced by yet other patches" (Kauffman, 1995).

Relationship binaries are social relationships constituted by and which constitute related attractors which in that process, generate the emotional energy to drive changes or sustain relationships in the current basin of attraction. Thus, teams may drift or spiral into or out of them in a nonlinear manner, when nudged by the forces of the emergent relationship binary dynamics. For instance, forming a "conflicting assumptions" binary where there are divergent cultural assumptions acting like memes, with one or more other binaries in any negotiations, and feeding energy into that sub-system where one may be potentially convergent towards collaboration but the other divergent and opposed to collaboration or seeking to constrain the levels of collaboration or seeking more assurances and guarantees of good faith negotiating. The result is often confusion, frustration, and barriers to further progress. These binary attractors may also drift into a **loop attractor** if they are not helped to overcome the confusion continually circling around the opposite one tending towards stalemate.

In fact, sensitivity to initial conditions may mean that due to some minor, initial differences of "energy input," the emotions in binaries in different negotiating teams or at different times have a different type of impact or are of a different order of magnitude through positive, or negative feedback amplification, or dampening as is currently the case with the French negotiators and government regarding the AUKUS pact. A binary may be composed of other binaries which may be either positive or negative, or both positive and negative, convergent, and divergent at different times, conditions, or contexts. Battram (1992: 37–38, 48–49) points out other countervailing tendencies within complex adaptive systems, composed of independent, but interdependent, self-organizing teams of individual agents. That is, there are tendencies towards individualism versus collectivism inherent in teams as living social systems. The "individualism" tends to promote "boundary-setting" or "autopsies" of the discussions, whereas the interdependence within the negotiating team encourages team collectivism, dissipating or weakening the boundary between the individual agents or actors in the network. The amplification of emergent, collective emotions into a stable attractor loop can form part of a social process of "emotional contagion" reflected in the negotiator's behavioural communication. This "contagion" forms a dynamic part at the "Edge of chaos."

The **edge of chaos** is a non-pejorative term describing a sharp change occurring when a tipping point in a complex system is reached. That is, when "ordered behaviour" gives way to "turbulent" behaviour: it is a "phase transition" like the change from ice to water or water to steam in physical sciences. It is an example of one of four classes of behaviour which occur in complex systems. These are, **Class I** behaviour, or stasis (death or freezing), **Class II** behaviour, or "order" (i.e., routine, predictable behaviour in the system), **Class III** disordered or chaotic behaviour, and fourth, "the edge of chaos" or complexity is a zone where turbulent changes are accelerating but where creative "branching out" is part of the possibility space i.e., poised between chaos and order, where the systems are still stable enough to allow novelty and learning within the network and negotiating teams as Stacey (1996) suggests. George et al. (cited in Barsade et al., 2003) showed that group emotions exist and affect work outcomes. That is, they amplify or dampen the teams' trust and anxiety as they occur, energizing centres of attraction across and between teams or within the network cohort. Thus, as Arrow et al. research (2000, pp. 44, 158–159) suggested, there are several noticeable peaks and troughs in the commitment to the BRI project as it proceeds.

Although this approach provides a more comprehensive account, recognizing the intricacies in dynamic complexity of the global system of "partnerships" envisioned in the BRI and the potential for unintended as well as accounting for both "known unknowns" as well as "unknown unknowns" emerging as potentially disruptive "surprises" in a network like the BRI. So, in this chapter, we propose extending Rost's conceptualization of a divide between twentieth and twenty-first-century paradigms to support the usefulness of scenarios in preparing for a change in these uncertain times.

5 Potential Attractor Basins Within Project Negotiations for the BRI Initiative

Since President Xi Jinping announced his grand plan to connect ASIA, Europe, and Africa, the initiative has become a broad catch-all term applied to a wide range of initiatives in countries from Panama to Madagascar, South Africa to New Zealand (Kuo and Kommenda, 2018). As Belt and Road expands in scope, so do concerns by some governments that it is a form of economic imperialism that gives China too much leverage over other countries, often those that are smaller and poorer. Some observers worry that expanded Chinese commercial presence around the world will eventually lead to expanded military presence. Last year, China established its first overseas military base in Djibouti, Africa. Analysts say almost all the ports and other transport infrastructure being built can be dual-use for commercial and military purposes. "If it can carry goods, it can carry troops," says Jonathan Hillman, director of the Reconnecting Asia project at CSIS (cited in Kuo & Kommenda, 2018, *Guardian* newspaper online).

Jane Golley, an associate professor at Australian National University, describes the BRI as an attempt to win friends and influence people which may backfire. "They've presented this very grand initiative which has frightened people," says Golley. In particular, it is seen as a form of debt-trap diplomacy by some following the Sri Lankan government's ceding control of the Hambantota port to China for 99 years (*New York Times*). "Rather than using their economic power to make friends, they've drummed up more fear that it will be about influence" (Kuo & Kommenda, 2018, *Guardian* newspaper online).

However, according to Shan Wenhua, a professor at Jiaotong University in Xi'an, Xi's signature foreign policy is "the first major attempt by the Chinese government to take a proactive approach toward international cooperation… to take responsibility" (Kuo & Kommenda, 2018, *Guardian* Newspaper online). Nevertheless, the AUKUS pact has infuriated the Chinese as it is seen by them as an attempt to circumvent the BRI and, according to recent news reports on CNN, China and some other BRI partner governments such as Indonesia, see the agreement between the three governments of Australia, UK, and US, to enable the Australian navy to build a nuclear-powered submarine fleet rather than a diesel-powered one, as increasing the Pacific arms race and related tensions, for instance, those with Japan where China has claimed some islands and Taiwan which China wants to annex? AUKUS leaders argue that the submarines are not nuclear-armed merely nuclear-powered and actual construction of the submarines will not occur immediately as it could mean a ten to twenty-year project for Australia and the others to facilitate and inaugurate processes and resources required to enable the construction and deployment of the submarines in Australia. On the other hand, the French government—a NATO ally of the UK and US has now lost a $65million submarine-building contract with Australia and thus France is unhappy and that has prompted a complaint from the European Commission to the AUKUS leadership too.

6   Building Projective Scenarios

So, what are the critical determinants in building scenarios? There are several critical questions and criteria that are often used to determine the scope and features in potential scenarios. The nine questions below are typical ones considered by panels of experts and professionals before developing scenarios for businesses, NGOs, and governments. These areas are often developed in discussions between experts in the discipline whether that is in economics, business, medicine, politics, or social studies, some combination of disciplines and skills, and so on.

1. What are the anticipated and prioritized issues-including both assumed and tacitly expressed ones as well as the explicitly announced issues?
2. Has there been Sufficient Analysis of the current situation?
3. Has the Peoples' Republic of China's (PRC) organizational position been adequately articulated, prepared, and facilitated?
4. Have the priority publics been identified?
5. Have Identified behavioural goals and objectives been prepared?

6. Are there well-developed, adequate, and relevant strategies, messages, and tactics to apply?
7. Are actors able to successfully implement the plan?
8. How will the progress of the plan be evaluated as it is rolled out? What have we learned?
9. How might the dynamic complexity of the global environment impact the ongoing project evolution?

7 From Domains to Ports, Portals, and Scenarios

In leadership terms, strategic vision and associated future projections are widely recognized as important for strategic development. Their centrality is succinctly summarized in Kouzes and Posner's (1997, p. xxv) statement: "The domain of leaders is the future." Earlier, Rost (1993) identified a clear divide between what he called the twentieth-century industrial leadership paradigm and that of the twenty-first. The old paradigm he described as "rationalistic, technocratic, linear, quantitative, and scientific in language if not entirely in its methodology in all cases" (Rost, 1993, p. 27). This chapter presents a matrix based on axes indicating levels of perceived trust and levels of unease or anxiety among the partners in the proposed BRI network initiative as the basis for suggesting an applicable scenario and we conclude by recommending that scenario's methodology becomes an accepted part of preparing the diverse publics across the BRI and elsewhere for the potentially disruptive or contested relationships evolving as the nonlinear, business-as-unusual future continues to be insufficiently addressed in much of the leadership and PR professional field's current thinking. In order to move away from the characteristics of that "business as usual" paradigm referred to above by Rost, and so also to thereby improve the discussion of technical, social, and political enactment of the BRI, it is advocated here that scenarios can be used as a portal—to use a more up-to-date metaphor in line with the growth of social media and information technology—to enable and encourage a less linear, less positivist, less certain, and more creative set of future projections accounting for Volatile Uncertain Complex and Ambiguous environments (VUCA) globally and dynamic complexity as well as disruptive "surprises" in the years ahead.

At the turn of this century, in *Net Future: The 7 Cybertrends That Will Drive Your Business, Create New Wealth, and Define Your Future*, for instance, Martin (1999) accompanied his trend analysis with five key associated adjustments including a top three of: "Capturing the hearts and minds of consumers"; "Changing corporate culture and authority"; and "Integrating personal and work lives." All three overlap significantly with traditional and contemporary issues we face in the current pandemic and future post-pandemic return to "normality" of a world under a major climate change emergency, while trying to be greener as well as addressing necessary re-skilling for new types of green employment and cushioning for anticipated unemployment among those in older industries as well as mass migrations which are set to increase significantly, in part, due to the climate threat. As Smith and Cockburn have indicated in a series of books (2013, 2014, 2016, 2020) dynamic complexity in the environment and striving for sustainability require new leadership models and mindsets involving achieving greater collaboration and "buy in," or consensus from followers and teams in order to "think the unthinkable" as futurist Hermann Kahn, formerly director of the Hudson Institute suggested, about addressing the possibility of nuclear war (Kahn, 1962). There are many further impacts to consider from a host of newly emerging digital technologies, autonomous Artificial Intelligence systems, trans-disciplinary applications, and "surprise" issues such on the horizon, such as unforeseen viral pandemics like COVID-19, realigned seen as "asymmetric threats" that may well become the final straw that breaks the proverbial political alliances within and between blocs such as ASEAN, ANZUS, EU, NATO, which can be "camel's back" for many organizations and potentially, for national economies (Smith & Cockburn, 2013, 2020; Wolfowitz et al., 2018).

8 Imagined Projections: Three Previous Examples of Influential Scenarios

In the first part of this concluding section of the chapter, we present a few examples of scenarios previously applied by the Global consulting corporation PWC to the EU, South Africa, and New Zealand as a brief introduction to the scenario that this chapter will suggest is potentially useful means for considering the current BRI. These exemplars begin from the point where reiterations of the old style "business as usual" perspectives end and COVID-19-pandemic/climate threat and change, surprise and complexity begin to impact the world of today and tomorrow. One well-known set of scenarios is that published in Allen Hammond's et al. (1998) *Which World: Scenarios for the 21st Century* offers three scenario options. The first is called "Market World" and, in brief, it envisages a situation where economic reform and technological innovation fuel rapid growth, where developing regions are integrated into the global economy, where the global market brings modern techniques and products to virtually all countries, and where the result is widespread prosperity, peace, and stability. The latter broadly fits with the explicit aims of the Belt and Road Initiative albeit from a free-market capitalist perspective. The second more pessimistic vision, "Fortress World" is based on the failure of market-led growth to address social wrongs and environmental crises. It projects the view that unconstrained markets will exacerbate these problems and lead to the destruction of the environmental and social fabric on which growth depends. The result will be uneven development internationally, and inside nations, as enclaves of prosperity coexist with widening misery and desperation. The third more visionary, and optimistic, future, "Transformed World," foresees radical social and political (including cultural values and norms) changing rapidly. It predicts that power will be more widely shared and that grass roots will influence governments towards new arrangements to improve society in terms of equality and contentment and to better protect the environment.

In opening up multiple visions, these three scenarios set up distinctly different futures. How scenarios operate in practice can be seen in South Africa's move away from apartheid. During that period the *Mont Fleur* scenarios were widely credited with assisting in a peaceful transition to greater democracy and offering a richer metaphorical base. In brief summary they projected four options: (1) *Ostrich*—which imagined a future where the government refused to face the realities of change; (2) *Lame Duck*—which imagined a protracted transition like bird with a broken wing unable to take off properly; (3) *Icarus*—which saw a popular elected government trying to achieve too much too quickly and burning in the global economic sun of the new world order; and (4) *Flight of the Flamingoes*: Which imagined a peaceful transition in which the whole country would take off slowly, fly high, and fly together.

In retrospect, the remarkable post-Apartheid developments had, in many important respects, their roots in the discovery by the South African people that the course they were on was unsustainable. As well as providing evidence of past success, the *Mont Fleur* scenarios offered a rich, if mixed, metaphor base for speculation. This chapter sees this richness as helpful in stimulating a more imaginative approach to both public relations and to potential leadership approaches to envisioning futures. More recently, on a more global scale, the four scenarios put up by a Canadian government roundtable have the requisite richness to invite public relations participation. Following many of the same drivers of Hammond's tripartite vision, Rossell's shipping forecasts run as follows:

1. *Starship Enterprise*: As with Hammond's *Market World*, the Enterprise vision sees existing capitalism, just like the famous *Star Trek* spaceship, as going boldly forth and spreading the economic success of the developed world internationally in an ongoing global movement;
2. *Titanic*: A more pessimistic forecast than any of Hammond's three visions. As its title graphically suggests, this projection sees major economic, environmental, and social catastrophes;
3. *HMS Bounty*: Close to Hammond's *Fortress World*, this scenario predicts major internal and external conflicts between the haves and have-nots of a socially and economically divided world; and
4. *Windjammer*: Aligning with Hammond's *Transformed World*, this more environmentally friendly craft would herald a transition to a friendlier more equitable world with less of a gulf between the information and technologically rich and the information and technologically poor.

9 Waving or Drowning? Taking Account of Catastrophic Potentials

The start of the heading is the title of global consulting firm PricewaterhouseCooper's (PwC) booklet of scenarios for European futures. Although offering a dramatic binary choice, its title is more optimistic than its probable source, Stevie Smith's *Not Waving but Drowning*, in which the poet observes that someone is trying to attract attention because they are in serious difficulties rather than because they narcissistically seek attention. Nevertheless, PwC's imaginative vision of a future is one where, in three of the four scenarios, business is not anything like the usual but merits attention as a corporate player of PwC's size and stature would not have committed its resources to the exercise without strategic intent.

Their four scenarios are the Golden Triangle, On the Edge, the Last Castle, and Drowning Spires. *Golden Triangle*, as the name implies, is the most promising of the scenarios. It envisages prosperity and improved public services promoting harmony. The prosperity is based on rapid technological advances in digital technology and biotechnology with strong economic growth in stable and open markets. In addition, the world order is stable, the EU enlargement is proceeding unabated, and there are no worrying environmental problems.

Scenario two, *On the Edge*, outlines a similarly strong economic growth but in this case accompanied by instability with boom-and-bust cycles and very little trickle down of the benefits amidst chaotic technological advances. Worrying changes in world leadership, fragmentation in EU power, and environmental concerns all feature prominently.

In the third vision, *The Last Castle*, the welfare state is alive but unwell. It has become an increasing burden as the European population and migration rises significantly. Moreover, technological regulation, due in part to environmental concerns, stifles and slows advance and growth in development throughout the European Union. The boom-and-bust cycles continue and there are politically powerful losers, which leads to the formation of rival power blocs, US and EU protectionism, and mounting worries, resulting in demands for further restrictions about immigration into the EU.

In the fourth scenario, *Drowning Spires*, the Greens are ascendant politically as the result of severe climate change that is wrecking the economy of the EU and the world and causing increasing food shortages and famines. Unrest is widespread and there are major population migrations. The rival power blocs remain and there is an increasingly desperate search for technological solutions. All in all, future business is clearly seen by PwC to be more likely to be *un*usual and environmental issues are positioned as too important to ignore.

It is suggested in this chapter that the BRI project—already delayed by COVID-19 may yet be viewed as a flop if not a catastrophe, and therefore we add a new 2021 scenario matrix, Table 1, of potential and key relational aspects among BRI project participants and its success built around relational trust and anxiety coordinates which suggest a range of possible future directions for the BRI project and evolving adaptation based upon potential partners' views of their relationship with the BRI, perceived Chinese intentions and/or the political position of Xi Jinping. The different scenario quadrants in the table relate to a range of positions between wholehearted trust of up to 100% descending to low trust quadrants, i.e., between 25% and 0% shown on the vertical axis and consequential anxiety levels of each position on the horizontal axis shown for the prospective or actual partners.

The positions in the quadrants in the matrix are described as follows:

High trust in Chinese government intentions (75–100%) with low anxiety about terms (levels 1–3 on a 10-point scale where 1 represents mild anxiety to 10) describes

Table 1 This Matrix shows potential locations of diverse partnership types and relationships that can be used for building scenarios for the Belt and Road project. The partnership types use axes of explicitly expressed trust and unease or anxiety concerning BRI project contract terms, conditions, and the potential level of Chinese involvement in the project host country or region. No complete and independent research and analysis have so far been published but the set of Partnership Power Relationship Asymmetry scales shown below are adapted to potentially suit some empirical testing of those relationships among the negotiators and public and private sector members of the BRI partnerships if researchers are granted access to do so by the BRI leadership

		High	Trust	
100%				
	Trusty Followers		**Wary Professionals**	
75%				
Skeptics				
			Equivocals	
Weak Anxiety				**Strong anxiety**
50%				
	fractious coupling			
25%			**Suspicious Mercenaries**	
			Resistance	
	Policentrist insurers	Low	Trust	
1	2 3 4	5	6 7 8	9 10

This table, devised by Tom Cockburn, 2021

the "*Trusty Followers*," the most willing collaborators and allies within the BRI project network, in the lower part of the same quadrant are the "*sceptics*," who range between 50 and 75% trust and on the horizontal scale exhibit anxiety levels of 1–3 about the network and actions in the BRI project to date. They still see potential benefits in being in the network so they will give some variable, limited support on a conditional, case-by-case basis—subject to any possible adverse PR or lowered outcomes in future.

In contrast to the "*Trusty Followers*" in the top left quadrant, the "*Wary professionals*" have similarly high levels of trust in principle and a pragmatic willingness to collaborate despite retaining some caution as they have anxieties in the 5–7 range. Therefore, they will confer with other similarly inclined partners and seek continued reassurances on key terms, and conditions such as the secrecy they are told they must keep about the contract terms of any Chinese direct investments made in their areas.

If they detect growing discontent from others within the quadrant, they may slip into the attractor basin below, i.e., to the *equivocals* or else to defect.

The *"Equivocals"* who are equivocating and located in the 50–75% trust and willingness to collaborate range but have given only notional or conditional support to BRI and they tend to vacillate a lot when adverse PR or negative commentaries emerge such as the 2019 report on the BRI and growing issues of decarbonization (from dissidents within or those outside the project, offering alternatives to support, such as the Western powers like the US; or EU).

In the bottom left and right halves of Table 1, lies the groups with less than 50% trust and anxiety fluctuating across the scale from 1 to 10.

The 4 scenarios posited for the BRI are as below:

Thus, for inclusive gains, the BRI needs to hold, sustain, and build the partnerships in top two quadrants, while reducing the other quadrants in the matrix. If that occurs, then the BRI may yet be hailed as the *"Long march to liberation from want and oppression"* for those included as partners, and prosperity will diffuse and spread outwards to the rest of the world as the project partners' economies grow and they trade with others outside the BRI.

However, if the US, UK, Japan, Russia, Australia, and India, especially the three major powers in the BRI regions begin to enact more "spoiler" plans beyond the AUKUS pact, progress for the BRI may falter. Russia and India have both attempted to minimize perceived Chinese influence ideologically and in the past—including by military means in the case of India over disputed territory—and may do so again if the impact and spread of the BRI project is seen as a counterweight to their own influence in the same region. Pakistan has an interest in controlling the Chinese overtures to the Taliban government in Kabul, to minimize any further impact in terms of migration or incursions at the borders, as have other states bordering Afghanistan. Thus, plans to thwart the emergence and growth of Chinese interests may attract a number of recruits and the project may then become a *Dictatorship of Development* by default, if it forces the Chinese investment terms to be tightened up or supplemented with other measures to entice or threaten the subordinate partners.

The lower left quadrant can be seen as a fractious area and a source of growing numbers of mainly small pinpricks or needling issues troubling or delaying the progress of the projects turning the project into a kind of long, slow *"Death by a 1000 cuts,"* eroding any overall gains from the other quadrants, increasing costs of management of Public relations to defuse adverse commentaries, bad press, building up barriers to recruiting new partners to join while increasing internal pressures on Xi in China for rapid disinvestment. On the other hand, the rise of social media has increased these threats as they are communicated easily across vast areas globally as well as locally and socio-digital technology enables rapid proliferation of protests and recruitment of activists. Further, social media, as indicated in the protests in Hong Kong in the last two years enables dissenters to bypass governments and official gatekeepers, enabling alternative views and opinions or facts to be disseminated, thereby increasing debate and discussion (Cockburn et al, 2015, pp. 425–426). Such viral voices online may not always be well-informed or even rational, but can often be very loud and vociferous in generating antipathy or activist protesters nonetheless. Thus, building movements rapidly and spreading far and wide like #Extinction Rebellion, #BlackLivesMatter movement, and #MeToo activism as noted above.

The lower right quadrant, with highest unease and distrust, is about an ideological approach akin to the politics of "*NIMBYISM*" *(Not-In-My-Backyard –ism)*, BRI is seen as a current and future polluter unless action is taken to be more green, as Ma and Zadek (2019) comment "The results indicate that, based on historical infrastructure investment patterns and growth projections, key B&RCs are currently on track to generate emissions well above 2-Degree Scenario ('2Ds') levels, the upper limit of the Paris Agreement's temperature increase target."

Chinese economic imperialism has been a fact and a feature of long-standing political and cultural distrust of Chinese intentions in parts of south Asia such as Vietnam, Taiwan, Malaysia, and India while, in the Balkans, many populations also hold negative views of communism. Thus, the seeds of active campaigns of resistance and sabotage have already been planted, some harking back to earlier wars, conquests, or campaigns such as the Malaysian Communist revolt in the 1950s, which the British government ensured was seen as a purely Chinese revolt and not a guerilla campaign supported by the majority of native Malay or Malaysian Indian people and so ultimately prompted resistance to the revolt by those ethnic groups with some localized violence or conflicts against the Chinese.

In conclusion, therefore, there is no excuse for ignoring the shifting of power towards Asia which has been flagged in many reports for some time and which requires more specificity (especially with regard to China) and a more distinct treatment than being aggregated—under general discussions of diversity and Randers' book (2013). Increasingly, according to a diverse range of informed observations, **"The West needs the East a lot more that the East needs the West"** [original in bold], and China has a strong chance of being the superpower of the third millennium if their approach to development is made greener and they are willing and able to meet the somewhat diluted climate targets such as those established at Cop26 (Ma & Zadek, 2019). The qualitative scenarios outlined in the matrix using Table 1 illustrate how hard it may be for the Chinese to overcome current concerns about perceived potential economic imperialist intentions, using debt entrapment methods, for instance, as seen in Sri Lanka to acquire control of territory. Further, their long-standing wish for reunification of Taiwan and other disputed land makes the PR objectives about development and inclusivity objectives in the BRI initiative seem hollow to many and thus engendering even more resistance to partnering with China while resistance and counter-initiatives by blocs such as AUKUS seem even more likely to act as a force for resistance to BRI overtures among potential partner countries and organizations by a process metaphorically similar to the so-called death by "1000 cuts" executions of the past.

The recent issues with the Chinese tennis star Peng Shuai and the WTA's publicly voiced concern for her welfare is a PR problem for the promotion of BRI. The latter issue has been exacerbated with the recent, publicly announced decision of the US and allies to raise a diplomatic boycott of the upcoming 2022 Beijing Olympics is another example of the same, i.e., "spoiling" efforts directed at China and BRI bolstering the continuing calls in the UK and US to block any involvement of Chinese technology organizations in these countries' 5G project development. To Chinese leaders, these are attempts to cause the BRI to flop but they may also cause other "knock on" issues at home in terms of disrupting the economy, reducing efforts to productively utilize excess domestic production of goods and services and that could then precipitate an economic crisis at home not seen since the days of the Maoist Cultural revolution. There may also be some latent Chinese concerns about the new Taliban government in Afghanistan or others, such as the US promoting Islamic style Uyghur resistance in China (Duchatel, 2019) although some other writers suggest that is unlikely in a mainly secularized population in China (Yehan, 2021) and the last time the US assisted resistance (to the Russian presence) in Afghanistan, it evolved into post-Soviet resistance by Osama bin laden's followers and their allies to the influence and presence of the US and their allies and to result in what current president Joe Biden has called the "Forever war" in Afghanistan from which the US and allies have just departed in what appeared to be an unseemly haste and shameful debacle akin to the earlier retreat from Vietnam according to the likes of US army General Milley (BBC News, General Mark Milley admits "anger and pain" over Afghanistan, September, 2021).

Bibliographic References

ABC TV News Broadcast. (2019, November 8). By Max Walden, *What is the Blue Dot Network and is it really the West's response to China's Belt and Road project?* Retrieved on August 28, 2021.

Arrow, H., McGrath, J. E., & Berdahl, J. L. (2000). *Small groups as complex systems.* Sage.

Barsade, S. G., Brief, A. P., & Spataro, S. E. (2003). The affective revolution in organizational behavior: The emergence of a paradigm. In J. Greenberg (Ed.), *Organizational behavior: The state of the science* (pp. 3–52). Lawrence Erlbaum Associates Publishers.

Bateson, G. (1979). *Mind and nature: A necessary unity.* Wildwood House.

Battram, A. (1992). *The complexicon—A lexicon of complexity.* LGMB.

BBC News. (2021). *General Mark Milley admits 'anger and over Afghanistan pain'.* Retrieved on January 2022, from https://www.bbc.com/news/av/world-us-canada-58416207

Blanchette, J. (2021, July 7). The race to consolidate power and stave off disaster. *Foreign Relations.*

China Daily. (2013, September 7). President Xi proposes Silk Road economic belt. Astana, Xinhua News Agency. Retrieved on August 2020. https://www.chinadaily.com.cn/china/2013xivisitcenterasia/2013-09/07/content_16951811.htm

China Daily Press Release. (2013). Retrieved on April 2021, from https://www.chinadaily.com.cn/china/2013xivisitcenterasia/2013-09/07/content_16951811.htm

Clement, V., Rigaud, K. K., de Sherbinin, A., Jones, B., Adamo, S., Schewe, J., Sadiq, N., & Shabahat, E. (2021). *Groundswell Part 2: Acting on internal climate migration.* World Bank. Retrieved on August 2021, from https://openknowledge.worldbank.org/handle/10986/36248

Cockburn, T. (2006, September 28–29). *A complexity-based typology of emotional regimes in teams.* ITPNZ conference paper, Napier, New Zealand.

Cockburn, T. (2008a, November 28–29). *Webs of emotion: A study of the formation of team identity.* 3rd Asia Pacific Symposium on Emotions in Worklife, University of Newcastle, Australia.

Cockburn, T. (2008b, March 17–19). *The emotional landscape of action learning MBA teams.* International Action Learning Conference, Action Learning: Practices, Problems & Prospects, Henley Management College, UK.

Cockburn, T. (2020, September 22). *Citizen learner discourse and emergent global knowledge societies.* Peter Lang. Available at SSRN https://doi.org/10.2139/ssrn.3703694

Cockburn, T., Desmarais, F., & Desmarais, M. (2007). The tale of a thousand needles. In D. Kantarlis (Ed.), *Global business and economics journal Anthology* (Vol. I, pp. 90–99).

Cockburn, T., Jahdi, K. S., & Wilson, E. G. (2015). *Responsible governance-international perspectives for the new era.* Business Expert Press.

Cordis UK Papers. (2003). *Education and training for governance and active citizenship in Europe: Analysis of adult learning and design of formal, non-formal and informal educational intervention strategies.* ETGACE Project, Fact Sheet, FP5, CORDIS, European Commission (europa.eu).

Cornwell, R., Coonan, C., McRae, H., & Walton, G. (2011, February 14). The year of the tiger: The Chinese century. *The Independent.*

Duchatel, M. (2019). *China's foreign fighters' problem.* Retrieved on April 2021, from https://warontherocks.com/2019/01/chinas-foreign-fighters-problem/

Fukuyama, F. (2020). *The pandemic and political order. It takes a state.* Retrieved at https://www.foreignaffairs.com/articles/world/2020-06-09/pandemic-and-political-order

Hammond, J. S., Keeney, R. L., & Raiffa, H. (1998). *The hidden traps in decision making.* Retrieved at https://hbr.org/1998/09/the-hidden-traps-in-decision-making-2

Hass, R. (2021, March 3). China is not ten feet tall-how alarmism undermines American strategy. *Foreign relations Journal.* Retrieved on August 2021, from https://www.foreignaffairs.com/articles/china/2021-03-03/china-not-ten-feet-tall

Jackson, T. (2016). *Prosperity without growth-foundations for the economy of tomorrow* (2nd ed.). Routledge.

Jenkins, J. (2001, June 10–13). *Imfundo: Partnership for IT IN education.* Paper presented at European Distance Education Network, 10th anniversary conference, Stockholm, Sweden.

Kahn, H. (1962). *Thinking about the unthinkable.* Horizon Press.

Kauffman, S. (1995). *At home in the universe.* Oxford University Press.

Khanna, P. (2011). *How to run the world: Charting a course to the next renaissance.* Random House.

Kouzes, J. M., & Posner, B. Z. (1997). *The leadership challenge: How to keep getting extraordinary things done in organizations* (pp. xv–31). Jossey-Bass.

Kuo, L., & Kommenda, N. (2018) What Is China's Belt and Road Initiative? *Guardian Online.* Retrieved on August 2021, from https://www.theguardian.com/cities/ng-interactive/2018/jul/30/what-china-belt-road-initiative-silk-road-explainer

Lissack, M., & Roos, J. (1999). *The next common sense.* Nicholas Brealey.

Mahon, C. J. (1999). *Charting complexity: Analysing how strategy emerges in organisations.* Copenhagen Business School Press.

Ma, J., & Zadek, S. (2019). *Decarbonizing the Belt and Road—A green finance road map.* Retrieved on August 2021, from http://www.vivideconomics.com/publications/decarbonizing-the-belt-and-road-initiative-a-greenfinance-

Martin, C. (1999). *Net future: The 7 Cybertrends that will drive your business, create new wealth, and define your future.* McGraw-Hill.

Naisbitt, J. (1997). *Megatrends Asia: The eight Asian megatrends that are changing the world.* Simon and Schuster.

Nye, J. (2010). China's century is not yet upon us. *Financial Times,* Comments Section. Retrieved on August 2021, from http://www.ft.com/intl/cms/s/0/649e807a-62aa-11df-b1d1-00144feab49a.html#axzz2OLFGTSdz

Ogilvy, J., & Schwartz, P. (2008). *China's futures: Scenarios for the world's fastest growing economy, ecology, and society.* Jossey Bass.

Randers, J. (2013). *2052—A global forecast or the next 40 years.* Chelsea Green.

Reuters. (2021). Retrieved at https://www.reuters.com/world/china/chinas-belt-road-plans-losing-momentum-opposition-debt-mount-study-2021-09-29/

Rost, J. (1993). *Leadership for the twenty-first century*. Praeger.

Sanders, T. I. (1998). *Strategic thinking and the new science: Planning in the midst of chaos, complexity and change*. Free Press/Simon Schuster.

Sha Song. (2021). *Belt and Road green investment that delivers on climate action*. Retrieved on August 2021, from https://www.weforum.org/agenda/2021/11/belt-and-road-green-investment-delivers-on-climate-action/

Sherman, H., & Schultz, R. (1998). *Open boundaries: Creating business innovation through complexity*. Perseus Books.

Smith, P., & Cockburn, T. (2013). *Dynamic leadership models for global business: Enhancing digitally connected environments*. IGI Global.

Smith, P., & Cockburn, T. (Eds.). (2014). *Impact of emerging digital technologies on leadership in global business*. IGI Global.

Smith, P., & Cockburn, T. (2016). *Developing and leading emergence teams*. Routledge.

Smith, P., & Cockburn, T. (Eds.). (2020). *Global business leadership development for the fourth industrial revolution* (Part of the advances in business strategy and competitive advantage book series). IGI Global.

Smith, P. A. C., & Cockburn, T. (2021). *Global business leadership development for the fourth industrial revolution*. IGI Global.

Stacey, R. D. (1996). *Complexity and creativity in organizations*. Berret-Koehler.

Wolfowitz, P., Rivera, K., & Ware, G. (2018). Planning for the unexpected. *Strategy + Business*. Retrieved on September 2021, from https://www.strategy-business.com/article/Planning-for-the-Unexpected

Wong, A. (2021, May/June). How not to win allies and influence geopolitics. *Foreign Affairs*.

Xi Jinping. (2013). *China Daily news report: China—Central Asia ties facilitate regional development*. Retrieved on August 2021, from https://www.chinadaily.com.cn/china/2013xivisitcentera sia/2013-09/08/content_16952970.htm

Yehan. (2021). Calls for independence may not help the Uyghur cause. *Foreign Policy*. Retrieved on August 2021, from The Uyghur movement needs to recalibrate away from calls for independence. https://foreignpolicy.com/2021/07/27/uyghur-independence-hurting-case-xinjiang/

Zhao, L. (2015). Retrieved at https://www.fmprc.gov.cn/eng/topics_665678/2015zt/xjpcxbayzlt2 015nnh/201503/t20150328_705553.html

Chapter 12
China's Ambition in Promoting Green Finance for Belt and Road Initiative

Berna Kirkulak-Uludag

1 Introduction

It was right before our eyes that we witnessed how China has transformed itself gradually from a manufacturing hub to an industrial powerhouse over the last few decades. Unless the rise of China was perceived as a threat by the developed countries recently, namely the US, EU together with Commonwealth countries, and Japan, almost all nations used to enjoy accessing and using the cheap products and services provided by China, in which the prosperity was partially built on the workers' shoulders. However, this understanding is abandoned gradually and all the cards are shuffled again for different types of cooperation and alliances following the US–China trade war.

In fact, the trade war between US and China might have come to the forefront before 2018. The obvious tension between these two countries somehow was postponed due to Global Financial Crisis (GFC), which was a severe portent of global economic stagflation in later years. The trade deficit against China has long been an elephant in the room for the policymakers and politicians not only in the US but also in other countries. However, like the US, the other countries enjoyed trade deficits against China due to fear of rising inflation. It was not until Huawei's advanced 5G technology, which was accused of being used in spying against the US, the sprouts of tension between the US and China became worldwide evident. It is not only the US, which treats China as a strategic rival but also the EU sees China as a systematic rival albeit its strategic partnership since 2003. According to the EU-China Factsheet (2022), China is defined as simultaneously a cooperation partner, a negotiation partner, an economic competitor, and a systematic rival. Nevertheless, the technology and trade-based tension between the US and China is taking place in a political dimension. In early 2021, the Alaska summit was an inflection point for US–China relationship. As both parties pushed an envelope to each other, it was

B. Kirkulak-Uludag (✉)
Faculty of Business, Dokuz Eylül University, İzmir, Turkey

the first time that China explicitly exposed itself as a counterattack country rather than a low profile country. In order to communicate amid tension, the leaders of two countries had a virtual meeting in late 2021. While the US prioritized climate diplomacy between two countries, however, yet, China seemed vacillated to have long-term commitments in terms of environment and climate change.

While China has been accused of maintaining status quo and not taking urgent actions on environmental issues, it is particularly worthy to note that it uses its own diplomatic tools to cooperate with region-specific countries. China more focuses on taking steps towards greening the Belt and Road Initiative (BRI) in order to promote low-carbon development, increase climate governance cooperation and capacity building in green. For example, the climate cooperation with African countries on green recovery and green sustainable development can be evaluated in this context (Kaneti, 2021). In fact, China tries its utmost to stay competitive against the recently launched Build Back Better World (B3W) of the US and the Global Gateway Strategy of the European Union. Isn't the backdrop of the efforts of China at greening the BRI just a reflection of this? Climate change and environmental degradation will occupy more and more of our agenda in the near future. Accordingly, China will draw more attention in the context of environmental diplomacy rather than debt-trap discourse or vaccine diplomacy. China's aspiration in greening the BRI cannot be explained simply by saying that it aligns with the core interests of BRI countries. The key question here is to understand what kind of responsibility China can take in the international community and whether China can be trusted to take responsibilities. China's determination and sincerity to promote green finance for BRI should also be evaluated in this context. Only in this way can the concerns of the international community about cooperating with China on climate change and environment be alleviated.

This chapter addresses China's ambition in greening the Belt and Road Initiative (BRI). The current study delves into the green credit and green bond policy of Chinese banks. It is a particular interest of this study to understand the role of state-owned banks, which are at the forefront of financing the BRI. Unlike the existing literature, which mainly focus on BRI beyond the "debt-trap" discourse (Brautigam, 2020; Dwyer, 2020; Lai et al., 2020; Shaikh & Chen, 2021), the author puts emphasis on how China promotes green finance for BRI and also opens the floor to discuss whether China is determined and sincere enough in this ambition. To this end, the current study provides blended views selected out from several policy and academic papers with the aim of contributing to this limited research area. This study has five sections. Following the introduction, Sect. 2 provides insights into environmental diplomacy and BRI. Section 3 describes China's green financing legal background. Section 4 depicts the Chinese banking industry and the role of banks in green financing. Finally, Sect. 5 concludes.

2 Environmental Diplomacy and BRI

In fact, the reason why China has become more visible in terms of environmental diplomacy can be somehow attributed to BRI. In 2013, China launched BRI, a contemporary silk road, to connect itself with the rest of the world through two new trade routes. While China avidly demonstrates an assertive foreign policy in international infrastructure and promoting global connectivity, mounting concerns about the environmental practices of Chinese companies make particularly Western societies raise questions regarding the environmental dimensions of overseas investments of China under the BRI umbrella. The controversial arguments view BRI as a poorly coordinated branding effort and exemplify it as a Chinese version of "Make America Great Again" (Freymann, 2019). Furthermore, some other arguments posit that China's FDI outflow stock is much weaker in comparison to those of developed countries. Table 1 clearly shows that the share of China's FDI outflow to its GDP is lacking behind many European countries. This implies the fact that China's overseas investments are much weaker relative to its domestic investments. In addition to this, While China encourages overseas investment, it fails to inhibit investment in carbon-intensive and fossil fuel industries. The majority, almost 80%, of China's overseas energy investments are in fossil fuels in comparison with 3% in solar and wind. It is confusing that China is aggressive in green finance policy, in particular, for its domestic market, while maintaining low-cost and carbon-intensive fossil fuel projects. This leads to a discrepancy between domestic and overseas investments of China. Furthermore, the Chinese companies are accused of being not transparent and not disclosing information about their overseas investments. Although China has been adopting a series of green measures in infrastructure, energy, and finance to support BRI participant countries, the majority of Chinese policies in this regard are derived from voluntary guidelines rather than mandatory provisions. In case of non-compliance with the host country regulations, the consequences of sanctions remain ambiguous. BRI's environmental policies appear to consist of soft governance and non-binding regulations (Gallagher & Qi, 2021).

Even when the COVID-19 outbreak emerged, unlike the Middle Ages, people no longer believe that this outbreak is a punishment from God. Rather, people started questioning whether the COVID-19 outbreak would be the outcome of environmental degradation, namely climate change or not. In particular, scientists started investigating how climate change alters other species on Earth that matters to our health and our risk of infections (Bernstein, 2020). Yet, there has been no crystal-clear answer to this question but it appears that the issue of environment within the scope of BRI together with the emergence of COVID-19 pandemic have increased pressure and taken a toll on China. It is possible that in the wake of COVID-19, balancing required economic growth and reductions in carbon emissions would bring multifaceted challenges to China. Another important issue is the role of China in the international community through the BRI. China seems reluctant to take on responsibilities in expanding its role in international organizations such as the World Bank and IMF over the years. Rather, China has been energizing its own resources to transform itself

Table 1 FDI Stocks Outward, % of GDP, 2020

Top 15 countries with high FDI stocks outwards		Top 15 countries with low FDI stocks outwards	
Luxembourg	1319.28	Lithuania	18.94
Netherlands	411.37	Saudi Arabia	18.39
Ireland	281.11	China	16.24
Switzerland	182.63	Slovenia	16.14
Canada	119.36	Mexico	13.59
Belgium	112.88	Argentina	10.71
European Union	85.93	New Zealand	9.92
Sweden	83.78	Indonesia	8.16
United Kingdom	78.94	Latvia	7.67
Denmark	69.76	Greece	7.40
South Africa	61.18	India	7.36
France	58.85	Turkey	7.04
Chile	58.35	Costa Rica	5.39
Norway	57.88	Poland	5.05
OECD-Total	57.05	Slovak Republic	5.01

Source OECD (2020). International Foreign Direct Investment

as a rule-maker than a rule-taker such as the establishment of the Asian Infrastructure Investment Bank (AIIB) in 2015, which was established few months later than the New Development Bank (NDB) by BRICS countries (Preston et al., 2016). It is important to note that while AIIB strongly focuses on financing BRI, NDB focuses on sustainable and green finance. In a very recent study, China was scrutinized under the spotlights in terms of its international lending. It is well documented that China surpassed the World Bank and IMF in terms of lending and has become the world's largest official creditor. However, it appears that the Chinese state-driven loans are more commercial than official. It is because almost half of China's official lending to the developed countries are hidden debts implying the fact that they are not reported in the most widely used official debt statistics (Horn et al., 2021). Furthermore, in spite of increasing discussions and COVID-19 pandemic, the BRI campaign has gone global in such a short time. On one hand, many countries have embraced China's BRI with enthusiasm. On the other hand, the implications of China's ambition in BRI have been increasingly subject to several debates. Mainly the US and some Western European countries are very much concerned about debt diplomacy and lack of transparency of the Chinese overseas investments (Wemer, 2019). Despite the scepticism of the EU, the countries of Poland, Greece, Italy, Hungary, Czechoslovakia, Croatia, Bulgaria, Latvia, Portugal, Romania, and Slovakia joined the BRI in Europe. China has been making significant inroads not only in Europe but also in Africa, Southeast Asia, Middle East, and also in Latin America. Despite no immediate gains associated with BRI, the attraction of BRI is so immense that even countries like Israel, which strongly allied with the US, started to curry favour with China regardless of attracting the anger of the US.

Less pessimistic, but equally detailed analyses on the BRI argue that there is nothing wrong in China's infrastructure investment and promoting global connectivity particularly in the developing world. Indeed, the US also has an interest in supporting a more developed world. It is only a matter of where BRI intersects with US interests. In particular, the regions like Africa and Latin America, which lack adequate infrastructure, can harness the BRI for their growth and development. Further, the BRI can support local economies and promote connectivity in some places like Tajikistan and Laos, where relatively draw less international interest and attention (Fujun et al., 2019). Furthermore, greening the BRI may also help to alleviate poverty in less developed countries. It is highly likely that more people may live in poverty due to climate change. However, China's greening ambition of the BRI should be accompanied with significant policy reforms that increase transparency and improve sustainability (World Bank, 2019; Zhou et al., 2018). China's aggression in greening BRI including the financial markets may also have a positive impact on the entire global financial system. For instance, in their study, Choi and Escalante (2020) reveal that green credits in China have performed better than the conventional credits. This implies that China has embraced green finance in response to regulatory pressures and green credits are perceived less risky than other traditional credits. Further, technology is disrupting traditional financial practices through artificial intelligence, big data, and block chain. China is becoming a global testing ground to explore how Fintech applications can be harnessed to achieve its green finance ambition. To end this, the Green Credit Management System, a cloud platform, was introduced to identify, evaluate, and classify green projects to have more accurate information for the banks. Using AI and machine learning, this system recognizes whether a financial transaction meets green standards or not (Paulson Institute, 2020). These innovative technological solutions associated with BRI can both change the lives of many people and force other countries to produce humanitarian and environmental friendly solutions. The idea of a multipolarized world is on the table for balancing the overwhelming power of the US. Exactly, at this point, BRI could be instrumental in making new economic and political allies in the neglected part of the world and help in creating an alternative particularly for developing nations to articulate themselves and make their voices more visible.

3 China's Green Financing Legal Background

In recent years, China has attracted significant attention due to its ambition in launching the largest green finance initiative to promote clean air, water, and safe soil. The first green finance policy of China dated back to 1995, when The People's Bank of China (PBOC) issued a notice on "Credit Policy for Environmental Protection" (PBOC, 1995). In order to stimulate financial institutions and raise the awareness of environmental risk when lending, the Ministry of Environmental Protection

Table 2 Milestones in China's green financing

Year	Actions
1995	Notice on Credit Policy for Environmental Protection by PBOC
2007	Notice on Implementing Environmental Protection Policies and Regulations to Prevent Credit Risks by the Ministry of Environmental Protection together with the PBOC and the China Banking and Insurance Regulatory Commission
2012	Green Credit Guidelines by China Banking Regulatory Commission
2013	Notice of Submission of Green Credit Statistics by China Banking Regulatory Commission
2014	Establishment of the Green Finance Task Force by the PBOC and the UN Environment Program
2016	Launch of the Guidelines for Establishing A Green Financial System, jointly developed by the PBOC and six other ministry-level agencies
2018	Guidelines for Green Investment by Asset Management Association of China supervised by China Securities Regulatory Commission

together with the PBOC and the China Banking and Insurance Regulatory Commission (CBIRC) released a notice on "Implementing Environmental Protection Policies and Regulations to Prevent credit risks" in 2007. Another important milestone in China's green financing is the Green Credit Guidelines issued by CBRC in 2012. The guidelines require banks to disclose ESG reports and encourage energy saving, low-carbon emission, and environment protection by managing environmental and social risks of their clients. The guidelines apply to state-owned policy banks, commercial banks, rural banks, and cooperatives.

In 2016, China pushed promoting green finance and green credit through establishing a green financial system, which addresses green bonds, green lending, green development funds, green insurance, markets for pollution control rights, local government initiatives, and international cooperation. Another important milestone is Guidelines for Green Investment, which is the first official policy guidance for Chinese investors on integrating ESG factors. It is a moot point for China to transform itself into green without a green transition in its financial sector. In this regard, it appears that the guidelines in green investment will play a crucial role to transform the funds, which are still invested in traditional industries. Therefore, it is important for China to include financial institutions and mobilize them together to achieve this task. Table 2 summarizes the milestones in China's green financing.

4 The Chinese Banking Industry and the Role of Banks in Green Financing

China has been adapting its financial system into a greener and a low-carbon economy. To end this, the Chinese Central Bank (CBC) together with pioneering state-owned banks support green development to tackle environmental and climate related financial risks to safeguard financial stability and restore its notorious image in terms of environmental degradation. China's financial market is dominated by the banking industry and state-owned banks give direction to its financial market. Bailey et al. (2011) underscore how state-owned banks are constrained by the long-lasting government interventions at different levels. China has a three-tier structured banking system and it opened up its banking industry in the early 1980s and allowed five state-owned banks to accept deposits and conduct banking activities. These banks are Industrial and Commercial Bank of China (ICBC), the China Construction Bank (CCB), the Bank of China (BOC), the Bank of Communications (BOCOM), and the Agricultural Bank of China (ABC). Among them, ICBC, BOC, CCB, and ABC are known as the "Big Four." In the early 1990s, the Chinese government established three policy banks including the Agriculture Development Bank of China (ADBC), the China Development Bank (CDB), and the Export–Import Bank of China (EXIM). The regulatory body of the banking system is the China Banking and Insurance Regulatory Commission (CBIRC), which replaced the China Banking Regulatory Commission (CBRC) in 2018 (Qian, 2020). In their study, Yin et al. (2019) investigate the impact of green credits on the profitability and credit risk of Chinese banks over the period 2011–2018. Their findings posit that green-lending practices reduce the profitability for state-owned banks. In line with the government policy, state-owned banks play crucial roles in green lending at the forefront even at the expense of their profitability. Interestingly, green-lending practices appear to be a driving force for private banks to improve their performance by increasing their profit while reducing their risk. In another study, Yin et al. (2021) examine the determinants of the green credit ratio and the impact of green credits on the profitability and credit risk of Chinese banks. Their findings indicate that Chinese state-owned banks play a crucial role in lending green credits and state-owned banks provide green credits at the expense of their profitability. This can be attributed to the Chinese government's ambition to push state-owned banks in green lending (Fig. 1).

Table 3 presents ICBC's green bond issuance. China has become the world's second-largest green bond issuing country following the US. The green bonds have become an important tool to earmark for BRI projects. Among China's big four state-owned banks, the Industrial and Commercial Bank of China (ICBC) has a dominant role as the largest underwriter in issuing BRI Green Climate Bonds. Having close ties with the state, ICBC plays a crucial role in adopting the green practices across China's banking industry. For instance, ICBC is the first Chinese commercial bank to implement the Green Credit Policy and ICBC is aggressive not only in green credit policy but also in building a positive image for China to be recognized as a green finance leader in the world.

China, as the biggest emitter of carbon dioxide, has heavy financial obligations (roughly $21 trillion) to meet net-zero emission targets. State-owned banks are aggressively pushed to issue bonds to align with government priorities. There has been no domestic market support for green bonds. In particular, domestic investors hesitate to purchase green bonds due to the risk and uncertainty embedded, as they are long-term investment tools. The green bonds account for less than 1% of China's

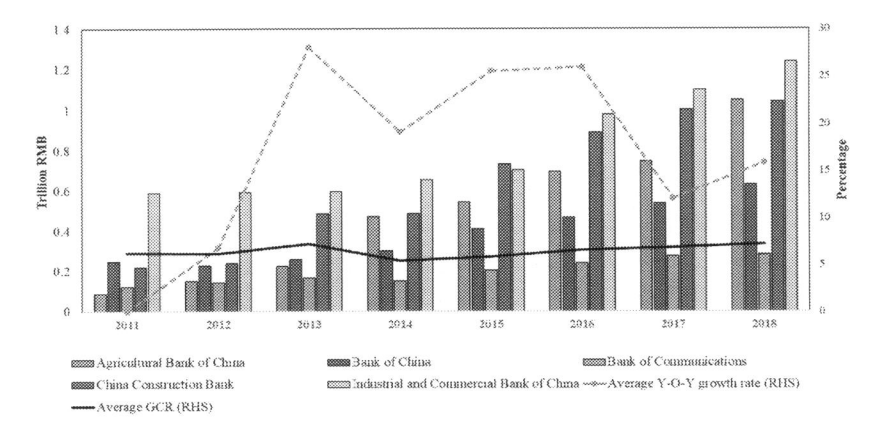

Fig. 1 The green credit balance of the big five state-owned commercial banks 2011–2018 (*Source* Yin et al. [2021]. Data was compiled from CSR Report and Annual Report from ABC, BOC, BOCom, CCB, and ICBC, 2011–2018)

Table 3 Green bond issuance by ICBC

Name	Place	Currency	Date	Proceeds (USD)	Aim
BRI Green Climate Bond I	Luxemburg	USD	2017	850 million	Wind generation and electrified railway projects in China, solar power projects in several other countries
	Luxemburg	Euro	2017	1.3 billion	
BRI Green Climate Bond II	London	USD	2018	1 billion	Clean transportation, renewable energy, and offshore wind
	London	Euro	2018	578 million	
	Hong Kong	HKD	2018	330 million	
	Hong Kong	USD	2018	400 million	
BRBR Bond	Singapore	SGD	2019	2.2 billion	
Greater Bay Area Green Bond	Hong Kong	USD, HKD, CHN	2019	3.15 billion	

Source Choi and Escalante (2020) and ICBC (2017, 2018, 2019)

bond market (Reuters, 2021). Table 3 shows that ICBC issued its first certified climate bond through its Luxembourg branch in 2017 and this was followed by a second certified climate bond via its London, Hong Kong, and Singapore branches in 2018 and 2019, respectively.

Figure 2 presents the overall performance of 21 major banks based on the green credit statistics of CBIRC. While the quantitative assessment depends on green credit metrics used by CBIRC, qualitative assessment depends on organizational and strategic commitments used by PBOC. The maximum total score is 22, made up of 10 for the quantitative and 12 for the qualitative assessment (Choi & Escalante, 2020). As clearly indicated in Fig. 2, top green lenders by proportion are state-owned banks including Bank of China (BOC). Agriculture Bank of China (ABC), and China Construction Bank (CCB). State-owned banks play a crucial role in the green bond market. Moreover, the policy banks including CDC, EXIM, and ADBC are involved in development loans. Their establishment objectives of these banks comply with developing certain green technologies and they are large enough to have significant influence on the green credit market. In particular, the China Development Bank (CDB) is the largest policy bank in lending domestically and internationally. For instance, the total asset size (approximately $2.55 trillion) is even larger than other international policy banks including the World Bank (CDB, 2021). The CDB plays a crucial role in financing large-scale development projects and has an agile focus on the infrastructure of social, green, and emerging industries and the BRI. Another development Bank of China, EXIM, is involved in supporting foreign trade, investment, and international cooperation. Unlike CDB, EXIM can provide concessional loans for China's foreign aid. The majority of EXIM's lending aims to address infrastructure connectivity of China with neighbouring countries (Zhao, 2017). It is important to note that unlike commercial banks, policy banks are funded through bond issuance and government funding. Moreover, two new multilateral banks, the Asian Infrastructure Investment Bank and New Development Bank, where China has substantial involvement, have similar roles for overseas investments.

Figure 3 presents that China's overseas lending is in line with its strategic ambitions and energy needs to sustain its economic growth. Chinese finance is highly concentrated in a few countries. In particular, oil-producing countries such as

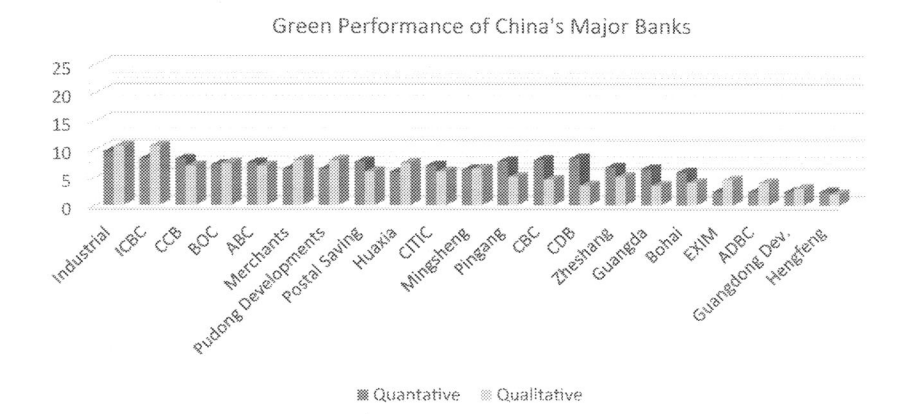

Fig. 2 The green performance of china's major banks (*Source* Author's own visualization based on the data provided by the report prepared by Choi and Escalante [2020] for Climate Policy Initiative. The original data is from Wind Data. ICBC: Industrial and Commercial Bank of China, ABC; Agriculture Bank of China, CCB; China Construction Bank, CITIC; China International Trust Investment Cooperation, CDB; China Development Bank, ADBC; Agricultural Development Bank of China)

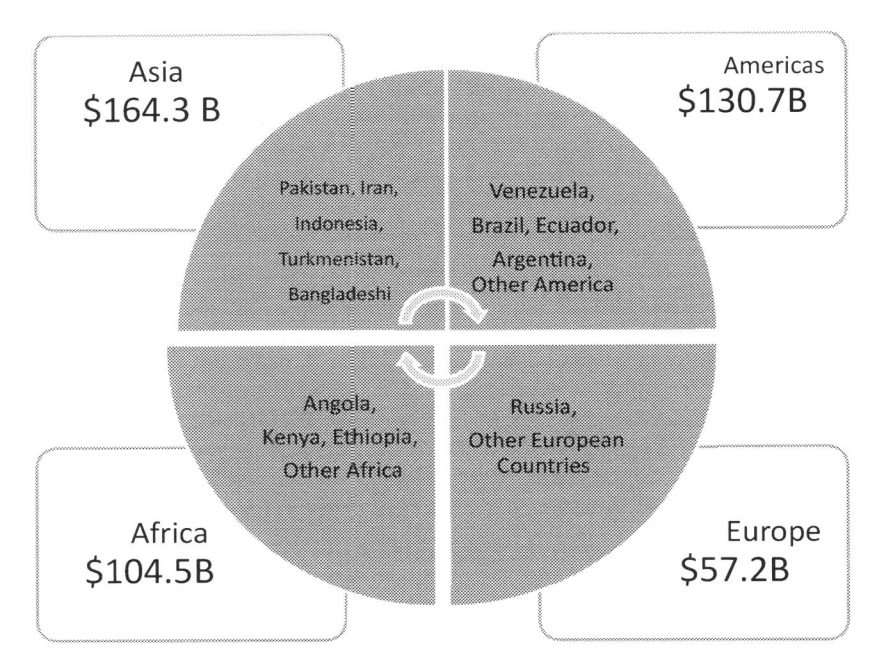

```
┌─────────────────┐                    ┌─────────────────┐
│      Asia       │                    │    Americas     │
│    $164.3 B     │    Pakistan, Iran,     Venezuela,    │    $130.7B      │
└─────────────────┘    Indonesia,         Brazil, Ecuador,└─────────────────┘
                       Turkmenistan,      Argentina,
                       Bangladeshi        Other America

                       Angola,            Russia,
                       Kenya, Ethiopia,   Other European
┌─────────────────┐    Other Africa       Countries      ┌─────────────────┐
│     Africa      │                                      │     Europe      │
│    $104.5B      │                                      │    $57.2B       │
└─────────────────┘                                      └─────────────────┘
```

Fig. 3 Financial Commitments of CDB and EXIM 2008–2019 (*Source* Global Development Policy Center [2020])

Venezuela, Angola, and Russia come to the forefront in overseas lending. The CDB together with EXIM were involved in totaling 615 development projects over 2008 and 2019. Out of 615 projects, 124 projects are within national protected areas, 261 are within critical habitats, and 133 are within indigenous people's land. The total Chinese overseas development finance amounted to almost $452 billion, whereas the World Bank spent roughly $467 billion through sovereign lending during the same time (Ray & Simmons, 2020).

5 Conclusion

The current study stems from the curiosity to understand China's commitments to global development. As China pulls up its sleeves to contest America's global leadership and expands its regional role, some fundamental questions arise behind its ambition. For example, some of them are: What kind of responsibilities can China take in the international community? To what extent can China be trustable in responding to its commitments or not? Exactly at this point, China's policy to promote green finance can be used as an instrument to understand the questions posed above. In this context, the current study discusses the green credit and green bond policy of Chinese banks. While concluding this chapter, the author of this study will not follow a mainstream approach. Instead, having an intellectual curiosity and avid scepticism, the author prefers raising some multifaceted questions that the readers of this chapter are more than welcome to ponder.

Two main areas stand out, where China has been criticized harshly, particularly, by the Western societies. The first of these is the destruction of the environment for the sake of its economic development. The other is the inability to access information on China's overseas loans and hence the lack of transparency regarding China's overseas loans to particularly developing or less developed countries. Is it a conscious policy of China to protect the data it produces in the age of Dataism[1] or Is it a problematic reality that China is trying to sweep under the carpet with the potential to lead us to another global financial crisis?

China embraces green finance through directing state-owned banks to take initiative in lending green credits and issuing green bonds in order to accomplish green BRI projects. While China is accused of weaponizing overseas lending and conducting a debt-trap diplomacy in the developing part of the world (Farley, 2021; Kaplan, 2018; Kinyondo, 2019; Singh, 2020), isn't it a big dilemma to witness fragility of its financial system (i.e., Even Grande and shadow banking)? What about domestic financial policy responses of China in dealing with surge in inflation, slowdown in economic growth, COVID-19 pandemic, discrepancy in wages and equality, rapid urbanization with ghost cities? Isn't it the communist ideology to prioritize the communes first? If this is the case, will some generations suffer until China's ambition in green finance along with BRI bears its fruits? In this context, is China similar to the US, which has been backing up its power by military force and ignoring its problems of fundamental healthcare and free access to higher education? What about climate change and the likelihood of new trade routes? Why are some countries recently involved in expeditions in the Arctic region and Antarctica intensively? Will it be important to talk about the BRI when trade routes change through the Arctic region and Antarctica? So the author of this chapter ends up leaving these mind-blowing questions unanswered, hoping that readers will discuss and perhaps provide some answers to help us get a better grasp of realities around us.

Bibliographic References

Bailey, W., Huang, W., & Yang, Z. (2011). Bank loans with Chinese characteristics: Some evidence on inside debt in a state-controlled banking system. *Journal of Financial and Quantitative Analysis, 46*, 1795–1830.

Belliconi, S. (2020). *5 reasons the coronavirus hit Italy so hard, the Conversation*. Retrieved on December 2021, from https://theconversation.com/5-reasons-the-coronavirus-hit-italy-so-hard-134636

---

[1] David Brooks first used this term in the *New York Times* in 2013. Dataism became popular by Yuval Noah Harari, who has described it as an emerging ideology or even a new form of religion, in which information flow is the supreme value.

Bernstein, A. (2020). Coronavirus, climate change, and the environment a conversation on COVID-19. *Harvard School of Public Health*. Retrieved on December 2021, from https://www.hsph.harvard.edu/c-change/subtopics/coronavirus-and-climate-change/

Brautigam, D. (2020). A critical look at Chinese debt trap diplomacy: The rise of a meme. *Area Development and Policy, 5*(1), 1–14.

Brooks, D. (2013-02-04). Opinion | The philosophy of data. *The New York Times*. Retrieved on December 2021, from https://www.nytimes.com/2013/02/05/opinion/brooks-the-philosophy-of-data.html

CBRC (China Banking Regulatory Commission). (2012, February). *Green credit guidelines*.

CDB (China Development Bank). (2021). *About CDB*. Retrieved on December 2021, from http://www.cdb.com.cn/English/gykh_512/khjj/

Choi, J., & Escalande, D. (2020). Green banking in China—Emerging trends with a spotlight on the industrial and commercial bank of China (ICBC). *Climate Policy Initiative*. Retrieved on December 2021, from https://www.climatepolicyinitiative.org/wp-content/uploads/2020/08/081220Green-Bankin-trends.pdf

Dwyer, B. M. (2020). They will not automatically benefit: The politics of infrastructure development in Laos's northern economic corridor. *Political Geography, 78*, 1–12.

EU-China Factsheet. (2022). *EU China relations*. https://www.eeas.europa.eu/sites/default/files/documents/EU-China_Factsheet_01Apr2022.pdf

Farley, R. (2021, July 1). Does China weaponize lending? *The Diplomat*. Retrieved on December 2021, from https://thediplomat.com/2021/07/does-china-weaponize-lending

Freymann, E. (2019, August 17). One belt one road' is just a marketing campaign. *The Atlantic*.

Fujun, Y., Gabuyev, A., Haenle, P., Bin, M., & Dimitri, T. (2019). *The Belt and Road Initiative: The views from Washington, Moscow, and Beijing*. Carnegie Endowment for International Peace. Retrieved on December 2021, from https://carnegieendowment.org/2019/04/08/belt-and-road-initiative-views-from-washington-moscow-and-beijing-pub-78774.

Gallagher, K. P. (2020). *China's global energy finance database*. Global Economic Governance Initiative. Retrieved on December 2021, from http://www.bu.edu/gdp

Gallagher, K. S., & Qi, Q. (2021). Chinese overseas investment policy: Implications for climate change. *Global Policy, 12*(3), 260–272.

Global Development Policy Center. (2020). *China's Overseas development finance*. Retrieved on December 2021, from https://www.bu.edu/gdp/chinas-overseas-development-finance/

Harari, Y. N. (2017). *Homo Deus: A brief history of tomorrow* (p. 428). Vintage Penguin Random House. ISBN 9781784703936.

Ho, V. H. (2018). Sustainable finance & China's green credit reforms: A test case for bank monitoring of environmental risk. *Cornell International Law Journal, 51*(3), 609–681.

Horn, S., Reinhart, M. C., & Trebesch, C. (2021). China's overseas lending. *Journal of International Economics, 133*, 103539.

ICBC. (2018). *Annual green bond report*. Retrieved on December 2021, from http://v.icbc.com.cn/%20userfiles/Resources/ICBCLTD/download/2019/GreenBondReport20191031.pdf

ICBC. (2019). *ICBC successfully issued the world's first green BRBR bond*. Retrieved on December 2021, from, https://www.icbc.com.cn/icbc/en/newsupdates/icbc%20news/ICBCSuccessfullyIssuedtheWorldsFirstGreenBRBRBond.htm

ICBC. (2017). *Annual green bond report*. Retrieved on December 2021, from http://v.icbc.com.cn/%20userfiles/Resources/ICBCLTD/download/2018/2017lvzhainiandubaogao_en.pdf

Kaneti, M. (2021). China's vision for environmental leadership, *The Diplomat*. Retrieved on December 2021, from https://thediplomat.com/2021/12/chinas-vision-for-environmental-leadership/

Kaplan, B. S. (2018). *The rise of patient capital: The political economy of Chinese global finance, institute for international economic policy* (Working Papers). The George Washington University.

Kinyondo, A. (2019). Is China recolonizing Africa? Some views from Tanzania. *World Affairs, 182*(2), 128–164.

Lai, K. P. Y., Lin, S., & Sidaway, J. D. (2020). Financing the Belt and Road Initiative (BRI): Research agendas beyond the "debt-trap" discourse. *Eurasian Geography and Economics, 61*(2), 109–124.

OECD. (2020). *International foreign direct investment.* Retrieved at https://data.oecd.org/fdi/fdi-stocks.htm)

Paulson Institute. (2020, September). *Fintech to go green.* Retrieved on December 2021, from https://www.paulsoninstitute.org/green-finance/green-scene/how-a-local-chinese-bank-used-fintech-to-go-green/

PBOC (The People's Bank of China). (2016). *The people's bank of China and six other agencies jointly issue "Guidelines for Establishing the Green Financial System* Retrieved on December 2021, from http://www.pbc.gov.cn/english/130721/3131759/index.html.

PBOC (The People's Bank of China). (1995). *Notice on implementing credit policies and enhancing environmental protection.*

Preston, F., Bailey, B., Bradley, S., Wei, J., & Zhao, C. (2016). *Navigating the New normal: China and global resource governance.* Development Research Center of the State Council of the People's Republic of China and The Royal Institute of International Affairs Chatham House, 87.

Ray, R., & Simmons, A. B. (2020). *Tracking China's overseas development finance.* Boston University Global Development Policy Center.

Reuters. (2021, April). *China leads global green-bond sales boom but faces headwinds.* Retrieved on December 2021, from https://www.reuters.com/article/us-china-bond-green-idUSKBN2BO4FP

Qian, J. (2020). *The Chinese banking system: Structure, potential risks, and reforms.* Fanhai International School of Finance, Fudan University and Peterson Institute Online Forum. Retrieved on December 2021, from https://www.piie.com/system/files/documents/qian2020-07-22ppt.pdf

Shaikh, D., & Chen, K. C. (2021). China's debt trap in Pakistan? A case study of the CPEC project. *South Asia Research, 41*(3), 399–414.

Singh, A. (2020). The myth of 2 debt-trap diplomacy 2 and realities of Chinese development of finance. *Third World Quarterly, 42*(2), 239–253.

Wemer, A.D. (2019, April 25). *Skepticism casts a shadow over China's Belt and Road summit.* Atlantic Council. Retrieved on December 2021, from https://www.atlanticcouncil.org/blogs/new-atlanticist/skepticism-casts-a-shadow-over-china-s-belt-and-road-summit/

World Bank. (2019). Millions could be lifted out of poverty but countries face significant risks, Success of China's Belt and Road Initiative Depends on Deep Policy reforms. Press Release. Retrieved on December 2021, from https://www.worldbank.org/en/news/press-release/2019/06/18/success-of-chinas-belt-road-initiative-depends-on-deep-policy-reforms-study-finds

Yin, W., Kirkulak-Uludag, B., & Zhang, S. Y. (2019). Is financial development in China green? Evidence from city level data. *Journal of Cleaner Production, 211*, 247–256.

Yin, W., Zhu, Z., Kirkulak-Uludag, B., & Zhu, Y. (2021). The determinants of green credit and its impact on the performance of Chinese banks. *Journal of Cleaner Production, 286*, 1–11.

Zhao, M. (2017, April 27). *China Eximbank—Striving to be a Pioneer in supporting the financing of BRI projects,* Financial News. Retrieved on December 2021, from https://www.financialnews.com.cn/yh/shd/201704/t20170427_116630.html

Zhou, L., Gilbert, S., Wang, Y., Cabré, M.M., & Gallagher, K. (2018). *Moving the green Belt and Road Initiative: From words to actions* (Working Paper). World Resources Institute.

Chapter 13
Liability of Emergingness of Emerging Market Banks Internationalizing to Advanced Economies

Anna Lupina-Wegener, Frank McDonald, Juan Shan, Gangfeng Zhang, and Güldem Karamustafa-Köse

1 Introduction

Over the past 10 years, the internationalization of Emerging Economy Multinational Corporations (EMNCs) has received extensive attention by management scholars (de Mello et al., 2015; Guillén & García-Canal, 2009). The findings of these studies reveal that EMNCs are generally smaller in size, with considerably less resources and international experience, than MNCs from industrialized countries, and they often do not have the ability to transfer management practices to their subsidiaries (Guillén & García-Canal, 2009). Moreover, key stakeholders in advanced markets often hold a poor image of the EMNCs' home countries (Thite et al., 2012). These circumstances, especially the lack of experience in conducting cross-frontier economic transactions, lead to the possibility of liability of emergingness. This liability adds to the costs and risks associated with engaging in cross-frontier activities such as foreign direct investment (Madhok & Keyhani, 2012). Liability of emergingness may particularly

A. Lupina-Wegener (✉) · G. Karamustafa-Köse
School of Engineering and Management Vaud (HEIG-VD), HES-SO University of Applied Sciences and Arts Western Switzerland, Yverdon-Les-Bains, Switzerland
e-mail: annaaleksandra.lupina-wegener@zhaw.ch

A. Lupina-Wegener
ZHAW School of Management and Law, International Management Institute, Winterthur, Switzerland

F. McDonald
University of Leeds, Leeds, UK

J. Shan
Faculty of Business and Economics (HEC Lausanne), University of Lausanne, Lausanne, Switzerland

G. Zhang
Department of Leadership and Organization Management, School of Management, Zhejiang University, Hangzhou, China

© The Author(s), under exclusive license to Springer Nature Singapore Pte Ltd. 2023
P. A. B. Duarte et al. (eds.), *The Palgrave Handbook of Globalization with Chinese Characteristics*, https://doi.org/10.1007/978-981-19-6700-9_13

be an issue in a context of high institutional distance, which has been shown to increase liability of foreignness (Eden & Miller, 2004).

However, few studies have examined how liability of emergingness affects EMNCs (de Mello et al., 2015; Hashai & Buckley, 2014). Understanding liabilities of EMNCs is particularly relevant in the political context in China where the central and municipal governments often have a powerful impact on Chinese firms (Deng, 2009). In 2013, China proposed the Belt Road Initiative as a national strategy to support the Chinese firms go global. The establishment of a financing platform (e.g., Asian Infrastructure Investment Bank), as well as the pronouncement of a series of relevant policies, created favourable conditions for Chinese firms to undertake overseas M&A. Compared with their counterparts in other countries, Chinese firms are more susceptible to political influences when engaging in overseas M&A. For instance, the central government policies can influence both Chinese firms' M&A decisions and IFDI by increasing or decreasing the financial support to the relevant companies. Increased financial support may encourage Chinese firms to seek strategic assets through overseas expansion. With the Belt and Road Initiative, the local government at all levels has shown strong willingness to promote overseas M&A in the Belt and Road countries. According to a research report release by the Chinese Academy of Social Science, Chinese firms were involved in 2,996 overseas M&A cases from 2000 to 2016 (Li, 2017). Among them, 196 M&A cases occurred in Belt and Road countries. In 2017, China's overseas M&A in economies related to the Belt and Road Initiative achieved a record high of $48.2 billion, up 81% year-on-year, according to a global accounting and consulting firm EY report (Jiang, 2018).

To address this gap, we draw from neo-institutional theory (DiMaggio & Powell, 1983) to explore how an organization engages in mimetic, coercive, and normative isomorphism to gain legitimacy in a host market (Björkman et al., 2007; Kostova & Zaheer, 1999). We use existing literature on how EMNCs entering the markets of advanced economies seek legitimacy by engaging in institutional isomorphism (Marchand, 2015; Salomon & Wu, 2012; Wei & Lau, 2008; Wu & Salomon, 2016). Building on insights from this literature, we suggest that EMNCs mitigate the liability of emergingness in host markets by engaging in isomorphism.

Drawing on collected data between 2012 and 2015, this chapter aims to provide insights into how EMNCs seek to mitigate their liability of emergingness to bridge the institutional distance between home and host markets. We focus on emerging market banks (EMBs), i.e., a particular type of a service industry which has less experience in internationalization than industries in the manufacturing sector (Wells, 2009). Drawing from extensive research on banks from industrialized countries (Focarelli & Pozzolo, 2005; Mutinelli & Piscitello, 2001; Parada et al., 2009; Qian & Delios, 2008), we argue that the low international experience of EMBs might expose them to the liability of emergingness. To examine this issue, two research questions were formulated. First, how do EMBs engage in isomorphism in advanced economy host markets? Second, what are the implications of how EMBs' engage in isomorphism for their internationalization objectives?

To answer these research questions, we conducted an exploratory qualitative investigation, using data from semi-structured, face-to-face interviews, focus groups, and "off-the-record" discussions that focused on Brazilian and Chinese banks. We also collected secondary data as for example: press articles, websites, industry reports, annual reports. We find indications that the liability of emergingness is stronger for Chinese than Brazilian banks due to a strong coercive isomorphism from their HQs.

The chapter is divided as follows. First, we discuss the literature review on internationalization of EMNCs and emerging market banks. Second, we present the qualitative methodology we applied to collect data on Brazilian and Chinese banks. Third, we follow with the results of our field work and conclude with the discussion.

2 Literature Review

2.1 Internationalization of EMNCs

The rise of Emerging Economy Multinational Corporations (EMNCs) has revealed internationalization processes which are sufficiently different from those of MNCs based in developed economies to warrant the development of new theories (de Mello et al., 2015; Guillén & García-Canal, 2009). Notably, EMNCs' internationalization strategies in advanced economies tend to contradict some international management theories. One, for example, is the Uppsala model, according to which firms internationalize incrementally, starting in proximal markets and gradually moving to institutionally distant markets (Johanson & Vahlne, 1977). However, as EMNCs often lack a competitive edge afforded by technology, brand, and management practices (Buckley & Hashai, 2014; Buckley et al., 2012), they tend to rapidly internationalize into industrialized countries to overcome the liability of newness in global markets. Liability of newness affects new ventures which must rapidly learn how to manage new roles and social relationships with relevant stakeholders such as customers (Stinchcombe, 1965). Like new ventures, EMNCs often seek access to the resources and assets needed to effectively compete with multinationals from advanced, often Western markets (Luo & Tung, 2007). Developing an EMNC's competitive advantage in advanced markets can be a difficult task. This was demonstrated in a quantitative investigation of a sample of 112 new foreign ventures which found that local banks often considered banks from emerging markets as ineffective competitors (Petrou, 2007). This study indicates that emerging market banks face the liability of foreignness, i.e., a low capacity to gain legitimacy in the host market (Zaheer, 1995).

To address the liability of foreignness, EMNCs could instead focus on acquiring know-how located in host, advanced markets. They can also use the increased competitive advantage in the home market before focusing on the business in the host market (Boehe, 2015). This is in line with the revised Uppsala model, wherein access to technologies or resources in the host market can be facilitated if a foreign firm is perceived as an insider by local stakeholders. Becoming an insider might be possible through prior exchanges between the foreign firm and local partners, establishing mutual commitments, relationships, and trust. Otherwise, a firm risks facing the liability of outsidership, i.e., challenges in the host market if the firm does not have a position in a relevant network and is thus perceived as an outsider (Johanson & Vahlne, 2009).

EMNCs that are pursuing a strategy of internationalization may face difficulties when there is a high institutional distance between the home and host markets, which increases an EMNC's liability of foreignness (Eden & Miller, 2004). For example, a quantitative study on Chinese overseas investments between 1984 and 2001 reveals that cultural proximity, market familiarity, and access to a network are important factors in internationalization (Buckley et al., 2007). This might result from the fact that many EMNCs, both Asian as well as Brazilian (Cuervo-Cazurra et al., 2014), often lack experience in dealing with the institutional distance between the host and home markets. This is referred to in the literature as a liability of emergingness, defined as "the additional disadvantage that EMNCs tend to suffer by virtue of being from emerging economies" (Madhok & Keyhani, 2012, p. 28).

Specifically, EMNCs are smaller in size with considerably less resources and international experience than MNCs from industrialized countries, and they often do not have the ability to transfer management practices to their subsidiaries (Guillén & García-Canal, 2009). Moreover, stakeholders in advanced markets may hold a poor global image of an EMNC's home country (Thite et al., 2012). This is especially true for Chinese firms, which often face resistance in Western societies due to the perception that they offer low-quality services, as demonstrated in a case study of Shanghai Pengxin's attempt to acquire bankrupted Crafar farms in New Zeland (Yu & Liu, 2018).

We argue that the liability of emergingness is likely to add to the costs associated with the liability of foreignness. However, scant research has been devoted to exploring how EMNCs might actually mitigate the liability of emergingness to cope with the institutional distance between home and host markets, with the exception of (Buckley & Hashai, 2014; de Mello et al., 2015).

2.2 *Neo-Institutional Theory Approach to Internationalization*

To address this research gap, we will refer to the neo-institutional theory which focuses on how institutions relate to organizations, especially how the latter legitimize their activities to comply with regulatory and social norms and values reflected in institutional systems (DiMaggio & Powell, 1983; Haunschild & Miner, 1997; Powell & DiMaggio, 2012). According to the neo-institutional theory, a major factor in MNCs' internationalization strategies is gaining acceptance (legitimacy) within the milieu in which they operate (Xu & Shenkar, 2002). This is often connected to the concept of institutional isomorphism (DiMaggio & Powell, 1983) whereby diverse pressures, namely mimetic (imitation of practices of other organizations), coercive (pressures from other organizations), and normative (influence from professions), provide the means of gaining legitimacy (Björkman et al., 2007; Kostova & Zaheer, 1999). Neo-institutional theory suggests that new entrants in host locations with ambitious goals and a low competitive advantage may seek legitimacy by engaging in isomorphic processes, that is respond to the three isomorphic pressures in the host market: coercive, normative, and mimetic. This was confirmed by a quantitative study of 89 foreign banks whose subsidiaries imitate the practices of local banks, especially when there is a large institutional distance between the home and host markets (Salomon & Wu, 2012; Wu & Salomon, 2016).

Interestingly, in their quantitative study of 600 Chinese firms from various industries, Wei and Lau (2008) found that firms which engage in mimetic isomorphism through human resource management could better achieve strategic goals in the host market. In the same vein, in the context of a high institutional distance, Chinese firms tend to grant autonomy to their local subsidiaries to better respond to isomorphic pressures in the host market, such as, for example, coercive pressures from host market regulators (Klossek et al., 2012; Zheng et al., 2016). Mimetic isomorphism, through the granting of autonomy and a partnering approach, also has been found in a multiple case study of Chinese acquisitions in France (Marchand, 2015). She demonstrates that when a Chinese acquirer focuses on obtaining the technology know-how of a French firm, the latter tends to experience high autonomy in the post-merger integration. However, when a Chinese firm already has accumulated prior experience in the advanced market, it is more likely to adopt a more interventionist approach in the post-merger integration of the Western firm. Thus EMNCs with experience in advanced markets may be less likely than MNCs without prior experience, to respond to isomorphic pressures from relevant stakeholders or to mimic local competitors in host markets (Oehme & Bort, 2015).

Building on these insights, we will investigate how EMNCs engage in isomorphism in the host market to overcome their liability of emergingness. We link the liability of emergingness with an EMNC's engagement in isomorphism because prior research has documented that firms with less international experience are likely to imitate other players in host markets (Oehme & Bort, 2015). We will focus on emerging market banks (EMBs), a particular type of a service industry which has less experience in internationalization than manufacturing or high-tech industries (Wells, 2009). We will investigate how they mitigate their liability of emergingness in the context of advanced host markets and address the following questions: (i) how do EMBs engage in isomorphism in advanced host markets? (ii) what are the implications of EMBs' engagement in isomorphism on their internationalization objectives in the host market?

3 Methodology

A qualitative methodology is used in this exploratory study to provide insights into an institutional context which is often overlooked in international management research (Peng et al., 2008; Xu & Meyer, 2013). We refer to primary data we collected in China, Brazil, and Europe, as well as our extensive secondary data analysis.

3.1 Data Access and Collection

To maximize the range and diversity of empirical settings, we employed a purposive sampling strategy (Miles & Huberman, 2019; Patton, 1990). We selected participants who could provide insights into EMBs in host markets. As data collection in the banking industry is difficult due to concerns of confidentiality, we relied on our personal networks and used snowball sampling, which is relevant in situations where respondents are difficult to access (Weiss, 2005). In the first stage, we conducted interviews with bankers from EMBs in Switzerland. We also seized an opportunity to interview bankers from a Chinese bank in Poland, which, like Switzerland, is considered to be a high-income country (OECD & European Commission, 2020). Moreover, the Polish banking sector is dominated by foreign-owned institutions; 45% of banks in Poland are subsidiaries of foreign, global banks (Kotowicz, 2018). We, therefore, thought it would be relevant to complement the Swiss-based interviews with three additional interviews from Poland and Polish secondary data analysis. Finally, at the time of the investigation, there was just one Chinese bank in Switzerland, which soon afterwards left. The integration of Chinese banks in Poland thus makes our case studies more anonymous and complements data gathered in Switzerland.

In-depth interviews took place with banks from China and Brazil as these two countries have the most global impact on banking compared to other emerging market players (Frieda, 2015). However, the internationalization of Brazilian MNCs might follow different internationalization patterns than Asian MNCs, and EMBs consequently should not be considered as a homogeneous category. While Chinese MNCs are more focused on know-how development (Luo & Tung, 2007), an empirical study by Amal and Tomio (2015) reveals that Brazilian MNCs may be more focused on growth opportunities in host, advanced markets, where they seek to benefit from stable and positive institutional environments. Our interviews were conducted only with banks that have international activities in OECD classified high-income countries. We also interviewed senior bankers from European banks who were specialized in emerging market clients and executives to learn the perceptions of key players in developed countries concerning the activities and behaviours of EMBs, in other words, to understand how key local players perceived the legitimacy of EMBs in the host market.

The research design, therefore, allowed the internationalization of EMBs to be explored through a double lens on the liability of emergingness. Altogether, 40 semi-structured, face-to-face interviews were conducted and lasted on average of 60 minutes. All of the interviewees were top or upper middle managers: 28 bank executives, 12 bankers from bank associations such as the Swiss Association of Foreign Banks and the Federation of Brazilian Banks. Interviews were conducted in the language the interviewee was most comfortable, i.e., English, Polish, Portuguese, or Chinese. We also conducted eight "off-the-record" discussions with the bankers in informal settings and without recording the conversation in order to get further insights and triangulate interview data (Schouten & McAlexander, 1995). Indeed, developing relationships with the people being researched can help one gain richer data and enable deeper insights into the phenomena of interest (Langley & Royer, 2006). Finally, two focus groups were organized in China upon the request of the participants.

Table 1 gives an overview of the background of the interviewees. For reasons of confidentiality, we cannot indicate the names of their employers, and instead provide the information on the type of the financial institution.

Interviews were recorded or, if this was not possible, the second interviewer took notes. Moreover, after each interview, "off–the-record" discussion and focus group, the interviewers noted down their impressions of the key points that emerged.

Table 1 Overview of the background of the interviewees

Interviewees	Number of interviews
Host market: Poland Chinese bank	3 bankers
Host market: Switzerland (i) Swiss institutions (banks and bank associations), (ii) EMBs	17 interviews and 5 "off-the-record" discussions: – 9 bankers in Swiss banks – 8 bankers in Brazilian and Chinese banks – "Off–the-record" with 5 Swiss bankers
Home market: China Chinese: (i) investment banks, (ii) state-owned banks, and (iii) commercial banks	10 interviews: – 4 bankers in investment banks – 6 bankers in commercial banks 2 focus groups
Home market: Brazil (i) bank associations, (ii) commercial banks	10 interviews and 3 "off-the-record" discussions: – 7 bankers in Brazilian – 3 bankers in bank associations – 1 "off-the-record" discussion in a Brazilian bank association – 3 senior bankers and 2 "off-the-record" discussions in Brazilian banks
	40 interviews, 8 "off-the-record" discussions, 2 focus groups

Source Data collected by the authors

This approach involves inductive logic to gain insights into managers' experiences (Corley & Gioia, 2004).

We compared the data with primary and secondary information and all the data were transcribed. Portuguese and Chinese audio files were transcribed and subsequently translated into English. Polish transcripts were coded directly, without prior translation into English. The verbatim data were organized, coded, and analysed using NVIVO software to keep track of emerging categories. Finally, we carried out an extensive press review and exchanged informally with banking experts.

3.2 Data Analysis

We followed the qualitative grounded-theory approach to theorize from process data to identify generative mechanisms. A process is an ongoing interaction that responds to situations or problems, often with the target of reaching a goal or handling a problem, and process data can offer many opportunities for grounded theorizing (Corbin & Strauss, 2008; Langley, 1999). We, therefore, looked for interactions (engagement in isomorphism) that may help shape subsequent consequences (EMBs' internationalization outcomes). This approach allows analytical generalization by providing insights into an under investigated phenomena of EMBs' internationalization. Table 2 illustrates the coding scheme of the data structure of the findings.

4 Findings

Our primary and secondary data analysis provide insights into EMB's engagement in isomorphic processes, and EMB's legitimacy in host and home markets. To ensure confidentiality promised to the interviewees, we provide anonymous quotes with fictional names and do not provide the exact date of the interview (all data was collected between 2012 and 2015).

4.1 EMBs' Engagement in Isomorphic Processes

Subsidiary Granted Low Autonomy by the Head Office

European managers in EMBs often complain that the subsidiary's autonomy is limited. They mention that the parent organization often puts considerable pressure on the local office to perform without providing necessary human and financial resources. The parent organization in question may be either the corporate Head Office or the founding family based in the home country. Many banks lament that

Table 2 Data structure

First order codes	Second order codes	Third order codes
– Low autonomy of the subsidiary vs experience of the HQs – HQ pressure for high performance, despite a lack of resources	Subsidiaries granted low autonomy	Engagement in isomorphic processes
– Challenges in collaboration local vs. expat staff – Inappropriate profile of a Chinese banker – Expatriates in key positions	HQ managers' limited understanding of the host market	
– Career risk for local bankers – Difficulty in collaboration with foreign counterparts	Difficulty to attract and retain local staff	
– Statements of local and home identity – Presenting identity of the acquired, European partner – Banking—beyond national boundaries – EMBs maintain home country identity – EMBs do not become players in the local community	Efforts to develop a dual identity	Legitimacy in host and home markets
– Aiming to increase a competitive advantage in the domestic market – High competition in the domestic market – Opportunistic entry mode of EMBs	Efforts to improve a home market position	

Source Data analysis conducted by the authors

they do not possess sufficient autonomy to run the business, noting the need to obtain authorizations from the parent organization (some products need prior authorization from the parent to be offered to clients and at times this authorization is not received or arrives late). Autonomy might be also impacted if a subsidiary is managed by a Head Office that does not agree with the strategy of the subsidiary. The following quote illustrates a commonly evoked challenge in EMBs:

> In Beijing, they wanted to handle (mentions name of the European subsidiary, and the country) just like a normal branch, like they do in Shanghai. But obviously the European environment (…) with all its history and the background and everything, which is condensed into a very small place, you cannot handle things in the same way and you need to get people who actually have knowledge about this kind of environment. Local executives need a free hand to achieve success. For me, this is really the biggest source of failure because they

> [Chinese Head Office] wanted to control things very closely and they wanted to do things like they do with their other branches in mainland China.
>
> Sylvain (+5 years seniority), European, Chinese bank, Europe

Like their Chinese counterparts, Brazilian bank executives consider it necessary to maintain influence over their overseas subsidiaries by using incentives to encourage the type of work ethos prevailing in the home base, as for example evident from the following quote:

> ... we will put [mentions name of the acquired bank] on the treadmill; you know, a small diet. It's good for everyone. It's healthy for everyone. But the idea is not to do a revolution inside [mentions name of the acquired bank], but rather encourage the evolution of the business. We don't expect to change the [mentions a specific country where acquisition took place] culture immediately but we do expect to put a bonus incentive in the [mentions a specific country] culture. We are not going to lower their salaries. We're never going to do that. However, we think that if we put a bonus incentive in the end of the year, it might make them think: 'Ah look, if I work more, this is better for me.'
>
> Adriana (+30 years seniority), Brazilian, Brazilian bank in Brazil

The autonomy of senior managers in Chinese banks is also limited by a failure to permit compliance with legal frameworks that impede the banks' ability to compete with local competitors. European interviewees claim that to gain clients, their bank sometimes needs to offer a higher number of competitive products and services. However, the parent company often fails to support the change in the legal status of the subsidiary that would allow them to increase the services they were permitted to offer. After a Brazilian acquisition of a European bank, its autonomy was reduced by layoffs of the top and senior executives, and the top management team was replaced by members of the acquiring bank. Interviews reveal that parent companies tend to attribute a lack of success in the host market to lower competence on the part of the local team, which is exacerbated by a failure to understand that a strong position in the domestic market is not necessarily an advantage in host, developed markets. Among others, the following quote illustrates a commonly expressed "superiority syndrome" by Western bankers:

> The Chinese have this kind of a bias; the Chinese consider themselves to be wonderful and fantastic, they do not thoroughly understand [mentions a specific country] market and corporate banking other than the Chinese. They think that [mentions name of the bank] ...that if [mentions name of the bank] has such a power in China, then it simply should be perceived as powerful everywhere else too...
>
> Monique (+10 years seniority), European, Chinese bank in Europe

HQ Managers' Limited Understanding of the Host Market

This is the second issue highlighted by our results. EMBs often find it challenging to recruit both expatriate and local employees. Chinese banks in particular face difficulties to secure talented workers. The interviewees reveal that a good Chinese banker in China might not necessarily be a good banker in Europe. Chinese state-owned banks (SOBs), which are particularly encouraged to internationalize, frequently hire government-connected executives whose skills often are unsuited to the institutional systems of a developed economy. Moreover, salaries at SOBs are less performance-driven, and tend to be lower than the market average in the Chinese banking industry.

Interviews with European managers in Chinese subsidiaries reveal that Chinese expatriates are often perceived to prioritize a good relationship with the Chinese government over business results in their subsidiary and they avoid taking business initiatives unless they are aligned with the expectations of the parent organization. For example, a European banker at a Chinese subsidiary revealed:

> Chinese bankers at [mentions name of his bank] are risk adverse, which slows down business of [mentions name of his bank]. It is not enough to offer credit to Chinese companies only; [insert name of the European country] banking is highly competitive. For example, the most important Chinese MNCs, like [mentions name of a leading Chinese company in [insert name of the European country], are clients of leading [insert name of the European country] banks and it is neither BOC nor ICBC [two leading Chinese SOBs]. At [mentions name of his bank] there is no growth strategy, objectives change all the time, so it is difficult to understand what is individually expected; work at [mentions name of his bank] is unpredictable.
>
> Robert (+10 years seniority), European, Chinese bank in Europe

Brazilian banks, like Chinese banks, often place senior executives from the parent organization in their European subsidiaries as testified by one interviewee, closely linked with the owner:

> You are here, because you like to be with the Family. It is your culture. It is the same. Family and senior management have the same culture.
>
> Nadia (+25 years seniority), European, Brazilian in Europe

However, Brazilian and European bankers have similar educational profiles, professional experience, and knowledge of international banking. Thus, although key decision-makers in Brazilian banks are often HQ executives, there seems to be less cross-cultural friction between local and home executives than in Chinese banks.

Difficulty to Attract and Retain Local Staff

Chinese and Brazilian banks also face difficulties in recruiting local talent with the necessary banking and cross-cultural expertise. EMBs are often not well known in developed country markets, their country of origin is stigmatized by corruption scandals (Brazil) or a different political system (China). For example, soon after a Brazilian bank, Pactual, acquired a Swiss Italian bank, BSI, Pactual's CEO was arrested due to his involvement in a massive corruption affair (Dubas, 2015) and Pactual had to sell BSI to a Swiss bank—EFG (ATS, 2016). The image of EMBs remains low and this leads to a tendency for people who wish to enter banking but cannot find jobs in local banks to join an EMB. This can lead to a lack of commitment to the EMB as these people regard employment in such banks as a necessary and hopefully temporary solution to a failure to obtain work in more highly regarded banks. Indeed, local bankers often associate working for such banks as risky. For example, one interviewee expressed this type of view:

> So most of the colleagues say: Okay, I'm out of the market. I can be back in the market, improve my saleability towards other employers so okay I do that for a few months, maybe two years, but whenever there's an opportunity, I'm out of here.
>
> Christopher, (+20 years seniority), Swiss, EMB, Switzerland

Finally, European interviewees reveal difficulties in collaborating with Chinese colleagues, for example, local employees dislike not having the opportunity to directly talk to their colleagues in the Head Office, as the latter often do not speak English. Communication between local and expatriate staff tends to be carried out through bi-cultural colleagues, e.g., a Chinese person educated in Europe. These difficulties appear to arise due to their less extensive knowledge of how banking operates in the host location and a reluctance to learn and adapt to local conditions.

The following quote illustrates some common problems:

> I think people, non-Chinese working for (mentions name of a Chinese bank) they were not considered by Chinese ... they basically don't exist, as 80% of the employees in the bank do not speak any other language than Chinese.
>
> Robert (+10 years seniority), European, Chinese bank in Europe

Language and cultural barriers appear less of an impediment for Brazilian banks, for instance, they often employ bilingual staff with prior international experience.

4.2 EMBs' Legitimacy in Host and Home Markets

Our interviews demonstrate only some divergence between managers based in the home market and those in host markets. While interviewees based in host markets lament the weak legitimacy of the EMBs' subsidiary in the host market, Head Office managers tend to be satisfied with the internationalization of their institution.

Efforts to Develop a Dual Identity

Host market-based managers note that EMBs mainly strive to acquire a dual identity (international and Chinese or Brazilian) in their business development. This dual identity is considered by the interviewees to strengthen EMBs' competitive advantage in the home market by leading to a perception that the banks are fit to be considered insiders in the host locations. This facilitates embedding into host locations, thereby permitting access to and utilization of often intangible assets that may enhance competitive advantages in both domestic and host markets. Having an "international reputation" also is viewed as facilitating talent attraction and retention, as well as the development of a local and compatriot client base. The importance of a dual identity is also often echoed in the press, as for example:

We are state owned – so our image is 'safe' [but] if something bad happens, we can no longer sell this image. There are 2 parts to it. You want to play up the 'European culture' as a starting point if you deal with a Chinese client. But if you look at a non-Chinese client, you want to sell the Chinese heritage.

Wang (+20 years seniority), Chinese, Chinese Bank, Europe

Similarly, after acquiring a local bank, Brazilian banks often maintain the local brand or introduce dual branding. There are, however, problems in establishing legitimacy and thereby achieving a good reputation in developed economy locations. EMBs often maintain their home identity and fail to effectively embrace the host one. Moreover, they rarely become legitimate players as they rarely integrate fully into host locations. They thus tend to remain outsiders and often are not taken seriously by developed economies and local competitors, which points to a weak ability of EMBs to acquire and exploit assets gained from investments in developed economies. Interviews also revealed that both European and emerging market executives consider that their main competitors in Europe are other compatriot banks rather than local players. Particular difficulties are faced in Switzerland, where EMBs would like to launch private banking activities, but as mentioned by a Swiss executive, it is a huge challenge to "*succeed in the heart of Swiss identity.*" Among different testimonies, a Swiss banker working with emerging clients in a traditional Swiss bank explained:

Within Switzerland it is difficult to enter certain circles. Use philanthropy and social engagement. Very hard to develop 'Swissness'. Look at Sarasin, it comes from the Basel aristocracy and joins now Banco Safra. As an outsider you cannot reproduce the culture!

Serge (+40 years seniority), Swiss, Swiss Bank

Due to these challenges, one preferred mode of entry of a Chinese bank in Switzerland and Poland is through a representative office or a branch with a basic service-product offer, e.g., trade finance, RMB (currency trading/policy of RMB internationalization), commercial and retail banking, raising corporate and project funding for overseas investment. Here, however, subsidiaries of Chinese banks in Poland and Switzerland face difficulties in attracting clients and developing a strong client base. Indeed, corporate and individual customers often prefer to work with local banks whose products and services are perceived as superior. Compared to Chinese banks, Brazilian banks have higher legitimacy, a greater tendency to refer to acquisitions as a market entry mode and they tend to have a stronger local–international client base, especially compatriot clients or Western clients doing business in Brazil. They face, however, some challenges in Europe due to corruption scandals in Brazil, e.g., Bank Pactual's failed acquisition in Switzerland. Summing up, Brazilian banks, in contrast to Chinese SOBs, engage more in mimetic isomorphism focused on economic objectives and, in addition to seeking know-how, aim for successful integration in host developed markets.

Efforts to Improve a Home Market Position

Data analysis of bankers based in China and Brazil reveals a strong desire to acquire knowledge to develop a new competitive advantage in developed economies, mainly to be used to further expand in home and in developing markets, but also to successfully access advanced economy host markets. Indeed, domestic clients become increasingly demanding, and they expect to access the same products and services available in foreign markets in their home market. Moreover, home market competition increases with stronger indigenous and foreign players. For example, wealth management products offered by Swiss private banks are significantly more competitive than those offered by EMBs. Chinese SOBs especially are increasingly threatened by commercial banks co-owned by local governments and online competitors. Interviews reveal that Chinese SOBs seem to be less competitive than other EMBs and are characterized by weaker client relationships, a poorer product/service offer, and stronger bureaucracy. In contrast, Brazilian banks often have competitive online products, but some remain underdeveloped, for example, wealth management products. Weaker experience of Chinese banks was often evoked, as for instance:

> For private banking, (Chinese state-owned bank 'X') is just like a child running a race with an adult. We're just like a child running in a competition with an adult. The most challenging part for us is to have the same service quality as our competitors.
>
> Zhen (+10 years seniority), Chinese, SOB, Beijing

In the same vein, Brazilian bankers stress improving their home market position, but also their position in other existing host locations, especially those which are geographically proximal:

> We only have two people in London [in wealth management]. In the Asian office there is no wealth management, but obviously with the acquisition of [insert name of the bank] and [insert name of the bank] in Chile and Colombia… and now we are having a strategy of expansion, there's [mentions the name of an acquired bank in Switzerland], right? First, it will become a different arm, which is our wealth management arm in Europe and Asia as well. Then, the expansion in the United States; and, as you may be aware there's the opening of the Miami office dedicated to wealth management. Continuing the expansion in North America…
>
> Camilla (+15 years seniority), Brazilian, SOB, Brazilian bank

5 Discussion

This chapter aims to provide insights into how EMBs mitigate their liability of emergingness (i.e., disadvantage of being from an emerging economy in terms of little experience in dealing with institutional distance) to bridge the institutional distance between home and host markets and, consequently, to reach their internationalization objectives in the host market. Specifically, referring to neo-institutional theory, we investigate how EMBs engage in isomorphism in the host market (i.e., respond to coercive, normative, and mimetic isomorphic pressures) in attempts to overcome their liability of emergingness. We find indications that the liability of emergingness is indeed a problem, one that is stronger for Chinese than Brazilian banks. Specifically, EMBs may fail to effectively engage in normative and mimetic isomorphism when they are subject to a strong coercive isomorphism from their HQs. We will explain this in the following section focusing on the three isomorphic processes: coercive, normative, and mimetic. We will conclude with the limitations of the study and outline future research to further develop our exploratory findings.

Coercive isomorphism. Our data analysis suggests that obstacles facing subsidiaries of EMBs in advanced markets might be strongly connected to unhelpful pressures from HQs that arise from the institutional conditions in the home base. This is a somewhat different idea than the standard concept of coercive isomorphism, where the agency exercising coercion is external to the firm (DiMaggio & Powell, 1983). Considering multinational enterprises as multi-organizational entities highlights the possibility of coercion arising from within the organizational system of the firm. In this view, HQs (which often have power over the multi-organizational system) exert pressure on subsidiaries to conform to strategies and operations that are common in the home locations rather than to adapt to the institutional conditions in the host location (Dörrenbächer & Gammelgaard, 2006). Coercive isomorphism thus arises from an "external" agency (HQs) forcing subsidiaries to conform to institutional conditions that prevail in the home location. This type of coercion is most likely to arise if the EMBs face liabilities of emergingness.

Interestingly, our data analysis reveals that this type of coercive isomorphism differs somewhat between Brazilian and Chinese banks. While Brazilian banks focus on pressuring their subsidiaries to perform well in host markets, Chinese banks tend to restrict their subsidiaries' autonomy, thereby hindering their ability to embed effectively in the host location. This in turn has repercussions in terms of acquiring and effectively utilizing assets from an advanced market to boost a competitive advantage in the home market. This echoes the findings of a qualitative study conducted by Marques et al. (2017) who found that the Brazilian Safra Bank was more successful in leveraging Swiss-based assets to its home market than the Bank of China. The different outcomes for the Brazilian and Chinese banks may be related to dissimilar approaches to institutional isomorphism in attempts to bridge the institutional distance between the home and host markets. The case of the Bank of China suggests a type of coercive isomorphism which arose because the Chinese headquarters did not understand the importance of the differences in the institutional systems of the home and host locations, nor the importance of this for acquiring necessary assets in host locations.

Safra's family-ownership model appeared to be better able to avoid this negative coercive isomorphism and allowed the bank to better fit into the traditional Swiss private banking culture (Marques et al., 2017). This highlights the role of managers in parent companies in understanding the importance of local isomorphism (Wu & Salomon, 2016). Specifically, the data reveals that the role of the government in many Chinese SOBs is pronounced and is likely to underpin the use of coercive isomorphism that is based on institutional conditions in China, but which is not suitable for host markets. The influence of the government appears to be perhaps the most significant factor behind the difference between Chinese and Brazilian banks. The findings support the view expressed in the literature wherein Chinese state-owned enterprises engaged in internationalization are more likely to face pressure from their headquarters to follow strategies in line with institutional pressure emanating from government sources (Amighini et al., 2013).

These coercive isomorphic pressures from the home base appear to reduce the ability of subsidiaries to effectively manage mimetic and normative isomorphic pressures to help them bridge the institutional distance between the home and host markets, and, consequently, to reach their internationalization objectives in the host market. HQs might be coercing subsidiaries to adopt policies and practices arising from the way the institutional systems in the home country affect the MNC, i.e., normative, mimetic isomorphism.

Normative isomorphism. Our findings reveal that EMBs tend to face difficulty in attracting talent in both home and host locations. First, both Chinese and Brazilian banks often make extensive use of expatriates in top management positions. However, talent attraction might be particularly difficult for Chinese banks as many Chinese bankers tend to have local careers, lack international experience, and face language issues in developed markets. In contrast, Brazilian bankers tend to have more international experience, language is less of a problem, and their education is similar to that of their Western counterparts. The similar education of host and home market managers may positively contribute to the successful internationalization of EMBs. These findings confirm quantitative research conducted by Lamotte and Colovic (2015), who reveal that the level of education of managers in emerging market firms is positively related to their successful internationalization. Moreover, the private ownership structure of many Brazilian banks compared to the strong state control of Chinese banks may also help to mitigate the liability of emergingness through the adoption of an entrepreneurial approach that is considered to be an effective means for EMNCs to alleviate the liability of emergingness (Madhok & Keyhani, 2012). These results echo findings of a quantitative study conducted by Amal and Tomio (2015) who demonstrate that Brazilian firms venturing into advanced markets tend to possess the necessary managerial abilities to successfully internationalize in those markets.

Attracting and retaining talent is also important to overcome the liability of foreignness (Thite et al., 2012; Wilkinson et al., 2014). Specifically, Western bankers are often reluctant to work for an EMB that does not have a strong reputation in the host location as they fear that it could have a negative impact on their careers. Research, however, suggests that talent management and granting autonomy to managers are important for the successful internationalization of banks (Parada et al., 2009). The results reveal that EMBs also face problems of talent retention. EMBs located in developed economies often have difficulties building a sufficient client base within a short period of time. The parent company in many EMBs often understands little about the problems faced by subsidiaries. Head Offices tend to attribute these problems to the low competence of the managerial team in the subsidiary and, in order to provide "support," the parent company imposes strong control over the subsidiary

(Björkman et al., 2007). This may contribute to problems in talent retention and at least partly explain the high turnover of staff revealed in the interviews.

Summing up, talent issues faced chiefly by Chinese banks are an example of how the pressures from HQs might limit the ability of EMB subsidiaries to embed in their host locations. This may indicate that the effect of home country's coercive isomorphic pressures arising from strong government influence hinders the development of entrepreneurial activities by subsidiaries that might help to mitigate the problems of liability of emergingness.

Mimetic isomorphism. The data analysis of home market bankers suggests that the primary objective of EMBs' internationalization is to develop their activities in a host location, but in basic banking services, supporting individual and corporate clients from their home countries operating globally. Second, interviewees based in the home market also highlight their institution's objective to acquire and utilize assets from advanced host markets to boost their competitive advantage in their home market. However, developing business in host locations is not an easy task, as revealed by the interviewees based in the host market. Indeed, EMBs tend to have many of the hallmarks of outsiders in the host market banking industry, indicating that they face the liability of emergingness (Madhok & Keyhani, 2012). The cases of the Bank of China and Safra bank illustrate the different approaches to using mimetic isomorphism (Marques et al., 2017). Safra bank adjusted to conditions in Switzerland through the acquisition of a private Swiss bank, Sarasin, and has become largely accepted within the Swiss wealth management industry. In contrast, the Bank of China remains an outsider, especially as senior executives do not possess sound knowledge of Swiss procedures, traditions, and know-how.

Interestingly, existing research provides evidence that some Chinese banks successfully engage in mimetic isomorphism. An example is provided by a qualitative multiple case study of Chinese firms in Germany, among which was the Chinese Bank of Communication (Klossek et al., 2012). Bank of Communication internationalized through simple banking services, i.e., currency trading and clearing, but faced institutional challenges in Germany, especially with regard to external relationships with public authorities. In contrast to the Bank of China in Switzerland (Marques et al., 2017) and to the majority of EMB cases that we investigated, a German national was in charge of external relationships with public authorities, while the branch had a Chinese managing director and the majority of senior positions were filled by both a Chinese and a German to deal with institutional complexities.

The Bank of Communications and Safra bank provide interesting insights into how EMBs might successfully engage in institutional isomorphism to mitigate a liability of emergingness. These findings are in line with existing research which points to the importance of mimetic and normative isomorphism to overcome liabilities of foreignness such as learning from other firms, and imitating their policies and practices to enable firms to gain legitimacy (Grant & Venzin, 2009; Parada et al., 2009). These companies, in contrast with some Chinese banks, appear to be able to engage in major entrepreneurial behaviour to develop subsidiary strategies and human resource policies that help them compensate for their liability of emergingness.

Future research. The following issues which emerged from our study may require further examination. First, the influence of the home country's institutional system on the views of HQ managers regarding how banks should operate in different institutional host markets. For example, liability of emergingness needs further investigation to assess how it might differ in more sophisticated institutional environments like Switzerland or Germany compared to other emerging or developing countries like certain ones in Africa. The views of HQ managers could be compared to the views of host country managers on how control by headquarters in the home market might influence their ability to achieve desired internationalization outcomes. Second, the influence of ownership modes should be investigated in the future (e.g., state-owned, private, or family-owned) in the light of EMBs' liability of emergingness.

Acknowledgements The authors would like to thank the audience at the 2016 BAM annual conference for their constructive comments as well as our colleagues from swissnex Brazil, swissnex China, and Greater Zurich Area in Shanghai for their support during the field investigations. The RCSO Economie & Management (HES-SO) supported this research with a grant (Nr 34218).

Bibliographic References

Amal, M., & Tomio, B. T. (2015). Institutional distance and Brazilian outward foreign direct investment. *M@n@gement, 18*(1), 78–101.

Amighini, A. A., Rabellotti, R., & Sanfilippo, M. (2013). Do Chinese state-owned and private enterprises differ in their internationalization strategies? *China Economic Review, 27*, 312–325.

ATS. (2016). *EFG International avale la banque tessinoise BSI.*

Björkman, I., Fey, C. F., & Park, H. J. (2007). Institutional theory and MNC subsidiary HRM practices: Evidence from a three-country study. *Journal of International Business Studies, 38*(3), 430–446.

Boehe, D. M. (2015). The internationalization of service firms from emerging economies: An internalization perspective. *Long Range Planning, 49*(5), 559–569.

Buckley, P. J., Clegg, L. J., Cross, A. R., Liu, X., Voss, H., & Zheng, P. (2007). The determinants of Chinese outward foreign direct investment. *Journal of International Business Studies, 38*(4), 499–518.

Buckley, P. J., Forsans, N., & Munjal, S. (2012). Host–home country linkages and host–home country specific advantages as determinants of foreign acquisitions by Indian firms. *International Business Review, 21*(5), 878–890.

Buckley, P. J., & Hashai, N. (2014). The role of technological catch up and domestic market growth in the genesis of emerging country based multinationals. *Research Policy, 43*(2), 423–437.

Corbin, J., & Strauss, A. (2008). *Basics of qualitative research: Techniques and procedures for developing grounded theory* (3rd ed.). Sage.

Corley, K. G., & Gioia, D. (2004). Defined by our strategy or our culture? Hierarchical differences in perceptions of organizational identity and change. *Human Relations, 57*(9), 1145–1177. Retrieved on December 2021, from http://search.proquest.com/docview/231490823?accountid=15920, http://linksolver.ovid.com/OpenUrl/LinkSolver?atitle=Defined+by+our+strategy+or+our+culture%3F+Hierarchical+differences+in+perceptions+of+organizational+identity+and+change&title=Human+Relations&aulast=Corley%2C+Kevin+G&date=2004-09-01&issn=00187267&volume=57&issue=9&spage=1145

Cuervo-Cazurra, A., Inkpen, A., Musacchio, A., & Ramaswamy, K. (2014). Governments as owners: State-owned multinational companies. *Journal of International Business Studies, 45*(8), 919–942.

de Mello, R. B., Ghauri, P. N., Mayrhofer, U., & Meschi, P.-X. (2015). Theoretical and empirical implications for research on South-South and South-North expansion strategies. *M@n@gement, 18*(1), 1–7.

Deng, P. (2009). Why do Chinese firms tend to acquire strategic assets in international expansion? *Journal of World Business, 44*(1), 74–84. https://doi.org/10.1016/j.jwb.2008.03.014

DiMaggio, P. J., & Powell, W. W. (1983). The iron cage revisited: Institutional isomorphism and collective rationality in organizational fields. *American Sociological Review, 48*(2), 147–160.

Dörrenbächer, C., & Gammelgaard, J. (2006). Subsidiary role development: The effect of micro-political headquarters–subsidiary negotiations on the product, market and value-added scope of foreign-owned subsidiaries. *Journal of International Management, 12*(3), 266–283.

Dubas, S. (2015). *Le patron de BTG Pactual a été arrêté au Brésil.*

Eden, L., & Miller, S. R. (2004). Distance matters: Liability of foreignness, institutional distance and ownership strategy. In M. A. Hitt & J. L. Cheng (Eds.), *Theories of the multinational enterprise: Diversity, complexity and relevance* (pp. 187–221). Emerald Group Publishing Limited.

Focarelli, D., & Pozzolo, A. F. (2005). Where do banks expand abroad? An empirical analysis. *The Journal of Business, 78*(6), 2435–2464.

Frieda, G. (2015). *China-Brazil link is top threat to global economy.*

Grant, R. M., & Venzin, M. (2009). Strategic and organisational challenges of internationalisation in financial services. *Long Range Planning, 42*(5), 561–587.

Guillén, M. F., & García-Canal, E. (2009). The American model of the multinational firm and the "new" multinationals from emerging economies. *The Academy of Management Perspectives, 23*(2), 23–35.

Hashai, N., & Buckley, P. J. (2014). Is competitive advantage a necessary condition for the emergence of the multinational enterprise? *Global Strategy Journal, 4*(1), 35–48.

Haunschild, P., & Miner, A. (1997). Modes of interorganizational imitation: The effects of outcome salience and uncertainty. *Administrative Science Quarterly, 42*(3), 472–500.

Jiang, X. Q. (2018). M&A deals in Belt and Road economies increase by 81%. *China Daily.* Retrieved on December 2021, from http://www.chinadaily.com.cn/a/201804/12/WS5acebb7ca3105cdcf6517c7d.html

Johanson, J., & Vahlne, J.-E. (1977). The internationalization process of the firm—A model of knowledge development and increasing foreign market commitments. *Journal of International Business Studies, 8*(1), 23–32.

Johanson, J., & Vahlne, J.-E. (2009). The Uppsala internationalization process model revisited: From liability of foreignness to liability of outsidership. *Journal of International Business Studies, 40*(9), 1411–1431.

Klossek, A., Linke, B. M., & Nippa, M. (2012). Chinese enterprises in Germany: Establishment modes and strategies to mitigate the liability of foreignness. *Journal of World Business, 47*(1), 35–44.

Kostova, T., & Zaheer, S. (1999). Organizational legitimacy under conditions of complexity: The case of the multinational enterprise. *Academy of Management Review, 24*(1), 64–81.

Kotowicz, A. (2018). *Raport o sytuacji banków w 2017 r.* Urzad Komisji Nadzoru Bankowego. Retrieved on August 16, 2018 from https://www.knf.gov.pl/knf/pl/komponenty/img/RAPORT_O_SYTUACJI_BANKOW_2017_12_61471.pdf

Lamotte, O., & Colovic, A. (2015). Early internationalization of new ventures from emerging countries: The case of transition economies. *M@n@gement, 18*(1), 8–30.

Langley, A. (1999). Strategies for theorizing from process data. *Academy of Management Review, 24*(4), 691–710.

Langley, A., & Royer, I. (2006). Perspectives on doing case study research in organizations. *M@n@gement, 9*(3), 81–94.

Li, Y. Q. (2017). *Annual report on development of the "belt and road" construction.* Social Sciences Academic Press.

Luo, Y., & Tung, R. L. (2007). International expansion of emerging market enterprises: A springboard perspective. *Journal of International Business Studies, 38*(4), 481–498. https://doi.org/10.1057/palgrave.jibs.8400275

Madhok, A., & Keyhani, M. (2012). Acquisitions as entrepreneurship: Asymmetries, opportunities, and the internationalization of multinationals from emerging economies. *Global Strategy Journal, 2*(1), 26–40.

Marchand, M. (2015). When the South takes over the North: Dynamics of up-market integrations by emerging multinationals. *M@n@gement, 18*(1), 31–53.

Marques, J. C., Lupina-Wegener, A., & Schneider, S. (2017). Internationalization strategies of emerging market banks: Challenges and opportunities. *Business Horizons, 60*(5), 715–723.

Miles, M. B., & Huberman, A. M. (2019). *Qualitative data analysis: A sourcebook of new methods* (4th ed.). Sage.

Mutinelli, M., & Piscitello, L. (2001). Foreign direct investment in the banking sector: The case of Italian banks in the '90s. *International Business Review, 10*(6), 661–685.

OECD & European Commission. (2020). *Cities in the world: A New perspective on urbanisation*. OECD Publishing. Retrieved on December 2021, from https://www.oecd-ilibrary.org/docserver/d0efcbda-en.pdf?expires=1638648270&id=id&accname=guest&checksum=07FA94E8C70B8B71B0C0BEAE44B82E69

Oehme, M., & Bort, S. (2015). SME internationalization modes in the German biotechnology industry: The influence of imitation, network position, and international experience. *Journal of International Business Studies, 46*(6), 629–655.

Parada, P., Alemany, L., & Planellas, M. (2009). The internationalisation of retail banking: Banco Santander's journey towards globalisation. *Long Range Planning, 42*(5), 654–677.

Patton, M. Q. (1990). *Qualitative evaluation and research methods*. Sage.

Peng, M. W., Wang, D. Y., & Jiang, Y. (2008). An institution-based view of international business strategy: A focus on emerging economies. *Journal of International Business Studies, 39*(5), 920–936.

Petrou, A. (2007). Multinational banks from developing versus developed countries: Competing in the same arena? *Journal of International Management, 13*(3), 376–397.

Powell, W. W., & DiMaggio, P. J. (2012). *The new institutionalism in organizational analysis*. University of Chicago Press.

Qian, L., & Delios, A. (2008). Internalization and experience: Japanese banks' international expansion, 1980–1998. *Journal of International Business Studies, 39*(2), 231–248.

Salomon, R., & Wu, Z. (2012). Institutional distance and local isomorphism strategy. *Journal of International Business Studies, 43*(4), 343–367.

Schouten, J. W., & McAlexander, J. H. (1995). Subcultures of consumption: An ethnography of the new bikers. *Journal of Consumer Research, 22*(1), 43–61.

Stinchcombe, A. (1965). Social structure and organizations. In J. March (Ed.), *Handbook of organizations* (Vol. 7, pp. 142–193). Rand McNally.

Thite, M., Wilkinson, A., & Shah, D. (2012). Internationalization and HRM strategies across subsidiaries in multinational corporations from emerging economies—A conceptual framework. *Journal of World Business, 47*(2), 251–258.

Wei, L.-Q., & Lau, C.-M. (2008). The impact of market orientation and strategic HRM on firm performance: The case of Chinese enterprises. *Journal of International Business Studies, 39*(6), 980–995.

Weiss, R. S. (2005). *Learning from strangers: The art and method of qualitative interview studies*. The Free Press.

Wells Jr., L. T. (2009). Third world multinationals: A look back. In R. Ramumurti & V. S. Jitendra (Eds.), *Emerging multinationals in emerging markets*. Cambridge University Press.

Wilkinson, A., Wood, G., & Demirbag, M. (2014). Guest editors' introduction: People management and emerging market multinationals. *Human Resource Management, 53*(6), 835–849.

Wu, Z., & Salomon, R. (2016). Does imitation reduce the liability of foreignness? Linking distance, isomorphism, and performance. *Strategic Management Journal, 37*(12), 2441–2462.

Xu, D., & Meyer, K. E. (2013). Linking theory and context: 'Strategy research in emerging economies' after Wright et al. (2005). *Journal of Management Studies, 50*(7), 1322–1346.

Xu, D., & Shenkar, O. (2002). Note: Institutional distance and the multinational enterprise. *Academy of Management Review, 27*(4), 608–618.

Yu, Y., & Liu, Y. (2018). Country-of-origin and social resistance in host countries: The case of a Chinese firm. *Thunderbird International Business Review, 60*(3), 347–363.

Zaheer, S. (1995). Overcoming the liability of foreignness. *Academy of Management Journal, 38*(2), 341–363.

Zheng, N., Wei, Y., Zhang, Y., & Yang, J. (2016). In search of strategic assets through cross-border merger and acquisitions: Evidence from Chinese multinational enterprises in developed economies. *International Business Review, 25*(1), 177–186. https://doi.org/10.1016/j.ibusrev.2014.11.009

Chapter 14
Chinese Health Strategy: A Tool Towards Global Governance

Anabela Rodrigues Santiago

1 Introduction

Health is a necessary condition for the humankind development. The People's Republic of China (PRC), as the world's second-largest economy and the most populated country in the world, has a huge responsibility towards global health. Global health diplomacy is more than ever a relevant component of an international system that needs to be multilateral to achieve a global state of health and well-being. The main role of global health diplomacy is to arrange consensuses that are scientifically valid and politically feasible to implement (Kickbusch et al., 2021).

The PRC health strategy is aligned to achieve the 2030 United Nations Sustainable Development Goals (SDG), namely those of cluster 3, dedicated to health. The main purpose of this cluster is to ensure healthy lives and promoting well-being at all ages (United Nations, 2021) by ensuring some specific targets such as: (i) the reduction of maternal and infant mortality and diseases; (ii) the implementation of Framework Convention on Tobacco Control in all countries; (iii) achieving universal health coverage and access to essential medicines; (iv) ensuring universal access to sexual and reproductive healthcare services, including for family planning, information, and education; (v) strengthening the capacity of all countries, in particular developing countries, for early warning, risk reduction, and management of national and global health risks; among others.

As a sign of commitment to international health standards, Chinese policies towards health are also very aligned with two main guidelines of the World Health Organization (WHO), which are: (i) Health for All and (ii) Health in All Policies. In fact, the PRC aims at implementing a universal health coverage—an objective almost already reached out—and to include the health component in transversal

---

A. R. Santiago (✉)
Research Unit on Governance, Competitiveness and Public Policies (GOVCOPP), DCSPT, University of Aveiro, Aveiro, Portugal
e-mail: anabela.santiago@ua.pt

policies outside the health domain as the PRC needs to deal with some health challenges caused by a series of health-related, political, or social factors (Wang et al., 2019). Among others, these health challenges are deriving from: (i) ageing population; (ii) accelerated rate of urbanization; (iii) change in lifestyle and diet habits; (iv) resistance to antibiotics and a new spectrum of diseases; and (v) pollution-related health issues.

The plan adopted for its internal health system development is the "Healthy China 2030," which is a national initiative to promote health and well-being, tracing the pathways to achieve these seven strategic goals (Zhuang, 2016): (i) Healthy living; (ii) Optimizing health services; (iii) Improving health security; (iv) Building healthy environment; (v) Develop healthcare industry; (vi) Build supportive mechanisms; and (vii) Strengthen organization and implementation.

Besides being committed to improve its health system internally, through the implementation of the "Healthy China 2030" plan, the PRC is also very engaged in global health through various actions towards global health governance, namely the recent development of the Health Silk Road integrated in the Belt and Road Initiative (BRI).

The point is what can we understood as health global governance? In this chapter, the concepts of "health global governance," "health diplomacy," and correlated ones will be revised through a literature review. Then, we will summarize the Chinese healthcare system transformations from 2009 until the present day and, lastly, we will discuss the Chinese position in terms of global health diplomacy by analysing the Health Silk Road as part of BRI. This is carried out with the intent of replying to the following research question: *Based on the PRC's internal reforms and external policies in the last two decades, how relevant is PRC's role in health global governance?*

2   Health Global Governance and Health Diplomacy—Theoretical Framework

The literature is not clear regarding the concept of health global governance, as it is highly dependent on the scientific perspective from which we look at it. In fact, from natural sciences to social sciences, through economics and politics, there are many different authors trying to define it. This chapter reflection is based on a definition proposed by David Fidler (2010, p. 3), which understands health global governance as "the use of formal and informal institutions, rules, and processes by states, intergovernmental organizations, and non-state actors to deal with challenges related to health that require cross-border collective action to address them effectively." The concept assumes that accrued globalization has brought not only a higher level of circulation of people and goods, but also a higher degree of potential circulation of infectious diseases. Therefore, it implies that the global community must join efforts to develop a coordinated response in order to fight against these potential health risks.

In order to be effective, this reaction must bring together the government actions from different countries around the globe, but it should also involve policies from different sectors and agents that have direct or indirect impact on health, which is why this is a matter of governance instead of a matter specific of any government.

According to Ilona Kickbusch et al. (2021, p. 22), "health is now part and parcel of global negotiations related to food, climate, energy and water, and is discussed at major global and regional summits." This statement points out the need for a multidisciplinary approach to health that puts it at the centre of all policies, considering the effective impact of the Social Determinants of Health (SDH). The WHO (2021) defines SDH as "the conditions in which people are born, grow, live, work and age (…). These circumstances are shaped by the distribution of money, power and resources at global, national and local levels." Therefore, the most common SDH referred to in literature are the following: income level, educational opportunities, employment status, workplace safety, food security, access to housing and utility services, social support and community inclusivity, neighbourhood conditions and physical environment, access to safe drinking water, clean air, toxin-free environments, and recreational and leisure opportunities (NEJM Catalyst, 2017). According to the County Health Ranking model below (Fig. 1), social and economic factors have a significant impact on the health outcomes (40%), reinforcing the idea that the need for multidisciplinary cooperation to shape health policies is crucial.

3 Chinese Healthcare System: Major Reforms from the 80s Until the Present day

In order to better understand the external position of the PRC in terms of global health diplomacy, we shall have an overall insight of how its healthcare system is structured, and how fast it has evolved. Thus, in this section we will briefly trace its evolution, from 1980 until the present day, focusing mainly on the structural reforms that occurred in 2009 and 2013. Then, the current plan "Healthy China 2030" and its purposes will be described. After the economic reform and opening-up of 1978, under the leadership of Deng Xiao Ping, the PRC slowly started to adopt market-based economic rules. The health sector followed the same trend and the government started to slightly reduce investment, more particularly in the hospital network. The source of revenue began being shared by the State and service charges were paid by patients. Medical institutions started to compete for more resources to support themselves and the final costs of healthcare began to increase substantially (Wang et al., 2019). Therefore, in the 90s, most of the Chinese population—particularly in rural areas—had limited access to health services and care as a result of the collapse of the cooperative system (Duckett, 2011). In the subsequent period, led by President Jiang Zemin, the healthcare system remained roughly as it had been in the previous decade. It was not marked by any major changes in this field, so access to healthcare in the PRC was extremely low due to the expensive costs of seeing a doctor or

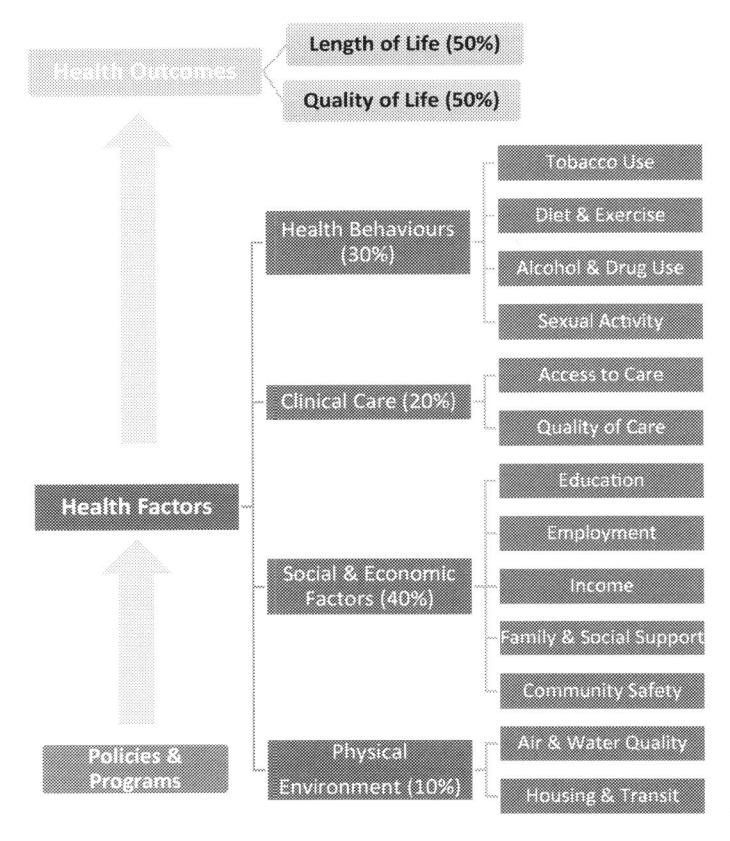

Fig. 1 Impact of socio-economic factors and health outcomes (*Source* County Health Ranking, 2014)

buying medicines, even those considered most basic. Social unrest began emerging, thus challenging the Chinese Communist Party's (CCP) higher motto of achieving a "harmonious society" (Chan, 2010). Consequently, the government began to think about possible healthcare reforms, which could improve access, quality of services, and healthcare costs. Thus, in 1998 and in 2000, health reforms were carried out to restore some of the health funds and insurance that existed in Mao's era. Such reforms were also intended to allocate more resources to primary care facilities, public hospitals, and so on, with the ultimate purpose of achieving wider access to healthcare services and more affordable prices for the population.

In 2003, the public health crisis triggered by the severe acute respiratory syndrome (SARS) highlighted the fragility of the health system in the PRC, which at the time was marked by a market-driven operating model and a wave of privatization. The discontent of the population was becoming more and more evident as it was reported in the media and as scientific studies (Huang, 2004). Technical opinions intensified regarding the state of the healthcare system and the impoverishment of the population, due to the sharp increase in personal healthcare expenses. The SARS public health crisis was the shock event that created the window of opportunity that had been latent since the 80s and particularly throughout the 90s (Thornton, 2009).

In the aftermath of SARS in 2003, many studies were commissioned by health sector experts, including the study of "China's Medical System Reform Study Group" under the Development Research Centre of the State Council (DRC), a semi-independent think tank supported by international organizations such as the World Bank and the WHO, whose report revealed that the reforms carried out and the measures implemented were a real failure (Hsiao et al., 2014; Wang, 2008). In 2005, these data found echoes in the media, as Wang (2008, p. 69) states: "(…) the Pandora's box had been opened and the public would not accept any further reform measures unless the government made big policy adjustments." Several measures would be implemented to meet this agenda, leading to the major reform in late 2003 with the reintroduction of health insurance for the entire population. By that time, 75% of the population was not covered by any insurance.

In 2004, the document with the "Scientific Principles for Development" was created, in which one of these principles refers precisely to the health field, with the aim of achieving universal primary healthcare coverage. In the pursuit of this goal, an interdisciplinary team was created in 2006, composed of national and international NGOs, experts from the World Bank, and the World Trade Organization, among others, to assess the measures necessary to reform the Chinese health system. As part of a two-day conference on the topic, the following conclusions emerged from the work conducted by the multidisciplinary expert group (Hsiao et al., 2014): firstly, the government should fund prevention as a public good; secondly, if equity is the nation's priority, the government should take responsibility in healthcare funding; in addition, since funding primary healthcare services to improve health is more efficient, the PRC should direct its budget on hospitals and redirect it to primary healthcare services; and finally there are severe shortcomings in the provision of healthcare services, either in supply by reputable pharmaceutical companies or in medical devices, and these should be tackled in terms of regulations. Based on these recommendations that were transmitted to the State Council, a proposal was drafted by the members of this interdisciplinary team that would lead, in 2009, to the latest health reform plan to be implemented at the national level. The procedure from the drafting of the proposal to its final approval that took effect in the implementation of the reform in 2009 was somewhat unprecedented in the PRC, as the proposal came from both internal and external agents who were considered "consultants" in the perspective of governmental authorities. Moreover, prior to the final version of the proposal, the draft was made public and subjected to comments and suggestions from civil society (Hsiao et al., 2014). Therefore, in 2009, healthcare became one of the top priorities of government action (Yip & Hsiao, 2015). This reform was designed in three phases: from 2009 to 2011 as the implementation phase, from 2011 to 2015 as the consolidation phase, and lastly from 2016 to 2020, when the objectives were expected to be achieved. The objectives were outlined according to five main categories: (i) expanding health insurance coverage; (ii) rendering public health services equally available to all; (iii) improving the efficiency and effectiveness of the basic primary healthcare system; (iv) establishing a well-regulated national essential medicines system; and (v) implementing pilot reforms in public hospitals (Hsiao et al., 2014; Meng et al., 2019). As part of this reform, with a focus on realigning the incentives for primary care providers, drug mark-ups that were previously in force were replaced by government subsidies, and a system of performance-based salary was introduced, in order to improve the quality of services (Xu et al., 2019).

In 2013, when Xi Jinping assumed the leadership of the PRC, a new reform of the healthcare system was initiated, with a slight shift in social values. In fact, Xi decided to deepen economic reform and rely more on market rules. According to Yip and Hsiao (2015, p. 58), "this pro-market approach also applies to the latest round of health reform. The goal now is to introduce market rules as a way to promote private investment, but also to motivate public hospitals to improve their performance as they would now face private competition." In addition, the PRC has designated health services and biomedicine as key-growth industries, benefiting these two areas from tax incentives.

According to Xu et al. (2019), during the 2013 reform, the Chinese government has pointed out the public hospital as one of the key domains of the healthcare system. As a matter of fact, they employ 64% of licensed doctors, deal with 82% of patient admissions, and account for half of China's total health expenditure (Xu et al., 2019). The public hospitals' network reform was mainly focused on the following areas of intervention: (i) increasing hospitals' budgets; (ii) adjusting prices of pharmaceuticals and medical services; (iii) reorganizing payment methods; (iv) reinforcing planning and governance; (v) re-establishing a referral system and redistributing hospitals' resources. We can point out that, at the outset, the healthcare system has always found itself between two main ideologies—the state-centred approach and the market approach—according to the predominant set of social values assumed by the CCP leader. The PRC has achieved a near-universal health insurance coverage and was able to reduce the heavy reliance of public hospitals on a drug sale incentives scheme. It managed to redirect outpatients from tertiary hospitals onto community health centres where the level of quality of primary care services was increased (Meng et al., 2019). Nonetheless, many challenges remain and a comprehensive assessment model should be implemented in order to evaluate if the policies had the expected outcomes.

4 The "Healthy China 2030" Plan

The "Healthy China 2030" strategic plan was released in 2016. It defines a range of goals to be achieved so that the Chinese society can be a prosperous society in all fields—especially in health and well-being. In practical terms, this implies that every citizen is able to access high-quality healthcare at affordable costs, everyone has health insurance and may be confident in the safety of food and medicines in the market. Health was deemed as a precondition for future economic and social development (Tan et al., 2017). The document is based on the following four core principles: (i) health priority; (ii) reforms and innovation; (iii) scientific development; and (iv) justice and equity.

According to Tan et al. (2017), the first core principle of health as a priority is translated into the positioning of health in a strategic place and role in the definition and implementation of public policies. The second core principle related to innovation is about enhancing the development of market mechanisms and fostering partnerships to develop innovative techniques in the healthcare industry, biotechnology, and biopharmaceutics. The third principle of scientific development is intertwined with the second one but also emphasizes the relevance of preventive medical practice and early diagnosis, as well as the need to reduce gaps in basic health services. Lastly, the principle of justice and fairness relates to an equitable access to basic healthcare services for the whole population reducing asymmetries deriving from the geographic location within the Chinese territory, for instance (Tan et al., 2017). A sum-up of the Chinese strategy for health was made in a discourse held by President Xi Jinping during the 19th Congress of CCP:

> We will, with emphasis on prevention, carry out extensive patriotic health campaigns, promote healthy and positive lifestyles, and prevent and control major diseases. We will initiate a food safety strategy to ensure that people have peace of mind about what they are putting on their plates. We will support both traditional Chinese medicine and Western medicine and ensure the preservation and development of traditional Chinese medicine. We will support the development of private hospitals and health-related industries. (China.org.cn, 2019)

We can observe that the "Healthy China 2030" plan mobilizes several sectors of economy: public health services, medical industry, food and drug safety, environment, and big data security. The outline stresses out that everyone should be responsible for their own health by adopting a healthy lifestyle and increasing their health literacy. The role of the government should be one of a facilitator, incorporating healthcare policy into all major policies, inviting all state and non-state actors to intervene in public health and in the definition of health policies and programmes in a "Health for All and All for Health" dynamics (Zhuang, 2016).

5 Development Assistance for Health: The Chinese Position

For decades, the PRC has been involved in Development Assistance for Health (DAH) namely *vis-à-vis* African countries. Since 2000, the contribution of the Chinese government has increased significantly. According to Lin et al. (2016), the PRC's current guide for foreign health assistance in Africa is the document entitled "China's African Policy" published in 2006. The document states that "China will increase its exchanges and cooperation with African countries in the prevention and treatment of infectious diseases including HIV/AIDS and malaria and other diseases, research and application of traditional medicine and experience concerning mechanism for public health emergencies" (Ministry of Foreign Affairs of the People's Republic of China, 2006). According to Liu et al. (2014), the main categories of Chinese aid include: (i) medical teams, (ii) construction of hospitals and health facilities, (iii) donation of drugs and medical equipment, (iv) training of health personnel, and (v) infectious diseases control with particular concerns regarding malaria.

In recent decades, healthcare assistance has been developing in many ways, despite with particular "Chinese characteristics." In fact, one of the basic pillars of Chinese foreign policy draws on the principles of the Bandung Conference, i.e., the key drivers of the whole foreign action of the Chinese government: (i) mutual respect for each other's territorial integrity and sovereignty, (ii) mutual non-aggression, (iii) non-interference in each other's internal affairs, (iv) equality and mutual benefit, and (v) peaceful coexisting (Vieira, 2019). Based on this premise, we note that the PRC follows a pattern frequently mentioned in literature as the "no strings" approach, which is translated into no interference in inner policies of each recipient of aid. At least in theory, PRC "never imposes ideology, values, and development models on other countries, especially African countries" (Lin et al., 2016, p. 3). However, when speaking about the practices implemented, it is possible to observe some phenomena of political influence such as the encouragement of diplomatic loyalty on issues like Taiwan, Tibet, and the Uyghur minority (Lin et al., 2016). In this sense and combined with other factors as, for instance, incipient global health organisms and institutions, the PRC still has a long path to walk towards a high-ranked role in health global governance. The country needs to develop the capacity to address global health issues effectively in a process of experimenting with new approaches in small-scale interventions (Husain & Bloom, 2020). It also needs to create financing support mechanisms in order to continue carrying out investments in high-technology equipment for healthcare purposes, including health personnel training. Besides these governmental, institutional, and financial capacities that need to be reinforced, the PRC also needs to foster expert counselling in the public health field. This is achieved by strengthening even more the cooperation between universities and scientific centres dedicated to global health issues and health emergencies. The PRC is already heading in this direction; and one of the supporting structures to achieve a significant role in global health governance is the BRI, which is to say the Health Silk Road, a concept that will be addressed in the next section.

6 Health Integrated into the Belt and Road Initiative: The Health Silk Road

Announced in 2013 by President Xi Jinping, the BRI first emphasized the goal of infrastructure connectivity, through five components: policy coordination, facility connectivity, free trade, financial integration, and people-to-people exchanges. These components are a well-coordinated arrangement of soft power and smart power elements. On a geographical perspective, the main scope of the BRI is Eurasia, although it is ambitious enough to extend its reach beyond Africa, Latin America, the polar regions, and the Pacific countries. The "people-to-people approach," based on a philosophy of shared prosperity, enables the BRI to address social topics such as health, digital economy, and sustainability (Tillman et al., 2021), which is the case of the Health Silk Road.

The expression "Health Silk Road" first came out in 2015 and was then reinforced by President Xi Jinping, in 2017, during the BRI Forum through the Beijing Communiqué of the Belt and Road Health Cooperation & Health Silk Road (National Health Commission of the PRC, 2017). The preliminary stage of the Health Silk Road was the programme established in a document titled "A Three-Year Implementation Plan for Advancing BRI Health Cooperation (2015–2017)." The document reflects on the increased risk of spreading diseases in a globalized world, which requires a global action: "Strengthening health cooperation between China and the BRI countries, and jointly working to encounter public health crises, will help protect the health security and social stability of China and BRI countries, which also protect the construction of the BRI" (Bing, 2020).

By the time it was issued, the document laid out a three-stage strategy for health promotion across the BRI. The first stage included the period from 2015 to 2017, the second from 2017 to 2020, and the third from 2020 to 2030, corresponding, respectively, to a focus on internal health issues, then on a regional sphere of influence, and lastly on global influence on health governance (Cao, 2020). Since its launch, the Health Silk Road has been based essentially on the promotion of China's high-tech healthcare model in Belt and Road countries. Such purposes are achieved through the realization of forums and summits on the subject of health, as a way of communicating to the world that the PRC intends to assume a prominent position in this field, demonstrating its concern for public health issues on a global scale (Wang et al., 2019). The main areas of intervention of the Health Silk Road encompass the (i) development of cooperation mechanisms; (ii) the control and prevention of infectious diseases; (iii) capacity building and personnel training; (iv) medical assistance and emergencies; (v) health systems and policies strengthening; and (vi) development of healthcare industry (Cao, 2020). In terms of foreign policy, soft diplomacy and people-to-people measures have become the focal point of Chinese external action. The Health Silk Road is a sign of Chinese "soft power" used not only as a nation branding and with the purpose of expanding PRC's overall ambitions, but also to enhance the already-existing soft power programmes and to capitalize new geopolitical opportunities (Su et al., 2021).

After the WHO declared the state of pandemic on March 2020, the Health Silk Road assumed a more prominent relevance and takes its prideful place in China's COVID-19 diplomacy era. This, specifically oriented to communicate the effective fight of China against COVID-19, was composed of the so-called "mask diplomacy" and "vaccine diplomacy." The "mask diplomacy" was the first to emerge and resulted in sending medical equipment and protective personal equipment to other countries struggling with COVID-19, namely ventilators, testing kits, and masks (Kowalski, 2021). "Mask diplomacy" is perceived as an attempt to change the COVID-19 narrative, boosting the PRC's geopolitical ambitions to take control of some strategic sectors in foreign markets and to gain the loyalty of some countries to lend their support to Chinese positions in international organisms (Verma, 2020). However, the "mask diplomacy" was rapidly turned into what is now known as the "vaccine diplomacy" (Gauttam et al., 2020).

"Vaccine diplomacy" is an expression coined by Peter Hotez (2014, p. 1) as "(…) the branch of global health diplomacy that relies on the use or delivery of vaccines, while vaccine science diplomacy is a unique hybrid of global health and science diplomacy." The same author (Hotez, 2014, p. 2) states that "(…) encompasses the important work of the GAVI Alliance, as well as elements of the WHO, the Gates Foundation, and other important international organizations." In fact, the WHO (2020) states that "global equitable access to a vaccine, particularly protecting healthcare workers and those most-at-risk is the only way to mitigate the public health and economic impact of the pandemic." In October 2020, after several months of indecision, the PRC finally joined COVAX, whose objective is to provide two billion doses of vaccine to the most vulnerable, especially in poor and developing countries (Lee, 2021). Moreover, authors like Su et al. (2021, p. 6) also speak about vaccine diplomacy as "a nation's vaccine efforts that aim to build mutually beneficial relationships with other nations ultimately" and that it "(…) might be a more sustainable solution to improve vaccine donations mainly because of its deeper and stronger roots in multilateral collaboration and cooperation." And, as Lee (2021, p. 1) advocates "with the advent of COVID-19 vaccines, home-grown national vaccines when distributed all over the world can play an integral role in nation branding as a technique for projecting soft power."

7 Conclusions

Health has been one of the areas that presents the greatest convergence in the acceptance of the need for global policies that meet global priorities. Collaboration is seen as indispensable, perhaps because of the essence of the health field, which deals with human life and its very survival. Those who study health sciences know that our own organism is a complex web of organs that cooperate in an extraordinary way, in a multidisciplinary logic that is essential to life—which is to say that global health governance matters a lot.

The Health Silk Road, under the scope of the Belt and Road Initiative is not a solo performance, it is supposed to be an orchestra effort. The logic behind it is to establish cooperation mechanisms to benefit the whole world's population with access to health, good national healthcare systems, and high-quality medical services in a logic of win–win situations in order to achieve what the Chinese President Xi Jinping designates as "community with a shared future for mankind" (Xiaochun, 2018, p. 23). This vision encompasses a view of the world in which multilateralism assumes a new preponderance in the face of the incapacity of the Westernized system in force leading to a new international order and a model where the geopolitics of health seems to play a significant role. In fact, at a time in which the US has been losing international influence and adopting a more self-centred economy approach and the EU is struggling to unify its different counterparts into a common ground of policies in different areas, PRC is gradually assuming a role that was somehow been left vacant by other nations. This is true not only, but also in health, preconfiguring a new world order based—in the words of President Xi Jinping—on multilateralism (Beeson, 2020). According to the same author (2020, p. 248), "it is quite possible that China's long-term influence will grow – despite its apparent role in causing the crisis in the first place." It is a fact that the PRC struggled with the emergence of the first cases of COVID-19—trying to "shoot the messenger"—but quickly shifted to mask diplomacy and then, vaccine diplomacy, to its advantage in order (i) to favourably change the western narrative, (ii) to not lose face, a concept very cherished by Chinese people, and (iii) legitimate the competency of the CCP. Indeed, there is a whole set of proposals for the PRC to become an important player in the health field: a focus on scientific cooperation, on health-related industry, on food safety, and on transparency in the production of pharmaceuticals; always in a partnership logic between the knowledge of so-called conventional medicine and Traditional Chinese Medicine. All this in a pragmatic approach that begins to favour public–private partnerships.

The Health Silk Road has a very relevant role in the definition of the Chinese strategy in terms of global health, as it is an important communication tool towards global partners, serving as a flag of its diplomatic soft power in an area that has been defined as the geopolitics of health. It can be perceived as a tool of soft and smart power in the PRC's way towards what Xi Jinping mentions frequently as the "building of a community of shared future for mankind." This shared future is the ultimate contribution of the PRC's to health global governance, trying to follow the path suggested by many specialists in global health and health diplomacy, such as Ilona Kickbusch et al. (2021), which is to "move beyond a charity model of foreign aid towards a global social contract one." The role of the PRC is undeniable.

Acknowledgements This work was supported by the doctoral grant SFRH/BD/151133/2021 from Foundation for Science and Technology, I.P. and Macau Scientific and Cultural Centre and by the Research Unit on Governance, Competitiveness and Public Policies (UIDB/04058/2020) + (UIDP/04058/2020) funded by national funds from Foundation for Science and Technology, I.P.

References

Beeson, M. (2020). A plague on both your houses: European and Asian responses to Coronavirus. *Asia Europe Journal, 18,* 245–249. https://doi.org/10.1007/s10308-020-00581-4

Bing, N. (2020). *COVID-19 speeds up China's 'Health Silk Road'*. East Asia Forum Special Issue. Retrieved on November 2021, from https://www.eastasiaforum.org/2020/05/26/covid-19-speeds-up-chinas-health-silk-road/

Cao, J. (2020). Towards a Health Silk Road. China's proposal for global health cooperation. *China Quarterly of International Strategic Studies, 6*(33), 19–35.

Chan, K. (2010). *Harmonious society. International encyclopaedia of civil society*. Springer. https://doi.org/10.1007/978-0-387-93996-4_101

China.org.cn. (2019). *The healthy China initiative (on governance)*. http://www.china.org.cn/english/china_key_words/2019-04/16/content_74687017.htm

County Healthy Rankings. (2014). *2014 rankings: Key findings reports*. Robert Wood Johnson Foundation & University of Wisconsin Population Health Institute.

Duckett, J. (2011). Challenging the economic reform paradigm: Policy and politics in the early 1980s' collapse of the rural cooperative medical system. *The China Quarterly, 205*, 80–95.

Fidler, D. (2010). *The challenges of global health governance*. Council on Foreign Relations.

Gauttam, P., Singh, B., & Kaur, J. (2020). COVID-19 and Chinese global health diplomacy: Geopolitical opportunity for China's hegemony? *Millennial Asia, 11*(3), 318–340. https://doi.org/10.1177/0976399620959771

Hotez, P. J. (2014). "Vaccine diplomacy": Historical perspectives and future directions. *PLoS Neglected Tropical Diseases, 8*(6), e2808.

Hsiao, W., et al. (2014). Universal health coverage: The case of China. *UNRISD* (Working Paper 2014–2015).

Huang, Y. (2004). *The SARS epidemic and its aftermath in China: A political perspective. Institute of Medicine (US) forum on microbial threats; Learning from SARS: Preparing for the next disease outbreak: Workshop summary*. National Academies Press (US).

Husain, L., & Bloom, G. (2020). Understanding China's growing involvement in global health and managing processes of change. *Global Health, 16*, 39. https://doi.org/10.1186/s12992-020-00569-0

Kickbusch, I., et al. (2021). *A guide to global health diplomacy. Better health—Improved global solidarity—More equity*. Global Health Centre. The Graduate Institute of Geneva.

Kowalski, B. (2021). China's mask diplomacy in Europe: Seeking foreign gratitude and domestic stability. *Journal of Current Chinese Affairs, 50*(2), 1–18. https://doi.org/10.1177/1868102621100 7147

Lee, S. (2021). Vaccine diplomacy: Nation branding and China's Covid-19 soft power play. *Place branding and public diplomacy*. Springer Nature. https://doi.org/10.1057/s41254-021-00224-4

Lin, S., et al. (2016). China's health assistance to Africa: Opportunism or altruism? *Global Health, 12*, 83.

Liu, P., et al. (2014). China's distinctive engagement in global health. *Lancet, 384*(9945), 793–804.

Meng, Q., Mills, A., Wang, L., & Han, Q. (2019). What can we learn from China's health system reform? *BMJ, 365*, l2349. https://doi.org/10.1136/bmj.l2349

Ministry of Foreign Affairs of the People's Republic of China. (2006). *China's African policy*. Retrieved on November 2021, from https://www.mfa.gov.cn/zflt//eng/zt/zgdfzzcwj/t230479.htm

National Health Commission of the PRC. (2017). *Beijing Communiqué of the Belt and Road Health Cooperation & Health Silk Road*. Retrieved on November 2021, from http://en.nhc.gov.cn/2017-08/18/c_72257.htm

NEJM Catalyst. (2017). *Social determinants of health (SDOH)*. Retrieved on November 2021, from https://catalyst.nejm.org/doi/full/10.1056/CAT.17.0312

Su, Z. et al. (2021). COVID-19 Vaccine donations-vaccine empathy or vaccine diplomacy? A narrative literature review. *Vaccines 2021, 9*(9), 1024.

Tan, X., et al. (2017). Healthy China 2030: A vision for health care. *Value in Health Regional Issues, 12C*, 112–114.

Thornton, P. M. (2009). Crisis and governance: SARS and the resilience of the Chinese body politic. *The China Journal, 61*, 23–48. Retrieved on November 2021, from http://www.jstor.org/stable/20648044

Tillman, H., et al. (2021). *Health silk road 2020: A bridge to the future of health for all*. Hong Kong Trade Development Council Research.

United Nations. (2021, September 19). *Ensure healthy lives and promote well-being for all at all ages*. https://sdgs.un.org/goals/goal3

Verma, R. (2020). China's 'mask diplomacy' to change the COVID-19 narrative in Europe. *Asia Europe Journal, 18*, 205–209.

Vieira, V. (2019). From third world theory to belt and road initiative: International aid as a chinese foreign policy tool. *Contexto Internacional, 41*(3).

Wang, S. (2008). Changing models of China's policy agenda setting. *Modern China, 34*(1).

Wang, L., et al. (2019). The development and reform of public health in China from 1949 to 2019. *Global Health 15*(45).

Wang, L., et al. (2019). The intentions, needs, advantages and barriers: A survey of twenty-nine countries participating in the "Belt and Road Initiative" health cooperation. *Global Health Research and Policy, 4*, 4. https://doi.org/10.1186/s41256-019-0109-z

World Health Organization. (2020). *COVAX—Working for global equitable access to COVID-19 vaccines*. Retrieved on December 2021, from https://www.who.int/initiatives/act-accelerator/covax

World Health Organization. (2021). *Taking action on the social determinants of health*. https://www.who.int/westernpacific/activities/taking-action-on-the-social-determinants-of-health

Xiaochun, Z. (2018). In pursuit of a community of shared future: China's global activism in perspective. *World Century Publishing Corporation and Shanghai Institutes for International Studies. China Quarterly of International Strategic Studies, 4*(1), 23–37. https://doi.org/10.1142/S2377740018500082

Xu, J., et al. (2019). Reforming public hospital financing in China: Progress and challenges. *BMJ,* 365.

Yip, W., & Hsiao, W. (2015). What drove the cycles of Chinese health system reforms? *Health Systems & Reform, 1*(1), 52–61.

Zhuang, N. (2016). *Outline of the healthy China 2030 plan*. National Health and Family Planning Commission.

Chapter 15
Digital China: Governance, Power Politics, and the Social Game

Dorothée Vandamme, Tanguy Struye de Swielande, and Kimberly Orinx

1 Introduction

In 2015, while China was launching the third-generation Beidou system for global coverage, Xi Jinping called on countries to respect each other's cyber sovereignty (Kolton, 2017). In 2016, it launched its National Cyber Security Strategy (Austin, 2018). That same year, TikTok went global, taking off first in the US and then worldwide. In 2017, Beijing revised its standardization law (Seaman, 2020), and then announced in 2018 that it would publish its "China Standards 2035" action plan over the next two years. In 2019, Chinese authorities proposed a new Internet Protocol (IP) developed by Huawei at the International Telecommunications Union. Meanwhile, Uganda acquired a nationwide surveillance system with recognition capabilities from Huawei. Last year, the COVID-19 pandemic outbreak was the theme of a major information operation campaign by Beijing. As of 2021, the Chinese social credit system is well implemented in several provinces and urban centres of the country (Creemers, 2018; Liang et al., 2018). The message from Chinese decision-makers is unequivocal: China is a major player in the cyber domain. Yet, while this very simple matter of fact is largely recognized in academic, political, and industrial circles, the extent of Chinese strategic thinking and its underlying processes remain little understood. Each example cited above is obviously linked to the cyber domain. If one focuses on each event, it appears as if China, playing a game of chess, moves its different pieces in the service of its overall objective. So far, the literature on China's digital politics has mainly focused on the country's economic power and its strategy in terms of geo-economics and geostrategy (Mattlin & Nojonen, 2015; Mattlin & Wigell, 2016; Zhao, 2019). Scholarly works have moved away from the no-strings-attached picture that dominated in the late 2000s (Chin & Helleiner, 2008; Foster et al., 2008), and in particular since the 2012 arrival of Xi Jinping as China's leader and his much more assertive diplomacy (Mattlin, 2021). Much has since been

D. Vandamme · T. S. de Swielande (✉) · K. Orinx
UCLouvain, Ottignies-Louvain-La-Neuve, Belgium

© The Author(s), under exclusive license to Springer Nature Singapore Pte Ltd. 2023
P. A. B. Duarte et al. (eds.), *The Palgrave Handbook of Globalization with Chinese Characteristics*, https://doi.org/10.1007/978-981-19-6700-9_15

written on China's foreign policy (Brautigam, 2007, 2020; Breslin, 2011; Cheng, 2016; Struye de Swielande, 2015), in particular the BRI and its Digital Silk Road component (Liu et al., 2018; Shen, 2018; Struye de Swielande and Vandamme, 2020; Xiao, 2019). Trying to make sense of China's increasing normative power and its role as norm-maker, emerging literature dwells on the Chinese characteristics of normative power and the tools it has at its disposal (Breslin, 2011; Forsberg, 2009; Zhao, 2018). Yet, while scientific literature provides us with ample literature on normative power processes per se (Diez, 2013; Manners, 2002; Zwitter & Hazenberg, 2020), there remains a gap between this literature and China's cyber policies in terms of normative process and international order structuration. More specifically, little has been written about the socialization process that underlies Chinese politics in the cyber domain and how these policies are part of a larger strategy. Indeed, the chess analogy is based on a confrontational strategy, overt actions that aim at reaching a well-known objective—to defeat the adversary and win. But China is not playing chess; it is playing a game of Go. All of its actions are well-orchestrated moves to covertly subvert the adversary, influence the entire game board so that every single piece of the game, including those of the adversary, acts to its own advantage.

The following analysis aims at identifying the process behind China's cyber policies and its objective to position itself as a central hub in the cyber domain, structuring cyber governance, norms, and rules to its image and values, shaping the domain structuration around the core principles of cyber sovereignty and authoritarianism. We seek to answer the following question: how are China's actions integrated into a linkage strategy that seeks to position the country as a central hub of the cyber domain and a structuring power in cyber governance? Focusing on the Xi era (from 2012), we answer this question by testing the hypothesis that China establishes a linkage strategy through the Digital Silk Road and by taking on standards and norms-setting role in international institutional fora. Using the method of interpretive phenomenological analysis (Vandamme, 2021) and building on socialization studies, we analyse official documents and discourses, technological innovations, and Chinese policies and norm-setting activities to identify the normative process that underlies China's cyber activities. The cases discussed in the chapter have been chosen to represent and cover the diversity of Chinese statecraft as it relates to the cyber domain.

The chapter first addresses the question of Chinese international policies and actions vis-à-vis technical standards in the cyber domain. It then links these policies to the "China Standards 2035" plan, demonstrating that China's policy in the cyber domain is part of an integrated vision. Looking at this integrated vision as a manifestation of China's international socialization process, the next section shows that China's strategy is built on normative foundations of standard-and-norms-setting. More specifically, the analysis identifies two core norms in which China aims at socializing with other states: cyber sovereignty and cyber authoritarianism. Our final section concludes our chapter by summarizing our argument and main findings. We expect to conclude that by implementing a linkage strategy, China adopts an integrated vision, combining international socialization through governance with power politics, structuring the norms and rules of cyber governance to its image and values, shaping the domain structuration around the core principles of cyber sovereignty and authoritarianism in a multilevel process that influences the social interactions of the system's actors and their values, norms, rules, and principles. In fine, China aims at shaping and influencing other states' socialization processes to defend and support its national objectives.

2   What's at Stake in Technical Standards

Whether in Brussels, Sydney, Islamabad, Shanghai, or San Francisco, your computer, smartphone, tablet, smartwatch, or any other related item connects to WiFi. One click, one password, and you are surfing the net. Amazing, isn't it? Well, not really. With the technological developments and the increase of exchanges of all kinds, the economic-industrial world had to adapt and facilitate interoperability of what surrounds us. Technological developments are certainly a glaring example, whether it is WiFi, Bluetooth, or the HDMI connection that allows a South Korean computer screen to be used in Argentina with a computer designed in the US and a cable made in Vietnam. But this is also the case for many everyday objects that have entered our lives, such as light bulbs. How did the multiple actors involved in the invention, creation, design, manufacture, and sale—of these products come to an agreement? Thanks to technical norms, or standards. These standards are at the heart of systems, networks, and objects interoperability, necessary to our daily lives. They enable the compatibility of new inventions and creations around the world. In doing so, they play a key role in the selection of technologies that become, or not, prevalent in the lives of citizens. Inconspicuous, unattractive because of their technicality, and often very complex, these technological and industrial standards are not much talked about. Yet, they occupy a central place in the technological and industrial structuring of the world. Therefore, having the capacity to influence the elaboration of these standards is a significant tool of power in the international system, since it guarantees a larger market share.

Technical standards are a set of technical specifications adopted and integrated by companies that enable global connectivity and interoperability of products. They ensure that products seamlessly work together, for example that an iPhone user can reach a Nokia or Samsung user. Despite widespread disregard for their political dimension, technical standards are fundamental to twentieth and twenty-first-century globalization. Rühlig thus points out that "technical standardization is the engine of connectivity, interdependence and globalization" (Rühlig, 2020, p. 7) which enables the deployment and smooth functioning of networks around the world. "Great things happen when the world agrees," proclaims the International Organization for Standardization, or ISO, on its website.

Because connectivity has long been taken for granted, the political dimension of international standards has long been either neglected or ignored; standards are merely the technical specification of connectivity, and their formulation results from a consensus of experts on finding the most effective and efficient technical solution to a given problem. And yet, the formulation of technical standards is an important political issue that allows a company to increase its market share. Formulating technical standards contributes to shaping the economic and industrial landscape of a given field, thus allowing it to gain a significant competitive advantage over competitors. For example, in the field of telecommunication technology standards, technical specifications are determined by fundamental standards of information and communication technologies, thereby shaping the ongoing information revolution. Therefore, countries that develop these standards will own intellectual property, training, development, and control of the corresponding supply chains. These supply chains in turn allow access to and control over extended economic and commercial systems, including some control over access to technology and services by other countries. As a result, in a globalized and highly connected economy, the stakes are high.

3 "China Standards 2035" and the Digital Information Revolution

The crucial issue of technical standards explains why the "China Standards 2035" action plan launched by China's SAC (Standardization Administration of China) in 2018 should be understood in the context of the geopolitical and geo-economic competition with the US. Far from being a simple political formulation of technical issues, this action plan is conceived as a real power tool in China's grand strategy,[1] whose primary objective is to become the world leader by the PRC's centenary in 2049. "China Standards 2035" aims at increasing and improving the number of international standards created by Chinese companies, both quantitatively and qualitatively, in order to increase Beijing's influence and become a key player in the global market, especially in the field of new technologies related to the information revolution. In 2019, the Chinese developed two platforms to facilitate standards cooperation, namely the Belt & Roads' Co-constructed National Standard Information Platform, and the Standardization CN-EN Bilingual Intelligent Translation Cloud Platform (Seaman, 2020, p. 27).

This strategy is particularly focused on specific sectors: blockchain, the Internet of Things, new forms of cloud computing, big data, 5G, artificial intelligence and machine learning, geographic information systems, and biotechnology, among others. In short, all the core technologies in the digital economy and information age, two major structural forces that are transforming our societies at a fundamental level and affecting all levels and sectors of activity. From Beijing's point of view, having missed the last technological revolution and having been relegated to a secondary

---

[1] For a detailed analysis of the Chinese grand strategy, see Struye de Swielande T., & Vandamme, D. (2020). The new silk roads: defining China's grand strategy. In F. J. Leandro & P. A. B. Duarte (Eds.), *The belt and road initiative: An old archetype of a new development model* (pp. 3–22). Springer.

role behind the US, or even the West more generally (Wilson, 2020), requires a surge of research and investment in the coming revolution. China therefore intends to "rebalance" the order by positioning itself at the heart of the global geo-economic *goban* and by (re)taking its natural status and position as a world leader.

It is worth noting that China did not wait for its "China Standards 2035" action plan to influence technical standards; standardization is integral to the Belt and Road Initiative (BRI) and Digital Silk Road (DSR) programme, which incorporate agreements on standardization with partner countries. The 2019 BRI Progress Report from the Office of the Leading Group for Promoting the BRI reported that same year 85 standards cooperation agreements with 49 countries and regions, a number increasing with the expansion of the BRI and the signing of partnership agreements. The development and adoption of Chinese technical standards in partner countries and regions are key to the BRI project to open up the markets of participating economies to Chinese products and companies (Ming Cheung et al., 2016). As Wen emphasizes by noting the importance of offshore communication networks (2020, pp. 184–193), the Digital Silk Road, or digital component of the BRI, is crucial to Beijing's standardization strategy. Infrastructures around the Internet of Things (smart cities, autonomous cars, electrical networks …), e-commerce (Alibaba, jd.com, Pinduoduo), or geolocation services (Beidou satellite) are particularly noteworthy. In this regard, economic and technological competitions have significantly been underpinned by the geopolitical race that characterizes the deployment of 5G networks, a key driver for these technological developments. China Telecom Corporation, China Module, and China Unicom are heavily investing and working with Huawei and ZTE, not only to develop the infrastructure, but to determine the technical and industry standards that will underpin 5G network deployment. If standards creation processes result from a consensus on finding the best technical solution to enable interoperability, players holding the intellectual property rights to the technological innovation clearly hold a strategic position to influence their formulation and to receive royalty payments granting access to the patents filed. In other words, the company or state that first develops the technology is the actor most likely to shape the standards around that technology and to financially benefit from the deployment of said technology. However, technical standardization in China is a state-driven process, unlike in Europe or the US, where the process is more industry-driven, by a market-oriented logic for the former, or resulting from a private–public partnership for the latter (see Rühlig, 2020). This divergence in process illustrates the politicized nature of technical standardization: technical standards are now an integral part of global geopolitical and geo-economic competition.

Moreover, these technical standards at the heart of China's strategy should also be placed within the standards requirements of the Military-Civil Fusion (MCF), a national strategy of the CCP whose goal is to "enable the PRC to develop the world's most technologically advanced military" (Department of State, 2020) and to transform the PLA (People's Liberation Army) into a world-class military by 2049. As a long-term strategic effort, the MCF aims to turn China into a technological superpower by leveraging dual-use technologies in a process of mutual support and barrier removal between industrial and commercial research on one hand, and military development on the other. Ultimately, this process merges China's commercial and defence economies (See Bitzinger, 2021, pp. 5–24). This is a long-term strategy that accompanies and combines with the BRI project. The coordination, even harmonization, of Chinese technical standards, carried out by the SAC, incorporates this dual-use requirement to provide a foundation for China's international power projection. For example, the 2017 Thirteenth Five-Year Action Plan for the Development of MCF in Science and Technology states that "by 2020, military-civilian standards will be compatible and dual-use" (Quoted in Ray Bowen II, 2020). Despite many technical, legal, or cultural obstacles, the MCF strategy could, in the medium to long term, represent a major challenge for the US, and more globally for the maintenance of the liberal institutional order, by positioning China as a major military power, thanks to the numerous BRI and DSR projects.

4 Norms and Global Power Structures

Beyond the strictly commercial and military dimensions surrounding technical standards, "China Standards 2035" is ultimately nothing more than a specific and concrete manifestation of China's power projection and its adoption of the role of standard-and-norms-setter at the international level. As pointed out above, the US–China competition includes norms and standards for three main reasons: (1) key enabling technologies are at the heart of the US–China competition; (2) China develops a state-driven approach to technical standards; and (3) the political dimension and power potential of technical standards are often neglected (see also Rühlig, 2021, p. 2). China has thus clearly stated the importance of the power of standards: "*Standards support acceleration of our domestic economic reform and our international status. […] Technical standardization will help spread Chinese wisdom to the world and contribute to the construction of a multipolar world*" (Quoted in Rühlig, 2021, p. 2).

Typically associated with the status of a leader, or at least with that of leading power, the role of standard-setter enables a political actor to project its vision and perception of the international scene, shaping the behaviours, rules, and relational habits of states and international actors. It is now recognized that the US' status as a world leader is not only due to its military and commercial power, but relies also on its discursive and normative power. By shaping an institutional order centred around liberal values central to American culture and institutions, such as respect for human rights, freedom of expression, individual rights, and democratic norms, the US has structured a system of global governance that regulates cooperation and the mediation and resolution of tensions and conflicts between countries based on rules, norms, and institutions, the primary representative of which being the United Nations. However, as long as the world governance system revolves around liberal and democratic values and norms, China cannot claim the highest rank in the international order because of its lack of normative legitimacy.

By norms, we mean the set of behaviours considered to be typical ("normal") and in conformity with what is expected of an actor, in this case a state, in a given system. A normative international system such as the one shaped by the US—and the West more broadly—thus means that states are expected to behave in a certain way, to respect specific norms, values, and rules. International institutions are the backbone of this system, as they are the main place for cooperation, exchange, and dispute settlement at the international level. It is therefore significant to note China's massive commitment to the UN, its specialized agencies, and other international institutions—including institutions in charge of international management of technical standards. China has increased its budgetary contribution to the UN, becoming the second-largest contributor after the US. It is widely recognized that a significant financial contribution provides leverage over the operations of a given organization. In addition, international organizations have an increasing number of Chinese nationals in their management: out of the 19 UN specialized agencies, 4 are headed by Chinese nationals, including the International Telecommunication Union which specializes in information and communication technologies. While the UN's operating principle is that its leaders and international staff should be independent of their countries and work exclusively for the service and benefit of the organization, reality has shown that Chinese leaders do not hesitate to use these positions to defend Chinese interests and advance their agenda (*The Economist*, 2019; see also Mazarr et al., 2018): in 2020, "the telecoms group Huawei, together with state-run companies China Unicom and China Telecom, and the country's Ministry of Industry and Information Technology (MIIT), jointly proposed a new standard for core network technology, called "New IP," at the UN's International Telecommunication Union (ITU)" (Gross & Murgia, 2020). The objective appeared to be the decoupling of the internet and the promotion of cyber sovereignty (regulations, sovereignty, and control in opposition to an open internet). China is pushing for standards reinforcing the role of the state (multilateral instead of multistakeholder).

In other words, rather than accepting the American or Western vision of the world and its structuration, China creates and proposes alternative norms of functioning, and then socializes other states into these norms and rules. Central to this alternative project is the learning of norms, rules of behaviour, and operation that are no longer based on liberal values, but on the Westphalian principles of sovereignty and non-interference in the internal affairs of states. Thus, China opposes democratic values to the free choice of each state's political system, the respect of human rights to social and civic rights that place public order and the interest of the state above individual rights, international law to a more Westphalian system of cooperation—in fact regulated by the most powerful because of the absence of specific pre-established rules. Chinese leaders have learned from the discursive and normative power of the US, and hold today a discourse of "rebalancing," of a more "just" order, in which the exceptional character of each state is recognized. This rhetorical spin, reinforced by Confucianism and economic power, would allow each state to choose its own model, however authoritarian and dictatorial. The implication is that by adopting the Chinese model of authoritarian capitalism, states will be able to achieve a level of economic development equivalent to that of China while maintaining their political stability. This is enough to seduce authoritarian leaders who are regularly targeted and stigmatized by Western countries that defend liberal democratic values.

This rhetoric of rectifying the international system from what is condemned as Western liberal deviance is in fact only part of a much larger (normative discourse and) strategy which builds on normative features of the international system. Beijing is now acting on the entire spectrum of norms that govern international relations, redefining the way states and non-state actors operate and relate to each other. On closer inspection, it is interesting to note that China does not really propose an alternative model of systemic organization: behind the rhetoric, one finds in fact a system of governance in which China, at the centre, updates a form of tributary system similar to the one in place in imperial China. This system is based on the centrality of Beijing to which other states owe allegiance—in short, they must adopt policies that do not run counter to China's power position, and which in fact reinforce its power. Through the BRI and its infrastructure development, investment, and financial cooperation projects, links are being forged that allow China to bring partner states closer to, or even bind them to Beijing. The rhetorical use of harmony, peaceful development, and Chinese benevolence is little more than a discursive tool to avoid suspicion and mistrust, and to promote the acceptance and implementation of Chinese norms and rules.

Establishing Chinese rules and norms and encouraging their implementation and adoption by other states through a socialization process allows Beijing to anchor other states in a position and a mode of operation that is favourable to China (Grusec & Hastings, 2015, p. xi), convergent with Chinese norms and values. Despite its reciprocal nature between China and the other states,[2] this structuring process is clearly backed-up by Chinese material power. As the world's second-largest economy, Beijing can easily convince and persuade other states to adopt its norms and values. Yet, this process should not be seen as unilateral and automatically successful on the part of China, which faces many obstacles. Socialization is indeed not entirely predictable; it does not force actors to move in a specific direction without choice or voice (Sandstrom et al., 2014, p. 86). In addition to the downward verticality inherent to the process (the most powerful has a structuring impact on the less powerful) the upward verticality (the less powerful or the new member also socializes the more powerful or older ones) as well as the horizontality of the process should also be taken into consideration. The final objective is to reach harmony in the rules of conduct, values, norms, and behaviours of the actors at the international level, thereby bringing fluidity and minimizing the unpredictable character of international relations.

Let us make no mistake: socialization, despite its multidirectional and reciprocal character, is in fact a means of establishing and perpetuating a specific social system according to a specific hierarchical order. The more powerful a state is, the more it holds the capacity to influence the socialization process of others. The US remains the primary socializer on the international scene. This normative dimension of power also characterizes the European Union, a leading normative and regulatory power,

---

[2] In the sense that China also learns from the modus operandi and standards of the states with which it cooperates.

which influence stands out very clearly in the economic sector (Bradford, 2020). The construction of an institutional architecture framing an ecosystem according to norms and regulations is a tool of power that makes it possible to influence the international structure. The influence of a normative power is exercised through its capacity to generate interactions that it deems appropriate. By influencing the adoption of certain norms and behaviours, the regulating agent socializes others into a system that it determines and defines according to its own values. The degree of integration of the socialized actor into a given social system depends on this socialization process. In other words, the state that conforms to the behavioural and relational expectations of the socializing state will have more opportunities and will be perceived more favourably than a non-conforming or deviant state.

5 Setting the Norms of Cyber Sovereignty and Authoritarianism

One might have thought that the development of smartphones and other connected objects would undermine Beijing's control over information; yet, the Chinese government has managed to use new technologies to increase its surveillance and influence over its own population. To this end, it has developed the norm of cyber sovereignty. This concept is based on two main principles: first, unwanted influence in a country's (in this case China's) "information space" should be prohibited; second, Internet governance should shift from the current bodies (which include academics and the private sector) to an international forum such as the United Nations, which would imply a transfer of power to states alone—a strict Westphalian-based architecture. According to China, "respecting cyber sovereignty" implies:

> respecting each country's right to choose its own internet development path, its own internet management model, its own public policies on the internet, and to participate on an equal basis in the governance of international cyberspace — avoiding cyber-hegemony, and avoiding interference in the internal affairs of other countries. (…) [We must] build a multilateral, democratic and transparent governance system for the global internet. (Xi, 2015)

For President Xi, cyber sovereignty equals the right of a nation to choose the development and regulation of its "own" Internet (Iasiello, 2017, p. 1). China seeks to avoid any risk of interference with its national audience (e.g., the *Great Firewall, Canon*, the social credit system established on a coercive logic of reward and punishment).

At the national level, the CCP wants to shape the domestic political arena and maintain the legitimacy of the Party. In a 2013 report commonly referred to as "Document No. 9" (officially titled "Communiqué on the Current State of the Ideological Sphere"), the PRC asserted that "Western constitutional democracy is an attempt to degrade the current leadership and socialism with the Chinese characteristics of the governance system" and that the Western universal values are "an attempt to weaken the theoretical basis of the party leadership" (Document 9, 2013). The last paragraph of the document also states: "We must strengthen the management of all types and levels of propaganda on the cultural front, perfect and implement the associated administrative systems and leave no possibility or means of disseminating information, incorrect ideas or views" (Ibidem).

At the international level, China wants to influence cyber authoritarianism by imposing its model of cyber sovereignty. According to President Xi Jinping, "respecting cyber sovereignty" implies.

> respecting the right of each country to choose its own path to internet development, its own internet business model, its own public policies in matters of internet, and participate on an equal footing in the governance of international cyberspace – avoiding cyber hegemony and avoiding interference in the internal affairs of other countries… [We must] set up a multilateral, democratic and transparent system of governance for the global internet. (Xi, 2015)

The key term here is "multilateral." In opposition to the current multistakeholder approach to cyberspace, which is the "involvement on an equal footing of all actors with a vested interest in the Internet including businesses and civil society," China vigorously defends multilateral or intergovernmental internet governance that considers states as the main decision-makers (Raud, 2016). In this regard, cyber sovereignty was described in 2015 by Xu Lin, the head of the Cyberspace Administration of China at the time, as the difference between the multistakeholder approach and the multilateral approach (Gady, 2016). The underlying idea behind the logic of cyber sovereignty is to develop an Internet system completely closed and controlled by the authorities, and to bring state sovereignty into the cyberspace, in a system that strikingly resembles Orwell's famous *1984*. As Xi put it in 2017, China's model offers "a new option for other countries and nations who want to speed up their development while preserving their independence."

Since 2014, Beijing hosts the yearly World Internet Conference in Wuzhen (Zhejiang province). This conference, which gathers officials and CEOs from all around the world, aims at legitimizing the Chinese vision of norms and cyber sovereignty (Kerry, 2018). Following the 2018 Freedom House Report on the Freedom of the Net, China has "hosted media officials from dozens of countries for two- and three-week seminars on its sprawling system of censorship and surveillance" (Shahbaz, 2018). Digital authoritarianism is encouraged as a way for government authorities to control their populations via technology, thus inverting the philosophy of the Internet as an engine of human emancipation (Ibidem). AI surveillance technology and facial-recognition software are accordingly exported to a growing number of developing countries. AI at the disposal of authoritarian regimes facilitates surveillance (monitoring and tracking) of the population and the opposition: "Beyond narrowing the space for civil society, authoritarian states are also learning to use digital tools to quell dissent. Although technology has helped facilitate protests, today's digitally savvy authoritarian regimes are using some of the same technological innovations to push back against dangerous popular mobilizations. … Digital repression not only decreases the likelihood that a protest will occur but also reduces the chances that a government will face large, sustained mobilization efforts" (Kendall-Taylor et al., 2020).

China is thus increasingly defending and promoting its authoritarian model, intending to export "socialism with Chinese characteristics" and therefore to propose an alternative model that departs from the liberal order. To this end, it strengthens its discursive power by proposing new ideas, concepts, norms, and institutions in order to reinforce regional and international control of agenda-setting at the political, economic, and security levels. In doing so, Beijing attempts to persuade other states to adopt its vision of a new world order; some success is already visible in some African, Middle Eastern, or Central Asian countries (Egypt, Algeria, Ethiopia, Saudi Arabia, UAE, Tajikistan, Kazakhstan). Through this process of socialization, states appropriate the norms defined by China, which source of leadership lies in the norms and values that it has managed to internationalize and, to a certain extent, to institutionalize.[3] Thus, by openly positioning itself as an alternative, China de facto attracts powers dissatisfied with the international order, but that cannot directly oppose it.

The Digital Silk Road, launched in 2015, provides in this context the full package of the "digital authoritarianism playbook" (Lilkov, 2020, p. 27): "Through its Belt and Road Initiative and separate economic partnerships, Beijing is rolling out technological infrastructure, data centers, fiber-optic cables and telecommunications networks—essentially building the digital backbone of these states" (Ibidem, p. 10). Furthermore, by emphasizing its successful management of the COVID-19 pandemic and the fact that its particularly restrictive measures have proven effective in containing the virus, China hopes to better sell its surveillance system to other countries. During the coronavirus crisis President Xi said in 2020: "This is a crisis and it is also a major test…The effectiveness of the prevention and control work has once again showed the significant advantages of the leadership of the Communist Party of China and the socialist system with Chinese characteristics" (Zheng, 2020).

Chinese ambitions do not stop here. To impose its digital authoritarianism and become a digital power, China also invests forcefully, among others, in submarine cables, Beidou, 5/6G, data, semiconductors, and raw materials. For instance, undersea cables make instant communications possible, "transporting some 95 percent of the data and voice traffic that crosses international boundaries. They also form the backbone of the global economy" (Schadlow & Brayden, 2020), and play a key role in data routing. Beidou was finalized in 2020 and offers an alternative to GPS, allowing China to have a greater hold on infrastructures, the internet of things, norms, and standards. The deployment of 5/6G will boost the internet of things (smart cities, smart cars…) accelerating communication and data sharing among devices. The purpose of these digital infrastructures is the transfer, storage, and processing of data. Big data provides the fuel for the expansion of artificial intelligence. In this regard, through their social credit system, Chinese authorities have amassed a considerable amount of data, which will be useful in both studying consumer behaviour and

---

[3] For more details on socialisation read (Struye de Swielande, T., & Vandamme, D. (2015). Power in international relations: Modernizing holsti into the twenty-first century. In T. Struye de Swielande & D. Vandamme (Eds.), *Power in the 21st century. determinants and contours* (pp. 9–32). Louvain-la-Neuve: Presses universitaires de Louvain and Struye de Swielande, T. (2015). *Duel entre l'aigle et le dragon pour le leadership mondial*. Brussels: Peter-Lang).

political profiling. The Chinese government is also developing its semiconductor industry, a key stage for processing data at high speeds and for storing data; currently they are lagging behind in this domain, when compared to the US or Japan. Finally, all these technologies are energy consuming and include rare earths in their components. China controls the rare earth market, a vital part of advanced technologies' chain of production: 80% of world production and 40% of world reserves are in Chinese hands. By the 1990s, China had understood the importance of rare earths, as evidenced by Deng Xiaoping's words in 1992: "The Middle East has oil and China has rare earths." The quasi monopoly on the production of rare earths allows China to control the market. Among others, this position enables Beijing to reduce exports to exert pressures on certain states, or lower prices to avoid other mines elsewhere in the world from becoming profitable.

6 Conclusion

Bridging the gap between international socialization processes and China's policies in the cyber domain, this chapter aimed at identifying China's linkage strategy and its normative features. The analysis reveals an active and assertive standards- and norms-setting role that Beijing enacts to position itself as a central hub in the cyber domain and its related international governance structures and institutions. This behaviour shapes and structures the international socialization process underlying China's strategy to influence other states' behaviour into accepting its position. This is revealed by two main findings: first, Beijing uses the international institutional framework to socialize other states into its technical standards and norms in the cyber domain. Whether through existing institutions (such as 3GPP, ETSI, ITU), or new ones (Digital Silk Road) when the former is not pliable to its influence, China builds on the global principle of multilateralism and institutional processes, thereby subverting the liberal international order through its own devices, to shape its own role as a standard-setter in the cyber domain. China intends to move from being a manufacturing country, to being a technology developer ("Made in China 2025" action plan), to leading standards creation and norm-setting among industrialized countries. Since standards determine the world's technological and industrial language, and norms shape the actors' visions, sense of appropriateness, and behaviour, structuring and influencing them would undoubtedly enable Beijing to strengthen its global position vis-à-vis the US. Second, these multilateral fora and systems of governance are complemented by bilateral mechanisms of material and social power in order to build a narrative of China as an alternative model for cyber governance, growth, and development. Beyond the financial gain, far from minimal,[4]

---

[4] Standards-setting and technology-producing states generally hold patents that are purchased by other states that produce products. China is currently a major purchaser of patents, and through this "China Standards 2035" action plan, intends to reverse the curve and become a holder of patents

this will allow Beijing to become a key player in this field, a hub of the cyber domain around which other players gravitate.

But China's ambition does not stop at becoming *a* key player: it seeks to become *the* world leader. Validating our hypothesis, the chapter demonstrates that China's socialization process links together every aspect of the domain, including the norms and values that underlie the digital era. If China puts forward standards, institutions, and governance, these domains are in fact directly linked to the promotion of an authoritarian model, cyber sovereignty, the control of big data and resources, and the development of new technologies (AI, 5/6G, semiconductors, etc.). In other words, China not only positions itself as a standard-setter, but it also plays the role of norm-setter as part of its linkage strategy. It participates in existing institutions and creates new ones in order to try and impose its own norms and standards, thereby delegitimizing those of the West. Grounding its arguments and norm-setting in a Westphalian logic of the international system, Beijing turns Western values, institutions, and norms against Western states and proposes an alternative model for those countries that are dissatisfied with the current world order and discontent of being stigmatized because of their (poor) democratic and human rights performance. This Westphalian-based discourse emphasizes sovereignty and nonintervention in the internal affairs of a country, thereby encouraging a decoupling logic in the cyber domain, in particular of the Internet.

The survival of the CCP and respect for China's sovereignty, and territorial and political integrity, are essential if China is to become a world leader by 2049. Thus, the socialization and normative strategies that China implements are at the service of Chinese national interests and are means of power mobilized to achieve that goal. Yet it does so not by openly confronting its adversaries in an open war with military means—chess game logic—but by weakening said adversaries from the inside, targeting weaknesses, and amplifying discontent, while offering an alternative model—game of Go logic. To this end, all tools of power are mobilized, following a holistic logic and linkage strategy. Indeed, the state that will control not only the development of new technologies (5G and 6G, Data, AI…), but also the norms and standards concerning them and their underlying philosophical conception, will dominate the international system. Beijing seeks to position itself at the centre of the technological economic-industrial ecosystem as its primary regulatory interface. This strategy lays the ground for China (and other like-minded states) to remake the world in its "techno-dystopian image" (Freedom House, 2018, p. 5). *In fine*, China seeks to shape the international system in ways that favour its own model of development and governance.

---

that will then be bought by other states. As of 2019, China has become the world's leading country in terms of the number of patents filed with the World Intellectual Property Organization.

Bibliographic References

A New battleground: In the UN, China uses threats and cajolery to promote its worldview. (2019, December 7). *The Economist*. Retrieved on November 2021, from https://www.economist.com/china/2019/12/07/in-the-un-china-uses-threats-and-cajolery-to-promote-its-worldview

Austin, G. (2018). *Cybersecurity in China: The next wave*. Springer.

Bitzinger, R. (2021). China's shift from civil-military integration to military-civil fusion. *Asia Policy, 28*(1), 5–24.

Bradford, A. (2020, February 3). When it comes to markets, Europe is no fading power. The EU sets the standards for the rest of the world. *Foreign Affairs*. Retrieved on November 2021, from https://www.foreignaffairs.com/articles/europe/2020-02-03/when-it-comes-markets-europe-no-fading-power.

Brautigam, D. (2007). China, Africa and the international aid architecture. *African Development Bank Group Working Paper Series, 107*, 37–40.

Brautigam, D. (2020). A critical look at Chinese "debt-trap diplomacy": The rise of a meme. *Area Development and Policy, 5*(1), 1–14.

Breslin, S. (2011). The "China model" and the global financial crisis: From Friedrich list to a Chinese mode of governance? *International Affairs, 87*(6), 1323–1343.

Cheng, J. Y. (2016). *China's foreign policy: Challenges and prospects*. World Scientific Publishing.

Chin, G. T., & Helleiner, E. (2008). China as a creditor: A rising financial power? *Journal of International Affairs, 62*(1), 87–102.

Creemers, R. (2018). *China's social credit system: An evolving practice of control*.

Department of State. (2020). *Military-civil fusion and the People's Republic of China*. Retrieved on November 2021, from https://www.state.gov/wp-content/uploads/2020/05/What-is-MCF-One-Pager.pdf.

Diez, T. (2013). Normative power as hegemony. *Cooperation and Conflict, 48*(2), 194–210.

Document 9: A china file translation—How much is a hardline party directive shaping China's current political climate? (2013, November 8). Retrieved on November 2021, from https://www.chinafile.com/document-9-chinafile-translation.

Forsberg, T. (2009). Normative power Europe, once again: A conceptual analysis of an ideal type. *Journal of Common Market Studies, 49*(6), 1184–1204.

Foster, V., Butterfield, W., Chen, C., & Pushak, N. (2008). *Building bridges: China's Growing role as infrastructure financier for Sub-Saharan Africa*. World Bank.

Freedom House. (2018). *The rise of digital authoritarianism. Freedom on the net 2018*. Retrieved on November 2021, from https://freedomhouse.org/report/freedom-net/2018/rise-digital-authoritarianism

Gady, F.-S. (2016, January 14). The Wuzhen summit and the battle over Internet governance. *The Diplomat*. Retrieved on November 2021, from https://thediplomat.com/2016/01/the-wuzhen-summit-and-the-battle-over-internet-governance/.

Gross, A., & Murgia, M. (2020, March 27). China and Huawei propose reinvention of the Internet. *Financial Times*.

Grusec, J. E., & Hastings, P. D. (2015). Preface. In J. E. Grusec & P. D. Hastings (Eds.), *Handbook of socialization: Theory and research* (2nd ed., pp. xi–xiii). The Guilford Press.

Iasiello, E. (2017). China's cyber initiatives counter international pressure. *Journal of Strategic Security, 10*(1), 1–16.

Kendall-Taylor, A., Frantz, E., & Wright, J. (2020, February 6). The digital dictators: How technology strengthens autocracy. *Foreign Affairs*. https://www.foreignaffairs.com/articles/china/2020-02-06/digital-dictators.

Kerry, C. (2018). *Can China have difficult conversations about the Internet*. Brookings Institution. China's World Internet Conference. Brookings Institution. https://www.brookings.edu/blog/techtank/2018/12/06/can-china-have-difficult-conversations-about-the-internet/.

Kolton, M. (2017). Interpreting China's pursuit of cyber sovereignty and its views on cyber deterrence. *The Cyber Defense Review, 2*(1), 119–154.

Liang, F., Das, V., Kostyuk, N., & Hussain, M. M. (2018). Constructing a data-driven society: China's social credit system as a state surveillance infrastructure. *Policy & Internet, 10*, 415–453.

Lilkov. D. (2020). *Made in China: Tackling digital authoritarianism*. Wilfried Martens Centre for European Studies. Retrieved on November 2021, from https://www.martenscentre.eu/publication/made-in-china-tackling-digital-authoritarianism/.

Liu, W., Dunford, M., & Gao, B. (2018). A discursive construction of the belt and road initiative: From neo-liberal to inclusive globalization. *Journal of Geographical Sciences, 28*(9), 1199–1214.

Manners, I. (2002). Normative power Europe: A contradiction in terms? *JCMS: Journal of Common Market Studies, 40*, 235–258.

Mattlin M. (2021). Normative economic statecraft: China's quest to shape the world in its image. In Ch. Shei & W. Wei, *The Routledge handbook of Chinese studies* (pp. 24–40). Routledge.

Mattlin, M., & Nojonen, M. (2015). Conditionality and path dependence in Chinese lending. *Journal of Contemporary China, 24*(94), 701–720.

Mattlin, M., & Wigell, M. (2016). Geo-economics in the context of restive regional powers. *Asia Europe Journal, 14*(2), 125–134.

Mazarr, M., Heath, T., & Stuth Cevallos, A. (2018). *China and the international order*. RAND Corporation.

Ming Cheung, T., Mahnken, Th., Seligsohn, D., Pollpeter, K., Anderson, E., & Yang, F. (2016). *Planning for innovation. Understanding China's plans for technological, energy, industrial, and defense development*. Report prepared for U.S.-China Economic and Security Review Commission.

Office of the Leading Group for Promoting the Belt and Road Initiative. (2019). *The belt and road initiative progress, contributions and prospects*. Foreign Languages Press Co.

Raud, M. (2016). *China and cyber: Attitudes, strategies, organization*. NATO Cooperative Cyber Defence Centre of Excellence. Retrieved on November 2021, from https://ccdcoe.org/library/publications/china-and-cyber-attitudes-strategies-organisation/.

Ray Bowen II, J. (2020). *A 'China model'? Beijing's promotion of alternative global norms and standards*. Testimony before the US-China Economic and Security Review Commission.

Remarks by H. E. Xi Jinping President of the People's Republic of China at the Opening Ceremony of the Second World Internet Conference. Wuzhen. (2015, December 16).

Rühlig, T. M. (2020). *Technical standardisation, China and the future international order. A European perspective*. Heinrich Böll Stiftung. Retrieved on November 2021, from https://eu.boell.org/en/2020/03/03/technical-standardisation-china-and-future-international-order.

Rühlig, T. (2021). *China, Europe and the new power competition over technical standards*. U Brief. the Swedish Institute of International Affairs.

Sandstrom, K. L., Lively, K. J., Martin, D. D., & Alan Fine, G. (2014). *Symbols, selves, and social reality: A symbolic interactionist approach to social psychology and sociology* (4th ed.). Oxford University Press.

Schadlow, N., & Brayden H. (2020, July 1). *Protecting undersea cables must be made a national security priority*. DefenseNews.com.

Seaman, J. (2020). *China and the new geopolitics of technical standardization*. Notes de l'IFRI. Retrieved on November 2021, from https://www.ifri.org/en/publications/notes-de-lifri/china-and-new-geopolitics-technical-standardization.

Shahbaz, A. (2018). *The rise of digital authoritarianism: Freedom on the net 2018*. Freedom House.

Shen, H. (2018). Building a digital Silk Road? Situating the Internet in China's belt and road initiative. *International Journal of Communications, 12*, 2683–2701.

Struye de Swielande, T. (2015). *Duel entre l'aigle et le dragon pour le leadership mondial*. Peter-Lang.

Struye de Swielande, T., & Vandamme, D. (2015). Power in international relations: Modernizing Holsti into the 21st century. In T. Struye de Swielande & D. Vandamme (Ed.), *Power in the 21st century. Determinants and contours* (pp. 9–32). Presses universitaires de Louvain.

Struye de Swielande, T., & Vandamme, D. (2020). The New Silk Roads: Defining China's grand strategy. In F. J. Leandro & P. A. B. Duarte (Eds.), *The belt and road initiative: An old archetype of a new development model* (pp. 3–22). Springer.

Vandamme D. (2021). Bringing researchers back in: Debating the role of interpretive epistemology in global IR. *International Studies Review, 23*(2), 370–390.

Wen, Y. (2020). *The Huawei model. The rise of China's technology giant.* University of Illinois Press.

Wilson, N. (2020). *A 'China model'? Beijing's promotion of alternative global norms and standards.* Testimony before the US-China Economic and Security Review Commission. Retrieved on November 2021, from https://www.uscc.gov/hearings/china-model-beijings-promotion-alternative-global-norms-and-standards.

Xi, J. (2015). *Remarks by H.E. Xi Jinping President of the People's Republic of China.* Opening Ceremony of the Second World Internet Conference, Wuzhen, China: Ministry of Foreign Affairs of the People's Republic of China. Retrieved on November 2021, from https://fmprc.gov.cn/mfa_eng/wjdt_665385/zyjh_665391/t1327570.shtml.

Xiao, Q. (2019). The road to digital unfreedom: President Xi's surveillance state. *Journal of Democracy, 30*(1), 53–67.

Zhao, S. (2018). A revisionist stakeholder: China and the Post-World War II world order. *Journal of Contemporary China, 27*(113), 643–658.

Zhao, S. (2019). China's belt-road initiative as the Signature of President Xi Jinping diplomacy: Easier Said than done. *Journal of Contemporary China, 29*(123), 319–335.

Zheng, W. (2020, February 25). Why Chinese President Xi Jinping called 170,000 Cadres about the coronavirus epidemic. *South China Morning Post.* Retrieved on November 2021, from www.scmp.com/news/china/politics/article/3052159/why-chinese-president-xi-jinping-called-170000-cadres-about.

Zwitter, A., & Hazenberg, J. (2020). Cyberspace, blockchain, governance: How technology implies normative power and regulation. In B. Cappiello & G. Carullo (Eds.), *Blockchain, law and governance* (pp. 87–97). Springer.

Chapter 16
The New Face of Multilateralism: The Case of "Chinese" Forums

Pedro Paulo dos Santos, Yichao Li, and José Alves

1 Introduction

It is widely recognized that Deng Xiaoping was the driving force behind the "internationalization" of the People's Republic of China (PRC). In the 1980s, China's foreign policy was reformed and adjusted to be in pursuance of "an independent, peaceful diplomacy" (Di, 2007, p. 8). As part of this new path, Chinese went on to modernize its domestic industries and markets, innovate its institutions, elevate its citizens' capabilities, and accelerate its technological advance (Aftah, 2014, p. 135). In the ensuing decades, China slowly but surely set itself up to partake in the world economy and to become a powerful player in global relations. A measure that exemplifies this vision is the creation of multilateral platforms between China and other nations, which we designate as Chinese Forums.

In 1990, China became the sixth dialogue partner of the Pacific Islands Forum (PIF), which was founded in 1971 (PIF, n.d.). China was accorded full dialogue partner status at the 29th ASEAN Ministerial Meeting (AMM) in 1996. This status was also extended to a broader ASEAN-led framework—the ASEAN Regional Forum (ARF) (ASEAN, 2020). Subsequently, China started to seek to deepen bilateral and multilateral cooperation by initiating and/or leading forums. For example, it co-established the Forum on China–Africa Cooperation (FOCAC) and the Boao Forum for Asia (BFA) in 2000; the Forum for Economic and Trade Cooperation between China and Portuguese-speaking Countries (Forum Macao) in 2003; the China–Arab States Cooperation Forum (CASCF) in 2004; the China–Community of Latin America and Caribbean States Forum (CCF) in 2014; and the Belt and

P. P. dos Santos (✉) · Y. Li
Institute for Research on Portuguese-Speaking Countries, City University of Macau, Macao, China
e-mail: pedropaulosantos79@hotmail.com

J. Alves
Faculty of Business, City University of Macau, Macao, China

© The Author(s), under exclusive license to Springer Nature Singapore Pte Ltd. 2023
P. A. B. Duarte et al. (eds.), *The Palgrave Handbook of Globalization with Chinese Characteristics*, https://doi.org/10.1007/978-981-19-6700-9_16

Road Forum for International Cooperation (BRF) in 2017, among other international, regional, and national forums.

Our review of existing literature on Chinese Forums shows that the majority of current research has focused on one forum each; not much has been done from a comparative angle, and certain forums, such as the FOCAC (Enuka, 2010; Naidu, 2007; Zeng & Shu, 2018), CASCF (Jalal, 2014; Yao, 2014), CCF (Bonilla Soria & Herrera-Vinelli, 2019), and Forum Macao (Costa, 2020), have been researched more considerably than others. Most of these articles are centred around reviewing their development history, summarizing their achievements, and identifying the challenges and visions that they are facing or expecting. In other published articles, for the most part, the forums are only mentioned as points of interest or case studies when they do fit into the context of bilateral and multilateral relations or cooperative frameworks between states. Scholars do, however, recognize how the forums form a series. Alden and Alves in particular call the series "China's regional forum diplomacy" (2017). Using FOCAC and Forum Macao—which constitute the beginning of the series—as case studies, they believe that the creation of these forums "reflects China's aspirations to shape the rules of regional cooperation…while simultaneously dispelling concerns about China's rise" (p. 156). Stephen's research (2020), on the other hand, has a broader scope, surveying multilateral institutions founded between 1990 and 2016. It was indeed during this timeframe that China had a leading role in creating or being a founding member of such forums as FOCAC, BFA, CASCF, and CCF. The main purpose of Stephen's research is "to bring together [] policy-oriented and theory-driven research strands to sketch an emerging research agenda on China's new institutions" (p. 4). Nevertheless, few academic publications have considered bringing these forums together as one research object to explore their commonalities and characteristics and/or analyse China's vision and international strategy for these forums as a whole.

In this chapter, we select six forums, which have been initiated and/or led by China, namely the FOCAC, BFA, Forum Macao, CASCF, CCF, and BRF, for a comparative analysis. We refer to them as Chinese Forums, though they should not be considered as being "owned" by China (it is in fact commonly (mis)understood that it is China that finances and oversees these forums). Indeed, China has played a major role in their inception, with greater protagonism in some forums (e.g., Forum Macao, BFA) than in others, but other member nations have also played significant roles in setting up these frameworks, and as the forums operate, a multinational effort can be observed. Therefore, this chapter queries two particular questions: *To what extent do these forums present elements of multilateralism in their structure? How do Chinese Forums serve the purposes of China's foreign affairs agenda?*

To answer these questions, we compare and contrast the forums, discussing in particular their practice of multilateralism, with a view to examining the role of these Chinese forums in pursuing China's foreign policy. Our analysis suggests that the forums not only intently welcome a broad range of member nations, but they also have significant functional flexibility to promote dialogue among the nations and to reframe foreign policy debates with China, thereby facilitating bilateral economic cooperation and addressing regional and global issues multilaterally. It is from the perspective of multilateralism and through these international organizations that we aim to contribute to understanding China's foreign policy. This chapter includes five parts: (1) an introduction; (2) an overview of Chinese Forums; (3) a comparative analysis of said Chinese Forums; (4) a discussion on the role of Chinese Forums in China's foreign policy; and (5) the conclusion.

2 Overview of Chinese Forums

The Forum on China–Africa Cooperation (FOCAC), established in 2000 in Beijing, promotes collaboration between China and 53 African countries. China has maintained long-term political relationships with nations in Africa since as far back as their independence movements. This particularly highlights a firm commitment to Sino-African relations that continues to be prevalent (Taylor, 2011). The official launch of FOCAC took place in the form of the 1st Ministerial Conference in Beijing in October 2000, with the theme "building a new international political and economic order and China-Africa economic and trade cooperation for the twenty-first century" (Zeng & Shu, 2018, p. 90). The primary objectives of FOCAC are to promote equal consultation, enhance understanding, expand consensus, strengthen friendship, and promote cooperation between all member nations (FOCAC, n.d.).

In 2000, the governments of 26 initial countries agreed to establish the Boao Forum for Asia (BFA). The Chinese government launched it in Boao in Hainan Province, followed by a preparatory meeting attended by representatives of various parties. BFA regularly holds annual conferences in Boao, with the first being held on 26–27 February 2001. Subsequently, the number of initial countries increased to 29. BFA is committed to contributing to the peace, prosperity, and sustainable development of Asia and the world (BFA, 2020).

The Forum for Economic and Trade Cooperation between China and the Portuguese-speaking Countries, commonly referred to as Forum Macao, is headquartered in the Macao Special Administrative Region (MSAR). It was the Chinese Ministry of Commerce (MOFCOM) that established it with support from the Macao Government in 2003 (Alves, 2008). The forum's permanent secretariat has been established and stationed in Macao since 2004—the particular locational choice had much to do with Macao's historical and cultural relationships with the Portuguese-speaking countries (PSCs). As agreed upon during the retrocession of the territory to China (1999), Macao has inherited a judicial system which maintains solid elements of the Portuguese law structure, encapsulated in what is called the Basic Law. The fact that the Portuguese language has kept its official status together with Cantonese in Macao makes the 30 km^2 city the perfect crossroads to host the forum that brings together China and Portuguese-speaking countries. In fact, by the time Forum Macao was established, China had long firmly chosen the tiny city of Macao to be the geographic link for promoting its relations with PSCs and Latin America (Costa, 2020).

After the establishment of FOCAC in 2000, ambassadors from the Arab states wished to develop relations between the Arab League and China (Jalal, 2014). In 2004, then Chinese President Hu Jintao visited the headquarters of the Arab League in Cairo, Egypt. After this visit, the China–Arab States Cooperation Forum (CASCF) was established. In the communiqué issued by China and the Arab League in 2004, Hu put forward four principles for developing a new type of partnership between China and Arab countries: to promote political relations based on mutual respect; to forge closer trade and economic links to achieve joint development; to expand cultural exchanges to draw upon each other's experiences, and to strengthen cooperation in international affairs to safeguard world peace and promote joint development (Xinhua, 2004).

The Community of Latin America and Caribbean States (CELAC) was established in 2010, and encompasses all sovereign nations in the Americas except the US and Canada. Four years later, the Forum of China and Community of Latin American and Caribbean States (a.k.a. China-CELAC Forum or CCF) was announced during the China–Latin America and the Caribbean Summit in Brasilia in 2014 and came into effect via a joint statement. The launch of the forum took place during its first ministerial meeting on 8–9 January 2015 in Beijing (Ministry of Foreign Affairs of China, 2016). The CCF aims to promote the development of cooperation based on equality, mutual benefits, and development in different fields between China and Latin American countries (Ministry of Foreign Affairs of China, 2016).

As of 2021, the Belt and Road Forum for International Cooperation (BRF), launched in 2017, has met twice, in 2017 and in 2019. It is intrinsically linked to the Belt and Road Initiative (BRI) which was put forward in 2013. The BRF is the highest-level, largest-scale multilateral diplomatic gathering initiated and organized by China. Its objective is to build consensus, better align development strategies, and strengthen partnerships and international cooperation in search of win–win results (China.org, 2018).

3 Comparative Analysis of Chinese Forums

To understand the structure, organization, and objectives of the various Chinese forums, we model their key areas. The model collects and presents organized data that not only overviews but also supports comparisons and analysis of the forums. In particular, we have chosen six categories that address the research questions we have posed in this study. The six categories are: political configuration, geographic range, membership affiliation, focus, highest operational mechanism, and organizational process.

- **Political configuration** pertains to the degree of governmental involvement from a forum's member nations. The degrees are either intergovernmental, intragovernmental, non-governmental, or a hybrid of these. An intergovernmental forum hosts meetings between governmental bodies of various member nations. An

intragovernmental forum is governed by different levels of the government of each member, for example, foreign ministers and commerce ministers of the same government working in unison. Non-governmental forums have no observable influence from governmental actors, in structure or in management. A hybrid forum accepts two or more political configurations, e.g., Intergovernmental, intragovernmental, and/or non-governmental, to be at play.
- The **geographic range** dimension shows the geographic scope of a forum's objectives, focuses, and projects. Having a global range means that a forum's reach extends to any continents, while a forum with a regional range reaches only one or two continents.
- **Membership affiliation** indicates a forum's degree of openness to members. An inclusive membership means that any nation can become a member of the forum; an exclusive membership imposes a set of conditions and/or criteria on nations to become members.
- **Focus** refers to the forum's primary area of purpose. A single focus indicates that a forum has one primary purpose, while having diverse focuses shows that the forum has multiple purposes and objectives in various areas.
- The **highest operational mechanism** dimension identifies the order and periodicity at which a forum's highest-level convenes. In other words, this parameter indicates how often and at what level such meetings occur, as well as what form of outcome (e.g., agreements, action plans, etc.) the meetings will output.
- An **organizational process** is one through which members engage in and contribute to making selections and decisions for the forum's main projects. It relates to the process through which development plans and cooperation agreements get passed to the highest operational mechanism, and how their implementation is certified by follow-up systems. An organizational process is multilateral if it is inclusive of all members throughout all stages. It can also be bilateral when two member nations oversee, negotiate, and make decisions throughout the entire process, or unilateral when only one member is responsible.

In terms of these six categories, we analyse the similarities and dissimilarities between the forums. The data thus obtained is presented in Table 1. The information has been collected from the forums' respective charters, statutes, operating rules, official websites, and existing literature.

3.1 *Political Configuration*

Four of the forums discussed here are intergovernmental-level forums: Forum Macao, FOCAC, CCF, and CASCF. At Forum Macao, sovereign states are represented by delegates and/or representatives appointed by their respective governments. As stated in the Intergovernmental Cooperation section of the Action Plan for Economic and Commercial Cooperation, all members agree on improving bilateral relations at the governmental level (Encarnação, 2013). The FOCAC runs on a multilateral system

Table 1 Comparative analysis of Chinese forums

Chinese forums	Political configuration Inter-/Intra-/Non-governmental/ Hybrid	Geographic range Global/Regional	Membership affiliation Inclusive/Exclusive	Focus Single/Diversified	Highest operational mechanism Summits/Conferences/Meetings	Organizational process Multilateral/ Bilateral/Unilateral
FOCAC	Intergovernmental	Regional	Exclusive	Diversified	Ministerial Conferences (3 years)	Multilateral & Bilateral
BFA	Non-governmental	Regional	Inclusive	Diversified—with a focus on economic development	Annual Conferences (1 year)	Multilateral
Forum Macao	Intergovernmental	Global	Exclusive	Diversified—with focuses on economy, commerce, and culture	Ministerial Conferences (3 years)	Multilateral
CASCF	Intergovernmental	Regional	Exclusive	Diversified	Ministerial Meetings (2 years)	Multilateral & Bilateral
CCF	Intergovernmental	Regional	Exclusive	Diversified	Ministerial Meetings (3 years)	Multilateral & Bilateral
BRF	Hybrid	Global	Inclusive	Diversified	The Leaders Roundtable Summits (2 years)	Multilateral & Bilateral

Source Authors' compilation

under an intergovernmental framework where foreign affairs ministers of the member states attend, approve, and sign agreements, memoranda of understanding, and/or action plans via the highest operational mechanism—ministerial conferences. It has mechanisms to put forward such action plans or agreements on a bilateral basis, to be monitored by a follow-up committee (Mackinnon, 2013). As for the case of the CCF, it is stated in its Institutional Arrangements and Operating Rules that it is "defined as the platform for intergovernmental cooperation led by the Foreign Ministries of China and the member countries of CELAC…" (CCF, 2015). Meanwhile, the CASCF has established a long-term mechanism composed of foreign ministers from all member states and the Secretary-General of the League of Arab States, according to CASCF's, 2004 Action Plan (CASCF, 2004). These senior governmental figures meet yearly in senior official meetings, and every two years during their highest operational mechanism—ministerial meetings.

The BRF has a hybrid political configuration. It welcomes the participation of different levels of government and members from the private sector. According to its *Joint Communique of the Leaders Roundtable of the Belt and Road Forum for International Cooperation* (BRF, 2017), BRF encourages "the involvement of governments, international and regional organizations, the private sector, civil society and citizens in fostering and promoting friendship, mutual understanding, and trust." The BFA is the only forum covered in this study that operates entirely on a non-governmental level. As with some of the other forums, it also welcomes different levels of involvement. Nevertheless, BFA's charter clearly states that it "shall be a non-government and non-profit international organization with a permanent principal location and shall hold meetings regularly" (BFA Charter, Article 2). The analysis above suggests that, despite being designed to operate on an intergovernmental platform, most forums can be observed to engage in non-governmental activities on some level. Some of these platforms comprise several sub-forums, organization of events, cultural exchanges, promotion of national products, training, and other undertakings under the supervision and development of private entities and/or individuals without official relation to their governments.

3.2 *Geographic Range*

Forum Macao and BRF each have a global range, meaning that their focuses and projects can be observed across several continents. FOCAC and BFA each cover a specific continent, Africa and Asia, respectively. All plans, agreements, and partnerships resulting from their operational mechanism are aimed at projects solely on those continents. CASCF also focuses on one specific geographic region, the Middle East, while CCF covers Central and South America as the scope for their plans and projects. The BFA counts among its members two non-Asian nations (Australia and New Zealand), so it could be presumed that its range extends beyond just the continent of Asia. But because it is stated in its mission as a founding purpose that the BFA promotes economic integration in Asia, we have decided to treat it as focusing on plans and projects pertaining to only one continent, and consider it as a regional forum.

3.3 Membership Affiliation

BRF and BFA have inclusive memberships. BRF is intrinsically associated with the BRI and is open to nations that have signed onto this framework, as well as to "international and regional organizations, the private sector, civil society and citizens" (BRF, 2017). BFA focuses on promoting economic cooperation among Asian nations and therefore has a regional geographic range. Nevertheless, its annual conferences are open to full and partial individual, corporate, and organization members from outside Asia. Therefore, we conclude that it has inclusive membership. The remaining forums have exclusive member affiliations that entail a set of eligibility criteria. Forum Macao only admits representation of PSCs, while FOCAC only accepts African nations as members. CCF is limited to South and Central American nations that are members of another international organization, CELAC. In the case of CASCF, it is restricted to Middle Eastern countries who must also be member of the Arab League.

3.4 Focus

The focuses of these six forums are very diverse, which means that they do not have a single, limited goal, but emphasize all-round development and cooperation. As can be concluded from each ministerial conference/meeting of FOCAC, CCF, and CASCF, their action plans are structured very similarly. They present many different dimensions, for example, political cooperation, economic development, social development, cultural and people-to-people exchanges, as well as peace and security cooperation. Meanwhile, BRF's priorities are aligned with the BRI, and include policy consultation, trade promotion, infrastructure connectivity, financial cooperation, and people-to-people exchanges (BRF, 2017). While we can observe diverse focuses on different areas in the cases of Forum Macao and BFA, their charters and/or mission objectives do contain specific focuses. Forum Macao emphasizes economic, commerce, and cultural relations between China and PSCs, while the BFA spotlights economic development (BFA Charter, Article 6; BFA, 2020).

3.5 Highest Operational Mechanism

The highest operational mechanism for Forum Macao, the FOCAC, CCF, and CASCF are conferences, meetings, and/or summits at the ministerial level, of which there are some noteworthy differences: Firstly, in the case of Forum Macao, each ministerial conference always takes place in the MSAR (where its permanent secretariat is). The other three forums hold regular ministerial conferences, meetings, and summits, but their organizers/hosts rotate—in fact, the duty alternates between China and another member (for FOCAC, African member countries; for CCF, either the current presidency country or another agreed-upon member country of CELAC; for CASCF, in the headquarters of the Arab League or another member of the forum). Secondly, only CASCF holds its highest-level meeting every two years; Forum Macao, FOCAC, and CCF all hold their highest-level meetings every three years. BFA, as its name suggests, is held every year with a specific theme to connect Asia to the world. BRF's highest operational mechanism—named the Leaders Roundtable Summit—is organized every two years, and has only been held twice so far.

3.6 Organizational Process

The central bodies of BFA include general meetings of members, board of directors, secretariat, research and training institute, and council of advisors (BFA Charter, Article 14). The organizational process of BFA appears to be multilateral. As for Forum Macao, it is a multilateral, intergovernmental cooperation mechanism that contributes to collaboration between PSCs and China via the platform of Macao.

The remaining four forums also exhibit elements of multilateralism in the development and implementation of their action plans and agreements, but some bilateral decision-making is observable along the process. FOCAC's negotiations of its action plans involve all of its member states during relevant ministerial conferences. However, after the conferences, policies are carried out bilaterally between countries and are monitored by a follow-up committee (Mackinnon, 2013, p. 1). For CCF, different procedures occur, where action plans only need to be reviewed and adopted in relevant ministerial meetings and jointly (bilaterally) implemented by member states and a follow-up committee (CCF, 2015). In the case of CASCF, it provides a platform between China and the Arab League to promote, complement, and develop multilaterally and bilaterally (Yao, 2014, p. 26). The ministerial meetings of CASCF focus on regional and international matters of common interest, paying particular attention to following up on action plans that the forum has published previously, as well as looking forward to drafting future ones (Giffoni et al., 2016, p. 2). The BRF also provides a platform for multilateral dialogue. Nonetheless, since China put forward the BRI, the forum's outcomes have mainly been based on bilateral consultations through the signing of memoranda of understanding and/or agreements (Ministry of Foreign Affairs, 2019; Xinhua, 2017).

Figure 1 presents the results of the comparative study as organized into the six above categories to elucidate the similarities and dissimilarities between forums. The next section also summarizes our findings.

In short, the six categories chosen for the comparative analysis model present a picture that helps understand the inner workings, structures, visions, and purposes of these frameworks. After the model data analysis, some patterns and correlations are

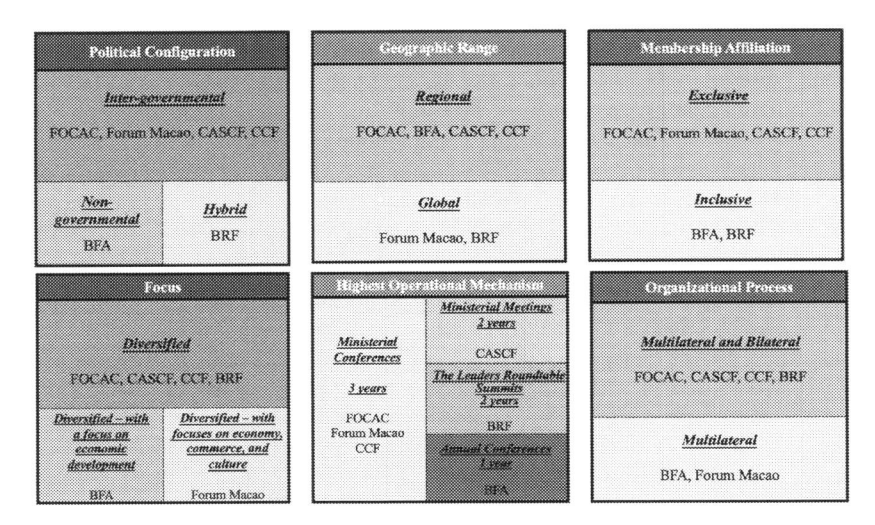

Political Configuration		Geographic Range		Membership Affiliation	
Inter-governmental		*Regional*		*Exclusive*	
FOCAC, Forum Macao, CASCF, CCF		FOCAC, BFA, CASCF, CCF		FOCAC, Forum Macao, CASCF, CCF	
Non-governmental	*Hybrid*	*Global*		*Inclusive*	
BFA	BRF	Forum Macao, BRF		BFA, BRF	
Focus		Highest Operational Mechanism		Organizational Process	
Diversified		*Ministerial Conferences*	*Ministerial Meetings 2 years*	*Multilateral and Bilateral*	
FOCAC, CASCF, CCF, BRF			CASCF	FOCAC, CASCF, CCF, BRF	
Diversified – with a focus on economic development	*Diversified – with focuses on economy, commerce, and culture*	*3 years*	*The Leaders Roundtable Summits 2 years*	*Multilateral*	
		FOCAC Forum Macao CCF	BRF	BFA, Forum Macao	
BFA	Forum Macao		*Annual Conferences 1 year*		
			BFA		

Fig. 1 Visual model of Chinese forums (*Source* Authors)

visible between the forums; however, dissimilarities are also present. We first deduce that BFA and BRF are the only forums that are inclusive and are not configured into an intergovernmental structure. These mechanisms can be considered as having the most Chinese influence. BFA's annual conference in Boao on Hainan island, China is the highest level at which the forum convenes. To some extent, the authors believe that BFA is very similar in organization and structure to the World Economic Forum (Davos Forum). In the form of an annual conference, many political and academic representatives, as well as those from non-governmental organizations and the media convene to discuss issues related to Asian economic development. BRF was created to facilitate China's most international project to date, the BRI, which welcomes bilateral, triangular, regional, and multilateral cooperations (BRF, 2017). The remaining forums are all run under an intergovernmental structure with exclusive memberships. In fact, a clear correlation between these two factors is observed, potentially raising the question of whether the forums can only operate in an intergovernmental framework if they adhere to membership exclusivity.

Another inference is how most of the forums have a regional geographic range, meaning that their objectives and projects are aimed at a particular continent or region. Forum Macao and BRF are exceptions, as they have a global range. In the case of the BRF, as it is closely associated with the PRC's largest international project, the BRI, it sets out to welcome members from all regions of the globe to discuss and approve various agreements and partnerships in diverse areas. This forum can be perceived as a platform where China can showcase the massive framework that is the BRI, while encouraging any nation-state to join and become part of this initiative as well as a member of the forum.

In the case of Forum Macao, its global reach is directly influenced by a language. It is the only forum where a criterion for membership is to share a particular official language, in this case, Portuguese. We think that this in fact shows China's ability and capacity to embrace different perspectives and opportunities in developing international frameworks. With the Macao Special Administrative Region, China has a special and unique location within its sovereign territory. The roughly 30 km^2 Macao was once part of a global empire—it was either administered or ruled by the Portuguese for roughly 450 years; in fact, Portuguese footprints are still evident in Macao 22 years after its retrocession to the PRC. This history presents an exceptional opportunity to create a platform where representatives from PSCs can meet with Chinese officials in an environment which is welcoming to all parties. Hence, the establishment of Forum Macao in fact illuminates China's ability to access its internal capabilities and establish a forum with different characteristics and structure from other such initiatives.

A noteworthy fact drawn from our analysis is that some forums, namely the FOCAC, CCF, and CASCF, are interlinked with other international organizations: the African Union,[1] CELAC, and the Arab League, respectively. Member nations of FOCAC are required to be affiliates of the African Union, CCF members have to be affiliates of CELAC, and CASCF members belong to the Arab League in parallel. Furthermore, the forums' cooperation frameworks, operational mechanisms, and organizational processes are generally similar. We surmise that it is because China could not be a full-fledged member of these establishments due to their membership criteria, so the creation of what can be conceived as "twin forums" is a testament to China's willingness to adapt to whatever circumstances and change their modus operandi when creating new forums.

The fact that our analysis can clearly observe a similarity in the cooperation framework shared by the forums is reflected in the action plans and/or documents that they have issued after their highest-level meetings. The six forums present diverse focuses and objectives, with the most prevalent being the economy, trade, and culture. This can be seen either through their various activities and events that they organize, or as stated in their charters and/or objective missions. In addition, it is also worth noting

---

[1] Eswatini is a member of the African Union instead of a member state of Forum on China–Africa Cooperation, since it does not have diplomatic relation with the People's Republic of China.

that FOCAC,[2] CASCF,[3] CCF,[4] and BRF[5] refine and deepen their cooperation fields in the form of sub-forums within their respective frameworks. These sub-forums usually have only singular focuses, such as youth, women, health, media, legal, think tank, enterprise and investments, science and technology, agriculture, and infrastructure, among others. Our model also reveals how multilateral practices are common in all of the forums. The data in the organizational process category reveals that when dealing with agreements pertaining to the highest level of these forums, either as action plans or declarations produced during their operational mechanisms, or as cooperation plans agreed by their members, we observe that their secretariats, councils, and/or committees are responsible for following through with appropriate implementation procedures, multilaterally or multilaterally-bilaterally. A more detailed and vivid description of the concepts of multilateralism at play in these forums will be given in the following section.

4 Role of "Chinese" Forums in China's Foreign Policy

This study has added to the predominant view that these forums operate under a multilateral perspective, and they can be seen as an integral part of the PRC's foreign strategy. China has been developing these mechanisms for two decades, accepting dozens of sovereign nations either as members or to be represented. These Chinese forums have evolved to become internationally recognized. They are now so widespread that hardly any nations have not been involved at least in some capacities. No one will deny that *multilateralism* is an attribute of the United Nations (Tago, 2017, p. 1). Likewise, many international organizations established after World War II, such as the World Bank and the International Monetary Fund, are considered

---

[2] Sub-forums in FOCAC include China-Africa People's Forum, China-Africa Young Leaders Forum, Ministerial Forum on China-Africa Health Cooperation, Forum on China-Africa Media Cooperation, China-Africa Poverty Reduction and Development Conference, FOCAC-Legal Forum, Forum on China-Africa Local Government Cooperation, and China-Africa Think Tanks Forum. Retrieved on August 22, 2021, from http://www.focac.org/eng/ltjj_3/ltjz/

[3] Sub-forums in CASCF include China-Arab Reform and Development Forum, Entrepreneur Conference and Investment Seminar of China-Arab States Cooperation Forum, China-Arab Media Cooperation Forum, China Arab Towns Forum, China-Arab States BDS (BeiDou Navigation Satellite System) Cooperation Forum, China-Arab Women's Forum, China-Arab States Health Cooperation Forum, China-Arab TV Cooperation Forum. Retrieved on August 22, 2021, from http://www.chinaarabcf.org/chn/ltjz/ggjzlzzdh/dlcggjzlzdh/

[4] Sub-forums in CELAC include China-LAC Agricultural Ministers' Forum, China-LAC Scientific and Technological Innovation Forum, China-LAC Business Summit, China-LAC Think-Tanks Forum, China-LAC Young Political Leaders' Forum, China-LAC Infrastructure Cooperation Forum, China-Latin America and Caribbean Region People-to-People Friendship Forum, China-CELAC Political Parties Forum. Retrieved on August 22, 2021, from http://www.chinacelacforum.org/eng/

[5] Sub-forums in BRF focused on policy, infrastructure, trade, financial and people-to-people connectivity, think-tank exchanges, clean silk road, digital silk road, green silk road, silk road of innovation, sub-national cooperation, and economic and trade cooperation zone promotion. Retrieved on August 22, 2021, from https://www.beltandroad.gov.hk/activities_20190423.html.

multilateral entities. A more recent and exemplary instance of multilateralism has to be 1994's multilateral trade agreement, negotiated among 123 countries, which successfully established the World Trade Organization (WTO) (Brummer, 2014, p. 1).

The most obvious characteristic of multilateralism is the participation of three or more states. Keohane (1989, p. 731) further defines it as "the practice of coordinating national policies [...] through ad hoc arrangements or by means of institutions." In turn, Ruggie (1992, pp. 570–571) believes that "multilateral" modifies the term "institution." Thus, "multilateralism depicts a generic institutional form in international relations" (ibidem). It is based on the "generalized" principles of consensus rather than any special interests of each state (ibidem). Furthermore, Moreland (2019, p. 2) believes that multilateralism is an instrument that functions "through architectures of organizations, institutions, and bespoke mechanisms, often based in treaties and international law and grounded, fundamentally, in the U.N. Charter." Therefore, multilateralism refers to a diplomatic practice based on cooperation among states, through specific principles, norms, rules, and/or organizations (UN News, 2020). El-Ghalayini (2017, p. 57) points out that current research on multilateralism has not been conducted thoroughly, which may be related to the relatively new emergence or to the new role of organizations (which the authors believe can be linked with Chinese forums) in the international system.

The forums create opportunities for international cooperation based on flexible arrangements. Among the six forums examined, Forum Macao, FOCAC, CCF, and CASCF issue action plans and declarations regularly to lay down specific directions and operational procedures, whereas after BRF meetings, usually memoranda of understanding are issued. For BFA, on the other hand, its annual conferences only provide a platform for individuals, enterprises, and states to communicate and exchange ideas with no written closure. Moreover, the above issued documents—action plans, declarations, and memoranda of understanding—all have non-binding status. As Barrett and Beckman (2020, p. 101) state, such documents "are normally (and should) be [*sic*] regarded by those who enter into them as binding in a political or moral sense." In other words, these documents are formed on the basis of consensus, and will be expected to be implemented based on practicality and consensuality. China is committed to multilateralism. The above forums in turn offer a flexible, multilateral mechanism for cooperation that represents a new form of multilateralism. For the PRC, these forums connect China and different sovereign states through specific geographical or historical ties. They also endeavour to facilitate values being shared and consensus being reached among states. Meanwhile, global or regional issues cannot be solved alone sans cooperation. Thus, a group of states with the same objectives or facing the same challenges will find it easy to come together and work together through such multilateral forums. Brummer (2014, p. 2) describes such cooperation as having distinct minilateral strategies, which is a modest form of multilateralism—modest in size, formality, inclusiveness, etc. He further states that "minilateralism is frequently exclusive" (p. 20), which is, to some extent, characteristically similar to Chinese forums.

Moreover, during the twentieth century, diplomacy evolved to accommodate the activities of intergovernmental organizations in the international arena. Pajtinka (2017) defines these activities as actions of non-governmental entities and supranational corporations involved in diplomatic efforts. These "outside" interventions in state foreign affairs have come to be coined as *paradiplomacy*, which is short for "parallel diplomacy." Paradiplomacy is defined as "a direct continuation, and to varying degrees, from sub-state government, foreign activities" (Mitchelmann & Soldatos, 1991, p. 34). For Duchacek (1990), the term defines the role of sub-state transnational policies as coordinated and complementary to the central government's diplomatic efforts. He points out that these non-state actors and subnational entities possess limited competencies and legal power in the scope of foreign policy. Paradiplomacy and diplomacy are not incompatible. There is an argument that the models in fact complement and reinforce each other (Joenniemi & Sergunin, 2014).

The forums are neither managed nor operated by officially appointed diplomats in Beijing, they are therefore in the margins of diplomatic protocols and political oversight. Although diplomats and high-government agents are present at some of the meetings of the highest level and in their decision-making process, the forums are organized by appointed representatives with no diplomatic designation or governmental association. In Forum Macao's case, there is a permanent secretariat, based in Macao, which comprises 15 members who are appointed by either the government of each member state, the government of the Macao SAR, or MOFCOM, and the Macao SAR government covers the secretariat's budget; this is an example of transnational parties working in unison under a subnational umbrella. These operational systems, structures, and working environments show how the role of paradiplomacy is intertwined with elements of soft power and people-to-people engagements.

Nye describes soft power as "the ability to get what you want through attraction rather than coercion or payments" (2004, p. 256). Hard power, in diplomatic terms, describes a scenario where a nation uses military coercion or economic capability to convince or pressure another state to agree to its requests, or exerts influence at the decision-making level. In contrast, soft power focuses on a nation's ability to use its appeal to achieve its goals. It is manifested through cultural values and output, business practices, news media, education, diplomacy, normative values, and people-to-people interactions (Tsoi, 2012). In diplomatic terms, people-to-people interactions are transboundary/transnational communication interactions between people that can impact foreign policies. The people-to-people dimension is integral to any soft power, whose purpose is to seek peaceful, sustainable, cooperative common ground between nations. It can resolve tense situations that hard diplomacy often cannot; this ability is what gives people-to-people exchanges its intrinsic appeal (Wang, 2016, p. 1).

China has been utilizing people-to-people diplomacy to influence and foster relations with other states. For example, China considers its massive overseas community a highly valuable asset, capable of strengthening cultural ties and promoting Chinese ideals (Soares, 2019). The concept of a "people-to-people bond" can enhance relations between nations, and is in fact central to the BRI framework (National Development and Reform Commission, 2015). As China's economy grew in the 1990s, so did its capability to use hard power whenever needed. However, so far, the PRC has decided instead to resort to good-neighbour policy so as not to present a threat to the balance of power in any regional political arena. The Communist Party of China emphasizes that although China is a global power, its foreign policy remains peaceful (Aydin & Yüce, n.d.). Such policy is realized through exchange programmes, public diplomacy, investment, humanitarian aid, and contributing to or setting up multilateral institutions (Fazil, 2014). The creation of multilateral Chinese forums represents China's response and approach to globalization. Moreover, these forums present an opportunity to gather governmental officials and/or representatives from member states in a less formal environment where other global powers such as the US or the European Union cannot interfere. These frameworks, which allow developing nations to join, in fact invite them to engage directly with Chinese officials and strengthen their diplomatic ties with China.

5 Conclusion

The rising number of Chinese forums in several global regions and their perceived inclusivity and multilateral approach have attracted many states to participate since the turn of the twenty-first century. This flexible cooperation framework provides another new pathway and platform for cooperation and dialogue between China and other groups of states who share common characteristics and/or goals. "Chinese" forums share common elements in structure, membership, range, focus, and political alignment, but they are not all identical. As mentioned, Table 1 and Fig. 1 present specific similarities and dissimilarities across forums. The differences revealed in our analysis showcase the forums' flexibility. Their locations, structures, organizations, memberships, and even focuses depend on the interests and priorities of individual parties. By promoting and engaging in various dimensions, these forums are far-reaching especially in terms of facilitating regional development, and are therefore more appealing to member states.

Recalling the research questions posed in this chapter—*To what extent do Chinese forums present elements of multilateralism in their structure? How do Chinese forums serve the purposes of China's foreign affairs agenda?*—we present some final thoughts: As demonstrated in the model in Fig. 1, in terms of organizational process, these six forums have characterized a multilateral platform, and two of them have presented bilateral initiatives. Clearly, multilateralism might not be prevalent throughout the entire decision-making process, but it is present on some level, and to most members, that is more than can be said of their respective "weight" in other international organizations. These forums also allow their members to have an additional line of communication with the second-largest economy in the world—an environment where they can communicate with Chinese representatives directly, without diplomatic protocols or the bureaucracy that comes with it. Perhaps the initial intention was not for these forums to have a massive impact on trade or economic figures, but significant economic transactions, trade agreements, and larger projects continue to occur on a diplomatic bilateral level, mainly through embassies in Beijing. Nevertheless, indirect impact that the forums might have in building goodwill and letting member nations feel more at ease, confident, and respected when they negotiate with the second-strongest economy in the world should not be underestimated. Chinese forums can catalyze China's foreign affairs agenda for maintaining long-term, sustainable cooperation. For China, these forums are in essence subnational agents that provide support for foreign policies. These international frameworks have also helped soften the image of might and strength that might otherwise intimidate other nations, thereby promoting peaceful diplomacy. The forums have also created opportunities for intercultural understanding, providing insight into China's business practices and models, offering an outlet for donations and charitable contributions, letting smaller-scale projects be presented and financed, and allowing implementation of initiatives that might otherwise take years to materialize through existing institutions and diplomatic tools.

Lastly, as Naim (2009) states, "we should bring to the table the smallest possible number of countries needed to have the largest possible impact on solving a particular problem." The successful implementation of Chinese forums suggests the emergence of new institutional mechanisms that are rooted in pragmatism. When consensus is difficult to reach among many states, a group of states sharing certain similarities and/or common interests presents a good starting point to facilitate the process. At this juncture, we suggest these further research directions: (1) Will "Chinese" forums evolve towards minilateralism? (2) How does the decision-making process in Chinese forums affect and facilitate bilateral/multilateral cooperation and projects? (3) How many other nations set up their own similar forums and/or initiatives and ensure viability and success? Are these forums only practical under the Chinese model, operated with Chinese characteristics?

Bibliographic References

Aftah, C. (2014). China's international strategy and how to pursue it. *Indonesian Journal of International Studies (IJIS), 1*(2), 133–138.

Alden, C., & Alves, A. C. (2017). China's regional forum diplomacy in the developing world: Socialisation and the 'sinosphere.' *Journal of Contemporary China, 26*(103), 151–165.

Alves, A. (2008). *China's Lusophone connection.* The South African Institute of International Affairs.

ASEAN. (2020). *Overview of ASEAN-China dialogue relations.* ASEAN Secretariat Information Paper. Retrieved on November 3, 2021, from https://asean.org/wp-content/uploads/2012/05/Overview-of-ASEAN-China-Relations-22-Apr-2020-00000002.pdf

Aydin, G., & Yüce, M. (n.d.). China's hard power versus soft power in central Asia: An analysis of the 'One Belt-One Road Initiative' as a soft power instrument. *Caucasus International, 8*(2), 63–76.

Barrett, J., & Beckman, R. (2020). *Handbook on good treaty practice.* Cambridge University Press.

BFA Charter. Retrieved on August 3, 2021, from https://english.boaoforum.org/newsDetial.html?navId=1&itemId=1&permissionId=117&detialId=2124

BFA. (2020). *Overview.* Retrieved on August 27, 2021, from https://english.boaoforum.org/new sDetial.html?navId=1&itemId=0&permissionId=118&detialId=2090

Bonilla Soria, A., & Herrera-Vinelli, L. (2019). CELAC como Vehículo Estratégico de Relacionamiento de China Hacia América Latina (2011–2018). *Revista CIDOB d'Afers Internacionals, 124,* 173–198.

BRF. (2017). *Joint Communique of the leaders roundtable of the Belt and Road Forum for international cooperation.* Retrieved on August 20, 2021, from http://2017.beltandroadforum.org/eng lish/n100/2017/0516/c22-423.html

Brummer, C. (2014). *Minilateralism: How trade alliances, soft law, and financial engineering are redefining economic statecraft.* Cambridge University Press.

CASCF. (2004). *Action plan of the China-Arab states cooperation forum.* Retrieved on July 11, 2021, from http://www.chinaarabcf.org/chn/lthyjwx/bzjhywj/dijbzjhy/t866307.htm (in Chinese).

CCF. (2015). *Institutional arrangements.* Retrieved on July 11, 2021, from http://www.chinacela cforum.org/eng/zywj_3/t1230941.htm

China.org. (2018). *Belt and road forum for international cooperation.* Retrieved on August 27, 2021, from http://keywords.china.org.cn/2018-11/30/content_74227052.html

Costa, C. M. (2020). O Discurso Chines para os Países Africanos de Língua Portuguesa: O Papel do Fórum Macao. *Relações Internacionais, 65,* 43–55.

Di, D. (2007). Continuity and changes: A comparative study on China's new grand strategy. *HAOL, 12,* 7–18.

Duchacek, I. D. (1990). Perforated sovereignties: Towards a typology of new actors in international relations. In H. J. Michelmann & P. Soldatos (Eds.), *Federalism and international relations: The role of subnational units.* Clarendon Press.

El-Ghalayini, Y. (2017). Multilateralism: Theoretical perspectives on the policy framework. *Public Policy and Administration Research, 7*(11), 53–58.

Encarnação, J. M. (2013). *Fórum Macau — Evolução dos Planos de Acção para a Cooperação Económica e Comercial entre a China e os Países de Língua Portuguesa; perspectivas e objectivos para a 4.ª Conferência Ministerial.* Administração No. 100, vol. XXVI, pp. 471–486. Retrieved on July 28, 2021, from https://www.safp.gov.mo/safppt/download/WCM_022053

Enuka, C. (2010). The forum on China-Africa cooperation (FOCAC): A framework for china's re-engagement with Africa in the 21st century. *Pakistan Journal of Social Sciences (PJSS), 30*(2), 209–218.

Fazil, M. D. (2014). China's increasing soft power; Implications for the United States. *The International Journal of Engineering and Science (IJES), 3*(6), 61–67.

FOCAC. (n.d.). *FOCAC mechanisms.* Retrieved on August 27, 2021, from http://www.focac.org/eng/ltjj_3/ltjz/

Giffoni, C., Veras, F., Gomes, G. Z., Gomes, M. F., Penido, L. N., Esteves, P., & Lopes, P. (2016). *The China-Arab states cooperation forum (CASCF).* Retrieved on August 20, 2021, from https://www.google.com.hk/url?sa=t&rct=j&q=&esrc=s&source=web&cd=&ved=2ahUKEwif oMfamLDzAhVLAmMBHUyhDj4QFnoECAUQAQ&url=http%3A%2F%2Fwww.bricspoli cycenter.org%2Fdownload%2F6153&usg=AOvVaw2UWmcfAcsMfj_tNExdASh-

Harvard Law School. (n.d.). *Intergovernmental organizations.* Retrieved on August 20, 2021, from https://hls.harvard.edu/dept/opia/what-is-public-interest-law/public-service-practi cesettings/public-international-law/intergovernmental-organizations-igos/

Jalal, M. N. (2014). The China-Arab states cooperation forum: Achievements, challenges, and prospects. *Journal of Middle Eastern and Islamic Studies (in Asia), 8*(2), 1–21.

Joenniemi, P., & Sergunin, A. (2014). Paradiplomacy as a capacity-building strategy. *Problems of Post-Communism, 61*(6), 18–33.

Keohane, R. O. (1989). Multilateralism: An agenda for research. *International Journal, 45*(4), 731–764.

Mackinnon, T. (2013). *The forum on China-Africa cooperation (FOCAC).* Retrieved on August 20, 2021, from https://bricspolicycenter.org/publicacoes/o-forum-de-cooperacao-china-africa-focac/

Ministry of Foreign Affairs of China. (2016). *Basic information about China-CELAC forum*. China-CELAC Forum. Retrieved on September 15, 2021, from http://www.chinacelacforum.org/eng/ltjj_1/P020161207421177845816.pdf

Ministry of Foreign Affairs. (2019). *List of deliverables of the second belt and road forum for international cooperation*. Retrieved on August 22, 2021, from https://www.fmprc.gov.cn/mfa_eng/zxxx_662805/t1658767.shtml

Mitchelmann, H. J., & Soldatos, P. (1991). *Federalism and international relations: The role of subnational units*. Clarendon Press.

Moreland, W. (2019). *The purpose of multilateralism: A framework for democracies in a geopolitically competitive world*. Foreign Policy at Brookings.

Naidu, S. (2007). The forum on China-Africa cooperation (FOCAC): What does the future hold? *China Report, 43*(3), 283–296.

Naim, M. (2009). *Minilateralism: The magic number to get real international action*. Retrieved on September 20, 2021, from https://foreignpolicy.com/2009/06/21/minilateralism/

National Development and Reform Commission. (2015). *Visions and Actions on jointly building Silk Road economic belt and 21st-century maritime Silk Road*. Ministry of Foreign Affairs and Ministry of Commerce of the People's Republic of China.

Nye, J. S. (2004). Soft power and American foreign policy. *Political Science Quarterly, 119*(2), 255–270.

Pajtinka, E. (2017). Between diplomacy and paradiplomacy: Taiwan's foreign relations in current practice. *Journal of Nationalism, Memory & Language Politics, 11*(1), 39–57.

PIF. (n.d.). *Forum dialogue partners*. Retrieved on November 3, 2021, from https://www.forumsec.org/dialogue-partners/

Ruggie, J. G. (1992). Multilateralism: The anatomy of an institution. *International Organization, 46*(3), 561–598.

Soares, L. (2019). Overseas Chinese, Soft power and China's people-to-people diplomacy in Timor-Leste. In A. McWilliam & M. Leach (Eds.), *Routledge handbook of contemporary Timor-Leste*. Routledge.

Stephen, M. D. (2020). *China's new multilateral institutions: A framework and research agenda* (WZB Discussion Paper, No. SP IV). Wissenschaftszentrum Berlin für Sozialforschung (WZB), Berlin.

Tago, A. (2017). Multilateralism, bilateralism, and unilateralism in foreign policy. In C. G. Thies (Ed.), *The Oxford encyclopedia of foreign policy analysis*. Oxford University Press.

Taylor, I. (2011). The forum on China-Africa cooperation (FOCAC). In T. Weiss & R. Wilkinson (Eds.), *Global institutions*. Routledge.

Tsoi, S. (2012). *Confucius goes global: Chinese soft power and implications for global governance*. John W. McCormack Graduate School of Policy and Global Studies, University of Massachusetts.

UN News. (2020). *About multilateralism*. Retrieved on September 20, 2021, from https://multilateralism100.unog.ch/about

Wang, S. (2016). China's people-to-people diplomacy and its importance to China-EU relations: A historical institutionalism perspective. *Journal of China and International Relations, 4*(1).

Xinhua. (2004). *China, Arab league issue communique on establishment of cooperation forum*. Retrieved on August 27, 2021, from http://www.china.org.cn/english/features/FbiCh/85842.htm

Xinhua. (2017). *List of deliverables of Belt and Road forum*. Retrieved on August 22, 2021, from http://www.xinhuanet.com//english/2017-05/15/c_136286376.htm

Yao, K. (2014). China-Arab states cooperation forum in the last decade. *Journal of Middle Eastern and Islamic Studies (in Asia), 8*(4), 26–42.

Zeng, A., & Shu, Z. (2018). Origin, Achievements, and prospects of the forum on China-Africa cooperation. In *China International Studies* (pp. 88–108).

Chapter 17
Secular Stagnation and World Leadership: China's Rising Path

Henrique Morais

1 Introduction

The world is experiencing unique moments that simultaneously create fears and anxieties, and also offer opportunities to rethink a good part of the paradigms that guided society and the economy after World War II. The dismemberment of the Bretton-Woods International Monetary System in the 70s, the unprecedented currency crises in Asia in 1997 and in Russia in 1998, and a period of some euphoria associated with the dotcom bubbles, were followed by disruptive movements in the twenty-first century. These included the 2007/2008 financial crisis, the most significant and probably the most devastating the 1929/1930 one. It was soon followed by the 2009 Great Recession and then, when we were recovering, the COVID-19 pandemic and an economic crisis that promises to rival, in size and impact, the 1929/1930 Great Depression.

We believe that these phenomena are no more than occasional movements in a long, more structural, and worrying path of stagnation of economic growth in a significant part of the world economy, specifically in the group of countries known as "advanced economies." And this path has already come a long way, since at least the last quarter of the twentieth century, when, together, these advanced economies represented around three quarters of the world's gross domestic product and were the nerve centre and engine of global growth. Since then, with a vigour difficult to imagine even for the most credulous of what globalization would mean in terms of greater international balance in wealth creation, there has been a strengthening of emerging economies such as China. This has come hand in hand with a progressive stagnation of growth in these advanced economies.

The theme of stagnation, or rather "secular stagnation," is not universal, but is spatially well determined. The origin of the scientific debate is easily identified in the 1930s, with the introduction of that concept by Alvin Hansen (1939). Although

H. Morais (✉)
Universidade Autónoma de Lisboa, Lisbon, Portugal

there has been a long interruption in scientific debates immediately after Hansen's outstanding contribution, with the exception of some Keynesian economists and the North American neo-Marxist school (among others, Sweezy, 1994), the topic resurfaced in the twenty-first century, associated in particular with the interventions of Lawrence Summers (2014).

This chapter briefly examines the scientific debates concerning the concept of secular stagnation and the influence of economic power on global power dynamics, thus evaluating the multiple impacts of the economy and its evolution at political and social levels. The problem is, in short, the eventual existence of stagnation in world economic growth and the consequences that it may have on world power balances. No radical changes are foreseen in the near future, such as a reversal of the processes of globalization and digitization of societies that could naturally have significant impacts on the entire current economic order. Rather, it is possible to predict that these movements will intensify. Thus, we ask ourselves about the consequences that may result from this fact on global power, its actors and instruments, its balances and instabilities. This being said, the first objective of this chapter is to determine whether the secular stagnation scenario, more than merely theoretical, is an identifiable phenomenon today in any country or region in the world. The second objective, even more challenging, is to assess the extent to which that phenomenon might have implications for power balances.

The argument is that secular stagnation is not a widespread phenomenon in contemporary society, but rather localized in advanced economies. Therefore, its asymmetric consequences are likely to jeopardize the balances of instituted world powers and, perhaps, the dominant power, itself possibly one of the most affected by the stagnation.

To achieve the aforementioned goals, this chapter comprises four sections. The first is the introduction. The second focuses on the theoretical and conceptual framework and the state of the art, and examines the hypothesis of the appearance of the secular stagnation of economic growth and its consequences on the global power structure. It argues that this stagnation is asymmetric, does not affect all regions and countries of the globe in the same way, and, therefore, is likely to cause changes in global power balances in the coming decades. In turn, the third-second section characterizes the secular stagnation phenomenon, presenting it in terms of a massive set of economic indicators, namely gross domestic product, the output gap, the productive capacity utilization rate, the interest and inflation rates, savings, and investment. In addition, this section places special emphasis on demography, as it is central to the secular stagnation phenomenon. The fourth section identifies the consequences of secular stagnation on global power structures, promoting a critical, but necessarily very limited, analysis of the changes envisaged in those structures through the impacts of the economic and financial aspects, as well as the dimensions of hard power and soft power in international relations. Finally, the conclusions present the main findings regarding the characterization of secular stagnation and its effects on the structures of world power in its various dimensions.

2 Theoretical and Conceptual Framework

In March 1939, one of the most prestigious economists of his time, Professor Alvin Hansen, in a speech entitled "Economic Progress and Declining Population Growth" and referring to the economic situation of the late thirties of the twentieth century, stated: "This is the essence of secular stagnation – sick recoveries which die in their infancy and depressions which feed on themselves and leave a hard and seemingly immovable core of unemployment" (1939, p. 4). Hansen argued that the US was going through an intermediate period, after the era of growth and expansion of the nineteenth century, which "no man, unwilling to embark on pure conjecture, can as yet characterize with clarity or precision" (ibid., p. 1). He referred to a huge change in the thirties: from a population increase of sixteen million people in the twenties, there was a halving in the following decade and forecasts pointed to less than a third in the 1940s (ibid., p. 2). Implicit in the apparent stagnation of the population were "serious structural maladjustments which can be avoided or mitigated only if economic policies, appropriate to the changed situation, are applied" (ibid., p. 2).

And what would be changing in the US economy? Hansen began by pointing out three factors that were at the origin of strong investment flows in the first decades of US economic history, thus ensuring abnormally high levels of gross domestic product growth, compared to the standards of the rest of the world in previous centuries: inventions, the discovery and development of new territories and resources, and population growth (ibid., p. 3). These "external forces" were changing and the economy saw the fundamental problem arising: underemployment, that is, the inability to achieve full employment (ibid., p. 4). Hansen suggested that weak population growth was crucial because it held back the increase in demand, generating the potential danger of stagnation and an effective underemployment of productive factors, capital, and labour. As indicated by Backhouse and Boianovsky (2016, p. 946), Hansen used the expression "secular stagnation" to refer to a historical movement, based on the US experience, a thesis on the consequences of economic maturity. Hansen began by explaining the cycles of prosperity and depression as a result of changes in money and credit, looking from the beginning for a dynamic model and showing that a slowdown in consumption growth can induce an absolute fall in investment (ibid., p. 949).

During the 1920s, he began to see fluctuations in investment, generated by population changes and waves of innovation, as the cause of the cycle: although monetary factors were still present, they were no longer an independent factor, but something that exponentiated these others forces. He argued that there were investment opportunities available and that when they run out, investment must fall, causing growth to slow (ibid., p. 949).[1] And yet, in only an apparent contradiction to some devaluation of monetary factors, Hansen considered that the Great Depression was particularly profound because it resulted from strong monetary and technological shocks that acted simultaneously.

---

[1] Thus sharing the idea initially presented by Arthur Spiethoff (1925, English version in 1953).

Backhouse and Boianovsky further argued (ibid., p. 950) that Hansen added to his notion of the steady state the idea that a decelerating population growth would lead to a fall in investment if there was no technical progress. He believed that the accelerator mechanism was central, allowing the increase in public investment in human and natural resources and in consumers (Hansen, 1939, p. 12) to offset the fall in private investment. However, if government spending was taken too far, it could change the cost structure and prevent full employment from being achieved. In his time, Hansen was criticized on two levels: the first group of authors rejected the concept of steady state, with Knight (1936) stating that there was no tendency for the reduction of capital returns to zero. Simons (1942) argued that the demand for durable assets increases rapidly if interest rates are very low (but always positive) and Pigou (1943) accepted the classic steady state notion but rejected Hansen's reformulation (Backhouse & Boianovsky, 2016, p. 952). In a second group, there was empirical criticism of the thesis of secular stagnation, namely by Terborgh (1945), for whom the decline in the population growth rate and the closing of the geographic frontier in the US were present at the end of the nineteenth century without having led to depression. On the other hand, a slowdown in population growth would alter the age structure and reduce savings, offsetting some drops in investment (ibid., p. 953). Nevertheless, it was Hansen who started the path to a series of debates about what secular stagnation actually means, the real possibility of occurring and even the different approaches depending on the various schools of thought of the authors who defend it. These approaches often differ even within the same school of thought, the most expressive example being Keynesians.

Among the authors who believe in the emergence of secular stagnation and point to the prevalence of demand factors as its main determinants, separating them from those who point to supply factors, Summers (2014) stands out. He shares with Krugman, Blanchard, and Bernanke the view that at the genesis of stagnation lies the fundamental imbalance between savings and investment and the liquidity trap, and had three levels of analysis: the difficulty of economic policy in achieving multiple goals, that is, good use of productive capacity and financial stability. This, in turn, is closely related to the decline in the equilibrium real interest rate and the need for different approaches to economic policies (ibid., pp. 65–66). As for the causes of this stagnant economic growth, Summers (2014) argues that structural changes in the economy have led to profound changes in the natural balance between savings and investment, causing a fall in the real equilibrium rate associated with full employment (ibid., p. 69). For Summers (2016), the main question is: what causes the increase in savings and the decrease in investment, creating this downward pressure, this tendency towards stagnation? (ibid., p. 100). The increase in savings is associated with changes in income distribution and profit sharing (more inequality would imply greater savings), the accumulation of reserves or capital flows, and deleveraging and preparation for retirement, in a context in which greater life expectancy would generate more resistance to indebtedness[2] (ibid., p. 100 and p. 102). The decline in

---

[2] Summers notes that household deleveraging and early repayment of debt are forms of savings (ibid., p. 102).

the propensity to invest (ibid., pp. 102–103) results from lower population and/or technology growth, lower economic massification, and, finally, the lower price of capital goods.

In the contributions focusing on the supply-side factors, there are authors who defend the possibility of the occurrence of stagnation, namely because they admit a strong decrease in potential long-term growth (Gordon and Crafts), while others point to the evolution of the price of investment goods (Thwaites). Some do not accept secular stagnation based on the analysis of potential growth (Mokyr), others advocate the existence of an anti-business climate created by the increase in political uncertainty and regulation which depress investment (Taylor, Baker, and Bloom) or defend the assumption of a secular unemployment scenario (Glaeser). Gordon (2015), for example, states that potential long-term growth has been significantly decreasing in recent decades, given the difficulties experienced by human capital in the face of changing demography and the less significant effects of technological changes on economic growth. Focusing on supply-side factors, he says that the lower potential growth of economies reflects the slowdown in growth in labour productivity and working hours and that the latter is due, simultaneously, to lower population growth and the decline of the labour participation rate (2015, p. 54). Although he considers his view of secular stagnation from a "supply-side" perspective, he concludes that "slower growth in potential output from the supply side, emanating not just from slower productivity growth but from slower population growth and declining labour-force participation, reduces the need for capital formation, and this in turn subtracts from aggregate demand and reinforces the decline in productivity growth.

In the end, secular stagnation is not about just demand or supply but also about the interaction between demand and supply" (ibid., p. 58), making evident his defence of an integrated vision (supply/demand) of the conditions that can contribute to the occurrence of secular stagnation. The central reasons given by Gordon for secular stagnation in the US are the slowdown in productivity and working hours, demonstrating that the average annual growth rate of total factor productivity from 1972 to 2014 is just over a third of that recorded between 1920 and 1972, in a movement closely related to the deceleration of labour productivity.

3 Characterization and Conceptualization of Secular Stagnation

Having briefly carried out the main revisited the main literature on secular stagnation, we will analyse the empirical evidence supporting the assessment of the existence of secular stagnation, which tends to be focused on four main dimensions. The first is associated with the behaviour of the wealth generated, measured namely by gross domestic product. However, it is demonstrated that advanced economies show a long tendency towards a slowdown in economic growth and its approximation to a zero annual growth rate. On its part, in the last four decades, China has maintained, like other emerging markets, a very strong economic growth. It is possible to perceive negative output gaps in advanced economies for more than a decade and a half. They have been growing below their respective potential, a clear sign of this stagnation.

The second dimension that is very detailed in authors who discuss secular stagnation is the need for negative real interest rates in order to match savings and investment with full employment. Inflation has been at least two decades below the equilibrium (or target) levels defined by the respective central banks. This trend is not exclusive to advanced economies. Some economists argue that it is "imported" precisely from some emerging economies. It is still indisputable that the real interest rates, and in a large part of the maturities also the nominal interest rates, are in the red.

The third dimension is associated with this negative real interest rates, that is, the relationship between savings and investment. One of the foundations of macroeconomics is the idea that income deducted from expenditure, therefore, savings, must equal physical investment (thus excluding the financial one). It seems that this fundamental equality of the economy is being called into question, with extremely high levels of savings associated with the aforementioned contribution from China, but also from petrodollar countries. It also involves other phenomena, such as population ageing in advanced economies, who put these savings above investment, which is also conditioned to a drop due to falling real interest rates and yields.

Finally, we have the demographic issue, an absolutely decisive factor in justifying and demonstrating the secular stagnation that will be plaguing some advanced economies.

Ferrero et al. (2017) provide a good summary of contributions on the relationship between demographic factors and, respectively, real interest rates and inflation. The authors consider that the significant persistence of demographic factors makes them extremely relevant from the perspective of monetary and financial policy stability, insofar as they affect the medium-term trends in nominal and real interest rates. The demographic factor had a significant impact on the downward movement of real interest rates, for example, in the euro area, as the age structure in many European countries evolved adversely, hampering economic growth and placing further downward pressure on real interest rates (ibid., p. 2). On the other hand, potential GDP growth depends positively on total factor productivity growth and negatively on the dependency ratio, so that a smaller percentage of young people may imply less innovation and less investment in research and development, reducing potential growth over the long term.

Cervallati et al. (2016) hypothesize that the slowdown in recent economic growth may be associated with important demographic changes and the heterogeneity of transition dynamics in the world (ibid., pp. 426–428). They argue that the demographic transition is endogenous and presents a very consistent cycle, common to most countries, characterized by a first phase when there is a brutal decline in mortality, followed by a reduction in fertility. Between these two periods, a temporary population growth occurs, which begins to slowdown in the third and last phase of the transition process (ibid., pp. 411–412). Goodhart and Pradhan (2017) point out the importance of the demographic factor in economic dynamics that do not necessarily translate into a scenario of secular stagnation. They argue that between 1980 and 2000, there was the biggest shock ever in the labour supply, causing a decrease in real income from work, greater inequalities within countries and smaller between countries, and falling real interest rates (ibid., pp. 1–2). In turn, Gordon (2012) recognizes that "no one should step into the trap of predicting that innovation will come to an end" (ibid., p. 9), giving some excellent examples of uninspiring predictions about technological evolution, which the lack of validity time took care of showing.[3] Nevertheless, it presents a set of "headwinds" that have contributed to a very faltering innovation process in the last two decades, with consequences for the already mentioned evolution of productivity in the US, and which may continue in the future.

The first of these headwinds is the demographic dividend (ibid.) and its reverse movement: the original, between 1965 and 1990, was the opening of the labour market to women and the baby boom, which caused working hours and per capita income to increase more than the hourly income. But now that the baby boomers are retiring and per capita working hours are declining. This will be accentuated if the retirement age does not keep pace with the increase in average life expectancy, causing per capita income growth slower than that of productivity.

Empirical analysis shows us that the two greatest economic powers of the twenty-first century are going through a demographic transition marked by the stabilization of net population growth: between 1950 and 2020, the average life expectancy at birth in the US and China went, respectively, from 68 and 43 years to 79 and 77 years. Mortality underwent a strong decrease between 1950 and 2008, especially in China, where this rate went from 23 deaths per thousand inhabitants to 6.8, while in the US it dropped from 9.6 to 8.1 deaths per thousand inhabitants. The drop in the birth rate is very expressive and it is estimated that this trend will continue throughout the current century, given the evolution of fertility. Thus, the ageing/non-rejuvenation of the population is a striking feature of this demographic transition and should remain a reality in both states in the medium and long term. This is reflected in the decreasing growth of the working population, an especially significant trend because it is accompanied by a very sharp increase in expectations regarding the years that women and men will remain in retirement. In the case of the former it went from 14.6 to 22.5 years between 1970 and 2018 and, in men, from 10.6 to 17.8 years. Despite these circumstances, the average retirement age is not rising. This increases dependency ratios, both in China and in the countries of the Organization for Economic Co-operation and Development (OECD), although in the case of China, the levels are much lower than those recorded in the OECD as a whole or in the US.

Contrary to what would be believed due to the stabilization of the working population, the increase in the years people will remain in retirement and the increase in dependency ratios, labour relations in OECD countries favour the reduction of working hours. This in itself would not be a significant problem if it was offset by productivity gains that would mitigate the negative effects of this demographic

---

[3] Examples include: in 1876, an internal Western Union (telegraph monopolist) document stated: "The telephone has too many shortcomings to be considered as a serious means of communication". In 1927, the head of Warner Brothers said (about Jazz): "Who the hell wants to hear actors talk?". In 1943, the *IBM* chairman said "I think there is a world market for maybe five computers". And in 1981, Bill Gates stated "640 *Kilobytes* ought to be enough for anyone" (Gordon, 2012, p. 9).

transition on economic growth. Still, these gains did not exist. Another stabilizer of the negative effects for economic growth and for the stabilization of social security would be the increase in the migratory flow towards advanced economies where the demographic transition is being more expressive. This would make up for an ageing population, a decrease in the employed population in relative terms, and its unwillingness to increase the number of working hours. However, none of this has happened, quite the contrary. If, to this scenario, we add the very strong increase in health expenses, which an ageing population naturally entails, it is very clear how the demographic transition is probably one of the most decisive factors for secular stagnation. If any country has already entered it, the solution to leave it will need to encompass measures that combat or attenuate the effects of the demographic transition described earlier.

In view of all this, policy measures to avoid or escape secular stagnation must inevitably address demographic issues and attempt to rejuvenate the population to find solutions. From this characterization of secular stagnation, we can empirically validate the strong deceleration of economic growth in some of the main advanced economies in the last two decades, as well as the falling nominal and real interest rates in these economies, in some cases with real interest rates stubbornly negative for a very long period of time. Finally, it was shown how valid demographic transition and its consequences for secular stagnation are. With a high degree of probability, the US will be very close to the beginning of a predictably long period of secular stagnation. Most European countries will experience it too, while China will be, at least for now, far from that scenario.

4 Consequences of Secular Stagnation in Global Power Structures

Assuming the above argument is valid, i.e., the existence of secular stagnation in the US but not in China, we will try to show how this can affect global power structures. In other words, the clear asymmetry between the patterns of economic growth in the US and China is progressively contributing to changes in the organization of global power and the relative strength of its main actors. We see the clear rise of China and its global influence, accompanied by consistent signs of the loss of influence of the US, and in some aspects even of its hegemony.

On the economic front, the evolution of the gross domestic product demonstrates without a doubt the rise of China to the top of the world scale and the more than probable departure of the US from that top position. In the last forty years, the weight of the Chinese economy has gone from 3 to 18% of the world GDP measured in current prices, while in the US there has been a stabilization of the gross domestic product of around 25% of the world total. In purchasing power parity, China has been the world's leading economy since 2017, dethroning a long US reign.

The budget, trade, and household debt components must be added to this macroeconomic scenario, taking into account the gigantic triple deficits of the US economy, increasingly financed from abroad in the form of the purchase of US public and corporate debt, although with a still not very significant weight, as most of the financing of the US economy is generated in the domestic market. The second impactful aspect of the global power balance is the financial one. The bubble behaviour, perhaps speculative, of the stock market both in the US and in China, is a very curious phenomenon (Koo, 2014). This is strange in the context of the fragility of the economy, namely in the US. In the public debt bond market, there is a very clear trend towards a sharp decrease in yields, facilitating the financing by the states of their financing needs, but favouring income demand movements. The latter, as a consequence, will promote risk behaviours and the formation of speculative bubbles in the financial markets.

It is not clear that emerging markets are immune to these behaviours that can jeopardize the stability of the financial sector and contribute to changes in geopolitics and global power. The example of the 2007/2008 financial crisis seems to bring a clear message: perhaps for the first time, we witnessed a financial crisis in which the "cold" of the advanced economies did not translate into a "pneumonia" of the emerging economies, which, on the contrary, seem to have "got round" the crisis. In short, emerging markets will now be more immune to the problems that more sophisticated financial engineering creates for advanced economies, and perhaps less dependent on international capital flows that, in the recent past, were likely to cause massive damage to these emerging markets.

At social level, extreme poverty has been significantly reduced over the last forty years and the evolution of inequality and the sharing of prosperity also seem to point towards a more inclusive society globally where global well-being is improving. However, major geographical differences remain, which would be even more evident if it were not for the extremely strong economic performance of two giants, also population-based, China and India. This fact evidently had an impact on the extreme poverty levels of a third of the world's population.

In addition, the fragility of the aforementioned recovery, in a context such as the present pandemic or increased pressure on scarce resources, such as water supply, or armed conflicts, can at any time cause a very significant reversal of this more balanced scenario of society, with possible impacts on the balance of power on a global scale. Changes in global power structures can also be evaluated with regard to the two main powers through hard power indicators, namely the military one regarding the evolution of expenses, the sale of arms, and its historical evolution (SIPRI, 2020). In this context, the US is the country in the world with the highest military expenditure, although in 2019 China's military expenditure reached about 37% of the US one and was by far the second largest in the world, when at the end of the twentieth century it was only 8.8%. However, the relative weight of US and Chinese military expenditures, when evaluated in terms of their respective GDP, is closer, 3.4% and 1.9%, respectively. China is of little importance, when compared to the US, in the world market for the sale of weapons, clearly dominated by the Americans, followed by Russia. Another aspect is the research and development (R&D) indicators, such as the investment made in R&D, the number of existing researchers per thousand inhabitants, the patents that each country has registered (and their importance in the information technology and communication sector), and the market shares in exports of some of the most significant sectors in technological terms, namely the pharmaceutical, aerospace, and information and communication technology industries.

With regard to research and development, it seems reasonable to conclude that there are three major trends in recent decades (among other, OECD, 2020). The first corresponds to the consistent increase in Chinese investment in this area and also in terms of research and development carried out by the private sector. Secondly, in a specific and cutting-edge sector, information and communication technologies, which is very important in the digital society that has been consolidating itself this century, China today has the primacy of research and development. This catapulted the country to the leadership of the export market, with more than a quarter of total world exports. Finally, despite the Chinese rise, it is undeniable that the US remains the great power in terms of research and development. In addition, there are composite hard power indicators, namely the composite indicator of national capacity, the global firepower indicator, and the global militarization index that also allow us to perceive the evolution of global power structures and the weight of each of the nations analysed (among others, ITU and United Nations, 2020).

We find very different information in these indicators: in some cases, China takes a top position, to the detriment of the US, as is the case of the Composite Index in National Capacity. This is certainly due to the weight that this indicator attributes to economic and demographic factors (besides the military component). In other cases, they show not only the maintenance of the US primacy but also the less favourable position of China in recent years. This is the case of Global Firepower, which evaluates the conventional air, sea, and land military force (excluding nuclear capacity). Other cases, like the global militarization indicator, show that these two nations are in very modest positions at the global level. This basically means that the weight of the military aspect in their societies and economies is much more balanced than in much of the rest of the world.

In the soft power component, there is a set of composite indicators that bring together the various dimensions of the phenomenon and their most appropriate indicators, namely the so-called Soft Power 30 (Portland, 2020). It includes a set of objective indicators such as governance, digitization, culture, companies, commitment, and education, as well as indicators obtained in more subjective opinion surveys on topics as diverse as local gastronomy, technological products, friendliness of the people, culture, luxury goods, foreign policy, and the attractiveness of the country to live, work, or study. Another important indicator, the Global Soft Power Index, is based on familiarity, influence, and reputation, ranging from business and commerce to culture, and including governance, education, and science. In the set of analysed indicators, we can identify a greater annual volatility of results and of the hierarchy of nations with regard to soft power, when compared to hard power indicators. Although this conclusion is not surprising, it nevertheless requires countries, especially those that dispute the world power leadership, to have a constant concern. This must be translated into active policy measures, to avoid that, circumstantially or in a more structural way, the world's perception of itself deteriorates. Regardless of epiphenomena such as the Trump presidency or COVID-19, which conditioned the assessment of the soft power of states, it still seems that the analysis carried out provides us with a dynamic but sustained vision, based on the idea that China has evolved favourably in this increasingly important global power component but which the US undoubtedly continues to lead.

5 Conclusions

In recent decades, geo-economics has evolved very intensely, at a pace difficult to find earlier and clearly directed regarding spaces and actors. It possibly has somewhat surprising characteristics compared to what would be the prevailing expectations and predictions, for example, on the eve of the first oil crisis of the 1970s. The information analysed in this chapter, namely the long series of GDP growth, the evolution of the productive capacity utilization rate, the gap between effective growth vis-à-vis potential growth, the behaviour of inflation and interest rates, or the evolution of savings and investment and demographic behaviour, confirms what the literature identifies as symptoms of secular stagnation in the US but not in China.

Starting from the previous conclusion, the second aspect of our work offers a perspective on how the economic developments described may affect the balances of world power. As a direct reflection of economic changes, the consequences of the current monetary order and globalization, demography or the new challenges posed to monetary policy, or the sum of all this, we find in the characterization of the various dimensions of power empirical evidence that can be summarized in a few lines: on the one hand we have the US, a stable power in the classic military dimension, expressed in defence budgets and military capacity, but falling, signalled by a vast set of hard power and soft power composite indicators. On the other hand, we find China on the rise in the most varied dimensions of power.

Does this mean that we are facing a change of paradigm or even of positions in the geography of world power? Not at all. The superiority of the US continues to be a reality, at military level but also in research and development, in the financial aspect, in the composite hard power indicators, in the social component, and also in the soft power indicators. In some of these dimensions, very often in soft power indicators, China is not even close to the top thirty in the hierarchy of nations, having a long way to go in these matters. Indeed, it often happens that the true counterpoint to the hegemonic dimension of the US is played by other nations or common economic spaces, namely the European Union, for example in terms of research or its importance as a commercial partner of other countries. What we infer from the analysis carried out is the appearance of a new actor in the dynamics of world power, an actor that less than three decades ago could not be expected to become a key player in those dynamics. China is increasingly an unavoidable actor in the balances of world politics, in their multiple dimensions.

Bibliographic References

Backhouse, R. E., & Boianovsky, M. (2016). Secular stagnation: The history of a macroeconomic heresy. *The European Journal of the History of Economic Thought, 23*(6), 946–970. Retrieved on October 2021, from https://www.tandfonline.com/doi/full/10.1080/09672567.2016.1192842?scroll=top&needAccess=true

Bernanke, B. (2015). *Why are interest rates so low, part 3: The global savings Glut.* Brookings. Retrieved on October 2021, from https://www.brookings.edu/blog/ben-bernanke/2015/04/01/why-are-interest-rates-so-low-part-3-the-global-savings-glut/

Blanchard, O., Lorenzoni, G., & Huillier, J. P. (2017). *Short-run effects of lower productivity growth: A twist on the secular stagnation hypothesis.* Peterson Institute for International Economics. Retrieved on December 2021, from https://www.piie.com/system/files/documents/pb17-6.pdf

Bloom, D. (2020). *Demography is destiny–really?* IMF Podcast. Retrieved on December 2021, from https://www.imf.org/en/News/Podcasts/All-Podcasts/2020/03/11/david-bloom-on-demographics

Caballero, R., Farhi, E., & Gourinchas, P. (2016). *Global imbalances and currency wars at the ZLB.* Retrieved on December 2021, from www.suerf.org/doc/doc_3295c76acbf4caaed33c36b1b5fc2cb1_4953_suerf.pdf

Cervallati, M., Sunde, U., & Zimmermann, K. F. (2016). Demographic dynamics and long-run development: Insights for the secular stagnation debate. *Journal of Population Economics, 30*, 401–432. Retrieved on December 2021, from https://link.springer.com/article/10.1007/s00148-016-0626-8

Crafts, N. (2014). Secular stagnation: US hypochondria, European disease? In C. Teulings & R. Baldwin (Eds.), *Secular stagnation: Facts, causes, and cures.* CEPR Press. https://voxeu.org/article/secular-stagnation-facts-causes-and-cures-new-vox-ebook

Eggertsson, G. B., Mehrotra, N. R., & Robbins, J. A. (2019). A model of secular stagnation: Theory and quantitative evaluation. *American Economic Journal: Macroeconomics, 11*(1), 1–48. Retrieved on December 2021, from http://pubs.aeaweb.org/doi/pdfplus/10.1257/mac.20170367

Favero, C. A., and Galasso, V. (2015). *Demographics and Secular Stagnation Hypothesis in Europe.* Conf. Growth in Europe. Marseille. Retrieved on December 2021, from http://www.greqam.fr/sites/default/files/demography_marseille.pdf

Ferrero, G., Gross, M., & Neri, S. (2017). *On secular stagnation and low interest rates: Demography matters* (ECB Working Paper 2088). Retrieved on December 2021, from https://www.ecb.europa.eu/pub/pdf/scpwps/ecb.wp2088.en.pdf?a6b4c0ab4102556cb4a52dcd26ac30aa

Goodhart, C., & Pradhan, M. (2017). *Demographics will reverse three multi-decade global trends* (BIS Working Papers n° 656). http://www.bis.org/publ/work656.pdf

Gordon, R. J. (2012). *Is US economic growth over? Faltering innovation confronts the six headwinds* (NBER WP No. 18315). Retrieved on December 2021, from https://www.nber.org/system/files/working_papers/w18315/w18315.pdf

Gordon, R. J. (2015). Secular stagnation: A supply-side view. *American Economic Review: Papers & Proceedings, 105*(5), 54–59. Retrieved on December 2021, from https://pubs.aeaweb.org/doi/pdfplus/10.1257/aer.p20151102

Hansen, A. (1939). Economic progress and declining population growth. *The American Economic Review, 29*(1). American Economic Association.

International Telecommunication Union. (2020). *ITU publications.* Retrieved on December 2021, from https://www.itu.int/en/ITU-D/Statistics/Pages/publications/default.aspx

Knight, F. H. (1936). The quantity of capital and the rate of interest. *Journal of Political Economy, 44*, 433–463.

Koo, R. C. (2014). *The escape from balance sheet recession and the QE trap: A hazardous road for the world economy.* Wiley.

Krugman, P. (2013). Bubbles, regulation, and secular stagnation. *The New York Times.* Retrieved on December 2021, from blog. https://krugman.blogs.nytimes.com/2013/09/25/bubbles-regulation-and-secular-stagnation/

Krugman, P. (2014). *Four observations on secular stagnation, in Secular Stagnation: facts, causes and cures* (C. Teulings & M. Baldwin, Eds., pp. 61–68). CEPR Press. https://voxeu.org/article/secular-stagnation-facts-causes-and-cures-new-vox-ebook

Krugman, P. (2016). Trade and tributation. *New York Times.* Retrieved on December 2021, from https://www.nytimes.com/2016/03/11/opinion/trade-and-tribulation.html.%20Accessed%2016%20September%202016

Mokyr, J., Vickers, C., & Ziebarth, N. L. (2015). The history of technological anxiety and the future of economic growth: Is this time different? *Journal of Economic Perspectives, 29*(3), 31–50. Retrieved on December 2021, from https://pubs.aeaweb.org/doi/pdfplus/10.1257/jep.29.3.31

Nye, J. S. (1990). The changing nature of world power. *Political Science Quarterly, 105*(2), 177–192. Retrieved on December 2021, from https://kwilliamson3.weebly.com/uploads/8/9/9/1/89912375/nye-_changing_nature_of_world_power-_reading.pdf

Nye, J. S. (2004). The decline of America's soft power (Why Washington should worry). *Foreign Affairs, 83*(3). Retrieved on December 2021, from https://www.jstor.org/stable/20033972

Organization for Economic Cooperation and Development. (2020). *OECD.* Retrieved on December 2021, from https://stats.oecd.org/

Pigou, A. C. (1943). The classical stationary state. *Economic Journal, 53*, 343–351.

Portland. (2020). *The soft power 30, a global rating of soft power.* Retrieved on December 2021, from https://softpower30.com/wp-content/uploads/2019/10/The-Soft-Power-30-Report-2019-1.pdf and https://portland-communications.com/pdf/The-Soft-Power_30.pdf.

Rachel, L., & Summers, L. (2019). *On secular stagnation in the industrialized world* (NBER Working Papers 26198). National Bureau of Economic Research. Retrieved on December 2021, from https://www.nber.org/system/files/working_papers/w26198/w26198.pdf

Rogoff, K. (2015). *Debt supercycle, not secular stagnation.* voxEu.org. http://voxeu.org/article/debt-supercycle-not-secular-stagnation

Simons, H. C. (1942). Hansen on fiscal policy. *Journal of Political Economy, 50.*

Stockholm International Peace Research Institute. (2020). *SIPRI military expenditure database.* Retrieved on November 2021, from https://www.sipri.org/databases/milex

Spiethoff, A. (1953). Business cycles, with a preface by the author. *International Economic Papers, 3*, 75–171.

Summers, L. (2014). US economic prospects: Secular stagnation, hysteresis, and the zero lower bound. *Business Economics, 49*(2), 65–73. Retrieved on November 2021, from http://larrysummers.com/wp-content/uploads/2014/06/NABE-speech-Lawrence-H.-Summers1.pdf

Summers, L. (2016). *Secular stagnation and monetary policy.* Federal Reserve Bank of St. Louis, Vol. 98(2), 93–110. Retrieved on November 2021, from https://files.stlouisfed.org/files/htdocs/publications/review/2016-06-17/secular-stagnation-and-monetary-policy.pdf

Summers, L. (2020). Accepting the reality of secular stagnation: New approaches are needed to deal with sluggish growth, low interest rates, and an absence of inflation. *Finance & Development, 57*(1). Retrieved on November 2021, from https://www.imf.org/external/pubs/ft/fandd/2020/03/larry-summers-on-secular-stagnation.htm

Sweezy, P. (1994). The triumph of financial capital. *Monthly Review, 46*(2).

Taylor, J. B. (2016). *The economic hokum of secular stagnation redux.* Economics One Blog. Retrieved on November 2021, from https://economicsone.com/2016/01/24/the-economic-hokum-of-secular-stagnation-redux/

Terborgh, G. (1945). *The bogey of economic maturity.* Chemical and Allied Products Institute.

Thwaites, G. (2015). *Why are real interest rates so low? Secular Stagnation and the relative price of investment goods* (Staff Working Paper No. 564). Bank of England. Retrieved on November 2021, from https://www.bankofengland.co.uk/-/media/boe/files/working-paper/2015/why-are-real-interest-rates-so-low-secular-stagnation-and-the-relative-price-of-investment-goods.pdf?la=en&hash=A280D3BB721387BC3EB09676FA27EAC30143E404

Chapter 18
Visuality and Infrastructure: The Case of the Belt and Road Initiative

Dennis Zuev

1 Introduction

The Belt and Road initiative (BRI) has become the largest infrastructure programme in history, and has become a symbol in itself of growing significance of China and its (soft) power. Schindler et al. (2021) go as far as calling BRI a "meta megaproject," which consists of multiple initiatives, which in itself is emblematic of contemporary megaprojects and their sublime nature (see Flyvbjerg, 2014). "Reading" or translating the politics, or indeed "technopolitics" of infrastructure (Larkin, 2013) is not an easy task, as larger logics and *infra* politics behind the visible materiality of the technological objects should be uncovered. These entanglements of materiality and "technopolitics" are directly linked to human affect, fantasy, and desire. The important part of the infrastructural political address is the representation of the possibility to become and be modern.

At the same time, massive infrastructural projects may be used to represent state power to the citizens (Harvey, 2012) or project that representation of state power to the citizens of other nations. BRI is an important element of the Chinese global imaginary, where different ideas related to global connectivity and prosperity, "inclusive globalization" (Liu & Dunford, 2016), Chinese leadership and modernity, "global entrepreneurship," and a missionary role of Chinese capital and knowledge in civilizing and modernizing (the backward) rurality are articulated. To some extent, China defines its external politics and "going out" via BRI. As an imaginary, it is constituted of significations and desires (Castoriadis, 1975) that make up an ideational (policy) superstructure of the BRI, whereas its material realizations of the infrastructure remain on the visible surface as rational, functional production of these ideas/policies.

D. Zuev (✉)
CIES-ISCTE, IUL, Lisbon, Portugal

University of St. Joseph, Macau, China

© The Author(s), under exclusive license to Springer Nature Singapore Pte Ltd. 2023
P. A. B. Duarte et al. (eds.), *The Palgrave Handbook of Globalization with Chinese Characteristics*, https://doi.org/10.1007/978-981-19-6700-9_18

How can we see the nuanced superstructure of the imaginary of the BRI? This chapter aims to address this question and via exploratory analysis of visual representations of the BRI and will attempt to bring more light on the politics of the spatial imaginary of the Belt and Road Initiative. Considering BRI as a *representational discourse* (Sykes & Shaw, 2018) the chapter will interrogate the immediate materiality of the BRI and symbolism or "spectacular" promise of its multiple infrastructure projects. Being a multivalent formation, BRI needs to be considered discursively (Wong, 2021), where particular attention needs to be paid to the "construction, framing, maintenance and dissemination of the sign systems that enable them" (ibid., p. 711). The symbolism and imaginary of the BRI have received relatively scarce attention from scholars. At the same time, BRI itself received a huge amount of attention, and most of the coverage has been positive (Liu & Dunford, 2016). However, here and there one encounters imagery that indicates at BRI and this visual dimension creates its own discourse about BRI. Due to ambivalence of images, the reading of the meanings can be multiple and this chapter will fill the existing gap by focusing on the visualization of BRI, identifiying iconic elements (successes and failures), and putting them to a visual sociological scrutiny (Zuev & Bratchford, 2020).

BRI is a unique mega-infrastructure and an economic collaboration project launched by China in 2013 that aims to connect China with multiple (primarily) Eurasian and African countries along ancient trade routes via infrastructure building. It has received an immense attention already from scholars in security and international relations (Pechlaner et al., 2020) and political geography (Bennett, 2020; Han & Webber, 2020) but also increasingly from anthropologists (see multi-sited ethnographic study on trade by Rippa, 2020). However, still many aspects of BRI remain understudied, for instance little research has been done on "Digital Silk Road," and impact of infrastructure on the local communities of the partner countries (Fung et al., 2018; Shen, 2018).

Very few studies interrogated Belt and Road Initiative from visual perspective, as a collection of representations or a social imaginary. Which is even more surprising, considering that the discipline of international relations has clearly embraced the importance of insights stemming from visual analysis and visual communication (Crilley et al., 2020) as part of a larger aesthetic turn. And it is also surprising considering the importance of visual communication in promoting such a "brand" as Belt and Road. Thus, this study for the first time will present and analyse primary visual data that will reveal the complexity of visual representation of BRI. These are the visuals found within the printed media (*The Economist* magazine) and visual imagery within the multimodal media (documentary films in YouTube). The images chosen for the empirical case study come from various sources, both non-Chinese and Chinese media, and have no definite time range (but mostly since 2018), and rather have been sampled purposefully by the researcher aiming to show the variety and diversity of representations.

In this chapter it will be argued that we need to delve deeper into the multiple visual narratives of BRI, and thus seeing it as a visual phenomenon that will help better understand its visual political messages and complex discourse which in its turn allows uncovering hidden mechanisms of power.

The structure of the chapter is as follows: to follow the introduction is the literature review on infrastructure, which will be followed by the section on the methodology of visual interrogation and specifically, visual analysis of the infrastructure. After that the section on the visual communication regarding BRI will follow by two instances of empirical analysis (vignettes) that better illustrate how BRI can be approached visually.

2 BRI and Enchantment of Infrastructure

While BRI is not only about infrastructure (bridges, flyovers, digital corridors, and port terminals), but also cooperation, investment, security, trade, and symbolic production of civilizational cultural exchanges, it is the very materiality of the built environment that will be the subject in this chapter as it is the infrastructure that most often becomes the visual object in media representations of BRI. To follow is a brief overview of some literature regarding the "promises of infrastructure," which will help to contextualize the object of this study. Building upon the literature of the aesthetic turn and visual sociology, as well as studies of infrastructure (Anand et al., 2018; Larkin, 2013; Schindler et al., 2021; Zuev & Habeck, 2019) this study approaches the visual dimension of BRI with a much more focus on the actual visual communication as has been done by previous (few) scholars.

BRI no doubt is a unique project of planetary scale and remains a "seductive" and hot research subject. While it has its own value to the scholars of international relations, security, and political studies, it is also fascinating for the study of mobility and connectivity, that this initiative implies. Belt and Road Initiative is an interesting example of what Harvey and Knox (2012) in their analysis of roads as infrastructure call "enchantment of infrastructure." Infrastructure is not only a "grand project" of the state, it is also a fundamental element for social cohesion, availability of which limits the range of lifestyles (Zuev & Habeck, 2019). Following Bennett (2001), Harvey and Knox (2012) argued against the notion, that the post-enlightenment world has been characterized by a process of disenchantment (Blumenberg, 1983; Weber, 1958).

Peter Schweitzer et al. (2017) remind us that in the study of infrastructure it is the deep structures beyond the observable that really matter and should constitute the task of the researcher. Schweitzer et al. (2017) also warn us about the danger of neglecting the *infra* in the infrastructure, and simply focusing on the infrastructure as materials, practices, and meanings. The authors believe that anthropologists should explore the materiality of the built environment along with its becoming, consumption, and entanglement with politics, historical contexts, and globalization. Part of the politics of the infrastructure is the social promises, which in the case of the BRI are related to technological modernity and sociotechnical imaginary. In the latter the key narrative is of China as a potent agent of technological modernization of the already-existing infrastructure or the creator of the new, desired one. It is exactly this narrative of technological leadership that China assumes in shaping the "built environment" and appearance of technoscapes that causes concerns among other leading Western and Asian nations, dubious about the intentionality of the Chinese technological endeavour. A major factor in this is the debate surrounding the claims that China engages in debt-trap diplomacy through the BRI, ensnaring developing countries with debt dependence and then translating that dependence into geopolitical influence. China's actions in Sri Lanka, Pakistan, and Malaysia are central to the debt-trap debates. The Center for Global Development classifies eight countries as having a "particular risk of debt distress" as a result of their involvement in China's BRI.

Infrastructure is an important concept for understanding not only the changing relationship between humans and nature, but what is of most relevance in this chapter—understanding the changing notion of the human–nature interaction in the modern Chinese culture. As Larkin suggested, "infrastructures are matter that enable the movement of other matter" (2013, p. 329) and it can be centred on built things, knowledge things, or people things. Not all the elements of infrastructure are however appropriate subjects for the visual analysis, but visual analysis can allow to elucidate the changing social practices and politics related to specific socio-material assemblages (Zuev, 2018). However, as Coller suggested (2011), we can see infrastructures as significations of the "biopolitical" ordering, a mixture of political rationality, administrative techniques, and material systems that can tell us a lot about and see better the practices of government. Decaying or ruined infrastructure facilities can at the same time signify the lack of political cohesion and become the source of unending sadness for the population (Walker, 2012).

Until now very few efforts have been made in applying visual analysis to the transforming built environment and sociotechnical assemblages. However, this has been changing with technological advances and specifically with the availability of drone technologies, that facilitated optical analysis of the spaces, landscapes, and vast *hyperobjects* (Fish, 2020). Visuality and analysis of infrastructure and technologies nevertheless remain a rather untouched domain (see Sinclair, 2017; Zuev, 2018). In the following section, the focus is on the relationship between infrastructure and specifically BRI and its social visuality. As I will show further the visuality of the BRI is constituted by various visual data: cartographic, satellite imagery as well as visual media discourses in popular magazines and films.

3 Seeing the Infrastructure-Induced Changes Along the BRI

In this section I wish to review several studies that can be a starting point for analysis of the visual dimension of BRI. The visual dimension in this sense means not only the analysis of representations and visual communication, but also the visual data-knowledge assemblage that relates to discourse on BRI. The visual data can be cartographic or satellite imagery, but also observations of the researchers collected over time via "slow ethnographies" with the dispersed mode of inquiry and thus diversity of ways of seeing (Woodworth & Joniak-Lüthi, 2020).

Interestingly, a project involving multiple countries and territories—BRI still lacks an official cartographic representation with areas, routes, and projects (Narins & Agnew, 2022). As Bennett suggests (2020)—the seduction of the initiative might be flowing from its "amorphous and ever-changing scope" (Oliveira et al., 2020). While cartographic imagery is scarce, Chinese government is increasingly relying on aerial imagery, which provides "rational" representation. Mia Bennett (2020) used nightlight imagery to see the differences in development along the BRI. By locating emerging hot and cold spots of development along the border of China and other nations one can see the actual reality and not the "imaginary" impact of the BRI. The study suggests that hot spots indicate clusters of high values, which may signal increases in socio-economic activity. And emerging cold spots are spatially significant clusters of low values, potentially indicating the decrease in economic activity. According to Bennett (ibid.), despite the much fanfare Pakistan-Chinese border is represented by a cold spot, while less known in public activity in the North-East (Near Russian Far East and North Korea) borders is a hot spot.

While aerial imagery allows to "rationally" assess the activity along the borders and thus see the impact of BRI-induced change, for the large audience BRI remains a multi-territorial project, which is promoted by means of maps (used and seen by scholars and lay public) showing the ambition and connectivity delivered by the BRI. An insightful study by Galen Murton (2021) shows that the maps of BRI are characterized by "invisibility" and the presence of blank spaces. Murton identifies the cartographic invisibility of particular Chinese regions (Tibetan Plateau and Himalayan valleys) as a distinct form of visual argument to assert that what goes missing from the map reflects power. The "cartographic silence" of conspicuously missing Tibetan Plateau and Himalayan valleys from large-scale cartographic representations of the BRI indexes that such "omissions" may obscure the specificities of the place or render the regions invisible, where certain social issues (such as human rights) are conspicuous (Murton, 2021). Interestingly, BRI maps leave blanks not only in the sensitive internal regions in China, but also beyond its borders, where many projects related to BRI are underway (such as "Sky Train extension").

Carolijn van Noort (2020) in one of the few studies that deal with the visual dimension of strategic narratives related to BRI explores visual narratives of the Maritime Silk Road at MSRI portal. She presents her findings (in a surprisingly non-visual way) as follows: the visual communication is much less about the projects, but the "political figures" behind them. Infrastructure projects are implied and not directly shown. Importantly, the image of Xi Jinping connotes the continuity and stability of the BRI, as he is the person who embodies the vision of the BRI. Van Noort (2020) reminds us that in the digital age it is imperative to analyse the intersection of strategic narratives and visual media, primarily as visual media are omnipresent. Her study shows how infrastructure is associated with key political actors (Xi Jinping), especially as they appear in public (raising a toast or depicted in a group photo in the centre). This section includes a review of several works that are important in bringing in BRI as a visual phenomenon. These are diverse aspects of the visuality of BRI: (in)visibility, and strategic visualization, the next section will review some methodological issues related to the analysis of actual visual representations of the BRI.

4 Visual Analysis: Some Methodological Notes

The stories emanating from different news channels constantly remind us that we are living in an ever-increasingly digital hyper-visual world awash with antagonistic ideologies and ideological movements. These movements are laden with images, image-events, and politically charged symbols and emblems that contribute to the gradual "symbolic thickening" (Kotwas & Kubik, 2019) of public culture through the intensification of national and religious visual displays and social performance.

While this chapter is exploratory and does not aim at systematic or full (or quantitative) analysis of imagery related to BRI, it will present and analyse several images qualitatively that will allow to show the complexity of visual representation of BRI—the illustrations in *The Economist* and the visual imagery within the multimodal media, such as documentary films in YouTube. The images chosen for the empirical case study come from various sources, both non-Chinese and Chinese media. Another important point is that sole visuals have never been considered as a single type of data in visual studies (Zuev & Bratchford, 2020), instead visuals help to elicit information, and also require a wide sociohistorical context. While images do not speak for themselves, they can allow to approach the issue at stake from a different perspective and identify "in-between invisibilities" that allow to pose questions: why peculiar images have been chosen and others have been omitted? Why a particular sequence of images has been presented?

G. Rose, introduced three types of modalities suitable for the study of visual texts: social, compositional, and technological (2001). "Social modality" refers to the economic, social, and political relations and practices, that surround the image and through which it is seen and used, "technological modality"—how the image is made, and "compositional modality" which relates to the material qualities, as well as content and composition in the visual text (Rose, 2001, p. 17). The three modalities matter in the area of the "site(s) of the production of an image, the site of the image itself, and the site(s) where it is seen by various audiences" (Ibid., p. 16). Researchers can structure their analysis using one or more modalities to study how meaning is constituted in the production of the image, the image itself, and through its interpretation by various audiences.

A visual methodology is best approached as a multimodal perspective, where the visual is but one feature along with auditory and textual ones that allow the holistic understanding of visual data and materiality (Pauwels, 2012). Following the view that visuality is communicated through mixed media, it is important to analyse the relations of the "verbal text with photographs, images, drawings and/or graphs." Documentaries unlike photographs or drawings should be approached as multimodal texts, as they use historical imagery, drawings, graphs, and combine musical and textual narrative, they also blend special effects for a more artistic portrayal. As van Noort (2020) suggested as methodological caveats in her study mentioned above, an analysis of strategic narrative success (or failure) needs to consider several variables, such as image selection (why a particular image depicting or representing an infrastructure project and not another), juxtaposition (choosing one image or a selection of carefully framed images), and the medium (from traditional to digital platforms). The following section will draw on these methodological suggestions and present two cases of visual analysis related to printed media and documentary films.

5 Visual Analysis Case 1: *The Economist* Representations of the BRI

While we may think that the same medium can give the same illumination of a social issue, by looking at selected images of the *Economist* journal we can discover, that the depiction of the New Silk Road or BRI is far from being unilaterally negative or positive. *The Economist* can be considered as an elite media platform that offers insightful information on developments across the world with perhaps a skewed or more than critical reflection in non-Western nations. The key images in this chapter are the graphic illustrations by European artists, which are associated with texts. While we tend to pay attention more to the text, these illustrations however are the important visual accompaniment of the messages. Each image represents a "plot." The following "plots" found in several images of *The Economist* may be a useful exploratory launching point for deconstructing the key tensions and anxieties behind the BRI. While the images can be ambivalent, they offer a rather insightful and fresh perspective on what kind of narratives cause key suspicion and should be countered by the authorities in their further "re-branding" or promotion of the BRI.

One of the common ingredients of representation is the image of the planet Earth or a map (terrain) suggesting the significance (impact) and the scale of the project to the planet.

5.1 Plot 1: China Gets Rich

For instance, in the drawing by Jac Depczyk for *The Economist*,[1] BRI is depicted as a New Silk Road with the flow of goods and money. Where there is no indication

---

[1] Will the China's Belt and Road Initiative outdo the Marshall Plan? *The Economist*. Retrieved on January 2022, from https://www.economist.com/finance-and-economics/2018/03/08/will-chinas-belt-and-road-initiative-outdo-the-marshall-plan.

Fig. 1 BRI representations (*Source* Jac Depczyk [2018])

of the "infrastructural promise" of the BRI, but rather a metaphoric suspicion or anxiety about one-way enrichment for China. A sort of incisive depiction of the Chinese "threat by infrastructure," and implications of impoverishment of the local population. At the same time, small heaps of coins represent the local treasures (resources), that are being carried away by boats and trucks. The camels depicted may be iconic animals of the Silk Road, an idealization that helps to sell BRI and promote it as a rejuvenated old trade route. At the same time, the roads are depicted as fragments, with projected ones connecting these bits and this projectification is one of the positive connotations of the drawing. The map here representing geographical terrain is the ground of turbulent trade and construction that is implied by the infrastructure built-up (Fig. 1).

5.2 Plot 2: Planetary Infrastructure

The image by Luca D'Urbino appeared on the cover of *The Economist* with the title Planet China,[2] and is a more metaphoric and caricature reference to the promise of the planetary infrastructurization. Indeed, the Earth is depicted as Saturn with its rings, where the roads—symbol of infrastructure are circling the Earth. The image is suggesting the scale of the ambition and the scale of the venture. The ring with the characters 中国 (China) however may be interpreted ambivalently as control or leadership, and at the same time can be a simple reference to the builder, as an ancient marker of the builder that was often left on the edifice. This image also suggests the

---

[2] Planet China: What to make of the Belt and Road Initiative. *The Economist*. Retrieved on January 2022, from https://www.economist.com/weeklyedition/2018-07-28.

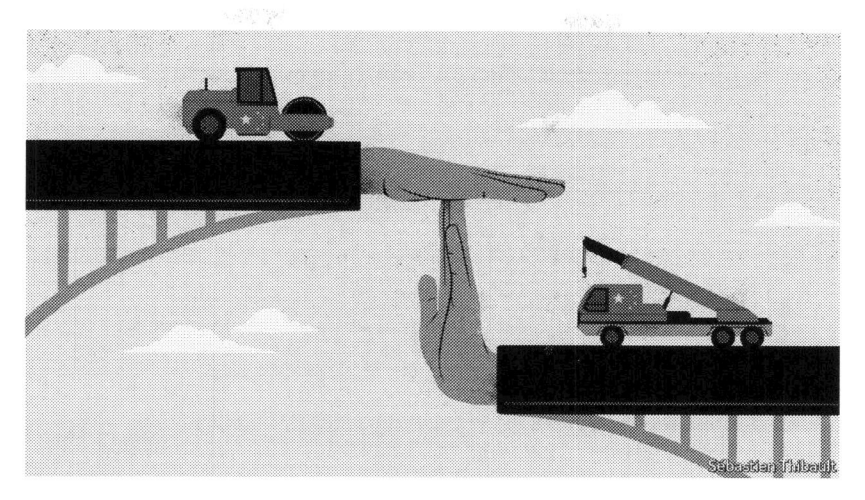

Fig. 2 BRI representations (*Source* Sebastien Thibault [2020])[3]

linearity of the road—not a rhizomatic network, that serves different purposes and destinations, but rather a principal line—two lane-traffic, serving just in one principal direction.

5.3 Plot 3: Perpendicular Mutuality and Complexity of Transactions

The image by Sebastian Thibault (Fig. 2) provides a reference to the common icon of the BRI—the highway (railway) bridge. In this drawing the road construction equipment is positioned on two different levels that may stand for the receiving party and the construction party. As was mentioned earlier, the incongruences between the parties involved lead to the common plot of the BRI discussions—the lack of mutuality between China and the receiving countries. The common mutuality or mutual agreement would be depicted with a handshake, however here the bridge is connected in a less, also suggesting unanticipated tensions and disagreements. The image is a metaphor for the transactions in the BRI or any other meta projects, which are characterized by a complicated geometric condition of power, non-linearity, and relationality (depicted here by two hands which could also represent two geometrical or (power) planes).

Related to this plot is an important sub-narrative of the infrastructure as a "debt-trap." BRI represents two opposites in the development of infrastructure—the nightmare of a debt-trap and the dream of connectivity. Importantly, the connectivity in

---

[3] The pandemic is hurting China's Belt and Road Inititative. *The Economist*. https://www.economist.com/china/2020/06/04/the-pandemic-is-hurting-chinas-belt-and-road-initiative

BRI is a dream for the two parties engaged (the recipient country and the executor (China). The same applies to the "debt-trap" nightmare (Lai et al., 2020)—which works against the positive image of BRI and the discourse that China is increasingly working to counter (Murton & Lord, 2020) and the debt as an economic turmoil for the recipient country (and its current government).

Related to this plot is a concrete case of the recent tensions over the highway in Podgorica. One of the images that has circulated widely recently been that of the new highway bridge near Podgorica in Montenegro. An image of a brand new, shining piece of road engineering is presented as a "luxury," that the customer can not pay for. While the discussion involves the previous government that explicitly suggests that this decision was the mistake of the Montenegro government and not the Chinese, the highway becomes a visual reminder of unaffordability of infrastructure and megaprojects (see Flyvbjerg, 2014). Indeed, any unpaid project within BRI becomes a luxury product bought with an average salary and concern of not having enough money to use and maintain it.

5.4 Plot 4: Prosperity for All Brought by China

The centrepiece of the illustration by Nathalie Lees[4] is the paper lantern in the shape of the globe and the central position of China on it. The graphic illustration in red and yellow colours on the black background is based on a popular symbol of "Chineseness," especially in the West—the paper lantern灯笼 (denglong), often associated with Chinatowns in the Western cities or popular Lunar New Year celebrations. The paper lanterns are common symbols of vitality and good luck (fortune), thus the wealth here is brought by the BRI to the whole world (depicted on the lantern). The red lanterns here can be illuminating and giving light (via creation of essential infrastructure), but also symbols of Chinese (aesthetic) or technical standard imposition, a sort of "paper lantern colonialism." They can also symbolize "red lights"—as in the red light district, connoting invisibility, secrecy of transactions, and hidden outcomes. Launching lanterns into the sky during Lantern Festival is an important part of the Lunar Year celebration, which is a family reunion holiday, and indeed an important solidarity ritual. Thus, the illustration to some extent also echoes the one by Luca D'Urbino on the Chinese central (planetary) role in the global map.

---

[4] China Wants to Put itself back in the centre of the World. *The Economist*. Retrieved on January 2022, from https://www.economist.com/special-report/2020/02/06/china-wants-to-put-itself-back-at-the-centre-of-the-world.

5.5 *Plot 5: BRI as Digital Control Room*

The image that would represent plot 5 is again by Nathalie Lees,[5] and we can see a less celebratory, "prosperity for all" vision of BRI via a centralized control space (CCTV surveillance room). The illustration depicts a graphic setting of one human figure in white shirt and black hair, looking at five screens showing different pieces of the world map. The image represents BRI as a digital surveillance control room with one supervising "key operator" in the manager's chair overlooking the movements on multiple screens between various dots related to important projects and hubs along the BRI, with the central screen showing the big picture of China and Beijing. While one supervisor control room suggests that there is a powerful singularity behind the project, it also makes us think—about the sustainability of the project beyond the "great supervisor"—will it cease to exist or it will be upheld by a follower? The pandemic crisis suggests that while thinking strategically is still valid, we are really living in one day and such future projections are no longer valid.

As a summary of these five images, one could suggest the far from univocal representation of the BRI and the New Silk Road even in one particular medium (*The Economist* magazine). The multiple images show the variety and wide range of connotations regarding the BRI by different authors—from visions of dystopian space of exploitation and surveillance to the visions of prosperity and planetary infrastructure, with hybrid visions of conflicting but connecting partnerships, led by China and thus slightly awkward ways of coping. The images may be alluding to different problems or content of the programme and thus it can be instrumental in decoding them as texts. The sets of symbols incorporated in them can be very simple but capable to symbolize visions and counter-visions of a particular project or an issue at hand. While images are drawn by individual (mostly European artists) they circulate far and wide via global networks of the media distribution and have a powerful impact on the reception of BRI among the general public (in this case English speaking, Western, educated elite). As a method for reflection images allow us to further conceptualize the features of the BRI—as a vision of prosperity and planetary infrastructure but at the same time of "perpendicular mutuality" and one supervisor control room.

---

[5] The digital side of the Belt and Road Initiative is growing. *The Economist*. Retrieved on January 2022, from https://www.economist.com/special-report/2020/02/06/the-digital-side-of-the-belt-and-road-initiative-is-growing.

6 Visual Analysis Case 2: Infrastructure and Connectivity Discourse in Documentaries

In this second instance the focus is on the imaginary presented in the official CCTV documentary *One Belt One Road, "Common Destiny"*,[6] the first documentary about BRI as a made in China "collaboration model" (合作模式) for "creating a brand new Asia." The narrative line starts with the historical references to the world mapmaking and the resulting human endeavour to connect via trade routes, nourished by the imagination of unknown territories and the thirst for discovery, wealth, and sea trade. Throughout the video politicians from some participating countries (majority European and Chinese, with only one leader of a North African country) share their positive visions of participating in the BRI.

The dynamic storyline is supported by the 55 minutes of epic music connoting a heroic undertaking, while the visual syntax of the documentary is highly relying on the aerial views providing the bird's eyeview perspective through a kaleidoscope of urban landscapes, industrial sites and largely showing the transformation of the empty scapes with the newly built environment features. Some of the common signifiers of this dynamic narrative are rhythmically edited with insertions of the winding roads with the two CCTV crew cars and the rushing high-speed rail trains, as well as with another frequent image of the seaports with containers and cargo cranes. The documentary finishes with the sequence of images of yet unconquered nature—mountains, valleys, and the ocean reminding that the common destiny is the "common dream" of commanding the resources of the planet.

The documentary is a glamorous or more romantic presentation of the Chinese "thinking big" in terms of metaphors of "common dream" or "common destiny," but at the same time careful reminder that this is a rejuvenation of a centuries-old exchanges along the Silk Road, which are now revived and led by an innovative "platform vision" from China. At the same time, the BRI in the documentary is depicted as a transformation outside China beyond its borders and gives little reference to the changes domestically. Several distinctive groups of images (visuals) convey the message of the documentary, these are the images of the rationalistic planning and management (e.g., graphs and maps), important people (politicians), who symbolize international endorsement of the project, the images of operatives and construction workers indicate the reality and tangible outcomes (e.g., railway) behind the policies, the final group of images refers to the future—the images of nature represent the work at the edge, future horizons, and resources to be tapped and taken advantage of along with the future prospects of development (represented by the global night time light map) (see Fig. 3).

BRI is not merely a political platform or ambition, but is an important cultural product and signifier of the modern Chinese culture—the symbol of going beyond the borders and effort of active exchange with the West. It also symbolically combats the cultural trauma of being dependent on the Western technologies, and reverts from

---

[6] One Belt One Road, part 1, "Common Destiny," 共同命运。Retrieved on January 2022, from https://www.youtube.com/watch?v=YgUJX5X_xNE.

Fig. 3 Common destiny. Collage of screenshots from the documentary "common destiny" (*Source* https://www.youtube.com/watch?v=YgUJX5X_xNE&t=102s. The Belt and Road EP 1 Common Destiny CCTV [2022])

China being the object of globalization to China being the main agent of globalization via technological domination and leadership. It is also a revision of the postcolonial imaginary and reminds the visual narratives of the 50s where Soviet engineers were shown on the posters of the Sino-Soviet collaboration as teachers (see Fig. 4), where posters glorified the Soviet Union's advanced economy to build up Chinese nation.

In the documentary Common Destiny—it is implied that a Chinese 大哥 (big brother, both as "surveiler" and a "knowledgeble expert" or consultant) becomes the key operative agents in the execution of the planetary connectivity dream. But in the CCTV documentary, the BRI is portrayed as a highly efficient techno-dream stimulated by the visual grammar of time-lapse shots of the urban landscapes and characterized by the automation and powerful machines, that manage the scale and natural challenges. The human dimension is reduced to the acceptance of the initiative by the national leaders as well as Chinese and Western experts, the only ones who are given a voice in the video.

A very different and much more critical vision is given in the *Deutsche Welle* documentary *One Belt One Road*,[7] which travels along the Maritime Silk Road and the Overland Silk Road to show the relational complexity of the undertaking. The key message in the German documentary is a less glamorous depiction of the "perpendicular mutuality" in the BRI, where the receiving countries lacking their own resources for modernization need China but are unable to fully take advantage

---

[7] The New Silk Road, Part 1: From China to Pakistan. DW Documentary. Retrieved on January 2022, from https://www.youtube.com/watch?v=cUxw9Re-Z-E&t=18s.

Fig. 4 Study the Soviet Union's advanced economy to build up our nation (*Source* Ding Hao [1953]. Landsberger Collection. Retrieved on January 2022, from www.chineseposters.net)

of this. Unlike CCTV documentary, the DW film uses insertions with the down-to-earth characters—farmers, artisans, and Chinese construction workers—the new kind of "missionaries" far away from their homeland.

7 Conclusion

The objective of this chapter was to underline some points crucial for understanding the visual communication surrounding the BRI and thus see BRI as a unique discursive domain, where different producers set parameters around the presentation of particular social or cultural bodies. Visual analysis has not been the key dimension in the understanding of BRI. However, it is crucial to deconstruct and contextualize the meanings and iconicity brought and promoted via official visual representations, and counter-representations of the BRI. The study of the visual representations of the BRI allows us to better examine not only the intricate relationships between China and the countries involved and affected by the politics of infrastructure but to see the visual communications about the grand project of China-led "inclusive globalization" (Liu, 2019), or globalization with Chinese characteristics. Following previous studies on the aerial visibilities (Bratchford & Zuev, 2020) in this chapter it is stressed that some technologies are becoming important not only as they provide a new vision from above, adding a poetic touch to the "boring" infrastructure, but they also remind us that visibilities are controlled in order to gain wider acceptance among the public.

The two cases of the *Economist* magazine illustrations and the documentaries demonstrate that we can uncover much deeper discursive tensions than the visuals allow us to see. Western representations are far from being critical or diminishing of the BRI, while perhaps touching upon multiple facets and latent symbolism of the BRI—its promise of prosperity and connectivity via planetary infrastructure, but also hidden tensions in the concept of mutuality—who eventually becomes the winner and looser in the partnership. While the BRI is the subject of various scholarly discourses it is crucial that further interrogations embrace the affordances of visual media to provide a multifaceted, more complex imaginary of the BRI not as a given-truth reality, but as a project as much in imagination and dreams as a collage of diverse visions and images. It is also essential for both the receiving parties and China to see how these imaginaries embrace different symbolic and expressive meanings, some enabled by new technologies (remote sensing or drones).

Acknowledgements I extend my gratitude for the right to reproduce the artwork by Jac Depczyk and Sébastien Thibault which is used in this article and allows to better see the world around us. I also thank Paulo Duarte for his valuable comments on this chapter.

Bibliographic References

Anand, N., Gupta, A., & Appel, H. (2018). *The promise of Infrastructure*. Duke University Press.
Bennett, M.K. (2020). Is a pixel worth 1000 words? Critical remote sensing and China's Belt and Road Initiative. *Political Geography, 78*.
Bennett, J. (2001). *The enchantment of modern life: Attachments, crossings, and ethics*. Princeton University Press.
Blumenberg, H. (1983). *The legitimacy of the modern age*. MIT Press.
Bratchford, G., & Zuev, D. (2020). Aerial visibilities: Towards a visual sociology of the sky Introduction to the special issue. *Visual Studies, 35*(5), 402–416.
Castoriadis, C. (1975). *The imaginary institution of society*. The MIT Press.
Coller, S. J. (2011). *Post-Soviet social: Neoliberalism, social modernity, biopolitics*. Princeton University Press.
Crilley, R., Manor, I., & Bjola, C. (2020). Visual narratives of global politics in the digital age: An introduction. *Cambridge Review of International Affairs, 33*(5), 628–637.
Fish, A. (2020). "Drones". In P. Vannini (Ed.), *The Routledge international handbook of ethnographic film and video*. Routledge.
Flyvbjerg, B. (2014). What you should know about megaprojects and why: An overview. *Project Management Journal, 45*(2), 6–19.
Fung, K. C., et al. (2018). Digital Silk Road, Silicon Valley and connectivity. *Journal of Chinese Economic and Business Studies* (Online first).
Han, X., & Webber, M. (2020, March). From Chinese dam building in Africa to the Belt and Road Initiative: Assembling infrastructure projects and their linkages. *Political Geography, 77*.
Harvey, D. (2012). *Rebel cities: From the right to the city to the urban revolution*. Verso.
Harvey, P., & Knox, H. (2012). The enchantments of infrastructure. *Mobilities, 7*(4), 521–536.
Kotwas, M., & Kubik, J. (2019). Symbolic thickening of public culture and the rise of right-wing populism in Poland. *East European Politics and Societies, 33*(2), 435–471.
Lai, K., Lin, S., & Sidaway, J. D. (2020). Financing the Belt and Road Initiative (BRI): Research agendas beyond the 'debt-trap' discourse. *Eurasian Geography and Economics, 61*(2), 109–124.

Larkin, B. (2013). The politics and poetics of infrastructure. *Annual Review of Anthropology, 42*, 327–343.

Liu, W. (Ed.). (2018). *China's Belt and Road Initiative*. Springer.

Liu, W. (2019). *The Belt and Road Initiative. A pathway towards inclusive globalization*. London.

Liu, W. D., & Dunford, M. (2016). Inclusive globalization: Unpacking China's Belt and Road Initiative. *Area Development and Policy, 1*(3), 323–340.

Murton, G. (2021). Power of blank spaces: A critical cartography of China's Belt and Road Initiative. *Asia Pacific Viewpoint, 62*(3), 274–280.

Murton, G., & Lord, A. (2020). Trans-Himalayan power corridors: Infrastructural politics and China's Belt and Road Initiative in Nepal. *Political Geography, 77*, 102100.

Narins, T. P., & Agnew, J. (2022). Veiled futures? Debt burdens, the Belt Road Initiative, and official Chinese lending after coronavirus. *Human Geography* (Online first).

Oliveira, G. L. T., Murton, G., Rippa, A., Harlan, T., & Yang, Y. (2020, October). China's Belt and Road Initiative: Views from the ground. *Political Geography, 82*, 102225.

Pauwels, L. (2012). A multimodal framework for analyzing websites as cultural expressions. *Journal of Computer-Mediated Communication, 17*, 247–265.

Pechlaner, H., Erschbamer, G., Thees, H., & Gruber, M. (2020). *China and the New Silk Road. Challenges and Impacts on the regional and local level*. Springer.

Rippa, A. (2020). *Borderland infrastructures. Trade, development, and control in western China*. Amsterdam University Press.

Rose, G. (2001). *Visual methodologies: An introduction to the interpretation of visual materials*. Sage.

Schindler, S., Fadaee, S., & Brockington, D. (2021). *Contemporary megaprojects. Organization, vision, and resistance in the 21st century*. Berghahn.

Schweitzer, P., Povoroznyuk, O., & Schiesser, S. (2017). Beyond wilderness: Towards an anthropology of infrastructure and the built environment in the Russian North. *The Polar Journal, 7*(1), 58–85.

Shen, H. (2018). Building a Digital Silk Road? Situating the Internet in China's Belt and Road Initiative. *International Journal of Communication, 12*, 2683–2701.

Sykes, O., & Shaw, D. (2018). Unpacking the spatial imaginaries of "One Belt, One Road": From representation to performativity. *Town Planning Review, 89*, 120–124.

Sinclair, K. (2017). Arctic political imaginaries: Crafting technologies and inhabiting infrastructures. *Visual Studies, 32*(2), 156–166.

van Noort, C. (2020). Strategic narratives, visuality and infrastructure in the digital age: The case of China's maritime Silk Road Initiative, *Cambridge Review of International Affairs* (Online first).

Walker, J. (2012). Olympic ghosts in a former warzone: What the legacy of 1984 means for Sarajevo today. *Visual Studies, 27*(2), 174–177.

Weber, M. (1958). *The protestant ethic and the spirit of capitalism* (Trans. T. Parsons). Charles Scribner's Sons.

Wong, A. (2021). Mapping signs and making them stick: Discursive power and the semiotic construction of a 'world's leader'. *Discourse: Studies in the Cultural Politics of Education, 42*(5), 699–715.

Woodworth, M. D., & Joniak-Lüthi, A. (2020). Exploring China's borderlands in an era of BRI-induced change. *Eurasian Geography and Economics, 61*(1), 1–12.

Zuev, D. (2018). *Urban mobility in China: The growth of the E-bike*. Palgrave.

Zuev, D., & Habeck, O. J. (2019). Implications of infrastructure and technological change for lifestyles in Siberia. In J. O. Habeck (Ed.), *Lifestyle in Siberia and the Russian North*. Open Book Publishers.

Zuev, D., & Bratchford, G. (2020). *Visual sociology: Politics and practice in contested spaces*. Palgrave.

Chapter 19
The Belt and Road Initiative: Can It Signalize a New Pendulum Movement?

Margarida Proença

1 Introduction

In the last decades, the growing interconnectedness of people, resources, markets, and institutions in the global markets, the diffusion of information technologies, the fragmentation of production processes, the increase of geopolitical tensions, and financial and pandemic severe crises, all contributed to more volatility and uncertainty. Moreover, there are potential changes in world power dynamics. Trade has been an engine of growth for so long. The United States (US) emerged from World War II with a stronger economic base, and a leadership and hegemonic position based on a liberal international economic set of institutions. Efficiency gains from multilateral trade liberalization allowed some social progress. Between 1990 and 2013, the number of people living in extreme poverty—with an income below €1.6 person/day—decreased from 35% to 10.7% of the world population; in Southeast Asia, the reduction in extreme poverty was drastic, having fallen from almost 60% to 3.5% of the population (World Bank, 2018).

The surprising expansion of the Chinese economy has been associated with a mixed of political and structural reforms. Being the country with the largest world population, a low-wage labour market, and a strategic location, China had all the initial conditions for growth. On the other hand, the implementation of structural strategic reforms followed a quite pragmatic approach since the end of the 70s, to improve efficiency and competitiveness. Other strategic vectors were macroeconomic stability, trade opening, investment growth, and improvements in education, science, and technology. The global pattern of consumption is also changing. In China, by 2030, 70% of the population could be part of the middle class (Tanzi, 2021). In 2021, 10 Chinese universities were ranked in the top 100. Chinese universities perform strongly in the Research Dimension, with over 70% of all indicator scores better than average (QS World University Rankings, 2021).

M. Proença (✉)
Retired Full Professor, University of Minho, Braga, Portugal

On December 11, China joined the World Trade Organization (WTO) and made its way from the periphery of world trade to become a global trade titan. By 2020, it had the largest share of global exports in goods (15.2% of the total), while the US' share was 8.1%. Chinese exports are dynamic and diversified, gradually shifting from mature low-value-added to sophisticated products. By 2007, Chinese exports were already more technological (medium and high) than the OECD average, representing 60% of their total exports (OECD, 2009).

In the 1990s, with the collapse of the Soviet Union and the German reunification, the signing of the Maastricht and Amsterdam Treaties in the European Union, the trend towards a growing insertion of China in the market economy, despite the Gulf Wars, among others, there was illusion and optimism. The political influence, reinforced and hegemonic of the US, reflected the victory of capitalism. Nevertheless, the international order became more uncertain and fragile. With time, China became stronger and richer; direct investment of the US in China rose from 11.14 to 123.88 billion dollars (2000–2020). Both countries engage in rivalry and competition. In 2013, President Xi Jinping launched the New Silk Road, one of the most ambitious infrastructure projects ever conceived. The plan was two-folded: the overland Silk Road Economic Belt and the Maritime Silk Road. Its implementation would reshape global networks of trade and people, but also political ties within and between countries, reinforcing global Chinese dominance. China's rise to the status of a major global economic power took place simultaneously with a decline of the US and a loss in importance of other powers such as Europe or Japan, creating objective conditions for a world economic realignment. One might ask whether these events are likely to lead to the end of unipolarity, and if so, what might be the contours of a new system. This chapter discusses the likelihood of a potential movement of the economic and political pendulum, back to Orient. The global impact might certainly involve a transformation of the entire system.

This chapter is organized as follows. Section 2 draws some of the key lessons from the relevant literature on the game changers along history and the competing perspectives on the evolution of hegemony and leadership. Section 3 describes the overall approach and actions to analyse and interpret information applied to understand the research question. Section 4 highlights the empirical evidence of the trends and patterns of recent Chinese economic evolution, and examines the opportunity for a change in power dynamics based on a duopoly model under network effects.

2 Game Changer and Power Dynamics

Game changers are macro trends that may shape the course of history. The Chinese strategic move over the design and investment of The Belt and Road Initiative might be one of those: appears as a form to induce further development over Asia and an effective leadership strategy in the consolidation of China's insertion in the globalization process. Throughout history, geopolitical reasons and innovation shocks have been able to reverse or interrupt the trend towards a deeper integration, eventually changing power dynamics in the international context. A good example of an archaic globalization period (Hopkins, 2002) was the Silk Road, a network of communication routes that has been enormously important, between the seventh and thirteenth centuries, in connecting Asia and Western Europe. The fall of the Roman Empire and the growing Arab influence made the Silk Road increasingly dangerous and less used, but it became a myth for centuries. By then Europe was not the richest region in the world; the pendulum was on the east side, where agriculture was more productive, and technology and product quality were superior. Chinese, Arabs, Persians, and others moved and traded freely throughout Asia. By contrast, European ships did not sail far beyond the Mediterranean, the Baltic Sea, or the Black Sea. During part of the fifteenth century, and throughout the following century, the discoveries of Vasco da Gama, Colombo, and many others brought important changes in political-economic rivalries and managed to transform a small and very peripheral country as Portugal into a remarkable centre of an empire, "one of the greatest enigmas in history" (Plum, 2017, p. 11). By then, for the first time in a systematic way, Europe became "the centre of a world-economy" (Wallerstein, 2004, pp. 4–6). In 1474, was signed the Treaty of Tordesillas established the division of the world between the areas of influence of the two Iberian countries—Portugal being responsible for the "discovered and undiscovered" lands situated before the imaginary line that delimited 370 leagues (1770 km) west of the Cape Verde Islands, and Castile the lands beyond this line. Its signature took place at a time of transition between the hegemony of the Papacy, and the affirmation of a new leadership cycle in world politics, although quite unstable (Table 1). However, over the course of the eighteenth century, with the advent of capitalism, mercantilist constraints slowly disintegrated. Portugal had already lost the hegemonic position in the world markets due to technical progress and more stable political institutions. With the Industrial Revolution and a marked technological progress, was also possible a greater efficiency of capital markets, free trade, and the advent of new ideas. Two additional vectors were also important: a more educated, more open, and more demanding society from the point of view of scrutiny and political control, and the creation of political institutions non-absolutist, stable and mature. All these factors contributed to promote innovation and economic growth, justifying England as a new, stable hegemonic power. By 1820, England still maintained its hegemony in the world economy, despite the growing threat by France and Germany.

The development of societies and economies is potentially contingent on accidents of history and reveals some empirical regularities. Economists and historians have long sought to know when changes in living standards between Asia and Europe will have occurred and what the reasons are for this. Maddison's (1995) GDP per capita estimates indicate that, by 1800, Europe was already more developed than the rest of the world, although Pomeranz (2000) or Brandt et al. (2012) argued that during the seventeenth and eighteenth centuries the standard of living in China were not very different from the most advanced regions in Europe. In a quite extensive work, Broadberry (2021, p. 34) accounted for the Great Divergence between Asia and Europe. The author examines the proximate and ultimate sources of growth, and concludes that growth in the factors of production, TFP growth, state capacity, and institutions

Table 1 Competing perspectives on hegemony and leadership

World economy			World politics		
	Hegemony cycle	Hegemony		Leadership cycle	World leader
Hapsburg/Genoa	1450–1575	1526–1556	Portugal	1494–1580	1516–1540
Netherlands	1575–1672	1620–1650	Netherlands	1580–1688	1609–1640
No Hegemon	1672–1798	No Hegemon	England I	1688–1792	1714–1740
England	1798–1897	1850–1873	England II	1792–1914	1815–1850
United States	1897–	1945–1967	United States	1914–	1945–1973

Sources Kwon (2011, p. 594). Hegemonies and hegemonic cycles are from Hopkins and Wallerstein (1979); world leadership and leadership cycles from Modelski (1987)

allowed creating the adequate incentives for accumulation and innovation. Finally, the technological progress in transports and infrastructural developments stimulated agglomeration economies and the British hegemonic role.

World War I contributed to the emergence of the US as the world's leading economy, reinforced after 1945 both on economic and military grounds. The scope and objectives of the Bretton Woods Agreement were remarkable—to establish a new global international monetary order and a fixed exchange rate system, based on the so-called gold-dollar standard. It was about creating the multilateral institutions capable of allowing the evolution of the world economy to a multilateral system, "a new kind of an open system – which the capitalist world had never seen" (Ikenberry, 1993, p. 155). The actual debate over the potential decline of American hegemony is not new. The hegemonic stability theory argues that international economic openness and stability are most likely when there is a single dominant state, unipolar; this occurred between 1820 and 1870 with the British hegemony, and between 1945 and 1973 with the American hegemony. In both cases, hegemony was stable, based on a set of universal rules and supranational institutions, and the world economy expanded, associated with a free trade orientation (Wallerstein, 1984).

The literature underlines the need for capabilities to enforce the rules of the system, the relevance of being a large and growing economy, holding military power and a leader in technology (Max Corden, 1990). In any case, the concept is not as clear as it may seem. Hegemony entails some sort of leadership, but the two concepts are different. Modelski and Thompson (1988) consider that leadership is mainly a military concept, while hegemony, in line with Gramsci (1971), has an economic focus, through economic growth and innovation. The realist tradition tends to identify hegemony with unipolarity and material power, ignoring the deliberate exercise of leadership. Gilpin (1987), in line with Kindleberger (1973) and Keohane (1984) analysed the relevance of hegemony in the international setting, under the point of view of the provision of international public goods, as free trade. Hegemony is approached as the interplay between states and markets (Gilpin, 1987). "A stabilizer, one stabilizer" (Kindleberger, 1973, p. 305) is a precondition for a stabilized world economy. In this sense, it was the relative loss of industrial dynamism, the diffusion of technology, and the rise of Japan, in a certain sense a loss of leadership capacity, that undermined the American hegemony (Gilpin, 1987). On the other hand, it allowed the increase in economic closure and protectionism, the development of three political and competing regional economic blocs (Northern America, Europe, and East Asia), and so the increase in volatility and uncertainty. In this context, the sound economic growth of a country as large as China might induce the end of a unipolar world. The local and regional hegemony in Asia might be translated into direct competition towards a global hegemony: " a recipe for trouble" (Mearsheimer, 2021). In this context, one might argue that it is fundamental to maintain the international status quo to prevent destabilization and eventually a nuclear conflict (Gilpin, 1981; Keohane, 1984). Gilpin (1987) associates hegemony with the top hierarchic prestige and reputation for power position, which will allow the possibility to enforce the rules of the game, both economic and military. However, given the presence of diminishing returns, one can expect ever-increasing costs to control or even avoid challenges from new entrants; then, attractive strategies might be to try to eliminate potential rivals before they become too strong. Gilpin's optimism over the future is limited, depending on the potential economic benefits of international interdependence and the fear of a nuclear war.

To Susan Strange (1987), the US lost hegemony is just a "persistent myth," far from the truth. Strange (1987, pp. 553–554) agrees that the game of the states changed over the last quarter century for reasons that are economic, not political. The advantages of restoring a US-led liberal world order are defended by many authors such as Ikenberry (2020), Niblett and Vinjamuri (2021), or Blackwill and Wright (2020). The main argument is that it was able to create a space for democracy, with rights and protections, while ensuring the balance between conflicting values such as liberty, equality, openness, social solidarity, sovereignty, and interdependence (Ikenberry, 2020).

To Keohane (1984) the hegemony concept is based on economic interdependence. It underlines the discussion of the conditions that enable potential sustentation of stable configurations of cooperation within a capitalist economic system. Rational self-interest explains why countries choose to cooperate; as it happens in repeated games of prisoner's dilemma, stability is the expected outcome of cooperation in the context of a clear hegemonic power. However, even in the absence of a hegemonic power, it is possible to obtain this outcome, given that the lower the cost of international transactions, the lower will be the costs of adjustment and the overall uncertainty. The self-interest of the participants and the expected benefits obtained through agreements will be maximized through cooperation (Gill & Law, 1986; Keohane, 1984).

Other authors align more with an idiosyncratic Marxist tradition. Cox (1987), for example, discusses hegemony as being related to a balance of social forces channelled by the political leadership. The neoliberal order created after 1945, under US leadership, mediated between oligopolistic world markets and domestic political forces, enabled the globalization process. The major international factors behind the so-called *pax American* have been the gold-dollar system, the multilateral international institutions led by the US, cheap energy, and military power, while in the context of OECD must be underlined the reconstruction of neoliberal states and the mediation of class conflicts through welfare. However, since then, a diffusion of power opened the possibility of a counter-hegemonic set of social forces allowing a progressive transformation. Cox (1987) recognizes that, since the sixties, there has been a weakening of global hegemony. Moreover, in the aftermath of the economic crises in the 70s, it started the mobilization of social forces into alternative blocks, potentially with a new identity of interests between workers and transnational corporations. Historically, there have always been alternatives to prevailing hegemony, and they will continue to exist.

Wallerstein (1984) refers to hegemony as the capacity to impose power and establish rules in economic, political, military, and cultural terms. Although in 1945 the US had, in fact, an economic capability unique in the world, the military dominance made all the difference, and allowed the creation of strong alliances, as NATO for example. A cultural world dominance reinforced those factors. For Wallerstein (2019), the US decline was a result of the Vietnam War, the sixties cultural transformation, and the rise of economic rivals. The strategies followed to try to overcome the loss, with relative success, reinforced cooperation through American leadership in the G7, the Washington Consensus, and globalization, supported by an ideological neoliberal consensus-building process at Davos. The Soviet Union was certainly a challenger, and the Cold War divided the world into zones economically separate, but later, its collapse removed an important political weapon, and in a way contributed to show the US vulnerability (Wallerstein, 1980, 2019). He considers that China, Korea, and Japan might move together, both in political and economic terms—but in the chaotic and uncertain world we live in now, control of any country would be very difficult. Also, Arrighi (1990, p. 366) departs from Gramsci to define world hegemony as the "power of a state to exercise governmental functions over a system of sovereign states," a phenomenon which emerged from the disintegration of medieval Europe and the emergence of capitalism.

H. Wagner (1986) approaches the balance of power debate using game theory. The objective is not to discuss hegemony, but stability and peace. The analysis is based on an n-person non-cooperative game in extensive form. Wagner shows that, quite paradoxically, stability is encouraged by conflicts of interest among states. In his model, if states are expansionists, they will be able to preserve independence as a function of their ability to make binding agreements.

To Weissmann (2015) both Chinese foreign policy and their self-perception, a mix of superiority and inferiority, are closely related. The 2007–2009 financial crisis, which had consequences for both Europe and the US, and the fast economic growth, were able to change the perception of their role in world politics and economy. China behaved as a leader in the Non-Aligned Movement, searched for alliances and partnerships with other emerging economies, and since 1971 is one of the United Nations's Security Council five permanent members (Shambaugh, 2013, p. 45). Several authors stressed the change in Chinese foreign policy, moving from a low profile to a more aggressive one, "striving for objectives" (Yan, 2014).

In a certain way, China acted to provide an alternative to the existing international order (Breslin, 2009, p. 822), expressed in principles and slogans as "Peaceful

Rise/Development," or "Harmonious World" (Weissmann, 2015, p. 154). Ikenberry and Lim (2017) called the attention to the building of new, counter-hegemonic institutions and the way they can serve to gain more control over its geopolitical environment. They argue that China, in fact, displays a willingness to allow loans that bypass namely World Bank multilateral mechanisms and controls and widen its impact in developing and emerging economies, in Asia, Latin America, or Africa (Weissmann, 2015, p. 163). The *One Belt One Road Initiative* might be an instrument of opposition to the international order created by Bretton Woods and demonstrated that it is possible to challenge the hegemonic power of the US. Some authors focus on specific institutional involvement. Schweller and Pu (2011) consider that with the Asian Infrastructure Investment Bank (AIIB), China got a primary leadership role over a major institutional player, and a first step in the exercise of influence and leadership, to "delegitimate the old order."

Brands and Sullivan (2020) list some strategic behaviours that support the idea that China is challenging American hegemonic power. It is the case of the Chinese ambitious naval shipbuilding programme, the campaign to control waterways off China's coast, or the systematic efforts to increase economic influence and coercion in the Asia–Pacific. The authors discuss two alternative potential roads to arrive at a superpower status: focus on building, first, a regional primacy, becoming a dominant player, or instead proceed directly to develop an economic, diplomatic, and political influence on a global scale. The Belt and Road Initiative, as well as the investment in military technology, and the promotion of ideas as "Asia for the Asians" are just examples of that first alternative, but at the same time they are important pieces for the second strategy. In 2013, Wang Yi, China's Minister of Foreign Affairs delivered a speech in Brookings, US, where defended a model of major-country relations "between China and the United States – each country should remain on each side of the Pacific, in a kind of win–win cooperation." Also, Wang Dong (2021) advocates this ideal of sound cooperation between the US and China as "the two pillars in an evolving new global order." China is increasing its level of participation and engagement in the building of new institutions; and since the second decade of XXI there have been strategic moves towards the establishment of potential free trade agreements in the Asia–Pacific Region. To pursue a leadership, or even a hegemonic position in the world markets, China must reinforce economic and technological instruments, more than traditional military power. After all, the US has done that after 1945: with the revealed capacity to shape the key international institutions, to convert military power into political dominance, and to create and maintain a technological gap with the rest of the world (Brands & Sullivan, 2020). The authors argue that China is behaving to mimic this past strategic American behaviour.

Mearsheimer (2021) considers the rivalry between the US and China as "inevitable." In his opinion, the US strategy, supported by liberalism ideas and the accommodation to a hegemonic role, acted in a way that reinforced China's wealth and a new position in the world trading system, creating a new kind of cold war. However, according to the author, China is a more powerful competitor than the Soviet Union, and thus "this cold war is more likely to turn hot." China looks forward to dominating Asia and becoming the dominant world power, following strategic lines very much like the US have done in the past, while the US "sees China's ambitions as a direct threat" (Mearsheimer, 2021). The author remembers that Asia is highly unstable, with armed and religious conflicts, and concludes that the rivalry between the US and China presents real dangers. Other authors contest the assumption, as premature, of the inevitability of a power transition from the US to China. Zhang (2004, p. 89) argues that the only realistic policy choice for China is a cooperation strategy, based on the recognition of a balance of power largely favourable to the US. While China made real progress in export-oriented industries, the US maintained, or even enlarged, a technological gap and military advantages. A study conducted in 1997 by the China Institute of Contemporary International Relations ranked the global powers. US and China occupied, respectively, the first and the seven relative positions; in between Japan, France, Britain, Germany, and Russia. Nevertheless, Zhang suggests that China should not just wait for a greater participation in world power, let's say blessed by the US. Instead, the author defends that China should "actively seek to expand participation in all kinds of global and regional regimes" (Zhang, 2004, p. 107), integrate the G-8 group (now G7), use its financial resources, and, in general, play a more aggressive leadership role.

Given the present level of uncertainty it is hard to anticipate the future. Balances of power will change over time, with new problems requiring new solutions. Going from a rigid bipolarity or a "winner-take-all" approach to hegemony there are several possible outcomes. This is the point of view of Rodrik and Walt (2021, pp. 4–6); they propose a "meta-regime," based on minimal initial agreements between the two major powers on a "basic operating system," a set of rules to manage global economy and diplomacy. The future global order will also depend on the capacity of the global community, non-state actors, to go "beyond the stark antinomy of conflict versus cooperation" (Rodrik & Walt, 2021, p. 35).

3 Methodology

The study design has a potential for bias and justifies a careful methodological description. We propose to think of the future as subject to waves and cycles, swinging back and forth as a pendulum. Sorokin (1957) used the pendulum to show that "nations and organizations tend to oscillate between extremes of two poles (centralization or decentralization, modernity and religion, civilian or military rule)." Imagine a massive object, *the pendulum bob*, hanging vertically in its equilibrium position. When the bob is displaced from equilibrium and then released, it begins its back-and-forth vibration about its fixed equilibrium position.

In physics, there are two dominant forces: the force of gravity and a tension force acting upwards and towards the pivot point of the pendulum. In fact, there are another force, air resistance, but it is relatively weak. Establishing the parallel with economic theory, in a similar way to the gravity theory of trade (Deardorff, 1998), we can take GDP and TFP as accounting for the force of gravity. On the other hand, innovation and mixed strategies account for the tension force; the Belt and Road

Initiative, among others, exemplifies these strategies. A mix of variables such as state capacity, locational advantages, agglomeration and dispersion forces, distance, culture, or tariffs can represent air resistance. It is not easy to access detailed statistical information. In what concerns the Belt and Road projects (BRI), information was directly obtained from Reconnecting Asia Project Database (December 2020), compiled by the Center for Strategic and International Studies; several alternative studies were checked, and some differences were found. The option was to accept the most recent information, including the number of BRI projects, and as well as other infrastructural projects, financed through the Chinese financial system and AIIB. For a moment, return to the parallel with the pendulum. In physics, symmetry breaking is a phenomenon in which even infinitesimally small fluctuations acting on a system crossing a critical point decide the system's fate, by determining which branch of a bifurcation can be taken. Those fluctuations, in economic terms, can be defined as game changers—technological advances, innovation, economic growth, institutional development, new ideas, the design of mixed strategies. The Belt and Road Initiative acts as a game changer that can deepen integration, create agglomeration economies, increase rates of GDP growth, and eventually contribute to a new reconfiguration of global power dynamics. In a complementary way, it will be considered competition in a duopoly model under network effects, a framework that might allow to capture horizontal differentiation and the pattern of bilateral connections among competing players.

4 Empirical Evidence: Lofty Ambitions

4.1 *China vs. US: Trends and Patterns*

Alongside the significant globalization of economic activities, the recent decades witnessed a change in the centre of gravity, with a shift in dynamism from the Atlantic to the Pacific axis. By 1995, most global value chains were organized around a regional hub. Japan or the US functioned as the key hub for Asia or America; in Europe, the situation was more diffuse. However, between 1995 and 2007, there was a decline in the importance of Japan, replaced by the greater centrality of China. This contributed to a loss of US leadership in the world markets.

First-generation industrialized countries accounted for nearly two-thirds of world trade by 1991 (OECD), but their market share has gradually declined in favour of new industrialized countries. The countries of East and Southeast Asia, which, in the 1960s, followed a very rapid process of industrialization and development, with a remarkable capacity for transforming the industrial structure and the pattern of foreign trade, recorded the most successful cases. In these countries, investment in human capital and effective economic policies reinforced comparative advantages. There are some major characteristics of modern economic growth (Kuznets, 1973). It is expected an increase in the nonagricultural sector and in the proportion of the labour force employed in those sectors, along with a redistribution of the population between rural and urban areas and an increase in the capital labour ratio. These structural changes should be associated with greater efficiency in the capital market, as well as a more open and a more demanding society from the point of view of scrutiny and political control. In short, more stable institutions, the formation of a middle class, greater human capital, and higher real wages will encourage the emergence of industrialization and innovation.

In the last twenty years, China's economic and societal transformations have been remarkable. Between 1978 and 1990, in China, the share of the primary sector in GDP increased from 28.2% to 41.7%, while the share of the secondary sector fell from 47.9% to 43.1%. Since then, the contribution of agriculture to the GDP growth fell sharply to 9.1%, quickly decreasing to 7.7% in 2020. From 1978 to 2004, the share of total Chinese employment in the primary sector dropped from 69.3% to 31.8% (Brandt & Zhu, 2010). These figures indicate a rapid growth and industrialization process. Kuijs and Wang (2005) estimated an increase in the capital labour ratio, going from a 3.2% average annual increase between 1978 and 1993 to 5.1% between 1993 and 2004. Finally, during the last decade, the reduction in rural population was drastic; the degree of urbanization in China increased from 19.39% in 1980 to 63.89% in 2020. Chaolin Gu et al. (2017) classified the Chinese urbanization process as "stunning."

Figure 1 shows the evolution of both China and the US GDP on a purchasing-power-parity basis; China is clearly set to be the world's largest economy. The World Bank described the pace of the real annual GDP growth as "the fastest sustained expansion by a major economy in history." China's GDP surpassed Japan's in 2010, Germany's in 2007, and the UK's in 2005. In 2021, the size of the Chinese economy was 5.4 times as large as the UK's, and 3 times as large as Japan's. The latest GDP reports show that the US fell by 2.3% in 2020, while China grew by 2.3% amid the coronavirus pandemic (2021). China will likely overtake the US as the world's largest economy earlier than anticipated. However, given the differences in the historical path, economic structures, and population, China's per capita GDP is still far below that of the US (Fig. 2). In 2021, China's GDP reached $16,640 trillion, and per capita GDP exceeded $18,931 (PPP) for the first time. Between 1988 and 2008, the global distribution of income changed, particularly due to economic growth in China, where the increase in individual income was dramatically higher than the world average increase (Lakner & Milanovic, 2016). During this period, the gains of globalization were clear, translated into a growth in real income of around 80% for a very broad set of people, between 40 and 60% percentiles of the world, in most cases belonging to emerging middle classes in Asian economies.

Based on Pew's income band classification, China's middle class has been among the fastest growing in the world, swelling from 39.1 million people in 2000 to roughly 707 million in 2018. By 2022, more than 75% of China's urban consumers will have a disposable income, in real terms, between $9000 and $34,000 a year (Barton et al., 2013). In purchasing-power-parity terms, that range is between the average income of Brazil and Italy. By 2030, China and India may come to represent 66% of the world's middle class and 59% of world consumption. Broadberry (2021) pointed

Fig. 1 GDP current international dollar (PPP), China and US (*Source* WB [2021])

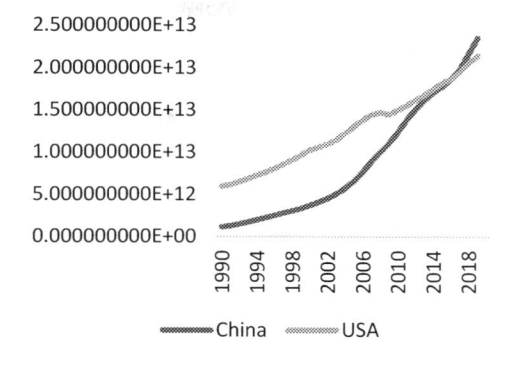

Fig. 2 GDP per capita current international dollar (PPP), China and US (*Source* WB [2021])

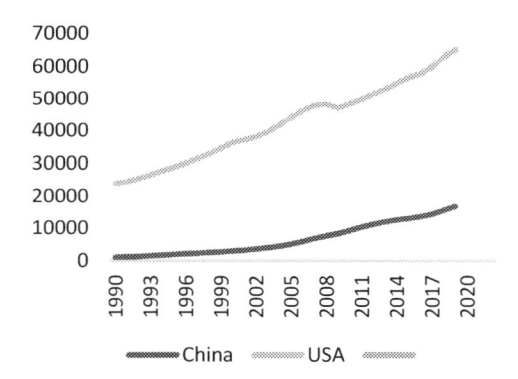

out the relevance of British labour productivity, driven by total factor productivity (TFP) to explain the so-called Great Divergence between Europe and China. Figure 3 shows the pattern of TFP. The US showed a consistent pattern, increasing since the mid-fifties, whereas China's pattern is unclear. Tian and Yu (2012) argued that the TFP evolved in ten-year cycles, being an average growth rate since 1978 of about 2.0%, contributing just to 20% of economic growth in China. Regional and sectorial disparities are significant, but since the last decade, both national trends appear to be quite close; given the time span and the marginal returns to investment in R&D, education level, and infrastructure, it might be expected an upsurge in TFP in China in the present decade.

If we recall the role of the US in creating the international institutional framework in the post-war period, the similarity of China's strategic behaviour is clear. Since 2001, China has agreed to liberalize its regime to better integrate into the world economy and offer a more predictable environment for trade and foreign investment. By the end of 2012, it launched the Regional Comprehensive Economic Partnership trade agreement, the largest trade deal in history, covering 30% of the global economy. The objective was to create a free trade zone covering about 30% of world GDP, trade, and population, eliminate tariffs on 91% of goods, induce the establishment of supply chains in Asia, and introduce rules on investment and intellectual property. It covers

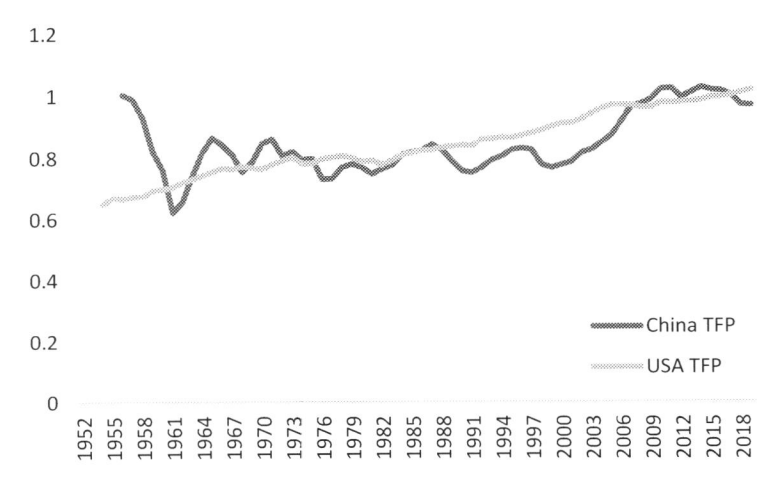

Fig. 3 Total factor productivity, constant national prices (2017 = 1) (*Source* Data from Penn World Table, version 10.0, 2021 [vd. Feenstra et al., 2015])

15 members, including China, Japan, and South Korea. The Comprehensive and Progressive Agreement for Trans-Pacific Partnership (TPP11), with 11 members, entered into force (December 2018); China filed an application to join the TPP11 in September 2021.

In 2016, the New Development Bank (NDB) became operational. The objective was to mobilize resources for infrastructure and sustainable development projects in BRICS and other emerging economies, as well as in developing countries. Perhaps a more prominent case is the multilateral development lending institution, first proposed by Chinese President Xi Jinping in 2013. As of January 2021, the Asian Infrastructure Development Bank (AIIB) has 103 members; the IMF and the World Bank have 119 members countries. The US declined. China Development Bank is the world's largest development finance institution. By the end of 2015, it had set up a business presence in 115 countries and regions worldwide. The Bank has contributed to the establishment of the Silk Road Fund and supported the preparation of the Asian Infrastructure Investment Bank. Another important source of loans is the Export–Import Bank of China, dedicated to supporting China's foreign trade, investment, and international economic cooperation. The Silk Road Fund is a medium to long-run development and investment fund established in China in 2014. Provides investment and financing support for trade, economic cooperation, and connectivity under the framework of the Belt and Road Initiative. The Fund cooperates with multilateral international institutions as the European Investment Bank among many others.

Finally, China has signed the most Authorized Economic Operator (AEO) agreement in the world to facilitate customs clearance for enterprises. Among all the 42 countries and regions holding AEO agreements with China, 18 are BRI countries and regions. Since the late 70s, China has received a significant amount of foreign direct investment and became the second-largest FDI host economy in the world.

FDI inflows to China rose by 6% in 2020 mainly due to economic growth and investment liberalization. In regional terms, developing Asia is the largest FDI recipient, more than half of global FDI. Despite the sizable influence of the pandemic, by 2020 outward FDI from China was 133 billion USD, making China the largest investor in the world. On the other hand, Asia was the only region where FDI was resilient during 2020 given it benefited from the Belt and Road Initiative, growing markets, and regional and global FDI linkages (UNCTAD, 2021, p. 18). Multinationals continue to invest strongly in China, and investment promotion agencies show optimism. One year and a half since the COVID-19 pandemic, China's economy did not contract and it is expected to grow by 8.5%, more than the US (6.5%). China maintains a dominant position, in global terms, in international development finance, propelled by the BRI strategy. It is the largest official creditor, surpassing the IMF or the World Bank. Currently, it spends at least twice as much on international development finance as the US and other major economic powers (AidData's, 2021). Horn et al. (2019) found out that Chinese lending has always had a strategic element, but the big push was the result of the going global strategy and the drastic increase in China's GDP. China has become the world's largest economy, manufacturer, merchandise trader, and holder of foreign exchange reserves; ranks second among the world's largest importers. The country is the largest commercial partner of the US, the biggest source of imports, and the third-largest US export market. Despite its strict policies, the country is fairly open to foreign trade, which represented 35.7% of its GDP in 2019 (World Bank, 2018). The evolution of the share of exports in China surpassed the US (Fig. 4); IMF forecasts a rebound of 7.8% in the volume of exports of China's goods and services in 2021. China's ten main exports include mobile and smart phones, integrated circuits, computers, tablets, computer peripherals manufacturing, software development, clothing, and steel rolling. The specialization pattern in mature and low-value-added industries is already history. China is also the second-largest foreign holder of US Treasury securities and US government debt, which help fund the federal debt and keep US interest rates low. The tensions in the US–China economic relationship increased the degree of business uncertainty in 2020, given that the US is the country's main trade partner. Similar tensions were at play with Australia although with less consequences for China. However, the Chinese government has been adopting looser economic policies to mitigate mounting risks to future growth.

4.2 China and the BRI Strategy

When China launched the BRI Strategy, the central objective was to connect countries in Central, South, and Southeast Asia with China; in the first two years, only ten countries had formally joined the initiative. The number of countries grew very quickly; seventeen other countries joined in 2015. Two years later, the Initiative was extended to Latin America. As of 23 June 2021, 140 countries and 132 international organizations had joined BRI by signing a Memorandum of Understanding (MoU)

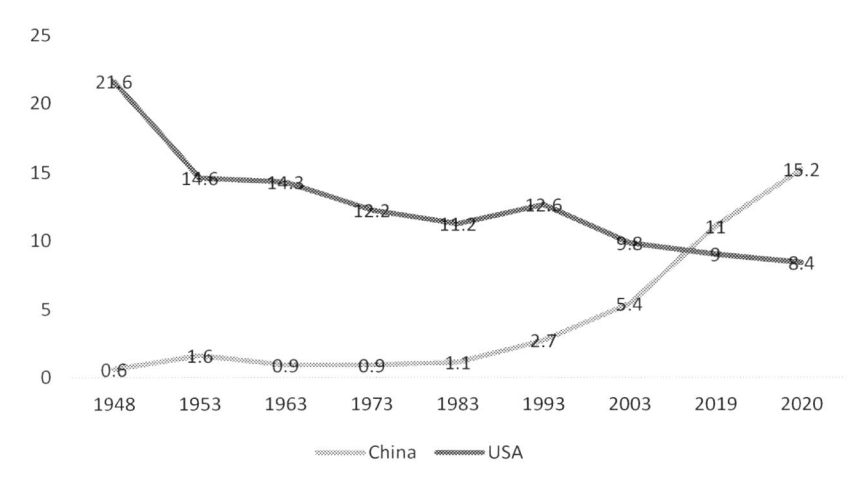

Fig. 4 Share of World Merchandise Exports—China and US 1948–2020 (%) (*Source* WTO [2021])

with China. They are spread across all continents; 40 are in Sub-Saharan Africa. BRI is now a truly global endeavour (Annex 1). BRI's countries account for about 40% of global GDP, and sixty-three per cent of the world's population. They are heterogeneous. 46% can be considered to have low or lower/middle per capita income; 25% are rich countries. When we consider population, in general, BRI countries are larger than the world average (Fig. 5). Trade value between China and Belt and Road countries between 2014 and 2019 almost doubled, from 0.7 trillion to 1.34 trillion USD (Statista, 2021), with an average annual growth of 6.1%. China has become the biggest trade partner of 25 BRI countries.

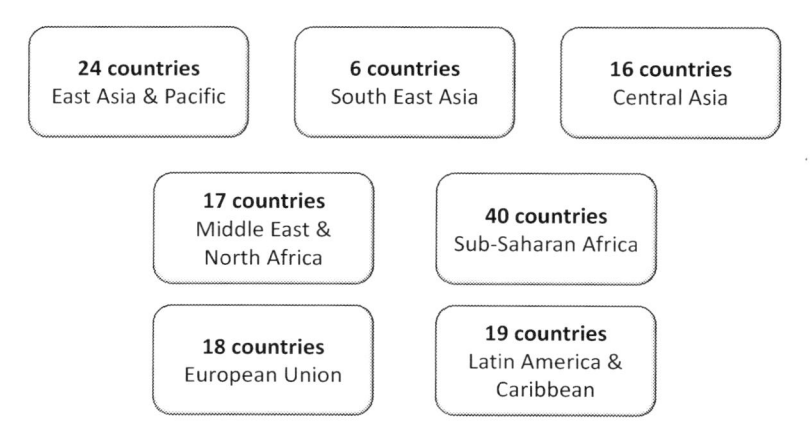

Fig. 5 Countries of the Belt and Road Initiative, 2021 (*Source* The author, based on information from Reconnecting Asia Project Database [see Annex 1])

China and other developing BRI countries are short of capital, advanced technologies, and an adequate supply of infrastructure services, essential for economic development. Infrastructures contribute to generate higher incomes, facilitate the access to productive opportunities, can improve health and education outcomes, and allow trade opening and higher productivity (Calderón & Servén, 2014, p. 2). It is, without doubt, a policy priority. For the poorest countries, it does have a transforming impact; the overall benefits to the society are larger than private returns. Several studies have estimated the global infrastructural needs, going from a cumulative investment gap of $5.2 trillion USD until 2030 (McKinsey report, 2016) to an average annual infrastructure spending requirement of $3.2 trillion USD per year between 2016 and 2040 (GI Hub, 2021, p. 24). Hard infrastructure (roads, ports, railways, power supplies, or other) determine the transaction cost of obtaining inputs, access final markets, and the capacity to realize economies of scale. Soft infrastructure includes institutions, capital social, and economic arrangements. They also determine transaction costs through social networks and legal and financial institutions.

Asia accounts for some 54% of global hard infrastructure investment needs by 2040; China alone accounts for 30% of global infrastructure needs. China's BRI aims to build connectivity and cooperation across six main economic corridors (Annex 2). Per se, BRI Initiative is a powerful strategy, with the capacity to increase global rates of growth, and decrease poverty. In the process, it can contribute to put China on the launch pad for a global hegemonic position, already underway. Global infrastructure investment in Asia, between 2007 and 2015, increased by more than 50%. China contributed more than half of this increase (GI Hub, 2021). In this same period, European investment fell. Annex 3 provides information on a large set of projects under the general umbrella of the BRI Initiative, as well as others related, but financed, in some way, by China. The overall impact is connected to the global development financial investment effort led by various Chinese institutions. This is, for example, the case of a road under construction in Afghanistan (Qauisar-Bala Mur) with a total cost of 55,304,000 USD, financed by the Asian Development Bank, or a road network in Azerbaijan, with a total estimated cost of 249,000,000, also financed by ADB. Data provides information on the status of each project, namely if they are completed, under construction, or instead still in the process of negotiation. Although the corridors, there are no obvious geographical patterns. Given the infrastructure investment gap for Africa, 39% larger than the one forecasted under current trends (GI Hub, 2021, p. 4), the number of African countries that signed BRI agreements are significantly large. Chinese loans to Africa rose from a total of 138 million US dollars to 7.6 billion USD in 2019; the peak was reached in 2016 (29.5 billion USD). Most of the financed projects have been in transport and power plants (China Africa Research Initiative, 2021).

China's global construction projects are very high. By 2017, the cumulative total was 480.3 billion dollars (OECD, 2009) for the BRI participating economies. It is not easy to distinguish, in terms of economic impact, the infrastructural projects directly supported by the BRI Initiative, and related projects. The Reconnecting Asia Project lists hundreds of them in the second decade of the twentieth century; besides the very large Chinese financial institutions, the World Bank and the European Union are also present.

4.3 Testing the Speed of Convergence for the BRI Countries

The present study tests a conditional form of convergence to compare the growth performance within and across BRI economies, in several regions, controlling for their heterogeneity. As expected, economic growth varies across different regions, namely the ones included in the Belt and Road Initiative (Tables 2 and 3).

Given these countries are competing for resources, one can ask how they are doing relative to one another. Is there a sense of network? The speed of convergence for the BRI countries was estimated using a specification of the following form (Barro & Sala-i-Martin, 1995):

$$\frac{1}{T}\log\log\left(\frac{Y_{iT}}{Y_{i0}}\right) = a - \frac{\left(1 - e^{-\beta T}\right)}{T}\log Y_{i0} + \mu \quad (1)$$

where Y_{i0} and Y_{iT} represent the per capita income in country i at time 0 and T. T is also the length of the interval; β is the speed of convergence and the last term is the error term. We estimate β nonlinearly for the periods 2000–2011, 2011–2021, and 2000–2021. The point estimate of β for the first period is 0.0079 (standard

Table 2 Per capita income levels and growth rates across regions (BRI Countries)

Regions	Average GDP per capita 2021 (in current USD)	Average GDP pc 2021 (in current PPPs)	Average annual per capita GDP growth rates 2000–2011	Average annual per capita GDP growth rates 2010–2020	Average annual per capita GDP growth rates 2000–2020
South Asia (7)	2985.9	5406.7*	4.40	3.30	1.7
European Union (12)	22,735	35,375	3.38	1.67	2.67
Europe & Central Asia (18)	6895.17	16,532.48	5.70	2.52	4.18
East Asia & Pacific (13)	11,358	22,137	4.50	3.23	3.74
Middle East & North Africa (9)	18,083.55	31,614.44	1.29	−1.02	0.15

Source The author, based on World Bank Development Indicators data (2021); Annual percentage growth rate of GDP per capita based on constant local currency. Aggregates are based on constant 2010 US dollars; * denote significance at 5% level

Table 3 Impact of the Belt and Road Initiatives on GDP

Independent variables	Dependent variable: $\frac{1}{T}\log(\frac{Y_{iT}}{Y_{i0}})$
Economic potential	367.57* (2.78)
Demographic advantage	−71.11 (−0.55)
Institutional effectiveness	90.20 (0.98)
Infrastructure development	544.83* (4.24)
Market accessibility	−138.91* (−2.08)
Resilience to natural disasters	274.45* (3.09)
R^2	0.62
N	55

Source Author calculations; this table shows the results of estimating equation (2); * denote significance at 5% level; t-statistics are shown in parentheses

error = 0.0032); for the period 2011–2021 it is 0.0361 (standard error = 0.00237), and finally for the whole sample it is 0.0061 (standard error = 0.0019). The main conclusion is that BRI countries tended to converge at a speed of about 3.6% per year in the period 2011–2021. It was also tested for conditional convergence across countries and regions with other variables, namely the log of the infrastructural BRI development index.

$$\frac{1}{T}\log\log\left(\frac{Y_{iT}}{Y_{i0}}\right) = a + b_1 \log\log(Y_{i0}) + b_2 \log\log(\text{infrast}) + \mu_{iT} \quad (2)$$

Coefficients were all statistically significant, and the estimated $b_1 < 0$; then it is possible to say that data exhibits conditional beta convergence, implying that countries further away from the steady state will grow at a faster rate than countries which are nearer to it. We also test the causal relationship between GDP per capita and a measure of the BRI, an index elaborated by Knight Frank (2018), disaggregated into six categories: economic potential, demographic advantage, institutional effectiveness, infrastructural development, market accessibility, and resilience to natural disasters. Each country's market was assessed to these criteria, and later the values in each category have been normalized. According to information available (2018), Singapore, Qatar, and the United Arab Emirates top the index. The dependent variable is real GDP per capita in 2021, for the BRI countries. As expected, infrastructural development exerts a more significant impact on GDP.

Competition between the European Union, the US, and China is increasing and diversifying. By December 2021, the European Union announced a plan to invest $340 billion globally by 2027 as an alternative to China's BRI. The scheme, Global Gateway, is to strengthen Europe's supply chains, boost EU trade, focusing on digitalization, health, climate, energy, and transport sectors, as well as on education and research. According to Von der Leyen (2021), this would be "a true alternative," offered "under fair and favorable terms" so as not to leave governments of third countries with a debt problem. The US also revealed interest in adopting a strategy based on an effective alternative to BRI to ensure American companies operate on a level playing field, including advanced technologies and business practices.

4.4 Networks and Market Shares

By 3 December 2021, as a BRI project, China launched its first cross-border train from Laos. A 1.035 km electrified passenger and cargo railway, it assumed a great significance to bilateral economic, social, and cultural exchanges. Besides China, Laos shares borders with Vietnam, Thailand, Myanmar, and Cambodia, which offered Beijing to extend the train to those countries. With the train, Laos turns into a land-linked hub, boosting regional connectivity and supply chain resilience. The larger the number of countries involved in the Initiative, the larger the presence of product-specific network effects. It allows direct networks through establishing and reinforcing interconnections among consumers and firms along supply chains, but also indirectly diplomatic relationships. As more countries conclude infrastructural projects and investments, more countries will be interested to enter in new negotiations towards BRI projects and to accept Chinese economic and political influence. Following Church and Gandal (2005), as the number of a given hardware brand consumers increase, more software will be written for that specific brand, and the final equilibrium will depend on the number of users rather than software applications.

Supply chains have become networks that span across countries and continents supplying goods and services, involving the flow of information, processes, and resources. Over the next decade, companies that engage with more success with customers, wherever they are, will capture about 90% of industry growth. Marketplaces become more and more connected, going beyond the linear paradigm of the value chain of the past, and require integrated transport systems and emerging technologies, partners, and access to financial and legal institutions—and a sense of integration. Network externalities can be assumed as a mechanism to analyse the evolution of market shares (Skrzypacz & Mitchell, 2005). Our approach is close to Griva and Vettas (2004); they employ the standard Hotelling "linear-city" model with quadratic transportation costs to capture horizontal differentiation, and then introduce a network effect. We propose to depart from a static Cournot duopoly model. We assume two heterogeneous players, China, and the United States (C; US), employing different strategies; no other players can enter the market, and it is not allowed collusive behaviour. Both players compete in quantities, and act strategically based on product differentiation with respect to variety, and quality. Accounting for quality, we assume vertical differentiation to be the set of non-price competition incentives, including institutional regulation, or military leadership. As usual, each player aims to maximize its expected profit, corresponding in our model to the recognition of a dominant or hegemonic position in global markets.

19 The Belt and Road Initiative: Can It Signalize a New Pendulum Movement?

Some individual states, taken as heterogeneous consumers, might prefer to be included in one or another sphere of influence, and accept or not to sign agreements towards investment flows or infrastructural projects. They are assumed to have different preferences over the products, but they always prefer the largest network. There are positive network externalities given that they will benefit from an increase in the adoption rate. Given the differential BRI strategy, the increase in the number of infrastructural projects directly or indirectly supported by China financial institutions, with local and regional impact through borders, will tend to generate additional positive externalities and induce more negotiations. It will work as if more consumers look after more products, direct construction, or FDI. Even assuming player the US as holding an initial competitive advantage, being the leader, intuition suggests that network externalities will tend to encourage a divergence in the market shares allowing C to grow relative to the leader, given this one it will not adopt such a strategy.

We start from a Hotelling type model. Firm's location is given. Suppose two firms, competing between them, located at the ends of a linear city, populated by a uniform distribution of consumers. Both firms sell an identical product, and given price is the same, consumers would buy from the closest seller. Consumers act to maximize their surplus. To maximize profits, both firms will move from their initial location to the centre of the city, which is the Nash equilibrium. This result is commonly used to explain, for example, why political parties, as product attributes, are many times very similar to each other. However, let's consider that consumers of each firm's product form a network; everyone derives utility from the network size of the firm he has chosen. That is to say, the surplus that a consumer derives from buying the good depends on the number of other consumers of the same, or alike goods, who join the network. Following Griva and Vettas (2004, p. 5), we assume that consumers' choice and the decision is based on expectations about each firm's (C, US) network size; all consumers can form identical expectations. To allow for ideological, political, or diplomatic loyalty inside each network, we consider that brands are incompatible. Each consumer is allowed to choose to integrate just one network. As in Katz and Shapiro (1985, p. 426), the output game then generates a set of prices. Formally, let $q_{i,t}$ be the quantity sold by firm i in time t. Let also $P_{i,t} > 0$. A given consumer located at point $x \epsilon [C, US]$ will be indifferent between the two firms when their costs are the same

$$P_C + tx^2 - \beta x^e = P_{US} + t(1-x)^2 - \beta(1-x^e)$$

where P_i, is the firm i's price, $i = C$, US. t is an index of cultural and political distance. $\beta > 0$ measures the network effect induced by the assumed strategy. x^e is the number of consumers expected to buy firm C product. Solving for x, the location of a consumer indifferent between C or US came to be

$$x = \frac{P_{US} - P_C + \beta(2x^e - 1) + t}{2t}$$

Each firm's strategy is conditional on the history of the game; the US tries to maintain the hegemonic position based on military leadership and information technology control, while China tries to maximize international trade, FDI flows, and infrastructural projects. Individual states, independent from their geographic location, are potential consumers, each one choosing a product that maximizes his utility. Every consumer will adhere, or not, to the player's C strategy (or US), and derives welfare maximization given the network size based on the expectation about each country's network.

$$U_i^t + U^{Nn}(q_{i,t}) + U^{no}(q_{i,t-1}) - p_i$$

The utility of a consumer located at x and buying the product, let's say accepting the integration on BRI projects, depends on the transportation cost or the index of cultural distance (U_i^t), representing the value of the product in itself. Depends also on the set of network effects from new consumers (Nn), and finally from the network effects from old consumers, U^{no}. U_i^t is strictly decreasing in distance, but the network effects from new ($U^{Nn}(q_{i,t})$) and old consumers ($U^{no}(q_{i,t-1})$) are strictly increasing.

Griva and Vettas (2004, p. 8) showed that if expectations, exogenously given, "are that market share differences exceed a given threshold, then the firm expected to have a larger market share captures the entire market." Allowing manipulation of consumer's expectations by any, or both players, through prices, with strong network effects, Griva and Vettas (2004, pp. 12–14) derived that only one of the two firms will capture the entire market.

Given players compete on quantities, and produce unequal levels of output, intuition suggests that multiple equilibrium is possible. If the network is strong, the equilibrium market share of each one of the players will increase as β (network effect induced by the assumed strategy) increases. The expectation formation process, being rational, will depend on each player's reputation. Therefore, each of the players will be interested in investing in strengthening their reputation, namely by proposing new programmes of horizontal strategic support, or even vertical differentiation. For example, see the recent competition between the US and China over political influence (Summit for Democracy, US, December 2021; International Forum on Democracy, Beijing, December 2021). As firms compete to control the links that are created between flows of people, goods, finance, and data, these flows cut across spheres of influence creating new maps of geopolitical power and reinforcing expectations.

5 Conclusion

Forecasting the future is too demanding and ambitious. Throughout history, several countries maintained a world hegemonic position. This occurred between 1820 and 1870 with the British hegemony, and between 1945 and 1973 with the American hegemony. In both cases, hegemony was stable, based on a set of universal rules and supranational institutions, and the world economy expanded, associated with a free trade orientation. Throughout history, game changers associated with technological progress, economic growth, geopolitical reasons, and new ideas have been able to change power dynamics in the international context. Things are not forever.

Nowadays, the centre of gravity of economic activities shifted in its dynamism from the Atlantic axis to the Pacific. We developed an approach to discuss the likelihood of a potential movement of the economic and political pendulum, back to Orient. Despite its simplicity, some general points emerge. China was able to emerge as the leading country in the global markets, and it was very quick, and pragmatic, to be able to do it. The increase in the nonagricultural sector, namely in the proportion of the labour force employed and in the capital labour ratio should be associated with changes in social institutions, more efficient capital market, the formation of a middle class and greater human capital, the emergence of industrialization, innovation, and success in international trade. In the same direction as the US, China worked to create multilateral and global financial institutions, as well as a network of economic and political influence, based on a strategy of differentiation like BRI. The influence of a large infrastructural investment contributed to economic growth, relative conditional convergence, and reputation. If economic growth will be real, if political influence will be consistent, and if transition in China to market mechanisms and institutions will be complete, then it will be possible for a new movement in the pendulum, back to Orient—and eventually, in the future, a new homogenous world power. Recent competitive movements from the US and Europe recognize this.

6   Annex 1: List of BRIC Countries (2021)

Income level per capita	Countries	Region
Low-income economies ($1036 or less) Main instruments of lending*** • Direct loans • FDI in commodity producing industries, transport, and energy ** 240 total infrastructural projects, 7 financed in the context of the Belt and Road Initiative (twenty-first century). 29.6% under construction. BRI projects financed by Asian Development Bank **22% in power plants, 46% in roads, 16.9% in railways, 5.1% in transmission	Afghanistan** Burundi Chad Congo, Dem Rep Ethiopia The Gambia Guinea Liberia Madagascar Mali Mozambique Niger Rwanda Senegal Sierra Leone Somalia South Sudan Tajikistan** Tanzania Togo Uganda Yemen, Rep.** Zimbabwe	South Asia Sub-Saharan Africa Sub-Saharan Africa Sub-Saharan Africa Sub-Saharan Africa Sub-Saharan Africa Sub-Saharan Africa Sub-Saharan Africa Sub-Saharan Africa Sub-Saharan Africa Sub-Saharan Africa Sub-Saharan Africa Sub-Saharan Africa Sub-Saharan Africa Sub-Saharan Africa Sub-Saharan Africa Sub-Saharan Africa Europe & Central Asia Sub-Saharan Africa Sub-Saharan Africa Sub-Saharan Africa Middle East & North Africa Sub-Saharan Africa

(continued)

(continued)

Income level per capita	Countries	Region
Lower middle-income economies ($1036 to $4045) Main instruments of lending*** • Direct loans • Sovereign bond • Swap lines • FDI, mainly in energy and transport ** 5756 total infrastructural projects, 155 financed in the context of the Belt and Road Initiative (twenty-first century). 41% under construction. 52% of total BRI projects financed by Asian Development Bank **72% in power plants, 18.6% in roads, 4.8% in railways, 2.2% in seaports construction	Angola Bangladesh** Benin* Bhutan** Comoros* Bolivia Cabo Verde Cambodia** Cameroon Côte d'Ivoire Djibouti Egypt, Arab Rep El Salvador Georgia** India** Indonesia Iran, Islamic Rep.** Kenya Kiribati Kyrgyz Republic** Lao PDR** Lesotho Mauritania Micronesia Fed Sts Moldova Mongolia** Morocco Myanmar** Nepal** Nigeria Pakistan** Papua New Guinea Philippines** Solomon Islands Sri Lanka** Sudan Tajikistan** Timor-Leste Tunisia Ukraine** Uzbekistan** Vanuatu Vietnam** Zambia Zimbabwe	Sub-Saharan Africa South Asia Sub-Saharan Africa South Asia Sub-Saharan Africa Latin America & Caribbean Sub-Saharan Africa East Asia & Pacific Sub-Saharan Africa Sub-Saharan Africa Middle East & North Africa Middle East & North Africa Latin America & Caribbean Europe & Central Asia South Asia East Asia & Pacific Middle East & North Africa Sub-Saharan Africa East Asia & Pacific Europe & Central Asia East Asia & Pacific Sub-Saharan Africa Sub-Saharan Africa East Asia & Pacific Europe & Central Asia East Asia & Pacific Middle East & North Africa East Asia & Pacific South Asia Sub-Saharan Africa South Asia East Asia & Pacific East Asia & Pacific East Asia & Pacific South Asia Sub-Saharan Africa Europe & Central Asia East Asia & Pacific Middle East & North Africa Europe & Central Asia Europe & Central Asia East Asia & Pacific East Asia & Pacific Sub-Saharan Africa Sub-Saharan Africa

(continued)

(continued)

Income level per capita	Countries	Region
Upper middle-income economies ($4046 to $12,535) Main instruments of lending*** • Direct loans • Sovereign bond • Swap lines • FDI, mainly in energy and transport ** 6526 total infrastructural projects, 209 financed in the context of the Belt and Road Initiative (twenty-first century). 18.2% under construction. Most part of total BRI projects financed by Asian Development Bank **77% in power plants, 7.8% in roads, 12% in railways construction	Albania**	Europe & Central Asia
	Algeria	Middle East & North Africa
	Armenia**	Europe & Central Asia
	Azerbaijan**	Europe & Central Asia
	Belarus**	Europe & Central Asia
	Bosnia & Herzegovina**	Europe & Central Asia
	Botswana	Sub-Saharan Africa
	Bulgaria**	Europe & Central Asia
	Brunei Darussalam	East Asia & Pacific
	Dominica *	Latin America & Caribbean
	China**	East Asia & Pacific
	Cook Island	East Asia & Pacific
	Costa Rica	Latin America & Caribbean
	Cuba	Latin America & Caribbean
	Dominican Republic	Latin America & Caribbean
	Ecuador	Latin America & Caribbean
	Equatorial Guinea	Sub-Saharan Africa
	Fiji	East Asia & Pacific
	Gabon	Sub-Saharan Africa
	Grenade	Latin America & Caribbean
	Guyana	Latin America & Caribbean
	Iraq**	Middle East & North Africa
	Jamaica	Latin America & Caribbean
	Jordan**	Middle East & North Africa
	Kazakhstan**	Europe & Central Asia
	Lebanon	Middle East & North Africa
	Libya	Middle East & North Africa
	Malaysia**	East Asia & Pacific
	Maldives**	East Asia & Pacific
	Montenegro**	Europe & Central Asia
	Namibia	Sub-Saharan Africa
	North Macedonia**	Europe & Central Asia
	Peru	Latin America & Caribbean
	Russia Federation**	Europe & Central Asia
	Samoa	East Asia & Pacific
	Serbia**	Europe & Central Asia
	South Africa	Sub-Saharan Africa
	Suriname	Latin America & Caribbean
	Thailand**	East Asia & Pacific
	Tonga	East Asia & Pacific
	Turkey**	Europe & Central Asia
	Turkmenistan**	Europe & Central Asia
	Venezuela, RB	Latin America & Caribbean

(continued)

(continued)

Income level per capita	Countries	Region
High-income economies ($12,536 or more) Main instruments of lending*** • Large-scale sovereign bonds purchase • Central bank swap lines • FDI in high-tech, finance, energy, and transport ** 3950 total infrastructural projects, 199 financed in the context of the Belt and Road Initiative (twenty-first century). 25.2% under construction **55.8% in power plants, 22.8% in roads, 15.8% in railways construction	Antigua & Barbuda Austria*, ** Bahrain** Barbados Brunei Darussalam** Chile Croatia** Cyprus** Czech Republic** Estonia** Greece** Hungary** Israel** Italy** Korea, Rep Kuwait Latvia** Lithuania** Luxembourg Malta New Zealand Nieu Oman** Panama Poland** Portugal Qatar** Romania** Saudi Arabia** Seychelles Singapore** Slovak Republic Slovenia Trinidad and Tobago United Arab Emirates Uruguay	Latin America & Caribbean Europe & Central Asia Middle East & North Africa Latin America & Caribbean East Asia & Pacific Latin America & Caribbean Europe & Central Asia Europe & Central Asia Europe & Central Asia Europe & Central Asia Europe & Central Asia Europe & Central Asia Middle East and North Africa Europe & Central Asia East Asia & Pacific Middle East & North Africa Europe & Central Asia Europe & Central Asia Europe & Central Asia Middle East & North Africa East Asia & Pacific East Asia & Pacific Middle East & North Africa Latin America & Caribbean Europe & Central Asia Europe & Central Asia Middle East & North Africa Europe & Central Asia Middle East & North Africa Sub-Saharan Africa East Asia & Pacific Europe & Central Asia Europe & Central Asia Latin America & Caribbean Middle East & North Africa Latin America & Caribbean

Source Constructed by the author, based on World Bank data (2021) and Green Finance & Development Center, 2021)
* The information concerning these countries and the Belt and Road Initiative is contradictory; ** countries with available data in the Reconnecting Asia Project DataBase; *** Horn, Reihart, and Trebesch, 2019.

7 Annex 2: Silk road economic belt: development corridors

Corridor	Core objectives
New Eurasian Land-Bridge Economic Corridor (NELBEC)	Link between China and Europe (11,870 km). Infrastructural investments in high-speed railway, as well in a 7200 km long multi-mode network of ship, rail, and route road for moving freight between India, Iran, Afghanistan, Azerbaijan, Russia, Central Asia, and Europe
China–Mongolia–Russia Economic Corridor (CMREC)	Entered into force on 21 September 2018. Infrastructural projects in transport sector and energy
China–Central Asia–West Asia Economic Corridor (CCWAEC)	Links China and the Arabian Peninsula, covering the trajectory of the ancient Silk Road
China–Indochina Peninsula Economic Corridor (CICPEC)	Links China and Indochina Peninsula, through Vietnam, Laos, Cambodia, Thailand, Myanmar, and Malaysia. Investments on a network of railways and highways
Bangladesh–China–India–Myanmar Economic Corridor (BCIMEC)	It links ASEAN Free Trade Area, ASEAN–China Free Trade Area, and ASEAN–India Free Trade Area. A combination of road, rail, water, and air linkages
China–Pakistan Economic Corridor (CPEC)	Pilot project of the Belt and Road Initiative. It focuses on road, port, energy, transportation infrastructures, and connectivity

8 Annex 3: BRI and related projects

19 The Belt and Road Initiative: Can It Signalize a New Pendulum Movement?

Countries	Number of projects		BARI index**	Type of projects					
	BRI	BRI & related*	BRI	Inter modal	Road and railways	Power plants	Seaport	Pipeline	Transmission
Afghanistan	4	41	27.63	5	28	5	0	0	5
Albania	2	29	48.09	0	24	9	3	0	0
Armenia	1	35	39.88	4	18	13	0	0	0
Austria	1	50	–	0	1	49	0	0	0
Azerbaijan	8	37	39.12	1	27	3	3	3	0
Bahrain	1	13	54.64	1	3	6	3	0	0
Bangladesh	31	216	40.91	15	137	56	6	0	0
Belarus	7	42	34.41	3	28	9	0	0	2
Benin*	–	11	–	–	–	–	–	–	–
Bhutan	1	66	54.21	1	54	10	0	0	0
Bosnia & Herzegovina	6	54	39.76	0	29	24	1	0	0
Brunei	1	3	53.32	0	2	0	1	0	0
Bulgaria	33	74	–	0	31	31	2	0	0
Burundi*	–	8	–	–	–	–	–	–	–
Cambodia	33	74	44.74	4	67	20	3	0	0
Chad*	–	5	–	–	–	–	–	–	–
China	23	3431	57.09	21	145	3260	14	1	0
Comoros*	–	3	–	–	–	–	–	–	–
DR Congo*	–	55	–	–	–	–	–	–	–
Croatia	8	46	46.22	0	17	17	15	0	0
Cyprus	0	7	–	0	1	6	0	0	0
Czech Republic	0	103	51.51	0	79	24	0	0	0
Ethiopia	–	52	43.36	–	–	–	–	–	–

(continued)

(continued)

Countries	Number of projects		BARI index**	Type of projects						
	BRI	BRI & related*	BRI	Inter modal	Road and railways	Power plants	Seaport	Pipeline	Transmission	
Estonia	3	20	55.42	1	2	17	4	0	0	
Gambia*	–	1	–	–	–	–	–	–	–	
Georgia	6	78	49.63	5	50	21	2	0	0	
Greece	1	39	–	0	20	17	2	0	0	
Guinea*	–	16	–	–	–	–	–	–	–	
Hungary	3	56	50.49	1	37	18	0	0	0	
India	18	1991	52.46	9	184	1768	29	1	0	
Indonesia	15	317	47.48	1	71	225	20	0	0	
Iran	6	285	35.88	10	63	209	3	0	0	
Iraq	2	79	26.45	0	3	73	3	0	0	
Israel	3	36	53.15	0	1	33	0	0	0	
Italy	1	181	–	0	1	179	1	0	0	
Jordan	10	47	44.96	0	0	46	1	0	0	
Laos	11	121	46.94	0	37	83	0	0	1	
Latvia	2	19	50.14	0	5	10	4	0	0	
Liberia*	–	2	–	–	–	–	–	–	–	
Lithuania	1	18	51.19	0	4	14	1	0	0	
Kazakhstan	26	52	44.45	6	18	26	0	1	0	
Kyrgyzstan	21	72	39.49	2	56	13	0	0	1	
Macedonia	2	26	42.78	0	20	6	0	0	0	
Madagascar*	–	6	–	–	–	–	–	–	–	
Malaysia	4	169	55.50	1	82	78	7	0	0	

(continued)

(continued)

Countries	Number of projects		BARI index**	Type of projects						
	BRI	BRI & related*	BRI	Inter modal	Road and railways	Power plants	Seaport	Pipeline	Transmission
Maldives	1	3	51.70	0	1	0	1	0	0
Mali**	–	11	–	–	–	–	–	–	–
Mongolia	8	57	51.72	3	27	26	0	0	1
Montenegro	4	20	47.41	0	14	6	0	0	0
Mozambique*	–	19	–	–	–	–	–	–	–
Myanmar	4	123	42.74	5	36	78	4	0	0
Nepal	8	183	32.58	4	40	135	0	0	4
Niger*	–	6	–	–	–	–	–	–	–
Oman	2	58	53.04	1	35	18	4	0	0
Pakistan	107	285	38.07	2	84	187	9	1	2
Philippines	5	268	39.78	3	39	204	21	0	0
Poland	1	282	51.59	1	174	97	10	0	0
Qatar	2	17	59.98	0	4	9	4	0	0
Romania	3	118	45.63	1	56	57	4	0	0
Russia	19	778	37.67	15	497	236	25	3	2
Rwanda*	–	13	–	–	–	–	–	–	–
Saudi Arabia	8	105	48.59	0	13	90	2	0	0
Senegal*	–	17	–	–	–	–	–	–	–
Serbia	9	81	43.50	3	55	22	1	0	0
Sierra Leone*	–	7	–	–	–	–	–	–	–
Singapore	1	39	69.85	0	15	19	6	0	0
South Sudan*	–	2	–	–	–	–	–	–	–

(continued)

(continued)

Countries	Number of projects		BARI index**	Type of projects					
	BRI	BRI & related*	BRI	Inter modal	Road and railways	Power plants	Seaport	Pipeline	Transmission
Sri Lanka	12	78	42.44	3	38	31	6	0	0
Tajikistan	16	56	36.38	5	47	25	0	2	2
Tanzania*	–	12	–	–	–	–	–	–	–
Thailand	6	188	46.45	2	54	126	6	0	0
Togo*	–	17	–	–	–	–	–	–	–
Turkey	8	420	46.33	18	50	338	13	1	0
Turkmenistan	1	20	41.80	0	11	7	1	1	0
Uganda*	–	17	–	–	–	–	–	–	–
Ukraine	4	82	35.81	2	16	63	7	0	0
Uzbekistan	5	52	37.75	2	32	18	0	0	0
Vietnam	21	349	51.45	7	45	295	11	0	0
Zimbabwe*	–	29	–	–	–	–	–	–	–
Yemen	1	12	26.67	0	0	11	0	1	0

Bibliographic References

AidData's. (2021). AidData's Global Chinese Development Finance Dataset, Version 2.0. *AIDDATA, A Research Lab at William and Mary.* https://www.aiddata.org/data/aiddatas-global-chinese-development-finance-dataset-version-2-0.
Arrighi, G. (1990, Summer). The three hegemonies of historical capitalism. *Review (Fernand Braudel Center), 13*(3), 365–408.
Barro, R. J., & Sala-i-Martin, X. (1995, June). *Technological diffusion, convergence and growth* (Working Paper No. 5151). NBER National Bureau of Economic Research.
Barton, D., Chen, Y., & Jin, A. (2013, June 1). Generational change and the rising prosperity of inland cities will power consumption for years to come, Mapping China´s middle class. *McKinsey Quaterly.* https://www.mckinsey.com/industries/retail/our-insights/mapping-chinas-middle-class.
Blackwill, R., & Wright, T. (2020). *The end of world order and American foreign policy.* Council on Foreign Relations.
Boswell, T. (2004, Summer). American world empire or declining hegemony. *Journal of World-System Research, 10*(2), 516–524.
Brands, H., & Sullivan, J. (2020, May). And a lot is riding on whether Washington can figure out which strategy Beijing has chosen. *Foreign Policy.*
Brandt, L., & Rawski, T. (Eds.). (2008). *China's great economic transformation.* Cambridge University Press.
Brandt, L., Van Biesebroeck, J., & Zhang, Y. (2012). Creative accounting or creative destruction? Firm-level productivity growth in Chinese manufacturing. *Journal of Development Economics, 97*(2), 339–351.
Brandt, L., & Zhu, X. (2010). *Accounting for China's growth* (IZA Discussion Papers, No. 4764). Institute for the Study of Labor (IZA), Bonn.
Breslin, S. (2009). Understanding China's regional rise: Interpretations, identities and implications. *International Affairs, 85*(4), 817–835.
Broadberry, S. (2021). Accounting for the great divergence: Recent findings from historical national accounting. University of Oxford, *Oxford Economic and Social History Working Papers* Number 187.
Calderón, C., & Servén, L. (2014). Infrastructure, growth, and inequality: An overview. *Policy Research Working Paper,* 7034, *World Bank.*
China Africa Research Initiative. (2021). *School of advanced international studies.* John Hopkins University.
Church, J. R., & Gandal, N. (2005). Platform competition in telecommunications. *Amsterdam Handbook of Telecommunications, 2.*
Clark, I. (2009). Bringing hegemony back in: The United States and international order. *International Affairs, 85*(1), 24.
Corden, W. M. (1990, Summer-Fall). American decline and the end of hegemony. *SAIS Review, 10*(2), 13–26.
Cox, R. (1987). *Production power and world order: Social forces in the making of history.* Columbia University Press.
Cugat, G., & Narita, F. (2020). How COVID-19 will increase inequality in emerging markets and developing economies. *IMF Blog.*
Deardorff, A. (1998). Determinants of bilateral trade: Does gravity work in a neoclassical world?. *The Regionalization of the World Economy.*
Dollar, D. (2019). Understanding China's Belt and Road infrastructure projects in Africa. *Global China.* Brookings.
Dong, W. (2021, May). The world could look like this. *China Focus.* https://www.chinausfocus.com/videos/the-world-could-look-like-this-wang-dong.
Feenstra, R. C., Inklaar, R., & Timmer, M. P. (2015). The next generation of the penn world table. *American Economic Review, 105*(10), 3150–3182.

Frank, K. (2018, January). *The belt and road index.* https://www.knightfrank.com/blog/2018/01/30/the-belt-and-road-index.

Friedman, M., & Savage, L. J. (1952). The expected utility hypothesis and the measurability of utility. *The Journal of Political Economy, 60*(6), 463–474.

Gelpern, A., Horn, S., Morris, S., Parks, B., & Trebesch, C. (2021). *How China lends: A rare look into 100 debt contracts with foreign governments.* Peterson Institute for International Economics, Kiel Institute for the World Economy, Center for Global Development, and AidData at William & Mary.

GI Hub. (2021). *Global infrastructure hub, non-profit organization formed by G20.* Retrieved on December 2021, from https://www.gihub.org/about/about/.

Gill, S., & Law, D. (1986). Global hegemony and the structural power of capital. *International Studies Quarterly, 33*(4), 475–499.

Gilpin, R. (1981). *War & change in world politics.* Cambridge University Press.

Gilpin, R. (1987). *The political economy of international relations.* Princeton University Press.

Gramsci, A. (1971). *Selections from the Prison notebooks.* International Publishers.

Griva, K., & Vettas, N. (2004). Price competition in a differentiated products duopoly under network effects. *CEPR Discussion Papers* 4574.

Gu, C., Hu, L., Cook, I. G. (2017). China's urbanization in 1949–2015: Processes and driving forces. *China Geographic Science, 27*(6), 847–859.

Hass, R. (2021, August 12). *The "new normal" in US-China relations: Hardening competition and deep interdependence.* Retrieved on December 2021, from https://www.brookings.edu/blog/order-from-chaos/2021/08/12/the-new-normal-in-us-china-relations-hardening-competition-and-deep-interdependence/.

Hopkins, A. G. (2002). *Globalization in world history.* W.W. Norton & Company.

Hopkins, T. K., & Wallerstein, I. (1979). *Processes of the world-system.* Sage.

Horn, S., Reinhart, C., & Trebesch, C. (2019). China's overseas lending. NBER working paper 26050.

Ikenberry, J. G. (1993). The political origins of Bretton woods. In M. Bordo, & B. Eichengreen (Eds.), A *retrospective on the Bretton woods system: Lessons for international monetary reform* (Chapter 3). University of Chicago Press.

Ikenberry, J. G. (2020). *A world safe for democracy: Liberal internationalisms and the cries of global order.* Yale University Press.

Ikenberry, J. G., & Lim, D. J. (2017). *China's emerging institutional statecraft The Asian Infrastructure Investment Bank and the prospects for counter-hegemony.* Project on International Order and Strategy at Brooking.

Jie, J., Hou, J., Wang, C., & Liu, H. Y. (2021). COVID-19 impact on firm investment—Evidence from Chinese publicly listed firms. *Journal of Asian Economics, 75*, 1–16.

Katz, M. L., & Shapiro, C. (1985). Network externalities, competition, and compatibility. *The American Economic Review, 75*(3), 424–440.

Kennedy, P. (1988). *The rise and fall of the great powers: The economic change and military conflict from 1500–2000.* Random House.

Keohane, R. (1984). *After hegemony: Cooperation and discord in the world political economy.* Princeton University Press.

Kindleberger, C. P. (1973). *The world in depression: 1929–1939.*

Kuijs, L., & Wang, T. (2005). "China's pattern of growth: Moving to sustainability and reducing inequality. *World Bank.* Working Paper 3767.

Kuznets, S. (1973). Modern economic growth: Findings and reflections. *The American Economic Review, 63*(3), 247–258.

Kwon, R. (2011, December). Hegemonies in the world-system: An empirical assessment of hegemonic sequences from the 16th to the 20th century. *Sociological Perspectives,* 593–617.

Lakner, C., & Milanovic, B. (2013). Global income distribution from the fall of the berlin wall to the great recession. *World Bank, Policy Research Working Paper* 6719.

Lakner, C., & Milanovic, B. (2016). *Global income distribution: From the fall of the berlin wall to the great recession*. Oxford University Press on behalf of the World Bank. https://openknowl edge.worldbank.org/handle/10986/29118. License: CC BY-NC-ND 3.0 IGO.

Latham, A. (2012). *Managing China's rise: Lessons from 1914*. Retrieved on December 2021, from https://www.e-ir.info/2021/08/16/managing-chinas-rise-lessons-from-1914/.

Lin, J. Y. (2011). China and the global economy. *China Economic Journal, 4*(1), 1–14.

Liu, D., Xiao, X., Li, H., & Wang, W. (2015). Historical evolution and benefit–cost explanation of periodical fluctuation in coal mine safety supervision: An evolutionary game analysis framework. *European Journal of Operational Research, 243*(3), 974–984.

Loorbach, D., Frantzeskaki, N., & Avelino, F. (2017). Sustainability transitions research: Transforming science and practice for societal change. *Annual Review of Environment and Resources, 42*(1), 599–626.

Maddison, A. (1995). *Monitoring the world economy 1820–1992*. OECD Development Centre Studies.

Mahbubani, K. (2021, January 27). Why attempts to build a new anti-China alliance will fail. *Foreign Policy*.

McKinsey report. (2016, June). *Bridging global infrastructure gaps*. McKinsey & Company. https://www.un.org/pga/71/wp-content/uploads/sites/40/2017/06/Bridging-Global-Infrastru cture-Gaps-Full-report-June-2016.pdf.

Mearsheimer, J. J. (2021, November/December). The inevitable rivalry: America, China, and the tragedy of great-power politics. *Foreign Affairs*.

Modelski, G. (1987). *Long cycles in world politics*. Macmillan.

Modelski, G., & Thompson, W. R. (1988). *Seapower in global politics*. University of Washington Press.

Nedopil, C. (2021). *Countries of the Belt and Road initiative*. Shanghai, Green Finance & Development Center, FISF Fudan University. Retrieved on December 2021, from www.greenf dc.org

Niblett, R., & Vinjamuri, L. (2021). The liberal order begins at home. In C. A. Kupchan & L. Vinjamuri (Eds.), *Anchoring the world: International order in the twenty-first century*. Council on Foreign Relations/Royal Institute of International Affairs.

OECD. (2009). *OECD Economic Outlook* (Vol. 2009, Issue 2). China.

Plum, J. H. (2017). Introdução. In C. R. Boxer (Ed.), *O Império Marítimo Português* (Vol. 70). Edições.

Pomeranz, K. (2000). *The great divergence: China, Europe, and the making of the modern world economy*. Princeton University Press.

Qin, Y. (2014). Continuity through change: Background knowledge and China's international strategy. *The Chinese Journal of International Politics, 7*(3), 285–314.

Qs World University Rankings. (2021). https://www.topuniversities.com/university-rankings/world-university-rankings/2021.

Rodrik, D., & Walt, S. (2021). How to construct a new global order. *HKS Faculty Research Working Paper* Serie n°13, Harvard Kennedy School.

Schmidt, B. (2019). *The debate on American hegemony*. Doc Research Institute. Retrieved on December 2021, from https://doc-research.org/2019/06/the-debate-on-american-hegemony/

Schweller, R., & Pu, X. (2011). After unipolarity: China's visions of international order in an era of U.S. decline. *International Security, 36*(1), 41–72.

Shambaugh, D. (2013). *China goes global: The partial power*. Oxford University Press.

Silva-Ruete, J. (2006). *The development of China's export performance*. Retrieved on December 2021, from https://www.imf.org/en/News/Articles/2015/09/28/04/53/sp030706.

Skrzypacz, A., & Mitchell, M. F. (2005). Network externalities and long-run market shares. *Stanford GSB Research Paper* No. 1879.

Sorokin, P. (1957). *Social and cultural dynamics*. Porter Sargent.

Strange, S. (1987, Autumn). The persistent myth of lost hegemony. *International Organization, 41*(4), 551–574.

Tanzi, A. (2021, September). More than 1 billion Asians will join middle class by 2030, in market economics. *Blomberg.* https://www.bloomberg.com/news/articles/2021-09-02/more-than-1-billion-asians-will-join-global-middle-class-by-2030?leadSource=uverify%20wall.

Tian, T., & Yu, X. (2012). *The enigmas of TFP in China: A meta analysis* (Discussion Papers, No. 113). Georg-August-Universität Göttingen, Courant Research Centre - Poverty, Equity and Growth (CRC-PEG), Göttingen.

UNCTAD. (2021). *World investment report 2021.* https://unctad.org/system/files/official-document/wir2021_en.pdf.

Von der Leyen, U. (2021, December 1). European Commission. *EuroNews.*

Wagner, R. H. (1986). The theory of games and the balance of power. *World Politics, 38*(4), 546–576.

Wallerstein, I. (1974). *The modern world-system I: Capitalist agriculture and the origins of the European world-economy in the sixteenth century.* Academic Press.

Wallerstein, I. (1980). *The capitalist world-economy.* Cambridge University Press.

Wallerstein, I. (1984). *The three instances of hegemony in the history of the capitalist world-economy.* Pp. 100–108 in Current Issues and Research in Macrosociology.

Wallerstein, I. (2004). *World-systems analysis: An introduction.* John Hope Franklin Center.

Wallerstein, I. (2019). U.S. weakness and the struggle for hegemony. *Monthly Review, 71*(6).

Weissmann, M. (2015). Chinese foreign policy in a global perspective: A responsible reformer "striving for achievement." *Journal of Interdisciplinary Cycle Research, 3*(1), 151–166.

World Bank. (2018). *The world bank annual report 2018.* Washington, DC: World Bank. © World Bank. https://openknowledge.worldbank.org/handle/10986/30326. License: CC BY-NC-ND 3.0 IGO.

World Bank national accounts data, and OECD national accounts data files. (2021). https://data.worldbank.org/indicator/NY.GDP.PCAP.CD?locations=CN.

Yan, X. (2014). From keeping a low profile to striving for achievement. *The Chinese Journal of International Politics, 7*(2), 153–184.

Zhang, B. (2004). The changing face of chinese politics and international relations. *Asian PersPective, 28*(3), 87–113.

Part II
The Mutual Perceptions and the Changing Contours of Globalisation

Chapter 20
The EU–China Geo-Economic Equilibrium in a World of Uncertainty

Enrique Feás and Federico Steinberg

1 Introduction

The COVID-19 pandemic has accelerated the decline of the so-called liberal economic order and has made it clear that realism might be more useful than liberal institutionalism in the analysis of the international political economy.[1] We are witnessing the consolidation of a new multipolar world where geopolitical rivalry between the US and China makes multilateral cooperation more difficult. The rules-based system that the countries of the European Union (EU) have traditionally defended is being eroded by mercantilist national strategies. China is trying to play a much more assertive role, deploying its influence in East and Central Asia through the Belt and Road Initiative (BRI) and in other emerging economies like Africa (through other instruments). In the meantime, the EU, who refuses to be relegated to the periphery now that a role of mere normative power is not enough to be influential, is upgrading its foreign policy toolkit and trying to become more autonomous. Finally, there is ambiguity regarding the Biden Administration's future foreign policy after the isolationist and mercantilist years of the Trump administration. Within this framework, the EU and China are interested in avoiding trade and currency conflicts and managing their differences in a diplomatic manner. Moreover, both would like to avoid a substantial economic decoupling that might endanger globalization and

---

[1] See Ikenberry (2018) and Mearsheimer (2018) for a discussion.

E. Feás (✉)
University of Alcalá, Madrid, Spain
e-mail: efeas@rielcano.org

F. Steinberg
Universidad Autónoma de Madrid, Madrid, Spain
e-mail: federico.steinberg@uam.es

E. Feás · F. Steinberg
Elcano Royal Institute, Madrid, Spain

© The Author(s), under exclusive license to Springer Nature Singapore Pte Ltd. 2023
P. A. B. Duarte et al. (eds.), *The Palgrave Handbook of Globalization with Chinese Characteristics*, https://doi.org/10.1007/978-981-19-6700-9_20

reduce prosperity.[2] They share the understanding that cooperation is required to ensure the provision of global public goods in areas of common interest, but they are also aware that they are rivals and competitors, and that collaboration is not granted.

The EU, who would like to increase its autonomy and learn to use the "language of power" (Borrell, 2019), has made it clear that rebalancing its bilateral economic relationship with China is essential. This requires reciprocity, a better access for European companies to the Chinese market, and a level playing field in the multilateral arena. This has become more urgent considering the European vulnerabilities exposed by COVID-19. China, on the other hand, would prefer a continuation of the *statu quo*, which has proven enormously useful for its economic growth. However, the fact that both the US and the EU have made it clear that they find several Chinese economic practices unacceptable, has made China's authorities realize that they may have to change certain features of its economic model in order to avoid a dangerous economic confrontation with "the West."

Moreover, global—especially Western—public opinion is increasingly critical towards China because of its management of COVID-19. Therefore, the Comprehensive Investment Agreement (CAI) between the EU and China, in which China has made concessions, is a building bloc in which to cement this new economic relationship. In addition, if China were to show its willingness to go down this path and the Biden Administration were willing to join forces with the EU, Japan, and others, putting pressure on China to trigger the reform of the World Trade Organization (WTO), the economic interests of the EU would be well served. Nevertheless, since this scenario is quite unlikely, the EU would probably have to continue constructing its bilateral relation with China in an autonomous manner, as it has started doing with CAI. It should also cooperate with China through the G-20 to create a more sustainable open economy.

This chapter analyses this bilateral economic relation from a European perspective. First, we disentangle the concept of European open strategic autonomy and its instruments. We deconstruct its meaning by looking at its implications in security and defence, trade and investment, finance, technology, and industrial capacity. Secondly, we explore the EU–China relation in the wider international context, specifying areas of cooperation and conflict in light of COVID-19. Thirdly, we analyse the CAI as a brief case study, which shows how the bilateral relation could improve to generate more trust and collaboration. Finally, we will present our conclusions.

---

[2] Bilateral economic relations are deep and wide. In the last two decades, the volume of trade multiplied by almost eight to EUR 560 billion a year and China is now the EU's second most important trading partner after the US (Zenglein, 2020).

2 Conceptualizing European Strategic Autonomy and Its Instruments

2.1 The Concept and Scope of Strategic Autonomy

The concept of "European strategic autonomy" is not new: it started being used by the European Council in November 2013 in relation to the European defence industry. It was later extended to the field of foreign policy with the 2016 EU Global Strategy. Finally, it entered the economic field in 2020, although modulated with an adjective ("open strategic autonomy").

In general terms, it refers to the capacity of Europeans to live by their own laws without interference, risk of attack, or destabilization from the outside. In other words, European strategic autonomy should ensure that the EU (and its member states) is not forced by others to do what it does not want to do (Tocci, 2021). President Macron referred to it in his 2017 Sorbone Speech as the ability to "being able to make decisions and act freely in a world of mutual dependencies." Later the concept has been widely discussed and re-elaborated (sometimes interchangeably with sovereignty, especially in the economic sphere), especially since the EU was forced to adapt to a more complex and less cooperatively international system.

In the post-World War II period, the multilateral rule-based framework, the technological prowess of many European businesses and the solid transatlantic relationship allowed EU countries to prosper. But the 'good old days' are gone: the resurgence of nationalism and geostrategic rivalry among major powers—above all the US and China—has made international relations less cordial and cooperative for a "herbivore" power like the EU, jeopardizing the sustainability of the so-called liberal international order. Within this context, the EU risks becoming an "object" instead of a "subject" of international relations (Simon, 2019). It can be blackmailed by others or suffer the negative externalities of the erosion of the rules-based system. It might also be incapable of pursuing its own interests and values just by being a soft normative power. As the EU's High Representative for Foreign and Security Policy puts it, "As EU, we face rougher seas and risk getting caught in the cross-currents of major powers telling us to 'pick a side'" (Borrell, 2020b). Developing autonomy and learning to "speak the language of power" (Borrell, 2019) are therefore more essential for the EU now than in the past.

There has been some debate about to what extent European strategic autonomy might lead to mercantilism and to a "fortress Europe," a vision historically associated with French foreign economic policy. However, European history, laws, and values are not protectionist or autarchic. Trade has been a fundamental part of the EU's identity from its inception. The integration of the community began with trade and economic integration that has paved the way for political integration.[3] That ensures

---

[3] The EU is home to just 7% of the world's population but the largest exporter and importer, responsible for one-third of global trade (more than the US and China). Around 30 million (one in seven) of its workers depend directly or indirectly on exports to the rest of the world. This figure has

that autonomy does not mean protectionism or even independence. In fact, the European Commission (2021) has started to talk about "open strategic autonomy" and the need for a more resilient Europe, which can be interpreted as a foreign policy strategy based on multilateralism and cooperation when possible, but that makes explicit that the EU might need to act autonomously (i.e., unilaterally) in certain cases.[4] Therefore, autonomy would be a means to achieve resilience, security, and prosperity, and not a goal in itself. Moreover, by becoming capable of acting alone, the EU is also expected to be better equipped to work effectively with partners.

The goal of autonomy is therefore not to act against, but rather to act *with* partners on an equal standing to reinforce interdependence and promote an adequate governance of the different aspects of globalization. The ambition to be autonomous affects all spheres of external action. It includes security and defence, which in turn implies having the necessary planning and decision-making capacity, civilian and military capabilities, as well as the joint willingness to use them. This is the most difficult area for the EU. First, because it has lived under the American security umbrella for decades. Second, because many of its member states (particularly those of the East, but also Germany) are keen to still depend on NATO and the US for security issues, especially once Trump left the White House in 2021.

However, the march towards autonomy is not limited to defence and security. Other areas stand out, such as the economy—including trade, finance, and investment—technology, energy, and—because of COVID-19—health. Whereas in trade the EU is already autonomous, when it comes to financing and investment work remains to be done, from developing the international role of the euro (Claeys & Wolff, 2020)—to avoid being forced to break European laws under the weight of secondary sanctions—to ensuring a level playing field with China in the bilateral economic relation. In addition, as it becomes clearer that technology and digitalization (and even security) will be the key drivers of growth in the twenty-first century, the EU needs to improve its capabilities—and thus reduce its dependency—in data, communications, artificial intelligence, semiconductors, digital industries, or 5G and 6G.

In energy and climate—especially regarding energy security, carbon pricing, and climate finance—the EU needs to upgrade its toolbox and be more willing to use it, even if this generates tensions with other powers. Finally, autonomy in healthcare matters has to be reconsidered as part of the conversation about what the strategic sectors in the economy of the twenty-first century will be. Overall, "the EU needs a change of mindset to address threats to its strategic sovereignty. It needs to learn to think like a geopolitical power" (Leonard & Shapiro, 2019). This requires putting its foreign economic policy not just at the disposal to the pursuit of wealth (as it has done historically), but to the pursuit of power.

---

risen by almost 50% since 1995, with European companies strongly integrated in global production chains, especially in the service sector.

[4] When discussion its trade strategy, the European Commission refers to Open Strategic Autonomy as *"strengthening the EU's capacity to pursue its own interests independently and assertively, while continuing to work with partners around the world to deliver global solutions to global challenges."* (Schmucker & Mildner, 2020).

2.2 Trade Dependence and Global Value Chains After COVID

The concept of strategic autonomy has also profound economic implications. The problem is that it can be easily linked to protectionism. The COVID pandemic has reinforced the risk element involved in the evaluation of global value chains (GVC), i.e., the need to decide the optimal configuration of GVC of a particular product not only in terms of efficiency, but also weighing in the risk of disruption.

Strictly speaking, increasing autonomy could be seen just as a reduction of risk concentration, which can be reached through an adequate diversification of sources of supply. In this case, the key element to minimize disruptions in GVC would continue to be trade and trade policy. This was, for instance, the strategy of Toyota after the 2011 earthquake in Fukushima: to create a database of suppliers and use it to diversify its supply chain. These efforts proved to be useful after the Kumamoto earthquake in 2016, when Toyota recovered much faster than in 2011 (Cernat & Guinea, 2020), and probably also after the second earthquake in Fukushima in February 2021 (which halted nine factories for several days). However, the COVID-19 crisis showed us once again that GVC benefits must be weighted by the risk of disruption, and it is not an easy task: even China had to import masks at the beginning of the pandemic. Moreover, since the boom of GVC, imports are closely linked to exports. In the case of COVID-19-related goods, for instance, for every euro of German exports, it imports EUR 0.72; the US, similarly, exports USD 0.75 for every dollar of imports (OECD, 2020).

In any case, measuring the vulnerability of GVCs is virtually impossible, as there is not enough firm-level data. Cernat and Guinea (2020) analyse EU imports of over 9000 different products at 8-digit level to check the number of countries where these products are sourced, and they find that most EU imports come from more than one supplier country, and 50% of the products have more than 25 suppliers. However, there are 250 specific products for which all EU imports come from just one country (although they account for just 1% of the value of total imports). We should, however, carefully consider these results because the value is not necessarily the best indicator of dependence: sometimes small products are key for production. The same authors analyse the available firm-level data and find that, for some countries[5] more than 50% of their importers (essentially SMEs) are reliant on a single supplying country. This means that, even if a country is adequately diversified, its economy might be seriously damaged by a disruption.

Therefore, in some cases geographical diversification might not be enough, and autonomous production could be convenient. In fact, the COVID pandemic has also reshuffled the map of "strategic sectors," For instance, after decades of liberalization of the EU's Common Agricultural Policy (CAP), the food sector has proven to be strategic in case of sanitary emergencies. It has provided, at the same time, a perfect excuse for the French government to block the acquisition of Carrefour by the

---

[5] Spain, France, Netherlands, Italy to Romania, Sweden, and Estonia.

Canadian company Couche-Tard (using a resuscitated concept of "food sovereignty" which seemed almost forgotten in the twenty-first century). Who would have said that the EU's vilified CAP would regain momentum sixty years after its creation?

In any case, the protectionist temptation has always been there. The key issue is to guarantee that GVC are resilient (i.e., able to recover quickly after disruption), and that crucial elements of the value chain are sufficiently diversified or, if this is not possible, produced in Europe. The COVID-19 vaccine management is a good example of "open strategic autonomy." Regardless of the initial confusion and mistakes by some member states and the clumsy negotiation of some vaccine contracts, the Commission was clever enough not to promote a general export restriction,[6] unlike the US (by law) or the UK (by contract). This would have had fatal consequences, as vaccines are the perfect example of a complex product embedded in GVC (therefore dependent on crucial imports[7]). But, at the same time, the Commission worked to reduce its dependence on third countries, promoting the manufacture in Europe of a key component for RNAm vaccines (nanolipids) initially produced only in the US. Therefore, a good example of open strategic autonomy was promoting three things at the same time: a joint supply of vaccines, a fine-tuned industrial policy to reduce excessive dependence, and free trade.

2.3 Trade Routes and Strategic Autonomy: The Belt and Road Initiative and Beyond

Strategic autonomy requires a strong transportation network. Today nearly 80% of the volume of international trade in goods is transported by sea. In the case of the EU-27, sea transport accounted for 46% of its exports and 56% of its imports in 2019, whereas by road the figure was 20% and 16%, respectively, and by rail less than 2% (Eurostat, 2020). As for trade between the EU and Asia, total maritime freight (westbound and eastbound) amounted to 16 million TEUs in 2016, but could reach 40 million in 2040, according to forecasts of the EU Parliament (European Parliament, 2018). Air freight between the EU and Asia, in turn, amounted to 3.3 million tons in 2016, but could grow to 5 million tons by 2040.

The need for the EU to gain strategic autonomy will entail a reinforcement of its trade routes with the rest of the world. Therefore, the EU's attitude towards other blocks' strategies (such as the BRI) will depend, among other things, on the real interest of the EU to reinforce its interdependence or its independence from Asia and, in particular, from China. In this regard, despite the tensions with China, the EU's need to reduce the emissions of greenhouse gases in the transportation sector could turn into an unexpected ally for the BRI, through the need to develop

---

[6] It allowed, though, the possibility of blocking specific exports, but this only materialized once (blocking of a lot of Astrazeneca in Italy bound to Australia).

[7] As an example, a single-dose of the BioNTech-Pfizer vaccine requires 280 components produced by 25 suppliers located in 19 different countries.

alternative—and less polluting—railway routes across Europe and Central Asia. A study by the European Parliament has assessed the extent to which cargo currently carried by maritime and air modes between Europe and the Far East will in future shift to rail as a result of improved services attributed to the BRI. The results of the analysis indicate that by 2040 around 2.5 million TEUs could be transferred to rail from maritime transport and 0.5 million from air transport (equivalent to 50 to 60 additional trains daily, or 2 to 3 trains per hour, in each direction), with rail services targeting "higher value and more time-sensitive goods than the current maritime transport" (European Parliament, 2018).

In addition, the EU could also reinforce its trade routes with Latin America or with Africa to increase its strategic autonomy through diversification. In the case of Latin America, the successful ratification of the EU–Mercosur trade agreement might have a geopolitical dimension, which was not considered when negotiations started twenty years ago. Even though political-economy constraints threaten to derail this process (as there are voices in Europe criticizing the agreement both because of its environmental risks and for its impact on the European agricultural sector), geopolitical elements could play an important role in the final decision. At the same time, geographical proximity and historical and cultural ties make Africa a good candidate as source of diversification of EU inputs. First, the EU could take advantage of the 2000 Cotonou Agreement with African, Caribbean, and Pacific (ACP) countries. However, more importantly, China's Ya-Fei-La strategy clearly shows the order of preference for a progressive increase of China's influence in the South–South sphere: Asia first, then Africa, and only later Latin America (García-Herrero & Casanova, 2016). Therefore, the EU's implication in Africa becomes not only a source of risk diversification for its inputs, but at the same time a way of asserting an alternative geopolitical role to China in the African continent.

2.4 Technological and Industrial Autonomy

As the fourth industrial revolution accelerates, it becomes clear that national production of strategic components—in particular—and industrial policy—more broadly— are deeply linked to strategic autonomy. In the old days, the disruption of GVC appeared only linked to natural disasters. In the current geopolitical context of weaker rules and institutions, disruptions can also be caused by geopolitical clashes and the need to guarantee the sanitary safety of citizens or access to key components. At the same time, it has been a few decades since technology and patents have become a key element in determining industrial supremacy. But the robotics and artificial intelligence revolution must now guarantee not only industrial competitiveness, but also data security. This is particularly true for all technological aspects involving telecommunications, especially 5G, cloud computing, and cybersecurity. In this regard, the concept of digital sovereignty becomes not only related to the mere availability of intermediate products or technologies, but also to security: controlling essential components in areas such as Telecommunications (including 5G), cybersecurity, or cloud computing becomes then essential to reduce the vulnerability of national networks (Hobbs, 2020). The problem is that the EU is lagging behind not only the US and Japan, but also China in key technological patents, and also in the production of more advanced semiconductors. So far, the EU seems ill prepared for the latest wave of globalization derived from artificial intelligence and robotics (Baldwin, 2016), and pretending to be competitive in most technological areas seems more wishful thinking than anything else.

3 The EU–China Relation in the Wider International Context: Areas of Cooperation and Conflict

3.1 China in the Eyes of the EU: The Awakening

The vision of China as an increasingly integrated actor in the economic world by Western parameters has profoundly changed in the past decade. The accession of China to the WTO in the early 2000s provoked an initial "China fever," but experience later proved that China's economic and trade practices have not (and will not) converge with those in the West, as some optimists in Washington and Brussels expected. The EU Trade Policy Strategy of 2021 clearly stated that "China's accession to the WTO has not led to its transformation into a market economy. The level at which China has opened its markets does not correspond to its weight in the global economy, and the state continues to exert a decisive influence on China's economic environment with consequent competitive distortions that cannot be sufficiently addressed by current WTO rules" (European Commission, 2021).

The disillusion has been doubled. Politically, some reforms have been reversed and there has been a concentration of power in the Party leader and a deterioration of human and political rights. Economically, and from a European perspective, there are increasing concerns related to the lack of a level playing field in the bilateral economic relation. The EU regards the lack of reciprocity in both trade and investment as not only unfair, but also dangerous.

Since economics and politics increasingly go hand in hand, the EU has begun to perceive the rise of China as a growing threat to its citizens and companies. This has led to an upgrading of its China strategy and to the gradual development of a number of defensive instruments. In 2019, the European Commission argued that "China is, simultaneously, in different policy areas, a cooperation partner with whom the EU has closely aligned objectives, a negotiating partner with whom the EU needs to find a balance of interests, an economic competitor in the pursuit of technological leadership, and a systemic rival promoting alternative models of governance." (European Commission, 2019). Therefore, the distrust, discrete at the beginning, has eventually become open: the consideration of China as a "systemic rival" (more or less modulated or softened for practical reasons) represents a new era in bilateral relations.

At the same time, understanding the Chinese challenge does not necessarily mean to confront China. If the EU Strategy on China specifically calls for "a flexible and pragmatic whole-of-EU approach," the EU's Trade Policy Strategy published two years later qualifies the trade and investment relationship with China as both "important and challenging" (European Commission, 2021). The Trump administration is for the EU the best example that a correct diagnosis does not necessary imply sharing the same opinion about the policy response. The failure of Trump's "trade war" (whose main objectives are far from fulfilled) shows that a purely conflictive attitude might not be the best course of action. After twenty years, China has become an industrial superpower, and this has made the bilateral economic relation between the EU and China deep, strong, and varied (Zenglein, 2020). Both powers understand their share in the responsibility for the management of globalization and the provision of key public goods, its risks and, perhaps more importantly, both would prefer to maintain active engagement with each other and avoid economic and political decoupling. So far, the attitude of the US has been of direct confrontation. The EU, despite cooperating with the US in 2021 created Trade and Technology Council with the implicit objective of containing the rise of China, does not share the US confrontational approach.

3.2 Room for Autonomy and Room for Cooperation

The EU recognizes that China is a key partner for tackling the enormous challenges of the twenty-first century but, at the same time, admits that Chinese values will never be aligned with those of the EU, and that economic competition is likely to increase. Moreover, European authorities seem to understand that they cannot substantially modify China's economic practices, but they are confident that given the high level of interdependence, active engagement will enable some changes in Chinese economic policy to avoid a damaging economic decoupling.

However, not all member states share the same view vis-à-vis China (Esteban & Otero-Iglesias, 2020) and Chinese authorities have tried to exploit these differences with a strategy of "divide and conquer." On the surface, almost all EU countries would prefer to continue enjoying the US security umbrella while making as much business with China as possible to take advantage of its economic dynamism. However, geopolitics has made this option virtually impossible. Security and economics are increasingly connected, and the US–China trade and technology "war" has modified European constraints and opportunities. While Germany (and especially other "northern" and more free trade-oriented EU countries) are keener on maintaining economic ties with China and overlook human rights and other politically sensitive issues, France, who is less dependent on exports to China and less interested on the US security umbrella, has fostered a concept of European sovereignty that it aspires to lead. Finally, Southern and Easter European countries have had more eclectic views, with some signing MoUs with China to be part of the BRI. Within this cacophony, however, the EU has been successfully able to forge and maintain a common position towards China (as it did with Brexit), most recently in the 2020 CAI negotiations. And it has become clear that elements like 5G or even the "Five Eyes Alliance" (of which no EU country is part after Brexit) would imply that on security and technology issues, the EU must be much less naïve towards China regardless of the future of the transatlantic relationship.

In practice, and especially in the light of COVID-19, this has translated, as we have explained, into a recognition of the need to reduce European economic and technological dependency on China (and to a certain extent on the US) by diversifying providers, shortening value chains, and opening more trade routes. The goal, however, is not independence, but a new trade and investment geography that would reduce risks and augment resilience. This defensive approach also requires more reciprocity, a concept that is well understood in China. The end of innocence should mean that the EU will not be ready to open its economy unless China reciprocates. Presenting a purely defensive mechanism ("we will close our market if you do not open yours") reduces potential conflicts. Unlike other trade agreements, where liberalization in one sector might be compensated by other advantages, in the case of China, reciprocity should be considered stricter, in order to avoid quid pro quo in aspects which could endanger the fundamental values or interests of Europe. Finally, after creating its investment screening mechanism in 2020, the EU will introduce more defensive tools by monitoring subsidies for companies that operate in the single market and by creating and anti-coercion instrument. Although these measures are not explicitly designed for China, they are part of the China strategy.

Beyond these defensive approaches, the EU and China have lots of room for cooperation (Zenglein, 2020). First, is the financing for development issue, which is now linked to vaccine diplomacy and to the need to improve the multilateral financial safety net to avoid sovereign debt crisis in emerging and developing countries. Here, the EU should try to coordinate within the OECD the response to China's financing of developing countries, where the OECD Consensus might not be the right framework anymore. It should also promote an increase in the financing of the COVAX initiative, which would strengthen (and potentially promote the reform) of the World Health Organization and make sure that the 2021 agreement to increase IMF's Special Drawing Rights materializes in generous financing for developing countries under stress. This last initiative should contribute to a peaceful coexistence of the Bretton Woods institutions with the recently created China-led development banks and financing mechanisms, in particular the Asian Infrastructure Investment Bank (AIIB). Moreover, within this financial collaboration, both powers are interested in the use of the euro and the yuan as alternatives to the dollar, in an adequate regulation for cryptocurrencies that ensures financial stability and in the effective implementation of the minimum 15% tax on the profits of large multinational corporations.

Multilateralism is another area where there is room for cooperation. Maybe it is utopian to think that a new WTO with decisions by a qualified majority can be accepted by China, or even by the US. Superpowers do not want to give up veto powers. But it would be feasible to concentrate efforts in a few areas where all parties might agree to collaborate, for instance in the definition of basic rules regarding protectionism, such as State trade, subsidies, dumping, and countervailing measures or other areas. That is, improving the already-existing codes, upgrading them to a world of GVC, and, above all, creating a dispute settlement mechanism sufficiently independent but respected by all (Rodrik & Walt, 2020). Finally, it would be important to try to have the regulatory conversation about trade and climate change within the WTO to avoid unilateral actions (like the proposed European Carbon Adjustment Mechanism) that might trigger additional trade conflicts.

As for preferential trade agreements, the evolution of globalization has shown that multilateral deals are difficult to achieve because when tariffs have almost disappeared and services trade is booming, trade protectionism consists mainly in regulation, and harmonizing regulations is complicated. The alternative of trade agreements among groups of countries that are more similar and share common social values is probably easier. The EU–Mercosur agreement and the China-led Regional Comprehensive Economic Partnership are good examples of how multilateralism finds its way through preferential trade agreements. Of course, in some cases preferential strategies might prove faster and more efficient. And they are always better than the lack of norms or unilateral actions. In any case, it is important that China and the EU understand this complex reality and are willing to work to avoid an increased divergence in standards and regulations that might endanger globalization.

4 The Comprehensive Agreement on Investment: A Step in the Right Direction?

Given the previous discussion, it is clear that the EU and China would like to avoid economic decoupling and make sure that what the EU perceives as unfair Chinese practices changes. In this section, we argue that the CAI, which has not been ratified yet because of the Chinese sanctions on members of the European Parliament, is the best way forward to achieve these goals.

After seven years and 35 negotiating rounds, on 29 December 2020, the EU and China finalized the CAI. It is striking that the agreement was both praised (Esteban & Otero Iglesias, 2021; Sandbu, 2021) and criticized (García Herrero, 2021) even before its full text was made public.[8] Probably Skovgaard Poulsen (2021, p. 1) provides a balanced assessment when he states that: "In substance, however, both critics and proponents should be under no illusion: the agreement is limited in nature (…). This is not because EU negotiators are weak or naive (they are not), but because they could never have hoped for more."

The CAI is not a trade agreement, but by covering wide aspects of bilateral investment and regulations, it serves as a building bloc in the attempt to make the Chinese economic model more compatible with "the West" (for the time being, with the EU) through constructive engagement and diplomacy. It establishes regulations and

---

[8] Retrieved on November 2021, from https://trade.ec.europa.eu/doclib/press/index.cfm?id=2237.

increases the transparency about investment, subsidies, state-owned companies, technology transfer, forced labour, and environmental issues. The agreement, however, does not create an investor-to-state dispute settlement mechanism. From the European perspective, it should serve to rebalance the bilateral economic relationship by opening some services sectors of the Chinese economy to European companies, start cementing the rule of law, increase reciprocity, and consolidate the limited openness of the Chinese economy, whose authorities will not be able to roll back some of the reforms implemented in the last decades. In addition, it shows that the EU strategy has delivered better results than the Trump Administration's aggressive diplomacy (Biscop, 2021). For China, whose higher authorities decided to give the green light to the agreement after years of negotiating paralysis, it shows its willingness to compromise and accept rules in a context of increased erosion of the multilateral rules-based system, declining trust in China in most Western countries and growing tensions between China and the US.

The agreement probably falls short of what the EU aspired to obtain in the first place. However, it seems to be a step in the right direction. It shows the willingness and the capacity of the EU to conclude ambitions agreements and it is part of the new China strategy. In sum, one could argue that it is a concrete illustration of the concept of European Open Strategic Autonomy. Some observers have presented the CAI as unexpected or even hasty. They have accused the EU of not getting enough concessions from China and of not consulting with the US. However, these criticisms are unconvincing. First, the EU had been negotiating with China for more than six years. It was the change in the Chinese negotiating position that made the deal possible. Following the deterioration of its public image in Europe and North America due to the lack of transparency in the management of COVID-19 and the situation in Hong Kong, China was eager to conclude the agreement to increase its international reputation. Borrowing from the economics terminology, when in a negotiation one of the two partners has a higher opportunity cost of not reaching an agreement, it has an incentive to make more concessions. A similar dynamic has recently taken place with the Brexit negotiations. It would therefore have been unwise for the EU to refuse these new offers or to postpone the conclusion of the negotiations. Second, the critique according to which Chinese commitments are insufficient does not recognize the reality of international relations. Believing that Europe could impose its own agenda on China, as it did with the UK, without an assessment of the balance of power is certainly Western-centric and naive. The EU strategy towards China is based on constructing engagement and dialogue, just the opposite of the one followed by the US in the last years. That requires moving forward in small steps, and the CAI is an important one. Finally, there is the geopolitical argument that suggests that the EU should have waited for the Biden Administration to define a common strategy and thus extract more concessions. This argument has its merits. However, the CAI is a bilateral agreement. There cannot be a trilateral investment agreement between the US, the EU, and China. In addition, Europe has an autonomous strategy vis-à-vis China, which it followed actively and without haste. It coldly assessed its position with regard to its interests without neglecting or prejudicing the interests of its allies. Moreover, it is unlikely that this agreement will hinder Euro-American collaboration towards China, as shown by the launching of the US–EU Trade and Technology Council.

In any case, it is important to highlight that the CAI will not resolve all the EU–China differences. There might be problems with the effective implementation of the agreement by China, especially in relation to its commitments regarding transparency, labour rights, and sustainability. However, the agreement has created a formal process to discuss differences, and this is a step in the right direction if the goal is to avoid that the Chinese economy follows the isolationist American path. Western suspicion about China is reasonable, but the only way to tackle it—if one believes in the benefits of economic integration and interdependence—is through binding rules that contribute to increase trust in small steps. The CAI seems to do precisely that.

5 Conclusion

The BRI and the pursuit of Strategic Autonomy are China's and Europe's foreign policy strategies to increase their influence abroad and adapt to the changing balance of power in world politics. Unlike the US, both the EU and China are interested in avoiding economic decoupling and direct confrontation. They are also interested in more balanced and sustainable globalization. It might be true that some degree of economic disintegration between China and the West is inevitable, especially in areas related to technology and the fourth industrial revolution. Moreover, the COVID-19 pandemic has shown the need to increase economic, climatic, social, and sanitary resilience, most notably for European countries. However, multiple areas require international cooperation and the provision of global public goods. And the pandemic has made this even more evident. Fighting infectious diseases and climate change or taxing large multinational corporations requires international cooperation, reinforced institutions, and clear and legitimate rules. Even in the areas in which economic competition will intensify, rules will always be necessary. Therefore, upgrading the governance of globalization to make it politically more sustainable is a goal shared by both the EU and China (and hopefully also by the Biden Administration). This means that constructive engagement, exemplified by the CAI, seems to be an appropriate way to proceed.

As this chapter goes to press, the CAI has not been ratified yet, the EU is upgrading its foreign economic policy toolkit, and China's BRI is still under implementation. Moreover, it is still unclear to what extent global value chains will be transformed or how achievable reforms of global economic institutions like the WTO are. This means that the research agenda related to the EU–China bilateral economic relation, in particular, and to the role of both powers in global economic governance will only broaden in the future.

Bibliographic References

Anghel, S. E., Immenkamp, B., Lazarou, E., Saunier, J. L., & Wilson, A. B. (2020). *On the path to 'strategic autonomy': The EU in an evolving geopolitical environment*. Retrieved on December 2021, from http://www.europarl.europa.eu/RegData/etudes/STUD/2020/652096/EPRS_STU(2020)652096_EN.pdf

Baldwin, R. (2016). *The great convergence: Information technology and the new globalization*. Harvard University Press.

Baldwin, R., & Evenett, S. (Eds.). (2020). *COVID-19 and trade policy: Why turning inward won't work*. CEPR Press. Retrieved on December 2021, from https://voxeu.org/system/files/epublication/Covid-19_and_Trade_Policy.pdf

Biscop, S. (2021). EU-China: Drop the masks, back to real diplomacy. *Egmont Commentaries*. Retrieved on December 2021, from https://www.egmontinstitute.be/eu-china-drop-the-masks-back-to-real-diplomacy/

Borrell, J. (2019, October 7). *High representative/Vice President-designate of the European Commission: Opening statement*. European Parliament. Retrieved on December 2021, from https://multimedia.europarl.europa.eu/en/hearing-of-josep-borrell-fontelles-high-representative-vice-president-designate-of-the-european-commission-opening-statement_I178140-V_v

Borrell, J. (2020a). China, the United States and us. [online] *Blog post*. European External Action Service. Retrieved on December 2021, from https://eeas.europa.eu/headquarters/headquarters-homepage/83644/china-united-states-and-us_en

Borrell, J. (2020b). In rougher seas, the EU's own interests and values should be our compass. [online] *Blog post*. European External Action Service. Retrieved on December 2021, from https://eeas.europa.eu/headquarters/headquarters-homepage_en/80854/In%20rougher%20seas,%20the%20EU%E2%80%99s%20own%20interests%20and%20values%20should%20be%20our%20compass

Cernat, L., & Guinea, O. (2020). On ants, dinosaurs, and how to survive a trade apocalypse. [online] European Centre for International Political Economy. Retrieved on December 2021, from https://ecipe.org/blog/how-survive-trade-apocalypse/

Claeys, G., & Wolff, G. 2020. Is the COVID-19 crisis an opportunity to boost the euro as a global currency? [online] *Bruegel Policy Contribution*, n. 11. Retrieved on December 2021, from https://www.bruegel.org/2020/06/is-the-covid-19-crisis-an-opportunity-to-boost-the-euro-as-a-global-currency/

Esteban, M., & Otero-Iglesias, M. (Eds.). (2020, January). *Europe in the face of US-China rivalry*. European Think-tank Network on China (ETNC). Retrieved on December 2021, from https://merics.org/sites/default/files/2020-04/200123_ETNC_Report.pdf

Esteban, M., & Otero-Iglesias, M. (2021). *El Acuerdo de Inversiones UE-China: Un paso en la dirección correcta*. Elcano Royal Institute. Expert Comment.

European Commission. (2019). *EU-China—A strategic outlook*. Retrieved on December 2021, from https://ec.europa.eu/info/sites/default/files/communication-eu-china-a-strategic-outlook.pdf

European Commission. (2021). *Trade policy review—An open, sustainable and assertive trade policy*. Retrieved on December 2021, from https://eur-lex.europa.eu/legal-content/ES/TXT/?uri=CELEX:52021DC0066

European Parliament. (2018). *Research for TRAN Committee: The new Silk Route: Opportunities and challenges for EU transport [Study]*. European Commission. Retrieved on December 2021, from http://www.europarl.europa.eu/RegData/etudes/STUD/2018/585907/IPOL_STU(2018)585907_EN.pdf

Eurostat. (2020). *International trade in goods by mode of transport*. Eurostat Statistics Explained. Retrieved on December 2021, from https://ec.europa.eu/eurostat/statistics-explained/index.php?title=International_trade_in_goods_by_mode_of_transport

García-Herrero, A. (2021). Europe's disappointing investment deal with China. [online] *Bruegel*. Retrieved on December 2021, from https://www.bruegel.org/2021/01/europes-disappointing-investment-deal-with-china/

García-Herrero, A., & Casanova, C. (2016). Africa's rising commodity export dependency on China. *SSRN Electronic Journal*. https://doi.org/10.2139/ssrn.2842566

Hobbs, C. (Ed.) (2020). *Europe's digital sovereignty: From rule maker to superpower in the age of US-China rivalry*. Retrieved on December 2021, from https://ecfr.eu/publication/europe_digital_sovereignty_rulemaker_superpower_age_us_china_rivalry/

Ikenberry, J. (2018, January). The end of liberal international order? *International Affairs, 94*(1), 7–23. https://doi.org/10.1093/ia/iix241

Keating, D. (2019). *Europe waking up to raw materials 'criticality'*. Retrieved on December 2019, from https://www.euractiv.com/section/circular-economy/news/europe-waking-up-to-raw-materials-criticality/

Leonard, M., & Shapiro, J. (2019, June 25). Strategic sovereignty: How Europe can regain the capacity to act. *ECFR Policy Brief*. Retrieved on December 2021, from https://www.ecfr.eu/publications/summary/strategic_sovereignty_how_europe_can_regain_the_capacity_to_act

Leonard, M., Pisani-Ferry, J., Woolf, G., Ribakova, E., & Shapiro, J. (2019, June). *Redefining Europe's economic sovereignty* (Issue no. 9). Bruegel Policy Contribution.

Mearsheimer, J. (2018). *The great delusion*. Yale University Press.

OECD. (2020). *Trade interdependencies in COVID-19 goods*. Retrieved on December 2021, from http://oecd.org/coronavirus/policy-responses/trade-interdependencies-in-covid-19-goods-79aaa1d6/

Rodrik, D., & Walt, S. (2020). *Constructing a new global order: A project framing document*. Mimeo. Retrieved on December 2021, from https://j.mp/3iasSCL

Sandbu, M. (2021, January 25). EU has a chance to change from negotiator to political enforcer. [online] *Financial Times*.

Schmucker, C., & Mildner, S.-A. (2020). EU trade policy reform: Levelling the playing field in a new geo-economic environment (DGAP Analysis No. 70). *German Council on Foreign Relations*. Retrieved on December 2021, from https://dgap.org/sites/default/files/article_pdfs/dgap-analysis-2020-07-en_0.pdf

Simon, L. (2019). *Subject and object: Europe and the emerging great-power competition*. Real Instituto Elcano Expert Comment. Retrieved on December 2021, from http://www.realinstitutoelcano.org/wps/portal/rielcano_en/contenido?WCM_GLOBAL_CONTEXT=/elcano/elcano_in/zonas_in/commentary-simon-subject-object-europe-and-the-emerging-great-power-competition

Skovgaard Poulsen, L. N. (2021, January 25 and 26). *The EU-China investment deal and transatlantic investment cooperation*. Prepared for the Shapiro Geopolitics Workshop on Transatlantic Disruption, Perry World House, University of Pennsylvania.

Tocci, N. (2021). *European strategic autonomy: What it is, why we need it, how to achieve it*. IAI. Retrieved on December 2021, from https://www.iai.it/sites/default/files/9788893681780.pdf

Weyand, S. (2020, September 15). *EU open strategic autonomy and the transatlantic trade relationship* [Speech]. Speech before the American Institute for Contemporary German Studies, Johns Hopkins University. Retrieved on December 2021, from https://eeas.europa.eu/delegations/united-states-america/85321/eu-open-strategic-autonomy-and-transatlantic-trade-relationship_en

Zenglein, M. (2020, November 18). Mapping and recalibrating Europe's economic interdependence with China. *MERICs China Monitor*. Retrieved on December 2021, from https://merics.org/sites/default/files/2020-11/Merics%20ChinaMonitor_Mapping%20and%20recalibrating%20%281%29.pdf

Chapter 21
A Shifting Current: Europe's Changing Approaches vis-à-vis China, the Belt and Road Initiative, and the COVID-19 Pandemic

Vassilis Ntousas and Stephen Minas

1 Introduction

Launched in 2013 by Xi Jinping, the President of the People's Republic of China, the Belt and Road Initiative (BRI) is, and has been widely understood as, a centrepiece of Beijing's foreign policy and domestic economic strategy. BRI encompasses both Chinese outbound financing, industrial output and infrastructure projects, but also the pursuit of wider strategic objectives which are not limited to economic and trade dimensions.

As the geographic end point of many of the trading roots created, facilitated, or revitalized by the BRI lies in Europe, the initiative over time attracted the attention of Europeans. The long-standing willingness on the part of many EU member states to cultivate and deepen their bilateral ties with Beijing found in the BRI a tangible opportunity for doing so. Coinciding with a moment where Europe was still in the throes of the economic and financial crises of the late 2000s and early 2010s and the self-inflicted dogma of austerity, with BRI's advent several national capitals, especially in Southern and Eastern Europe, vied to attract related trade and investment, aiming to gain economic benefits linked to the promise of Beijing's concrete economic backing. While this intra-EU competition to secure China's support made the creation of a concerted EU strategy towards BRI difficult, the goal of exploring potential synergies with the BRI was also pursued at the EU level. Efforts under the Juncker Commission to create complementarity between its own Investment Plan for Europe—the so-called Juncker Plan—and BRI (Valero, 2015) demonstrated Europe's initially open approach to the initiative and an interest in reaping benefits from it, where possible.

V. Ntousas (✉)
German Marshall Fund of the United States (GMF), Brussels, Belgium

S. Minas
Peking University School of Transnational Law, King's College London, London, UK

Yet, as BRI's contours and impact became clearer over time, European attitudes towards Beijing and towards the initiative in particular shifted. Step by step, lingering questions over the social and environmental repercussions of Chinese investments across the continent, criticisms focused on the lack of reciprocity and access to the Chinese market, and reservations related to Beijing's purchase of key European industrial assets and its takeover of critical infrastructure in a number of member states all translated into an EU approach that was decidedly more balanced. China's increasingly assertive approach to domestic and foreign policy under President Xi also contributed to this trend, as did the pressures of the US under President Trump on its transatlantic partners for limiting European dependency and use of Chinese products and services.

These factors were reinforced by the arrival of COVID-19. As the coronavirus spread across the European continent, several of the emerging tendencies in Europe were intensified, "including increased contestation and polarization on links with China; securitization of a relationship traditionally analysed from a business perspective; and pressure from the China-US strategic rivalry" (Esteban & Armanini, 2021). Against this backdrop, EU decision-makers applied greater scepticism to BRI-related investments and attitudes towards the initiative hardened. Trying to delve more deeply into this critical period for Sino-European relations, this chapter offers an overview of the dynamics that have been at play in the run-up to and during the pandemic. In so doing, the chapter will argue that the pandemic may have strengthened the EU narrative for rebalancing the relationship between Brussels, national capitals, and Beijing both at a policy-making and a societal level, but that this shift has still not translated into a meaningful change in policy terms. This attitudinal and policy discrepancy might be expected given the traditionally slow pace of policy change at the EU level, but could be seen as a signal of the direction of travel in the Sino-European relationship at large. Equally, given the well-known effect of crises in accelerating intra-EU cooperation and galvanizing new initiatives and approaches (notably through the mechanism of the European Council: (Van Middelaar, 2018), the pandemic may well turn out to be an inflection point in EU approaches to China and its BRI. The remainder of the chapter is structured as follows. Section 2 provides a brief introduction to the BRI. Section 3 discusses the EU's uneven initial response to the BRI. Section 4 tracks the growth of scepticism in EU member states and institutions concerning the BRI. Section 5 considers the impact of the COVID pandemic on the topic under study. Section 6 concludes.

2 What Is the Belt and Road Initiative?

BRI—or "One Belt, One Road" (一带一路) as it is known in China—was unveiled by President Xi Jinping in the fall of 2013. The Silk Road Economic Belt concept was presented by Xi Jinping in a speech at Nazarbayev University in Kazakhstan in September 2013 (Ministry of Foreign Affairs of the People's Republic of China, 2013), referring to a network of land routes that would connect China with Central

Asia, Eastern and Western Europe. The Twenty-First-Century Maritime Silk Road was first introduced during Xi's state visit to Indonesia in October 2013 (ASEAN–China Center, 2013), encapsulating the idea for a network of sea routes that would span from the east coast of China to Europe and Africa through the South China Sea and the Indian Ocean. Taken together, the objective behind this initiative was presented as creating mutually beneficial arteries of unimpeded infrastructure, trade and investment routes, and networks in one coherent web of connectivity stretching from South, East, and Central Asia all the way to the Middle East, Africa, and of course Europe.

In March 2015, the Chinese government presented an action plan on the intended ways in which this initiative would be operationalized. This was included in the document "Vision and Actions on Jointly Building Silk Road Economic Belt and 21st-Century Maritime Silk Road," which was jointly prepared by China's National Development and Reform Commission, the Ministry of Foreign Affairs, and the Ministry of Commerce (National Development and Reform Commission, 2015).The Action Plan highlighted five key areas in which connectivity links were to be created, ranging far beyond physical infrastructure: Enhancing and promoting policy coordination, facilities connectivity, unimpeded trade, financial integration, and people-to-people bonds. As explained in the document "the connectivity projects of the Initiative will help align and coordinate the development strategies of the countries along the Belt and Road, tap market potential in this region, promote investment and consumption, create demands and job opportunities, enhance people-to-people and cultural exchanges, and mutual learning among the peoples of the relevant countries, and enable them to understand, trust and respect each other and live in harmony, peace and prosperity" (National Development and Reform Commission, 2015).

For an initiative of this magnitude, however, BRI arrived at the global geopolitical landscape high on ambition but nebulous in its specifics. As Ekman indicated, "the concept was launched before its concrete content was defined, and China's partners were and still are frequently encouraged to provide ideas to the Chinese government on how to make it concrete" (2019, p. 1). It is noteworthy—and presumably intentional—that an initiative launched and pursued with such commitment on the part of the Chinese authorities was characterized by such lack of clarity in its early stages of development. The 2015 Action Plan, for instance, only provided a blueprint of application, but left a great deal to be operationalized in practice. While a degree of this ambiguity was to be expected, not least given the project's constantly evolving nature and Beijing's preference to gradually flesh out its geographical footprint, the fact remained that awareness about BRI and appreciation of its full scope took a long time to build in many of the targeted countries, including in Europe. Indeed, the announcement of the BRI and subsequent periodic high-level statements and action plans from Beijing can be seen to have foregrounded the need for joined-up thinking on China relations in various EU circles, more than actually resulting in particular practical changes to China's economic footprint in the EU. This is because the BRI gave a name to Chinese trade, investment, and diplomatic outreach that had, in fact, been underway for years, including in the EU.

What was unambiguous, though, since the very first announcements regarding the initiative, was its significance for China. Beijing might have framed the BRI as a "win–win" project for all countries, businesses, and actors involved (Xinhua, 2015), but the initiative was also clearly designed to serve domestic and foreign policy objectives. Indeed, the Chinese authorities saw tremendous upside in pursuing BRI, "ranging from creating new markets through economic penetration, widening the trading and commercial horizons to export Chinese surplus, improving the innovation and competitiveness of Chinese industries, whilst providing the necessary impetus, vision, and know-how for a more coherent regional policy aimed at alleviating internal inequalities amongst provinces and for a more active and better-founded foreign policy that will promote the Chinese interests in a more reliable and efficient manner" (Ntousas, 2016). BRI was therefore also designed to achieve wider objectives than connectivity promotion; through it, Beijing wanted to boost its diplomatic reach, cultivate important relationships and/or dependencies with said countries, and ultimately more clearly reinforce China as a major power with gravitas and an important role to play at the international level.

3 Europe's Uneven Initial Response to the BRI

The announcement of the BRI coincided with a time during which Europe was still very much struggling with the profoundly negative impacts of the 2008/2009 economic and financial crisis. Backed by China's strong infrastructure development capabilities and extensive financial firepower, the promise of the BRI appealed to several European countries, while perceptions of risk varied. Indeed, as the crisis affected EU member states in profoundly different ways, the divergence in historical ties, government policies, business dynamics, and degree of exposure to the crisis translated into a landscape of uneven responses to the BRI and China's financing and investment capacity in general. This was strengthened by Beijing's own strong preference for bilateral outreach directly to national capitals, instead of a more holistic engagement with the EU framework. This meant that while richer countries like the Netherlands have viewed BRI with a degree of caution or scepticism since the very onset, the crisis-stricken states of the South tended to show a clear and sustained interest in what the initiative had to offer.

Plunged into recession and plagued by skyrocketing unemployment, Greece provides a highly illustrative case study of this trend. Having to operate under the stringent fiscal supervision of the "troika" of the European Commission, the European Central Bank, and the International Monetary Fund, Athens found itself in dire need of external economic support and under immense pressure to implement a radical programme of privatization of public assets. Chinese investments in strategic sectors of the economy such as transportation, energy, and infrastructure were therefore viewed by the Greek authorities as an important lever towards addressing this challenge. By far the most emblematic of these investments, and highly controversial within Greek society at the time, was the purchase of a majority stake in the

Piraeus Port Authority by the Chinese state-owned COSCO Shipping in 2016, a highly significant move in Beijing's plan of creating a trade route to the European continent through this critical gateway. Continuing investment on the part of COSCO in Piraeus has led to the transformation of the port to a major trans-shipment hub and its elevation to one of the busiest ports in Europe (Kokoromytis & Chryssogelos, 2021), not however without significant and ongoing tensions between the Chinese investor and Greek authorities.

Dealing with similar fiscal restraints and supervision by international creditors, Portugal also demonstrated an open stance towards Chinese investment. Lisbon's growing realization of the opportunities presented by these streams of investment preceded Beijing's announcements regarding BRI in 2013, but it was certainly emboldened by the economic hardship related to the eurozone crisis that coincided with them. As Ferreira-Pereira and Duarte explain, "the 'foul weather' of the Portuguese recession and the desire to overcome the economic crisis and eventually get rid of the troika's austerity measures created favourable conditions for the Chinese presence that started to be particularly felt as of 2012" (2021, 223). Over time, Portugal became the recipient of a flow of expansive, calibrated, and highly diversified investments by a variety of Chinese state-owned enterprises (SOEs) and private firms, *inter alia* in the areas of energy, telecommunications, banking, renewable energy, and real estate. Indicatively, in 2012, China Three Gorges, a Chinese SOE, purchased 21.35% of the capital of Electricity of Portugal, while in 2014, FOSUN, a privately owned Chinese company, acquired Fidelidade, the most significant insurance firm in the country, and became the largest stakeholder of Banco Comercial Português, the largest private bank (Ibid., p. 224). China's growing footprint in the country was facilitated by the receptive approach sought by consecutive Portuguese governments, which viewed such support as firmly in line with the country's national interest.

Italy also demonstrated a similar posture, owing to a desire to address its own longstanding investment needs. Rome's gradual embrace culminated in the signing of a BRI Memorandum of Understanding (MoU) with Beijing in March 2019, heralding bilateral willingness to cooperate in areas including policy dialogue; transport, logistics, and infrastructure; trade and investment; fiscal, financial and structural reform policies; and people-to-people connectivity (Governo Italiano, 2019). Although this development was mostly linked to a nexus of internal political dynamics (Amighini, 2021), Italy's signing of the MoU—the first G7 and NATO member to do so—underlines the perception of tangible opportunities that BRI presented for several EU member states.

Concerning the Franco-German engine, the approaches were decidedly more balanced. As France was initially not perceived as a target for BRI projects, the French authorities followed a cautious stance of conditional engagement. In practice, this meant that "[w]hile France [was] reluctant to endorse the Chinese initiative in its entirety, it [was] fully aware that it cannot afford to antagonize China. As a result, the favored option [was] to stress the need for sustainability (both environmentally and financially) and to favor punctual cooperation through projects in third countries" (Nicolas, 2021, p. 153). Due to the historically close economic partnership of the German state as well as German business and industry with China, Berlin on the other hand allowed economic interests to continue being the key factor in driving bilateral ties forward. The concept of "Wandel durch Handel"—or "change through trade"—was based on the assumption that "China's authoritarian politics would morph into a free, open, and more democratic system through ever-tightening economic ties" (Barkin, 2020), and which long guided German strategy vis-à-vis China, translated into a cautiously optimistic take on the BRI. Berlin initially "welcomed the initiative's stated aims of closing existing infrastructure gaps in Eurasia and its potentially positive effects on trade and regional economic development" (Mair & Schaff, 2021, pp. 178–179). This variety of approaches to the BRI across the EU raised obstacles against the creation of a truly unified European response to the initiative. These particular obstacles are in addition to the EU's general challenge of speaking with a single voice on most topics in external affairs. Europe's traditional view of China as an economic and trading partner provided the general parameters of engagement and member states differed in their individual responses, acting according to perceptions of national interest. This diversity was also linked to the kind of Chinese investments, the level of dependence on the Chinese export market as well as the strength of each country's relations with Beijing. As suggested above, this meant that especially in the early years of BRI there was considerable intra-EU policy divergence and at times competition among member states to attract Chinese finance, trade, and investment.

4 An Increasingly Sceptical Europe Facing a Changing China and BRI

As time went by, however, and despite these differing interests, European attitudes seem to have converged towards a more sceptical outlook vis-à-vis Beijing and the BRI. For reasons that will be presented below, this change does not fall into a neat time category, given that it took place in varied ways, at different speeds, across various national contexts. As BRI continued being built in a piecemeal manner and bilateral interactions between China and European countries continued to shape perceptions of the initiative, differing national positions persisted. Notwithstanding this plurality, however, the general direction of travel across the continent did undergo a nuanced, but important, course correction towards a greater degree of scrutiny and concern. There were three crucial reasons why this happened.

4.1 The Increased Clarity of BRI Objectives and Elements

First, BRI's rise in importance was very much aligned with growing awareness and visibility of its full scope and concrete impacts. As Nicolas observes, "beyond the physical (hard) infrastructure, the intangible (soft) dimension of the project became increasingly conspicuous, suggesting that China's objectives were more far-reaching than initially anticipated and encompassed the promotion of new standards, courts, customs, policy co-operation mechanisms" (2021, p. 159). As the first trains connecting China and Europe started arriving in 2015 and 2016, and as the acquisition by Chinese SOEs of critical infrastructure across the EU became increasingly evident, so European concerns grew. China's economic expansion into South-Eastern Europe and beyond, which was facilitated by its purchase of the port of Piraeus as a key point of entry into Europe, raised alarms, not least due to the added direct competition Chinese exports presented for European companies. What is more, China's interest in gaining an economic foothold via BRI-related investment in the Western Balkans was also seen as increasingly problematic given the region's strategic importance for Europe and the problems impeding EU accession talks. A poorly conceived and managed highway project in Montenegro, which was financed by Chinese loans and has sent the country's debt soaring (Barkin & Vasovic, 2018) brought such issues directly to the fore. The first phase of this project was expected to be completed in November 2021, but its implementation and financing led to serious accusations of corruption and financial mismanagement (Kajosevic, 2021) as well as calls by the Montenegrin government for the EU to help the country repay the massive Chinese loan (Von der Burchard, 2021).

Within the EU, it was also not long before the inextricable links between the political and economy dynamics were laid bare. For example, Hungary, a significant recipient of Chinese investment, repeatedly blocked EU statements criticizing China's rights record (Emmott & Koutantou, 2017). These instances were only some of the most public examples where Beijing's economic outreach, either related to BRI or not, undermined the EU's capacity to craft unified positions. More generally, these fissures also underscored the growing unease felt in Europe over China's widening political influence within the bloc and its immediate periphery. Beijing's own modalities of engagement within the framework of its investment outreach to Europe added to this growing impression. Indeed, the Chinese authorities' penchant for a predominantly bilateral *modus operandi* targeting EU member states individually—rather than engaging with the EU as a whole—gradually raised alarms as to the difficulties this fragmentation signified in creating a unified strategy vis-à-vis China, its second-largest trade partner. When acting at a plurilateral, instead of purely bilateral, level, Beijing also chose to bring together EU member states, EU applicants, and non-EU member states in a single grouping.

The 16 + 1 initiative, as this sub-regional cooperation format became known,[1] was launched in 2012 with a view to expanding Chinese cooperation with Central

---
[1] The initiative was called "17 + 1" with the addition of Greece in 2019 and again the "16 + 1" following Lithuania's withdrawal in 2021.

and Eastern European countries. Nevertheless, the nature of this configuration and Beijing's preference for engagement outside of the EU framework fed concerns in Brussels and certain national capitals. In a September 2018 resolution, the European Parliament echoed these concerns, calling on all EU member states "to urgently and decisively step up collaboration and unity on their China policies" and those member states participating in the format "to ensure that their participation in this format enables the EU to have one voice in its relationship with China" (European Parliament, 2018). This was a sentiment crucially and increasingly shared not only in Brussels corridors but in other key capitals as well; in 2017, for instance, then German Foreign Minister Sigmar Gabriel argued—in a transparent riff on the "one China policy"—that China should have "a 'one Europe' policy that doesn't attempt to divide us" (Associated Press, 2017). A 2018 report that the EU's 27 ambassadors to Beijing (except for Hungary) allegedly compiled that sharply criticized BRI (Heide et al., 2018), as well as the remarkably speedy adoption (by EU standards) of the foreign direct investment screening framework (Official Journal of the European Union, 2019), which mostly had BRI in mind, started setting the tone of this change in the political outlook.

As Mair and Schaff explain, "[i]t was in this context that Germany together with France pushed the EU to step up its efforts for its own comprehensive strategy for connectivity between the EU and Asia" (2021, p. 180). As a result, in 2018, the EU adopted its own Europe–Asia connectivity blueprint in the form of a Joint Communication on "Connecting Europe and Asia – Building blocks for an EU strategy" (European Commission, 2018) that set out the EU's vision for a new and comprehensive strategy to better connect the two continents. While the then High Representative of the Union for Foreign Affairs and Security Policy and Vice President of the European Commission (HR/VP) Federica Mogherini indicated that it was "not a reaction […] to another initiative" (European External Action Service, 2018), most analysts identified the strategy as the EU's first attempt at a united response to BRI (D'Ambrogio, 2021). The concerns that were linked to the potentially corrosive impact of the BRI on European unity were amplified by the bloc's growing apprehensiveness not least over the negative economic, social, human rights, labour, and environmental consequences of many of the projects subsumed under the BRI umbrella. The EU increasingly voiced these concerns both at the EU and member state level. The first Belt and Road Forum held in Beijing in 2017 saw then European Commission Vice President Jyrki Katainen stressing that any scheme to connect Europe and Asia should adhere to principles such as openness, transparency, and sustainability (European Commission, 2017). In his first state visit to China in 2018, French President Emanuel Macron also warned that the Belt and Road could not be a "one way" project, implying the need to ensure that these principles are met in the design and implementation of the initiative (Rose, 2018). This sentiment was over time echoed by several other EU leaders.

4.2 The General Trajectory of EU–China Relations

A second point that influenced Europe's attitudes towards the initiative was the wider framework of EU–China relations. The two could not be conceivably separated, anyhow, given the BRI's inextricable links to the broader parameters of China's foreign policy and external relations, and the porous boundaries between BRI-specific projects and other streams of Chinese investment. Considering this, European wariness over aspects of the BRI very much matched a growing awareness of the complexity of the overall relationship between the two sides. According to Mair and Schaff, "[w]ith China's influence on global markets expanding rapidly—a development decisively supported by the BRI—there has also been an increasing sense of urgency about asymmetries in market access and distorted competition" (2021, p. 171). Chronic grievances among European policymakers and businesses alike concerning the slow pace of China's "opening up," the lack of reciprocity in access to the Chinese market, the uneven treatment of European investors in China, and the promise fatigue over the lack of change in this domain all synthesized the basis for this gradual shift. As did the solidifying perception of unfair practices employed by Beijing in its economic *modus operandi*, such as the deep involvement of the state in economic and financial matters and the heavy state support and subsidization of much of the exported goods outflow.

China's growing confidence in pursuing its political and policy goals only emphasized the need for a firm and concerted European stance. Despite the existing cleavages and complications, such as the aforementioned signing of Italy's MoU with China drawing the country into the BRI, the unveiling of a strategic reflection paper that was presented to the European Council by the European Commission and the European External Action Service in March 2019 has been widely seen as epitomizing the dynamics of this complex effort towards solidifying the EU position vis-à-vis Beijing. The document, titled "EU-China – A Strategic Outlook" was striking in that it went so far as to call China not only a "partner," but also an "economic competitor" and for the first time "a systemic rival promoting alternative models of governance" (European Commission, 2019). In it, the EU also recognized that China's wider geopolitical objectives "present security issues for the EU, already in a short- to mid-term perspective," and accused Beijing of "withholding its domestic market for its national champions and restricting European companies" access to it; subsidizing domestic competitors; and failing to protect intellectual property rights (Casarini, 2019). The shift towards a more realist approach encapsulated in the strategy reflected the sense of movement in the EU's balance of assumptions about the Sino-European relationship and was in turn reflected in the EU leaders' tone during the 21st EU–China Summit that took place in April 2019. 2019 constituted a year of change in the European approach; not fixing all existing intra-bloc differences over BRI, but substantiating this nuanced, but meaningful step change. As French President Macron declared in a press conference after the Strategic Outlook's presentation, "The time of European naïveté" towards Beijing is over, since "[f]or many years we had an uncoordinated approach and China took advantage of our divisions" (Peel et al., 2019).

4.3 The Transatlantic Dimension

The role of the US should be seen as an additional facilitator of this adjustment in the European outlook. Washington's intense pressure on European allies to bar Huawei, a Chinese company that is the largest provider of telecoms equipment in the world, from being involved in the rollout of the 5G digital infrastructure in many EU member states is the most illustrative case of this. Citing severe risks to data privacy, security, and human rights if Chinese companies were allowed to develop this new generation of telecom network systems, the Trump administration unleashed an intense, months-long diplomatic offensive towards several European countries to roll back and/or exclude the Chinese tech giant from participating in these processes. Over time, this strategy bore fruit in that most EU member states either banned or placed almost insurmountable restrictions on Huawei (Gramer, 2020). Beyond this, however, the pressures applied had two additional important effects: first, they further raised the European public's awareness over potential risks that might come part and parcel with Chinese investment; second, they forced many European capitals to confront the important policy dilemmas that existed in this balancing act between the US and China.

Indeed, while Europe had come to share many of the concerns with the US on what China's growing presence and influence entailed for international affairs, European opposition to many of Beijing's initiatives was nowhere near as sturdy or monolithic as Washington's. Owing to the very political-economy dynamics described above, most EU member states were therefore disinclined to follow a more confrontational stance vis-à-vis Beijing than what the Strategic Outlook implied. This is why Washington's pressures also acted as a reminder to Brussels and many European capitals of the need for Europe to form its own, distinctive approach to the matter.

5 The COVID-19 Pandemic and Its Impact

The advent of COVID-19 found the Sino-European relations amidst this steady hardening shift. The public health crisis that ensued served as an accelerator both of long-term frustrations, but also of EU suspicions vis-à-vis Beijing. Looking back, it is now clear that the coronavirus led to the rebalancing described above gaining greater velocity and urgency. The pandemic's first cataclysmic months inescapably forced many issues of the bilateral relationship to the forefront of attention for European political leaders and citizens alike. The virus shed an unforgiving light on Beijing's handling of the crucial early weeks of the outbreak, but also exposed the EU's high degree of dependence on imports from China for critical medical, protective, and sanitary supplies.

As early as February 2020, the EU along with several member states expressed their readiness to "provide any assistance necessary to assist China in its efforts to contain the spread of the Coronavirus" and mobilized to send protective equipment and other supplies (European Commission, 2020a). In turn, as the spread of the virus reached Europe, and the vast need for similar equipment became obvious across the continent, Beijing reciprocated, utilizing various modalities and avenues of engagement: through direct mobilization of Chinese SOEs, companies, and other private actors, bilaterally with individual national capitals and authorities, and—to a smaller extent—centrally with the EU. Echoing the early years of the BRI's development, the severe shortages in necessary equipment and supplies to battle the pandemic within the EU combined with China's position as a major supplier of them, thrust many EU member states onto a sort of intra-bloc competition courting Chinese aid. Key European countries tried to capitalize on their (perceived) privileged relations vis-à-vis Beijing, aiming to establish quick and reliable flows of said supplies in order to match the meteoric rise in demand. Lacking competence on health issues, the European Commission could not prevent national governments from acting in an uncoordinated manner; many states' attempts at meeting the needs of their own hospitals, patients, and medical staff were often at the expense of other member states. This amplified a sentiment and a reality of initial fragmentation observed across the EU, whereby a disjointed set of restrictions were imposed along national lines, including state border closures, and state-to-state medical export bans.

Sensing an opportunity, Beijing responded to this by implementing a "charm offensive" strategy of aid towards Europe. In an attempt to leverage its position as a critical supply hub and to mobilize one of the pillars of the BRI, the so-called Health Silk Road (Amighini, 2021), shipments of face masks, sanitizers, and ventilators, among other pertinent equipment, started arriving in Europe in a highly publicized fashion. Countries like Italy (Poggioli, 2020), Estonia, Spain (Crawford et al., 2020), France (Reuters, 2020a), and Czechia (Moritsugu, 2020) were only some of the struggling recipients. Beijing's eagerness to provide desperately needed support in vital health equipment and expertise was clearly aimed at restoring its image across many European societies. Furthermore, through this massive international operation—that took place in over seventy countries in the world—China wanted to boost its profile as responsible global leader (Verma, 2020), at a time when the US under the Trump administration opted for a more transparently self-serving stance.

What is critical, though, is that although shipment operations of this kind were organized in most European states, an implicit prioritization of countries that had hitherto been closer to Beijing was conducted on the part of the Chinese authorities. As Luettge et al. (2020) illustrate, this prioritization did not fully align with coronavirus infection rates; rather, purely medical considerations aside, targeting those countries with the highest perception-shaping potential of the donations in an effort to strengthen China's soft power footprint and influence was key.

As the epicentre of the pandemic in Europe during the first few months, Italy was the clearest example of this. Overwhelmed by the virus' rapid and expansive outbreak, Rome initially turned to European partners for support, *inter alia* by asking to activate the EU's Civil Protection Mechanism, which then forwards this request to other member states for voluntary assistance (Beaucillon, 2020). Yet, this request was left unanswered. Making matters worse, reports emerged that countries like Germany blocked shipments of surgical masks "en route from China to Italy ... due to a ban [...] on exporting essential medical goods used in the fight against COVID-19" (Cui, 2020). Europe's insufficient solidarity towards Italy meant that Beijing's subsequent continuous shipments of medical equipment to help with the emergency were warmly welcomed by Rome. Italian Foreign Minister Luigi Di Maio publicly thanked Beijing on multiple occasions, even going so far as suggesting that "those who laughed at the Silk Road, in this moment they must admit that investing in that friendship allowed us to save lives in Italy" (quoted in Chen, 2021).

5.1 *The Turn of the Tide*

As the pandemic gradually stabilized across Europe, however, Beijing's efforts did not bring about the intended results. Notwithstanding a shared view of China as a necessary partner in overcoming the COVID-19 crisis, European views instead became more critical of Chinese actions and rhetoric over time. As Pierre Haski explains, "China thought it was coming out on top from the crisis by sending planes with face masks and medical equipment. Beijing thought it could reap the benefits from being the only power with the capability for this. It's a very weird thing that it has instead provoked a backlash" (Jacinto, 2020). Five interlinked reasons seem to have been most prominent in this regard. First, and at the most basic level, the equipment shipped itself often did not meet quality standards and was rejected by the relevant national authorities. This led to a high number of headlines about substandard Chinese medical aid pouring into countries like Belgium (Sánchez Nicolás, 2020), Finland (Yle News, 2020), the Netherlands, and Spain (BBC, 2020).

Second, China's "mask diplomacy"—understood as a combination of aid shipments, proactive political messaging, and use of other soft power means—was conducted in a very uneven manner in many EU member states, and was itself faced with a very uneven level of receptiveness across the bloc. Indeed, Beijing's overtures might have been perceived more sympathetically in counties like Italy and Hungary, whose populist leaders nurtured close ties with Beijing, but the heavy-handed way they were conducted in others had the opposite effect than that envisioned. As a Reuters investigation revealed, "from Berlin to Bratislava," China often "sought to pressure European countries that criticise[d] its handling of the outbreak" of COVID-19 (Baker & Emmott, 2020). Intent on controlling the pandemic's narrative across Europe, Beijing also assumed a far more proactive, if not belligerent, tone in its public outreach in certain countries, which expectedly did little to polish its tarnished image, but stirred unease instead. The most striking example of this was France, where China's diplomatic offensive included sharing an article on the Chinese embassy website that criticized the West's handling of the coronavirus crisis and in part suggested Western countries had left their pensioners to die in nursing homes (Reuters, 2020b). This led to the French Foreign Minister Jean-Yves Le Drian summoning the Chinese envoy, only to be followed by another article posted on the website, claiming that "some Westerners are beginning to distrust liberal democracy" and that "in the response to the epidemic, socialism with Chinese characteristics has demonstrated its ability to concentrate resources in the service of great achievements" (Ambassade de La Republique Populaire de Chine en Republique Française, 2020).

Third, the transition from "mask diplomacy" to "wolf warrior" diplomacy—as this new, no-holds-barred approach to the outside world—was combined with a series of disinformation and propaganda campaigns that stoked further anger in many member states. In March 2020, Swedish Defense Minister Peter Hultqvist warned publicly that Chinese and Russian media were engaged in a disinformation campaign to discredit his own country's handling of the crisis (Hutt, 2020). Italian media reported that China had deployed armies of twitter bots to spread COVID-19 propaganda, including anti-EU messaging (Bechis & Carrer, 2020), whereas Chinese media outlets also promoted stories based on conspiracy theories that aimed to sow confusion over the coronavirus's origins, suggesting it came from the country (Quartz & Li, 2020). An official report by the European External Action Service named China as a source of disinformation, arguing that it "continued to widely target conspiracy narratives and disinformation both at public audiences in the EU and the wider neighbourhood" (EUvsDisInfo, 2020). Although the report was heavily criticized due to reported pressures by China to soften its criticisms in it (Myers, 2020), it did signal a considerable change in the EU's very real doubts and concerns over the Chinese PR efforts. Indicating this shift, HR/VP Josep Borrell also warned that "there is a geo-political component including a struggle for influence through spinning and the 'politics of generosity'" (European External Action Service, 2020).

Fourth, China's politicization of its position as a supply hub and its efforts to use aid to its own advantage at a time when EU-wide solidarity was found missing, combined with the controversial tactics and belligerent diplomacy it sometimes involved, were gradually seen as attempts to divide Europe. Further doubt was cast on Beijing's motivations when the Chinese authorities attempted to capitalize on the crisis moment that Europe was experiencing, not solely to "win the hearts and minds" of European citizens but promote Chinese economic interests as well. For instance, despite considerable European criticisms, in April 2020, Hungary and China signed a loan agreement to finance the construction of a railway link project between Budapest and Belgrade, as part of BRI, yet classified the project's information for a decade using emergency legislation that was put in place due to the pandemic (Euractiv, 2020).

Fifth, exacerbating things further, China's greater assertiveness in its own regional affairs, including skirmishes with India, the sweeping national security law that was adopted for Hong Kong, as well as the rising criticisms over the treatment of ethnic minorities in Xinjiang, all reinforced Europe's negative views. All these developments made the set of values-based issues that underpinned the 2019 Strategic Outlook's tripartite scheme of "partner, competitor, rival" even more visible in the European mindset, despite the well-trodden economic tracks of cooperation between China and many European countries.

The confluence of these factors turned 2020 into "an annus horribilis for China's image in Europe" (Dams et al., 2021, p. 5). What used to be a more technical list of items predominantly discussed behind closed doors was suddenly replaced by a range of wider, urgent, and sensitive issues that directly affected the lives and livelihoods of European citizens. As argued above, Beijing's coercive practices and assertive handling in terms of both the spread and the management of the pandemic exposed Chinese words and actions to a much higher degree of public scrutiny. Polling released by the European Council on Foreign Relations during the pandemic (April–May 2020) demonstrated this growth of unfavourable views of China across Europe. Almost 50% of the survey's respondents indicated their worsening view of China as a consequence of the pandemic, and in eight of nine surveyed countries, the share of respondents who held a more negative view of China increased by between a factor of two and a factor of ten (Dennison & Zerka, 2020). A wide-scale survey of public opinion on China in thirteen countries in Europe (including Russia, Serbia, and the UK) conducted in September and October 2020 also confirmed this trend (Turcsányi et al., 2020). As the survey's findings indicate "Populations in Western and Northern Europe tend to have the most negative views, Eastern Europe holds positive views, and Southern and Central Europe find themselves in between, while still being predominantly negative. [...] Chinese investments are perceived somewhat more negatively, with only a minority of countries leaning to the positive—such as Serbia, Russia, Latvia, and Poland. Chinese investments are the most negatively perceived by respondents in Sweden, France, and Germany. Similarly, the Belt and Road Initiative is perceived somewhat positively in Serbia, Russia, Latvia, Italy, and Poland, while the remaining countries lean towards negative perceptions" (Ibid.).

6 Conclusion: A Tense Equilibrium

There can be very little doubt that the pandemic has served as a sobering episode in the EU–China relationship, in a way hardening its context and content but also moving its centre of gravity. As Small explains "Beijing's handling of the pandemic has changed long-standing European assumptions about its reliability as a crisis actor and its approach to the European project. [...] [O]n issues ranging from supply chains to ideological competition, European governments have rebalanced their view of what dynamics with China should look like in the aftermath" (2020, p. 1). Although not uniformly felt in each EU member state and across the bloc, the combination and acceleration of accumulated criticisms, fresh concerns over China's actions during the pandemic, and tangible perception shifts among both European elites and the public made the promotion of key tenets in the bilateral agenda an extremely thorny affair. The frosty atmosphere during the 22nd EU–China summit in June 2020, which took place over video conference, was underscored by the fact that no joint statement was released (Grieger, 2020). As underscored during the summit by Commission President von der Leyen, "the Summit was only a starting point. Progress implies cooperation by both sides, implies reciprocity, and implies trust" (European Commission, 2020b). This was also confirmed in subsequent high-level meetings between the two sides, including the September 2020 leaders meeting that took place under the German presidency (European Commission, 2020c).

As an exception to this rule, the only item where progress was made was the negotiations over the long-stagnant Comprehensive Agreement on Investment (CAI) between the two sides. On 30 December 2020, negotiators reached an agreement in principle over a text that is aimed at establishing a uniform legal framework for EU–China investment ties by replacing the 25 outdated bilateral investment treaties China and EU member states had concluded prior (Grieger, 2021). This was made possible after considerable pressures exerted by Germany, which held the rotating EU presidency at the time, even if the agreement's "in principle" nature meant that considerable legal work remained to be done before it would be formally submitted to the Council for approval and to the European Parliament for consent (Ibid.).

Notwithstanding CAI's merits, however, this step could not mask the general negative climate in the bilateral relationship. Confirming this reality, in March 2021, the EU imposed sanctions on several Chinese individuals citing serious violations of human rights in Xinjiang (Council of the European Union, 2021), and China reciprocated by announcing counter-sanctions on a number of individuals and entities in the EU, including Members of the European Parliament, that it said "severely harm China's sovereignty and interests and maliciously spread lies and disinformation" (Reuters, 2021). This has effectively frozen CAI's prospects for adoption (Emmott, 2021), but it also underlined the downward spiral and increasing distrust in the bilateral relationship. Against this backdrop, the question of whether China's economic outreach, including under the BRI along with other streams of Chinese outbound investments and loans, constitutes "a vehicle for EU–China collaboration, a threat to be fended off or some uneasy combination of the two" (Ntousas & Minas, 2021, p. 237) remains ripe for debate. Indeed, the general framework in Europe's approach and attitudes towards China has unmistakably moved, accelerated by a pandemic that widened, furthered, and expedited the repertoire of grievances felt within the EU vis-à-vis Beijing. Yet, this does not mean that intra-EU differentiation has been eliminated. "Either by choice or need, each EU member state [still] sees in the BRI a different balance of economic opportunity and risk" (Ibid., p. 238). Countries such as Portugal still see ample added value in Chinese capital and technology opportunities, whereas others like Lithuania have taken a markedly more confrontational stance. Vilnius exited the 17 + 1 initiative in 2021 and has recently advised against the purchase and use of Chinese mobile phones, after reports revealed built-in censorship technology in many of them (Bateman, 2021). As mentioned above, most European countries have taken active steps to preclude or impede Huawei from participating in their 5G network development processes, but the Greek Court of Audit has recently approved the sale of another 16% stake in Piraeus Port Authority to COSCO (Glass, 2021).

At the EU level, the bloc has still not presented concrete plans as to what the Strategic Outlook's tripartite "partner, competitor, rival" schema of engaging with China would entail in practice, and several member states still pursue "what they consider a pragmatic policy towards [the country], considering it both a competitor and a partner" (Bergsen, 2021, p. 16; see also Oertel, 2020). This means that growing wariness over China's practices has still not translated into tangible changes at the policy level. At the same time, as much of the workability of the tripartite vision of "partner, competitor, rival" is still at a very embryonic level, China's own orientation about and strategic thinking over Europe and the BRI matters as well. Despite the country's rapid economic recovery from the pandemic, COVID-19 has had a huge impact on the Chinese government's planning. China's 14th Five-Year Plan for the years 2021–2025 was presented in 2021 (State Council of the People's Republic of China, 2021), *inter alia* setting objectives in the areas of environmental standards and carbon neutrality, manufacturing, technology, and urbanization. It is still unclear how these would translate in Beijing's overall calculus about the Belt and Road, and in turn how Beijing's overall approach towards Europe would shift, if at all.

Looking at the wider framework of international affairs, China and the EU still confront a common set of collective action problems, such as climate change. While the specifics of the future bilateral relationship remain unknown, the preceding analysis has served to explore the important dynamics that has shaped its current trajectory. The COVID-19 pandemic has served to strengthen the narrative for rebalancing the relationship between Brussels and national capitals on one side and Beijing on the other, both at a decision-making and a public opinion level. So far, there has been limited evidence as to how this shifting attitudinal current might translate into a meaningful change in the EU's policy direction.

In preparing this chapter, we faced the now-familiar challenge of the sprawling and contested nature of the BRI. In current international politics, the BRI may be a uniquely challenging phenomenon to study, differing as it does not just from international organizations and from national policies and initiatives with more coherent and conventional characteristics. To capture the BRI's complexity and *sui generis* nature, we have relied largely on the empirical work presented in our co-edited volume and other recent publications. The analysis of this chapter suggests opportunities for further research including: the intra-EU treatment of "outlier" member states regarding the BRI (i.e., member states whose approach to the BRI is either significantly more welcoming or more hostile than the EU mainstream); the impact on the future development of the BRI of a more restrictive EU policy environment towards it; and the agency of private sector actors within EU–China BRI engagement.

Bibliographic References

Ambassade de La Republique Populaire de Chine en Republique Française. (2020, April 26). *"Pourquoi l'épidémie de covid-19 est-elle à ce point politisée?" Observations d'un diplomate chinois en poste à Paris*. Retrieved on December 2021, from http://www.amb-chine.fr/fra/zfzj/t1773585.htm

Amighini, A. (2021). Italy's Embrace of the BRI and the role of internal political dynamics. In V. Ntousas & S. Minas (Eds.), *The European Union and China's Belt and Road*. Routledge.

ASEAN-China Center. (2013, October 3). *Speech by Chinese president Xi Jinping to Indonesian Parliament*. Retrieved on December 2021, from http://www.asean-china-center.org/english/2013-10/03/c_133062675.htm

Associated Press. (2017, August 31). *China questions German minister's 'One Europe' comments*. AP NEWS. Retrieved on December 2021, from https://apnews.com/89191e6f61cc4f3cb9f3dabda1ea3bcf

Baker, L., & Emmott, R. (2020, May 14). *As China pushes back on virus, Europe wakes to 'wolf warrior' diplomacy*. Reuters. Retrieved on December 2021, from https://www.reuters.com/article/us-health-coronavirus-europe-china-insig-idUSKBN22Q2EZ

Barkin, N. (2020, March 25). *Germany's strategic gray zone with China*. Carnegie Endowment for International Peace. Retrieved on November 2021, from https://carnegieendowment.org/2020/03/25/germany-s-strategic-gray-zone-with-china-pub-81360

Barkin, N., & Vasovic, A. (2018, July 16). *Chinese 'highway to nowhere' haunts Montenegro*. Reuters. Retrieved on November 2021, from https://www.reuters.com/article/us-china-silkroad-europe-montenegro-insi-idUSKBN1K60QX

Bateman, T. (2021, September 27). *'Throw away your Chinese phone,' says Lithuania in new report*. Euronews. Retrieved on November 2021, from https://www.euronews.com/next/2021/09/22/throw-away-your-chinese-phone-says-lithuania-after-new-report-reveals-built-in-censorship

BBC. (2020, March 30). *Coronavirus: Countries reject Chinese-made equipment*. Retrieved on November 2021, from https://www.bbc.com/news/world-europe-52092395

Beaucillon, C. (2020, April 25). *International and European emergency assistance to EU member states in the COVID-19 crisis: Why European Solidarity is not dead and what we need to make it both happen and last*. European Papers. Retrieved on November 2021, from https://www.europeanpapers.eu/en/europeanforum/international-and-european-emergency-assistance-eu-member-states-during-covid-19-crisis

Bechis, F., & Carrer, G. (2020, March 31). *How China unleashed twitter bots to spread covid-19 propaganda in Italy*. Formiche.net. Retrieved on December 2021, from https://formiche.net/2020/03/china-unleashed-twitter-bots-covid19-propaganda-italy/

Bergsen, B. (2021, July 9). *The EU's unsustainable China strategy*. Chatham House, The Royal Institute of International Affairs, Research Paper. Retrieved on December 2021, from https://www.chathamhouse.org/2021/07/eusunsustainable-china-strategy

Casarini, N. (2019, October). *Defend, engage, maximise: A progressive agenda for EU–China relations*. FEPS Policy Paper. Retrieved on December 2021, from https://www.feps-europe.eu/attachments/publications/feps%20policy%20paper%20on%20eu-china%20relations%20-%2011102019.pdf

Chen, W. A. (2021). Covid-19 and China's changing soft power in Italy. *Chinese Political Science Review*. https://doi.org/10.1007/s41111-021-00184-3

Council of the European Union. (2021, March 22). *EU imposes further sanctions over serious violations of human rights around the world*. Consilium. Retrieved on December 2021, from https://www.consilium.europa.eu/en/press/press-releases/2021/03/22/eu-imposes-further-sanctions-over-serious-violations-of-human-rights-around-the-world/

Crawford, A., Martin, P., & Bloomberg. (2020, March 19). *'Health silk road:' China showers Europe with coronavirus aid as both spar with trump*. Fortune. Retrieved on December 2021, from https://fortune.com/2020/03/19/china-europe-coronavirus-aid-trump/

Cui, M. (2020, March 24). *Covid-19: China steps in to help Italy battle the virus*. DW. https://www.dw.com/en/covid-19-china-steps-in-to-help-italy-battle-the-virus/a-52901560

D'Ambrogio, E. (2021). *Prospects for EU-Asia connectivity—European Parliament*. Briefing. EPRS | European Parliamentary Research Service. Retrieved on December 2021, from https://www.europarl.europa.eu/RegData/etudes/BRIE/2021/690534/EPRS_BRI(2021)690534_EN.pdf

Dams, T., Martin, X., & Kranenburg, V. (Eds). (2021). *China's soft power in Europe: Falling on hard times*. Clingendael. Retrieved on December 2021, from https://www.clingendael.org/publication/chinas-soft-power-europe-falling-hard-times

Dennison, S., & Zerka, P. (2020, June 29). *Together in trauma: Europeans and the world after covid-19*. ECFR. https://ecfr.eu/publication/together_in_trauma_europeans_and_the_world_after_covid_19/

Ekman, A. (Ed). (2019). *China's Belt & Road and the world: Competing forms of globalization*. Études de l'Idri, Ifri. https://www.ifri.org/en/publications/etudes-de-lifri/chinas-belt-road-and-world-competing-forms-globalization

Emmott, R. (2021, May 20). *EU Parliament freezes China deal ratification until Beijing lifts sanctions*. Reuters. Retrieved on December 2021, from https://www.reuters.com/world/china/eu-parliament-freezes-china-deal-ratification-until-beijing-lifts-sanctions-2021-05-20/

Emmott, R., & Koutantou, A. (2017, June 18). *Greece blocks EU statement on China human rights at U.N.* Reuters. Retrieved in December 2021, from https://www.reuters.com/article/us-eu-un-rights-idUSKBN1990FP

Esteban, M., & Armanini, U. (2021). COVID-19 and EU-China relations. In V. Ntousas & S. Minas (Eds.), *The European Union and China's Belt and Road*. Routledge.

Euractiv. (2020, April 24). *Hungary, China sign classified loan deal for Budapest-Belgrade Chinese rail project*. Retrieved on December 2021, from https://www.euractiv.com/section/china/news/hungary-china-sign-classified-loan-deal-for-budapest-belgrade-chinese-rail-project/

European Commission. (2017, May 15). *Speech by Jyrki Katainen, Vice President of the European Commission at the leaders' roundtable of the Belt and Road Forum for International Cooperation*. Retrieved on December 2021, from https://ec.europa.eu/commission/presscorner/detail/fr/SPEECH_17_1332

European Commission. (2018, September 19). *Joint Communication to The European Parliament, The Council, The European Economic and Social Committee, The Committee of The Regions and The European Investment Bank: Connecting Europe and Asia: Building blocks for an EU strategy*. JOIN (2018) 31 final. Retrieved on December 2021, from https://eeas.europa.eu/headquarters/headquarters-homepage_en/50708/Connecting%20Europe%20and%20Asia:%20Building%20blocks%20for%20an%20EU%20Strategy

European Commission. (2019, March 12). *European Commission and HR/VP contribution to the European Council. EU-China—A strategic outlook*. https://ec.europa.eu/info/sites/default/files/communication-eu-china-a-strategic-outlook.pdf

European Commission. (2020a, February 1). *Statement by Commissioner for Crisis Management Janez Lenarčič on EU support to China for the Coronavirus outbreak*. Retrieved on December 2021, from https://ec.europa.eu/commission/presscorner/detail/en/statement_20_178

European Commission. (2020b, June 22). *Statement by President von der Leyen at the joint press conference with President Michel, following the EU-China Summit videoconference*. Retrieved on December 2021, from https://ec.europa.eu/commission/presscorner/detail/en/STATEMENT_20_1162

European Commission. (2020c, September 14). *EU-China Leaders' Meeting: Upholding EU values and interests at the highest level*. https://ec.europa.eu/commission/presscorner/detail/en/IP_20_1648

European External Action Service. (2018, September 19). *Remarks by HR/VP mogherini at the press conference on the Joint Communication: Connecting Europe and Asia—Building blocks for an EU strategy*. Retrieved on December 2021, from https://eeas.europa.eu/headquarters/headquarters-Homepage/50736/remarks-hrvp-mogherini-press-conference-joint-communication-connecting-europe-and-asia-%E2%80%93_fr

European External Action Service. (2020, March 23). *EU HRVP Josep Borrell: The coronavirus pandemic and the new world it is creating*. Retrieved on December 2021, from https://eeas.europa.eu/headquarters/headquarters-homepage/76379/corona-virus-pandemic-and-new-world-it-creating_en

European Parliament. (2018, September 12). *European Parliament resolution of 12 September 2018 on the state of EU-China relations*. 2017/2274 (INI). Retrieved on December 2021, from https://www.europarl.europa.eu/doceo/document/TA-8-2018-0343_EN.html?redirect

EUvsDisInfo. (2020, April 24). *EEAS special report update: Short assessment of narratives and disinformation around the COVID-19/coronavirus pandemic.* Retrieved on December 2021, from https://euvsdisinfo.eu/eeas-special-report-update-2-22-april/

Ferreira-Pereira, L. C., & Duarte, P. A. (2021). China and the Belt and Road Initiative in Europe: The case of Portugal. In V. Ntousas & S. Minas (Eds.), *The European Union and China's Belt and Road.* Routledge.

Glass, D. (2021, August 24). *Cosco shipping raises stake in Piraeus Port to 67%.* Seatrade Maritime News. Retrieved on December 2021, from https://www.seatrade-maritime.com/ports-logistics/cosco-shipping-raises-stake-piraeus-port-67

Governo Italiano. (2019). *Memorandum of understanding between the Government of the Italian Republic and the Government of the People's Republic of China on cooperation within the framework of the Silk Road Economic Belt and the 21st Century Maritime Silk Road Initiative.* Retrieved on August 21, 2021, from https://www.governo.it/sites/governo.it/files/Memorandum_Italia-Cina_EN.pdf

Gramer, R. (2020, October 27). *Trump turning more countries in Europe against Huawei.* Foreign Policy. Retrieved on December 2021, from https://foreignpolicy.com/2020/10/27/trump-europe-huawei-china-us-competition-geopolitics-5g-slovakia/.

Grieger, G. (2020). *EU-China relations taking stock after the 2020 EU-China summit.* Briefing. EPRS | European Parliamentary Research Service. Retrieved on December 2021, from https://www.europarl.europa.eu/RegData/etudes/BRIE/2020/651987/EPRS_BRI(2020)651987_EN.pdf

Grieger, G. (2021). *EU-China comprehensive agreement on investment.* Briefing. EPRS | European Parliamentary Research Service. Retrieved on December 2021, from https://www.europarl.europa.eu/RegData/etudes/BRIE/2021/679103/EPRS_BRI(2021)679103_EN.pdf

Heide, D., Hoppe, T., Scheuer, S., & Stratmann, K. (2018, April 17). *China first: EU Ambassadors band together against Silk Road.* Handelsblatt. Retrieved on December 2021, from https://www.handelsblatt.com/english/politics/china-first-eu-ambassadors-band-together-against-silk-road/23581860.html

Hutt, D. (2020, March 25). *China's 'mask diplomacy' in pandemic-hit Europe stirs unease.* Nikkei Asia. Retrieved on November 2021, from https://asia.nikkei.com/Spotlight/Coronavirus/Chinas-mask-diplomacy-in-pandemic-hit-Europe-stirs-unease

Jacinto, L. (2020, May 1). *Can the unmasking of China's covid-19 'mask diplomacy' stem Beijing's global power grab?* France 24. Retrieved on November 2021, from https://www.france24.com/en/20200501-can-the-unmasking-of-china-s-covid-19-mask-diplomacy-stem-beijing-s-global-power-grab

Kajosevic, S. (2021, November 16). *Montenegro authorities exaggerated cost of highway, surveys show.* Balkan Insight. Retrieved on November 2021, from https://balkaninsight.com/2021/11/16/montenegro-authorities-exaggerated-cost-of-highway-surveys-show/

Kokoromytis, D., & Chryssogelos, A. (2021). Greece between crisis, opportunity and risk as a key BRI node. In V. Ntousas & S. Minas (Eds.), *The European Union and China's Belt and Road.* Routledge.

Luettge, F., Soula, E., Ladner, M., & Reuter, M. (2020, July 7). *Masks off: Chinese coronavirus assistance in Europe.* GMFUS. Retrieved on November 2021, from https://www.gmfus.org/news/masks-chinese-coronavirus-assistance-europe

Mair, S., & Schaff, F. (2021). Between commerce and geopolitics: Is there a German China strategy? In V. Ntousas & S. Minas (Eds.), *The European Union and China's Belt and Road.* Routledge.

Ministry of Foreign Affairs of the People's Republic of China. (2013, September 07). *President Xi jinping delivers important speech and proposes to build a Silk Road Economic Belt with Central Asian countries.* Retrieved on November 2021, from https://www.fmprc.gov.cn/mfa_eng/topics_665678/xjpfwzysiesgjtfhshzzfh_665686/t1076334.shtml

Moritsugu, K. (2020, March 21). *China, on virus PR offensive, sends masks and experts abroad.* AP NEWS. Retrieved on November 2021, from https://apnews.com/article/ap-top-news-virus-outbreak-international-news-china-health-eca869390e67736df891003862e1aeae

Myers, S. L. (2020, March 13). *China spins tale that the U.S. Army started the coronavirus epidemic. The New York Times*. Retrieved on November 2021, from https://www.nytimes.com/2020/03/13/world/asia/coronavirus-china-conspiracy-theory.html

National Development and Reform Commission, Ministry of Foreign Affairs, and Ministry of Commerce of the People's Republic of China. (2015, March 03). *Vision and actions on jointly building Silk Road Economic Belt and 21st-century Maritime Silk Road*. Retrieved on November 2021, from https://en.ndrc.gov.cn/newsrelease_8232/201503/t20150330_1193900.html

Nicolas, F. (2021). France, China and the BRI: The challenge of conditional engagement. In V. Ntousas & S. Minas (Eds.), *The European Union and China's Belt and Road*. Routledge.

Ntousas, V. (2016, March). *Back to the future: China's 'One Belt, One Road' initiative*. FEPS Policy Brief. Retrieved on October 2018, from https://www.feps-europe.eu/assets/6b12aa95-9d47-466f-a791-fa02a5d5c7d3/backtothefuture-feps-policybriefpdf.pdf

Ntousas, V., & Minas, S. (Eds.). (2021). *The European Union and China's Belt and Road*. Routledge.

Oertel, J. (2020, September 7). *The New China consensus: How Europe is growing wary of Beijing*. ECFR. Retrieved on October 2018, from https://ecfr.eu/publication/the_new_china_consensus_how_europe_is_growing_wary_of_beijing/

Official Journal of the European Union. (2019, March 21). *Regulation (EU) 2019/452 of the European Parliament and of the Council of 19 March 2019 establishing a framework for the screening of foreign direct investments into the Union*. Document 32019R0452. Retrieved on October 2021, from https://eur-lex.europa.eu/eli/reg/2019/452/oj

Peel, M., Mallet, V., & Johnson, M. (2019, March 22). *Macron hails 'end of Europe Naïveté' towards China*. Financial Times. Retrieved on October 2021, from https://www.ft.com/content/ec9671ae-4cbb-11e9-bbc9-6917dce3dc62

Poggioli, S. (2020, March 25). *For help on Coronavirus, Italy turns to China, Russia and Cuba*. NPR. Retrieved on October 2021, from https://www.npr.org/sections/coronavirus-live-updates/2020/03/25/821345465/for-help-on-coronavirus-italy-turns-to-china-russia-and-cuba?t=1632637823195

Quartz, S., & Li, J. (2020, April 2). *An Italian doctor is now key to China's efforts to sow confusion over the coronavirus's origins*. Quartz. Retrieved on October 2021, from https://qz.com/1823417/italy-now-key-to-china-coronavirus-origin-propaganda-efforts/

Reuters. (2020a, March 18). *China sends masks, gloves to help France fight virus—French minister*. Retrieved on October 2021, from https://www.reuters.com/article/us-health-coronavirus-france-china/china-sends-masks-gloves-to-help-france-fight-virus-french-minister-idUSKBN2152GF

Reuters. (2020b, April 14). *France summons Chinese envoy after comments on Coronavirus handling*. Retrieved on October 2021, from https://www.reuters.com/article/us-health-coronavirus-france-china-idUSKCN21W2TC

Reuters. (2021, March 22). *China hits back at EU with sanctions on 10 people, four entities over Xinjiang*. Retrieved on October 2021, from https://www.reuters.com/business/aerospace-defense/china-hits-back-eu-with-sanctions-10-people-four-entities-over-xinjiang-2021-03-22/

Rose, M. (2018, January 8). *China's new 'Silk road' cannot be one-way, France's Macron says*. Reuters. Retrieved on October 2021, from https://www.reuters.com/article/us-china-france/chinas-new-silk-road-cannot-be-one-way-frances-macron-says-idUSKBN1EX0FU

Sánchez Nicolás, E. (2020, April 2). *EU fighting shortages and faulty medical supplies*. EUobserver. Retrieved on October 2021, from https://euobserver.com/coronavirus/147958

Small, A. (2020, May 13). *The meaning of systemic rivalry: Europe and china beyond the pandemic*. ECFR. Retrieved on October 2021, from https://ecfr.eu/publication/the_meaning_of_systemic_rivalry_europe_and_china_beyond_the_pandemic/

State Council of the People's Republic of China. (2021). *Major targets in 14th five-year plan*. Retrieved on December 2021, from http://english.www.gov.cn/w/14thfiveyearplan/

Turcsányi, R. Q., Šimalčík, M., Kironská, K., Sedláková, R., Čeněk, J., Findor, A., Buchel, O., Hruška, M., Brona, A., Bērziņa-Čerenkova, U. A., Esteban, M., Gallelli, B., Gledić, J., Gries, P., Ivanov, S., Jerdén, B., Julienne, M., Matura, T., Rühlig, T., & Summers, T. (2020). *European public opinion on China in the age of covid-19: Differences and common ground across the continent*. Ifri. Retrieved on December 2021, from https://www.ifri.org/en/publications/publicati ons-ifri/european-public-opinion-china-age-covid-19-differences-and-common

Valero, J. (2015, October 6). *China uses Juncker plan to boost involvement in Europe*. www.eur activ.com. Retrieved on December 2021, from https://www.euractiv.com/section/global-europe/ news/china-uses-juncker-plan-to-boost-involvement-in-europe/

Van Middelaar, L. (2018). *Quand l'Europe improvise. Dix ans de crises politiques*. Gallimard.

Verma, R. (2020). China's 'mask diplomacy' to change the COVID-19 narrative in Europe. *Asia Europe Journal, 18*(2), 205–209. https://doi.org/10.1007/s10308-020-00576-1

Von der Burchard, H. (2021, April 12). *EU rebuffs Montenegro plea to help repay $1b Chinese highway loan*. Politico. Retrieved on December 2021, from https://www.politico.eu/article/eu-montenegro-billion-dollar-china-unfinished-highway-loan/

Xinhua. (2015, March 29). *Full text of Chinese president's speech at Boao Forum for Asia*. Retrieved on December 2021, from http://news.xinhuanet.com/english/2015-03/29/c_134106145.htm

Yle News. (2020, April 11). *Finland not alone in medical supplies scam*. Retrieved on December 2021, from https://yle.fi/uutiset/osasto/news/finland_not_alone_in_medical_supplies_scam/11303307

Chapter 22
China in Central and Eastern Europe: New Opportunities for Small States

Vladimir Milić

1 Introduction

The founding of the Belt and Road Initiative (BRI) in 2013 clearly signalled China's intention to shift towards a more proactive foreign policy. Preceding this global initiative, the "16 + 1" mechanism was created in 2012 to promote and deepen economic and cultural exchanges between Central Eastern European (CEE) countries and China. Although the mechanism predates the BRI by a year, it was absorbed by the BRI and its objectives aligned with the latter. The CEE represents a strategic gateway to Europe from Asia. It is an entry point for the BRI's maritime road through Greece and the land route through Poland. Additionally, it is a significant market, with more than 110 million middle-income consumers. The mechanism originally included 16 countries from the CEE region: 11 members of the European Union (EU) (Bulgaria, Czech Republic, Croatia, Estonia, Latvia, Lithuania, Hungary, Poland, Romania, Slovakia, and Slovenia), and five countries aspiring to become part of the EU (Albania, Bosnia and Herzegovina, Montenegro, North Macedonia, and Serbia). All countries except Serbia and Bosnia and Herzegovina are members of the North Atlantic Treaty Organization (NATO). In 2019, with the addition of Greece (an EU and NATO member), the platform changed its name to 17 + 1 (China–CEE, 2019). However, in May 2021, the platform was downsized to 16 members again as Lithuania decided to leave (Lau, 2021). Moreover, all countries signed the Memorandum of Understanding (MoU) of the BRI and supported the Initiative from the beginning (Sacks, 2021).

Speculation questioning the basic aim and purpose of the 17 + 1 mechanism has existed since its foundation. As we will see next in this section, current literature describes it either as a platform used to strengthen cooperation between China and Europe or as a tool that could threaten to divide Europe. So far, those predictions

V. Milić (✉)
An Independent Researcher, Megatrend University, Belgrade, Serbia
e-mail: milic.vlada@gmail.com

have not been realized, but critics remain convinced of these narratives (Duan et al., 2021). Unhelpful to the situation has been the profusion of analysis from a great power perspective (Cumpănaşu, 2019; Eggleton, 2021; Pepe, 2017). Therefore, our analysis tries to address the gap in the literature by providing an alternative view from the smaller CEE states' motivations and perspectives. The timeframe considered for this analysis spans from the establishment of the mechanism in 2012 to the exit of member state Lithuania in May 2021. This analysis of the relations between China and CEE countries argues that two new trends are emerging. First, countries are using the newly forged connections with China to get closer to Western alliances and to reaffirm their affiliation. Second, countries are trying to leverage their links with China for quasi-balancing purposes or concessions in addition to domestic gains.

Once in place, the 17 + 1 mechanism aimed at forging economic ties in the fields of infrastructure, transportation, trade, and investment along with growing ties in the areas of culture, education, and tourism. In an attempt to explain the motives underpinning cooperation between China and CEE region, Song (2018) claims that Chinese expansion towards CEE was a logical outgrowth of the People's Republic's developmental state model and that it showed the country's desire to be a global leader. Vangeli (2018) also attaches China's regional involvement to a broader process of China's shifting global role, in which CEE serves as a land bridge and a partner in the expansion of production capacity. Liu (2018) goes on to suggest that CEE countries help link European and Asian economies by promoting cooperation between China and the EU.

Since the 17 + 1 mechanism is limited to the CEE region, suspicions have been raised over China employing a "divide and conquer" strategy at Europe's expense. The simple notion that a country from Asia established a sub-regional organization inside European Union has caused great concerns (Gerstl, 2020). These concerns are clear and abundant not only throughout the media but also throughout academic publications (Benner & Weidenfeld, 2018; Oertel, 2020). Pepermans (2018) claims that the BRI and 16 + 1 mechanism offered China the opportunity to expand its influence in Central and Eastern Europe utilizing economic incentives and soft power acquired by cultural exchange and diplomatic dialogue. Jakimów (2019) agrees with this view and claims that desecuritized BRI narratives deployed by China are an effective soft power strategy in China's engagement with Europe. These narratives are then deliberately used and reproduced by CEE countries aiming to negotiate domestic interests with EU institutions, rendering the cooperation neither apolitical nor benevolent.

However, in reality, the geopolitical situation is more complex since great powers' influence is a determinant factor in the region. While W. Song and L. Song (2020) acknowledge that China is a dominant player vis-à-vis CEE countries, its dominance is constrained by the other great powers in the region, namely the EU and the US. Furthermore, regarding the evident asymmetry in the relations between China and CEE countries, Song and Pavlićević (2019) argue that although China retains overall agenda-setting control in the relations, it tries to share leadership in the platform through sectoral cooperation to participating countries based on their perceived advantages, preferences, and strategic interests. Nonetheless, Malinowski

(2019) warns that Chinese cooperation proposals are caught up in geopolitical narratives. As a result, cooperation that was supposed to bring gains for less developed countries has turned into a point of contention between the major powers. Turning the focus to Chinese economic practices, Garlick (2019) asserts that they are not hostile and detrimental to Europe, but allow for the scenario in which Western Europe's influence may experience a downturn in absolute terms, whereas China and CEE economies will rise.

As opponents to the idea that China is trying to break up Europe, W. Song and L. Song (2020) point out that there is no concrete indication that China wants to use the 17 + 1 mechanism to exploit or politically divide European countries, as this would be ineffective and detrimental to Chinese interests. As Gerstl (2020) found, China acted far more as a norm-taker than a norm-setter in the CEE so far. Pavlićević (2019) also finds that China not only lacks the ability but also the desire to influence CEE countries, especially at the expense of the EU. Using the Western Balkans as an example, Pavlićević (2019) refutes the notion that China has made substantial strides at the detriment of the EU, demonstrating that the EU can easily reassert itself by exercising structural power. The naïve vision of China splitting Europe using 17 + 1 should be dismissed according to Karásková et al. (2020) since it infantilizes CEE countries and denies their power. Instead of endorsing Beijing's agenda, they advise that CEE countries should "hijack" the platform and use it to advance their interests.

However, governments and the public in the West have remained unconvinced of Chinese benign intentions. The EU has repeatedly questioned the motives for cooperation between China and CEE countries, especially since the EU has been changing to a more confrontational posture towards China (European Parliament, Committee of Foreign Affairs, 2021). BRI and consequently the 17 + 1 mechanism are still vague initiatives that have inspired suspicion and lack of trust in the Chinese's intentions. The EU is distrustful since the proclaimed economic cooperation in the long term could bring the CEE region under China's sphere of influence (Cumpănașu, 2019). This narrative has been amplified by member countries' politicians who have exaggerated the cooperation with China for their own domestic goals of self-promotion or to assert some degree of independence from Brussels (Lau, 2020).

Moreover, the competition between the US and China has added another dimension to an already complex relationship. Since the launch of the trade war, the US policy towards China has progressed to a new level of hostility and containment. In this environment, the US has increased its engagement in Central and Eastern Europe, putting direct pressure to limit China–CEE collaboration (Speranza & Huntington, 2021).

This chapter will proceed as follows. First, it will present the different ways CEE countries and China understand each other and demonstrate that almost 10 years after the foundation, 17 + 1 remains a loose setting that member countries perceive and use differently. Second, it will describe how misunderstandings and diverging expectations have resulted largely in CEE countries' disappointment with the attained levels of economic cooperation. Third, as the tepid political relations have shown, fears that China is using the mechanism to split Europe remain unfounded. However, closer scrutiny of the relations reveals that the COVID-19 outbreak along with the

US–China rivalry exacerbated political views across the region, compelling some countries to forgo newly developed relations with China for security or economic benefits elsewhere. As a result, this analysis finds that two new trends are emerging. In the first, countries are using newly forged connections with China to get closer to Western alliances and to reaffirm their affiliation. In the second, countries are trying to leverage links with China for quasi-hedging purposes or concessions, in addition to domestic gains. The road ahead for the 17 + 1 mechanism will be discussed in light of the emerging trends concluding that the initiative's future will be determined by the countries' capacity to adjust original expectations and handle their relationships in the face of mounting external pressures.

2 Forming Unrealistic Expectations

Historically, CEE countries have not had significant levels of interaction with China. They were among the first to recognize the People's Republic of China after its founding in 1949, yet the development of closer relations did not come to fruition. Until the collapse of the Union of Soviet Socialist Republics (USSR), their relations were conditioned by USSR–China relations, except for Albania, Romania, and Yugoslavia. After the Cold War, both China and CEE were burdened by domestic priorities and the subsequent search for a new development model. Both sides prioritized developing relations with Western countries, albeit for different motives. CEE countries were searching for a new role model to follow, and China was searching for a lucrative market and sources of technology and capital. Consequently, during the 1990s and early years of the twenty-first century, CEE was virtually missing from China's foreign policy, while the majority of CEE countries saw EU and NATO integration as key components of their political and economic direction (Pavlićević, 2018; Turcsányi & Qiaoan, 2019).

With renewed vigour in foreign diplomacy and the formation of 17 + 1, China has tried to conceptualize CEE as a region; however, those countries have never perceived themselves as such. The shared communist past they were trying to shed off was the main factor connecting them. So, when China approached the region with an outdated rhetoric about communist comradery, it did not find the expected acceptance (Turcsányi & Qiaoan, 2019). Strategically, this approach was one of the first oversights in trying to deepen the relationship. The absence of meaningful relations has caused a lack of understanding on both sides. For example, China saw these countries as a former communist block and part of the global south, whereas only Serbia, North Macedonia, and Bosnia and Herzegovina identified themselves with the global south. On the other hand, CEE countries' misperception of China can be ascertained by their belief of China mainly being a potential source of direct investments and export opportunities. Right from the beginning, a knowledge gap was displayed quite visibly on both sides, and perceptions of China and its increasing presence in the area fluctuated between positive and negative extremes, even though neither positive nor negative assessments were based on empirical evidence or guided by a thorough understanding of the relationship's context (Pavlićević, 2018). The apparent lack of understanding was exacerbated by diverging interests. European countries were concentrated on short-term economic gains, such as rising exports or attracting Chinese FDI, while China was more interested in forging long-term relations with political benefits (Song & Song, 2020). Nonetheless, while these misunderstandings laid the foundation for the relationship, the relationship has proceeded and continued to date.

Except for 2020 (due to COVID-19), yearly 17 + 1 summits have taken place, where several additional coordinating institutions and mechanisms for cooperation have been established. However, despite these efforts for setting more meaningful structures, 17 + 1 has remained a loose institutional setting. China built this mechanism using its previous experience working with developing countries in Latin America (CCF) and Africa (FOCAC) and envisioned it as an "adaptable and fluid institutional framework" which would allow it to mix multilateral and bilateral cooperation (Jakóbowski, 2018). The final result was a China-led organization where the agenda-setting is in Chinese hands with sectoral cooperation open for leadership from CEE countries. This was an attempt to blend multilateral and bilateral approaches to the region to overcome differences inside the region while keeping countries in the framework (Song & Pavlićević, 2019). As a result, the mechanism proved to be effective in gathering all countries in one place but ceding priority to bilateral ties. Almost 10 years of interaction between CEE and China through the 17 + 1 mechanism have resulted in the creation of new connections across all levels of government, new economic ties, and cultural exchanges (Vangeli & Pavlićević, 2019). Throughout the course of this period, 17 + 1 has generally avoided stronger institutionalization and countries were mostly collaborating through bilateral ties. However, the mutual lack of geopolitical acumen and misunderstandings have put a heavy load on the relationship and have continued to burden the cooperation.

3 Sluggish Economic Cooperation

Economic cooperation was emphasized as one of the main goals of the 17 + 1 mechanism and is often asserted as its most noteworthy achievement. From 2012 to 2020, trade between the 17 CEE countries and China rose by 8% annually on average, more than double the growth of China's trade with the EU, topping the $USD 100 billion thresholds for the first time in 2020 (Xinhua, 2021). In percentage terms, economic results look substantial and can signal continued growth in the future. However, when taking into account the starting low base, results fall short of CEE countries' prior expectations. Moreover, imports from China have risen much faster than CEE exports, resulting in rising trade deficits (Xu, 2021). The lack of strong export growth and expanding deficits have caused disappointment regarding the platform, in turn often causing its results and potentials to be downplayed (Brînză, 2021).

CEE countries had expected to serve as a bridge connecting China and Western Europe, an idea that was often promoted by domestic politicians. Noteworthy is the Hungarian Prime Minister Victor Orban's declaration that Hungary would be an "entry gate" for Chinese companies towards Western markets and Czech Republic's President Milos Zeman's statement referring to the Czech Republic as an "unsinkable aircraft carrier of Chinese investment" (Barboza et al., 2018; The Economist, 2018). Such politicians and their statements were completely neglecting the fact that Chinese companies were already present in Western markets and that majority of Chinese Foreign Direct Investment (FDI) went to Western countries. This trend is likely to continue into the future.

Despite high growth in percentage terms, trade with China has remained a small part of the overall trade of the 17 countries. Comparing the Chinese economic engagement with other parts of the world, the CEE region has one of the lowest levels of interactions with China in the world. Less than 2% of the region's exports go to China and less than 9% of its imports come from China (Turcsányi, 2020). As one of the pillars in the promised growth in economic activity, trade figures indicate lethargic cooperation. The amount of Chinese investments, as with trade, have mostly been directed towards Western Europe. From 2000 to 2019, China invested USD 126 billion in the EU (excluding the UK), with less than USD 10 billion coming to the CEE region, including USD 5.5 billion to V4[1] countries (MERICS, 2017). Chinese FDI in CEE countries accounted for less than 1% of total FDI. The situation is even more grim-looking from the Chinese side since the region constitutes much less than 1% of total FDI, and around 3% of total Chinese exports flow to the region (Duan et al., 2021; Turcsányi, 2020). Despite the initial touting of investments growth, investments have not satisfied CEE countries either.

In terms of economic cooperation, infrastructure projects stand out. It is worth noting that most of the infrastructure projects promoted as success stories of the mechanism are based on loans given by the Chinese side and could be counted as investments by local governments. Nevertheless, by this measurement, Serbia ranks first in the region with (EUR 9.7 billion) of Chinese investments and loans, followed by Hungary (EUR 5.4 billion), Romania (EUR 2.8 billion), Poland (EUR 2.7 billion), and Bosnia and Herzegovina (EUR 1.9 billion) (Matura, 2021). While infrastructure projects have seen some growth, these projects have materialized only in a few countries with many disparities. Assessing the economic cooperation so far Chinese exports and loans for infrastructure projects (in Western Balkans countries) have been the only economic success stories. To help stimulate trade, China announced in 2021 plans to import more than USD 170 billion of agricultural products in the next 5 years to reduce the trade deficit and bolster trade cooperation (Xinhua, 2021). Although a welcome announcement, it portrayed well the mismatch in expectations. CEE countries had hoped that the cooperation would bring investment and export

---

[1] The Visegrád Group or V4 is a cultural and political alliance of four Central European (Czech Republic, Hungary, Poland, and Slovakia), all of which are members of the EU and of NATO, to advance cooperation in military, cultural, economic, and energy matters with one another and to further their integration to the EU.

opportunities to upgrade their economies, while China dominantly offers loans and, more recently, increased agricultural exports.

Due to the economic structure of CEE countries, observed trends do not appear to be changing anytime soon. Generally, CEE countries are not resource-abundant and lack advanced technologies that could attract Chinese capital. They are situated between developed and developing countries, trying to move up the supply chain in advanced manufacturing and basic services. These are overlapping sectors China is trying to develop at home, thus making them competitors more than complementary trading partners (Turcsányi, 2020). So even if the agricultural exports met established targets, the economic cooperation would be far from the initial expectations of an influx of Chinese FDI into the region and export success to the Chinese markets. So far, Chinese economic engagement through loans has predominantly concentrated in the Western Balkans focusing heavily on energy and transportation (Vladimirov & Gerganov, 2021). Although countries in the EU are economically bigger and more developed, the focus on non-EU members has been mostly due to various EU regulations (Song, 2018). Coming to the region, China had made similar bargains as with the rest of the developing world, entailing state-to-state agreed and negotiated credits, without a transparent bidding process and with a requirement to employ a Chinese company with its employees and importing large quantities of Chinese goods (Grgić, 2017). EU member countries were less interested due to their access to alternative sources of funding within the EU, such as structural funds, which are more appealing than the Chinese bid, and because this method of deal-making is incompatible with EU regulations (Malinowski, 2019). As a result, Western Balkans countries have seen the most materialization of the cooperation albeit in bilateral terms.

Economic interactions so far have been notable; however, they have been unable to match the often-unrealistic expectations that CEE countries have had. China remains an important source of capital to countries outside of the EU and will remain an important trading partner for all countries. Compared to Western Europe, the Chinese economic footprint in CEE has been relatively small but implies further potential for growth (Duan et al., 2021). Relations in the future will be strongly influenced by the way members of the 17 + 1 platform handle and adjust their expectations versus the economic realities.

4 Recommitment to Western Allies Versus Strategic Autonomy

Since the beginning of the new century, China has made an effort to upgrade political relations with almost every country across Europe (Horváth, 2020). Western European countries such as France, Portugal, and Italy, as well as the EU signed a "Comprehensive strategic partnership" with China, and Germany even upgraded its relation with China to "all-around strategic partnership." From Central and Eastern Europe

Bulgaria, Serbia, Greece, Poland, and Hungary stand out as having a "Comprehensive strategic partnership" (Li & Ye, 2019) with China. These documents illustrate the point that China is trying to create deeper partnerships and forge connections all around the continent.

With the foundation of the 17 + 1 mechanism, many observers have raised their concerns regarding China's attempt to acquire political influence in the European Union by forging political ties with the smaller eastern European states (Stojanovic, 2019; Vladimirov & Gerganov, 2021). According to this narrative, the weaker economies in CEE are more susceptible and easier to influence by China. The deepening of relations in these states would subject them to Chinese influence and hurt European unity.

In the first few years since establishing the 17 + 1 mechanism, CEE countries' high expectations amplified Western narratives that accused CEE countries of being too accommodating of China and taking its side over supporting EU interests. For a moment, it looked like CEE countries were going to sacrifice Europe's political cohesion in exchange for Chinese economic benefits (Mitchell, 2020). However, it has become clear that the economic benefits were exaggerated, as well as the political influence that was supposed to follow. More than just opportunities for deepening Chinese influence in CEE, 17 + 1 meetings allowed leaders of small CEE countries to brag about their countries' advantages to China. Leaders were presenting themselves as capable of forming closer ties with the rising power and trading powerhouse (Xinhua, 2017). This narrative was mostly intended for domestic political gains or to exert independence vis-à-vis Brussels (Ghincea et al., 2021), but it also found a global audience (Politico, 2018; The Diplomat, 2017).

As lagging economic cooperation and weak institutional settings gave priority to bilateral ties, only a few countries took this advantage and developed political ties. The most significant development in bilateral cooperation between China and states in the region, which has been characterized by high-level visits, political and economic cooperation, can be observed in Hungary and Serbia. In contrast, states such as Slovenia and Slovakia have not managed to increase the intensity of their relationship with China. Countries like Poland, Czech Republic, and Romania have changed their initial attitudes considerably, mainly towards taking a less active stance as their participation in the mechanism has not brought on the anticipated gains and as a response to the EU and the US pressure to limit their interaction (CSIS, 2020a, 2020b; Karásková et al., 2020). So far, Hungary and Serbia are the only countries that have demonstrated a constant interest in closer political ties with Beijing. Notably, their interest has been motivated by domestic factors and an attempt to form strategic autonomy vis-à-vis Brussels (Ghincea et al., 2021). Serbian engagement with China can be understood as a balancing act, trying to bolster its position between great powers. As the EU membership prospect is faltering and the pressure to accept the independence of its runaway province Kosovo is increasing, political elites are searching for potential partners (Milić, 2020). On the other hand, the Hungarian actions can be traced back to the decade-old change in a foreign policy called "Eastern opening." Although it failed to bring the anticipated economic gains, the strategy often fulfilled a political purpose, allowing Hungary to assert its independence from Brussels (Paszak, 2021).

More broadly across the region, the COVID-19 pandemic caused several issues in the relationship that slowed the cooperation further. Some initiatives had to be postponed while people-to-people exchanges came to a standstill (Jing, 2021). At the start, China did use the 17 + 1 mechanism to offer help to countries in need, but final deals were made at the individual level where each country made a separate request and negotiated cooperation on a bilateral level. Additionally, the perception of China in the region during the pandemic largely took a negative turn with the notable exception of Serbia (Turcsányi et al., 2020).

Worsened attitudes towards China were also exacerbated by the US–China rivalry, as the US has started using its influence in the region to gather support for schemes intended to limit China's reach. Often under pressure or in exchange for security or financial investment, almost every CEE country except for Hungary, Bosnia and Herzegovina, and Montenegro subscribed to the US-led initiative "Clean Network" (Lee, 2019). The initiative is understood to limit the expansion of Chinese telecommunication giant Huawei by excluding it from telecommunication networks. For example, Serbia pledged to exclude untrusted vendors from its telecommunication networks as a part of the broader deal called the "Washington Agreement," a US-led attempt to normalize relations between Serbia and Kosovo with promised US investment in the region (Bjelotomic, 2020; Muharremi, 2021). Poland also became part of the initiative in exchange for additional security guarantees (through the Enhanced Defense Cooperation Agreement) that strengthened the US military presence in the region (Ministry of National Defense—Republic of Poland, 2020). Additionally, all countries except the Western Balkans are part of the US-backed "Three Seas Initiative" which is supposed to balance the BRI's influence in the regions, especially in the infrastructure sector (Brînză, 2019; Grgić, 2021; Rakštytė, 2021). Historically, the region has been a battling ground for great powers, and it has become apparent that this has not changed.

The effects of these global issues have easily trickled down to affect the domestic politics of 17 + 1 members. Recent political changes in several member countries have pointed towards more confrontational relations with Beijing (Turovski, 2021). Different governments have different agendas, and the succeeding one does not have to follow in the footsteps of the previous one. As the existing ruling elite portray themselves as a provider of economic benefits that never materialize, the opposition can exploit this to erode the existing government's legitimacy. An example is the Czech Republic, where opponents of President Zeman, who has been a strong supporter of cooperation with China, have questioned this cooperation. They have even called for stronger ties with Chinese Taipei and suggested a change in foreign policy with a stronger emphasis on human rights (AP News, 2020). In another instance, Budapest's mayor campaigned against Viktor Orban by attacking the cooperation with China and recently went against the agreement to build a Fudan University campus in Budapest by naming 4 streets around the proposed location with the names that go against the "One China" policy (BBC News, 2021). In turn, these localized actions may have regional aftershocks in other countries.

Already, some countries have also exhibited China-alienating behaviours to gain support from other allies. For example, after a historic change of government in Montenegro in 2020, ruling elites used the real danger of sovereign debt default to show their commitment to the EU and to get closer to the EU's orbit by refinancing Chinese credit with the help of Western countries, thus eliminating Chinese influence in the process (Baczynska & Vasovic, 2021; Ruge & Shopov, 2021). Romania has been observed to abandon previous contracts with Chinese companies under the pressure from the US, thus signalling the change from its low-level participation in the platform to a more active distancing from the cooperation with China (Brînză, 2021). In the case of Baltic countries, change has been even more visible. As their primary concern is security due to their proximity to Russia and after disappointing economic results with the 17 + 1 platform, they have used the Chinese presence in the region to attract more attention from the US. Notable in the region was Lithuania, which acted as the *tip of the spear* in the confrontation between the US and China as it left the 17 + 1 mechanism and called for a united EU and Western front when dealing with China (Andrijauskas, 2021; Kramer & Binnendijk, 2021). The case of Lithuania could point to a shift in the relations between CEE and China. As the anticipated economic gains did not materialize, other countries might also sacrifice their relations with China to reap a reward in the future, whether through financial assistance from the US or increased American security presence to counterweight Russian influences. These countries have slowly but surely shifted their foreign policy posture regarding China, making themselves even more unavailable to the latter.

Warnings regarding China's gain of influence in the EU through CEE countries have so far fallen short as the expansion of influence has failed to materialize even ten years after the platform's establishment. Even in the Western Balkans, a region that is not formally part of the EU, Brussels could quickly reassert itself exercising its structural power (Pavlićević, 2019a). In parallel, China lacks both the intention and the capacity to alter the strategic and policy choices of CEE countries specially to gain influence inside the EU (Pavlićević, 2019b). The concern that China will influence these countries politically has proven to be excessive. Even in the case of Hungary or Serbia, their closer political ties with China were guided by domestic motives or in an attempt to assert a degree of independence from Brussels. A new trend emerging from the disappointment in the economic cooperation and in search of other benefits from the EU or US stimulated some CEE countries to sacrifice relations with China and bring the future of 17 + 1 to question.

5 Conclusion

The rise of China is drawing concern for the changing power distribution around the globe. However, this power shift has not been so pronounced in CEE as in other regions. The 17 + 1 mechanism has generally avoided stronger institutionalization and kept a low profile by focusing on economic cooperation. While it has succeeded in forging a certain level of connections between CEE countries and China, these relationships have remained shallow and uneven across the bloc. Initial warnings that China was creating a sphere of influence in CEE have thus proven to be inapplicable. CEE remains too far away geographically, deeply anchored into the EU and Western alliances with rising, but still not substantial, economic or political relations with China.

The mechanism's mixed success almost a decade after its formation could be explained by the misunderstanding or mutual lack of knowledge which caused diverging expectations since the beginning. In this scenario, these "growing pains" could be overcome along the way as the cooperation develops. This would require willing partners ready to cooperate and recalibrate their overly ambitious expectations and plans in the future. On the Chinese side, there has been a clear desire to stabilize the cooperation. Conversely, CEE countries have varying visions for cooperation. As noted before, 17 + 1 is a heterogeneous region, with countries pursuing diverse interests. Lithuania's exit from the platform might prelude other countries' similar shift where they would be willing to abandon the entire or sacrifice certain parts of the cooperation with China in exchange for closer relations to the US or Western allies. The most likely scenario is that CEE countries may just downgrade their involvement in the platform and switch to maintaining bilateral relations as this position might put them under less pressure. Lastly, there are still countries such as Poland, Hungary, Serbia, or Greece who expect to benefit from the cooperation and will try to continue attracting Chinese investments and benefitting from the rising trade and connectivity between Europe and China.

China will remain present across Europe. It is the biggest trading partner of the European Union, and as the EU is searching for a new approach towards China, CEE will be an important part of any future strategy since it is a physical link between Western Europe and Asia. The future of China–CEE cooperation will depend on countries' ability to find common ground for cooperation and to navigate around the EU and emerging US–China rivalry. The number and diversity of countries in the mechanism limit the ability to capture and single out exact variables that shape relations. Additionally, the lack of analytical frameworks that could encompass structural factors as well as individual actors both inside and outside the region makes rigorous analysis difficult. Further research may expand on the growing burdening effects of US–China rivalry on the region. Additionally, future research could focus on China's response to a more negative posture of some CEE countries and the EU itself. New tools and initiatives introduced by the EU are certain to change the relations and influence the way CEE countries interact through the mechanism.

Bibliographic References

Andrijauskas, K. (2021). Lithuania's decoupling from China against the backdrop of strengthening transatlantic ties. *Eastern Europe Studies Centre*. Retrieved on December 2021, from https://www.eesc.lt/wp-content/uploads/2020/07/RESC.-Lithuanias-decoupling-from-China_2021_EN.pdf

AP News. (2020). Czech officials visit Taiwan as China threatens retaliation. *AP News*. Retrieved on December 2021, from apnews.com/article/asia-pacific-europe-904801e00c28e1204dde11c1b3380bf0

Baczynska, G., & Vasovic, A. (2021). Montenegro counts on EU aid, asset sales to ease burden of China debt-officials. *Reuters*. Retrieved on December 2021, from https://www.reuters.com/world/exclusive-montenegro-counts-eu-aid-asset-sales-ease-burden-china-debt-officials-2021-06-11/

Barboza, D., Santora, M., & Stevenson, A. (2018). China seeks influence in Europe, One Business Deal at a Time. *The New York Times*. Retrieved on December 2021, from www.nytimes.com/2018/08/12/business/china-influence-europe-czech-republic.html.

BBC News. (2021). Budapest roads renamed in protest against Chinese university. *BBC News*, www.bbc.com/news/world-europe-57333270

Benner, T., & Weidenfeld, J. (2018). Europe, don't let China divide and conquer. *Politico*. Retrieved on December 2021, from https://www.politico.eu/article/europe-china-divide-and-conquer/

Bjelotomic, S. (2020). Brnabic: 'No 5G Network in Serbia, people not interested.' *Serbian Monitor*. Retrieved on November 2021, from www.serbianmonitor.com/en/brnabicno-5g-network-in-serbia-people-not-interested/

Brînză A. (2021). How China's 17 + 1 became a Zombie mechanism. *The Diplomat*. Retrieved on December 2021, from https://thediplomat.com/2021/02/how-chinas-171-became-a-zombie-mechanism/

Brînză, A. (2019). The "17 + 1" mechanism: Caught between China and the United States. *China Quarterly of International Strategic Studies, 5*(2), pp. 213–231. Retrieved on December 2021, from https://doi.org/10.1142/s237774001950009x

Brînză, A. (2020). China and Romania: Old friends drifting apart. In T. Matura (Ed.), *China and Central Europe: Success or failure?* (pp. 164–188).

Budapest Business Journal. (2018). Orbán: If EU doesn't pay, Hungary will turn to China. *Budapest Business Journal*. Retrieved on December 2021, from https://bbj.hu/economy/orban-if-eu-doesnt-pay-hungary-will-turn-to-china_143836

Center for the Study of Democracy. (2021). Chinese Economic Influence in Europe. *Center for the Study of Democracy*. Retrieved on December 2021, from https://csd.bg/publications/publication/chinese-economic-influence-in-europe/

China-CEE. (2019). The Dubrovnik guidelines for cooperation between China and Central and Eastern European Countries. Retrieved on December 2021, from https://www.ceec-china-croatia.org/files/dubrovnik-guidelines.pdf

CSIS. (2020a). What do overseas visits reveal about China's foreign policy priorities?" CSIS. Retrieved on November 2021, from https://chinapower.csis.org/diplomatic-visits/

CSIS. (2020b). Chinese economic activities in the Western Balkans. *Center for Strategic and International Studies*. Retrieved on November 2021, from https://reconasia.csis.org/analysis/entries/chinas-hub-and-spoke-strategy-balkans/

Cumpănașu, B. L. (2019). China's linkages and leverages in Central and Eastern Europe—A new challenge for EU. *CES Working Papers, 6*(3), 185–197. Retrieved on December 2021, from https://www.proquest.com/openview/9d1d92875b78b3792ba2620b3b936c5f/1?pq-origsite=gscholar&cbl=2035671

Ding, S., & Garver, J. W. (2017). China's Quest: The history of the foreign relations of the People's Republic of China. *Journal of Chinese Political Science, 22*(2), 303–304. https://doi.org/10.1007/s11366-017-9479-6

Duan, C., Zhou, Y., Shen, D., Lin, S., Gong, W., Popp, J., & Oláh, J. (2021). The misunderstanding of China's investment, and a clarification: "faustian bargain" or "good bargain"? On the OFDI data of Central and Eastern Europe. *Sustainability, 13*(18), 10281. https://doi.org/10.3390/su131810281

Economist. (2018). Chinese investment, and influence, in Europe is growing. *The Economist*. Retrieved on December 2021, from https://www.economist.com/briefing/2018/10/04/chinese-investment-and-influence-in-europe-is-growing

Eggleton, O. (2021). The great game of the twenty-first century: Can Europe compete? *Australian and New Zealand Journal of European Studies, 13*(1). https://doi.org/10.30722/anzjes.vol13.iss1.15484

European Parliament, Committee of Foreign Affairs. (2021). On a new EU-China strategy. *European Parliament*. Retrieved on December 2021, from https://www.europarl.europa.eu/doceo/document/A-9-2021-0252_EN.html

Garlick, J. (2019). China's economic diplomacy in Central and Eastern Europe: A case of offensive mercantilism? *Europe-Asia Studies, 71*(8), 1390–1414. https://doi.org/10.1080/09668136.2019.1648764

Gerstl, A. (2020). Governance along the New Silk Road in Southeast Asia and Central and Eastern Europe: A comparison of ASEAN, the EU and 17 + 1. *Jebat: Malaysian Journal of History, Politics & Strategic Studies, 47*(1). Retrieved on December 2021, from https://ejournal.ukm.my/jebat/article/view/39015/10387

Ghincea, M., Volintiru, C., Nikolovski, I. (2021). China's demand-driven influence in Central-Eastern Europe and the Western Balkans: A political and economic regional comparison. *Global Focus*. Retrieved on December 2021, from https://www.global-focus.eu/wp-content/uploads/2021/04/GlobalFocus_China's-demand-driven-in-uence-in-CEE-and-WB.pdf

Grgić, G. (2021). The changing dynamics of regionalism in Central and Eastern Europe: The case of the three seas initiative. *Geopolitics*. https://doi.org/10.1080/14650045.2021.1881489

Grgić, M. (2017). Chinese infrastructural investments in the Balkans: Political implications of the highway project in Montenegro. *Territory, Politics, Governance*. Retrieved on December 2021, from https://www.tandfonline.com/doi/abs/10.1080/21622671.2017.1359106

Horváth, L. (2020). The geopolitical role of China in the CEE region. *Contemporary Chinese political economy and strategic relations, 6*(2), 617-VIII. Retrieved on December 2021, from https://icaps.nsysu.edu.tw/var/file/131/1131/img/CCPS6(2)-Horvath.pdf

Jakimów, M. (2019). Desecuritisation as a soft power strategy: The Belt and Road Initiative, European fragmentation and China's normative influence in Central-Eastern Europe. *Asia Europe Journal, 17*(4), 369–385. https://doi.org/10.1007/s10308-019-00561-3

Jakóbowski, J. (2018). Chinese-led regional multilateralism in Central and Eastern Europe, Africa and Latin America: 16 + 1, FOCAC, and CCF. *Journal of Contemporary China, 27*(113), 659–673. https://doi.org/10.1080/10670564.2018.1458055

Jing, L. (2021). Post-pandemic cooperation between China and Central and Eastern Europe. *China Quarterly of International Strategic Studies, 6*(2), 1–16. https://doi.org/10.1142/s2377740020500098

Karásková I., Bachulska, A., Szunomár, Á., Vladisavljev, S., Bērziņa-Čerenkova, U. A., Andrijauskas, K., Karindi, L., Leonte, A., Pejić, N., & Šebok, F. (2020). Empty shell no more: China's growing footprint in Central and Eastern Europe. *Association for International Affairs (AMO)*. Retrieved on December 2021, from https://chinaobservers.eu/wp-content/uploads/2020/04/CHOICE_Empty-shell-no-more.pdf

Kramer, F., & Binnendijk, H. (2021). The China-Lithuania rift is a wake-up call for Europe. *Foreign Policy*. Retrieved on December 2021, from https://foreignpolicy.com/2021/09/22/china-lithuania-taiwan-eu-nato/

Lau, S. (2020). Serbia reaches out for China's helping hand in coronavirus fight. *South China Morning Post*. Retrieved on December 2021, from https://www.scmp.com/news/china/diplomacy/article/3075511/serbia-reaches-out-chinas-helping-hand-coronavirus-fight

Lau, S. (2021). Lithuania pulls out of China's '17 + 1' bloc in Eastern Europe. *Politico*. Retrieved on December 2021, from https://www.politico.eu/article/lithuania-pulls-out-china-17-1-bloc-eastern-central-europe-foreign-minister-gabrielius-landsbergis/

Lee, M. (2019). Pompeo warns European partners that US may scale back cooperation over Huawei concerns. *The Diplomat*. Retrieved on November 2021, from https://thediplomat.com/2019/02/pompeo-warns-european-partners-that-us-may-scale-back-cooperation-over-huawei-concerns/

Li, Q., & Ye, M. (2019). China's emerging partnership network: What, who, where, when and why. *International Trade, Politics and Development, 3*(2), 66–81. https://doi.org/10.1108/ITPD-05-2019-0004

Liu, Z. (2018). The '16 + 1 Cooperation' under the 'Belt and Road' Initiative. In W. Song (Ed.), *China's relations with Central and Eastern Europe: From 'Old Comrades' to new partners*. Routledge.

Malinowski, G. (2019). China, geopolitics and geoeconomics: How not to fall into the trap of narration? *Acta Oeconomica, 69*(4), 495–522. https://doi.org/10.1556/032.2019.69.4.2

Matura, T. (2021). Chinse investment in Central and Eastern Europe: A realty check. *Central and Eastern European Center for Asian Studies*. Retrieved on December 2021, from https://bird.tools/wp-content/uploads/2021/04/72d38a_373928ea28c44c7f9c875ead7fc49c44.pdf

MERICS. (2017). Chinese investment in Europe: Record flows and growing imbalances. *MERICS*. Retrieved on December 2021, from https://www.merics.org/en/merics-analysis/papers-on-china/cofdi/cofdi2017/

Milić, V. (2020). Serbia's balancing act on China. *China Observers in Central and Eastern Europe*. Retrieved on December 2021, from https://chinaobservers.eu/serbias-balancing-act-on-china/

Ministry of National Defence - Republic of Poland. (2020). New U.S.-Poland enhanced defense cooperation agreement signed. *Ministry of national defence—Gov.pl website*. Retrieved on December 2021, from www.gov.pl/web/national-defence/new-us-poland-enhanced-defense-cooperation-agreement-signed.

Mitchell, A. W. (2020). Central Europe's China reckoning. *The American Interest*. Retrieved on December 2021, from https://www.the-american-interest.com/2020/04/23/central-europes-china-reckoning/?fbclid=IwAR36yV2hmkrvabJe5jR-R29pEIYQwrDxmAZuY2xVBHW89wC5HoQjF7EOpTE

Muharremi, R. (2021). The 'Washington Agreement' between Kosovo and Serbia. *The American Society of International Law (ASIL)*. Retrieved on December 2021, from www.asil.org/insights/volume/25/issue/4/washington-agreement-between-kosovo-and-serbia

Oertel, J. (2020). The new China consensus: How Europe is growing wary of Beijing. *European Council on Foreign Relations (ECFR)*. Retrieved on December 2021, from ecfr.eu/publication/the_new_china_consensus_how_europe_is_growing_wary_of_beijing/

Paszak P. (2021). Hungary's 'Opening to the East' hasn't delivered. *The Center for European Policy Analysis*. Retrieved on December 2021, from https://cepa.org/hungarys-policy-of-opening-to-the-east-is-more-than-a-decade-old-but-it-hasnt-delivered-much-chinese-investment/

Pavlićević, D. (2018). "China threat" and "China opportunity": Politics of dreams and fears in China-Central and Eastern European relations. *Journal of Contemporary China, 27*(113), 688–702. https://doi.org/10.1080/10670564.2018.1458057

Pavlićević, D. (2019a). Structural power and the China-EU-Western Balkans triangular relations. *Asia Europe Journal, 17*, 453–468. https://doi.org/10.1007/s10308-019-00566-y

Pavlićević, D. (2019b). A power shift underway in Europe? China's relationship with Central and Eastern Europe under the Belt and Road Initiative. In L.Xing (Ed.), *Mapping China's 'One Belt One Road' Initiative*. International Political Economy Series. Palgrave Macmillan, Cham. https://doi.org/10.1007/978-3-319-92201-0_10

Pepe, J. M. (2017). China's in-roads into Central, Eastern, and South Eastern Europe: Implications for Germany and the EU. *Forschungsinstitut der Deutschen Gesellschaft für Auswärtige Politik e.V.* (pp. 1–11). Retrieved on December 2021, from https://nbn-resolving.org/urn:nbn:de:0168-ssoar-56045-3

Pepermans, A. (2018). China's 16 + 1 and Belt and Road Initiative in Central and Eastern Europe: Economic and political influence at a cheap price. *Journal of Contemporary Central and Eastern Europe, 26*(2–3), 181–203. https://doi.org/10.1080/25739638.2018.1515862

Politico. (2018). Beware Chinese Trojan horses in the Balkans, EU warns. *Politico*. Retrieved on December 2021, from https://www.politico.eu/article/johannes-hahn-beware-chinese-trojan-horses-in-the-balkans-eu-warns-enlargement-politico-podcast/

Rakštytė, A. (2021). How can the Baltic states support 5G security through transatlantic cooperation? *Center for European Policy Analysis (CEPA)*. Retrieved on December 2021, from cepa.org/how-can-the-baltic-states-support-5g-security-through-transatlantic-cooperation/

Ruge, M., & Shopov, V. (2021). The EU's Montenegro dilemma. *European Center on Foreign Relations (ECFR)*. Retrieved on December 2021, from https://ecfr.eu/article/the-eus-montenegro-dilemma/

Sacks, D. (2021). Countries in China's Belt and Road Initiative: Who's in and who's out. *Council on Foreign Relations*. Retrieved on December 2021, from https://www.cfr.org/blog/countries-chinas-belt-and-road-initiative-whos-and-whos-out

Song, L. (2018). China is uniting, not fracturing, Europe. *East Asia Forum*. Retrieved on December 2021, from http://www.eastasiaforum.org/2018/08/11/china-is-uniting-not-fracturing-europe/

Song, L., & Pavlićević, D. (2019). China's multilayered multilateralism: A case study of China and Central and Eastern Europe cooperation framework. *Chinese Political Science Review, 4*(3), 277–302. https://doi.org/10.1007/s41111-019-00127-z

Song, W., & Song, L. (2020). Assessing China's '16 + 1 cooperation' with Central and Eastern Europe: A public good perspective. In F. Leandro & P. Duarte (Eds.), *The Belt and Road Initiative*. Palgrave Macmillan. Retrieved on December 2021, from https://doi.org/10.1007/978-981-15-2564-3_17

Speranza, L., & Huntington, C. (2021). China's failures in CEE open the door for the U.S. *Center for European Policy Analysis (CEPA)*. Retrieved on December 2021, from cepa.org/chinas-failures-in-cee-open-the-door-for-the-u-s/

Stojanovic, D. (2019). China's spreading influence in Eastern Europe worries West. *AP News*. Retrieved on December 2021, from apnews.com/article/eastern-europe-ap-top-news-international-news-croatia-china-d121bfc580f04e73b886cc8c5a155f7e

The Diplomat. (2017). One China—One Europe? German Foreign Minister's Remarks Irk Beijing. *The Diplomat*. Retrieved on December 2021, from https://thediplomat.com/2017/09/one-china-one-europe-german-foreign-ministers-remarks-irk-beijing/

Turcsányi, R. (2020). China and the frustrated region: Central and Eastern Europe's repeating troubles with great powers. *China Report, 56*(1), 60–77. https://doi.org/10.1177/0009445519895626

Turcsányi, R., & Qiaoan, R. (2019). Friends or foes? How diverging views of communist past undermine the China-CEE "16 + 1 platform." *Asia Europe Journal, 18*(3), 397–412. https://doi.org/10.1007/s10308-019-00550-6

Turcsányi, R., Šimalčík, M., Kironská, K., Sedláková, R., Čeněk, J., Findor, A., Buchel, O., Hruška, M., Brona, A., Aleksandra U., Bērziņa-Čerenkova, M. E., Gallelli, B., Gledic, J., Gries, P., Ivanov, S., Jerdén, B., Julienne, M., Matura, T., Rühlig, T., & Summers T. (2020). European public opinion on China in the age of COVID-19 differences and common ground across the continent. *Central European Institute of Asian Studies*. Retrieved on December 2021, from https://ceias.eu/wp-content/uploads/2020/11/COMP-poll-report_3.pdf

Turovski, M. (2021). Estonia and Lithuania to attend 17 + 1 summit on lower level. *Eesti Rahvusringhääling*. Retrieved on December 2021, from https://news.err.ee/1608100870/estonia-and-lithuania-to-attend-17-1-summit-on-lower-level.

US Department of State, Office of Treaty Affairs. (2020). *Poland (20-1113)—Enhanced defense cooperation agreement*. Retrieved on November 2021, from https://www.state.gov/poland-20-1113-enhanced-defense-cooperation-agreement/

Vangeli, A. (2018). Global China and symbolic power: The case of 16 + 1 cooperation. *Journal of Contemporary China, 27*(113), 674–687. https://doi.org/10.1080/10670564.2018.1458056

Vangeli, A., & Pavlićević, D. (2019). Introduction: New perspectives on China—Central and Eastern Europe relations. *Asia Europe Journal, 17*(2019), 361–368. https://doi.org/10.1007/s10308-019-00560-4

Vladimirov, M., & Gerganov, A. (2021). Chinese economic influence in Europe: The governance and climate conundrum. *Center for the Study of Democracy*. Retrieved on

December 2021, from https://csd.bg/fileadmin/user_upload/publications_library/files/2021_09/Chinese_EI_Europe_ENG_WEB.pdf

Xinhua. (2017). Central and Eastern European parties initiate closer ties with China. *Xinhua*. Retrieved on December 2021, from http://www.xinhuanet.com//english/2017-07/15/c_136445861.htm

Xinhua. (2021). Cooperation between China, Central and Eastern Europe bears fruit. *Xinhua*. Retrieved on December 2021, from http://www.xinhuanet.com/english/2021-02/09/c_139732684.htm

Xu, Y. (2021). Race to the east? China revives the 17 + 1 summit. *The American Institute for Contemporary German Studies, John Hopkins University*. Retrieved on December 2021, from www.aicgs.org/2021/02/race-to-the-east-china-revives-the-171-summit/

Chapter 23
China and the European Union: Inside the Economic Dynamics of a Challenging Relationship

Martina Basarac Sertić, Anita Čeh Časni, and Kosjenka Dumančić

1 Introduction

Today's world is undergoing a profound change. On the one hand, multipolarity, economic globalization, cultural diversity, and information technology are extending their reach, and on the other side, peace and development remain the themes of the times. At the same time, deep-seated problems are apparent throughout the world, with increasing instability and uncertainties (The State Council Information Office of the People's Republic of China, 2019). In 2020, COVID-19 spread around the world, bringing humanity together in a common experience that highlighted the fragility of our societies. As the first country to grapple with the crisis, China has been on the frontlines both of post-COVID-19 economic recovery, and of the societal changes the pandemic has precipitated (McKinsey Global Institute, 2020). The efforts to stabilize the domestic economy are already well underway. As that recovery takes shape, several important shifts in the make-up of China's economic landscape have already become apparent. COVID-19 has accelerated pre-existing trends, ushering in the arrival of a future we were likely already on track to realize (McKinsey Global Institute, 2020). Moreover, relatively impoverished, isolated, and cut off from global innovation and technology a mere generation ago, China, with its 1.3 billion population, has dramatically re-emerged to become one of the world's great manufacturing centres, a vibrant commercial marketplace, a vital source of global finance, and a central node in the global economy of the twenty-first century (Deloitte, 2014). Additionally, according to Credit Suisse Research Institute (2020), the pandemic eradicated the expected growth in North America and caused losses in every other region, except mainly China and India. Importantly, the worldwide distribution of wealth will change in response to the changing pattern of household wealth across

M. B. Sertić
Croatian Academy of Sciences and Arts, Zagreb, Croatia

A. Č. Časni (✉) · K. Dumančić
Faculty of Economics and Business, University of Zagreb, Zagreb, Croatia

© The Author(s), under exclusive license to Springer Nature Singapore Pte Ltd. 2023
P. A. B. Duarte et al. (eds.), *The Palgrave Handbook of Globalization with Chinese Characteristics*, https://doi.org/10.1007/978-981-19-6700-9_23

countries and regions, with China very likely to be among the countries to benefit most (Credit Suisse Research Institute, 2020). On this track, China has a grand strategy for realizing its dream of national rejuvenation through achieving the "Two Century Goals," i.e., becoming a "moderately well-off society" by 2021, the 100th anniversary of the Chinese Communist Party, and becoming a fully developed nation by 2049, the 100th anniversary of the founding of the People's Republic of China (Lu, 2016). However, limited evidence demonstrates influential observers in and out of government viewed China's rise as an opportunity to enlarge the world market and thereby benefit all nations through increased global commerce (U. S. Department of State, 2020). How to respond to the Chinese long-term growth trajectory?

To answer this question, the purpose of this paper is twofold. First, to investigate China's powerful growth momentum by reaching a new level of tourism, industrial, trade, and investment maturity. To this aim, this chapter provides a comprehensive analysis that points to the fact that China in many areas. Other studies generally observe only one or few of these features; tourism, industry, trade, or economic relations between China and the EU (McKinsey Global Institute, 2019). Second, this chapter provides a reference point in time and a window on some of the issues that are increasingly important in the relationship between the EU and China based on the Belt and Road Initiative (BRI). Among other things, depriving the EU of its economic advantage. Hence, the aim is not offering an innovative theoretical argument on the notion of EU and China relationship. Rather, this chapter aims to map and identify Chinese expediency and recent leadership on the world stage.

Section 2 highlights China's economic significance in the world economy by providing key facts on how China is contributing to global growth. Namely, within this chapter we note that China is a global tourism, industrial, trade, and investment superpower, while assessing the opportunities and challenges that this new role played by China poses for the EU. Section 3 discusses the implications of the bilateral economic relationship between China and the EU, as well as the significance of the BRI for the EU. Final section outlines the main recommendations and suggests emerging trends for future research.

2 China as a Global Economic and Tourism Superpower

There is no economic success story that has captured the world's imagination more convincingly than the stirring transformation of China and its path to the central pivot of the world's economy (Deloitte, 2014).

2.1 China's Ascending Trajectory in the World

Prior to the initiation of economic reforms and trade liberalization nearly 40 years ago, China's policies did not succeed in departing from an economy that was very poor, stagnant, centrally controlled, vastly inefficient, and relatively isolated from the global economy (US Congressional Research Service, 2019). Since opening up to foreign trade and investment and implementing free-market reforms in 1979, China has been among the world's fastest-growing economies, with real annual gross domestic product (GDP) growth averaging 9.5% through 2018, a pace described by the World Bank as "the fastest sustained expansion by a major economy in history" (US Congressional Research Service, 2019). In this way China has been a leading contributor to Asia Pacific's rise into global prominence, with market-oriented reforms and rapid industrialization playing a key role in generating robust economic growth for the country since the 1980s (PWC, 2020). In the 70 years since the founding of "New China," China's economy and society have undergone earth-shaking historical changes (National Bureau of Statistics, 2019). The Chinese position in the world's rankings of major economic and social indicators has increased significantly and its international status and international influence have increased significantly.

Hence, China's growth took off when it began to connect its economy to those of the rest of the world, and when it embraced a market-based system and global best practices of foreign partners (McKinsey Global Institute, 2019). Such growth has enabled China, on average, to double its GDP every eight years and helped raise an estimated 800 million people out of poverty (US Congressional Research Service, 2019). China has become the world's largest economy on a purchasing power parity (PPP) basis (as can be seen on Graphs 1 and 2), manufacturer, merchandise trader, and holder of foreign exchange reserves (US Congressional Research Service, 2019). If we analyze the growth rates from 1990 onwards (Graph 2), it can also be concluded that China's economic rise as today's world's largest economy has been impressive. Hence, China has transitioned from low-income to upper-middle-income status in the past four decades as the result of these sequential and structured reforms, considering lessons from the experience of earlier phases, current and likely future circumstances, and any adjustment of goals (Hepburn et al., 2020). In that context, in 1962, Mao Zedong had pointed out that, while "it took Western countries more than three hundred years to develop a great capitalist economy (…) it will take China 50 to 100 years to develop a strong socialist economy" (Hu et al., 2021). According to these authors, "it now appears that we will achieve our goal to complete the building of a moderately prosperous society in all respects by 2021, the year the Communist Party of China celebrates its centenary."

Therefore, it can be read that "the world economy is turning East" (ESPAS, 2019). Namely, as a manufacturing powerhouse (as illustrated on the Graph 3) and a major consumption hub, China today represents the largest economy in Asia-Pacific, and features among leading nations worldwide in terms of Foreign Direct Investment (FDI) and trade flows (PWC, 2020). Besides, technology adoption has become a new growth driver in recent years—marked by fast-growing presence of digitally consumers and increasing focus among government and business stakeholders to boost innovation (PWC, 2020). As McKinsey Global Institute (2021) research suggests "in a relatively short span of time, China has transitioned from a technological backwater to become one of the world's largest digital economies."

■ China ■ United States ■ European Union ■ Rest of the World

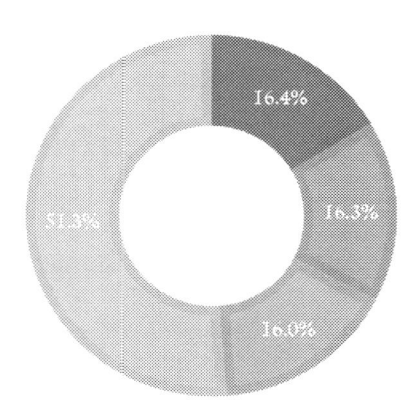

Graph 1 Shares in world's GDP in PPP, 2017 (*Source* Eurostat [2020])

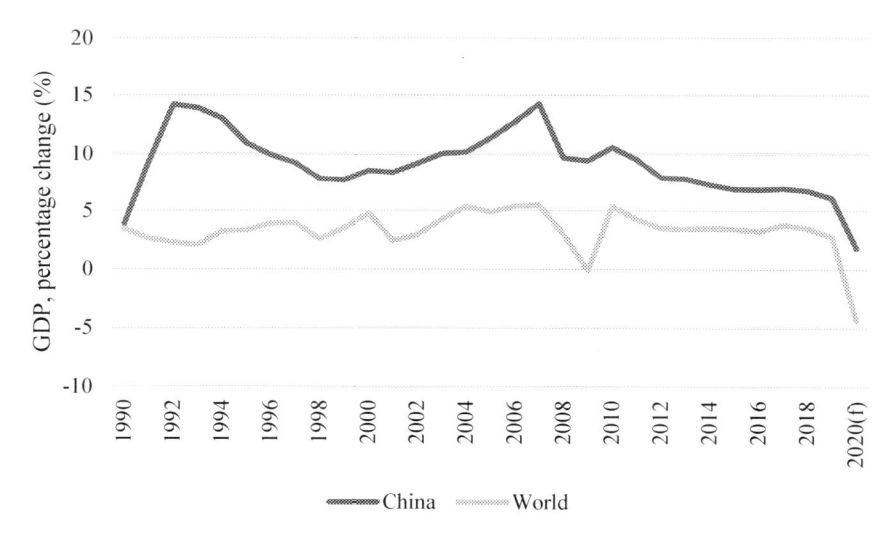

Graph 2 Economic growth trends for China compared to the world (*Notes* (f) forecast. *Source* International Monetary Fund [2020])

These factors are also proving crucial to the country's COVID-19 response, enabling China to feature among few global economies expected to register positive economic growth in 2020 (PWC, 2020).

Furthermore, during the last two decades China has become crucial to the global economy. China's rising importance in the global economy is not only related to its status as a manufacturer and exporter of consumer products (UNCTAD, 2020). China

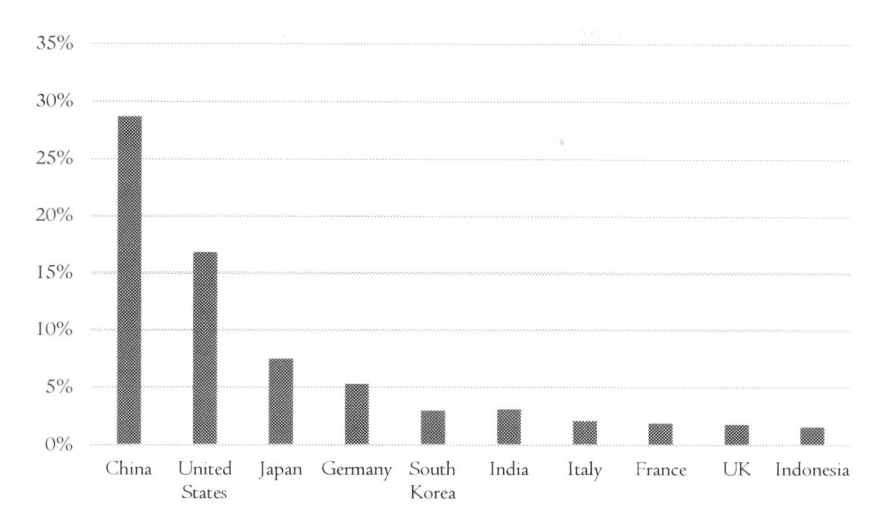

Graph 3 China is the world's manufacturing superpower. Top 10 countries by share of global manufacturing output in 2019*. (*Note* *Output measured on a value-added basis in current US dollars [USD]. *Source* Richter [2021])

has become the main supplier of intermediate inputs for manufacturing companies abroad (UNCTAD, 2020). As of today, about 20% of global trade in manufacturing intermediate products originates in China (UNCTAD, 2020). In 2009, China became the world's largest exporter of goods and second-largest importer of goods. In 2013, China became the world's largest trader in goods (The State Council Information Office of the People's Republic of China, 2019). More precisely, when ranking the top export countries worldwide, China ranked first in exports with an export value of about USD 2.5 trillion in 2019 (according to Statista, 2021a). Since reform and opening up in 1978, foreign investment in China has seen a substantial increase, and China has become very attractive to global investment (The State Council Information Office of the People's Republic of China, 2019). China has become the world's second-largest economy, largest manufacturer, largest trader in goods, second-largest consumer of commodities, second-largest recipient of FDI, and largest holder of foreign exchange reserves. Table 1 shows the relative nominal growth observed in China for many of these indicators.

It follows from the above that the relationship between China and the world is changing. On the new McKinsey Global Institute (2019) China-World Exposure Index, China's exposure to the world in trade, technology, and capital has fallen in relative terms. Conversely, the world's exposure to China has increased.

Next, when it comes to research and patents for new technologies, China and the US (US) are in the process of defining the future of not just the digital market—but of the future market altogether, and indeed geopolitics and warfare, too (ESPAS, 2019). Moreover, according to PWC (2017) analysis, China could be the largest economy in the world, accounting for around 20% of the world GDP in 2050, with

Table 1 Relative nominal growth in major indicators of China's economic strength

Category	1952	2018
GDP	RMB 67.9 billion	RMB 90 trillion
Fiscal revenue	RMB 6.2 billion (in 1950)	RMB 18.33 trillion
Industrial added value	RMB 12 billion	RMB 30.5 trillion
Per capita GDP	RMB 119	RMB 64,644
Final consumption rate	78.9%	54.3%
Non-financial FDI	USD 920 million (in 1983)	USD 135 billion
Trade in goods	USD 1.9 billion	USD 4.6 trillion

Source The State Council Information Office of the People's Republic of China (2019)

India in second place and Indonesia in fourth place (based on GDP at PPP). The US and the EU will steadily lose ground to China and India. That being said, China's notable achievements in developing a sophisticated manufacturing base, higher living standards, a more secure social safety net, and focused investments in education and health, have laid a strong foundation for the country's future dynamism (Deloitte, 2014). China has the opportunity to be a global leader in a number of important areas that will be cornerstones of global growth in the next decades (Deloitte, 2014).

The most prevailing global economic news recently is the EU and China announced the accomplishment of a long-awaited EU–China Comprehensive Agreement on Investment (EU–China CAI) on 30 December 2020, in a move to open up more investment opportunities between two economies (Dong, 2020). Economically, the meanings of the EU–China CAI are multi-faceted, from alleviating China–US tensions to constructing an EU–China reciprocity investment relation, from prompting China's domestic structural reform and opening up policy to stimulating economic growth in both regions (Dong, 2020). However, despite its remarkable success, China still has plenty of room for improvement. Namely, China's economic expansion over the past four decades was intrinsically linked to a spatial reconfiguration of economic activity (World Bank, 2020). The forces of urbanization and agglomeration of economic activity played a critical role in unleashing rapid industrialization and productivity gains, which fuelled China's overall economic success (World Bank, 2020). But these very forces also led to widening income gaps between swiftly growing coastal and lagging interior provinces and between rural and urban areas within provinces (World Bank, 2020). Today, Shanghai's per capita GDP is almost five times that of the north western province of Gansu, the poorest province (World Bank, 2020). In that context, China's 14th Plan (2021–2025) will, in large measure, chart the course for the new era in the country (Hepburn et al., 2020). China has highlighted structural reform within the new growth model and concentrated on various types of capital other than physical capital, as well as innovation and technology. As such, China will transform itself again in the next 30 to 40 years (Hepburn et al., 2020).

When it comes to China's success, it is necessary to mention that China shares land borders with as many as 14 countries, and has eight maritime neighbours, which means China and its neighbours are closely bound by geography (Zhang & Wang, 2017). But to adequately understand China's neighbourhood relations, one must look beyond geography to consider how history, culture, geopolitics, and geo-economics have shaped and will continue to shape, these relationships. Serious consideration must also be given to their competitive national interests in the evolution of their increasingly interdependent social, economic, and geopolitical relationship (Zhang & Wang, 2017). Guided by the vision that the unprecedented level of interconnection and interdependence among countries binds them into a global community of shared future, China's international development cooperation in the new era has a more profound philosophical basis and clearer goals, which could lead to more concrete actions (The State Council Information Office of the People's Republic of China, 2019).

2.2 China's Reshaping Global Tourism Industry

When it comes to Chinese market capture, tourism has become an essential contributor to China's domestic economy since the beginning of reform and opening in the early eighties (Statista, 2021b). The Chinese tourism market has transformed into one of the world's most-watched inbound and outbound tourist markets (Statista, 2021b). Through a range of tourism growth strategies and their implementation, China's tourism industry has gradually ushered and become "the number one source market for international tourism" (FTN News, 2020). More precisely, the BRI, as a strategic transcontinental long-term and investment programme, has, as explained above, among other things, "deepened cultural exchanges in the region" (OECD, 2018). Further, "515 Strategy," published in 2015 referred to the five objectives of tourism development (civility, order, safety, convenience and national prosperity), 10 actions and 52 measures adopted to promote tourism development in China from 2015 to 2017. Next, "Tourism+," a concept that has encouraged new competitive and innovative forces by mixing tourism with other industries. This notion of holistic tourism was proposed by Li Jinzao, Chairman of the China National Tourism Administration, during the National Tourism Work Conference in 2016, according to which China has entered a new era of mass tourism, with travel no longer a luxury for the few but a necessity for all (Li et al., 2017). Finally, in 2016, China National Tourism Administration launched a nationwide All-for-One-Tourism—a complete concept that should guide the modification and upgrading of the country's regional tourism industry. Hence, according to Feng (2017), in the nearly forty years of China's reform and opening up, tourism industry started from scratch and experienced the rapid development process from small to large.

The number of domestic trips reached six billion in 2019, indicating an exponential increase compared to the number of trips made in China ten years ago (Statista, 2021b). Namely, with the continuous improvement of the country's comprehensive strength and national living standards, China's tourism industry has achieved leapfrog development (Zhao & Liu, 2020). More precisely, in recent years, China's tourism industry's focus has begun to shift from quantity to quality, continuously deepening the reform of the tourism industry, improving the quality of tourism development, and promoting the coordinated economic and social development (Zhao & Liu, 2020). Hence, the tourism industry has become a pillar industry of China's economy (Zhao & Liu, 2020). Not only the tourism industry itself promotes the rapid development of China's economy, but also promotes the development of elements that can be integrated with tourism, such as technology, culture, and sports (Zhao & Liu, 2020). In 2019, the comprehensive contribution of tourism to China's GDP reached RMB 10.94 trillion (USD 2.61 trillion in PPP), accounting for approximately 11.05% of China's total GDP (Zhao & Liu, 2020). According to Statista (2021c), the total revenue generated by the travel and tourism industry in China amounted to around RMB 6.6 trillion as of 2019, indicating a firm growth over the past decade (in 2008, revenues amounted to 1.1 trillion).

According to World Economic Forum (2019), China is by far the largest travel and tourism (T&T) economy in Asia-Pacific and the 13th most competitive globally (up two spots from 2017). It welcomes more international visitors than any other country in the region and its T&T industry benefits from a large and growing domestic market (Table 2). The cornerstone of China's competitiveness according to the Travel and Tourism competitiveness report is its exceptional natural resources as well as its highest score for cultural resources according to the Travel and Tourism Competitiveness Index (TTCI). The nation has the greatest number of UNESCO Natural World Heritage sites in the world as well as impressive wildlife (World Economic Forum, 2019). Meanwhile, Europe was home to half of the top 10 countries with the highest direct contribution to GDP globally (through travel and tourism) (Statista, 2021d).

More precisely, the EU is the most visited destination in the world and for many members, European regions, and cities; tourism is a key contributor to the economic and social fabric (European Commission, 2020). However, the rise of Chinese tourism has caused huge changes in the global travel industry. Therefore, for those in charge of tourism in Europe, the increase in tourist arrivals from China has not been neglected. The initiative named EU–China Tourism Year (ECTY) was launched in Venice on 19 January 2018, aimed at supporting the development of new and better travel itineraries, promoting intercultural understanding, and enhancing travel and tourism experiences, including greater promotion and more sustainable tourism.

Nevertheless, competition from emerging destinations is getting bigger. Based on World Tourism Organization (UNWTO) UNWTO data, in 2000, the EU had 58% of the world's market (according to world's international arrivals indicator). According to data for 2019, Europe holds a share of 51% (World Tourism Organization, 2021). On the contrary, Chinese tourism grew every year despite the impact of the economic

Table 2 Direct contribution of travel and tourism to GDP in leading countries worldwide—2019 (in USD billion)

Country	Year 2019
United States	580.7
China	403.5
Germany	143.4
Japan	126.3
Italy	119.7
France	112
United Kingdom	109.4
India	108.3
Mexico	101.8
Spain	82.3

Source Statista (2021d)

and financial crisis. In 2000, Asia and the Pacific recorded 16% of the world's international arrivals (World Tourism Organization & Global Tourism Economy Research Centre, 2014). However, in 2019, this region achieved 25% of global arrivals and significantly increased its share in the world market (World Tourism Organization, 2021). Besides, although the EU represents 39% of international tourism receipts, Asia and the Pacific with almost one-third—30% follow it in 2019. It is therefore evident that Asian countries, and above all China, are climbing the competitiveness ladder and occupying an increasing share of the world tourism market.

2.3 China Powerful Growth Momentum—Industry, Trade and Investment

The relationship between EU member states and China is evolved due to the coronavirus crisis. Even though efforts to enhance trade and other economic links remain having a major role in the relationship, countries across Europe are ever more sceptical of Beijing's intentions. They are discussing reducing their dependence on China for supplies of critical goods, and are concerned about the future of the relationship in a hastily shifting geopolitical environment marked by growing US–China enmity (Oertel, 2020). In the last decade, we could witness an exceptional widening and deepening of bilateral economic and, to some degree, also non-economic relations between the EU and China. This process can be attributed to several factors, starting from China's entry into the WTO as of 2001, through the dramatic increase of bilateral trade relations and partly of direct investments as well as a large number of institutional forms of bilateral cooperation, up to identifying common areas of global commitments, responsibilities and cooperation opportunities (Inotai, 2013). Despite China and the EU having an extensive and growing economic relationship, the relationship has growing more problematic because of the distortions caused by China's state-capitalist system and a range of interests within the EU. China's size and dynamism, and its new shift from an export-led to a domestic demand-led growth model, mean that the opportunities for trade and investment are likely to grow with time (Dadush et al., 2019). Since China joined the World Trade Organisation back in December of 2001, the EU's goods exports to China have grown on average more than 10% a year and service exports by over 15% a year. This has resulted in ample benefits for EU producers and consumers but, as imports from China have also grown rapidly, it has also caused some degree of disruption in EU labour and product markets (Dadush et al., 2019). Additionally, the EU and China announced a comprehensive strategic partnership in 2003 that was intended to uplift their relationship from the economic to the political and even security spheres. Even if that strategic partnership has not lived up to expectations (Maher, 2016), it has enabled much larger and profounder contacts between EU and Chinese officials across many different policy domains, including economic, diplomatic, and even security (Christiansen, 2015; Christiansen & Maher, 2017). As for any twosome of trading partners, the trade relationship between China and the EU is best understood in a general equilibrium context, rather than from a narrow bilateral perspective. The essential point is that even if China does not buy as much from the EU as it sells to the EU, the EU runs an overall trade surplus, and this is made possible to some extent by the EU's exports to third parties which have, in turn, seen their exports to China surge. In fact, China is now the largest export destination for 33 countries out of 186 for which data is available (McKinsey Global Institute, 2019). The changing composition of trade between China and the EU reflects the economic transformation China has undergone since the beginning of the millennium. As China has moved up the value chain, the share of machinery and electrical equipment imported by the EU that comes from China has grown (Dadush et al., 2019).

While public opinion in most EU countries still identifies imports from China with textiles and clothing, the statistics clearly reveal (as evident from Table 3) the modest role of these commodities in total imports from China (one-eighth of total EU imports but one-fourth of total EU deficit). Other manufacturers (from plastics and toys through furniture to household goods) arriving from China represent a higher share in EU imports (Inotai, 2013). China's top exports to the EU are telecommunications equipment, computer parts, baby carriages, electrical machinery, apparel, and footwear. The inflow of these products from China has undoubtedly expanded the range available to EU consumers, while large quantities of intermediate goods or inputs have also been supplied at low prices, improving the productivity and international competitiveness of EU industries (Dadush et al., 2019). No wonder that the EU became the major export market for China and the EU is the second largest supplier of the Chinese economy. In turn, China clearly leads the list of extra-EU imports and ranks third in extra-EU exports. EU–China trade volume is only slightly less than that of EU–US trade (Inotai, 2013), as evident from Table 4.

The current situation provides an excellent area of mutual learning and, simultaneously, of making use of new fields of cooperation, partly identified both in the current Five-Year Plan of China (until the end of 2015) and in the EU 2020 strategy.

Table 3 EU trade with China top 5- HS Sections of Imports in 2019

	Products	Value in € million	% Total
XVI	Machinery and appliances	186,622	51.6
XI	Textiles and textile articles	32,975	9.1
XX	Miscellaneous manufactured articles	28,993	8.0
XV	Base metals and articles thereof	23,514	6.5
VI	Products of the chemical or allied industries	17,524	4.8

Source European Commission, European Union trade in goods with China (2019)

This automatically results from the fact that, together, the EU and China represent more than one-fourth of the world population, produce more than one-third of the global GDP and more than two-fifth of global exports and imports including intra-EU trade and more than one-fourth, if intra-EU trade is excluded from the calculation. Although rapidly developing EU–China relations have been covering almost all areas of activities, trade remains the centre piece of bilateral cooperation (Inotai, 2013). Moreover, FDI flows between the EU and China are closely related to trade, complementing trade because FDI results in the development of marketing networks provides financial and transport services and lead to production with a view to selling in global markets. FDI flows can also substitute for trade, for example when investors establish facilities to produce and sell in the same market. Furthermore, the purchase by investors of controlling interests in competitors or suppliers, including raw materials, often fosters global or regional value chains that tend to stimulate trade. Not surprisingly, as trade between the EU and China has surged, FDI has also increased. However, bilateral FDI flows remain small in relation to the size of both economies and have been volatile (Dadush et al., 2019). However, European FDI in China has fallen in recent years, and European players have complained of the many obstacles faced in China where investor protection is poor and market access highly uneven and sometimes arbitrary. A key concern has been joint venture requirements in many sectors. These have often involved transfers of intellectual property to Chinese counterparts, making an investment in Chinese operations less attractive. Increased competition from Chinese companies, and rising wages, have also reduced incentives to invest in China (Dadush et al., 2019; Garcia-Herrero & Jianwei, 2019).

It is evident that both the EU and China share a lot of common interests. Recent developments in trade, and partly also in direct investment relations helped not only identify latent common positions but also strengthened bilateral cooperation in several fields. Still, each other's perception is far from "balanced" (Inotai, 2013). The economic relationship between China and the EU is already extensive. The sustained growth of the Chinese economy and its integration into global supply chains have put China on a path to be the world's largest trader and its largest economy measured at market exchange rates—as it already is on purchasing power parity measures. China's size and the rapidity of its rise have been the cause of much disruption, but have also led to the opening up of many opportunities (Dadush et al., 2019).

Table 4 Top 10 client and supplier countries of the EU27 in merchandise trade (value %) (2020, excluding intra-EU trade)

	Total EU Trade with…	EUR million	Share (%)	EU imports from…	EUR million	Share (%)	EU exports to…	EUR million	Share (%)	EU trade balance with…	EUR million
	Extra EU27	3,645,933	100.0	Extra EU27	1,714,224	100.0	Extra EU27	1,931,709	100.0	Extra EU27	217,484
1	China	585,967	16.1	China	383,397	22.4	USA	352,911	18.3	USA	150,292
2	USA	555,530	15.2	USA	202,619	11.8	UK	277,651	14.4	UK	110,336
3	UK	444,967	12.2	UK	167,315	9.8	China	202,570	10.5	Switzerland	33,753
4	Switzerland	250,990	6.9	Switzerland	108,618	6.3	Switzerland	142,372	7.4	Australia	22,148
5	Russia	174,309	4.8	Russia	95,335	5.6	Russia	78,975	4.1	UAE	17,303
6	Turkey	132,408	3.6	Turkey	62,551	3.6	Turkey	69,857	3.6	Hong Kong	15,851
7	Japan	109,389	3.0	Japan	54,917	3.2	Japan	54,473	2.8	Canada	13,291
8	Norway	90,868	2.5	South Korea	44,075	2.6	Norway	48,600	2.5	Egypt	11,744
9	SouthKorea	89,343	2.5	Norway	42,268	2.5	SouthKorea	45,268	2.3	Mexico	10,168
10	India	65,178	1.8		34,413	2.0	Canada	33,339	1.7	Saudi Arabia	9,447

Source European Commission (2021b)

The large untapped opportunities for increased trade, investment, and movement of people between China and the EU are evident, and these opportunities are likely to grow with China's rising weight. As the EU is in a relatively mature phase of its development, the growth opportunities of a closer relationship with China, and the boost that China can indirectly provide to Europe's traditional markets elsewhere, cannot be ignored. At the same time, the EU must insist that economic relations with China be based on as level a playing field as possible, or, in the technical jargon, should aim for something close to "competitive neutrality." Based on that premise, the EU should raise its level of ambition with respect to closer ties with China. That will require stepping up its efforts to understand China, to coordinate its approach to China internally, and to establish a prioritized list of actions and approaches (Dadush et al., 2019).

A discussion of geopolitical tensions between China and the EU, which are part of the reason for the paucity of institutional arrangements to govern the China-EU economic relationship, is outside the scope of this chapter. It is clear, however, that even though the EU is not locked in a global power struggle with China, the escalating competition between China and the US, Europe's historical ally, have made China–EU relations more complicated. A March 2019 communication from the European Commission referred to China as a "systemic rival promoting alternative models of governance" (European). China's BRI and the 16 + 1 framework that governs BRI cooperation between China and 16 central and eastern European countries (11 of which are EU members) are cases in point. Baltensperger and Dadush (2019) addressed the BRI's potential benefits and limitations, while a recent paper by European Parliament Research Service (2017) concluded that the initiative has had limited success and has not resulted in institutions (formal and informal) conducive to closer ties.

3 The Belt and Road Initiative in the Context of the European Union

Although the BRI primarily refers to the partnership between China and the Central and Eastern countries of Europe, the trade relationship between the EU and the China is one of the most important relations for both China and the EU (Ping & Zuokui, 2019). In the very beginnings of China's opening to the world, it was necessary to find a partner with whom it was possible to establish long-term, quality, trade, and diplomatic relations. According to the data available, the EU is China's largest trading partner, and China is the EU's second-largest trading partner. The diplomatic relations between the EU and China were established on 6 May 1975, the strategic partnership began in 2003. Previously, in 1985, an agreement on trade and economic cooperation between the European Economic Community (EEC) and China was signed. From these facts to infer how the economic relations between these two trade giants proceeded to the mutual satisfaction. Moreover, the EU and China pledged at the EU–China Summit on 9 April 2019 to commit to further building economic relations based on openness, non-discrimination, and fair competition. The main idea of the BRI is to connect China and EU by transportation infrastructure. That is achieved by land and sea corridors through three main routes: Northern, Central, and Southern, as well as by some minor secondary routes (Plevnik, 2016). A comprehensive investment agreement between the EU and China has not yet been reached. The fact that 28 rounds of negotiations have been conducted so far speaks volumes about the importance and scope of this agreement. The European Commission highlights 2016 as one of the most important years for negotiations because at the time both sides agreed that this type of agreement would go beyond traditional agreements. In the EU–China Strategic Review, the European Commission (2019a, 2019b) positions this agreement as a key instrument for restoring the balance in the investment relationship and obtaining fair and equal treatment for EU companies operating in China, while providing legal certainty to Chinese companies in doing business throughout the EU market. At the summit on April 9, 2019, the EU and China pledged to make significant progress under this agreement, which happened in 2019. During 2019, there was a significant shift in negotiations, while 2020 is marked as the year of concluding the agreement. In a joint statement of the EU–China summit held on 9 April 2019 in Brussels, the EU and China pledged to build their economic relationship on openness, non-discrimination and fair competition, ensuring a level playing field, transparency while ensuring mutual benefit. The 28th round of negotiations was held on 24 April, 2020 via videoconference. The focus was on investment liberalization and a level playing field, especially in state-owned enterprises. Also, in this round of negotiations, progress has been made in the chapter on resolving disputes between states.

In December 2020 new CAI between EU–China was signed. The Agreement will create a better balance in the EU–China trade relationship. The EU has traditionally been much more open than China to foreign investment. Three main level playing fields were accentuated: state-owned enterprises, forced technology transfers, and transparency in subsidies. This CAI is strongly connected with the former agreement in which the improvement of the market access conditions for European companies was one of the cornerstones of the joint action. Regarding the state-owned companies there is a need for them to act in accordance with commercial considerations and not to discriminate. The state-owned companies are these entities that are controlled by the state through minority ownership legal title as well as state-designated monopolies or entities vested with special rights or privileges. The goal is to contribute to fairer competition on the market and have a favourable effect on investor confidence. Regarding the transfer of technology, the CAI will lay very clear rules against forced transfers of technology, such as the prohibition of several types of investment requirements that compel the transfer of technology, as well as prohibitions to, directly or indirectly, interfere in contractual freedom in technology licencing. These rules would also include disciplines on protection of confidential business information collected by administrative bodies from unauthorized disclosure.

The third pillar concerning the transparency of subsidies will set out in the existing multilateral rules on subsidies related to goods by imposing transparency obligations on subsidies related to services. A specific consultation procedure will apply requiring either side to engage in consultations in order to provide additional information on any subsidies that could have a negative effect on the investment interests of the other side and to seek to address such negative effects (European Commission, 2020). The agreement also calls for commitments to state-owned enterprises in China and increased transparency of subsidies, as well as emphasizing that sustainable development is the overarching goal of bilateral investment relations. The agreement should ensure a high level of protection for European companies, while preserving the Chinese government's right to regulate business. The agreement should also include a variation of the European Investment Court system, which, through its prescribed and clear procedure, helps resolve disputes between investors and the state.

Chinese investments across Europe are not randomly selected, but consciously planned by a long-term development strategy. Through numerous initiatives, the Chinese government wants to increase China's influence in Europe, taking advantage of every country with which, it cooperates to the best of its ability. China invests significantly more in its investments in Western developed European countries such as Germany, France, and the UK compared to investments in Southeast Europe. Due to a wide range of investment opportunities, the People's Republic of China has a strategy that has seemingly divided Europe into regions in terms of development. The Chinese, as already mentioned in the less developed countries of Central and Eastern Europe, are investing in road infrastructure, railways, and the production of electricity from coal and outdated technologies. In the first place, investments in Central and Eastern Europe in the framework of cooperation between China and Central and Eastern European countries and the BRI are viewed through investment in transport infrastructure by which the Chinese government seeks to bring trade flows closer to Europe. By implementing such projects, China is creating a foundation for the development of logistics centres in the south-eastern countries that would facilitate trade between China and Europe. The further we go west, we can see that investments are also increasingly focused on more profitable activities. Taking a stake in the ownership of major European airports, seaports, and sports clubs are becoming a major forte for Chinese investors in highly developed countries.

A study by Kratz et al. (2020), for Rhodium Group and MERICS states that the cumulative value of Chinese foreign investment transactions in EU countries in the period from 2000 to 2019 is mostly affected by four European countries. In the first place is the UK, which has attracted over 50 billion euros of Chinese direct investment, followed by Germany with EUR 22.7 billion, Italy with EUR 16 billion, and France with EUR 14.4 billion. If we compare this with Chinese direct investment in Southeast Europe, it is clear what is in the main interest of the China and its investors. Austria, Bulgaria, Croatia, the Czech Republic, Estonia, Greece, Hungary, Latvia, Lithuania Poland, Romania, Slovakia, and Slovenia, together attracted EUR 10.5 billion in the same period.

Crucially, the EU is seeking to move beyond the 2018 EU–Asia connectivity strategy and is vowing to build a "globally connected" EU which would allow the bloc to turn its attention to Africa and Latin America, key destinations for Chinese investments. The EU strategy, called "A Globally Connected Europe," doesn't mention

China which is also significant. Since 2013, China has launched construction projects across more than 60 countries, seeking a network of land and sea links with Southeast Asia, Central Asia, the Middle East, Europe, and Africa. China denies any intention to project power and has said the infrastructure corridor focuses on the needs of ordinary people.

4 Conclusion

China, as the world largest economy, creates the biggest contribution to global growth, which has sparked a rethinking of the other top world's economies strategic dimensions. On the other side, the expectation for the EU remains open to numerous risks and challenges that could contribute to a significant lagging in development. However, the EU has a strong platform on which to base its renewal and future progress. Therefore, the aim of this chapter was twofold. First, we examined the economic importance of China on the global stage and highlighted the outstanding performance of China as a tourism superpower, both as origin as the destination. Furthermore, China's aspiration for world industrial, trade, and investment dominance were also the subject of our analysis. Next, we analyzed the economic relationship of China and the EU, as well as the opportunities offered by the BRI. According to our analysis, there is great untapped growth potential for trade, investment, and tourism between China and the EU. However, this conclusion is based on an exploratory statistical data analysis and may be affected by certain statistical problems due to the quality of the underlying data series. In any case, they shed significant light on the sectoral behaviour in analyzed groups of countries in a qualitative manner.

Consequently, this chapter has documented the key role that China has primarily on the global arena, since, according to McKinsey Global Institute (2019)—the Asian Century has begun. Furthermore, Asia is the world's largest regional economy and, as its economies are integrating further, so it has the potential to fuel and shape the next phase of globalization. China is the anchor driving the development of intraregional trade in Asia.

We consider our research to be relevant because of the following reasons: (i) it captures the outlook for China's growing role on the world stage as well as in the EU; and (ii) it contributes to exploring the China's rapid economic development pattern and offers a feature in time and a window into some of the issues that are increasingly important in the bilateral EU–China relations. Further studies should tackle more sophisticated statistical analysis of available data and produce significant policy recommendations accordingly.

Bibliographic References

Baltensperger, M., & Dadush, U. (2019). The Belt and Road turns five. *Russian Journal of Economics, 5*, 136–153.

Christiansen, T. (2015). A liberal institutionalist perspective on China–EU relations. In J. Wang & W. Song (Eds.), *China, the European Union, and the international politics of global governance* (pp. 29–50). Palgrave Macmillan.

Christiansen, T., & Maher, R. (2017). The rise of China—Challenges and opportunities for the European Union. *Asia Europe Journal, 15*(2), 121–131.

Congressional Research Service. (2019, June 25). *China's economic rise: History, trends, challenges, and implications for the United States, RL33534*. Retrieved on January 2022, from https://fas.org/sgp/crs/row/RL33534.pdf

Credit Suisse Research Institute. (2020, October). *Global wealth report 2020*.

Dadush, U., & Guntram, W. (2019). *The European Union's response to the trade crisis* (p. 5). Policy Contribution.

Dadush, U., Domínguez-Jiménez, M., & Tianlang, G. (2019). The state of China European Union economic relations. *Bruegel Working Working paper*, 9. Retrieved on January 2022, from https://www.bruegel.org/wp-content/uploads/2019/11/WP-2019-09-China-final.pdf

Deloitte. (2014). *Competitiveness: Catching the next wave—China*. Retrieved on January 2022, from https://www2.deloitte.com/content/dam/Deloitte/global/Documents/About-Deloitte/gx-china-competitiveness-report-web.pdf

Dong, J. (2020). China | EU–China comprehensive agreement on investment: A game-changer to superpower game. *China Economic Watch*. BBVA Research.

ESPAS. (2019). *Global trends to 2030—Challenges and choices for Europe*. Retrieved on January 2022, from https://ec.europa.eu/assets/epsc/pages/espas/ESPAS_Report2019.pdf

European Commission. (2019a). *China challenges and prospects from an industrial and innovation powerhouse*.

European Commission (2019b). *Communication: EU–China—A strategic outlook*.

European Commission. (2020). *Tourism and transport in 2020 and beyond Brussels, 13. 5. 2020 COM(2020) 550 final*. Retrieved on January 2022, from https://eur-lex.europa.eu/legal-content/EN/TXT/PDF/?uri=CELEX:52020DC0550&from=EN

European Commission. (2021a). *European Union, trade in goods with China*. https://webgate.ec.europa.eu/isdb_results/factsheets/country/details_china_en.pdf

European Commission. (2021b, March). *European Union trade in goods with China*. Retrieved on January 2022, from https://ec.europa.eu/eurostat/statistics-explained/index.php?title=International_trade_in_goods&oldid=541694

European Parliament Research Service. (2017). *China, the 16+1 cooperation format and the EU*. Retrieved on January 2022, from https://www.europarl.europa.eu/thinktank/en/document.html?reference=EPRS_BRI(2018)625173

European Union Chamber of Commerce in China. (2020). *Decoupling severed ties and patchwork globalisation*.

Eurostat. (2020). *Purchasing power parities in Europe and the world*. Retrieved on May 2021, from https://ec.europa.eu/eurostat/statistics-explained/index.php?title=Purchasing_power_parities_in_Europe_and_the_world

Feng, X. (2017). All-for-one tourism: The transformation and upgrading direction of regional tourism industry. *Journal of Social Science Research, 11*(2), 2374–2378.

FTN News. (2020, November 18). *China still no. 1 international tourism source market in 2020, Özgür Töre*. Retrieved on November 2021, from https://ftnnews.com/tours/40695-china-still-no-1-international-tourism-source-market-in-2020

Garcia-Herrero, A., & Jianwei, X. (2019). 'Countries' perceptions of China's Belt and Road Initiative: A big data analysis. *HKUST IEMS Working Paper*, 59. Retrieved on November 2021, from https://ssrn.com/abstract=3430318 or https://doi.org/10.2139/ssrn.3430318

Hepburn, C., Stern, N., Xie, C., & Zenghelis, D. (2020). *Strong, sustainable and inclusive growth in a New Era for China—Paper 1: Challenges and ways forward*. Grantham Research Institute on Climate Change and the Environment.

Hu, A., Yan, Y., Tang, X., & Liu, S. (2021). *2050 China becoming a great modern socialist country*. Springer.

Inotai, A. (2013). Economic relations between the European Union and China. *L'europe En Formation, 4*(370), 47–84.

International Monetary Fund. (2020). *World Economic Outlook 2020*. Retrieved on November 2021, from https://www.imf.org/en/Publications/WEO/weo-database/2020/October

Kratz, A., Zenglein, M. J., & Sebastian. G. (2020). *Chinese FDI in Europe 2020 update investments falls to 10-year low in an economically and politically challenging year*. A report by Rhodium Group and the Mercator Institute for China Studies (MERICS).

Li, M., Wu, B., & Guo, P. (2017). Holistic tourism: A new norm of the industry. *Journal of China Tourism Research, 13*(4), 388–392.

Lu, D. (2016). China's "two centenary goals": Progress and challenge. *East Asian Policy, 08*(02), 79–93. https://doi.org/10.1142/S1793930516000222

Maher, R. (2016). The elusive EU–China strategic partnership. *International Affairs, 92*(4), 959–976.

McKinsey Global Institute. (2019). *China and the world: Inside the dynamics of a changing relationship*. Retrieved on November 2021, from https://www.mckinsey.com/~/media/McKinsey/Featured%20Insights/China/China%20and%20the%20world%20Inside%20the%20dynamics%20of%20a%20changing%20relationship/MGI-China-and-the-world-Full-Report-Feb-2020-EN.pdf

McKinsey Global Institute. (2020). *China consumer report 2021: Understanding Chinese consumers: Growth engine of the world* (Special ed.). Retrieved on November 2021, from https://www.mckinsey.com/~/media/McKinsey/Featured%20Insights/China/China%20Still%20the%20worlds%20growth%20engine%20after%20COVID%2019/McKinsey%20China%20Consumer%20Report%202021.pdf?shouldIndex=false

McKinsey Global Institute. (2021). *The future of digital innovation in China—Megatrends shaping one of the world's fastest evolving digital ecosystems*. Retrieved on November 2021, from https://www.mckinsey.com/~/media/mckinsey/featured%20insights/china/the%20future%20of%20digital%20innovation%20in%20china%20megatrends%20shaping%20one%20of%20the%20worlds%20fastest%20evolving%20digital%20ecosystems/future-of-digital-innovation-in-china.pdf

National Bureau of Statistics. (2019). Retrieved on November 2021, from http://www.stats.gov.cn/tjsj/zxfb/201908/t20190829_1694202.html

OECD. (2018). The Belt and Road Initiative in the global trade, investment and finance landscape. In *OECD business and finance outlook 2018*. OECD. Retrieved on November 2021, from https://www.oecd.org/finance/Chinas-Belt-and-Road-Initiative-in-the-global-trade-investment-and-finance-landscape.pdf

Oertel, J. (2020). The new China consensus: How Europe is growing wary of Beijing. *ECFR, policy brief*. European Council of Foreign Relations.

Pieke, F. N. (2020). China through European eyes. *Institute for Chinese Studies, Occassional Paper Series, 4*.

Ping, H., & Zuokui, L. (2019). *The cooperation between China and Balkan Countries under the framework of the "Belt and Road" Initiative*. China-CEEC Think Tank Book Series.

Plevnik, J. (2016). *The "Belt and Road" Initiative and its implications for Southeast Europe*. Center for international relations and sustainable development.

PWC. (2017). *The long view how will the global economic order change by 2050?* Retrieved on November 2021, from http://www.iberglobal.com/files/2017/pwc-world-in-2050-2017.pdf

PWC. (2020). *Time to act: China*. Retrieved on December 2021, from https://www.pwc.com/gx/en/asia-pacific/asia-pacific-time-china.pdf

Richter, F. (2021). *China is the world's manufacturing superpower [Digital image]*. Retrieved on 10 November 2021, from from https://www.statista.com/chart/20858/top-10-countries-by-share-of-global-manufacturing-output/

Statista. (2021a). *Leading export countries worldwide in 2020 (in billion U.S. dollars)*. Retrieved on December 2021a, from https://www.statista.com/statistics/264623/leading-export-countries-worldwide/

Statista. (2021b). *Travel and tourism industry in China—Statistics & facts*. Retrieved on July 2022, from https://www.statista.com/topics/1210/tourism-industry-in-china/#dossierKeyfigures

Statista. (2021c). *China's revenue from tourism from 2011 to 2021c (in billion yuan)*. Retrieved on July 2022, from https://www.statista.com/statistics/236040/revenue-from-tourism-in-china/

Statista. (2021d). *Direct contribution of travel and tourism to GDP in leading countries worldwide in 2019 (in USD billion)*. Retrieved on December 2021d, from https://www.statista.com/statistics/292461/contribution-of-travel-and-tourism-to-gdp-in-select-countries/

The State Council Information Office of the People's Republic of China. (2019). *China and the world in the new era*. Retrieved on December 2021, from http://english.www.gov.cn/archive/whitepaper/201909/27/content_WS5d8d80f9c6d0bcf8c4c142ef.html

UNCTAD. (2020). *Global trade impact of the coronavirus (COVID-19) epidemic, trade and development report update*. Retrieved on December 2021, from https://unctad.org/system/files/official-document/ditcinf2020d1.pdf

US Congressional Research Service. (2019, June 25). *China's economic rise: History, trends, challenges, and implications for the United States, RL33534*. Retrieved on December 2021, from https://fas.org/sgp/crs/row/RL33534.pdf

U. S. Department of State. (2020) *The elements of the china challenge, office of policy planning*. Retrieved on December 2021, from https://www.state.gov/wp-content/uploads/2020/11/20-02832-Elements-of-China-Challenge-508.pdf

World Bank. (2020). From recovery to rebalancing: China's economy in 2021. *China Economic Update*. Retrieved on December 2021, from http://pubdocs.worldbank.org/en/264421608625565168/ceu-December-2020-Final.pdf

World Economic Forum. (2019). *The travel & tourism competitiveness report 2019: Travel and tourism at a tipping point*. Retrieved on December 2021, from http://www3.weforum.org/docs/WEF_TTCR_2019.pdf

World Economic Outlook. (2020, October). Retrieved on December 2021, from https://www.imf.org/en/Publications/WEO/weo-database/2020/October

World Tourism Organization. (2021). *International tourism highlights, 2020 edition*. UNWTO. https://doi.org/10.18111/9789284422456. Retrieved on December 2021, from https://www.e-unwto.org/doi/pdf/10.18111/9789284422456

World Tourism Organization and Global Tourism Economy Research Centre. (2014). *UNWTO/GTERC annual report on tourism trends*. UNWTO. Retrieved on December 2021, from https://www.e-unwto.org/doi/pdf/10.18111/9789284419470

Zhang, Y., & Wang, Y. (2017). *ASEAN in China's grand strategy*. In: ASEAN @ 50 building ASEAN community: Political-security and socio-cultural reflections, 4: Retrieved on December 2021, from https://www.eria.org/ASEAN_at_50_4A.9_Zhang_and_Wang_final.pdf

Zhao, Y., & Liu, B. (2020). The evolution and new trends of China's tourism industry. *National Accounting Review, 2*(4), 337–353.

Chapter 24
A Review of China's Contribution to the Sustainable Development of the European Tourism Industry: A Case Study of Economic Effects and Sustainability Issues in Albania

Klodiana Gorica and **Ermelinda Kordha**

1 Introduction

The global travel industry has experienced a recent boom from the Chinese tourism as rapid urbanization and higher disposable incomes are allowing more and more Chinese tourists to explore their country and beyond. Although the vast majority of Chinese tourists in 2019 travelled domestically within China the two and a half per cent of tourists who travelled outside of the country was an amount to be considered significantly. According to statista.com (2021) the share of travellers who do visit destinations outside of China show a steady growth of the number of outbound journeys of Chinese tourists, in the last decade (2009–2019). Of the around 170 million outbound trips from China in 2019, nearly all were for private purposes rather than business trips. Chinese tourists spending on international tourism has also increased dramatically over the last ten years, reaching a peak of over 277 billion US. dollars in 2018. In 2019, around 28% of tourists travelling abroad from China visited Europe. Around 6.33 million trips were made from China to Central and Eastern Europe alone in 2019, outnumbering trips to Western European destinations.

Chinese tourists make up one-fifth of global tourism, and only in 2018, 12.4 million Chinese visited Europe,[1] which is why Central and Eastern European countries see a big potential for growth from Chinese tourism. EU was the second-largest region after Asia for Chinese tourists at the beginning of the decade (Andreu et al.,

---

[1] Europe includes all European countries of the continent, while where there are data related to the European Union, this will be detailed in the chapter.

K. Gorica
COST Action CA18215 - "China in Europe Research Network", Brussels, Belgium

K. Gorica (✉) · E. Kordha
Faculty of Economy, University of Tirana, Tirana, Albania

2013). The number of Chinese tourists in the European Union was projected to reach 3 million in 2019, showing an increase of 7.4% compared to 2018 (China Outbound Tourism Research Institute, COTRI, 2018). In the air travel sector, over 600 aircraft travelled from China to Europe each week in 2018 (UNWTO & CTA, 2019). As a result, 10 air routes were expected to be opened in 2020 between provinces of China and European countries, shortening travel time. According to the Civil Aviation Administration of China (CAAC). There were 11 applications to CAAC for route launches to Europe and one for an additional frequency. If approved, there will be 10 new routes from China to Europe of which seven will be to Italy. Non-traditional tourist destinations are lacking direct air routes from China though. According to European Travel Commission (ETC, 2019 barometer), Chinese tourists went to these destinations by train, in tours that cover several stops in one trip, showing interest for long trips covering a large number of destinations.

The economic effect is of course an important matter after the need for resilience in tourism industry. Many authors have dedicated their work to the contributions of tourism to national, regional, and local economies. The work includes spending estimates of tourists, which generates economic activity directly in the form of output or sales, labour earnings, and employment (Bull, 1998; Fletcher, 1994; Frechtling, 1994; Lundberg et al., 1995). On the other hand, many authors have dedicated work to sustainability issues of a destination (Munoz et al., 2016, Spenceley & Meyer, 2012). So, the sustainability issues together with the economic effect must be considered to understand ways of improving destination management, to achieve such an equilibrium that economic results will not have a negative impact from the sustainability perspective and its three societal-environmental-economic pillars. However, the tourist inflows create sustainability challenges. The resources and infrastructures of several European tourist destinations, particularly those based on cultural heritage, are stretched during peak seasons.

This study tries to analyze the effects of Chinese tourism demand in Europe from both general sustainability perspective and more specific economic perspective, with a focus on impact on relatively small and unknown destinations that can tailor their tourism product through Chinese tourist profiles and requests. Section one concentrates in the literature review, with a list of authors that have dedicated work to the Chinese outbound tourism. The aim is to identify trends and tourist segments within this market, which is not always simple with the latest developments. The literature review confronts the current trends of Chinese outbound tourism with the characteristics of the most demanded destinations in Europe, the importance for the sustainable tourist destinations, and the need for the involvement of travel agencies and tour operators as important intermediaries in the market towards the goal of sustainability. Section two explains the methodology of the study, compounded by two main pillars. In the first phase, the study takes in consideration secondary data from reports and statistics and 20 Interviews from Tourism operators in Albania. Qualitative analyses of interviews and secondary data tries to answer the research questions related to Chinese market in European destinations, in Albanian case and the related sustainability issues. In the second phase the multiplier effect is studied to measure economic effects and opportunities for sustainable policies. Section three relates to data and case study research to show the trends and the characteristics of Chinese outbound tourism market in relation to the destinations in case. The data will show how is raising this market and how it is developing in Europe and in Albania. Section four includes the discussion related to three main points, How Europe will cope with the massive inflows of Chinese tourists, Chinese outbound tourism in Europe and in Albania, and the Assessment for target segment identification. At the end of the chapter, the conclusions and recommendations' section try to give some orientation in relation to the research questions raised at the beginning of the study.

2 Literature Review

Europe is becoming one of the most popular long-haul destinations, which may be considered more than six hours flying time, for Chinese tourists (Lui et al., 2011). Chinese tourists come from a past culture of travelling in destinations geographically and culturally close to home, that is more related to Asian destinations (Andreu et al., 2013). There is a change to this trend from more than two decades now (Lojo, 2016) with a growing number of mainland Chinese tourists more than any other countries. In today's world, China is the leading market of tourism industry worldwide (Lojo, 2016). According to China Daily and Chinese Tourism Academy statistics, in 2019 Chinese tourist peak made Europe their primary destination. In the first six months of 2019, Chinese travellers made almost 3 million visits to European countries.

A large number of scholars and media have already written about the Chinese outbound tourism (Kwek & Lee, 2013; Nyiri, 2006; Ryan & Huang, 2013; Tse, 2015), due to its particular characteristics, and also specifically to Chinese travel to Europe (Fugmann & Aceves, 2013; Pendzialek, 2016; Prayag et al., 2015; Zhu et al., 2016). Tourism was quickly adopted in China since the mid-1990 and affluent families got to experience leisure travel massively, because of factors such as the growth in the household incomes and the government's policies to promote tourism (Andreu et al., 2013; Lojo, 2016). After the 90s, the raising desire to consume different products, including tourism products demand in the middle-class population of China, depends on government action related to the new international situation and conditions and desires of the population, related to consumerism (Lojo, 2016). While authors mention also the raising household income, the abundance of consumer goods, and the official government promotion as drivers of consumption in the large group of middle-class population (Bui & Trupp, 2019). The tourism industry in Europe has experienced some very important changes during the last decades, related to the way destiantions are conceived and the new tourism era, with a special attention to resource consumption. The concept of destination within Europe is also shifting from geographical and territorial concept in a "new Europe" and sustainable tourism destinations concept, which is based on *networking* and *communities* (Gorica, 2020).

In regard to Chinese outbound tourism market, there is a trend to plan and book through tourism operators and agencies, mostly offering the tourism product to the related agencies in China. There is a high importance of studying the characteristics of this potentially raising market. Studies have taken in consideration the motives for which Chinese tourist travel through the last decades, evaluating the developments in market segments (Bui & Trupp, 2019). One of the reasons for this market-raised demand stated by De Graaff et al. (2019), is the concept of the "tailor-made tour" packages, which are customized in accordance with travellers.

China has been regulating outbound group travel through its approved destination status (ADS) policy, which by 2005 included all European Union member states (Arlt, 2006). The strengthening in trade and political relationships between EU and China has been accompanied with an increase in the number of the Chinese visiting Europe. A more opened market from regulatory point of view to promote outbound Chinese tourism resulted in a first evaluation of raising demand. Furthermore, other factors appeared to influence the raising demand, such as higher wages and the desire for consuming prestigious brands (Davis, 2000). Since luxury goods are associated with the social status (Davis, 2000), some international destinations were seen as brands to consume (Arlt, 2006). Chinese consumers also compete for prestige and style, by not being satisfied only with actual followed fashions and trends. As a result, tourism is seen by them as a positional good among the middle and upper class with purchasing power, as it happened in Europe (Garay & Cànoves, 2011).

Another study of Andreu et al. (2013) identified, through 47 European countries, that Chinese outbound tourism raised demand is related to factors such as greater cultural distance from China, a large number of World Heritage Sites, a large ethnic Chinese population, and a large number of flight connections to China. Since Cultural attractions such as monuments and museums have become crucial objects of international travel and constitute the largest sector of the European attraction market (Richards, 1996), and of course are related with Chinese tourism motives to travel, the authors here focus more on cultural tourism and heritage sites while analyzing Chinese tourism demand. For example, the Chinese middle class prefers components of traditional culture (as reflected in Confucianism) to be part of tourist consumption and it shows a way how tourism is culturally framed as a form of consumptionn (Fu et al., 2017). The growth of elite tourism consumption, as elite forms, reflects new patterns of transnational class stratification, and is illustrated in the growth of outbound travellers from China, who increasingly seek to consume cultural capital in Western countries (Arlt, 2006; Wong et al., 2016). "Experience economy" on the other hand is also very important to identify economic effects and it is closely allied to cultural consumption, which has recently been identified as a major tourism trend in the Asia Pacific region (Tolkach et al., 2016). Material consumption in the form of shopping has gained increasing interest in recent years (Zaidan, 2016). Tourists who seek novelty, uniqueness, and unusual or exotic goods and experiences often engage in luxury shopping (Park & Reisinger, 2009), which is a major motivation for Chinese outbound travel to satisfy its consumers' focus on materialism (Tsai et al., 2013). Importantly, luxury shopping generates prestige and value of places (Correia et al., 2019).

Within the context of identifying Tourism demand segments, new trends are showing even in the aspect of Chinese tourism demand. Even though the first generation has been characterized as travellers who book through the tourism operators and who take package tours by visiting tourist site one by one, parts of the second generation are more sophisticated and individualistic and more interested in experiences than in counting visited attractions or countries. The latter group has shown increasing interest in European second-tier destinations with a preference for deeper experiences and intangible lifestyle-related attractions (Jørgensen et al., 2018). But which are the economic effects and the impact on sustainable tourism destinations? A great deal has been published about the contributions of tourism to national, regional, and local economies (Fletcher, 1994, US Travel Data Center, 1996; World Travel & Tourism Council, 1996). Most of these studies include estimates of what tourists or visitors spend to an area while there, which generates economic activity directly in the form of output or sales, labour earnings, and employment. Many of these studies have presented estimates of the so-called multiplier impact of tourism expenditures: the total sales, output, or other measures of economic benefits generated once the initial visitor spending has worked its way through the economy under study through interindustry transactions (the "indirect impact") and through employee consumption expenditures (the "induced impact"). This study would serve not to calculate multiplier effect, but mainly to identify the most sources of income and give an example of how the multiplier effect may be used in further developing calculations for the region and for similar studies in the future.

3 Methodology

Methodology used to answer the three research questions is qualitative and quantitative, with two phases. In the first phase, the study takes in consideration secondary data from reports and statistics, to answer the first and the second question related to the main factors of Chinese tourist demand in regard to European destinations, and how they promote sustainability in relatively small destinations such as Albania. Then, the interview to tourism agencies and tour operators in the country, is used as an instrument, for the qualitative study to answer the third question related to the main Chinese tourist segments and their drivers that promote sustainability. 20 interviews are administered face to face and further it is accepted from the interviewed to give information through an online form for tourism expenditures in case of Chinese tourists. Main parts of the interviews relate to Chinese outbound tourism demand in agencies, main motives, and segments, according to operators' point of view and sustainability issues related to this demand for destinations. A critical qualitative analysis is developed.

The second phase of the study analyzes the sources of contribution to the economic effect that Chinese tourism has in Europe in general and in specific destinations, as part of factors that bring sustainable development, such as in the Albanian case. In the case of assessing the economic impact of tourism, many authors suggest to use a variety of research methods. One of the most important is the evaluation of multiplier effect. Many research methods are suggested to measure the impact of Chinese outbound tourism in Europe, for example through concrete case studies according to the most preferred destinations by Chinese tourists as well as using the multiplier effect. The latter will directly determine the effect that every euro or dollar spent by Chinese tourists will have on the local economy, which makes the multiple effect directly related to communities. A detailed analyses of Interviews for the most preferred Albanian destinations for the Chinese tourists (as a case within Europe) will strongly orient the design of a typical model to guide the sustainable tourism development for communities. If so, the multiplier effect would be as large as possible and the effects of tourism due to Chinese inflows in the local economies would remain within the country. The case of Albania is taken in consideration since data for tourist expenditures were provided by the survey with the biggest tour operators and agencies responsible for fulfilling the Chinese tourists demand in Albania.

4 Data and Case Study Research

This section is following with the data taken from the first step, secondary data, and evaluation of interviews from Tour operators and agencies. Qualitative analyses of interviews have shown that the trend of Chinese tourism in Europe and in Albania has its own characteristics. They, not only prefer trips to see tourist spots, but also want to get acquainted with European culture. According to the requests of tourists, the theme of tourism is honeymoon, tourism for delicious food, skiing, horseback riding, getting to know local towns, football, culture, enjoying the holidays, etc. 2018 was the "Year of China–Europe Tourism." In this scene, tourism cooperation between China and Europe Chinese tourists gained visa facilitation policies, airlines, tourism products, and consumer services. In the field of tourist activities, the cooperation has increased to the number of products where over 1 thousand tourist products are counted in different ways, such as group tourist packages, individual tourism, cruise, study tours, custom trips, local activities, etc. In the service field, the number of bodies receiving the "Welcome Chinese" standard presented by the China Tourism Institute has increased. These agencies can provide Chinese-speaking escorts who can speak Chinese, recognize Chinese menus, Chinese-language information, provide Internet and "UnionPay" card payments from Chinese banks (UNWTO, 2019).

The most attractive destinations to the Chinese are Russia, Italy, Britain, Germany, France, Spain, Greece, Czech Republic, Switzerland, and Portugal (UNWTO, 2019). In addition, attention was also paid to Turkish and Dutch destinations. According to TTRW (2018),[2] traditional destinations continue to remain attractive and are the first choice of Chinese tourists in Europe. It is worth mentioning that in 2018 Italy improved Chinese-language services and security guarantee and opened over 10 visa offices in China as well as followed the visa insurance policy within 36 h, in order for Chinese tourists to visit Italy. Albania, Montenegro, Serbia, Croatia, Russia, etc., have provided facilities for the entry of Chinese tourists.

---

[2] Retrieved in December 2021, from www.ttrweekly.com.

The number of Chinese tourists raised in Russia as a result of world cup organization. Serbia and Montenegro have also been the newest attractive destinations because of Natural landscapes, cultural heritage as well as the low cost (Raspor et al., 2018). In Croatia, the Chinese compound is the fourth largest group of tourists. A big advantage is that the Chinese, conditioned by the holidays, prefer to travel non in the peak season, traditionally differently from Western travellers who choose the peak of the summer season. This increases the number of tourists throughout the year (TTRW, 2018). In 2018, the Albanian government also pursued easing policies for Chinese tourist citizens in April–May. After the announcement of this policy, the number of Chinese tourists in Albania increased by 60% more (INSTAT, 2019). In addition to Eastern European countries, 5 Northern European countries are also attractive to Chinese tourists. The number of Chinese tourists in Denmark increased by 120%, while in Finland by 77%. Chinese tourists mainly went to see the village of Santa Clause (Nielsen, 2017). According to the study of 32-Nielsen in 2017, in terms of gender and age, females occupy 60%, while males 40%. Tourists born in the 80s of the last century occupy 22%, tourists born in the 70s and 50s occupy 19% and those born in the 60s occupy 18%. According to the data, travelling with the family was the most attractive choice. Of average consumption, a Chinese tourist travelling in a tourist group spends 11,823 yuan, a figure lower than 2018. The increase in the number of airlines is another reason for this reduction in the cost of tourism. A new phenomenon in tourism in Europe is that the Chinese find a companion who speaks Chinese well and knows the situation of the country they are going to visit. Group tourism still remains the main way, while personalized tourism, thematic tourism, etc., as well as various consumption has increased a lot. Tourists want to increase consumption in the field of hospitality, restaurants on the basis of product change (Nielsen, 2017).

4.1 The Tourism Potential Demand in the Chinese Outbound Market

Chinese tourists continue to put Europe at the top of their favourite destinations despite the relative slowdown of the Chinese economy and any concerns about BREXIT or even the impact of covid. Quotations made by important international organizations and authorities are directly related. "Chinese tourists are the single most powerful source of change in the tourism industry." Taleb Rifai, Secretary-General of the World Tourism Organization (UNWTO, 2011), emphasizes every word. He explains: "Not only is it the largest domestic market in the world, with 4.4 billion trips made each year, but it is also the world's leading outbound market, with over 135 million international departures in 2016." This number has been growing in double-digit figures since 2010 as it passes 2020, and is simply the tip of the iceberg. "The potential of the Chinese market is much greater because only 6% of the Chinese people have a passport. So, we expect 200 million Chinese to travel abroad within just a few years."

Speaking on the sidelines of the 22nd UNWTO General Assembly, which was held in September in Chengdu, Sichuan province, Rifai stressed that, even more important than the number of Chinese tourists—those from Hong Kong and Macau were not included in these statistics—is the fact that they lead the world in terms of spending: 261.1 billion US dollars last year, according to the United Nations agency. According to Rifai "Chinese travelers spend twice as much as the international average, so their impact on local economies can be huge." Eduardo Santander, executive director at the European Travel Commission stays that given such big number of tourists, it seems strange in terms of sustainability but industry may still be sustainable because of Chinese tourist travel patterns and tastes.

5 Discussion

6 How Europe Will Cope with the Massive Inflows of Chinese Tourist

According to Statista.com (2021), outside of Asian countries, which are very popular among outbound tourists from China, one of the primary destinations for Chinese tourists travelling abroad is the European continent. In 2019, around 28% of tourists travelling abroad from China visited Europe. Around 6.33 million trips were made from China to Central and Eastern Europe alone in 2019, outnumbering trips to Western European destinations. Southern Europe and regions around the Mediterranean were the least visited areas by Chinese tourists that year. Within Western Europe, the UK in particular experienced a significant rise in journeys from China starting in 2015. Prior to the COVID-19 pandemic, tourism from China remained high, firmly placing the country as an important inbound market for Britain, with the number of Chinese tourist trips reaching a record high of 883 thousand visits in 2019. Figure 1 shows the data for European regions outbound tourism.

The impact of Chinese Tourists on the destination Europe, in the macroeconomic level, but also in the context of achieving the objectives of sustainable development, is relatively positive because:

It can contribute in fighting seasonality. The Chinese extend their travel time throughout the year. In the supply–demand ratio, the tourist demand coming from China is oriented towards a time stretch throughout the year. The Chinese help to do this because they travel when Europe is not on holiday—the weeks of May and October, or the Lunar New Year—and many go to unconventional places.

There is a need to avoid the massive tourism, which is challenged due to the Chinese inflows. In the wake of the so-called "tourism phobia" phenomenon, which exists in places like Venice and Barcelona, the concentration of crowds in certain places may be avoided by diversifying products and services in such a way as to

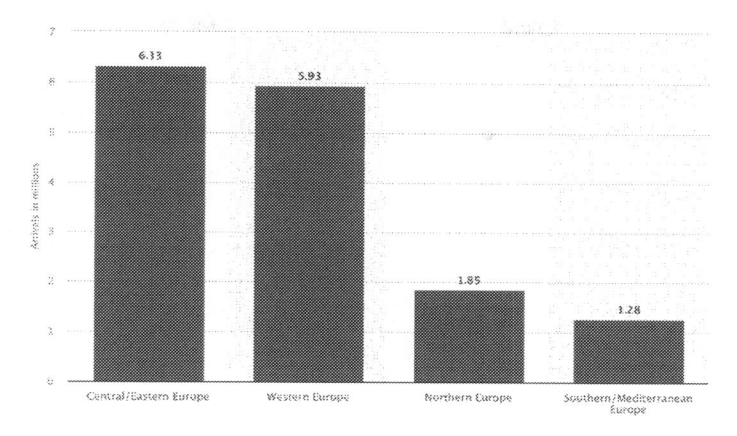

Fig. 1 Chinese Outbound tourism according regions in Europe (*Source* Statista.com [2021])

give benefits to the community by having an all-inclusive tourism approach. Chinese tourism segments can serve as good drivers towards more sustainable destinations of these kinds.

Tourism in Europe Influenced by Chinese flows encourages the development of the Community Based Tourism model. For example, the place the Chinese visit most in Germany is not Berlin or Frankfurt but a small town in the [Rhineland-Palatinate] region called Trier. Why? Because this is the birthplace of Karl Marx, a man who is in every Chinese student's textbook, which is related to cultural heritage. Hallstatt could have shared the fate of many picturesque European cities, where just a decade ago, new residents were relocating, while older generations were left behind. The tourism boom changed everything. Small destinations can be approached by tour operators because of their characteristics related to what Chinese tourist segments are demanding (BBC Travel, 2018).

6.1 Chinese Outbound Tourism in Europe

The secondary data show that the outbound tourism from China is growing exponentially and is becoming one of the industry's main fragment development opportunities due to China's advantaged situation of the primary tourism outbound marketplace in the world. According to China Tourism Academy (UNWTO & CTA, 2019) Chinese tourists mostly travelled to 20 destinations, which are part of the Eastern Europe and also part in China's Belt and Road Initiative. The number of Chinese tourists in Europe is increasing year by year with a growth rate of 20% due to:

- **Pleasing visa policies,**
- **Exchange rates:** as the exchange rates of some European countries like Iceland, Norway, Hungary, Sweden, Russia, and the UK have fallen in 2019 compared with 2018, making them affordable destinations.
- **Customer service and new flight directions:** direct flights were opened facilitating the travelling of Chinese tourists to European cities.

According to CTA, in the first six months of 2019, the number of Chinese outbound tourists is increased by 14% compared with 2018. According to CTA and HCG (2019) data, 10% of the outbound trips for Chinese tourists are made towards Europe in 2019 (Figs. 2, 3).

The situation of EU–China affairs has been radically transformed over the past years and China's attention to Europe has extended geographically and significantly

Fig. 2 Chinese arrivals in Europe (*Source* China Tourism Academy & HCG Travel Group)

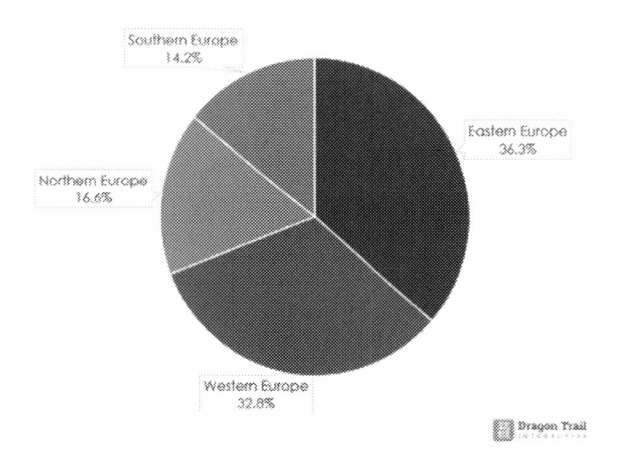

Fig. 3 Destinations of Chinese tourists in 2019 (*Source* CTA and HCG [2019])

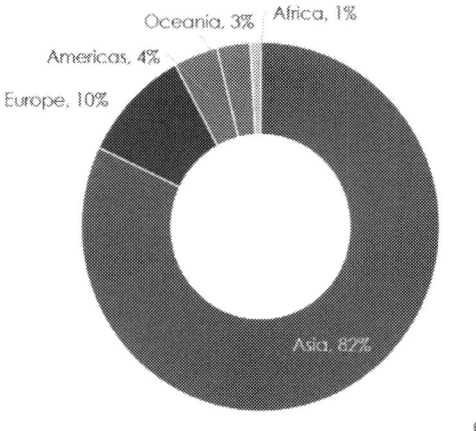

since Chinese presence in Europe is uprising into every sector in the global economy. Extended secure political negotiations and financial interactions of substantial worth as well, have happened in times of good relations between China and Europe, even though they have not been continuous. According to Rhodium Group: "Chinese direct investment into the European Union in 2010 totaled just 2.1 billion euros. That climbed rapidly to 20.7 billion in 2015 and then jumped to 37.2 billion in 2016." Opening to the outside world has changed the Chinese economic structure and the peoples' social/cultural values. This change has also impacted the tourism industry. "Tourism is the third largest socio-economic activity in the European Union (EU), and makes an important contribution to the EU's gross national product and to employment. Europe is also the world's number one tourist destination." stated the Tourism and European Union. Therefore, China outbound tourism plays an important role in the EU and worldwide economy.

6.2 Chinese Outbound Tourism in Albania

Albania is a small country, in the Western Balkans, part of European Continent, actually in the process of Integration in EU. From resources point of view, Albania is an attractive country with significant tourism growth prospective, because of a gorgeous coastline, presence of mountainous areas and a rich cultural and natural heritage (INSTAT, 2019). As such, it proposes endless potential to investors who aim to benefit from untapped opportunities in tourism industry, contributing as a result in its growth as an important strategic economic sector. Albania has a relatively young population, with a relatively high level of education, which can help in tourism growth, due to very good communication with foreigners, since most Albanians speak more than one language and are considered hard working hospitable people (INSTAT, 2019). Tourism development in Albania is also driven by the perfect location in short distances from the main European capital cities and by the ongoing development and growth of the infrastructure, inside and outside the country. Actually Albania is improving the airports' infrastructures and air transportation in general, as well as inside road and train infrastructure, which encourages investors to further develop tourism infrastructure.

The number Chinese outbound tourism arrival is increasing year by year, not only in EU countries, but also in WB as part of European Continent. As part of WB, Albania is mostly visited by Chinese tourists, as stated by the tourism operators in their interviews, mostly for the beautiful South coastline and rich cultural and the rich historical heritage. the interviews also state that Chinese outbound tourist demand has a big potential for Albanian, since it is one of the poorest countries in Europe. The current flourishing in Chinese tourism has formed a tempest through the worldwide travel business including Albania. One important decision that shows the trend of investing in Albanian tourism and tourist inflows increase, is the improvement of visa free travel for 7 countries from the eastern nations. The tourism inflows especially from the eastern countries are important part of all tourists in Albania (INSTAT,

Table 1 European destinations—Chinese tourism flows in 2019

Country	Growth rate (%)
Croatia	**540**
Latvia	**522**
Slovenia	**497**
Bulgaria	**459**
Estonia	**321**
Albania	**300**
Serbia	**295**
Malta	**281**
Ireland	**220**
Denmark	**212**

Source CTA and HCG Travel Group

2019). This is a reason why Albanian tour operators are inciting business relationship to attract visitors especially from China because of being the key country that congregates in highest statistics to the European investments and capitals every year (Table 1).

However, there are still a lot of challenges that Albania needs to face to increase its growth from Chinese outbound tourism demand. Albania has benefited from China's impact in Europe by bringing more visitors to Albania through Europe airports and transportation, but yet there are still many issues to consider.

First of all, the new and upgraded air transport infrastructure must be accompanied with business deals to attract more appropriate airlines, to increase competition and lower the prices. Second, it must invest more in promoting cultural heritage, since Albania is rich in existing artefacts, heritage objects, museums, and old traditions, which could be valorized through tourism supply. According to Albanian tourist operators, a systematic market approach must be followed not only by the private sector but also by public institutions in the endeavour of promoting and developing traditional and new tourism products, to serve and attract a growing number of tourists in the outbound Chinese tourist market. An important issue is that the public transport and the light infastructure as well should be improved, so they can easily orient tourists to find the key points of cities (Oxford, 2014). Improvement of promoting through digital media especially social media is considered an important part of marketing strategy, since Chinese travelers are particularly drawn to experiences they can participate in socially and then share via Instagram or WeChat (BRINK 2019). The report by Nielsen (2017) and Alipay shows that "for Chinese tourists who are generally well-off, tourist attractions and the travel experience are more important factors than the costs that might be incurred."

6.3 Assessment for Target Segment Identification

As previously analyzed, Tourism in Albania is considered to be an essential economic sector with a great impact in employment and development trends. *How China's outbound tourism demand is segmented and how these segments influence growth in tourism aiming to achieve sustainable development?* With outbound tourism from China, rising exponentially, Chinese tourists are becoming one of Albanian industry's major segment growth chances and there is a growing interest from Albanian Tour operators to comprehend how adjusting to meet the needs of this innovative marketplace will affect the tourism industry for the extended period. The supply–demand ratio in the tourism sector is specific and difficult to balance, for these reasons:

1. Demand is very elastic and variable. Crises like covid 19 or natural disasters, cause changes in travelling ways, growing the demand for new destinations that offer an attractive mix of resources and benefits.
2. The tourist supply is rigid and not elastic. Investments in tourism should be well planned and strongly calculated on the basis of observed trends and preliminary studies. This means that if China's influence on European (and Albanian) tourism is projected to be very optimistic in the next 10 years, then national governments should review tourism infrastructure development policies in their countries (Birn, 2020). For example, Albania in this context needs to make some preliminary studies to test and verify the potential of Chinese tourists as a growing market segment for the country, the WBs, and Europe.
3. Furthermore, tourism investment policies should be top-down oriented: regional policies should orient and support national (and Balkan) policies, which further orient local investments in tourism. It is the duty of Albanian politics (and of every Balkan country) to orient and support local domestic investors towards financial investments and capacity-building Chinese tourists. In this way the state becomes a guarantor and supporter of operators and tourist structures in every Balkan country.
4. Furthermore, Balkan governments and public levels should join efforts to strengthen and unify the growing demand for European-oriented tourism in the Balkans, as well as to unify their support policies for operators shaping tourism supply.

6.4 The Multiplier Effect

The economic impact of Chinese tourists' arrivals in Europe will be variable in terms of:

- Level of tourist expenditures;
- employees in tourism;
- Level of salaries;

- The rate of tourist revenue flow from the local community to outside the community. The issue of revenue stream leads further to another specific discussion on the application of sustainable tourism, in that of multiple effect. The following discussion deals with the link between the level of out-of-destination flows experienced by Chinese tourists and the level of development of European destinations. Thus, regarding the income generated by the inflows of Chinese tourists: High-income streams will occur in those European destinations that make up areas in developing countries with economies based mainly on production such as agriculture, where tourism is a relatively new phenomenon. Low-income streams will be in the main well-established tourist destinations in developed countries.

Whenever the costs and benefits of tourism in the local economy are considered, the principles of multiple effect must be analyzed. It basically consists of the idea that every dollar, euro or pound paid by tourists affects the local economy in different ways. In terms of sustainable tourism in Europe, the goal is to maximize tourism spending from the Chinese tourists' inflows, and then minimize the outflow of tourism revenue from the local economy. The multiple effect created and coming from Chinese tourists, varies between different countries and economies. The multiple effect is related to a single indicator: Chinese tourist spending in each European locality or destination. The level of income that remains in the local economy depends on the type of economy. However, this effect is intended to determine the impact generated on a tourist destination for every dollar spent by the Chinese tourist in Europe on the purchase of the tourism product or its components. The higher the use of local/regional European resources, the lower the ratio of use of imported goods that are part of local consumption and production costs, the greater the multiplier effect. The theory of multiplier effects of tourism is important in terms of analyzing the impact of tourism expenditures on the country's national income. The multiplier effects of income show the relationship between an additional unit of expenditure and changes in the income level of the economy. Tourism multipliers represent the relationship between three types of expenditure:

- direct costs resulting from the expenditures of Chinese tourists to purchase a range of goods and services in European destinations;
- indirect costs that are money that remains in the tourist area and can be spent on other business transactions, thus increasing the area's output, employment opportunities, staff income, etc.;
- inductive expenses which is the addition of personal income that brings further consumption expenses.

This is the way to understand the positive, generative, direct, and indirect impact that 1 USD/dollar spent by 1 Chinese tourist in Europe, brings. Every element in the analysis starts from the structure of tourist expenditures without including transport costs. Table 2 represents the case of accommodation and stay of a Chinese couple for a period of 7–10 days in a European locality. The approximate cost structure according to data taken from the interviews, and also a desk research about the average prices, is illustrated in the table. Let us analyze the turnover of expenses of 1000 dollars in

Table 2 Assessment of yearly turnover of 1000 $ from tourism expenses

Expenditure structure	Number of transactions (in $)					Total arrivals	Yearly turnover of 1 $
	First	Second	Third	Fourth	Fifth		
Accommodation	250.0	250.0	178.0	112.0	64.5	854.5	3.42
Food	320.0	320.0	211.0	137.0	63.5	1051.5	3.28
Buying	250.0	250	149	89.5	48.5	787.0	3,15
Entertainment	100.0	100	70.5	41.0	25.0	336.5	3.30
Local transportation	50.0	50	29.0	16.5	7.5	153.0	3.06
Other	30.0	30	16.5	9.0	4.5	90.0	3.00
Total	**1000**	**1000**	**654.0**	**405.0**	**213.5**	**3272.5**	**3.27**

Source authors

some transactions according to the structure of expenses for a year. The results of this analysis are given in the Table 2

From Table 2 we see that the tourist expenditure of $1000 during a year has passed into five transactions. The first transaction is the payment of these $1000 by foreign tourists for the services received as specified in the table. In the second transaction begins the spending of $1000 from the country's economy without any loss. In the third transaction they lose $346 for various reasons (import) and $654 remain in circulation. In the fourth transaction they lose 249 $ and 405 $ remains in circulation. In the fifth transaction they lose $191.5 and remain in circulation $213.5. After this transaction, the effects of $1000 are 3272.5 $, so the first value of 1000 $ has been circulated 3.27 times. This means that every dollar of foreign tourists in that resort country has additional effects on the country's 3.27 $ economy over the course of a year. Although the effect of leakage (for loan payments, fuel, etc.) is inevitable, the effect that leaves 1 $ for a Chinese tourist after 5 years is such that it generates 3.27 $ in the European locality. The difference of 5 USD that should have left with 3.27 is flowing abroad.

7 Conclusions and Recommendations

Chinese outbound tourism has been on the rise in European tourism in recent decades, and despite the COVID-19 crisis, it is still projected to continue to grow when tourism returns to its new post-crisis normality. In addition to the increase in numbers, it has also changed in quality and in market segments that have developed related to their motives, reasons, age groups, and demands, regarding the tourism product. Although they remain in the segment of traditional cultural tourism, lately they are experiencing new trends in shopping, as well as requesting visits to specific destinations, and looking for tailored products.

In this context, the European tourism industry can benefit in economic aspect, from their expenditures and expenditure structure, and especially from sustainable development point of view, because of the fulfilled standards for sustainable tourism. Building the right strategies to avoid disadvantages such as bad implementation in such forms as mass tourism or even other forms such as ecotourism, will support sustainable tourism development in terms of all the three pillars, the economic, and the environment. Adjusting the tourism supply to the demand of different segments of the Chinese market demand, will also support sustainability and the community development.

Smaller communities and destinations, but with a rich cultural tourism offer can benefit from the increase, not only in quantity but also in the diversification of Chinese outbound tourism demand. Such countries and their communities, as in the Albanian case, will benefit not only from the economic point of view, but also from the inclusion of the community in an all-inclusive tourism development approach. The economic effect that is identified and measured by the multiplier effect methods will help build a model for further tourism development by Chinese tourist demand in small destinations or in destinations that include also communities in their tourism development, in Europe. Difficulties related to this study are found mainly in the use of secondary data, which are not appropriate to study main segments in the Chinese outbound tourism. It is also difficult to directly relate this demand with sustainability issues in tourism development. The tourist behaviour of the market and the interviews have helped in this direction, but further quantitative studies are needed. The multiplier effect is also difficult to be measured in Countries like Albania with problems in data reliability, which need time to gather data from primary sources.

The study did not take in consideration the COVID-19 Pandemic effect, because a totally whole study should be dedicated to the same issues related to economy and sustainability pillars after the Pandemic, where identification of changed activities, experiences, and consumption habits for many products and services, tourism included, should be taken in consideration. So this is a suggestion for further research that may serve also as a comparative study, before and after the Pandemic.

Bibliographic References

Andreu, R., Claver, E., & Quer, D. (2013). Chinese outbound tourism: New challenges for European tourism. *Enlightening Tourism: A Pathmaking Journal, 3*(1), 44–58. ISSN 2174-548X

Andreu, R., Claver, E., Quer, D. (2014). Destination attributes and Chinese outbound tourism to Europe. *Journal of China Tourism Research, 15*(4), 4–28. Retrieved on December 2021, from https://rua.ua.es/dspace/bitstream/10045/44415/3/2014_Andreu_etal_JCTR.pdf

Arlt, W. G. (2006). *China's outbound tourism*. Routledge.

BBC Travel. (2018). Retrieved on December 2021, from http://www.bbc.com/travel/story/20180725-the-german-city-beloved-by-chinese

Birn. (2020). *Balkan countries put an eye on Chinese tourism, in Reporter.al*. Retrieved on December 2021, from https://www.reporter.al/vendet-e-ballkanit-i-vene-syrin-turizmit-kinez

Brink Editorial. (2019). *Chinese tourists are going international—And their travel habits are evolving*. Retrieved on December 2021, from https://www.brinknews.com/chinese-tourists-are-going-international-and-their-travel-habits-are-evolving/

Bui, H. T., & Trupp, A. (2019). Asian tourism in Europe: Consumption, distinction, mobility, and diversity. *Tourism Recreation Research*. https://doi.org/10.1080/02508281.2019.1634305

Bull, A. (1998). *The economics of travel and tourism* (2nd ed.). Addison Wesley Longman Australia.

CAAC. (2019). Retrieved on December 2021, from https://centreforaviation.com/analysis/airline-leader/chinas-airlines-turn-their-attention-to-europe-routes-470307

China Outbound Tourism Research Institute, COTRI. (2018). *COTRI Chinese market segment: High spending fits opportunities and challenges for nordic destinations*.

China Tourism Academy (CTA). (2021). *Annual Report of China outbound tourism development*. Tourism Education Press. ISBN 978-7-5637-2132-0.

Correia, A., Kozak, M., & Kim, S. (2019). Investigation of luxury values in shopping tourism using a fuzzy-set approach. *Journal of Travel Research, 58*(1), 77–91.

CTA. (2019). *Big data: Chinese tourism to Europe keep growing in H1 2019*. Retrieved on December 2021, from http://news.travel168.net/focus_on/20190830/53053.html

CTA and HCG. (2019). *China tourism academy and HCG travel group Chinese tourism to Europe H1 2019 report*.

DAVIS, D. (2000). Introduction. In D. Davis (Ed.), *The consumer revolution in Urban China* (pp. 1–24). University of California Press.

De Graaff, N., Henderson, J., Gledić, J., Magli, R., Warenghien. (2019). *CA18215—China in Europe research network*. Retrieved on December 2021, from https://www.cost.eu/actions/CA18215/

ETC – European Travel Commission. (2019). *Chinese tourists flock to Europe. Increase confirms success of EU-China Tourism Year*. Report.

Fletcher, J. E. (1994). "Economic Impact." In Stephen F. Witt & Luiz Moutinho (Eds.), *Tourism marketing and management handbook* (2nd ed., pp. 475–479). Prentice Hall.

Fletcher, J. E., & Archer, B. H. (1991). The development and application of multiplier analysis. In C. P. Cooper (Ed.), *Progress in tourism, recreation and hospitality management* (Vol. 3, pp. 28–47). Belhaven Press.

Frechtling, D. C. (1994). Assessing the impacts of travel and tourism—Measuring economic benefits. In J. R. B. Ritchie & C. R. Goeldner (Eds.), *Travel, tourism and hospitality research: A handbook for managers and researchers* (pp. 359–365). John Wiley.

Fu., X., Cai, L., & Lehto, X. (2017). Framing Chinese tourist motivations through the lenses of confucianism. *Journal of Travel & Tourism Marketing, 34*(2), 149–170. https://doi.org/10.1080/10548408.2016.1141156

Fugmann, R., & Aceves, B. (2013). Under control: Performing Chinese outbound tourism to Germany. *Tourism Planning & Development, 10*(2), 159–168.

Garay, L., & Canoves, G. (2011). Life cycles, stages and tourism history: The Catalonia Case, Spain. *Annals of Tourism Research, 38*, 651–671.

Gorica, K. (2020). China: investing and touristing in Europe. *Journal of Tourism Hospitality, 9*, 434. https://doi.org/10.35248/2167-0269.20.9.434

Icoz, O., & Icoz, O. (2019). *Economic impacts of tourism from: The Routledge handbook of tourism impacts, theoretical and applied perspectives*. Routledge.

INSTAT. (2019). *Tourism in figures Albania 2019, Editor Republic of Albania*, Institute of Statistics.

Jørgensen, M. T., Law, R., & King, B. E. (2018). Beyond the stereo-types: Opportunities in China inbound tourism for second- tier European destinations. *International Journal of Tourism Research, 20*(4), 488–497.

Kwek, A., & Lee, Y. (2013). Consuming tourism experiences: Mainland Chinese corporate travellers in Australia. *Journal of Vacation Marketing, 19*(4), 301–315.

Liu, W. X. (2008). China-turismo receptive. In *Proceeding of I Congreso Internacional sobre Turismo Asiático*, Barcelona, 25th–26th September.

Lojo, A. (2016). Chinese tourism in Spain: An analysis of the tourism product, attractions and itineraries offered by Chinese travel agencies, *Cuadernos de Turismo, 37*, 243–268. Universidad de Murcia ISSN: 1139-7861. https://doi.org/10.6018/turismo.37.256231

Lui, V., Kuo, Y., Fung, J., Jap, W., & Hsu, H. (2011). *Tacking off: Travel and tourism in China and beyond*. Retrieved May 15, 2012, from http://www.bcg.com

Lundberg, D., Stavenga, M., & Krishnamoorthy, M. (1995). *Tourism economics*. John Wiley.

Muñoz, D. R. M., Muñoz, R. D. M., & Pérez, F. J. G. (2016). A sustainable development approach to assessing the engagement of tourism enterprises in poverty alleviation. *Sustainable Development, 24*, 220–236.

Nielsen. (2017). *Outbound Chinese tourism and consumption trends*. Retrieved on December 2021, from https://www.nielsen.com/wp-content/uploads/sites/3/2019/05/outbound-chinese-tourism-and-consumption-trends.pdf

Nyiri, P. (2006). *Scenic spots. Chinese tourism, the state and cultural authority*. University of Washington Press.

Oxford. (2014). Tourism economics, an Oxford economics company—The future of Chinese travel, The Global Chinese travel market, A report by Oxford Economics for InterContinental® Hotels Group (IHG®).

Park, K. S., & Reisinger, Y. (2009). Cultural differences in shopping for luxury goods: Western, Asian, and Hispanic tourists. *Journal of Travel & Tourism Marketing, 26*(8), 762–777.

Pendzialek, B. (2016). Mainland Chinese outbound tourism to Europe: Recent progress. In *Chinese outbound tourism 2.0* (pp. 189–206). Apple Academic Press.

Prayag, G., Cohen, S. A., & Yan, H. (2015). Potential Chinese travelers to Western Europe: Segmenting motivations and service expectations. *Current Issues in Tourism, 18*(8), 725–743.

Raspor A., Lasmanovic, D., & Popovic, M. (2018). Chinese tourists in Western Balkan: Facts and forecast, Perfectus, Svetovanje in izobraževanje, dr. Andrej Raspor s.p. ISBN: 978-961-94220- pp. 7-6 (pdf), as part of the Project: The development of integrated and sustainable tourism offer of Slovenia and Montenegro for Far Eastern Market (China).

Richards, G. (1996). *Introduction: Culture and tourism in Europe cultural tourism in Europe*. CABI.

Ryan, C., & Huang, S. (Eds.). (2013). *Tourism in China: Destinations, planning and experiences*. Bristol.

Spenceley, A., & Meyer, D. (2012). Tourism and poverty reduction: Theory and practice in less economically developed countries. *Journal of Sustainable Tourism, 10*(3), 297–317.

Statista. (2021). Retrieved on December 2021, from https://www.statista.com/topics/4805/chinese-tourism-in-europe/#dossierKeyfigures

Tolkach, D., Chon, K. K. S., & Xiao, H. (2016). Asia Pacific tourism trends: Is the future ours to see? *Asia Pacific Journal of Tourism Research, 21*(10), 1071–1084.

Tsai, W. S., Yang, Q., & Liu, Y. (2013). Young Chinese consumers' snob and bandwagon luxury consumption preferences. *Journal of International Consumer Marketing, 25*(5), 290–304.

Tse, T. S. M. (2015). A Review of Chinese outbound tourism research and the way forward. *Journal of China Tourism Research, 11*(1), 1–18.

TTR Weekly. (2018). Retrieved on December 2021, from https://www.ttrweekly.com/site/2018/11/chinese-tourists-flock-to-europe/

UNWTO and CTA. (2019). *Guidelines for success in the Chinese outbound tourism market*.

U.S. Travel Data Center. (1996). *Impact of tavel on state economies 1994*. Travel Industry Association of America.

Wong, I. A., McKercher B., & Li, X. (2016). East Meets West: Tourist interest in hybrid culture at postcolonial destinations, 2014. *Journal of Travel Research, 55*(5), 628–642. https://doi.org/10.1177/0047287514563984

World Tourism Organization. (2019). *Guidelines for the success in the Chinese outbound tourism market*. UNWTO. https://doi.org/10.18111/9789284421138

World Tourism Organization (UNWTO). (2011). *Tourism Highlights 2011*. Retrieved on December 2021, from http://mkt.unwto.org/en/content/tourism-highlights

World Travel and Tourism Council. (1996). *The 1996/7 WTTC travel & tourism report*. Insight Media.

Zaidan, E. A. (2016). Tourism shopping and new urban entertainment: A case study of Dubai. *Journal of Vacation Marketing, 22*(1), 29–41.

Zhu, D., Xu, H., & Jiang, L. (2016). Behind buying: The Chinese gaze on European commodities. *Asia Pacific Journal of Tourism Research, 21*(3), 293–311.

Chapter 25
A Greater Eurasian Partnership? Xi and Putin's Road to Integrate and Lead

Ana Isabel Xavier

1 Introduction

"We acted resolutely and consistently to uphold our national interests and the security of the country and our citizens. We took swift action to restore the economy, and, in many areas, we are close to achieving our strategic development objectives." The statement is quoted from Vladimir Putin's New Year Address to the Nation[1] and clearly anticipates how the (national) interests act as an indispensable prerequisite for (national) security.

Also in Beijing, the 2022 New Year address by President Xi Jinping flagged complete unification of Chinese Taipei with the mainland as an "aspiration" for the nation's survival at the international level. One particular statement is important to quote: "The prosperity and stability of Hong Kong and Macao is always close to the heart of the motherland. Only with unity and concerted efforts can we ensure sound implementation of One Country, Two Systems in the long run. The complete reunification of our motherland is an aspiration shared by people on both sides of the Chinese Taipei Strait. I sincerely hope that all the sons and daughters of the Chinese nation will join forces to create a brighter future for our nation."[2]

Both statements converge on the importance of an integrated nation to compete for the shift in the balance of power and leadership within a greater Eurasian Partnership. The day of the Opening Ceremony for the Winter Olympics in China's capital, in early February 2022, marked an important step into the enhancement of the bilateral relation between Vladimir Putin and his Chinese counterpart Xi Jinping,

---

[1] Retrieved on December 2021, from http://en.kremlin.ru/events/president/news/67514.
[2] Retrieved on December 2021, from http://www.chinadaily.com.cn/a/202112/31/WS61cee9c5a310cdd39bc7e98b.html.

A. I. Xavier (✉)
Universidade Autónoma de Lisboa, Lisbon, Portugal
e-mail: aixavier@autonoma.pt

as well as in the official partnership between Beijing and Moscow. As relations with the West deteriorate for both parts, pressured by Ukraine's and Taiwan's concerns, reciprocal sympathy and support were raised in the bilateral talks at the Diaoyutai State Guesthouse in Beijing around international strategic security and stability.

The joint statement in English,[3] entitled "International Relations Entering a New Era and the Global Sustainable Development," includes two important declarations. First, the Western liberal order established in the wake of the Second World War (Frye, 2021; Friedberg, 2017; Grosse et al., 2021; Ikenberry, 2018; Mearsheimer, 2019) is responsible for world's disruption, as the two countries "believe that certain States, military and political alliances and coalitions seek to obtain, directly or indirectly, unilateral military advantages to the detriment of the security of others."

The second is a major proof of harmony and solidarity of the two powers, as Russia and China "oppose further enlargement of NATO and call on the North Atlantic Alliance to abandon its ideologized cold war approaches, to respect the sovereignty, security and interests of other countries, the diversity of their civilizational, cultural and historical backgrounds, and to exercise a fair and objective attitude towards the peaceful development of other States."

The joint statement also bridges an increasing integration and leadership of Central Asia and the Eurasian Economic Union to streamline investments in the region (Rolland, 2019; Stent, 2020; Sutter, 2019), despite the prolonged period of uncertainty and fluctuations in political power (Secrieru & Shkliarov, 2018) that Russia is facing. Also, the South Korean president launched a "Eurasian Initiative," which seeks to connect transportation, electrical, gas, and oil links from Western Europe to East Asia which echoes China's long-standing "New Silk Road" project or Belt and Road Initiative (Emerson, 2014; Karaganov, 2016; Shakhanova & Garlick, 2020). In fact, Klein (2019, p. 7) holds that "At a global level, Russia is seeking to position itself as an independent pole in the multipolar world order. While it claims a say on all important global issues, it pursues hegemonic ambitions in the post-Soviet space. This is because, in Moscow's traditional understanding, control of its own sphere of influence is considered an indispensable prerequisite for acting as a great power."

Bearing in mind these introductory remarks, this chapter will explore to which extent the Eurasian Economic Union (EAEU) and the Belt and Road Initiative (BRI), position an ambitious Russia and a rising China, questioning if a greater Eurasian partnership is taking place in the context of both initiatives. First section will assess the Eurasian Economic Union, and second section will elaborate on the belt and road, to explore to which extent these two initiatives are instrumental to both Russia and China cooperating to compete. A third section will be devoted to measuring the strategic and operational asset with a detailed analysis of maps, figures, and graphs for a comparative assessment of both countries' capabilities. The concluded paragraphs will stress how Russia and China are cooperating within Eurasia region to compete for global leadership, as the current *status quo* in Ukraine and Chinese Taipei keeps triggering unanimous reactions from the West.

---

[3] Retrieved on December 2021, from http://en.kremlin.ru/supplement/5770#sel=1:21:S5F,1:37:3jE.

1.1 The Eurasian Economic Union (EAEU)

The dramatic decline in GDPs[4] of Russia and post-Soviet Republics faced harsh economic issues right after the Soviets were dismembered (Troitskiy, 2020; Vicari, 2016), leading to an intense consideration for an alternative way of economic cooperation. In 1991, Russia, Belarus, and Kazakhstan agreed on going through shared and deepening economic reforms within the establishment of the Commonwealth of Independent States (CIS) that has been the foundational rationale behind Eurasian Economic Union. In fact, the CIS clearly initiated a process quite like the European Union (Kinyakin & Kucheriavaia, 2019) as institutions and policies were triggered around free movement, coordination of policies and regulation of activities.

Back in 1994, at Moscow State University, Nursultan Nazarbayev, the first president of Kazakhstan, gave his vision of creating a regional trading bloc to connect to and profit from the growing economies of Europe and East Asia (Mostafa & Mahmmod, 2018) implementing a truly Eurasian trading bloc facilitating trade and investment flows across central Asia, Armenia, and Belarus. After that, numerous treaties have been signed to gradually establish a Eurasian Customs Union and the Single Economic Space (Mostafa & Mahmood, 2018) on goods, services, capital, and labour with open borders and no passport controls among member states to increase economic integration among different Eurasian countries having Russia as a common ground (Yarashevich, 2020).

In turn, in October 2011, Vladimir Putin gave a speech entitled "A new integration project for Eurasia: the future in the making," suggesting that Eurasian countries should lean on European Union's experience, take advantage of refraining from mistakes and the burden of heavy bureaucracy[5] and accelerate the Eurasian Integration. The official kick off for the Eurasian Economic Union has just been released. On 29 May 2014, the presidents of Kazakhstan, Belarus, and Russia formally signed the treaty on the Eurasian Economic Union, which came into effect on 1 January 2015 (Madiyev, 2021). Armenia (signed on 9 October 2014 and entered into force on 2 January 2015) and Kyrgyzstan (the accession treaty of Kyrgyzstan was signed on 23 December 2014 and came into force on 6 August 2015) soon followed. Compared with the EU's bloc of 50 million of people, Vladimir Putin highlighted the "powerful, attractive centre of economic development, a big regional market that unites more than 170 million people."[6] According to its official database,[7] the EAEU has currently the tenth-largest economy in the world by nominal GDP and has major

---

[4] Asia Report N°201—3 February 2011—Central Asia: Decay and decline. International Crisis group. Retrieved on December 2021, from https://www.crisisgroup.org/europe-central-asia/central-asia/central-asia-decay-and-decline.

[5] Retrieved on December 2021, from https://russiaeu.ru/en/news/article-prime-minister-vladimir-putin-new-integration-project-eurasia-future-making-izvestia-3-.

[6] Retrieved on December 2021, from https://soulfreesociety.org/EurAsianUnion/Headquarter.html.

[7] Retrieved on December 2021, from http://www.eurasiancommission.org/ru/Documents/2797_1_EEK_%D0%A6%D0%98%D0%A4%D0%A0_%D0%B0%D0%BD%D0%B3%D0%BB__sait_rasv.pdf.

potential within the energy sector (it produces about 20.7% of the world's natural gas and 14.6% of the world's oil and gas condensate. It is the third producer of the world's electrical energy (9%) and the fourth producer of the world's coal (5.9%), and it produces 18.6% of the world's sugar beet and 22.7% of the world's sunflowers. This economic union of Eastern Europe, Western Asia, and the Central Asian States integrates a single market (Kostem, 2019; Turarbekava, 2019) consisting of free movement of goods, capital, services, and people, ambitions for a common currency unit in a span of five to ten years, a common electricity market (Zemskova, 2018) as well as a single hydrocarbons market by 2025. One of the main similar features is the supranational and intergovernmental dimension, as the EAEU comprises, on one hand, a Supreme Eurasian Economic Council (consisting of the Heads of the member states) and, on the other, and Eurasian Intergovernmental Council (Heads of the governments of member states) and a Eurasian Economic Commission (the executive body).

As Fig. 1 illustrates, China is not a EAEU member state but a non-preferential free trade agreement country, providing no reduction of duties. In May 2018, an Agreement on Economic and Trade Cooperation among the Eurasian Economic Union and its member states and the People's Republic of China[8] was signed, entering into force in October. This legal framework was aimed to regulate the entire structure of trade and economic relations, increasing the transparency of regulatory systems, simplifying trade procedures as well as developing cooperation ties across a wide range of issues, such as customs cooperation, technical barriers to trade, sanitary and phytosanitary measures, trade protection measures, e-commerce, or intellectual property.

1.2 The Belt and Road Initiative (BRI)

Also known as "One Belt One Road," "Silk Road Economic Belt and the twenty-first-century Maritime Silk Road," or "New Silk Road," the Belt and Road Initiative (BRI) is anchored in the Chinese constitution as the main international cooperation and economic strategy. It is enshrined in "five goals": policy coordination, facilities connectivity, unimpeded trade, financial integration, and people-to-people bonds. The BRI initiative was first unveiled in 2013 by China's president and in 2015 released by the National Development and Reform Commission, the Ministry of Foreign Affairs, and the Ministry of Commerce of the People's Republic of China. As of January 2022, the number of countries that have joined the Belt and Road Initiative (BRI) by signing a Memorandum of Understanding (MoU) with China is 137 to 144: 42 countries are in Sub-Saharan Africa; 34 BRI countries are in Europe & Central Asia (including 18 countries of the European Union (EU) that are part of the BRI); 25 BRI countries are in East Asia & pacific; 18 BRI countries in the Middle East &

---

[8] Retrieved on December 2021, from http://www.eurasiancommission.org/en/nae/news/Pages/25-10-2019-5.aspx.

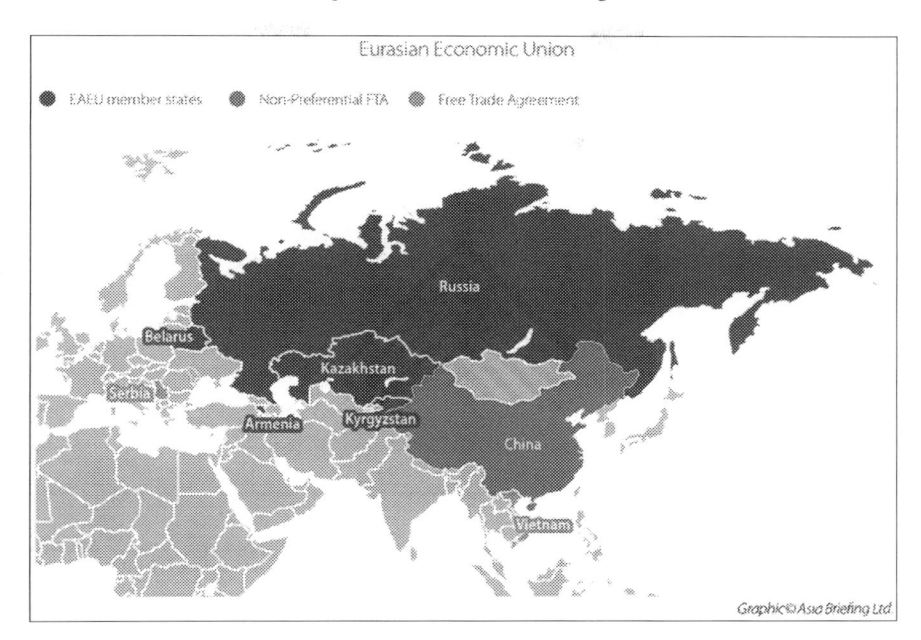

Fig. 1 Countries of Eurasian Economic Union (*Source* Retrieved on December 2021, from https://www.silkroadbriefing.com/news/2019/08/22/russias-eurasian-economic-union-free-trade-area-gets-first-foothold-europe)

North Africa; 19 BRI countries are in Latin America & Caribbean and 6 countries are in South East Asia (Fig. 2).

Fig. 2 Countries of the Belt and Road Initiative (*Source* Retrieved on December 2021, from https://www.cfr.org/blog/countries-chinas-belt-and-road-initiative-whos-and-whos-out)

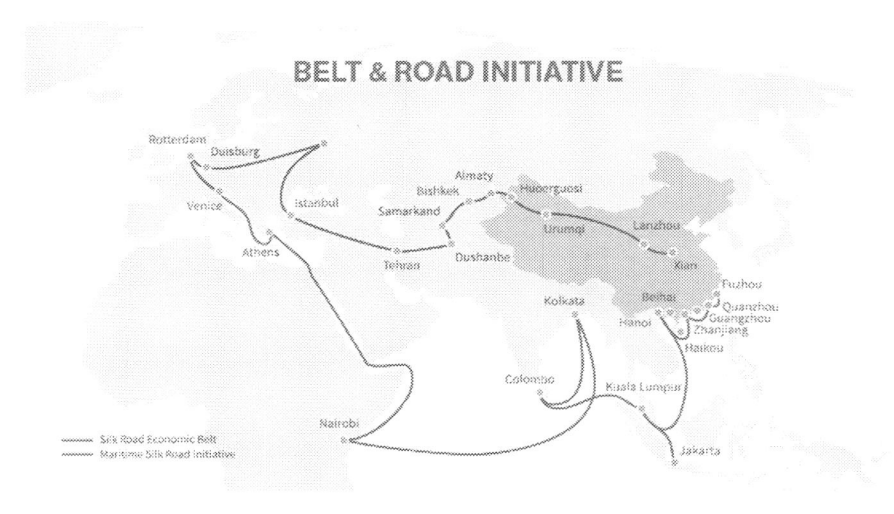

Fig. 3 Belt and Road Initiative's Silk Roads (*Source* Retrieved on December 2021, from https://www.beltroad-initiative.com/belt-and-road/)

Hailed as a transformative effort to deploy China's economic might in service of its strategic goals (Small, 2018), the land corridors include the New Eurasian Land Bridge (which runs from Western China to Western Russia through Kazakhstan) and the Silk Road Railway (through China's Xinjiang Autonomous Region, Kazakhstan, Russia, Belarus, Poland, and Germany).

Both Figs. 3 and 4 illustrate the transcontinental nature of this long-term policy and investment programme, as well as the geographical importance of European Union member states in the destination of those flows.

1.3 Measuring the Strategic and Operational Assets

Russia and China's positions in the international system are widely studied in the academic literature. Krickovic (2017) recognizes Russia as a declining power, while China as the most dynamic rising power. If Russia is "dissatisfied with the order and determined to change it to reverse its decline and maintain its great power status" and therefore arises as the most assertive challenger to the US-led global order has emerged, China "can grow and prosper by free-riding on the hegemonic order established by the US and is thus cautious about challenging it" (2017, p. 299). In turn, Person (2020, p. 9) claims that "there is little doubt that Russia has a grand strategy, regardless of whether it is reflected in foundational national security documents." He also suggests that taking Russia's statements and actions, it is obvious that Moscow has spent tremendous efforts to coordinate a considerable resource for that grand strategy (Person, 2020, p. 9). Russia's military-modernization

Fig. 4 Land and maritime routes of the Belt and Road Initiative (*Source* Bloomberg)

efforts (Lindley-French, 2019) are providing Moscow with a credible military tool for pursuing national policy goals[9] both based on nuclear (the ultimate security guarantor) and ground forces (at a very high level of readiness). The Russian military bases abroad and in disputed territories also show how targeted the priorities are.

In what concerns Russia's military bases in the post-soviet space, the extent of the Kremlin's presence in the neighbourhood is crystal clear (Klein, 2019, p. 23). Russia prioritizes a considerable operational group of forces in Sevastopol, on the disputed Crimean Peninsula, not only as a base of the Russian Navy but as the main base of the Black Sea Fleet (Zaborsky, 1995). Besides Crimea, the Russian military base in Dushanbe, Tajikistan, part of the Central Military District, is its largest abroad. The Transnistria separatist region hosts the Operational Group of Russian Forces in Transnistria (OGRF), an overseas military task force of the Russian Armed Forces for peacekeeping purposes and to guard a decommissioned arms depot in Cobasna. Russia also keeps sizable troops based in South Ossetia and Abkhazia, both disputed territories in the Caucasus. As Russian Military built up its capabilities along the separatist provinces of Donetsk and Luhansk in the eastern part of Ukraine, it also becomes clear the geopolitical interest of controlling Azov Sea (Coffey, 2020; Urcosta, 2018) and Mariupol Port, bridging Crimea Peninsula to the Black Sea.

In the same token, Person (2020, p. 1) emphasizes that, by analysing Russian strategic documents, the fundamental aim of the nations has been based on defence and deterrence, and thus Russian economic, political, information, and military power are entirely employed for this purpose. Proof of this is the fact that the military

---

[9] The International Institute for Strategic Studies (IISS) Strategic Dossier Russia's Military Modernisation: An Assessment.

expenditure has been increasing until 2016 and from 2018 to 2019 a small annual nominal expansion is also registered. In a longer perspective and when prospecting 2030, Rácz (2020, p. 57) sets three scenarios for Russia's military power: first, "calm after the storm" (after a nuclear crisis, Russian elites turn their back on Putin and new leadership disengages from Eastern Ukraine but not Crimea); second, "tired Golliath" (Russian armed forces fail to keep pace with the military capabilities of China and the US and focuses on core tasks and winds down much of its international presence); and third, "Military superpower" (disengaged US and internally weakened EU create space for Russia to build up military dominance).

As the second scenario also depends on China's capabilities, it is important to recall that it is in the Southern Sea area that China has established numerous military installations, primarily in the Spratly Islands (Fig. 5), where airfields and potential missile, radar, and helicopter infrastructure project its power (Grossman, 2019). In the horn of Africa, China is strategically deployed in the Bab-el-Mandeb Strait, "(…) a vital strategic link in the maritime trade route between the Mediterranean Sea and the Indian Ocean via the Red Sea and the Suez Canal" (Calabrese, 2020). In this particular strait, the Chinese People's Liberation Army Navy operates a military base for anti-piracy operations, intelligence, non-combat evacuation operations, peacekeeping operations support, and counterterrorism. Also, in Djibouti (Fig. 5), the Chinese People's Liberation Army Support Base is the PLAN's second overseas military base. This increase of military movements and power projection in the Horn of Africa and the Indian Ocean is a clear illustration of China's investment in Africa, as well as ambitions to gradually expand to all continent's Atlantic coast (Beauchamp-Mustafaga, 2020; Tanchum, 2021).

Chinese Taipei, the Philippines, Indonesia, Vietnam, Japan, India, South Korea, North Korea, Singapore, Brunei, Nepal, Bhutan, Laos, Mongolia, and Myanmar all

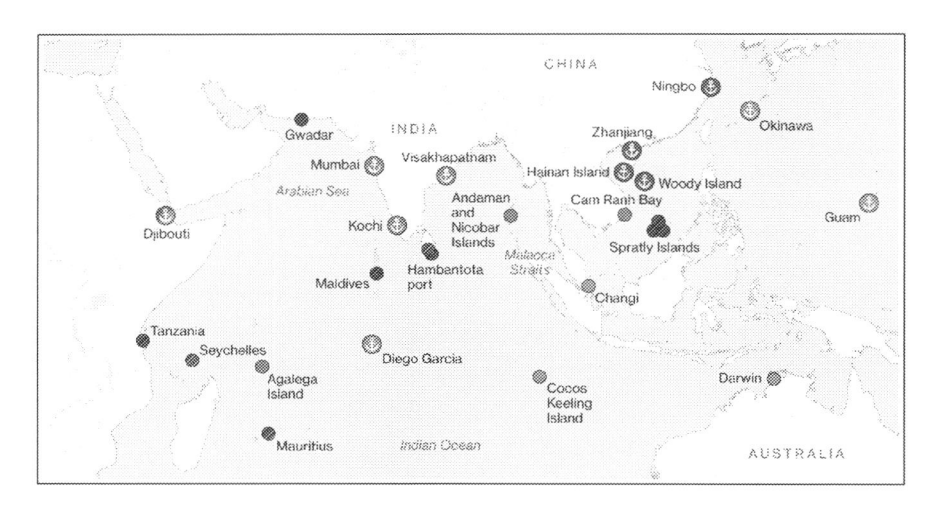

Fig. 5 China: Military Bases Abroad (*Source* Retrieved on January 2022, from https://www.bloomberg.com/graphics/2018-china-navy-bases/)

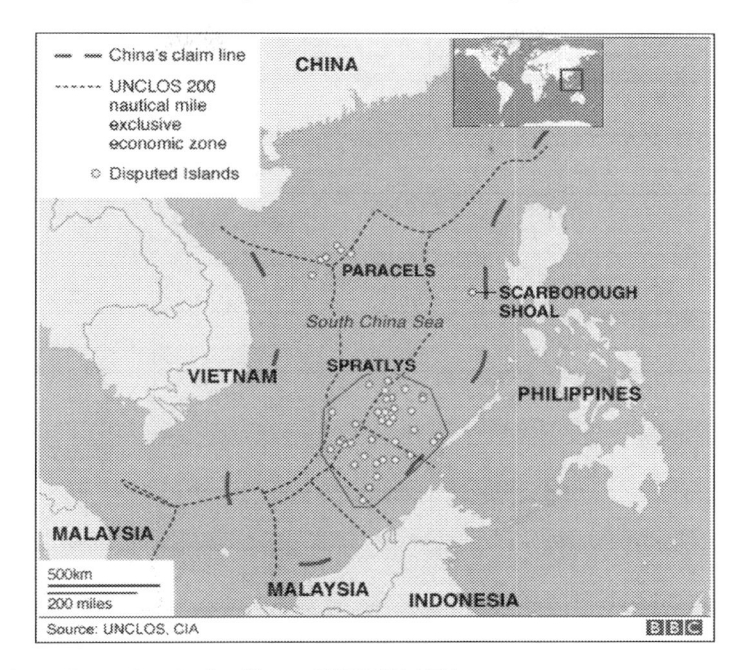

Fig. 6 China disputed territories (*Source* UNCLOS, CIA)

comprise the list of disputed territories by China. Chinese Taipei ranks the list, as China aims to reunify it with the mainland in the future by force if needed, as the claim line of Fig. 6 illustrates. Xi Jinping has been regularly showing that reunification with Chinese Taipei must be fulfilled peacefully (Zhao, 1999–2000), although all means must be considered in opposing separatism.

On what concerns Russian and Military spending, there is a common ambition regarding budget increasing. According to the SIPRI military expenditure database on Russian and Chinese military spending (1988–2015), both China and Russia have been constantly increasing the figures, as China rises up to 200 billion USD and Russia 80 billion USD in 2015.

When assessing the evolution of their military spending since 2007 (Fig. 7), both China and Russia lead the two first rows.

In addition, Russia is ranked among the world's top five military big spenders since 2010, according to SIPRI Military Expenditure Database[10]: the fifth-largest spender in 2018 and the fourth in 2019, after the US, China, and India. Still, Fig. 8 recalls that US military spending in 2019 is 11 times greater than Russia's. China spends four times more, but Russia spends about 30% more than France, Germany, and the UK. The military burden can be slightly higher than that of the US and China when we look at the weight of national defence in the overall budget. For

---

[10] Retrieved on December 2021, from https://www.sipri.org/commentary/topical-backgrounder/2020/russias-military-spending-frequently-asked-questions.

How Military Spending Has Changed Since 2007
% change in military spending among major powers between 2007 and 2016

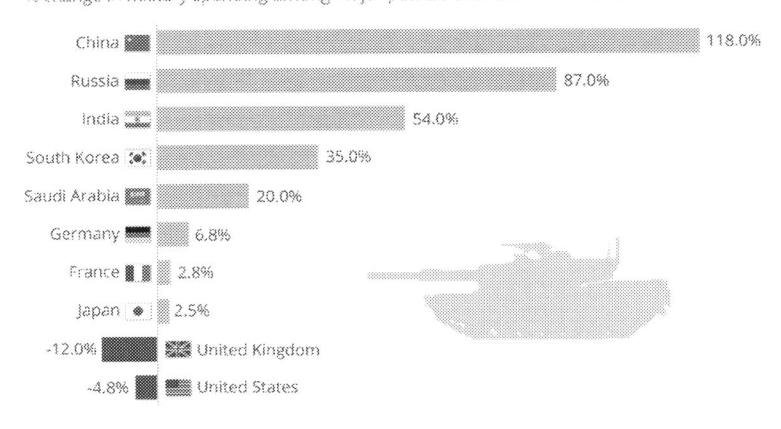

- China: 118.0%
- Russia: 87.0%
- India: 54.0%
- South Korea: 35.0%
- Saudi Arabia: 20.0%
- Germany: 6.8%
- France: 2.8%
- Japan: 2.5%
- United Kingdom: -12.0%
- United States: -4.8%

Fig. 7 Evolution of the military spending since 2007 (*Source* SIPRI/Statistica)

Rank 2019	Rank 2018	Country	Military expenditure, 2019 (US$ b.)	Change in military expenditure (%) 2018–19	Change in military expenditure (%) 2010–19	Military expenditure as a share of GDP (%) 2019	Military expenditure as a share of GDP (%) 2010	Share of world total, 2019 (%)
1	1	United States	732	5.3	-15	3.4	4.9	38
2	2	China	(261)	5.1	85	(1.9)	(1.9)	(14)
3	4	India	71.1	6.8	37	2.4	2.7	3.4
4	5	Russia	65.1	4.5	30	3.9	3.6	3.4
5	3	Saudi Arabia	(61.9)	-16	14	(8.0)	8.6	(3.2)
6	6	France	50.1	1.6	3.5	1.9	2.0	2.6
7	9	Germany	49.3	10	15	1.3	1.3	2.6
8	7	United Kingdom	48.7	0.0	-15	1.7	2.4	2.5
9	8	Japan	47.6	-0.1	2.0	0.9	1.0	2.5
10	10	South Korea	43.9	7.5	36	2.7	2.5	2.3

Fig. 8 The 10 Countries with the highest military expenditure in 2019 (*Source* Retrieved on December 2021, from https://www.sipri.org/commentary/topical-backgrounder/2020/russias-military-spending-frequently-asked-questions)

2021, Russia is ranked 2 of 140 out of the countries considered for the annual GFP review.[11]

China is placed in second in all the figures and facts in the last few years. In the 2021 annual meeting of the National People's Congress, China's 2021 defence

---

[11] Retrieved on December 2021, from https://www.globalfirepower.com/country-military-strength-detail.php?country_id=russia.

budget was set at 1.36 trillion yuan or $209.16 billion, a 6.8% increase from the 1.27 trillion-yuan budget set for 2020. In addition, a modernization of the People's Liberation Army (PLA) was clearly anticipated.

According to Matthew P. Funaiole and Brian Hart, the increase in the 2021 defence budget is hardly surprising, but closely linked to its economic development and alleged security demands.[12] In what concerns the current year, the strengthening of the US's position in the Indo-Pacific region has raised the projections of defence spending growth by 7.1%, expected to achieve 1.45 trillion yuan ($229 billion) in 2023.[13]

2 Conclusion

In this chapter, we aimed to assess how Russian led Eurasian Economic Union and China's Belt and Road Initiative, envisage a greater Eurasian perspective. On one hand, the Eurasian Economic Union represents an integrated single market of 183 million people and a gross domestic product of over 4 trillion US dollars. From the perspective of the Eurasian region, Russia has the world's largest natural gas, the 8th largest oil, and the second-largest coal reserves, it is the world's leading natural gas exporter and the second-largest natural gas producer.[14]

On the other hand, the Belt and Road Initiative is a major investment, trade, and infrastructure development plan for Chinese stakeholders to access and explore markets in the Middle East and Europe for building materials, high-voltage equipment, machinery, and petroleum equipment. Most of these investments are concentrated in the highly attractive Suez Canal Economic Zone, where more than 10 per cent of global trade passes every year and around 120 km (75 miles) concentrates the majority of Chinese investments in the east of Cairo. Both initiatives include Russia and China as privileged partners and allies and, therefore, a greater Eurasian partnership is actively increasing based mostly in trade, but highly supported by a reciprocal synergy on competing for global leadership. Still, in the current escalation of the security environment in Ukraine, the reaction of Beijing authorities towards its Russian ally is still unclear. At the 58th Munich Security Conference (MSC), in February 2022, Chinese State Councillor and Foreign Minister Wang Yi urged the international community via video link to reject attempts to start a new Cold War and called for efforts to build lasting peace in the world. Also, the security of one country should not be achieved at the expense of the security of other countries, and regional security should not rely on strengthening military blocs. This was a clear-cut message to Chinese Taipei's prospects for autonomy and a powerful statement

---

[12] Retrieved on December 2021, from https://www.csis.org/analysis/understanding-chinas-2021-defense-budget.

[13] Retrieved on March 2022, from https://www.bloomberg.com/news/articles/2022-03-05/china-s-defense-budget-climbs-7-1-fastest-pace-in-three-years.

[14] Retrieved on December 2021, from https://www.gecf.org/countries/russia.

on national unity. In addition, several phone calls have been allegedly made by Xi Jinping to Vladimir Putin to convince him to retreat in face of an unprecedented humanitarian tragedy in Ukraine's borders and neighbourhood.

In turn, in late 2021, the European Union launched the Global Gateway initiative to boost sustainable links around the world. According to the European Commission, €300 billion in investments between 2021 and 2027 will be displayed for sustainable and trusted connections that work for people and the planet, to tackle the most pressing global challenges, from climate change and protecting the environment, to improving health security and boosting competitiveness and global supply chains. Previously, on June 2019, the Council adopted a new EU strategy on Central Asia strengthening of relations between the EU and Kazakhstan, the Kyrgyz Republic, Tajikistan, Turkmenistan, and Uzbekistan since the adoption of the first EU strategy for Central Asia in 2007. This strategy clearly aims to enhance partnership in economic development ("prosperity"), comprehensive security ("resilience") and in strengthening cooperation with and within Central Asia (Saari, 2019). Those are topics for further research, as both the European Commission denies that the global gateway encompasses a deliberate response to China's expansion (specially in Africa) and the green deal is a strategic tool to manage the constraints created by the suspension of Nord Stream 2 pipeline for Russia's suppliance for the West. In addition, the further démarches at Ukraine by Russia and the impact on China's intimidation towards Chinese Taipei shows room for manoeuvre in further analysis on the extent of the debate of liberal democracies vs autocratic regimes. Still, it seems evident that the Eurasian region is the common ground for Russia and China to cooperate for competing for global leadership at grand pace. Xi and Putin's road to integrate and lead is on the way and will inevitably change Globalization patterns, shifting the geoeconomical balance to the Eurasian region.

Bibliographic References

Abrahamyan, E. (2017). *Russia mulls new role for its Post-Soviet military bloc*. Black sea strategy papers. Retrieved on December 2021, from https://www.fpri.org/article/2017/12/russia-mulls-new-role-post-soviet-military-bloc/

Barros, G. (2020). *Belarus warning update: Upcoming CSTO exercise could support Russian military deployment to Belarus*. Institute for the Study of War.

Beauchamp-Mustafaga, N. (2020). Where to next? PLA considerations for overseas base site selection. *China Brief, 20*(18), 27–35.

Bordyuzha, N. (2011). The collective security treaty organization: A brief overview. In IFSH (Ed.), *OSCE yearbook 2010* (pp. 339–350). Baden-Baden.

Brzezinski, Z. (2009). Towards a security web. *Politique Étrangère, 5*, 41–55.

Bugajski, J. (2008). *Expanding Eurasia—Russia's Europe ambitions*. Center for strategic and International Studies.

Calabrese, J. (2020). The Bab el-Mandeb Strait: Regional and great power rivalries on the shores of the Red Sea. Policy analysis. *Middle East Institute*. Retrieved on December 2021, from https://www.mei.edu/publications/bab-el-mandeb-strait-regional-and-great-power-rivalries-shores-red-sea

Coffey, L. (2020). Russian dominance in the Black Sea: The Sea of Azov. Policy analysis. *Middle East Institute*. Retrieved on December 2021, from https://www.mei.edu/publications/russian-dominance-black-sea-sea-azov

Emerson, M. (2014). Toward a greater Eurasia: Who, why, what, and how? *Global Journal of Emerging Market Economies, 6*(1), 35–68.

Friedberg, A. L. (2017). The authoritarian challenge—China, Russia and the threat to the liberal international order. *The Sasakawa Peace Foundation*.

Frye, T. (2021, May/June). Russia's weak strongman—The perilous bargains that keep Putin in power. *Foreign Affairs*.

Gorenburg, D. (2020). *Russia and collective security: Why CSTO is no match for Warsaw Pact*. Retrieved on December 2021, from https://www.russiamatters.org/analysis/russia-and-collective-security-why-csto-no-match-warsaw-pact

Grosse, R., Gamso, J., & Nelson, R. C. (2021). China's rise, world order, and the implications for international business. *Management International Review, 61*, 1–26.

Grossman, D. (2019). Military build-up in the South China Sea. In L. Buszynski, & D. T. Hai (Eds.), *The South China Sea: From a regional maritime dispute to geo-strategic competition* (Chapter 12, pp. 182–200). Routledge. https://doi.org/10.4324/9780429331480

Grossman, D. (2020). Military build-up in the South China Sea. In L. Buszynski, & D. T. Hai (Eds.), *The South China Sea: From a regional maritime dispute to geo-strategic competition* (Chapter 12, pp. 182–200). Routledge. https://doi.org/10.4324/9780429331480

Ikenberry, J. G. (2018). The end of liberal international order? *International Affairs, 94*(1), 7–23.

Karaganov, S. A. (2016). From east to west, or greater Eurasia. *Russia in Global Affairs*. Retrieved on January 2022, from https://eng.globalaffairs.ru/articles/from-east-to-west-or-greater-eurasia/

Karimov, N. (2021). Effectiveness of the CSTO in the context of the changing regional security system. *Central Asian Bureau for Analytical Reporting*. Retrieved on December 2021, from https://cabar.asia/en/effectiveness-of-the-csto-in-the-context-of-the-changing-regional-security-system#_ftn2

Keaney, J. (2017). *CSTO: A military pact to defend Russian influence*. Retrieved on December 2021, from https://www.americansecurityproject.org/csto-a-military-pact-to-defend-russian-influence/

Kinyakin, A. A., & Kucheriavaia, S. (2019). The European Union vs. the Eurasian Economic Union: "integration race 2.0"? *Przegląd Europejski, 2019*(3), 135–153.

Klein, M. (2019). Russia's military policy in the Post-Soviet space: Aims, instruments and perspectives, SWP Research Paper. *Stiftung Wissenschaft und Politik*. German Institute for International and Security Affairs.

Kortunov, A., & Timofeev, I. (2017). Report—Russia's foreign policy: Looking forwards 2018. *Russian International Affairs Council*.

Köstem, S. (2019). *Russia's search for a greater Eurasia: Origins, promises, and prospects*. Kennan Cable No. 40 l February 2019.

Krickovic, A. (2017, Autumn). The symbiotic China–Russia partnership: Cautious riser and desperate challenger. *The Chinese Journal of International Politics, 10*(3), 299–329. Retrieved on December 2021, from https://doi.org/10.1093/cjip/pox011

Kropatcheva, E. (2016). Russia and the collective security treaty organisation: Multilateral policy or unilateral ambitions? *Europe-Asia Studies, 68*(9), 1526–1552.

Lindley-French, J. (2019). Complex strategic coercion and Russian military modernization: Policy perspective. *Canadian Global Affairs Institute*.

Madiyev, O. (2021). The Eurasian Economic Union: Repaving Central Asia's road to Russia? Migration information source. *The Online Journal of the Migration Policy Institute*. Retrieved on December 2021, from https://www.migrationpolicy.org/article/eurasian-economic-union-central-asia-russia

Marocchi, T. (2018). *EU-Russia relations: Towards an increasingly geopolitical paradigm*. Retrieved on December 2021, from https://eu.boell.org/sites/default/files/uploads/2017/07/eu-russia-relations_towards-an-increasingly-geopolitical-paradigm.pdf

Mearsheimer, J. J. (2019, Spring). Bound to fail: The rise and fall of the liberal international order. *International Security, 43*(4), 7–50.

Mostafa, G., & Mahmood, M. (2018, July). Eurasian Economic Union: Evolution, challenges and possible future directions. *Journal of Eurasian Studies, 9*(2), 163–172.

Mowchan, J. A. (2009, July). *The militarization of the collective security treaty organization* (Vol. 6-09). Issue Paper Center for Strategic Leadership, U.S. Army War College.

Person, R. (2020). *Four myths about Russian grand strategy*. https://www.csis.org/blogs/post-soviet-post/four-myths-about-russian-grand-strategy

Rácz, A. (2020, August). Russia's military power: Fast and furious—Or failing? Russian futures—The shape of things to come. In S. Saari & S. Secrieru (Eds.), *Chaillot Papers 159*. EUISS—European Union Institute for Security Studies.

Rolland, N. (2019). A China–Russia condominium over Eurasia. *Survival: Global Politics*. Retrieved on January 2022, from https://www.iiss.org/publications/survival/2019/survival-global-politics-and-strategy-februarymarch-2019/611-02-rolland

Saari, S. (2019, June). Connecting the dots: Challenges to EU connectivity in Central Asia. *Brief 6*. EUISS—European Union Institute for Security Studies.

Saari, S., & Secrieru, S. (Eds.). (2020, August). *Russian futures 2030—The shape of things to come*. Chaillot Paper/159. EUISS—European Union Institute for Security Studies.

Schneider, U. (2020). Rapprochement between the EU and the EAEU offers more than economic benefits. *European Leadership Network*. Retrieved on December 2021, from https://www.europeanleadershipnetwork.org/commentary/rapprochement-between-the-eu-and-the-eaeu-offers-more-than-economic-benefits/

Secrieru, S., & Shkliarov, V. (2018, November). Putin's fourth term—The twilight begins? *Brief Issue, 11*. EUISS—European Union Institute for Security Studies.

Shakhanova, G., & Garlick, J. (2020). The Belt and Road Initiative and the Eurasian Economic Union: Exploring the "greater Eurasian partnership". *Journal of Current Chinese Affairs*. GIGA—German Institute for Global and Area Studies—Institute for Asian Studies.

Small, A. (2018). The Backlash to Belt and Road—A south Asian Battle over Chinese economic power. *Foreign Affairs, Council on Foreign Relation*.

Stent, A. (2020, February). Russia and China: Axis of revisionists? In *Global China—Assessing China growing role in the world*.

Sutter, R. (2019). Testimony before the U.S.-China Economic and Security Review Commission Hearing on an Emerging China-Russia Axis? Implications for the United States in an Era of Strategic Competition.

Tanchum, M. (2021). *China's new military base in Africa: What it means for Europe and America*. European Council on Foreign Relations. Retrieved on December 2021, from https://ecfr.eu/article/chinas-new-military-base-in-africa-what-it-means-for-europe-and-america/

Troitskiy, E. (2020). The Eurasian Economic Union at five: Great expectations and hard times. *The Russia file—A blog of the Kennan Institute*. Retrieved on December 2021, from https://www.wilsoncenter.org/blog-post/eurasian-economic-union-five-great-expectations-and-hard-times

Turarbekava, R. M. (2019). Eurasian integration: From post-Soviet to new regional projects. *Journal of the Belarusian State University. International Relations,* (2), 11–18.

Urcosta, R. B. (2018). Russia's strategic considerations on the sea of azov. *Warsaw Institute*. Retrieved on December 2021, from https://warsawinstitute.org/wp-content/uploads/2018/12/Russias-Strategic-Considerations-on-the-Sea-of-Azov-Warsaw-Institute-Special-Report.pdf

Van der Togt, T. (2020). *EU & Eurasian Economic Union: A common Chinese challenge, Clingendael*. Retrieved on December 2021, from https://www.clingendael.org/publication/eu-eurasian-economic-union-common-chinese-challenge

Vicari, M. S. (2016). The Eurasian Economic Union—Approaching the economic integration in the Post-Soviet space by EU-emulated elements. *Revue Interventions économiques, 55 | 2016 - D'un régionalisme à l'autre: Intégration ou interconnexion?* Open Editions Journal.

Weitz, R. (2020). Absent with leave: Moscow's deficient Eurasian military alliance. *Middle East Institute Policy Analysis.* mei.edu/publications/absent-leave-moscows-deficient-eurasian-military-alliance

Yarashevich, V. (2020). The Eurasian Economic Union as a regional development project: Expectations and realities. *Area Development and Policy*, 1–24.

Zaborsky, V. (1995, September). *Crimea and the Black Sea fleet in Russian-Ukrainian relations.* CSIA Discussion Paper 95–11, Kennedy School of Government, Harvard University.

Zemskova, K. (2018). The common energy market of the Eurasian economic union—Implications for the European Union and the role of the Energy Charter Treaty (ECT). Occasional paper series. International Energy Charter.

Chapter 26
Health, Road, and Russia: Perspectives on Russian Involvement with China's Health Silk Road

Una Aleksandra Bērziņa-Čerenkova

1 Introduction

China harvested the COVID-19 momentum as a supportive measure to BRI making and made a play for the revival of its Silk Health Road (HSR) (赵磊, 2020). Also, immediately signalled the wish for Russia to be on board with it. China's activity is understandable, as the cooperation in health is generally non-abrasive, yet it can present economic potential on two levels. First, China saw the no-contact economy ushered in by COVID-19 as an opportunity for its telecommunications and online commerce companies to gain a stronger foothold in Russia (Чжан, 2020). Second, the pandemic was expected to open doors for China's high-value-added medical sectors such as medtech, biotech, and pharma. From a Chinese perspective, these arguments were deemed to work well for Russia, too, because they could contribute to driving the Russian public opinion away from the critical views of China as a predatory and low-value-added partner in energy and infrastructure, and selling the public on the "equal partnership" and the innovation-driving higher value-added messages.[1]

The Health Silk Road, designed to breathe more life into BRI cooperation in the post-pandemic setting, also holds dual implications for the Sino-Russian "comprehensive strategic partnership of coordination for a new era." On one hand, it could add value to the economic relationship by giving substance to innovative cooperation in IT, medtech, biotech, and pharma, but on the other hand, the multilateral setting robs Russia of exclusivity and importance and does not fully align with the Russian vision of connecting Eurasia. Therefore, Russia is not unquestionably on board with

---

[1] More on the Chinese and Russian attempts to spread the "innovation" narrative, see Chapter 1 Relationship Status: Official Narratives of Russia and China, in: Bērziņa-Čerenkova, U. (2022). *Russia and China: Perfect Imbalance*. World Scientific Publishing.

U. A. Bērziņa-Čerenkova (✉)
Riga Stradins University, Riga, Latvia

Beijing's plan: The Russian minister of foreign affairs Sergei Lavrov was not among the high-level officials who participated in the BRI conference "Belt and Road International Cooperation: Combating COVID-19 with Solidarity" in June, 2020, limiting himself to a written statement of support instead (Hatem, 2020).

As Russia significantly downgraded China in its list of priorities in the new 2021 Security Strategy (President of Russia, 2021), at the same time highlighting population sustainability, the need to re-examine Russia's approach to Sino-Russian cooperation in general and its outlooks towards BRI in particular arises, and one of its faucets—health—is particularly pertinent, exacerbated by the pandemic realities faced by both nations. The chapter aims to explore the official messaging surrounding the Health Silk Road in Russia, as well as to analyse the surrounding policies in order to establish the degree of the Russian buy-in. Adopting a constructivist conceptual lens, the chapter sets political discourse analysis as the theoretical research framework, and employs qualitative methodology—official discourse analysis, as well as secondary source textual analysis in Russian, Mandarin, and English languages.

Section 1 of the chapter offers an overview of the existing scholarship along two lines: by benchmarking Russia's engagement with the Belt and Road Initiative in general, and by analysing the research on regional implications of the HSR. The section concludes that research on Russia's role in and the approach to HSR in particular remains scarce. Section 2 presents a document analysis to trace the Chinese framing and the origins of any Russian involvement in the HSR framework, concluding that, Chinese domestic messaging aside, there is nothing to point towards Russian engagement with HSR. Section 3 aims to establish the degree of Russian participation as seen by Moscow. The section concludes that the Russian reluctance to engage with China via HSR is driven neither by lack of substance in Sino-Chinese medical exchanges nor by aversion to multilateral formats, but stems from the distaste for BRI in particular, as well as from Russia's ambition to be an equal, if not a leading partner in such exchanges. The final section presents future outlooks and provides the responses to the research questions. It argues that future perspectives of any Russian contribution to the Chinese-led multilateral health initiative remain bleak, given the non-existent Russian involvement with HSR to date. Ultimately, HSR could have been a positive agenda point and an opportunity of high-value-added cooperation, especially in the face of a common enemy—COVID-19, but it resulted in driving Russia further away from China.

2 Existing Research: Literature Review

In light of lacking analysis of Russia's involvement with HSR proper, it is helpful to assess the state of affairs from two sides: first, by benchmarking Russia's engagement with the Belt and Road Initiative in general, and second, by gauging the research on regional implications of the HSR. Several authors have tackled the scope, evolution, motivation, and prospects of Russia and BRI. In 2016, Igor Denisov provided an early-days comprehensive analysis of BRI for the Russian-speaking audience, mentioning Russia's unease over some aspects of the project and concluding that "capacity for constructive interaction" between the two Eurasian powers would determine its future (Денисов, 2016). Sebastien Peyrouse tracked the early evolution of the Kremlin position towards BRI in his 2017 article (Peyrouse, 2017), pointing out push–pull cyclicality rather than steady cohesion in Russo-Chinese engagements.

Ladislav Zemánek in his examination of BRI cohesion with Eurasian Economic Union (EAEU) promoted by Russia provides a more optimistic outlook, stating that "the degree of mutual trust and agreement in national interests makes the convergence of the BRI with the Russian-promoted EAEU feasible" (Zemánek, 2020). Zemánek refers to earlier analysis by Timofeev et al., also asserting Russian ambition in acquiring China's endorsement of EAEU: "Deep and progressive integration of the EAEU is definitely a condition for its advancement in co-development with the Belt Initiative" (Timofeev et al., 2017). The findings of narrative analysis of Russian major newspapers conducted by Kuteleva and Vasiliev (2020) support this conclusion. In an explanation of EAEU-BRI connection, Alexander Gabuev and Ivan Zuenko write that Russia's drive to find a linkage with BRI was connected to the 2014–2015 events: "the Crimean crisis," the fall of the rubble, and anti-Russian sanctions: "[The discourse on BRI] was used to articulate foreign policy ideologemes important for Moscow's efforts to assert itself as one of the centers of the world order and regain the status of great power… the geopolitical component continues to have a decisive influence on the content of the 'Belt and Road' discourse and was the key factor in making the decision in May 2015 to 'couple' the EEU and SREB" (Gabuev & Zuenko, 2020). Kaneshko Sangar et al. (2017) provide a similar argument, adding that "one of the major challenges for Moscow is to get Beijing to cooperate at a multi-lateral level," as that is more beneficial for Russia. However, even a multi-lateral setting does not guarantee success for the Russian vision. Shakhanova and Garlick (2020) focus on Kazakh elites' perception of BRI and EAEU, concluding that they in fact hold BRI in higher regard.

Li Yongquan (2018) admits that one shouldn't say that it is easy to reach "agreement on questions regarding a partnership between China and Russia in conjunction with the EAEU. In fact, just the opposite might be closer to the truth," in the meantime stating that the Chinese and Russian "economies complement each other greatly, including in the areas of resources, market, technology, commodity structure, etc."—the argument used by the Chinese side also in the context of HSR. Gaye Christoffersen (2018), on the contrary, makes a point that reaching a well-defined Eurasian connectivity partnership is in fact not the goal of either Russia or China, as both engage in construction and reconstruction of the boundaries of Eurasian regional integration. Significantly less research is available on HSR and its regional implications. Cao Jiahan (2020) presents an on look onto the Chinese HSR aspirations and motivations, tracing the origins of HSR from 2015. He argues that China has been developing the HSR framework consistently since then. Lancaster et al. (2020), however, point out the HSR was "resurrected" to solve economy and image problems caused by COVID-19: "CCP may be dusting off the Health Silk Road concept to take advantage of this moment of global upheaval." Writings on China's HSR rollout and regional and national-level reactions and involvement features are of particular use, as they provide a solid benchmark of HSR regional logic. e.g., a recent chapter by Yahia H. Zoubir and Emilie Tran (2021) looks at HSR-related activities in the MENA region. Nader Habibi and Hans Yue Zhu (2021) have examined the role of HSR in China's BRI strategy in Africa, concluding that "Health Silk Road has become a key pivot in the China–Africa bilateral relationship, and the transformation of China's Belt and Road Initiative in general." With that in mind, however, research on Russia's role in and the approach to HSR in particular remains scarce.

3 HSR and Russia: Tracing the Origins

The first PRC document containing a mention of the Health Silk Road was the "National Health and Family Planning Commission Three-Year Implementation Plan on Promoting the 'Belt and Road' for Health Exchanges and Cooperation (2015–2017)" (henceforth—the Plan), which spoke of "promoting the development of health services in my country [China] and countries along the [Belt and Road] route, building a 'Health Silk Road' to provide strong support and make due contributions to the construction of the 'Belt and Road'" (National Health [and Family Planning] Commission of the People's Republic of China,[2] 2015). The Plan mentions Russia on several occasions. One cannot help but notice the centrality of Russia in the document, as Russia and Czechia are the only two countries at the centre of two separate sub-chapters.

First, the Plan names Russia among the key countries for carrying out health exchanges and cooperation. Second, a separate sub-chapter on "Association of Sino-Russian Medical Universities" speaks of a cooperation mechanism established bilaterally in 2014—that is, before BRI or HSR. Perhaps unsurprisingly, and in a demonstration of the disconnect between the Chinese and the Russian discourse on BRI, the Association documents on the Russian side contain no mention of China's "roads," describing the exchanges in strictly bilateral terms (Sechenov University). Third, in a separate sub-chapter on the "Sino-Russian Disaster Medicine Cooperation Project," the Commission singles out the September 2015 disaster health emergency drill in the border area jointly carried out by Russia and China, and names Russia to be the "fulcrum country" in bringing more Central Asian partners into the fold. Just like in the case of the "Association of Sino-Russian Medical Universities," official Russian reports of the endeavour, including the Russian Ministry of Health, contain no mention of BRI or HSR, and speak of the drill in strictly bilateral terms (Ministry of Health of the Russian Federation, 2015). Interestingly, the Plan also names the Shanghai Cooperation Organization as one of the main cooperation mechanisms for health exchanges, thus possibly trying to avoid hinging the dialogue on health with

---

[2] The National Health and Family Planning Commission of the People's Republic of China was reorganized into National Health Commission in 2018. The documents refer to the pre-reform period, therefore, the original name of the issuing institution is kept in square brackets for precision purposes.

Russia just on the BRI formats and to balance the uncertainties of Russia's participation in the then early-days BRI. In hindsight, the approach proved correct, as Russia's outlook on SCO is much more engaging than BRI.

A further HSR milestone followed in January 2017, as the World Health Organization and China signed a Memorandum of Understanding to jointly implement a Belt and Road Initiative that focuses on health with China, and ties HSR to the WHO 2030 sustainable development agenda. *China Daily* called the MoU a "pact" and underscored that the WHO had become "the first global organization under the United Nations to have signed such an agreement with China" (An, 2017). In August 2017, the "Belt and Road" Forum for Health Cooperation: Towards a Health Silk Road was held in Beijing, and, along with representatives from over 30 countries and international organizations, the WHO was represented as well (Страны…, 2017). The Organization's Director-General Tedros Adhanom Ghebreyesus spared no praise for the initiative: "President Xi's proposal for a Health Silk Road, which strengthens and renews ancient links between cultures and people, with health at its core, is indeed visionary. But how can we accomplish this? Her Excellency [Liu Yandong] has said most of them. First, we must put in place systems to contain outbreaks or crises where they start, and prevent them from becoming epidemics. Second, health is a human right. Third, women, children, and adolescents must be at the centre of global health and development. China has much to teach us about these issues" (World Health Organization, 2017). The Belt and Road High Level Meeting on Health Cooperation towards Health Silk Road of the Forum saw the adoption of the Beijing Communiqué of the Belt and Road Health Cooperation & Health Silk Road, listing WHO, the Joint United Nations Programme on HIV/AIDS (UNAIDS), Organization for Economic Cooperation and Development (OECD), the Global Alliance for Vaccines and Immunization (GAVI), and Global Fund among the attendees, but without naming specific countries as its signatories (National Health [and Family Planning] Commission of the People's Republic of China, 2017). Although Russia was not explicitly listed as a participant of the event or among the signatories of the Communiqué, a media event held by the organizing body—the National Health and Family Planning Commission of the PRC—nevertheless mentions Russia when speaking on the anticipated outcomes of the event: "In order to build more consensus, this high-level seminar intends to achieve the following three types of outcomes. The first category is the planned release of the conference outcome document 'Beijing Communiqué'. The second category is cooperation agreements. Before and after the meeting, national-level health cooperation agreements will be signed with Mongolia, Iran, and other countries. Beijing, Anhui, Hunan, Sichuan, and other places will cooperate with local governments and related institutions in Russia, Singapore, Sri Lanka, and Germany. The third category is the 'Belt and Road' cooperation network alliance" (National Health & Family Planning Commission of the People's Republic of China, 2017). On a side note, the exact relationship between BRI and HSR is open to interpretation. Calling HSR "a rhetorical extension of China's Belt and Road Initiative," Kirk Lancaster, Michael Rubin, and Mira Rapp-Hooper explain: "Like the BRI itself, the Health Silk Road is not a well-defined term, and it is not clear which of China's activities fall under the banner" (Lancaster et al., 2020). HSR is often perceived to be in direct subordination to BRI akin to the Polar Silk Road and the Digital Silk Road, and the 2017 Beijing Communiqué of The Belt and Road Health Cooperation & Health Silk Road seems to lend proof to this perception, as Clause 15 states: "Our joint endeavor on the Belt and Road health cooperation, forging a Health Silk Road will provide new opportunities and impetus for international cooperation, serve as a model for other cooperation platforms such as BRICS and the G20" (National Health [and Family Planning] Commission of the People's Republic of China, 2017). However, Cao Jiahan (2020) of Shanghai Institutes of International Affairs introduces nuance into the reading: "Rather than a new geopolitical strategy within the BRI framework, the HSR is an emerging diplomatic initiative for promoting health cooperation in a world increasingly threatened by proliferating public health emergencies." One can argue that HSR was originally equipped with even more elasticity that BRI, and this built-in design feature meant that HSR could involve countries without evident BRI connection, if need be.

The PRC government moved to a new level of HSR promotion in the early 2020, as China saw HSR as an opportunity to counter the unfavourable narratives surrounding the COVID-19 outbreak in Wuhan, including inaction and delay. Attempting to point the proverbial gun right back on its attackers, China made "a push for global health leadership" (Lancaster et al., 2020) and gave new life to HSR, famously mentioned by Xi Jinping in his March 2020 phone call with Italy's Giuseppe Conte. (Xi…, 2020). HSR served the purpose well, because it provided proof of China's initiative to bring countering infectious disease to the international agenda five years prior to the outbreak. It is no wonder, then, that also in 2020, Beijing stepped up HSR mentions in the Russian context. According to the PRC messaging, it would appear that Russia is a supporter and a member of HSR. "In recent years, my country's health cooperation and exchanges with countries along the 'Belt and Road' have been continuously deepened, and the areas of cooperation have been expanded. 41 major projects have been implemented… cooperation in health emergency response with the World Health Organization, ASEAN countries, Russia, Israel, etc." (China International Development Cooperation Agency, 2017). One should immediately note, however, that China's official communication in the Russian information space places accents differently. E.g., the ambassador of the PRC to the Russian Federation Zhang Hanhui in his Russian newspaper op-ed is careful not to push, as he uses future tense and avoids any emphasis on China's leading role: "China will continue to contribute to the creation of HSR" (Чжан, 2021). China is well aware that in fact there is nothing to point towards Russian engagement with HSR.

4 Health Silk Road—Nowhere Near Russian Sights

What, then, is the degree of Russian participation as seen by Moscow? To answer this question, prior to moving to HSR in particular, first the Russian buy-in into BRI in general needs to be established. As the literature review has already demonstrated,

Russia's buy-in into BRI is in fact contested. Moscow, as Igor Denisov and Aleksandr Lukin puts it, "keeps persistently explaining to Beijing that it is participating in BRI not as an ordinary partner who signed a bilateral document with Beijing on cooperation within the framework of the initiative, but as a member of the Eurasian Economic Union (EAEU). The EAEU, which consists of five members, interacts not with BRI, but with one of its parts—the Silk Road Economic Belt (SREB) within the framework of documents signed by the Eurasian Economic Commission and the Chinese Ministry of Commerce. That is to say, Russia did not join the Chinese initiative" (Денисов & Лукин, 2021). The same conclusion can also be extended to HSR. Cooperation in health has a stable presence in the Sino-Russian bilateral agenda, e.g., in the Joint Statement following the upgrade of the official partnership to "comprehensive strategic partnership of coordination for a New Era" between the countries tied to the 70 years of diplomatic relations in 2019. The Joint Statement contains all cooperation points mentioned in the Chinese "National Health and Family Planning Commission Three-Year Implementation Plan on Promoting the 'Belt and Road' for Health Exchanges and Cooperation (2015–2017)," including catastrophe medicine and the "Association of Sino-Russian Medical Universities," and many other points, but, of course, in no relation to HSR (President of Russia, 2019). Even when Russian officials do make reference to BRI in their statements, HSR is absent from them, e.g., during 19th meeting of the Russian-Chinese Commission on Humanitarian Cooperation, the head of the Russian delegation, Deputy Prime Minister of Russia Tatyana Golikova proposed to jointly hold an "international forum of associations of specialized universities within the framework of the EAEU member countries and the Belt and Road Initiative" (Government of Russia, 2018), but, as Golikova spoke of cooperation in health, neither BRI nor HSR came up. Of course, one can argue that HSR had not been "revived" yet in 2018, however, no high-level mentions have appeared in the period since 2020, either. As opposed to China's reporting making it seem as if Russian officials express support to HSR (e.g. 颜欢, 曲颂, 2020), there currently are no documents affirming Russia's commitment to Health Silk Road. Still, health as such is a stable presence on Sino-Russian talk itinerary, and is driven by both sides. It is understandable for several reasons, both countries feel it is beneficial for them. For China, the cooperation in health has economic potential on two levels. First, the no-contact economy ushered in by COVID-19 is an opportunity for China's telecommunications and online commerce companies to gain a stronger foothold in Russia (Чжан, 2020). Second, the pandemic opens doors for China's high-value-added medical sectors such as medtech, biotech, and pharma. For Russia, such cooperation serves the "equal partnership" with China's message, because it capitalizes on the points of pride of the Russian medical establishment, including medical education, catastrophe medicine, sanitary control, pharma production control, and ophthalmology (Ministry of Health of the Russian Federation, 2013). Given the turn towards population sustainability in the 2021 Security Strategy (President of Russia, 2021), health and medicine are becoming even more streamlined into the Russian international exchanges. So, high-value-added medical cooperation, unlike energy extraction projects, can spare Russia the embarrassment of being perceived as a junior partner to China.

One can conclude that a significant number of bilateral exchanges connected to the medical and health fields do exist between Russia and China. In general, health presents the perfect point of positive cooperation agenda and allows for an optimistic atmosphere during talks, but chalking it up to the HSR would be unfounded. Can one deduce, then, that the Russian emphasis on framing Sino-Russian cooperation in bilateral rather than BRI/HSR terms speaks to the Russian dislike of using multilateral formats for health agenda in general? It does not appear to be the case. In fact, Russia has been using other multilateral formats, including SCO and BRICS, for health-related agendas. In 2020, a BRICS meeting on spread of tuberculosis during the COVID-19 pandemic was called at Russia's behest (Ministry of Health of the Russian Federation, 2020, October 7), demonstrating the Federation's intent not just to participate, but to lead on certain agenda points. Furthermore, Russia has opted for an active use of the COVID-19 momentum to reaffirm itself, perhaps sensing an opportunity arising from China's PR struggles due to the pandemic. A claim can be made that Russia's multilateral statements on COVID-19 are also due to the perception of China as an unstraightforward partner, with China's unwillingness to provide Russian doctors with a live strain of coronavirus in early 2020 (Китай..., 2020); and the Beijing Organising Committee for the 2022 Olympic and Paralympic Winter Games denying recognition of the Russian "Sputnik V" coronavirus vaccine (Лисин, 2021) serving as the loudest displays. Moscow has even shown active signs of unhappiness over China's handling of the pandemic, e.g., by moving to stop issuing electronic visas to the citizens of the neighbouring country in January, 2020 and calling upon Russian citizens to abstain from visits to the PRC (Ministry of Foreign Affairs of the Russian Federation, 2020).

In 2020, during the chairmanship of the Russian Federation in the SCO, the meetings of the health ministers were resumed, with the Outcome Statement highlighting the importance of the SCO 2011 Agreement on cooperation in health in the light of the COVID-19 pandemic (Shanghai Cooperation Organisation, 2020). Coordinating within SCO, Russia produced a document on "Comparative measures relating to the production of COVID-19," and only then presented its translation into Chinese and English, thus symbolically demonstrating the primacy of the Russian initiative (Ministry of Health of the Russian Federation, 2020, September 14). The Russian minister of health Mikhail Murashko actively shaped the narrative of Russia's leading role in the fight against COVID-19, somewhat over China, in the BRICS context as well: "The World Health Organization assumed a coordinating role for the world at large, providing information support, and in the early stages forming expert groups that were sent to the People's Republic of China. Subsequently, the Russian Federation, having gained experience and determined approaches to treatment in the framework of the interaction of the BRICS countries, the SCO, formed the best practices for the World Health Organization that are used in the treatment of patients with a new coronavirus infection. Moreover, Russia has assumed a leading role in the framework of interaction this year" (Ministry of Health of the Russian Federation, 2020, December 24). Thus, the Russian reluctance to engage with China via HSR is driven neither by lack of substance in Sino-Chinese medical exchanges nor by aversion to multilateral formats, but stems from the distaste for BRI in particular, as well as from Russia's ambition to be an equal, if not a leading partner in such exchanges. Indeed, Russia has a history of medical exchanges with China, and is even driving further engagement on multilateral fora, most notably SCO and BRICS, however, HSR is not one of its outlets.

5 Russia and Health Silk Road: Perspectives and Conclusions

The chapter aimed to answer several research questions in relation to Russia's HSR role: How has the format developed vis-à-vis Russia so far? What is the degree of Russian engagement and what are its perspectives in the future? And, to zoom out: How does HSR measure against Russia's BRI outlooks overall? As to the first question, the chapter traces two distinct periods of HSR promotion by the Chinese side: first, in 2015–2017, at which point Russia was described as an important partner in the initiative and the agenda included traditional Russian strong-points in health and medicine; and starting from 2020, when COVID-19 took centre stage. During the first period, Russia, albeit cautiously, appeared more open towards future engagement in China-shaped formats, whereas during the second period, Russia is actively attempting to shape bilateral and multilateral cooperation in health away from HSR. In connection to the previous point and in response to the second question, Moscow simply does not see HSR serving its interests. Just like in the case of other BRI offshoots, Russia is cautious—it fears the risk of a junior role, distrusts China, and even engages in open competition with it.[3] Russia perceives the main agenda of the HSR to be that of mitigating the negative impact of COVID-19 on China's international image, which is reported to be the lowest in years as a result of the handling of the pandemic (Silver et al., 2020). On top of that, Russia does not believe China to be a straightforward partner on COVID-19, either. In other words, Russia sees no point in helping China to shield itself from bad COVID-19 PR through HSR, because to some extent it believes the bad PR to be justified. Given the non-existent Russian involvement with HSR to date, the perspectives of any Russian contribution or participation in the Chinese-led multilateral health initiative remain bleak. With this in mind, however, one should remember that Russia in principle is not opposed to bilateral and even some multilateral cooperation with China on health-related issues—just not within HSR. Conversely, and in response to the final research question, Moscow's reluctance to engage with HSR attests to the bigger picture—it is consistent with Russia's general approach to the Belt and Road Initiative, reaffirming the Russian disregard of BRI. One can conclude that HSR, something that could have been a positive agenda point and an opportunity of high-value-added cooperation, especially in the face of a common enemy—COVID-19—resulted in driving Russia further away from China. HSR, however, still presents an interesting case of the Chinese approach of talking something into existence. China is indeed

---

[3] E.g. regarding the COVID-19 vaccines in Serbia.

drumming up the level of Russian participation in the initiative for domestic audiences to demonstrate a united front against the West, but knows not to go beyond its internal public information space with this narrative. Still, regardless of the reality of Russia's non-engagement with HSR, the cooperation narrative is already out there.

In the course of the research, the scarcity of materials on Russian health cooperation with China, both bilateral and multilateral, proved to be a limitation. Further research assessing Sino-Russian engagement in health, as well as its comparison against China's health agenda with other partners regionally and globally, should be conducted before deeper conclusions on the scale, scope, and future of Russian engagement with China's HSR can be made.

Bibliographic References

An, B. (2017, January 19). WHO, China sign pact establishing 'health silk road'. *China Daily*. Retrieved on December 2021, from https://www.chinadaily.com.cn/business/2017wef/2017-01/19/content_27993857.htm

Bērziņa-Čerenkova, U. (2022). *Russia and China: Perfect imbalance*. World Scientific Publishing.

Cao, J. (2020). Toward a health silk road, China's proposal for global health cooperation. *China Quarterly of International Strategic Studies, 6*(1), 19–35. https://doi.org/10.1142/S2377740020500013

China International Development Cooperation Agency. (2017, August 16). "健康丝绸之路"造福民生. http://www.cidca.gov.cn/2017-08/16/c_129972358.htm

Christoffersen, G. (2018). Sino-Russian accommodation and adaptation in Eurasian regional order formation. *Asian Perspective, 42*(3), 439–462. https://doi.org/10.1353/apr.2018.0019

Gabuev, A., & Zuenko, I. (2020). The "Belt and Road" in Russia: Evolution of expert discourse. *Russia in Global Affairs*. Retrieved on December 2021, from https://eng.globalaffairs.ru/wp-content/uploads/2020/02/19915.pdf, https://doi.org/10.31278/1810-6374-2018-16-4-142-163

Government of Russia. (2018, October 30). *Татьяна Голикова совершила рабочий визит в Китай*. Retrieved on December 2021, from http://government.ru/news/34510/

Habibi, N., & Zhu, H. (2021, February 16). *The health silk road as a new direction in China's Belt and Road Strategy in Africa (2021)*. General Development Studies Working Paper Series. No. 2021.01. Retrieved on December 2021, from https://heller.brandeis.edu/gds/pdfs/working-papers/china-africa-2021.pdf

Hatem, M. (2020, June 20). Ministers of 'Belt and Road Initiative' issue joint statement on combating COVID-19. *Emirates News Agency*. Retrieved on December 2021, from https://wam.ae/en/details/1395302850046

Kuteleva, A., & Vasiliev, D. (2020). China's belt and road initiative in Russian media: Politics of narratives, images, and metaphors. *Eurasian Geography and Economics*. Retrieved on December 2021, from https://doi.org/10.1080/15387216.2020.1833228

Lancaster, K., Rubin M., & Rapp-Hooper, M. (2020, April 10). *Mapping China's health silk road*. Council on Foreign Relations [Source: Asia Unbound]. Retrieved on December 2021, from https://www.cfr.org/blog/mapping-chinas-health-silk-road

Li, Y. (2018). The greater Eurasian partnership and the Belt and Road Initiative: Can the two be linked? *Journal of Eurasian Studies, 9*(2), 94–99. Retrieved on December 2021, from https://doi.org/10.1016/j.euras.2018.07.004

Ministry of Foreign Affairs of the Russian Federation. (2020, January 30). *В связи со вспышкой в Китае новой коронавирусной инфекции*. Retrieved on December 2021, from https://www.mid.ru/ru/foreign_policy/news/-/asset_publisher/cKNonkJE02Bw/content/id/4013950

Ministry of Health of the Russian Federation. (2013, September 24). *Делегация Минздрава России приняла участие в работе Российско-Китайской Комиссии по гуманитарному сотрудничеству, которая проходила в КНР*. Retrieved on December 2021, from https://minzdrav.gov.ru/news/2013/09/24/1441-delegatsiya-minzdrava-rossii-prinyala-uchastie-v-rabote-rossiysko-kitayskoy-komissii-po-gumanitarnomu-sotrudnichestvu-kotoraya-prohodila-v-knr

Ministry of Health of the Russian Federation. (2015, September 15). *В Хабаровском крае пройдут Российско-китайские учения медико-санитарных служб*. Retrieved on December 2021, from https://minzdrav.gov.ru/special/news/2015/09/15/2535-v-habarovskom-krae-proydut-rossiysko-kitayskie-ucheniya-mediko-sanitarnyh-sluzhb

Ministry of Health of the Russian Federation. (2020, September 14). *Минздрав России публикует перевод на английский и китайский языки сводный Обзор передовых мер, предпринимаемых государствами-членами ШОС по противодействию распространения COVID-19*. Retrieved on December 2021, from https://minzdrav.gov.ru/news/2020a/09/14/14916-minzdrav-rossii-publikuet-perevod-na-angliyskiy-i-kitayskiy-yazyki-svodnyy-obzor-peredovyh-mer-predprinimaemyh-gosudarstvami-chlenami-shos-po-protivodeystviyu-rasprostraneniya-covid-19

Ministry of Health of the Russian Federation. (2020, October 7). *Эксперты исследовательской сети БРИКС по туберкулезу обсудили ситуацию по борьбе с туберкулезом во время пандемии COVID-19*. Retrieved on December 2021, from https://minzdrav.gov.ru/news/2020b/10/05/15120-eksperty-issledovatelskoy-seti-briks-po-tuberkulezu-obsudili-situatsiyu-po-borbe-s-tuberkulezom-vo-vremya-pandemii-covid-19

Ministry of Health of the Russian Federation. (2020, December 24). *Брифинг Министра здравоохранения России Михаила Мурашко*. Retrieved on December 2021, from https://minzdrav.gov.ru/news/2020c/12/24/15748-brifing-ministra-zdravoohraneniya-rossii-mihaila-murashko

National Health [and Family Planning] Commission of the People's Republic of China. (2015, October 23). 国家卫生计生委关于推进"一带一路"卫生交流合作三年实施方案 *(2015–2017)*. Retrieved on December 2021, from http://www.nhc.gov.cn/wjw/ghjh/201510/ce634f7fed834992849e9611099bd7cc.shtml

National Health and Family Planning Commission of the People's Republic of China. (2017, August 11). 国家卫生计生委就"一带一路"暨"健康丝绸之路"高级别研讨会相关情况举行媒体吹风会. Retrieved on December 2021, from http://www.china.com.cn/zhibo/2017-08/11/content_41391900.htm

National Health [and Family Planning] Commission of the People's Republic of China. (2017, August 18). *Beijing Communiqué of The Belt and Road health cooperation & health silk road*. Retrieved on December 2021, from http://en.nhc.gov.cn/2017-08/18/c_72257.htm

Peyrouse, S. (2017). The evolution of Russia's views on the Belt and Road Initiative. *Asia Policy, 24*, 96–102. Retrieved on December 2021, from https://www.jstor.org/stable/26403207

President of Russia. (2019, June 5). *Совместное заявление Российской Федерации и Китайской Народной Республики о развитии отношений всеобъемлющего партнерства и стратегического взаимодействия, вступающих в новую эпоху*. Retrieved on December 2021, from http://kremlin.ru/supplement/5413

President of Russia. (2021, July 2). *Стратегия национальной безопасности Российской Федерации, (Указ Президента Российской Федерации О стратегии национальной безопасности Российской Федерации)*. Retrieved on December 2021, from http://static.kremlin.ru/media/events/files/ru/QZw6hSk5z9gWq0plD1ZzmR5cER0g5tZC.pdf

Sangar, K., Bader, M., & Lane, D. (2017). Russia and China in the age of grand Eurasian projects: Prospects for integration between the Silk Road Economic Belt and the Eurasian Economic Union. *Cambridge Journal of Eurasian Studies, 1*, 1–15. https://doi.org/10.22261/YDG5KF

Sechenov University. *Российско-Китайская ассоциация медицинских университетов (РКАМУ)*. Retrieved on December 2021, from https://www.sechenov.ru/univers/structure/department/otdel-mezhdunarodnykh-svyazey/rkamu-/

Shakhanova, G., & Garlick, J. (2020). The Belt and Road Initiative and the Eurasian Economic Union: Exploring the "Greater Eurasian Partnership." *Journal of Current Chinese Affairs, 49*(1), 33–57. https://doi.org/10.1177/1868102620911666

Shanghai Cooperation Organisation. (2020, July 27). *ИТОГОВОЕ ЗАЯВЛЕНИЕ Третьего Совещания Министров здравоохранения государств-членов Шанхайской организации сотрудничества*. Retrieved on December 2021, from https://sco-russia 2020.ru/images/43/08/430848.pdf

Silver, L., Devlin, K., & Huang, C. (2020). *Unfavorable views of China reach historic highs in many countries*. Pew Research Center. Retrieved on December 2021, from https://www.pewresearch.org/global/2020/10/06/unfavorable-views-of-china-reach-historic-highs-in-many-countries/

Timofeev, I., Lissovolik, Y., & Filippova, L. (2017). Russia's vision of the Belt and Road Initiative: From the rivalry of the great powers to forging a new cooperation model in Eurasia. *China & World Economy, 25*(5), 62–77. https://doi.org/10.1111/cwe.12214

World Health Organization. (2017, August 18). *Towards a health silk road*. Retrieved on December 2021, from https://www.who.int/director-general/speeches/detail/towards-a-health-silk-road

Xi Says China to Send More Medical Experts to Italy. (2020, March 17). *Xinhua*. Retrieved on December 2021, from http://www.xinhuanet.com/english/2020-03/17/c_138886179.htm

Zemánek, L. (2020). Belt & Road initiative and Russia: From mistrust towards cooperation. *Human Affairs, 30*(2), 199–211. Retrieved on December 2021, from https://doi.org/10.1515/humaff-2020-0019

Zoubir, Y., & Tran, E. (2021). China's health silk road in the Middle East and North Africa amidst COVID-19 and a Contested World Order. *Journal of Contemporary China*. Retrieved on December 2021, from https://doi.org/10.1080/10670564.2021.1966894

Денисов, И. (2016). Поднебесная смотрит на Запад. *Контуры глобальных трансформаций*, 6, том 9. Retrieved on December 2021, from https://doi.org/10.23932/2542-0240-2016-9-6-20-40

Денисов, И., & Лукин, А. (2021). Коррекция и хеджирование. *Russia in Global Affairs*. 4, July/August. https://globalaffairs.ru/articles/korrekciya-i-hedzhirovanie/

Китай так и не предоставил российским медикам живой штамм коронавируса. (2020, February 16). *Interfax*. Retrieved on December 2021, from https://www.interfax.ru/russia/694320

Лисин, С. (2021, September 30). МОК не подтвердил признание российской вакцины «Спутник V» на олимпиаде в Пекине. *Match TV*. https://matchtv.ru/winter/matchtvnews_NI1413382_MOK_ne_podtverdil_priznanije_rossijskoj_vakciny_Sputnik_V_na_Olimpiade_v_Pekine

Страны "Пояса и пути" укрепляют сотрудничество в области здравоохранения. (2017, August 21). *Russian News Cn*. [Source: Xinhua]. Retrieved on December 2021, from http://russian.news.cn/2017-08/21/c_136542828.htm

Чжан, Вэйкан. (2020, March 24). Специальный репортаж: Строительство Шелкового пути к здоровью -- как китайско-российские отношения укрепляются в ходе борьбы с COVID-19. *Xinhua Russian*. Retrieved on December 2021, from http://russian.news.cn/2020-03/24/c_138912130.htm

Чжан, Ханьхуэй. (2021, January 16). «Один пояс, один путь»: открыть дорогу взаимному выигрышу. *Embassy of the People's Republic of China to the Russian Federation* [Source: "Trud"]. Retrieved on December 2021, from http://ru.china-embassy.org/rus/zgxw/t1846717.htm

颜欢, 曲颂. (2020, April 27). 打造健康丝绸之路正当其时. *People's Daily Online*. Retrieved on December 2021, from http://world.people.com.cn/n1/2020/0427/c1002-31688854.html

赵磊. (2020, October 19). 建设健康丝绸之路 助力人类卫生健康共同体. *Qiu Shi Theory*. [Source: Guangming Daily.] Retrieved on December 2021, from http://www.qstheory.cn/llwx/2020-10/19/c_1126628513.htm

Chapter 27
India's Challenge to the BRI: Shaping the Global Normative Consensus

Harsh V. Pant and Anant Singh Mann

1 Introduction

The trajectory of the Sino-Indian relationship over the last seven decades has remained erratic with manifold uncertainties out of which the twenty-first century's focus on global connectivity has arguably formed its contemporary core. It is from this focus on connectivity that China rolled out its "One Road, One Belt" (OBOR) initiative in 2013, later rephrased as the more benign and multilateral sounding "Belt and Road Initiative" (BRI), which has now come to be one of the central bones of contention in the Sino-Indian relationship. India's policies regarding connectivity and its aversion to participating in the BRI initially stood out in the pre-COVID-19 era to be incongruous with most of the globe which had welcomed BRI as a vehicle facilitating the strengthening of global connectivity. New Delhi's abstinence from the BRI was seen at the time as a direct result of competing strategic interests within the South Asian region which were forcing *pragmatism* to supersede the mutual benefits from heightened connectivity within the region. However, the onset of COVID-19 pandemic in the beginning of 2020 saw the rise of a markedly different global arena in which countries that had earlier consented to the BRI, like Italy, the first major European economy to subscribe to the BRI in 2019, beginning to show signs of hesitation and reluctance in continuing their participation (Gyu, 2021; Mouritz, 2020). Although there exists a combination of both internal and external factors guiding Italy's choice to review its participation in the BRI in the post-COVID-19 era (Ghiretti, 2021), the evident scarcity of conflicting Sino-Italian strategic interests does indicate that among other factors the widening normative gap remains a key explanatory factor.

Furthermore, the widespread global disaffection with China's BRI in the post-COVID-19 era (Ellis, 2021) does not only vindicate New Delhi's original stance against the BRI, but it also throws into question the traditional and much subscribed

H. V. Pant · A. S. Mann (✉)
Observer Research Foundation, New Delhi, India

to explanation of India's original opposition based on its *realpolitik* pragmatism caused by its underlying conflicting strategic interests with China. This chapter aims to fill this prevailing gap by focusing on the widening normative gap within the Sino-Indian relationship which remains foundational in understanding *how* and *why* India's policy towards the BRI was spot-on right from its inception, with New Delhi finding itself at the vanguard of this geopolitical transition, with its policies representing the new playbook for the twenty-first-century policy towards China and its BRI.

This chapter essentially proposes that while much of India's position in respect to China over the past couple of decades—including New Delhi's noted stance against the China–Pakistan Economic Corridor (CPEC) under the BRI—has been attributed to its *realpolitik* pragmatism based on underlying conflicting interests, the widening normative gap in the Sino-Indian relationship remains the pivotal explanatory variable and the central causative factor in explaining this increasingly strained affair. The chapter begins with a brief review of literature locating the BRI in the Sino-Indian relationship, before focusing on the importance of the normative gap. The study then explores the trajectory of the widening Sino-Indian normative divergence. Finally, the analysis traces the trajectory of New Delhi's counterstrategies to the BRI, to explore how India has collaborated with other smaller nations in providing viable alternatives, effectively representing a new playbook for the international community. To carry out this study, the chapter employs a mixed methodology and relies on both quantitative and qualitative analysis.

2 BRI and the Sino-Indian Relationship: An Arena of Conflicting Interests?

For the last decade, the general shadow which has been cast over India's response to the BRI has been fixated on New Delhi's strong protest against the CPEC, a combination of infrastructure projects and investments that would eventually connect China's Xinjiang province to Pakistan's Gwadar port (Khan & Khan, 2019). In its essence, India's sovereignty comes into question since CPEC runs through the contested territories of Pakistan-occupied Kashmir due to which India was forced for the first time to officially oppose the BRI and its CPEC design in 2017 (Pant & Passi, 2017). Unfortunately, India's objection to the CPEC based on strategic interests and issues of sovereignty has generally coloured the general perspective of New Delhi's approach to the larger BRI as one of *realpolitik* pragmatism, suggesting that India's opposition to the BRI is based on its narrow self-interest, and is not aligned to the general global interest of better connectivity and its resultant mutual economic gains. This perception is further strengthened by perspectives that bracket the responses of nations to the BRI into the rigid categories of "utilitarian," "pragmatic," and "revisionist" (Bhardwaj, 2017; Sharma, 2019), altogether a rather nondescript paradigm which threatens to oversimply highly complex interstate relationships. Through this model and other similar frameworks New Delhi's position on the BRI has been vastly typified as being based on its narrow security and self-interests.

Notwithstanding this problematic reductionism, the Sino-Indian relationship has inherited the burden of a nearly 3,500 kms long undefined border loosely bound by convention and historical tradition. Adding to this the Sino-Indian relationship has the unfortunate antecedent of the Sino-Indian War of 1962 which has maintained its gory legacy through frequent periods of high-tension, among others, like the border standoff at Doklam in 2017 and the border skirmishes of 2020/2021. Naturally, the strategic angle exposes New Delhi's justifiable anxieties regarding Beijing's extended influence through its development initiatives of ports, roads, and railways in its immediate vicinity. The concerns of being hemmed in by China's massive infrastructure projects appear valid given the wide array of plans being designed apart from the CPEC like the Trans-Himalayan Economic Corridor, which aims to connect Nepal and India through the Tibetan plateau, the Bangladesh-China-India-Myanmar Economic corridor, which strengthens the Chinese presence in India's eastern neighbourhood, and the Maritime Silk Road, which aims to create a sea route from Europe to China, threatening India's naval presence in the Indian Ocean (Baruah, 2018, p. 5).

However, there are several important features of India's response which need to be reappraised to challenge the overemphasis on strategic concerns. Most importantly, while the Government of India's (GOI's) press release cited "sovereignty and territorial integrity" in justifying its opposition to the CPEC, it crucially highlighted the widening normative gap between New Delhi and Beijing in their approaches to enhancing connectivity in their neighbouring region as the primary reason for New Delhi's continued indifference with China's BRI (MEA, 2017). Notably, the release asserted that the GOI is a firm supporter of connectivity initiatives as long as they subscribe to the prevailing normative values of the international community, described as,

> international norms, good governance, rule of law, openness, transparency, and equality ... [adhering to strict] financial responsibility to avoid projects that would create unsustainable debt burdens for communities; balanced ecological and environmental protection and preservation standards; transparent assessment of project costs; and skill and technology transfer to help long term running and maintenance of the assets created by local communities. (MEA, 2017)

The above excerpt sheds light on the importance of the normative gap in explaining New Delhi's scepticism of Beijing's BRI, right from its genesis in 2013, much before ideas such as the CPEC were conceptualized. Furthermore, the events that unfolded after the outbreak of the COVID-19 pandemic revealed the true picture of the widening normative gap between China and the rest of the global community. The era of the pandemic proved that it was not India that was misaligned with the global interest of connectivity and mutual economic prosperity, but it was indeed China that has been actively aiming to revise the prevailing normative values of the rules-based global order. Manifested in Beijing's wolf warrior diplomacy (Pant & Mann, 2020a, 2020b), China had contradicted any semblance of the infamous peaceful rise narrative, providing global community with insight for the first time of its revisionist mindset for the global rules-based world order.

Beijing's knee-jerk reaction in response to the global community's outcry regarding the lack of transparency on Beijing's part in determining the cause and origin of the COVID-19 virus in Wuhan led to a heretofore unseen display of an imprudent diplomatic offensive under which Beijing aimed to influence the global narrative through its "aid blitz," which was widely publicized through a slew of official press releases (MFA, 2020b, 2020c). Notwithstanding the various reports questioning the quality of this aid (BBC, 2020), what the global community found more concerning was resurgence of the BRI's "Health Silk Road" (HSR) (MFA, 2020a), which brought the focus on one of the most salient features of the BRI which is to provide and build alternative institutions mechanisms based on vastly different norms to the prevailing rules-based order.

The HSR did not only provide an alternative for the languishing World Health Organization (WHO), but it also innately transformed the prior-to multilateral institutional mechanisms of the WHO governing global health-related coordination to the new "hub-and-spoke model" in which China is at the core of a vast amalgam of bilateral treaties and agreements, subordinating the rest of the countries as merely its spokes (Wang, 2019). Described accurately as "multilateralism with Chinese characteristics" (Pal & Singh, 2020), the HSR manifested all that the global community had tried so hard to overlook of the BRI, smashing the delicate bridges of trust that had been built so carefully between China and the rest of the world. These new institutional normative values, which are clearly "of China, by China, and for China," circumvent the prevailing democratic decision-making that has governed international institutional mechanisms since the Second World War to ensure that in the era of the twenty-first century eventually *all roads will lead to the Middle Kingdom.*

3 The Widening Normative Gap

It is the BRI's disregard for the rules-based global order that India rejected right at its genesis in 2013. Beijing's desire to transform its role on the global stage from a norm-taker to a norm-maker is perhaps the central point of contention for the Sino-Indian relationship with India strongly supporting the prevailing rules-based order and its associated normative values. New Delhi has made it abundantly evident that its central area of concern is maintaining the rules-based liberal multilateral order which was moulded out of the insufficiencies of international cooperation prior to the Second World War. The prevailing rules-based world order, which has often-times been described as the "liberal international order," is essentially what John Ikenberry (2010, 2012, 2018a, 2018b) describes as a system founded at the Peace of Westphalia in 1648, evolving ever since with new layers being added over time, eventually seeing the rise of democratic liberal states (Kundnani, 2017). A key aspect of this liberal project was the organic development of various global norms, conventions, ideals, and values which have for the last half-century guided international relations.

Multilateralism in global governance is one of the foremost norms of the liberal order which, as mentioned earlier, has been questioned and weakened by China's new hub-and-spoke model, which fundamentally reduces the ability of smaller and weaker nations to have a voice on the international stage, or the ability to hedge and maintain their strategic autonomy (Lim & Mukherjee, 2019). The "Bilateralisation" of global governance by the BRI effectively lessens the bargaining power of the smaller nations in question by reducing their ability to leverage multilateral mechanisms to their advantage by lobbying other nations to pressurize larger economies like China (Tarp & Hansen, 2013). Crucially, India has right from its independence been at the forefront of democratization process of the international order, effectively being an integral part of the evolution of the liberal rules-based world order (Lall, 1978: 449). Whether it has been its fight for policy autonomy on behalf of the global south through its Non-Alignment Movement (NAM), or through its championing the establishment of a more equitable international economic order through the New International Economic Order (NEIO) movement, a key feature of Indian foreign policy has been to leverage multilateral mechanisms and strengthen them not only for the newly decolonized nations but also for the rest of the global community.

As an original founder member of the United Nations (UN), this legacy of utilizing multilateral platforms to magnify the voice of oppressed nations and protect the rights of suppressed people has continued with India being the largest contributor of troops for the UN Peace Keeping Missions, supplying over 200,000 troops since its establishment (MEA, 2019). This, of course, pales in comparison to the 2.5 million troops supplied to protect the liberal order during the Second World Order (MEA, 2019). Naturally, China's willingness to replace this age-old liberal order, the evolution of which India has been an integral part of, does raise serious concerns. Unlike China, which only began being socialized into this rules-based order towards the late twentieth century, India truly has a stake and legacy to protect.

Aligned to Beijing's new hub-and-spoke model is the rise of a "Beijing consensus" (Vadell et al., 2014; Williamson, 2012). This new developmental consensus epitomizes Beijing's willingness to depart from liberal rule-based norms of development finance, the structuring of loans, and their conditionalities, which thus far had been carefully controlled and managed by multilateral organizations like the World Bank, and International Monetary Fund (IMF). Although these Western institutions have been widely criticized for monopolizing the arena of developmental finance, the marketing of the Beijing consensus as a viable alternative is a serious issue as it lacks multilateral democratic checks and balances that are vitally essential to guard against hidden geopolitical agendas and known fault lines. The lack of incorporation of institutional safeguards like blacklisting of corrupt firms, citizen feedback mechanisms, competitive bidding, and instead supporting and strengthening existing socio-economic frameworks which benefit only the elite is a dangerous combination to say the least (Parks & Strange, 2019).

Representational of the lack of these checks and balances is the much talked about debt-trap diplomacy practiced by Beijing in which it acquires strategic real estate for long leases in place of debt repayments which its partner states are often unable to make. Sri Lanka is one of its famous victims with it being forced to lose its strategic

Hambantota port to a 99-yearlong lease to China's BRI (Gangte, 2020). Recently the Centre for Global Development reported that out of the 23 nations studied 8 were at high risk of debt traps laid by the projects under the BRI (Hurley et al., 2018). Other projects in Malaysia[1], and Cambodia[2] have reported rises in corruption and significant increases in environmental, ecological, and human risk (Cordell, 2020). Moreover, China's involvement in development assistance has led to situations in which even China has ultimately borne losses from, including its involvement in the developmental fiasco in Venezuela over the last couple of decades (Mann, 2020).

Beyond Beijing's opposition to the rules-based liberal order, New Delhi's apprehensions are only exacerbated by Beijing's scarcity of consistent normative framework in its approach to its connectivity initiatives with the often-cited "trial and error" method signifying that Beijing is willing to go to any length, disregard existing frameworks, create ad hoc norms, to ensure the success of its BRI design (Song, 2020). Wang (2019, pp. 45–47) describes this unscrupulous demeanour as one of "maximised flexibility," with Beijing relying primarily on ad hoc soft law (legally non-binding bilateral agreements), while continuing to forum shop from existing hard law as and when convenient and conducive to the BRI (legally binding treaties and international agreements).

The far-reaching effects the BRI has on international trade governance are perilous given its approach of "infrastructure development first, institution next" (Zhou, 2020). This complete disregard for the normative order and this fixated rhetoric of infrastructure development has led to an extensive amount of reports from the ground level regarding the neocolonial practices carried out by its Special Economic Zones (SEZs) throughout its partner states like discrimination in its SEZs in Nigeria (Adunbi, 2019), adverse impacts on the Kenyan economy (Newcomb, 2020), allegations of "digital-colonialism" (Gravett, 2020), and the widespread displacement of indigenous producers in South Africa (Edwards & Jenkins, 2015), to mention a few. Naturally, the general disregard of international normative values by Beijing is a threatening prospect for New Delhi as it puts into question, and the potential renegotiation of, nearly all of New Delhi's global interactions and pre-existing conventional practices (Basrur, 2019), be it the protection and continued access to a "free and open Indo-Pacific," or the global effort against climate change, or the international fight against terrorism, or the access to energy resources, or simply the facilitation of economic activity through adherence to global financial, trade, and investment governance. Nearly every international-oriented activity of New Delhi is potentially threatened by Beijing's disregard for global normative values and its expanding BRI interests.

---

[1] See (Shepard, 2020).
[2] See (Horton, 2020).

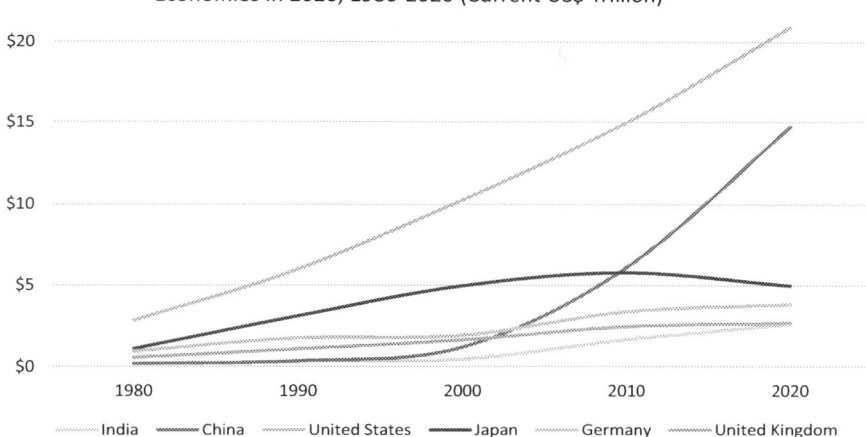

Graph I: Gross Domestic Product for the World's 6 Largest Economies in 2020, 1980-2020 (Current US$ Trillion)

Graph 1 GDP for world's 6 larger economies (*Source* Data sourced from the World Bank [2021])

4 Appraising New Delhi's Policy Playbook for the BRI

A key aspect for India's policy playbook to be adopted by other countries is its tactfulness in working with other nations to provide alternatives to BRI for smaller and economically weaker nations. It must be noted that although New Delhi has over the past three decades attempted to match China's BRI with a myriad of bilateral agreements for projects in its immediate neighbourhood,[3] these projects have been largely unsuccessful in challenging China's BRI with inefficiencies in project implementation, administrative coordination, and financial and economic capacity being consistently faced (Xavier, 2020). The sheer financial gap in capabilities is made evident with the fact that even though India was part of the six largest economies of the world in 2020, it remains dwarfed by China's Gross Domestic Product (GDP) which is nearly 6 times larger (See Graph 1). In fact, Japan, which was the third-largest economy in 2020, fell short of China's GDP by nearly 3 times. Least to say, it appears that apart from the US there exists no economy that can individually match China's financial capacity in competing for Asian connectivity projects. Consequently, combining financial capacities with nations with similar normative values is crucial in understanding the foundations of New Delhi's policy playbook for the BRI. It is quite clear that frantic individual attempts at out-competing Chinese connectivity projects are not the answer and have not paid significant dividends to nations that have attempted it so far.

---

[3] For a comprehensive analysis on India's various bilateral connectivity projects see (De, 2014; Jacob, 2020; Pulipaka et al., 2017; Purushothaman and Unnikrishnan, 2019).

Stage 1 — plurilateral Participation: Participation in plurilateral connectivity initiatives, like the INSTC, BCIM, BIMSTEC, BBIM, etc.

Stage 2 — Individual Initiatives: Individual efforts at providing solutions to connectivity challenges, like IDEAS strategy, Project Mausam, etc.

Stage 3 — Formation of like-minded coalitions: Formation of coalitions with like-minded nations to combine resources and provide viable connectivity alternatives to the BRI for smaller nations, like AAGC, Quad, etc.

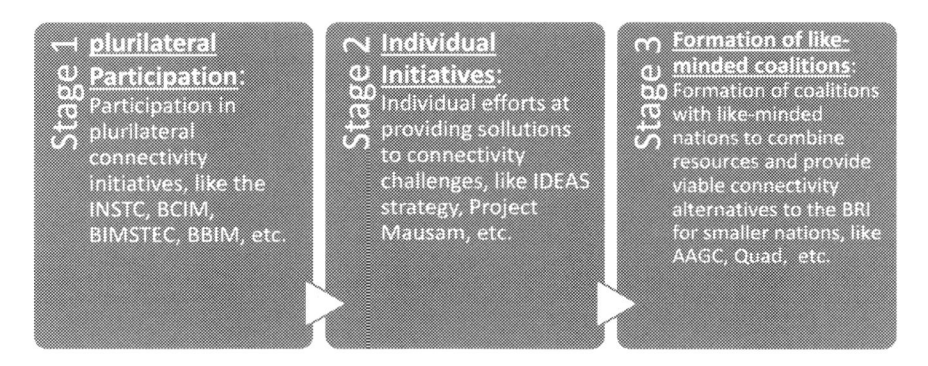

Fig. 1 The evolution of India's connectivity initiatives (*Source* Authors)

New Delhi's policy playbook based on its combined connectivity efforts is already being adopted widely with a post-COVID-19 coalition being announced by the Group of Seven (G7)[4] in June 2021, at which India was invited as an observer, of a new scheme phrased as the "Build Back Better World" or the B3W initiative (G7, 2021). The B3W has been formed precisely for providing the developing nations with a viable alternative to the BRI, aiming to strengthen the normative values of the prevailing rules-based liberal global order (Holland & Faulconbridge, 2021). Considering that India now finds itself at the vanguard of this geopolitical transition, it is worth tracing the trajectory of its continued efforts to draw out other elements that can be adopted by other similarly positioned nations.

It is no coincidence that New Delhi today finds itself at the cutting-edge of this global transition towards the BRI policy. Over the last few decades, India has through trial and error attempted a variety of methods of providing efficient connectivity solutions that appear to have a chronological transition with the initial focus being on actively participating in the connectivity efforts of other nations, to attempting to provide individual answers to connectivity challenges, to finally attempting to form coalitions of like-minded and similarly placed nations to provide efficient alternatives to the BRI. Although the initiatives that began at each of these stages have continued to exist, their speed of progress and enthusiasm have differed with the most recent stage naturally receiving the most enthusiasm (See Fig. 1). Although, quite evidently, these stages are not mutually exclusive, this framework does provide insight into the general direction of New Delhi's policy approach to connectivity. Moreover, this framework provides the general understanding of India's connectivity efforts with a certain chronological and thematic order under which New Delhi's policy playbook for the BRI and evolution can be better evaluated and exported.

In its initial stages New Delhi participated in a wide variety of plurilateral connectivity engagements like Russia's International North–South Transport Corridor (INSTC) which aims to provide the crucial link between Western India to the

---

[4] A group of the seven largest Western democratic economies which includes France, US, UK, Canada, Italy Germany, and Japan.

larger Eurasian continent through Russia and eventually into Europe (Sharma, 2021). Conceived through an agreement between Iran, Russia, and India in 2000, the INSTC involves around 14 countries, reducing shipping costs and time by 40 and 30%, respectively (Purushothaman & Unnikrishnan, 2019, p. 79). The INSTC promises to not only strengthen connectivity on the Eurasian continent but also crucially provide India with the access to Iran's strategic Chabahar port, countering BRI's control of the proximate Gwadar port in Pakistan. Although New Delhi's hold on the Chabahar project appears to be increasingly slipping due to bureaucratic inefficiencies, the INSTC project appears highly promising in not only connecting the Eurasian region, but also in providing the smaller nations within this geography with viable alternatives to the BRI.

The Bangladesh-China-India-Myanmar Economic Corridor (BCIM) was another plurilateral effort which began in 1990 to enhance Southeast Asian regional connectivity. This is perhaps the only BRI project that India has been officially a part of, primarily due to the path dependence created by the initial decision taken more than two decades before the BRI was unveiled (Sharma & Rathore, 2015). Following the BCIM, in 1997 the Bay of Bengal Initiative for Multi-Sectoral Technical and Economic Cooperation (BIMSTEC) was established which included a larger portion of Southeast Asia than the BCIM, including Bangladesh, India, Myanmar, Nepal, Thailand, and Sri Lanka, sans China and Pakistan. Naturally, New Delhi has approached BIMSTEC with a great amount of more enthusiasm. The expanse and strategic involvement by BIMSTEC is also remarkable for New Delhi's context with it bringing together its strategic peripheral sub-regions of the Himalayan sector, the Mekong sector, and the Bay of Bengal sector (Yhome, 2016). Other sub-regional connectivity efforts in this sector include the Bangladesh, Bhutan, India, and Nepal (BBIN) initiative. The accumulated effect of India's plurilateral participations like INSTC, BCIM, BIMSTEC, and BBIM, among others, does indeed provide the initial infrastructure and frameworks to provide BRI alternatives for smaller nations. However, one of the pivotal weaknesses of New Delhi's initial plurilateral agreements was that they were not initially created with the underlying intent to compete with China's BRI. Apart from the relative contemporaneity of the BRI's formulation in 2013, these plurilateral efforts lack the expanse, the financial opportunity, infrastructure investment, and technical know-how that the BRI offers. New Delhi's reaction to the post-2013 rapid rise and domination of the BRI brings this study to the second stage which incorporates India's frantic individual attempts and initiatives to counter what China offers through its BRI. Representational of these efforts is perhaps New Delhi's "Indian Development Assistance Scheme" (IDEAS) created in 2015 and relaunched in 2018 with expanded resources with the mandate to increase the Lines of Credit already extended to nations in Asia, Latin America, and Africa (GOI, 2015). Facilitated by the Indian Export–Import Bank, the IDEAS initiative is designed to provide smaller nations throughout the world with alternative to the BRI for sources of infrastructure investment and connectivity solutions. Post the 2018 announcement, it is estimated that India has opened nearly 18 new diplomatic missions across Africa (Devonshire-Ellis, 2019).

"Project Mausam" is another much-publicized initiative which started around the same time as the IDEAS programme. Launched in mid-2014, it was created to strengthen the cultural linkages across the littoral regions of the Indian Ocean Region (IOR) and promote economy and commerce, to help India regain its ancient role at the helm of connectivity and trade in the Indian Ocean (Ministry of Culture, 2021). Quite evidently this project has been structured to directly counter China's MSR, in an effort to increase India's soft power and presence in the IOR in order to not only stimulate more exchange but also to reawaken India's ancient legacy and highlight its capabilities of providing alternative platforms for connectivity, other than the BRI (Pillalamarri, 2014). Notwithstanding the extensively clearer objectives of such individual initiatives and their focus on directly countering China's BRI, the massive discrepancy in financial resources, the sheer size of China's economy, and China's first-mover advantage considerably weaken the chances of these individual efforts in successfully competing with the BRI. Considering the weaknesses of these first two stages, it becomes apparent that the keystone for India's policy to challenge the BRI is to formulate coalitions of normatively like-minded and similarly placed nations to combine resources and coordinate activities to provide alternative platforms to enhance regional connectivity and provide smaller nations with safer alternatives to the BRI. Accordingly, New Delhi has made several overtures to nations with similar normative values out of which perhaps its strongest coalition so far has been made with Japan. With both nations strongly supporting the rules-based liberal multilateral order, Japan and India jointly announced in 2017 to develop "quality infrastructure" in the Indian Ocean basin and to link Asia to the Africa's eastern coast through the Asia–Africa Growth Corridor (AAGC) (Harris, 2019). India has also reportedly in April 2021 begun strategizing with the European Union (EU) a so-called "global infrastructure deal" specifically focusing on the IOR (Peel et al., 2021).

Perhaps most remarkably has been the development of the Quadrilateral Security Dialogue (Quad) between India, the US, Australia, and Japan over the past one and a half decades. Initially beginning in 2007, the Quad was revived in 2017 meeting biannually ever since and released for the first time a joint statement after the meeting in September 2021 (The White House, 2021). Although the agendas for the meetings have changed marginally, a central feature has remained to maintain a "free and open Indo-Pacific" and strengthen the "rules-based order" (Pant & Mann, 2020a, 2020b). It is quite clear that one of the fundamental purposes the Quad serves is to provide nations of the littoral regions of the IOR with safer and better connectivity in line with the normative values of the rules-based liberal order, offering a better alternative to protecting global commons than the BRI. The formation of coalitions and their initiatives such as the AAGC and the Quad, among others, have a clear advantage in achieving common objectives simply due to the extent of resources that can be pooled together. Deconstructing New Delhi's policy playbook, it appears that there exist clear concentric circles of the importance and centrality of different avenues of policy in countering the BRI. At the core is New Delhi's ability to formulate like-minded coalitions, followed by its individual initiatives, and with its plurilateral participations at the periphery (See Fig. 2).

Fig. 2 The concentric circles of India's policy playbook for challenging the BRI (*Source* Authors based on Fig. 1)

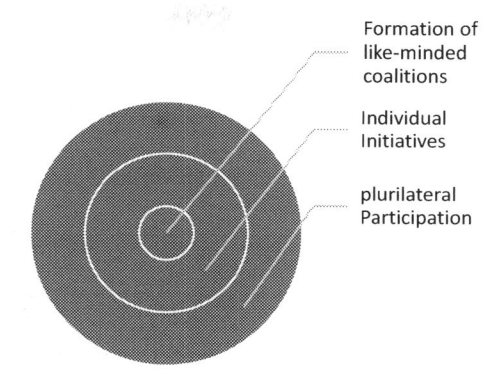

Formation of like-minded coalitions

Individual Initiatives

plurilateral Participation

5 Conclusion

To conclude, this chapter started out with two central puzzles. The first attempted to understand *how* and *why* India's policy towards the BRI was highly accurate right from the beginning, with New Delhi finding itself at the vanguard of this geopolitical transition. The second built from the first to deconstruct and trace India's policy trajectory towards the BRI to understand the development of New Delhi's policy playbook for the BRI which seems to increasingly be adopted by nations across the world. The chapter began by briefly appraising the trajectory of Sino-Indian relations and their different takes on connectivity. The analysis then explored the evidently widening normative gap in the Sino-Indian relationship and its consequences for regional connectivity initiatives. Finally, the study deconstructed and reviewed the trajectory of India's policy towards connectivity and the BRI to locate New Delhi's BRI policy playbook.

Essentially this chapter found that while much of India's position in respect to China over the past couple of decades—including New Delhi's noted stance against the China–Pakistan Economic Corridor (CPEC) under the BRI—has been attributed to its *realpolitik* pragmatism based on underlying conflicting interests, the widening normative gap in the Sino-Indian relationship remains the pivotal explanatory variable and the central causative factor in explaining this increasingly strained affair. More importantly, the study unpacked India's policies towards the BRI and connectivity to find that there does exist a clear direction in its policy trajectory which can tangibly be adapted to by other nations with similar normative values. The analysis of this chapter essentially highlights that the centrality of norms cannot be disregarded in understanding the BRI. Beijing's rhetoric of regional connectivity and its resultant economic and social benefit do worryingly appear to have certain similarities with the British imperial machine which used the same validations as expanding connectivity in its colonies for the overarching purpose to ultimately exploit them. China's disregard for the rules-based liberal order and their associated values and norms of the twenty-first century which are designed to guard against similar occurrences, does raise the question of whether China's actions are purely for the good of the region or if China simply wants to inherit the imperial legacies of the so-called British and American empires that preceded it.

Furthermore, the normative alignment of India and China has only diverged since the 1950s, when both nations came together to propagate the Five Principles of Coexistence and champion the cause of the "third world." Much has changed since 1960 and their normative divergence appears to be reaching new heights every decade. Under these circumstances it is not surprising that India continues to warn the world of the BRI and its ad hoc norms and superficial values. For the time being New Delhi's position at the vanguard of this global transition of perspectives is pivotal as much can be learned and adopted from its policy playbook for the BRI and regional connectivity. Notwithstanding the innovative contributions and findings of this study, this chapter did indeed face the limitations of its word count, and the recentness of the global transitions and geopolitical re-adjustments caused by the disruption of the COVID-19 era. However, the most pertinent contribution of this chapter, its schematic representation of India's BRI policy (See Figs. 1 and 2), merits future research and would be useful in providing insight in a variety of areas relating to the evolution and trajectory of India's foreign and connectivity policies.

Bibliographic References

Adunbi, O. (2019). (Re)inventing development: China, infrastructure, sustainability and special economic zones in Nigeria. *Africa, 89*(4), 662–679. Cambridge Core. https://doi.org/10.1017/S0001972019000846

Baruah, D. M. (2018). *India's answer to the belt and road: A road map for South Asia* [Working Paper]. Carnegie Endowment for International Peace: India. Retrieved in December 2021, from https://carnegieendowment.org/files/WP_Darshana_Baruah_Belt_Road_FINAL.pdf

Basrur, R. (2019). The BRI and India's grand strategy. *Strategic Analysis, 43*(3), 187–198. https://doi.org/10.1080/09700161.2019.1598082

BBC. (2020, March 30). Coronavirus: Countries reject Chinese-made equipment. *BBC*. Retrieved in December 2021, from https://www.bbc.co.uk/news/world-europe-52092395

Bhardwaj, A. (2017). Belt and road initiative: An idea whose time has come. *China International Studies, 64*, 101.

Cordell, K. A. (2020, October). The evolving relationship between the international development architecture and China's belt and road: Who is making the rules? *Brookings Institute*. Retrieved in December 2021, from https://www.brookings.edu/articles/the-evolving-relationship-between-the-international-development-architecture-and-chinas-belt-and-road/

De, P. (2014). *India's emerging connectivity with Southeast Asia: Progress and prospects* (ADBI Working Paper 507). Asian Development Bank Institute. Retrieved in December 2021, from http://www.adbi.org/working-paper/2014/12/19/6520.india.connectivity.southeast.asia/

Devonshire-Ellis, C. (2019, July 19). What is India's "IDEAS" belt & road alternative project? *Silk Road Briefing*. Retrieved in December 2021, from https://www.silkroadbriefing.com/news/2019/07/17/indias-ideas-belt-road-alternative-project/

Edwards, L., & Jenkins, R. (2015). The impact of Chinese import penetration on the South African manufacturing sector. *The Journal of Development Studies, 51*(4), 447–463. https://doi.org/10.1080/00220388.2014.983912

Ellis, E. (2021, July 20). Northeast Asia: BRI 2.0: China adapts to post-covid world. *Asia Money*, ir.

G7. (2021). *G7, United Kingdom 2021: Build back better*. Retrieved in December 2021, from https://www.g7uk.org

Gangte, L. (2020). The debt-trap diplomacy revisited: A case study on Sri Lanka's Hambantota port. *Artha Journal of Social Sciences, 19*(2), 53–66. https://doi.org/10.12724/ajss.53.4

Ghiretti, F. (2021, March 23). The belt and road in Italy: 2 years later two years after the signing of the memorandum of understanding, where does the BRI stand in Italy? *The Diplomat*. Retrieved in December 2021, from https://thediplomat.com/2021/03/the-belt-and-road-in-italy-2-years-later/

GOI. (2015). *IDEAS* [Government]. Department of economic affairs: Government of India. Retrieved in December 2021, from https://www.dea.gov.in/divisionbranch/ideas

Gravett, W. (2020). Digital neo-colonialism: The Chinese model of internet sovereignty in Africa. *African Human Rights Law Journal, 20*(1), 125–146. Retrieved in December 2021, from https://doi.org/10.17159/1996-2096/2020/v20n1a5

Gyu, L. D. (2021). The belt and road initiative after COVID: The rise of health and digital silk roads. *Asian Institute for Policy Studies, Issue Brief* (2021–02(S)).

Harris, T. (2019, April 9). 'Quality infrastructure': Japan's robust challenge to China's belt and road. *War on the Rocks*. Retrieved in December 2021, from https://warontherocks.com/2019/04/quality-infrastructure-japans-robust-challenge-to-chinas-belt-and-road/

Holland, S., & Faulconbridge, G. (2021, June 13). G7 rivals China with grand infrastructure plan. *Reuters*. Retrieved in December 2021, from https://www.reuters.com/world/g7-counter-chinas-belt-road-with-infrastructure-project-senior-us-official-2021-06-12/

Horton, C. (2020, January 9). The costs of China's belt and road expansion. *The Atlantic*. Retrieved in December 2021, from https://www.theatlantic.com/international/archive/2020/01/china-belt-road-expansion-risks/604342/

Hurley, J., Morris, S., & Portelance, G. (2018). *Policy papers: Examining the debt implications of the belt and road initiative from a policy perspective*. Center for Global Development. Retrieved in December 2021, from https://www.cgdev.org/publication/examining-debt-implications-belt-and-road-initiative-a-policy-perspective

Ikenberry, G. J. (2010). The liberal international order and its discontents. *Millennium: Journal of International Studies, 38*(3), 5, 09–521. https://doi.org/10.1177/0305829810366477

Ikenberry, G. J. (2012). *Liberal leviathan: The origins, crisis, and transformation of the American world order*. Princeton University Press. https://doi.org/10.1515/9781400838196

Ikenberry, G. J. (2018a). Why the liberal world order will survive? *Ethics & International Affairs, 32*(1), 17–29. https://doi.org/10.1017/S0892679418000072

Ikenberry, G. J. (2018b). The end of liberal international order? *International Affairs, 94*(1), 7–23. https://doi.org/10.1093/ia/iix241

Jacob, J. T. J. (2020). China, India, and Asian connectivity. In K. P. Bajpai, S. Ho, & M. C. Miller (Eds.), *Routledge handbook of China-India relations*. Routledge.

Khan, M. Z. U., & Khan, M. M. (2019). China-Pakistan economic corridor. *Institute of Strategic Studies Islamabad, 39*(2), 67–82.

Kundnani, H. (2017, May 3). What is the liberal international order? *German Marshal fund of the United States: Foreign policy*. Retrieved in December 2021, from https://www.gmfus.org/news/what-liberal-international-order

Lall, K. B. (1978). India and the new international economic order. *International Studies, 17*(3–4), 435–461. Retrieved in December 2021, from https://doi.org/10.1177/002088177801700305

Lim, D. J., & Mukherjee, R. (2019). Hedging in South Asia: Balancing economic and security interests amid Sino-Indian competition. *International Relations of the Asia-Pacific, 19*(3), 493–522. Retrieved in December 2021, from https://doi.org/10.1093/irap/lcz006

Mann, A. S. (2020, October 21). Venezuela, the pink tide and China. *Observer Research Foundation*. Retrieved in December 2021, from https://www.orfonline.org/expert-speak/venezuela-the-pink-tide-and-china/

MEA. (2017, May 13). Official Spokesperson's response to a query on participation of India in OBOR/BRI forum. *Ministry of External Affairs, Government of India, Media Center: Media Briefings.* Retrieved in December 2021, from https://mea.gov.in/media-briefings.htm?dtl/28463/Official+Spokespersons+response+to+a+query+on+participation+of+India+in+OBORBRI+Forum

MEA. (2019, November 8). UN peacekeeping: India's contributions: By: Ambassador (Retd.) Asoke Kumar Mukerji. *Ministry of External Affairs, Government of India, Media Center: Media Briefings.* Retrieved in December 2021, from https://www.mea.gov.in/articles-in-indian-media.htm?dtl/32014/UN_Peacekeeping_Indias_Contributions

MFA. (2020a, March 16). President Xi Jinping talked with Italian Prime Minister giuseppe conte over the phone. *Ministry of Foreign Affairs, the People's Republic of China.* Retrieved in December 2021, from https://www.fmprc.gov.cn/mfa_eng/zxxx_662805/t1756887.shtml

MFA. (2020b, March 21). The Chinese government sends a team of medical experts on COVID-19 to Serbia. *Ministry of Foreign Affairs, the People's Republic of China.* Retrieved in December 2021, from https://www.fmprc.gov.cn/mfa_eng/xwfw_665399/s2510_665401/2535_665405/t1759175.shtml

MFA. (2020c, March 23). The Chinese government sends a team of medical experts on COVID-19 to Cambodia. *Ministry of Foreign Affairs, the People's Republic of China.* Retrieved in December 2021, from https://www.fmprc.gov.cn/mfa_eng/xwfw_665399/s2510_665401/2535_665405/t1759571.shtml

Ministry of Culture. (2021). *Project Mausam.* Ministry of Culture, Government of India. Retrieved in December 2021, from http://www.indiaculture.nic.in/project-mausam

Mouritz, F. (2020). Implications of the COVID-19 pandemic on China's belt and road initiative. *Connections: The Quarterly Journal, 19*(2), 115–124. https://doi.org/10.11610/Connections.19.2.09

Newcomb, C. S. (2020). *The impact of Chinese investments on the Kenyan economy* [Masters Thesis, Wilkinson College of Arts, Humanities, and Social Sciences, Chapman University]. Retrieved in December 2021, from https://www.proquest.com/openview/6f0e09c7c64801fc11ee52ab9a66d5d7/1?pq-origsite=gscholar&cbl=44156

Pal, D., & Singh, S. V. (2020, July 10). Multilateralism with Chinese characteristics: Bringing in the hub-and-spoke: Beyond capturing border territories and changing narratives, China wants to reshape global governance. New Delhi and the world must realize this. *The Diplomat.* Retrieved in December 2021, from https://thediplomat.com/2020/07/multilateralism-with-chinese-characteristics-bringing-in-the-hub-and-spoke/

Pant, H. V., & Mann, A. S. (2020a, July 26). Wolf warrior vanguard: The global times is a perfect metaphor for China's rise and current adventurism. *The Times of India.* Retrieved in December 2021, from https://timesofindia.indiatimes.com/blogs/toi-edit-page/wolf-warrior-vanguard-the-global-times-is-a-perfect-metaphor-for-chinas-rise-and-current-adventurism/

Pant, H. V., & Mann, A. S. (2020b). India's malabar dilemma. *Observer Research Foundation, ORF Issue Brief No. 393.* Retrieved in December 2021, from https://www.orfonline.org/research/indias-malabar-dilemma/

Pant, H. V., & Passi, R. (2017). India's response to China's belt and road initiative. *Asia Policy, 24*, 88–95.

Parks, B. C., & Strange, A. M. (2019). *Autocratic aid and governance: What we know, don't know, and need to know* (AidData Working Paper #75). AidData: William and Mary. Retrieved in December 2021, from https://www.aiddata.org/publications/autocratic-aid-and-governance-what-we-know-dont-know-and-need-to-know

Peel, M., Fleming, S., & Findlay, S. (2021, April 21). EU and India plan global infrastructure deal. *Financial Times.* Retrieved in December 2021, from https://www.ft.com/content/2e612c38-aba9-426a-9697-78e11ab1c697

Pillalamarri, A. (2014, September 18). Project mausam: India's answer to China's 'maritime silk road.' *The Diplomat.* Retrieved in December 2021, from https://thediplomat.com/2014/09/project-mausam-indias-answer-to-chinas-maritime-silk-road/

Pulipaka, S., Antara, G. S., & Sircar, S. (2017). *India and connectivity frameworks* (H. K. Singh, Ed.). Delhi Policy Group.

Purushothaman, U., & Unnikrishnan, N. (2019). A tale of many roads: India's approach to connectivity projects in Eurasia. *India Quarterly: A Journal of International Affairs, 75*(1), 69–86. https://doi.org/10.1177/0974928418821488

Sharma, A., & Rathore, C. K. (2015). *BIMSTEC and BCIM initiatives and their importance for India.* CUTS Centre for International Trade, Economics & Environment (CUTS CITEE). Retrieved in December 2021, from http://www.cuts-citee.org/pdf/BIMSTEC_and_BCIM_Initiatives_and_their_Importance_for_India.pdf

Sharma, M. (2019). India's approach to China's belt and road initiative—Opportunities and concerns. *The Chinese Journal of Global Governance, 5,* 136–152. https://doi.org/10.1163/23525207-12340041

Sharma, N. (2021). Energy security of India: Role of international North-South transport corridor. *Electronic Journal of Social and Strategic Studies, 02*(02). https://doi.org/10.47362/EJSSS.2021.2204

Shepard, W. (2020, January 31). Inside the belt and road's premier white elephant: Melaka gateway. *Forbes.* Retrieved in December 2021, from https://www.forbes.com/sites/wadeshepard/2020/01/31/inside-the-belt-and-roads-premier-white-elephant-melaka-gateway/?sh=414e8590266e

Song, W. (2020). China's normative foreign policy and its multilateral engagement in Asia. *Pacific Focus, 35*(2), 229–249. https://doi.org/10.1111/pafo.12163

Tarp, M. N., & Hansen, J. O. B. (2013). *Size and influence: How small states influence policy making in multilateral arenas: Vol. DIIS Working Paper 2013:11.* Danish Institute for International Studies.

The White House. (2021, September 24). *Fact sheet: Quad leaders' Summit.* US Government. Retrieved in December 2021, from https://www.whitehouse.gov/briefing-room/statements-releases/2021/09/24/fact-sheet-quad-leaders-summit/

Vadell, J., Ramos, L., & Neves, P. (2014). The international implications of the Chinese model of development in the global South: Asian consensus as a network power. *Revista Brasileira de Política Internacional, 57*(spe), 91–107. https://doi.org/10.1590/0034-7329201400206

Wang, H. (2019). China's approach to the belt and road initiative: Scope, character and sustainability. *Journal of International Economic Law, 22*(1), 29–55. https://doi.org/10.1093/jiel/jgy048

Williamson, J. (2012). Is the "Beijing consensus" now dominant? *Asia Policy, 13,* 1–16. JSTOR.

World Bank. (2021). *GDP (current US$)—India, United States, United Kingdom, Germany, Japan, China.* The World Bank: Data. Retrieved in December 2021, from https://data.worldbank.org/indicator/NY.GDP.MKTP.CD?locations=IN-US-GB-DE-JP-CN

Xavier, C. (2020). *Sambandh as strategy: India's new approach to regional connectivity* (Brookings India Policy Brief 012020–01). Brookings Institution India Center.

Yhome, K. (2016, October 3). BIMSTEC and India's shifting diplomatic calculus. *Observer Research Foundation.* Retrieved in December 2021, from https://www.orfonline.org/expert-speak/bimstec-india-shifting-diplomatic/

Zhou, J. (2020). A new multilateralism? A case study of the belt and road initiative. *The Chinese Journal of Comparative Law, 8*(2), 384–413. https://doi.org/10.1093/cjcl/cxaa022

Chapter 28
China–Pakistan Economic Corridor (CPEC): India's Conundrum and Policy Options

S. Y. Surendra Kumar

1 Introduction

Having realized that India's growth and prosperity is connected with the development of the South Asian region, successive Indian prime ministers have attempted to give due importance to India's neighbours and continue to engage with them, despite the ups and downs they have experienced in such bilateral ties. But in this endeavour, Pakistan remains a difficult nut to crack and the challenges are further deepened with the commencement of the China–Pakistan Economic Corridor (CPEC), which is one of the six core economic corridors under the China's Belt and Road Initiative (BRI) and is regarded as a fate-changer/game-changer for Pakistan. The CPEC was launched in April 2015, with China pledging to invest around US$46 billion in Pakistan (enhanced to US$62 billion in 2017) and providing preferential loans in key sectors. However, this corridor has been out rightly opposed by India on the grounds that it threatens its sovereignty and security. In this context, there are several studies by policymakers, academics, and business groups that analyse India's position and response to CPEC. But, there are fewer studies (from an Indian perspective) on the prospects of CEPC for both China and Pakistan, as well as the impact of CEPC on India's strategy. Subsequently, scholars and policymakers have yet to undertake studies on identifying areas for India's (at least restricted) engagement in BRI/CPEC. Nonetheless, this study contends that India must reconsider its CPEC responses and plans, and China must address India's concerns in order for both countries to participate in the BRI. Subsequently, Pakistan's economic expansion will benefit both India and China, as well as the region.

In this context, the twin objective of the chapter is to: first, examine the socio-economic/geostrategic prospects of CPEC for both China and Pakistan and its implications for India. Second, analyse India's responses so far and identify the viable policy options for India to overcome the CPEC dilemma. In order to understand the

S. Y. Surendra Kumar (✉)
Department of Political Science, Bangalore University, Bengaluru, Karnataka, India

dynamics of CPEC and its implications for India, the study attempts to argue from a realistic and liberal international relations perspective. The methodology consisted of interpretive view focusing on the political, economic, and strategic aspects of CPEC from 2015 to till now. The study is deductive in nature as the economic, political, and security-related aspects are reviewed, analysing the perspectives of Pakistan and China as well as India. Subsequently, it examines the qualitative and narrative characteristics of the data, and uses exploratory research methodology to enhance the understanding of the strategic importance of CPEC for both China and Pakistan.

The study is divided into four sections—the first portion provides an overview of China–Pakistan relations and focuses on the reasons that led to the development of the CPEC. It also identifies the prospects and benefits of CPEC for both the countries and examines "India factor" in pushing for CPEC. The second section discusses the CPEC's implementation issues as well as its influence on both Pakistan and China. The third section focuses on India's perspective, as well as the reasons that influenced its attitude to CPEC. The final portion is the conclusion, which identifies India's policy alternatives, highlights the study's limitations, and suggests prospective research areas.

2   CPEC: A *Win–Win Situation and All-Round Cooperation?*

China and Pakistan's relations since the 1950s have deepened politically, economically and, recently, even strategically. Despite both countries having different culture, beliefs, and geographical proximity, they have emerged as all-weather friends or regarded as "Iron brothers." The strong roots of the bilateral ties were laid with Pakistan being the first Muslim nation and the third non-communist country to recognize People's Republic of China (PRC) after the 1949 revolution. The diplomatic ties between the two nations began formally in May 1951, as a result of India's devaluation of currency, which affected the overall bilateral trade between India and Pakistan, and later was severely affected, as it depended on India for coal to sustain its industries. China used this as an opportunity and immediately signed the "coal for cotton" trade deal with Pakistan (Riaz et al., 2020, p. 68). This laid the strong foundation between the two countries, such that Pakistan pitched for China's inclusion in the United Nations Security Council (UNSC).

The 1960s is regarded as a milestone in bilateral ties, with the visit by head of states and signing of several economic and political agreements, including the settlement of territorial demarcation. China stood behind Pakistan even during the India–Pakistan war in 1965, i.e., China expressed that its people and leaders were fully committed to support Pakistan's "national independence sovereignty and national integrity" (Pande, 2011). At the same time, China's aid to Pakistan also increased and from 1965–1971, it provided approximately US$ 445 million as well as military equipments (Allauddin et al, 2020, p. 77). In the 1980s and 90s, the areas of cooperation were expanded to trade, investment, technology, defence sector and also in the nuclear programme. Furthermore, economic ties got a big boost, with Free Trade

Agreement (FTA) signed in 2006 and subsequently, another FTA on trade in service (2009) (Riaz et al., 2020, p. 68). As a result, China emerged as the largest trading partner for Pakistan and the bilateral trade has increased from just US$ 1 billion (1998) to US$ 17.49 billion (2020) (*Global Times*, 2021), and now China has also emerged as the key investor in telecommunications, energy, ports, and infrastructure.

Despite the COVID-19 pandemic, bilateral ties continue to be strong, with the two-day visit by Pakistan President Arif Alvi to Beijing (March 2020) on the invitation by Chinese President Xi Jinping. Both leaders had expressed solidarity in fighting the pandemic and China even pledged to offer Pakistan the much-needed support to battle COVID-19. As a result, from March 2020, China provided millions of surgical masks and key medical equipment, which was rightly acknowledged by the Pakistan Senate through a resolution (15 May 2020) thanking China for the help, not just for its mask diplomacy, but for repatriating hundreds of Pakistani students stranded in Wuhan province (Afzal, 2020, p. 6). At the same time, China consented to the request made by the Pakistani government, due to the impact of COVID-19, for easier repayment terms of the power project loans worth US$30 billion (Afzal, 2020, p. 6). Thus, the challenges posed by COVID-19 have also been used by both the nations as opportunities to strengthen the bilateral ties. Nevertheless, it is CPEC which is bonding both the countries in recent times.

Initially, the proposal for the economic corridor—CPEC was put forward by Li Keqiang, the Chinese premier, during his visit to Islamabad in May 2013. The intention was that the economic corridor could be a solution to key problems faced by Pakistan, i.e., huge power shortage, weak economic growth, unemployment, and serious internal insecurity. In June 2013, during Prime Minister Nawaz Sharif's visit to Beijing, a Memorandum of Understanding (MOU) was signed to finalize the modalities of CPEC. Although, it was supposed to be launched in 2014, but was pushed to 2015, due to stiff opposition from Imran Khan-led Tehreek-e-Insaf (TTK) party. Thus, during President Jinping's visit to Pakistan in 2015, the CPEC was launched with the signing of MoUs; financial agreements and press releases were done with wide mass media coverage in Pakistan. Even at the project sites, huge billboards were placed of both President Jinping and Prime Minister Sharif, to project CPEC as beneficial for both the nations. At the same time, Prime Minister Sharif also argued that CPEC would be a "game changer" for Pakistan, as it would improve infrastructure, reduce its blackouts, create jobs, and boost economic growth.

Under the CPEC, China pledged to invest US$46 billion in Pakistan (enhanced to US$ 62 billion in 2017), which exceeds the Foreign Direct Investment (FDI) to Pakistan. The CPEC was agreed for 1 + 4 structure of corridors, i.e., the project would be the hub of Port (Gwadar), energy, transport infrastructure, Special Economic Zones (SEZ), high-speed internet connectivity, and industrial cooperation. Subsequently, it was decided to implement in three stages—the short-term projects (also known as ready to harvest projects) and to be accomplished by 2020; medium- and long-term projects to be accomplished by 2025 and 2030, respectively (Khursheed et al., 2019, p. 7). Moreover, the first phase (2014–2020) primarily dealt with the development of Gwadar port city, with regard to energy and infrastructure building in the period 2021–2025. The second phase focuses on projects to boost trade, market access, "development of global values chains, building Gwadar oil city and blue economy, regional connectivity and third-party participation" (Chinoy, 2021, p. 4).

Some of the key projects include Orange Line Metro Lahore, New Gwadar International Airport, Gwadar East-Bay Expressway, Motorway M-5 (Sukkur–Multan), Infrastructure Development for Free Zone Gwadar, Construction of Breakwaters, Gwadar Port, Havelian Dry Port, Cross Border Optical Fibre Cable Pakistan-China Friendship Hospital, Karot Hydropower Plant, Karachi-Peshawar Line, Karakoram Highway Suki Kinari Hydropower Project, Sahiwal Coal Power Project, Port Qasim Power Project, Dawood Wind Power Project. An investment (since 2015) of US$ 18.9 billion was allocated for 22 projects, of which 11 have been completed and the rest are ongoing. In addition to these there are 20 more projects in the pipeline (CPEC Portal, 2021a).

Despite the launch, leader Imran Khan and his TTK party continued to oppose and even went to the extent of making it a key issue during the 2018 parliamentary elections, by emphasizing that he would review the terms of CPEC if his party comes to power. He opposed CPEC on the ground that there was serious allegation of corruption during the Nawaz Sharif government and increasing Pakistan's external debt that stood at US$ 96 billion, was a result of unfair negotiations done during the Sharif regime. With Imran Khan forming the government in August 2018, one of his Union Minister Abdul Razzak Dawood stated that "the previous government did a bad job negotiating with China on CPEC, they didn't do their homework correctly and didn't negotiate correctly so they gave away a lot" (Anderlini et al., 2018). But he backtracked on this statement and clarified that it was taken out of context.

Despite this, the Pakistan Army Chief, Qamar Javed Bajwa, undertook a three-day visit to Beijing (September 2018), during which he stated: "BRI with CPEC as its flagship is destined to succeed despite all odds and the Pakistan Army shall ensure security of CPEC at all costs" (Inter Services Public Relations, 2018). On similar lines, Imran Khan during visit to Beijing (April 2019) at the Second BRI Forum Summit stated that the CPEC as a major component of BRI "has made substantial progress… and next phase will focus on social economic uplift, poverty alleviation, agriculture cooperation and industrial development"(Patranobis, 2019). Thus, at present it looks like the Imran government and Pakistan's army are on the same page with regard to the CPEC, as it provides opportunities for both the countries.

2.1 Pakistan's Advantages and Benefits

Although CPEC was launched in 2015, efforts to secure this kind of economic project from China were initiated during the Pakistan People's Party (PPP)-led government and by the former President Asif Ali Zardari (2008–2013) and then it was taken forward by Nawaz Sharif government and later on with initial opposition, Imran Khan's regime also endorsed CPEC and went on to state that CPEC was the "gateway to prosperity" (CPEC Portal, 2021b). Apart from this, the backing by the Pakistan Army boosted the success of CPEC, as the army perceived the project from a geopolitical and strategic angle and believed that this could counterbalance US' frequent diplomatic and economic pressure/sanctions. Thus, there has been a political consensus in Pakistan both among the civilian and the army favouring CPEC, due to its potential economic and strategic benefits for the country. Some of them are: (a) Given that Pakistan has the potential of becoming one of the world's largest economies, with a huge population (fifth largest) and a formidable purchasing power parity (24th largest), it is argued that CPEC will boost its economy by developing and also modernizing the critical sectors like transportation, energy networks, road and rail; agricultural productions, rural development, which, in turn, would enhance economic growth. (b) CPEC will address the prevailing domestic energy crisis, which has hit the industrial production. It is argued that there is a shortfall of 4000 megawatts (MW) to 7000 MW per year and its current production on an average is just 25,000 MW (Aziz, 2019). The World Bank Report (December 2018), emphasized on the inefficiencies in Pakistan's power sector, effecting its economy worth US$ 18 billion (6.5% of GDP) and around 50 million people lack access to grid electricity (*Press* Release, 2018). Thus, under the CPEC, many projects based on wind, solar, coal, and hydro power generation have/are coming up to meet the energy shortage in the country. As a result, it is estimated that these projects could add 3240 MW (11% to total capacity) to Pakistani national grid (CPEC Portal, 2021c). (c) It is the golden opportunity for transforming Baluchistan, which is regarded as the most backward province, deeply affected with insurgency, despite regular army operations. It is perceived that under the CPEC thousands of jobs would be created; by providing quality education, the socio-economic backwardness of the province would improve naturally. Moreover, with the development and modernization of Gwadar Port, Baluchistan would eventually become the hub for processing industries, handling both cargo and passengers, and accommodating the recreational and tourism industries (Riaz et al., 2020, p. 70). Apart from this, Baluchistan is blessed with rich natural resources like coal, chromite, sulphur, barites, marble, limestone, iron ore, gas reservoirs and oil reserves, which will not only meet the requirements of China, but other Central Asian countries as well. (d) Successive governments have stressed on the fact that CPEC will not only improve the socio-economic conditions of people, but it will promote bilateral connectivity, investment, trade, logistics, and infrastructure development and promote people-to-people contact for regional connectivity. Moreover, Pakistan's urge to become self-sufficient with regard to its energy resources could be addressed through CPEC, as the corridor would connect Pakistan through Gilgit-Baltistan to Tajikistan, which is rich in natural resources; China would also help the geo-economics of Pakistan. (e) CPEC has also promised of creating 2.3 million jobs (2015–2030), and so far it has been estimated to have created more than 75,000 direct jobs and 200,000 indirect jobs in for medium- high-skilled, and blue-collar workers (CPEC Portal, 2021c). Even the subcontracting of projects by the Chinese companies has created more jobs for the local populations with the participation of Pakistan's small and medium scale enterprises. (f) Over the decades, Pakistan's dependence on the United States (US), United Arab Emirates (UAE), and Saudi Arabia for its economic and military assistances has also come with a huge cost. Thus, CPEC has emerged as a vital step to reduce over dependency.

At the same time, the global image of Pakistan has been overshadowed by political instability, weak economy, internal security threats due to religious extremist and terrorist outfits, perpetuating human rights violations, fragile democratic institutors due to military influence/intervention and prolonged tensions with India. In this context, it is important to boost Pakistan's positive image at the global arena, and CPEC has come at the right time. (g) Unlike the US, it is always beneficial for Pakistan to deepen its ties with China and be part of BRI, as the latter follows a policy of non-interference, peaceful coexistence, emphasis on dialogue and negotiation and does not support separatist movements in Pakistan. Hence, CPEC would be a game changer for Pakistan's economy and global ambitions, as perceived by its political establishments. As a result, Pakistani government claims that CPEC would reduce poverty, create more jobs, and minimize the prevailing inequality in the provinces through trade and economic activity, which will bring wealth to both Pakistan and China.

2.2 *China's Advantages and Benefits*

Even China will equally benefit through the success of CPEC. For instance, (a) through CPEC, China intends to deepen its ties with Pakistan by investing in transportation, modernization of ports, power sector, and other infrastructure projects, thereby contributing towards making Pakistan economically stronger, which is not only good for China, but also for the region. Apparently, it will boost people-to-people contact and increase cultural cooperation, as emphasized by President Jinping: "We should use the platforms of sister cities, cultural centres, and media organizations to conduct diverse events of celebration. China and Pakistan should continue to send 100-member youth groups to visit each other's country and encourage more contacts and exchanges between young Chinese and Pakistanis. In the next five years, China will provide 2,000 training opportunities for Pakistan and train 1,000 Chinese language teachers for Pakistan" (Sharif & Rabbani, 2015). (b) The Xinjiang Uyghur Autonomous Region (XUAR) in China continues to be economically backward due to perpetuating militancy and separatism, thus this can be addressed through CPEC and it will also reduce the geographical distance to Baluchistan. Moreover, China also wants a stable Pakistan, without much influence of religious extremist and Jihadi forces that poses a threat to China's interest in XUAR. The bomb attack in Tiananmen Square, Beijing (October 2013), for which the Turkistan Islamist Party claimed responsibility and similar attacks at Kunming and Urumqi railway stations (March 2014) killed close to 15 people and injured more than hundred indicates the that roots of Islamic terrorism in Xinjiang province are deepening (Hameed, 2018, p. 2). (c) China is an energy-dependent country and most of its energy imports have to pass through the Malacca strait, a vulnerable choke point which is 500 nm narrow waterway between Indian Ocean and South China Sea (SCS). Moreover, it is estimated that around 80% of its energy supply (crude oil and natural gas) pass this strait. Thus, by developing the Gwadar Port (Pakistan), it will emerge as an alternative energy route [for China] instead of passing through the Malacca strait in Indian Ocean. At the same time, the route will be most secured and shortest, as the present transportation of energy through Malacca strait takes 45 days, but will be reduced to less than 10 days via Gwadar port. In addition, in China, the coal accounts for approximately 70% of total energy consumption, hence, it will shift its power generation (use of coal) out of its country through CPEC. (d) China realizes that CPEC is the gateway to Afghanistan and Iran, where it can increase its political, economic, and strategic influence in Central Asia and West Asia. With the withdrawal of US-led forces from Afghanistan (August 2021) and China already engaging with the Taliban regime, the extension of CPEC [from Pakistan] will be highly beneficial for China. Overall, for China, the CPEC is not just an economic cooperation to improve its ties with Pakistan through trade, connectivity, and infrastructure building, but it is also the former's grand strategy to achieve its dream of becoming the largest economy of the world by 2049 and be the superpower.

2.3 Undermining India's Interest?

Generally, the Sino-Pak relations are shaped by the regional security architecture and economic imperatives and CPEC is regarded as mutually beneficial for both, but CPEC is also to a certain extent guided by the "India factor" i.e., the development of Gwadar Port is regarded by many Indian policymakers and strategists as China's strategy to encircle India (string of pearls strategy), through commercial ports in the Indian Ocean region. However, in response, the Chinese have argued that being an energy importing (70% of its oil) country, has to pass through the Indian Ocean region and the objective remains necessary refuelling, commercial purpose, and sea lane security, and not to threaten or contain India. Nevertheless, the ports (including Gwadar) can also be used by Chinese naval base in future for military purpose. At the same time, the CPEC projects are not far away from Siachen glacier and Ladakh and with projects in Gilgit-Baltistan give an advantage for China to station its paramilitary construction crops/troops and expanded if necessary in near future. This will obviously affect India's security interests. For Pakistan, development of Gwadar Port is vital, as it will be an alternative base, if the Indian government imposes a naval blockade on Karachi in the near future. Subsequently, Pakistan through CPEC is helping China to come closer to Iran, which in a way reduces India's influence in Iran and the region. With CPEC and now it is being extended to Afghanistan, India's interest would be further threatened, which will be an advantage for Pakistan. Overall, the BRI would inevitably lead to a geopolitical competition between India–China and Pakistan in Central Asia and South Asia and CPEC will be beneficial for China and Pakistan at the cost of India's interest. In a nutshell, CPEC is emerging as potential economic counterbalance to India and will enhance the China–Pakistan military ties against India. At the same time, CPEC is promoted by both the nations in South Asia to undermine India's geopolitical interest in the region.

3 CPEC: The Challenges

From time to time, the Chinese and Pakistani leaders have attempted to project the CPEC as a win–win situation. For instance, the Chinese ambassador to Pakistan Yao Jing (2018) stated "iron brother relations... will forge a new model of state-to-state relations, the project is projected to be complimentary to promoting people-to-people exchange, tourism, healthcare, agriculture and so on" (Chinoy, 2021, p. 4). Even the official website of CPEC also emphasizes that CPEC will boost the bilateral ties, promote socio-economic development, and improve connectivity (CPEC Portal, 2021d). Despite this, there are several challenges that threaten the success of CPEC, some of them are as follows

3.1 Security Concerns

For several decades, Pakistan continues to fight terrorism and religious extremism in the country, which also threatens the CPEC projects. For instance, there are several extremist outfits such as Tehreek-e-Taliban Pakistan (TTP), Lashkar E-Jhangvi, Daesh, Balochistan Lashkar E-Tayyiba, Liberation Front, East Turkestan Islamic movement (ETIM), United Baloch Army (UBA), and other militant wings of political parties. These groups operate from Xinjiang to Gwadar and have opposed CPEC on the grounds that Punjab province is given more preference over other provinces like Baluchistan which is the largest, least residential, and urbanized, but forms the main trade, connecting the Gwadar port with Kashgar city. Thus, the rebel groups believe that CPEC is threatening the sovereignty and could become urbanized, making it attractive for outsiders. In this regard, in recent times, several attacks at the gas pipelines and even on Chinese engineers have been perpetuated by the rebel groups. For example, in August 2018, a suicide bomb killed six people, in South-Western Pakistan of which three were Chinese engineers. Subsequently, in November 2018, the Chinese consulate in Karachi was targeted, but was prevented by the security forces, with minimum causalities. In order to address the security concerns, Pakistan has deployed 32,000 security personnel in Baluchistan and Sindhi province, dedicated only to protect CPEC and guard over more than 15,000 Chinese workers engaged in various projects concerning CPEC (Hameed, 2018, p. 7). Despite these measures, 14 July 2021, there was bomb attack targeting the Chinese workers at Dasu Hydro project killing 13 people of which nine were Chinese citizens. Again in August 2021, a suicide bomber injured Chinese workers, as a result, the Chinese embassy in Pakistan requested the Pakistan government to ensure the safety of its citizens by "undertaking effective measures and upgrade security cooperation mechanisms" (Krishnan, 2021, p. 11). Hence, ensuring the safety of the Chinese nationals continues to be a major challenge for Imran Khan's regime.

3.2 Opposition Within Pakistan

From time to time, some of the political parties and rebel groups in Pakistan have opposed CPEC projects like TTP (while they were in opposition), Baluchistan Liberation Front (BLF) and Daesh (ISIS); they have claimed that the projects will immensely benefit Punjab and Sind province and less for Baluchistan. Moreover, they argue that the exploitation of natural resources in Baluchistan is intended to benefit the elite and not the local population and Pakistan companies may not gain much due to high tax breaks and concessions given to Chinese companies (Anderlini et al., 2018). These arguments were retreated by Senator Tahir Mashhadi saying that the "[CPEC] another East India Company in the offering… and Pakistan's national interests are not being protected" (Amir, 2019).

In May 2017, the leading newspaper *Dawn* had reported that allowing China's involvement in Pakistan [in long term] would have vast repercussions on the agricultural supply chain and China would promote its culture and pitch for visa-free entry for the Chinese. However, apprehensions raised in the report were rejected by the then Nawaz Sharif government that it was "one sided and factually incorrect… there was definite angling in [the] story to malign CPEC by promoting fears" (Afzal, 2020, p. 3). Despite this, *Dawn* report continued to haunt the successive government. As a result, Imran Khan-led government, in August 2019, constituted a committee of nine members for power sector audit, circular debt reservation, and future roadmap. The committee submitted its report in April 2020 and emphasized that the Lahore-Matiari power transmission line project (US$ 1.7billion) was 234% expensive than a similar project in India, which had better technology as provided by a Swiss company and that some of the Chinese companies had inflated their set-up costs and it is also alleged that the Chinese contractors were overcharging Pakistan by US $3 billion to two CPEC power plants (Haq, 2019; Rana, 2020). But Imran Khan's government is yet to act on the recommendation of the report.

Some of the other allegations include—planning of CPEC being highly centralized with limited opportunities for consultation with the provincial government. Although a parliamentary committee was formed to ease the tensions in Baluchistan, not much consultation has been done so far and even the people and leaders of Gilgit-Baltistan province perceive that they have not got the due share in CPEC. Furthermore, no commercial shipping calls have been made at Gwadar; the Lahore metro project is considered as economically unviable, and Pakistan continues import materials worth billions of dollars for the projects.

Apart from this, the attacks on Chinese employees are becoming more regular; one of the reasons has been reports of Chinese trafficking of Pakistani women to China under the guise of marriage and forcing them into prostitution, with prices ranging from US$ 12,000 to US$ $25,000 per woman. According to reports from the Associated Press, there is an increase in the trafficking of Pakistani women who marry Chinese men. Overall, the claims and criticism levelled at CPEC continue, jeopardizing the project's prospects as a game changer for Pakistan's economy.

3.3 Increasing External Debts

Pakistan's external debt continues to affect the stability of the economy, and it is now regarded that it has increased due to CPEC. For instance, in June 2013, Pakistan's external debt was around US $44.35 billion of which it owned 9.3% to China. According to the IMF, the external debt has shot up to US $ 90.12 billion (April 2021) of which Pakistan owns US $24.7 billion to China; CPEC-related investment and loans would amount to US$ 3.5 billion (2024–2025) (Younus, 2021). On similar lines, some of the media report, "Pakistan external debt and liabilities stood at US$110 billion (March 2020), an increasing of US$ 3.6 billion in the first nine months of FY 2020" (Chinoy, 2021, p. 19). Thus, the growing external debts due to CPEC is the key concern for Pakistan, but it is also argued that unlike the IMF/World Bank/ADB, China does not fiddle/influence in the economic policies of Pakistan, thereby giving a breathing space to the Pakistani government. With the pandemic, Pakistan has already requested China to allow a delayed repayment and a time period of a decade so that the interest loan is reduced; China has responded positively to a certain extent.

3.4 Other Concerns

Both the governments are yet to resolve irritants over the tax issues, electricity price and power tariff and reduction in tariff on renewable energy. Further delay in negotiations will have negative effects on CPEC projects. Even the critiques of projects have pointed out that the Chinese funding is not to be seen as aids, but as a loan and other forms of financing that is non-concessional with profit guarantees for Chinese state-owned enterprises. At the same time, the Chinese investors and companies have also raised concerns that Pakistan follows unclear and arbitrary policies in several sectors, often not receiving a proactive support from the Imran government. Hence, some of the projects are delayed; there have been reports of corruption, despite the presence of security forces; regular terrorist attacks on Chinese workers continue; and CPEC projects have slowed down due to procedural delays. Thus, in order to address these concerns, Pakistan's government has also set up a "CPEC Authority" mainly to implement the projects on fast track, though some of the issues still persist from the Chinese point of view. Overall, peace, security, and stability continue to be the vital factors for the success of CPEC.

4 India's BRI Conundrum

India's resistance to the BRI and CPEC is louder and more conspicuous than those advocating for India's participation in the BRI. India's concerns, however, are as follows.

4.1 Security Concerns

Security concerns have been the driving force behind India's opposition to the BRI in general and the CPEC in particular. For instance, China's ambitious plan to connect its Xinjiang autonomous region with Baluchistan Province (in Pakistan), which passes through the part of Jammu and Kashmir (J&K) known as Pakistan-occupied Kashmir, undermines India's sovereignty and is further threatened with the presence of both Chinese and Pakistani security forces in POK to protect CPEC projects (Singh, 2017, p. 2). Moreover, both India and Pakistan have yet to recognize the existing Line of Control (LOC) as the international border, which, if done, would validate the CPEC projects in J&K and diminish India's long-standing claim during negotiations with Pakistan. Union Minister for External Affairs Muraleedharan reaffirmed this position in February 2020, saying: "CPEC as a flagship project of BRI, directly impinges on the issue of sovereignty and territorial integrity of India … and government has conveyed its concerns to the Chinese side about their activities in areas illegally occupied by Pakistan in the Union Territories of J&K and Ladakh and has asked them to cease such activities" (Ministry of External Affairs, 2017a).

The development of Gwadar Port, a vital component of CPEC, poses a maritime threat to India, as the corridor will not only boost Sino-Pak military ties, but also enhance naval cooperation and challenge India's maritime dominance in the Indian Ocean. Furthermore, China's Maritime Silk Route (MSR) would strengthen its regional presence and footprint in nations such as Sri Lanka, the Maldives, Myanmar, Bangladesh, and Pakistan (Chung, 2018). India's policymakers and strategists see this as an encircling or "stings of pearls" approach. However, China has rejected the charge, claiming that it is a matter of energy security (70% of its oil imports), refuelling, economic purposes, and sea lane security, rather than an attempt to control India in the region. These arguments, however, have not persuaded India, and they pose a threat to India's future naval force projects and regional dominance. Furthermore, being an energy-dependent country, India has big ambitions to supply its needs from the Central Asian region. India's energy hunt has been aided by China's completion of the CPEC, which extends to Afghanistan and seizes chances in Central Asia. Thus, India believes the BRI projects are unclear, and it is dissatisfied with the unilateral decisions taken without input.

4.2 BRI—Is It a Debt Trap?

Apart from its resistance to CPEC, India is also concerned about BRI which is leading to a possible debt trap of smaller nations and neighbouring countries. Apparently, countries like Ukraine, Zimbabwe, Cambodia, Pakistan, and Sri Lanka are struggling to pay back the debts it owns to China. One of the IMF reports in 2016, highlighted that Cambodia owned US$ 3.9 billion bilateral public debts, of which it owns 80% to China (Singh, 2017, p. 2). As part of the BRI, Sri Lanka got significant Chinese funding and was unable to repay its debts; as a result, the Sri Lankan government surrendered the Hambantota port (which China owns 70%) to a Chinese corporation for 99 years in December 2017 (Darshana, 2018). In this context, India is concerned that a similar situation could develop in Pakistan, as China's percentage of Pakistan's total debt is increasing rapidly. Some Chinese leaders and policymakers, however, counter the narrative by claiming that the debts are less than 10% of Pakistan's total debts, and even the Pakistan Foreign Office (May 2020) stated that debt in CPEC-related projects is less than 10% of total public debts, and defended that such projects have "helped to address development gaps in energy, infrastructure, industrialization, and job creation" (Press Trust of India, 2020). At the same time, studies show that Sri Lanka's external obligations to China amount to less than 6% of its GDP, with the rest owed to multilateral institutions and nations such as Japan. The same may be said for Nepal and the Maldives (Pal, 2021). Nonetheless, India's warnings about the debt trap are supported by a number of news reports and studies conducted by Western governments on the possibility for Chinese businesses to take over infrastructure projects or get access to natural resources in host countries. Such occurrences would damage the economy and have a significant impact on local communities, as host countries are frequently unable to repay their massive debts. Prime Minister Narendra Modi (July 2020) underlined this as well; he warned that neighbours should avoid debt-trap diplomacy of China and stated that "historically, nations were being forced into dependence partnerships in the name of development partnerships. This in turn had given rise to colonial and imperial rule and humanity suffered" (Bhaumik, 2020, p. 1).

4.3 Other Concerns

In addition to the foregoing, there are additional major issues, including: (a) India has followed the same path as Europe and the US in terms of the BRI, namely, lack of transparency and non-compliance with the rule of law and good governance standards. The Ministry of External Affairs (MEA) voiced these concerns in 2018; "we are of the firm belief that connectivity initiatives must be based on universally recognised international norms, openness and equality, and must be pursued in a manner that respects sovereignty and territorial integrity" (Ministry of External Affairs, 2018). (b) India has contended that the BRI was a unilateral decision by

China, with no opportunity for consultation [with India] prior to its introduction to address its security concerns. As a result, people who are investing in BRI are still unclear. However, because it is said that 90% of the investment comes from Chinese banks and enterprises, India is wary and cautious. (c) India has traditionally seen the South Asian region as its sphere of influence, and any other player challenging India's interests has caused it uneasy. However, as China's impact in the area grows—politically, economically, culturally, and militarily, and now through BRI—the three primary corridors—CPEC, BCIM, the Trans-Himalayan Economic Corridor, have direct impact on India's economic and security interests. As a result, India views Chinese developments in the region as a broad strategy to confine and challenge India, rather than as economic undertakings. (d) Given China's opposition to blocking India's membership in multilateral organizations such as the Nuclear Suppliers Group (NSG), becoming a permanent member of the UNSC, Asia–Pacific Economic Cooperation (APEC), and imposing United Nations (UN) sanctions on Pakistan-based terror outfits, among other things, but expecting India to endorse BRI or cooperate on CPEC projects is not fair. As a result, India seeks to use its opposition as a bargaining chip with China in order to address its concerns about the BRI/CPEC.

5 India's Response

India's response to BRI, in general, and CPEC, in particular, can be summarized as follows.

5.1 Expressed Its Concerns

India has not been shy in expressing its concerns about the consequences of the BRI for India and the area (South Asia and the Indian Ocean), and has highlighted these issues at most multilateral meetings/forums. Prime Minister Modi, for example, discussed CPEC issues during the 2015 BRICS and SCO summits. India maintained its momentum by refusing to sign the BRI joint declaration at the 2018 SCO summits, and Prime Minister Modi added that India embraces connectivity both within and outside the region "which are sustainable and efficient and which respect territorial integrity and sovereignty of the countries" (Sengupta, 2018, p. 1). More recently, India's representative Priyanka Sohoni stated at the second UN Global Sustainable Transport Conference (October 2021) that "inclusion of the so-called CPEC as a flagship project impinges on India's sovereignty and no country can support an initiative that ignores its core concerns of sovereignty and territorial integrity" (*The Hindustan Times*, 2021). She also stated that China must adhere to openness, transparency, and fiscal responsibility ideals. Furthermore, the ramifications of the BRI are conveyed in joint statements even at bilateral meetings. In June 2017, for example, during bilateral meetings between India and the US, a joint declaration called for greater transparency, responsible debt financing processes, respect for sovereignty and territorial integrity, and adherence to universal values (Darshana, 2018, p. 7). In a similar spirit, the joint statement issued after the India–Japan bilateral meeting in September 2017 stressed the importance "quality infrastructure and safety, resilience, social and environmental impacts and job creation"(Ministry of External Affairs, 2017b), Although, China extended invitation to India to attend the successive BRI summits (May2017 and April 2019), unlike countries like the US, Australia, and some of the EU nations who sent their representatives (despite reservation over BRI) for the Summit, India rejected the invitation and did not even send any representative continuing to keep the pressure on China.

5.2 Countering MSR/BRI

India has made measures to resist MSR and BRI from time to time. For example, in May 2016, India, Iran, and Russia announced an agreement to launch the International North–South Corridor (INSTC), an ambitious trilateral corridor project with the primary goal of developing Iran's Chabahar port with a US $500 million initial investment. The port's expansion was strategically important for India's energy and economic interests., i.e., (a) connect West Asia and Central Asia; and provide opportunities for Indian businessmen (from Kandla, Kochin, Mumbai) to export to Iran, Afghanistan, and also Central Asia and even European markets in the long run (Conference Proceedings, 2016). (b) reduce dependence on Pakistan's land route to export to Afghanistan and Central Asia countries. Moreover, the Chabahar port is less than 80 km from Gwadar Port, focal point for BRI core projects, thus enabling India to move close to Gwadar port. (c) Given that the basic infrastructure in Chabahar port was already developed, India was expected to invest minimum, and not as China did to develop Gwadar port. Keeping these benefits, the project INSTC was developed on a faster scale, as a result, India was able to ship wheat to Afghanistan through Chabahar port in October 2017 and again in May 2020. Thus, INSTC has emerged as successful investment for India in recent times and Chabahar port as India's Oceanic gateway to Central Asian region (Wagner & Tripathi, 2018, p. 3).

To counter China's Maritime Silk Route (Chung, 2018), India has made significant efforts to strengthen its long-standing ties with the Indian Ocean's littoral, including bilateral visits by Prime Minister Modi (since 2015) and the launch of flagship projects such as Mausam in 2014, with aim to "explore the multi-faceted Indian Ocean 'world'–collating archaeological and historical research in order to document the diversity of cultural, commercial and religious interactions in the Indian Ocean" (Press Information Bureau, 2017). The Modi government's project like *Mausam* is argued as a cultural one, primarily initiated by the Union Ministry of Culture and implemented by the Archaeological Survey of India (ASI) as the nodal agency with research support of the Indira Gandhi National Centre for the Arts (IGNCA) and National Museum as associate bodies. However, it also attempts to limit

Chinese influence in the Indian Ocean region, as once a place receives a UNSECO heritage tag, no other country (including China) may interfere with the project. Ironically, since its commencement, the Mausam project has made only a fraction of the progress predicted at the time of its inception. On the other hand, China has made greater headway in forging relationships with countries in the Indian Ocean region, leveraging its status as an Observer member of the Indian Ocean Rim Association (IORA). During a visit to Mauritius in March 2015, Prime Minister Modi proposed the SAGAR project (security and growth for all in the region). The idea's main goals were to protect marine interests, stimulate more economic activity, take collective action to address common challenges in the region, ensure rule of law prevails through peaceful conflict settlement, and create trust among the region's littoral states. At the UNSC debate on Maritime Security (May 2021), Modi reaffirmed SAGAR's vision. Modi also announced Mission SAGAR as part of Vision SAGAR, which provides aid to littoral states in the region in the fight against COVID-19. Ironically, SAGAR, like Mausam, has yet to realize its objectives.

Generally, the Asia–Africa Growth Corridor (AAGC) was seen as a game changer or a counter to the BRI, which was launched jointly by India and Japan in May 2017 as a vision document. This corridor focussed on connecting Asia and Africa through development projects, building critical infrastructure, promoting people-to-people and institutional contacts (Singh, 2017, p. 6). AAGC is described by many Indian academics and policymakers as a hybrid of India's Act East Policy and Japan's ambition of connecting Asia and Africa. Unfortunately, the AAGC has made little progress, and it now does not even appear in the successive joint statement issued by the two countries at bilateral meetings. Overall, India is making genuine attempts to guarantee its strategic interests in the region, but unlike China, it is failing to carry out ambitious programmes to their logical conclusion.

6 Conclusion

Given India's limited ability to challenge or prevent countries from joining the BRI at this time, some policy alternatives for India include the following:

- Former Foreign Secretary Shyam Sharan correctly observes that "it's worth giving a chance to BRI, given that India do not have capacity to provide an alternative in either scale or scope on the grounds that it might help India to regain some cultural and strategic leverage by advancing its own SAGAR mala project and cotton and spice routes via the MSR" (Kumar, 2019, p. 39) Thus, India can think of engaging with China on BRI, before it formally decides to send a representative to the BRI Summit.
- India should not compromise on its sovereignty claims in J&K, but it should consider taking a more selective approach to the BRI project outside the South Asian region, particularly in Central Asia and the Middle East, such as connecting Afghanistan and Iran, which will benefit India's energy and economic interests.

- China's influence in the region has grown since the 1990s; aside from India's own policy mistakes, neighbouring countries have also backed China's presence as a counterbalance to India. In this scenario, India's refusal to join the BRI is neither a response nor a plan. The BRI has attracted international backing, including from adversaries such as the United States, Australia, and European countries. As a result, India must accept reality and begin discussions on identifying areas of mutual interest in the BRI.
- Many Indian critics have argued that India and China may be economic partners because they have a common position/strategy on global commons and are founding members of the New Development Bank (NDB) and Asian Infrastructure Investment Banks (AIIB), which have boosted South-South cooperation. Furthermore, with both nations having the capacity to make important contributions to integrating South Asia and Central Asia, India needs to reconsider its blanket approach to the BRI. At the same time, India must insist on transparency in both the BRI and the CPEC to ensure that China does not exert undue influence on Pakistan.
- The twenty-first century is regarded as 'Asia Century' due to the peaceful rise of India, China, Japan and other Asian countries. Thus, both India and China have a critical role to play in maintaining this trend, and they must engage with one another on global commons as well as issues relating to the BRI and CPEC. As a result, sustaining constructive relations with China is necessary for economic and regional stability.
- India should recognise that having an unstable Pakistan, as well as its inability to repay Chinese debts, will lead to a surge in religious extremism, as well as severe national security challenges to both China and India. As a result, India should engage with Pakistan and make efforts to address its reservations over the CPEC. Pakistan should also oblige in the interest of region and its own economic growth.
    - Overall, the study suggests that in this situation, India must reconsider its approaches and policies towards CPEC, and China must resolve India's concerns in order for both countries to participate in the BRI. At the same time, economic expansion of Pakistan through CPEC will be beneficial for both India and China and also to the region. Due to the lack of a field visit to Pakistan or China to collect primary data and interview policymakers, scholars, and stakeholders of CPEC, the study's comprehensive viewpoint of CPEC and its implications for India has been limited. Nevertheless, there is still scope for further research, such as (a) analysing the major CPEC projects in terms of actual investment, employment, and outcomes. (b) finding areas {within or outside BRI} of bilateral and trilateral cooperation among the three to improve relations benefit the people of the region through CPEC.

Bibliographic References

Afzal, M. (2020, June). *At all costs: How Pakistan and China control the narrative on the China Pakistan Economic Corridor*, p. 6. Retrieved in December 2021, from https://www.brookings.edu/research/at-all-costs-how-pakistan-and-china-control-the-narrative-on-the-china-pakistan-economic-corridor/

Ahmad, R., Mi, H., & Fernald, L. W. (2020). Revisiting the potential security threat slinked with the CPEC. *Journal of the Internal Council for Small Business, 1*(1), 64–80.

Allauddin, Liu, H., & Ahmed, R. Q. (2020). The changing dynamics and new developments of China-Pakistan relations. *India Quarterly, 76*(1), 73–88.

Amir, A. (2019, February 15). The Baluchistan insurgency and the threat to Chinese interests in Pakistan. *China Brief, 19*(4) [online]. Retrieved in December 2021, from https://jamestown.org/program/the-balochistan-insurgency_and-the-threat-to-chinese-interests-in-pakistan/

Anderlini, J., Sender, H., & Bokhari, F. (2018, September 9). Pakistan rethinks its role in Xi's belt and road plan. *Financial Times*. Retrieved in December 2021, from https://www.ft.com/content/d4a3e7f8-b282-11e8-99ca_68cf89602132

Aziz, S. (2019, June 12). Can China solve Pakistan's energy crisis? *The Diplomat*. Retrieved in December 2021, from https://thediplomat.com/2019/06/can-china-solve-pakistans-energy_crisis/

Bhaumik, A. (2020, July 31). India subtly warns Nations of China's debt trap diplomacy. *Deccan Herald*, p. 1.

Chinoy, S. R. (2021). *China-Pakistan Economic Corridor (CPEC) the project and its prospects*. IDSA Occasional Paper, No. 58, 1–45.

Chung, C.-P. (2018). What are the strategic and economic implications for South Asia of China's maritime silk road initiative? *The Pacific Review, 31*(3), 315–332.

Conference Proceedings. (2016, December 18–19). *International relations conference: India and Indian Ocean: Sustainability, security and development*, Symbiosis International University, Pune. Retrieved in December 2021, from http://www.irconference.in/assets/archive16/IRC%20Report.pdf, p. 43

CPEC Portal. (2021a). *CPEC facts vs fiction*. Retrieved in December 2021a, from http://cpecinfo.com/cpec-facts-vs-fiction/

CPEC Portal. (2021b). *CPEC: A gateway to prosperity*, at http://www.cpec.gov.pk

CPEC Portal. (2021c). *Progress on CPEC*. Retrieved in December 2021c, from http://cpecinfo.com/latest-progress-on-cpec/

CPEC Portal. (2021d). *10 fundamentals of CPEC*. Retrieved in December 2021d, from http://cpecinfo.com/10-questions-on-cpec/

Darshana, B. M (2018, August 21). *India's answer to the belt and road: Road map for South Asia*. Retrieved in November 2021, from https://carnegieindia.org/2018/08/21/india-s-answer-to-belt-and-road-map-for-south-asia-pub-77071

Global Times. (2021, July 29). Pakistan could overtake India in trade with China in eight years: Official. Retrieved in December 2021, from https://www.globaltimes.cn/page/202107/1230056.shtml#:~:text=In%202020%2C%20the%20total%20trade,from%20the%20Ministry%20of%20Commerce.

Hameed, M. (2018). The politics of China-Pakistan economic corridor. *Palgrave Communications, 4*(64), 1–10.

Haq, S. (2019, August 18). Govt forms committee for power-sector audit. *The Express Tribune* (Islamabad). Retrieved in December 2021, from https://tribune.com.pk/story/2036265/govt-forms-committee-power-sector-audit

Inter Services Public Relations. (2018, September 19). *General Qamar Javed Bajwa, Chief of Army Staff (COAS) called on Chinese President Xi Jinping on special invitation*. Retrieved in December 2021, from https://www.ispr.gov.pk/press-release-detail.php?id=4940

Khursheed, A., Haider, S. K., Mustafa, F., & Akhtar, A. (2019). China-Pakistan economic corridor: A Harbinger of economic prosperity and regional peace. *Asian Journal of German and European Studies, 4*(1), 1–15.

Krishnan, A. (2021, August 21). Suicide bombing casts doubt on China's Pakistan projects. *The Hindu*, p. 11

Kumar, S. Y. S. (2019). China's belt and road initiative: India's concerns, responses and strategies. *International Journal of China Studies, 10*(1), 27–45.

Ministry of External Affairs, Government of India. (2017a, May 13). *Official spokesperson's response to a query on participation of India in OBOR/BRI forum*. Retrieved in December 2021, from https://mea.gov.in/media-briefings.htm?dtl/28463/Official+Spokespersons+response+to+a+query+on+participation+of+India+in+OBORBRI+Forum

Ministry of External Affairs, Government of India. (2017b, September 14). *India-Japan joint statement during visit of Prime Minister of Japan to India*. Retrieved in December 2021, from https://www.mea.gov.in/bilateral-documents.htm?dtl/28946/IndiaJapan_Joint_Statement_during_visit_of_Prime_Minister_of_Japan_to_India_September_14_2017b

Ministry of External Affairs, Government of India. (2018, April 5). *Official spokesperson's response to a query on media reports regarding possible cooperation with China on OBOR/BRI*. Retrieved in December 2021, from https://www.mea.gov.in/mediabriefings.htm?dtl/29768/Official+Spokespersons+response+to+a+query+on+media+reports+regarding+possible+cooperation+with+China+on+OBORBRI

Pal, D. (2021, October 13). *China's influence in South Asia: Vulnerabilities and resilience in four countries*. Retrieved in December 2021, from https://carnegieendowment.org/2021/10/13/china-s-influence-in-south-asia-vulnerabilities-and-resilience-in-four-countries-pub-85552

Pande, A. (2011). *Explaining Pakistan's: Foreign policy*. Routledge.

Patranobis, S. (2019, April 27). Pak, China to begin CPEC second phase meet, says Imran Khan in Beijing. *The Hindustan Times*. Retrieved in December 2021, from https://www.hindustantimes.com/world-news/pak-china-to-begin-cpec-second-phase-meet-says-imran-khan-in-beijing-as-india-stays-away/story-OzKQMe3ynAywhiYuAzw6GP.html

Press Information Bureau. (2017, July 24). *Project Mausam*. Ministry of Culture, Government of India. Retrieved in December 2021, from http://pib.nic.in/newsite/PrintRelease.aspx?relid=168923

Press Release. (2018, December 12). *Power sector distortions cost Pakistan billions*. Retrieved in December 2021, from https://www.worldbank.org/en/news/press-release/2018/12/11/power-sector-distortions-cost-pakistan-billions

Press Trust of India. (2020, May 22). *Pak says debt in CPEC—Related projects is just 10%, rejects US concern*. Retrieved in December 2021, from https://www.business-standard.com/article/pti-stories/pak-says-debt-in-cpec-related-projects-is-just-10-rejects-us-concern-120052200937_1.html

Priyanka, S. (2017). India's participation in CPEC: The Ifs and buts. *IDSA Issue Brief*, 17 February, 1–9.

Rana, S. (2020, April 21). Umar wants explosive power sector inquiry made public. *The Express Tribune*. Retrieved in November 2021, from https://tribune.com.pk/story/2203143/2-umar_wants-explosive-power-sector-inquiry-made-public

Sengupta, R. (2018, June 10). Modi rules out joining China's mega belt and road initiative. *The New Indian Express*, p. 1

Sharif, N., & Rabbani, R. (2015). *Full text of President Xi Jinping's speech to the joint session of parliament in Pakistan*. Retrieved in December 2021, from http://issi.org.pk/wp-content/uploads/2015/07/Pak-China_Year_of_Friendly_Exchange_Doc-1.docx.pdf

Singh, K., & Kumar, A. (2017). Unpacking China's white paper on maritime cooperation under BRI. *IDSA Issue Brief*, 28 June, 1–10.

The Hindustan Times. (2021, October 20). Technical glitch' hits India's strong response to China-led BRI at UN meet, p. 1

Wagner, C., & Tripathi, S. (2018). India's response to the Chinese belt and road initiative. *SWP Comment No., 7*(January), 1–4.
Younus, U. (2021, May 26). Pakistan's growing problem with its China economic corridor. *USIP Analysis and Commentary*. Retrieved in December 2021, from https://www.usip.org/publications/2021/05/pakistans-growing-problem-its-china-economic-corridor

Chapter 29
China in Latin America: To BRI or not to BRI

Ana Tereza L. Marra de Sousa⃝, Giorgio Romano Schutte⃝, Rafael Almeida F. Abrão⃝, and Valéria Lopes Ribeiro⃝

1 Introduction

The launch of the *One Belt, One Road project* in 2013 caused concern in LAC. The subcontinent had no relationship with the history of the ancient Silk Road, and the question was whether this could mean a reduction in the importance that China was giving to LAC in favour of prioritizing investments in Eurasia and Africa. The initiative expanded its scope and dropped the reference to "one" belt, being renamed in March 2015 to Belt and Road Initiative (BRI). The BRI expanded its horizons from a geographical point of view to potentially cover any country interested in signing a Memorandum of Understanding and was increasingly seen as the main vehicle for introducing globalization with Chinese characteristics. It also opened the range of activities, while maintaining the focus on physical infrastructure, to be able to include investments in other sectors, provided that it involves Chinese companies and financing.

In recent years, BRI has begun to be identified more and more with the overall global expansion of Chinese capital and foreign policy (Rolland, 2019). Pre-existing projects, even those already executed, were included in BRI (Jones & Zeng, 2019). In this context, it is not surprising that Chinese diplomacy has begun to seek the formal integration of its Latin American partners in the initiative. In any case, as we will explore in this chapter, most Latin American countries were incorporated into the BRI model, with or without formal membership. Countries like Brazil or Argentina, which did not join the initiative, remained a priority for Chinese expansion (Dreyer, 2019). This model will be presented in three sections, exploring the quantitative data, and reviewing existing literature for each section. In the first section, we offer an overview of the growing Chinese economic presence in LAC. This presence created opportunities for LAC countries, despite the asymmetries and

A. T. L. M. de Sousa (✉) · G. R. Schutte · R. A. F. Abrão · V. L. Ribeiro
Federal University ABC, Santo André, Brazil

complexity of relations. In the second section, we will discuss the political relationships that have been established between China and LAC countries. China operates following objectives and long-term goals related to the expansion of its influence as a political actor, while LAC countries' strategy is mainly focused on overcoming short-term challenges. Three specific challenges in China´s relation with LAC will be highlighted. First, the difficulties in establishing a regional articulation mechanism with LAC. Second, the potential for dispute with the US. And, third, the Chinese Taipei issue. The third section will present four case studies: Brazil, Chile, Ecuador, and Panama. The last three are members of the BRI, and Panama is one of the countries that recently exchanged Chinese Taipei's diplomatic recognition for that of the People's Republic of China (PRC). Chile is part of the Pacific Alliance and the Asia–Pacific Economic Cooperation (APEC), while Ecuador, at the time when the country began to receive Chinese investments and financing in 2010, was a member of the Bolivarian Alliance for the Peoples of Our America (Alba). Brazil, although it did not join the BRI, is the country with the largest Chinese presence and was the first country in the world to establish a Strategic Partnership with China in 1993. Thus the four countries can be seen as a representative cut of LAC diversity. In the country analysis, the focus is again on the combination of the political and economic dimensions, while attention is paid to the changes in these dynamics over the years. The final section offers some preliminary conclusions.

Most of the literature on the BRI focuses on Asia, Africa, and Europe in many cases with no mention of the LAC. Recently several contributions were made especially by Latin American authors (Myers, 2018; Pires, 2020; Jauregui, 2020) mostly focusing on a single-specific dimension. This chapter presents an integrated approach, combing the economic data with political analyses and discussing the BRI in the light of the overall expansion of Chinese presence in the region considering simultaneously Chinese, LAC, and US interests.

2 Chinese Economic Expansion in Latin America

The Chinese presence in LAC takes place mainly on four fronts that have expanded at different rates: trade, financing, Foreign Direct Investment (FDI), and infrastructure projects. This mix is composed differently in each country in the region. Thus, for example, in 2019 Venezuela ranks first in terms of stock of financing from Chinese banks and state funds, while Brazil is the country that attracts the most FDI. Economic relations between China and LAC deepened strongly in the 2010s. As shown in Fig. 1, China's share in the region's exports went from just over 1% in 1995 to 12% of the total exported in 2019. In the same year, imports also grew, corresponding to 18% of the total imported. As a result, trade reached USD 324 billion, with a regional trade deficit with China of USD 68 billion, despite Brazil's expressive surplus (USD 20 billion).

By 2020, China had established free trade agreements with Chile, Costa Rica, and Peru was in the process of negotiating an agreement with Panama and was studying

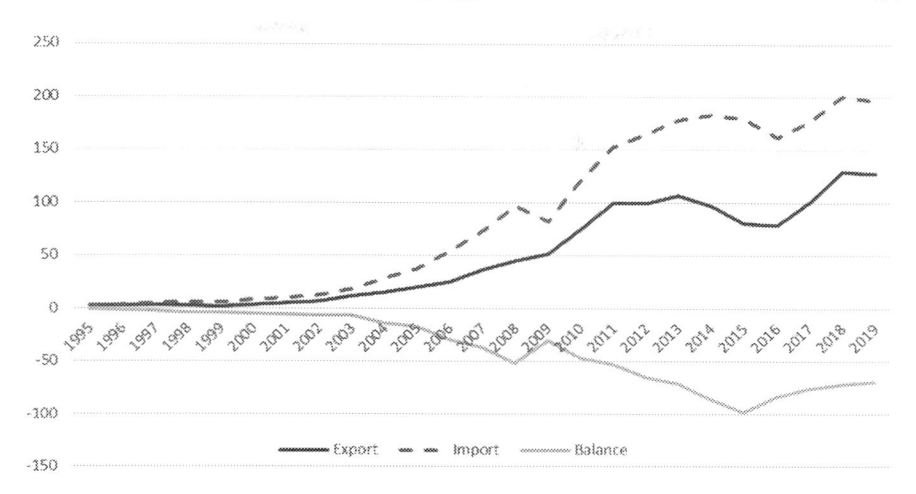

Fig. 1 Latin America and the Caribbean—exports to and imports from China (1995–2019) in billions of US dollars

the feasibility of an agreement with Colombia (Casas et al., 2020). In addition, state-owned companies, integrated into BRI, are making investments with the support of Chinese state-owned banks, either through participation in public service concessions or as FDI. With this, China is making a significant contribution to the expansion of infrastructure in the region and, along with that, to the exploitation of natural resources. Between 2005 and 2019, there were 86 infrastructure projects carried out by Chinese companies in LAC, totalling USD 76.8 billion. Most of these projects are energy and transport: 89% in value and 71% in number of projects (Peters, 2020, p. 8). Regarding FDI flows classified by China Global Investment Tracker as part of the BRI in LAC between 2013 and 2019 operations in South America and Central America, these add up to a total of US$ 54.7 billion. Of this total, 39.9% are in the energy sector and 35.8% in the metals sector, with 13% in transport. The biggest investment is Peru, which accounts for 36.41% of the total FDI via BRI in LAC; followed by Chile, with 16.47% of the total; and Venezuela with 14.86% (China Global Investment Tracker, 2020).

The financing of these projects was mainly the responsibility of the China Development Bank (CDB) and Exim Bank, the same ones that oversee the global financing of the BRI projects. In LAC, they were responsible for almost US$140 billion in loans in the period between 2005 and 2020. This volume was higher than the portfolios of the World Bank and the Inter-American Development Bank (IDB) (Gallagher and Myers, 2020). In the case of smaller economies, in particular Bolivia and Ecuador, the impact of these projects is very significant. In addition to oil, there was also a strong interest in projects related to lithium, a strategic item for the electrification of individual transport, with around 75% of its global reserves located in South America (Pires, 2020). One feature of Chinese operations in infrastructure is the mounting of specific funds. In Latin America, it established the

CLAI Fund (China Latin American Investment Fund for Industrial Cooperation and the CLAC Fund (China Latin American Cooperation Fund), with the participation of the China Development Bank (CDB), China Exim Bank, and the State Administration of Foreign Exchange (SAFE). These funds were created in the period 2014–2015, with an announced funding capacity of US$ 40—US$55 billion, mainly, but not exclusively, in infrastructure projects. CLAI Fund was approved by the Chinese State Cabinet in June 2015, but the concrete investments were less than expected and were mainly to support Chinese companies, for example, the acquisition of hydroelectric Paraná and assets of Duke Energy in Brazil by the *China Three Gorges* (CTG) (Rosito, 2020). In addition to the three regional funds, a specific project was created for Brazil. In June 2017 the China–Brazil Cooperation Fund for the Expansion of Production Capacity capitalized at US$ 20 billion. Although announced on several occasions, this Fund was never operationalized (idem). Likewise, is worth mentioning is the region's involvement in Chinese initiatives to set up the Asian Infrastructure Investment Bank (AIIB), a multilateral development bank created by China in 2015, designed to finance infrastructure to the benefit and connectivity of Asia. Argentina, Brazil, Chile, Ecuador, and Uruguay were AIIB shareholders as of 27 July 2021, while Bolivia, Peru, and Venezuela at that time were *nonregional prospective members*, awaiting ratification of membership. Brazil was a founding member of the BRICS-related New Development Bank (Asia Infrastructure Investment Bank, 2021). This complex web of investment and financing mechanisms at the bilateral, regional, and multilateral levels raised concerns in the US. "This multi-layer financing has weakened the ability of the US and of and multilateral organizations to influence LAC governments' behavior" (US–China Economic and Security Review Commission, 2018).

China generated great expectations by limiting the financial vulnerability of the region and expanding the limits of existing financing structures. Further, we should note the downsizing of the infrastructure portfolio by traditional financing banks, IDB and World Bank (Gallagher & Myers, 2020). Notwithstanding the difficulties in operationalizing the projects in the quantity and at the speed desired by both parties, they benefitted from the fact that several financing actors of the region had since 2000 been organizing themselves to generate a portfolio of infrastructure projects. Originally, the financing of the projects would be the responsibility of IDB, the Development Bank of Latin America (CAF), and Brazil's National Development Bank (BNDES). Several of these projects that had been complemented, or not even started, entered into negotiations with Chinese banks and funds (Pires, 2020).

China also established investment agreements with 12 countries in the region (CEPAL, 2019). More than 50% of Chinese investment stock in LAC was directed to the energy sector (Petrol & Gas and electricity), with mining (30%) in second place (Peters, 2019). The share of energy in the portfolio is mainly due to operations in Brazil. The LAC without Brazil shows mining in the first place. The role played by Huawei and ZTE in the expansion and modernization of telecommunications should also be noted. These investments also provoked concern on the part of the US. Bernal-Meza (2016) challenged the thesis of a *win–win relationship* -

often claimed by representatives of Chinese governments and companies when characterizing the China-LAC relationship. The author believes it is advantageous for everyone, but more for some than for others.

In the second half of the 2010 decade the flow of investment and financing stabilized. For Peters (2019), Chinese companies entered a period of consolidation of their operations. He forecast an increase in Chinese investments in the service sectors and, to a lesser extent, in manufacturing. Furthermore, the trend would be for an increase in the participation of private companies. The pandemic caused a widespread reduction in investment and financing, with consequences felt by the LAC, but there are still expectations regarding a focused growth in the Chinese presence in the region in a post-pandemic future (Cariello, 2021).

3 Chinese Diplomacy and Political-Institutional Relations

The Chinese preference for the construction of multilateral spaces in which the main rules of the game are bilateral also applied to LAC (Rosito, 2020). China is betting on the Community of Latin American and Caribbean States (CELAC), formalized in December 2011, to provide the framework for articulation with the 33 LAC countries. During Xi Jinping´s visit to the region in 2014, the Forum China—CELAC (CCF) was created with the Chinese-style formula 1 + 3 + 6 Cooperation Framework. In this case, "1" refers to the China-CELAC *Joint Plan of Action for Cooperation on Priority Areas*. "3" are the drivers of cooperation: trade, investment, and finance. And "6," the priority areas: energy and resources, infrastructure construction, agriculture, manufacturing, scientific and technological innovation, and information technologies (IT).

In 2009, China's State Council published *China's Policy Paper on Latin America and the Caribbean*, in which it suggested South–South cooperation: "The development of China cannot be possible without the development of other Developing Countries, including Latin America and the Caribbean" (LAC Policy Paper, 2009). Alongside the CCF, the policy paper placed the institutional frameworks for deepening cooperation to reproduce the institutional experience that China had with Africa (Vadell, 2018). The first CCF ministerial meeting took place in Beijing in 2015. However, Brazilian diplomacy maintained its preference for negotiating with China bilaterally, diminishing the importance of the CCF as an instrument of regional articulation, and rejecting any formulation in the Summit Declaration that affirmed the region's adhesion to the BRI. Thus, it has been through bilateral negotiations that China has sought the accession of LAC to the BRI. By the end of 2020, 19 countries had joined.[1] However, these did not include the four major economies in the region in terms of Gross Domestic Product (Brazil, Mexico, Argentina, and Colombia). At

---

[1] Antigua and Barbuda, Barbados, Bolivia, Chile, Costa Rica, Cuba, Dominica, Dominican Republic, Ecuador, El Salvador, Grenade, Guyana, Jamaica, Panama, Peru, Surinam, Trinidad and Tobago Uruguay, Venezuela.

the same time, China has developed other ways of structuring its cooperation at the regional level by joining existing organizations such as the Caribbean Development Bank (CDB) and the IDB (2009). The country gained observer status at the Organization of American States (2004), the Latin America Parliament (2004), and the Pacific Alliance (2013) (Jauregui, 2020). In the diplomatic sphere, new strategic partnerships were established (Bolivia, Costa Rica, and Uruguay). In the case of Brazil, it was upgraded to "Global Comprehensive Strategic Partner." These names have nebulous meanings, but Li and Vicente (2020) conclude that the greater the number of words, the greater the importance and the comprehensiveness of the partnership. Another feature of the country's strategy of expanding its influence is the value given to high-level meetings, with several visits to President Xi Jinping's region in 2013, 2014, 2016, and 2018 (Rosito, 2020). LAC countries understood the importance of accepting China´s political initiatives to take advantage of economic opportunities. Left-wing nationalist governments were also interested in approaching China to show greater autonomy from the US, something that remained in the case of Venezuela.

The challenge was above all to understand this new actor who gained importance in a short space of time. The Economic Commission for Latin America and the Caribbean (ECLAC) began providing analysis on Latin America's strategies towards China with a series of publications and tracking data on investment, trade, and finance.[2] These documents show the concern with commercial asymmetry and the deepening of the region as a supplier of raw materials. In the case of the BRI, smaller economies understood formal participation as a window of opportunity that could provide access to new funds and attract investments. In any case, with or without a Memorandum of Understanding (MoU), all LAC countries have high expectations regarding the potential of investments in infrastructure in railways, ports, roads, airports, ultra-high-voltage lines, maritime cables, and communication networks, in particular 5G (Pires, 2020).

LAC is considered, however, to be an area of US influence, the famous *backyard*. China's expansion, even more so under the BRI, tends to foster competition between China and the US in the region for the simple fact that, in a zero-sum game view, the increase in Chinese influence would automatically lead to a reduction in US hegemony (Flint & Zhu, 2019). China was careful at first not to be perceived as a rival by the US. In 2006, during the presidencies of George W. Bush and Hu Jintao, a bilateral dialogue on LAC was established, without the presence of the region itself. During the Obama administration, these meetings were continued, albeit more sporadic (Magnotta, 2019). There are no reports of similar meetings during the Trump administration.

Baiyi (2016) analysed the advance in the China-LAC relationship in the context of an alleged decline in US and EU influence in the region. It was also observed that the expansion of China's presence had not been the target of a counteroffensive by Western countries, but warned that "when the general influence of China exceeds a

---

[2] All publications are retrieved in December 2021, from https://www.cepal.org/en (English, Spanish and Portuguese).

certain critical point of Western tolerance, Latin America may become a new frontier for geopolitical arm-wrestling between powers." Until then, he believes there is a "period of strategic opportunity" (Baiyi, 2016, p. 19). During the Trump government, as the Chinese presence continued to advance in the region, things began to change. In the report of the US–China Economic and Security Review Commission (2018, p. 28) it was clearly said that "China is eroding US economic dominance in the region." While Secretary of State John Kerry had declared the end of the Monroe Doctrine[3] in 2013, his successor, Rex Tillerson, reinvigorated it in early 2018 with a clear reference to Chinese expansion (Pires & Nascimento, 2020). While the tone of President Joe Biden's team may be different, concerns about the Chinese presence remain. And the US weight in LAC increases caution on the part of the major economies in the region regarding further collaboration with the BRI.

The first major diplomatic conflict between China and the US in LAC took place in 2019, over the IDB. As mentioned above, the PRC became a nonregional member in 2009 to integrate its infrastructure financing strategies with those of the regional bank. Chinese diplomacy had invested a lot to celebrate its ten years of participation in the IDB and the 50 years of the IDB's existence during the annual meeting of the Board of Governors of the Bank initially scheduled for March 2019, in Chengdu. However, when the Chinese government refused to allow the participation of Ricardo Hausmann, a newly appointed member of the Bank's Board of Directors in the delegation of the Venezuelan parallel government, led by Juan Guaidó, in the event, the US insisted that Venezuela should be represented on the board by Ricardo Hausmann, the economy minister appointed by Juan Guaidó lobbied for the cancellation of the annual meeting. Given this impasse, the event was cancelled 48 h before the General Assembly began (Wroughton & Rampton, 2019).

Since the beginning of the 1970s, LAC has also been the region with the greatest number of countries having diplomatic relations with Chinese Taipei.[4] Between 2000 and 2008, during the first Democratic Progressive Party (DPP)[5] governments in Chinese Taipei, there was a shift in Chinese diplomacy in Beijing that resulted in a change of recognition by Costa Rica, Dominica, and Grenada. With the return of the DPP to the government in 2016, there was another shift, resulting in three more countries changing their position: Panama in 2017 and the Dominican Republic and El Salvador in 2018.[6] To achieve this goal, the PRC signalled the availability of further resources for those countries changing their position. For example, in the case of the Dominican Republic, US$ 3.1 billion in investments and loans. The change of position by Panama will be one of the case studies discussed in the next section.

---

[3] "The Monroe Doctrine" refers to President James Monroe's 1823 annual message to Congress when he warned European powers not to interfere by military means in the Americas. Later it would become symbol of the US hegemony over LAC and the right to consider it as their backyard.

[4] Out of a total of 15 countries, nine are from the LAC region: Belize, Grenadines, Guatemala, Haiti, Honduras, Nicaragua, Paraguay, Saint Kitts and Nevis, Saint Lucia, and Saint Vincent.

[5] The DPP governments are seen by Beijing as pro-independence, contrary to the Kuomintang (KMT) that defends the one China policy.

[6] Note the curious fact that the US, which itself does not formally maintain diplomatic relations with Chinese Taipei, called the Ambassadors of the three countries to consult in protest.

4 Case Studies

4.1 Brazil

Brazil–China relations date back to the 1970s, in the context of the Brazilian government's pragmatic foreign policy. Although little progress was made in the economic area, in the 1980s there was an exchange in the hydroelectric sector because China wanted to learn from the Brazilian experience for the construction of the Three Gorges Dam. In 1988, a partnership was established in the space sector that went through ups and downs until it regained prominence again from the mid-2000s onwards (Barbosa, 2018). In 1993, Brazil was the first country in the world to set up a Strategic Partnership Agreement with China. In the mid-2000s, the two nations established an institutional framework that Brazil does not have with any other nation outside Mercosur (Rosito, 2020). In 2004, the Sino-Brazilian Commission of High Level of Concertation and Cooperation (Cosban) was created, headed by the vice presidents of the two countries, to identify opportunities for further partnerships. Consequently, there was an expansion of economic relations, especially in terms of the common goal of overcoming the 2007–2008 global financial crisis, and in 2012, Brazil and China upped their Strategic Partnership to the level of Global Strategic Partnership. In the context of the set of bilateral, regional, and global forums in which both countries participate (BRICS and G20 in particular), there was an intensification of contacts between the two governments for over the decade, which has been accompanied by a growth in business opportunities, academic and subnational government contacts (Schutte, 2020). This demonstrates China's ability to attract by offering opportunities: real, potential, and imagined. Cosban became more dynamic in the 2010s, with a series of high-level meetings that resulted in ambitious Joint Plans. While not always following the real conditions for their materialization, they signalled the desire to expand the partnership (Rosito, 2020).

Beginning in 2010, in addition to being the main destination for Brazilian exports, China became one of the country's main investors and providers of financial assistance (Cariello, 2021). The presence of Chinese companies, especially state-owned companies, expanded rapidly. While Venezuela was the great recipient of Chinese financing in the region, in the first decade of the twenty-first century, by 2010 Brazil started to assume the position as the principal destination (Biato Jr, 2010). Regarding trade, there are two constant characteristics: a) the existence of a surplus due to the export of raw materials that hides the deficit in manufacturing and b) the concentration in the export basket of three products (soybean, oil, and iron ore), which consistently accounted for almost 80% of the total over the years (Brazil, 2021).

In the second decade of the century, Brazil became one of the top five Chinese destinations of FDI (Schutte, 2020). Between 2007 and 2020 Chinese FDI totalled US$ 66.1 billion (Cariello, 2021). Also, Chinese FDI was heavily concentrated on large projects, especially in the areas of energy (oil) and electricity. In both cases, Chinese state-owned companies managed to position themselves as one of the main players in the country in a short time. For State Grid and CTG, Brazil is the main destination of foreign investment and is a priority for its internationalization strategies (Schutte, 2020). In the case of financing, the main agents in Brazil were the CDB and China Exim. According to the China–Latin America Finance Database (2021), these two institutions lent US$ 28.9 billion to companies/projects in Brazil between 2005 and 2017, with the CDB being responsible for 95% of the amount.

In addition, China-LAC Cooperation Fund (CLAC) invested in several projects in Brazil, with smaller stakes, but important enough to make some acquisitions or expansions feasible. One example is the acquisition of the Paraná Container Terminal (TCP), the second-largest in Brazil, by China Merchant (Jiang, 2020). The fund also played an important role in the design of the Brazil–China Cooperation Fund for the Expansion of Productive Capacity ("Brazil–China Fund"), signed by the governments of Brazil and China in 2015, with the commitment to allocate US$ 15 billion on the Chinese side and US$ 5 billion on the Brazilian side. Since then, however, this mechanism has not advanced, frustrating expectations. There are several reasons: the difficulty of qualifying those projects that would be of bilateral interest, planning and structuring deficiencies, and, to a lesser degree, political instability in Brazil (Rosito, 2020).

Finally, there were expectations regarding the potential to finance infrastructure projects by the NDB and the AIIB, both of which have Brazil as a founding member and prospective founding member, respectively.[7] In addition to frustrations regarding financing announcements that were not put into operation afterwards, there were a few large projects that were not put into practice because they were not in tune with the country's economic situation. One example is the announcement of the bi-oceanic railway project linking Brazil (Atlantic) to Peru (Pacific) by the China Railway Eryuan Engineering Group (Creec), designed to improve the flow of soy and ores. Although the project had been part of Cosiplan's portfolio, the Chinese agents failed to grasp the political, environmental, and economic complexities involved. On the Brazilian side, on the other hand, there was an exaggerated expectation regarding the Chinese capacity to overcome these problems (Schutte, 2020). Another element of the learning curve that was not addressed was the Chinese frustration with the rules for public–private partnership projects, which must go through a competitive bidding process and cannot be implemented by direct contracting (Rosito, 2020).

It was evident that China had a clear strategy aimed at guaranteeing raw materials and exploring markets in which its companies can have a competitive advantage. The economic problems that affected Brazil from 2015 did not have a significant impact on these investments, contrary to what happened with projects aimed directly at the consumer market, many of which were rescheduled. Examples are the investments by Chinese carmaker Chery planned in 2014 but scaled down drastically considering the fall in demand. The company ended up selling part of its assets in 2017 to a local

---

[7] Brazil intended to be a prospective founding member of the AIIB at the beginning of 2015. However, immediately afterwards the country went through a severe political and economic crisis with the impeachment of the president the following year. This had several negative side effects on Brazil's international commitments, one of which was the AIIB membership. According to the Bank's formula for membership, Brazil should have bought US$ 1 billion in shares. In the negotiations Brazil ended up pledging just 10% and did not officially become a member until 2020.

company (Reuters, 2017). With all these initiatives connecting the two countries, one question becomes obvious: why did Brazil not join the BRI to consolidate this intense economic and institutional partnership?

Everything indicates that it did not join because it did not see the added value of a bilateral relationship that already has an important specific weight. Nor is it part of the Brazilian diplomatic tradition to sign on to multilateral projects in which the country has not actively participated in the construction. Furthermore, there is the aforementioned element of equidistance needed to be able to seize opportunities with the US and even with the European Union (Caramuru et al., 2019).

There is no doubt that China would like to see progress towards an explicit accession by Brazil to give greater weight to the initiative. However, it can be concluded that the Chinese way of acting and presence in the country follows the same logic as in the BRI signatory countries, generating the same opportunities and challenges.

4.2 Chile

Chile was the first South American nation to establish diplomatic relations with China in 1970, the first country to support Chinese entry into the World Trade Organization (WTO) in 1999, the first to recognize China as a market economy in 2004, and, again, the first to sign a free trade agreement with China in 2005. Since then, the economic relations between the two countries have been strengthened through the signing of successive trade treaties and agreements, such as the Supplementary Agreement on Trade in Services, in 2008, and the Supplementary Agreement on Investment, in 2012. As a result, by 2015, almost 100% of tariffs on Chilean products in the Chinese market were eliminated and China consolidated itself to be Chile´s main trading partner (Casas et al., 2020). At the multilateral level, both are part of the Asia–Pacific Economic Cooperation (APEC). In addition, Chile is a member of the Pacific Alliance—along with Colombia, Mexico, and Peru—which has been consolidated as a bloc to promote trade relations with Asia (Toro-Fernandez & Tijmes-Ihl, 2020). With an economy historically focused on commodity exports, China is the main market for Chilean mineral products, especially copper, as well as forest products, wines, and fresh fruits. Thus, Chinese demand has become one of the main factors behind the growth of Chilean GDP (Casas et al., 2020) and the maintenance of a positive trade balance. It should be noted that, according to UN Comtrade (2019), in 1995, the country's exports to China accounted for just over 1% of the total, while in 2019, 39% of Chilean exports were directed to China. China has also achieved a leading position in Chilean imports, representing 23% of the total.

Various Chilean governments have sought to strengthen relations with China. Thus, the priority given to the BRI was manifested by the presence of centre-left President Michelle Bachelet at the first Belt and Road Forum for International Cooperation in Beijing, in 2017, and at the second Forum, held in 2019, with the participation of the centre-right President Sebastián Piñera (Moreno et al., 2020). With the signing of the MoU, formalizing Chile's membership of the BRI, in 2018, Piñera got even closer to China. In this context, the Chinese Ministry of Science and Technology and the Chilean Commission for Scientific and Technological Research formed a partnership for technological cooperation entitled the Action Plan on Cooperation in Science and Technology (2017–2019) (Casas et al., 2020). With regard to the AIIB, joining the bank was seen by the Chilean government as an opportunity to occupy the forefront of relations once again between China and the region (Casas et al., 2020; Urdinez, 2020). At the domestic level, some sectors had to be convinced of the benefits of joining a multilateral institution whose geopolitical emphasis was on Asia, but the possibility of boosting investments by Chinese multinationals, increasing cooperation with Asian countries, and strengthening political ties with China accelerated the proceedings in the House and Senate[8] (Urdinez, 2020).

Two infrastructure projects would potentially be financed by the AIIB on the bilateral agenda of the two countries (Urdinez, 2020). The first is the expansion of the port of San Antonio, Chile's largest port city and a key facility for the country's trade relations with the Asia–Pacific region. The second priority project on the agenda is an underwater fibre-optic cable to support the installation of 5G technology in Chile and, if implemented, would become the first direct undersea link between South America and Asia. Huawei was the main candidate to execute this project, having participated in the construction of another 2,800 km fibre -optic project in the south of the country, in 2019. In addition, since 2017 the company has participated in the implementation of studies of the cable in partnership with the Chilean regulatory agency. The development of the project was financed by the CAF, and several possible routes to Shanghai were designed.

Moreno et al. (2020) highlight that Chilean domestic policy has shown little resistance to closer relations with China, making the political cost of signing up for the BRI relatively low. Thus, the points of friction in relations with China have been caused by external determinants. The execution of the bilateral agenda of joint projects between Chile and China has been hampered by US pressure, with the argument that there is an alleged Chinese threat in the technologies developed by Huawei, putting Chilean citizens at risk (Bangar, 2020). After US pressure, Chilean authorities announced in 2020 that Sydney would be the final stop for the route chosen for the fibre-optic project. As a result, the original project for a direct interconnection with China was abandoned with arguments of cost-efficiency. And Huawei was excluded from the project as it was banned from Australia for the benefit of Japanese suppliers (BNAmericas, 2020).

Other projects within the scope of the BRI were successful, with emphasis on the acquisition of a 26% stake in Sociedad Química y Minera (SQM) by Chengdu Tianqi Lithium, one of the largest lithium producers in the world, for a US$ 4.51 billion, and the purchase of another 30% of the SQM of Canadian Nutrien (Zhu & Tilak, 2018). Lithium is an essential raw material in the manufacturing process for electric batteries, a booming sector in which China aims to be a world leader (Criekemans, 2011).

---

[8] However, the accelerated process was interrupted by large social protests that took over the country in 2020, frustrating the Chilean diplomacy's desire to be the first in the region in the AIIB, a position that remained with Ecuador.

Table 1 Chinese investments in Chile under the BRI

#	Investor	Millions (USD)	Share size	Transaction partner	Sector
2016	Chengdu Tianqi	$ 210	2%	Sociedad Quimica y Minera	Metals
2016	State Power Investment Corporation	$ 140	n.d	n.d	Energy
2018	Southern Power Grid	$1.300	28%	Transelec	Energy
2018	Chengdu Tianqi	$ 4.070	24%	Sociedad Quimica y Minera	Metals
2018	China Three Gorges	$ 240	100%	Cornelio Brennand	Energy
2018	Legend	$ 830	94%	Australis Seafoods	Agriculture
2019	Huawei Technologies	$ 100	n.d	n.d	Technology
2019	State Grid	$ 2.230	n.d	Sempra	Energy
2020	State Grid	$ 3.030	96%	Naturgy	Energy
2021	China Railway Construction	$ 800	n.d	n.d	Transport

Source China Global Investment Tracker (2021)

In addition to lithium, the most important projects are State Power Investment's greenfield investments in the energy sector, carried out in 2016; the purchase by Chinese Southern Power of 28% of Transelec, a Chilean energy company, for US$ 1.3 billion, in 2016; and, finally, the purchase by CTG of the entire capital of Chilean Cornelio Brennand, in 2018 (China Global Investment Tracker, 2020). By 2021, there were a total of 10 projects in Chile listed under the BRI, as seen in the Table 1.

The Chilean case shows that the justifications for joining BRI and related institutions, such as the AIIB, are commonly linked to the idea that this will increase investments and the financing of infrastructure projects. On the other hand, recent US actions to contain Chinese advance in the region demonstrate that relations between China and LAC have entered a new phase, whose deepening will depend on the ability of Latin American nations to maintain their interests and relative autonomy in the face of the dispute between the two powers.

4.3 Ecuador

Although the Chinese presence in investments and financing began during the government of Rafael Correa (2007–2017), it was during the term of his successor that, in December 2018, Ecuador signed the MoU that marked its adhesion to the BRI. On the occasion, President Lenín Moreno stated that the MoU was an "initial instrument" through which investments and trade between countries could be boosted, as well as the "construction of a more efficient, modern and interconnected Latin America" (Xinhua, 2018, p. 1). The country's entry into such an initiative must be understood within a framework of deepening China-Ecuador relations. Traditionally, the US is the country of greatest importance to Ecuador, which was still its biggest trading partner in 2020 (Trade Map, 2021). However, in the twenty-first century, China has significantly expanded its presence. Trade Map (2021) data show that, in 2019, China was the destination of 13% of Ecuadorian exports (while, in 2000, it was only 1.2%) and the source of 19% of imports (against only 2.1% in 2000), having become Ecuador's second leading trading partner. Similar to the pattern in the region, trade has been marked by asymmetry. Ecuador's main exports are fish, oil, fruits, wood, and minerals, while imports are concentrated in machinery and equipment, with a bilateral deficit of US$ 753 million in 2020 for the South American nation (Trade Map, 2021). What has drawn the most attention, however, are investments and financing.

China Global Investment Tracker (2020) shows that from 2005 onwards, Chinese investments in Ecuador began to intensify, focused in the energy and mineral sectors. The entry of more Chinese investments and financing reflected, on the one hand, the internationalization strategy of Chinese companies and banks, guided both by the microeconomic logic and by China's strategic objectives. On the other hand, there were the results of the new guidelines of the Rafael Correa government, which chose to develop a foreign policy of diversification aimed at making the country more independent of the US and international organizations, such as the World Bank (Garzón & Castro, 2018).

Concerning financing, between 2010 and 2018, Ecuador was the country to receive the third most Chinese resources in the region (only behind Venezuela and Brazil). According to data from the China–Latin America Finance Database, US$ 18.4 billion were allocated to the country, with an emphasis on projects in the energy and infrastructure sector (Gallagher & Myers, 2020). Of the eight largest hydropower projects in Ecuador, China was involved in seven, through financing and participation of Chinese companies in construction, especially the Coca Codo Sinclair and Sopladora hydroelectric plants—the two largest projects in the country, both financed by the Chinese Exim Bank (Garzón & Castro, 2018). These contracts received US$ 1.7 billion in 2010 and US$ 509 million in 2014.

China's participation in such projects has contributed to the diversification of the Ecuadorian energy matrix, helping to fulfil the government's electrification plan, in addition to generating employment and local infrastructure. However, environmental, technical, and budgetary problems arose. One criticism was that the Chinese financing offered to carry out the projects had interest rates above those charged by other official institutions (Garzón & Castro, 2018). In particular, the controversies surrounding the Coca Codo Sinclair dam ended up damaging the Chinese reputation (Bullock, 2020; Dreyer, 2019). Concerning copper, the Panantza-San Carlos and Mirador mining projects are the largest ever carried out in Ecuador in the mining sector. The initial Chinese investment was made in 2018, with the first ore exports to China from

2020 (Mendoza, 2020). Criticism of the environmental aspects and the impact on indigenous populations are more related to the project than to Chinese companies, although they end up getting mixed up. The project was considered by the government as one of the most important for Ecuador in the medium and long term, mainly due to its potential to contribute to the desired diversification of the economy beyond oil (MINGA, 2019). For China, the project aims to provide greater diversification of its copper sources.

In 2009, China began to offer financing to Ecuador, conditioned to the payment in oil. This strategy is designed to diversify import sources and contribute to the internationalization of Chinese oil companies. On the Ecuador side, there was a need for financing the extraction of natural resources and the development of infrastructure (Luzuriaga, 2017). In 2010, Chinese firms started to act more directly in the exploration of Ecuadorian oil. In 2010, CNPC and SINOPEC took over Andes Petroleum, through which they began to control exploration blocks in the Ecuadorian Amazon and, beginning in 2016, in the Province of Pastaza. As of 2013, more than 80% of Ecuadorian oil exports were provided by Chinese companies (Luzuriaga, 2017).

Ecuador's entry into the BRI in 2018, however, did not represent a change in the pattern of economic relationship that already existed between the two countries, since Chinese investments and financing in Ecuador were already focused on activities that were embraced as priorities by the BRI. Previous projects were even classified as part of the Initiative (Castro, 2021). The space for the expansion of projects within the BRI framework is small due to the volume of previous Chinese investments and financing and the indebtedness that this caused. In 2020, in the context of the economic crisis caused by the pandemic, Ecuador managed a renegotiation of its debt with the Chinese Exim Bank that provided US$ 474 million in relief between 2020 and 2021 and reprogramming with the CBD that allowed the country to achieve a moratorium on payments for 12 months (between August 2020–2021), which represented a relief of US$ 891 million (Ministerio de Economia y Finanzas, 2020). There was an expectation that China could grant new loans (US$ 1.4 billion from the Industrial and Commercial Bank of China and US$1 billion from the CDB) that were frustrated. These loans would be based on oil, but in the international framework of low oil prices, and given the disagreements over the determination of the value of the product in the agreement, negotiations did not progress (Lucero, 2020).

On the other hand, Ecuador closed, in early 2021, with the new Development Finance Corporation (DFC) of the US, a credit of US$ 3.5 billion for projects aimed at the productive sector and for the payment of its external debt. This raised concerns on the part of some internal actors due to the suspicion that such an agreement could harm relations with China (Ângulo, 2021). Thus, the deepening of relations with China and the full integration of Ecuador into BRI are issues that will depend on: (i) the countries dealing with the impact that the indebtedness with China has on Ecuador and finding space for new projects in this scenario, and (ii) the pressures that the US may offer to create embarrassments to Chinese operations in the region.

4.4 Panama

In recent years, there has been little US interest in the region, represented, for example, by the cuts in financial aid, according to Granados and Rodriguez (2020). Even so, Central American nations maintain a strong relationship of dependence, including through free trade agreements with the US. In this context, according to Mendez and Alden (2019), Panama is the most important country for China in the sub-region, mainly due to the Panama Canal. Regarding trade relations, trade between China and Panama increased mainly from 2000 onwards, according to UNCTAD (2020). In 2019, total trade was US$ 4.7 billion, with Chinese imports taking on significant importance, with US$ 4.2 billion. Panama has been running a constant trade deficit with China, reaching US$3 billion in 2019 (UNCTAD Stat, 2020). This scenario of growing imports reflects the fact that China is currently in first place as a supplier to the Free Trade Zone of Colon, one of the largest free ports for the re-export of goods in the world. On July 13, 2017, Panama stopped recognizing Chinese Taipei as an independent state, establishing diplomatic relations with the PRC. As a result of this recognition, the relationship between Panama and China has become increasingly close, with a historic state visit to China by Panamanian President Juan Carlos Varela in November 2017. According to Méndez (2018), this visit produced more progress in China-Panama relations in one year than other Latin American countries have achieved in many years of diplomacy. In July 2018, Panama signed 28 bilateral agreements with Beijing, from free trade to infrastructure development, tourism, and cultural exchange. In December 2018, President Xi Jinping visited Panama, signing another 19 new agreements. In total, 47 agreements were signed between 2017 and 2018, which can be divided into areas such as diplomacy; BRI; merchant marine; air transport; cooperation for human development; infrastructure; electricity; agriculture; phytosanitary actions; banking; tourism, cooperation for economic and commercial zones; science and technology and innovation (Herrera et al., 2020). This large number of agreements reveals an ambitious bilateral agenda that shows an effort on the Panamanian side, and at the same time on the Chinese side, to recruit Panama into the BRI, reflecting the Chinese maritime security strategy and a bold bet on the Chinese global strategy to extend its area of influence (Mendez & Alden, 2019). Thus, amid the strengthening of relations between the two countries, Panama became, in December 2018, the first LAC country to join the initiative through a MoU. In the Memorandum itself, the centrality of the Canal was clear, as Garzón (2017) emphasizes: "Panama joins the China Silk Road Initiative, reinforcing its role as 'the great connection' with the Panama Canal."

According to China Global Investment Tracker (2020), China´s FDI and infrastructure financing in Panama between 2015 and 2018 totalled US$ 3.1 billion. Of this, several were incorporated into the BRI, like the investments made by the Chinese State Construction Engineering in the construction sector, totalling US$ 330 million. This company invested, in 2016, another US$ 180 million in the education sector.

An important investment was made by Shandong Landbridge Group, one of the largest Chinese private companies in the field of logistics and energy, owned by businessman Ye Chang. The company invested US$ 900 million in 2016 in the construction of a new deepwater port and container terminal in the Colón free zone facing the Atlantic (Tam, 2016). Other large-scale investments related to the expansion of the Panama Canal were carried out by China Communications Construction Corp (CCCC) in 2017 and 2018. The company invested a total of US$ 1.6 billion in infrastructure (transport) projects, such as that of the Atlantic Bridge and the design of the new bridge newly opened in 2019 on the Pacific side of the Channel. In 2018, the Chinese company Power Construction Corporation of China teamed up with a local company to become the first Chinese company to win a bid for a public facility, in the case related to water supply in Panama City.

The advance of Chinese companies in Central America provoked a reaction from the US. In 2018, US Secretary of State Mike Pompeo visited Panama City to warn against "predatory economic activity" by Chinese companies. Then, diplomatic pressure on the government of Laurentino "Nito" Cortizo, who assumed the presidency in May 2019, appeared to be having an effect. A Chinese proposal for a US$ 4.1 billion high-speed train linking Panama City to the north of the country was cancelled. The same thing happened a few months later with a large electrical transmission project off the Caribbean coast in which a Chinese group was one of the two qualified bidders. The processing of the Panama-China free trade agreement was also delayed and, according to Youkee (2020), there are strong indications that pressure from the US was also responsible for the refusal to build a new Chinese embassy at the mouth of the Canal.

5 Conclusion

Data analysis shows a significant advance in the Chinese economic presence in a relatively short period in LAC, with different intensities and emphases among the various countries, but reaching all. This movement reflects not only the geo-economic and geopolitical aspirations of the Chinese actors but also of Latin American governments looking for financing and investment for their projects, particularly in the area of infrastructure and for the monetization of their mining wealth. An alternative to globalization driven by the Washington Consensus had been opened. The pattern of Chinese activities in the region is common to what prevails throughout the BRI: a combination of state-owned companies, financing banks, cooperation agreements, and strong asymmetry in trade relations, with manufacturing exports and imports of raw materials. As a whole, the region's trade balance with China is in deficit, despite Brazil's expressive and constant surpluses.

China's move towards LAC predates BRI and, at first, intensified in parallel with the more ambitious new policy of the Xi Jinping administration. Later, LAC was integrated into the BRI, based on two movements. On the one hand, the Latin American countries themselves have signalled their desire to stay out of Beijing's priorities since the launch of the initiative. On the other hand, BRI itself changed its scope to become a proposal intended to cover every country in the world. An attempt by the Chinese diplomacy to coordinate this participation at the regional level failed due to Brazil's resistance and the weakening of the regional integration structures themselves, in particular CELAC.

The differences in Chinese performance and presence among countries in the region reflect a set of factors of each nation: their economic structure and the existence of natural resources, government policies, the impact of US policy to reduce Chinese influence, and in some cases, a certain path dependency, as in Venezuela. In the case of Brazil, there is also an interest in establishing a partnership that involves the global action of both countries, in particular in the BRICS and the G20.

The adherence or not to the BRI is not, therefore, an independent variable or determining factor that explains the intensity of the relationships. Thus, the non-adherence of Brazil does not seem to be an obstacle to the deepening of economic relations. In the cases presented, it was observed that Panama's adhesion to BRI was part of a broader and bolder process by China to have a strong presence in a country that for more than a century was a symbol of US influence in the region.

In the case of Ecuador, participation in BRI did not guarantee access to new Chinese financing, which opened a possibility for the US to present a concrete alternative, something that is still rare in the region. In the Chilean case, however, a permanent policy is identified aiming at the greatest possible openness and participation in the BRI. The objective is to be able to make the most of the opportunities generated by the Chinese economy, but with care not to oppose US interests.

The 2020s began with a slowdown in investments and financing, largely related to the pandemic. But there is also some reflection on both sides about the experience of the past decade. On the Chinese side, there is a maturing and rising learning curve, which tends to result in a more focused approach. This is true for investment banks as well as for state and private companies, the latter largely due to the economic difficulties that most countries in the region are experiencing. And on the side of the LAC nations, there was also learning, in two ways. First, on the part of governments, a greater understanding of the limits of what can be expected from the relationship with China. Or, the "Santa Claus-doesn't-exist" effect. Second, a growing understanding in some countries about the negative impacts of investment and trade with China, concerning the environment and the deepening re-primarization of economies. In this sense, both sides and the various agents involved maintain an interest in consolidating and deepening the relationship but seeking to adjust its operationalization.

Another factor that should be more present in the 2020s is the US reaction. The intensification of the dispute between the two powers will increase US pressure in the region to align itself with its strategic positions. This was already happening at the end of the Trump administration. On the other hand, there may be disputes over countries that maintain diplomatic relations with Chinese Taipei, such as Paraguay and Nicaragua, among others. It is up to the region to find a way to take advantage of what both powers can offer the best for their development and maintain the proper equidistance to the geopolitical dispute.

Future research on China´s presence in LAC should take into account the changes in the US stance in the context of the global rivalry between the two superpowers. After a surprising lack of reaction to the advance of Chinese influence in the region, a bipartisan consensus seems to have been formed around the need to maintain control over what they consider to be their direct area of influence. However, so far it has been difficult to identify a comprehensive strategy and this by itself should be object of further investigation.

Bibliographic References

Ângulo, S. (2021). *Ecuador firma un acuerdo de créditos con DFC de Estados Unidos por $ 3.500 millones para prepagar deuda cara*. Retrieved in December 2021, from https://www.expreso.ec/actualidad/economia/ecuador-firma-acuerdo-creditos-dcf-estados-unidos-3-500-millones-prepagar-deuda-cara-96975.html#:~:text=Cortes%C3%ADa.,%2C%20por%20hasta%20%24%203.500%20millones.

Asia Infrastructure Investment Bank. (2021). *Members and prospective members of the bank*. Retrieved in December 2021, from https://www.aiib.org/en/about-aiib/governance/members-of-bank/index.html

Baiyi, W. (2016). *Oportunidades em meio à transformação: uma análise multidimensional das perspectivas de cooperação entre China e América Latina*. Instituto Confúcio na UNESP/Cultura Acadêmica.

Bangar, R. (2020, July 27) Will Huawei weather 5G storms in Latin America? [online] *Financial Express*.

Barbosa, P. H. B. (2018). CBERS: 30 anos de parceria do programa aeroespecial sino-brasileiro. *Carta Brasil-China*. Rio de Janeiro, edição 21, pp. 9–12.

Bernal-Meza, R. (2016). China and Latin America relations: The win-win rhetoric. *Journal of China and International Relations*. Special Issue.

Biato Jr, O. (2010). *A parceria estratégica sino-brasileira: origens, evolução e perspectivas (1993–2006)*. Funag.

BNAmericas. (2020). How geopolitics shaped Chile's trans-pacific cable route. [online] *BNAmericas*. Retrieved in December 2021, from https://www.bnamericas.com/en/analysis/how-geopolitics-shaped-chiles-trans-pacific-cable-route

Brazil, Federal Government. *Comércio exterior do Brasil*. Retrieved in August 2021, from https://comexstat.mdic.gov.br/pt/

Bullock, G. (2020). The belt and road initiative: China's rise, America's balance, and Latin America's Struggle. *History Honors Papers*, n. 7.

Caramuru, M., Lins, C., & Ferreira, G. (2019). *Brasil-China: O estado da relação, Belt and Road e lições para o futuro*. CEBRI, Rio de Janeiro.

Cariello, T. (2021). *Investimentos Chineses no Brasil*. Histórico, Tendências e Desafios Globais (2007–2020). CECB.

Casas, A. O., Freitas, C. D., & Bascuñán, D. R. (2020) The imminence of the belt and road initiative in Latin America: Commentary from Brazil, Chile and Mexico. In A. O. García (Ed.), *China: The belt and road initiative—A global transformation*. UNAM.

Castro, D. (2021). Ecuador. *The people´s map of global China* [online]. https://thepeoplesmap.net/country/ecuador/

CEPAL. (2019). *La Inversión Extranjera Directaen América Latina y el Caribe*. Nações Unidas.

China Global Investment Tracker. (2020). Retrieved in December 2021, from https://www.aei.org/china-global-investment-tracker/

China Global Investment Tracker. (2021). Retrieved in December 2021, from https://www.aei.org/china-global-investment-tracker/

China–Latin America Finance Database. (2021). Retrieved in December 2021, from https://www.thedialogue.org/map_list/

Criekemans, D. (2011, March 19). The geopolitics of renewable energy: Different or similar to the geopolitics of conventional energy? *ISA Annual Convention*, Montreal: ISA, pp. 1–52.

Dreyer, T. J. (2019, January 16). The belt, the road, and Latin America. *Foreign Policy Research Institute*.

Flint, C., & Zhu, C. (2019). The geopolitics of connectivity, cooperation, and hegemonic competition: The belt and road initiative. *Geoforum, 99*, 95–101.

Gallagher, K. P., & Myers, M. (2020). *China-Latin America finance database*. Inter-American Dialogue.

Garzón, P. (2017). China's silk road reaches the Panama Canal. *Dialogo chino*. https://dialogochino.net/en/infrastructure/10233-chinas-silk-road-reaches-the-panama-canal/

Garzón, P., & Castro, D. (2018). China-ecuador relations and the development of the hydro sector: A look at the Coca Codo Sinclair and Sopladora hydroelectric projects. In E. D. Peters, A. Armony, & C. Shoujun (Eds.), *Building development for a new era: China's infrastructure in Latin America and the Caribbean*. Asian Studies Center.

Granados, U., & Rodríguez, X. A. (2020). Avance de China en Centroamérica: Oportunidades y obstáculos". *Working Paper Series* de REDCAEM, n. 14.

Herrera, L. C., Montenegro, M., & Torres–Lista, V. (2020). El contexto diplomático entre China y Panamá y sus acuerdos. *SENACYT–FID–18–034 Working Paper*.

Jauregui, J. G. (2020). Latin American countries in the BRI: Challenges and potential implications for economic development. *Asian Education and Development Studies, 10*(3).

Jiang, J. (2020, January 17). China merchants sells stake in Brazilian terminal to state funds. Splash247. Retrieved in December 2021, from https://splash247.com/china-merchants-sells-stake-of-brazilian-terminal-to-state-funds/

Jones, L., & Zeng, J. (2019). Understanding China's 'belt and road initiative': Beyond 'grand strategy' to a state transformation analysis. *Third World Quarterly, 40*(8), 1415–1439.

LAC Policy Paper. (2009). *China's policy paper on Latin America and the Caribbean*. USC US-China Institute. https://china.usc.edu/chinas-policy-paper-latin-america-and-caribbean

Li, Y., & Vicente, M. B. (2020). The Chinese partnerships and "the belt and road" initiative: A synergetic affiliation. In F. Leandro & P. Duarte (Eds.), *The belt and road initiative* (pp. 203–235). Palgrave Macmillan.

Lucero, K. (2020). China no prestará un dólar más al Ecuador sin petróleo de por médio. [online] *Revista Gestion*. Retrieved in December 2021, from https://www.revistagestion.ec/economia-y-finanzas-analisis/china-no-prestara-un-dolar-mas-al-ecuador-sin-petroleo-de-por-medio

Luzuriaga, M. F. (2017). Inversiones chinas en el Ecuador: Andes Petroleum y los bloques 79 y 83. *CDES*. Retrieved in December 2021, from https://www.redalc-china.org/monitor/images/pais/Ecuador/investigacion/197_Ecuador_2006_China_Petroleum__chemical_Corp.pdf

Magnotta, F. (2019). A Política dos Estados Unidos para a China no início do século XXI: acomodação versus confrontação. Tese (Doutorado em Relações Internacionais), UNESP/UNICAMP/PUC-SP, Programa San Tiago Dantas. Retrieved in January 2022, from http://hdl.handle.net/11449/183594

Méndez, A. (2018). Panama could soon become China's gateway to Latin America thanks to an imminent free trade agreement. *The London School of Economics and Political Science*.

Mendez, A., & Alden, C. (2019). China in Panama: From Peripheral Diplomacy to Grand Strategy. *Geopolitics*, pp. 1–23.

Mendoza, M. (2020) Exportación de concentrado de cobre empieza en Ecuador. [online] *Diario El Comercio*. Retrieved in December 2021, from https://www.elcomercio.com/actualidad/exportacion-cobre-ecuador-china-mineria.html

MINGA. Proyecto Mirador de Ecuacorriente en producción. (2019). *Minga service*. Retrieved in December 2021, from https://www.mingaservice.com/web/noticia/item/proyecto-mirador-de-ecuacorriente-en-produccion.

Ministerio de Economia y Finanzas. (2020). Ecuador totaliza alivio financiero por USD 891 millones con China. Retrieved in December 2021, from https://www.finanzas.gob.ec/ecuador-totaliza-alivio-financiero-por-usd-891-millones-con-china/

Moreno, S., Telias, D., & Urdinez, F. (2020). Deconstructing the belt and road Initiative in Latin America. *Asian Education and Development Studies, 10*(3).

Peters, E. D. (2019). *China's foreign direct investment in Latin America and the Caribbean*. Universidad Nacional Autónoma de México.

Peters, E. D. (2020). Monitor de la Infraestructura China en América Latina y el Caribe. RED ALC-China. Retrieved in December 2021, from https://www.redalc-china.org/monitor/

Pires, M. C. (2020). A Iniciativa Cinturão e Rota: Suas derivações políticas, econômicas e culturais e seus vínculos com o futuro da América Latina. *Mundo e Desenvolvimento, 1*(2), 81–102.

Pires, M. C., & Nascimento, L. G. (2020). The Monroe doctrine 2.0 and the US-China-LAC trilateral relations. *Journal of Latin American Studies, 42*, 33–48.

Proyecto Mirador de Ecuacorriente en producción. (2019). *Minga service*. Retrieved in December 2021, from https://www.mingaservice.com/web/noticia/item/proyecto-mirador-de-ecuacorriente-en-produccion

Reuters. (2017). Caoa compra 50% da Chery no Brasil e anuncia investimento de R$ 6,5 bi. *Folha de São Paulo*. Retrieved in December 2021, from https://www1.folha.uol.com.br/mercado/2017/11/1934723-caoa-chery-vai-investir-ate-r-65-bilhoes-no-brasil-nos-proximos-5-anos.shtml

Rolland, N. (2019). Beijing's response to the belt and road initiative's 'pushback': A story of assessment and adaptation. *Asian Affairs, 50*(2), 216–235.

Rosito, T. (2020). *Bases para uma estratégia de longo prazo do Brasil para a China*. CEBC.

Schutte, G. R. (2020). *Oásis para o capital—solo fértil para a corrida de ouro*: a dinâmica dos investimentos chineses no Brasil. Appris.

Tam, N. (2016). *China's landbridge group acquires Panama port*. Infrastructure Investor. Retrieved in December 2021, from https://www.infrastructureinvestor.com/chinas-landbridge-group-acquires-panama-port/

Trade Map. (2021). *Trade statistics for international business development*. Retrieved in December 2021, from https://www.trademap.org/Index.aspx.

Toro-Fernandez, J., & Times-Ihl, J. (2020). The pacific alliance and the belt and road initiative. *Asian Education and Development Studies*, v. ahead of print.

Unctad Stat. (2020). Retrieved in December 2021, from https://unctadstat.unctad.org/

UN Comtrade Database. (2019). Retrieved in December 2021, from https://comtrade.un.org/data/

Urdinez, F. (2020). The accession of Latin American countries to the Asian Infrastructure Investment Bank: lessons from Brazil and Chile. *Asian Education and Development Studies*, Vol. ahead-of-print.

US-China Economic and Security Review Commission. (2018). *Staff research report*. China's Engagement with Latin America and the Caribbean.

Vadell, J. A. (2018). El Foro China-CELAC y el nuevo regionalismo para un mundo multipolar: desafíos para la Cooperación ´Sur-Sur´. *Carta Internacional, 13*(1).

Wroughton, L., & Rampton, R. (2019, 22 March). IADB cancels China meeting after Beijing bars Venezuela representative. *Reuters*. Retrieved in August 2021, from https://www.reuters.com/article/us-venezuela-politics-china-iadb-exclusi-idUSKCN1R32NU

Xinhua. (2018). Lenín Moreno: Ecuador busca promover inversiones y comercio con China a través de la Franja y la Ruta [online]. *Xinhua*. Retrieved in December 2021, from http://spanish.xinhuanet.com/2018-12/14/c_137674549.htm

Youkee, M. (2020). *Has China's winning streak in Panama ended?* Dialogo Chino.

Zhu, J., & Tilak, J. (2018) *Exclusive: China's Tianqi nears $4.3 billion deal to buy stake in Chile's SQM*. Retrieved in December 2021, from https://www.reuters.com/article/us-tianqi-lithium-m-a-sqm-idUKKCN1IG2TW

Chapter 30
Why America Opposes the Belt and Road Initiative (BRI)

Robert Sutter

1 Introduction

The context for this assessment seeking to answer the above question is influenced by the "whole government" American pushback against a wide range of challenges seen posed by rising China underway since mid-2018 when the National Defense Authorization Act mandated such a policy as a matter of law (Sutter, 2021a, 2021b, pp. 2–3). Countering China's egregious trade, investment, and other economic challenges has involved punitive tariffs, import restrictions, and export controls encompassing the so-called US trade war with China. Relations became even more contentious in 2020 with President Donald Trump targeting China for responsibility for devastation caused by the coronavirus that spread from China to other countries. American public opinion joined the bipartisan consensus in Congress and the administration viewing China as America's primary international danger. In response, the Chinese government gave tit for tat in the trade war and remained uncompromising in the face of US pressure. Many observers forecast a new cold war (Sutter & Limaye, 2020, pp. 2–23).

Though preoccupied with domestic priorities and much more consistent than the Trump administration with carefully worded policy statements, the incoming Joseph Biden government endorsed the bipartisan concerns in Congress and the Trump government with Chinese malign practices endeavouring to undermine America. Seeking closer relations with allies and partners in order to deal with China from "a position of strength" (Glaser & Price, 2021, p. 30), President Biden repeatedly warned that China sought dominance in future high-technology industries defining global economic and military leadership, arguing that "we can't let them win" (US–China Policy Foundation, 2021). He cooperated closely with an enormous congressional

R. Sutter (✉)
Elliott School of George Washington University, Washington D.C., United States

enterprise demonstrating remarkable bipartisan support to pass multifaceted legislation in 2021 to improve US high-technology industries and advance other measures to counter China (US–China Policy Foundation, 2021).

Against this background, assessments of US opposition to President Xi Jinping's signature foreign policy stratagem, the Belt and Road Initiative (BRI), tended to focus on the two powers' competition for international influence. China was taking a major initiative which greatly enhanced Chinese influence and diminished US influence. Given acute US–China rivalry, both sides sought to avoid being positioned at a disadvantage. Thus, the US worked to preserve its international influence by criticizing the BRI and fostering competing initiatives such as the Blue Dot Network involving initially the US, Japan, and Australia and the Build Back Better Initiative launched by the G7 countries that would blunt the Chinese advantage (Arha, 2021; Geraci, 2020).

In fact, this kind of competition has been taking place between the US and China. However, this line of assessment gave little attention to a wide range of factors in BRI and in related Chinese statecraft employed in support of the initiative that was deemed seriously objectionable by Americans. Many of these factors concerned newly prominent unconventional aspects of Chinese foreign behaviour and levers of influence abroad that were heretofore disguised, hidden, denied, or unexamined. These unconventional Chinese actions and levers were featured in recent investigations carried out by the US government and the governments of US allies and partners; by progressive, moderate, and conservative think tanks in the US and those in allied and partner countries, and by investigative journalists and scholars from those states (Babbage, 2018; Diamond & Schell, 2018; Foxall & Hemmings, 2019; Harrell et al., 2018; Hart & Johnson, 2019; Hart & Magsamen, 2019; Hillman, 2018; Hoffman, 2019; Kliman et al., 2019; McDonald & Burgoyne, 2020; Mahnken et al., 2018; Roland, 2019; Rolland, 2020; Russel & Berger, 2019; Schrader, 2020; Shullman, 2019; Tellis et al., 2020). What the investigations and qualitative and sometimes quantitative evidence showed was that BRI, despite Chinese rhetoric to the contrary, was part of a wide-ranging effort by the Chinese government to undermine those many interests of the US and its allies and partners that stand in the way of China's determined international ascendance. Those interests include: (a) the rule of law; (b) the rights of small nations in contested issues with large nations, including the rights to join with other powers in protecting themselves and their interests in the face of dominance; (c) transparent, free, and fair economic dealings in line with governance accountable to the populations concerned; (d) sustainable international lending and development practices in the broad interests of the recipient country; (e) popular political rights—including the rights to dissent and popular empowerment leading to government accountable to the people, political freedom, human rights, and democracy; and (f) religious freedom and non-discrimination of minorities (Sutter, 2021a, 2021b, pp. 16–20; 312–314). Based heavily on the findings of these investigations, this chapter argues that the US opposition to the BRI is motivated not just by competition for economic advantage and related influence. It is also motivated by a determination to thwart those many elements associated with the Chinese advance in the BRI that undermine a wide range of important American interests. Without considering such American concerns, analysts will be dealing superficially with this key area of dispute in the emerging US–China rivalry. This chapter examines key US objections to BRI under several headings and concludes with an overall assessment of their significance.

2 Features of BRI Challenging America

2.1 Legitimating China's Growth Model, Huawei Expansion

Beijing has succeeded in having the BRI widely endorsed by the United Nations, with the UN Secretary General playing a prominent role in China hosting international forums on the BRI in 2017 and 2019. An internationally prominent Chinese company associated with the BRI is the information and communications technology (ICT) firm Huawei. It along with other Chinese ICT firms have the dominant position in Africa's 4G communications systems and have prominent position in other world regions, with the strong support of Chinese government officials under the auspices of the BRI (Lee & Sullivan, 2019; Sutter, 2021a, 2021b, pp. 262–263; Rotberg, 2019).

Such endorsements of BRI and expansion of Huawei are major problems for US leaders in Congress and the administration seeing Americans enduring major losses because of Chinese unfair economic practices very much out of line with WTO norms. Beijing's surplus capital for financing BRI deals comes as a result of China's Communist Party-state employing neo-mercantilist practices. Beijing's mendacity and hypocrisy espouses economic globalization while it doubles down in a three-decade-long effort using state-directed development policies which plunder foreign intellectual property rights and undermine international competitors. Beijing does so with hidden and overt economic coercion, massive state subsidies, import protection, and export promotion using subsidized products to drive out foreign competition in key industries. The profits flow into efforts to achieve dominance in major world industries, build military power, and support the BRI in order to secure China's dominance in Asia and world leadership. The Chinese economic practices allow companies like Huawei to attempt to dominate international communications enterprises; the profits support the top priority state-directed Chinese efforts to lead high-technology industries that will define economic and eventually military leadership in world affairs (Hart & Magsamen, 2019; Sutter, 2021a, 2021b, pp. 85–86).

Examples of substantial Chinese erosion of economic norms of open and free markets in globalization involved the Chinese government supporting Chinese industrial firms to gain access to US advanced technology through state-backed funding, espionage, required joint ventures, and/or coerced technology transfers. This step supported developing of competing industries in China without permitting the US or other foreign competition. These Chinese firms then emerged on the international market with heavily state-subsidized products that wiped out international competition and placed China in the lead of a key new industry. Huawei was a prime example of this predatory Chinese government practice (Hart & Magsamen, 2019, pp. 17–19; Sutter, 2021a, 2021b, pp. 58, 61–64). US industry complaints risked losing access to China's market. Past authoritative US estimates of the loss of US wealth to Chinese cyber theft and other espionage ranged around several hundreds of billions of dollars annually. In 2015, Beijing released the "made in China 2025" plan, which called for Chinese firms to supplant their foreign competitors in China and in global markets, and provided massive financial and regulatory support to achieve these goals. Beijing also implemented a new cybersecurity law requiring foreign firms to expose US data and intellectual property to misuse and theft. In March 2018, the US Trade Representative (USTR) laid out a long list of Chinese practices out of line with its WTO commitments at the time of entry in 2001 and at odds with international economic norms, asserting that they represented an "existential threat" to the American economy—a view that came to define US government policy (Morrison, 2019, pp. 36–37; Lynch, 2018).

In sum, China's strong efforts in seeking ever broader international endorsement of BRI and the expansion of its leading ICT partner Huawei legitimated the above negative Chinese economic practices that undergird the BRI. Such international support made it harder for the US to counter the many negative features of Chinese economic practices for US interests. The prevailing international economic order was viewed as under serious threat coming from China's determined efforts to weaken and undermine restrictions on the egregiously mercantilist state capitalism prevalent in China today (Lynch, 2018).

2.2 BRI and Corruption

The BRI is not a multilateral organization. Its basis is nontransparent bilateral agreements between China and Chinese firms and various countries and their firms. Corruption remains a serious problem in China, where there are serious government countermeasures; there are no such countermeasures in many other countries. Chinese firms and supporting Chinese government representatives work effectively with corrupt foreign leaders seeking mutual advantage. As a result, pervasive corruption has occurred in the nontransparent BRI deals in all parts of the world. Such practices undermine long-standing US-led efforts to reduce corrupt practices weakening good governance and disadvantaging the public interest (Sutter, 2021a, 2021b, pp. 46, 58–59, 209, 238, 288–289).

In Africa, one source using diplomatic language described corruption in the BRI occurring this way: "Chinese companies in Africa cultivated relationships with local politicians and elites through personal ties, favors, and personal benefits. The practice allowed Chinese state-backed industrialists and entrepreneurs to make inroads in the largely under-regulated African political and business environment where personal ties often trump regulations and accountability" (McDonald & Burgoyne, 2020, p. 110).

A comprehensive study by the Asia Society of China's BRI being implemented in Southeast Asia recalled the extraordinary scale of corruption in the Najib Razak government (2009–2018) in Malaysia making deals with enormous payoffs in railway and other very expensive Chinese projects in the country. The study advised that the Malaysian case was an exception only in that corrupt practices were exposed and publicized, concluding "the pervasive use of bribery, cost padding, and kickbacks was also indicated in numerous other BRI projects in the region." It judged there were no operational anti-corruption mechanisms for monitoring, enforcement, and accountability in BRI projects (Russel & Berger, 2019, pp. 16–17).

Cambodia is ranked as the most corrupt nation in Southeast Asia. Chinese statecraft abetted such corrupt practices as a basis for Beijing's ever stronger relationship with Phnom Penh. Notably, the International Republican Institute (IRI) linked pervasive corruption to Cambodian leader Hun Sen awarding a Chinese company a 99-year lease of territory over half as large as New York's Manhattan Island along the South China Sea. IRI said Chinese firms seeking and implementing BRI-related agreements in Cambodia worked through the corrupt networks of Hun Sen's Cambodian People's Party. The deals remained unaccountable to those outside a small circle centred on Hun Sen (Shullman, 2019, pp. 11–16).

Corruption prevailed in China's deep involvement with the Venezuelan government of Hugo Chavez (1999–2013) and Nicolas Maduro (2013-). For better or worse, it saw China become the country's main source of external financing (Guevera, 2020). From 2007 to 2017, Beijing provided more than $60 billion in financing to Venezuela, representing more than 40% of total Chinese lending in Latin America. The financing involved mining research and exploration, housing projects, communication satellites, and a railway company. Maduro signed many more bilateral agreements with China during a Beijing visit in 2018 (Koleski & Blivas, 2018, pp. 23–24).

In Ecuador, corrupt practices of President Rafael Correa (2007–2017) and his government in deals with China were shown as the regime turned away from the country's traditional sources of financing requiring transparency and accountability. The government leaders relied heavily on China in concluding massive infrastructure and other deals for the personal benefit. For example, building the Coca Coda Sinclair hydroelectric facility saw a Chinese contractor as the required bidder. The interest rate of Chinese loans of $1.7 billion for the project was high at 7%. Chinese construction of the project led to major flaws which meant the dam did not produce the anticipated electricity and was not commercially viable. Corrupt practices throughout showed that almost every top Ecuadorian official involved in the dam's construction was later convicted on bribery charges. The project represented about 9% of Ecuador's $19 billion repayments to China until 2024, involving 80% of the country's oil exports (Koleski & Blivas, 2018, p. 27; Shullman, 2019, pp. 31–32).

In Europe, the government of Montenegro (population 631,000; GDP $4.7 billion in 2017) contracted with the Chinese state-owned enterprise China Road and Bridge Corporation (CRBC) to construct a controversial highway connecting Montenegro's port with landlocked Serbia. The first stage of construction began in 2015 and the second stage in 2020. The first stage cost about 1.3 billion Euros, which was financed mainly by a loan from the Export–Import Bank of China. The small country's debt dependence on China became enormous, and as profits from the road remained uncertain, Montenegro's debt dependence on Beijing grew. The debt reportedly reached a stage in mid-2021 where the Montenegro government sought help from the European Union to refinance almost $800 million in Chinese debt (Reuters, 2021). The outcome met Chinese ambitions in its BRI to carry out lucrative infrastructure projects abroad, while China diplomatically devoted special attention in recent years to 16 central and eastern European (CEE) countries, including Montenegro, under the so-called 16 + 1 dialogue. The dialogue became 17 + 1 when Greece joined in 2019. That dialogue focused on China fostering and building closer ties with a European group apart from existing leading groups such as the EU and NATO, and encouraging the group members to adopt positions in support of China's interests including BRI. Four heads of state or government of the 16 + 1 group were among those participating in the Chinese Belt and Road summits of 2017 and 2019. For their part, European Union officials were outspoken in criticizing the Chinese moves as designed to weaken European unity (Sutter, 2021a, 2021b, pp. 263–264).

Why Montenegro would support this continuing and growing dependence on China rested with the usual nontransparent arrangements in Chinese deals under the BRI rubric? Montenegro's President Milo Đukanović was either president or prime minister nearly uninterruptedly since 1991 and was known for notorious corruption. He arranged for the deals with China to ensure that a third of the work must be done by local contractors. This arrangement reportedly allowed dispersing patronage in the president's sophisticated and effective patronage network (Doehler, 2020; Sutter, 2021a, 2021b, p. 263). Beijing's Belt and Road Initiative came at an opportune time for Serbian President Aleksandar Vučić (2012-). Increased Chinese financing and investment backed the strongman ruler and his political party. The timing of the deals and quickly provided Chinese funding in nontransparent ways supported Vucic and his party during election campaigns. The deals also mandated provision of material and labour from Serbia for the Chinese-funded projects and enterprises, which were useful for President Vucic and his party for patronage purposes (Shullman, 2019, pp. 25–28).

In South Asia, Beijing in recent years built much more substantial relations with Sri Lanka and the Maldives using corrupt practices, elite capture, and unsustainable loans in nontransparent BRI agreements. The Sri Lankan government of President Mahinda Rajapaksa (2005–2015) followed ruthless pursuit of final victory in the long-running war with the separatist Tamil Tigers in 2009 with unsustainable large-scale Chinese- financed and built development projects, featuring corruption and rent seeking by Sri Lankan leaders focused on political and personal gain. The loans proved to be impossible for Sri Lanka to support, resulting in the Chinese taking over control of a large port and airport in compensation. With a change in leadership in Sri Lanka in 2015, the incoming government endeavoured to renegotiate terms but the costs of reneging on the loan payments and commitments of equity proved too much. And by 2019, Mahinda Rajapaksa returned to power as prime minister with his brother as president, reassuring China that its past commitments to these leaders would pay dividends in the years ahead (McDonald & Burgoyne, 2020, pp. 75–76;

Ramachandran, 2019; Shullman, 2019, pp. 21–25). During the strong man rule of President Abdulla Yameen in the Maldives, 2013–2018, the government focused on infrastructure projects financed and built by China under the rubric of BRI. The projects involved kickbacks and what later Maldives rulers called "willful corruption." The regime also enabled the Chinese Communist Party (CCP) to cultivate government officials who saw Chinese money as a means of personal enrichment (Shullman, 2019, pp. 59–64).

2.3 BRI Supports Authoritarian Rule

There was a widespread symbiosis between Chinese deal makers and authoritarian leaders using BRI to sustain authoritarian rule. Such practices ran against US interests in good governance with accountability to the people of the country. They promoted an alternative international order accommodating leaders who suppressed the rights of their people for the sake of maintaining their power. BRI often found such leaders very interested in Chinese communications and surveillance technologies and equipment for use in controlling their populations. The authoritarian leaders also found adopting Chinese journalistic practices served their priorities by influencing their people to support authoritarian rule. China in turn benefited from the sales and much greater access to the communications, surveillance, and media of the recipient country. Outwardly, the result was often public media discourse in the country supporting China's government and its priorities as well as those of the authoritarian government. Those experienced in espionage and penetration of a state's information, communications, and surveillance networks also saw great opportunities for Chinese covert operations in these cases in order to monitor developments in the state and take actions in the case of adverse developments not yet publicly disclosed (Sutter, 2021a, 2021b, pp. 88, 237–238, 262, 280–281, 287–289).

Cambodia's Hun Sen was an avid consumer of Chinese media and information control mechanisms and surveillance equipment. Greater Chinese control over Cambodian communications networks by the Chinese firm Huawei added to deep Chinese penetration of Cambodian domestic operations of interest to China (Ciorciari, 2014; Shullman, 2019, pp. 11–16). China provided the Maduro government with technological assistance for surveillance and social control through the "homeland card." The card was inspired by China's national identity card programme, and was used by the Venezuelans to provide surveillance in areas of state concern (Koleski & Blivas, 2018, pp. 23–24).

The Serbian regime also was moving forward with contracts for Huawei to provide both communications equipment and technology along with traffic and "safe city" surveillance systems which also facilitated control of the sometimes restive opposition and broader public (Shullman, 2019, pp. 25–28). The Yameen-ruled Maldives allowed Chinese state-owned enterprises to control information regarding the Maldives' infrastructure plans, leaving local media reliant on Chinese newspapers and contractors' websites for information (Shullman, 2019, pp. 59–64). Huawei was in the lead among Chinese information and communications technology firms with a growing presence in Central Asia, a region where authoritarian leaders prevailed. Central Asia authoritarian rulers were well aware of how those networks were used in restive areas of China as a political tool with facial recognition and other technologies feeding information about possible dissidents or other troublemakers challenging authoritarian rule. In 2019, Huawei signed a $1 billion deal with Uzbekistan to further its surveillance operations in the country. There were similar Chinese deals with Kazakhstan and Tajikistan. On the whole, Central Asian leaders anxious to enhance domestic control against oppositionists and others disrupting local order welcomed the enhanced technical capacity provided by Chinese firms. An added benefit for China was said to be the fact that the Chinese provided surveillance and communication capacity allowing hidden access for interested Chinese authorities seeking intelligence and information in influencing the host countries (Sutter, 2021a, 2021b, pp. 237–238).

2.4 BRI Fosters Unsustainable Lending, Dependency, Leverage, and Control

On the one hand, under the rubric of BRI, Chinese officials held out offers of trade, investment, funding, and other economic benefits to encourage countries to align more closely with China on issues of importance to the Chinese government. This represented a common and conventional practice to expand influence in international affairs. On the other hand, Beijing also steadily used these economic relations to develop strong dependency on China. A graphic example was the debt dependency for a number of states brought about by excessive and unsustainable borrowing from Chinese state banks, which did not abide by responsible lending guidelines of the developed countries and the international lending and financial institutions they supported. The Chinese agreements with the borrowing country often capitalized on and severely disrupted Western efforts through the Paris Club and other means to assist poor countries with debt management, allowing China to exploit these newly solvent states to take on often insupportable debt from China. A prevailing pattern saw the excessive debt sought by short-sighted, selfish, and corrupt foreign leaders; their successors found that easing the debt burden was impossible without China's close cooperation as the costs of cancelling overly ambitious Chinese-financed infrastructure projects often precluded this action. Such debt dependency on China made these states more accommodating regarding Chinese demands for equity (e.g., land, ports, and airfields) for repayment and/or Chinese requests for access to military facilities or other favours. Salient examples explained above are Sri Lanka, Cambodia, Malaysia, The Maldives, Ecuador, Venezuela, and Serbia. Others included Djibouti, Laos, Myanmar, Pakistan, Zambia, and Ethiopia. The disadvantages for the US from this kind of Chinese behaviour ranged widely across US security, economic, and governance issues. At bottom, the Chinese actions fostered a world order at odds with prevailing rules with China free to manipulate vulnerable states for its own advantage, leading to economic stalling of these countries that will require costly intervention by existing international economic institutions (Sutter, 2021a, 2021b, pp. 59, 88; Morris, 2021).

Pakistan was an example of the pattern of a developing country which repeatedly relied on US-backed international organizations (notably the International Monetary Fund (IMF) for economic support to deal with economic insolvency. And recently China and Pakistan have taken advantage of these IMF-backed periods of solvency to take on greater and seemingly unsustainable debt in the form of loans from Chinese government banks as part of Beijing's BRI. Pakistan figured prominently in the Chinese BRI plan known as the China–Pakistan Economic Corridor, featuring many proposed Chinese-financed and built infrastructure projects in Pakistan. The cost of the planned projects was said to be $60 billion. Problems soon arose with several of the projects, notably because Pakistan's ability to pay seemed in doubt especially with the latest of a series of IMF bailouts of Pakistan in 2019 and its impact on growth in the country. The terms of agreements governing most of the projects were hidden, with such nontransparency widely seen as leading to the broad corruption and rent seeking by various interest groups taking advantage of the incoming economic assistance (Shullman, 2019, p. 18).

One result of the corridor was a key port developed by China at Gwadar, which has the potential for military use by China against India and for providing more secure lines of communications from the Middle East. China gaining rights for its first military base in Djibouti in 2017 occurred after the Djibouti government became heavily indebted to China over a Chinese-constructed railway among other projects. Analysts outside of China judged that it was only a matter of time for Beijing to use its economic leverage over Pakistan to gain military access to base facilities at Gwadar (Iwanek, 2019).

Laos was involved in another episode in what critics called predatory lending. Chinese negotiators backed by top-level government and party officials used China's strong leverage as Laos' most important neighbour and investor to create the funding and construction capacity to build the China-Laos Railway project with a cost of $6 billion. China's role in the project was already so deep that official Chinese media sometimes characterized the railway as China-owned. Indeed, about 60% or US$3.5 billion for the project was in the form of borrowing from the Export–Import Bank of China. A further 40%, amounting to US$2.4 billion, was funded with equity in the form of a joint venture company comprising three Chinese state-owned firms and one Laotian state-owned enterprise. The latter enterprise held a 30% stake. To fund this, the Laotian government committed US$250 million from the national budget and took a second loan of US$480 million from the Export–Import Bank of China (Freeman, 2019).

Beijing needed the rail link in Laos to complete the long sought high-speed railway from Kunming to Singapore. The feasibility for Laos was seriously questioned. One result for Laos was a mountain of debt with no sure means of repayment. Unfortunately, some estimates predicted that the railway would lose money for at least the first decade of operation instead of the annual 4.35% profit anticipated by the joint venture company. Laos already made tax and land concessions to support the Kunming–Vientiane Railway project, significantly undercutting the benefits it will derive. Past experience suggested that further concessions may be necessary. In 2008, the Lao government had to cede land to a Chinese developer as compensation for back debts from a Chinese-built sports stadium in Vientiane (Russel & Berger, 2019, p. 14).

Throughout the BRI were many of those countries that relied heavily on exports to China. They included those selling advanced equipment and manufactured goods and components and those selling oil, gas, iron ore, agricultural products, and other raw material. And many states depended on Chinese imports and the inflow of Chinese tourists and students to their countries. And many of China's neighbours involved with BRI invested heavily in China. In dealing with many of these states and others, China endeavoured to influence them to support Chinese interests and to defer to Chinese demands by putting aside or manipulating WTO norms to use such dependence as leverage. The coercion was applied or threatened by the Chinese government directly or through party channels mobilizing boycotts, demonstrations, and other pressures in China against foreign targets. The many foreign economies subject to these kinds of threats in recent years included those affiliated with the BRI such as Argentina, Czech Republic, The Philippines, and South Korea and other prominent examples of such application of Chinese pressure as Australia, Canada, France, Germany, Great Britain, Japan, New Zealand, Norway, Taiwan, and the US (Harrell et al., 2018).

A notable episode began in 2020 when Australia's support for an independent investigation of the origins of the coronavirus in China prompted Chinese cutoff of Australian beef imports. The dispute soon grew with an array of Chinese trade restrictions on Australian exports explicitly linked by Chinese diplomats to 14 categories of Australian government policies that China opposed (Sutter & Huang, 2021, p. 73). A very costly and ostensibly non-government Chinese boycott of South Korean business and tourism came in retaliation to the deployment of the US THAAD anti-missile system in South Korea which Beijing deemed against its interest. And Chinese officials warned Germany and other European countries that their large trade interests in China would be seriously impacted if they did not favour the Chinese company Huawei for their telecommunications modernization, despite strenuous opposition from the US. Meanwhile, Chinese interference increasingly targeted foreign businesses, carrying out or threatening retaliation for the statements or actions deemed offensive to China by the enterprises or their representatives, including large sports groups like the National Basketball Association. The Chinese demands concerned the foreign firms' handling of Taiwan, Hong Kong, Tibet, and other issues sensitive to China, including support for the BRI and support for Huawei's international expansion (Sutter, 2021a, 2021b, pp. 84, 86).

The BRI fostered close cooperation in building by Huawei and other Chinese companies Chinese communications and surveillance systems along with robust interchange with media outlets in various states. Those outlets pursued news coverage and information that was positive concerning the government leadership and China. The expensive and complicated communications and surveillance systems along with

Chinese-provided hydroelectric dams, railways, and port operations caused recipient countries to rely ever more on Chinese firms for management and maintenance. Such connections made the Chinese ties difficult and expensive to replace by another provider. As noted above, communications and surveillance systems also were seen serving the purposes of Chinese intelligence collection and manipulation of opinion in the country in ways favourable to China (Sutter, 2021a, 2021b, pp. 85–88, 313).

Other unconventional coercive methods used to intimidate neighbouring states involved Chinese officials stressing the beneficence of the BRI as they employed usually unpublicized Chinese deployment of Maritime Militia and Coast Guard vessels to deter and intimidate governments challenging China's expansive claims in the South China Sea and the East China Sea. In tandem with such deployments, China privately warned Vietnam and The Philippines that countering China on these matters would lead to their decisive military defeat. Repeated shows of force by Chinese naval and air forces in the South and East China Sea and around Taiwan were used for similar purposes of deterring these governments from countering China's demands for deference. Beijing bombers in 2019 and 2020 teamed up with Russian bombers to probe and challenge the air space of South Korea and Japan, thereby serving notice of China–Russia cooperation against the claims of these US allies (Sutter & Huang, 2019, p. 55).

Meanwhile, despite China's decades-long avowal that it does not interfere in other countries' internal affairs, Chinese practices interfered in often gross ways in the political, social, and related affairs of targeted countries, many of which were involved with the BRI and others China sought to join the BRI. They included the mobilization of the ethnic Chinese and Chinese students. These practices involved embassy and consulate officials and other agents to recruit, monitor, and control ethnic Chinese abroad, employing them for purposes in line with Chinese interests. A subset involved efforts to control and influence Chinese students abroad to counter perceived anti-China forces in various countries. The scope of such efforts focused on the many countries with large ethnic Chinese and Chinese student populations. South Korea and New Zealand were examples of this kind of pressure among BRI-affiliated countries while Australia and the US were prominent examples among non-BRI states. The efforts became more prominent when developments in the country concerned moved in directions opposed by the Chinese government (Babbage, 2018; Diamond & Schell, 2018; Mahnken et al., 2018).

Related Chinese influence operations involved substantial financial and other assistance to key individuals and institutions that were prepared to support China's interests. This included large campaign contributions to political parties in some democracies, employment of recently retired or active government or political leaders in paid positions in organizations backed by the Chinese government favouring Chinese interests; and recruitment of local business leaders with high salaries and benefits to work in organizations backed by China to pursue Chinese interests. Examples among BRI-affiliated states involved Italy, New Zealand, and Tonga among many others (Babbage, 2018; Foxall & Hemmings, 2019).

Recent in-depth investigations showed the impressive and expanding scope of the Chinese overseas united front influence operations carried out by the Chinese

Communist Party, its overt International Liaison Department, and various disguised or hidden influence and espionage operations, many under the direction of the United Front Department of the Communist Party with others directed by the military and the espionage agencies. These efforts seemed relatively benign in countries closely aligned with China's interests but they appeared very much focused on interfering in the internal affairs of countries that seem opposed or resistant to Chinese interests (Sutter, 2021a, 2021b, pp. 259–266).

Some other influence operations related to BRI involved building support in foreign media, seeking media control in some developing countries (e.g. Kenya) with poor media infrastructures, and greater influence in more developed countries (e.g. Italy) (Hart & Johnson, 2019, pp. 16–17; Foxall & Hemmings, 2019). Others fostered pro-China views in educational institutions such as the Confucius Institutes and the wide-ranging training and educational opportunities provided by the Chinese government and party. The expulsion from Belgium on charges of conducting espionage of a prominent Chinese expert on European affairs who headed a major Confucius Institute in Brussels indicated that the institutes serve more than an educational purpose (Sutter, 2021a, 2021b, pp. 265–266). Indeed, behind the various influence operations rested strong efforts to penetrate high-technology centres for desired information through the Chinese government's thousand talents programme and other means including common IPR theft. And also active were Chinese agents recruiting foreign individuals to serve the purposes of Chinese espionage.

3 Conclusion

Competition for economic and political influence represents only some of the reasons why Americans oppose the BRI. The Chinese initiative has a wide range of negative implications and challenges for US interests. And there is no easy answer for the US in countering these kinds of often disguised or hidden unconventional applications of Chinese power. It is clear that these practices have become more active and important with China's rise. Under the rubric of BRI and employing the wide range of instruments of influence in Beijing's foreign policy tool kit, China has advanced its sway. Beijing is determined in pursuit of key ambitions, and in Asia as elsewhere in much of the world, there are many authoritarian and/or corruptible leaders inclined to side more with an enabling China. What this conundrum means for America is that it weighs heavily on the side of those who are wary of China and its multifaceted challenges. Recent experience with the BRI widens Sino-American differences adding support to the forecast that relations between the two powers will remain acutely competitive and tense.

Looking forward, further in-depth case studies and other research will reveal more of the practice in Chinese lending and interchange with recipients of Chinese financing in the now opaque dealings of the BRI. It remains to be seen how salient the BRI will continue to be in coming years, particularly in the event that

Western-led lending increases substantially under the Build Back Better and Blue Dot programmes, among others.

Bibliographic References

Arha, K. (2021, June 12). A hidden key to the G7's infrastructure ambitions: The blue dot program. *New Atlanticist*. Retrieved in November 2021, from https://www.atlanticcouncil.org/blogs/new-atlanticist/a-hidden-key-to-the-g7s-infrastructure-ambitions-blue-dot-network/

Babbage, R. et al. (2018). *Winning without fighting: Chinese and Russian political warfare campaigns*. Center for Strategic and Budgetary Assessments.

Campbell, K., & Doshi, R. (2021, January 12). How America can shore up Asian order. *Foreign Affairs*. Retrieved in November 2021, from https://www.foreignaffairs.com/articles/united-states/2021-01-12/how-america-can-shore-asian-order

Ciorciari, J. (2014). A Chinese model for patron-client relations? The Sino-Cambodia partnership. *International Relations of the Asia-Pacific, 15*(2), 8–21.

Diamond, L., & Schell, O. (2018). *Chinese influence and American interests*. Hoover Institution Press.

Doehler, A. (2020, March 25). Montenegro moves on to next phase of highway project and further into China's debt-trap. *National Interest*. Retrieved in November 2021, from https://nationalinterest.org/feature/montenegro-moves-next-phase-highway-project-and-further-china%E2%80%99s-debt-trap-137242

Foxall, A., & Hemmings, J. (2019). *The art of deceit*. The Henry Jackson Society.

Freeman, N. (2019, December 10). Can Laos profit from China rail link. *South China Morning Post*. Retrieved in November 2021, from https://www.scmp.com/week-asia/opinion/article/3041394/can-laos-profit-china-rail-link-despite-being-us15-billion-debt

Geraci, M. (2020, January 23). *An update on American perspectives on the belt and road initiative*. ICAS Issue Primers. Retrieved in November 2021, from https://chinaus-icas.org/research/an-update-on-american-perspectives-on-the-belt-and-road-initiative/.

Glaser, B., & Price, H. (2021). Continuity prevails in Biden's first 100 days. *Comparative Connections, 23*(1), 29–37.

Guevara, C. (2020, January 13). *China's support for the Manduro regime: Enduring or fleeting*. The Atlantic Council.

Harrell, P. et al. (2018, June 11). *China's use of coercive economic measures*. Center of New American Security.

Hart, M., & Johnson, B. (2019, February). *Mapping China's global governance ambitions*. Center for American Progress.

Hart, M., & Magsamen, K. (2019, April). *Limit, leverage and compete: A new strategy on China*. Center for American Progress.

Hillman, J. (2018, January 25). *China's belt and road initiative: Five years later*. Center for Strategic and International Studies.

Hoffman, S. (2019). *Engineering global consent*. APSI Policy Brief.

Iwanek, K. (2019, November 19). No, Pakistan's Gwadar port is not a Chinese naval base (just yet). *The Diplomat*. Retrieved in November 2021, from https://thediplomat.com/2019/11/no-pakistans-gwadar-port-is-not-a-chinese-naval-base-just-yet/.

Kliman, D. et al. (2019, April). *Grading China's belt and road*. Center for New American Security.

Koleski, K., & Blivas, A. (2018, October 17). *China's engagement with Latin America and the Caribbean*. US-China Economic and Security Review Commission.

Lee, K., & Sullivan, A. (2019, May). *People's Republic of the United Nations*. Center for New America Security.

Lynch, D. (2018, July 21). Trump's raise the stakes strategy. *Washington Post*, A. 14.

McDonald, S., & Burgoyne, M. eds. (2020). *China's global influence*. Asia-Pacific Center for Security Studies.

Mahnken, T., Babbage, R., & Yoshihara, T. (2018). *Countering comprehensive coercion*. Center for Strategic and Budgetary Assessments.

Morris, S. (2021, May 18). *Testimony on Chinese lending practices and the international debt architecture*. Center for Global Development. Retrieved in November 2021, from https://www.cgdev.org/publication/testimony-chinas-lending-practices-and-international-debt-architecture

Morrison, W. (2019, June 25). *China's economic rise*. Library of Congress. Congressional Research Service Report RL33534.

Ramachandran, S. (2019, November 18). Sri Lanka's Rajapaksas are back in power. *The Diplomat*. Retrieved in May 2021, from https://thediplomat.com/2019/11/sri-lankas-rajapaksas-are-back-in-power/

Reuters. (2021, June 18). *Montenegro in final phase with Europe to refinance US$809 million in debt to China*. Retrieved in November 2021, from https://www.scmp.com/news/world/europe/article/3137748/montenegro-final-phase-talks-europe-refinance-us809-million-debt?module=perpetual_scroll&pgtype=article&campaign=3137748

Roland, N. (Ed.). (2019, September 3). *Securing the belt and road initiative*. National Bureau of Asian Research.

Rolland, N. (2020, January). *China's vision for a new world order*. National Bureau for Asian Research.

Rotberg, R. (2019, April 4). *Strengthening network reception in Africa, China-US focus*. Retrieved in November 2021, from https://www.chinausfocus.com/society-culture/strengthening-network-reception-in-africa

Russel, D., & Berger, B. (2019, June). *Navigating the belt and road initiative*. Asia Society Policy Institute.

Schrader, M. (2020, April 22). *Friends and enemies: A framework for understanding Chinese political influence in democratic countries*. German Marshall Fund.

Shullman, D. (Ed.). (2019). *Chinese malign influence and the corrosion of democracy*. International Republican Institute.

Sutter, R. (2021a). *Chinese foreign relations: Power and policy of an emerging global force*. Rowman & Littlefield.

Sutter, R. (2021b, January 8). Will congress be a 'spoiler' in Biden's China policy? *The Diplomat*. A Retrieved in November 2021b, from https://thediplomat.com/2021b/01/will-congress-be-a-spoiler-in-bidens-china-policy/

Sutter, R., & Huang, C. (2019, May). China-Southeast Asia relations. *Comparative Connections*, *21*(1).

Sutter, R., & Huang, C. (2021, January). China-Southeast Asia relations. *Comparative Connections*, *22*(3).

Sutter, R., & Limaye, S. (2020). *A hardening US-China competition: Asia policy in America's 2020 elections and Asian responses*. East-West Center.

Tellis, A. et al. (Eds.). (2020). *Strategic Asia, 2020: US-China competition for global influence*. National Bureau of Asian Research.

US-China Economic and Security Review Commission. (2021, January 28). U.S.-China relations at the Chinese communist party's centennial. *Hearing*. Retrieved in August 2021, from https://www.uscc.gov/hearings/us-china-relations-chinese-communist-partys-centennial

US-China Policy Foundation Newsletter. (2021, May 21). US view of China competition. *US-China policy foundation newsletter*. Retrieved in June 2021, from https://uscpf.org/v3/2021/05/21/us-china-competition/

Chapter 31
The Belt and Road Initiative's Security Challenges: The Chinese Globalization Project and Sino-American Rivalry

Diego Pautasso and Tiago Soares Nogara

1 Introduction

Chinese President Xi Jinping unveiled in the second half of 2013 the One Belt, One Road Initiative, also known as the New Silk Road. Later called the Belt and Road Initiative (BRI), it had its first forum, the Belt and Road Forum, in May 2017. The initiative is a massive project based on integrating transport infrastructure, communication, and energy, opening a path for productive investments, expanding regional trade volume, and strengthening diplomatic agreements. It is an ambitious, complex, and multifaceted initiative we sought to understand through several prisms (Pautasso, 2019; Pautasso & Ungaretti, 2017; Pautasso et al., 2020a, 2020b, 2020c). This chapter suggests that the New Silk Road faces security challenges intertwined with Washington's strategic interests in containing China as its primary challenger. In this sense, the Chinese initiative represents a fundamental step in a *Chinese globalization project*, forging alternatives for integration and development projects on a global scale and affecting the neoliberal order driven by the US. This framework follows the premise that the world is going through a *systemic transition* process (Arrighi, 2008), with profound rearrangements in interstate and inter-business relations and geopolitical and economic dynamics. The first section provides a brief overview of the New Silk Road and its role as a stage in a Chinese globalization project. In the second, we discuss how the Chinese strategy has modulated the paths of Eurasian

---

"This study was financed in part by the Coordenação de Aperfeiçoamento de Pessoal de Nível Superior—Brasil (CAPES)—Financial Code 001".

D. Pautasso
Federal University of Rio Grande Do Sul, Rio Grande Do Sul, Brazil

T. S. Nogara (✉)
Shanghai University, Shanghai, China

University of São Paulo, São Paulo, Brazil

integration. Finally, we analyze the security challenges posed to the New Silk Road, emphasizing the role played by Washington in containing the Chinese initiative.

2 The New Silk Road as a *Chinese Globalization Project*

The New Silk Road is just intelligible as part of the broader and sinuous process of *national reconstruction* initiated in China after the revolution in 1949. The revolution had decisive impacts in forging the conditions of this current process, considering that it imposed the end of the Chinese political submission to foreign powers; restored the integrity of the national territory; restored political unity after decades of civil war, and developed the main structures that allowed the opportunity for substantial economic development.

After the setbacks of the policies of the Great Leap Forward and the Cultural Revolution, as well as the complications arising from international isolation after the Sino-Soviet schism, the second generation of Chinese communist leaders, headed by Deng Xiaoping, has driven a correction of direction in the national reconstruction process. In this sense, the implementation of the Reform and Opening policies guidelines, from the third plenary session of the 11th Central Committee of the Communist Party of China, held in 1978, established the main vectors of a new and vigorous politically controlled economic opening process, with aggressive industrial modernization (Kissinger, 2011). In this context, the country reoriented its international insertion, aiming to attract foreign investments and technologies, open markets, and allow progressive Chinese integration into multilateral institutions of regional and global scope. This movement contributed to overcoming the relative political isolation of the past in favour of greater engagement in the international system.

However, as it expanded its economic capacities over the decades, China began to act with a reformist bias in the face of hegemonic power structures forged in the post-war period under Washington's leadership, such as the International Monetary Fund (IMF), the World Bank and the World Trade Organization (WTO). Simultaneously, Beijing started to promote institutional mechanisms alternative to those linked to the dominance of Western powers, such as the New Development Bank (NDB), operated by Brazil, Russia, India, China, and South Africa (BRICS), and the Asian Infrastructure Investment Bank (AIIB); the China International Payment System, an alternative to the Society for Worldwide Interbank Financial Telecommunication (SWIFT); China UnionPay, rival of Visa and Master; and the Universal Credit Rating Centre, which antagonizes Moody's and Standard and Poor's. In addition, the Chinese government has simultaneously promoted multilateral instruments for political cooperation, such as the Comprehensive Regional Economic Partnership, the BRICS, the SCO, the Boao Forum for Asia, and the New Silk Road (Stuenkel, 2018).

In the same way, Chinese diplomacy has shown decisive action in favour of fostering the deepening of bilateral relations with key countries in the global political and economic arena, as it seeks to establish alternatives to the difficulties of exercising leadership and defending the national interest within the multilateral institutions (Shambaugh, 2013). Faced with the proliferation of obstacles in some of the multilateral forums, the implementation of the New Silk Road aims to explore ways of lesser resistance, considering the need for infrastructure investments in peripheral countries and the enormous Chinese capabilities to provide funding and *expertise* in engineering and production of inputs and machines. Consequently, the promotion of infrastructure projects enables commercial flows and strengthens the gravitational effect of the Chinese economy, contributing to the re-creation of a *Sinocentric system*. In this context, some discursive adequacy of the Communist Party of China (CPC) can be observed. If, until the beginning of the twenty-first century, rhetoric was centred on strong ideas emphasizing the defence of strictly national development, from the twenty-first century onwards, concepts of broader territorial coverage appeared, such as *going global*, the *Chinese dream,* and the *Harmonious World*, among others, reflecting the Chinese projection on a worldwide scale. In this sense, such rhetoric is intertwined with propositions relevant to the New Silk Road, representing an important initiative in favour of a global order aligned with the perspectives coming from the Chinese decision-making centres (Ferdinand, 2016). Therefore, it is precisely for these reasons that such conceptions clash with the goals of the globalization process led by the US.

The main project that shapes the current paradigm of Chinese international insertion undoubtedly resides in the efforts to implement the New Silk Road. This paradigm finds its roots in the model of the Sino-Angolan relation, later expanded to the rest of Africa, based on the implementation of infrastructure works with the counterpart of deepening trade relations and export of natural resources linked with Chinese economic demands. Its operationalization involved unprecedented agreements in law, foreign direct investment, and development. The maturing of such a relationship emulated other cooperation mechanisms, strengthening cooperation projects covering governance, sustainability, and other areas of social development. The New Silk Road also affects multilateral political agreements, incorporating its parameters into the 2030 Agenda for Sustainable Development, boosting Beijing's participation in the prominent institutions of global governance (Ly, 2020). Thus, the dynamics of development and integration are driven by the New Silk Road in contrast with those mechanisms intrinsic to the neoliberal globalization process led by Washington (Yiwei, 2016). The institutionalization of the first *Belt and Road Forum for International Cooperation* (BRF) in 2017 in Beijing was attended by thirty world leaders and official representatives of more than thirty governments. In the opening speech, President Xi Jinping reiterated BRI's principles and highlighted the advances from 2013 to 2017, underlining the deepening of cooperation in diplomacy, culture, trade, finance, and infrastructure (Xinhua, 2017). The Chinese president also defended that the initiative constitutes a path to peace, prosperity, openness, innovation, and connection between different civilizations. In the mutual communication of the roundtable of BRF leaders, including representatives of multilateral organizations,[1] the principles, objectives, and measures of international cooperation were reinforced (Belt & Road Forum, 2017).

In April 2019, China hosted the second BRF, also in Beijing, with the participation of forty world leaders and representatives from several international multilateral institutions. In the mutual communication of the second BRF roundtable of leaders, they highlighted the strengthening of political synergy for development, the increase of connectivity in infrastructure, promotion of sustainable development, strengthening of practical cooperation, and promotion of cultural exchanges (Belt & Road Forum, 2019). The economic corridors and projects catalyzed by the initiative,[2] the sectoral platforms for a multilateral cooperation,[3] and other relevant efforts brought by the participants were listed in the annex to that communication.

Since 2013, there have been more than US$ 755 billion in investments from countries that formally joined the Chinese initiative. Between 2014 and 2019, foreign direct investment and construction contracts summed up more than $100 billion annually, peaking at $127.47 billion in 2015 (Graph 1). The New Silk Road has further boosted Chinese foreign investment, strengthening the *going global* strategy with the logic of continuity in state policies (Rodrigues & Hendler, 2018). Not surprisingly, China surpassed the US in *Fortune's* 2020 report, with 133 Chinese companies on the world's top 500 list compared to 121 from the US, and three quarters of them were public companies (Yang, 2020), revealing the profound link between the state and economic enterprises in China.

The leading destinations of the Belt and Road investments are energy and transport in terms of sectoral distribution. Combined, both totalized US$ 482.34 billion since 2013 and represented more than 63% of Chinese investments in countries involved in the BRI. Graph 2 shows the sectoral distribution of these investments in construction agreements.

Asia's energy and transport sectors also stand out when identified with the New Silk Road infrastructure projects. According to the Reconnecting Asia platform, there are 374 infrastructure projects associated with the Chinese initiative on the continent (Oh, 2018). These projects are separated into the following categories: (i) intermodal (13); (ii) gas/oil pipelines (7); (iii) power generating plants (146); (iv) railways (75); (v) highways (102); (vi) ports (25); and (vii) power transmission lines (6). The energy and transport sectors stand out, in line with the initiative's purpose of promoting connectivity and physical integration, especially in Eurasia.

Regarding loans and financing, it is worth highlighting the prominent role of Chinese public banks, such as the China Development Bank (CDB), which by 2019 had already committed US$ 190 billion in financing for projects related to the Chinese initiative (Staff, 2019). Considering only the energy sector and the countries that are

---

[1] Took part in the forum with the Secretary-general of United Nations António Guterres, the President of World Bank, Yong Kim, and IMF directress Christine Lagarde.

[2] In total, 35 initiatives were listed, including economic corridors and development and infrastructure projects of countries composing the New Silk Road.

[3] In total, fourteen sectoral multilateral cooperation platforms were listed that support the achievement of the initiative, such as the Belt and Road Energy Partnership and the Digital Silk Road Initiative.

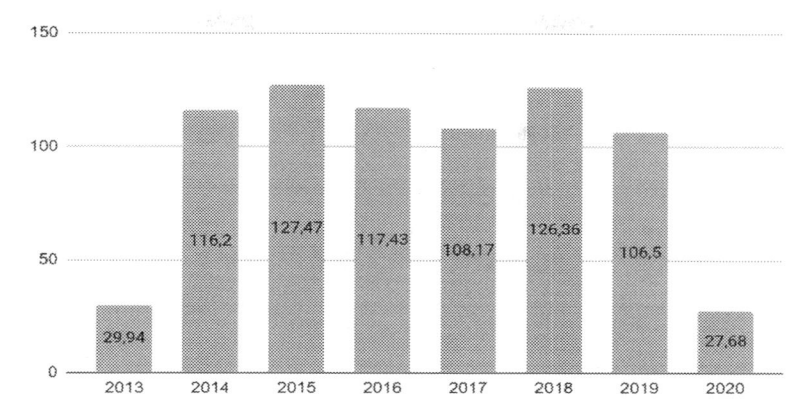

Graph 1 Chinese investments and construction agreements in countries of the new silk road between 2013 and 2020 (in the US $ billion) (*Source* American Enterprise Institute (AEI) [2020] Authors' elaboration)

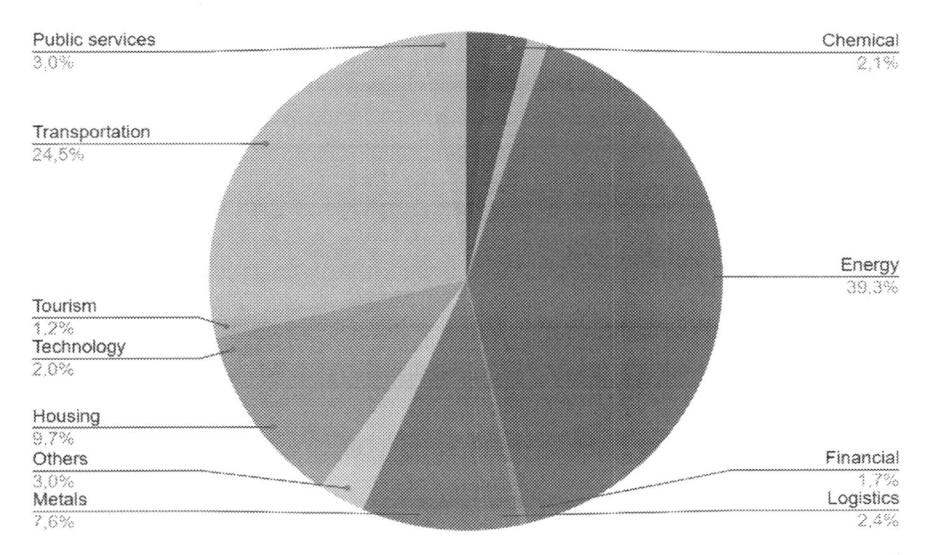

Graph 2 Distribution of Chinese investments agreements on the new silk road (2013–2020) (*Source* AEI [2020] Authors' elaboration)

part of the initiative, the CDB and the Export–Import Bank of China carried out financing operations that exceeded, between 2013 and 2019, the amount of US$ 114 billion (Global Development Policy Center, 2019). Also of great importance, the Multilateral Development Banks (MDBs) have been created under the leadership or with the participation of China, complementing the efforts to boost investments in infrastructure in Asia and other regions. The AIIB, for example, already has more than 100 member countries, more than 90 projects approved, and more than US$ 19.80 billion in financing for regional works of regional infrastructure.[4]

With the financial crisis of 2008 and the current coronavirus pandemic, the systemic transition process appears to have accelerated. Faced with the rise of disruptive forces, China has demonstrated greater accountability from multilateral institutions. The 18th CPC Congress in 2012 reinforced the speech aimed to contribute to the development of the continent (Jiemian, 2015). In other words, it is great power diplomacy with Chinese characteristics and a strategy loaded with greater proactivity (Kekin & Xin, 2015), combining tremendous power responsibility with the defence of fundamental interests such as economic development and territorial integrity (Zhao, 2011).

3   Implementation in the Greater Eurasian Region and Its Contradictions

The concept of Eurasia is polysemic and has been redefined throughout history (Vasylieva & Lagutina, 2016). We can define as Eurasia a vast region between the Middle East and East Asia, crossing Central Asia, whose role in human history has been fundamental. As Diamond (2009) highlighted, the main domesticated animal and vegetable species were Eurasian, favouring the agricultural revolution through the offer of meat, milk, wool, leather, transport, labour, fertilizer, etc. Agrarian transformations allowed the production of surpluses, the formation of cities, the emergence of writing, the development of techniques and weapons, the shape of political organizations, and even the strengthening of immunity. Some of the most long-lived and complex civilizations have developed there, including Chinese, Indian, Persian, Turkish, Mongolian, and Russian. It was also marked by the spread of significant religions, such as Zoroastrianism, the three monotheistic Abrahamic faiths (Judaism, Christianity, and Islam), Hinduism, Buddhism, and Shintoism.

The first major transcontinental commercial network in the world was the ancient Silk Road. Extensive and diverse routes linking East Asia to the Mediterranean, passing through South Asia, Central Asia, and the Middle East. It survived the upheavals and collapse of the Han and Roman Empires, reaching its peak when the Byzantine Empire and the Tang Empire flourished. In addition to goods, its routes transacted new ideas, religions, and genetic material (Liu, 2010). It can be said that it was the embryo of current global integration processes, which is neglected by Western ethnocentric approaches.

As Amin (2006) highlights, China represented the most vigorous and continuous political centre in the last two millennia among these civilizations, destabilized only by disorders in the inter-dynastic periods. According to him, at the beginning of the Christian era, it had 28% of the world's population, remaining in this proportion until 1700, reaching 35% at the beginning of the nineteenth century. China was an

---

[4] Retrieved in November 2021, from https://www.aiib.org/en/index.html.

epicentre of exchanging goods, technologies, and ideas through several routes. The Chinese regions of Gansu and Xinjiang were one of the starting points, crossing Central Asia (via Samarkand, Bokhara and Khiva, Fergana, Syr, and Amou Daria valleys) until reaching Persia and then European markets, which were a backward periphery of the pre-modern system until the year 1000 (Amin, 2006).

China's demographic weight meant that the Middle Kingdom represented around 32.8% of world manufacturing production in 1750, against 1.9% in the UK—even with similar per capita levels of industrialization, respectively 8 and 10% (Kennedy, 1989). After the period of foreign domination, its demographic and economic weights decreased in the world: the population passed from 36.6% in 1820 to 21.6% in 1950, the GDP from 33 to 4.6%, and the GDP per capita from 50.2 to 7.1% of total Western Europe and Western branches in the same period (Nayyar, 2014). The shaping of modern states and the penetration of extraregional powers have intensified competition and conflict in Eurasia. The Russian Revolution of 1917 and the subsequent establishment of the Soviet Union constituted a challenging socialist experiment in the epicentre of the Eurasian landmass. Paradoxically, it updated the Anglo-Saxon fear of control of the heartland originally inspired by Napoleonic power and later replicated with the Nazi experience. For this reason, the US formulated the Containment Doctrine as a vector of post-war foreign policy (Kissinger, 1997).

The creation of the Truman Doctrine and the Marshall Plan, as well as the military organizations in the Soviet environment, such as NATO (North Atlantic Treaty Organization), SEATO (Southeast Asia Treaty Organization), and CENTO (Central Treaty Organization), as well as bilateral military alliances with Japan, South Korea, Chinese Taipei, and the Philippines, represented the encirclement and containment of the Soviet Union. It is the reason why they correspond to the three primary strategic fronts for containing the Soviet bloc: The Far West, the Populous South, and the Far East (Brzeznski, 1987). During the Cold War, several interventions were carried out in the Soviet and Eurasian environment, including Greece, the Korean Peninsula, Indonesia, and Vietnam. Furthermore, the intelligence services were a central part of international politics and political and economic wars. The policy of containing Soviet influence was, however, global, as illustrated by the cases of US sponsorship of anti-communist guerrillas in Nicaragua (Contras), Afghanistan (Taliban), Angola (UNITA), and Mozambique (RENAMO), which in the 1980s were emblematic of the proxy war strategy.

This panorama triggered the first wave of Cold War coups, using the military widely without giving up other elements. The political-diplomatic sponsorship of the US and its allies took place through the National Security Doctrine, the promotion of anti-communist rhetoric by the mainstream media and the cultural industry, and the instrumentalization of the military in the School of the Americas in Panama, etc. Internal destabilization, inflationary spiral, the moralistic denunciation of corruption by conservative sectors, institutional paralysis, and the economic crisis were preconditions built to execute military coups (Losurdo, 2016). This situation combined the military siege with the mobilization of an entire intelligence system, unleashing covert action to impose strategic objectives in other countries. In this sense, instruments, such as the financing of media bodies, NGOs, parties, unions, social movements, etc., were used to shape public opinion with misinformation. On the other hand, actions using force, sponsoring, training, and offering information to insurgent groups of all kinds (from paramilitaries to guerrillas and terrorist organizations) encourage civil wars, assassinations, sabotage, etc. (Bandeira, 2013). Thus, Eurasia was the target of several splits and overlapping rivalries during the Cold War. Initially, the one that configured the structure of the bipolar order was hegemonized by the US and its challenging pole, the Soviet Union. However, another split was intertwined with the bipolar order due to the Sino-Soviet split from the 1960s onwards. The divisions in the socialist bloc were, in fact, skillfully exploited by Washington, especially when it came closer to Beijing at the turn of the 1960s–1970s. The Sino-US axis was decisive for the outcome of the Cold War and the temporary unipolarity of the US in the 1990s. However, the unstoppable growth of China transformed the Asian country from an ally to a challenger of Washington, exacerbating bilateral and systemic contradictions and impacting the ongoing new power configurations. Indeed, the Chinese globalization project represented by the New Silk Road joins other regional integration initiatives, notably the Shanghai Cooperation Organization (SCO). The SCO has assumed immense regional prominence, enlarged with India and Pakistan's entry in 2017, featuring four observer states (Afghanistan, Belarus, Iran, Mongolia) and six dialogue partners (Azerbaijan, Armenia, Cambodia, Nepal, Turkey, Sri Lanka). It began working with strict priority under security scope, as illustrated by the Anti-Terrorism Regional Structure (RATS-2002), and today has advanced to other political and economic dimensions of interstate cooperation. In this sense, the Chinese initiative of the New Silk Road drives regional development and integration and hence the multilateral institutional processes in Eurasia. Besides having its strategic core in China, a main emerging power, and the Russian Federation, relevant geopolitical power (territorial, military, and energy), this Beijing initiative involves about 65 countries representing collectively more than 30% of global GDP, 62% of the population and 75% of known energy reserves, according to the World Bank. Furthermore, unlike the neoliberal paradigm, the Chinese initiative leverages what Yiwei calls the "five factors of connectivity," namely: (a) political communication; (b) infrastructure connectivity; (c) unimpeded trade; (d) currency circulation; (e) understanding between people (Yiwei, 2016)

The Chinese initiative has several fundamental objectives. First is the creation of demand for the idle overcapacity of the Chinese domestic industry. Second, a guarantee of security and expansion for the routes that supply natural and food resources, especially energy, avoiding possible strangulation through maritime straits and overcoming the so-called Malacca Dilemma. Third, the promotion of the internationalization of Chinese companies and the export of services (especially engineering ones). Fourth, the strengthening of regional trade and the gravitational role of China, recreating the Sinocentric system. Fifth is the contribution to political stability in neighbouring countries based on regional economic development and integration. Sixth is the promotion of convertibility to the renminbi (RMB), making the Chinese currency a reserve of value and a means of current trade. For this reason, we suggest that the BRI is a Chinese globalization project compartmentalized in different circles of gradual expansion.

The emphasis on investments in heavy infrastructure works (communication, transport, energy) makes Beijing develop capacities to deal with vulnerable and unstable countries, seeing opportunities where other powers have been prescribing institutional solutions based either on neoliberal adjustments or on military interventions (euphemistically called "humanitarian aid" or "state-building"). That is why the initiative results do not concern only the directions of the Sino-US rivalry but different and disputed globalization projects, whose consequences will shape the new world order. The US resumes the logic of containment typical of the Cold War, while the Eurasian heartland returns to the recurring and permanent Great Game scene.

4 Security Challenges of the New Silk Road and the New Cold War

As the New Silk Road consolidates itself as the materialization of a Chinese globalization project, it is evident that Eurasia is its priority region. The regional Sinocentric leadership has been remarkable and tends to deepen with advances in infrastructure integration processes. In this context, the security challenges of this integration initiative led by China should be assessed, considering the contradiction it entails with the global hegemony of the US. Reactively, Washington has mobilized multiple strategies to contain the success of the initiative process of international integration.

We suggest that such a dynamic deepens the Sino-US rivalry, increasing a systemic crossroads panorama resulting from a complex transition of power and civilization. If China accounted for just over 10% of GDP (PPS) of the US in 1980, in 2020 already surpassed the US, representing 116% of the American amount (Knoema, 2020), strengthening its ability to intervene in the course of new world order in gestation. However, the ambition of the New Silk Road is compatible not only with the challenges to development and regional integration but also with the addressing of relevant security issues.

The *first arc of security challenges* refers to China's territorial integrity. Separatist movements in Xinjiang, Taipei, and Tibet and waves of destabilization in Hong Kong are linked with foreign interests. As highlighted by Allison (2020), it is not difficult to infer from the assertions of members of the US establishment that the objective of such activities is precisely to encourage dissidents, accentuating internal Chinese contradictions. The dismemberment of China is the new American Great Game in the region (Losurdo, 2012), replicating the contention and objective of territorial disintegration of the challenging power that had once occurred with the Soviet Union.

The *second arc* concerns the regional neighbourhood. In Central Asia, it can be perceived through regions where transnational organized crime radiates linked to drug and arms trafficking in Afghanistan, Pakistan, and other countries in the area, as well as in disputes over territorial enclaves—such as Vorukh, Tajik enclave in Kyrgyzstan, Barak, Kyrgyzstan enclave in Uzbekistan, and the Uzbek enclaves of Sokh and Shakhimardan in Kyrgyzstan. In the Pacific Basin, it ranges from the division of the Korean Peninsula, the disputes in the South China Sea, especially in the Spratly Islands, and the domination of the Senkaku/Diaoyu Islands. Furthermore, the US military presence punctuates the region in South Korea, Japan, Thailand, Malaysia, the Philippines, Guam, and Hawaii. In addition to its existence, the Pacific Commands (PACOM), the European Command (EUCOM), and the Central Command (CENTCOM) were consolidated, configuring part of the *full spectrum dominance* goals. The map below clearly expresses Washington's presence in the Chinese territorial neighbourhood and its initiative to contain the Eurasian integration process led by Beijing (Fig. 1).

The *third arc* covers the so-called *String of Pearls*. China gives rise to the construction and modernization of the ports of Colombo and Hambantota in Sri Lanka; Gwadar in Pakistan; Chittagong in Bangladesh; Meday Island in Myanmar; and Port Victoria in Seychelles. Such a large infrastructure project was entitled the *String of Pearls* and is perceived by Indians as a challenge to its regional hegemony, especially the China–Pakistan Economic Corridor. The Chinese String of Pearls thus competes with the already established presence of the US and India in the region. On the one hand, the US continues as a guarantor of regional security schemes, anchored in military alliances extending from the Persian Gulf to Southeast Asia, exemplified by the Quadrilateral Security Dialogue, an informal strategic dialogue between the US and Japan, Australia, and India, started in 2007. On the other hand, India has sought to strengthen its regional presence with initiatives such as the creation in 2014 of the IO-5 group—involving Maldives, Mauritius, Seychelles, and Sri Lanka—and new bilateral partnerships in East Africa (Mozambique and Madagascar), in the Persian

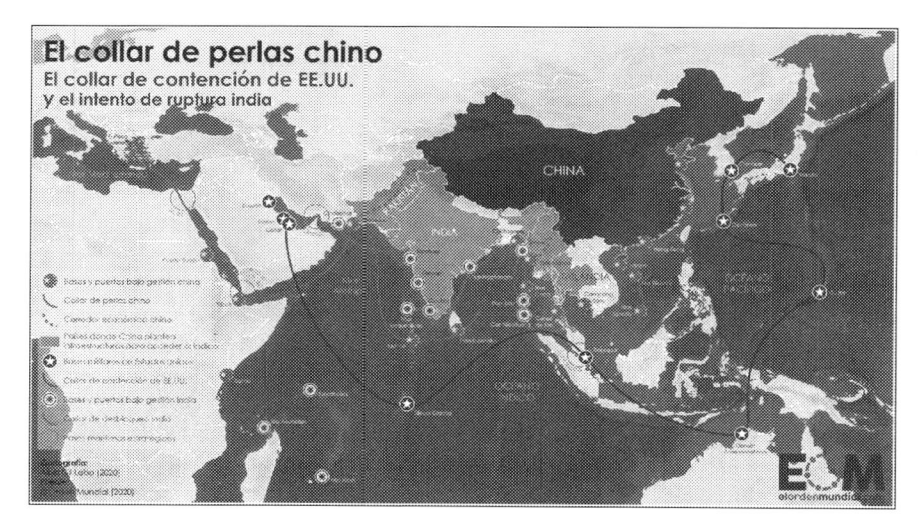

Fig. 1 The siege against China (*Source* Arancón [2014] and El Orden Mundial in Pautasso, D., Nogara, T. S., & Ribeiro, E. H. Mural Internacional, Rio de Janeiro, Vol. 11, p. 8)

Gulf (Oman and Qatar), and in Southeast Asia (Indonesia, Singapore, and Vietnam), and the establishment of logistical agreements with the US and France. Another hotspot was the creation, in 2012, of the *Indian Ocean Naval Symposium* (IONS), with the presence of navies from 24 countries and eight external observers, including Diego Garcia Island, as far as Ethiopia and countries with critical positions in the Persian Gulf; the *Indian Ocean Rim Association* (IORA), with 21 members and ten dialogue partners, including the US, China, Japan, and South Korea; the rebirth of the Bay of Bengal Initiative (BIMSTEC), created in 1997, with nearly all South Asian countries, except Pakistan, plus Myanmar and Thailand (Xavier, 2018); and the Malabar naval exercises (India, US, and Japan); and the strengthening of ties with ASEAN countries (Chan, 2020).

The *fourth arc* spans the Western edges of Eurasia, encompassing NATO's expansion into Eastern Europe, covering the military interventions dating from the disintegration of Yugoslavia to the Global War on Terror, with the invasion of Afghanistan and subsequently Iraq; the proxy wars and aggressions against Syria; the siege and threats against Iran; as well as the systematic anti-Russian policy, which ranges from military raids to sanctions; and the colour revolutions in Serbia in 2000, Georgia in 2003, Kyrgyzstan in 2005, and Ukraine in 2004 and 2014 (Bandeira, 2013). The latter encompasses a new wave of coups d'état, which reinvigorated *regime change* policies through multimedia campaigns, including internet operations and social networks, deepening Psywar and PsyOps methodologies (Losurdo, 2016).

Against the intensification of contradictions between the advance of the Chinese globalization project, which has the New Silk Road as its main stronghold, and US strategic interests on a global scale, the idea of a new Cold War increasingly emerges. Despite the polysemy of theories about the period, the Cold War was an intersystemic conflict that marked the consolidation of US hegemony under the aegis of a strategy of containing the socialist anti-systemic rival pole (Halliday, 1994). On the US side, the heart of the Cold War was the Soviets' containment strategy, launched with the Long Telegram, the Marshall Plan, and the NSC-68 memo.

Currently, we witnessed a gradual reissue of containment strategy, adapted to the reality of the conflict with China and seeking to demoralize the regime in Beijing and accentuate the contradictions at the heart of the Chinese communist ideology (Allison, 2000). The resurgence of anti-Chinese rhetoric—fueled by Mike Pompeo's recent speech on *Communist China and the Future of the Free World*—has called for "a struggle between the free world and tyranny" and accused the Chinese Communist Party of being a "national oppressor" and a "dishonest international agent." In this sense, the US replicates the logic of containment to unite its allies and prevent the rival's expansion, giving coherence to events such as the Trade War, support for separatist movements in China, and the military siege. On China's side, academic and political elites have debated the US strategy for containing China. The prevailing view is that US–China strategic competition will likely intensify as Washington sees the erosion of its global hegemony. They also consider that Sino-US economic and technological rivalry increases while the Pacific Basin becomes the focal competition point (Zhao, 2019). But China, unlike the Soviet Union, has economic-commercial synergy with the US and the capacity for global technical-productive competition.

The ongoing economic and geopolitical reorganization has involved complex and intertwined processes, such as the neoconservative and neoliberal reaction, the emergence of new productive paradigms, the end of the Cold War, the spread of US power, and an increasing multi-polarization of the international system. This situation boosts the geopolitical and economic competition between the most powerful countries, with the reduction of the arbitral and unilateral capacity of the US, the rapid fragmentation of the world system, bankruptcy and emptying of multilateral organizations, the return of the struggle for regional supremacy, and the increasing degree of uncertainty in the world (Fiori, 2007). The pandemic deepened this panorama. Thus, the Sino-US competition tends to intensify during the implementation of the New Silk Road and the disputed globalization projects, transforming the security challenges into disruptive movements for the initiative, certainly explored by Washington in its strategy to contain China.

5 Conclusion

The systemic transition pushes the world into multiple-dimensional shocks. The intensification of US foreign policy, the multiplication of failed states after interventions supported by foreign forces, the humanitarian and migratory crises, the strengthening of xenophobia and centrifugal forces in Europe, and the tensions in several Asia–Pacific localities increase the risks of military escalations. Concurrently, these trends are sharpened by a global economic crisis in 2008 in the system epicentre, the loss of legitimacy of democracies and institutions in the West, and the pandemic crisis since 2020. The predominance of irrationality, a typical systemic transition symptom, is intertwined with the new potentials of the Scientific-Technological Revolution and the rise of new economic and geopolitical power configurations.

The security challenges, arranged in *four arcs*, are crucial both for the achievement of the New Silk Road and for the definition of the rise of China. The conflicts that dot Eurasia—some dating back to the beginning of the Cold War, as in the Korean Peninsula—gain another logic for Washington in the twenty-first century. In other words, they adapt to the dynamics of containment of its main challenging power (China) and its primary means of global projection (the New Silk Road), establishing the parameters of a New Cold War. Thus, the current systemic crossroads results from the interaction dynamics between the established power (US), the leading emerging power (China), and their disputed globalization projects, whose consequences will inform the degree of conflict in this global reordering of power.

Acknowledgements This study was partially financed by: Coordenação de Aperfeiçoamento de Pessoal de Nível Superior—Brazil (CAPES)—Financial Code 001.

Bibliographic References

Allison, G. (2000). *A caminho da guerra*. intrínseca.
American Enterprise Institute (AEI). (2020). *China global investment tracker*. https://www.aei.org/china-global-investment-tracker/
Amin, S. (2006). *Os desafios da mundialização*. Idéias & Letras.
Arancón, F. (2014, March 28). El colar de perlas de China: Geopolítica en el Índico. *El Orden Mundial*. Retrieved on 8 April 2022, from https://elordenmundial.com/el-collar-de-perlas-chino/
Arrighi, G. (2008). *Adam Smith em Pequim*. Boitempo.
Bandeira, L. A. M. (2013). *A Segunda Guerra Fria*. Civilização Brasileira.
Belt and Road Forum. (2017, 16 May). *Joint communique of the leaders roundtable of the Belt and Road Forum for international cooperation*. Belt and Road Forum report. Retrieved on 24 March 2021, from http://2017.beltandroadforum.org/english/n100/2017/0516/c22-423.html
Belt and Road Forum. (2019, April 27). *Joint communique of the leaders' roundtable of the 2nd Belt and Road Forum for international cooperation*. Belt and Road Forum report. Retrieved on 24 March 2021, from http://www.beltandroadforum.org/english/n100/2019/0427/c36-1311.html.
Belt and Road Initiative. (2022). *Belt and Road Initiative*. Retrieved on 8 April 2022, from https://www.beltroad-initiative.com/belt-and-road/
Brzezinski, Z. (1987). *EUA x URSS: O grande desafio*. Nórdica.
Chan, L. (2020). Can China remake regional order? Contestation with India over the Belt and Road Initiative. *Global Change, Peace & Security, 32*(2), 1–19.
Diamond, J. (2009). *Armas, germes e aço*. Record.
Enghdal, F. (2009). *Full spectrum dominance*. Progressive Press.
Ferdinand, P. (2016). Westward ho—The China dream and 'one belt, one road': Chinese foreign policy under Xi Jinping. *International Affairs, 92*(4), 941–957.
Fiori, J. L. (2007). *O poder global e a nova geopolítica das nações*. Boitempo.
Friedman, T. (2009). *O mundo é plano*. Objetiva.
Global Development Policy Center. (2019). *China's global energy finance*. Global Development Policy Center report. Retrieved on 24 March 2021, from http://www.bu.edu/cgef/#/2019/Country.
Halliday, F. (1994). *Rethinking the international relations*. Macmillan Press.
Jiemian, Y. (2015). China's new diplomacy under the Xi Jinping administration. *China Quarterly of International Strategic Studies, 1*(1), 1–17.
Kejin, Z., & Xin, G. (2015). Pursuing the Chinese dream: Institutional changes of Chinese diplomacy under president Xi Jinping. *Quarterly of International Strategic Studies, 1*(1), 35–57.
Kennedy, P. (1989). *Ascensão e queda das grandes potências*. Campus.
Kissinger, H. (1997). *Diplomacia*. Francisco Alves.
Kissinger, H. (2011). *On Chins*. Penguin Books.
Knoema. (2020). *China—Produto Bruto Doméstico baseado na paridade do poder aquisitivo (PPA)* (billion international dollars). Knoema report, Retrieved on 24 March 2021, from https://knoema.com/atlas/China/GDP-based-on-PPP?compareTo=US.
Liu, X. (2010). *The silk road in world history*. Oxford University Press.
Losurdo, D. (2016). *A esquerda ausente*. Anita Garibaldi.
Losurdo, D. (2012). *A não violência: Uma história fora do mito*. Revan.
Losurdo, D. (2010). *A linguagem do Império*. Boitempo.
Ly, B. (2020). China and global governance: Leadership through BRI. *Cogent Social Sciences, 6*(1), 1–22.
Nayyar, D. (2014). *A corrida pelo crescimento*. Contraponto.
Oh, E. (2018, June 29). *Mapping the China-Pakistan economic corridor's environmental impacts*. Reconnecting Asia. Retrieved on 24 March 2021, from https://reconnectingasia.csis.org/map.
Pautasso, D., Nogara, T., Ungaretti, C., & Doria, G. (2020a). A Iniciativa Cinturão e Rota e os dilemas da América Latina. *Revista Tempos do Mundo, 24*(1), 77–106.

Pautasso, D., Nogara, T., & Ribeiro, E. H. (2020b). A Nova Rota da Seda e as relações sino-indianas: o desafio do 'Colar de Pérolas'. *Revista Mural Internacional, 11*, 1–14.

Pautasso, D., Doria, G., & Nogara, T. (2020c). A Nova Rota da Seda e o projeto chinês de globalização. *Insight Inteligência, 90*, 106–115.

Pautasso, D. (2019). A Nova Rota da Seda e seus desafios securitários: Os EUA e a contenção do eixo Sino-Russo. *Estudos Internacionais, 7*, 85–100.

Pautasso, D., & Ungaretti, C. (2017). A Nova Rota da Seda e a recriação do sistema sinocêntrico. *Estudos Internacionais, 4*, 25–44.

Rodrigues, B., & Hendler, B. (2018). Investimento externo chinês na América Latina e no Sudeste Asiático: Uma análise de escopo, valores e setores-alvo. *Estudos Internacionais, 6*(3), 5–25.

Shambaugh, D. (2013). *China goes global: The partial power*. Oxford University Press.

Staff, R. (2019, March 27). *China development bank provides over $190 billion for Belt and Road projects*. Reuters.

Stuenkel, O. (2018). *O mundo pós-ocidental*. Zahar.

Trenin, D. (2002). *The end of Eurasia*. Carnegie Endowment for International Peace.

Vasylieva, N., & Lagutina, M. (2016). *The Russian project of Eurasia integration*. Rowman & Littlefield Publishing.

Xavier, C. (2018). *Bridging the Bay of Bengal: Toward a stronger BIMSTEC*. Carnegie Endowment for International Peace.

Xinhua. (2017, May 14). *Full text of President Xi's speech at the opening of the Belt and Road forum*. Belt and Road Forum report. Retrieved on 24 March 2021, from http://2017.beltandroadforum.org/english/n100/2018/0306/c25-1038.html.

Yang, Y. (2020, November 8). Chinese companies listed on fortune global 500. *China Daily*. Retrieved on 24 March 2021, from https://www.chinadaily.com.cn/a/202008/11/WS5f324861a31083481725f9fe.html.

Yiwei, W. (2016). *The Belt and Road initiative*. New World Press.

Zhao, M. (2019). Is a new cold war inevitable? Chinese perspectives on the US-China strategic competition. *The Chinese Journal of International Politics, 12*(3), 1–24.

Zhao, S. (2011). *China's new foreign policy assertiveness: Motivations and implications*. ISPI.

Chapter 32
Sino-Iranian Cooperation in Artificial Intelligence: A Potential Countering Against the US Hegemony

Mohammad Eslami, Nasim Sadat Mosavi, and Muhammed Can

1 Introduction

Over the past four decades, the Iranian government has recognized the United States (US) as its main enemy and has defined a major part of its foreign policy based on confronting this enemy (Eslami et al., 2021). This confrontation took on different dimensions during the leadership of Ayatollah Khamenei and compared to the time of Ayatollah Khomeini (1979–1989) when the slogan "neither the East nor the West" was the cornerstone of Tehran's foreign policy; it changed direction to the policy of "looking at the East" (Avdaliani, 2020). In this new policy, China, due to its high economic power, has played a decisive role in Iran's foreign policy, and Tehran, especially in the face of Washington's sanctions, has relied more on it than any other country (Gentry, 2005; Tabatabai & Esfandiary, 2018). While the antagonizing relations between Iran and the US have caused the former to face various problems, China has played a critical role in offering strategic support through growing bilateral relationships, particularly in the area of knowledge and technology transfer for military purposes (Mandelbaum, 2019). After the Iranian revolution in 1979 and reforming China and Iran's political relation, both countries have continued their beneficial relationship in various areas such as science, technology, energy, and trade, where this partnership has challenged their common threat; US hegemony in the contemporary world politics (Tabatabai & Esfandiary, 2018).

The US views China as a state disturbing balance of power via various involvements such as increasing its military power and political influence. China aims to limit US regional access by modernization of its military and also economic empowerment (Saniabadi, 2019). Based on that policy, Iran's growth as a regional power has provided a unique opportunity for China to develop the policy via empowering Iran under different strategic plans such as the Belt and Road Initiative (BRI), which is the Chinese version of globalization. One of the dimensions of BRI is breaking the

M. Eslami (✉) · N. S. Mosavi · M. Can
University of Minho, Minho, Portugal

US hegemony and alliance with the anti-US countries such as Iran. Whereas Iran, as the first-class threat for the US and its allies, is pushing forward with its drone capabilities and emerging other technologies for coordinating ballistic missiles, speedboats, planes, tanks, many analysts attribute Iran's technological advances to China's support (Ajili & Rouhi, 2019).

The bilateral partnership between Iran and China not only influences sectors such as trade, economy, politics, culture, and security but also influences the military industries through the emergence of Artificial Intelligence (AI) applications. Indeed, today AI has implications not only in the military realm but also it is possible to expect that these implications will determine the national power of any given country in the near future (Daniels & Chang, 2021). Yet still, progress in AI depends predominantly on key factors such as data, AI talent, and computing power that are even challenging for the US and China. Therefore, any prediction regarding the long-term implications of AI in global politics might fall short and be misleading. For instance, Feijoo et al. (2020) created a framework regarding possible scenarios on technological development in AI. They compared potential pathways of the US, the European Union (EU), and China in ways in which these actors intervene the trajectory of AI development. Regardless of the type of industry, one of the major areas in using AI, is decision-making. Where AI techniques (e.g., robotics, machine learning) perform over data, using powerful componential techniques and mathematical algorithms for proposing transparent and accurate outcomes (Rasch et al., 2003).

Emerging AI in the military influences not only the accurate military decision-making process (Rasch et al., 2021) but also pioneers adopting autonomous and automatic warfare such as autonomous weapons and vehicles where it performs the substance of human's absence. AI applications projected in military support targeting, surveillance, observation, cyber security, detection, and operations (e.g., logistics, administration) aiming to copy human's intelligence with high-componential power for performing faster, optimized and accurate (Jiang et al., 2020). Considering the huge investment in developing AI applications in the military, still, the reliability and credibility of such technological innovations need to be seen in the future. Like any other technological diffusion, AI adopted in the military demands more practical evidence, research work, restructuring ethical policies, and setting new ethical aspects (Mosavi & Santos, 2021).

Drawing on the strategic documents signed by Iran and China during the last decade and focusing on the military and technological agreements between the two countries, this chapter argues that China's cooperation with Iran is a potential opportunity for the latter to strengthen its military power via projecting advanced technologies and adopting related training as well as assistance offered by Chinese experts. This strategic plan will remarkably influence the Middle East's military balance in favour of China and Iran. We, therefore, seek possible answers to the following question: Can Sino-Persia's cooperation in artificial intelligence counter the US hegemony? Furthermore, we argue that Iran–China cooperation in technology (specifically in AI) can be a key factor for regional dynamics in the Middle East. In addition to this, given the rising competition in emerging technologies along with polarization in global technology policies (Democracies vs. Authoritarian governments), we assess that Iran is a key actor to counter the US technology hegemony considering Iran's huge influence in the Middle East.

The present contribution is structured as follows. Section 1 discusses the historical background of China–Iran relations explaining how the anti-US ideology of these actors led to their cooperation on AI technology. Section 2 discusses the role of AI in military sectors. Section 3 looks into the global implications of China's AI strategy. Section 4 discusses the role of AI in Iran's defence and security policy. Section 5 demonstrates the potential uprising of the Sino-Persian partnership against the US hegemony by adopting artificial intelligence technology. The final section concludes.

2 Sino-Persian Relations: From Anti-US Ideology to Anti-US Technology

Iran's strategic relations with China dates back to 2600 years ago. However, in the recent decades and following the Islamic Revolution in Iran in 1979, the relation between China and Iran has changed to a strategic partnership due to the anti-US nature of both countries (Azad, 2017; Park & Glenn, 2010). Being in an economic war with the US, China has shown its tendency towards Iran as a country that can contribute to China's anti-US goals. During Ayatollah Khomeini's era (1979–1989), the most important strategic issue in Tehran-Beijing relations was the export of weapons to Iran. Iran's relations with both the US and the Soviet Union were overshadowed due to the specific ideology of Ayatollah Khomeini during the Eight-Year War. The country had difficulty meeting its military needs. As a result, during the war, Iran entered into arms deals with countries other than the two superpowers and bought more weapons from China than from any other country (Eslami, 2021). In addition to these direct purchases, the export of North Korean surface-to-surface missiles to Iran at the end of the war, which was important in Iran's retaliatory attacks during the "War of the Cities," was, in fact, Chinese-made missiles assembled in Korean factories and exported to Tehran with the green light of Beijing. In addition, China sold several anti-ship "silkworm"[1] missiles to Iran. In fact, China's key exports to Iran during the war were the same missiles that played a key role in Iran's retaliatory attacks on oil and merchant ships for Iraq, the so-called "War of Tankers" (Eslami & Sotoudehfar, 2021).

Iran–China relations have seen many ups and downs in recent years, especially with China's positive voting for a number of UN Security Council resolutions (Perteghella, & Talbot, 2020). In spite of enjoying the veto power, Beijing voted in favour of Resolutions n. 1696, 1737, 1747, 1803, 1835, 1887, and 1929, most of

---

[1] There has always been a debate about China's reliability within Iranian political elites. According to official documents, China's military support to Iraq during the war with Iran was more than China's weapon export to Iran. In this way, Saddam received even more missiles than Iran from China.

which included extensive sanctions against Tehran. Iran's development of its nuclear programme, Ballistic Missile Program (BMP) and Unmanned Combat Aerial Vehicles (UCAV) programme, as well as its Artificial Intelligence (AI) and Cyber Security Technologies (CST), promoted Iran as a "regional power" and made western countries to prevent Iran's domination over the Middle East (Eslami & Vieira, 2020). However, China decided to approach Iran and improve its relationship with the latter as an anti-Western country that can contribute to China's comprehensive cold war with the US and the Western bloc (Tabatabai & Esfandiary, 2018).

The relation between the two countries has been improving due to their cooperation under a joint comprehensive plan of action (JCPOA) as well as their economic partnership in the oil and gas industries. More recently, Iran signed a 25 years agreement with China, which includes the sectors such as trade, economy, politics, culture, and security, as well as military industries, Artificial Intelligence (AI), and Robotics and cyber technologies (Belal, 2020). One of the dimensions of the China–Iran coalition is military and warfare technology exchanges. While Iran is isolated due to international sanctions, such an action seems perfectly reasonable (Bazoobandi, 2015; Dorraj & Currier, 2008). The two countries have a comprehensive strategic partnership that emphasizes defence cooperation. They have long-standing diplomatic ties and historical ties dating back centuries. Iran is a huge potential market for Chinese industries. China, a US$ 13 trillion economy, receives only a few million dollars in the form of resuming arms sales to Iran. At the same time, it also provokes US hostility and dissatisfaction with Iran's rivals in the Middle East. Many of these competitors are also China's strategic partners (Osiewicz, 2018). While Iran's arms embargo expired in October 2020, the US efforts to extend it have drawn widespread international criticism (Eslami, 2022). This is at a time when relations between the US and China have declined to their lowest level in decades, making Beijing's views on Iran even more important. To the extent that some of the experts believe that China will be Iran's first weapon and warfare technology supplier.

3 The Role of AI in Military Power

Although there is no unique and agreed definition of AI, the general concept is defined as the capability of computer systems to perform tasks in a way that requires human intelligence. for instance, decision-making, speech recognition, and visual perception (Delen, 2020). The fast development of AI has offered advanced capabilities and opportunities in both military and non-military (e.g., transportation, healthcare, manufacturing, business, education, entertainment) areas (Li et al., 2018). Substituting AI regardless of the type of industry improves human performance in terms of accuracy, speed, and machine decision-making (Mosavi & Santos, 2020) in a complex environment (Maas, 2019).

During the years, many countries have developed military applications using AI in defence, warfare, and security where accurate operation with less human involvement is required (Yan, 2020). According to Fig. 1, from a general point of view

Optimization	Optimizing Automated Processing
Example: Improving signal to noise ratio in detection.	

Decision Support	Assisting humans to make sense of complicated and large data
Example: Situation awareness.	

Autonomy	The system acts when specific conditions are met
Example: Autonomous weapons.	

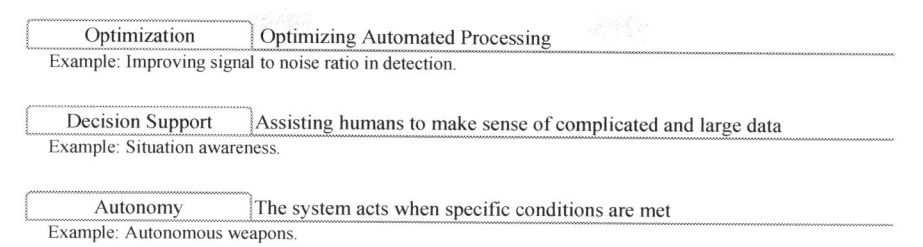

Fig. 1 Major categories of AI applications in military 2020 (*Source* Klijn and Okano-Heijmans [2020])

the major AI applications in the military includes: optimizing automated processing (e.g., improving signal to noise ratio in detection), decision support (automated data analysis and assisting human to make sense of complicated and large data) and autonomy (system performs when specific conditions are met).

Although Machine Learning (ML) as a category of AI has attracted the military domain for developing autonomous systems such as weapon platforms in the air, on land, and underwater, the successful outcome of such adoption depends on the progress in developing other technologies such as sensors and robotics. AI applications that project ML are effective for predicting future behaviour and optimization where precise and high-componential decision-making is required. ML uses data to train algorithms to propose the best possible performance. Predicting behaviour/situation is an example of using ML algorithms (Masuhr, 2019). Besides, robotics is another category of AI, where utilizing this technology in the military supports tasks such as mine detection and destruction where human involvement is minimized. According to Tom Ryden, iRobot, director of sales and marketing in industrial division of US government: "We're happy that the robot could be in a situation so that a soldier didn't have to be—one robot lost means one soldier was not." The PackBot is an example of an autonomous robot that was deployed for the Afghanistan war in 2002 for investigating reconnaissance missions in caves and buildings (Voth, 2004).

As Fig. 2 presents, AI has been emerged in the military through various projects and for different purposes such as Automatic Target Recognition (ATR), for example, identification of legitimate threats that targeting presupposes strategic nuclear missiles where the accuracy calculate, Cyberwarfare, surveillance such as situation awareness, (Suchman, 2020), Robotic Autonomous Systems (RAS) such as strategic armed race or even "new cold war" between countries such as China and the US (Maas, 2019). Furthermore, for predictive performance such as predictive maintenance and also optimization operations such as improving logistics, transport, and administrative tasks (Klijn & Okano-Heijmans, 2020; Masuhr, 2019; Mori, 2018).

Over the past years, surpassing the US's military power has been a strategic policy for China to challenge the hegemony of the US, particularly in the area of "weapons." With a US$ 175 billion allocated budget in 2019, China has the second-largest military budget, where this value is only one third of the US military. China, in fact,

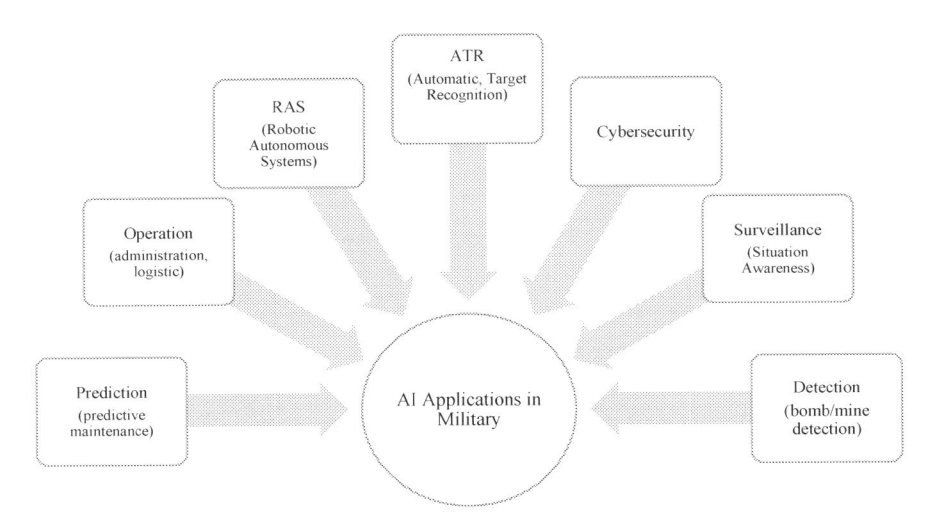

Fig. 2 Examples of AI applications in military 201820192020 (*Source* Authors, based on Mori [2018]; Masuhr [2019]; and Klijn and Okano-Heijmans [2020])

views AI as an opportunity to overtake the US over military modernization (Roberts et al., 2021a, 2021b). Chinese research for developing AI and robotics in the military sector backs to the mid-1980. Between the 1980s and 1990s, adopting expert systems and decision support systems in the military was actively launched many projects. In the mid-2000, Research & Development (R&D) efforts shifted to developing weapons and applying advanced algorithms to work on hypersonic glide vehicles and make cruise and ballistic missiles more 'intelligent equipped within Automatic Target Recognition (ATR) that is the major concern for autonomous weapons (). The urgent need to project AI and ML in the US military was announced in April 2017 by the US Department of Defense (DoD) under the project initiation of Maven. This project aimed to use AI for object detection, classification, and alert mainly to automate weapon targeting via using data generated by DoD (Johnson, 2019). Obtaining perfect accuracy in threat identification was the major purpose of launching this project. In the area of automated operation, the US adopted object recognition techniques for targeting aerial strikes or aerial surveillance in Afghanistan and Iraq and for undeclared war in Yemen, Somalia, and Pakistan. Furthermore, automatic data analysis to discover patterns and actionable Information (Suchman, 2020). Whereas AI is projected to create automated systems in different areas (commercial, military), several countries such as the US, China, and the EU present incredible progress for developing autonomous systems (underwater, air, ground vehicles) for modernizing the military sector. Different types of autonomous helicopters controllable by smartphone is an example (Cummings, 2017).

The future of AI in the military is strong links with designing and developing autonomous systems and robots where the independence of knowledge, expert, and reasoning is the key. (Cummings, 2017) Autonomous systems are those that perform via generating alternatives/behaviour and choosing the best possible outcome. In other words, where autonomous systems perform through understanding and decision-making, automated systems follow rule/base structure and if–then-else scenarios to propose output. Some examples of AI world models for autonomous systems are Radar, GPS, and Computer vision, where sensing (collecting information and processing), optimization & verifications (generating options and evaluating alternatives) lead to action (proactive decision) (Yan, 2020). Although autonomous and automated systems applied in the military provides accuracy, faster reaction, optimization, and carry componental power, the technology needs reliability and transparency to be utilized (Mosavi & Santos, 2021). Furthermore, as mentioned above, the speed of other technological development is an influential factor for AI's effective and successful use. Moreover, where the control of humans is absent, restructuring policies, regulations, and standards are required. For instance, developing and using autonomous weapons or killer robots are cases that caries doubts in terms of moral standards (Klijn & Okano-Heijmans, 2020; Li et al., 2018).

4 Chinese AI Strategy and Global Political Implications

The term 'ganchao' in Chinese refers to 'catch and surpass' that has long been one of the Chinese Communist Party's (CCP) ultimate goals not only in global politics but also in technological development (Gewirtz, 2019). From the beginning of supreme leader Mao Zedong to Xi Jinping, technology was an important end for CCP (Gewirtz, 2019). Exponential growth in AI technologies has strengthened this posture and led China to reify robust AI strategies to become competitive in the emerging technology realm. CCP's support for AI development traces back to 2006 when the State Council launched the 'National Medium-and Long-Term Plan' (MLP) for the Development of Science and Technology (Ding, 2018). Xi Jinping has continuously encouraged AI development along with domestic innovation. He pointed out the need for a comprehensive approach: "We must strengthen deliberations and decisions, plan matters comprehensively, coordinate and innovate, move ahead steadily, and make strengthening original innovation capability into a focus point" (Kania & Creemers, 2018, para. 5). As for the importance of AI, he stressed that in his speech, "AI is a vital driving force for a new round of technological revolution and industrial transformation, and speeding up AI development is a strategic issue to decide whether we can grasp opportunities" (Xin & Chi-Yuk, 2018, para.6). A large and growing body of literature has investigated AI development in China (Lee, 2018; Horowitz et al., 2018; Kania, 2019a, 2019b; Roberts et al., 2021a, 2021b). For instance, Ahmed et al. (2018) compare three great powers' AI policies, notably the US, China, and Russia. They focus on how regime types differ in AI development and how AI has shifted the security policies of these three countries. Like them, Fischer (2018) and Webster et al. (2019) focus on state-led development and the enhanced technological capacity of China. Indeed, capacity and capabilities are key factors for China to challenge US tech hegemony partly because what determines AI development capacity is not merely depending on a mighty economy. Rather, other variables include social capital/epistemic communities, comprehensive funding schemes, structured R&D activities, and specific inputs mostly related to the AI stack (data, computing power, talent) (Buchanan, 2020; Ding, 2019). Therefore, China takes a 'whole government' approach in AI development and different strategies such as 'Military-Civil Fusion' that distinguish China from its major counterparts.

Starting from the Alpha GO's success over world champion (ancient Chinese game GO) Lee Sedol in 2016, which is mostly presented as 'sputnik moment' for China in the literature, great powers have realized the potential of AI not only its socio-economic benefits but also its game-changer characteristics in the battlefield (Johnson, 2019; Kania, 2021; Schiavenza, 2018). In 2017, the State Council of China released its first structured plan, and even the most ambitious one for some, titled 'New Generation Artificial Intelligence Development Plan' although previous plans such as "Internet + " or "Made in China 2025" included projections related to AI development (Ding, 2018). Through 'New Generation Artificial Intelligence, China set the goal of becoming a world leader in AI by 2030, investing US$ 150 billion into the AI industry, and setting standards and ethical norms (Roberts et al., 2021a, 2021b). In addition to these actions, China started to expand its global digital reach through 'Digital Silk Road' (DSR) projects under the banner of the BRI, which prompted Western powers to reconsider their strategies to offset Chinese digital expansion (Kurlantzick, 2020). For instance, establishing 'Global Partnership on Artificial Intelligence' (GPAI) with fifteen founding members, notably democratic countries, such as Australia, Canada, the US or the United Kingdom (UK), was merely a reflection of aspiration to counter Chinese digital expansion harness the trajectory of AI. It is worth noting that all these developments were not a coincidence; rather, they were consequences of three distinct factors (technological breakthroughs, particularly in ML, rising Chinese economy, and global power vacuum during the Trump administration) that slightly signifies coming global technological bipolarity (Can & Kaplan, 2020). Since the establishment of the DSR initiative in 2015, China has signed an agreement with at least sixteen different countries DSR-related technologies ranging from artificial intelligence, surveillance technology, mobile payment systems to cloud computing that accounted for a US$ 79 billion investments (Ghiasy & Krishnamurthy, 2021; Kurlantzick, 2020). Africa is a hotspot for China that has actively engaged through technology trade with underdeveloped/developing countries. Take, for instance; it has established twenty-four different data centres, for the time being, provided surveillance technologies to fourteen countries, built up more than twenty-five smart city projects, set up fourteen overseas offices along with five different R&D labs according to estimates (Australian Strategic Policy Institute, 2021). Apart from DSR, China boosted its global technology network through foreign direct investments such as German robot maker 'Kuka' or the ongoing acquisition of the UK's largest semiconductor manufacturer Newport Wafer Fab (NWF) (Sweney, 2021). Semiconductors are key for China since its reliance on foreign technology exports and the significance of semiconductors for AI development. More importantly, China has invested in critical US tech companies such as Cohesity, a security and data management company with close business relationships with several US departments (US-China Economic & Security Review Commission, 2019). Hence, there are compelling reasons to argue that China will continue expanding its global technology network in the near future though it is difficult to assess for now the overall success of these ambitious projects. Given the recent rift between the US and China and their different approach to technology in terms of regulations and setting standards, it is likely to witness bipolarity in global technology policy shortly. However, again it is hard to foresee the trajectory of coming bipolarity—even though the Biden administration has taken a similar approach to President Trump in terms of China—since the level of interdependence. There are other precarious points regarding what extent AI will continue to diffuse and grow given its well-known 'winter-spring cycles, and it is not clear whether China's economic growth will remain at the same pace. Moreover, allies and partners of both countries' role is also a significant factor that will impact global political implications of AI, particularly in their balancing or bandwagoning strategies.

5 Artificial Intelligence and Iran's Defence and Security Policies

During the last decade, Iran has always been among the top countries in the fields of artificial intelligence (Mehr-News, 2020). Today, traces of artificial intelligence, robots, and cognitive sciences, many of which are based on computer science, can be seen in various industries in Iran, including medicine, software, weather forecasting, robots, and even the humanities. However, the impact of artificial intelligence on Iran's defence and security industries has been much greater (Fetzer, 1990; Gordon & Matsumura, 2013).

Iran's approach towards artificial intelligence is similar to China in some senses. As we argued in the previous section, focusing on artificial intelligence technology, China intends to extend its domination over the world and be the number one economic, military and political actor in the world (Mosher, 2000). Iran has a similar ambition for developing its AI technologies, but on a smaller scale. Post-revolutionary Iran has always been trying to establish its role as the Islamic world leader and regional power in the Middle East (Eslami et al., 2021). This superiority and domination over the region is not considered to be possible without a strong and modern army (Kreps & Zenko, 2014). Besides the ambitions for superiority, the sense of threat also is one of the driving factors that pushed Iran to develop its defence capabilities. Nowadays, the strategic challenges Iran's faces are beyond the attack of Iraq (Adib-Moghaddam, 2006). Saudi Arabia's assertiveness as a regional power and Israel and the US increasing military and political domination over the Middle East, and the emergence of terrorist groups in the region can be considered good examples of Iran's strategic challenges (Adib-Moghaddam, 2007). Something that pushes the country to describe the conflicts and hostility with the US and Israel as part of its national interest (Eslami & Vieira, 2022). As a country that has been in a long-lasting conflict with Israel and is surrounded by several US military bases, Iran has a special focus on its defence and security policy. However, due to the existence of international sanctions after the revolution of 1979, the country was not able to buy new warfare, renovate its military forces and especially its antiquated air forces (Adib-Moghaddam, 2012). Therefore, Iran put its main effort into developing ballistic missiles, military drones, speed-boats, and other modern warfare that necessarily work with artificial intelligence (Ajili et al., 2019).

Nowadays, Iran has the largest missile power and the biggest squadron of military drones in Western Asia (Brookes, 2019; Eslami, 2021). Accordingly, the country has the potential capability to challenge its enemies in the region. The Iranian Revolutionary Guards Corps (IRGC) recently used artificial intelligence in a military exercise called "The Great Prophet 15" (Salami, 2021). Emphasizing that "the use of artificial intelligence applications in Iran's military industry has created a new capability for the Iranian armed forces," Hajizadeh said the exercise used a combination of missile and UAV power to attack ground targets tested. He went on to claim that the use of "artificial intelligence technology in combined operations using ballistic missiles and attack drones has given the Revolutionary Guards new powers" (Hajizadeh, 2021).

Contrary to extensive studies on Iran's BMP and UCAV programme, research on Iran's navy forces, especially speed-boats are rare. High-speed boats are the most prominent feature of the Islamic Republic of Iran's naval power in the Persian Gulf and the Strait of Hormuz, which are controlled by artificial intelligence (Ajili et al., 2019). The very serious challenge that the presence of speed-boats in the Persian Gulf poses to American forces can be considered a strong reason for the investment and development of speed-boats. The use of unmanned surface vehicles, or USVs, is a relatively new and influential area in the creation of naval power that has received worldwide attention in recent years. It is considered the greatest operational and tactical challenge for the US Navy in this region. A challenge that both the West and the Americans have acknowledged sees Iran's naval warfare tactics as increasing operational capability in asymmetric combat by using speed-boats and "mass attack" tactics against targets (Ajili et al., 2019).

Iranian anti-missile systems, including the surface-to-air missile launchers as well as all radars and cyber warfare, work with artificial intelligence. The precision and advancement of such systems can be found from the shootdown of the US surveillance drone RQ4 (global hawk) in the Strait of Hormuz by Iranian missile systems (Eslami & Vieira, 2020). In addition, Iran is developing several versions of fighter robots that are capable of increasing the power of Iran's ground forces. All we mentioned above are the applications of artificial intelligence in Iranian military programmes, which helped the country to survive in the international system and preserve its territorial integrity contrary to the high level of tensions and conflicts in the Middle East.

6 Opposing the US by Adopting Artificial Intelligence Technology

The US is considered to be the first-class threat for both China and Iran, and the roots of hostility between the US and these two countries have gone deeper during recent years. During the Trump era (2016–2021), China faced an economic confrontation with the US (Conduit & Akbarzadeh, 2019). Imposing sanctions for different reasons on the one hand and restricting Chinese production in the US market by putting a high tax, on the other hand, influenced China's economy (Bazoobandi, 2015; Itakura, 2020; Mikheev & Lukonin, 2019). Iran also deals with an old enmity with the US following the coup of 1953, US support of Saddam Hussein in the Iran–Iraq War (1980–1988), imposing economic sanctions on Iran (1979-present), withdrawal from the nuclear deal (2018), and the most recent assassination of General Qasem Soleimani (2020) (Eslami, 2021).

All mentioned above was considered as the US declaration of war for China and Iran. Having a common threat brought Iran and China together to cooperate for a common national interest, "breaking US hegemony" (Tabatabai & Esfandiary, 2018). To break the US hegemony and oppose the US in the international arena, economic and military power play a key role, and the first precondition for a big economy and a strong army in the twenty-first century is artificial intelligence technology. Although both China and Iran have invested in developing Intelligent warfare technologies, particularly in the defence sector, via strategic cooperation with academia and private sectors and recruiting AI talent, the success of such technological diffusion needs to be analyzed in the future. The defence sector is one of the areas in which China has supported Iran to strengthen since the Iran–Iraq war (Bhat, 2014). Beijing has become one of the major sources of warfare supplies for Iran, providing 80% of Iran's arms (Conduit & Akbarzadeh, 2019), exporting thousands of tanks, artillery pieces' combat aircraft, and dozens of small warships. Building missile factories in Isfahan and Semnan, training Iranian scientists, and administrative assistance is areas where China cooperates with Iran (Eslami, 2021). While missile and weapon export from China has been terminated or suspended under the US pressure and sanction, the cooperation efforts have shaped to empower Iran's military with technology and knowledge transfer for Iran to build ballistic missiles and nuclear technology independently (Garver, 2011; Hughes, 2015).

In October 2020, all sanctions on Iran's military sectors were lifted under the United Nations Security Council Resolution 2231. Accordingly, Iran can buy all types of conventional weapons and export its military products without any limitations. Is China about to be Iran's first weapon supplier? In an isolation situation, such a thing seems perfectly reasonable (Bazoobandi, 2015). Especially after the signing of a comprehensive strategic partnership in 2021, the countries emphasized defence cooperation. They have long-standing diplomatic ties and historical ties dating back centuries. Iran is a huge potential market for Chinese products, not only in weapons but also in the field of consumer and industrial goods. However, Iran's approach towards China is different. Iranian officials have repeatedly declared that they are only interested in importing technology from China and not the products. In this line, Iran counts on importing modern weapons from China and the knowledge and the technology to build the same products in a few years. Therefore, joint projects with China to produce autonomous weapons and AI-based warfare are among Iran's top priorities. China but has a different vision for this issue. China needs an ally in the Middle East to preserve its national interest including, energy security and opposing the US unipolarity (Garver, 2015). However, in China's cost and benefit calculations, a partnership with Iran is not as important as with the US. China has a mutual interdependence with the US. Therefore, it is not possible to predict to what extent the China–Iran partnership will be successful.

Nonetheless, this partnership has the potential to challenge the US hegemony in the long term. The result of our study demonstrates that challenging US supremacy is strongly dependent on the development of modern technologies, including artificial intelligence. Something that Iran and China are planning for in their recent cooperation.

7 Conclusion

In this chapter, we focused on Iran and China's potential cooperation in the field of AI to oppose the US hegemony. We started with historical relations between Iran and China dating back to 2600 years ago and explained how their positive approach towards their historical relations made the two countries trust each other once again and try to balance the US unipolarity. We then continued by introducing the anti-US ideology of Iran and China as one of the main driving factors of their relations, which can even bring them closer in the near future. While pointing to the source of hostility between these two countries, we argued that Trump's economic war with China and his withdrawal from JCPOA and assassination of Iran's Soleimani reinforced the possibility of a confrontation between the two parties. Securing the economic interest of China in the Middle East and preserving Iran's territorial integrity requires a very strong and modern military power. In the contemporary era, consolidating military power without the development and employment of artificial intelligence is impossible.

Middle East's energy resources and rich market are important for China's economic plans, including Belt and Road Initiatives and New Silk Road. Thus, US domination over the region is against China's national interests. However, due to China's economic interdependency with the US, China's priority is not to confront the US directly. Accordingly, the country considers consolidating Iran's military power as a possible way to balance US power in the Middle East. Artificial intelligence plays a key role in military power. China has modernized its army with several new warfares utilizing AI China's nuclear programmes, ballistic missiles, military drones, and China's other military capabilities are synchronized with AI. Moreover, the country is planning to develop a fully automatic army working with robots instead of soldiers. Iran's new style of war depends on AI Ballistic missiles, military drones, and Iran's space programme, which are considered key factors that deter the US from attacking Iran using AI technology. The advantages of AI for Iran's military programmes push Iran towards the development of AI technology, and there is no country willing to support Iran with technology transfer but China.

In recent years, Iran's relation with China has had a special focus on AI as far as the issue of technological exchanges and Artificial intelligence has been changed to the most important elements of Iran and China after energy exchange and COVID-19. The case of AI has been mentioned three times in Iran's 25 years deal with China, and the countries agreed on cooperation in IA and military sectors. Therefore, we argue that Iran–China cooperation in technology (specifically in AI) can be a key factor for regional dynamics in the Middle East. In addition to this, given the rising competition in emerging technologies along with polarization in global technology policies (Democracies vs. Authoritarian governments), we assess that Iran is a key actor to counter the US. Notably, AI as an emerging field in science and technology is not known in all academic debates, especially inter-disciplinary fields. Accordingly, there are still some ontological and epistemological ambiguities in the employment of AI as a new phenomenon in international relations. In addition, the applications of AI in military sectors are a secret issue, and therefore, most official documents and agreements are not accessible. All in all, AI as a new field that can influence economic, security, and political relations between countries should not be underestimated. The impact of AI on implementing the digital Silk Road can be an interesting topic for future studies. Furthermore, future studies might examine the role of actors (states) but also non-state agencies and their effects on specific policy-making.

References

Adib-Moghaddam, A. (2006). *The international politics of the Persian Gulf: A cultural genealogy.* Routledge.
Adib-Moghaddam, A. (2007). Inventions of the Iran–Iraq war. *Critique: Critical Middle Eastern Studies, 16*(1), 63–83.
Adib-Moghaddam, A. (2012). What is radicalism? Power and resistance in Iran. *Middle East Critique, 21*(3), 271–290.
Ahmed, S., Bajema, N. E., Bendett, S., Chang, B. A., Creemers, R., Demchak, C. C., & Kania, E. (2018). *AI, China, Russia, and the global order: Technological, political, global, and creative perspectives.* NSI Boston United States.
Ajili, H., & Rouhi, M. (2019). Iran's military strategy. *Survival, 61*(6), 139–152.
Australian Strategic Policy Institute. (2021). *Mapping China's tech giants* [online]. China Tech Map. Retrieved on 17 July 2021, from https://chinatechmap.aspi.org.au/#/homepage/
Avdaliani. E. (2020). *Why is Iran turning east* [online]. Armynow. Available at: https://armynow.net/iran-turn-to-east/
Azad, S. (2017). *Iran and China: A new approach to their bilateral relations.* Rowman & Littlefield.
Belal, K. (2020). China-Iran relations: Prospects and complexities. *Policy Perspectives, 17*(2), 47. https://doi.org/10.13169/polipers.17.2.0047
Bazoobandi, S. (2015). Sanctions and isolation, the driving force of Sino-Iranian relations. *East Asia, 32*(3), 257–271.

Bhat, M. A. (2014). Iran-China relations: A challenge for US hegemony. *Quarterly Journal of Chinese Studies, 3*(2), 113.

Brookes, P. (2019). The growing Iranian unmanned combat aerial vehicle threat needs US action. *Heritage Foundation Backgrounder, 3437*.

Buchanan, B. (2020). *The AI Triad and what it means for national security strategy* [online]. CSET. Retrieved in December 2021, from https://cset.georgetown.edu/wp-content/uploads/CSET-AI-Triad-Report.pdf

Can, M., & Kaplan, H. (2020). Transatlantic partnership on artificial intelligence: Realities, perceptions and future implications. *Global Affairs, 6*(4–5), 537–557.

Conduit, D., & Akbarzadeh, S. (2019). Great power-middle power dynamics: The case of China and Iran. *Journal of Contemporary China, 28*(117), 468–481. https://doi.org/10.1080/10670564.2018.1542225

Cummings, M. L. (2017). *Artificial intelligence and the future of public relations. 12* (January), 1–16. Retrieved in December 2021, from https://www.icaew.com/-/media/corporate/files/technical/information-technology/technology/artificial-intelligence-report.ashx?la=en

Currier, C. L., & Dorraj, M. (2010). In arms we trust: The economic and strategic factors motivating China-Iran relations. *Journal of Chinese Political Science, 15*(1), 49–69. https://doi.org/10.1007/s11366-009-9082-6

Daniels, M., & Chang, B. (2021). *National power after AI* [online] Retrieved on 3 August 2021, from https://cset.georgetown.edu/publication/national-power-after-ai/

Delen, D. (2020). *Prescriptive analytics: The final frontier for evidence-based management and optimal decision making*. Pearson FT Press.

Ding, J. (2018). Deciphering China's AI dream [online]. *Future of Humanity Institute Technical Report*.

Ding, J. (2019). *China's current capabilities, policies, and industrial ecosystem in AI*.

Dorraj, M., & Currier, C. L. (2008). Lubricated with oil: Iran-China relations in a changing world. *Middle East Policy, 15*(2), 66–80.

Eslami, M., & Vieira, A. V. G. (2020). Iran's strategic culture: The 'revolutionary' and 'moderation' narratives on the ballistic missile programme. *Third World Quarterly, 42*(2), 312–328.

Eslami, M., & Vieira, A. V. G. (2022). Shi'a principles and Iran's strategic culture towards ballistic missile deployment. *International Affairs, 98*(2), 675–688.

Eslami, M. (2021). Iran's ballistic missile program and its foreign and security policy towards the United States under the Trump administration. *Revista Española De Ciencia Política, 55*, 37–62.

Eslami, M. (2022). Iran's drone supply to Russia and changing dynamics of the Ukraine war. *Journal for Peace and Nuclear Disarmament*, 1–12.

Eslami, M., Bazrafshan, M., & Sedaghat, M. (2021). Shia geopolitics or religious tourism? Political convergence of Iran and Iraq in the light of Arbaeen pilgrimage. In F. J. B. S. Leandro, C. Branco & F. Caba-Maria (Eds.), *The geopolitics of Iran* (pp. 363–385). Palgrave Macmillan.

Eslami, M., & Sotoudehfar, S. (2021). Iran–UAE relations and disputes over the sovereignty of Abu Musa and Tunbs. In F. J. B. S. Leandro, C. Branco & F. Caba-Maria (Eds.), *The geopolitics of Iran* (pp. 343–361). Palgrave Macmillan.

Feijóo, C., Kwon, Y., Bauer, J. M., Bohlin, E., Howell, B., Jain, R., Potgieter, P., Vu, K., Whalley, J., & Xia, J. (2020). Harnessing artificial intelligence (AI) to increase wellbeing for all: The case for a new technology diplomacy. *Telecommunications Policy, 44*(6), 101988.

Fetzer, J. H. (1990). What is Artificial Intelligence? In J. H. Fetzer (Ed.), *Artificial intelligence: Its scope and limits* (pp. 3–27). Springer.

Fischer, S. (2018, July 16). Artificial intelligence: China's high-tech ambitions. *CSS Analyses in Security Policy*, ETH Zürich. Retrieved in December 2021, from https://css.ethz.ch/content/dam/ethz/special-interest/gess/cis/center-for-securities-studies/pdfs/CSSAnalyse220-EN.pdf

Garver, J. W. (2011). Is China playing a dual game in Iran? *Washington Quarterly, 34*(1), 75–88. https://doi.org/10.1080/0163660X.2011.538296

Garver, J. (2013). China-Iran relations: Cautious friendship with America's nemesis. *China Report, 49*(1), 69–88. https://doi.org/10.1177/0009445513479247

Garver, J. W. (2015). The US factor in Sino–Iranian energy relations. *Sino-US Energy Triangles: Resource Diplomacy under Hegemony*, 207.

Gentry, J. B. (2005). The Dragon and the Magi: Burgeoning Sino-Iranian relations in the 21st century. *The China and Eurasia Forum Quarterly*, 3(3) (November), 111–125.

Gewirtz, J. (2019). China's long march to technological supremacy [online]. *Foreign Affairs*. Retrieved in December 2021, from https://www.foreignaffairs.com/articles/china/2019-08-27/chinas-long-march-technological-supremacy

Ghiasy, R., & Krishnamurthy, R. (2021). China's digital silk road and the global digital order [online]. *The Diplomat*. Retrieved on 17 July 2021, from https://thediplomat.com/2021/04/chinas-digital-silk-road-and-the-global-digital-order/

Gordon, J., & Matsumura, J. (2013). *The army's role in overcoming anti-access and area denial challenges*. RAND Corporation. Retrieved in December 2021, from https://www.rand.org/content/dam/rand/pubs/research_reports/RR200/RR229/RAND_RR229.pdf.

Hajizadeh, A. (2021, January, 25). *Releasing artificial intelligence technologies in Iranian military industries* [online]. Hoosho. Retrieved in December 2021, from https://hooshio.com/

Horowitz, M. C., Allen, G. C., Kania, E. B., & Scharre, P. (2018). *Strategic competition in an era of artificial intelligence*. Center for a New American Security.

Hughes, L. (2015, November). The energy and strategy of China—Iran relations [online]. *Future Directions International*, 1–6.

Itakura, K. (2020). Evaluating the impact of the US–China trade war. *Asian Economic Policy Review*, 15(1), 77–93.

Jiang, X., Coffee, M., Bari, A., Wang, J., Jiang, X., Huang, J., & Huang, Y. (2020). Towards an artificial intelligence framework for data-driven prediction of coronavirus clinical severity. *Computers, Materials & Continua*, 63(1), 537–551.

Johnson, J. (2019). Artificial intelligence & future warfare: Implications for international security. *Defense and Security Analysis*, 35(2), 147–169. Retrieved in December 2021, from https://doi.org/10.1080/14751798.2019.1600800

Kania, E. B. (2019a). *Center for a new American security*, 76–76. Retrieved in December 2021, from https://doi.org/10.1007/978-1-349-67278-3_123

Kania, E., & Creemers, R. (2018). *Xi Jinping calls for 'healthy development' of AI (translation)* [online]. New America. Retrieved 18 July 2021, from https://www.newamerica.org/cybersecurity-initiative/digichina/blog/xi-jinping-calls-for-healthy-development-of-ai-translation/

Kania, E. B. (2019b). Chinese military innovation in the AI revolution. *The RUSI Journal*, 164(5–6), 26–34.

Kania, E. B. (2021). Artificial intelligence in China's revolution in military affairs. *Journal of Strategic Studies*, 1–28, https://doi.org/10.1080/01402390.2021.1894136

Klijn, H., & Okano-Heijmans, M. (2020). Managing RAS : The need for new norms and arms control. *The Hague Centre for Strategic Studies*, 1–29.

Kreps, S., & Zenko, M. (2014). The next drone wars preparing for proliferation. *Foreign Affairs*, 93, 68.

Kurlantzick, J. (2020). China's digital silk road initiative: A boon for developing countries or a danger to freedom? *The Diplomat*. Retrieved 17 July 2021, from https://thediplomat.com/2020/12/chinas-digital-silk-road-initiative-a-boon-for-developing-countries-or-a-danger-to-freedom/

Lee, K. F. (2018). *AI superpowers: China, silicon valley, and the new world order*. Houghton Mifflin Harcourt.

Li, S., Wang, Y. & Wu, Z. C. (2018). Artificial Intelligence and unmanned warfare. *IEEE International Conference on Cloud Computing and Intelligence Systems*, pp. 336–339.

Maas, M. M. (2019). How viable is international arms control for military artificial intelligence? Three lessons from nuclear weapons. *Contemporary Security Policy*, 40(3), 285–311. https://doi.org/10.1080/13523260.2019.1576464

Masuhr, N. (2019). AI in military enabling applications. *ETH Zürich Research Collection* (251), 1–4. Retrieved from https://doi.org/10.3929/ethz-b-000367663

Mehr-News. (2020, October 10). Iran's ranking in artificial intelligence [online]. *Mehr News*. Available at: https://www.mehrnews.com/news/5051394/

Michael, M. (2019). *The new containment: Handling Russia, China, and Iran*.

Mikheev, V. V., & Lukonin, S. A. (2019). China–USA: Multiple vector of trade war. *Mirovaia Ekonomika i Mezhdunarodnye Otnosheniia, 63*(5), 57–66.

Mori, S. (2018). US defense innovation and artificial intelligence. *Asia-Pacific Review, 25*(2), 16–44. https://doi.org/10.1080/13439006.2018.1545488

Mosavi, N. S., & Santos, M. F. (2020). How prescriptive analytics influences decision making in precision medicine. *Procedia Computer Science, 177*, 528–533.

Mosavi, N., & Santos, M. (2021). *Characteristics of the intelligent decision support system for precision medicine (IDSS4PM)*. Computer Science & Information Technology (CS & IT); pp. 1–16

Mosher, S. W. (2000). *Hegemon: China's plan to dominate Asia and the world*.

Osiewicz, P. (2018). The Belt and Road Initiative (BRI): Implications for Iran-China Relations. *Przegląd Strategiczny, 8*(11), Retrieved in December 2021, from 221–232.

Park, J. S., & Glenn, C. (2010). Iran and China [online]. *The Iran Primer*, 182–185.

Perteghella, A., & Talbot, V. (2020). Russia's relations with Iran, Saudi Arabia, and Turkey: Friends in need, friends indeed? In C. Lovotti, E. T. Ambrosetti, C. Hartwell & A. Chmielewska (Eds.), *Russia in the Middle East and North Africa* (pp. 77–103). Routledge.

Purdy, M., Jing Qui, S., & Chen, F. (2017). *How artificial intelligence can drive China's growth | Accenture*. Retrieved in December 2021, from https://www.accenture.com/cn-en/insight-artificial-intelligence-china

Rasch, R., Kott, A., & Forbus, K. D. (2003). Incorporating AI into military decision making: An experiment. *IEEE Intelligent Systems, 18*(4), 18–26.

Rasch, M. J., Moreda, D., Gokmen, T., Le Gallo, M., Carta, F., Goldberg, C., ... & Narayanan, V. (2021, June). A flexible and fast PyTorch toolkit for simulating training and inference on analog crossbar arrays. In *2021 IEEE 3rd International Conference on Artificial Intelligence Circuits and Systems (AICAS)* (pp. 1–4). IEEE.

Roberts, H., Cowls, J., Morley, J., Taddeo, M., Wang, V., & Floridi, L. (2021a). The Chinese approach to artificial intelligence: An analysis of policy, ethics, and regulation. *AI and Society, 36*(1), 59–77. https://doi.org/10.1007/s00146-020-00992-2

Roberts, H., Cowls, J., Morley, J., Taddeo, M., Wang, V., & Floridi, L. (2021b). The Chinese approach to artificial intelligence: An analysis of policy, ethics, and regulation. *AI & SOCIETY, 36*(1), 59–77.

Salami, H. (2021, 25). The 15th military exercise of the great prophet [online]. *Entekhab News*. Retrieved in December 2021, from: https://www.entekhab.ir/fa/news/596301/

Saniabadi, E. R. (2019). Comparative analysis of U. S. 2017 national security strategy document towards China and Iran. *Geopolitics Quarterly, 14*(4), 188–208.

Suchman, L. (2020). Algorithmic warfare and the reinvention of accuracy. *Critical Studies on Security, 8*(2), 175–187. Retrieved in December 2021, from https://doi.org/10.1080/21624887.2020.1760587

Schiavenza, M. (2018). China's 'sputnik moment' and the Sino-American battle for AI supremacy [online]. *Asia Society*. Retrieved on 17 July 2021, from https://asiasociety.org/blog/asia/chinas-sputnik-moment-and-sino-american-battle-ai-supremacy

Sweney, M. (2021). Chinese-owned firm acquires UK's largest semiconductor manufacturer [online]. *The Guardian*. Retrieved on 17 July from https://www.theguardian.com/business/2021/jul/05/chinese-owned-firm-acquires-uks-largest-semiconductor-manufacturer

Tabatabai, A., & Esfandiary, D. (2018). *Triple-axis: Iran's relations with Russia and China*. Bloomsbury Publishing.

US-China Economic and Security Review Commission. (2019). *Annual Report to Congress* [online]. Washington DC. Retrieved on 8 July 2021, from https://www.uscc.gov/annual-report/2019-annual-report-congress

Voth, D. (2004). A new generation of military robots danna. *IEEE Intelligent Systems, 19*(4), 15–41.

Webster, G., Grotto, A., Wallace, I., Laskai, L., Toner, H., & Nelson, M. et al. (2019). *AI policy and China realities of state-led development*. Stanford University- New America Retrieved in December 2021, from https://d1y8sb8igg2f8e.cloudfront.net/documents/DigiChina-AI-report-20191029.pdf

Xin, Z., & Chi-Yuk, C. (2018). *Develop and control: Xi urges China to use AI in race for tech future* [online]. SCMP. Retrieved 10 June 2020, from https://www.scmp.com/economy/china-economy/article/2171102/develop-and-control-xi-jinping-urges-china-use-artificial

Yan, G. (2020). The impact of artificial intelligence on hybrid warfare. *Small Wars and Insurgencies*, *31*(4), 898–917. Retrieved in December 2021, from https://doi.org/10.1080/09592318.2019.1682908

Part III
The Potential of the BRI as a Cross-Border Initiative

Chapter 33
China and the Wave of Globalization Focusing on the Middle East

Flavius Caba-Maria

1 Introduction

The end of the Cold War brought on a new set of changes to the international world. At that moment, the international milieu transformed from a bipolar world, focusing more on trade links, various aspects of technological advances, and a revolution in communications. The world has become increasingly interconnected, encroached in a nexus of new links, where the economy dictates centres of power. In the light of these changes, there was cemented an enhanced interdependence between regional systems and fragmentation of former power centres. In the specific case of the Middle East, a new layer of changes took place in the wake of the Arab Spring—between the first and second decade of the twenty-first century. This enabled the presence of interdependence and the rise of relatively new players in the arena, as it is the case for China. The Popular Republic in its contemporary form benefits from its immense economic development and tries to respond to the necessities of the newly shaped Middle East. In fact, "China's economic penetration of the Middle East inevitably has far-reaching foreign policy and security implications" (Rózsa, 2020). The chapter addresses the new realm of the international milieu, together with China's relatively new role as a participant to the Middle East and North Africa's development.

In terms of theory, interdependence is a concept that values reciprocity, economic connectivity over military responses (the classical superpower attributes). Keohane and Nye elaborated in the late 1970s the postulate of interdependence from the premises that politics is mimicking reality. Interdependence in global affairs relates to "situations characterized by reciprocal effects among countries or among actors in different countries" (Keohane & Nye, 1977, p. 8). A complex interdependence is happening under three conditions, namely, the absence of force, a lack of hierarchy among issues, and growing contacts between societies. The new wave of globalization

---

F. Caba-Maria (✉)
Middle East Political and Economic Institute, Bucharest, Romania

corresponds to such conditions, especially as the communications' revolution diminished the space between interactions. In addition, there are no strict lines between domestic and foreign policy goals, which can be found exactly in the Chinese case, as the administration in Beijing mixes domestic and foreign policy goals.

Multidimensional interactions with Middle Eastern and African countries are part of an interdependence paradigm that is taking place globally, thus the presence of China in the Middle East and North Africa (MENA). China cultivates a vision for shared destiny for humanity, giving new meanings to cooperation between China and the rest of the world (China Intercontinental Press, 2014). China launched an updated version of the Silk Road, adapted to the twenty-first-century circumstances. It is entitled the Belt and Road Initiative (BRI). It links Africa, Asia, and Europe into one circle of cooperation (through land and sea), for the sake of mutual benefits. Africa is a continent that enjoys enormous untapped reserves of natural resources and represents a growing market, while the Middle East is abundant in hydrocarbon reserves specifically, and a young labour force, without many job prospects. The Middle East displays advantages for connectivity between the European and Asian landmasses. It could link China to its African projects, where it has several strongholds (in Central and East Africa). Europe and Asia form the two landmasses that have continuous exchanges, notably economic contacts, due to new shifts in the global markets. While Europe is eroding its financial power, Asia is rising. For these reasons, Ehteshami coined the term Asianization (2020), defined as an Eastwards shift in the global balance of power. As a result, the Middle East that always looked westwards has started to turn towards the East. Therefore, Middle Eastern States have systematically engaged with the Asian powers, based on economic reasoning, since it has become more appealing to do business with Asia, especially under the Chinese lead (Ehteshami & Bahgat, 2019).

In addition, we are witnessing the globalized world providing a channel for revived regionalism. Ever since the end of the Cold War, regionalization has gained strong momentum in the developing world (Asia, Africa, Latin America, the Arab world). As such, more forums and formats for regional cooperation have emerged, such as the Asia-Pacific Economic Cooperation, the Southern Common Market in South America (MERCOSUR), the Caribbean Community and Common Market (CARICOM), forums in South and East Asia, and two forums promoted by China with developing countries, namely the Forum on China–Africa Cooperation (FOCAC), and the China–Arab States Cooperation Forum (CASCF). The latter was inaugurated in 2004, by the former President Hu Jintao during a visit to the Arab League in Cairo. It upholds the principles of cooperation and coordination on foreign policy matters (Benabdallah, 2018).

China under President Xi Jinping pursues many geostrategic goals, both globally and regionally. Since 2013, Xi has set the tone for great projects in pursuit of attaining China's leadership in Asia, eroding the United States of America (US) prominence in international affairs (Yang, 2015, pp. 9–10). China has elaborated an overall geostrategic plan consisting of several circles: going out strategy (El-Shafei & Metawe, 2021), periphery strategy (working closely with neighbors for secure borders), Belt and Road Initiative, and Asian Infrastructure Investment Bank

(Di Donato, 2021). All of them serve the purpose of maximizing the Chinese competitive advantage obtained through manufacturing at a large scale and capitalizing on stocks. BRI has been described as China's *grand strategy* for a model of global governance steered by the Chinese leadership (Di Donato, 2021). In a way, we witnessed a new model put forward for global powers interrelations. These are part of the aspirations to reach the higher ladder of global power. Xi Jinping has accelerated the pace for Chinese leadership goals and acted accordingly in a swifter manner, by abandoning the previous "hide and bide" principle. He adopted instead the slogan of "strategic opportunity," which gives Chinese characteristics to an eventual regional or global interplay (Blackwill & Campbell, 2016, pp. 16–17; Mccahill, 2017, pp. 1–4).

In the pursuit of its development, China remains energy thirsty, for the reasons of huge domestic consumption that give China primacy in many industries. The great pace of development was highlighted in 2003 when it replaced Japan as the second world consumer of oil just behind the US (Lanteigne, 2009). The large necessities imply a sound supply system and finding markets for the finished products. In practice, it was translated into acquiring more ground in the African resource-rich countries, as well in countries on the road of international trade, such as the Persian Gulf countries. These ends of course force China to limit the influence of its competitors or limit their advantage in world affairs, especially the US, with whom it clashes at the ideological level. During the last few years, the Middle East has entered a period of crises and upheavals that took the tool on the regional balance, while prompting regional actors to search for forging new alliances or at least to adjust the existing ones. This occasion granted China the opportunity to display some of its newly acquired geostrategic plans, with a far-reaching sight of security goals, going beyond the traditional economic impact.

2 China in Relation to the Broader Middle East

We can name several reasons for China's engagement with the extended Middle East, first, driven by energy consumption, the Middle East being rich in oil and gas resources; stability in its Asia-Pacific neighbourhood; expanding the influence in a Eurasian context; while displaying and consolidation China's ambitions as a global player (Kamrava, 2018). Due to its abundant energy reserves and geostrategic importance, the Middle East has acquired an increasingly salient position in China's diplomacy since the beginning of the twenty-first century. When Chinese President Xi Jinping proposed the BRI, we could notice the Middle East was not mentioned per se as a strategic point, but it was implicit China needs it as a lynchpin between its grand projects. On this account, early in 2016, China produced its first "Arab Policy Paper." The document focuses on energy cooperation between China and Arab states within the BRI (China's Arab Policy Paper, 2016). In this vein, China has formulated a contemporary strategy for policies of the Middle East, although some aspects are remnants of the previous periods. For instance, the 1950s were represented by the "Big Bloc," whereas the "big export market" is a legacy of the 1980s, the "leverage in China-US relations" belongs to the 1990s, while the "vital energy supplier" has been the core of the 2000s (Retrieved on October 2021, from www.manaramagazine.org, 2021).

For China, the Middle East has obtained a more attractive status, whereas Middle Eastern leaders find more interest in the economic trend bouncing towards the East, which means we can witness a level of interdependence. BRI is the nexus between the projects envisaged by both parties, ultimately shaping the Eurasian context in the decades to come. For Middle Eastern countries, China's comparative economic advantage means new partnerships and opportunities for job creation (which are highly needed in the region); for China, the cooperation with Middle Eastern countries will bring economic benefits through oil and gas trade as well as investment in the petrochemical industry and infrastructure construction. The Middle East region brings together the land and maritime Silk Road, in a strategic location with diverse and complex religious, ethnic, and humane aspects. The fact that MENA is so abundant in hydrocarbon reserves, plays a decisive role in China's steps for engagement in a new format of diplomacy for the region. In the quest of China to obtain stability, the broader Middle East would play a security role in China's strategies and the consecrated economic cooperation and cultural exchanges framed under the BRI (Chaziza, 2020). According to the Asianisation trend, China's importance to the Middle East has risen considerably and not the contrary (Retrieved on October 2021, from www.manaramagazine.org, 2021). The indicators used by United Nations Conference on Trade and Development (UNCTAD) and the American Enterprise Institute (AEI) help us draw a comparison (Table 1). If in 2010, the Middle East accounted for 6.6% of China's foreign trade, it went up to 7.1% in 2019. In 2010, the Middle East accounted for 53.93% of China's total crude oil imports, accounting for 47% in 2019. China is increasingly important for crude oil exports from the Middle East (rising exponentially): in 2010, China accounted for 3.9% of, 22.6% in 2012, and 31.2% in 2019. As for the Foreign Direct Investments (FDI) inflow to the Middle East, China went from 3.3% in 2010 to 10.1% in 2019 (aei.org; UNCTAD, 2020).

As mentioned previously, as an overall aim, China had an incentive to go outside China and find markets for its manufactured goods and domestic companies, the Middle Eastern countries being ideal in this sense. From a strategic point of view, in the Middle East, the sea-lanes (Miyake, 2017) can obtain noticeable advantages over the US and can reduce costs significantly for delivering products elsewhere, mainly in Europe. Some of the countries important on the routes of BRI are the Gulf

Table 1 Economic figures regarding trade, imports, exports, and FDI

Indicators	2010 (%)	2019 (%)
Foreign trade	06.6	07.1
Total crude oil imports	53.93	47.0
Middle Eastern crude oil exports	03.9	31.2
FDI inflow to the Middle East from China	03.3	10.1

Source Author's adaptation from aei.org and UNCTAD

Cooperation Council (GCC) States, namely, Saudi Arabia, Kuwait, Oman, Bahrain, Qatar, and the United Arab Emirates (UAE). These relations do not hamper a special status in the relation with Iran, the Arab Gulf countries' rival.

China organizes its priorities in the region, noting that the GCC's location is a shortcut to reach the Indian Ocean, a place where it aims to reach a dominant position (Dana, 2017). In addition, the GCC countries are very close to the "China-Pakistan Economic Corridor" that has multiple benefits, at geo-strategic level, including undermining the Indian presence in the region (Xuewen, 2016, pp. 27–28). In addition, through the corridor, China will block some of the US's pressure and impose its dominance over the strategic distribution of energy in Asia (Liangxiang & Janardhan, 2018, p. 5). Links with the GCC allow a maritime route for China's military presence in Africa and the Gulf of Aden. China enjoys a strong economic presence in Africa. Under the Presidency of Xi Jinping, China tried to maximize such opportunities. Hence, the Military Strategy of 2015 is acknowledging the presence in the Gulf of Aden "the country's armed forces will continue to carry out escort missions in the Gulf of Aden and other sea areas as required" (China's Military Strategy, 2015).

The strategic goals are far-reaching, but they took the shape of economic advantages first. This resulted in cementing a gradual mutual interdependence. By the mid-2000s, the Gulf-China relations started to deepen thanks to the "Looking East Policy" (Almujeem, 2021), which is adopted by the GCC States, as the Western countries started to look more critically at the political environment in the region, together with a decline of their demand on oil (Gao, 2018). In 2012, China has become the biggest exporter of GCC countries and the main oil and commercial partner to the GCC countries (Karasik, 2016, p. 3). This is the seed of an Asianisation process. In the context of the looking *east* policy, China and the GCC countries have started in 2004 negotiations on a free trade agreement. This has not been finalized, because of different political implications, but in 2021, there were talks regarding its revival (Retrieved on October 2021, from www.xinhuanet.com, 2021). However, China has managed to conclude bilateral agreements, Memorandums of Understanding, particularly with Saudi Arabia (Andersen & Jiang, 2014, pp. 26–27). Within the BRI, the United Arab Emirates signed 13 memorandums of understanding concerning various fields of coordination with China in 2018. The UAE with its ports and developed infrastructure constitutes an important lynchpin under the BRI framework (Abdul Ghaffar, 2018, pp. 522–525). In 2013, Qatar has signed already a strategic partnership with China, highlighting gas cooperation, Qatar being very rich in gas resources (Saidy, 2017, p. 447). In 2014, China National Petroleum Corporation has been granted its first contract for exploration in the United Arab Emirates. The vastest sums for investment are in deals with Saudi Arabia. For instance, China signed with Saudi Arabia an agreement for bilateral energy cooperation amounting to a value of $65bn (Almujeem, 2021). Energy lubricates China's expansion and the GCC stays at the heart of an energy corridor. By 2018, China has become the biggest energy player in the Gulf through investment contracts.

Beyond energy goals, the GCC countries viewed the BRI as a great chance to promote their new economic visions that are based mainly on diversifying the economy by lessening the dependence on oil revenues (Bodetti, 2019). The diversification plans are laid out in National visions (documents that are endorsed by Gulf leadership in the view of sustainability). Saudi Arabia merges its National Vision 2030 with BRI's goals. In this context, Saudi Arabia signed in February 2019, 12 cooperation agreements with China touching upon several domains. In addition, the initiative merges also with Kuwait's Vision 2035. Under the auspices of the Vision, in 2017 the relationship was a heightened to strategic one, with plans for building "Silk City"—a hub for technology, infrastructure, and transport. Bahrain also treats the BRI as a part of a national vision for future development. For the same reasons, and as well as in the interest of proximity to the China-Pakistan corridor, China built the "Duqm port" in Oman (Fulton, 2019) emphasizing Oman's role on the maritime part of the BRI (Chaziza, 2019, p. 48).

In parallel with maintaining these higher-profile relations with Saudi Arabia and the GCC bloc, China is determined to deepen relations with Iran, Saudi Arabia's rival in the region. Iran accounts for a reliable partner in the BRI's architecture. Calabrese (2018, p. 181) explained Iran's crucial part for the Chinese strategy, as it represents "the only East–West and North–South intersection for Central Asian trade." China and Iran have reached recently a comprehensive partnership agreement, signed in Tehran, on 27 March 2021. This document paves the way for deepening strategic cooperation and extending China's involvement in developing Iranian infrastructure. Caba-Maria assesses (2021) the potential of this relationship through the lens of a great power game.

The vast economic development of China juxtaposed with its strategic aims is slightly problematic, especially in the event of intense geopolitical competition between China and the US, or Iran and Saudi Arabia at a regional level, or the Israeli–Palestinian conflict. The Middle East is approached by China as a vital crossroads, but is acknowledged is also an arena for world powers' games. China has navigated its own way, in the wake of a new wave of interdependence at the global and regional levels. Under Xi Jinping, China has been engaged in a rebalancing of forces, prior to President Barack Obama's "rebalance" to the Asia-Pacific. The Chinese approach is different from the American one. China's rebalance is comprehensive, comprising more domestic interests combined with foreign policy, and having economic and energy goals at the forefront.

The footprint of China in the extended Middle East plays a role not only for energy security, but also is an example of the new international dynamics, engaging regionally and globally, and efforts to pacify its nationalist and Islamic minorities. The strategic changes in the Middle East—notably the US relative disengagement with the region allowed created a multipolar arena of confrontation. Global powers like the US, Russia, China, European Union (EU) have their own vulnerabilities when engaging with the region, whereas the regional players: Iran, Saudi Arabia, the UAE, Qatar, Turkey, and Israel, have their own assets. One can consider multipolarity is beneficial for China; it gives it space to determine its priorities in the region (Retrieved on October 2021, from www.manaramagazine.org, 2021).

China has a diverse portfolio of partnerships in the extended Middle East, its relations expanding at different paces, converging currently with the BRI's goals.

The original choice had a very strong ideological motivation, whereas the economic part was not as developed as nowadays. Beijing's non-aligned status, its communist ideology, and anti-imperialism were key in the 1950s and 1960s (Rózsa, 2020). Thus, it implied a political choice, based upon an anti-colonial (very vivid in those times in the Middle East and Africa) and anti-imperialist narrative. However, China's newly acquired status at the economic level has definitely transformed its priorities in the Middle East (Rózsa, 2020). Its level of influence is on rising, as China's activities in the broader Middle East are a translation of the evolution of Chinese foreign policy thinking, aligning China to its economic power, hence the enhanced status of cooperation with the GCC bloc. Nonetheless, compared with the US, the European Union member states, and Russia, China is a new player in the Middle East. Officially, China is still applying the non-interference principle, explaining its presence in the Middle East as an economic driver. Its long-standing official adherence to the principle of non-interference in the domestic affairs of others dates back to the era of Mao Zedong (Dorsey, 2018). In practice, China is realizing it cannot stay away from the tumult of Middle Eastern and South Asian rivalries, conflicts, and politics, mainly influenced ideologically and by external powers (most of them reticent to China's role).

Nonetheless, China prioritizes official diplomacy in which it invested a lot. From the Chinese perspective, socio-economic development should be at the forefront, as it can alleviate security problems in the Middle East, because "development means the greatest security and the master key to regional security issues" (www.china.org.cn., n.d.). The very essence of the promotion of the BRI is economic development; instead of filling power voids, China is preparing a transnational framework of cooperation in a win–win manner.

3 Discussion

Nowadays, the international arena faces mixed views regarding the main approaches. China, the Middle East, and the West have different political ideologies and goals. Therefore, there are many clashes, which affect stability. Currently, the postulates of pragmatism and utilitarianism are dominant (Degang, 2019). China's Middle East policy has been formulated with reference to the great power competition and the overall goal of China's diplomacy, neglecting aspects of specific regional dynamics, a feature that can be amended. This is a place where Beijing might feel the need to adapt especially that under Xi Jinping goals needs to be achieved at a speedier pace (Ang, 2021). China is not willing to replace the US as a hegemon, as it acknowledges it makes the Middle Eastern States difficult to engage with such an approach. China is present in the Middle East as a desire to go outside, promoting BRI as Xi Jinping's most important project and China's desire to engage differently, in a multipolar setting, discussing directly with regional players. Beijing needs to project its goals by not offending Middle Eastern partners or replicating the US role while pursuing its interests. In fact, Chinese diplomacy has seized the opportunity to penetrate space in order to build economic relations in a methodical way, while the US security plans for the region ensure a certain leeway for China to promote its lower-cost approach to the markets (Chaziza, 2020).

One has to mention one unpredicted element in 2020—the novel coronavirus pandemic. Given its geographical location and centrality to Eurasian trade networks, the Middle East has not been spared by the rapid spread of the virus. The Middle East—notably the GCC—hosts workers who frequently travel to and from their home countries. These extensive economic links create a dynamic pattern for a pandemic. Considering that Dubai and Abu Dhabi are both global financial centres and major hubs for international travel, the pandemic arrived early in the Emirates and ultimately to the GCC. On the other side of the Gulf, Iran was among the most affected countries at the initial phase. Thus, here it came into play the Chinese strategic diplomacy for tackling health crises. When mask stocks were low in 2020, China delivered packages to Middle Eastern countries. It repeated the efforts again in 2021 with respect to the vaccines. It was a good opportunity to impose a model of Chinese soft power—engagement while solving problems (Chaziza, 2020). China has managed to reframe itself in the Middle East through "Infrastructure Diplomacy," "Loan Diplomacy," "Mask Diplomacy," and "Vaccination Diplomacy" (Retrieved on October 2021, from www.manaramagazine.org, 2021), which goes against the US interventionist image in the Middle East. This coronavirus diplomacy is meant to counter initial reactions to the fact that the pandemic started in China. It also tests the credibility of Chinese policies, including the BRI (Rózsa, 2020). Actually, China strives to present Arab–African relations as fruitful cooperation South—South. It is slowly overcoming the challenge of the previous stereotype that China providing low-quality goods, flooding markets, while the West has technologically superior capacities. The Coronavirus pandemic has proven China and Asia, in general, resisted better the provocations caused by the virus. which prompted Arab leaders to engage more with Chinese counterparts for enabling resilience, and prospective plans. COVID-19 is still unfolding, with disruptions at a financial level, work, and societal models, the temptation being to say China has managed it better. The economic outlook of the Western world is not promising, and we can expect worse than the financial crisis of 2008–2009 (www.valdaiclub.com, 2020). It might be in Beijing's assessment that the power and influence of the West have eroded, and as a result, a new era of multipolarity has begun (Ang, 2021). Hence, China is riding a new wave of international relations, seizing the opportunities of a new type of globalization, with strong regional accents. As for what lays ahead, China needs to get a tailor-made approach to engagement with Middle Eastern countries. China can try to consolidate its network of strategic partnerships, as it did with Iran, based on bilateral collaboration and multilateral cooperation (inviting Iran as a member of SCO in September 2021). This is a test for its policy of not making enemies. China's positions and eventual response, yet, will dwell on Beijing's consecrated plans, along the lines of the non-interference principle to which it adheres strictly.

4 Conclusion

With the US dwindling presence in the Middle East and a rearrangement of the regional order, almost all countries in the Middle East orientate themselves towards China as an economic lifeguard. This is part of an Asianisation trend, encouraged by the Chinese success in economic development. To this layer, we add external elements- such as a global pandemic (COVID-19) unreeling. In this context, the crises in the Middle East are looming, the region being in the need of structural economic and social reforms, as well as reducing their dependence on oil and gas revenues (Dorsey, 2021). Furthermore, competition between states remains an issue in the Middle East, as the regional states/blocs often resent each other and are mingled in global power struggles. There are moments when the tensions reshuffle and the hopes for pacifying the neighbourhood diminish. As a result, China remains a cautious player; as it tries to avoid the US mistakes, which created havoc in some parts of the region and a rejection of hegemonic power. China is not a fan of a sanctions policy or the creation of military bases all over the place—instead it chose some strategic places (presence in ports in Iran, Gulf of Aden). For instance, China conducted a four-day naval drill with Russia and Iran in the northern part of the Indian Ocean at the end of 2019 (27 and 30 December), but it always presented such exercises as a form of joint cooperation meant to guarantee general security. China puts forward a general benefit/profit when it advances its diplomatic and strategic goals. Overall, China displays a "Middle East policy with Chinese characteristics," promoting non-alignment, non-interference, and economic development, and multilateralism as solutions to existing problems (www.manaramagazine.org, 2021). China seeks to create a bilateral strategic partnership with individual countries, often placed in antagonistic positions, as it is the case with Saudi Arabia and Iran. Furthermore, China does not intend to neglect the already existing regional platforms (Bingbing, 2020).

For the sake of its interests, China advanced a holistic type of diplomacy in the Middle East, being more obvious after 2010 and mostly once the BRI was launched in 2013. China maintains its collaborative ties with Middle Eastern countries in a variety of multilateral organizations and mechanisms, the scope being agenda beyond a simple China–Arab world relation. This highlights the holistic approach, being in both China and MENA's States interest to solve problems in multilateral formats. For this purpose, we notice the platforms provided by the CASCF, Shanghai Cooperation Organization (SCO), Asian Infrastructure Investment Bank (AIIB), the United Nations Security Council (UNSC), the International Monetary Fund (IMF), the World Bank, the Group of Twenty (G20), the P5 + 1 Talks on the Iranian nuclear file and the Vienna Conference on Syria. These interplays help China to generate a constructive approach with Middle Eastern leaders. China still believes that it can be a trusted friend of parties in conflict, though this is the toughest challenge in the Middle East. Such interactions also help to increase China's international profile, in relation to the US, the EU, Russia, Japan, and India (Degang, 2019). China has not held decisive positions on global crises, yet it thought it contributed to restraint from an international spillover in the cases of Syria and Libya.

The Middle East is known for its conglomerate of religious, ethnic divides, which are challenging any major power to reap benefits from a foreign policy agenda. All the great powers faced difficulties, as the Middle East is fragmented and chaotic, on the verge of conflicts. The outlook for the region remains bleak (Liangxiang, 2020). The complexity of the ethnic-religious and external milieu of the region impedes China to consolidate a decisive role beyond energy and economics for the moment. One can wait and see the direction of the comprehensive partnership with Iran and its future concrete realization in order to assess the fruits of China-MENA cooperation.

In this context of globalized relations, with regional twists, it is worth mentioning that China should try to adapt its policies for the extended Middle East, in a manner that fits sub-regions. Therefore, it will be a distinct approach for the Gulf region, a specific one for the Red Sea region, another for the Eastern Mediterranean region, and the North African part would be treated accordingly (Degang, 2019), based on the local colour, hereby including politics and the specific needs for socio-economic development (Degang, 2019). Such an approach implies that regional actors guarantee security through political dialogue (Liangxiang, 2020), with an emphasis on economic coordination. It better reflects the realities on the ground and mirrors the BRI's goals. The avenues of collaboration would be based on interactions that require less hard power (military—at least from a classical understanding), but better synergism at the economic and political levels. Based on these findings, the study admits its limits, as the events in the broader Middle East are always in the making and would recommend future in-depth and follow-up of the tangible global influence of China. It should assess the outcome of grand economic strategic games in the Middle East, accompanied by the BRI, with the accent on developments of the Sino-Iranian relations in parallel with China-GCC relations.

Bibliographic References

Abdul Ghaffar, M. M. (2018). Strategic development of Sino-GCC relations: Visions of Arabian Gulf economic development and the Belt and Road Initiative. *Asian Journal of Middle Eastern and Islamic Studies, 12*(4), 517–532.

Almujeem, N. (2021). GCC countries' geoeconomic significance to China's geopolitical ends. *Review of Economics and Political Science, 6*(4), 348–363. https://doi.org/10.1108/reps-11-2019-0152

Alterman, J. B. (2017). *The other side of the world: China, the United States, and the struggle for Middle East security* (p. 1). The Center for Strategic and International Studies.

American Enterprise Institute. (2020). *China is not the Middle East's high roller*. Retrieved on October 2021, from https://www.aei.org/op-eds/china-is-not-the-middle-easts-high-roller/

American Enterprise Institute. (2021). *China global investment tracker*. Retrieved on October 2021, from https://www.aei.org/china-global-investment-tracker/

Amineh, M., & Guang, Y. (2018). China's geopolitical economy of energy security: A theoretical and conceptual exploration. *African and Asian Studies, 17*, 9–39.

Andersen, L. E., & Jiang, J. (2014). *Is China challenging the US in the Persian Gulf?* (DIIS Report, No. 29, pp. 26–27). Danish Institute for International Studies.

Ang, Y. Y. (2021). *Decoding Xi Jinping*. [online] www.foreignaffairs.com. Available at: https://www.foreignaffairs.com/articles/china/2021-12-08/decoding-xi-jinping. Accessed April 18 2022.

Benabdallah, L. (2018). *China's relations with Africa and the Arab World: Shared trends, different priorities*. South African Institute of International Affairs.

Bingbing, W. (2020, July 14). *Gulf-Asia relations within the changing global order*. Middle East Institute Singapore.

Blackwill, R. D., & Campbell, K. M. (2016). *Xi Jinping on the global stage: Chinese foreign policy under a powerful but exposed leader* (Council Special Report, No.74).

Blackwill, R. D., & Harris, J. (2016). *War by other means—Geoeconomics and statecraft*. The Belknap Press of Harvard University Press.

Bodetti, A. (2019). *The Gulf's balance between the US and China*. Gulf State Analytics. https://gulfstateanalytics.com/the-gulfs-balance-between-the-us-and-china/

Caba-Maria, F. (2021). Iran–China relations: A game changer in the Eastern World. In F. J. Leandro, C. Branco, & F. Caba-Maria (Eds.), *The geopolitics of Iran*. Springer Nature.

Calabrese, J. (2018). China's "One Belt, One Road" (OBOR) Initiative: Envisioning Iran's role. In A. Ehteshami & N. Horesh (Eds.), *China's presence in the Middle East: The implications of the One Belt, One Road Initiative (Durham Modern Middle East and Islamic World Series)* (1st ed.). Routledge.

Chaziza, M. (2019). The significant role of Oman in China's Maritime Silk Road Initiative. *Contemporary Review of the Middle East, 6*(1), 44–57. https://doi.org/10.1177/2347798918812285

Chaziza, M. (2020). *Coronavirus, China, and the Middle East*. Begin-Sadat Center for Strategic Studies. Retrieved on October 2021, from https://besacenter.org/coronavirus-china-middle-east/

Chen, K., Ding, X., & You, T. (2014). *Interpretation on new philosophy of Chinese diplomacy*. China Intercontinental Press.

China's Arab Policy Paper. (2016, January). Retrieved on October 2021, from www.fmprc.gov.cn/fra/wjdt/gb/W020160115345916404312.pdf

China's Military Strategy. (2015). *The state council information office of the People's Republic of China*. Retrieved on October 2021, from https://jamestown.org/wp-content/uploads/2016/07/China%E2%80%99sMilitary-Strategy-2015.pdf

Dana, J. (2017). *How the GCC and China stand to benefit from a deeper 'belt and road' partnership*. Retrieved on October 2021, from www.thenational.ae/opinion/how-the-gcc-and-china-stand-to-benefitfrom-a-deeper-belt-and-road-partnership-1.665346

Daojiong, Z., & Meidan, M. (2015). *China and the Middle East in a new energy landscape* (pp. 2–3) (Research Paper). The Royal Institute of International Affairs.

Degang, S. (2019). China's whole-of-region diplomacy in the Middle East. *World Century Publishing Corporation and Shanghai Institutes for International Studies China Quarterly of International Strategic Studies, 5*(1), 49–64. https://doi.org/10.1142/S2377740019500015

Di Donato, G. (2021, June 24). *China's approach to the Belt and Road Initiative and Europe's response*. ISPI. Retrieved on October 2021, from https://www.ispionline.it/en/pubblicazione/chinas-approach-belt-and-road-initiative-and-europes-response-25980

Diesen, G. (2017). *Russia, China and 'balance of dependence' in greater Eurasia* (Valdai Papers, No. 63).

Diesen, G. (2020). *Analytics*. Retrieved November 23, 2020, from https://valdaiclub.com/a/highlights/the-international-economic-system-after-covid-19/

Dorsey, J. M. (2018). *China and the Middle East: Venturing into the maelstrom*. Springer.

Dorsey, J. M. (2021). *Middle East futures: Defiance and dissent* (Mideast Security and Policy Studies No. 192). Begin-Sadat Center for Strategic Studies.

Ehteshami, A. (2020, July 14). *Gulf–Asia relations within the changing global order*. Middle East Institute Singapore.

Ehteshami, A., & Bahgat, G. (2019). Iran's Asianisation strategy. In A. Perteghella (Ed.), *Iran looking East: An alternative to the EU?* (Ispi Publications). Ledizioni.

El-Shafei, A. W., & Metawe, M. (2021). China drive toward Africa between arguments of neo-colonialism and mutual-beneficial relationship: Egypt as a case study. *Review of Economics and Political Science, 7*(2), 137–152. https://doi.org/10.1108/reps-03-2021-0028

Fulton, J. (2019). *China is becoming a major player in the Middle East.* Marsh and McLennan Insights. Retrieved on October 2021, from www.brinknews.com/china-is-becoming-a-major-player-in-the-middle-east/

Gao, H. (2018). *Beyond energy: The future of China-GCC economic ties.* Arab Gulf States Institute in Washington, DC. Retrieved on October 2021, from https://agsiw.org/beyond-energy-the-future-of-china-gcceconomic-ties

Kamrava, M. (2018). Hierarchy and instability in the Middle East regional order. *International Studies Journal (ISJ), 14*(4), 1–35.

Karasik, T. (2016). *The GCC's new affair with China.* MEI Policy Focus (Middle East Institute, No. 6, p. 2).

Keohane, R. O., & Nye, J. S. (1977). *Power and interdependence: World politics in transition.* Little, Brown.

Lanteigne, M. (2009). China in the world economy. In *Chinese foreign policy: An introduction* (pp. 39–55). Routledge.

Lee, S. O., Wainwright, J., & Glassman, J. (2018). Geopolitical economy and the production of territory: The case of US-China geopolitical-economic competition in Asia. *Environment and Planning A: Economy and Space, 50*(2), 416–436.

Liangxiang, J. (2020). *China and Middle East security issues: Challenges, perceptions and positions.* Retrieved 13 October 2021, from https://www.iai.it/sites/default/files/iaip2023.pdf

Liangxiang, J., & Janardhan, N. (2018). *Belt and Road Initiative: Opportunities and obstacles for the Gulf* (p. 5). EDA Insight, Emirates Diplomatic Academy.

Liu, Z. (2016). Historical evolution of relationship between China and the Gulf region. *Journal of Middle Eastern and Islamic Studies (in Asia), 10*(1), 11.

Mccahill, W. C. (2017). *China's new era and XI Jinping thought* (pp. 1–4). NBR Commentary, The National Bureau of Asian Research.

Miyake, K. (2017). *China as a Middle East power.* Retrieved on October 2021, from https://www.cnas.org/publications/reports/china-as-a-middle-east-power

Rózsa, E. N. (2020). *Deciphering China in the Middle East.* European Union Institute for Security Studies (EUISS). Retrieved on October 2021, from http://www.jstor.org/stable/resrep25023

Saidy, B. (2017). Qatar and rising China: An evolving partnership. *China Report, 53*(4), 447–466.

UNCTAD e-Handbook of Statistics. (2020). *Foreign Direct Investment.* Retrieved on October 2021, from https://stats.unctad.org/handbook/EconomicTrends/Fdi.html

www.china.org.cn. (n.d.). *Xi: Asia needs sustainable, durable security—China.org.cn.* [online] Available at: http://www.china.org.cn/world/2014-05/21/content_32449834.htm. Accessed December 12 2022.

Xinhua | English.news.cn. (2021). *China, GCC discuss resuming free trade talks.* Retrieved 13 October 2021, from http://www.xinhuanet.com/english/2021-03/25/c_139833915.htm

Xuewen, Q. (2016). The new Silk Road in west Asia under the Belt and Road Initiative. *Journal of Middle Eastern and Islamic Studies (in Asia), 10*(1), 27–28.

Yang, J. (2015). China's "new diplomacy" under the Xi Jinping administration. *China Quarterly of International Strategic Studies, 1*(1), 1–17. https://doi.org/10.1142/s2377740015500013

Chapter 34
China–Iran's 25-Year Deal: The Implication for the Belt and Road Initiative and Joint Comprehensive Plan of Action (JCPOA)

Mohammad Eslami and Joel Anthony Kemie

1 Introduction

China's progress in various political and economic fields over the past half-century has been very rapid, and it seems that it has focused all its efforts and will on becoming the next superpower in the world. This position has gone so far that President Xi Jinping has made it clear that the country will lead the world until 2050. In connection with China's plans to expand its power around the world, the country's foreign policy has also undergone significant changes, and huge and ambitious projects in the political, economic, military, and security fields have been launched by this country. Belt and Road Initiative (BRI) and the new Silk Road is a Chinese comprehensive plan which is going to guarantee China's domination over the world in the coming years. The BRI is a combination of The Silk Road Economic Belt, and the Maritime Silk Road. It was announced by Xi Jinping in 2013. Official documents in China defined the Initiative as a way for a win–win cooperation that promotes common development and prosperity and a road towards peace and friendship through the enhancement of mutual understanding and trust. The Road runs through the continent of Asia, Europe, and Africa, connecting the vibrant East Asia economic circle at one end and developed European economic circle at the other end; all of these will include countries with enormous potential for economic development.

Alongside the entire parts of the world, China's activism in the Middle East has been growing rapidly in recent years (Scobell & Nader, 2016; Yetiv et al., 2007). Accordingly, its relation with the Middle Eastern countries has been expanded under different agreements, contracts, and partnerships (Kemp, 2012). The so-called "Comprehensive Strategic Partnership" (CSP) agreement with Iran which is attributed to the BRI has attracted attention in political and academic debates. The agreement is meant to pursue a formalized partnership that will cover cooperation in economic, political, cultural, and military spheres for the next 25 years (Anonymous, 2021a).

M. Eslami (✉) · J. A. Kemie
University of Minho, Braga, Portugal

© The Author(s), under exclusive license to Springer Nature Singapore Pte Ltd. 2023
P. A. B. Duarte et al. (eds.), *The Palgrave Handbook of Globalization with Chinese Characteristics*, https://doi.org/10.1007/978-981-19-6700-9_34

The "Comprehensive Strategic Partnership" (CSP) is a unique and special document for both China and Iran. Contrary to regular protocols for the development and implementation of international agreements, the negotiations of the CSP were signed in the presence of a direct representative of Iranian Supreme Ayatollah Khamenei. To this end, the agreement was signed between China and Iran's regime and not Iran's government (Anonymous, 2021b). Moreover, while the total value of the BRI project is estimated to be four trillion US dollars, China's investing 400 billion USD in Iran's infrastructures (which represents 10% of the total BRI budget) is a demonstration of the uniqueness of the agreement and the importance of Iran in the future of China's quest for global dominance, as well as redefining the International Order (Alef, 2021).

While highlighting the importance of the China–Iran 25-years agreement, the present contribution argues that CSP is the result of a significant change in Iran's foreign and security policy following the US withdrawal from the Joint Comprehensive Plan of Action (JCPOA) and imposing new sanctions on Iran. Accordingly, following the failure in cooperation with the western countries and reinforcing the sense of mistrust and scepticism of international cooperation, Iran's foreign policy is witnessing a shift towards the East (Eslami & Papageorgiou, 2021). Something that pushed Iran to get closer to China as the biggest energy client in the world in order to neutralize the sanctions and survive in the international system (Belal, 2020).

The agreement is as important to China as it is to Iran. Iran has a large area and is a strategic actor in the heart of the Middle East located between the Straits of Hormuz and the Caspian Sea (Eslami & Sotudehfar, 2021). Iran is also a counterweight to undermining the influence of the US in the Persian Gulf, plummeting the US hegemony as well as redefining the International World Order (Katzman, 2010), which is one of the dimensions of the Belt and Road Initiative. While Iran's geographical location is pivotal to the implementation of the Belt and Road Initiative, the present contribution argues that China's investment in Iran is a matter of reconstructing the Silk Road and promoting the Belt and Road Initiative. Aiming to understand the implications of China's 25 years deal with Iran for the future of nuclear deal (JCPOA) and reconstruction of the Silk Road and the implementation of the Belt and Road Initiative across the globe, the present contribution draws on official and semi-official documents published by the Ministry of Foreign Affairs in Iran and China (Including the official document of BRI and document of 25 years deal as well as other agreements between the two countries.

This research is structured as follows. We begin by discussing the historical background of China–Iran relations. In addition, by introducing the Belt and Road Initiatives and the new Silk Road, we examine China's posture of extending its domination over the world and changing to the new superpower by economic investments in different countries and establishing a new partnership pattern. We then look into the value of China's investments in different countries around the world under BRI to analyze the importance and uniqueness of China's 25 years-deal with Iran. We then focus on China–Iran's 2021 deal and explain how this agreement can lead to the implementation of Belt and Road Initiatives. Finally, we demonstrate how Sino-Persian partnership can be replaced with JCPOA to preserve Iran's national interests by relying on energy trade, currency exchanges, and neutralizing international sanctions.

2 China–Iran Relations (A Historical Background)

The history of China–Iran relations dates back to the Achaemenid Empire era and reaches more than two thousand and six hundred years (Park et al., 2010). The interaction of these two ancient countries has continued since the Sassanid era, and during the construction of the Silk Road, these relations reached their peak (Azad, 2017).

The Silk Road as a Persian-China global route thus constitutes an accurate alternative model of globalization and a significantly early form of capitalism that is reliant on trade that has ushered in the "trade policy," significant capital formation, the introduction of financial norms and institutions, and, perhaps, most importantly, the spread of ideas, knowledge and technology transfer, not least the major innovation of paper and paper-based societies, and gunpowder (Balding, 2017). The "Silk Road" was not one road but many; it was actually a network of roads, generally going East and West, but with spurs into southern Iran, the northern Eurasian steppe, and south over the Hindu Kush to the Indian subcontinent. The ancient Silk Road trade routes connecting Asia, Europe, and Africa lay behind the development of many great civilizations (Duarte & Xing, 2018).

While the image of the ancient Silk Road is a recent product coming into being in the mid-nineteenth century (1877), the Silk Road itself began when traders and explorers found theory passage from China to Europe and the Middle East in the second century BCE, mostly as a trade based on silk and silk products but also including precious stones and jewellery. The Silk Road was not a permanent link between the East and West, and yet it existed for over 1000 years (Azad, 2017).

In contemporary times, the history of Iran–China relations goes back to the early years of the twentieth century. The first step in this direction was taken in 1911, when a consular and judicial treaty was signed between the two governments in Rome. At the beginning of the twentieth century, specifically in the year 1911, the democratic revolution of the Chinese bourgeoisie took place, and at the same time, the constitutional revolution took place in Iran (Munoz et al., 1982). The revolutionaries of the two countries watched the developments of each other from afar, especially the Chinese revolutionaries who were inspired by it after learning about the constitutional revolution. The Constitutional Revolution shook the foundations of the Qajar government, and the Chinese 1911 Revolution toppled and overthrew the Qing Dynasty scroll. Since then, the history of China and Iran has progressed almost simultaneously and in the same way (Salmanipour et al., 2017).

In 1949, when China was humiliated by Western powers at the Paris Peace Summit and the Qajar monarchy was collapsing in Iran, a "Friendship Agreement between

China and Persia" was signed in Rome, Italy, and the two countries appointed ambassadors, ministers, and caretakers (Mohajer, 1991). However, diplomatic relations between the countries did not take effect at that time due to the weakness of the two countries' forces and their involvement in the civil war and the handling of their relations with the Western powers. Hence, this agreement was not implemented, so no progress was made in relations between the two countries (Azad, 2017).

During World War II, the US helped China in its anti-Japanese war, and the two countries allied themselves. In 1942, Iran also entered the US Alliance bloc after being occupied by the forces of the allied countries (Steele, 2020). In September 1945, Iran established its autonomous ministry in Chongqing, the interim capital of China, but this was not seen as an act of sovereignty between the two countries and was more a sign of the two allies (Mohajer, 1991). Naturally, at a time when the world was witnessing great changes and the logic of militarism had prevailed in the relations between the countries, Iran and China had inadvertently fallen victim to the political and military greed of the belligerent powers (Green, 2015). Therefore, not only cultural relations but also political relations were interrupted. To this end, no cultural activities and exchanges took place between the two countries (Mohajer, 1991; Steele, 2020).

In 1979, China pursued a policy of reform and open doors and established political relations with the US (Huan, 1987). In the same year, under the leadership of Ayatollah Khomeini, the Islamic Revolution took place in Iran and the Islamic Republic was established (Daneshvar, 2016). These two events changed the international political structure at the end of the Cold War and also transformed Sino-Iranian relations. China moved from closed-door to open-door conditions and established political relations with the US (Sung & Song, 1991), while the Iranian political community's approach shifted from full orientation and dependence on the West, especially the US, to independence and severing ties with foreigners and religious affiliations. In this vein, the revolutionary and Islamic movements evolved, and as a result, US-Iranian relations and alliances became enmity after 30 years (Ramazani, 1992). In other words, the policies of China and Iran in this period, almost simultaneously, moved in opposite directions. Therefore, the relations between China and Iran have been redundant for a while. The occupation of the US embassy by the Muslim Students Followers of Imam's Line, the start of the Iraq–Iran war, and Iraq support of world powers, and China's declaration of neutrality at the start of the war (Tabaar, 2017), signalled a new relationship between Iran and China. Concerned about the course of events in Iran that led to the victory of the Islamic Revolution, Chinese politicians became convinced that the Islamic Revolution of Iran would increase Soviet influence in Iran by announcing and pursuing a "neither the East nor the West" policy (Noroozi, 1999; Taghizadeh, 1991).

According to the common views that emerged between the leaders of the two countries, since then, Iran and China have sympathized and supported each other in the fight against the hegemony of the Western powers (Tabatabai & Esfandiary, 2018). Iran supported China in the field of human rights and the Taiwan issue, and China resisted in international forums, especially against international sanctions and the issuance of UN Security Council resolutions issued under US pressure against

Iran (Perteghella & Talbot, 2020). The visit of high-ranking officials of the two countries and the increase of trade and economic exchanges in these conditions also provided the ground for cultural cooperation.

3 Iran–China 25-Years Agreement: Comprehensive Strategic Partnership (CSP)

In March 2021, a strategic document for long-term cooperation in dozens of areas, including banking, telecommunications, ports, railways, healthcare, and information technology, over the next 25 years was signed between Iran and China. The Comprehensive Strategic Partnership (CSP) between the People's Republic of China and the Islamic Republic of Iran "consists of 9 clauses and 3 annexes." The context of this document, prepared by the "Secretariat of the Supreme Mechanism for Comprehensive Strategic Partnership between Iran and China." Having a glance at the CSP official document which was published in Persian, Chinese, and English, some key points can be inferred. First, in accordance with this draft, China will invest 400 billion US dollars in all Iranian infrastructures, especially in the energy and transit sectors. In addition, the country will transfer knowledge and technology to Iran to develop Iran's scientific infrastructures. This amount of investment by China, while in the current situation, China does not release investment or foreign exchange resources of tens of billions of dollars to prevent sanctions even in Iran's huge oil industries, is surprising and will be a fundamental change for Iran's economy if implemented. This contract is mainly in the form of a memorandum of understanding and does not include numbers and amounts. In fact, this cooperation document reflects the long-term strategy of Iran–China cooperation, and each paragraph of the original text or the three annexes requires separate agreements to be implemented, which contain the details of this agreement; Therefore, it strongly depends on the contracts that will be concluded later after the approval of this contract for the implementation of different parts between Iran and China. This 25-year agreement does not provide an executive guarantee for either Iran or China. Therefore, the objectives set out in this contract and the annexes may not be fulfilled by the parties at any stage, and their implementation may be suspended, unless later in the framework of each clause of the cooperation agreements are executed, which normally require separate evaluations.

4 Iran–China Comprehensive Strategic Partnership: Implications for BRI and Silk Road

How is this deal important to China and the Belt and Road Initiative? By 2013, Chinese President Xi Jinping was assertively articulating his own vision for a China-led Silk Road that would streamline foreign trade, ensure stable energy supplies, promote Asian infrastructure development, and consolidate Beijing's regional influence (Balding, 2017; Duarte & Xing, 2018). The BRI put forward by the Chinese was no accident. The momentum has always been there but has been limited temporarily by diverse factors. After the end of the Cold War, there have been several attempts to revive the overland Silk Road that has been disconnected from the rest of the global system (Balding, 2017; Chen, 2015; Duarte & Xing, 2018; Rudolph, 2016). The BRI has been tagged as a response to a fast-changing world in the twenty-first century where the centre of gravity seems to be shifting to the east. This is evidenced by the rising shares of global GDP of countries in Asia and by China, whose economy has grown geometrically since 2001 (Duarte & Xing, 2018; Dugué-Nevers, 2017; Ibrahim & Bibi-Farouk, 2020). About US$1 trillion has been committed to almost a thousand projects across Asia since the launch of the Initiative in 2013. The projects have been linked to China's strategic interests in the construction of ports, pipelines, roads, and railways that will pave easy ways for Chinese goods to get to new markets faster, as well as in the energy sector, where consumption is expected to treble by 2030 (Duarte & Xing, 2018; Dugué-Nevers, 2017; Ibrahim & Bibi-Farouk, 2020; Mayer & Zhang, 2020; Mirire, 2019; Robert, 2020).

Over time, there have been various studies that argue about China's global dominance quest. While some argue that China's quest is primarily to undermine the USA's international power with a view to emerging as the new hegemonic power, some argue that the quest is influenced by the traditional strategic recipes which include strengthening Chinese blue water sea power to gain control of global trade and to undermine the top position of the USA within the international system. Order narrative revolves around the claim that China's main geopolitical goal is to organize Eurasia along the lines of Mackinder traditions. This narrative fits the Belt and Road Initiative because, based on the grand strategy, it could usher in hegemony over the World Island and global political leadership (Duarte & Xing, 2018; Garlick, 2020; Leandro & Duarte, 2020).

Since the launch of the Initiative, there have been arguments among scholars that the Initiative is a grand strategy with a geo-economic undertone. Still, the Chinese government has refuted that the BRI is not a geopolitical strategy but an initiative by which the Chinese leadership calls for an action geared towards the common good and is open to any state who constructively wish to build economic and political relationship between the three continents captured in the Initiative (Leandro & Duarte, 2020). China has shown a keen interest in the Iranian energy sector. The country is reputed to have the world's second-largest natural gas reserves and the fourth-largest oil reserves in the world (Ehteshami & Horesh, 2018; Garlick, 2020). This puts Iran in a strategic position that would make China put in its efforts to secure sustainable sources of energy which is pivotal to its economic growth. Experts have argued that the various projects and initiatives associated with China's Belt and Road Initiative (BRI) have in recent years boosted Iran's potential value as a critical nodal point in an evolving regional network that would also connect the Arabian Sea and the Indian Ocean to the project. The new deal viewed from within the context of increasing US-China conflict over issues ranging from the COVID-19 pandemic, maritime disputes in the South China Sea, political repression in Hong Kong, and issues relating to human rights violations in Xinjiang, will help China send a clear message to the Biden administration that it is accelerating its influence in the Middle East and as such is prepared to support a regime whose policies are antithetical to traditional US allies in the region (Belal, 2020; Ehteshami & Horesh, 2018; Englund & Holmquist, 2020; Garlick, 2020; Mehdi, 2021; Vakuchuk & Overland, 2019).

The Belt and Road Initiative cuts across Asia, Africa, Middle East, Europe, South America, and North America (Wang, 2020). Since the launch of the Initiative in 2013, China has invested in 138 countries that cover the Initiative across the globe. The Chinese investment under the BRI revolves around different sectors. They include: infrastructure development, transport and logistics, and energy. However, the primary focus of the Initiative is and has continued to centre around infrastructure, with an emphasis on energy and transport (Baruzzi, 2021; Lavery & Menon, 2021; Wang, 2020). This is evident in the share investments in transport and energy that have increased significantly from about 70% in 2019 to over 80% in 2020. The logistic sector has also witnessed a significant increase in investment, with more than 25% in 2020 than what was obtainable in 2019 (Baruzzi, 2021; Lavery & Menon, 2021; Wang, 2020). However, there is a decline of 54% to investment value in 2019, and about US$78 billion less than 2015 when the Initiative was at its peak. It should be noted that the decline was more moderate in countries under the BRI compared to countries that are not. The countries that have no linkage to the BRI witnessed about a 70% decline in Chinese investments. This decline could be due to the COVID-19 pandemic (Baruzzi, 2021; Lavery & Menon, 2021; Wang, 2020).

The energy sector constitutes the largest investments and deals of the BRI. Within the year 2020, most of the Chinese investment in this sector went into hydropower which is approximately 35%. This is followed closely by coal, which is around 27% (though there was a decline in coal mining investment, the year 2020 saw a resurgence. To this end, there was an upward investment that went up from 15% coal-related investment in 2018 to 27% in 2020), and solar which is about 23%. Within 2020, a large chunk of investment went into renewable energies. A close look at the Chinese investment in the energy sector in different countries, it can be observed that Pakistan received the most investment in the energy sector since the launch of the Initiative in 2013 down to 2020. In total, Pakistan attracted over 50% of renewable energy investment, with 47% of the investment in hydropower. This is closely followed by Russia and Indonesia who received an appreciable investment in the energy sector (Baruzzi, 2021; Lavery & Menon, 2021; Wang, 2020).

The transport sector remains key for trade between China and the countries under the BRI. To this end, China has invested in the construction of roads, rail, aviation, shipping, and related logistics. The investment in the aviation subsector is primarily focused on the building of airports across countries in Africa. A clear example is the upgrade and expansion of the Abuja and Lagos international airports in Nigeria. Another clear example is the upgrade of the Osmani International Airport in Sylhet city, which is located in the northeast of Bangladesh (Ibrahim & Bibi-Farouket, 2020). Investments in the rail subsector are also enormous. There are rail projects that are connecting China through Malaysia to Singapore. China is also building a high-speed rail at the cost of US$6 billion. It is a high-speed rail connecting about

142 kilometres between Jakarta and Bandung in Indonesia. The rail investments have also been extended to Kenya, Nigeria, Ethiopia in Africa. Europe is also not left out. There is the Budapest- Belgrade railway built by China under the BRI. The investment also includes several urban rail transport projects, for example, the US$900 million subway constructed in Hanoi, Vietnam, as well as the US$1.6 billion metro line built in Lahore, Pakistan (Baruzzi, 2021; Lavery & Menon, 2021; Wang, 2020).

In the road transport subsector, there has also been a huge Chinese investment. Some of the notable investments here include: the Karakoram Highway connecting China and Pakistan. However, there was a sharp decline in investment in this sector to the tune of about US$4 billion. This is due to the COVID-19 pandemic. The Port subsector has also witnessed a huge investment, with Pakistan being the recipient of the highest investment. The Gwadar port in Pakistan is operated by the Chinese Overseas Port Holding Company. Other strategic port investments of China across the globe include: Piraeus in Greece, Lamu and Mombassa Ports in Kenya, as well as in Djibouti (Baruzzi, 2021; Lavery & Menon, 2021; Mirire, 2019; Wang, 2020).

The BRI, according to the Chinese, is premised on some underlying principles. They are: Connectivity which revolves around political coordination. This means coordinating the policies of individual state actors, regional, as well as international institutions. Hard infrastructure which consists of the interconnection of new and existing roads, rails, pipelines, optical networks, accompanied by the construction of industrial parks, logistics centres, and ports (Chen, 2015). It is expected that these will foster economic relations between centres of productions, markets, and sources of raw materials. Ensuring barrier-free trade which will help to eliminate barriers brought about by bureaucracy, thus leading to free trade areas in the long term. Financial integration is aimed at harmonizing and jointly regulating financial services and the exchange of currencies in the regions concerned. Strengthening human relations while placing a strong emphasis on cooperation in the area of culture, research, a development that covers areas like the awards of scholarship and exchange opportunities, students, technocrats and experts, etc. Based on the well-articulated claims by the Chinese that the BRI is designed to promote international cooperation and to encourage globalization, some scholars have argued otherwise. (Chen, 2015) termed the Initiative as "China's strategic initiative" with many more objectives that makes the Initiative more than meets the eyes. They identified nine objectives in this regard, and they include: the development of China is at a crossroad and thus restructuring and upgrading its economy from factor intensive to export orientation. This has necessitated the need to pursue a new and active role in global markets. The BRI becomes a veritable tool in promoting national economic development by boosting exports, enhancing access to natural resources. In this regard, the BRI becomes an avenue of relieving the overcapacity in some Chinese capital goods industries, especially in the construction-based industrial sector. A glance at articles of Iran–China 25 years agreement, it can be observed that the CSP is totally in line with the goals of BRI and designed to pave the way of China's supremacy in the world by providing access to Iranian energy resources (Chen, 2015; Ibrahim & Bibi-Farouk, 2020).

China hopes to build prosperous political and economic relations with its neighbours so as to ensure a peaceful environment for its continuing economic growth. China is the world's second and fourth-largest importer of crude oil and natural gas. This means it requires a constant and undisrupted supply of energy and reduces its dependence on the Strait of Malacca, which is susceptible to the US blockade in order to sustain its rising economic growth (Chen, 2015). The BRI will provide an alternative energy corridor and improve its safe access to vital energy resources by constructing pipelines between China and Central Asian countries, and also building railway lines, pipelines, and road networks through China–Pakistan Economic Corridor to transport sustainable fuel from the Middle East and Africa. While BRI is one of China's plans to produce and export more, they would need to have constant access to more and secure energy sources. Comprehensive Strategic Partnership with Iran, therefore, provides China the opportunity to maintain the constant supply of energy to meet its demands (Chen, 2015).

By and large, the BRI is China's strategic push towards fulfilling the "Chinese dream" of the greater role of China in global governance. Thus, the grand strategy of the BRI becomes very clear: to deepen connectivity with the states participating in the Initiative in a way that serves China national interests, while at the same time meets China's long-term geopolitical interests, which is to overcome US hegemony in the international system. As a regional power with a strong anti-US ideology located in one of the most important points of the world, Iran can play a significant role in China's rivalry with the US. Owing to Iran's political influence in the Middle East, the deal gives great political leverage to China within the region.

Summarily, the BRI is intertwined with geo-economics and geopolitical goals developed to displace Western globalization with a view to limiting the US global dominance and to strengthen China's influence globally. This view is in contradiction to China's perspective that revolves around the notion that the BRI is a "win-win" outcome that will bring about a new phase of globalization and will usher in a new engine that will stimulate economic and industrial growth through infrastructural development and regional connectivity.

Within the Persian Gulf, the need to obtain energy supplies to maintain China's economic growth also dominates China's relation with BRI in the region. The region is rich in oil and natural gas. While there are other aspects to China's engagement in the Persian Gulf, oil has to be placed at the heart of the analysis as China attempts to navigate Saudi-Iranian regional rivalry and US sanctions on Iran. But the Silk Road spirit of peace, mutual benefit, and learning has been revived in an ambitious plan to bridge East and West, launched in 2013 by Chinese President Xi Jinping. The main aim is socio-economic development through improving the routes for land and sea trade (Ehteshami & Horesh, 2018; Vakulchuk & Overland, 2019).

China developed grand diplomatic and economic strategies in the form of BRI not only to sustain its economic growth but also to improve its political and economic stance in the global governance system by undermining the US dominance of the global economy and reducing its influence to contain China's regional and global interests. These motives indicate that the time is right for China to demonstrate shared globalization for equity, economic growth, poverty reduction, human development, and social and cultural respect. China seeks to resuscitate global geopolitics through the BRI with a view to returning Eurasia to its historical and significant position as the centre of human civilization (Chen, 2015; Ehteshami & Horesh, 2018). Official documents in China defined the Initiative as a way for a win–win cooperation that promotes common development and prosperity and a road towards peace and friendship through the enhancement of mutual understanding and trust. The Road runs through the continent of Asia, Europe, and Africa, connecting the vibrant East Asia economic circle at one end and the developed European economic circle at the other end. All of these will encompass countries with enormous potential for economic development. The core of the BRI is the interconnectivity of infrastructure development. By and large, the Belt and Road Initiative can be described as a large-scale vision that seeks to further deepen the connection between Asia, Europe, and Africa hinging on the principles of mutual benefits (Chen, 2015; Ehteshami & Horesh, 2018).

5 Iran–China's Comprehensive Strategic Partnership as an Alternative for JCPOA

JCPOA and the Iran–China Long-Term Cooperation agreement are completely different in nature and in terms of negotiation and decision-making (Tabatabai & Esfandiary, 2018). However, these two important events in Iran's foreign policy are not unrelated, and the initial steps of the Iran–China Strategic Cooperation agreement were taken after the implementation in early 2015. JCPOA was a response to the years-long dispute between Iran and the West over Iran's peaceful nuclear programme, which began in Washington in 2002 (Eslami, 2021). Subsequently, referring to the non-proliferation treaty (NPT), the US and Western countries opened Iran's case in the International Atomic Energy Agency (IAEA). Despite extensive inspections and negotiations between Iran and Britain, France and Germany, the case was sent to the International Atomic Energy Agency in 2006 and led to the approval of resolution 1696, 1737, 1747, 1803, 1835, 1887, and 1929 against Iran (Tarock, 2016). In addition, the US imposed unprecedented sanctions on Iran in various areas, including oil exports and financial exchanges (Fayazmanesh, 2003). Of course, the main instrument for imposing these sanctions was the US economic power and the position of the dollar as the main global currency, which was able to make US domestic law a global rule (Tabatabai et al., 2017). JCPOA can be attributed to Iran's resistance to international pressure and the Obama administration's fear of increasing Iran's nuclear capabilities. In fact, increasing Iran's enrichment capacity to 20% like a "game-changer" has increased the US desire for a deal with Iran to impose severe restrictions on the growth of nuclear capabilities in the face of no further pressure on Iran and some pressure reduction (Rivlin, 2018). Accordingly, Iran was also able to engage with the international community and preserve its national interests, including energy trade and currency exchanges.

However, due to domestic evolutions in the US, including the rise to power of Donald Trump, this agreement could not be successful (Eslami, 2021; Eslami & Vieira, 2022). The Trump administration's approach to withdrawing from international institutions and serious pessimism about JCPOA success in curbing Iran's regional movements eventually led to the withdrawal of the US from JCPOA and the return of sanctions despite European Countries' efforts to prevent the US from withdrawing (Eslami & Vieira, 2020). Consequently, Iran began to reduce its commitments under the nuclear deal after a one-year "strategic patience." In this line, Iran revived its nuclear reactors and started uranium enrichment at the level of 63% (Kamalvandi, 2021).

While the reduction of nuclear commitments and uranium enrichment was considered as a necessary condition for preserving Iran's national interests, it was not a sufficient condition. The country needed clients for its oil as well as partners for trade to neutralize international sanctions and allies for possible war as sufficient conditions for the survival of the regime. Iran, which is facing the pressure of unilateral US economic sanctions and no longer has any hope for the West, at least in the medium term, has chosen China as an economic partner with which it can have strategic relations.

As one of the largest energy sources in the Middle East and connecting Asia to Africa, Iran is a stronghold for China to maintain energy security (Eslami et al., 2021). Moreover, Beijing, as an economic superpower that will become the world's number one GDP power in the future, could be the driving force behind Iran's economic growth. Improving the economic situation was the same hope that Iran had for the nuclear deal for economic reconciliation with the West (Tabatabai & Samuel, 2017). Something that has never been materialized, and now Iran is seeking to develop its economy with a big change in its foreign policy, which is called "turning to the east" (Avdaliani, 2020). While CSP is a massive and long-lasting agreement that can preserve Iran's national interests for the next 25 years and does not impose any restriction on Iran's nuclear and military sectors, it is safe to argue that the Iran–China deal has a negative impact on the development of Iran's nuclear negotiations with the Western Countries. Iran's new government under Ebrahim Raeisi, who is an anti-American actor, has originally a sceptical view towards JCPOA and nuclear negotiations. Therefore, the new government considers CSP as an alternative for JCPOA, which allows Iran to follow its economic goals on the one hand and develop its nuclear and ballistic missile programmes on the other hand.

6 Conclusion

In March 2021, a strategic document for long-term cooperation in dozens of areas, including banking, telecommunications, ports, railways, healthcare, and information technology, over the next 25 years was signed between Iran and China. The strategic memorandum of cooperation between Iran and China can be considered the result of both countries' realistic view of the international situation. The fact is that over the past 40 years, Iran and China have established extensive cooperation in various fields in military and strategic issues, the starting point of which goes back to the victory of the Islamic Revolution and the formation of the Islamic Republic of Iran. However, the recently signed deal between both countries under the auspices of the BRI means a lot remains to be seen regarding the impacts the deal would have on Iran's position in the Middle East and China's quest for global dominance.

The Comprehensive Strategic Partnership (CSP) with Iran is important to China because the deal will in no small measure help in the implementation of the Belt and Road Initiative as well as the reconstruction of the Silk road. The BRI is portrayed as a revival of the ancient Silk Roads which is linked China with Europe through Central Asia. It is a twenty-first-century reincarnation of the ancient Silk Road that connects the Pacific coast of China to the Mediterranean. China's thirst for fossil fuels plays a very key role in the reconstruction of the Silk Road. While Iran has one of the largest energy resources in the world, the CSP will become a veritable tool in helping China quench this thirst. However, aside from the thirst for fossils, there are other views that point to the fact that the Belt and Road initiative to the Chinese goes beyond building economic integration but a quest for global dominance and expansion. The ancient Silk Road is now an image and metaphor that has been revived into a project that President Xi Jinping has described as 'the project of the century, and can otherwise be referred to as the Belt and Road Initiative' (BRI).

The CSP is important to Iran as it is also important to China. Iran's failure in cooperating with the Western countries under the JCPOA changed Iran's approach towards its foreign policy. After the US withdrawal from the JCPOA and the imposition of new sanctions on Iran's economy, Iranian leadership took a step to shift towards the East. CSP is one of the most important strategic decisions of Iran during the last years, especially after the failure of the nuclear deal. The country seeks to secure its national interest under new agreements and in cooperation with new countries. While China is considered to be one of the strongest economic powers in the world, which is in a trade war with the US, Iran's tendency for approaching China seems to be rational. Accordingly, CSP is an alternative for JCPOA, and by signing this strategic document, Iran intends to gain what the country lost after the US withdrawal from JCPOA.

Bibliographic References

Alef, G. (2021). *China invests 400 billion in Iran's economy*. Alef Groups. Retrieved on December 2021, from https://www.alef.ir/news/3980619051.html

Anonymous. (2021a). *Comprehensive strategic partnership between Islamic Republic of Iran and Republic of China*. Official Website of the President. Retrieved on December 2021, from https://president.ir/EN/91435

Anonymous. (2021b). *Presence of Ayatollah Khamenei's representative in negotiations with China*. RadioFarda. Retrieved on December 2021, from https://www.radiofarda.com/a/two-high-ranking-iranian-officials-defend-the-signing-of-a-25-year-contract-with-china/31181462.html

Arifon, O. (2018). Comparing Chinese and EU soft power: The credibility factor. *Languages Cultures Mediation Journal, 5*(2), 35–50.
Avdaliani, E. (2020). *Why is Iran turning east? Army now.* Retrieved on December 2021, from https://armynow.net/iran-turn-to-east/
Azad, S. (2017). *Iran and China: A new approach to their bilateral relations.* Rowman & Littlefield.
Balding, C. (2017). *Can China afford its belt and road?* Bloomberg Opinion. Retrieved on December 2021, from https://www.bloomberg.com/opinion/articles/2017-05-17/can-china-afford-its-belt-and-road
Baruzzi, S. (2021). *The Belt and Road Initiative: Investments in 2021 and future outlook.* Silk Road Briefing. Retrieved on December 2021, from https://www.silkroadbriefing.com/news/2021/02/09/the-belt-road-initiative-investments-in-2021-and-future-outlook/
Belal, K. (2020). China-Iran relations: Prospects and complexities. *Policy Perspectives, 17*(2), 47–66.
Brown, K., & Bērziņa-Čerenkova, U. (2018). Ideology in the era of Xi Jinping. *Journal of Chinese Political Science, 23*(3), 323–339.
Buzan, B. (2010). China in International society: Is 'peaceful rise' possible? *The Chinese Journal of International Politics, 3*(1), 5–36.
Calabrese, J. (2018). China's One Belt, One Road (OBOR) Initiative: Envisioning Iran's role. In A. Ehleshami & N. Horesh (Ed.), *China's presence in the Middle East: The implication of the One Belt, One Road Initiative.* Routledge.
Chan, S., & Song, W. (2020). Telling the China story well: A discursive approach to the analysis of Chinese Foreign Policy in the 'Belt and Road' Initiative. *Chinese Political Science Review, 5*(3), 417–437.
Chen, D. (2015). *The rise of China's new soft power.* Retrieved on December 2021, from https://thediplomat.com/2015/06/the-rise-of-chinas-new-softpower/
Chen, Z. (2016). China, the European Union, and the fragile world order. *Journal of Common Market Studies, 54*(4), 775–792.
Chen, Z., & Song, L. (2012). The conceptual gap on soft power between China and Europe and its impact on bilateral relations. In Z. Pan (Ed.), *Conceptual gaps in China-EU relations: Global governance, human rights and strategic partnerships* (pp. 50–64). Palgrave.
Courmont, B. (2015). Soft power debates in China. *Academic Foresights, 13*, 1–6.
Daneshvar, P. (2016). *Revolution in Iran.* Springer.
Dreyer, J. (2015). The 'Tianxia trope: Will China change the international system? *Journal of Contemporary China, 24*(96), 1015–1031.
Duarte, P., & Xing, L. (2018). Conclusion: The One Belt One Road in the politics of fear and hope. In L. Xing (Ed.), *Mapping China's One Belt One Road Initiative* (pp. 279–289). Palgrave.
Dugué-Nevers, A. (2017). China and soft power: Building relations and cooperation. *Contemporary Chinese Political Economy and Strategic Relations, 3*(1), 71–101.
Ehteshami, A., & Horesh, N. (2018). *China's presence in the Middle East: The implications of the One Belt.* Routledge.
Englund, J., & Holmquist, E. (2020). *China and Iran-an unequal friendship.* Swedish Defence Research Agency. Retrieved on December 2021, from https://www.foi.se/en/foi/research/security-policy/asia-and-the-middle-east.html
Eslami, M. (2021). Iran's ballistic missile program and its foreign and security policy towards the United States under the Trump Administration. *Revista Española De Ciencia Política, 55*, 37–62.
Eslami, M., Bazrafshan, M., & Sedaghat, M. (2021). Shia geopolitics or religious tourism? Political convergence of Iran and Iraq in the light of Arbaeen pilgrimage. In F. Leandro (Ed.), *The geopolitics of Iran* (pp. 363–385). Palgrave Macmillan.
Eslami, M., & Papageorgiou, M. (2021). *Iran's relations with Russia and India: Under the American sanctions.* Indrastra Global.
Eslami, M., & Sotudehfar, S. (2021). Iran–UAE relations and disputes over the sovereignty of Abu Musa and Tunbs. In F. Leandro (Ed.), *The geopolitics of Iran* (pp. 343–361). Palgrave Macmillan.

Eslami, M., & Vieira, A. V. G. (2020). Iran's strategic culture: The 'revolutionary' and 'moderation' narratives on the ballistic missile programme. *Third World Quarterly, 42*(2), 312–328.

Eslami, M., & Vieira, A. V. G. (2022). Shi'a principles and Iran's strategic culture towards ballistic missile deployment. *International Affairs, 98*(2), 675–688.

Fayazmanesh, S. (2003). The politics of the US economic sanctions against Iran. *Review of Radical Political Economics, 35*(3), 221–240.

Garlick, J. (2020). The regional impacts of China's Belt and Road Initiative. *Journal of Current Chinese Affairs, 49*(1), 3–13.

Green, N. (2015). From the Silk Road to the Railroad (and back): The means and meanings of the Iranian encounter with China. *Iranian Studies, 48*(2), 165–192.

Huan, G. (1987). *China's "open door" policy: 1978–1984* (Doctoral dissertation). Princeton University.

Ibrahim, S. G., & Bibi-Farouk, F. I. (2020). Nigeria-Africa in the Belt and Road Initiative: Major benefits, challenges and prospects. *North Asian International Research Journal of Social Science & Humanities, 6*(5), 6–27.

Kamalvandi, B. (2021). *Iran will enrich its Uranium even above 20 percent if needed*. Mehr. Retrieved on December 2021, from https://www.mehrnews.com/

Katzman, K. (2010). *Iran: US concerns and policy responses*. Diane Publishing.

Kemp, G. (2012). *The east moves west: India, China, and Asia's growing presence in the Middle East*. Brookings Institution Press.

Lavery, C., & Menon, A. (2021). China's BRI spends down 54% in 2020 but "green" funding up. *World Economy News*. Retrieved on December 2021, from https://www.hellenicshippingnews.com/chinas-bri-spend-down-54-in-2020-but-green-funding-up/. Accessed August 10 2021.

Leandro, F., & Duarte, P. (Eds.). (2020). *The Belt and Road Initiative—International perspectives on an old archetype of a new development model*. Palgrave.

Mayer, M., & Zhang, X. (2020). Theorizing China-world integration: Socio-spatial reconfigurations and the modern Silk Roads. *Review of International Political Economy*. Retrieved on December 2020, from https://doi.org/10.1080/09692290.2020.1741424

Mehdi, S. Z. (2021). *Iran, China sign deal on 'Belt and Road' project* [Online]. https://www.aa.com.tr/en/asia-pacific/iran-china-sign-deal-on-belt-and-road-project/2190154

Mirire, D. (2019, October 16). *Kenya opens $1.5 billion Chinese-built railway linking Rift Valley Town and Nairobi*. Reuters. Retrieved on December 2020, from https://www.reuters.com/article/us-kenya-railway-idUSKBN1WV0Z0

Mohajer, P. (1991). Chinese-Iranian relations v: Diplomatic and commercial relations, 1949–90. *Encyclopaedia Iranica, 5*(4), 438–441.

Munoz, N., Grassi, A., Qiong, S., Crespi, M., Qing, W. G., & Cai, L. Z. (1982). Precursor lesions of oesophageal cancer in high-risk populations in Iran and China. *The Lancet, 319*(8277), 876–879.

Noroozi, T. (1999). *Islamic utopianism and international relations: A reflection on the symbolism of Khomeini's "neither east, nor west" doctrine* (Ayatollah Ruhollah Khomeini, Iran).

Park, J. S., & Glenn, C. (2010). Iran and China. In R. Wright (Ed.), *The Iran Primer* (pp. 182–185). United States Institute of Peace Press.

Perteghella, A., & Talbot, V. (2020). Russia's relations with Iran, Saudi Arabia, and Turkey: Friends in need, friends indeed? In *Russia in the Middle East and North Africa* (pp. 77–103). Routledge.

Ramazani, R. K. (1992). Iran' foreign policy: Both North and South. *Middle East Journal, 46*(3), 393–412.

Rivlin, P. (2018). Leverage of economic sanctions: The case of US sanctions against Iran, 1979–2016. In *Geo-Economics and power politics in the 21st century* (pp. 99–113). Routledge.

Robert, T. L. (2020). The Belt and Road Initiative and Africa's regional infrastructure development: Implications and lessons. *Transnational Corporations Review, 12*(4), 425–438.

Rudolph, J. (2016). XI's state media tour: News must speak for the party. *China Digital Times*. Retrieved on December 2021, from https://chinadigitaltimes.net/2016/02/191569/

Salmanipour, T., & Mahmudov, Y. (2017). An analysis of the history of cultural and political relations with Iran and Britain in the Naseri Era (Qajar Era). *The Turkish Online Journal of Design, Art and Communication TOJDAC, 7,* 1597–1605.

Scobell, A., & Nader, A. (2016). *China in the Middle East: The wary dragon.* Rand Corporation.

Steele, R. (2020). *The Shah's imperial celebrations of 1971: Nationalism, culture and politics in late Pahlavi Iran.* IB Tauris.

Strategiczny, P. (2018). The Belt and Road Initiative (BRI): Implications for Iran-China Relations. *Przeglad Strategiczny, 8*(11), 221–232.

Sung, Y. W., & Song, E. (1991). *The China-Hong Kong connection: The key to China's open-door policy.* Cambridge University Press.

Tabaar, M. A. (2017). Causes of the US hostage crisis in Iran: The untold account of the communist threat. *Security Studies, 26*(4), 665–697.

Tabatabai, A., & Esfandiary, D. (2018). *Triple-Axis: Iran's relations with Russia and China.* Bloomsbury Publishing.

Tabatabai, A. M., & Samuel, A. T. (2017). What the Iran-Iraq war tells us about the future of the Iran nuclear deal. *International Security, 42*(1), 152–185.

Taghizadeh, M. R. (1991). *Neither east nor west: Iran, the USSR, and the USA.* Yale University Press.

Tarock, A. (2016). The Iran nuclear deal: Winning a little, losing a lot. *Third World Quarterly, 37*(8), 1408–1424.

Vakulchuk, R., & Overland, I. (2019). China's Belt and Road Initiative through the lens of Central Asia. In M. C. Fanny & H. Ying-Yi (Eds.), *Regional connection under the Belt and Road Initiative.* Routledge.

Wang, C. N. (2020). *Investments in the Chinese Belt and Road Initiative (BRI) in 2020 During the Covid19 pandemic.* International Institute of Green Finance. Retrieved on December 2021, from https://www.researchgate.net/publication/343333141

Yetiv, S. A., & Lu, C. (2007). China, global energy, and the Middle East. *The Middle East Journal, 61*(2), 199–218.

Chapter 35
China's New Maritime Silk Road Cooperation: Why Malaysia, Indonesia, and the Philippines Are Clings in Disagreement?

Muhamad Azwan Abd Rahman● and Sufian Jusoh

1 Introduction

Compared to previous years, the China–Southeast Asia relationship was critical in 2002 because of severe and concerted efforts by the Association of Southeast Asia Nations (ASEAN) member states to secure political, economic, and mutual security benefits. Since 2002, China-ASEAN relations have been more optimistic and friendly, with ASEAN calling for consensus and a deeper understanding of maritime cooperation. The existence of a consensus was further strengthened by Pempel (2007) and Sohn (2010), who argued that China strengthened its close relationship with ASEAN through four major agreements signed in 2002: the Declaration on the South China Sea, the Joint Declaration on the Cooperation of Non-Traditional Security Issues, the Framework Agreement on Comprehensive Economic Cooperation, and the Memorandum of Understanding in Agriculture Cooperation.

The selection of ASEAN as a trading partner is part of China's plan to achieve inclusive trade boosts similar to those received by the US and Japan in Southeast Asia. China's efforts have taken nearly a decade, resulting in the establishment of the twenty-first-Century Maritime Silk Road in Southeast Asia in 2013, which was intended to strengthen the country's economy. The policy approach process, as well as the five pillars towards the strengthening of the Belt and Road Initiative (BRI), showcased China by, for example, strengthening strategic communications policies; ensuring financial cooperation and the use of currency in trading and investment; improving relationships between countries; and promoting more open trade. Exchanges and displays of cooperation have gradually convinced ASEAN member countries to participate in this mega project. Nevertheless, there has been criticism that this action is intended to expand China's political and economic influence in Southeast Asian countries such as Malaysia and Indonesia. Many China watchers

---

M. A. A. Rahman (✉) · S. Jusoh
The Institute of Malaysia and International Studies (IKMAS), National University of Malaysia (UKM), Bangi, Malaysia

© The Author(s), under exclusive license to Springer Nature Singapore Pte Ltd. 2023
P. A. B. Duarte et al. (eds.), *The Palgrave Handbook of Globalization with Chinese Characteristics*, https://doi.org/10.1007/978-981-19-6700-9_35

and commentators have pushed the view that China's BRI, launched in 2013, is a tool being used by China to expand its geopolitics and economic interest in the region and the world (Vltchek, 2020). The truth of this must be assessed based on hard facts, given that there are many geopolitical rivalries and conflicts between the US and rising China. For ASEAN member states, including Malaysia, Indonesia, and the Philippines, the stand must be active neutrality. As stated in the ASEAN Zone of Peace, Freedom, and Neutrality, ASEAN member states should maintain active neutrality and not be drawn into conflicts between the superpowers.

China has made a clear assertion of claims in the South China Sea that come into conflict with littoral states such as Malaysia, the Philippines, Vietnam, Brunei, and Indonesia. This position remains even after China offered vaccination diplomacy through BRI networks; Xi announced in his speech on 18 May 2020 that China would provide inexpensive COVID-19 vaccinations for the global public good (Rudolf, 2021). However, though the framework of cooperation and friendship remains, there are still strains and misunderstandings. This unease is most profound when China makes what is seen as excessive claims over the South China Sea (the 9-dotted line map) by sending its aeroplanes and patrol ships into the space of neighbouring countries that are still battling the pandemic. The US has stood against the BRI since its establishment, particularly in situations involving territorial disputes.

Additionally, the US has established the Department of Justice's China Initiative (DoJCI) to counter China's BRI (USDJ, 2020). President Biden of the US announced the development of new strategic cooperation between the US, Australia, and the UK to reinforce Indo-Pacific stability as China develops its military might and dominance. However, when Australia–the United Kingdom–the United States pact (AUKUS) announced, they anticipated that China would be hostile and that France would be upset because they were not invited. Furthermore, the AUKUS treaty, lauded by the presidents of the three countries as historic and forward-thinking, is intended to offset China's growing influence in the Indo-Pacific and the region, where it has steadily grown its military power. Nevertheless, ASEAN still hoped that China's BRI would facilitate the genuine joint development of the Southeast Asian states. However, issues of distrust continue to emerge, and if prolonged, these could impact the development prospects for the region.

This chapter is divided into four parts. The first section will explain the fluctuation of Malaysia–China's recent development. The following section will look into the bumpy road of wealth creation for Indonesia–China. The subsequent discussion will involve the multifaceted Philippines–China relations. The final section considers the ongoing discussion and policy implications. Whatever the implications, cooperation between Malaysia and Indonesia with China is unique, having never been offered by any Western country before, and true collaboration could boost Southeast Asia's economic growth to make it a global twenty-first-century maritime hub.

2 The Fragility of the Recent Strategic Development in Malaysia–China

Since normalization of relations between Malaysia and China in 1974, trading has gradually increased, and when China became a member of the World Trade Organisation (WTO) in 2001, Malaysia–China trade dramatically increased. From 2001 until 2013, as shown in Table 1, while Malaysia continued to trade with its traditional partners—the US, Japan, and South Korea—Malaysia–China trade showed tremendous achievement. Nevertheless, as shown in Table 2, trade relations show an imbalance that favours China (Blanchard, 2019).

Table 1 Malaysia trade according to the destination of selected countries (2001–2011) (amounts in RM million)

State/Year	China	US	Japan	South Korea
2001	14,683	67,618	44,393	11,107
2002	20,008	74,131	39,707	11,866
2003	25,791	77,872	42,507	11,555
2004	32,286	90,254	48,499	16,948
2005	35,153	105,238	50,509	18,329
2006	42,620	110,135	52,475	21,388
2007	53,038	94,485	55,648	23,165
2008	63,435	82,700	70,688	26,956
2009	67,359	60,811	53,345	20,318
2010	80,105	60,951	66,763	24,300
2011	91,551	57,653	81,368	26,252
2012	88,793	60,791	83,401	25,368
2013	97,043	58,055	79,197	26,199

Source Economic Planning Unit Malaysia (2017)

Table 2 Malaysia–China trade, 2010–2017 (amounts in US$ billion)

	2010	2011	2012	2013	2014	2015	2016	2017
Exports (Freight on Board-FOB) to China	24.91	29.95	28.78	30.71	28.20	25.99	23.72	29.40
Imports (Cost, Insurance and Freight-CIF) from China	20.68	24.75	29.76	33.74	35.33	33.16	34.29	38.31
China Trade balance	4.23	5.21	−0.98	−3.03	−7.12	−7.17	−10.57	−8.91

Source Blanchard (2019)

Table 3 China Gross Domestic Product (US$)

Year	GDP (US$)
1980	191.149 billion
1990	360.85 billion
2000	1,211.0 billion
2006	2,712.0 billion
2010	6,0870.0 billion
2015	11,062.0 billion
2016	11,233.0 billion
2019	14,280.0 billion

Source World Bank (n. d)

Before the BRI was launched in 2013, Malaysia's exports to China expanded. For example, exports from Malaysia to China in 2010 totalled US$24.91 billion, compared to China's exports to Malaysia of US$20.68 billion. In the previous decades, China's increasing demand had enabled Malaysia to expand its exports of manufactured goods to this enormous market at an impressive rate (Hong et al., 2019), allowing it to increase its investment in China. However, the situation changed once China shifted its strategy policy under BRI in 2013. Since then, the trade balance between Malaysia and China has affected the value of Malaysia's exports, with the balance of trade favouring China.

China's rapid economic growth and expansion of its GDP have been awe-inspiring, and many countries are taking note, including Malaysia. As shown in Table 3, China's GDP has increased by leaps and bounds since 1980, with China's GDP in 2019 being 74.7 times bigger than 40 years earlier. With such bountiful wealth accumulated through rapid economic growth, China is in a strong position to invest overseas and work more closely with small states, such as Malaysia, through the Maritime Silk Road to facilitate regional development.

As indicated above, Malaysia has taken note of China's growth and rising prosperity, as well as the strategic role it now plays in the ASEAN region, Asia, and the world. Malaysia welcomed the Regional Cooperation and Economic Partnership (RCEP) proposed by China's President Xi Jinping in 2013 when he visited Kuala Lumpur during Mohd Najib Abdul Razak's premiership. The warm welcome by the Malaysian people and their appreciation of the China–Malaysia relationship were evident in a 2016 survey in which 70% of the respondents had a favourable impression of China, and only 22% were unfavourable (Yeoh, 2018). At the same time, 67% of respondents felt that Malaysia–China relations had a bright future, while 22% expressed feeling the quiet development of friction between the countries (Yeoh, 2018). This is of ongoing concern for Malaysia regarding the trade and investment imbalance that began in 2013. The balance of trade was in favour of China throughout 2014 (−US$7.12 billion), 2015 (−US$7.17 billion), 2016 (−US$10.57 billion), and 2017 (−US$8.91 billion) (Blanchard, 2019).

Based on the above analysis, there are three parts to the relationship between Malaysia and China's efforts to remain in this cooperation. The first is financial infrastructure, which involves financial assistance from the Asian Infrastructure Investment Bank (AIIB) and China Bank for investment in technical infrastructure. The second is the social infrastructure, which includes the relationship between the people of the two countries in terms of culture, history, moral values, geography, migration, education, and others. The third is the technical infrastructure, which applies cluster strategies combining ports, railways, technology expertise assistance, gas pipelines, industrial estates, and condominiums (Evers & Menkhoff, 2018). However, in recent developments, China has struggled to gain trust from ASEAN member countries, particularly Malaysia, for reasons related to the changing political landscape, scandals such as 1Malaysian Development Berhad (1MDB), disproportionate geopolitical and regional developments in the water, and China's stance on humanitarian and health issues. Moreover, Xi Jinping has not shown any change in policy position on the dispute in the South China Sea (Mohammad Zaki & Mohd Azizuddin, 2017; Ngeow, 2018).

Recently, there have been two incidents in the South China Sea involving China. On 17 April 2020, China survey vessel Haiyang Dizhi 8 moved in formation with four Chinese Coast Guard ships and nine militia vessels entering Malaysia's maritime zone of exclusive economy and continent shelf illegally (Sumathy, 2020). On another occasion, 16 air crafts of the People's Liberation Army–Air Force (PLAAF), China, moved in tactical formation to enter the Malaysia Maritime Zone, Kota Kinabalu Flight Information Region (FIR). Then, they changed course to be illegally close to the Beting Patinggi Ali on 31 May 2021. The Royal Malaysian Air Force (RMAF) was able to intercept and make visual identification of the Ilyushin Il-76 and Xian Y-20, which are capable of executing any military mission (RMAF, 2021). Hishammuddin Hussein, Ministry of Defence Malaysia (MinDef), was summoned to China and stated that even though Malaysia has a good relationship with China, this action is regarded as intolerable (Tarrence, 2021). The public urged Hishammuddin Hussein to send a diplomatic note to China objecting to China's intrusive behaviour in the South China Sea. These two incidents have created uneasy feelings among Malaysians regarding China, which have become more obvious as Malaysia is fighting the COVID-19 pandemic and negotiating with China to procure the Sinovac Sinopharm vaccine.

Although the strategy has implications for settlement in South China Sea, Malaysia is maintaining their low-key policy position and strengthening cooperation with China in multiple areas, such as politics, education, economy, tourism, defence, and military training. In addition, Malaysia's continued attempts to preserve a special relationship with China are intended to balance US dominance in Asia. The positive message of the BRI, as stated by Xi Jinping, should be applied to the South China Sea dispute, and new forms of bilateral cooperation can be considered for certain cases, as Malaysia and Thailand did with the Malaysia–Thailand Joint Authority (MTJA) in 1978, which had the theme "brothers drinking from the same well."

3 Indonesia–China: Creating Wealth on a Bumpy Road

For Indonesia and China, 10 October 2013 is an important date, as it was the day when Xi Jinping announced his intention to restore the 21st Century Maritime Silk Road in the Indonesian Parliament (Jacob, 2015; Zhao, 2015). The announcement received a positive reaction from the newly appointed President of Indonesia, Joko Widodo, who replaced Susilo Bambang Yudhoyono in 2014. This is because one of Jokowi's administration's agenda items was to strengthen Indonesia as a fulcrum in maritime activities as well as to advance the economy of the country and the income of the people. Through this doctrine, Jokowi predicted that the Indonesian economy would rise from a country with a low middle income of US$3,592 in terms of population per capita to an upper middle income of US$10,000 by 2045 (Nainggolan, 2015). The Indonesia–China partnership is widespread and complex, covering not only business and national networks but other aspects as well. In terms of tourism, the Indonesian government has recorded that tourist from China spends on average US$1,107 each in Indonesian, contributing to the country's revenue of US$2 billion; thus, Jokowi set a target to attract approximately 20 million Chinese tourists by 2020 (FMPRC, 2017). The two presidents have also agreed to synergize the idea of the World Maritime Axis and the 21st Century Maritime Silk Road to realize maritime relations in strategic areas, primarily through infrastructure development (HUMAS, 2014).

However, based on Table 4, the investment conditions between Indonesia and China are a bit fluctuate. In terms of Chinese investments in Indonesia, the figures increased from 2013–2017, but the situation changed in the following year, decreasing from US$2.38 million in 2018 to US$2.29 million in 2019 (Lalisang & Candra, 2020). According to the The ASEAN Secretariat (2021), Foreign Direct Investment (FDI) inflows into Indonesia fell by 22% to $19 billion in 2020, owing to a 58% drop in investment in the manufacturing sector, although this was also affected by the pandemic (The ASEAN Secretariat, 2021). In 2014, the impact of the Maritime Silk Road cooperation that China introduced motivated Jokowi to sign the agreement, suggesting that the geopolitics strategy under Jokowi was coordinated. Meanwhile, China was one of Indonesia's most prominent donors and trading partners, and President Xi's offer of maritime partnerships, financial assistance, and infrastructure projects under the Maritime Silk Road umbrella had the potential to greatly help Jokowi achieve his maritime goals (Lai, 2019).

According to HUMAS (2015), both leaders witnessed the approval and signature of eight forms of cooperation by the ministries of state-owned enterprises (SOEs) of Indonesia and China, including the following:

1. Memorandum of Understanding (MoU) on Economic Cooperation between the Coordinating Ministry for Economic Affairs of the Republic of Indonesia and the National Commission on Development and Reform of the People's Republic of China;
2. MoU on Industrial and Infrastructure Development Cooperation between the National Commission on Development and Reform of the PRC with the Minister of State-Owned Enterprises (BUMN);

Table 4 Chinese investment in Indonesia

Year	Investment (Thousand USD)
2010	173,646
2011	128,229
2012	140,969
2013	296,882
2014	800,029
2015	628,337
2016	2,665,297
2017	3,361,227
2018	2,376,536
2019	2,289,890

Source Lalisang and Candra (2020)

3. MoU between the Minister of SOEs and China's National Commission for Development and Reform for the Jakarta-Bandung High-Speed Rail Development Project;
4. MoU between Indonesia's National Search and Rescue Agency (BASARNAS) and China's Minister of Transport;
5. Cooperation Agreement between the Government of Indonesia and China for the prevention of double taxation;
6. MoU between the National Space Development Agency (LAPAN) and the National Space Agency of China;
7. MoU on Cooperation between the Minister of SOEs and China Development Bank Corporation (CDBC).

Zhao (2015) explained that Indonesia is among China's economic destinations in FDI because of its huge market potential. However, considering that this cooperation will make Indonesia one of China's largest natural resources providers, China is risking capital resources, expertise, and technology as a distributor of products to the user country. In turn, Indonesia will be forced to depend on Chinese goods and products. Indonesia's experience has also influenced concerns about China's cooperation in the ASEAN-China Free Trade Area (ACFTA) agreement 2005. However, John Lee (2013) argued that China is a small player compared to the manufacturing sector in Indonesia, which Indonesia itself dominated the flow of FDI by 45.5% in 2012, 42% in 2011, and 37% in 2010. Moreover, China's FDI flow to Indonesia became less stable, declining from 2004 to the first quarter of 2012, providing evidence that Chinese investors are still a long way from dominating Indonesia. At the same time, Indonesia is one of the ASEAN member states that forged ahead with the 4.0 industry initiatives prior to attracting FDI (The ASEAN Secretariat, 2021). Although evidenced by statistics from social, political, and economical memories such as the ACFTA impact, the repeated influence of communism and the impact of China-generated deficits have the most influence on domestic perceptions of cooperation with the country. For example, since the ACFTA agreement was signed, Indonesia's export–import sector has contracted, with parts of the textile industry in Indonesia having shut down its operation and competition from other Free Trade Areas (FTAs) has increased (Gatra Priyandita, 2015; Yang Mu & Heng, 2011).

In 2019, Jokowi proposed that China establish a special BRI fund in Indonesia. That tacit endorsement led to expansion talks, with Indonesia inviting China to invest in 28 more projects worth US$9.1 billion (Lai, 2019). As a result, several projects have been financed and built under the Chinese initiative, the most important of which is Jakarta-Bandung High-Speed Rail (JBHSR), which is currently being built on the island of Java and will be completed by 2023 (Goulard, 2021).

The slow implementation of BRI projects is due to Indonesia's prudent approach to project financing and not the problematic debt trap. Nevertheless, anti-Chinese prejudices have exacerbated criticism of the project in Indonesia and hampered further Chinese investment, particularly for bringing migrant workers from China to complete the megaprojects (Lam, 2020; Muhamad Azwan, 2018). The cases of Jakarta-Bandung High-Speed Rail (HSR) show how China's BRI projects are shaped by their embedding in certain countries (Tritto, 2020). This is also related to the problem of the dumping of cheap goods and products from China to Indonesia, which is affecting local enterprises in Indonesia. What is clear is that economic cooperation with China is necessary because Indonesia's economic capacity alone is not enough to cover the development expenditure of megaprojects in Indonesia. However, the ongoing deficit in the trade balance between Indonesia–China affects the domestic situation, especially in economic matters, and matters of strategic cooperation, such as that in the South China Sea.

Unlike other ASEAN countries, it is so clear that, since Jokowi took exception in the Yudhoyono era, Indonesia will not be involved as a claim country, as even Indonesia admits (Calleja, 2016; Ramadhani, 2015). However, this does not mean Indonesia is free to confront China on issues in the South China Sea, specifically tensions on Natuna Island.

The approval of the pressure received by Jokowi at the domestic level has led to his administration making decisions that surprised China on a series of Natuna Island issues.[1] First, this invasion had become a major national issue that was widely discussed in public spaces in relation to Jokowi's subsequent actions with China (Suryadinata, 2017). Second, the insistence of various parties also influenced Jokowi's soft stance with China on this issue. These two justifications were important to Jokowi, considering the importance of maintaining domestic political continuity and support at the cabinet level.

The evidence for this argument is that, after the Natuna issue and all the domestic debates, the cabinet under Jokowi provided a new map that included the renaming of the Natuna Sea and was in the planning stage for six months, since October 2016 (Suryadinata, 2017). Thus, Indonesia's decision to rename the South China Sea looks

---

[1] Rizal Ramli, while holding the post of Ministry of Maritime Affairs, asserted that Natuna is rich in natural resources and needs to be maintained. Natuna is also firmly the territory of Indonesia, and its sovereignty must be held and should not be challenged by any party. See The Maritime Minister: The Government Wants to Make Natuna a Fishing City as well as a 'Hub' of Gas and Industry, 2016; Retrieved on December 2021, from http://www.setkab.go.id.

dramatic and responsive because the planning took only six months after the crisis occurred in March 2016. This reinforces the proposal that the strong nationalistic attitude of the Indonesian people influenced local leaders in a decision that increased the length of Jokowi's political power. The move prompted Jokowi, several cabinet ministers and[2] agencies, and research bodies to support the renaming of the South China Sea to the North Natuna Sea, which also overlaps with the demarcation of the nine-dash lines as demanded by China.

The different historical, political, and economic backgrounds of Indonesia, China, and Malaysia provide interesting dimensions to consider in relation to new phases of cooperation. First, the discussion at the domestic level is in terms of the amount of anti-Chinese attitudes in Indonesia and the impact of diplomatic relations with China. The second dimension is the reaction of investors, multinational corporations, and local companies regarding the presence of large investments, products, goods, and workers from Chinese-owned companies into Indonesia on the space and economic opportunities in new maritime cooperation. The third dimension is the introduction of the Global Maritime Fulcrum proposed by Jokowi that encourages more focus on maritime activities and infrastructure development, creating dynamism in Indonesia's economic and political systems at the regional and international levels, particularly with China. Thus, the close and mutual relationship of trust between the two countries has succeeded in setting a target, and the benchmark for the long-term surge in GDP, production, energy, investment, infrastructure, and productivity will be at a mega-scale in the long run.

4 The Multifaceted Relationship of the Philippines and China in the BRI

The Whitsun Reef is 175 nautical miles from the Philippine province of Palawan and 638 nautical miles from China's southern island of Hainan, according to Manila's statement, issued after the country's arbitration ruling in 2016 that invalidated China's expansive claims in the South China Sea (Venzon, 2021). In response to China's assertive presence in the region, Japan sold military ships and equipment to the Philippines and Vietnam to enhance their maritime security capabilities and deter Chinese aggression (CFR, 2021). Under President Rodrigo Duterte's administration, the Philippines has been one of the United States' most important strategic partners in the Indo-Pacific and has moved closer for close relationship with China. Close military ties between the US and the Philippines in the form of bilateral defence exercises, military aid, and information sharing are aimed at strengthening maritime

---

[2] International relations analyst from State Islamic University (UIN) Syarif Hidayatullah, Teguh Sentosa explained that the decision to change the name to the North Natuna Sea may have caused China to protest, but Jokowi would stick with his stance. This is clearly Teguh, because maritime control is the main issue in Indonesia and the primary force behind national development. See Bilal Ramadan in 'China Protests North Natuna Sea Name, Jokowi Will Not Be Daunted', 2017; Retrieved on December 2021, from http://republika.co.id.

security against Chinese threats, which seems to contradict Duterte's pro-Beijing foreign policy (Brenda, 2020). In addition, Aquino, obtained a US$13 billion Chinese promise to increase FDI and development finance projects. Nonetheless, as territorial tensions between China and the Philippines over Scarborough Shoal escalated into a 2012 confrontation in the South China Sea, Aquino and his team searched for local political approval and placed government-to-government transactions on hold. This resulted in China imposing sanctions on Philippine fruit exports and restricting the Chinese tourist influx (Camba, 2017).

As a result, Philippine relations with China fluctuated from one extreme to the other. For example, China did not actively deal with the Philippines' claims in the South China Sea under Duterte and was slow to invest in new industrial and infrastructure projects (Chang, 2021). On the other hand, President Xi Jinping has noted that China and the Philippines have seen a turnaround in recent years in terms of consolidating and deepening their relations and establishing extensive strategic cooperation, which has brought tangible benefits to both countries as well as stability in the region (FMPRC, 2021).

In recent months, the diplomatic relationship between the Philippines and China was made closer after President Rodrigo Duterte signed approval for several business projects that would secure his transformational programme of improving infrastructure in the Philippines, particularly the country's transportation systems (Rubiolo, 2020). Despite ongoing disputes over the South China Sea, the Philippines government is willing to compromise and focus on establishing a bilateral relationship and greater cooperation for the country's best interests. On the other hand, China is keen on securing a business deal for joint exploration in the South China Sea. As a result, both countries have arranged to work offshore oil and gas exploration based on the so-called appropriate legality context (Heydarian, 2018). However, the road ahead seems unclear if we consider that the Philippine constitution stresses that a country that rejects the Philippines' Exclusive Economic Zone (EEZ) and its sovereignty should be barred. Consequently, many analysts and critics have argued that the Philippines may end up repaying loans given for government projects earlier than planned and eventually falling into a debt trap.

In 2015, in its maritime dispute with China over the West Philippines Sea, a disputed stretch of the South China Sea off the east coast of the Philippines, the Philippines became the last founding member of the China-led AIIB, which serves as a source of finance for China's BRI. The BRI project was expected to create jobs for 21,000 Filipinos, while other deals with Chinese companies have brought $12 billion worth of investment to the country (Fernando, 2020). Fernando (2020) also stated that this resulted in bilateral trades between China and the Philippines reaching close to US$50 billion in 2019, growing at an average of 17% in the last five years.

In 2017, during Duterte's state visit to China, the countries agreed on 24 major investments, with China signing memoranda of understanding worth US$1.5 billion and pledging US$9 billion in loans to Philippine companies (Camba, 2017). For example, Duterte agreed to play down tensions between China and the US in an effort to improve economic ties between the two countries. Two major projects in the Philippines (as illustrated in Table 5) that have made substantial progress under

Table 5 Majors Chinese capital projects in the Philippines

	Kaliwa Dam	Chico River Pump Irrigation Project
Location	Infanta Quezon to Teresa, Rizal	Cordillera
Type of Project	Dam	Irrigation Pump
Developers	China Energy Engineering Corporation Limited	China CAMC Engineering Company Limited
Contractors	Metropolitan Waterworks and Sewerage System	NIA
Financiers	Export-Import Bank of China	Export-Import Bank of China
Loan Amounts	Approximately $US211 million	Approximately $US62 million
Project Status	Ongoing	Ongoing
Interest Rates	2%	2%
Commitment Fee	0.30	0.30
Management Fee	0.30	0.30

Source Camba (2017)

Duterte's watch with the backing of Chinese financing and Chinese project involvement are the Kaliwa Dam and the Chico River Pump Irrigation Project (Camba, 2017). Additionally, China stands ready to strengthen ties and mutual trust with the Philippines to keep bilateral relations on the right track and obtain steady long-term development (FMPRC, 2021).

Faced with global challenges, such as the changing international situation and the COVID-19 pandemic, both countries are at a historic crossroads. They have reason to believe that a new era of friendship will shine through the mitigation of time under the leadership of President Xi Jinping and President Duterte and the concerted efforts of the governments and people of both countries to forge closer strategic cooperation (China Embassy, 2021). Despite optimistic talks between China and the Philippines over the flare-up of the maritime crisis, improving relations is seen as crucial in the dispute over the sovereignty of the South China Sea (Jennings, 2021).

However, Secretary of State Mike Pompeo's announcement on July 13 that the US would change its policy in the South China Sea to recognize maritime counter-claims at sea, including Manila's maritime claims settled by international arbitration in 2016, prompted China's Foreign Minister Wang Yi to contact Philippine Foreign Minister Locsin the next day (Grossman, 2020). The Chinese Foreign Ministry said that the country's sixth bilateral consultation mechanism on the dispute over the sovereignty of South China Sea waters would promote the healthy and stable development of Sino-Philippine relations and support peace and stability in the region (Jennings, 2021). According to Xu Liping (2021), Locsin stressed that the South China Sea is 'the only pebble in the broader avenue of bilateral relations' between China and the Philippines because it is part of the two countries' relationship. Meanwhile, the Philippines also accused Beijing of spreading a false narrative that it has illegitimate claims in the disputed South China Sea, marking Manila's last step in a weeks-long feud that strained diplomatic relations (Venzon, 2021). Philippine President Rodrigo

Duterte barred Philippine officials from commenting on the naval dispute, but he has since backed away from this position (Chang, 2021). Nevertheless, according to Kurlantzick (2021), since the beginning of May 2021, hundreds of Chinese ships have entered the Philippines' exclusive economic zone in the sea, where Beijing has made vast maritime territorial claims.

China's response was to reaffirm the progress in bilateral relations since the election of Duterte in order to prevent further erosion of his position against the US and to make a favourable turning point in the South China Sea (Grossman, 2020). Duterte also had the opportunity to clarify the Philippines–US mutual defence agreement terms, as the Biden administration continued its hard line with China (Chang, 2021). Furthermore, in contrast to the aggressive policies of his predecessors, Duterte announced the military and economic separation of the Philippines from Britain at the 2016 Philippines–China Trade and Investment Forum between the Philippines and Beijing, downplaying his government's diplomatic victory at the Permanent Court of Arbitration and describing the 2016 arbitration ruling on China's claims in the South China Sea as 'a piece of garbage with four corners' (Brenda, 2020).

Chinese leaders also hope to put the South China Sea back on the Philippines agenda before the presidential election of next year (Jennings, 2021), as concerns cover the Philippines claims in the South China Sea, China and its underlying problems, China's current situation and characteristics in terms of politics, the international community, the growing role of the US as a superpower, the challenges facing both parties, and the possible solutions for better relations between the Philippines and China (Asia Society, n.d.). Clarifying these agenda will broaden the range of options available to the incoming Philippine president as Duterte pursues relations with China.

5 South China Sea as a Sea of Friendship: Policy Implications

The Australia–United Kingdom–United States pact (AUKUS) is expected to have an important impact on Southeast Asia, an area at the heart of the Indo-Pacific region. However, those who seek to whitewash Southeast Asia and the region point out that Japan and India, the two biggest regional powers, support AUKUS. Moreover, China's ambassador to Malaysia recently stated that the South China Sea is a 'sea of friendship'. This statement may be an indication of friendly actions and cooperation in the South China Sea in the future. Thus, this chapter contributes in terms of encouraging policy within certain limits, especially policy involving cooperation in the field of strategic and economic communication between Malaysia and Indonesia with China, which could be applied by all littoral states that have disputes in the South China Sea. Some analysts welcome the AUKUS pact in Southeast Asia, while others are concerned that it will make the existing issues in Southeast Asia less stable. Thus, a new maritime strategy approach that incorporates strategic communication and intensive joint development efforts from the various actors involved should be considered on the part of ASEAN and China and could act as a model to other countries in ASEAN. The approach is for the benefit of historical networks for the advancement of future development and involves using historical value for tomorrow's success. Therefore, the China–ASEAN High-Level Economic Friendship Policy (CAHLEFP) recommendation in this chapter is apparent in response to China's state-led BRI policy of safeguarding the interests of not only ASEAN member states but of all three parties in economic cooperation, as well as strengthening effective strategic communications as expressed by Xi Jinping. Table 5 shows the level of ties between Malaysia and Indonesia with China.

Thus, and as illustrated in Table 6, evoking historical memories is not a magic wand. Historical memories between China and Malaysia will lose their appeal if China clings to geopolitical posturing in the South China Sea. In a survey conducted among ASEAN citizens, 76.3% regard China as the most influential economic power in Southeast Asia (Seah et al., 2021), but there is a trust deficit towards China. The results from Malaysia, for example, show a slight decline in trust in China from 67.2% to 63.3% (Seah et al., 2021). In fact, the synergy between China and the ASEAN member countries should be preserved and combined with strengthened effectiveness of national policy coordination, the contribution of other domestic support systems, such as organizations and business bodies, and the collective voices of the people, while avoiding overly centralized policy-making (Surin Pitsuwan, 2017). For example, the spirit of the sea of friendship was demonstrated by ASEAN members such as Malaysia and Thailand through the Malaysia–Thailand Joint Authority (MTJA) on 21 February 1978. According to the mutual consensus agreement, the function of the MTJA is to jointly coordinate and manage the development, heritage, and profit from the seabed and overlapping offshore area. This coordination of this event proves that discontent, such as that between Malaysia and Thailand, over territorial overlapping can be changed to the benefit of both countries in terms of contemporary development. This shared investment is the most important determinant in shaping the future well-being of these countries. Thus, the results of this chapter are significant in that they demonstrate an important policy of the ASEAN organization that encourages member countries to engage in strategic communication and cooperation with China as well as to showcase and maintain the context of diplomatic and contemporary economic uniqueness. This policy focuses both on the economy and on bilateral communication between ASEAN countries and China, especially in terms of long-term Maritime New Silk Road cooperation. The success of the Maritime New Silk Road and the agreed Action Plan 2016–2020 requires mutual respect between the parties involved.

In addition, in order to strengthen the implementation of the proposed friendship policy, this chapter also proposes the establishment of a special committee to evaluate the progress of the ASEAN-China Maritime New Silk Road called her the ASEAN-China Special Evaluation Committee on Maritime Silk Road (ACSEC-MSR). This special committee is necessary to monitor, regulate, and advise the

Table 6 Strong and weak relationship dimensions in the context of G2G, B2B + P2P between Malaysia and Indonesia with China

Dimensions	Strength level of relationship	Description	ASEAN Countries
G2G and B2B + P2P High	Strong Ties	High government interaction + strong encouragement between countries and business communities and citizens	Malaysia
G2G High but B2B + Medium P2P	Strong Ties	High government interaction + business community and people relations are gradually improving	Indonesia
G2G Low and B2B + P2P Low	Weak Ties	Both foundations are sceptical about political issues	Philippines

Source Revised from Granovetter (1973, 1983) and Chan (2015)

ASEAN countries involved in this megavision. The objective is to refine the strategies that have been formulated between China and ASEAN to avoid misunderstandings in communication and unhealthy competition within ASEAN countries. While this special committee cannot completely resolve issues relating to communication, competition, and inequality, it will help create positive gradual developments in terms of mutual understanding and tolerance in economic partnerships. The benefits of this joint regional development should be publicized through strategic and effective communication among ASEAN member countries and China. Through the proposed policies, as well as clear and orderly communication, the committee could also be beneficial to other countries that are participants in the Maritime New Silk Road project.

6 Conclusion

The future of ASEAN countries requires a new paradigm of thinking in order to weather the prosperity and challenges of China's rise to a new maritime vision. China has focused on ASEAN as the world's largest maritime hub of the twenty-first century with offers of sophistication in terms of communication, infrastructure development, and inter-people exchanges. Hence, there are two actions that ASEAN countries need to take so as not to be exposed to political, social, or economic risks. First, they must strategize closely to resolve existing conflicts. Second, they must develop and strengthen their social infrastructure and use it to create opportunities and resolve disputes between parties. The first action requires ASEAN member countries and China to focus on shared interests. That is to say, China cannot put its wants above those of the small and medium countries in ASEAN. Although the task will be challenging given China's status as a superpower, whether or not China should respect and accept ASEAN member states as a benefit to China's strategy in the country's long-term maritime cooperation is unconditionally burdened. The second action ensures that each side can make the issues of dispute in the South China Sea an opportunity rather than a threat. Also, China and ASEAN should stick to the principle of togetherness to solve a regional problem in an Asian way. Such actions will enable ASEAN countries to move forward by injecting policy values based on those elements in response to China's policy. Additionally, policymakers in each ASEAN country should thoroughly examine the communication network spaces and social infrastructure that can be used to develop new strategies for dealing with China. It has been quite difficult for China to negotiate multilaterally with ASEAN on this issue, as the issues that arise between member countries also pressure ASEAN to act, either through collective solutions or through member states, because they are firmly bound by the principle of not interfering in the affairs of other countries.

A proposed policy, CAHLEFP, based on a new perspective, as well as the establishment of the ACSEC-MSR committee, is needed for future bilateral relations between China and ASEAN member countries. The establishment of this policy and committee will distribute responsibility for negotiation among the collective voice of ASEAN and individual countries with the capacity to establish a partnership that benefits China–ASEAN relations in this new phase of cooperation. These policies and committees will not only safeguard the interests of ASEAN member states from the negative impact of China's projects but will also prevent exploitation by outside parties, including other major powers of interest in the Southeast Asian region. However, it is essential not to rule out the possibility that the implication of AUKUS pact will play an important role in driving the hostility and also the economic development of ASEAN member countries, and in their protection from China. The goal is that each ASEAN country should have closer ties to superpowers other than China that can provide greater cooperation. The effectiveness of the policy would be increased if combined with gradual improvements to identify weaknesses in cooperation. Thus, this chapter anticipates that the twenty-first-century Maritime Silk Road can restore the glory of Asia if it truly collaborative.

Bibliographic References

Asia Society. (n.d.). *A Filipino in China: A perspective on Philippine-China relations a talk by veteran journalist Chito Sta.* Romana. https://asiasociety.org/philippines/filipino-china-perspective-philippine-china-relations

Blanchard, J. M. F. (2019). Malaysia and China's MSRI: The road to China was taken before the (Maritime Silk) road was built. In J. M. F. Blanchard (Ed.), *China's Maritime Silk Road Initiative and Southeast Asia: Dilemmas, doubts and determination* (pp. 95–132). Palgrave Macmillan.

Brenda, T. (2020, October 8). *Friend or foe? Explaining the Philippines' China policy in the South China Sea*. Retrieved on December 2021, from https://www.e-ir.info/2020/08/10/friend-or-foe-explaining-the-philippines-china-policy-in-the-south-china-sea/

Calleja, N. P. (2016, February 16). *Widodo pushes for dialogue to resolve South China Sea conflict*. Retrieved on January 2022, from http://globalnation.inquirer.net/136563/widodoproposesdialoguetoresolvesouthchinaseaconflict

Camba, A. (2017). Inter-state relations and state capacity: The rise and fall of Chinese foreign direct investment in the Philippines. *Palgrave Communications, 3*(1), 1–19.

Chan, I. (2015, March 12). *China's Maritime Silk Road: The politics of routes*. https://www.rsis.edu.sg/rsis-publication/rsis/co15051-chinas-maritime-silk-road-the-politics-of-routes/#.Wel4x2iCzIU

Chang, F. K. (2021, July 7). *Hot and cold the Philippines relations with China and United States*. Retrieved on January 2022, from https://www.fpri.org/article/2021/07/hot-and-cold-the-philippines-relations-with-china-and-the-united-states/

China Embassy. (2021, June 9). *China-Philippines relations shine brighter in the tempering of time*. Retrieved from http://ph.china-embassy.org/eng/sgdt/t1882350.htm

Council on Foreign Relations. (2021, October 27). *Territorial disputes in the South China Sea*. Retrieved on January 2022, from https://www.cfr.org/global-conflict-tracker/conflict/territorial-disputes-south-china-sea

Economic Planning Unit. (2017). *Eksport Mengikut Negara Destinasi*. http://www.epu.gov.my/ms/statistik-ekonomi/dagangan-luar

Evers, H. D., & Menkhoff, T. (2018). China's Belt and Road initiative and ASEAN's maritime cluster. *Southeast Asian Social Science Review, 3*(2), 8.

Fernando, J. O. (2020). *China's belt and road initiative in the Philippines*. Asia Pacific Bulletin.

FMPRC. (2017, February 13). *China and Indonesia stand together to promote win-win cooperation*. http://www.fmprc.gov.cn/ce/ceindo/eng/xwmtfw/xwgbtz/t1437808.htm

FMPRC. (2021, August 27). *Xi Jinping speaks with Philippine President Rodrigo Duterte on the phone*. Retrieved on January 2022, from https://www.fmprc.gov.cn/mfa_eng/zxxx_662805/t1902941.shtml

Gatra Priyandita. (2015, November 7). *Don't expect too much from growing Sino–Indonesia ties*. https://www.eastasiaforum.org/2015/11/07/dont-expect-too-much-from-growing-sino-indonesia-ties/

Goulard, S. (2021, February 7). *China's BRI in some ASEAN countries (2/4): Indonesia's GMF*. Retrieved on January 2022, from https://www.oboreurope.com/en/chinas-bri-asean-indonesia/

Granovetter, M. S. (1973). The strength of weak ties. *American Journal of Sociology, 78*(6), 1360–1380.

Granovetter, M. S. (1983). The strength of a weak ties: A network theory revisited. *Sociological Theory, 1*, 201–233.

Grossman, D. (2020, July 22). *China refuses to quit on the Philippines*. Retrieved on January 2022, from https://thediplomat.com/2020/07/china-refuses-to-quit-on-the-philippines/

Heydarian, R. J. (2018, April 6). Are China and the Philippines agreeing to share the South China Sea? *The National Interest*. Retrieved on January 2022, from http://nationalinterest.org/blog/the-buzz/are-china-the-philippines-agreeing-share-thesouth-china-sea-25229?page=show

Hong, M., Sun, S., Beg, R., & Zhou, Z. (2019). Malaysia's exports to China: Does diplomatic relationship matter? *The Economic Society of Australia*, 1–17. https://doi.org/10.1111/1759-3441.12270

HUMAS. (2014, November 14). *Pidato Presiden RI Joko Widodo Pada KTT ke-9 Asia Timur, di Nay Pyi Taw, Myanmar*. Retrieved on January 2022, from http://setkab.go.id/pidato-presiden-ri-joko-widodo-pada-ktt-ke-9-asia-timur-di-nay-pyi-taw-myanmar-13-november-2014/

HUMAS. (2015, March 26). *Disaksikan Presiden Jokowi dan Presiden Xi Jinping, RI—RRT Tandatangani 8 Kerjasama*. Retrieved on January 2022, from http://setkab.go.id/presiden-rrt-xi-jinping-sambut-presiden-jokowi-dengan-upacara-kenegaraan/

Jacob, J. T. (2015, March 13). Pothole potential on China's Silk Road. *Asia Times Online*.

Jennings, R. (2021, May 28). *Relations between China, Philippines seen smoothing after upbeat talks*. Retrieved on January 2022, from https://www.voanews.com/a/east-asia-pacific_relations-between-china-philippines-seen-smoothing-after-upbeat-talks/6206314.html

Kurlantzick, J. (2021, June 2). *Duterte's ingratiating approach to China has been a bust*. Retrieved on January 2022, from https://www.worldpoliticsreview.com/articles/29697/duterte-s-approach-to-china-philippines-relations-has-been-a-bust

Lai, H. (2019, October 4). *Indonesia: The Belt and Road Initiative and relations with China*. Retrieved on January 2022, from https://theasiadialogue.com/2019/10/04/belt-and-road-initiative-in-indonesia-and-relations-with-china/

Lalisang, A. E. Y., & Candra, D. S. (2020). *Indonesia's global maritime fulcrum & China's Belt Road Initiative a match made at sea?* Friedrich Ebert Stiftung.

Lam, A. (2020, October 15). *Domestic politics in Southeast Asia ad local backlash against the BRI*. Retrieved on January 2022, from https://www.fpri.org/article/2020/10/domestic-politics-in-southeast-asia-and-local-backlash-against-the-belt-and-road-initiative/

Lee, J. (2013). *China's economic engagement with Southeast Asia: Indonesia*. IISEAS.

Muhamad Azwan, A. R. (2018). *Laluan Sutera Baharu Maritim China*. UKM Press.

Mohammad Zaki, A., & Mohd Azizuddin, M. S. (2017). China's assertive posture in reinforcing its territorial and sovereignty claims in the South China Sea: An insight into Malaysia's stance. *Japanese Journal of Political Science, 18*(1), 67–105.

Nainggolan, P. P. (2015). Kebijakan Poros Maritim Dunia Joko Widodo dan implikasi internasionalnya. *Politica, 6*(2), 167–190.

Ngeow, C-B. (2018). A "model" for ASEAN countries? Sino-Malaysian relations during the Xi Jinping era. In A. Cheng-Hin Lim & F. Cibulka (Eds.), *China and Southeast Asia in the Xi Jinping era* (pp. 103–122). Lexington Books.

Pempel, T. J. (2007). Japanese strategy under Koizumi. In G. Rozman, K. Togo, & J. P. Freguson (Eds.), *Japanese strategic thought toward Asia* (pp. 109–136). Palgrave Macmillan.

Pitsuwan, S. (2017). *Good governance: Challenges for the ASEAN community*. Universiti Kebangsaan Malaysia.

Ramadhani, M.-A. (2015). An Indonesian perspective toward maritime version: Is pursuing national interest while maintaining neutrality in the South China Sea possible? *European Scientific Journal, 11*(10), 381–400. https://eujournal.org/index.php/esj/article/view/6546

RMAF. (2021). *Royal Malaysian air force press statement: 10/2021*. RMAF Public Relations Department.

Rubiolo, M. F. (2020). The South China Sea dispute: A reflection of Southeast Asia's economic and strategic dilemmas (2009–2018). *Revista de Relaciones Internacionales, Estrategia y Seguridad, 15*(2). https://doi.org/10.18359/ries.4336

Rudolf, M. (2021). China's health diplomacy during Covid-19: The Belt and Road Initiative (BRI) in action. *Stiftung Wissenschaft Und Politik* January (9). https://doi.org/10.18449/2021C09

Seah, S., Ha, H. T., Martinus, M., & Thao, P. T. P. (2021). *The state of Southeast Asia: 2021 survey report*. ISEAS-Yusof Ishak Institute.

Sohn, Y. (2010). Japan's new regionalism: China shock, values, and the East Asian community. *Asian Surveys, 50*(3), 497–519.

Sumathy, P. (2020, April 20). *Maritime flashpoints and the COVID-19 pandemic*. Retrieved on January 2022, from https://thediplomat.com/2020/04/maritime-flashpoints-and-the-COVID-19-pandemic/

Suryadinata, L. (2017). What does Indonesia's renaming of part of the South China Sea signify? *ISEAS Perspective, 64*, 1–6.

Tarrence, T. (2021, June 1). *Wisma Putra to summon Chinese envoy, issue diplomatic note of protest over airspace intrusion*. Retrieved on January 2022, from https://www.thestar.com.my/news/nation/2021/06/01/wisma-putra-to-summon-chinese-envoy-issue-diplomatic-note-of-protest-over-airspace-intrusion

The ASEAN Secretariat. (2021). *ASEAN Investment Report (AIR): Investing in industry 4.0*. ASEAN Secretariat.

Tritto, A. (2020, May 6). *Contentious embeddedness: Chinese state capital and the belt and road initiative in Indonesia.* https://madeinchinajournal.com/2020/05/06/contentious-embeddedness-chinese-state-capital-indonesia/

Unit Perancang Ekonomi. (2017). *Eksport Mengikut Negara Destinasi.* http://www.epu.gov.my/ms/statistik-ekonomi/dagangan-luar

USDJ. (2020, September 1). *China initiative.* Retrieved on January 2022, from https://www.justice.gov/usao-edtx/china-initiative

Venzon, C. (2021, April 5). *Philippines and China intensify war of words over South China Sea.* Retrieved on January 2022, from https://asia.nikkei.com/Politics/International-relations/South-China-Sea/Philippines-and-China-intensify-war-of-words-over-South-China-Sea

Vltchek, A. (2020). *China's Belt and Road Initiative: Connecting countries, saving millions of lives.* PT Badak Merah Semesta.

World bank. (n.d.). *China gross domestic product (Current US$).* Retrieved on January 2022, from https://data.worldbank.org/indicator/NY.GDP.MKTP.CD?end=2019&locations=CN&start=1961&view=chart

Xu Liping. (2021, January 19). *China-Philippines ties can overcome US factor.* https://www.globaltimes.cn/page/202101/1213281.shtml

Yang, Mu, & Heng-Siam Heng. (2011). China-ASEAN relations after AFTA. In Mingjiang Li & Chong Guan Kwa (Eds.), *China-ASEAN sub-regional cooperation: Progress, problems & prospect* (pp. 125–142). World Scientific Publishing Co. Pte. Ltd.

Yeoh, E. K. (2018). Malaysia: Perception of contemporary China and it is economical, political, and societal determinants. *The Pacific Review.* https://doi.org/10.1080/09512748.2018.1480522

Zhao, H. (2015). *China's New Maritime Silk Road: Implications and opportunities for Southeast Asia.* ISEAS.

Chapter 36
The Belt and Road Initiative and the Uneven Triangle of Latvia, Belarus, and China

Māris Andžāns and Una Aleksandra Bērziņa-Čerenkova

1 Introduction

The uneven triangle of the People's Republic of China (hereafter—China), Belarus, and Latvia in the context of the Belt and Road Initiative provides a peculiar case for analysis. In the past few years Belarus fostered close political and economic ties with China. It became a notable hallmark of the Belt and Road Initiative in Europe. While the youngest son of the Belarusian leader in Mandarin greeted the "respected Uncle Xi Jinping" in the Chinese spring festival (CCTV Video News Agency, 2018), freight trains from China crossed Belarus and the Great Stone Industrial Park was developed near the capital Minsk. Belarusian own cargo and Belarus' quest to become China's manufacturing and logistical hub in the region captivated Latvia, Belarus' northern neighbour. Thus, Belarus became an integral part of Latvia's economic perspective towards China. But the two European neighbours could not be more different. Both were in similar positions in 1991, the year the Soviet Union ceased to exist. Since then they have gone along entirely different paths. Latvia, now a vibrant democracy, became a member of the North Atlantic Treaty Organization (NATO), the European Union (EU), and the Organisation for Economic Co-operation and Development. Belarus, led by "the last dictator of Europe" A. Lukashenko, as he was known even before the 2020 post-electoral violence, chose a complex but close engagement with Russia. That included membership in the Commonwealth of Independent States, the Eurasian Economic Union (EAEU), and the Collective Security Treaty Organization (CSTO). The EAEU and CSTO can be regarded as essentially antitheses of the EU and NATO respectively. Notwithstanding the contrasting Latvian and Belarusian foreign policy vectors and their domestic foundations, Latvia tended to see its immediate neighbour, like China, in predominantly economic terms. That was about to change in the end of 2010s and the beginning of 2020s.

M. Andžāns · U. A. Bērziņa-Čerenkova (✉)
Riga Stradins University, Riga, Latvia

2 Literature Review

Analysis of Latvia–China surged after the 16+1, also known as Cooperation between China and Central and Eastern European Countries, the summit was held in Riga in November 2016. Prior to that event, China has not been visible and active in Latvia, nor was it the focus of academics, save for sinologists and Mandarin linguists and some other researchers of social science disciplines (e.g., a study on prospects of Latvian entrepreneurs in the Chinese market (Bulis et al., 2016). Latvian and Chinese relations since then have been approached in the context of 16+1 format (known also as 17+1 since 2019) and/or the Belt and Road Initiative. Such publications include pieces both in China and Europe, e.g., Huang and Liu (2017, 2018), Seaman et al. (2017), Brocková et al. (2020), Esteban and Otero-Iglesias (2020), and Karásková et al. (2020). One of the main reasons is that Latvia was not among the most active members of the format prior to the Riga 16+1 summit and after the drive of the summit winded down.

Latvian-centric publications multiplied following the 16+1 summit held in Latvia. One of the comprehensive opening publications in Latvia was a follow-up collection of assessments from the think tank forum that accompanied the Riga 16+1 summit (Andžāns, 2016). Other following publications include an analysis of Latvia's cautious and pragmatic approach to the Belt and Road Initiative and 16+1 (Andžāns & Bērziņa-Čerenkova, 2017a), on Latvia's dilemmas with China between interests and values (Andžāns & Bērziņa-Čerenkova, 2017b; Bērziņa-Čerenkova & Andžāns, 2018), the lack of Chinese investment in Latvia (Andžāns & Bērziņa-Čerenkova, 2017c; Bērziņa-Čerenkova, 2018), the perception of China in Latvia (Bērziņa-Čerenkova, 2021a; Struberga, 2020), as well as Latvia's geopolitical dilemmas and China's place among them (Bērziņa-Čerenkova, 2021b, 2021c, 2021d). As it can be judged from the list of publications, also the Latvian research community on China is rather thin, which is even more so from the Chinese angle.

Belarus as an immediate neighbour of Latvia often hit the headlines. It also has received considerable attention from scholars. Much of the attention to the country was given as a part of the EU's Eastern Partnership initiative, e.g., Bruģe (2018, 2020, 2021), Kuzņecova et al. (2013), Potjomkina (2017), Potjomkina (2015, 2016), and Sprūds et al. (2016). Given that Belarus was among the least active participants of the initiative and in 2021 it announced its departure from it, the country has not been the central point in such studies. Research has been devoted also to the bilateral relations of Latvia and Belarus, e.g., on economic and other cooperation aspects both before and after the 2020 crisis, e.g., Livdanska (2021), Potjomkina (2013), Sprūds (2012), Šteinbuka and Avetisjana (2021), and Vizgunova (2020). A separate study on Belarusian foreign policy from the viewpoint of Latvia was produced in 2017 (Kudors, 2017). Recently, a study devoted to the Baltic and Nordic countries' responses to the Belarusian 2020 post-electoral violence was commissioned (Sprūds et al., 2021). Finally, publications looking at both China and Belarus from the Latvian perspective have been few. These include some studies on economic aspects and transport of goods between Asia and Europe, noting there also the possible role of Latvia, e.g., Andžāns (2017) and Gubins (2017).

3 Methodology

To take on the research question—how Latvia's perception of the Belt and Road Initiative has evolved in the context of Latvian relations with China and Belarus—the next chapters build on the preceding literature review, having already elaborated on the main issues and tendencies in Latvia's relations with China and Belarus. The following chapters trace the evolution of Latvia's perception and engagement with China and Belarus. The first of the following chapters revisits tendencies of Latvia's engagement with both China and Belarus. The second chapter reviews, compares, and visualizes Latvia's economic interaction in terms of statistical data. The remaining chapter reviews the cooperation with both countries in the logistics sector and thus more directly touches upon the Belt and Road Initiative. The timeframe of analysis is 2013 through 2021. In 2013, the Belt and Road Initiative, initially called the One Belt One Road Initiative, was announced by the Chinese president Xi Jinping. It took time for the initiative to gain recognition and impact. Therefore, the year 2013 and the first two to three following years serve not only as the time of inception of that initiative but also as a benchmark of the engagement before and after the initiative was launched.

4 Latvia's Perception and Engagement with China and Belarus in Retrospective

Perception of China in Latvia has gone through ups and downs. In 2013, its image was relatively obscure. For example, the 2013–2014 annual report by the Latvian minister of foreign affairs paid attention to China in primarily economic terms. The essence of a 2013 minister's meeting with the Chinese premier was summarized as "… to discuss, among other things, transit opportunities and trade volumes, as well as [the minister] submitted projects for potential China investments …" The 16+1 format was mentioned in the report. However, it paid no attention to the One Belt One Road Initiative, as it was then called (Ministry of Foreign Affairs of Latvia, 2014, pp. 23, 24). Cooperation became more active after 2014 as several developments followed. First of all, China expedited import permits for Latvian produce (it became the first Baltic state to gain a dairy export permit to China, and a speedy accreditation process for individual companies followed). Secondly, during the 2015 Suzhou 16+1 summit, Latvia obtained the rights to hold the fifth 16+1 summit and the first transport minister's meeting of the same format. Third of all, also during the Suzhou 16+1 summit, the establishment of China-CEEC Secretariat on Logistic cooperation in

Riga was backed. Consequently, the interaction with China peaked in 2016 with the landmark 16+1 summit, encompassing various other events and hosting the Chinese premier Li Keqiang. (Regardless of the fact that Belarus was not a party to the 16+1 format, it was invited as an observer to the gathering.) During the summit, the Latvian Prime Minister M. Kučinskis, in a speech largely sympathetic to China, among other things noted that "... the 16+1 is a productive format that facilitates growth of our countries," as well as Latvia's "determination to realize the Silk road initiative together with China" (Kučinskis, 2016).

Sino-Latvian engagement continued actively in 2017 and extending also in 2018. Frequent visits in both directions took place, accompanied by the signing of cooperation memorandums across different fields. Also the exchange of entrepreneurs, academics, and artists, many of them taking part in 16+1 or Belt and Road themed events, were rife. As summarized in the annual report by the foreign minister, "[i]nterest in China remains consistently high: trade promotion, development of cooperation in transport and logistics, and in tourism are priorities for economic cooperation ..." (Ministry of Foreign Affairs of Latvia, 2018, p. 22). However, starting from 2018 and more so in 2019, the perception of China gradually transformed from rather positive and open to more cautious and even negative. In contrast to previous years, the annual 2019 foreign minister's report addressed China not only comprehensively but also in a soberer tone than before. It also expressed caution regarding the Belt and Road Initiative, calling for "[a] comprehensive analysis ... and a ... strategy formulated at the European Union level concerning this major project and the influence of its implementation in all dimensions" (Ministry of Foreign Affairs of Latvia, 2019, p. 3). The next edition of the foreign minister report did not address the initiative at all and was more critical on China. It also quite precisely formulated the state of the Latvian-Sino relations: "[o]n the whole, the relations can be characterised as pragmatic, seeking possibilities for cooperation where it is mutually beneficial" (Ministry of Foreign Affairs of Latvia, 2020, p. 16).

The aforementioned turn in part was related to the unmet initial high expectations from the benefits in cooperation with China. These were mostly seen in terms of lower trade barriers for export of goods, investment from China and a new impetus to the Latvian transit sector. But it resulted in modest deliverables. This factor triggered a China-fatigue both among entrepreneurs and policymakers alike. Another factor was the gradual fortification of China and its increasingly assertive approach abroad, along with its human rights record domestically. This set of factors led policy makers to rethink the Latvian approach to China, further reinforced by a more assertive China policy adopted by the US, Latvia's strategic partner.

Latvia's relations with Belarus have also gone through ups and downs. Compared to China, though, the turning points have been stark and thus easier to identify unambiguously. Since 2004, the year Latvia joined the EU, the Union imposed and henceforth gradually reinforced sanctions against Belarus over violations of human rights and other issues. Against that background, the economic interests were put in forefront in Latvian-Belarussian bilateral engagement.

In February 2016, the bulk of the EU's sanctions were lifted "... while acknowledging the steps taken by Belarus that have contributed to improving EU-Belarus relations" (Council of the European Union, 2021). The lifting of most of the sanctions gradually expanded also the political dialogue with Latvia, with a symbolic thaw in 2019. In July of that year, the Belarussian leader A. Lukashenko hosted Latvia's minister of foreign affairs E. Rinkēvičs. In Minsk the minister "… expressed pleasure over the active political dialogue between Latvia and Belarus …," and, among other things, noted that "Latvia sees potential in cooperation with Belarus in development of the Eurasian transport corridors, and we offer Latvian transit infrastructure for the industrial park "Great Stone" cargo servicing" (Rinkēvičs, 2019). In January of the following year, the Latvian prime minster K. Kariņš also paid a visit to the Belarusian leader. The premier underlined that "Latvia and Belarus are bound by good and friendly neighbour relations" (Kariņš, 2020). As a part of the visit, he paid a visit to the Great Stone industrial park.

Things changed quickly in the follow-up of the Belarussian presidential election in August 2020. In the West, the election was widely seen as rigged in favour of A. Lukashenko. Latvia was among the countries to refuse to recognize the election results and Lukashenko as the president. A. Lukashenko along with other Belarusian officials was declared persona non grata. The national parliament issued a statement where it, inter alia, "… strongly condemns actions by the Belarusian authorities against the peaceful protesters …" and "… does not recognize Alexander Lukashenko as legitimate president of Belarus" (Saeima, 2020). In October, the EU imposed sanctions on Belarus over "… the fraudulent nature of the … elections …, and the intimidation and violent repression of peaceful protesters, opposition members and journalists" (Council of the European Union, 2021). In stark contrast, the Chinese leader "… Xi extended warm congratulations and best wishes to President Lukashenko on his re-election on behalf of the Chinese government and people as well as in Xi's own name" (Xi, 2020). It sent a clear signal as to where China stands in relation to Belarus, as well as in a wider context of values and principles.

In 2021, Minsk and Riga were supposed to jointly host the World Ice Hockey Championship. Due to the situation in Belarus, Riga became the only host of the event. As a response to another incident caused by Belarus—forced landing of a civilian aircraft travelling from Greece to Lithuania—among the flags of the ice hockey championship participant-nations in the centre of Riga, the mayor of the capital M. Staķis replaced the official Belarusian flag with the one used by the Belarusian opposition. "One thing, of course, is sanctions … but such symbolic steps sometimes say more than 101 condemnation or 101 statement," said the Latvian minister of foreign affairs who was present (Rinkēvičs, 2021). Following this, Belarus expelled almost all Latvian diplomats, including the ambassador, and Latvia reciprocated. Thus, the bilateral diplomatic relations were essentially suspended. Furthermore, in June 2021 the EU imposed further sanctions on Belarus over the forced landing of a civilian aircraft, this time banning Belarusian air carriers from the EU airspace and airports.

Further deterioration of the Latvian-Belarusian relations followed in summer 2021. Belarusian authorities begun deliberately sending migrants from the Middle East and other regions over the Lithuanian and later also over the Latvian border. Such Belarussian actions were condemned jointly by the Estonian, Latvian, Lithuanian, and Polish presidents as "hybrid attack" of the "Lukashenko's regime" (Kaljulaid et al., 2021, p. 1). In response to the influx of migrants, a state of emergency was declared on the Latvian side of the border, and fence-building was commenced.

5 Latvia's Engagement with China and Belarus in Trade and Investment

Statistics on trade of goods, as exemplified in detail in the Graph 1, allow us to provide several observations. First, neither Belarus, nor China has been a top trade partner of Latvia. In 2013 China with 1.8% of total Latvia's trade of goods was the 13th biggest partner, while Belarus was 12th with 2.2% of total trade of goods; in 2020 China was the 11th biggest partner with 2.8% of total trade and Belarus the 14th with 1.7% of total trade. Second, Latvia's balance in trade of goods with both countries was negative throughout the entire review period, i.e., Latvia exported less than it imported from both. The imbalance was more pronounced with China. Third, the trade of goods with China gradually expanded from 2013 to 2020, mainly because of the import from China, though trade in the opposite direction expanded as well. However, the Latvian-Belarusian trade of goods fluctuated around similar levels in the review period (in 2020 its total monetary value was slightly below the 2013 level). Fourth, while in 2013 and 2014 Latvia's trade of goods with Belarus was larger than that with China, from 2015 on, the trade with China superseded that with Belarus (National Statistical System of Latvia, 2021).

Another statistical indicator—foreign direct investment—provides a similar though slightly different picture. First, the mutual investment levels with both China and Belarus are rather modest. No closing value year by year produced one hundred million euros in either direction. Furthermore, the current Latvian official

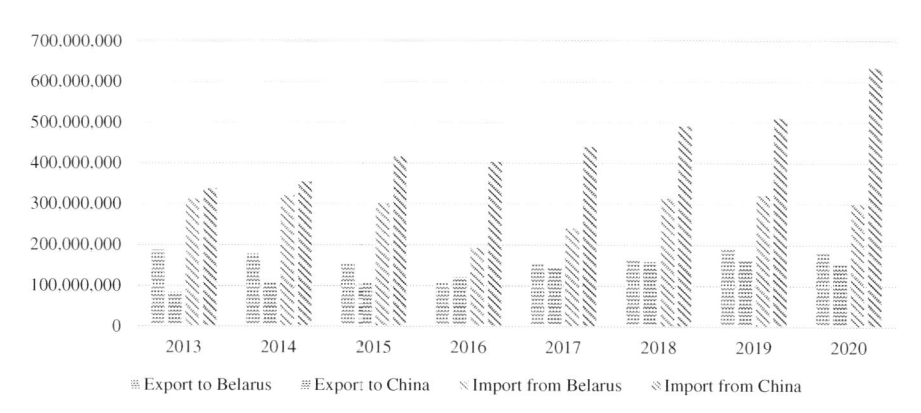

Graph 1 Latvia's trade of goods with China and Belarus, 2013–2020, EUR (*Source* National Statistical System of Latvia [2021])

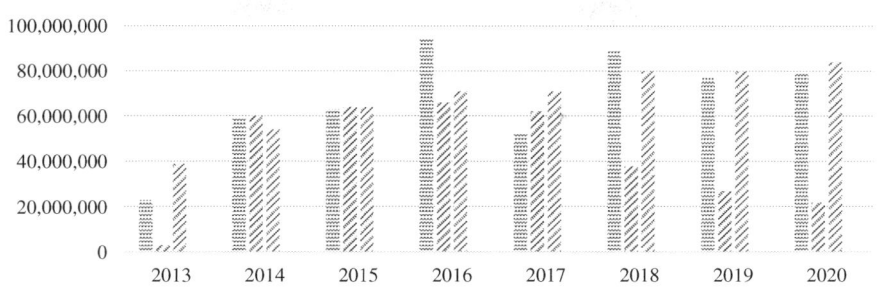

Graph 2 Latvia's foreign direct investment with China and Belarus, 2013–2020, EUR (*Source* Bank of Latvia [2021a, 2021b])

statistics provide no records of direct investment to China in 2013 through 2020. Second, Latvia's investment engagement with Belarus was more balanced and stable compared with that of China. Investment from China increased from 2013 to 2016 before taking a downward turn. Third, investment to Belarus was a somewhat notable part of the entire Latvian foreign direct investment—it constituted 3.4% of total in 2013 and 4.1% in 2020. But both Belarusian and Chinese investments in Latvia were negligible—they did not near even one per cent of total foreign direct investment in Latvia (Bank of Latvia, 2021a, 2021b) (Graph 2).

The data is significant, as one of the arguments in favour of Latvia contemplating joining the Belarus' Belt and Road branch was the perception of Belarus as a historically familiar trade partner—hence, Latvia would know how to do business with it, in contrast to China. The data show that the expectations that Belarus' active engagement with China in trade would have a spillover effect for Latvia have not materialized, perhaps leading to conclude that the hopes had been overly optimistic to begin with.

6 Latvia's Engagement with China and Belarus in Logistics

Latvia was motivated to develop new logistics, or cargo transit, routes by the fact that the transit over its railroads and ports was one of the very few sectors still dominated by (cargo from) Russia. Latvian-Russian relations have traditionally been jittery (Andžāns & Bērziņa-Čerenkova, 2021), and Russia has tended to direct its own cargo to its own ports. And indeed, in the recent years the amount of rail and port cargo transit volume plummeted, especially so in 2020 (Ministry of Transport of Latvia, 2021, pp. 2, 15). In this respect, the landlocked Belarus has traditionally been the second most significant partner for Latvia, though with a notable distance in terms of cargo volume. E.g., in 2020, Russian cargo constituted 61.2% and Belarusian 27.0% of the external cargo moved by the main rail carrier of Latvia (Valsts akciju sabiedrība

"Latvijas dzelzceļš", 2021, p. 6). With China and its Belt and Road Initiative, there was a prospect of cargo running between China and Europe via Latvian railroads and ports. The centrality of Belarus for China had been highlighted time and again by Chinese officials and state media publications alike, e.g.: "Belarus, located in the Eastern European Plain, is the geographic center of Europe. It is adjacent to Russia, Ukraine, Poland, Lithuania, and Latvia. It is the gateway for China's "Belt and Road" initiative to enter Europe from Central Asia" (China.org.cn, 2019). Prior to the Latvia-Belarus-China idea in the Belt and Road context, it was hard to justify the practical role of Latvia in the Chinese Eurasian connectivity and infrastructure outlooks due to being too far North-East from the major envisaged routes. (There was some Chinese interest in the Rail Baltica railroad megaproject that is mostly funded by the EU, though it has not materialized.) The BRI projections and visualizations usually did not include Latvia. Under these circumstances, the Belarus link sounded like a rare, if not the only viable solution—hence the opportunity.

In 2015 Suzhou 16+1 summit Latvia received the green light to establish the CEEC-China Secretariat on Logistic Cooperation. The China–Belarus–Latvia link was emphasized both in 16+1 format, as well as in the Latvian-Belarusian engagement. E.g., the declaration of the first 16+1 transport ministers meeting in Riga, a side event of the 16+1 summit, underlined the "… the significance of development of supply chains and strengthening of transport links between such major investment projects … as the China-Belarus industrial park "Great Stone" in Belarus … with logistics centers, maritime and inland ports and airports in CEEC" (Riga Declaration, 2016). In practical terms, a few so-called test container trains have been launched between China and Latvia. Most famously, a test train from China arrived in Latvia in 2016 during the 16+1 summit. Latvia's transport minister enthusiastically greeted the train and expressed hope "… that in the near future the arrival of such a train to Riga will not be a celebration, but an everyday event!" (Augulis, 2016). However, no permanent container train traffic crossing Latvia has been established neither from Belarus, nor via other routes.

Following the attempts to utilize the CEEC-China Secretariat on Logistic Cooperation, especially following the 2016 Riga 16+1 summit, its activities and relevance winded down since around 2019, as exemplified by the most recent events covered on its website (CEEC-CHINA Secretariat on Logistic Cooperation, n.d.). This rather coincides also with the disillusionment of the Latvian logistics sector with China: the participation in various events in China, the work surrounding cooperation agreements, etc., demanded much input, but led to limited output. Nevertheless, such names as Chengdu, Yiwu, Urumqi, and Xian are still marked on Latvian prospective transit maps (Freeport of Riga, 2021, p. 5; Secretariat of Latvian Ports, Transit and Logistics Council, 2021).

7 Conclusion

The early enthusiastic Latvian economic-centric approach towards China until around 2018–2019 transformed in disillusionment and fatigue—both towards China and its cooperation formats, the 17+1 and the Belt and Road Initiative. Meanwhile, the 2020 post-electoral crisis in Belarus resulted in a critical deterioration of the Latvian–Belarussian relations that culminated in the mutual expulsion of almost the entire diplomatic corps and migrant crisis on the Latvian-Belarusian border. The worsening of the relations significantly downgraded not only the Latvian-Belarussian links but also the prospects of the Belt and Road Initiative leg via Latvia. Also, the Chinese approach of the supposed abstinence from domestic affairs of other countries played a role. In the case of Belarus, the unambiguous support to the authoritarian Belarusian leader A. Lukashenko estranged it from Latvia further. Thus, ironically, the China-Belarus link, which was perceived as a solution and the missing piece of the puzzle to boost practical Sino-Latvian Belt and Road cooperation, turned out to be yet another factor contributing to the loss of the momentum of the Belt and Road Initiative in Latvia. One can thus conclude that not one particular factor, but rather a set of mutually enforcing factors contributed to the change in the initial Latvian optimistic outlook on the Belt and Road prospects. All in all, the uneven triangle of Latvia-Belarus-China has proven to be an unstable construct precisely because of the overwhelming number of differences between the partners opposed to only one commonality—the interest in economic engagement. To zoom out, the case of Latvian engagement with China and its Belt and Road Initiative serves as an illustration of the swings between pragmatism and values that small democracies experience in their foreign policy, and the importance of the outside factors and actors, including the US, in tipping the scale.

Finally, the current trends in Latvia's bilateral and multilateral approach—as a part of the EU and in concert with the US, Latvia's strategic partner—does not leave much space for optimism with the Belt and Road Initiative. Unless the political regime in Belarus will change, its confrontation with Latvia and the West will probably endure. There are also no practical or even rhetorical signs that China and Latvia might engage in the Belt and Road Initiative otherwise, including no need for new infrastructure megaprojects in Latvia save for the EU-backed Rail Baltica. With that, also the prospects of a Belt and Road via the Chinese-Belarussian-Latvian triangle diminishes further still.

Bibliographic References

Andžāns, M. (2016). *Afterthoughts: Riga 2016 International Forum of China and Central and Eastern European countries.* Latvian Institute of International Affairs.

Andžāns, M. (2017). A bridge between the East and the West? The case of the Latvian Cargo Transit Sector. In A. Sprūds & D. Potjomkina, *Riga dialogue afterthoughts 2017: Transforming Euro-Atlantic security landscapes* (pp. 116–127). Latvian Institute of International Affairs.

Andžāns, M., & Bērziņa-Čerenkova, U. A. (2017a). Perception of the 16+1 and the Belt and Road Initiative: A perspective from Latvia. In P. Huang & Z. Liu (Eds.), *How the 16+1 Cooperation promotes the Belt and Road Initiative* (pp. 124–131). China Social Sciences Press.

Andžāns, M., & Bērziņa-Čerenkova, U. A. (2017b). "16+1" and China in Latvian Foreign Policy: Between values and interests. In A. Sprūds, I. Bruģe, & K. Bukovskis, *Latvian foreign and security policy yearbook 2017* (pp. 163–171). Latvian Institute of International Affairs.

Andžāns, M., & Bērziņa-Čerenkova, U. A. (2017c). Assessing (the lack of) Chinese investment in Latvia. In J. Seaman, M. Huotari, & M. Otero-Iglesias, *Chinese investment in Europe: A country-level approach* (pp. 87–92). French Institute of International Relations, Elcano Royal Institute, and Mercator Institute for China Studies.

Andžāns, M., & Bērziņa-Čerenkova, U. A. (2021). The COVID-19 pandemic and Latvia–Russia relations: Landscape for desecuritization or further securitization? *Social Sciences, 10*(9), 323. https://doi.org/10.3390/socsci10090323

Augulis, U. (2016, November 7). *Latvijas Vēstnesis*. Retrieved on 15 July 2021, from Rīgā svinīgi sagaida pirmo testa vilcienu no Ķīnas pilsētas Yiwu: https://lvportals.lv/dienaskartiba/283108-riga-svinigi-sagaida-pirmo-testa-vilcienu-no-kinas-pilsetas-yiwu-2016

Bank of Latvia. (2021a). *Bank of Latvia*. Retrieved on 12 July 2021, from 01 DI data by country tables (closing position): https://statdb.bank.lv/lb/Data/128

Bank of Latvia. (2021b). *Bank of Latvia*. Retrieved on 12 July 2021, from 01 DI data by country tables (closing position): https://statdb.bank.lv/lb/Data/129

Bērziņa-Čerenkova, U. A. (2018). *Starting small—An emerging profile of Chinese SME investors in Latvia to challenge the preconceptions on Chinese FDI*. Central European University.

Bērziņa-Čerenkova, U. A. (2021a, April 7). *Foreign Policy Research Institute*. Go with the Devil You Don't Know? Retrieved on 15 July 2021, from Latvians Still Believe in Economic Cooperation with China: https://www.fpri.org/article/2021/04/go-with-the-devil-you-dont-know-latvians-still-believe-in-economic-cocperation-with-china/

Bērziņa-Čerenkova, U. A. (2021b, April 22). *RUSI Transatlantic Dialogue on China*. Retrieved on 15 July 2021, from A Baltic View on Transatlantic Tech Relations Towards China: https://www.transatlantic-dialogue-on-china.rusi.org/article/a-transatlantic-business-recent-developments-in-the-baltic-hi-tech-cooperation-with-china

Bērziņa-Čerenkova, U. A. (2021c). The Baltic CAI challenge: Reconciling transatlanticism with EU solidarity. *Asia Europe Journal, 19*(4), 511–515.

Bērziņa-Čerenkova, U. A. (2021d). The Baltic resilience to China's "Divide and Rule". *Lex Portus, 2*(7), 11.

Bērziņa-Čerenkova, U. A., & Andžāns, M. (2018). A pragmatic approach without making significant concessions to China. In T. N. Rühlig, B. Jerdén, F.-P. van der Putten, J. Seaman, M. Otero-Iglesias, & A. Ekman, *Political values in Europe-China relations* (pp. 55–59). European Think Tank Network on China (ETNC).

Brocková, K., Grešš, M., Karpenko, L., & Lipková, L. (2020). Qualitative changes in China's foreign trade in the era of "new normal". *Ekonomický časopis, 68*, 1126–1151.

Bruģe, I. (2018). The Eastern Partnership—Still a priority for Latvia. In A. Sprūds, & I. Bruģe, *The Latvian foreign and security policy yearbook 2018* (pp. 148–162). Latvian Institute of International Affairs.

Bruģe, I. (2020). The Eastern Partnership—10 years on. In A. Sprūds & S. Broka, *The Latvian foreign and security policy yearbook 2020* (pp. 154–162). Latvian Institute of International Affairs.

Bruģe, I. (2021). Latvia and the Eastern Partnership. In A. Sprūds & S. Broka, *The Latvian foreign and security policy yearbook 2021* (pp. 134–142). Latvian Institute of International Affairs.

Bulis, A., Škapars, R., & Šķiltere, D. (2016). *Latvijas ražošanas uzņēmumu konkurētspējas uzlabošana Ķīnas Tautas Republikas tirgū*. Latvijas Universitāte.

CCTV Video News Agency. (2018, February 15). *YouTube*. Retrieved on 15 July 2021, from Belarusian President's Son Nikolai Lukashenko plays piano, extending Spring Festival greeting: https://www.youtube.com/watch?v=yuQTL4qmIsA

CEEC-CHINA Secretariat on Logistic Cooperation. (n.d.). *CEEC-CHINA Secretariat on Logistic Cooperation*. Retrieved on 15 July 2021, from Events: http://www.ceec-china-logistics.org/en/events/

China.org.cn. (2019, March 29). *China.org.cn*. Retrieved on 15 July 2021, from 中国互联网新闻中心: http://www.china.com.cn/opinion/theory/2019-03/29/content_74625499.htm

Council of the European Union. (2021, June 18). *Council of the European Union*. Retrieved on 15 July 2021, from EU relations with Belarus. Sanctions following the August 2020 presidential elections: https://www.consilium.europa.eu/en/policies/eastern-partnership/belarus/

Esteban, M., & Otero-Iglesias, M. (2020). *Europe in the face of US-China Rivalry*. European Think-tank Network on China (ETNC).

Freeport of Riga. (2021). *Freeport of Riga*. Retrieved on 25 August 2021, from Freeport of Riga. Riga 2020: https://rop.lv/sites/default/files/2020-10/2020_ENG.pdf

Gubins, S. (2017). *Tranzīts: izaicinājumi un iespējas*. Certus.

Huang, P., & Liu, Z. (2017). *How the 16+1 Cooperation promotes the Belt and Road Initiative*. China Social Sciences Press.

Huang, P., & Liu, Z. (2018). *"16+1 Cooperation": Status quo, prospects and policy suggestions*. China Social Sciences Press.

Kaljulaid, K., Levits, E., Nausėda, G., & Duda, A. (2021, August 23). *President of Latvia*. Retrieved on 25 August 2021, from Igaunijas, Latvijas, Lietuvas un Polijas prezidentu kopīgais paziņojums par Baltkrieviju: https://www.president.lv/lv/media/91409/download

Karásková, I., Andrijauskas, K., Bachulska, A., Bērziņa-Čerenkova, U. A., Karindi, L., Leonte, A., Pejić, N., Szunomár, Á., Šebok, F., & Vladisavljev, S. (2020). *Empty shell no more: China's growing footprint in Central and Eastern Europe*. Association for International Affairs (AMO).

Kariņš, K. (2020, January 16). *Ministru kabinets*. Retrieved on 15 July 2021, from Kariņš uzsver nepieciešamību veicināt labās kaimiņattiecības ar Baltkrieviju: https://www.mk.gov.lv/lv/karins-uzsver-nepieciesamibu-veicinat-labas-kaiminattiecibas-ar-baltkrieviju

Kučinskis, M. (2016, November 5). *Ministru kabinets*. Retrieved on 15 July 2021, from Ministru prezidenta Māra Kučinska atklāšanas runa 5. Centrāleiropas un Austrumeiropas valstu un Ķīnas valdību vadītāju sanāksmē Rīgā: https://www.mk.gov.lv/lv/ministru-prezidenta-mara-kuc inska-atklasanas-runa-5-centraleiropas-un-austrumeiropas-valstu-un-kinas-valdibu-vaditaju-san aksme-riga

Kudors, A. (2017). *Belarusian Foreign Policy: 360°*. Centre for East European Policy Studies.

Kuzņecova, I., Vargulis, M., & Potjomkina, D. (2013). *From the Vilnius summit to the Riga summit: Challenges and opportunities of the Eastern Partnership*. Latvian Institute of International Affairs.

Livdanska, B. (2021). With caution towards change: Relations between Latvia and Belarus. In A. Sprūds & S. Broka, *The Latvian foreign and security policy yearbook 2021* (pp. 143–151). Latvian Institute of International Affairs.

Ministry of Foreign Affairs of Latvia. (2014). *Ministry of Foreign Affairs of Latvia*. Retrieved on 15 July 2021, from Annual Report by the Minister of Foreign Affairs on activities performed and planned in national foreign policy and European Union matters 2013–2014: https://www.mfa.gov.lv/en/media/2227/download

Ministry of Foreign Affairs of Latvia. (2018). *Ministry of Foreign Affairs*. Retrieved on 15 July 2021, from Annual Report of the Minister of Foreign Affairs on the accomplishments and further work with respect to national foreign policy and the European Union 2018: https://www.mfa.gov.lv/en/media/2223/download

Ministry of Foreign Affairs of Latvia. (2019). *Ministry of Foreign Affairs of Latvia*. Retrieved on 15 July 2021, from Annual Report of the Minister of Foreign Affairs on the accomplishments and further work with respect to national foreign policy and the European Union 2019: https://www.mfa.gov.lv/en/media/2222/download

Ministry of Foreign Affairs of Latvia. (2020). *Ministry of Foreign Affairs of Latvia*. Retrieved on 15 July 2021, from Annual Report of the Minister of Foreign Affairs on the accomplishments and further work with respect to national foreign policy and the European Union 2020: https://www.mfa.gov.lv/en/media/2221/download

Ministry of Transport of Latvia. (2021). *Ministry of Transport of Latvia*. Retrieved on 15 July 2021, from Statistika par kravu apgrozījumu Latvijas ostās un dzelzceļa pārvadājumos. Paplašinātā statistika par kravu apgrozījumu Latvijas ostās un dzelzceļā no 2011. gada janvāra līdz 2021. gada maijam: https://www.sam.gov.lv/lv/media/5260/download

National Statistical System of Latvia. (2021). *ATD020. Exports and imports by countries (CN at 2-digit level) by Flow of goods, Commodity CN at 2-digit level, Countries, Unit and Time period*. Retrieved on 12 July 2021, from National Statistical System of Latvia: https://data.stat.gov.lv/pxweb/en/OSP_PUB/START__TIR__AT__ATD/ATD020/

Potjomkina, D. (2013). Latvian-Belarusian relations in 2013: Multiple realities. In A. Sprūds, *The Latvian foreign and security policy yearbook 2013* (pp. 59–72). Latvian Institute of International Affairs.

Potjomkina, D. (2015). Latvia and the Eastern Partnership: Moving towards 2015 slowly but surely. In A. Sprūds & D. Potjomkina, *The Latvian foreign and security policy yearbook 2015* (pp. 121–133). Latvian Institute of International Affairs.

Potjomkina, D. (2016). Peace, trade, and European resources: Latvia and the Eastern Partners in 2015–2016. In A. Sprūds & I. Bruģe, *The Latvian foreign and security policy yearbook 2016* (pp. 43–58). Latvian Institute of International Affairs.

Potjomkina, D. (2017). *Eiropas Savienības Austrumu partnerības politika. Pētījuma publiskā daļa*. Latvian Institute of International Affairs.

Riga Declaration. (2016). *CEEC-CHINA Secretariat on Logistic Cooperation*. Retrieved on 15 July 2021, from The Declaration of the 1st Central and Eastern European Countries and China Transport Ministers' Meeting (CEEC-China TMM1). Riga Declaration. On Closer Cooperation in Logistics: http://www.ceec-china-logistics.org/databank/images/docs/9/70/Riga%20Declaration.pdf

Rinkēvičs, E. (2019, July 26). *E. Rinkēvičs tiekas ar Baltkrievijas prezidentu Aleksandru Lukašenko*. Retrieved on 15 July 2021, from Latvijas Vēstnesis: https://lvportals.lv/dienaskartiba/306512-e-rinkevics-tiekas-ar-baltkrievijas-prezidentu-aleksandru-lukasenko-2019

Rinkēvičs, E. (2021, May 24). *Lsm.lv*. Retrieved on 15 July 2021, from Hokeja čempionāta karogu rindā pie viesnīcas Baltkrievijas oficiālo karogu aizstāj ar vēsturisko: https://www.lsm.lv/raksts/sports/hokejs/hokeja-cempionata-karogu-rinda-pie-viesnicas-baltkrievijas-oficialo-karogu-aizstaj-ar-vesturisko.a405968/

Saeima. (2020, October 1). *Saeima*. Retrieved on 15 July 2021, from PAZIŅOJUMS: https://titania.saeima.lv/LIVS13/saeimalivs_lmp.nsf/0/837A4AAD0D65EC69C22585F40022B8E9?OpenDocument

Seaman, J., Huotari, M., & Otero-Iglesias, M. (2017). *Chinese Investment in Europe: A country-level approach*. European Think-tank Network on China (ETNC).

Secretariat of Latvian Ports, Transit and Logistics Council. (2021). *Secretariat of Latvian Ports, Transit and Logistics Council*. Retrieved on 15 July 2021, from CONTAINER TRAINS: https://transport.lv/en/dzelzcels/konteinervilcieni/

Sprūds, A. (2012). *The economic presence of Russia and Belarus in the Baltic States: Risks and opportunities*. Latvian Institute of International Affairs.

Sprūds, A., Andžāns, M., & Djatkoviča, E. (2021). *Baltic and Nordic responses to the 2020 post-election crisis in Belarus*. Latvian Institute of International Affairs.

Sprūds, A., Bruģe, I., & Austers, A. (2016). *Dilemmas of Europeanisation: Political choices and economic transformations in the Eastern Partnership countries*. Latvian Institute of International Affairs.

Struberga, S. (2020, May 13). *China Observers in Central and Eastern Europe (CHOICE)*. Retrieved on 15 July 2021, from The Unknown Other? Perceptions of China in Latvia: https://chinaobservers.eu/the-unknown-other-perceptions-of-china-in-latvia/

Šteinbuka, I., & Avetisjana, S. (2021). The effectiveness of the EU sanctions: The cases of Russia and Belarus. In A. Sprūds & S. Broka, *The Latvian foreign and security policy yearbook 2021* (pp. 110–121). Latvian Institute of International Affairs.

Valsts akciju sabiedrība "Latvijas dzelzceļš". (2021). *Valsts akciju sabiedrība "Latvijas dzelzceļš" Konsolidētais 2020. gada pārskats*. Retrieved on 10 August 2021, from Valsts akciju sabiedrība "Latvijas dzelzceļš": Retrieved on 15 July 2021, from https://www.ldz.lv/sites/default/files/LDZ_KONCERNS_2020.gada_parskats%20Final.pdf

Vizgunova, E. (2020). Latvian-Belarussian relations: Changes are inevitable. In A. Sprūds & S. Broka, *The Latvian foreign and security policy yearbook 2020* (pp. 163–177). Latvian Institute of International Affairs.

Xi, J. (2020, August 10). *Xinhua*. Retrieved on 15 July 2021, from Xi congratulates Lukashenko on re-election as Belarusian president: http://www.xinhuanet.com/english/2020-08/10/c_139279630.htm

Chapter 37
The Impact of Belt and Road Initiative on Asian Economies Along the Route

Badar Alam Iqbal, Mohd Nayyer Rahman, and Nida Rahman

1 Introduction

China's Belt and Road Initiative is one of the most awaited and grandiose projects of the present Chinese regime. It is projected to accentuate Chinese economic growth and development, and if the claim is taken into account, it will also benefit the Asian region in terms of growth, infrastructure development, and employment. OBOR project along with maritime silk road is known as Belt and Road Initiative (BRI). BRI is an important project for China and defines its economic aspirations and needs (Cai, 2016). BRI was named in 1877 by Richthofen Ferdinand Von. Historically, it was connected to Asia, Europe, and Africa (Wu, 2017). The old Silk Route on which BRI is based reached its peak in the period of Tang Dynasty and it ended in 1453 partly due to the operations of the Ottoman Empire (Mark, 2014). Initially, China granted permission to financial institutions for establishing the Asian Infrastructure and Investment Bank (AIIB) and the US$40 billion New Silk Road Fund as part of the BRI project (Chhibber, 2017). According to Leer and Yau (2016), the BRI programme unites 65 countries (with varied degrees of connectivity), spanning 4.4 billion people and encompassing 30% of the global economy, with a $5 trillion infrastructure need.

East Asia, Southeast Asia, Central Asia, Middle East and North Africa, South Asia, and Europe are the six key regions of the BRI project. China and Mongolia make up East Asia. Southeast Asia includes Vietnam, Timor-Leste, Thailand, Singapore, Philippines, Myanmar, Malaysia, Laos, Indonesia, Cambodia, and Brunei. The Central Asian region for the BRI consists of Uzbekistan, Turkmenistan, Tajikistan,

---

B. A. Iqbal
Faculty of Economics and Finance, Monarch Business School, Zug, Switzerland

M. N. Rahman (✉)
Department of Commerce, Aligarh Muslim University, Aligarh, India

N. Rahman
Indian Council for Research on International Economic Relations, New Delhi, India

© The Author(s), under exclusive license to Springer Nature Singapore Pte Ltd. 2023
P. A. B. Duarte et al. (eds.), *The Palgrave Handbook of Globalization with Chinese Characteristics*, https://doi.org/10.1007/978-981-19-6700-9_37

Kyrgyzstan, and Kazakhstan. Yemen, the United Arab Emirates, Syria, Palestine, Saudi Arabia, Qatar, Oman, Lebanon, Kuwait, Jordan, Israel, Iraq, Iran, Egypt, and Bahrain are among the Middle East and North African countries with the most natural resources. Sri Lanka, Pakistan, Nepal, Maldives, India, Bhutan, Bangladesh, and Afghanistan are all part of the South Asian region. Ukraine, Turkey, Slovenia, Slovakia, Serbia, Russia, Romania, Poland, Montenegro, Moldova, Macedonia, Lithuania, Latvia, Hungary, Georgia, Estonia, Czech Republic, Croatia, Bulgaria, Bosnia and Herzegovina, Belarus, Azerbaijan, Armenia, and Albania are among the nations connected by the BRI. There are six main BRI corridors: New Eurasia Land Bridge Economic Corridor (international railway line and bridges), China–Mongolia–Russia Economic Corridor (frontline trade and cross-border economic cooperation), China–Central Asia–West Asia Economic Corridor (railway networks and economic cooperation), China–Indochina Peninsula Economic Corridor (transportation network and sustainable socio-economic development), China–Pakistan Economic Corridor (trade and economic cooperation) and Bangladesh–China–India–Myanmar (connectivity and transportation infrastructure).

1.1 Belt and Road Initiative: China and Asia in Partnership

BRI project has been well accepted by the international community in praise. Analysts have labelled the project as one of the best to boost the growth of the Asian region and thus benefitting the global economy (Cai, 2016). The grandiose initiative aspires to restore Asia's economic grandeur in general, and China's in particular (Shull, 2017). The whole region can have a substantial impact on the global economy and can alter the dynamics of international trade and development. This can be gauged from the dynamics of the region covered in the BRI corridors (Table 1).

With BRI, China is aiming at the growth prospects of Asian region pushed by the industrial output of its own. One of the subtle aims is to achieve regional and global leadership in international trade and development and reforming the present international political economy dominated by the Western nations, particularly the United States of America (US). The growing operation and alliances of the US in the Asian region need a response from Asian countries and BRI will act as a game changer for the region (Blanchard, 2017). BRI will connect the markets of Central Asia, South Asia, Southeast Asia and would open up opportunities of trade and development for countries in the Asian and Eurasian region (Chung, 2017). China is building roads, railway networks, bridges in countries along the BRI initiative. China and Turkey are building a 7000 kms railway route to link all the main cities of Turkey to be completed till 2023 (Sen, 2016).

The East Asian region is prospering to become a market economy and thus will add to the growth of the region. China has invested and collaborated with Central Asian countries to develop multilateral partnerships in energy, trade, and transportation.

Table 1 Dynamics of the region covered by BRI (2019)

Region	Cumulative GDP (US$ trillion)	Cumulative land area (sq. km.)	Cumulative population (billion)
South Asia	3.597	4,770,754	1.836
Europe & Central Asia	22.828	27,447,887	0.921
Southeast Asia[a]	2,555,307	4,340,499	639,892
East Asia and Pacific	23,917	245,024,289	2.341

[a]Complete data not available

Source World Bank Database

Notes South Asia (Sri Lanka, Afghanistan, Bhutan, India, Maldives, Nepal, Bangladesh, Pakistan), Central Asia (Uzbekistan, Kazakhstan, Tajikistan, Turkmenistan, Kyrgyzstan), Southeast Asia (Vietnam, Brunei, Indonesia, Laos, Malaysia, Philippines, Singapore, Timor-Leste, Thailand, Cambodia, Myanmar), and East Asia (Vietnam, Brunei, Indonesia, Laos, Malaysia, Philippines, Singapore (Mongolia, China)

The 1100-mile gas pipeline from Turkmenistan to China is a significant arrangement between China and Central Asia (Sen, 2016).

The BRI project will improve the infrastructure of the region while focusing on the development of the region. This plan could be a game changer for small countries like Laos and Cambodia as well (Nataraj & Shekhani, 2016). Table 2 shows the achievements of BRI from 2013 to 2019 just after the launch of the project. From the table it is clear that BRI aspires to usher a new wave of economic growth and development for the participating Asian economies. China will become the largest trading partner of Asian economies as a result of the project, Pakistan stands testimony to it (Irshad et al., 2015). China has invested in ports and other facilities in Maldives, Sri Lanka, Bangladesh, and Pakistan that, apart from civilian use, may also be used for strategic goals of China (Baqai, 2015). There are bilateral implications of BRI for India, as the Asian economies participating in BRI will move strategically away from India or will demand more in strategic terms (Chung, 2017). Asian Development Bank has estimated that around US$8 trillion is required for funding the infrastructure need of Asia and China's project can be a prominent source (Lee, 2017). China has also assured investment for the ASEAN's Master Plan for Connectivity for those projects that are compatible with the initiative (Jetin, 2018).

2 Review of Literature

In the existing literature, a number of studies have been written on the BRI theme, but not all relates to the Asian region. Selected and relevant studies are reviewed in

Table 2 BRI: Achievements in the Asian region

Year	Economy	Projects
2013	Maldives	China Maldives Friendship Bridge
2014	Kazakhstan	Kazakhstan (Lianyungang)-China logistics base launched
	China	C-line Natural gas pipeline completed
	Kyrgyzstan	Bishkek power station reconstructed
2015	Tajikistan	Vahdat-Yovonrailway launched
	Vietnam	Construction of Hai Duong thermal plant and Yongxin coal-fired power plant begun while Yon Hydropower Station was completed
	Laos	China-Laos railway construction began
	Thailand	Thailand-China railway line started getting constructed
2016	Sri Lanka	Hambantota Port extension
	Pakistan	Construction of Karot hydropower project was started; Gwadar port launched
	Bangladesh	Construction of Padma Bridge
	Uzbekistan	Kamchiq tunnel in Uzbekistan completed
	Indonesia	Bandung-Jakarta high-speed rail started
	Cambodia	Sihanouk Ville Special Economic Zone (SSEZ) jointly initiated by Chinese and Cambodian enterprises
	Indonesia	Jakarta-Bandung High Speed Rail
	Laos	Vientaine-Boten Railway
2017	Sri Lanka	Colombo International Financial City
	Thailand	Kunming-Singapore Railway
2019	Turkey	Edime-Kars High Speed Train

Source Authors compilation from multiple sources

this section. Chung (2017) made an attempt to understand the implications of the Maritime Silk Road (MSR) initiative on India, Bangladesh, Sri Lanka, Maldives, and Pakistan. It was concluded that for countries like Pakistan, Maldives, Sri Lanka, and Bangladesh, to mitigate the dominance of India in the region, they have to take sides with China or at least an association with China. With respect to the case of India collaborating with China on BRI, it has been concluded that the relationship between India and China has been competitive yet collaborative, and therefore in the future conditionally India can be part of BRI (Chhibber, 2017). Peyrouse and Raballand (2015) identified the opportunities that will open with the OBOR project for the Asian region. Jetin's (2018) study identified that China needs to have smaller projects under OBOR to benefit local economies, without any direct benefit of China. This will ensure development as well as confidence building among countries involved in Belt Initiative, particularly the smaller ones. To bolster the BRI policies, China needs to reform the framework and talent selection of the bureaucracy so as to have a balanced foreign policy. This may change the view of "no preferential diplomacy for weak country" (Xue, 2016). BRI is a strategic project with huge implications for not just Asian region but the Eurasian region as well (Shukla, 2015). The projects under BRI in Russia indicate a long-term approach towards growth and development for the country as well as region. Because of OBOR, trade between Russia and China will continue to grow (Kralovicova & Zatko, 2016). Gabuev (2016) identified that OBOR unites Russia and China and it will be linked to European Economic Union with the support of Russia. China–Pakistan Economic Corridor (CPEC) as part of BRI is working successfully in the China–Pakistan region. The partnership is economic as well as strategic (Irshad et al., 2015). Recent studies on BRI focus on diverse issues and different dimensions. China's BRI must be seen in the broader context of promoting "multilayered multilateralism," an approach making use of a new set of institutions (Yuan, 2019). In a study conducted on the sample of 98 countries along the Belt, it was found that R&D and internationalization are important constraints for the Chinese companies. But they should learn from foreign experience and as a result avoid excessive internationalization. Chinese companies should invest more in Research and Development to benefit from the BRI (Lu & Mei, 2019). Impact of BRI on the six economic corridors will benefit the infrastructure facilities in the region. Improvement in border administration will boost exports and imports in the region. Trade facilitation needs to be focused upon for better and seamless international trade along the route (Ramasamy & Yeung, 2019). BRI is a global strategy and this strategy is also having a positive impact on Sino-African relations (Chen, 2016). BRI is promising for China and African relations, but there is an area of caution with respect to cooperation among China and African countries (Ndzendze & Monyae, 2019). Recent studies on the impact of BRI on Asian economies suggest that the dummy of BRI for 25 countries shows a positive impact on several macroeconomic variables of Asian countries (Iqbal et al., 2019). On many levels, the One Belt One Road programme will create doors for collaboration between China and Eurasia (Rahman & Rahman, 2019).

3 Methodology and Data

The study identifies eight macroeconomic variables to identify the impact of BRI on Asian economies along the route. After the identification of the economic variables, they are related with the economic growth across the economies under the project. Table 3 shows the data description and sources. The study is based on 25 countries of the Asian region and the sample period is from 2009 to 2020. Panel regression technique is applied to identify the impact of BRI on Asian economies.

The econometric methodology is adopted for the panel regression analysis. The data used is secondary and each variable is discussed theoretically before developing hypothesis pertaining to it.

Table 3 Variables description

Type	Variable	Measure with definition	Notation	Data source
Dependent	GDP Growth Rate	GDP growth (annual %) Annual percentage growth rate of GDP at market prices based on constant local currency. Aggregates are based on constant 2010 U.S. dollars. GDP is the sum of gross value added by all resident producers in the economy plus any product taxes and minus any subsidies not included in the value of the products. It is calculated without making deductions for depreciation of fabricated assets or for depletion and degradation of natural resources	GDP	World Development Indicators
Independent	Exports (Bilateral Trade)	Reporter: Asian Economy Partner: China	EXP	UN Comtrade
Independent	Imports (Bilateral Trade)	Reporter: Asian Economy Partner: China	IMP	UN Comtrade
Independent	Financial Development	Domestic credit to private sector by banks (% of GDP) Domestic credit to private sector by banks refers to financial resources provided to the private sector by other depository corporations (deposit taking corporations except central banks), such as through loans, purchases of nonequity securities, and trade credits and other accounts receivable, that establish a claim for repayment. For some countries these claims include credit to public enterprises	FDP	World Development Indicators

(continued)

Table 3 (continued)

Type	Variable	Measure with definition	Notation	Data source
Independent	Political Stability	Political Stability and Absence of Violence/Terrorism Political Stability and Absence of Violence/Terrorism measures perceptions of the likelihood of political instability and/or politically-motivated violence, including terrorism. Estimate gives the country's score on the aggregate indicator, in units of a standard normal distribution, i.e., ranging from approximately −2.5 to 2.5	POL	World Governance Indicators
Independent	Corruption	Control of Corruption Control of Corruption captures perceptions of the extent to which public power is exercised for private gain, including both petty and grand forms of corruption, as well as "capture" of the state by elites and private interests. Estimate gives the country's score on the aggregate indicator, in units of a standard normal distribution, i.e., ranging from approximately −2.5 to 2.5	COR	World Governance Indicators

(continued)

Table 3 (continued)

Type	Variable	Measure with definition	Notation	Data source
Independent	Infrastructure	Fixed telephone subscriptions (per 100 people) Fixed telephone subscriptions refer to the sum of active number of analogue fixed telephone lines, voice-over-IP (VoIP) subscriptions, fixed wireless local loop (WLL) subscriptions, ISDN voice-channel equivalents and fixed public payphones	INR	World Development Indicators
Independent	Geographic Distance	Distance between China and the reporting country	DIS	World Map Distance Calculator
Dummy	Belt and Road Initiative	Different values assigned for both periods (0 = dormant BRI 2009 to 2014, 1 = active BRI 2015 to 2020)	BRI	Own dummy

Source Prepared by the researcher

3.1 Bilateral Trade

BRI is a project focusing on trade ties between China and other Asian economies. This means that its focus is on bilateral trade. Bilateral trade also affects economic growth or rather it promotes it. Several studies have identified the importance of exports and imports as explanatory variables for assessing economic growth and vice versa (Irshad et al., 2015; Rahman, 2016; Ugochukwu & Chinyere, 2013; Yao, 2006). Exports and Imports also help to improve Foreign Direct Investment and the spillover effects contribute to the economic growth (Iqbal et al., 2016, 2018; Rahman & Grewal, 2017).

H01: *The relationship between Economic Growth and Bilateral Exports is positive for Asian economies along the BRI.*

H02: *The relationship between Economic Growth and Bilateral Imports is positive for Asian economies along the BRI.*

3.2 Financial Development

The degree to which industries are linked to the financial market is referred to as financial development. As the degree of connectedness improves, so does the region's financial development. Financial development can theoretically have a favourable impact on economic growth (Estrada et al., 2010).

H03: *The relationship between Economic Growth and Financial Development is positive for Asian economies along the BRI.*

3.3 Political Stability

With respect to political stability, a theoretical foundation stating a direct relationship with economic growth has been reviewed. It has been identified that political stability is a better indicator than economic freedom to achieve economic growth (Younis et al., 2008).

H04: *The relationship between Economic Growth and Political Stability is positive for Asian economies along the BRI.*

3.4 Corruption

Theoretically, corruption increases the cost of financing and is also related to political instability. A country with political instability will witness high level of corruption and in turn will see low economic growth. Empirical studies suggest both negative and positive relationships of Corruption with FDI. For India, Corruption has a negative impact on FDI, while for China it has a positive impact. FDI can become a mediating variable to influence economic growth originating from Corruption (Hasan et al., 2017). Thus, the impact of corruption varies for Asian economies (Thach et al., 2017).

H05: *The relationship between Economic Growth and Corruption is negative for Asian countries along the BRI.*

3.5 Infrastructure

A proxy for infrastructure in Asian economies is identified based on telephone mainlines (per 100 persons). It is hypothesized that there exists a positive relation between Infrastructure and Economic Growth.

H06: *The relationship between Economic Growth and Infrastructure is positive for Asian economies along the BRI.*

3.6 Geographic Distance

Geographic distance affects the transportation cost in international trade. One of the aims of BRI project is to minimize the transportation cost for exports and imports in the Asian region. This variable has been widely used in gravity models of trade as well as a determinant of economic growth. An inverse relation between distance and growth is hypothesized in H07.

H07: *The relationship between Economic growth and Geographic Distance (between reporting country and China) is negative for Asian economies along the BRI.*

3.7 Belt and Road Initiative

As discussed in detail the theoretical aspects of BRI, a positive impact of BRI on the Economic Growth of the Asian economies is expected. The hypothesis is stated as H08.

H08: *The relationship between Economic Growth and BRI is positive for Asian economies along the route.*

4 Econometric Analysis and Results

In this section, a model is developed based on the discussion under Sect. 3. After applying econometric analysis, results are reported followed by hypotheses testing. Panel regression is applied and therefore the specification of the model assumes the Guass-Markov properties (Rahman, 2018). The specified model is Ordinary Least Square model.

$$\begin{aligned} \text{GDP}_{it} = {} & \gamma_0 + \gamma_1 \text{EXP}_{it} + \gamma_2 \text{IMP}_{it} + \gamma_3 \text{FDP}_{it} + \gamma_4 \text{POL}_{it} \\ & - \gamma_5 \text{COR}_{it} + \gamma_6 \text{INR}_{it} - \gamma_7 \text{DIS}_{it} + \gamma_8 \text{BRI}_{it} + \varepsilon_{it} \end{aligned}$$

where,

GDP_{it} represents the economic growth panel, cross section countries i and time series years t
γ_0 is the intercept
$\gamma_1, \gamma_2 \ldots \gamma_8$ are the parameters of the independent variables
EXP_{it} represents the exports panel, cross section countries i and time series years t
IMP_{it} represents the imports panel, cross section countries i and time series years t
FDP_{it} represents the financial development panel, cross section countries i and time series years t
POL_{it} represents political stability panel, cross section countries i and time series years t.
COR_{it} represents the corruption panel, cross section countries i and time series years t
INR_{it} represents the infrastructure panel, cross section countries i and time series years t
DIS_{it} represents the distance panel, cross section countries i and time series years t
BRI_{it} represents the Belt and Road Initiative dummy panel, cross section countries i and time series years t

ε_{it} represents the stochastic error term for the panel of Asian economies

Panel Regression is performed followed by Hausman testing to decide whether Random or Fixed model fits. Based on Hausman test the identified model is used to draw inferences through hypothesis testing. The output of the Hausman test is presented in Table 4.

From Table 4, the probability value of Hausman test is 1.0000 that is more than 0.05. This means that null hypothesis is accepted. The null hypothesis of Hausman test if "Random Effect Model is correct," as per results this stand to be accepted. The next step is to move forward with Random Panel model for hypothesis testing.

For the sample of 25 Asian economies, the results of Random Panel regression are summarized in Table 5. The probability value of the model indicated by F-statistic is 0.000 (<0.05) indicating statistical significance of the model for hypothesis testing. Out of eight explanatory variables, three are having a significant impact on economic growth. Interestingly, the signs of the parameters reveal positive or negative impact between the variables. As hypothesized, positive relationship is indicated between exports and economic growth, while a negative relationship is revealed between imports and economic growth, though the hypothesized parameter sign was positive. Contrary to the hypothesized sign of the parameter for Financial Development, the analysis suggests a negative relationship between financial development and economic growth. Political Stability and Distance is having a positive relationship (as opposed to hypothesized negative for Distance), while for rest, that is, Corruption, Infrastructure and BRI, the parameter sign is negative.

Table 4 Hausman test output

Test summary	Chi-Sq. Statistic	Chi-Sq. d.f	Prob
Period random	0.0000	7	1.0000

Source Prepared by the researcher from the e-views output

Table 5 Random effect panel regression output

Variable	Coefficient	Std. error	t-Statistic	Prob
C	12.2646	2.1211	5.7822	0.0000[a]
EXP	4.31E-11	2.20E-11	1.9604	0.0509
IMP	−2.74E-12	2.01E-11	−0.1367	0.8913
FDP	−0.0690	0.01196	−5.7748	0.0000[a]
POL	1.3542	0.5381	2.5166	0.0124[a]
COR	−0.5526	0.8096	−0.6825	0.4954
INR	−0.0694	0.0474	−1.4634	0.1444
DIS	5.53E-05	0.0003	0.2028	0.8394
BRI	−2.3206	0.9525	−2.4361	0.0154[a]

[a]Indicates rejection of null hypothesis
Source Prepared by the researcher from the e-views output

Based on probability value, there is no significant relationship between bilateral exports and economic growth along the BRI ($p = 0.050 = 0.05$), though it is marginal. According to a lenient view, the hypothesis H01 may be accepted but in the study no rule of thumb is neglected. This signals that exports in the region under BRI will have no significant impact on the economic growth of Asian economies. Similarly, the results indicate no significant relationship between economic growth and bilateral imports as the probability value is more than 0.05 ($p = 0.8913 > 0.05$). With respect to financial development as an explanatory variable, the probability value indicates a significant relationship (negative) with economic growth ($p = 0.000 < 0.05$). Similarly, political stability as an explanatory variable is significant ($p = 0.0124 < 0.05$). Thus, the relationship between political stability and economic growth is supported by empirical testing. There is an insignificant relationship between corruption and economic growth along the BRI supported by the probability value ($p = 0.4954 > 0.05$). With respect to the relationship between economic growth and infrastructure, there is an insignificant relationship. This is supported by the probability value and coefficient values associated with the variable ($p = 0.1444 > 0.05$). Thus, the hypothesized relation between infrastructure and economic growth stands empirically null and void for BRI along the route. In the same manner, there is an insignificant relationship between geographic distance and economic growth for Asian economies along the route ($p = 0.8394 > 0.05$). The study has applied a dummy variable for BRI. As per the theoretical expectation, empirical testing indicates a significant but negative impact of BRI on the economic growth of the Asian economies along the route. This is supported by probability value ($p = 0.0154 < 0.05$) and coefficient value (-2.3). Table 6 summarizes the results of the hypotheses testing.

5 Conclusion

The present study has discussed in detail the implications and opportunities of the Belt and Road Initiative of China on the Asian economies along the route. BRI represents a great opportunity for the Asian economies who are participating and subdued opportunity for those not participating but benefiting through mediation. BRI will change the dynamics of Asian and Eurasian region in terms of geopolitics, economics, and environment. The empirical investigation reveals that bilateral trade with China is not associated with the economic growth of the Asian economies. However, this may be due to the recent origin of BRI. This indicates a lack of empirical evidence in favour of the relationship between BRI and bilateral trade. Inclusion of BRI as a dummy in the model, the results are reverting back to the theory that BRI will have a significant impact on the economic growth of the region. This empirical evidence can go a long way to promote BRI as well as convince other economies who have still not participated (e.g., India). Though, the negative sign is a concern for BRI dummy, this can be overcome in the future. Corruption is a major problem faced by developing and underdeveloped countries. All the Asian economies are developing or underdeveloped as per UNCTAD statistics (only two countries are

Table 6 Summary of hypotheses testing

Hypothesis	Parameter sign	Prob	Decision
H01: The relationship between Economic Growth and Bilateral Exports is positive for Asian economies along the BRI	+	0.0509	Parameter supported but insignificant relationship
H02: The relationship between Economic Growth and Bilateral Imports is positive for Asian economies along the BRI	−	0.8913	Parameter not supported and relationship insignificant
H03: The relationship between Economic Growth and Financial Development is positive for Asian economies along the BRI	−	0.0000	Parameter not supported but relationship is significant
H04: The relationship between Economic Growth and Political Stability is positive for Asian economies along the BRI	+	0.0124	Parameter supported but relationship is significant
H05: The relationship between Economic Growth and Corruption is negative for Asian countries along the BRI	−	0.4954	Parameter supported but relationship is insignificant
H06: The relationship between Economic Growth and Infrastructure is positive for Asian economies along the BRI	−	0.1444	Parameter not supported but relationship is insignificant
H07: The relationship between Economic growth and Geographic Distance (between reporting country and China) is negative for Asian economies along the BRI	+	0.8394	Parameter not supported and relationship is insignificant
H08: The relationship between Economic Growth and BRI is positive for Asian economies along the route	−	0.0154	Parameter not supported but relationship is significant

Source Prepared by the researcher from data analysis

developed in Asian region: Israel and Japan), and corruption is rampant. As the results reveal a negative relationship between economic growth and corruption, it is high time that countries associated with BRI make domestic policies to control and curb corruption. The relation between economic growth and distance is positive due to transportation costs associated with distance. This empirical evidence is also an eye opener for China to gradually reduce the transportation and transit costs for all Asian economies and not just for a selective few. This will build confidence among the Asian economies and will further push BRI in the region. The study has not included the qualitative and strategic issues of BRI and the future studies can incorporate variables such as Connectivity, Business Confidence Index, Ease of Doing Business *et cetera* for further investigations.

Bibliographic References

Baqai, H. (2015, June 10). CPEC: All to benefit Pakistan. *Pak Observer*.

Blanchard, J. M. F. (2017). China's Maritime Silk Road Initiative (MSRI) and Southeast Asia: A Chinese 'pond' not 'lake' in the works. *Journal of Contemporary China*, 1–15. https://doi.org/10.1080/10670564.2018.1410959

Cai, P. (2016, September 2). Why India is wary of China's silk road initiative. *The Huffington Post*. Retrieved on December 2021, from http://www.huffingtonpost.com/peter-cai/india-china-silk-road-initiative_b_11894038.html

Chen, H. (2016). China's 'One Belt, One Road' initiative and its implications for Sino-African investment relations. *Transnational Corporations Review, 8*(3), 178–182.

Chhibber, A. (2017). *China's One Belt One Road strategy: The new financial institutions and India's options*. Institute for International Economic Policy Working Paper Series Elliott School of International Affairs, the George Washington University. WP-7(Cross-listed with the National Institute of Public Finance and Policy). https://www2.gwu.edu/~iiep/assets/docs/Papers/2017WP

Chung, C. P. (2017). What are the strategic and economic implications for South Asia of China's Maritime Silk Road initiative? *The Pacific Review*, 1–18. https://doi.org/10.1080/09512748.2017.1375000

Estrada, G., Park, D., & Ramayandi, A. (2010). *Financial development and economic growth in developing Asia*. ADB Economics Working Paper Series.

Gabuev, A. (2016). Crouching bear, hidden dragon: "One Belt One Road" and Chinese-Russian jostling for power in Central Asia. *Journal of Contemporary East Asia Studies, 5*(2), 61–78. https://doi.org/10.1080/24761028.2016.11869097

Hasan, M., Rahman, M. N., & Iqbal, B. A. (2017). Corruption and FDI inflows: Evidence from India and China. *Mediterranean Journal of Social Sciences, 8*(4–1), 173–182. https://doi.org/10.2478/mjss-2018-0088

Iqbal, B. A., Rahman, M. N., & Hassan, M. (2016). MNCs and their role and contribution in Latin American countries. *Transnational Corporations Review, 8*(2), 151–164. https://doi.org/10.1080/19186444.2016.1197476

Iqbal, B. A., Rahman, M. N., & Sami, S. (2019). Impact of Belt and Road Initiative on Asian economies. *Global Journal of Emerging Market Economies*, 1–8. https://doi.org/10.1177/0974910119887059

Iqbal, B. A., Rahman, M. N., & Yusuf, N. (2018). Determinants of FDI in India and Sri Lanka. *Foreign Trade Review, 53*(2), 116–123. https://doi.org/10.1177%2F0015732517734751

Irshad, M. S., Xin, Q., & Arshad, H. (2015). One Belt and One Road: Dose China-Pakistan Economic Corridor benefit for Pakistan's economy? *Journal of Economics and Sustainable Development, 6*(24), 200–207.

Jetin, B. (2018). 'One Belt-One Road Initiative' and ASEAN connectivity: Synergy issues and potentialities. In *China's global rebalancing and the New Silk Road* (pp. 139–150). Springer.

Kralovicova, M., & Zatko, M. (2016). *One belt one road initiative in Central Asia: Implications for competitiveness of Russian economy* (No. 2016/9).

Lee, A. (2017). *A brilliant plan One Belt, One Road*. Retrieved on December 2021, from https://www.clsacom/special/onebeltoneroad/

Leer, Y. V. D., & Yau, J. (2016). *China's new silk route: The long and winding road* (p. 5). PWC's Growth Markets Centre.

Lu, J., & Mei, H. (2019, August). The influence of enterprise internationalization level and R&D input on enterprise performance under the background of "One Belt and One Road". In

International conference on management science and engineering management (pp. 177–188). Springer.

Mark, J. J. (2014). *Silk Road*. Ancient History Encyclopedia. Retrieved on December 2021, from https://www.ancient.eu/Silk_Road/

Nataraj, G., & Sekhani, R. (2016). *China's One Belt One Road initiative: Analysis from an Indian perspective*. Hong Kong Trade Development Council. Retrieved on December 2021, from http://china-trade-research.hktdc.com/business-news/article/The-Belt-and-Road-Initiative/China-s-One-Belt-One-Road-Initiative-Analysis-from-an-Indian-Perspective/obor/en/1/1X000000/1X0A5J3C.htm

Ndzendze, B., & Monyae, D. (2019). China's belt and road initiative: Linkages with the African Union's Agenda 2063 in historical perspective. *Transnational Corporations Review, 11*(1), 38–49.

Peyrouse, S., & Raballand, G. (2015). Central Asia: The new Silk Road initiative's questionable economic rationality. *Eurasian Geography and Economics, 56*(4), 405–420. https://doi.org/10.1080/15387216.2015.1114424

Rahman, M. N. (2016). Role of WTO in promoting merchandise trade of BRICS. *Transnational Corporations Review, 8*(2), 138–150. https://doi.org/10.1080/19186444.2016.1196867

Rahman, M. N. (2018). Macroeconomic variables of India and finite sample properties of OLS under classical assumptions. *Pacific Business Review International, 10*(8), 7–14. Retrieved on December 2021, from https://www.researchgate.net/profile/Mohd_Rahman8/publication/324107487_Macroeconomic_Variables_of_India_and_Finite_Sample_Properties_of_OLS_under_Classical_Assumptions/links/5abe177c45851584fa7088a5/Macroeconomic-Variables-of-India-and-Finite-Sample-Properties-of-OLS-under-Classical-Assumptions.pdf

Rahman, M. N., & Grewal, H. S. (2017). Foreign direct investment and international trade in BIMSTEC: Panel causality analysis. *Transnational Corporations Review, 9*(2), 112–121. https://doi.org/10.1080/19186444.2017.1326720

Rahman, N., & Rahman, M. N. (2019). One Belt One Road: Will it increase the gravity between China and Eurasia. *Journal of International Trade Law and Policy, 18*(3), 152–164. https://doi.org/10.1108/JITLP-06-2019-0037

Ramasamy, B., & Yeung, M. C. (2019). China's one belt one road initiative: The impact of trade facilitation versus physical infrastructure on exports. *The World Economy, 42*(6), 1673–1694.

Sen, G. (2016). *China-One Belt and One Road Initiative: Strategic & economic implications*. Vivekananda International Foundation.

Shukla, A. P. P. (2015). *Understanding the Chinese One-Belt-One-Road* (Occasional Paper, 3–28). Vivekananda International Foundation.

Shull, B. (2017). The hungry dragon. *Wall Street Journal*, A.17.

Thạch, N. N., Oanh, T. T. K., & Dương, M. B. (2017). Effects of corruption on economic growth-empirical study of Asia countries. *Imperial Journal of Interdisciplinary Research (IJIR), 3*(7), 2454–1362. Retrieved on December 2021, from http://www.onlinejournal.in

Ugochukwu, U. S., & Chinyere, U. P. (2013). The impact of export trading on economic growth in Nigeria. *International Journal of Economics, Business and Finance, 1*(10), 327–341.

Wu, S. (2017). *Understanding One Belt One Road initiative of China*. Teknologidagene E39 Session. Wuhan University of Technology, China. Retrieved on December 2021, from https://www.vegvesen.no/_attachment/2047173/binary/1214464?fast_title=Understanding+One+Belt+One+Road+Initiative+of+China.pdf

Xue, L. (2016). China's foreign policy decision-making mechanism and "One Belt One Road" strategy. *Journal of Contemporary East Asia Studies, 5*(2), 23–35. https://doi.org/10.1080/24761028.2016.11869095

Yao, S. (2006). On economic growth, FDI and exports in China. *Applied Economics, 38*(3), 339–351. https://doi.org/10.1080/00036840500368730

Younis, M., Lin, X. X., Sharahili, Y., & Selvarathinam, S. (2008). Political stability and economic growth in Asia. *American Journal of Applied Sciences, 5*(3), 203–208.

Yuan, F. (2019). The One Belt One Road Initiative and China's multilayered multilateralism. In *Mapping China's 'One Belt One Road' Initiative* (pp. 91–116). Palgrave Macmillan.

Chapter 38
The Belt and Road in the Kyrgyz Republic: Mapping Economic Risks and Risk Perceptions

Linda Calabrese and Olena Borodyna

1 Introduction

China's Belt and Road Initiative (BRI) has the potential to promote development through investment and infrastructure building, stimulating job creation and encouraging economic transformation. However, this is not a given—it requires effort and coordination to ensure that finance flows under the BRI framework provide a positive development impact. Existing debates and studies on infrastructure investment along the BRI have focused on investment deals and foreign investors, rather than host countries, and neglected the multifaceted effects which could undermine development efforts. Many BRI countries are vulnerable to various hazards, resulting in weak economic resilience and posing significant risks to the sustainability of BRI infrastructure projects. Therefore, the risk angle of the BRI needs to be further investigated. Political risk (and its subset of economic risk) is prominent in the Central Asia region.

The early economic and international business literature on political risks focused on risks *to investment* (Alon & Martin, 1988; Fitzpatrick, 1983; McKellar, 2016; Simon, 1984) rather than risks *to sustainable development*. Even when considering emerging markets and developing countries, scholars have focused on the risks to the companies rather than to the host country (Bilson et al., 2002; Busse & Hefeker, 2007; Diamonte et al., 1996; Sethi & Luther, 1986). However, risks do not only affect companies—they can also threaten development progress (Opitz-Stapleton et al., 2019). Not only risks, but *perceptions of risks* play a role in determining the course of action taken by governments, affecting development outcomes. Literature on risk perception also has limitations: when investigating how *risk perceptions* affect investment (Al Khattab et al., 2007; Barbosa et al., 2007; Thomas et al.,

L. Calabrese (✉)
ODI and King's College London, London, UK

O. Borodyna
ODI, London, UK

© The Author(s), under exclusive license to Springer Nature Singapore Pte Ltd. 2023
P. A. B. Duarte et al. (eds.), *The Palgrave Handbook of Globalization with Chinese Characteristics*, https://doi.org/10.1007/978-981-19-6700-9_38

2003), researchers have focussed on the business angle. More recently, the development literature has started considering risk perceptions, especially related to natural hazards (Janmaimool & Watanabe, 2014; Libarkin et al., 2018; Omanga et al., 2014; Peng et al., 2018), and recently expanding to include different types of hazards (Sullivan-Wiley & Short Giannotti, 2017). This study is embedded in that literature, considering political risks to development, their perceptions, and how these interact to elicit government responses.

Located along the BRI, Kyrgyzstan lies at the heart of the Initiative, first announced in 2013 in neighbouring Kazakhstan. The country is a major trading hub for goods coming from China and directed towards other Central Asian countries and Russia. Most Chinese infrastructure projects in Kyrgyzstan target the country's road network, with a handful focused on improving and upgrading the electricity network and developing the country's productive and trading capacity. Chinese investment in the country is also directed at the country's extractives sector. Given its significance in terms of infrastructure development, the BRI has the potential to support economic diversification and development in Kyrgyzstan. However, the BRI potentially entails risks to the country's development process through several channels—challenges to debt sustainability, limited spillovers, exacerbation of corruption.

This study aims to review the risks and perception of risks to the Kyrgyz economic development process brought about by the BRI and assess to what extent these are substantiated; and to the extent possible, understand how risk perceptions shape government responses. The study relies on a series of expert interviews conducted in Kyrgyzstan in May–June 2019, targeting government officials, academics, civil society, experts, and development partners. While the most prominent manifestation of the BRI is its infrastructure component, in reality, it's much broader than that, with its five areas of connectivity (trade, financial, infrastructure, political and people-to-people) encompassing a variety of activities. Moreover, the BRI is often considered by experts as an expansion of the earlier "Going Out" strategy, encouraging Chinese firms to invest abroad (Cabestan, 2019; Calabrese, 2021; Calabrese et al., 2021; Wang, 2016). In addition to this, many Kyrgyz stakeholders do not distinguish between the BRI and any other Chinese activity in the country, such as investment in extractives and trade. For this reason, this study does not only look at infrastructure construction and related lending but also includes trade with and investment from China. The study is structured as follows. Section 2 provides an overview of the context, focusing particularly on Kyrgyzstan's economic development. Section 3 provides an overview of the BRI in Kyrgyzstan. Section 4 reviews the risks to the development process and Sect. 5 concludes.

2 The Kyrgyz Context

To assess the impact of the BRI on development in Kyrgyzstan, the study frames it in the broader economic and political context of the country. This section reviews the status of the Kyrgyz economic and political context and provides an update of the additional challenges generated by COVID-19.

2.1 A Fragile Economic Model

A lower-middle-income economy with a GDP of US$8.5 billion and GDP per capita of US$1,309 in 2019, Kyrgyzstan has experienced uneven patterns of growth in the last few decades. Since 2014, however, GDP growth has hovered around 4% a year (World Bank, various years). The country's economic structure has diversified in the past two decades. In 2019 the construction and services sectors were booming, while agriculture, once the largest economic sector, contracted considerably (Asian Development Bank, 2020). There are three important sources of finance in the economy: extractives, remittances, and trade, particularly as a regional hub for trade with China. We examine the first two here, and the third one in the next section.

In 2014 the formal extractives sector represented over 50% of industrial output, 8.4% of GDP, and 17% of government revenues, accounting for 16,000 jobs (World Bank Group, 2018), in addition to contributing significantly to the country's exports. The sector is a significant source of foreign exchange: in 2017, gold represented over 18% of the country's total exports (second only to the travel and tourism sector, at 19% of exports). Activities related to extractives also dominate the manufacturing sector (NSC, n.d.). The main and most remunerative mineral product is gold. Gold extraction activities are strongly concentrated: the biggest gold mine, the Canadian-Kyrgyz-owned Kumtor, contributed 9.7% to the Kyrgyz GDP in 2017 (EITI, 2021). However, Kumtor's operations are planned to cease in 2031, and there appears to be no clear plan to offset this loss.

Remittances, primarily from Kyrgyz citizens in Russia, are another important source of capital (Dubashov et al., 2017). In 2018, remittances accounted for over 35% of GDP, making Kyrgyzstan the most remittance-dependent country in the world (International Organisation for Migration, 2018). While in the short-term remittances boost consumption and reduce poverty, in the long term they can weaken investment and growth (Dubashov et al., 2017). External public debt is another source of fragility for Kyrgyzstan. At the end of 2018, the total debt was at US$3.8 billion, which the most recent IMF Debt Sustainability Analysis puts at 48% of the GDP (IMF, 2019). 45% of this debt (or US$1.7 billion) is owed to China, the country's biggest lender. This is roughly the same amount the country owes to all multilaterals combined (National Bank of the Republic of Kyrgyzstan, 2019).[1]

Long-term development planning and economic diversification are a challenge for Kyrgyzstan. In 2018, the country published its first long-term development strategy—Strategy 2040, prioritizing economic diversification and industry, agriculture, and tourism as key to long-term sustainable development. Despite aspirations, our interviewees cited structural weaknesses in government ways of working, opportunistic foreign policy, and challenges with broader planning as constraints to realizing the Strategy. Indeed, the Strategy and accompanying Development Programme were

---

[1] Kyrgyzstan is no stranger to debt sustainability issues. In 2006, the country was considered eligible for debt relief under the Enhanced Initiative for Highly-Indebted Poor Countries (HIPC) (International Monetary Fund, 2006).

regarded as wishlists, with no real prioritization and costing. Meanwhile, government agencies approach development partners and financiers with uncoordinated and conflicting requests.[2]

2.2 Frequent Political Unrest Destabilizes the Investment Scene

Since independence in 1991, Kyrgyzstan has experienced periods of political unrest in 2005, 2010 and 2020. The most recent episode, after a parliamentary election in October 2020, led to a prompt resignation of the then-President Jeenbekov. During the unrest, several politicians were freed including Sadyr Japarov, a former MP who was serving a sentence on kidnapping charges (Wachtel, 2020). Japarov went on to win the presidential election in January 2021 by a large margin (*The Economist*, 2021; Wachtel, 2020).

Periodic political unrest followed by outbreaks of violence, combined with weak economic fundamentals, and development challenges creates a volatile environment for foreign investors. Following recent political unrest, Chinese companies, similarly to other foreign investors, have experienced disruptions to their operation and physical violence. Production on the Chinese-owned Ishtamberdy gold mine was disrupted by protests, though mines operated by other foreign investors were also affected (Pak, 2020). Investors were reportedly reluctant to resume work following protests owing to a lack of faith in the government's capacity to negotiate with protesters (Azzatyk, 2020). In response, the Chinese government prioritized the security of their citizens, holding several meetings with representatives of the Kyrgyz government to ensure the protection of their investors. More than other investors, Chinese businesses are often the target of protests, including the most recent wave in 2018–2019 and then again in 2020 (Elmer, 2020; Reuters, 2019). These protests often express both explicit anti-Chinese sentiments and dissatisfaction with the government's approach to China's economic presence in the country.

2.3 An Emerging Challenge: COVID-19

Kyrgyzstan detected the first official cases of COVID-19 on 18 March 2020, responding with countrywide lockdowns (ADB and UNDP, 2020). Restrictive measures to limit domestic and cross-border movement, including temporary restrictions on Kazakhstan and Uzbekistan borders and closure of the one with China, however, failed to halt the spread of the pandemic (ibid.). As of 8 October 2021, the country reported almost 180,000 cases of COVID-19, and 2,616 mortalities (WHO, 2021). The pandemic has taken a heavy toll on the Kyrgyz economy. ADB and UNDP

---

[2] Interview with independent consultants, July 2019.

(2020) estimate that in 2020 Kyrgyz GDP will shrink by 10% owing to a decline in main sources of revenues. Trade volumes fell by 15% in the first half of 2020, while a decline in domestic demand led to a GDP contraction of 5.3%. Tourism and travel revenues were also predicted to fall by 90%. Remittances, which in 2018 accounted for 35% of the country's GDP, fell 25% year-on-year for January–May 2020, and should the trend continue, it would cost the country an amount close to 4–5% of GDP by the end of 2020. Dependence on remittances leaves Kyrgyzstan vulnerable to macroeconomic changes in Russia, with lower economic activity as a result of weaker oil prices leading to fewer remittances to Kyrgyzstan (IMF, 2020). Significant numbers of Kyrgyz migrants were unable to return to the country of work owing to lockdowns, leading to a higher labour supply and creating pressures on employment. ADB and UNDP (2020) estimate that unemployment in 2020 can rise to between 13.8% and 21%, up from 6.8% in 2018.

3 The Belt and Road in Kyrgyzstan

3.1 *Kyrgyzstan-China Relations*

Following the disintegration of the Soviet Union, China quickly settled outstanding border disputes with newly independent Central Asian states and Russia. In the 1990s, shuttle trading and Kyrgyz entry to the WTO facilitated economic relations with China.[3] The country engaged Kyrgyzstan through high-level bilateral diplomacy and under the framework of the Shanghai Cooperation Organisation. After signing the Treaty of Good Neighbourliness in 2002, China and Kyrgyzstan have upgraded their cooperation several times, signing a Joint Declaration on Deepening of Comprehensive Strategic Partnership[4] in June 2019 (MFA, 2019). Chinese economic engagement with Kyrgyzstan predates the BRI, which Kyrgyzstan has since joined (*The Diplomat*, 2017). The scale and scope of bilateral trade, investment, and lending relationships have grown exponentially in recent years, with China becoming one of Kyrgyzstan's main economic partners.

Trade is possibly the most important aspect of the China-Kyrgyzstan economic relation. Since the early 2000s, Kyrgyzstan has been a transit hub for goods from China destined to other Central Asian markets and Russia (Mogilevskii, 2019). In

---

[3] Shuttle trading 'refers to the activity in which individual entrepreneurs buy goods abroad and import them for resale in street markets or small shops. Often the goods are imported without full declaration in order to avoid import duties' (OECD, IMF, ILO, Interstate Statistical Committee of the Commonwealth of Independent States, 2002).

[4] A Comprehensive Strategic Partnership is one of the closest types of partnership established by China with other countries or organizations. 'Comprehensive' indicates cooperation in the economic, technological, cultural and political domains; 'strategic' means that cooperation is not only important, but also stable and long-term; and 'partnership' indicates that the two parties cooperate on the basis of respect, trust and equality, for a relationship that is mutually beneficial (Li & Ye, 2019).

2018 China was the source of almost 60% of Kyrgyzstan's imports, though flows in the other direction are much smaller, with China absorbing a little over 3% of Kyrgyzstan's exports (Mogilevskii, 2012). Compared to trade in goods, trade in services is small, mostly covering tourism and construction, and some transport and logistics (Mogilevskii, 2019). China is also the largest provider of foreign direct investment (FDI) inflow terms to Kyrgyzstan, concentrated in geological explorations, mining, and production of refined petroleum products (Mogilevskii, 2019). FDI in geological explorations and mining focuses on the development of gold deposits. Investment in oil refineries entered the country in 2011 but face issues sourcing raw materials (Mogilevskii, 2019).

Finally, China is the main provider of development assistance to Kyrgyzstan, based on data provided by the Kyrgyzstan Aid Management Platform. This includes grants and concessional loans but also lending for infrastructure projects. By 2017, the lending by China Exim bank skyrocketed to US$1.7 billion, constituting 42% of total government external debt, or 24% of GDP (Mogilevskii, 2019). Kyrgyzstan has also requested debt relief from China, its largest creditor, though has not yet received a response to its request (van der Kley, 2020b). "Cloud" diplomacy allowed China and Kyrgyzstan to continue bilateral engagements even as the COVID-19 pandemic constrained opportunities for face-to-face meetings.[5] Since the start of the pandemic, the Chinese government, enterprises and business associations operating in Kyrgyzstan have all contributed humanitarian assistance to the country (Borodyna et al., 2022). China provided Kyrgyzstan with testing and protective equipment, as well as food donations to poor families in Bishkek (Kabar, 2021). After pandemic-induced lockdowns and border closures, China prioritized resuming economic activities and restarting the construction and production on existing projects. Chartered flights were organized to transport CRBC and PetroChina workers back to Kyrgyzstan. Chinese mining companies have continued production during the pandemic. Resuming freight functions at closed borders was another key priority (Embassy of the People's Republic of China in the Kyrgyz Republic, 2020).

3.2 The Belt and Road in Kyrgyzstan

As demonstrated, Chinese economic engagement in Kyrgyzstan takes different forms - trade, foreign direct investment, and development assistance. In terms of the energy sector, Chinese companies built two oil refineries in the north of Kyrgyzstan—Zhongda and Tokmok (Mogilevskii, 2019). These reportedly operate at one-third of their capacity owing to relatively high raw material and transportation costs (Mogilevskii, 2019). Chinese companies have invested in at least four gold mines (Borodyna et al., 2022), signing agreements for an additional $1,675 billion worth of projects during the China—Kyrgyzstan Business Forum in June 2019 (Kabar,

---

[5] 'Cloud diplomacy' refers to high-level engagements between foreign leaders and other members of the international community through phone calls, correspondence, and video conferences.

2019). During the aforementioned Business Forum, the two countries signed seven agriculture agreements worth a minimum of $2.7 billion (Kabar, 2019), though one project was already cancelled owing to community protests about alleged Chinese land ownership (Voice of America, 2020).

There are no major Chinese investments in communications and digital technology, but cooperation in this area may grow in the future as Kyrgyzstan seeks technology for digitalization. During the Business Forum, the two signed several agreements in the digital sector (Kabar, 2019) however the project timelines are unclear. Chinese companies have also reportedly installed facial recognition in the country (Azzatyk, 2019). Chinese companies have also been actively engaged in road and energy construction projects in Kyrgyzstan (Mogilevskii, 2019). China Road and Bridge Corporation (CRBC) and Tebian Electric Apparatus Stock (TBEA) worked on several projects financed through grants and concessional lending from China EXIM Bank, including road reconstruction, electricity transmission line, and heat plant modernization project in Bishkek (Mogilevskii, 2019). The latter, carried out by TBEA with financing from China EXIM Bank, was a source of great controversy. The plant broke down shortly after reconstruction, prompting allegations of corruption, and poor standards (Putz, 2018).

4 Economic Risks Deriving from the BRI

While the BRI, with its infrastructure offer and strengthening of economic ties, can be an engine of development, its actual impact depends on two main factors: the willingness of foreign investors to move into a country, and the ability of the infrastructure projects to generate economic growth. While Chinese (and other foreign) investors are mainly concerned with the risks to their investment, from the Kyrgyz side, the most important question is how will Chinese investment and infrastructure construction affect the development of the country and the welfare of its citizens. This section discusses the potential risks to the Kyrgyz development process in relation to China in general, and the Belt and Road in particular, as identified in the course of our interviews. It also reviews these risks on the basis of the available literature to gage whether they constitute a real threat to the Kyrgyz development process.

4.1 Reliance on China as an Economic Partner

Section 2 has shown that the Kyrgyz economy is fragile, with limited growth and reliant on remittances, gold extraction, and the import–re-export trade. Moreover, the revenue and export contribution of the Kumtor mine will be difficult to replace if it ceases production as currently planned in 2026, and the government has made limited plans in this sense. Section 3 has shown that China is the main trade, investment, and development finance partner for Kyrgyzstan. The fact that China is a prominent partner in so many areas that are important for Kyrgyzstan's economic development highlights a potential weakness, as it is an additional sign of a development model that is not focusing on diversification.

China's economic presence in Kyrgyzstan should also be read in conjunction with the fact that other foreign non-Chinese investors have shown limited interest in the country, given the challenges with the operating environment and infrastructure and the small size of the market. While mining and mineral processing remain potentially among the most attractive sectors of the economy, the long lead times, the highly politicized nature of the sector, pervasive corruption, and conflict with local communities have made investment challenging.[6] Several foreign investors have left the country in recent years.[7] Interviewees also pointed out that there does not seem to be a contingency plan for 2026 when Kumtor's operations are scheduled to close. Many also highlighted that the government is expecting foreign companies to invest, but activities to promote such investment have been limited.

The limited interest by foreign investors, coupled with the lack of active investment promotion by the government, has left Kyrgyzstan in a vulnerable position. Within the space of a few years, China has gained a prominent position as an economic partner. As one interviewee highlighted, "we need Chinese investors in mining because no one else is coming."[8] Relying heavily on one partner can accentuate vulnerability for a country such as Kyrgyzstan. As one commentator pointed out: "massive investment from any single country is a security threat regardless of country of origin."[9]

This contrasts sharply with another set of findings from our interviews. Some interviewees (in some cases, the same that were quoted above) mentioned that many perceived that China was not offering much to Kyrgyzstan in their partnership. The most common evidence offered for this was that Kyrgyzstan did not receive any significant finance or was not promised any large-scale project during the Belt and Road Summit, held in April 2019. However, during the Kyrgyzstan-China Business Forum that took place in Bishkek in June 2019, on the margin of the SCO Council of Heads of State, China and Kyrgyzstan signed deals worth over US$7 billion. Overall, there seems to be general unease with China's increased economic role in Kyrgyzstan, at the same time as an acknowledgement that Chinese investment is needed in a country where few others are willing to invest. The limited efforts of the government in finding and attracting new economic partners contribute to a general sense that the Kyrgyz economy is vulnerable.

---

[6] Interview with private sector association, May 2019.

[7] Interview with independent expert, May 2019.

[8] Interview with mining labour union representative, June 2019.

[9] Interview with independent expert, June 2019.

4.2 Debt Sustainability

Debt is one of the most debated issues around the Belt and Road. Allegations that China is creating a "debt trap" (Chellaney, 2017), even though widely debunked in the academic literature (Jones & Hameiri, 2020; Singh, 2020), have made many nervous about infrastructure borrowing from China. Kyrgyzstan's debt situation has evolved considerably recently with debt owed to China roughly equalling what Kyrgyzstan owes all the multilateral lenders combined (National Bank of the Kyrgyz Republic, 2019). Debt repayments amounted to US$144 million in 2016 but were due to increase to US$200 million in 2018 and US$308 million in 2024 (van der Kley, 2017).

A recent analysis by the IMF indicates that Kyrgyzstan is at moderate risk of debt distress. The country's capacity to carry debt is strong, but the economy remains vulnerable to external changes. While infrastructure investment is necessary, externally financed public investment could undermine debt sustainability (IMF, 2019). Other studies confirm the IMF's statements. Wignaraja et al. (2018) identify BRI-related debt in Kyrgyzstan as a cause of concern in terms of sustainability, estimating that Kyrgyzstan should grow at 27% per year to maintain a GDP-to-debt ratio of 60%, compared with the current forecast placing growth at 5%. Similarly, Hurley et al. (2019) identify Kyrgyzstan as high risk in terms of BRI-related debt.

The economic deceleration caused by COVID-19 threatens debt sustainability even further. To ease the burden, the government received two emergency loans from the IMF. Moreover, it has asked China for some form of debt relief twice in 2020 (van der Kley, 2020b), but at the time of writing it appears that China has not yet responded to this request. Our interviews with Kyrgyz stakeholders revealed a degree of unease around debt owed to China. There is a common perception that Kyrgyzstan is being "strangled" by Chinese debt, linked to the "debt trap" narrative. Rumours abound around allegedly similar cases in Sri Lanka, regarding the famous Hambantota port controversy, and neighbouring Tajikistan, which allegedly gave China rights over land and mining concessions in exchange for debt write-off (Reynolds, 2018). The example of Russia writing off debt in exchange for concessions on military bases (mentioned above) is also cited as evidence that infringements on sovereignty are not uncommon—though one interviewee also mentioned that this was in exchange for Kyrgyzstan joining the Eurasian Economic Union. One interviewee noted, China has not yet "called in the favour," implying that it may do so in the future.[10]

One interviewee noted that "Chinese money is too good to refuse" as it offered good financial conditions with no commitment to reform.[11] At the time of our interviews, the feeling from some senior government advisors was that Kyrgyzstan had too much debt from China and little room to borrow more from others. In response, the government was unwilling to provide any more government guarantee on debt, and it has not taken additional finance from China since 2018. Several interviewees raised doubts about the government's ability to critically assess loans and develop a

---

[10] Interviews with three political experts, and with one advocacy organisation, May 2019.

[11] Interview with government advisor, May 2019.

solid debt management strategy. The lack of critical discussion by the government around engagement with China, in particular on debt, emerged from our interviews.[12] Several interviewees also pointed to the limited options available to the government. In 2019, none of our interviewees considered it likely that China could restructure or forgive the debt, but given the recent requests for debt relief by the Kyrgyz government, the situation may have changed.

In reality, debt renegotiations are not uncommon for the debt owed to China (Kratz et al., 2019). One recent review shows that, since 2000, China has written off almost $10 billion in 96 rounds of cancellations (Development Reimagined and Oxford China-Africa Consultancy, 2019). However, as discussed above, two requests for debt relief by the Kyrgyz government to China have not yet yielded results.

Finally, it is worth highlighting that the Kyrgyz and Chinese governments appear to have taken a more prudent approach towards borrowing. We have no information of new loans being agreed from 2018 onwards, which seem to signal increased caution in contracting new debt. This slowdown in new borrowing predates COVID-19, suggesting that the issue is broader than just the pandemic.

4.3 Corruption

Corruption remains a serious issue in Kyrgyzstan, shaping the country's recent history. Political unrest and coups in 2005 and 2010 were both sparked by public discontent at government corruption and nepotism, though these practices continued under successor regimes (Ismailbekova, 2018). The country was characterized as "an investment market" where politicians and businessmen make investments through buying political positions and paying for political parties in exchange for access to resources and privileges (Engvall, 2016). Corruption takes many forms affecting bureaucracy and public administration, nepotism and cronyism, and political corruption leading to large-scale embezzlement (Martini, 2013). In terms of corruption control, in 2019 the World Bank Governance Indicators place Kyrgyzstan among 17% worse-performing countries in the world (World Bank, n.d.). The country ranks similarly poorly on Transparency International's Corruption Perception Index (Transparency International, n.d.). A fifth of investors in the country admit to having paid bribes (Kudryavtseva, 2016).

Corruption scandals such as the one with the Bishkek power plant prompted the Kyrgyz public to associate Chinese investment with corruption, contributing to a negative image for Chinese engagement in the country. TBEA was contracted to modernize the heat and power plant using a US$386 million loan from China Exim Bank. The power plant broke down shortly after its inauguration in 2017 prompting an investigation that revealed massively bloated costs and implicated high-level Kyrgyz officials, including two former prime ministers, a former mayor of Bishkek, a former energy minister, and a representative of TBEA (Alkanova, 2018; Radio Free

---

[12] Interview with political expert, May 2019.

Europe/Radio Liberty, 2018). One interviewee pointed to Chinese companies being more prone to corruption than Western investors, however, it is unclear to what extent such attitudes are shaped by historical mistrust which shapes perceptions of China, especially as the evidence points to corruption being a widespread phenomenon for foreign and domestic investors alike. Another interviewee points out that in contrast to other countries like the US which has the Foreign Corrupt Practices Act, which enables the prosecution of foreign officials, China lacks foreign bribery legislation. In reality, such legislation exists, it is often not applied.

Overall, Kyrgyzstan seems to lack incentives to invest in production activities (Engvall, 2016). While in the short-term corruption may contribute to the personal enrichment of corrupt individuals, providing them with access to public funding, in the long term is likely to discourage investment. Perception of China as contributing to corruption in Kyrgyzstan among the Kyrgyz public will likely affect aspects of relations between the two countries, potentially leading to further operational disruption, physical violence, and generally sowing distrust between the two sides.

4.4 Limited Spillovers

One common claim about Chinese-financed projects is that these have no requirements in terms of local procurement, and therefore have limited spillover on the local economy. In Kyrgyzstan, this discussion is often centred around labour market issues, in particular in relation to hiring Kyrgyz workers. As in other countries, Kyrgyz citizens see immigrants as "taking their jobs." Immigrants into Kyrgyzstan are predominantly from CIS countries (mostly Kazakhstan and Russia), but there is also a large and growing Chinese workforce.

Hiring foreign workers in Kyrgyzstan is regulated by a quota system. Quotas establish the maximum number of foreign citizens that can be granted work permits (labour quota) or permanent residence (immigration quota) on an annual basis. However, these quotas are never reached, and they mostly go to Chinese citizens. In 2014, Chinese migrants filled 72% of the quotas assigned to foreign workers, primarily in construction and gold mining (OECD and ILO, 2017). In addition to legal immigrants, there are a certain number of illegal immigrants who overstay their visas or do not go through the formal quota systems. Given their informal, estimating how many are in the country is difficult.

The workforce localization rate, or share of local workers hired by foreign companies, is a contentious issue for Chinese firms, both private and state-owned. Whether Chinese firms largely rely on expatriates or prefer to hire local workers has been widely debated (Oya & Schaefer, 2019; Sautman & Yan, 2015) before the emergence of the BRI.

In Kyrgyzstan, the belief that Chinese SOEs and private companies only or mostly hire Chinese workers is widespread and was one of the most common complaints flagged in our interviews. Interviewees identified low localization rates for Chinese companies both in more visible sectors (for example, in the construction of roads around Bishkek) and in less visible ones (for example, in the informal mines spread around the country). These concerns are also reported in the media (Asanov & Najibullah, 2013) and circulate widely on social media. For mid- to high-skilled jobs, many understand that, for some skill levels or selected specializations, Chinese workers may be necessary. However, interviewees also noted that some of these skills are available in Kyrgyzstan, and hiring foreign workers is not always necessary. For lower-skilled jobs in the construction and mining sectors, many mentioned that the working schedules and conditions that Chinese workers are prepared to accept would not be acceptable to Kyrgyz workers, and therefore that Chinese employers prefer to hire compatriots.

A contributing factor in Chinese companies mostly hiring Chinese nationals is language. In Chinese firms using Chinese machinery, processes, and manuals, Kyrgyz workers have no access to a large part of the information, which makes working together a complicated process. There is very little evidence on localization rates in Chinese companies in Kyrgyzstan, but even this does not support the claim that Chinese firms do not hire Kyrgyz workers. A recent study conducted on a handful of Chinese companies in Kyrgyzstan shows that these hire between 60 and 90% local workers and that their localization rates have increased over time (van der Kley, 2020a). Moreover, it seems that the overall number of Chinese workers remains very small, as confirmed by Mogilevskii (2019). Two interviewees reported that Altynken, a joint venture between state-owned Kyrgyzaltyn and China's Zijin Mining, signed a voluntary agreement to maintain a maximum ceiling of expatriate staff at 10%. However, one interviewee regarded this agreement as of little use given that the company would also hire several subcontractors for specific tasks, most of whom were Chinese companies mostly employing Chinese nationals. Overall, the data is scarce and there is no evidence supporting or contradicting the widespread perception that Chinese immigration is damaging employment prospects for Kyrgyz workers in Kyrgyzstan. Even so, the belief is widespread and contributes to anti-Chinese sentiment and unrest. In 2012, around 450 Kyrgyz protested against the presence of Chinese subcontractors at the Taldybulak Levoberezhny deposit, to be operated by Altynken, a joint venture between and a subsidiary of China's Zijin Mining (Dzyubenko, 2015; TCA, 2012). In January 2019, several hundred protesters gathered in Ala-Too Square in Bishkek to demand the deportation of illegal Chinese migrants (Eurasianet, 2019).

5 Conclusion

The Kyrgyz Republic lies at the heart of China's BRI and could therefore benefit from the initiative's infrastructure offer to further attract a variety of investors and diversify its growth model. However, this depends on whether the BRI contributes to improving productive infrastructure, or whether the risks it poses to the Kyrgyz development process translate into negative outcomes.

This study has shown that there exist threats to sustainable development linked to the Belt and Road in Kyrgyzstan, and that these are perceived in various ways by Kyrgyz stakeholders. The risk perceptions affect how stakeholders react, and shape the government's responses to risk. Regarding economic reliance on China, the risk is perceived as almost inevitable. There is a recognition that China is becoming increasingly important for the Kyrgyz economy, and that this may be a problem. However, there is also a perception that little can be done about this. In reality, the government has not managed to diversify its economic partnerships, and it does not seem to have a clear policy in place. Kyrgyzstan's "multivector foreign policy" (Kainazarova, 2018) does not seem to translate into an active multivector economic policy.

Secondly, while the "debt trap diplomacy" may not be grounded in reality, this narrative has acted as a cautionary tale, raising awareness against excessive borrowing. The country is indeed in a precarious situation in terms of external public debt, and the idea of potential asset grabs by China has discouraged further lending. In this case, perceptions are in line with the situation on the ground, and they have prompted the adoption of a more prudent approach by government officials.

Thirdly, corruption remains a major issue. Not only this can scare investors away, but large infrastructure projects are also a breeding ground for large-scale embezzlement. The potential benefits of the BRI may be hampered by the presence of corruption, limiting the gains for the population. As for the economic reliance on China, this is acknowledged by the government but not translated into effective anti-corruption policy actions.

Finally, there is a perception among Kyrgyz stakeholders that Chinese investment and infrastructure projects may have limited spillovers on the Kyrgyz economy. While there is little evidence to support claims of limited workers' localization, the fact that Chinese firms often subcontract other Chinese firms rather than local firms is a common tendency found in other locations as well. However, this speaks more to the lack of capacity in the domestic market rather than to a specific issue with Chinese firms, who may be willing to subcontract local firms if they found some with the right skills and prices.

Considering all these risks, real and perceived, one major point emerges: the Kyrgyz Republic lacks a clear approach to the BRI, and to the Chinese presence in the country in general. While the BRI can potentially generate benefits for the Kyrgyz economy by providing the much-needed infrastructure for economic diversification, it is unclear whether the government has a clear strategy on how to exploit these potential benefits. It is also unclear whether the government will seek to assuage concerns about greater reliance on China as identified in this paper through diversifying finance sources or any other strategy. In the meantime, the lack of a clear approach to the Initiative and its relationship with China leaves the government disadvantaged in seeking to leverage the potential benefits of the BRI.

Even more concerning is the fact that the government has no clear plan for economic diversification. The country's fragile economic model needs to be stirred in a direction of further structural transformation, supporting investment in new, more productive sectors. There seem to be limited plans to upgrade or replace the extractives sector. The COVID-19 pandemic has further exposed these sources of vulnerability, hitting many important sources of revenues such as trade and remittances. Along with the pandemic, at the end of 2020, Kyrgyzstan has experienced another period of political instability when the October parliamentary elections led to a third regime change in 15 years. As a result, President Jeenbekov resigned his position only three years into his term putting an end to hopes of a peaceful transfer of power at the next presidential election. His successor, Sadyr Japarov, a former MP who was serving a prison sentence at the time of the October election, was elected President by a majority in January 2021. The political unrest, though relatively short-lived, has disrupted the work at several mining sites, including those operated by Chinese companies. Since his election, Japarov carried out a protectionist policy when it comes to the extractives sector. Government measures targeted the future development of natural resources in the country, prohibiting foreigners from participation in large mining projects, and granted it powers to temporarily seize control of the Kumtor Gold Mine. While these measures did not necessarily target Chinese investors in the country, they speak to public and elite anxiety over ownership of the natural resources and the feeling that the country does not sufficiently benefit from their development. The Chinese government is acutely aware of the risks associated with an investment in the Kyrgyz extractives sector, including labour unrest and security concerns, to name but a few. It is unclear whether the recent policy pursued by the Kyrgyz government, coupled with continued disruption to their operations, will deter Chinese investors in the sector. The absence of concrete plans to finance long-term development strategy, coupled with economic ramifications of the COVID-19 pandemic and poor planning towards attracting and retaining foreign investment in the country, including that of Chinese investors, presents potent challenges for the new Kyrgyz government. It remains to be seen whether the new government can provide the vision and strategy the country requires to tackle these challenges and secure the long-term development of Kyrgyzstan.

Bibliographic References

ADB and UNDP. (2020). *COVID-19 in the Kyrgyz Republic: Socioeconomic and vulnerability impact assessment and policy response*. Asian Development Bank and United Nations Development Programme.

Alkanova, E. (2018, October 24). Abuse of power? On the trail of China's mystery millions in Kyrgyzstan. *openDemocracy*.

Al Khattab, A., Anchor, J., & Davies, E. (2007). Managerial perceptions of political risk in international projects. *IRNOP VII, 25*(7), 734–743. https://doi.org/10.1016/j.ijproman.2007.03.006

Alon, I., & Martin, M. A. (1988). A normative model of macro political risk assessment. *Multinational Business Review, 1988*(Fall), 10–19.

Asanov, B., & Najibullah, F. (2013, November 16). Kyrgyz ask why jobs at home are going to Chinese. *Eurasianet*.

Asian Development Bank. (2020). *Key indicators for Asia and the Pacific 2020*. Asian Development Bank.

Azzatyk. (2019, November 1). Face recognition cameras appeared on the streets of Bishkek. China installed them free of charge. *Azzatyk*.

Azzatyk. (2020, December 24). Investors are leaving Kyrgyzstan. The economy is losing hundreds of millions of dollars. *Azzatyk*.

Barbosa, S. D., Kickul, J., & Liao-Troth, M. (2007). Development and validation of a multidimensional scale of entrepreneurial risk perception. *Academy of Management Proceedings, 2007*(1), 1–6. https://doi.org/10.5465/ambpp.2007.26508257

Bilson, C. M., Brailsford, T. J., & Hooper, V. C. (2002). The explanatory power of political risk in emerging markets. *International Review of Financial Analysis, 11*(1), 1–27. https://doi.org/10.1016/S1057-5219(01)00067-9

Borodyna, O., Calabrese, L., & Nadin, R. (2022). *Risks along the belt and road: Chinese investment and infrastructure development priorities in Kyrgyzstan* (Research Report). ODI.

Busse, M., & Hefeker, C. (2007). Political risk, institutions and foreign direct investment. *European Journal of Political Economy, 23*(2), 397–415. https://doi.org/10.1016/j.ejpoleco.2006.02.003

Cabestan, J.-P. (2019). Beijing's "going out" strategy and Belt and Road Initiative in the Sahel: The case of China's growing presence in Niger. *Journal of Contemporary China, 28*(118), 592–613. https://doi.org/10.1080/10670564.2018.1557948

Calabrese, L. (2021). The BRI in Africa: Change or continuity in China-Africa relations? *Research Handbook on the Belt and Road Initiative, Political Science and Public Policy 2021*, 355–369. https://doi.org/10.4337/9781789908718.00041

Calabrese, L., Huang, Z., & Nadin, R. (2021). *Chinese enterprises in Ethiopia: Risks and opportunities for development* (Research Report). ODI.

Chellaney, B. (2017). China's debt-trap diplomacy. *Project Syndicate*.

Development Reimagined and Oxford China-Africa Consultancy. (2019). *China's debt relief along the Belt and Road—What's the story?* Development Reimagined. Retrieved on 29 July 2019, from https://developmentreimagined.com/2019/04/25/chinas-debt-relief-along-the-belt-and-road-whats-the-story/

Diamonte, R. L., Liew, J. M., & Stevens, R. L. (1996). Political risk in emerging and developed markets. *Financial Analysts Journal, 52*(3), 71–76. https://doi.org/10.2469/faj.v52.n3.1998

Dubashov, B., Kruse, A., & Ismailakhunova, S. (2017). *Kyrgyz Republic Economic Update: A robust recovery with underlying weaknesses* (No. 6). World Bank.

Dzyubenko, O. (2015, July 29). Kyrgyzstan launches Taldy-Bulak gold venture with China. *Reuters*.

Elmer, K. (2020, October 12). Kyrgyzstan unrest "may scare off" future Chinese, other foreign investors. *South China Morning Post*.

Embassy of the People's Republic of China in the Kyrgyz Republic. (2020). *Ambassador Du Dewen accepted an exclusive interview with Silk Road New Observation on China-Kyrgyzstan anti-epidemic cooperation*. Embassy of the People's Republic of China in the Kyrgyz Republic. Retrieved on 7 May 2021, from http://kg.chineseembassy.org/chn/dssghd/t1805775.htm

Engvall, J. (2016). *The state as investment market: An analytical framework for interpreting politics and bureaucracy in Kyrgyzstan*. University of Pittsburgh Press.

Eurasianet. (2019). Kyrgyzstan: Another week, another anti-China rally. *Eurasianet*. Retrieved on 8 May 2021, from https://eurasianet.org/kyrgyzstan-another-week-another-anti-china-rally

Extractive Industries Transparency Initiative (EITI). (2021). *Kyrgyz Republic, Extractive Industries Transparency Initiative*. Retrieved on 7 May 2021, from https://eiti.org/es/implementing_country/39

Fitzpatrick, M. (1983). The definition and assessment of political risk in international business: A review of the literature. *Academy of Management Review, 8*(2), 249–254. https://doi.org/10.5465/amr.1983.4284734

Hurley, J., Morris, S., & Portelance, G. (2019). Examining the debt implications of the Belt and Road Initiative from a policy perspective. *Journal of Infrastructure, Policy and Development, 3*(1), 139.

International Monetary Fund. (2006). *Kyrgyz Republic: Enhanced initiative for heavily indebted poor countries: Preliminary document*. International Monetary Fund.

International Monetary Fund (IMF). (2019). *Kyrgyz Republic: 2019 Article IV Consultation* (Press Release and Staff Report 19/208). International Monetary Fund.
International Monetary Fund (IMF). (2020). *Policy responses to COVID19—Policy tracker*. IMF. Retrieved on 5 November 2020, from https://www.imf.org/en/Topics/imf-and-covid19/Policy-Responses-to-COVID-19
Ismailbekova, A. (2018). *Informal governance and corruption—Transcending the principal agent and collective action paradigms in Kyrgyzstan*. Basel Institute on Governance.
Janmaimool, P., & Watanabe, T. (2014). Evaluating determinants of environmental risk perception for risk management in contaminated sites. *International Journal of Environmental Research and Public Health, 11*(6). https://doi.org/10.3390/ijerph110606291
Jones, L., & Hameiri, S. (2020). *Debunking the myth of "debt-trap diplomacy": How recipient countries shape China's Belt and Road Initiative*. Chatham House.
Kabar. (2019, June 13). 24 documents worth USD 7.7 billion are signed during the Kyrgyzstan-China Business Forum (list). *Kabar*.
Kabar. (2021, February 5). Kyrgyz Foreign Minister met with the Chinese Ambassador. *Kabar*.
Kainazarova, C. (2018). *New trends in Kyrgyz foreign policy* (MPRA Paper 86491). University Library of Munich.
Kratz, A., Feng, A., & Wright, L. (2019). New data on the "debt trap" question. *Rhodium Group*. Retrieved on 29 July 2019, from https://rhg.com/research/new-data-on-the-debt-trap-question/
Kudryavtseva, M. (2016). Corruption and unpredictability of government—Main problems for investors in Kyrgyzstan. *24.kg*. Retrieved on 7 May 2019, from https://24.kg/archive/en/economics/179047-news24.html/
Libarkin, J. C., Gold, A. U., Harris, S. E., McNeal, K. S., & Bowles, R. P. (2018). A new, valid measure of climate change understanding: Associations with risk perception. *Climatic Change, 150*(3), 403–416. https://doi.org/10.1007/s10584-018-2279-y
Li, Q., & Ye, M. (2019). China's emerging partnership network: What, who, where, when and why. *International Trade, Politics and Development, 3*(2), 66–81. https://doi.org/10.1108/ITPD-05-2019-0004
Martini, M. (2013). *Overview of corruption and anti-corruption in Kyrgyzstan*. Transparency International.
McKellar, R. (2016). *A short guide to political risk* (1st ed.). Routledge. https://doi.org/10.4324/9781315263632
Ministry of Foreign Affairs (MFA). (2019). *Joint Statement of the People's Republic of China and the Kyrgyz Republic on Further Deepening the Comprehensive Strategic Partnership*. Ministry of Foreign Affairs. Retrieved on 7 May 2021, from https://www.fmprc.gov.cn/web/gjhdq_676201/gj_676203/yz_676205/1206_676548/1207_676560/t1671981.shtml
Mogilevskii, R. (2012). *Trends and patterns in foreign trade of Central Asian countries* (Working Paper 1). University of Central Asia.
Mogilevskii, R. (2019). *Kyrgyzstan and the Belt and Road Initiative* (Working Paper 50). University of Central Asia.
National Bank of the Republic of Kyrgyzstan. (2019). *Annual Report 2018*. National Bank of the Republic of Kyrgyzstan.
NSC. (n.d.). *Manufacturing statistics*. National Statistical Committee.
OECD and ILO. (2017). *How immigrants contribute to Kyrgyzstan's economy*. ILO and OECD Publishing.
OECD, IMF, ILO, and Interstate Statistical Committee of the Commonwealth of Independent States. (2002). *Measuring the non-observed economy: A handbook*. OECD.
Omanga, E., Ulmer, L., Berhane, Z., & Gatari, M. (2014). Industrial air pollution in rural Kenya: Community awareness, risk perception and associations between risk variables. *BMC Public Health, 14*(1), 377. https://doi.org/10.1186/1471-2458-14-377
Opitz-Stapleton, S., Nadin, R., Kellett, J., Calderone, M., Quevedo, A., Peters, K., & Mayhew, L. (2019). *Risk-informed development: From crisis to resilience*. ODI.

Oya, C., & Schaefer, F. (2019). *Chinese firms and employment dynamics in Africa: A comparative analysis*. SOAS University of London.

Pak, M. (2020, October 7). Budget deficit, lawsuits in international courts, job losses—Trade union on the consequences of attacks on fields. *Economist.kg*.

Peng, Y., Zhu, X., Zhang, F., Huang, L., Xue, J., & Xu, Y. (2018). Farmers' risk perception of concentrated rural settlement development after the 5.12 Sichuan Earthquake. *Habitat International, 71*, 169–176. https://doi.org/10.1016/j.habitatint.2017.11.008

Putz, C. (2018, May 31). The Bishkek Power Plant Saga: Former Kyrgyz Prime Minister faces corruption charges. *The Diplomat*.

Radio Free Europe/Radio Liberty. (2018). *SECOND Ex-PM jailed as Kyrgyz power-plant corruption case grows*. Radio Free Europe/Radio Liberty.

Reuters. (2019, January 17). Kyrgyz police disperse anti-Chinese rally. *Reuters*.

Reynolds, S. (2018). For Tajikistan, the Belt and Road is paved with good intentions. *The National Interest*.

Sautman, B., & Yan, H. (2015). *Localizing Chinese enterprises in Africa: From myths to policies* (HKUST IEMS Thought Leadership Brief Series 2015-05). HKUST Institute for Emerging Market Studies.

Sethi, S. P., & Luther, K. A. N. (1986). Political risk analysis and direct foreign investment: Some problems of definition and measurement. *California Management Review, 28*(2), 57–68. https://doi.org/10.2307/41165184

Simon, J. D. (1984). A theoretical perspective on political risk. *Journal of International Business Studies, 15*(3), 123–143. https://doi.org/10.1057/palgrave.jibs.8490499

Singh, A. (2020). The myth of "debt-trap diplomacy" and realities of Chinese development finance. *Third World Quarterly*, 1–15. https://doi.org/10.1080/01436597.2020.1807318

Sullivan-Wiley, K. A., & Short Gianotti, A. G. (2017). Risk perception in a multi-hazard environment. *World Development, 97*, 138–152. https://doi.org/10.1016/j.worlddev.2017.04.002

TCA. (2012, October 24). Fight halts work at Altynken gold mine. *The Times of Central Asia*.

The Diplomat. (2017, May 12). Belt and Road Attendees List. *The Diplomat*.

The Economist. (2021, January 16). Sadyr Japarov is elected president of Kyrgyzstan in a landslide. *The Economist*.

Thomas, A. V., Kalidindi, S. N., & Ananthanarayanan, K. (2003). Risk perception analysis of BOT road project participants in India. *Construction Management and Economics, 21*(4), 393–407. https://doi.org/10.1080/0144619032000064127

Transparency International. (n.d.). *Corruption Perceptions Index*. Retrieved on 7 May 2021, from https://www.transparency.org/en/cpi/2020/index/nzl

van der Kley, D. (2017, December 1). Can Central Asia's poorest states pay back their debts to China? *The Diplomat*.

van der Kley, D. (2020a). Chinese companies' localization in Kyrgyzstan and Tajikistan. *Problems of Post-Communism, 67*(3), 241–250. https://doi.org/10.1080/10758216.2020.1755314

van der Kley, D. (2020b). COVID and the new debt dynamics of Kyrgyzstan and Tajikistan. *Eurasianet*.

Voice of America. (2020, February 18). Kyrgyzstan opposed Chinese investment. *Voice of America, Russia Service*.

Wachtel, A. (2020, October 29). Amid warning signs, the future of Kyrgyzstan's politics is wide open. *openDemocracy*.

Wang, H. (2016). *A deeper look at China's 'Going Out' policy*. Commentary. CIGI.

Wignaraja, G., Tyson, J., Prizzon, A., & te Velde, D. W. (2018). *Asia in 2025: Development prospects and challenges for middle-income countries* (Research Reports and Studies). ODI.

World Bank Group. (2018). *Kyrgyzstan—From vulnerability to prosperity: A systematic country diagnostic*. Systematic Country Diagnostic. World Bank.

World Bank Group. (n.d.). *Worldwide Governance Indicators*. Retrieved on 7 May 2021, from http://info.worldbank.org/governance/wgi/Home/Reports

World Bank Group. (Various Years). *World Development Indicators*.

World Health Organization (WHO). (2021). *Kyrgyzstan: WHO Coronavirus Disease (COVID-19) Dashboard*. WHO. Retrieved on 7 May 2021, from https://www.who.int/countries/kgz/

International Organization for Migration. (2018). *World migration report 2018*. International Organisation for Migration.

Chapter 39
Belt and Road Initiative's Economic Impact on Central Asia. The Cases of Kazakhstan and Kyrgyzstan

Jildiz Nicharapova

1 Introduction

The cooperation between China and the Central Asian republics, particularly as it relates to the Belt and Road Initiative (BRI) in Central Asia, has become a highly discussed subject in the region. Despite this, there is not much research discussing the impact of the BRI on the economies of the Central Asian countries. It is evident that Central Asia is the most important region for China in terms of economic, security, and social issues. The landbound leg of the BRI is the Silk Road Economic Belt (SREB), which passes through Central Asia before reaching its desired destinations, making the region critical to China's goals for the BRI (Yazdani, 2020, p. 189).

Central Asia thus forms a key component of the BRI (Dilleen, 2017), and many works discuss the reasons behind the importance of Central Asia for China. According to some scholars, Central Asia is valuable to China because of the region's energy and mineral resources (Duarte, 2019, p. 167; Garlick, 2020, p. 7; Sim & Aminjonov, 2020, p. 21). Central Asia's geographical and cultural proximity to China's restive Xinjiang also informs Beijing's focus on these states (Sim & Aminjonov, 2020, p. 22). Since the introduction of the BRI in 2013, all cooperation projects and any cooperation between China and other nations have been related to BRI projects. According to Aminjonov et al. (2019, p. 1), projects are regarded as part of the BRI if they meet the criteria of being publicly reported as a BRI project, regardless of whether projects are fully or partially financed by the BRI financial institutions, such as the Asian Infrastructure Investment Bank (AIIB), China Development Bank, Export–Import Bank of China or New Silk Road Fund, or are implemented and financed via a bilateral or multilateral format. The BRI provides opportunities for Central Asia in return for its use as a gateway connecting China with West Asia and Europe, namely through enabling the building of infrastructure with China's financial assistance, thereby reducing logistics costs, expanding trade, and attracting

---

J. Nicharapova (✉)
ESIC International University of Kyrgyzstan, Bishkek, Kyrgyz Republic

© The Author(s), under exclusive license to Springer Nature Singapore Pte Ltd. 2023
P. A. B. Duarte et al. (eds.), *The Palgrave Handbook of Globalization with Chinese Characteristics*, https://doi.org/10.1007/978-981-19-6700-9_39

foreign investment (Kitade, 2019, p. 2). Some scholars consider Chinese projects to exclusively serve Chinese interests and not the interests of the Central Asian countries. According to Taliga (2021, p. 8) a large share of the funds injected by China into Central Asia never leaves the Chinese system: a loan granted by a Chinese bank to a Central Asian government is reinvested in the Chinese company that gets the contract and which brings Chinese equipment and a Chinese workforce to Central Asia to carry out the project. A multi-regional study of the BRI conducted by Building and Wood Worker's International (BWI) indicates that more than 60% of the BRI projects funded by China are allocated to Chinese companies. Despite the importance of Central Asia to the BRI, with the exception of a handful of research papers (Sim & Aminjonov, 2020; Kitade, 2019; Mogilevski, 2019; Taliga, 2021; Vakulchuk & Overland, 2019; Yazdani, 2020), not much research has been done which analyzes the economic cooperation between China and Central Asia or which clarifies the impact of the BRI on the economies of Central Asia.

This chapter aims to analyze the cooperation of China with two Central Asian countries—Kyrgyzstan and Kazakhstan—within the BRI and the positive and negative impacts of this on the economies of those two countries. This chapter discusses what projects have been implemented within the framework of the BRI in the economic spheres, including FDI and infrastructure project, and also questions what role the BRI plays for the countries of Central Asia in the globalization processes. Analysis of economic cooperation with China and its impacts on these two Central Asian countries was done using qualitative analysis of secondary sources (articles, book chapters, research center reports) and primary data (interviews and statistical data), with the most recent data available used in order to answer our research questions.

This chapter has a twofold objective. The first objective is to discuss the cooperation between China and these two Central Asian Republics within the BRI and the spheres of cooperation and joint projects implemented successfully between them. The second goal of this chapter is to analyze projects realized within the BRI and their impact on the economies of the Kyrgyz and Kazakh Republics. The text is organized into three main sections, each dedicated to the aforementioned fields of research, and concluding remarks. In the first we analyze the notion of BRI, what it is and what its goals are in terms of theory and empirical data. In the second part we consider cooperation between China and both the Kyrgyz Republic and Kazakhstan within the BRI. The last section discusses the implementation of joint projects and their economic impacts on the Kyrgyz Republic and the Republic of Kazakhstan. In these sections we aim to clarify whether BRI projects serve only the interests of China, or those of the Central Asian republics as well.

2 What Is the Belt and Road Initiative?

President Xi best summarized the BRI: "China will actively promote international co-operation through the Belt and Road Initiative. In doing so, we hope to achieve policy, infrastructure, trade, financial, and people-to-people connectivity and thus build a new platform for international co-operation to create new drivers of shared development" (Xi, 2017, p. 61). This suggests that China is interested not only in its own development but also the development of all participating countries in the BRI, representing more than one-third of global GDP and over half of the world's population (OECD Business Report, 2018, p. 9), especially neighbouring countries. The BRI was created not only to serve Chinese national interests but for the interests of other countries that directly or indirectly impact Chinese national interests in terms of economy development, political stability, and security.

As stated by China, the focus on connectivity within the BRI is both about facilitating trade and investment, and thereby developing of neighbouring countries, and on strategically shoring up its own security of energy, resources and food by taking a regional leadership role with its most important neighbours. The BRI thus has a very broad scope encompassing economic, strategic, and cultural connectivity (OECD, 2018, p. 10). The Belt and Road Initiative may also have some geopolitical goals associated in the linking of its neighbours economically more closely to China (Chapter 2, 2018 edition of the OECD Business and Financial Outlook, p. 4). According to the China Global Investment Tracker, the total volume of Chinese investments and contracts within the BRI in 2013–2020 was USD 755.17 billion (as of November 20, 2020), of which USD 297 billion was in the energy sector, USD 185.34 billion in transport, USD 73.22 billion in real estate, USD 57.44 billion in metals, USD 22.58 billion in utilities and USD 15.67 billion in chemicals (Taliga, 2021, p. 8).

From the point of view of theory, Freeman's (2018) conception of China's "regionalism foreign policy" and Zhou and Esteban's (2018) "regional multi-lateral cooperation" are the best defining concepts of the BRI. Freeman interprets the BRI as a "comprehensive approach to regional security whereby it seeks to engage [a] region through multiple vectors as part of an overarching security strategy to advance China's power and influence" (Freeman, 2018, p. 92). Similarly, Zhou and Esteban (2018, p. 488) see China's focus on regions via the BRI as a multifaceted grand strategy promoting China's soft power and building its role as a normative power through the promotion of different ideas and norms to redesign global governance in a way that reflects China's values, interests, and status. Most of the scholars have stated that it is necessary to combine theoretical visions from realism, liberalism, and constructivism to analyze the complex material, ideational, and institutional factors that are being generated by the emerging BRI (Garlick, 2020, p. 8). It is not possible to cover China's approach to the BRI using only one theoretical approach. We should analyze BRI goals and activities by applying different theoretical approaches as the BRI was created to meet all these approaches. From a realist point of view, we can estimate that the BRI was created for and serves Chinese national interests, including economic, political and security issues. On the other hand, in such a globalized world China cannot guarantee economic development and security without the support of its neighbours or other countries. Thus, we can analyze the BRI from a liberalist point of view as well.

China's approach to regionalism and regionalization is different from the Western conception of the terms. Kavalski (2009, p. 10) points out "what distinguishes

Western and Chinese regionalization strategies is the former's territorial ramification of regions and the latter's emphasis on practices." In other words, China's approach involves developing a sense of co-constitutive regional identity through encouraging the mutualization of shared practices and attitudes. Such an approach constitutes an expression of normative power, defined as "the ability to define what passes for 'normal' in world politics" (Manners, 2002, p. 253). The aim is to persuade regional actors—the leaders of states—to adopt a Chinese understanding of the regionalization process, which increases Chinese influence in the region. Taking up Kavalski's idea of China as a regionalizing normative power, the article by Shakhanova and Garlick in this issue examines perceptions of Russian and Kazakh elites regarding the BRI to ascertain the extent to which they have absorbed and are validating the Chinese approach to Central Asia (Garlick, 2020 p. 9).

According to Garlick, China's regionalizing focus within the framework of the BRI, and Xi Jinping's flagship foreign policy strategy is a pragmatic, expansionist strategy of economic statecraft within which political and economic aspects dynamically interact. Beijing's regional strategies are multifaceted and flexible rather than monolithic, static, and one-size-fits-all. Thus, although there are commonalities in China's approach to promoting the BRI in each region, there are also clear differences depending on the geopolitical and geo-economic dynamics of a specific region (Garlick, 2020, p. 9). China is driven primarily by economic interests in Central Asian region, as well as an attempt to "rebalance" its domestic, foreign, and security policies, so that these are less skewed in favour of eastern China and East Asia. Greater interest and involvement in Central Asia are manifestations of growing dependence on energy resources from the region and Chinese efforts to "march West" into the region and beyond. Therefore, one can assume that China's commitment to Central Asia stems largely from its own national and international economic, energy, and security concerns (Yazdani, 2020, p. 181).

3 The Economic Cooperation of China and Central Asian States Within the BRI

In this section we analyze the economic cooperation of China with two Central Asian republics, Kazakhstan and Kyrgyzstan, within the framework of the BRI. Under the BRI, there are 261 Chinese projects in Central Asia. Trade promotion and industrial development are the sectors in which there is most BRI-related activity in the region. In terms of the number of implemented projects, roads are the second key sector, followed by energy. Nevertheless, due to larger project sizes, energy receives more funding than roads. The majority of these Chinese projects in Central Asia are bilateral (Yazdani, 2020, p. 192). Two of the six BRI corridors pass through the region, connecting China. These connect China to Europe and to Iran and West Asia, respectively. One of the routes of the New Eurasian Land-Bridge BRI corridor links China and Western Europe via Kazakhstan–Russia–Belarus–Poland–Germany.

Thus, regionally these transport corridors are not just for facilitating Chinese exports because, for most of the Central Asian economies, China offers the closest port (Taliga, 2021, p. 7).

In recent years, China has been developing infrastructure in the five Central Asian countries—Kazakhstan, Kyrgyzstan, Turkmenistan, Tajikistan, and Uzbekistan—under the BRI. The region is being transformed by China's infrastructure investments, with the launch of railway logistics routes connecting Central Asia and Europe, and the development of highways, oil and gas pipelines, transmission networks, and optical fibre cables (Kitade, 2019, p. 1). The infrastructure projects for Central Asian countries are not just investments but also a means to join global trade. The governments are expecting that investments, first in the infrastructure projects, will open the landlocked region economically and attract more diversified projects with greater global attention (Taliga, 2021, p. 6). The Asian Development Bank has estimated that over USD 30 billion needs to be spent annually on infrastructure modernization until 2030 in Central Asia (Sim & Amonjonov, 2020, p. 22) given the current conditions of infrastructure in Central Asia.

Central Asia, however, is trying to attract investment in not only the transport and logistics sectors, but also the areas of agriculture, food processing, and textiles, in addition to mining, supported by abundant natural resources. Each country is making efforts to maximize the benefits gained from the BRI (Kitade, 2019, p. 2). The highest investment need, in percent of GDP, within the region of Central Asia is 7.8%. The BRI is a global project of enormous scope which could help the Central Asian countries by providing an opportunity for these republics to gain investment in order to improve their economies, develop their industry and infrastructure, export energy and, accordingly, play an affective role in the global economy (Yazdani, 2020 p. 178).

Trade between China and Central Asian countries has been increasing year over year since the independence of the Central Asian states. In the 1990s, trade between China and Central Asia amounted to less than USD 1 billion, but by 2018 China-Central Asia trade had surged to almost USD 30 billion (Sim & Aminjonov, 2020, p. 20). Central Asia exports mainly raw materials and unprocessed products to China. The Belt and Road Initiative contributes to the fact that the Central Asian region is used as a large transit zone between Europe and China, a kind of transcontinental bridge (Nuryshev, 2017). In the area of energy cooperation within the framework of the BRI, new pipelines strengthen connectivity between China and Central Asia. An oil pipeline from Kazakhstan to China and three gas pipelines from Turkmenistan to China have been constructed so far. About 85% of China's total imports of natural gas in 2017 came from Central Asia, with Turkmenistan accounting for 76% of its total imports, indicating that Central Asia is an extremely important region for China in terms of energy security (Kitade, 2019, p. 3).

Kazakhstan is a major energy resource partner for China, while Kyrgyzstan offers important transit routes and acts as the region's wholesale market for affordable Chinese consumer goods (Toktogulova & Zhuang, 2020, p. 45). Kyrgyzstan is a very important neighbour for China since they have a common frontier of more than 1000 km and the history of friendly exchanges between two nations has lasted for more than 2000 years (Yichen, 2019). Some of the projects in Kyrgyzstan under the BRI include the alternative North–South artery, which leads from Balykchy in the Northeast to Djalal-Abad in the South, the refurbishment of the heat and power station, and the new high voltage power line to connect the north and south of the country that we discuss later (Toktogulova & Zhuang, 2020, p. 46).

Beijing and Bishkek agreed that the BRI, through implementation of major projects, is of key significance to bilateral ties and regional cooperation (Xiang, 2019). This was agreed to by both sides during Chinese President Xi Jinping's state visit to the Central Asian country, during which he also attended the 19th Shanghai Cooperation Organization summit in June 2019. There is great potential for cooperation to dock the China-proposed BRI within Kyrgyzstan's National Development Strategy 2018–2040. Overlapping interests may aid to realize common development based on the principle of mutual benefits and win–win outcomes by further expanding trade, transportation cooperation, bilateral agriculture cooperation, cooperation in investment and finance, protection of the legitimate rights of citizens and legal persons, and cooperation in commerce and tourism (Xiang, 2019). We can consider all Chinese-Kyrgyz economic agreements as a part of the BRI agenda (Mogilevski, 2019, p. 5). According to the leaders of the two countries, the BRI has become a new engine for the development of their relations (Han Yichen, 2019). The cooperation between the two countries within the BRI is based on reconstruction of existing railways and highways and construction of new railways and highways, pipelines and logistic infrastructure, ensuring the transportation of energy resources such as Turkmen and Uzbek gas to China, relocation of Chinese production facilities to Kyrgyzstan in order to meet the demand for Chinese goods in the EAEU, provision of Chinese investments, improving cooperation in many fields, and strengthening border cooperation by establishing a free trade zone (Taldybaeva, 2017).

According to Roman Vakulchuk and Indra Overland, Kyrgyzstan is of less interest to China due to the small size of its market and its geographic location (2019, p. 121). From the total 261 Chinese projects in Central Asia, 46 have been implemented in Kyrgyzstan, with the country coming just after Kazakhstan with 102 projects. From 46 BRI and bilateral projects between China and Kyrgyzstan, 17 of these have been related to trade and industrial development, including mineral extraction, industry, agriculture, food, finance, and IT, Of the remaining, 11 have been related to rail and road connectivity, 5 to energy and 13 to people-to-people projects. According to CADGAT, total Chinese investments to Kyrgyzstan were USD 5.3 billion by 2019, with USD 1.7 billion going to rail and road, USD 2.7 billion going to energy, USD 676 million to mineral and petroleum exploration, and USD 31.5 million to agriculture and food. China possesses more strategic projects in Kyrgyzstan (with 34 in the Kyrgyz Republic as compared to 32 in Kazakhstan) than commercial (of which there are 12, compared to Kazakhstan's 70) (Aminjonov et al., 2019, p. 4). Apart from loans and direct investments, China provided Kyrgyzstan with more than USD 300 million non-refundable aid to build roads and supply potable water to remote regions (Taliga, 2021, p. 8). There were about 400 Chinese companies and 170 joint Chinese–Kyrgyz ventures operating in Kyrgyzstan in 2019. Chinese investments and contracts in Kyrgyzstan have amounted to USD 4.34 billion since 2013, of which

USD 2.5 billion has been put into the energy sector, USD 1.69 billion into transport, and USD 150 million into metals (Taliga, 2021, p. 13).

In recent years, the Government of China has supported the implementation of several major infrastructure projects in Kyrgyzstan, with the total amount of loans at USD 2.1 billion. If one adds to this amount the grants and costs of "resources in exchange for investments" project, the total costs of infrastructure projects financed by China in Kyrgyzstan climb as high as USD 2.2 billion (Mogilevski, 2019, p. 5). These loans went mostly to road and energy system rehabilitation and development. From 2008 to 2017, 12 projects were implemented. Six of these were on road rehabilitation, valued at more than USD 1 billion. Four out of the twelve were on energy system rehabilitation, at more than USD 1.2 billion for the modernization of electricity transmission in the south of Kyrgyzstan, construction of the 500 kV Datka Kemin electricity transmission and 500 kV Datka substation, modernizing the Bishkek heat and power plant. More than USD 1 billion has been allotted to be spent for a Kyrgyzstan–China gas pipeline in the future. For the urban development of Bishkek, there has been USD 120 million allotted (China-Kyrgyzstan intergovernmental agreements). The road projects are part of the CAREC corridors that have been designed to improve transportation links in Central Asia and connect the region with China, South and West Asia, and Europe. The Bishkek-Naryn-Torugart Road is part of the CAREC Corridor 1c, the alternative North–South Road is the road connecting Corridors 1 and 3, and the Osh-Sarytash-Irkeshtam and Osh-Batken-Isfana Roads are parts of Corridor 2 (Mogilevski, 2019, p. 9). Significant progress has been made in the construction of the cross-border fibre optic cables for information transmission. Beijing and Bishkek have signed a cooperation agreement on fibre optic cables and have launched the project (Han Yichen, 2019). Chinese companies have built two petrol stations in Tokmok and Kara-Balta and participate in natural resource extraction (Vakulchuk & Overland, 2019, p. 122).

The Sino-Pipeline International Company Ltd started constructing Kyrgyzstan's section of the fourth arm (line D) of the Central Asia–China gas pipeline in 2019. Two oil refineries, one in Kara-Balta with a production capacity of around 800,000 tonnes a year and one in Tokmok with 450,000 tonnes, have been built by Chinese companies in the north of the country. Due to the lack of crude oil, neither refinery was operating at full capacity. Kara-Balta oil refinery suspended operations when the COVID-19 pandemic arrived. Before the stoppage, the refinery employed around 775 people—500 local staff with the rest from China (Imanaliyeva, 2020).

Reportedly, there are 11 companies operating in the mining and quarrying sector in Kyrgyzstan, each employing 500 or more people. Chinese investors own four of these companies. Zijin Mining Group, a Chinese multinational, third among the global gold corporations, owns 60% of shares in Altynken LLC, an operator of Taldybulak Levoberezhnyi, the third largest gold mine in Kyrgyzstan. Taldybulak Levoberezhny started commercial production in July 2015 and produced 133,335 oz of gold in 2019. Kyrgyzstan's Investment Promotion and Protection Agency signed a framework agreement with Daren Group, Lingbao Gold Group, and Full Gold Mining on the construction of a new gold processing plant in June 2019 (Taliga, 2021, p. 14).

Since 2012, China has become the largest source of foreign direct investments into the economy of Kyrgyzstan; for 2006–2017, the cumulative gross Chinese FDI inflow was equal to USD 2.3 billion. For this period, Chinese FDI constituted 25–50% of total FDI into Kyrgyzstan (National Statistic Committee of KR, 2017). Key Chinese FDI sectors are geological explorations, the mining industry, and the production of refined petroleum products. Mining-related FDI (geological explorations and the mining industry) concentrates on the development of gold deposits in Kyrgyzstan. Chinese companies operate some 10 medium-sized mines producing gold-copper concentrate, which is exported for refining to China. Chinese FDI in other sectors of the Kyrgyz economy (e.g. retail trade, construction materials production, food processing) is relatively minor. In 2009, Chinese Eximbank financed the construction of a large cement plant in southern Kyrgyzstan. Later, however, this plant was sold to Kazakh investors (Mogilevski, 2019, pp. 10–11). Chinese investors abandoned a plan to build a trade and logistics centre for about USD 280 million in the Naryn region in February 2020 due to the worsening business climate (Taliga, 2021, p. 13). The largest economic development programmes in Kazakhstan are in some way associated with China. At the end of 2014, Kazakhstan developed the "Nurly Jol" State Programme for Infrastructure Development for 2015–2019, which was specifically intended to fit with the projects allocated by China within the framework of OBOR (Izimov & Muratalieva, 2018, p. 131). Kazakhstan has already invested USD 5 billion in the development of the transport routes, railways, and highways within Kazakhstan itself and, in the next three years, has planned to invest another USD 9 billion so that Astana is connected with all regions via a large road and rail network (Nuryshev, 2017).

The New Eurasian Land Bridge, a rail route connecting China with Europe via Kazakhstan, is attracting particular attention as a major infrastructure project in the region. The number of freight trains between China and Europe has increased sharply from 17 in 2011 to 6,300 in 2018 (Kitade, 2019, p. 2). Pairing of the Nurly Zhol with the Chinese initiative of the Silk Road Economic Belt is very important for Kazakhstan to unite transport corridors that go from China through Kazakhstan to other regions. In September 2016, during the G20 summit in Hangzhou, a cooperation plan was signed between China and Kazakhstan to link the Nurly Zhol and the Silk Road Economic Belt programmes. The spheres of cooperation are transport, trade, industry, tourism, and energy (Nuryshev, 2017).

Kazakhstan is a leading country in attracting Chinese investment to Central Asia. The total amount of Chinese investments and contracts in Kazakhstan within the framework of the BRI (in 2013–2020) was USD 18.69 billion according to the China Global Investment Tracker (AEI, 2021). More than half of the total amount, USD 9.53 billion, was allocated to the energy sector, while USD 3.81 billion has been invested in transport, USD 2.65 billion in chemicals, and USD 1.91 billion in metals. China's dependence on oil and gas imports is expected to continue growing and China's share is about 24% of oil production and 13% of gas production in Kazakhstan (Taliga, 2021, p. 11). China's thirst for fossil fuels plays a key role in the implementation of the Silk Road Economic Belt in Kazakhstan (Garlick, 2020, p. 7). The government of Kazakhstan has talked about more than 50 Chinese investment projects (mining, chemicals, and petrochemicals among others) since 2015. In September 2019 an overview listed 55 joint Kazakh–Chinese projects worth USD 27.6 billion that have been or will be implemented in the country starting from 2015. Of them, 15 projects are complete, 11 are ongoing and 29 are under consideration (Taliga, 2021, p. 11). The main focus has been on the oil and gas industry where there are many joint ventures with Chinese shareholders. The main actor is the China National Petroleum Corporation (CNPC), which acquired a stake in Kazakhstan's AktobeMunaiGas in 1997 and owns 85.42% of shares in the company. In addition to several oilfield development projects in the country, CNPC is involved in two crude oil pipelines (one of them Kazakhstan-China) as well as a Kazakhstan–China gas pipeline (Taliga, 2021, p. 11).

One of the subsidiaries of CNPC in Kazakhstan is PetroKazakhstan—a group of companies 67% owned by CNPC and 33% owned by the national joint stock company KazMunaiGas. PetroKazakhstan is engaged in the acquisition, exploration, development, and production of oil and gas, in particular at Kumkol Resources in Kyzyl-Orda (in the south of the country), as well as in the sale of oil and refined products (Taliga, 2021, p. 11). The authorities in Kazakhstan, after discussion with social partners, later required that investors must recruit 70% of the workforce from Kazakhstan. Currently, Chinese companies control over a quarter of oil production in Kazakhstan and Beijing is interested in boosting the level of oil imports (Sim & Aminjonov, 2020, p. 22). Chinese companies have expanded their activities in agriculture in recent years. For example, of the 22 Chinese companies active in Akmola province, 17 are operating in agriculture. This is also true of 22 of the 59 Chinese companies in East-Kazakhstan (Taliga, 2021, p. 13). According to the Ambassador of Kazakhstan to China Nuryshev, when the idea of creating the Silk Road Economic Belt was voiced, the emphasis was on the corridors that pass through Kazakhstan, then to Russia and Europe. The corridor through Kazakhstan to the countries of Central Asia was also mentioned, as was another corridor that flows through the countries of Central Asia further into the Gulf region (Nuryshev, 2017). The launch of the China–Kazakhstan Railway and China–Kazakhstan International Border Cooperation Centre at Khorgos in December 2011 also tightened the business relationship between the two countries (Toktogulova & Zhuang, 2020, p. 45).

4 Impacts on the Economies of the Central Asian States

BRI projects are often presented as drivers of economic development by the Central Asian regimes. However, the unprecedented dependence of Central Asia on Chinese investments and infrastructure interconnectivity, and the fact that most of the national economic development programmes are now aligned with the BRI, masks several risks for China and, by extension, for the Central Asian regimes (Sim & Aminjonov, 2020, p. 23). In this part of the chapter, we analyze the impacts of implementing BRI projects on the Kyrgyz Republic and the Republic of Kazakhstan economies. Central Asian authorities perceive the physical infrastructure development projects promoted by BRI initiative to be critical for the growth of the local economies (Sim &

Aminjonov, 2020, p. 23). China is expecting to create stable economies through the construction of new roads, railroads, and gas and oil pipelines in territories endowed with natural resources (Yazdani, 2020, p. 190). According to Yazdani (2020, p. 191) Chinese credit in the framework of the BRI increases economic activity and facilitates trade growth in Central Asia. This can contribute to the globality of Central Asia.

The total trade turnover between China and Central Asia grew 60-fold between 1991 and 2016, from USD 0.5 billion to USD 30 billion (excluding significant informal trade by small-scale entrepreneurs) (Vakulchuk & Overland, 2019, p. 115). The BRI would provide the region's countries with the opportunity to advance in the development of their infrastructure and economy, and to expand their global and regional trade and transportation networks (Yazdani, 2020 p. 185). In 2011–2017, total money committed to project implementation in the Kyrgyz Republic was USD 4.1 billion, USD 2.2 billion for infrastructure projects and USD 1.9 billion in FDI; however, contribution to aggregate demand was much smaller according to Roman Mogilevskii since most of these resources went to the import of goods and services from China. According to him, the contribution of these projects to employment in Kyrgyzstan is not significant since it composes only 0.1–0.3% of the country's total employment. Enterprises with Chinese participation paid USD 3.2 millions of tax to the Kyrgyz budget. This composes 2.5% of state budget (Finance Ministry of Kyrgyz Republic). Concerning trade, Kyrgyz exports to China in 2016–2017 was 2% of the country's total exports (mostly gold exports), while imports of machinery and equipment from China in 2011–2017 was 6–10% of total imports (Mogilevski, 2019, p. 13).

All the infrastructure projects have been implemented by the Chinese companies CRBC and TBEA Co. Ltd which use mostly Chinese labour force as well as machinery, equipment, and materials which have been imported from China (Mogilevski, 2019, p. 9). The problem is that China provides loans to countries under the condition that they use Chinese technologies and hire Chinese workers. This does not address the high unemployment rates which push Kyrgyzstan and Tajikistan to send migrant workers to Russia (Kitade, 2019, p. 5). Central Asian authorities often highlight that the Silk Road Economic Belt will not simply transform Central Asia into a transit region but will also boost domestic economies and raise living standards. Current projects, however, suggest otherwise. Because Tajikistan and Kyrgyzstan do not have strong local content requirements, local workers often get short shrift and money goes to Chinese contractors. For instance, a workforce made up of 30% locals built Kyrgyzstan's Osh-Sarytash-Irkeshtam and Bishkek-Naryn-Torugat Roads, partly funded by China, and 70% Chinese workers, with 60% imported raw materials. Consequently, benefits for the local economy are tempered as mostly Chinese materials, technology, equipment, and labour force are used (Sim & Aminjonov, 2020, p. 25).

On people-to-people cooperation between the countries, the Director of the National Institute for Strategic Studies of the Kyrgyz Republic, Kuvanychbek Shadybekov, said infrastructure projects improve the quality of life of the population living in the region and, in this regard, the most important thing is to find common ground throughout this initiative in order to maintain the interests of all involved countries (Kabar, 2019). Bilateral cooperation in education, medical care, culture, and art continues to promote mutual understanding. China has established in Kyrgyzstan four Confucius Institutes and 21 Confucius Classrooms. More than 4,600 Kyrgyz students are currently studying in China (Yichen, 2019).

The construction of roads, modernization of the energy system, and development of urban spaces are the main benefits for Kyrgyzstan. The Bishkek road network reconstruction project started in October 2016, covering 49 streets and 10 bridges with a total length of 95.4 kms. By 2019, 47 roads had been constructed and restored. The wide and flat roads have given the city a facelift (Zhonghua et al., 2019). Only 500 of the more than 1,800 villages in the country had the access to centralized water supply. To tackle the issue, the Chinese Academy of Sciences (CAS) and the Kyrgyz National Academy of Sciences co-established the Research Center for Ecology and Environment of Central Asia (RCEECA) in Bishkek in 2014. In August 2018, RCEECA established the first drinking water safety technology demonstration site in Bishkek (Zhonghua et al., 2019). According to the World Bank (2020a) the BRI and the improved cross-border transport connections can provide an anchor for increasing growth and reducing poverty in Kyrgyzstan.

According to the World Bank (2020b) Kazakhstan is likely to be among the larger beneficiaries of the BRI. As a large landlocked country, its integration with the world is highly dependent on the quality of cross-border transport. This depends as much on its own transport network as it does on those of its neighbours. For more than a decade Kazakhstan has invested substantially to improve its own network, but due to more limited improvements in trade facilitation and the limitations of resources in many neighbouring countries, the gaps have been difficult to fill. The focus of the BRI on expanding transport infrastructure and economic integration, and China's drive to connect its western and central regions more effectively to Europe and to West Asia has provided an opportunity to address these gaps. Ultimately, however, conditions for loans to Central Asian countries which state the country should use Chinese technologies and hire Chinese workers do not contribute to the development of local industry or to a reduction in unemployment in the region (Toktogulova & Zhuang, 2020, p. 48).

China and Central Asia are bound together by geography, economy, and history. (Toktogulova & Zhuang, 2020, p. 48). The BRI provides opportunities for Central Asia by serving as a gateway connecting China with West Asia and Europe, expanding trade, building infrastructure, and attracting foreign investment. Infrastructure development and intraregional cooperation under the BRI have created an unprecedented environment in Central Asia (Toktogulova & Zhuang, 2020, p. 47). As declared by Chinese officials, the new Silk Road project complies with regional States' interests and is beneficial for Central Asia (Yazdani, 2020, p. 192). The BRI can provide an opportunity for Central Asian countries to gain investment in order to strengthen their economies, develop their industry and infrastructure, export energy and, accordingly, play an affective role in the global economy. According to the author (Yazdani, 2020, p. 193) the flow of investment and projects under the framework of the BRI would contribute to the development of the Central Asian republics and would position the Central Asian region as a crucial nexus for cross-regional long-distance loops of investment, trade, infrastructure, and cultural development. However, together with their positive impacts, projects within the BRI have been strongly criticized. According to Stuenkel, Chinese officials have privately acknowledged that up to 30% of their Silk Road Economic Belt investments in Central Asia are lost to corruption (2016). China also promotes no-tender procurement, such as exclusive rights granted to the Chinese company TBEA to refurbish the Bishkek Power Plant for USD 385 million. Corruption scandals have also dogged some projects (Sim & Aminjonov, 2020, pp. 23–24).

The Chinese model of investment creates some challenges for recipient states. It's already clear that the BRI will follow the traditional Chinese investment model of using expatriate Chinese workers and Chinese technology and equipment for funded projects. That approach arguably creates very few direct benefits for the recipient state, such as critical jobs creation and development of skills and expertise in the local population (Dilleen, 2017).

5 Conclusion

This chapter discussed the economic cooperation between China and two Central Asian republics—Kazakhstan and Kyrgyzstan—and the impacts that this cooperation has on the economies of these two Central Asian countries. Based on our analysis, since 2013, the BRI has been successfully implemented in Central Asia, facilitating trade and developing infrastructure in the region and ensuring that China remains the largest investor in Central Asia. Chinese influence, particularly on the region's economic growth, is increasing. Central Asia is the most important region for the implementation of BRI projects and this region plays a huge role in China's ability to achieve the goals of the BRI. Central Asia has been an important region for China in terms of security and economic issues, and continues to be important for attaining the main goals of the BRI.

Our second finding is that China is also the main significant partner country for landlocked Central Asian countries. After the launch of the BRI in 2013, economic cooperation between Central Asia and China has intensified. China has been playing a major role in the economic development of Central Asian countries. Trade between Central Asia and China is increasing, and China has been contributing massively to the infrastructure development of the countries of the region. These infrastructure projects are important for both China, as Central Asia is a key node in the BRI, and for Central Asia where these projects are considered vital for overall development. China has thus been playing a vital role in the development of the Central Asian countries.

Most scholars stress that BRI projects and cooperation between China and Central Asia Republics mostly serve China and not Central Asia, and our next finding reveals that the projects implemented within the BRI have no or little impact on the economies of Central Asia, and may even be considered harmful for some countries such as

Kyrgyzstan and Tajikistan. Chinese money never leaves China, and the result of Chinese investment thus produces debt dependency for countries such as Kyrgyzstan and Tajikistan. China has not contributed to employment and job creation through its infrastructure development, and China's investment is not welcomed by many Central Asian countries. China's projects have also led to some trouble in these countries and contributed to corruption and Sinophobia. It is said that, among the Central Asian countries, Kazakhstan is benefiting most from the BRI. Due to the pandemic, we could not visit this country in order to clarify this assumption and, in the future, would like to continue researching this question.

Thus, the impacts of the BRI and economic cooperation with China on the Central Asian Region requires further and deeper research. There is a lack of data on projects implemented within the BRI and their official impacts on the economies of the region. The BRI phenomenon should be further analyzed, especially with regard to China-Central Asia cooperation within BRI. The theorization of the role of the BRI in Central Asia could be the most thought-provoking dispute for academics in the region.

Bibliographic References

American Enterprise Institute (AEI). (2021). *China global investment tracker*. Retrieved in November 2021, from https://www.aei.org/china-global-investment-tracker/

Aminjonov, F., Abylkasymova, A., Aimée, A., Eshchanov, B., Moldokanov, D., Overland, I., & Vakulchuk, R. (2019). BRI in CA: Overview of Chinese projects, CADGAT Academy of OSCE Bishkek. *Central Asian Data Review, 20*, 1–5.

Dilleen, C. (2017). China's Belt and Road initiative in Central Asia: Insurmountable obstacles and unmanageable risks? In Australian Strategic Policy Institute ASPI (Ed.), *The strategist*. Retrieved in November 2021, from https://www.aspistrategist.org.au/chinas-belt-road-initiative-central-asia-insurmountable-obstacles-unmanageable-risks/

Duarte, P. (2019). *Central Asia's role in China's energy security: Challenges and opportunities* (Chapter 9). https://doi.org/10.4018/978-1-5225-4203-2.ch009

Freeman, C. P. (2018). China's 'regionalism foreign policy' and China-India relations in South Asia. *Contemporary Politics, 24*(1), 81–97.

Garlick, J. (2020). *The impact of China's Belt and Road initiative: From Asia to Europe*. Routledge.

Hashimova, U. (2018). *Why Central Asia is betting on China's Belt and Road*. Retrieved in November 2021, from https://thediplomat.com/2018/08/why-central-asia-is-betting-on-chinas-belt-and-road/

Imanaliyeva, A. (2020). *Kyrgyzstan: Living in the shadow of a sleeping Chinese oil refinery, the country's largest oil refinery is no stranger to scandals*. Retrieved in November 2021, from https://eurasianet.org/kyrgyzstan-living-in-the-shadow-of-a-sleeping-chinese-oil-refinery

Izimov, R., & Muratalieva, Z. (2018). The Central Asian track of the One Belt One Road initiative: Opportunities and risks. *International Organisations Research Journal, 13*(3), 128–142 (in English). https://doi.org/10.17323/1996784520180308

Kavalski, E. (2009). Do as I do: The global politics of China's regionalization. In E. Kavalski (Ed.), *China and the global politics of regionalization* (pp. 1–16). Ashgate.

Kitade, D. (2019). Central Asia undergoing a remarkable transformation: BRI and Intraregional cooperation, Mitsui & Co. Global Strategic Studies Institute Monthly Report August 2019,

EMEA & Russia Dept., Global Economic & Political Studies Div. Mitsui & Co. Global Strategic Studies Institute.

Manners, I. (2002). Normative power Europe: A contradiction in terms? *JCMS: Journal of Common Market Studies, 40*(2), 235–258.

Mogilevski, R. (2019). *Kyrgyzstan and BRI* (UCA, Working paper #50).

Nuryshev, S. (2017). *Interview with Shahrat Nuryshev, ambassador of Kazakh Republic to PRC* (Российская газета Спецвыпуск № 115(7281)). Retrieved in November 2021, from https://rg.ru/2017/05/29/posol-kazahstana-v-knr-rasskazal-o-dvustoronnih-otnosheniiah.html

OECD. (2018). *OCED Business and financial outlook* (Chapter 2). OCED.

Sim, C., & Aminjonov, F. (2020). Avoiding the Potholes along the Silk Road Economic Belt in Central Asia. In *China's Belt and Road Initiative in Central Asia: Ambitions, risks, and realities* (special issue 2). OSCE Academy in Bishkek.

Stuenkel, O. (2016, November 6). *The Political Economy of China's New Silk Road*. Post-Western World.

Taldybaeva, D. (2017, March 28). Prospects for China–Kyrgyzstan Economic relations in the framework of Silk Road Economic Belt project, Hong Kong Trade Development Council.

Taliga, H. (2021). BRI in Central Asia, Desk Study, Friedrch Ebert Stiftung and ITUC.

Today's Processes in Central Asia and BRI Can Be Complementary. (2019, February 21). Retrieved in November 2021, from http://kabar.kg/eng/news/todays-processes-in-central-asia-and-one-belt-one-road-initiative-can-be-complementary-kyrgyz-expert/

Toktogulova, D., & Zhuang, W. A. (2020, August). Critical analysis of the Belt and Road initiative in Central Asia. *International Journal of Managerial Studies and Research* (IJMSR), *8*(8), 42–51, ISSN 2349-0330 (Print) & ISSN 2349-0349. https://doi.org/10.20431/2349-0349.0808005. Retrieved in November 2021, from www.arcjournals.org

Vakulchuk, R., & Overland, I. (2019). China's BRI through the lens of CA. In F. M. Cheung & Y.-y. Hong (Eds.), *Regional connection under the BRI*. Routledge, TFG.

World Bank. (2020a). *South Caucasus and Central Asia: The Belt and Road Initiative Kazakhstan Country case study*.

World Bank. (2020b). *South Caucasus and Central Asia: The Belt and Road Initiative Kyrgyz Republic Country case study*.

Xi, J. (2017, October 18). *Secure a decisive victory in building a moderately prosperous society in all respects and strive for the great success of socialism with Chinese characteristics for a new era*. Delivered at the 19th National Congress of the Communist Party of China.

Xiang, B. (2019). *China, Kyrgyzstan agree BRI key to bilateral ties, regional cooperation*. Xinhua. Retrieved in November 2021, from http://www.xinhuanet.com/english/2019-06/13/c_138140839.htm

Yazdani, E. (2020, May). China-Central Asia relations and role of the Belt and Road Initiative. *Chinese Business Review, 19*(5), 178–195. https://doi.org/10.17265/1537-1506/2020.05.004

Yichen, H. (2019). *BRI pushed China-Kyrgyzstan relations to the fast track*. Retrieved in November 2021, from https://news.cgtn.com/news/2019-06-13/BRI-pushed-China-Kyrgyzstan-relations-to-the-fast-track-HsRW6djHxu/index.html

Zhonghua, L., Guangjiang, P., Pei, Q., & Xinxin, X. (2019, June 17). Belt and Road construction brings benefits to Kyrgyz people. *People's Daily*. Retrieved in November 2021, from http://en.people.cn/n3/2019/0617/c90000-9588596.html

Zhou, W., & Esteban, M. (2018). Beyond balancing: China's approach towards the Belt and Road Initiative. *Journal of Contemporary China, 27*(112), 487–501.

Chapter 40
How Does BRI Affect the Degree of Globalization in Southeast Asia?

Chien-wu Alex Hsueh

1 Introduction

How the rise of China and the different degrees of Globalization among states affect the world order are both important issues that shape contemporary global politics. While Western-style Globalization revealed its limitations in the 2008 financial crisis, the successful Chinese development model and the South-South Cooperation achievement have demonstrated that a non-Western way of Globalization is also a viable alternative. This competition between Eastern- and Western-led models has intensified following China's proposal of the Belt and Road Initiative (BRI) in late 2013.

According to the Chinese government's initial announcements about the BRI project in 2013, the BRI main projects include a Belt (the Silk Road Economic Belt) that links China with Europe like the Silk Road of the Middle Ages did, a Road (the 21st Century Maritime Silk Road) that links China's main ports with the main ports in Southeast Asia and the Indian Ocean, two financial agencies (the Asian Infrastructure Investment Bank and the Silk Road Fund) that provide funding to the participating countries in infrastructure building, and six economic corridors (the China-Mongolia-Russia Corridor, the New Eurasian Land Bridge, the China-West Asia-Central Asia Corridor, the China–Pakistan Corridor, the China–Bangladesh–India Corridor, and the China-Indochina Corridor) that facilitate land transportation between China and the surrounding countries. In China's official language, the BRI aims to "help promote the economic prosperity of the countries along the Belt and Road and regional economic cooperation, strengthen exchanges and mutual learning between different civilizations, and promote world peace and development" (Vision and Actions on Jointly Building Silk Road Economic Belt and 21st-Century Maritime Silk Road, 2015).

C. A. Hsueh (✉)
National Chengchi University, Taipei, Taiwan

In the official BRI announcement declared by the National Development and Reform Commission, Ministry of Foreign Affairs, and the Ministry of Commerce of the People's Republic of China with State Council authorization in March 2015, the Chinese government described BRI as:

> The initiative to jointly build the Belt and Road, embracing the trend towards a multipolar world, economic Globalisation, cultural diversity and greater IT application, is designed to uphold the global free trade regime and the open world economy in the spirit of open regional cooperation. It is aimed at promoting orderly and free flow of economic factors, highly efficient allocation of resources and deep integration of markets; encouraging the countries along the Belt and Road to achieve economic policy coordination and carry out broader and more in-depth regional cooperation of higher standards; and jointly creating an open, inclusive and balanced regional economic cooperation architecture that benefits all. (Vision and Actions on Jointly Building Silk Road Economic Belt and 21st-Century Maritime Silk Road, 2015)

As we can see from this announcement, the main goal of the project is to promote the development of the countries along the BRI through the benefits of more free trade and regional integration facilitated by the construction of new infrastructure. Thus, BRI can be deemed as a new wave of Globalization promoted or led by China (Berlie, 2020) in countries which, for the most part, have experienced only limited exposure to the previous Globalisation efforts led by Western countries.

Although promoting the common economic development by infrastructure building is the official goal of BRI, most analysts tend to think that BRI is a multidimensional solution to solve China's own economic and diplomatic problems. On the one hand, BRI is a solution package for many of China's economic predicaments. First, the BRI construction plans can help China export its excess production capacity in certain industries including steel, cement, aluminium, glass, and shipbuilding. Second, China can also find new overseas targets with a higher rate of return for its excess capital through the BRI investments. Third, China can also promote economic development in its inland and western regions through the transportation connections and links brought about by BRI. On the other hand, BRI is also a practical alternative that can ensure China the critical resource imports without the direct competition with the established Western-led supply chains. First, the transportation infrastructure that links China with the Middle East secures the imports of oil, gas, coal, and other minerals that China requires to sustain the rapidly increasing domestic demand resulting from its continued economic development. Second, by emphasizing the linkages with the developing countries of West and Central Asia, China can also avoid a direct confrontation with the US in the Asia–Pacific region to some degree. Overall, economically, politically, and even ethically, BRI is an ideal project that can solve many of China's problems and pave the road for its further development.

After being promoted for almost eight years, BRI has produced as many controversies as it has achievements that are emphasized by the Chinese government. For one thing, the Chinese government has already invested more than USD 795,140 million in the countries that have joined BRI and most of the main infrastructure projects, such as the railroads, ports, dams, and special economic zones, are under construction or even about to be finished.[1] For another, critics of BRI claim that it is Beijing's economic statecraft that aims to influence the policies of the participating countries or squeeze their natural resources by making them more economically reliant on China or by debt diplomacy. Besides, China's rapid rise in recent years has also initiated the debate about whether it is a revisionist power that aims to change the US-led world order. People who hold this attitude argue that BRI is one of the policy tools that China may use to build a pro-China alliance amidst its great power competition with the US. Due to the controversies above, investigating the influence of BRI on the participating countries is indispensable to understanding China's influence.

This chapter aims to investigate the influence of Chinese investments, including BRI and non-BRI ventures, on the degree of Globalization of the ten member states of the Association of Southeast Asian Nations (ASEAN). There are good reasons for choosing this region. Most importantly, there is a considerable proportion of China's total BRI expenditure invested in the ten ASEAN states. From the first announcement of BRI in October 2013 till the end of June 2021, China has invested close to USD 800,000 million 115 participating countries around the world for the BRI projects (American Enterprise Institute, 2021). This amount of BRI investment is equal to 5.4% of China's GDP and 3.8% of the US' GDP for the year 2020. Among this total investment of BRI, 23.7% go to the ten ASEAN countries (refer to Table 1). It is apparent that this region is the key area of BRI. ASEAN countries are important to China for reasons of both security and economics. First, with the rapid rise of China, the Sino-US competition has gradually emerged, and this region is one place where China and the US come into competition for asserting their influence (Friedberg, 2011; Shambaugh, 2018). Second, the ASEAN region, plus South Korea, Japan, Taiwan, and India, boasts half of the world's total population and high economic growth rates. Compared to Western industrialized countries with both low birth and growth rates together with a much smaller population, this so-called "Easternization" transition (Rachman, 2016) means that for China to sustain its development and consolidate its security, this region will be the one with the highest geopolitical importance. If China can successfully integrate the markets of the participating countries in this region with the BRI investments and infrastructure, it will not only secure the supply of critical resources to sustain its development but also serve as an important advantage in the competition with other great powers over geopolitical issues.

The rest of the chapter proceeds as follows. To begin with, the first section provides an overview of China's BRI projects in the ten ASEAN states. The second section investigates the relationship between the amount of Chinese investment and the degree of Globalization in various aspects of these countries, revealing different patterns of Chinese influence. The third section discusses how these different patterns may inform us about the different policies that the ASEAN states choose when

---

[1] All the information about the BRI investment and construction statistics is from the "China Investment Tracker" dataset (Spring 2021 Edition) provided by the American Enterprise Institute (AEI), a famous think tank located in Washington D.C (American Enterprise Institute, 2021).

Table 1 BRI investments in the 18 East and Southeast Asian countries, 2013/10–2021/6

Participating country	Population (million) (2020)	GDP[a]	Freedom score (0–100) (2020)	Trade openness (% GDP) (2020) (%)	Amount of total Chinese investment received[b]	Amount of total BRI investment received[c]	2020 GDP in current USD (million)	Total Chinese investment[d] (%)	Total BRI investment[e] (%)	Number of BRI invested items	BRI troubled transaction value[f]	Troubled transaction[g] (%)
Myanmar	544	1,478	28	56	9,880	5,700	76,186	13	7	16	910 (2)	16
Thailand	698	6,094	30	98	10,140	8,360	501,795	2	2	29	300 (1)	4
Cambodia	1,672	1,212	24	126	18,220	12,530	25,291	72	50	32	290 (1)	2%
Laos	728	1,836	13	75 (2016)	29,810	22,110	19,136	156	116	36	1,380 (1)	6
Vietnam	9,734	2,123	19	209	28,910	13,290	271,158	11	5	30	1,060 (2)	8
Malaysia	3,237	11,637	51	117	43,820	30,610	336,664	13	9	61	7,350 (4)	24
Singapore	569	56,349	48	321	50,700	38,730	339,999	15	11	84	0 (0)	0
Brunei	44	32,402	28	110	4,110	3,970	12,016	34	33	3	0 (0)	0
Philippines	10,958	2,980	56	58	17,680	13,860	361,489	5	4	23	0 (0)	0
Indonesia	27,352	4,312	59	33	55,070	39,550	1,058,424	5	4	81	2,460 (3)	6

[a] Per Capita in 2010 USD (2020)
[b] (Million) (2005–2021)
[c] (Million) (2013–2021)
[d] As a percentage of its 2020 GDP
[e] As a percentage of its 2020 GDP
[f] (Million)/(Number of Items)
[g] As a percentage of total BRI investment

Source American Enterprise Institute (2021) and World Bank (2021)

responding to China's influence. Lastly, the conclusion section addresses the implications of this chapter's findings to the ongoing situation in the ASEAN countries amidst the Sino-US competition.

2 BRI in Southeast Asia

BRI includes several important construction projects in the ASEAN states. Among these are the China-Indochina Corridor and the twenty-first-Century Maritime Silk Road. The largest-scale plan, however, is the extension of the Trans-Asian Railway (TAR). TAR starts from the city of Nanning in Guangxi Province and Kunming in Yunnan Province and consists of three main routes from Kunming, China to Bangkok, Thailand: The Eastern route via Vietnam and Cambodia; the Central route via Laos and Thailand, and the Western route via Myanmar. Then, these three routes merge in Bangkok, Thailand and continue south via Malaysia all the way to Singapore. The goal of the TAR extension is to connect China and Singapore directly by rail. The other important plans in this region include the construction of Kyaukpyu Port in Myanmar, the Jakarta-Bandung (and the possible extension to Surabaya) high-speed rail in Indonesia, and several special economic zones in most of the ASEAN participating countries. Even though in almost all the participating countries there have been skirmishes between local people and the Chinese construction firms over issues related to the environment and quality of construction, China's BRI projects are going well in general, especially in Laos, Cambodia, Singapore, and the Philippines, with the strong support of these countries' leaders. As we can see in Table 1, except for Malaysia and Myanmar that have slightly more troubled transactions in some BRI items, in all the other ASEAN countries China's BRI construction and investment plans are going smoothly.

Not surprisingly, China's large-scale investment of BRI in the ASEAN countries has aroused debate over whether China will garner more policy leverage through its "economic statecraft" (Bader, 2015; Kastner, 2016) or "debt diplomacy" (Gelpern et al., 2021; Huang & Brautigam, 2020) in this region. Especially in countries like Cambodia, Laos, and Brunei, where the cumulative Chinese investment (including BRI and non-BRI projects) has surpassed more than 30% of their annual GDP (refer to Table 1). Many studies demonstrated that, to balance China's influence, these ASEAN countries have adopted various policy tools to alleviate their dependency on China (Ikenberry, 2016; Zhao & Qi, 2016). Meanwhile, in an attempt to restore its influence on the Asia–Pacific region, the US has also adopted more active policies in the region since the Obama administration (2009/1~2017/1), such as the "America's Pacific Century" and the "Pivot to Asia" policy declarations (Clinton, 2011) and the promotion of the Trans-Pacific Partnership (TPP, which later became the Comprehensive and Progressive Agreement for Trans-Pacific Partnership [CPTPP] in 2017 after Trump withdrew from the TPP). Following Obama, the Trump administration (2017/1~2021/1) adopted a more antagonistic attitude towards China's influence in ASEAN. There is abundant research on Sino-US competition and how the ASEAN states have responded to it (Chung, 2009; Goh & Simon, 2008; Ikenberry, 2016; Kuik, 2016; Liff & Ikenberry, 2014; Lim & Cooper, 2015; Ross, 2006; Shambaugh, 2018). Essentially, this question is about how the ASEAN governments respond to the external economic and political pressures on their society—that is, Globalization—amid their pursuit of prosperity, security, and autonomy. Therefore, the next section analyzes this question from another point of view by discussing how BRI affects the degree of Globalization in the ASEAN states.

3   BRI and Globalization in the Ten ASEAN States

Globalization is a concept with diverse meanings and various dimensions. Most studies measure countries' degrees of Globalisation through economic dimensions such as trade openness, financial openness, and the internationalization of production (supply chains) when investigating the influence of Globalisation on the states (Garrett, 1998). However, looking at only the economic factors fails to capture the other important aspects of Globalisation because Globalisation also involves "the diffusion of government policies" and "the spread of trans-planetary or supra-territorial connections between people" (Gygli et al., 2019, p. 546). Besides, states will try to take advantage of economic Globalization and avoid the unwanted parts of it through political policy tools (Solingen, 2001). Therefore, a multidimensional measurement is needed to grasp states' degrees of Globalization.

According to a popularly used database in empirical research—the KOF Globalization Index developed by Axel Dreher at the Swiss Federal Institute of Technology Zurich in Switzerland (Dreher, 2006; Gygli et al., 2019), a state's Globalization score is determined by its degree of connection with other countries in economic, social, and political dimensions. The higher the connection between a certain country and other countries in economic (such as the volume of trade and capital flows), social (such as the frequency of interpersonal connections), and political issues (such as the interaction with international organizations), the more that state is globalized. To start, we will first investigate how BRI investments affect the overall degree of Globalization in the ASEAN states.

In this chapter, all Chinese investments—not only those that are included in BRI—are taken into consideration because of the following reasons. First, most of the Chinese investments in this region before the promotion of BRI were for similar projects such as railroads, highways, and minerals. Second, after 2017, the Chinese government has included almost all the previous investments as part of the BRI projects. Third, not only the Chinese investments in the name of BRI but also all the other Chinese FDI will provide the Chinese government with political and economic leverage over these countries. Thus, it is both practically impossible and theoretically unnecessary to clearly distinguish which items belong to BRI and which ones do not. Besides, since BRI has only been promoted for less than eight years, observing the Chinese investment projects for a longer period can provide us with a more complete picture to understand China's influence over the ASEAN countries.

Figure 1 demonstrates the correlation between cumulative Chinese investments and the overall degree of Globalization in the ten ASEAN states. Indonesia, Laos, Malaysia, Singapore, and Vietnam are the countries that have received the greatest amounts of Chinese investments. Most of their received investments belong to BRI projects after 2013. These countries are the members of the TAR Eastern route. As Fig. 1 shows, with the increase in Chinese investment, most of the ASEAN states' overall degrees of Globalization increase as well (except for Brunei, Indonesia, the Philippines, and Singapore, where the overall degrees of Globalization have remained stable before and after the influx of Chinese capital). This effect is partially the result of increased interactions with China on economic, social, and political issues after receiving significant Chinese investment. At first glance, Chinese investment, whether made in the name of BRI or not, seems to slightly positively correlate with the increased degree of Globalization in general in the ten ASEAN states.

In addition, Fig. 1 also shows that, before the announcement of BRI in late 2013, China had stably invested in the ASEAN states for many years. In all of the ten ASEAN states, there is no significant discontinuity (a sudden increase or decrease) in the fluctuations of Chinese investment. This fact suggests that China had paid attention to developing its relationship with the ASEAN states for a long time prior to BRI, which echoes the "four deployments" strategy that former Chinese President Hu Jintao declared in 2004: "Major powers are the key, surrounding (peripheral) areas are the first priority, developing countries are the foundation, and multilateral forums are the important stage" (*People's Daily*, 2004). China had actively managed its relationships with the ASEAN states long before the US announced its "Pivot to Asia" policy in 2012, India's "Act East" Policy was announced in 2014, Taiwan's

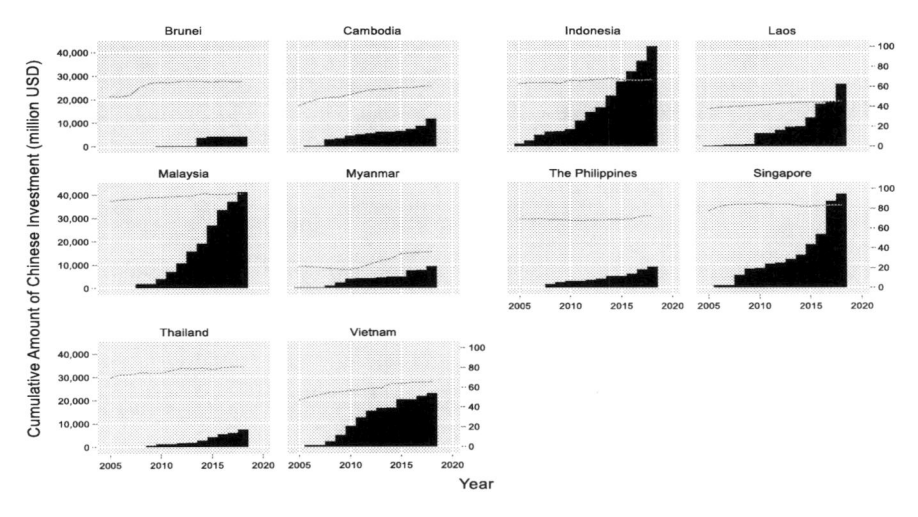

Fig. 1 Cumulative Chinese investment and the degree of globalization (Ten ASEAN States, 2005~2018) (*Note* Bars are the cumulative amount of Chinese investments since 2005. Lines are the value of the KOF Globalization index. *Source* American Enterprise Institute [2021], Dreher [2006] and Gygli et al. [2019])

New Southbound Policy came into effect in 2016, and South Korea's New Southern Policy was initiated in 2017.

However, the KOF Globalization index has some limitations if we want to further analyze the influence of Chinese investment in the ASEAN countries. First, the KOF index tends to have an increase trend over time because of the way it measures the degree of Globalization.[2] Thus, most of the time the results reveal a single-direction trend that shows the countries are becoming more and more globalized with the increase of time. This provides us only limited information to evaluate how Chinese investment changes the degree of Globalization of the target states. Second, the composite KOF index does not distinguish whether the target states' degree of Globalization is due to their increased connections with China or with other countries other than China. Therefore, this study further analyzes this question with the investigation of other stand-alone indexes to get a more complete picture of how Chinese investment affects Globalization in the ASEAN states. In addition, this chapter considers the relationship between Chinese investment and the changes in trade, FDI, and the number of international cooperation events—the most important indexes to measure a state's degree of interaction with other states—in each of the ASEAN states respectively to further find out how Chinese investment correlates with their interactions with other countries. This may provide us with a clearer picture to show how Chinese investment affects the ASEAN states' Globalization footprints.

4 Chinese Investment and Trade

Since China joined the World Trade Organization in 2001, the trade flows between China and other countries has increased rapidly year by year. In 2000, the total trade volume between China and the world was USD 481,469 million, and it soon reached USD 4,646,192 million in 2020 (UN, 2021), almost a ten-fold increase within a period of 20 years. Trade becomes the main engine that boosts China's rapid growth. The trade flows between China and the ASEAN states have also increased rapidly since 2001. In 2004, China surpassed the US to become the largest trade partner of the ASEAN states.

Figure 2 analyzes the correlation between cumulative Chinese investment and the ASEAN states' trade flows with China and with other countries. In contrast to the outcome of the overall degree of Globalization that the KOF index shows, with the increase of Chinese investment, ASEAN states see their trade relationships develop differently. We can easily distinguish three different types in Fig. 2. The first appears in Brunei, Cambodia, Laos, and Myanmar. Albeit receiving more and more Chinese investment, these countries do not further develop more extensive trade relationships with China or other countries. That is, their degree of Globalization in terms of trade

---

[2] For example, many of the KOF indexes have an increasing characteristic such as the volume of trade (which tends to increase year by year due to inflation) and the cumulative number of international organizations in which the state participates.

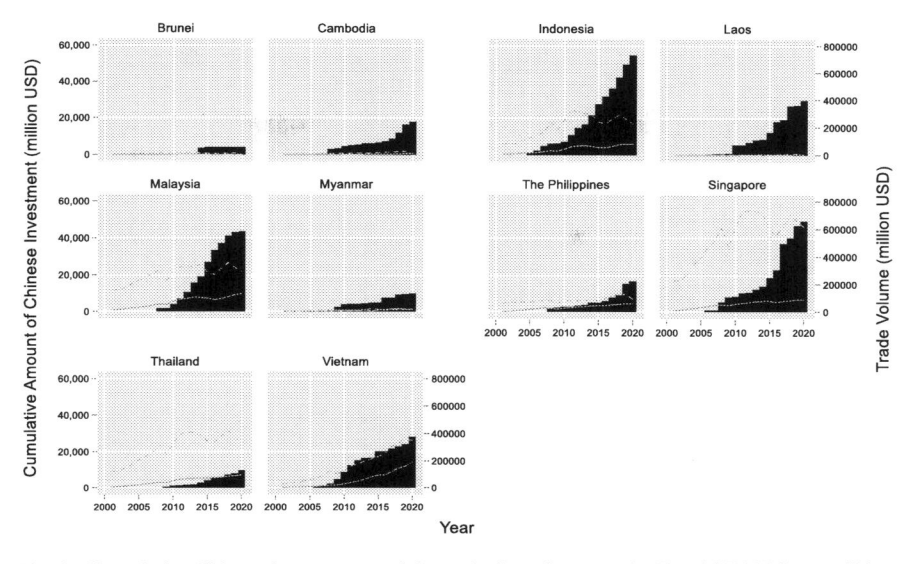

Fig. 2 Cumulative Chinese investment and the trade flows between the Ten ASEAN States, China, and Other Countries, 2001~2020 (*Note* Bars are the cumulative amount of Chinese investment since 2005. Solid lines are the trade volume between the country and China. Dash lines are the trade volume between the country and other countries. *Source* American Enterprise Institute [2021] and United Nations [2021])

does not see a notable increase after receiving Chinese investment. The second type is the case of the Philippines, which maintains a very similar degree in its trade relationship with China and other countries during these two decades. The last is the development of the other half of the ASEAN states, including Indonesia, Malaysia, Singapore, Thailand, and Vietnam, that with the increase in Chinese investment, they develop more and deeper trade relationships with both China and other countries. They become more and more globalized in terms of trade. It is worth noting that their trade relationships with other countries grow much faster than that with China. In sum, Chinese investment seems to result in different effects on the ASEAN states' trade Globalization.

5 Chinese Investments and FDI

The amount of foreign direct investment (FDI) that China invests overseas has also increased rapidly with its concurrent economic growth. In 2001, China had a USD 9,696 million net outflow of FDI,[3] which grew to about USD 109,922 million in 2020, an increase of more than 11 times within 20 years (World Bank, 2021). For the

---

[3] FDI net outflows/inflows are the value of outward/inward direct investment made by non-resident investors in the reporting economy.

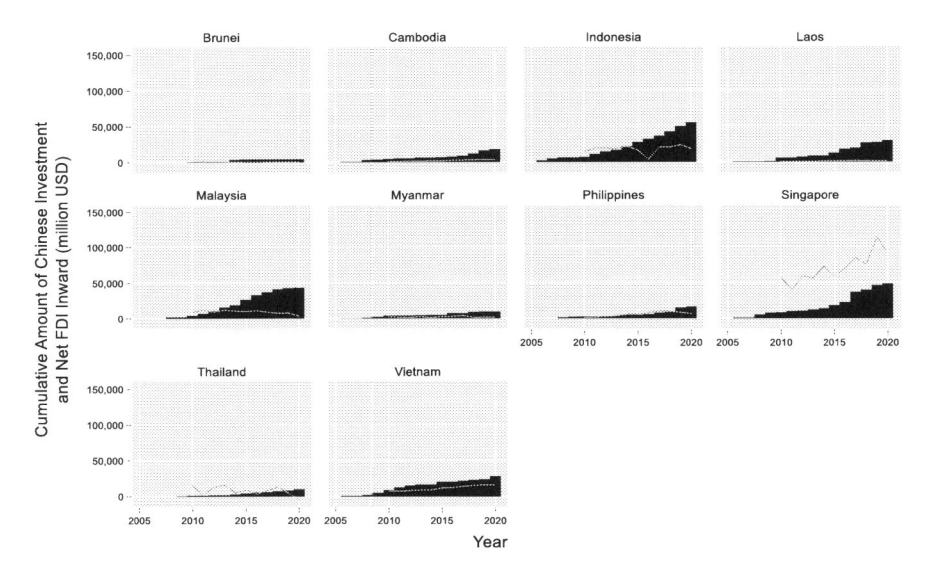

Fig. 3 Cumulative Chinese investment and net FDI inward of the ten ASEAN States, 2005~2020 (*Note* Bars are the cumulative amount of Chinese investment since 2005. Solid lines are the net FDI inward. *Source* American Enterprise Institute [2021], ASEAN [2021], and World Bank [2021])

ASEAN region, from 2015 to 2020, about 10% of the total FDI that the ASEAN states received came from the US, 9% from the other ASEAN states, 7% from countries in the European Union, 6% from Japan, 4% from China, 2% from South Korea, 1% from Taiwan, and the remaining 60% from other countries around the world (ASEAN Data Portal, 2021). Although the trade flows between ASEAN and China have grown rapidly in recent years, the US remains the most important source of FDI for the ASEAN states at this time (Fig. 3).

However, the correlation between cumulative Chinese investment and the net FDI inwards to the ASEAN states is different from the change in trade flows. With the increase of Chinese investments, only Singapore and Vietnam can attract more FDI. The other eight states remain at the same level or become an even less attractive destination for international capital. This situation does not improve even after their BRI infrastructure projects are in progress or completed. Thus, in terms of FDI, Chinese investment, albeit most of which is for developing infrastructure that is supposed to be helpful for improving their competitiveness and economic development, does not make these countries more competitive in attracting FDI. In sum, Chinese investment seems to have limited effects on improving the ASEAN states' degree of Globalization in terms of attracting international capital.

6 Chinese Investment and International Cooperation

We have seen that Chinese investment may influence ASEAN states differently when it comes to trade and their ability to attract FDI. Next, we investigate the correlation between Chinese investments and the ASEAN states' political relationship with China and other countries—the political dimension of Globalization. An intuitive way to gauge countries' political dimensions of Globalization is to see whether the countries have more international cooperation with other countries. To investigate this systematically, data from the Integrated Crisis Early Warning System (ICEWS) Dataset is used to calculate the number of events of international cooperation between each of the ASEAN states and China as well as with other countries. The ICEWS database is a big-data database, where the researchers use computers to automatically code all the events reported by the mainstream news media every second since the project's inception on January 1st, 1995 up through the present (Boschee et al., 2015). The advantage of using big data to count the number of interactions between countries is to alleviate researchers' potential selection bias. In ICEWS, each of the events is coded into the form of "who (senders) did what to whom (targets) at what time." Then, each coded event is transformed with the Conflict and Mediation Event Observations (CAMEO) categories and then calculated into numeric scores with the Goldstein conflict-cooperation scale (Goldstein, 1992). Each CAMEO event code is assigned a numeric score from -10 (the most conflictual behavior) to $+10$ (the most cooperative behavior), capturing the theoretical potential impact that type of event will have on the stability of a country. The entire CAMEO event taxonomy is ultimately organized under four primary classifications: Material Cooperation (Goldstein score of around -2 to 8), Verbal Cooperation (Goldstein score of around -2 to 10), Verbal Conflict (Goldstein score of around -7.5 to 0), and Material Conflict (Goldstein score of around -10 to 0), from left to right indicating an increasing conflictual posture. Only the number of the highest level of bilateral cooperation, namely Material Cooperation, is counted as the number of bilateral cooperation events. The number of Verbal Cooperation events is excluded to avoid taking trivial lip-service agreements into account. Figure 4 demonstrates the change of the number of international cooperation events of each ASEAN state with the Chinese investment they received. The solid lines denote the number of cooperation events between the country and China, while the dash lines are the number of cooperation events between the country and other countries. Thus, three clear-cut patterns emerge from among the ASEAN states.

The first pattern that comes to light is the situation in Brunei and Myanmar, both of which received relatively low investment from China and have a low number of cooperative interactions with China and other countries. The second is the situation in Cambodia and Laos. With the increase in Chinese investment, the number of their cooperative events with China and other countries remained at relatively similar levels. That is, Chinese investment seems to have no discernable impact on their number of cooperative events with China or other countries. The third pattern is the situation in the remaining six ASEAN states, namely Indonesia, Malaysia, the Philippines, Singapore, Thailand, and Vietnam. In these countries, with the increase

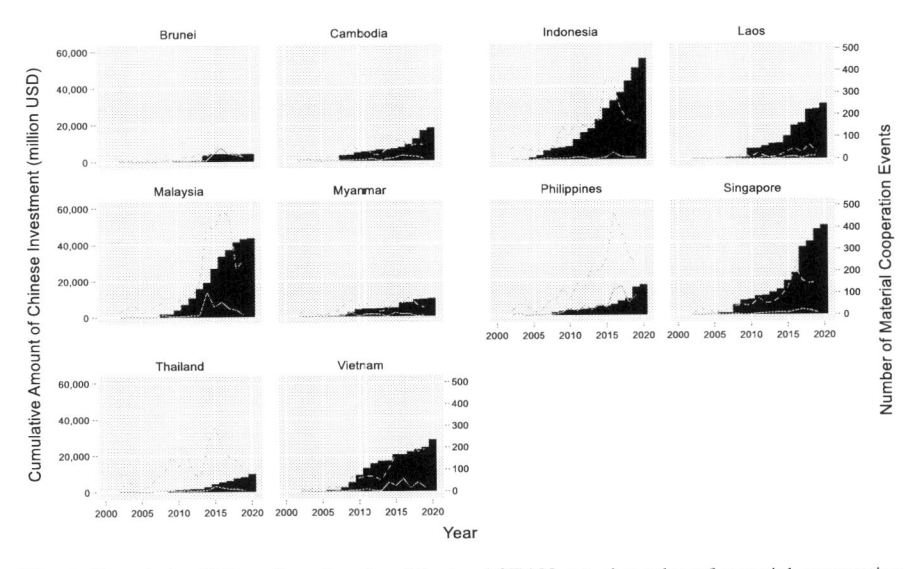

Fig. 4 Cumulative Chinese investment and the ten ASEAN states' number of material cooperation events with China and other countries, 2002~2019 (*Note* Bars are the cumulative amount of Chinese investment since 2005. Solid lines are the number of material cooperation events between the country and China. Dash lines are the number of material cooperation events between the country and other countries. 2021 *Source* American Enterprise Institute [] and ICEWS [2020])

in Chinese investment they received, the numbers of their cooperative interactions with China also increase. And furthermore, they have even more cooperative interactions with countries other than China. Chinese investment seems to largely increase their degree of Globalization in terms of their international interactions with other countries besides China.

In sum, the indexes investigated in this section demonstrate that Chinese investment can correlate with different patterns of Globalization in the ASEAN states. Generally, with the increase in Chinese investment, most of the ASEAN states' overall degrees of Globalization increase as well, except for Brunei, Indonesia, the Philippines, and Singapore, where the overall degrees of Globalization have remained at a stable level both before and after Chinese capital was introduced. If we look at the other main components of Globalization, then we will see that the ASEAN countries have different paths of development after receiving Chinese investment. In terms of trade, Brunei, Cambodia, Laos, and Myanmar do not engage in more trade with either China or other countries; the Philippines maintains a very similar degree of trade with China and other countries; and Indonesia, Malaysia, Singapore, Thailand, and Vietnam have deeper in increased trade relationships with both China and other countries, while their trade flows with other countries grow much faster. In terms of FDI, only Singapore and Vietnam can attract more FDI with the increase of Chinese investment, and the other eight ASEAN countries remain at similar degrees of attractiveness as a destination for FDI as they were before, despite the amount of Chinese investment they received. As for international interactions, Brunei, Cambodia, Laos, and Myanmar seldom interact with other countries despite the amount of Chinese investment they received, and Indonesia, Malaysia, the Philippines, Singapore, Thailand, and Vietnam have much more cooperative interactions with other countries after receiving significant Chinese investment. China's investment, including both BRI and non-BRI projects, may lead to different Globalization patterns in the ASEAN states. Thus, a question emerges. Since the ten Southeast Asian countries analyzed in this chapter all belong to ASEAN, why do they have such distinctive patterns of Globalization after receiving Chinese investment? The next section offers a possible explanation to this question.

7 Understanding the Relationship Between Chinese Investment and the Different Patterns of Globalization in the ASEAN Countries

According to most Globalization studies, Globalization is the connection between a certain country and the outside world, and this can be the result of both unintended and intended developments. The former is mostly caused by the country's natural economic, social, and political developments, while the latter is a deliberate policy choice, such as the decision between pursuing autarky and adopting a more *laissez faire* approach. These two sources of Globalization may provide a good hint in explaining the different Globalization paths that the ASEAN states have undergone after receiving Chinese investment.

Southeast Asia is well known for its diverse and heterogenous characteristics. In this region, there are poor countries as well as rich ones, non-democracies and democracies, maritime states and land states, closed countries, and open ones. Generally, there are two distinct groups of states in the diversified Southeast Asian region. One is the land states located in the Indochina Peninsula which tend to be less developed, open, and democratic such as Myanmar, Cambodia, and Laos, and the other is the maritime states which tend to be more developed, open, and democratic like Thailand, Malaysia, the Philippines, and Indonesia. The remaining countries in the region, Vietnam, Brunei, and Singapore, fall somewhere in between. Taking the first group, they have fewer trade connections with China and other countries, and Chinese investment does not seem to raise their degree of Globalization in a discernable manner. However, for the second group, which has more trade connections with both China and other countries, Chinese investment correlates with these countries' increased interactions with both China and other countries. And this is probably not mainly caused by their natural economic, social, or political developments that make them a more attractive destination for commercial investment, tourism, immigration, etc. according to the changes in their FDI (refer to Fig. 3). If this is the case, then the increasing numbers of international cooperative events are likely the result of their deliberate policy choices.

Based on the findings of the literature, these "deliberate policy choices" mainly come from both external international stimuli and their domestic policy goals. The external stimuli include not only the increasing Chinese investment that may make them more sensitive to China's economic fluctuations and political requirements, but also the increasing levels of the US' engagement in this region that may force them to make some sort of response amid the Sino-US competition (Ikenberry, 2016). Their internal policy goals are their pursuit of economic development, policy autonomy, and their leaders' own political survival (Hsueh, 2016, pp. 36–42). Therefore, the ASEAN states have developed different strategies as a response to the internal–external demands.

In Brunei, Cambodia, Laos, and Myanmar—those states with few trade connections with China and other countries—Chinese investment has not raised their degree of Globalization in any discernible manner. For Brunei, its abundant oil reserves and rather solitary foreign policy preference make it more independent from the pressures from China and the US, thus it is not forced to craft a corresponding policy response. For Cambodia, Laos, and Myanmar, they have much fewer economic connections with other countries, and Chinese investment is critical to their economy and their leaders' political survival. Therefore, these countries tend to maintain a more bandwagoning policy attitude towards China (Shambaugh, 2018). As a result, since Chinese investment does not have a clear correlation with these countries' increased or decreased connections with China and other countries, it does not affect their degrees of Globalization in a meaningful way.

In contrast, for those Southeast Asian states that have more trade connections with China and other countries, especially the US, they face pressure from both sides. Their high trade interdependence with China encourages them to seek economic profits by maintaining a good relationship with Beijing. Also, the fact that they depend on China economically and that the US has adopted a more hands-on approach to the Southeast Asia region also provides them the incentive to deepen their security ties to the US and work together in the name of ASEAN (Lim & Cooper, 2015; Zhao & Qi, 2016). That is, these countries adopt clear "hedging" and "grouping" strategies amid the Sino-US competition. As a result, since Chinese investment has raised the ASEAN states' connections and interactions with China, the US, and other countries as well, due to ASEAN states' "hedging" and "grouping" foreign policy choices and other countries becoming more active and engaged in this region, Chinese investment has considerably increased their degrees of Globalization. Putting these two influences together, Chinese investment, including non-BRI and BRI projects, makes Southeast Asia more unevenly globalized.

8 Conclusion

The ASEAN states play an important role in China's BRI project. The main BRI projects there include the TAR that connects China with all the Southeast Asian countries along the line until it reaches Singapore, the Kyaukpyu Port that enables

China to bypass the Malacca Strait, the highways that connect the main cities in the Southeast Asian countries, and several special economic zones that facilitate further bilateral private investment.

How BRI affects the political economy of its member states is a debatable issue. In terms of Globalization, there is a popular argument that BRI is a new form of Globalization led by China, since China wants to develop its own international order through its tremendous economic and market power that can be an alternative to the present US-led system. By analyzing the correlation between Chinese investment and the different dimensions of Globalizations in the ASEAN states, this chapter finds that the Chinese investment projects, including BRI and those not a part of BRI, lead to different Globalization paths in different countries. For countries that have more trade connections with China but fewer connections with other countries, Chinese investment does not raise their degree of Globalization in any discernable manner. However, for those that have more trade connections with other countries, Chinese investment increases their degree of Globalization likely because of their active hedging and grouping behaviour. The findings suggest that Chinese investment does have a political influence on the ASEAN states and is making this region more unevenly globalized.

For a long time, the effectiveness of ASEAN as an international organization that promotes development and harmony in Southeast Asia has been a topic of debate (Rüland & Jetschke, 2008). While some consider it to be merely a weak and ineffectual forum full of routine meetings and non-binding solutions, the supporters of ASEAN argue that it successfully gets the Southeast Asian states together to solve their differences through consensus building, which best matches the needs of the diversified Southeast Asian states (Acharya, 2001; Mahbubani & Sng, 2017). Whether this more unevenly globalized situation further erodes the consensus and effectiveness of ASEAN amid the Sino-US competition is another important question to consider in the future.

Bibliographic References

Acharya, A. (2001). *Constructing a security community in Southeast Asia: ASEAN and the problem of regional order*. Routledge.

American Enterprise Institute. (2021). *China global investment tracker*. https://www.aei.org/china-global-investment-tracker/

ASEAN States Data Portal. (2021). *Foreign Direct Investment Statistics (FDIS)*. https://data.aseanstats.org/

Bader, J. (2015). China, autocratic patron? An empirical investigation of China as a factor in autocratic survival. *International Studies Quarterly, 59*(1), 23–33.

Berlie, J. A. (2020). *China's globalization and the belt and road initiative*. Palgrave Macmillan.

Boschee, E., Lautenschlager, J., O'Brien, S., Shellman, S., Starz, J., & Ward, M. (2015). *ICEWS coded event data*. Harvard Dataverse.

Chung, J. H. (2009). East Asia responds to the rise of China: Patterns and variations. *Pacific Affairs, 82*(4), 657–675.

Clinton, H. (2011, October 11). America's pacific century. *Foreign Policy*. https://foreignpolicy.com/2011/10/11/americas-pacific-century/

Dreher, A. (2006). Does globalization affect growth? Evidence from a new index of globalization. *Applied Economics, 38*(10), 1091–1110.

Friedberg, A. L. (2011). *A contest for supremacy: China, America, and the struggle for mastery in Asia*. W. W. Norton.

Garrett, G. (1998). Global markets and national politics: Collision course or virtuous circle? *International Organization, 52*(4), 787–824.

Gelpern, A., Horn, S., Morris, S., Parks, B., & Trebesch, C. (2021). *How China lends: A rare look into 100 debt contracts with foreign governments*. Center for Global Development. https://www.cgdev.org/publication/how-china-lends-rare-look-into-100-debt-contracts-foreign-governments

Goh, E., & Simon, S. W. (2008). *China, the United States, and South-East Asia: Contending perspectives on politics, security, and economics*. Routledge.

Goldstein, J. S. (1992). A conflict-cooperation scale for WEIS events data. *The Journal of Conflict Resolution, 36*(2), 369–385.

Gygli, S., Haelg, F., Potrafke, N., & Sturm, J.-E. (2019). The KOF globalisation index - Revisited. *The Review of International Organizations, 14*(3), 543–574.

Hsueh, C. (Alex). (2016). ASEAN and Southeast Asian peace: Nation building, economic performance, and ASEAN's security management. *International Relations of the Asia-Pacific, 16*(1), 27–66.

Huang, Y., & Brautigam, D. (2020, June 24). Putting a dollar amount on China's loans to the developing world. *The Diplomat*. Retrieved in January 2022, from https://thediplomat.com/2020/06/putting-a-dollar-amount-on-chinas-loans-to-the-developing-world/

Ikenberry, G. J. (2016). Between the eagle and the Dragon: America, China, and middle state strategies in East Asia. *Political Science Quarterly, 131*(1), 9–43.

Kastner, S. L. (2016). Buying influence? Assessing the political effects of China's international trade. *Journal of Conflict Resolution, 60*(6), 980–1007.

Kuik, C.-C. (2016). How do weaker states hedge? Unpacking ASEAN states' alignment behavior towards China. *Journal of Contemporary China, 25*(100), 500–514.

Liff, A. P., & Ikenberry, G. J. (2014). Racing toward tragedy? China's rise, military competition in the Asia Pacific, and the security dilemma. *International Security, 39*(2), 52–91.

Lim, D. J., & Cooper, Z. (2015). Reassessing hedging: The logic of alignment in East Asia. *Security Studies, 24*(4), 696–727.

Mahbubani, K., & Sng, J. (2017). *The ASEAN miracle: A catalyst for peace*. National University of Singapore Press.

National Development and Reform Commission. (2015, March). Vision and actions on jointly building Silk Road Economic Belt and 21st-Century Maritime Silk Road, Issued by the National Development and Reform Commission, Ministry of Foreign Affairs, and Ministry of Commerce of the People's Republic of China with State Council authorization.

People's Daily. (2004, August 30). The 10th Conference of Chinese Diplomatic Envoys Stationed Abroad Held in Beijing. *People's Daily*.

Rachman, G. (2016). *Easternization: Asia's rise and America's decline from Obama to Trump and beyond*. Other Press.

Ross, R. S. (2006). Balance of power politics and the rise of China: Accommodation and balancing in East Asia. *Security Studies, 15*(3), 355–395.

Rüland, J., & Jetschke, A. (2008). 40 years of ASEAN: Perspectives, performance and lessons for change. *The Pacific Review, 21*(4), 397–409.

Shambaugh, D. (2018). U.S.-China rivalry in Southeast Asia: Power shift or competitive coexistence? *International Security, 42*(4), 85–127.

Solingen, E. (2001). Mapping internationalization: Domestic and regional impacts. *International Studies Quarterly, 45*(4), 517–555.

United Nations. (2021). *UN comtrade: International trade statistics database*. https://comtrade.un.org/

World Bank. (2021). *World development indicators*. Retrieved in December 2021, from https://datopics.worldbank.org/world-development-indicators/

Zhao, S., & Qi, X. (2016). Hedging and geostrategic balance of East Asian countries toward China. *Journal of Contemporary China, 25*(100), 485–499.

Chapter 41
Vietnam's Attitude Towards China's Belt and Road Initiative Amid Globalization

Vu Quy Son

1 Introduction

Since 1991, Vietnam has been integrating deeply into the international community at both the regional and global levels. Similarly, as Vietnam's huge neighbour, with its power rising, China has launched its Belt and Road initiative (BRI) to extend its globalization process. Vietnam–China relations, furthermore, have developed to the level of a Comprehensive Strategic Cooperation Partner (CSCP) since 2008. Logically, Vietnam should engage proactively with the BRI. In fact, Vietnam initially expressed ambitious views regarding this mega project. Additionally, many existing researches discuss Vietnam's strategy towards China's BRI at the structural level (Vu et al., 2021, p. 11). This means that those studies rarely consider issues in terms of Vietnam's domestic approach. In particular, Vietnam perceives that China's BRI is influencing Vietnam's goals amid globalization.

The aim of the chapter is to investigate why Vietnam appears to be adopting a cautious attitude towards the BRI through applying role theory to the state's expectations within its relations with other states amid globalization. It argues that Vietnam is adopting a cautious attitude towards the BRI because of its expectations that China will be a crucial partner to it, and Vietnam–China cooperative relations still demand the development of mutual trust. Such need reflects Vietnam's belief about the gap between China's statements and its behaviours regarding the BRI. To explore this issue, this chapter will proceed in the following manner. First, it will outline the existing discussion about the small state's external choice from different approaches, including Vietnam's expectations and responses to China amid globalization. Second, it will highlight Vietnam's views on the BRI and the factors shaping it. Finally, it will discuss several cases where Vietnam has responded cautiously to the BRI.

V. Q. Son (✉)
Institute of Chinese Studies (ICS), Vietnam Academy of Social Sciences (VASS), Hanoi, Vietnam

2 The Small State's Choice and Response to Other States Amid Globalization

2.1 The Small State's External Choice from Diverse Perspectives

Currently, various scholars are debating which factors (such as population size, territory, the economy, and the military) determine whether or not state is small (Godfrey & Wivel, 2020; Hey, 2003). Additionally, a small state is defined as being the weak component within an asymmetric relationship with the greater powers surrounding it (Criekemans & Duran, 2010, p. 32; Thorhallsson & Steinsson, 2017). Consequently, diverse views exist regarding the outcomes of a small state's external choices. For instance, realists contend that a small state may depend more on alliances to raise its voice in the international arena (Criekemans & Duran, 2010, p. 31). Furthermore, a small state is more prone to choosing to bandwagon with a larger state or become a satellite state to a great power (Galal, 2020, p. 39; Paul, 2019, p. 50). For example, Vu et al. (2021, p. 11) contend that Vietnam has adopted various policies in order to respond to China's BRI, such as hedging, hedging combining with resistance, balancing, and bandwagoning. Liberalists speculate that, because of its economic independence, a small state is more inclined to engage in multilateralism or regional cooperation agreements to mitigate its weakness and reduce its rate of deploying force in international relations (Galal, 2020, p. 41; Godfrey & Wivel, 2020, p. 5; Thorhallsson & Steinsson, 2017, p. 3). Furthermore, liberalists are not inclined to contend the member state's perception of the role of these international mechanisms and the feasibility of the member state complying with the norms and rules thereof. Note that the aforementioned approaches regarding the external choices of a small state still draw attention to the dominance of structural factors. Regarding asymmetric power, the goal of a small state is to obtain greater autonomy (Womack, 2006, p. 21). Such an approach still focuses more on the behaviours of the greater powers that impact on the behaviours of both sides (Chu & Huang, 2018, p. 312). Alternatively, asymmetric power hypothesizes that the state is a radical individual, ignoring the possibility that the state or government may shape the decision-making process of the policy actors to a certain extent (Chu & Huang, 2018, p. 312). As a result, this indicates that the choice of the state may not fit the model of rational choice but is formed by one or more people whose perceptions may be affected by their historical experience and/or personal emotions.

2.2 The Expectations and Responses of a Small State from the Role Theory Approach

The methods employed in this chapter are mainly document analysis of Vietnamese domestic materials and interviews with scholars of Vietnam. These materials allow the chapter to illustrate Vietnam's varying views. Interestingly, these views are affected by Vietnam's ideologies and domestic politics. This is consistent with the purpose of this chapter, that reflects the emotional stance and thought in Vietnam with regard to China, together with speculations and lessons regarding many historical incidents that have occurred within Vietnam–China relations (Chu & Huang, 2018, p. 314). Subsequently, this chapter highlights Vietnam's logical thoughts regarding China's BRI and Vietnam's responses to this mega project, based on a discussion of Vietnam's view of globalization and Vietnam–China relations amid globalization.

Theoretically, role theory is employed, and the term "altercasting" is used to explain Vietnam's perceptions of China's behaviours regarding the BRI and whether or not these meet Vietnam's expectations and needs amid globalization. In this respect, role theorists regard a state's interaction with others as a learning process, in which each individual actor (state) can play one or more roles. The previous interaction forms the behaviour and properties of an actor (i.e., its identities, interests, and capabilities) (Harnisch et al., 2011, p. 10), implying that the state has an expectation of the role of the others, and *vice versa*. Specifically, role expectations refer to social actors (state), who may be perceived differently in the eyes of others. Such expectations comprise domestic and/or individual expectations regarding what the role is and what it implies. Hence, roles, and particularly role sets, can lead to potential conflicts within and between roles (inter-role conflict) (Harnisch et al., 2011, p. 8). "Altercasting" refers to situations in which one state casts another state in a particular role. This learning process provides various signals to attain the corresponding behaviour. To a certain extent, "altercasting" is similar to "role expectation." Nevertheless, altercasting also explores whether or not the state that has a certain role accepts the rights and obligations associated with that role. If a state is unable to or fails to adopt such a role clearly, this results from itself, rather than from others. This indicates that altercasting focuses on the potential conflict that may arise between different roles. In practice, role theorists divide roles into self-roles and other-roles. Tangibly, self-roles refer to the extension of a cohesion culture and value system, as well as experiences arising from the interaction between the ego and the alter. These two concepts depend on the difference between the characteristics of the actor (namely, the state) and its self-perception. (Harnisch, 2012). Moreover, a social actor employs its self-perception and own comprehension about its self-role to advance its own expectations regarding others' roles. Similarly, this expectation is likely to be cast by others. The acts of others should meet such expectations, as another actor is unlikely to follow the aforementioned expectations to forge a bilateral interaction if such an interaction appears likely to produce negative outcomes or harm the national interest of any actor (state) (Chu & Huang, 2018, p. 315).

3 An Overview of Vietnam–China Relations

Intriguingly, Vietnam–China relations have fluctuated over the past few decades. In this respect, in the 1950s and 1960s, the bilateral relations became those of "comrades plus brothers," with China's offering immense support to Vietnam during the Vietnam War. Subsequently, in the 1970s and 1980s, Vietnam and China sank into "adversary relations," with the border war deployed by China in 1979 and the Vietnam–China skirmish over the South China Sea in 1988. Since the normalization of bilateral relations in 1991, Vietnam–China relations have witnessed fluctuations, as both sides engage in the globalization process. In this regard, in the 1990s and 2000s, the bilateral relations developed into a "golden period," with both sides signing delimitation agreements regarding the Tonkin Gulf in 1999. Moreover, in 2008, the CSCP strengthened a wide range of cooperative efforts, in fields such as politics, the economy, society, defence, diplomacy, and so on.

With regard to Vietnam–China relations amid globalization, since proposing the "Doi moi" in 1986, Vietnam has integrated deeply with the international community in a wide range of fields, such as politics, economic, defence, culture, and so on. Since 2011, Vietnam has been emphasizing economic globalization that is centred on comprehensive integration into the global community. Such international integration, that requires a high level of development of international cooperation, is likely to enhance Vietnam's national interests with regard to: protecting its territorial integrity and national sovereignty; promoting its economic development; maintaining an external peaceful environment; and safeguarding its regime legitimacy and internal stability (Tran, 2016). In order to achieve these goals, Vietnam expects that its bilateral relations will create a peaceful external environment that will enable it to comply with the international community's rules and principles, to gain mutual respect, and to adopt win–win principles.Interestingly, globalization has resulted in various conflicts, positive and negative effects, cooperation and struggles. Since 2010, Vietnam–China relations have developed, with the characteristics of both cooperation and struggle. Their bilateral cooperation has been demonstrated by several investment projects, high-level leader visits, a significant increase in the volume of trade between them as well as personal contacts between Vietnamese and Chinese citizens, whereas Vietnam and China have also struggled with each other due to the SCS tension, that is mainly caused by China's aggressive behaviours, such as the Haiyang oil rig incident in 2014, building artificial islands, disrupting Vietnam fishermen and so on.

Interestingly, the globalization process is an unavoidable trend that strengthens the relationships of a state with others, including its relations with a greater power. To a certain extent, this has caused various conflicts, positive and negative effects, cooperation, and struggles between Vietnam and China (Nguyen, 2021). To a certain extent, these reflect the expectations and responses of Vietnam with regard to China. Currently, Vietnam–China relations are characterized by both cooperation and struggle, under the CSCP framework. Such relations reflect the deep integration of both Vietnam and China in the globalization process. In such relations, Vietnam expects stable Vietnam–China relations that are likely to create an external peaceful environment that will enable both countries to comply with the international community's mutual rules and principles, to gain mutual respect, and to foster win–win principles. Only based on such expectations are Vietnam and China likely to develop in more predictable ways. Consequently, Vietnam–China relations have strengthened persistently.

Consequently, Vietnam's responses to China's behaviours under the BRI framework have been affected by these fluctuating bilateral relations, which stem from Vietnam's expectations regarding China's role. Vietnam regards China as a cooperative partner amid globalization. Such perceptions are formed by the hierarchical structure that is embedded in Vietnam's bilateral relations with China, together with its understanding of China's history and culture and how it itself is viewed by China. Vietnam interprets differently the cooperative partner in the Vietnam–China cooperation amid globalization due to China's actions and assertions regarding various issues, such as Vietnam–China trade and investment cooperation, South China Sea (SCS) issues and so on. Hence, these perceptions and related responses of Vietnam regarding China, that elucidate the reason why Vietnam is embracing China's BRI, will be explored in more detail in the following sections.

4 Vietnam's Perceptions of China's Role in the Belt and Road Initiative

4.1 An Overview of China's Belt and Road Initiative

China's BRI comprises the Silk Road Economic Belt (SREB) and the 21st Century Maritime Silk Road (CMSR), which was initiated by Chinese President Xi Jinping when he delivered speeches on two overseas visits. The first one was made at Nazarbayev University during his visit to Kazakhstan, on September 7, 2013, when President Xi proposed building a new SREB by promoting policy coordination, road connectivity, unimpeded trade, currency convertibility, and strengthened people-to-people ties. On October 3, 2013, President Xi further proposed, during a speech before the Indonesian parliament, that China was ready to work with the ASEAN members to build the 21st CMSR as a way of strengthening connectivity and promoting cooperative partnership. Note that BRI is seen as a blueprint for establishing a new type of globalization which clearly reflects several global characteristics of the economy, politics, and cultural aspects of international governance (Yilmaz & Li, 2020, pp. 2–6).

4.2 The Opportunities and Challenges Associated with the BRI for Vietnam

Currently, Vietnam regards China as a cooperative partner, with a need to boost their mutual trust. Vietnam's expectations of such a role can be seen in the BRI's opportunities and challenges that affect Vietnam–China relations. In this regard, the BRI's chances are interpreted as China's behaviours matching Vietnam's demands, whereas the BRI's challenges are perceived as China acting in such a way that it fails to meet the expectations of Vietnam, which would probably hinder the efforts to boost Vietnam and China's mutual trust.

4.3 The Opportunities

From Vietnam's perspective, China's BRI brings various types of prospective economic cooperation that meet Vietnam's expectations about the role of China as a cooperative partner amid globalization. First, to a certain extent, Vietnam regards China as a state that provides a model of economic development for Vietnam. This means that the development experience of China's economy fits the expectations of Vietnam regarding the role of other states amid globalization and also determines Vietnam's welcome response to the BRI. Tangibly, regarding integrating into the international community, China's economic achievement provides an example to the rest of the developing world (Legran, 2003, p. 16). In other words, China continues to open up its market to Vietnam's goods. Also, China remains Vietnam's largest trading partner and largest provider of tourists (Khánh, 2017). Regarding the infrastructure, Vietnam regards China as a partner that is likely to help to boost the development of its infrastructure connectivity, such as the transportation and communication networks within Vietnam. Moreover, Vietnam's connectivity to the BRI network is likely to boost the economic and social development of Vietnam's various regions, especially in the remote areas lying along the Vietnam–China border, through strengthening the development of Vietnam–China cross-border economic zones (Van Huy, 2020, pp. 154–155).

Second, Vietnam expects to mitigate the limitations of China's trade and investment in Vietnam through the BRI. This means that, through the BRI, China's enterprises are expected to improve the country's image. Through the BRI's implementation, China is likely to increase the need for China's domestic consumption that will create many opportunities for Vietnam to export products, such as agricultural ones. This may change the structure of Vietnam–China trade, in which Vietnam mainly exports raw materials to China. The BRI's implementation may increase the amount of products in many priority fields such as agriculture, environment protect, techonoly as well as transportation, and so on. This means that Vietnam's exports to China will not be limited solely to raw material but also include end products. By so doing the BRI would serve to mitigate the current deficit of bilateral trade between the two countries. Regarding infrastructure connectivity in Vietnam, because China is under pressure from competition by other developed states, such as Japan and France as, given Vietnam's infrastructure development, with the BRI's implementation, China might provide more advanced technology and management, as well as more financial loans with fewer conditions, to foster Vietnam's welcoming of Chinese contractors to work on its infrastructure projects in the coming years. By applying a high standard, which is likely to reduce Chinese enterprises' disadvantages in the BRI's framework, these enterprises' image in Vietnam's infrastructure development and Vietnam–China trade will be improved.

Third, Vietnam perceives China as adopting a responsible role in economic globalization through the BRI, that emphasizes the generation of mutual respect and trust, mutual benefits, and win–win cooperation (Ploberger, 2019). This means that Vietnam expects China to comply with the existing rules, norms, and principles of the international mechanisms. Specifically, as developing states, both Vietnam and China place huge attention on developing their respective national economy so, as a result, engage persistently in the global economy through joining the international economic cooperation mechanisms. Moreover, the state has not enacted its roles and responsibilities in the international community until it is able to do so more easily (Lampton, 2008, p. 12). It means that, with it rising power, China is in a better position to adopt its international responsibilities. These related responsibilties reveal that China needs to comply with the existing rules and norms of the international community, including the WTO and FTA agreements, whether the goal of the BRI is to mitigate the limitations of the existing international cooperative mechanisms or to create new rules or norms in China's favour. It is noteworthy that, as a small state, Vietnam persistently stresses the importance of respecting the international laws and resolving disputes via negotiation, as well as maintaining peaceful, stable, cooperative environments. Additionally, the BRI is regarded as China's globalization, as it contains a critique of its old forms of governance (Yilmaz & Li, 2020, p. 2). This mega project, based on China's rising power and confidence, is expected to contribute to the international community and help to resolve international trade disputes. This might help to reduce the disadvantages that Vietnam and China face in the globalization process. One of these is that both Vietnam and China need to conduct political reform along with economic reform to obtain the finance support of a certain international mechanism.

These aforementioned opportunities are affected by Vietnam's perception of the hierarchical structure embedded in bilateral relations with China, and Vietnam's understanding of China's history and culture. In this respect, the historical and cultural memory of Vietnam–China relations has significantly contributed to Vietnam's perception of China's role. On one hand, Vietnam's historical experience of interacting with China within a hierarchical bilateral relationship leads it to perceive the role of China in the BRI as one that fits Vietnam's economic expectations. Historically, China had supported Vietnam and provided it with many materials during the Vietnam War from the 1950s to the 1970s because of the shared ideology and the role of Vietnam. Such support by China is seen as the fundamental factor that enabled the

Vietnam–China relations to develop in an amicable, stable manner.[1] Additionally, Vietnam and China share various similarities in their history of national development, such as pursuing a free-market economy in a shift away from a planned economy, domestic politics being run by a Communist Party and forging economic reform, so China's successful economy offers a model for Vietnam's economic development. Especially during the 1990s–2000s, Vietnam–China relations developed significantly in the field of politics, economics, diplomacy, defence, and so on. Vietnam, hence, interprets the trade and investment cooperation as well as infrastructure connectivity in the BRI as an opportunity to learn from China's successful experience to develop its own economy.

4.4 The Challenges

The challenges that BRI poses to Vietnam can be seen from Vietnam's perception about the methods and legal framework of the BRI that make the shortcomings of the Vietnam–China relations more serious. In Vietnam's view, such shortcomings add greater uncertainty and complexity to the bilateral relations between the two countries.

First, Vietnam regards the method of implementing the BRI as consistent with China's traditional "going out" strategy, imposed in 1995. These similarities are based on the deficits in the Vietnam–China trade and investment, China's enterprise's role, and the conditions attached to China's loans. In particular, because China might put bilateral trade at the risk of a deficit, it has various statecraft tools at its disposal through which it may put pressure on Vietnam regarding many issues, especially security ones. For example, during the oil rig crisis, China suspended the importation of agricultural products from Vietnam and, in late 2016, China stopped importing live pigs from Vietnam due to "quality" concerns (Hiebert, 2020, p. 232). Furthermore, China may affect the development of Vietnam's industry through exploiting the imbalance of Vietnam–China trade. In particular, the dependence of Vietnam on China's economy is clearly manifested in the booming trade deficit with China, accounting for $34 billion in 2019 (Strangio, 2020). Regarding China's financial support, because the BRI's implementation will have to embrace the traditional methods of China's financial loans, China is likely to attach conditions when it offers financial support. It is noteworthy that China's loans are neither cheap nor easy to obtain (H. V. Le, 2018b), as already demonstrated by many existing infrastructure projects that have been funded by China's ODA loans in the past. In order to obtain China's financial support, Vietnam must accept the many associated conditions, that include the use of Chinese technologies, equipment, and contractors (H. Le, 2018a). This means that the dependence of Vietnam's economy on China is likely to reduce the autonomy of Vietnam with regard to resolving various difficult issues that exist between the two countries. For example, Vietnam is concerned that China will use

---

[1] Interview with an anonymous interviewee, 25 September 2019, Hanoi (Vietnam).

various economic tools to coerce it over the SCS. Note that the SCS is the biggest obstacle to Vietnam–China relations, that affects Vietnam's willingness to engage in the BRI

Additionally, the role of China's enterprises in the BRI also increases Vietnam's concern regarding these enterprises' potential interference in the infrastructure and trade activities of Vietnam. In the past, China's enterprises emphasized the pursuit of political rather than economic goals. Currently, Chinese state-owned enterprises (SOEs) at both the central and local levels are playing a leading role in promoting the BRI's connectivity (Zhang & Yin, 2019). Note that the bids for many of the investment projects in Vietnam have been won and are being overseen by China's SOEs. Many of those have poor records for using low-level technology, increasing the investment budget, and falling behind schedule on various infrastructure projects. Currently, China is strengthening the reform of it SOEs through "The State Advances, The Private Sector Retreats" policy, that improves the role of the SOE in China's national strategies to achieve both political and economic goals. One of the political goals is to propagandize China's stance on many issues, such as the SCS issue. Hence, the importance of the role of China's SOEs in the BRI has increased significantly. Whether or not these SOEs' investment in Vietnam, therefore, will be adjusted or changed remains to be seen.

Second, Vietnam is concerned about the methods and legal framework of the BRI. Note that China's implementation of the BRI project might not differ from that of other, Western-style projects, despite the fact that China's mainstream media and scholars frequently stress that the BRI is better than the Western-led cooperative projects and provides more commodities and services that will benefit many more people all over the world (Zheng, 2019, p. 49). In order to attract more states to support China's BRI, China emphasizes the advantages of BRI and limitations of the current international mechanism, to demonstrate that China's new style of globalization will bring much more benefits to other states with less requirements. The BRI promotes cross-country infrastructural connectivity and free trade, aiming to build large-scale, high-level, high-standard international/regional economic networks, as Chinese top leaders frequently emphazise during their speeches about the BRI, that foster other states' engagement (H. Y. Chun, 2021; Zheng, 2019, p. 49), This reflects the ambiguity of the BRI, which makes it harder for Vietnam to recognize the difference between the BRI approach and that of other, Western-style projects. Note that, due to globalization, as a developing state, Vietnam has become accustomed to following the rules, norms, and principles of the international mechanisms led by Western states. Furthermore, the BRI is primarily an economic and political project. Its legal aspect is underdeveloped (Crawford, 2021, p. 13). Hence, the ambiguous assertions and law deficits of the BRI make it difficult for Vietnam to maintain Vietnam–China relations in an appropriate and predictable way.

Third, the way in which China is implementing the BRI is likely to disrupt the existing principles, norms and rules, that are recognized mutually and prevalently by the international community, including respecting and abiding by the international laws. This might make the Vietnam–China relations regarding the SCS disputes more uncertain and complex. For example, although China is a member of the UNCLOS, the big power is unwilling to enact the whole rights and responsibilities of such a member. To date, China continues to adopt a power-oriented approach, disregarding its legal and judicial obligations under the UNCLOS (Petersmann, 2018, p. 56). In this respect, China's tactics for resolving the SCS disputes have remained unchanged. These pathways reflect China's emphasis on bilateral negotiations and inducement/coercion with regard to other SCS claimant states. Note that the BRI provides many mechanisms for SCS dispute settlement in China's favour. These related mechanisms aim to enact the role of China as a responsible state in global governance. In reality, China's provision of mechanisms for resolving international disputes serve to strengthen its control over the SCS.

The previous challenges result from Vietnam's perceptions about the history of Vietnam–China relations, understanding of China's history and culture, and perceptions of China's view of Vietnam. Tangibly, Vietnam's leaders and people view Vietnam as China's vassal state, that has been affected profoundly by Chinese civilization and China's mulitiple military invasions of Vietnam's territories in the past, whether China's power was strong or weak.[2] Vietnam's interaction with China during the socialist brotherhood period also leads Vietnam to adopt a negative view towards China. Historical incidents already demonstrate China's willingness to ignore other states in order to pursue its own interests. This implies that China's aforementioned behaviours hardly met the expectations of Vietnam regarding China's role during the 1970s and 1980s.

Vietnam interprets that, given its well-established history and culture, China has diverse pathways and tools for handling its external relations in its own favour. China is inclined to opt to use economic statecraft to put pressure on Vietnam regarding security issues. Over negotiation issues, China prefers to enhance bilateral methods with weaker states, as well as multilateral ones with greater states (Lampton, 2014, p. 206). For instance, regarding the SCS issues, China's firm stance is to negotiate bilateral methods to prevent the impact of a third party. Nevertheless, when other claimants agree to bilateral negotiations, China is likely to choose various tools to coerce them into acting in China's favour.[3] Hence, in order to maintain its superiority within the asymmetric power, China still prefers to strengthen its international relations through bilateral negotiations undertaken within the inclusive framework of the BRI. Furthermore, China is inclined to use ambiguous disclosures to create more room for manoeuvre in its bilateral relations. Such ambiguous assertions result from the characteristics of China's language and culture. For example, China has not yet elucidated, implicitly and explicitly, its stance regarding its sovereign claims based on the so-called "nine-dash line." In the BRI framework, China provokes many ambiguous accounts: such as "win-win"; "China's active efforts for win-win cooperation with its neighbors have brought real benefits to the countries and peoples in the region…" (Shang, 2019, pp. 19–20); or "Friendship, Good Faith, Mutual Benefit and Inclusiveness."[4] However, to date, China has rarely mentioned the disadvantages of

---

[2] Interview with an anonymous interviewee, 23 September 2019, Hanoi (Vietnam).

[3] Interview with an anonymous interviewee, 28 September 2019, Hanoi (Vietnam).

[4] Interview with an anonymous interviewee, 26 October 2019, Hanoi (Vietnam).

the BRI and how to handle these. Because of its experience of integrating into the regional and global communities, Vietnam understands that all globalization projects are similar in that they create both advantages and disadvantages. Hence, Vietnam is concerned about the BRI that is seen as China's globalization.

Also, Vietnam's expectations of China's role derive from its understanding of China's view of this small state. In particular, Vietnam shows that China does not appear to hold a positive view of Vietnam. Such a belief is derived from Vietnam's leaders and people's understanding of the characteristics of China's civilization and the asymmetric structure of the Vietnam–China relations. From Vietnam's perspective, with its long history and culture, China emphasizes its superiority persistently. In the past, China held influence over its neighbouring states in the East Asia region through the tribunal system, whereby China regarded itself as the "Middle Kingdom," and saw the other states as "Saga states." This indicates that China strove to bring the peripheral states under its own influence. Additionally, because of China's rising power and influence, its superiority and confidence have become more apparent. In order to maintain this superiority, China strives to keep Vietnam within its influential orbit. China is constantly concerned that its peripheral states may draw closer to extra-regional states in order to establish an alliance as a counterbalance against China. If Vietnam were to strengthen its bilateral relations with the US, especially in terms of military cooperation, China would criticize its neighbouring state. Vietnam should not regard China as an adversary and must control its domestic nationalist sentiments to avoid affecting the overall Vietnam–China bilateral relations (Xin, 2016, p. 82). In other words, China frequently calls Vietnam a "trouble-maker" regarding the SCS issues (Cun, 2012). This reflects China's negative view of Vietnam's behaviours regarding the SCS issues. This understanding reveals the lack of mutual trust between Vietnam and China, that impacts on Vietnam's perception of whether or not China will enact its role as a cooperative partner, as it asserts in reference to the BRI.

5 Vietnam's Connection with China's Belt and Road Initiative

Currently, Vietnam's engagement in the BRI is founded on a strategic connectivity between Vietnam's "Two Corridors, One Belt" (TCOB) and China's BRI. Note that the TCOB initiative, which embodies a successful model of Vietnam–China cooperation, was imposed by Vietnam during the 2000s, as Vietnam–China relations had entered "a golden period" since the normalization of the bilateral relations in 1991. Through the extension of the TCOB, Vietnam expects to expand the degree of cooperation within the Vietnam–China relations, reduce the risks associated with joining China's BRI, as well as to expand its traditional friendship with China. Within the cooperative framework of the BRI, Vietnam supports some policy connectivity, such as the Asian Infrastructure Investment Bank (AIIB), and Regional Cooperative Economic Partner (RCEP). In 2015, Vietnam and China signed the extension of the agreement on bilateral trade development in the period 2016–2020 (Nhandan, 2015a). Alternately, Vietnam has been a member of the AIIB since 2015 (Thư, 2015) and signed the RCEP in 2020 (Vietnamnews, 2020). This means that Vietnam expects to maintain friendly Vietnam–China relations and forge the development of the bilateral relations, stably and substantively.

Vietnam's cautious approach to the BRI reveals that it failed to express its respective stance initially, when the BRI was imposed in 2013. Only in November 2015 did Vietnam release an official statement about its ability to join China's BRI, when the highest leader of China paid an official visit to Vietnam. This document is considered an important milestone in promoting Vietnam's engagement in the BRI (Hoa & Nguyen, 2021). It was the first time that the initiative had been mentioned in a joint statement, showing that, to some extent, the two sides had agreed to promote the connectivity between the TCOB and the BRI (Nhandan, 2015b). Prior to that moment, the discussion about the feasibility of Vietnam's engagement with the BRI in its mainstream media and among its top leaders was random. It was only in 2017 that Vietnam and China signed a cooperative memorial about the strategic connectivity between TCOB and BRI (Ministry of Commercial, 2017). In this regard, Vietnam's concerns about which cooperative fields Vietnam and China should prioritize have still not been negotiated completely. During 2018–2019, no new agreement or deal labelled as the BRI was signed between Vietnam and China. This means that it took Vietnam a significant amount of time to respond to China's BRI, appropriately and cautiously.

There are a few China-funded projects labelled as an example of Vietnam–China strategic connectivity under the BRI. One is the Cat Linh-Ha Dong metro project, which has been under construction by the China Railway Sixth Group Co Ltd since 2011, funded by an ODA loan from China. In 2020, the Chinese ambassador in Vietnam stated that this project symbolized Vietnam–China friendship (Ha, 2020). Both Vietnam and China list this project in the framework of the BRI (H. Le, 2018a). Interestingly, because infrastructure connectivity is one of the most crucial pillars of the BRI, China implements such connectivity through the path of contract projects. Note that China's contractors, who are state- or province-owned enterprises, have participated in many transportation projects or power plants in Vietnam since the normalization of the Vietnam–China relations in 1991. Many of these infrastructure projects have fallen behind schedule, and their investment budgets have increased as well (Hiebert, 2020). The investment budget for the Cat Linh-Ha Dong metro project, for example, has increased several times and the project is now several years overdue. Additionally, to date, China's contractors who have taken part in building some sections of the North-South expressway road project in Vietnam have also caused various problems that affect the lives of local citizens. In 2020, Vietnam called for various new bids to build the remaining sections of its North-South expressway road project that attracted huge attention among Chinese enterprises, seeking to engage in joint ventures with Vietnam's construction companies (Diep, 2019). In fact, many Chinese enterprises or China–Vietnam joint venture firms failed to participate in these new bids (PL, 202). This is due to the efforts of Vietnam's central agencies to limit Chinese and Vietnamese contractors with low capabilities and low records regarding the existing infrastructure projects nationwide in Vietnam. By so doing, Vietnam expects to mitigate the situation of increasing investment budgets and late completion.

Regarding financial issues, Vietnam strives to diversify its financial sources across infrastructure development in order to reduce its dependence of China's loans, despite that fact that China is a crucial ODA source for Vietnam, and Vietnam is also a co-founder of the AIIB, which strives to access China-led bank loans. In reality, only in 2020 was the first AIIB loan approved, issued to a private Vietnamese bank (He, 2020). Additionally, many of Vietnam's policy actors at both the central and local levels still hesitate to accept such loans to improve their infrastructure system due to concerns about public debt. Specifically, various provinces substitute other financial support for China's ODA loans, especially those provinces which share a border with China. For instance, in 2018, Quang Ninh province, which is located on the northeastern Vietnam–China border did not choose an ODA loan from China to build the Van Don-Mong Cai section of the highway that connects the centre of Quang Ninh province (Ha long city) with the border area (H. V. Le, 2018b). Alternatively, Vietnam's local actors are seeking other public investment sources to reduce the country's dependence on government-to-government loans. This means that China's financial loans are no longer the top consideration of Vietnam's local policy actors for developing their infrastructure systems.

To summarize, Vietnam welcomes China's BRI because of the prospects it offers. To a certain extent, Vietnam's responses to the BRI reflect the prospect that it may enhance its economic development, and continue the history of friendly Vietnam–China relations. Furthermore, the responses of Vietnam to the BRI indicate its efforts to accommodate China appropriately as well as its expectations of China's in the BRI.

6 Conclusion

The chapter has discussed the reasons why Vietnam is adopting a cautious policy towards China's BRI. This reticence reflects the expectations of Vietnam regarding China's role as a cooperative partner. Vietnam interprets China's behaviours regarding the BRI as creating both opportunities and challenges for Vietnam. In this regard, while Vietnam perceives that the opportunity imposed by the BRI fits Vietnam's expectations regarding Vietnam–China cooperative relations, the challenges of the BRI create more uncertainty regarding whether Vietnam can display friendly relations towards China, peacefully and stably. These interpretations by Vietnam about China's behaviours mainly derive from Vietnam's experiences of the two countries' bilateral relations in the past, and Vietnam's understanding of China's history and culture. Vietnam reckons that China can hardly enact fully its role as a cooperative partner due to the gap between China's statements and its actions in regard to the BRI.

Bibliographic References

Chu, C. H., & Huang, C.-c. (2018). Li shi hou jian zhi ming zhong de xin xu shi: Cong Yue nan shi jiao chu fa de Zhong Yue guan xin fen xi, 1975–1991 [The new explaination of historical hindsights: An Analasys of Vietnam–China relations from Vietnam own perspective (1975–1991)]. In W. Y. Shan (Ed.), *Resurgence of China: A dialogue between history and international relations*. The Centre of Confucianism studies in East Asia, The Institute for Advanced Studies in the Humanities and Social Sciences (IHS).

Chun, H. Y. (2021). *Ji xu gao zhi liang gong jian "Yi dai, Yi lu" [to proceed to jointly construct "one belt, one road" in high quality level*. Retrieved in December 2021, from http://opinion.peo ple.com.cn/BIG5/n1/2021/0422/c1003-32084274.html

Crawford, J. (2021). China and international dispute resolution in the context of the 'Belt and Road Initiative'. In W. Shan, S. Zhang, & J. Su (Eds.), *China and international dispute resolution in the context of the 'Belt and Road Initiative'*. Cambridge University Press.

Criekemans, D., & Duran, M. (2010). Small state diplomacy compared to sub-state diplomacy: More of the same or different? In *Small states in Europe: Challenges and opportunities*. Ashgate Publishing Limited.

Cun, W. S. (2012). *Who are the real troublemakers in the South China Sea?* Retrieved in December 2021, from https://www.globaltimes.cn/content/742715.shtml

Diep, V. (2019). *Nhà đầu tư Trung Quốc muốn liên danh với Việt Nam làm cao tốc Bắc - Nam* [Chinese contractors want to cooperate with Vietnam partner to build Vietnam North - South highway]. Retrieved in December 2021, from https://vietnamnet.vn/vn/thoi-su/an-toan-giao-thong/nha-dau-tu-trung-quoc-muon-lien-danh-voi-viet-nam-lam-cao-toc-bac-nam-550005.html

Galal, A. M. (2020). External behavior of small states in light of theories of international relations. *Review of Economics and Political Science, 5*, 38–56.

Godfrey, B., & Wivel, A. (2020). *Handbook on the politics of small states*. Routledge.

Ha, N. (2020). *Đại sứ Trung Quốc: Đường sắt Cát Linh-Hà Đông là biểu trưng cho tình hữu nghị Việt Nam-Trung Quốc* [ambassador of China in Vietnam: Cat linh - Ha Dong metro is a icon of Vietnam-China frienship]. Retrieved in December 2021, from https://laodong.vn/giao-thong/dai-su-trung-quoc-noi-ve-du-an-duong-sat-cat-linh-ha-dong-815072.ldo

Harnisch, S. (2012). Conceptualizing in the minefield: Role theory and foreign policy learning. *Foreign Policy Analysis, 8*(1), 47–69. Retrieved in December 2021, from https://doi.org/10.1111/j.1743-8594.2011.00155.x

Harnisch, S., Frank, C., & Maull, H. (2011). *Role theory in international relations: Approaches and analyses* (Vol. 90). Routledge.

He, L. (2020). *AIIB approves first Viet Nam loan to help private sector COVID-19 response*. Retrieved in December 2021, from https://www.aiib.org/en/news-events/news/2020/AIIB-App roves-First-Vietnam-Loan-to-Help-Private-Sector-COVID-19-Response.html

Hey, J. A. (2003). *Small states in world politics: Explaining foreign policy behavior*. Lynne Rienner Publishers.

Hiebert, M. (2020). *Under Beijing's shadow: Southeast Asia's China challenge*. Center for Strategic and International Studies.

Hoa, N. T. P., & Nguyen, P. T. (2021). The reception and implementation of the Belt and Road Initiative in Vietnam. *Strategic Analysis, 45*(2), 128–143. https://doi.org/10.1080/09700161.2021.189 3507

Khánh, D. C. (2017). Quan hệ thương mại Việt - Trung từ năm 1991 đến nay: Thực tiễn, vấn đề và giải pháp. *Tạp Chín Nghiên Cứu Trung Quốc, 186*(2), 34–43.

Lampton, D. M. (2008). *The three faces of Chinese power: Might, money, and minds*: University of California Press.

Lampton, D. M. (2014). *Following the leader: Ruling China, from Deng Xiaoping to Xi Jinping*. University of California Press.

Le, H. (2018a). The Belt and Road Initiative in Vietnam: Challenges and prospects, perspective. *ISEAS Yusof Ishak Institute, 18*, 1–7.

Le, H. V. (2018b). *Quảng Ninh không vay ODA Trung Quốc làm cao tốc* [Quang ninh province does not receive China's ODA loans to build highspeed way]. Retrieved in December 2021, from https://tienphong.vn/quang-ninh-khong-vay-oda-trung-quoc-lam-cao-toc-post1062419.tpo

Legran, P. (2003). *Open world: The truth about globalization.* Abacus.

Ministry of Commercial. (2017). *Zhong Yue xieshou gongjian "Yi Dai Yi Lu" "Liang Lang Yi Juan"* [Vietnam and China buid "One Belt and One Road", "Two Corridors and One Circle"]. Retrieved in December 2021, from http://fec.mofcom.gov.cn/article/fwydyl/zgzx/201711/20171102669141.shtml

Nguyen, M. H. (2021). Về hội nhập quốc tế và tham gia tiến trình toàn cầu hóa của Việt Nam. *Tạp chí Cộng sản.* Retrieved in December 2021, from https://www.tapchicongsan.org.vn/web/guest/quoc-phong-an-ninh-oi-ngoai1/-/2018/821539/ve-hoi-nhap-quoc-te-va-tham-gia-tien-trinh-toan-cau-hoa-cua-viet-nam.aspx

Nhandan. (2015a). *Thông cáo chung Việt Nam - Trung Quốc.* Retrieved from https://nhandan.vn/tin-tuc-su-kien/thong-cao-chung-viet-nam-trung-quoc-229434/

Nhandan. (2015b). *Tuyên bố chung Việt Nam - Trung Quốc.* Retrieved in December 2021, from https://nhandan.vn/tin-tuc-su-kien/tuyen-bo-chung-viet-nam-trung-quoc-247099/

Paul, T. (2019). When balance of power meets globalization: China, India and the small states of South Asia. *Politics, 39*(1), 50–63.

Petersmann, E.-U. (2018). Trade and investment adjudication involving 'silk road projects': Legal methodology challenges. *EUI Department of Law Research Paper* (2018/02).

Ploberger, C. (2019). *Political Economic Perspectives of China's Belt and Road Initiative: Reshaping regional integration.* Routledge.

Strangio, S. (2020). *In the Dragon's shadow: Southeast Asia in the Chinese Century.* Yale University Press.

Thorhallsson, B., & Steinsson, S. (2017). Small state foreign policy. In W. R. Thompson (Ed.), *Oxford research encyclopedia of politics.* Oxford Unversity Press.

Thư, H. (2015). *Việt Nam gia nhập ngân hàng do Trung Quốc khởi xướng.* Retrieved in December 2021, from https://vnexpress.net/viet-nam-gia-nhap-ngan-hang-do-trung-quoc-khoi-xuong-3241071.html

Tran, T. T. (2016). Rebalancing: Vietnam's South China Sea Challenges and Responses. In T. T. T. Dr Christopher Roberts & T. Kotani (Series Ed.), *NASSP issue brief series.* UNSW Canberra at the Australian Defence Force Academy.

Van Huy, D. (2020). A Vietnamese perspective on China's Belt and Road Initiative in Vietnam. *Contemporary Chinese Political Economy and Strategic Relations, 6*(1), 145–VIII.

Vietnamnews. (2020). *World's largest trade pact signed by ASEAN countries and five partners.* Retrieved from https://vietnamnews.vn/economy/806645/worlds-largest-trade-pact-signed-by-asean-countries-and-five-partners.html

Vu, V.-H., Soong, J.-J., & Nguyen, K.-N. (2021). Vietnam's perceptions and strategies toward China's Belt and Road Initiative expansion: Hedging with resisting. *The Chinese Economy, 54*(1), 56–68.

Womack, B. (2006). *China and Vietnam: The politics of asymmetry.* Cambridge University Press.

Xin, Z. T. (2016). *Yan jin zhong de Yue Zhong guan xi: Zhuan xing and qianzhan* [Vietnam–China relations in development: Changes and Prospect]. *Crossroad: Southeast Asia Studies, 6.*

Yilmaz, S., & Li, B. (2020). The BRI-led globalization and its implications for East Asian regionalization. *Chinese Political Science Review, 5*(3), 395–416. https://doi.org/10.1007/s41111-020-00145-2

Zhang, D., & Yin, J. (2019). *China's Belt and Road Initiative, from the inside looking out.* Retrieved in December 2021, from https://www.lowyinstitute.org/the-interpreter/china-s-belt-and-road-initiative-inside-looking-out

Zheng, Z. (2019). The changing Asian perception of China's rising: A BRI context. In J. Syed & Y.-H. Ying (Eds.), *China's Belt and Road Initiative in a global context* (pp. 41–59). Springer.

Chapter 42
The South Atlantic in China's Global Policy: Why It Matters?

Laura C. Ferreira-Pereira and Paulo Afonso B. Duarte

1 Introduction

The projection of power at sea, the control of supply lines and the fight against piracy have captured the growing attention by key-international actors given that the great majority of world trade circulates by sea (Jacobsen & Larsen, 2019; Lane & Pretes, 2020). China is an illustrative case, as evinced by the developing assertive posture it has been adopting in the framework of the twenty-first Century Maritime Silk Road, which is an integral part of the Belt and Road Initiative (BRI). The twenty-first Century Maritime Silk Road has translated into investments in port infrastructure along the Indian Ocean, while covering several countries in Southeast Asia and the African coast (Chatzky & McBride, 2020).

The literature offers insightful analyses concerning the People's Liberation Army (PLA) Navy presence and assertive stance in the Pacific and Indian Oceans (Butt et al., 2020; He & Li, 2020; Liu, 2020; Mohan & Abraham, 2020). The Chinese engagement in the Arctic has stimulated some scholarly works, but only in recent years (Bennett et al., 2020; Zeng et al., 2020). Yet, literature dedicated to China's interests, presence and influence in the vast Atlantic Ocean remains thin on the ground. There are few analyses dealing specifically with Chinese presence in North Atlantic; and most of these have mainly discussed China's Atlantic maritime strategy in the making (Goldstein, 2017; Martinson, 2019; *South China Morning Post*, 2021a). Other scholarly works have bypassed China's discreet interests in the South Atlantic, while showing a preference for addressing NATO's concerns regarding Russia's increasing maritime assertiveness in the North Atlantic (Horrell et al., 2016; Olsen,

L. C. Ferreira-Pereira
Research Center in Political Science (CICP-UMinho), University of Minho, Braga, Portugal
e-mail: lpereira@eeg.uminho.pt

P. A. B. Duarte (✉)
Universidade do Minho & Universidade Lusófona, Braga & Porto, Portugal
e-mail: pauloduarte@eeg.uminho.pt

© The Author(s), under exclusive license to Springer Nature Singapore Pte Ltd. 2023, corrected publication 2023
P. A. B. Duarte et al. (eds.), *The Palgrave Handbook of Globalization with Chinese Characteristics*, https://doi.org/10.1007/978-981-19-6700-9_42

2018; Păunescu, 2020; Tardy, 2021). Hence, the lack of literature on Chinese interests and presence in the South Atlantic (except for Abdenur & Neto, 2013a, 2013b; Goldstein, 2017, 2021; Martinson, 2019; Vreÿ, 2017) remains a gap which the present study will help to narrow down.

This chapter will focus on the South Atlantic to appraise the emergent geostrategic relevance of this region for China; in other words, why it matters, as the title conveys. It argues that, despite its geographical distance from Beijing, the South Atlantic has emerged as a timely strategic extension of China's maritime assertiveness in its surrounding waters. As such, as some have already anticipated, this region might serve as a relief mechanism in view of the pressure exercised by the US on China's navy in the Indo-Pacific (Martinson, 2019, p. 31). Along these lines, the South Atlantic might be used as a laboratory for PLA Navy's attempts to build up China's coastal defence capacities (Ibidem). This is so, not only since activities in this area might enable the PLA Navy to test its developing blue-water means and assets, but also because they might provide China with resources to develop an offensive and more active strategy that complements the PLA Navy's defensive posture vis-à-vis the US in the East and South China Seas. Eventually, all this points to the interdependence in Chinese naval calculus and international power projection between the South Atlantic, on the one hand, and the Indian Ocean and the Pacific Ocean, on the other. This is an aspect which the available Anglophone literature, focused on Chinese foreign policy, has not hitherto fully explored.

While focusing on China's presence in the South Atlantic, this study will give particular attention to Brazil for being the most prominent coastal and naval power in the region. Both actors have been close allies in multilateral initiatives and structures designed to promote the Global South, notably the BRICS and BASIC (Brazil, South Africa, India and China). At the same time, although Brazil has not formally joined the BRI, it has established and consolidated a strategic partnership with China. As of 2019, under Donald Trump's Administration, the "US first" policy underpinning Jair Bolsonaro's presidential diplomacy has not been without consequences for Sino-Brazilian relations, in general (Amorim & Ferreira-Pereira, 2021).

This chapter's analysis spans largely from 2014, when the PLA Navy made its first exercises into South Atlantic waters, until the outbreak of the Coronavirus crisis in March 2020, after which the major focus of Chinese authorities shifted largely to the management of the pandemics, both at the domestic and foreign policy levels. The analysis of the topic will rely on primary sources, among which stand out China's official documents (e.g. China's 2013 and 2019 Defence White Papers, the 12th and 13th Five-Year Plans, and China's 2015 Military Strategy) and economic databases (e.g. Statista, World Economic Forum, and Trading Economics). Scientific articles and book chapters will be used as the main secondary sources.

The present study will start by outlining the key issues at stake in South Atlantic before examining the major contours of Chinese activities in the area. It then attempts to demonstrate China's shifting stance from a bystander towards an emerging South Atlantic naval power, in view of the perceived security and strategic relevance of the region for Beijing. Finally, this chapter gives attention to Brazil's reactions vis-à-vis Chinese engagement in the region. Underlying this chapter's conclusion is the idea that although China's naval presence in the South Atlantic is still modest, there is evidence pointing to its somewhat inevitable expansion due to the mounting importance of the South Atlantic for Chinese authorities.

2 The South Atlantic: A Changing Strategic Landscape

The Atlantic is a heterogeneous and fragmented space. Historically, the North Atlantic has been part of the area of influence of NATO and the Unites States (US). Although the Atlantic Community, as Lippmann envisioned it, transcended the North Atlantic in terms of space and concept, the creation of NATO and its interests and priorities have entailed the neglect of the Atlantic's Middle and Southern flanks (Aubourg et al., 2013; Lesser, 2010; Lesser & Aynaoui, 2014). The South Atlantic, encompassing the oceanic expanse and the full basin area (both the sea and the coastal lands) located south of the Tropic of Cancer, has remained outside NATO's area of jurisdiction and strategic interest (Adogamhe, 2019). On the other hand, diverging views on the role and scope of NATO flourished across the South Atlantic (Abdenur & Neto, 2014a, p. 8). Overall, throughout the twentieth and early twenty-first century, the South Atlantic, has been one of the least strategically relevant oceans. Yet, for some observers, the South Atlantic has witnessed a "strategic rebirth" (Guedes, 2012, p. 26); and this change cannot be dissociated from diverse Chinese interests in this region.

Three major reasons account for that strategic renaissance (Duarte & Barros, 2019a; Lesser, 2010). Firstly, there is the biodiversity, mineral, and energy resources that can be found in the South Atlantic, which match the demand and search for complementary sources on the part of China and other players. In this regard, it should be stressed that, in recent years, there has been a series of discoveries of vast oil and gas reserves on South American and African platforms (Cortinhas, 2019; Duarte & Barros, 2019a, 2019b). Secondly, there is the South Atlantic's relevance within global trade given that "twenty percent of all maritime routes to and from the US transit through the South Atlantic" (Soares & Leopoldino, 2019, p. 127) that should be borne in mind to understand the rising strategic importance of this geographical area. Finally, there are complex security regional challenges, posed by several threats plaguing the African shores, like piracy, drug trafficking, and illicit fishing that need to be addressed for the sake of international security and stability (Seabra, 2014, p. 332; Soares & Leopoldino, 2019, p. 127). For instance, the Gulf of Guinea—home to vast oil and gas reserves—is on the crossroads of maritime piracy. Also, due to its geostrategic location, Cape Verde has been used as a hub for the transshipment of drugs coming from South America, with Europe as final destination (Siqueira, 2021). As for the Latin American shores, the Chinese fishing activities have been perceived as having "geopolitical dimensions," with US officials being "wary of China's increasing presence" in the region (Business Insider, 2021, para. 22). Such US wariness and suspicion have led Washington to deploy "US Coast Guard (USCG), [more precisely] its new ship, USCGC Stone, to the South Atlantic to build regional maritime security partnerships and counter illegal, unreported, and unregulated fishing in the region" (Australian Institute of International Affairs, 2021, para. 4). Incidentally, the case of Argentina is an illustrative one. In the past years, numerous Chinese boats have been caught up due to suspicions of illegal fishing in Argentinean waters (*South China Morning Post*, 2021b, para. 1). The situation became particularly tense in March 2016, when this country's navy sank a Chinese-flagged boat that was reportedly fishing illegally in its national waters (Aljazeera, 2016, para. 1).

Besides the strategic revival of the South Atlantic, it is important to underline the power vacuum prevailing in this region, given the lack of both maritime governance structures in most littoral states and a multilateral system of governance (Richardson et al., 2012, p. 160). Barros warns that such a lack of governance may well foster "mutual suspicions and dilemma security behaviours," which in turn "undermine regional initiatives" such as those involving sharing information between countries facing maritime insecurity (2019, p. 195). At the same time, in order to prevent external powers from taking advantage of such governance vacuum (Cortinhas, 2019) some have noted that Brazil has tried to mobilize other states in the region, in an effort to make the Middle and South Atlantic "an area of predominantly South-South cooperation, in which Western powers ought to play a secondary role" (Abdenur et al., 2016, p. 1113). Hence the weight attributed by Brazil to the Zone of Peace and Cooperation in the South Atlantic (ZOPACAS), created in 1986, by the United Nations upon its initiative as the guarantor of a "shared South Atlantic identity" (Ibid., p. 1114).[1] This background is necessary to contextualize the projects China has developed in the South Atlantic as part of its *Going Out Policy*.

3 The Chinese Going Out Policy in the South Atlantic: An Assessment

China's initiatives and activities in the South Atlantic can be seen as part of its *Going Out Policy* (Parello-Plesner, 2016) which originally began in 1999 and, after 2013, was enshrined in the BRI. The *Going Out Policy* has been inspired by a threefold objective: diversification of energy sources[2] and investments abroad, and internationalization of Chinese companies. The BRI, which encompasses the land-based Silk

---

[1] Currently ZOPACAS includes 24 member states: Angola, Argentina, Benin, Brazil, Cameroon, Cape Verde, Congo, Cote d'Ivoire, Democratic Republic of Congo, Equatorial Guinea, Gabon, Gambia, Ghana, Guinea, Guinea-Bissau, Liberia, Namibia, Nigeria, Sao Tome and Principe, Senegal, Sierra Leone, South Africa, Togo and Uruguay.

[2] In a context in which it is imperative that China finds new sources to ensure its energy security (largely explained by the end of the One Child Policy, as well as the Chinese Middle-class expansion), the Gulf of Guinea has great advantages for Chinese oil imports, when compared to other regions of the world, such as the Middle East. In fact, with the exception of Nigeria which is a member of the Organization of Petroleum Exporting Countries, the other countries of this Gulf do not pose major restrictions to the exploration and export of oil directly by China (Onuoha, 2009).

Road Economic Belt and the sea-based twenty-first-Century Maritime Silk Road, is the world's largest multilateral infrastructure-building project (Mathews, 2019). At the same time, as Mendez and Alden posit, it is "the material basis of Chinese new world order," the piece of a grand strategy aimed at "promoting China's status as the centre and the leader of the global economy" (2021, p. 844). With the restoration of the millennial concentric distribution of power which served China in the so-called *Pax Sinica* in view (Duarte & Leandro, 2020), Beijing has sought to consolidate its power capabilities, both on land and sea, as well as to gain uninterrupted access to places and resources. Incidentally, the 12th (2011–2015) and the 13th (2016–2020) Five-Year Plans help to understand China's concern in adopting a hybrid land-sea strategy for the country's security, in the framework of which stand out China's goal of building a Blue Water Navy, that is, a navy able to operate anywhere in the ocean(s). To achieve this goal, the geographical expansion of China's maritime activities beyond the Pacific Ocean to increasingly distant waters (such as those of the Atlantic Ocean) is of crucial relevance (Martinson, 2016, 2019; The 2019 Defence White Paper).

Despite Chinese official documents have not established any geographical or conceptual delimitation of the South Atlantic so far (Parello-Plesner, 2016), a common twofold denominator characterizes the Chinese stance towards the Latin American and African shores of South Atlantic. This is the search for energy, natural resources, and new markets, and the politico-diplomatic endeavour to isolate Taiwan (Duarte, 2016; Grieger, 2019). In the process, China has provided loans to African and Latin American states in exchange for access to natural resources, something which is often referred to as the "Angolan Model" and still remains for such states as an alternative to Western string-attached loans (Fijałkowski, 2011; Grieger, 2019).

China is Africa's most important trading partner, "with trade growing 40-fold in the past 20 years" (Nantulya, 2021, para. 2). In 2019, Angola, South Africa, and the Republic of Congo were the largest exporters for China, while Nigeria was the largest buyer of Chinese goods, followed by South Africa and Egypt (China Africa Research Initiative, 2019). Raw commodities and unfinished goods account for most of China's imports from Africa, while finished goods represent the most important Chinese exports to Africa. In this regard, it is noteworthy that, according to Nantulya, China has become the "top supplier of weapons to sub-Saharan Africa," while diversifying its sales "from small arms and light weapons to tanks, armoured personnel carriers, maritime patrol craft, aircraft, missiles, unmanned aerial vehicles, and artillery." It also became increasingly concentrated on "building institutional capability in Africa's security sector" (2019, pp. 3 and 4). Equally important, in the African continent, the Gulf of Guinea has acquired a certain prominence in terms of Chinese investments (Yachyshen, 2020; Zhang, 2019). While some of the latter have already led to infrastructure building, others, such as the deep-water port in São Tome and Principe, that China expects to become a regional transshipment centre, are still waiting for materialization (Yachyshen, 2020).

In September 2017, Foreign Minister Wang Yi declared that "Latin America [was] the natural extension of the twenty-first-Century Maritime Silk Road, and the Belt and Road Initiative has become a new opportunity for current China-Latin America cooperation" (Ministry of Foreign Affairs of PRC, 2017, para. 1). Three months later, China managed to extend the BRI to Latin America, through the inclusion of Panama in the list of countries embraced by its Initiative. Besides this, between 2018 and 2019, BRI cooperation memoranda have been signed with several member states of ZOPACAS.[3] The extension of the BRI to Latin America evinced Chinese willingness to strengthen ties with more Latin American states and consequently further eroded the US hegemony in this region (Bayardo, 2019, para. 2). Here, although the US has been at the forefront in the sphere of trade, China has been rapidly catching up (World Economic Forum, 2021) given the US disinterest in the South Atlantic which, albeit prior to 2016,[4] remained very visible during the Trump Administration inspired in the "America First" motto. Among the most important goods that China has imported from Latin America are raw commodities, particularly soybeans, copper, petroleum, and iron (Global Development Policy Center, 2020), with the main partners being Brazil, Chile, Peru, and Uruguay (Statista, 2021). In turn, China exports have mainly comprised manufactured and finished goods to Latin America (Trading Economics, 2021).

The Chinese *modus operandi* has raised considerable criticism on both shores of the Atlantic. Among the most common ones, features the lack of transparency underlying "contracts predominantly allocated to Chinese firms without public tender" (Grieger, 2019, p. 3). Another frequent criticism lies in the debt-trap attached to Chinese funding and the resulting fear from host countries vis-à-vis China's economic and political influence (do Nascimento, 2020). There is also the recurrent observation that contracts signed require that the Chinese workforce be usually larger than the one of the host state, in addition to the criticism that Chinese goods are cheaper and of lower-quality, thereby undermining local economies. The debate on China's stance as win–win versus neo-colonialist power has also been recurrent (Brautigam & Zhang, 2013; Carrai, 2020), with states like Cape Verde, Guinea, and Mali perceiving Chinese presence in a very positive way (Statista, 2020).

Regardless of mixed feelings and criticism explored in the following section, there is evidence that China has been emerging as a naval power in South Atlantic, as a result of its departure from a role of mere bystander in this geographical area.

---

[3] In 2018, the cases in point are Angola, Cameroon, Cape Verde, Côte d'Ivoire, Gabon, Gambia, Ghana, Namibia, Nigeria, Senegal, Sierra Leone, Togo and Uruguay. BRI cooperation memoranda with Benin, Equatorial Guinea and Liberia were established in 2019. Beyond this chapter's timeframe, Guinea-Bissau, Sao Tome and Principe and the Democratic Republic of Congo signed similar arrangements in 2021.

[4] This deficit of interest explains, for example, the lack of progress following the 2008 US declaration on the willingness to revive the US Fourth Fleet (The North American Congress on Latin America, 2008).

4 China as an Emerging South Atlantic Naval Power: Where Now, What's Next?

Although China's main security concerns regarding sea lanes of communication have been more salient in the Indian Ocean and the East and South China Seas, in recent years the South Atlantic has attracted Chinese authorities' attention. There is a considerable Chinese diaspora living and working on both shores of the Atlantic, who is often the object of kidnapping, murder, and other forms of violence. This has contributed to raise awareness among Beijing's authorities about "diplomatic protection," that is to say the pressing need to protect national citizens, as well as investments and infrastructure in third countries, namely located along the African and Latin America shores (Parello-Plesner, 2016; The 2019 Defence White Paper). As a result of this, China has established an anti-terrorism law in 2005, which enables the PLA to undertake counterterrorist missions overseas "with the approval from the State Council and agreements from concerned countries" (The National People's Congress of the PRC, 2015, para. 3).

The Gulf of Guinea is particularly important, as the coastal states of this region, inhabited by an extremely young population, represent a vast consumer and investment market for China. In fact, across this region, about 60% of the people are under 25 years of age, thereby providing important human resources for the growth of new industries, like fishing and logging. In addition, these industries play a vital role in helping China to ensure its food security (Yachyshen, 2020). In 2015, the African Union and China signed a cooperation agreement to build transport infrastructure which would connect 54 African countries, including those in the Gulf of Guinea. Nigeria has played a significant role in this initiative, as evinced in the fact that China has been financing several projects in the country, such as a deep-water port and the construction of the so-called Lekki Free Zone (Babatunde, 2020).

Diverse factors have contributed to bring security issues in South Atlantic to the forefront of Chinese agenda. Among these stand out the threat perception(s) linked to piracy in the Gulf of Guinea and the Boko Haram activities, on the one hand, and China's new role conception as a responsible international power (Duarte & Ferreira-Pereira, 2021) on the other. To this, it should be added the considerable economic losses experienced by China in Libya and Sudan, which made the country aware of the necessity to expand its involvement in Africa's peace-support activities in order to secure national economic and strategic interests (Yu, 2018, p. 493). Consequently, since the end of the 2000s, various Chinese White Papers on defence have reflected a gradual moderation regarding the traditionally dogmatic principle of non-interference, in order to ensure the protection of both Chinese investments and diaspora abroad. The 2013 and 2019 Defence White Papers, as well as China's 2015 Military Strategy, are cases in point. These strategic documents have underlined the need for the PLA to develop capabilities in Military Operations Other than War (MOOTW). This encompasses, for instance, counter-piracy action, evacuation, and peacekeeping.

In 2014, PLA Navy's units undertook their first-ever joint drills with Tanzanian forces, and in the first half of 2018, the PLA Navy's anti-piracy escorted task forces and conducted joint military exercises with Cameroon, Gabon, Ghana, and Nigeria (Grieger, 2019, p. 8). In November of the following year, China has engaged in a first joint naval drill with two BRICS partners, Russia and South Africa (code-named MOSI), off the city of Cape Town (The Diplomat, 2019, para. 1). That being said, in order to ensure the basic conditions to protect Chinese diaspora and investments in the South Atlantic shores, the PLA Navy would need to become a resident naval actor in the region, instead of relying exclusively on the logistics of friendly ports, such as Cape Town, to conduct its operations. Djibouti, where China opened its first naval base in 2017, is too distant from the South Atlantic. The PLA Navy would take over 13 days to sail from Djibouti until Lagos, in Nigeria, should any need for evacuation of Chinese citizens in African shores arise (Martinson, 2019). Incidentally, the former's unprecedented rescue mission conducted in Libya, in 2011, through the deployment of the frigate "Xuzhou" (Collins & Erickson, 2011, para. 1), has further raised Beijing authorities' awareness to the need to be vigilant in unstable regions along the Atlantic shores, in order to act fast when the lives of Chinese citizens are in danger. This explains China's intention reported by US intelligence in establishing its first permanent military presence in the Gulf of Guinea, more concretely, in Equatorial Guinea (The Wall Street Journal, 2021, para. 1).

There is a fundamental political obstacle preventing the PLA Navy from establishing a naval base in the Gulf of Guinea: the regional states' reluctance and hostility "to open up their jurisdictional waters to policing by outside powers" (Martinson, 2019, p. 30). But according to some observers, Namibia's strategic access to the South Atlantic, together with its logistics facility and proximity to other hubs of the twenty-first-Century Maritime Silk Road, makes this country an attractive candidate to host the first Chinese naval base in the South Atlantic (Nantulya, 2019). As Robert O'Brien highlighted, Walvis Bay would allow the PLA Navy "to patrol the critical Cape of Good Hope around Africa and the Cape Horn around South America. The approaches to the key North Atlantic sea lanes linking the Americas, Africa and Europe would be nearby" (In The Diplomat, 2015, para. 1). Eventually, during an official event in February 2018, the Chinese Ambassador to Namibia, Zhang Yiming, recognized the plausibility of this scenario when noting that Namibia's port of Walvis Bay "will become the most brilliant pearl on the Atlantic Coast of southwest Africa" (The State Council Information Office of the PRC, 2018, para. 1). This statement is particularly telling for two main reasons. On the one hand, it is a clear acknowledgement that Namibia, with whom China shares a "special military relationship dating back to Chinese support for Namibia's independence war against South Africa" (Nantulya, 2019, p. 4), has the potential to play a crucial role in Chinese Atlantic MOOTW. On the other hand, it holds an implicit reference to China's String of Pearls in the Indian Ocean, in which Djibouti (the first Chinese naval base abroad) has played a critical role (Barton, 2021).

Time will tell about Chinese endeavours towards establishing a naval base in Walvis Bay, complementing Djibouti's assistance to the PLA Navy, which would result in the extension of China's String of Pearls to the South Atlantic. As for now, there is evidence that, in recent years, Walvis Bay has hosted numerous PLA Navy port visits and naval drills and that its infrastructure could support nearly all types of PLA Navy surface combatants (Peltier et al., 2020). Also, Namibian press (e.g. Hartman, 2014) has spread out rumours that China has attempted to build naval facilities in Walvis Bay, based on a similar approach previously adopted in Djibouti, entailing the initial construction of a deep-water port before opening the naval base. The pieces seem to fit well in the puzzle to the extent that, according to Nantulya "once complete, this port will connect Southern Africa to China Harbour Engineering Company ports and infrastructure in São Tome and Principe, Cameroon, Nigeria, Ghana, the Ivory Coast, and Guinea, and planned facilities in Gambia and Senegal" (2019, p. 4). As aptly noted by the same observer, all these maritime corridors have important security dimensions as critical nodes of the twenty-first-Century Maritime Silk Road (Ibidem).

China's concerns with the protection of its diaspora, investments, and infrastructure in third countries have been gradually accompanied by a developing long-term strategic calculus in which the South Atlantic became part of Beijing's equation to relieve US pressure in the East and South China Seas. So far, China has implemented what is called an "interior strategy,"[5] aimed at countering any possible threat posed by the US and its allies in the former's regional waters. At the same time, the South Atlantic has begun to provide China with a complementary "exterior strategy" of a more active and offensive nature, which has been endorsed by Chinese maritime planners. Such strategy consists of using the South Atlantic to "diffuse the attention of extra-regional powers away from China's maritime periphery," by mobilizing a "permanent fleet of 2–3 aircraft carrier strike groups" to the region, in an attempt to "deter and pin down US forces" (Martinson, 2019, p. 28). In other words, by becoming gradually more assertive in the South Atlantic, China would reduce the US encirclement in Asia, indirectly leading Washington to demobilize some of its naval means used in the Pacific, to better contain the newly perceived Chinese threat in the Atlantic. Incidentally, a top US general for Africa has warned that a mounting threat from China may come, not only from the Pacific region, but also from the waters of the Atlantic as well. US. In an interview given to the Associated Press, Gen. Stephen Townsend, observed that Beijing has already approached countries stretching from Mauritania to the south of Namibia in order to establish a large navy port capable of hosting submarines or aircraft carriers on Africa's western coast. If this prospect is materialized, China would be able to base warships in its expanding Navy in the Atlantic, as well as in the Pacific oceans (Associated Press, 2021).

Chinese visits and maritime drills in South Atlantic ports, as dating back to 2014 or so, are relatively recent when compared to the country's more active stance in other oceans. Yet, since that time, one has witnessed an evolution from ad hoc initiatives to more independent and long-term operations in this region. While such operations have allowed the PLA Navy to get more familiarized with South Atlantic underwater geography and operating conditions, they have also demonstrated a departure from

---

[5] This "interior strategy" is both passive and defensive to the extent that it enables China to react to US pressure on its Eastern flank.

the traditional bystander approach to an emerging proactive South Atlantic naval power. For example, China has already expressed its interest in "constructing the Antarctic Logistics Pole in Ushuaia, Tierra del Fuego" to support Chinese expeditions to the South Pole (Dialogo, 2019, para. 10). This logistical maritime hub has the potential to provide the PLA Navy with a foothold in the Strait of Magellan, which lies at the geostrategic convergence between the Atlantic and Pacific oceans, *en route* to Antarctica.[6] Also, it might benefit from the previous openness shown by Argentinean authorities towards Neuquen, a space station in Patagonia,[7] which further evinces China's military presence on the western shore of the Atlantic Ocean and its interest in protecting maritime lanes communication and reserves of natural resources in the South Atlantic (Boletim Geocorrente, 2020). Along these lines, Argentina might play an important role in China's Atlantic operations due to the Antarctica factor (Dialogo, 2019, para. 10).

However, considering that Brazil is the most prominent coastal and naval power in South Atlantic, it is important to shed light upon its posture vis-à-vis the developing presence of China in the region against the backdrop of the existing Brazil-China strategic partnership.

5 Brazil's vis-à-vis Chinese Emergence in South Atlantic

As of the early years of 2000s, Brazil and China have played a significant role in international trade, economy, and finance, domains within which they have attempted to redefine global governance. In their condition of emerging powers, they have promoted South-South cooperation at several international fora, notably the BRICS, G20, BASIC, and the also the United Nations, stressing the role of multilateralism and multipolarity (Amorim & Ferreira-Pereira, 2021). According to Trinkunas, they have stood together by criticizing "the degree to which the United States ignored the rules of the rules-based liberal order it purportedly championed" (2020, p. 5). Non-intervention, solidarity, and mutual respect have featured as the principal characteristics of their common stance in world affairs, most particularly within the Global South.

Their diplomatic ties, dating back to 1974, were elevated to a strategic partnership in 1993 and, as of 2004, to a so-called "all weather strategic partnership."[8] Overall, the latter is of major significance if one bears in mind that China is the largest country

---

[6] For more details about China's Antarctic engagement and strategy, see Chapter 46 entitled "Why Is China Going Polar? Understanding Engagement and Implications for the Arctic and Antarctica," in this Volume.

[7] This space station (concluded in 2016) is managed by China Satellite Launch and Tracking Control General, which reports to the Strategic Support Force of the PLA.

[8] According to Li and Ye, "the term All-weather suggests that the cooperation between [...] two countries would continue regardless of how the external environment changes" (2019, p. 67). An "all-weather strategic partnership" is seen by China as a superior form of cooperation between states, even above the official strategic partnership (Li & Ye, 2019).

of the developing world, while Brazil is the largest developing state in the Western hemisphere. Not unnaturally, Brazil was the first Latin American country that established, in 2012, a comprehensive strategic partnership with China. Under the Presidency of Dilma Rousseff (2011–2016), as it had been the case during Lula da Silva mandates, Brazil cultivated robust ties with China which featured as a foreign policy priority. On the other hand, in the domestic sphere, the "Chinese factor" has become increasingly noticed as it is the case with the domain of infrastructure building. For instance, the Chinese company CCCC has been operating Brazil's second-largest container port in Paranaguá, and China is planning to build an enormous port in São Luis (the capital of the state of Maranhão) (Espach, 2021, para. 3). Moreover, much of the potential existing in this bilateral relationship is still to be unleashed. According to Marcondes and Barbosa (2018), there is remarkable potential for Sino-Brazilian defence cooperation in areas ranging from defence industry and space technology, information technology, telecommunications, and remote sensing, among others.

Apparently, the growing presence of China in the African continent and its activities in South Atlantic waters performed by PLA Navy, as of 2014, did not affect the Sino-Brazilian relations. This is so although the Brazilian national defence documents have stressed the "strategic importance of South Atlantic," while placing this region among the priority areas for National Defence, where national Brazilian authorities should promote the security of the maritime lines of communication (*Política Nacional de Defesa e Estratégia Nacional de Defesa*, 2012, pp. 22, 23 and 31). The 2012 White Book of National Defence (*Livro Branco de Defesa Nacional*) has affirmed that Brazil's "strong bound to the sea moves it to exert a natural influence on the South Atlantic" (pp. 16 and 17) in which the country has a "special interest in peace and security" (Ibid., p. 35). Also, this key strategic document has stated clearly that: "Conflicts and rivalries strange to the South Atlantic should not be here projected by states situated in other regions" (Ibid., p. 26). The 2020 Brazil Navy Strategic Plan (*Plano Estratégico da Marinha*) and the 2020 White Book of National Defence reiterate this view, while ascribing particular importance to the need to ensure free lanes of communication in the South Atlantic. In this regard, Brazilian authorities perceive the Gulf of Guinea as playing a major role.

Besides recognizing that Brazilian "strategic environment [...] includes the South Atlantic and the countries bordering Africa, as well as Antarctica" (p. 21), the 2012 National Defence Policy and National Defence Strategy adds that "Brazil gives priority to the countries of South America and Africa, especially West Africa and the Portuguese-speaking countries, and seeks to deepen its ties with them" (p. 25). Incidentally, during Lula's Presidency, Brazil has prioritized the export of defence equipment to the Atlantic Africa, as exemplified by the sale of ships, *Super Tucano* aircraft and the development of advanced technology projects like the *A-Darter* Air-to-Air Missile (da Silva, 2020, p. 108). At the same time, Brazil has engaged itself in the training of military personnel from various African countries, notably Angola, Cape Verde, Guinea-Bissau, Namibia, Nigeria, and São Tome and Principe (Ibid., p. 102). Another example of Brazilian endeavours to ensure its leading role in the South Atlantic, thereby countering external powers' attempts to penetrate in the region, is the creation of a Navy mission centre in São Tome and Principe (in 2014) charged with the identification of the major needs of navies in the area (Mattos et al., 2017, p. 272). At the same time, the country has been competing with China in terms of military training and equipment sales to many states of the African Atlantic coast, including Lusophone Africa (Abdenur & Neto, 2014b; Grieger, 2019). Regarding the latter, Brazil has been aware of China's attempts to expand its influence in the South Atlantic Portuguese-speaking countries, whose geostrategic location is key within the BRI dynamics of enlargement in/across the South Atlantic. More concretely, Brazil has been attentive not only to Chinese critical investments on land, such as Dar es Salaam-Lobito railway system connecting Tanzania to Angola (in the making), but also on the establishment of "deep-sea ports and maritime installations in West African coast," which may help China to expand its twenty-first-Century Maritime Silk Road to South Atlantic (dos Santos & Lobo, 2020, p. 25).

According to some observers, arguably enough, "the sale of Chinese war material to African countries does not interfere with Brazil's strategic goals of preventing militarization of the South Atlantic by exogenous countries to the region" (da Silva, 2020, p. 122). China and Brazil's economic and military engagement in the Atlantic coast of Africa exhibits a major difference: while Chinese strategic interests in Africa are well-defined, continuous and projected for the long-run, Brazilian approach seems to be subject to cyclical changes, besides lacking a coherent and long-term oriented planning (da Silva, 2020). This could potentially damage Brazilian relationships with relevant countries, such as Namibia, which has already showed interest in diversifying military partners and suppliers. In this regard, China appears to be an interesting alternative. For instance, in 2012 "Namibian forces chose a Chinese company as an alternative naval hardware supplier" (Seabra, 2016, p. 99). Later, on 27th October, 2017, the Namibian President, Hage Geingob, "thanked China for its assistance to the southwestern African country in protecting its territory and maritime resources" (Xinhua, 2017, para. 5). Such assistance was substantiated in the donation by PLA of two state-of-the-art submarine chasers, Brukkaros and Daures, to Namibian army (Ibidem). Episodes like these might carry with them the seeds to undermine Brazilian interests, as Namibian support for any Brazilian-inspired South Atlantic conceptualization "remains open to question" (Ibidem). This, in turn, seems to pose a geostrategic challenge to Brazil's prominence in the region in the medium/long term, should Namibia be keen to offer the PLA Navy residency in South Atlantic waters, as we have discussed in the previous section.

6 Conclusion

Against the backdrop of the strategic revival of the South Atlantic, this chapter has attempted to shed light on the importance of this region for China's global policy. It has underlined that, since 2014, the PLA Navy has been more active in the South Atlantic. This was associated to Beijing's authorities need to protect both its diaspora and investments in the South Atlantic shores, in a context of globalization of world trade and increasing quest for natural resources. And it was not dissociated from the governance vacuum, as well as the longstanding US and NATO disinterest in the region, in contrast to what has been these actors' historical stance in the North Atlantic.

Moreover, this chapter has showed that, although China's naval presence in the South Atlantic remains considerably modest—when compared to its assertive stance in the East and South China Seas, and even in the Indian Ocean—, the continuous modernization of the PLA Navy, together with its willingness to operate in increasingly distant seas, have indicated a gradual shift in this state of affairs. Indeed, the PLA Navy's diversified activities in the South Atlantic have substantiated China's endeavours to evolve from its longstanding near-coast defence towards exploring possibilities in more distant waters of the South Atlantic. Overall, this region offers a twofold advantage. On the one hand, African and Latin American shores provide China with complementary energy, food, and mineral sources. On the other hand, it might be relevant in helping the country to relieve its Eastern flank from US pressure (Martinson, 2019). In fact, engagement in South Atlantic might enable Chinese authorities to foster a complementary offensive and more active naval strategy, thereby transcending the exclusive traditional attachment to a defensive strategy vis-à-vis US containment, both in the Indian and the Pacific Oceans.

This study featuring the still modest but significant China's engagement in South Atlantic gave particular attention to the Brazilian view of its prominence as a coastal and naval power in this region, which is of great national importance in strategic, security, and defence terms. Since the early 2000s, the country has developed an "all weather strategic partnership" with China. Yet, it has chosen to remain outside the realm of BRI. In view of the developing posture of China in South Atlantic, evidence regarding Brazilian (negative) response or reactive strategy is thin, fostering doubts about how Brazilian authorities have been "the facto" accommodating Chinese presence and influence in South Atlantic. Nonetheless, this is a matter expected to acquire even greater significance, as the South Atlantic develops into a critical gateway for an interconnected world marked by globalization trends with Chinese characteristics (see the Introduction of this Volume), designed to protect sea lanes of communication, as well as China's diaspora, interests, and investments worldwide.

Acknowledgements The authors acknowledge that this study was conducted at the Research Center in Political Science (UIDB/CPO/00758/ 2020), University of Minho/University of Évora, and that it was supported by the Portuguese Foundation for Science and Technology and the Portuguese Ministry of Education and Science, through national funds. The authors would like to thank Danilo Marcondes, Daniella Melo, and João Mourato Pinto for their valuable comments on earlier drafts.

Disclosure Statement No potential conflict of interest was reported by the author(s).

Bibliographic References

Abdenur, A., Mattheis, F., & Seabra, P. (2016). An ocean for the Global South: Brazil and the zone of peace and cooperation in the South Atlantic. *Cambridge Review of International, 29*(3), 1112–1131. https://doi.org/10.1080/09557571.2016.1230592

Abdenur, A., & Neto, D. (2013a). La creciente influencia de China en el Atlántico Sur. *Revista CIDOB D'afers Internacionals, 102–103*(2013), 169–197.

Abdenur, A., & Neto, D. (2013b). Brazil's maritime strategy in the South Atlantic: The Nexus between security and resources. *South African Institute of International Affairs. Occasional Paper no. 161.*

Abdenur, A., & Neto, D. (2014a). Regionbuilding by rising powers: The South Atlantic and Indian Ocean rims compared. *Journal of the Indian Ocean Region, 10*(1), 1–17. https://doi.org/10.1080/19480881.2014.896103

Abdenur, A., & Neto, D. (2014b). O Brasil e a cooperação em defesa: A construção de uma identidade regional no Atlântico Sul. *Revista Brasileira De Política Internacional, 57*(1), 5–21.

Adogamhe, P. (2019). Maritime security and governance of the South Atlantic: The Nigerian perspective. In E. Duarte, & M. Barros (Eds.), *Navies and maritime policies in the South Atlantic* (pp. 13–40). Palgrave Macmillan.

Aljazeera. (2016, March 16). *Argentina sinks Chinese boat for 'illegal fishing'*. https://www.aljazeera.com/news/2016/3/16/argentina-sinks-chinese-boat-for-illegal-fishing

Amorim, S., & Ferreira-Pereira, L. C. (2021). Brazil's quest for autonomy in Asia: The role of strategic partnerships with China and Japan. *Revista Brasileira de Política Internacional, 64*(2).

Associated Press. (2021, May 6). *General: China's Africa outreach poses threat from Atlantic.* https://www.usnews.com/news/politics/articles/2021-05-06/general-chinas-africa-outreach-poses-threat-from-atlantic

Aubourg, V., Bossuat, G., & Scott-Smith, G. (Eds.). (2013). *European community, Atlantic community?* Éditions Soleb.

Australian Institute of International Affairs. (2021, May 20). *Will great power competition in the South Atlantic spill into Antarctica?* https://www.internationalaffairs.org.au/australianoutlook/will-great-power-competition-in-the-south-atlantic-spill-into-antarctica/

Babatunde, M. (2020). Promoting connectivity of infrastructure in the context of One Belt, One Road Initiatives: Implications for Africa in the fourth industrial revolution. In G. Odularu, M. Hassan, & M. Babatunde (Eds.), *Fostering trade in Africa: Advances in African economic, social and political development*. Springer.

Barros, M. (2019). Conclusion. In E. Duarte & M. Barros (Eds.), *Navies and maritime policies in the South Atlantic* (pp. 187–196). Palgrave Macmillan.

Barton, B. (2021). Leveraging the String of Pearls for strategic gains? An assessment of the Maritime Silk Road Initiative's (MSRI) economic/security nexus in the Indian Ocean Region (IOR). *Asian Security, 17*(2), 216–235. https://doi.org/10.1080/14799855.2020.1844664

Bayardo, M. (2019). *Will Latin America become part of the New Silk Road?* EGADE Business School. https://egade.tec.mx/en/egade-ideas/research/will-latin-america-become-part-new-silk-road

Bennett, M. M., Stephenson, S. R., Yang, K., Bravo, M. T., & De Jonghe, B. (2020). The opening of the Transpolar Sea Route: Logistical, geopolitical, environmental, and socioeconomic impacts. *Marine Policy*. https://doi.org/10.1016/j.marpol.2020.104178

Boletim Geocorrente. (2020). Edição Especial: Zopacas. Escola de Guerra Naval. 15 de outubro. Ano 6.

Brautigam, D., & Zhang, H. (2013). Green dreams: Myth and reality in China's agricultural investment in Africa. *Third World Quarterly, 34*(9), 1676–1696.

Business Insider. (2021). *Fleets of fishing ships are going 'dark' in the South Atlantic, and China is the leading culprit.* https://www.businessinsider.com/chinese-fishing-vessels-going-dark-off-argentina-waters-2021-6

Butt, K., Kharl, S., & Bhatti, K. (2020). String of Pearls: Politics of ports in Indian Ocean. *South Asian Studies, 35*(1), 73–86.

Carrai, M. (2020). The China model and its Reach in Africa: Toward a new partnership? *Brown Journal of World Affairs, 27*(1), 135–149.

Chatzky, A., & McBride, J. (2020). China's massive Belt and Road Initiative. *Council on Foreign Relations.* https://www.cfr.org/backgrounder/chinas-massive-belt-and-road-initiative

China Africa Research Initiative. (2019). *Data: China-Africa trade.* http://www.sais-cari.org/data-china-africa-trade

Collins, G., & Erickson, A. (2011, March 11). Implications of China's military evacuation of citizens from Libya. https://jamestown.org/program/implications-of-chinas-military-evacuation-of-citizens-from-libya/

Cortinhas, J. (2019). Brazil and the construction of its power to defend the South Atlantic. In E. Duarte & M. Barros (Eds.), *Navies and maritime policies in the South Atlantic.* Palgrave Macmillan.

da Silva, M. (2020). Brazil and China interests in Atlantic Africa. *Journal of China and International Relations, 8*(SE), 98–132. https://doi.org/10.5278/jcir.v8iSE.4241

Dialogo. (2019). *China reaffirms strategic interest in Antarctica.* https://dialogo-americas.com/articles/china-reaffirms-strategic-interest-in-antarctica/#.Yb9ASGjMLIU

do Nascimento, L. (2020). The Beijing Consensus and the New Silk Road in Africa: Chinese investments in new disputes of hegemony. *Conjuntura Internacional, 17*(1), 27–38. https://doi.org/10.5752/p.1809-6182.2020v17n1p27-38

dos Santos, P., & Lobo, A. (2020). *Geo-political relations between China and South Atlantic Portuguese-speaking Countries: A blue evolving partnership.* https://www.researchgate.net/publication/354236358_Geo-political_Relations_between_China_and_South_Atlantic_Portuguese-speaking_Countries_A_Blue_Evolving_Partnership

Duarte, P. (2016). As Incursões da China na América Latina e no Atlântico Sul. *Brazilian Journal of International Relations, 5*(1), 98–123.

Duarte, É., & Barros, M. (Eds.). (2019a). *Maritime security challenges in the South Atlantic.* Palgrave Macmillan.

Duarte, É., & Barros, M. (Eds.). (2019b). *Navies and maritime policies in the South Atlantic.* Palgrave Macmillan.

Duarte, P., & Ferreira-Pereira, L. C. (2021). The soft power of China and the European Union in the context of the Belt and Road Initiative and global strategy. *Journal of Contemporary European Studies.* https://doi.org/10.1080/14782804.2021.1916740

Duarte, P., & Leandro, F. (Eds.). (2020). *The Belt and Road Initiative: An old archetype of a new development model.* Palgrave.

Espach, R. (2021, March 22). *A new great game finds the South Atlantic.* https://warontherocks.com/2021/03/a-new-great-game-finds-the-south-atlantic/

Fijałkowski, L. (2011). China's 'soft power' in Africa? *Journal of Contemporary African Studies, 29*(2), 223–232. https://doi.org/10.1080/02589001.2011.555197

Global Development Policy Center. (2020). *New China-Latin American economic bulletin, 2020.* https://www.bu.edu/gdp/2020/03/18/new-china-latin-american-economic-bulletin-2020/

Goldstein, L. (2017). Is China crafting an Atlantic maritime strategy? *The National Interest.* http://nationalinterest.org/feature/beijing-sea-china-crafting-atlantic-maritime-strategy-19622

Goldstein, L. (2021). That's weird: Could China be getting an Atlantic fleet? *The National Interest.* https://nationalinterest.org/blog/reboot/thats-weird-could-china-be-getting-atlantic-fleet-185492

Grieger, G. (2019, October). China's growing role as a security actor in Africa. *European Parliamentary Research Service.* https://www.europarl.europa.eu/RegData/etudes/BRIE/2019/642232/EPRS_BRI(2019)642232_EN.pdf

Guedes, A. (2012). Geopolitical shifts in the Wider Atlantic: Past, present, and future. In Richardson, J., Guedes, A. M., Gorce, X. D., Salvy, A. F. D., & Holthus, P. (Eds.), *The fractured Ocean: Current challenges to maritime policy in the wider Atlantic* (pp. 11–57). Wider Atlantic Series.

Hartman, A. (2014, November 19). Chinese naval base for Walvis Bay. *Namibian.* https://www.namibian.com.na/index.php?id=130693&page=archive-read

He, K., & Li, M. (2020). Understanding the dynamics of the Indo-Pacific: US–China strategic competition, regional actors, and beyond. *International Affairs, 96*(1), 1–7. https://doi.org/10.1093/ia/iiz242

Horrell, S., Nordenman, M., & Slocombe, W. (2016, July). *Updating NATO's maritime strategy.* Issue Brief. Atlantic Council.

Jacobsen, K., & Larsen, J. (2019). Piracy studies coming of age: A window on the making of maritime intervention actors. *International Affairs, 95*(5), 1037–1054. https://doi.org/10.1093/ia/iiz099

Lane, J., & Pretes, M. (2020). Maritime dependency and economic prosperity: Why access to oceanic trade matters. *Marine Policy.* https://doi.org/10.1016/j.marpol.2020.104180

Lesser, I. (2010). *Southern Atlanticism: Geopolitics and strategy for the other half of the Atlantic Rim* (pp. 3–23). The German Marshall Fund of the United States.

Lesser, I., & Aynaoui, K. (2014, October). Atlanticism in the 21st century: Convergence and cooperation in a wider Atlantic. In *Atlantic currents: An annual report on wider Atlantic: Perspectives and patterns* (pp. 3–14).

Li, Q., & Ye, M. (20219). China's emerging partnership network: What, who, where, when and why. *International Trade, Politics and Development, 3*(2), 66–81. https://doi.org/10.1108/ITPD-05-2019-0004

Liu, F. (2020). The recalibration of Chinese assertiveness: China's responses to the Indo-Pacific challenge. *International Affairs, 96*(1), 9–27. https://doi.org/10.1093/ia/iiz226

Livro. Branco de Defesa Nacional (White Book of National Defence). (2012). https://www.gov.br/defesa/pt-br/arquivos/2012/mes07/lbdn.pdf

Livro Branco de Defesa Nacional (White Book of National Defence). (2020). https://www.gov.br/defesa/pt-br/assuntos/copy_of_estado-e-defesa/livro_branco_congresso_nacional.pdf

Marcondes, D., & Barbosa, P. (2018). Brazil–China defense cooperation: A strategic partnership in the making? *Journal of Latin American Geography, 17*(2), 140–166. https://doi.org/10.1353/lag.2018.0025

Martinson, R. (2016). The 13th five-year plan: A new chapter in China's maritime transformation. *China Brief, 16*(1): 14–17. https://jamestown.org/program/the-13th-five-year-plan-a-new-chapter-in-chinas-maritime-transformation/

Martinson, R. (2019). China as an Atlantic naval power. *The RUSI Journal, 164*(7), 18–31. https://doi.org/10.1080/03071847.2019.1700684

Mathews, J. (2019). China's long term trade and currency goals: The Belt & Road Initiative. *The Asia-Pacific Journal, 17*(5), 1–23.

Mattos, B., Matos, F., & Kenkel, K. (2017). Brazilian policy and the creation of a regional security complex in the South Atlantic: Pax Brasiliana? *Contexto Internacional, 39*(2), 263–280. https://doi.org/10.1590/s0102-8529.2017390200004

Mendez, A., & Alden, C. (2021). China in Panama: From peripheral diplomacy to grand strategy. *Geopolitics, 26*(3), 838–860. https://doi.org/10.1080/14650045.2019.1657413

Ministry of Foreign Affairs of PRC (People's Republic of China). (2017). *Wang Yi: The Belt and Road Initiative becomes new opportunity for China-Latin America cooperation.* https://www.fmprc.gov.cn/mfa_eng/zxxx_662805/t1494844.shtml

Mohan, S., & Abraham, J. (2020). Shaping the regional and maritime battlefield? The Sino-Indian strategic competition in South Asia and adjoining waters. *Maritime Affairs: Journal of the National Maritime Foundation of India, 16*(1), 82–97. https://doi.org/10.1080/09733159.2020.1781374

Nantulya, P. (2019, January). Chinese hard power supports its growing strategic interests in Africa. *Africa Center for Strategic Studies, 17.* https://africacenter.org/spotlight/chinese-hard-power-supports-its-growing-strategic-interests-in-africa/

Nantulya, P. (2021, March 2). Reshaping African Agency in China–Africa relations. *Africa Center for Strategic Studies.* https://africacenter.org/spotlight/reshaping-african-agency-china-africa-relations/

Olsen, J. (Ed.). (2018). *NATO and the North Atlantic: Revitalising collective defence.* RUSI.

Onuoha, G. (2009). Energy and security in the Gulf of Guinea: A Nigerian perspective. *South African Journal of International Affairs, 16*(2), 245–264. https://doi.org/10.1080/10220460903269008

Parello-Plesner, J. (2016, March). *China's risk map in the South Atlantic.* Foreign and Security Policy Paper. The German Marshall Fund of the United States.

Păunescu, P. (2020). NATO encounters on 'High North' strategic direction. *Annals: Series on Military Sciences, 12*(2), 187–199.

Peltier, C., Nurkin, T., & O'Connor, S. (2020, April 15). China's logistics capabilities for expeditionary operations. *Janes* (prepared for the U.S.–China Economic and Security Review Commission). https://www.uscc.gov/sites/default/files/2020-04/China%20Expeditionary%20Logistics%20Capabilities%20Report.pdf

Plano Estratégico da Marinha do Brasil (Brazil Navy Strategic Plan). (2020). https://www.marinha.mil.br/pem2040

Política Nacional de Defesa e Estratégia Nacional de Defesa (National Defence Policy and National Defence Strategy). (2012). Ministério da Defesa.

Richardson, J., Guedes, A., Gorce, X., Salvy, A.-M., & Holthus, P. (2012). *The fractured Ocean: Current challenges to maritime policy in the wider Atlantic.* Wider Atlantic Series.

Seabra, P. (2014). A case of unmet expectations: Portugal and the South Atlantic. *Portuguese Journal of Social Science, 13*(3), 331–346.

Seabra, P. (2016). Defence cooperation between Brazil and Namibia: Enduring ties across the South Atlantic. *South African Journal of International Affairs, 23*(1), 89–106.

Siqueira, F. (2021, April). *The South Atlantic drug trafficking route as a threat to the regional security.* CEDIS Working Papers. https://cedis.fd.unl.pt/wp-content/uploads/2021/05/DSD_2021_ABR-01.pdf

Soares, R., & Leopoldino, C. (2019). Gateway and neighbourhood: Brazilian perspective on South Atlantic security. In É. Duarte & M. Barros (Eds.), *Navies and maritime policies in the South Atlantic* (pp. 125–149). Palgrave Macmillan.

South China Morning Post. (2021a). China's naval plans in Africa are threat in Atlantic, says US general. https://www.scmp.com/news/china/diplomacy/article/3132471/chinas-naval-plans-africa-are-threat-atlantic-says-us-general

South China Morning Post. (2021b). Chinese boats caught up in suspicions of illegal fishing in Argentina's waters. https://www.scmp.com/news/china/diplomacy/article/3136138/chinese-boats-caught-suspicions-illegal-fishing-argentinas

Statista. (2021). *China as share of total exports from selected countries in Latin America in 2019.* https://www.statista.com/statistics/1105815/latin-america-share-exports-china-country/

Statista. (2020). *Africans perception on positive influence of China in their countries between 2019 and 2020, by country.* https://www.statista.com/statistics/1189157/africans-perception-on-positive-influence-of-china-by-country/

Tardy, T. (2021). The risks of NATO's maladaptation. *European Security, 30*(1), 24–42.

The 12th Five-Year Plan. (2011). *The 12th five-year plan for economic and social development of the People's Republic of China.* Central Committee of the Communist Party of China. http://www.csrc.gov.cn/pub/csrc_en/newsfacts/release/201210/W020121010631355001488.pdf

The 13th Five-Year Plan. (2016). *The 13th five-year plan for economic and social development of the People's Republic of China 2016–2020.* Compilation and Translation Bureau, Central Committee of the Communist Party of China. https://en.ndrc.gov.cn/policies/202105/P020210527785800103339.pdf

The 2015 China's Military Strategy. http://english.www.gov.cn/archive/white_paper/2015/05/27/content_281475115610833.htm

The 2013 Defence White Paper. *The diversified employment of China's armed forces.* http://english.www.gov.cn/archive/white_paper/2014/08/23/content_281474982986506.htm

The 2019 Defence White Paper. *China's National Defence in the New Era.* http://www.xinhuanet.com/english/2019-07/24/c_138253389.htm

The Diplomat. (2015, March 28). *Is China secretly building a navy base in Africa?* https://thediplomat.com/2015/03/is-china-secretly-building-a-navy-base-in-africa/

The Diplomat. (2019, November 27). Chinese, Russian, South African navies conduct trilateral naval exercises. https://thediplomat.com/2019/11/chinese-russian-south-african-navies-conduct-trilateral-naval-exercises/

The National People's Congress of the PRC. (2015, December 28). *New law allows PLA to undertake counterterror missions overseas.* http://www.npc.gov.cn/englishnpc/c2763/201512/e0ee87d8a7a9456194b77567a7511d13.shtml

The North American Congress on Latin America. (2008, May 12). *US navy resurrects fourth fleet to police Latin America.* https://nacla.org/news/us-navy-resurrects-fourth-fleet-police-latin-america

The State Council Information Office of the People's Republic of China. (2018, February 18). *China's cranes to promote Namibia's port construction.* http://english.scio.gov.cn/beltandroad/2018-02/11/content_50483293_3.htm

Trading Economics. (2021). *China exports to Latin America.* https://tradingeconomics.com/china/exports-to-latin-america

Trinkunas, H. (2020, July 20). Testing the limits of China and Brazil's partnership. *Brookings.* https://www.brookings.edu/articles/testing-the-limits-of-china-and-brazils-partnership/

Vreÿ, F. (2017). A blue BRICS, maritime security, and the South Atlantic. *Contexto Internacional, 39*(2), 351–371. https://doi.org/10.1590/s0102-8529.2017390200008

Wall Street Journal. (2021, December 5). *China seeks first military base on Africa's Atlantic coast, U.S. intelligence finds.* https://www.wsj.com/articles/china-seeks-first-military-base-on-africas-atlantic-coast-u-s-intelligence-finds-11638726327

Wall Street Journal. (2022, February 11). *U.S. aims to thwart China's plan for Atlantic base in Africa.* https://www.wsj.com/articles/u-s-aims-to-thwart-chinas-plan-for-atlantic-base-in-africa-11644607931

World Economic Forum. (2021, June 17). *China's trade with Latin America is bound to keep growing. Here's why that matters.* https://www.weforum.org/agenda/2021/06/china-trade-latin-america-caribbean/

Xinhua. (2017, October 28). *Namibian president commissions Chinese-built naval vessels.* http://www.xinhuanet.com//english/2017-10/28/c_136712029.htm

Yu, L. (2018). China's expanding security involvement in Africa: A pillar for 'China–Africa community of common destiny.' *Global Policy, 9*(4), 489–500.

Zeng, Q., Lu, T., Lin, K. C., Yuen, K. F., & Li, K. X. (2020). The competitiveness of Arctic shipping over Suez Canal and China–Europe railway. *Transport Policy, 86,* 34–43. https://doi.org/10.1016/j.tranpol.2019.11.005

Zhang, P. (2019). Belt and road in Latin America: A regional game changer? *Atlantic Council.* https://www.atlanticcouncil.org/in-depth-research-reports/issue-brief/belt-and-road-in-latin-america-a-regional-game-changer/

Yachyshen, D. (2020). *The Chinese scramble for the Gulf of Guinea.* University of Colorado Boulder: College of arts and Sciences. https://www.colorado.edu/polisci/2020/01/22/chinese-scramble-gulf-guinea

Chapter 43
Belt and Road Initiative: Impact and Implications for Africa–China Relations

João Paulo Madeira, Ivete Silves Ferreira, and Nilton Fernandes Cardoso

1 Introduction

The Chinese government launched in 2013 one of the most ambitious infrastructure projects that had ever been seen globally—the Belt and Road Initiative (BRI).[1] The New Silk Road was initially suggested in September of that year by Xi Jinping while visiting Kazakhstan. The project was announced as a reinvigorated economic belt constructed across Central Asia and into Europe. A subsequent Maritime Silk Road was unveiled while the Chinese president was visiting Indonesia a month later. This one was aimed at linking China across the Indian Ocean to East Africa. With estimates putting the investment programme at $8 trillion over a 20-year period, the BRI finances project mainly in the energy, telecommunications, and transport sectors across Africa, Asia, and Europe. The aim is for these infrastructure projects to increase regional connectivity and economic integration. The financing modalities for the BRI come in various forms, ranging from "packaged loans," blended finance, and interest-free loans to projects funded at full commercial rates.

The BRI models of functioning contrast with those of the traditional globalization process, as its proposal has the potential to promote an inclusive rapprochement, without asymmetries between maritime and land, urban and rural, and developed and underdeveloped countries. Insertion and inclusion would be centred here on five factors, namely: (i) political coordination; (ii) infrastructure connectivity; (iii) free

---

[1] President Xi Jinping announced, in 2013, the Belt and Road Initiative. Two years after the National Development and Reform Commission (NDRC), the Ministry of Foreign Affairs and the Ministry of Commerce issued the Vision and Actions on Jointly Building Silk Road Economic Belt and twenty-first-Century Maritime Silk Road. This document emphasizes that more than two millennia ago, people from Asia, Europe, and Africa connected their civilizations through the Silk Road.

J. P. Madeira (✉) · N. F. Cardoso
University of Cabo Verde, Praia, Cabo Verde

I. S. Ferreira
National Institute of Land Management (INGT), Federal University of Pernambuco, Recife, Brazil

© The Author(s), under exclusive license to Springer Nature Singapore Pte Ltd. 2023
P. A. B. Duarte et al. (eds.), *The Palgrave Handbook of Globalization with Chinese Characteristics*, https://doi.org/10.1007/978-981-19-6700-9_43

trade; (iv) currency circulation; and (v) understanding between people (Yiwei, 2016). The strategic direction, articulated under facilities connectivity, signals China's desire to play a leading role in hard and soft transport infrastructure development, all stages of the infrastructure project development cycle, and all modes of transport (Lisinge, 2020).

Therefore, China's goal is to establish links between the main markets of the Middle East, Central Asia, and Africa through the Maritime Silk Road. Moreover, the country seeks to consolidate a port infrastructure to strengthen trade and energy corridors in the South China Sea, from the Persian Gulf to the Red Sea, encompassing the peninsulas of Indochina, Indonesia, Arabia, and the Horn of Africa. It is a way of increasing the Chinese presence in the chokepoints existing in the region (Bab el-Mandeb, between the Red Sea and the Indian Ocean; Hormuz, between the Persian Gulf and the Indian Ocean; and Malacca, between the Indian Ocean and the South China Sea).

2 Africa's Place in the Belt and Road Initiative

In Africa, the initiative has been promoted by the Chinese leaders as a symbol of the Chinese commitment to, as well as an opportunity for, the development of these countries, since many lack infrastructure in strategic sectors. In this context, the BRI aims to integrate Africa into an ambitious Chinese-constructed infrastructure network. This network is intended at promoting regional economic integration in order to enhance the commercial capabilities of African countries, as well as to enable the set-up of regional value chains and economic competitiveness. So far, China has listed forty-nine out of Africa's fifty-four countries as partners under the BRI.

Regarding the sectoral distribution, the most prominent sectors in Africa are energy and transport. Combined, both total US$482.34 billion since 2013 and represent more than 63% of Chinese investments in the BRI countries. In the African continent, energy and transport sectors also stand out when considering the BRI's infrastructure projects, which may take a large variety of programmes, from international rail and expressways to seaports; hydropower to carbon-based power; water supply and sanitation; and many others. Beijing began many of its investment activities in the East Africa region, given its access to ports and the need for rails and roads, but initiatives have since branched out to numerous projects across the continent. China is now the largest funder of infrastructure projects in Africa, financially backing around a fifth of all projects and constructing a third of them (Fu & Eguegu, 2021).

The infrastructure projects associated with the Chinese initiative on the continent are divided into the following categories: (i) intermodal, (ii) gas/oil pipelines, (iii) power plants and transmission systems, (iv) railways, (v) highways; (vi) ports and (vii) power transmission lines (TRALAC, 2019). The sectors of energy and transport stand out, in line with the initiatives' purpose of promoting connectivity and physical integration. This is one of the reasons why China is using its connectivity projects (20% of all its projects in Africa including rail and road lines), to link its industrial (10% of all its projects including minerals processing) and energy projects (15% of all its projects including oil and renewables) in the hinterland of Africa to the infrastructure projects (nearly 45% of all its projects including thirteen ports[2]) along the African coastline (Lokanathan, 2020).

The New Maritime Silk Road aims at consolidating port infrastructures and, thus, strengthening the commercial and energy corridors of the South China Sea, from the Persian Gulf to the Red Sea, encompassing the peninsulas of Indochina, Indonesia, Arabia, and the Horn of Africa. That is also why China is investing in ports and port areas along the coastline from the Gulf of Aden through the Suez Canal towards the Mediterranean Sea. Among the forty-nine countries that China claims have signed a Memorandum of Understanding (MoUs) or officially expressed support for the BRI,[3] thirty-four (nearly 70%) are located along the coast of Africa. The People's Liberation Army (PLA) Navy has built its first overseas military base in Djibouti, which has been in operation since 2017. To serve its strategic interests, China could use its influence over these ports for economic (transport of raw materials, finished goods, and labour) and military purposes (protection of its Sea lines of communication, abbreviated as SLOC) in the future (Lokanathan, 2020; Nantulya, 2019). For instance, the Chinese government-funded part of the construction of the mega port of Doraleh, in Djibouti, through the Eximbank, with the objective of establishing one of the largest free trade zones on the African continent. Such a port, opened in 2017, has the capacity to handle 220,000 containers. In this regard, China also financed the modernization of 752 km of the railway linking Addis Ababa to the port of Djibouti (Melvin, 2019).

The pros and cons of the BRI, which have been discussed extensively in the literature, are also worth noting. In terms of its advantages, the BRI is known to be attractive to developing countries for several reasons. For instance, concerning Africa, it could contribute to meeting the continent's huge infrastructure financing demand, estimated at US$130–170 billion per year (African Development Bank, 2018). This is vital to achieve the continent's trade, industrialization, regional integration, and economic transformation aspirations. The BRI is also associated with practical and affordable Chinese technology, available capital and equipment, and infrastructure construction. In addition, it is perceived to have increased competition for development projects, allowing developing countries to bargain more effectively for better economic returns with Western countries. Furthermore, the BRI is not associated with conditions that Western countries set in exchange for support in infrastructure development such as democracy, transparency, rule of law, and human rights (Zhao, 2020). Regarding the criticism of the BRI, many questions the economic sustainability of both the

---

[2] These include the Port of Djibouti; Port Sudan; the Said-Port, Tewfik, and the Port of El Sokhna in Egypt; Port Zarzis in Tunisia; and Port Centre El Hamdania in Cherchell, Algeria.

[3] There are only five African countries (Eritrea, Benin, Mali, Saint Thomas and Principe, and Eswatini) that have neither signed a MoU nor expressed support. In 2018, The African Union has also signed a MoU on BRI cooperation with China. In addition, their political leaders attended the First and Second BRI Forum for International Cooperation during which some of them signed huge infrastructure agreements with China.

projects themselves and of the levels of debt taken on by the countries.[4] Therefore, critics stress that the initiative is driven more by China's strategic ambition than an economic rationale. In the case of the African continent, while investment projects are helping to close its infrastructure gap, they have also raised fears of runaway debt levels. Overall, more research is needed on the development impact of Chinese investment activities on the continent, including the financial implications thereof. Furthermore, there are critiques concerning a lack of transparency and unfair procurement processes; limited or lack of technology transfer; limited job creation for the locals; non-compliance with national design standards; and the quality of the infrastructure delivered (Taylor & Zajontz, 2020; Zhao, 2020).

In any case, the *Belt and Road Initiative* brought new elements to the relations between China and Africa, revitalizing existing projects and investments and introducing new cooperation mechanisms. The BRI entails the opportunity of deepening relations and cooperation with China, which tends to fill important gaps that could leverage integration, infrastructure, and development projects in the countries of the region. An initiative that serves as a decisive strategic manoeuvre for China to ensure security and promote power status in the international order, moving from rule-taker to rule-maker (Zhou & Esteban, 2018). In this sense, they can coordinate their policies for the purpose of mutual benefit through enhanced connectivity and trade between Africa and China, on the one hand, and deepened African regional integration and intra-African trade on the other (Lisinge, 2020).

3 Restructuring of Chinese Interests in Africa

Concerning the historical and cultural relations between China and Africa, it can be said that they have intensified from the 1960s, particularly with the Chinese support in the struggle for independence. Since then, the Chinese interests in the African continent have undergone a restructuring process, more specifically from October 2000, when the first Forum on China–Africa Cooperation (FOCAC) took place. With eight editions carried out so far, this event is currently held every three years.[5] The Chinese interest in Africa has also raised some criticism, mostly regarding natural and mineral resources exploitation.

As a result of the several cooperation agreements signed between Beijing and the African countries, China became Africa's largest trading partner in mid-2009. Chinese investments have grown considerably since then, despite competing with other countries or blocs, notably, the USA, India, France, the UK, and the European

---

[4] According to the Johns Hopkins China Africa Research Initiative (2021), East African countries alone have borrowed more than $29 billion from China for various projects.

[5] The eighth edition of FOCAC took place in Dakar, Senegal, from 29–30 November 2021 under the theme "Deepen China–Africa Partnership and Promote Sustainable Development to Build a China–Africa Community with a Shared Future in the New Era".

Union, which, taken together, exceed the volume of Chinese commercial transactions with the African continent. Prospects point to a significant increase in Chinese investments, as well as to a shift in the approach of the partnership, which may be reconfigured to include interests of other spheres or domains to its primarily economic nature. Among the African countries with which China currently has strong commercial relations Angola, Djibouti, Ethiopia, Nigeria, Kenya, South Africa, Uganda, and Zambia stand out. Unlike traditional Western partners, China has shown interest even in countries like the Central African Republic, Somalia, and Sudan, which are in situations of great political or economic instability and have benefited from a considerable number of projects led by Chinese private companies (Chen et al., 2018).

The African continent witnessed the opening of more than 320 diplomatic and consular representations from extra-regional countries between 2010 and 2016 (The Economist, 2019). Probably the biggest to date since records exist. The relations of the various powers with African countries encompass the technological, commercial, financial, and military domains. China has embassies in all African countries, with the exception of the Kingdom of Eswatini, formerly Swaziland. The main studies on China–Africa relations show that China is increasingly strengthening its engagement with the African continent (Alden, 2005). On the one hand, this relation is positively evaluated by Africans and, on the other, there are some particularities that must be taken into account (Mlambo et al., 2016). The main observations concern the gap between China's direct investments and public investments in beneficiary countries. In the same sense, the criticisms are based on the fact that, instead of honouring its financial pledges with African countries, as they did in previous FOCACs, China has been offering less generous packages, because some deals have failed. Another point concerns the fact that China grants loans to countries that, from the outset, cannot pay them and, therefore, obtains advantages in other concessions. China is currently the largest creditor in Congo-Brazzaville, Djibouti, and Zambia.

In August 2017, China installed a military base in Djibouti, having carried out in 2018 military exercises under the People's Liberation Army (PLA) command in countries such as Cameroon, Gabon, Ghana, and Nigeria (Nantulya, 2019). Even in the field of linguistic and cultural promotion, despite the rapid growth, some centres and institutes have been closing their doors, after the universities that hosted them have considered their operating model as threatening some basic rules of academia, namely the freedom of thought (Horsley, 2021).

China has military and civilian contingents in UN Peacekeeping Operations in countries such as the Democratic Republic of Congo, Mali, Sudan, and South Sudan. The other members of the UN Security Council are in a smaller number. As a way to protect trade, Beijing considers East Africa part of the maritime silk road, with more than a million Chinese residing across the continent, a population whose protection is China's responsibility (Park, 2016). For instance, during the 2011 Libyan Civil War, a Chinese navy ship helped to evacuate 35,000 Chinese citizens from the country (Zerba, 2014).

China has assisted the new nations which have become independent with complementary financial and technical support. One of the strategies adopted in the relationship with Africa was to cultivate as many allies as possible, maintaining old alliances and consolidating its international recognition. This is why, in this regard too, China seeks to support countries with the aim of gaining their sympathy and, therefore, their commitment to recognizing Taiwan as an inalienable part of the Chinese mainland's territory (Yu, 2009). Currently, in Africa, only the Kingdom of Eswatini recognizes Taiwan, after Malawi in 2008, Gambia in 2013, Burkina Faso and Sao Tome and Principe in 2018, have broken diplomatic relations with that country.

The Sino-African relations were, as mentioned above, historically characterized by different phases, materialized in agreements, and public financial support. In the 1990s, the relationship underwent a process of reconfiguration according to the circumstances and China's interests. Currently, it's one of the most pragmatic relations compared with other countries or regional blocs. Regarding the Chinese trade policy, the economic benefits have become central, although China continues to support several African countries directly, without requiring the imposition of conditionalities, sanctions, warnings, and/or restrictions against the beneficiary countries. This is due to the fact that the formulation of Chinese foreign policy towards Africa is characterized by a plurality of approaches, opposing to a single dominant and enduring tradition (Large, 2008). In practice, this means that Chinese foreign policy is not a uniform, homogeneous or monolithic strategy, but rather that it is shaped by closely related internal and external factors. Ideology, economics, and political considerations equally contribute to the formalization and consolidation of partnership agreements, depending on the circumstances of the moment.

4 Impact and Implications for Africa–China Relations

As already mentioned, China outlined, in the Bandung Conference held in April 1955, a development aid policy to foster economic and cultural cooperation of an Afro-Asian nature (Kynge, 2006). To that end, it provided military, financial, and logistical support in the fight for independence. Since then, these forms of relationship have gone through different phases, focusing more, even before the 1990s, on the struggle against the hegemonic influence of the West (Looy, 2006). Beijing supported Africa on three fronts: (i) in nationalist movements in the decolonization process, providing military or logistical support in their respective territories; (ii) in the implementation of large construction projects such as the Tazara Railway, which links the port of Dar es Salaam in Tanzania to the city of Kapiri Mposhi in the Central Province of Zambia over an extension of 1860 km, or the railway line opened in October 2016, with 759 km connecting the Port of Dorale in Djibouti to Sebeta in Ethiopia; (iii) in health and education, sending medical teams and awarding scholarships so that African students can continue their studies in China.

In the 1960s and 1970s, Africa served as a field of dispute between China and Taiwan over the issue of Taiwan's sovereignty and, thus, who would be the Chinese official representative. However, since the beginning of the twenty-first century, economic issues have become central, such as the guarantee of access to energy and raw materials from Africa. However, the question is this: How did they manage it? In fact, Chinese past experience, in particular, the support for the struggle for independence in the 1960s, has been gradually translating, until today, into a relationship based on pragmatism, acceptance, and openness. To achieve its goals, China has been innovative in the use of foreign policy tools suited to the country's purpose, which has always been at the base of these relations. Among these tools, three stand out: official aid, trade, and influence (Rotberg, 2008). Cultural practices, processes, and tools have also been adopted through the creation of non-profit institutions such as the Confucius Institute with the aim of promoting the teaching of the Chinese language and culture. Currently, there are more than sixty delegations of this kind in African countries (King, 2017).

Several factors gave rise to this paradigm shift, in particular, the Chinese economic growth, which, from 1992 until today, has presented an annual growth rate above 9% (CEIC DATA, 2021). As the Chinese economy has been growing steadily, access to natural resources becomes the main priority. The port of Djibouti and the railways connecting it to Addis Ababa, Ethiopia, over a length of 752.7 km, are part of a large free trade zone. Also, the routes between Nairobi and Naivasha in Kenya (120 km) and between Abuja and Kaduna in Nigeria (312 km) are examples of projects financed by the Chinese. Another aspect that deserves particular attention concerns the permanent visits of senior officials from the People's Republic of China to Africa (Shinn & Eisenman, 2012). It is possible to note that, when the Chinese do not receive visits from African politicians, Chinese diplomatic delegations visit Africa instead. Moreover, Chinese state-backed companies helped to establish Special Economic Zones (SEZs) in countries such as Egypt, Djibouti, Ethiopia, Mauritius, Nigeria, Rwanda, and Zambia (Tao et al., 2016).

These discussions led to questions about the role and place of China in Africa. Hanauer and Morris (2014, pp. 5–6) highlight four strategic interests: (i) access to natural resources, especially oil and gas; (ii) Chinese export markets; (iii) political legitimacy in international forums and (iv) adherence to the "One China" policy. Regardless of the motivations that drive Chinese interests in Africa, experience has pointed out the infrastructure sector as one of China's main bets in Africa (Ferreira & Madeira, 2020).

Chinese investment in Africa is increasingly dynamic and diversified, mainly due to the growing role played by the private sector. Large state-owned companies have played leading roles in the infrastructure sector, with variations depending on the country in question. The private sector leads in the manufacturing industry, wholesale and retail trade of food products, civil construction, sale of auto parts, car rental, motorcycle maintenance and repair shops, mechanics, carpentry, metalwork, milling, and aluminium industry (Madeira, 2017). Despite the criticisms, the diversification of Chinese investment in Africa has played a relevant role in the development of Africa, contributing to its early industrialization and job creation. Therefore, there is a necessity for technology, and for the injection of flows of labour, capital, ideas, and knowledge, for this to be positively evaluated by African countries, as aforementioned (Shen, 2013).

Since 2000, China's relations with Africa, in terms of frequency and scope, have become what is commonly referred to as a Global Partnership for Development (Cissé, 2015). This actually represents a potential alternative to the Western-dominated global culture and its structures (Yu, 2009, p. 31). It is to be recalled that the private companies that invest in Africa are focused on obtaining profits, although sometimes they may have different motivations. We refer, more specifically, to the fact that the increase in Chinese private investment abroad reflects less on China's economic power than its integration into international trade and investment market, whose dynamics encourage all participants to move wherever they can produce with lower production costs, thus providing higher levels of efficiency (Shen, 2013, p. 42).

On the other hand, it is worth noting that while Western investments prioritize countries that match the principles of good governance, transparency, and accountability, the presence of Chinese investments in environments considered to be of poor governance also tends to have high implications and very clear consequences on African economies and their respective political cultures (Renwick et al., 2018). Thus, it seems to us that, although the Chinese may value social, economic, and political stability, China does not seem to give significant weight to the rules, laws, and regulations of the beneficiary countries, acting in a non-discriminatory way towards them, whether they are 'good' or 'bad' in terms of governance or respect to human rights (Osondu-Oti, 2016). In addition, Chinese companies, even the relatively small ones, are quick and flexible in their responses to the African market they target. The Chinese are, according to Shen (2013, p. 42) incredibly adventurous, hardworking, and practical, which ultimately helps them to deal with adverse conditions in emerging, bordering, or even developed countries. However, there are also negative aspects mainly due to the fact that Chinese private companies still have few years of experience in investing abroad; limited knowledge concerning the legal and political systems in the countries in which they operate; and, equally, difficulties concerning the languages and cultures of the host countries. Another aspect is related to the fact that entrepreneurs choose to maintain strong family business traditions, which may constitute a limitation in adapting to changes in the business and labour world.

Africa receives a small share of the total China's foreign direct investment. Chinese companies still have a negative image of Africa as a distant, poor, and unstable investment destination, resulting from real and misleading problems. Thus, in order to increase Chinese investments, several authors have suggested an "open and friendly" model of investment, which encourages competition and provides better infrastructure support, as the ultimate goal is not just to attract more Chinese private investment, but more benefits to African national economies (Shen, 2013, p. 43).

5 Conclusion

This chapter sought to ascertain the impact and implications of the Belt and Road Initiative on Chinese foreign policy towards Africa. From the analysis presented earlier, the initiative is widely considered to be the centrepiece of China's new foreign policy and a reflection of its ascendancy in the global arena, economically, politically, and strategically. BRI is a multifaceted and connectivity-oriented grand strategy designed to serve China's ambitious geostrategic and geo-economic interest. BRI reflects China's rise as a global power, industrial redeployment, increased outward investment, and need to diversify its energy sources and routes. For Africa, cooperation with China on infrastructure development started much earlier than the launch of BRI. As has already been said, China was involved in the construction of the Tazara railway linking Tanzania and Zambia in the 1970s. Being an inter-continental connectivity initiative, many expect BRI's benefits in Africa to be regional in nature.

On the other hand, the economic links between China and Africa have increased dramatically over the past 20 years. Trade has risen more than 40-fold since the mid-1990s, and China is now sub-Saharan Africa's largest trading partner. According to China's Ministry of Commerce, trade between China and Africa increased by 40.5% year-on-year in the first seven months of 2021 and was valued at a record high of USD 139.1 billion. Nevertheless, African countries make up less than 4% of China's global trade and less than 3% of China's global foreign direct investment (FDI) flows and stocks. Beijing is a major source of loan financing for public infrastructure projects, with available data suggesting that China is now Africa's largest bilateral creditor, holding at least 21% of African debt (CARI, 2021).

In general terms, China–Africa relations were initially driven by the accelerated development of the Asian country and, thus, by the increased demand for natural, energy, and food resources. With the exponential increase in commodity prices in the first decade of the twenty-first century, the Chinese market quickly became the largest importer of almost all countries in the region. According to our analysis, it is possible to note that the People's Republic of China is going through a process of the establishment of strategic partnerships abroad, especially with countries associated with the Economic Belt and the Maritime Silk Road. In this sense, Pautasso et al. (2020) argue that the New Silk Road is a Chinese globalization project and, in order to contain it, the US has reacted by articulating a geopolitical encirclement around the Sino-Russian axis (e.g., the US pivot to Asia), the structuring axis of the Eurasian integration process.

Bibliographic References

African Development Bank. (2018). *African Economic Outlook 2018*. Côte d'Ivoire: AfDB. Retrieved on 08 December 2021, from https://www.afdb.org/fileadmin/uploads/afdb/Documents/Publications/African_Economic_Outlook_2018_-_EN.pdf

Alden, C. (2005). China in Africa. *Survival: Global Politics and Strategy, 47*(3), 147–164.

CARI. (2021). Chinese loans to Africa database. In *China Africa Research Initiative*. China Africa Research Initiative and Boston University Global Development Policy Center. Retrieved on 08 December 2021, from https://chinaafricaloandata.bu.edu/

CEIC DATA. (2021). *China crescimento real do PIB*. CEIC Data (SG) Pte Ltd. Retrieved on 24 January 2022, from https://www.ceicdata.com/pt/indicator/china/real-gdp-growth

Chen, W., Dollar, D., & Tang, H. (2018). Why is China investing in Africa? Evidence from the firm level. *World Bank Economic Review, 32*(3), 610–632.

Cissé, I. (2015). Developing global partnership for development: Chinese investments in Africa and impacts on sustainable development. In N. Andrews, N. E. Khalema, & N. D. T. Assié-Lumumba (Eds.), *Millennium development goals (MDGs) in retrospect: Africa's development beyond 2015* (pp. 209–227). Palgrave Macmillan.

Ferreira, I. S., & Madeira, J. P. (2020). China and the Great Urban projects in Cabo Verde. In F. Leandro & P. Duarte (Eds.), *The Belt and Road Initiative: An old archetype of a new development model* (pp. 343–362). Palgrave Macmillan.

Fu, Y., & Eguegu, O. (2021). *China's BRI and the AfCFTA: Potential overlaps, complementarities and challenges*. South African Institute of International Affairs. Retrieved on 29 November 2021, from http://www.jstor.org/stable/resrep34100

Hanauer, L., & Morris, L. (2014). *Chinese engagement in Africa: Drivers, reactions, and implications for U.S. policy*. Rand Corporation. Retrieved on 08 December 2021, from https://www.rand.org/content/dam/rand/pubs/research_reports/RR500/RR521/RAND_R

Horsley, J. P. (2021, April 1). It's time for a new policy on Confucius institutes. *Brookings*. Retrieved on 08 December 2021, from https://www.brookings.edu/articles/its-time-for-a-new-policy-on-confucius-institutes/#cancel

King, K. (2017). Confucius Institutes in Africa: Culture and language without controversy? In K. Batchelor & X. Zhang (Eds.), *China–Africa relations building images through cultural cooperation, media representation and communication* (pp. 98–112). Routledge.

Kodzi, E. (2018). Live and let live: Africa's response options to China's BRI. In W. Zhang, I. Alon, & C. Lattemann (Eds.), *China's Belt and Road Initiative: Changing the rules of globalization* (pp. 155–178). Palgrave Macmillan.

Kynge, J. (2006). *A China Abala o Mundo—A Ascensão de uma Nação Ávida*. Bizâncio.

Large, D. (2008). Beyond 'dragon in the bush': The study of China–Africa relations. *African Affairs, 107*(426), 45–61.

Lisinge, R. T. (2020). The Belt and Road Initiative and Africa's regional infrastructure development: Implications and lessons. *Transnational Corporations Review, 12*(4), 425–438.

Lokanathan, V. (2020, August). China's Belt and Road Initiative: Implications in Africa. *ORF Issue Brief No. 395*. Observer Research Foundation. Retrieved on 08 December 2021, from https://www.orfonline.org/wp-content/uploads/2020/08/ORF_IssueBrief_395_BRI-Africa.pdf

Madeira, J. P. (2017). The dragon embraces Africa: Cape Verde–China relations. *Austral: Brazilian Journal of Strategy & International Relations, 6*(12), 123–141.

Melvin, N. (2019). *The foreign military presence in the Horn of Africa region*. Stockholm International Peace Research Institute (SIPRI). Stockholm, SIPRI Background Paper. Retrieved on 08 December 2021, from https://sipri.org/sites/default/files/2019-04/sipribp1904.pdf

Mlambo, C., Kushamba, A., & Simawu, M. B. (2016). China–Africa relations: What lies beneath? *The Chinese Economy, 49*(4), 257–276.

Nantulya, P. (2019, January). Chinese hard power supports its growing strategic interests in Africa. *Africa Center for Strategic Studies, 17*. Retrieved on 14 November 2021, from https://africacenter.org/spotlight/chinese-hard-power-supports-its-growing-strategic-interests-in-africa/

OECD. (2018). *China's Belt and Road Initiative in the global trade, investment and finance landscape*. OECD, 13. Retrieved on 08 December 2021, from https://www.oecd.org/finance/Chinas-Belt-and-Road-Initiative-in-the-global-trade-investment-and-finance-landscape.pdf

Osondu-Oti, A. (2016). China and Africa: Human rights perspective. *Africa Development / Afrique Et Développement, 41*(1), 49–80.

Park, Y. J. (2016, May 12). One Million Chinese in Africa. *Perspectives*. Retrieved on 14 November 2021, from http://www.saisperspectives.com/2016issue/2016/5/12/n947s9csa0ik6km km0bzb0hy584sfo

Pautasso, D., Nogara, T. S., Ungaretti, C. R., & Doria, G. (2020). A iniciativa do cinturão e rota e os dilemas da América Latina. *Revista Tempo Do Mundo, 24*, 77–106.

Renwick, N., Gu, J., & Hong, S. (2018). China and African Governance in the Extractive Industries. *International Development Policy*. Article 10.1. Retrieved on 08 December 2021, from https://journals.openedition.org/poldev/2547

Rotberg, R. I. (Ed.). (2008). *China into Africa: Trade, aid, and influence*. Brookings Institution Press, World Peace Foundation.

Shen, X. (2013). Private Chinese investment in Africa: Myths and realities. *The World Bank Development Economics Vice Presidency*. Policy Research Working Paper 6311. Retrieved on 20 November 2021, from http://documents.worldbank.org/curated/pt/488211468216585858/pdf/wps6311.pdf

Shinn, D. H., & Eisenman, J. (2012). *China and Africa: A century of engagement*. University of Pennsylvania Press.

Tao, Y., Yuan, Y., & Li, M. (2016). Chinese special economic zones: Lessons for Africa. In K. Kapoor, & C. Mollinedo (Eds.), *AfD*. Chief Economist Complex | AEB 7, 6, 1–16. AfD. Retrieved on 20 November 2021, from https://www.afdb.org/fr/documents/document/africa-economic-brief-chinese-special-economic-zones-lessons-for-africa-91559

Taylor, I., & Zajontz, T. (2020). In a fix: Africa's place in the Belt and Road Initiative and the reproduction of dependency. *South African Journal of International Affairs, 27*(3), 277–295.

The Economist. (2019, March 9). The new scramble for Africa. *The Economist*. Retrieved on 20 November 2021, from https://www.economist.com/leaders/2019/03/07/the-new-scramble-for-africa

TRALAC. (2019). *Joint statement of the coordinators' meeting on the implementation of the follow-up actions of the FOCAC Beijing Summit*. TRALAC. Retrieved on 08 December 2021, from https://www.tralac.org/news/article/14122-joint-statement-of-the-coordinators-meeting-on-the-implementation-of-the-follow-up-actions-of-the-focac-beijing-summit.html

van de Looy, J. (2006). Africa and China: A strategic partnership? *ASC Working Paper 67/2006*. African Studies Centre. Retrieved on 14 November 2021, from https://www.ascleiden.nl/pdf/wp67.pdf

Yiwei, W. (2016). *The Belt and Road Initiative: What will China offer the world in its rise*. New World Press.

Yu, G. T. (2009). *China, Africa, and globalization: The "China Alternative"*. Institute for Security and Development Policy. Retrieved on 14 November 2021, from https://isdp.eu/content/uploads/publications/2009_yu_china-africa-and-globalization.pdf

Zerba, S. H. (2014). China's Libya evacuation operation: A new diplomatic imperative—overseas citizen protection. *Journal of Contemporary China, 23*(90), 1093–1112.

Zhao, S. (2020). China's Belt-Road Initiative as the signature of President Xi Jinping diplomacy: Easier said than done. *Journal of Contemporary China, 29*(123), 319–335.

Zhou, W., & Esteban, M. (2018). Beyond balancing: China's approach towards the Belt and Road Initiative. *Journal of Contemporary China, 27*(112), 487–501.

Chapter 44
The Unequal Modalities of China's Intervention in Africa

Xavier Aurégan

1 Introduction

Actors and modalities of Chinese (PRC) intervention in Africa have considerably increased and evolved since the beginning of the 2000s with the sudden media coverage of the various forms of Chinese presence on the continent. After decades of state-centric relations, reforms, in the first instance, and atomization of Chinese actors, in a second, has led to the complexification of flows and exchanges. While these still primarily concern the Chinese State and its representatives or representations, they are also linked to a multitude of actors controlled or not by *Zhongnanhai*, the heart of power in Beijing.

Thus, only the understanding of the evolution of China-Africa relations can enlighten the current Chinese presence in Africa. These relations are rooted in the history of Asia–Africa links and in the respective chronologies of contemporary China and Africa. Accordingly, this chapter will first examine Sino-African historicity since 1949. Through the analysis of three periods (1949–1971; 1972–1993; 1994–2013), the first part of the chapter looks back at the main events that have impacted on current Sino-African relations. Within this framework, 1955, 1963, 1982, 1994, and 2003 are several key dates that embody both evolution and ruptures in the Sino-African relationship. The years 1994–2013 are a pivotal period: on one hand for Chinese economic actors who are encouraged to internationalize, on the other hand for the modalities of Chinese intervention in Africa which have been steadily increasing over the past thirty years.

Xi Jinping's accession to power in 2013 coincides with a fourth phase which is materialized, both in discourse and in statistics, by Belt and Road Initiative (BRI[1]).

---

[1] NSR's acronym expresses the New Silk Roads instead of the official Chinese formulas (OBOR, BRI).

X. Aurégan (✉)
Catholic University of Lille, Lille, France

Accordingly, our second part draws on several national and international databases to analyze the increases in various Sino-African flows. Our results support our premise: the nature and extreme concentration of Sino-African economic flows certainly leads to the forms of polarization, but above all to inequalities and dependencies that China, as a global actor, considerably increases. The capitalist and self-interested nature of Chinese interventions in Africa is far from trivial in the current context of this China-Africa relationship. On the one hand, this double function is now fully integrated into the official Chinese rhetoric which, since 2013, is embodied in the New Silk Roads project (Leandro & Duarte, 2020; NDRC, 2017). On the other hand, it generates de facto strong inequalities between African territories, seen as relays of extraterritorial growth supported by African elites.

2 Methodology

The first part is based on previous researches (Aurégan, 2016a, 2016b, 2019b) that has dealt with Sino-African relations from a historical perspective. Part 2 analyze them using descriptive statistics. While several economic flows are not included (development aid, debt forgiveness), trade (UNCTAD, 2021), contracts of Chinese enterprises in Africa (NBSC, 2021), loans to African governments (CARI, 2021), and outward direct investment (NBSC, 2021) allow for an assessment of the evolution of Sino-African economic relations.

The common period for the databases is 2003–2018. For trade flows, we compile data for "China," "Macao" and "Hong Kong," but exclude "Taiwan." In contrast, the statistical treatment of the Infrastructure Consortium for Africa (ICA) data covers the period 2006–2017. ICA has been publishing an annual report integrating African infrastructure finance since 2006. By convenience, only one year is included in the bibliography: 2019. Chinese investment flows (FDI) in Africa are generally favoured since they are easier to compare with other types of flows. Finally, Sudan expresses Northern Sudan (Khartoum).

3 First Part: China-Africa: The Long Story Today

3.1 The First Sino-African Era (1949–1971)

Between the proclamation of the PRC in 1949 and Beijing's accession to the United Nations Security Council as a permanent member in 1971, the first Sino-African period (Aurégan, 2019b) was characterized by China's threefold ideological, military, and diplomatic presence on the African continent.

During the first decade, i.e. the 1950s, Mao Zedong's China wanted to make up for a delay linked to internal factors (Qing dynasty, rebellions and floods) as well as external factors (European colonialism, opium wars and unequal treaties). This catching up was not only economic, but also diplomatic and political, since China was already asserting itself as a political power with an international aura at the Indonesian Bandung Conference in 1955. This meeting was the first to bring together some of the Third World States that would become non-aligned. The 29 delegations present at Bandung (including India and China for Asia, and Liberia, present-day Ghana, Libya, Sudan, Ethiopia, and Somalia, as well as the Algerian National Liberation Front and the Tunisian Destour for Africa) adopted the Five Principles of Peaceful Coexistence guiding the relationship of what would be called, today, South—South relations: mutual respect for each other's territorial; integrity and sovereignty; mutual non-aggression; mutual non-interference in each other's internal affairs; equality and mutual benefit; and peaceful coexisting.

In a Cold War context where the decolonisation process was certainly underway but not yet completed, this Conference emphasized respect for national sovereignty and, in a way, the right of peoples to self-determination. Bandung also represents the launch of Chinese foreign policy, specifically in Africa, and in a multilateral framework that intended to prioritize the needs and claims of these territories claiming independence. While officially a common position emerged from Bandung, unofficially, power rivalries were in full play between the main powers represented or not (such as the Union of Soviet Socialist Republics, USSR) in Indonesia. During the 1950s and 1960s, Beijing's foreign policy was influenced by these Sino-Indian and Sino-Soviet competitions. Several points and highlights characterize it, including Nehru's trip to Moscow in the summer of 1955: on the one hand, it was a diplomatic victory for India, since the Soviets ratified the five principles of peaceful coexistence; and on the other hand, it was a way for Moscow to integrate this movement. A few months later, at the 20th Congress of the Communist Party, the USSR distanced itself from certain Marxist principles and undertook a process of de-Stalinisation which led to the abolition of the *Kominform* in 1956. From then on, communism became polycentric and potential partners had to choose between Beijing or Moscow. In 1963, the rupture between China and the New Delhi-Moscow axis was consummated in Moshi, Tanzania, where the Third African Asian Peoples' Solidarity Conference was held. The impossible consensus made it necessary for both China and India to launch African policies based on bilateralism - and no longer on a potential multilateralism defined at Bandung (Aurégan, 2016a).

China-Africa relationship was born. Chinese posture materialized a few months later with the first trip to the continent of Zhou Enlai, Prime Minister, between December 1963 and January 1964. During this tour, Beijing formalized this bilateral cooperation when Zhou visited Bamako (Mali) and Accra (Ghana). In both speeches, 8 principles are stated: equality and mutual benefits; respect for sovereignty; economic aid in the form of interest-free or low-interest loans; no dependence, but autonomy and independent economic development; weak investment and quick results; best-quality equipment and material; qualified personnel for technical assistance, experts must have same standard of living as the experts of the recipient country. These principles were to compete with the Soviet and Indian Third World policies. Following China's lead, New Delhi (Aurégan, 2019a) is launching its International Technical and Economic Cooperation (ITEC). Chinese presence in Africa can be summarized in four types of actors until the early 1970s: Mao's Little Red Book, symbolizing the Chinese Communist Party (CCP), its revolution and its first representative; the barefoot doctors officiating in Chinese medical missions, starting with the Algerian one in 1963; the agricultural technicians (Aurégan, 2019c) working in the agricultural state farms; and the military support (Fig. 1) of the People's Liberation Army (PLA) to the African National Liberation Revolutions (Aurégan, 2019b). This first Sino-African period ended with the year 1971, which was the year of China's entry (PRC) into the UN. China won diplomatic victories (Fig. 1), including General de Gaulle's France in 1964, after a relative isolation on the international scene (between 1958 and 1968).

However, a number of African States did not vote in favour of Resolution 2758 (Fig. 1). These latter are mainly French-speaking, previously integrated into French West and Equatorial African territories (AOF and AEF). The historical picture of these African States opposed to the 'Reds' is to be combined with the one highlighting the African capitals that alternately played the game of Beijing and Taipei. These African States are once again predominantly French-speaking and the two maps therefore partially overlap. At that time, Africa did not yet vote as one in favour of Beijing in international organizations. China itself was competing with Taiwan, which took away diplomatic partners between 1958 and 1970 (and again between 1998 and 1998). Today, only Eswatini (former Swaziland) and Somaliland recognize

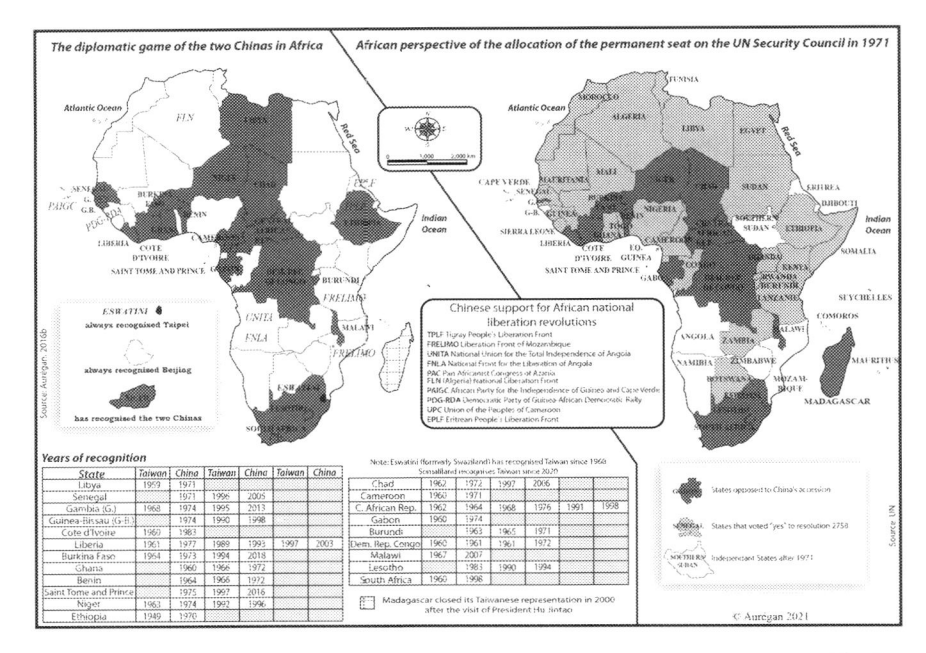

Fig. 1 The diplomatic game of the two Chinas and the UNSCR 2758 (*Source* Aurégan [2016b])

Taipei. In this context, the case of Burkina Faso is enlightening. In 1994, in order to oust Beijing, Taiwan paid former President Blaise Compaoré a substantial amount of money calculated according to Burkina's demographics, i.e., about $50 million (Aurégan, 2011). After 1971, it was paradoxically the beginning of an ideological retreat and a paradigm shift where economics was to take precedence over politics and solidarity. However, this second period was the time of China's biggest project ever in Africa: the railway linking Lusaka, Zambia, to Dar es Salaam, Tanzania.

3.2 The Second Sino-African Era (1972–1993)

This second phase of Sino-African relations begins with the main cooperation project carried out by China in Africa. Completed in 1976, a year ahead of schedule, the pharaonic Tazara is a 1,600 km railway that was intended to open up Zambian territory by exporting copper. The Zambian government, which had been refused twice by the World Bank and the British, then turned to the Chinese authorities who saw in the construction of this infrastructure the equivalent of the Egyptian Aswan Dam (built by the USSR). Financed by an interest-free loan of 400 million dollars (over 30 years, including 8 years free of charge), this railway line mobilized up to 50,000 Chinese workers. This infrastructure remains, in African perceptions like in Chinese discourses, as one of the main South–South collaborations. Tazara project can be compared to the other major railway infrastructure built by China, or rather a Chinese state-owned company (SOE), the new railway linking Addis Ababa to Djibouti. 750-km long, the latter is half the length, but is electrified and of standard gauge, while the Zambian corridor requires a break bulk with the Tanzanian network.

The following years coincided with a half-hearted African record despite this Tazara and the new international status acquired by China in 1971. This was the case until Tiananmen and the early 1990s. China's withdrawal from Africa which should be put into perspective, is less the result of African or international contexts (oil crises, fall in raw material prices, International Monetary Fund (IMF), socio-political crises and coups d'état) than of several factors that are mainly linked to China itself. Diplomatically, the record is mixed in these early post-UN years. The visits to Beijing by Kissinger in 1971 and Nixon in 1972 contrasted with the timid resumption of relations with the USSR in 1970. While the foreign policy was not shelved, resources and forces were concentrated on the domestic front, since the return of Deng Xiaoping in 1973 was to be seen in the context of the deaths of Zhou Enlai (8 January 1976) and Mao Zedong (9 September). In 1975, the National People's Congress also adopted the Four Modernisations (Agricultural, Industrial, Defence and Scientific) which contributed to the economic opening up of the country and the Special Economic Zones (SEZ) in 1979. The official end of the Cultural Revolution in 1977, and finally the victory of Deng Xiaoping at the 3rd Plenary Session of the 11th Central Committee in December 1978, prompted China to concentrate on its domestic policy by allocating the necessary resources.

This second period is therefore above all one of economic, social, and political reform. From decollectivization to international economic opening, China definitively closed the Mao chapter and opened the Deng one. The main events were the fourth constitution of 1982, the reform of the people's communes in 1983 and the economic reforms of 1984. Indeed, the reform of SOEs is at the heart of the new Chinese economic policy. Private law and the dematerialization of public assets are progressing, and the provinces are gaining responsibility and power. All these reforms will ultimately play a key role in how we analyze the role and influence of Chinese presence on the continent, limited until the third period. At the end of the 1980s, the normalization of relations with the USSR, the shortened visit of Mikhail Gorbachev, initiator of glasnost, the democratization of Taiwan, and above all the death of Hu Yaobang contributed to the outbreak of the events of April-June 1989 in Tiananmen Square. In contrast to the West, this repression is barely criticized in Africa. Many governments had to or would also have to deal with 'democratic impulses' orchestrated or desired by the 'Northern' donors, including France, which ratified the multi-party system in June 1990. From the point of view of some African governments, development and democracy are not interdependent as it is in the West, and there is no need to be a democrat to get rich.

Between 1971, year of Resolution 2758, and 1988, year of Taiwanese President Lee's accession to power, the Chinese government nevertheless continued its cooperation with States that recognized the One-China policy. It gained a certain prestige among the leaders and populations concerned, since on the one hand its achievements were symbolic and ostentatious (palaces, stadiums, hospitals or ports), and on the other hand, they were aimed at the rural populations neglected by the capitals (rice growing and medical missions). If the amounts allocated, except for the Tazara, did not rival those of the USSR and the former colonial powers, they were nevertheless generally well received in a moribund context of financial and social crises fuelled by the Structural Adjustment Programmes (SAPs) of the IMF and the World Bank. In parallel with these trusteeships of African government budgets and the victory of the Washington Consensus on development economics, China began a paradigm shift in 1982: the 8 principles of 1963 were replaced by Premier Zhao Ziyang's "Four principles for Sino-African Economic and Technical Cooperation." From an overall horizontal cooperation (not without verticality given the nature of the Chinese regime), China invested a double mercantile and vertical approach in its relationship with developing countries. According to Deborah Bräutigam (1998, pp. 49–50; 2009), the mutual benefit (win–win today) is above all a way of making Chinese cooperation profitable, and of linking development aid to contracts or purchases of Chinese goods. This new Chinese African policy is politically a failure since the Chinese operating methods are precisely an adaptation of those used by the Western or Soviet camps. The result is a relative but noticeable withdrawal from the continent. Most of the diplomats recalled during the Cultural Revolution never returned and their successors have neither the same training nor the same experience. With limited means, a wavering ideology and a strategy that lacked clarity, they struggled to exploit the international recognition that China had obtained in 1971.

44 The Unequal Modalities of China's Intervention in Africa

Chinese political and institutional reforms and evolutions will have a considerable impact on the outside world as they will create this economic and commercial bridge between China and Africa, and more generally between China and the world. Tiananmen and Chinese economic reforms, backed by energy needs, are therefore the real drivers or explanatory factors of the Chinese economic and political breakthrough on the African continent. After 1989, China is embarking on a new cycle of reforms that directly concern the African continent, or at least Africa in its relationship with China and vice versa. We are entering two decades of all-out development, with regard to trade, investments, services, and relations (cultural, economic and political): these are China's twenty glorious years in Africa.

3.3 The Third Sino-African Era (1994–2013)

A number of factors have therefore driven and promoted the growth of China's relationship with Africa. Two analytical frameworks can summarize the major developments that have led Beijing to see Africa as a strategic continent. The first is related to the set of reforms that affect Chinese enterprises and their legal status. The second is due to institutional and strategic changes. Both frameworks have allowed the development of the financial sector with the creation of instruments that enable economic actors and capital to go out China.

Between 1994, with the creation of the three Policy Banks (Export–Import Bank of China; Agricultural Development Bank of China; China Development Bank), and 2013, China has gone through countless highlights. For example, reforms related to the status of Chinese SOEs have partially aligned them with the Western liberal and capitalist model, have facilitated mergers and acquisitions capable of creating direct competitors to multinational companies (MNCs), and above all have allowed Chinese economic actors to "go out." This evolution can be represented by the promulgation of the General Principles of Civil Law establishing natural and legal persons in 1986, and by the increasingly preponderant place of private law: from work units before 1978 (*danwei*) to enterprises from 1988 and up to enterprises (limited liability, joint-stock and capital) from 1993.

This dematerialising public assets policy and transposing them into private law was enshrined ten years later, in 2003, with the creation of the State-owned Assets Supervision and Administration Commission of the State Council (SASAC). The latter manages the 96 main SOEs. These groups, frequently reaching one million employees and increasingly operating abroad, including in Africa, are excellently ranked in the Fortune Global 500, taking 3 of the top 4 places in 2020. These national champions, built for and by the Chinese Communist Party through SASAC, are, before African States, the main beneficiaries of Chinese aid and loans, which are mainly channelled through the Export–Import Bank of China. Juxtaposed with institutional and strategic reforms, these business-related reforms enabled China to regain its place in the IMF and the World Bank (in 1980), to join the General Agreement on Tariffs and Trade (GATT) in 1982, and to become a member of the Multi-Fibre

Agreement in 1983. The consecration of this policy came in 2001 when China joined the World Trade Organisation (WTO). The year 2001 also follows another key year in Sino-African relations: 2000 with the organization of the first Forum on China-Africa Cooperation (FOCAC). This reforming context of the 1980s, 1990s, and 2000s and the 7 series of reforms have led China to evolve towards the state capitalism described, for example, by Marie-Claire Bergère (2013) or Joshua Kurlantzick (2016).

Other factors must be taken into account in the rise of Chinese power in Africa. On the continent, in addition to resentments towards Western powers and financial institutions, these factors are essentially geopolitical. These include the search for alliances after Tiananmen and the second Taiwanese parenthesis in Africa (1988–1998), the fall of the Wall and the dissolution of the USSR, the challenge to US hegemony, and the subsequent multi polarization of economic and political powers, as well as the development of South–South relations up to the creation of the New (BRICS) Development Bank in July 2014. Added to these key points are economic factors, with the Asian economic crisis of 1997, the international economic shift towards the East and Asia, the reduction in European aid to Africa, which was redirected towards the countries of Central and Eastern Europe (CEECs), and above all China's energy dependence, with Beijing having to make strategic investments or investments geared towards the search for markets in the Middle East, Latin America and therefore in Africa since 1994. Hence the creation, in the same year, of the three Policy Banks.

For Africa and China in Africa, this set of elements has led to a spectacular increase in economic relations, with its five components: development aid, FDIs, loans, services (contracts) and trade. Among them, investments coupled with loans and services have a triple purpose: to open up new markets, to increase the turnover of enterprises, and/or to secure access to raw materials to supply Chinese production lines. Interdependent or not, entangled with political and economic strategies that are sometimes heterogeneous, disparate, or even antagonistic, these modalities must be separated in order to best break down the Sino-African relationship.

4 Second Part: China-Africa: Inequalities, Dependence, and Extroversion

4.1 The Fourth Sino-African Era and the Unequal Economic Relationship

Since the 1990s and especially the 2000s, the Sino-African relationship has been based on a classic capitalist model of financing and contracting (especially infrastructure) in exchange for natural resources and markets. Therefore, China's heterogeneous presence in Africa has similar objectives to its neoliberal corollary in terms of economics, stability, and development, but with different priorities: political stability, economic growth, and market- or resource-seeking investments for China; conditionalities, areas of influence and MNC's turnover for the traditional powers. After Hu Jintao's presidency (2003–2013), which made social peace and China's image abroad the administration's stated priorities, Xi Jinping's presidency is more distinct in three respects. First, Xi incorporates these principles while discarding the record of his predecessor. Second, he inserts a dose of protectionist and nationalist pragmatism. Finally, he prioritizes the factors of domestic economic growth.

In this context, the first years of Xi's presidency years are certainly those of the deepening of the major axes and doctrines launched since the 1990s, but also those of a new Sino-African temporality. Voluntarily or not, the Chinese government is granting more and more freedom to economic actors investing or winning contracts in Africa. These uninhibited economic actors are transforming an important part of the Bottom-up China-Africa relationship. They are both private (migrant-investors, private enterprises) and public (provincial as well as central) in this contemporary relationship where the Chinese State still orchestrates the overall Sino-African Topdown relationship.

In other words, we are witnessing the gradual privatization and financialisation of Sino-African relations, which remain driven by the Chinese state. The substantial increase in loans and the provision of services (Table 1) support this statement. Second modality of intervention in value after trade flows, Chinese services are, during both periods, for a third carried out in Africa. This situation demonstrates the (key) role of the African market for Chinese economic actors. Over the period 2003–2018, more than 60% of these contracts were signed and won from 2013 onwards. Moreover, contracts mainly concern 6 African States out of 54: Algeria, Angola, Nigeria, Ethiopia, Sudan, and Kenya. Loans are even more concentrated, as Angola (33%), Ethiopia (10%) and Zambia (8.5%) are only three needed to reach half of the Chinese loans granted between 2013 and 2018; years that together account for 51% of the total $143 billion granted since 2003. These two modalities are growing rapidly, more so than FDI which is better distributed in Africa. These findings are all the more striking as the second period covers only six years (ten for the first). Moreover, only five African countries (Angola, South Africa, Algeria, Nigeria and Sudan) account for 51% of all four modalities, and 13 countries for 76%. In Africa, this dual process of concentration (by modality) and polarization (geographic) of Chinese interventions has thus generally accelerated since 2013.

For the Chinese regime, the launch of the New Silk Roads in 2013 was most likely due to the fact that trade in goods and services has grown twice as fast as the international gross national product (GNP) since the 1990s (UNCTAD, 2021). With China having become the world's largest trading player since joining the WTO, there is no doubt that this element has weighed in the thinking of Xi Jinping and co. From a geoeconomic point of view, Chinese state capitalism has a mercantilist conception of territoriality. For the African continent, this capital's territorialization reveals historical intra- and extraterritorial inequalities (Démurger, 2001; Dobberstein et al., 2005; Fedderke et al., 2006), renewed and potentially exacerbated under the Sino-African overall economic partnership. The statistics speak for themselves (Table 1).

Table 1 Chinese intervention modalities in Africa (2003–2018)

Modalities	Africa in world (%)		Amount ($billion)		NB countries >50% of total		NB countries >75% of total		Total (%)		% without Trade	
Periods	2003/2012	2013/2018	2003/2012	2013/2018	2003/2012	2013/2018	2003/2012	2013/2018	2003/2012	2013/2018	2003/2012	2013/2018
Trade	2.9	3.8	952	1,193	4	4	10	12	78	74	/	/
Services	33.2	33.1	197	307	5	6	12	14	16.1	19	73.3	73.2
Loans	n.d.	n.d.	53	90	4	3	11	8	4.4	5.7	20	21.7
FDIs (flows)	3.9	2.4	17	21	4	8	10	15	1.5	1.3	6.7	5.1

Notes NB expresses the number of countries needed to reach 50% or 75% of total flows
Sources Trade (UNCTAD, 2021); Services and FDIs (NBSC, 2021); Loans (CARI, 2021)

Along with Chinese development aid flows, which are difficult to measure and even less comparable with those of OECD's Development Assistance Committee States, FDIs flows represent the weakest modality of Chinese intervention. Yet, in theory, FDIs are an essential lever for industrialization, GDP growth, and finally development (Gui-Diby & Renard, 2015; Ravallion, 2009; Sahoo et al., 2010). For Chinese economic players, this continent is therefore not the preferred region when it comes to creating or developing a subsidiary, or controlling a foreign company. FDIs reveals the lack of interest in African markets for Chinese enterprises, due to the risks and shortcomings (infrastructural, energy, logistical, or legal) assessed or even imagined by the former. With 3% of Chinese FDI stock between 2003 and 2018, Africa barely exceeds Oceania (2.5%). Moreover, the link between investment and African natural resources seems to be proven, since after South Africa, which accounts for 18.3% of the stock between 2003 and 2018, the following receiving countries are exporters of raw materials: Zambia (7.5%), Nigeria (7.4%), Democratic Republic of Congo (7.1%), Algeria (6.1%) and Sudan (4.9%). Logically, FDIs are more or less directed to China's main African trading partners, which are also the main suppliers of contracts to Chinese enterprises, and sometimes the main debtors (Angola, 29.8% of loans). This dual concentration-polarization of China-Africa flows has been growing since Xi Jinping came to power and the launch of the New Silk Roads. However, the diversification of Chinese and African actors involved in the overall partnership should have led to the opposite. Geographic concentration on the one hand, and the weight of services and loans in China-Africa flows on the other, both favour a highly unequal nature of relations that translate, on the continent, into an unequal process of international integration coupled with a geographical development that is just as unequal (Amin, 1977; Hirschman, 1985; Rist, 1996; Smith, 1990; Stiglitz, 2002). Does this mean that we are witnessing a form of unequal Sino-globalization of Africa through geographic, economic, and commercial, or even sectoral specializations?

4.2 Polarization, Concentration and Inequalities: The Consequences of NSR in Africa

New or reaffirmed dependencies are associated with these Chinese flows. Will the coastal areas with well-equipped ports, especially container terminals, and the territories structured by corridors (Amjadi & Winters, 1997; Doxiadis, 1978; Rodrigue, 2017), i.e., winning areas that are open and even extroverted, not further widen the gap with others territories? These latter are losing out to globalization, i.e., those spaces that are landlocked internally and/or externally, far from the coasts and dependent on the road, rail and port infrastructures that allow goods to enter and leave. Are they not already the territories abandoned by Chinese capital and the New Silk Roads project?

Will we see the progression of a form of specialization (Lefebvre, 1991) of the Chinese rent (Fig. 2) in Africa through these infrastructure projects opportunely and sometimes a posteriori stamped New Silk Roads? Politically, are we not going to see the intensification of several strategic Sino-African bilateral partnerships over the next few years, like the Angolan model, to the detriment of the greatest number of African States? Will Chinese capital create an economic and political clientele, turning a significant part of Africa into a political relay for the Chinese Communist Party? Are these scenarios not already at work in some African States (Ethiopia, Angola, South Sudan, etc.)? In any case, with these Chinese Spatial fixes (Harvey, 2001, 2006), China can help to aggravate metropolisation as well as territorial and socio-economic inequalities in Africa.

The above-mentioned classical capitalist model of financing and construction of infrastructures (Ayogu, 2007; Calderón & Servén, 2010), which characterizes a significant part of NSR and Chinese interventions in Africa, expresses in filigree the search for and securing of profits, resources, and markets. What about Africa? Through the NSR, Chinese interventions lead to an integrating character (Foster et al., 2009; Moller & Wacker, 2017; Schiere & Rugamba, 2011) of major Chinese works on the continent, which are now placed at the level of Regional Integration Communities (RECS). Often financed and/or carried out by Chinese groups, they do not seem likely to slow down and it is therefore necessary to take into account the

Fig. 2 The Chinese spatial fix in Africa (*Source* Author)

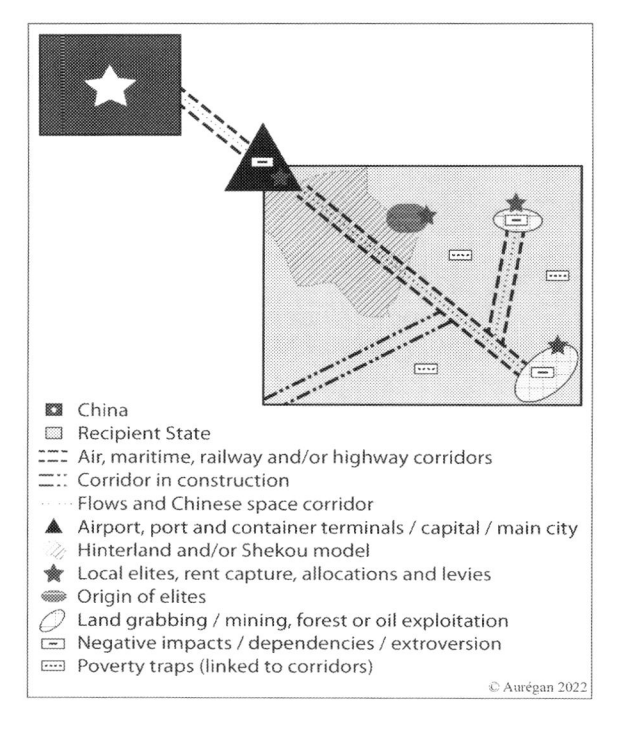

multi-layer (Notteboom & Rodrigue, 2007) territorial impacts as well as the diversification of Chinese actors and operating methods: by networking territories through infrastructures and investing in land-grabbing, China and its actors are materializing internal, but above all external, circulation and mobility. In this way, China is creating or rehabilitating the infrastructures that are lacking in the multiform and international integration of African States, and potentially, the multi-scale integration (Baldwin et al., 2003; Pedroni & Canning, 2004) of the eponymous territories.

This social and physical infrastructure which ensuring the continuity of flows generated by African States heavy investments should facilitate the movement of capital as well as goods, but primarily with the international scale, Asia and China in the first place. These infrastructures, including the corridors (ICA, 2012) of the African Union's Programme for Infrastructure Development in Africa (PIDA), partially overlap to form not a network as such, which dates back to the colonial period, but strategic axes whose vocation is supposedly reticular, and which are sometimes oriented towards the extraction of natural resources. These underpins numerous transformations of productive processes, mutations, and new dynamics, whether internal (African), external (Chinese), or more certainly mixed (Sino-African *at least*). These spatial dynamics are furthermore amplified by the presence of the infrastructures discussed above, since the development corridors, sometimes multimodal and always favoured by the African Union and China, generate as many positive consequences (speed, fluidity and security of flows) as negative ones with low-income trap, territorial marginalization, agglomeration versus diffusion, etc. (Limaõ & Venables, 2001; Shi & Huang, 2014; Zhang, 2014).

More specifically, what about China's financing of African infrastructure? According to our research based on data provided by the Infrastructure Consortium for Africa (ICA, 2019) and taking into account external (towards Africa) public financing, China's financing is 30.6% during the 2006–2017 period ($128 billion). France, ODA flows or not, would have financed these African infrastructures to the tune of 27 billion dollars (6%). Private flows amounted to $102 billion, i.e., $26 billion less than China. All funding sources combined, West Africa is the region that has obtained the most loans (23%), ahead of East Africa (21%) and North Africa (19%). China financed the same regions: 33% for West Africa, 31% for East Africa, and 15% for North Africa. The sectors favoured by all funders are transport infrastructure (41%), energy (35%), hydroelectricity (14%), "multisector" (3%), and finally telecommunications (2%). Chinese commitments are similar: transport (41%) and energy (37%) accounting for the bulk of the flows. Thus, China finances the same countries or regions in Africa and the same infrastructure sectors as other funders. These figures and information prove wrong those who believe (Cooper Ramo, 2004) that there is a Chinese model (in Africa or elsewhere). Nevertheless, Chinese actors are touting certain Chinese ways of doing things, but at different scales. This is the case, for example, of the Shekou model (前港-中区-后城), an integrated system also called "Port-Park-City" according to which the port, as an infrastructure generating flows, circulations and exchanges, embodies the integrating bridgehead of a space whose surface area amply exceeds the sole footprint of the port (Fig. 2).

What does this mean? Firstly, the statistics currently available can be improved upon and are by no means exhaustive. Second, China has partially replaced Japan, which until the mid-2000s could finance up to 10% of African infrastructure, including transport corridors. Third, in parallel with the increase in trade, official visits and more generally Chinese presence in Africa, Chinese actors are increasingly involved in the financing and/or implementation of the said African infrastructure, with a clear preference for transport and energy, especially in West Africa. These exploratory remarks confirm the findings on the ground (Aurégan, 2016b). If African governments ultimately provide the bulk of the commitments (42% of the total), are they not benefiting from Export and Import Bank of China loans under turnkey contracts that are supposed to participate in infrastructure projects promoted by the ruling elites? Will some of these supposedly low-profit projects become white elephants?

In this post-2013 context, these Sino-African flows, including loans, create debt and multiple dependencies since Beijing uses the same capitalist procedures as Westerners (Collier, 1995; Cooper, 2002). Is China then in the process of reproducing the Western mistakes that it never ceases to decry? This compression of flows with certain partners is de facto locking China and African countries into a pattern that China itself could denounce. In this, the political factor becomes the support for trade and this economic diplomacy is verified both through the New Silk Roads project and through the "health diplomacy" (Habibi & Zhu, 2021; Tang et al., 2017) observed during the COVID-19 epidemic. While NSR is very frequently mentioned or analyzed through infrastructure, culture, health, and agriculture are among the other sectors prioritized by Chinese actors. As a useful screen for the Chinese authorities, NSR cannot, however, hide Chinese interventions with Western characteristics that obey, a priori, logics superior to the formation of this officially presented and vaunted "win–win" infrastructure network.

5 Conclusion

Our premise was as follows: the nature and extreme concentration of Sino-African economic flows certainly lead to forms of polarization, but above all to inequalities and dependencies that China, as a global actor, considerably increases.

From our point of view, the Sino-African relations diachrony as narrated by the Chinese authorities is not as linear as it seems. It is made up of evolutions and ruptures. To simplify, the China-Africa relationship has gone from the spirit of Bandung (in 1955) to a mercantile approach (1982), and has definitely taken a financial path since 2013. These financialization and Chinese spatial fix in Africa allow Chinese authorities and Chinese enterprises to: increase their turnover; test equipment, labour, and standards in real conditions; acquire know-how through Sino-Western consortiums for large infrastructure projects; reinject (even partially) the foreign exchange reserve; secure the loyalty of African client States that have become dependent on Chinese loans; sell the qualitatively weaker part of Chinese manufacturing production; and finally, ensure the emergence of future Chinese MNCs (Gu et al., 2016; Kolstad & Wiig, 2012; Schortgen, 2009).

China has created a "win–lose" rather than a "win–win" partnership by exporting its excess productive capacity and tying infrastructure financing to the signing of contracts with Chinese enterprises. All the more so since the question of debt and its consequences, in particular, is not addressed here. Of course, these different polarisations by port centres or sub-regional powers can be seen as positive for the economic development of part of the African continent. In theory, this development can lead other States to follow in their wake. However, will these interventions not rather contribute to brutal forms of territorial, commercial, urban, political, and economic differentiation, leaving behind landlocked rural territories (Robinson & Conning, 2009) that are not endowed with exploitable resources? Is China not exacerbating the duality between a useful Africa, seen as an extraterritorial geopolitical relay for itself and its actors, and an excluded Africa? Finally, is this not the inevitable consequence of the New Silk Roads project?

In our view, NSR heralds a paradigm shift that is meant to be definitive. Development aid, its ideological corpus, its public actors and its means are marginalized to the NSR's benefit, which has the advantage of being able to integrate all Chinese intervention modalities. The other NSR's advantage is that it is broad-based: the project makes it possible to develop or integrate new areas of economic cooperation with the African countries concerned. In this context, the COVID-19 pandemic was a tremendous accelerator: it allowed the Chinese government and all those who identify with it to develop a global communication campaign based on the NSR narratives (connectivity, integration, people-to-people links, cooperation, harmonious environment, global community of shared destiny, new era). In the rhetoric, development aid is no more. NSR and its declensions have become omnipresent, omnipotent. This paradigm shift allows for the integration of the countless privately owned enterprises that used to wait behind the publicly owned ones, historically favoured by the party. Now authorized and armed, these private actors work with syncretic mean with the public ones, specifically in Africa. For the many Chinese actors present or interested in the continent on the one hand, and African elites on the other hand, the specialization of the NSR rent has only just begun.

Bibliographic References

Amin, S. (1977). *Unequal development: An essay on the social formations of peripheral capitalism.* Monthly Review Press.

Amjadi, A., & Winters, L. A. (1997). *Transport costs and "natural" integration of mercosur* (Working Paper). Washington, World Bank. http://documents.worldbank.org/curated/en/271551468773379871/pdf/multi-page.pdf

Aurégan, X. (2011). Le Burkina Faso et les « deux Chines » (Burkina Faso and the "two Chinas"). *Outre-Terre, 4*(30), 381–390.

Aurégan, X. (2016a). Temps et non-temps des relations sino-africaines (Time and non-time of Sino-African relations). *Géoéconomie, 4*(81), 177–195.

Aurégan, X. (2016b). *Géopolitique de la Chine en Côte d'Ivoire* (Geopolitics of China in Cote d'Ivoire). Riveneuve.

Aurégan, X. (2019a). L'Inde en Afrique ou l'impossible rattrapage vis-à-vis de la Chine (India in Africa or the impossible catching up with China). *L'espace politique, 36*. https://journals.openedition.org/espacepolitique/5516

Aurégan, X. (2019b). Les quatre temps de la Chine en Afrique (The four Eras of China in Africa). In X. Aurégan & S. Wintgens (Eds.), *Les dynamiques de la Chine en Afrique et en Amérique latine – Enjeux, défis et perspectives (China's dynamics in Africa and Latin America—Issues, challenges and perspectives)* (pp. 33–63). Academia.

Aurégan, X. (2019c). Les centres de démonstration agricoles chinois en Afrique: étude de cas en Côte d'Ivoire (Chinese agricultural demonstration centres in Africa: A case study in cote d'Ivoire). *Les Cahiers d'Outre-Mer, 70*(275), 63–92.

Ayogu, M. (2007). Infrastructure and economic development in Africa: A review. *Journal of African Economies, 16*(1), 75–126.

Baldwin, R., Forslid, R., Martin, P., Ottaviano, G., & Robert-Nicoud, F. (2003). *Economic geography and public policy*. Princeton University Press.

Bergère, M.C. (2013). *Chine: le nouveau capitalisme d'État* (China: The New State Capitalism). Fayard.

Braütigam, D. (1998). *Chinese aid and African development: Exporting green revolution*. Palgrave Macmillan.

Braütigam, D. (2009). *The Dragon's gift: The real story of China in Africa*. Oxford University Press.

Calderón, C., & Servén, L. (2010). Infrastructure and economic development in Sub-Saharan Africa. *Journal of African Economies, 19*(1). 13–87.

CARI. (2021). *Data: Chinese loans to Africa*. China Africa Research Initiative (CARI). http://www.sais-cari.org/data

Collier, P. (1995). The marginalization of Africa. *International Labour Review, 134*(4–5), 541–557.

Cooper, F. (2002). *Africa since 1940*. Cambridge University Press.

Cooper Ramo, J. (2004). *The Beijing consensus*. The Foreign Policy Center.

Démurger, S. (2001). Infrastructure development and economic growth: An explanation for regional disparities in China? *Journal of Comparative Economics, 29*(1), 95–117.

Dobberstein, N., Neumann, C. S., & Zils, M. (2005). Logistics in emerging markets. *The McKinsey Quarterly, 1*, 15–17.

Doxiadis, C. (1978). *Ecology and ekistics*. Westview Press.

Fedderke, J. W., Perkins, P., & Luiz, J. M. (2006). Infrastructural investment in long-run economic growth: South Africa 1875–2001. *World Development, 34*(6), 1037–1059.

Foster, V., Butterfield, W., & Chen, C. (2009). *Building bridges: China's growing role as infrastructure financier for Africa*. Trends and Policy Options, World Bank, 5. https://openknowledge.worldbank.org/handle/10986/2614

Gu, J., Zhang, C., Vaz, A., & Mukwereza, L. (2016). Chinese state capitalism? Rethinking the role of the state and business in Chinese development cooperation in Africa. *World Development, 81*, 24–34.

Gui-Diby, S. L., & Renard, M. F. (2015). Foreign direct investment inflows and the industrialization of African countries. *World Development, 74*, 43–57.

Habibi, N., & Zhu, H. Y. (2021). *The Health Silk Road as a new direction in China's belt and road strategy in Africa*. Center for Global Development and Sustainability, Brandeis University, GDS Working Paper Series, 1. https://heller.brandeis.edu/gds/pdfs/working-papers/china-africa-2021.pdf

Harvey, D. (2006). *Spaces of global capitalism: Towards a theory of uneven geographical development*. Verso.

Harvey, D. (2001). *Spaces of capital: Towards a critical geography*. Routledge.

Hirschman, A. (1985). *The strategy of economic development*. Yale University Press.

ICA. (2012). *Executive summary of the programme for infrastructure development in Africa (PIDA).* https://www.icafrica.org/en/news-events/ica-news/article/executive-summary-of-the-programme-for-infrastructure-development-in-africa-pida-3238/

ICA. (2019). *ICA Publications.* The Infrastructure Consortium for Africa (ICA). https://www.icafrica.org/en/knowledge-hub/ica-publications/

Kolstad, I., & Wiig, A. (2012). What determines Chinese outward FDI? *Journal of World Business, 47*(1), 26–34.

Kurlantzick, J. (2016). *State capitalism: How the return of statism is transforming the world.* Oxford University Press.

Leandro, F. B. S. J., & Duarte, P. A. B. (2020). *The Belt and Road Initiative—An old archetype of a new development model.* Palgrave Macmillan.

Lefebvre, H. (1991). *The production of space.* Blackwell.

Limão, N., & Venables, A. J. (2001). Infrastructure, geographical disadvantage, and transport costs and trade. *World Bank Economic Review, 15*(3), 451–479.

Moller, L. C., & Wacker, K. M. (2017). Explaining Ethiopia's growth acceleration—The role of infrastructure and macroeconomic policy. *World Development, 96,* 198–215.

NBSC. (2021). *Annual data.* National Bureau of Statistics of China (NBSC). http://www.stats.gov.cn/english/Statisticaldata/AnnualData/

NDRC. (2017). *Vision and actions on jointly building Belt and Road.* National Development and Reform Commission (NDRC). http://2017.beltandroadforum.org/english/n100/2017/0410/c22-45.html

Notteboom, T. E., & Rodrigue, J. P. (2007). Re-assessing port-hinterland relationships in the context of global commodity chains. In J. Wang et al. (Eds.), *Port, cities and global supply chains* (pp. 51–68). Ashgate.

Pedroni, P., & Canning, D. (2004). *The effect of infrastructure on long-run economic growth.* Department of Economics Working Papers, Williams College. https://web.williams.edu/Economics/wp/pedroniinfrastructure.pdf

Ravallion, M. (2009). Are there lessons for Africa from China's success against poverty? *World Development, 37*(2), 303–313.

Rist, G. (1996). *Le développement: histoire d'une croyance occidentale* [The development: History of a Western Belief]. Presses de Sciences Po.

Rist, G. (2008). *The history of development: From Western origins to global faith.* Zed Books.

Robinson, J. A., & Conning, J. H. (2009). Enclaves and development. An empirical assessment. *Studies in Comparative International Development, 44,* 359–385.

Rodrigue, J. P. (2017). *The geography of transport systems.* Routledge.

Sahoo, P., Dash, R.K. & Nataraj, G. (2010). *Infrastructure development and economic growth in China.* IDE-JETRO (Discussion Paper), 261. https://www.ide.go.jp/English/Publish/Download/Dp/261.html

Shi, H., & Huang, S. (2014). How much infrastructure is too much? A new approach and evidence from China. *World Development, 56,* 272–286.

Schiere, R., & Rugamba, A. (2011). *Chinese infrastructure investments and African integration* (Working Paper). African Development Bank Group, 127. https://www.afdb.org/fileadmin/uploads/afdb/Documents/Publications/WPS%20No%20127%20Chinese%20Infrastructure%20Investments%20.pdf

Schortgen, F. (2009). A contextual view of Chinese enterprise internationalization. In I. Alon, J. Chang, M. Fetscherin, C. Lattemann, & J. R. McIntyre (Eds.), *China rules. Globalization and political transformation* (pp. 15–45). Palgrave Macmillan.

Smith, N. (1990). *"Uneven development": Nature.* Basil Blackwell.

Stiglitz, J. E. (2002). *Globalization and its discontents.* Norton.

Tang, K., Li, Z., Li, W., & Chen, L. (2017). China's Silk Road and global health. *The Lancet, 390*(10112), 2595–2601.

UNCTAD. (2021). *Database. United Nations conference on trade and development (UNCTAD).* https://unctad.org/fr/en/Pages/statistics.aspx

Zhang, Y. (2014). From state to market: Private participation in China's urban infrastructure sectors, 1992–2008. *World Development, 64,* 473–486.

Chapter 45
Africa's Thirst for Infrastructure: Contemporary Phenomenon That Makes China the Trading Partner

Paulo Elicha Tembe

1 Introduction

The relationship between China and Africa has drawn attention from various spheres of society and has been currently the centre of research and studies that seek to understand the real motivations for China's engagement in Africa. Concern over whether China intensifies its cooperation with Africa, seeking in return access to the resources that Africa has in abundance, comes from sceptics on the African continent, Japan, and the West. On the one hand, there is some legitimacy in the concern of Africans regarding China's engagement in the continent, as there is evidence of pillaging and/or expropriation of its resources in the past by colonizing countries. On the other hand, Japan's narrative is motivated by its secular rivalry with China which has become a global phenomenon. Japan's approach in Africa has provided asymmetries in terms of the amount of investments and financing of these two countries in Africa, which makes the game competitive, good for Africa because, where there is competitiveness; there are gains in the market. Furthermore, it is the speech of the West that never moves away from classifying China as neocolonial. China's approach has been without equal intervention in the creation of infrastructures of all kinds in almost all of Africa, because that Asian tiger, in the design of its intervention plan with Africa, begins by identifying the real problems of the continent that has been par excellence, the lack of infrastructure, namely, roads, bridges, energy, telecommunications, among others. China's entry into the continent is seen as a timely and immediate solution because it resolves the issue of infrastructure that African countries are unable to build through domestic public investment programmes.

The economic growth that African countries have often observed has not been translated into development, which is the influence of economic growth indicators in creating economic and social well-being in the lives of citizens. It is recognized

P. E. Tembe (✉)
Center for Strategic and Internacional Studies, Joaquim Chissano University, Maputo, Mozambique

that any country, however poor it may be, draws, within its governance, an action plan to make its economy grow, aiming to distribute income among various sectors and its population. Such a claim is a utopia for Africa as the continent is undermined by the corruption that is characteristic of African countries where public projects are hostage to individual interests. On the other hand, in China the issue of corruption is treated seriously, different from the way the African counterpart deals with the problem. China realized that corruption undermines the development of a country and created a political strategy to eradicate it and hold the corrupt responsible in a severe and exemplary manner.

However, for this study we are not interested in discussing corruption. It is interesting to discuss in subsequent chapters the relationship between infrastructures lacking in Africa and China's objective of seeking access to raw materials on the continent to supply its industry. The idea of access to raw materials may be, on the one hand, because Chinese industries are beginning to resent the projected economic inefficiency in the long term, or because of the "less expensive" strategy China wants to be competitive on the continent and leave its mark and model. However, one of the best-known models designed by China in accessing raw material was the Angolan model, which consisted of exchanging barrels of oil for the creation of infrastructure, especially railways and public buildings and housing. This model was possible for Angola because, this country, did not have capital as a bargaining chip to have infrastructure installed in its country, and, for China, it was a great opportunity to directly access oil continuously in an exclusive contract signed by these two countries.

Given the above view, the following research question arises: Will China replicate the Angolan model across the continent and solve the continent's problems? To answer this question, the qualitative and quantitative method is adopted as a methodology, where several bibliography referring to what has been written in this field of research is consulted, from official documents, adopting the historical method. However, the research question is answered based on the general and specific objectives: a) Assess the relationship between Chinese infrastructure and access to African raw material; b) Analyze the basis of trade exchange mechanisms between China and Africa; Describe and characterize the cooperation programmes between China and Africa.

2 China-Africa Cooperation: An Overview

Cooperation between China and Africa is currently the epicentre in the field of international relations and in the field of international political economy. This cooperation has been of capital importance since the times of struggle for the independence of African countries, a period in which, china supported most of these countries in the conquest of their identity, sovereignty and economic independence. The relationship between the Asian country and Africa began in the political and diplomatic field and later, moved to cooperation in the commercial and business area, ranging from Chinese direct investment, granting Chinese government loans, humanitarian aid, and cooperation in access to raw materials in exchange for infrastructure. It is a situation in which the European Parliament, mentions that China is trying to "establish a firm control over Africa's natural resources," and its interest in Africa "seems confined to resource-rich (or "resource-cursed") countries," bypassing a large number of other African nations.

China commonly funds the construction of infrastructure such as roads and railroads, dams, ports, and airports. While relations are mainly conducted through diplomacy and trade, military support via the provision of arms and other modern technological equipment is also a major component (Manyeruke & Abegunrin, 2020, p. 27). Today, China's relations with sub-Saharan Africa are multifaceted and much of this activity is concentrated in a handful of African countries and in the extractive industries, such as oil and mining, but increasingly businesses from China are also pursuing strategies in Africa that are about far more than natural resources (Ziso, 2018, p. 108).

Chinese upstream investments help secure energy resources overseas to feed its growing energy demand, which is estimated to double over the next 30 years and, is the single most important driver of global energy demand growth (IEA, 2016, p. 10). Energy is an important part in China's cooperation with Africa and it is also, one of the most important things of the International Society (Aiqin & Jianhong, 2017, p. 107). Africa has solar, wind, and hydropower resources to solve its energy gap and to industrialize (Lahtinen, 2018, p. 87). As with infrastructure, China has a long history of providing African governments with loans for manufacturing, agro-industry, and other value-added productive sectors (Brautigam, 2019, p. 141). In the last few years Chinese FDI to Africa has diversified into sectors such as textiles, agro-processing, power generation, road construction, tourism, and communications (Moyo, 2009, p. 102). In the Johannesburg Declaration, Xi Jinping pledged to improve China-Africa relations in 10 sectors, namely: Industrialization, modernization of agriculture, infrastructure, financing, green development, trade and investment, poverty reduction, public health, culture, peace and security (Brautigam et al., 2018, p. 1). The improvement of these relations presupposed to guarantee that the sectors indicated by President Xi, created productive sustainability, institutional capacity to intervene with quality in the reduction of poverty and greater response to mutual interests. China's interest is undoubtedly, as it is often referred to, access to raw materials, given its position and responsibility in the world either as an exporter or importer of commodities (Tembe, 2021).

For example, Alves and Chichava (2019, p. 254) indicate that between 2000 and 2015, Mozambique received $1.87bn loans from China less than one-tenth of the extended loans to Angola. China Exim Bank was the one providing financial support to build transport infrastructure. Despite the other sector, the Chinese government has pledged to step up China–Africa cooperation in transportation, communications, water conservancy, electricity, and other infrastructure (Moyo, 2009, p. 102).

3 Relationship Between Chinese Infrastructure and Access to African Raw Materials

Various literatures on the direct link between Chinese investment infrastructure creation in Africa in exchange for access to the continent's raw materials has been discussed in accusatory manner. It is no less true that China's interest in Africa is intended to help the continent without a bargaining chip. Countries cooperate seeking to obtain mutual benefits or gains, but sometimes unequal. Since one of the first Chinese Premier Zhao Ziyang trip to 11 African countries, China wanted to emphasize the mutual benefits that should result from its engagement in Africa as opposed to simply giving aid (Brautigam, 2015, p. 50). Aid is not working in the view of Moyo (2009), because from the 1970's up to recent years, as many as thirty other developing countries, mainly aid-dependent in sub-Saharan Africa, have failed to generate consistent economic growth, and have even regressed. Her argument is consistent with China's engagement in Africa since the Chinese Premier Zhao Ziyang trip to Africa in which he stressed a win–win cooperation based on mutual benefits.

China wanted to make clear that any future relationship with Africa should be based on mutual interests, exploring areas of both sides' interests. The economic growth of the cooperating countries can only be achieved if there is an exchange of resources, whether natural, financial, or otherwise, from that partner who has in abundance in his possession, more competitive advantage of products or services, in relation to the cooperating country's economic. Thus, for China, the competitive advantage lies in having the financing that Africa needs, and, for the continent, its advantage lies in the existence of the resources that the Asian market needs to supply its industries. However, Jenkins (2019), states that acquiring resources, particularly oil and minerals, plays an important role in China's economic involvement in Sub-Saharan Countries (SSA), but it is not the sole explanation of its relations with the region.

Although other reasons for China's engagement in Africa are considered, the idea of interest in accessing raw materials in exchange for infrastructure seems to be the most prevalent of all. In some cases, infrastructure finance is packaged with natural resource development, making use of a mechanism known as the "Angola mode," (Foster et al, 2009). The demand for natural resources explains the tremendous increase in Chinese trade and investment in Africa. Of the majority of natural resources that capture China's interest in Africa, we can highlight: Oil, copper, iron, bauxite, uranium, aluminium, manganese, diamond, with the most important resource being oil, as mentioned ENUKA (2010, p. 210) in an assessment of China's engagement with Africa in the twenty-first century. With oil being the resource that captures China's most interest in Africa; Libya's Chinese investment indicators show that the country still provided in 2011, the conflict period, a large market for Chinese manufacturing products and was a profitable source of contracts for development Infrastructure for Chinese private and public companies (Hodzi, 2019, p. 109).

The Libyan conflict, which practically destroyed many infrastructures in that country, provided an opportunity for the Chinese government to apply its model of providing infrastructure in exchange for access to natural resources, which in this case is oil. The destruction of Libya by the armed conflict was a blank check for China, which had already identified in its strategic business plan for Africa, the solution of making new infrastructure available by winning post-conflict reconstruction contracts. It was based on this above scenario that Hodzi (2019) explains that Contracted infrastructure development projects funded by the Libyan government together with large Chinese private and state-owned enterprises, such as the Changshu Construction Group, a Jiangsu-based enterprise which was contracted to construct a university town in Libya. Another country that has also stepped up in infrastructure is Ethiopia where Chinese companies are currently behind 70 per cent of all road construction in Ethiopia. Chinese companies are involved in these practically all major infrastructure projects in Ethiopia, including the construction of roads, railways, airports, hydroelectric power dams, wind power plants, and upgrading of telecom networks (Skjerdal & Gusu, 2016, p. 150). However, African countries such as Djibouti, Ethiopia, Kenya, Namibia, and Tanzania as stated by contracted with China on major hydropower, logistics, railway, road, seaport, and other projects and, in many cases, received aid and loans from China to support these initiatives (Blanchard, 2021, p. 15). Figure 1 indicates the sectors of intervention for power plant construction projects in Sub-Saharan Africa.

Looking at the above indicators, it can be deduced that it is believed that Chinese infrastructure involvement in Africa focuses on the resource sector as mentioned by International Energy Agency (2016), which means that there is a relationship between the creation of infrastructure by Chinese investment aiming to have access to the abundant natural resources in Africa. In this case, the engagement of China in the energy sector shows its interest in modernizing this sector, so that, there is productive efficiency in African countries, thus making their resources available to the internal market and especially to the Chinese market. China will undoubtedly, directly or indirectly, intensify its formula better known as the Angola model because, as discussed and evidenced in this study, it would have already strategically identified in its approach to Africa, the problems facing most African countries, which is the lack of basic infrastructure and access to capital to promote their economic activities.

Fig. 1 Origin of financing for Chinese-built power projects in Sub-Saharan Africa (*Source* International Energy Agency [2021])

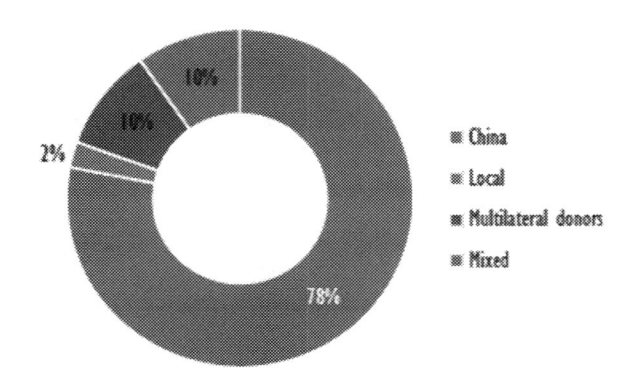

Therefore, as a way of guaranteeing access to natural resources, meaning that, the raw material will always have to design in its plans, credit granting packages at relatively low rates, as it has been part of its strategy for Africa and other countries under development.

4 China-Africa Trade Exchange Mechanism

The trade sector has also been a strong feature of trade relations between China and Africa. This characteristic is typical as, for example, in the last decade, China launched the Beijing Action Plan (2007–2009) focusing on political-economic cooperation with targets in terms of bilateral trade of up to 100 billion in 2010, lending $3 billion and preferential credits of around $2 billion to African countries, creation of the Sino-African development fund with a $5 billion subsidy to encourage Chinese firms to invest in Africa (Montenegro & Alves, 2016, p. 158). Meanwhile, China's strategy continued with the Johannesburg Declaration in South Africa and the Action Plan (2016–2018), according to FOCAC data. This declaration presented a financial package of 60 billion divided into preferential loans and credit lines for exports, subsidies, Capital for the CAD Fund, and loans aimed at the development of African small and medium enterprises.

If, on the one hand, the disbursement of the financial package contained in the action plan (2016–2018) was intended, for various sectors, including trade, China-Africa trade reached 170 billion US dollars in 2017, compared with 765 million US dollars in 1978, whereas in 2016, China's investment in Africa totaled 100 billion US dollars, and it has grown to US$149.1 billion (Duggan, 2020, p. 1). There is evidence that these trade exchanges are not only oriented in a sector as referred by the same author, evidencing that this trade is not based solely on the import of raw materials from Africa, by China or on the export of consumer goods into the African market by China. However, it is known that there are several sectors of commercial cooperation between China and Africa. In these sectors of trade, there is evidence of import and export of products on both sides.

Like Blanchard (2021) data show, Africa's exports to China were $40.85 billion in 2010, $37.86 billion in 2015, and $48.76 billion in 2017. On the other hand, Africa's imports from China ran $37.02 billion in 2010, $58.02 billion in 2015, and $54.30 billion in 2017. The trade mechanism between Africa and China has been mostly focused on oil and gas, although not exclusively on these commodities. In addition to the commercial performance between China and Africa in 2017, according to (Manyeruke & Abegunrin, 2020), after the Johannesburg declaration in which the financial package for Africa is announced, the Beijing Summit of 2018, also includes a $5 billion special fund for financing Chinese imports from Africa. The scenario of financial amount made available by China for trade with Africa already established until 2017, is a demonstration of that Asian country's commitment to the mechanism of trade cooperation with the continent. However, this suggests that in the medium and long term, China will remain Africa's main economic cooperation partner. Nevertheless, it is necessary to increase the levels of production and productivity in Africa so that, the situation of trade deficit in which most African countries find themselves is reversed. Taking into account the exchange currency based on the production line, it is stated (Brautigam, 2015) that the country has borrowed the most from China for production-oriented projects is Angola.

5 Instruments of Cooperation Between China and Africa

The cooperation instruments that are known in the relationship between China and Africa are mostly designed by China. There is no known strong African instrument, designed with particular attention to China-Africa cooperation, other than through particular initiatives by countries or bodies created by China. However, one of the great current cooperation mechanisms between China and Africa that has brought tangible results both for China and for Africa is the China–Africa-FOCAC Forum, created in 2000, according to data by Li et al. (2012, p. 9), as a multilateral exchange and cooperation platform between China and African countries that have a diplomatic relationship with that Asian country, covering various aspects from politics, trade, economy, society, and culture.

The authors point out how some of FOCAC's achievements have become a model of cooperation that could provide a new basis for solving poverty problems on the continent. The forum, for these authors, has become a new model of mutually beneficial cooperation, based on mutual respect and directly linked to the legitimacy of the current political-economic system in the world. This is a unilateral Beijing initiative that later, turned into an instrument of mutual cooperation where strategies, plans, approaches, and policies have mostly been unilateral, although it is recognized that there are panel discussions where major decisions are in the interest of both leave. In 2012, on the initiative of China, the China-Africa Cooperative Partnership for Peace and Security promising an integration of security into the FOCAC process is created (Barber & Alden, 2018, p. 2).

Another cooperation mechanism is the creation of Confucius Institutes throughout Africa, with the main role of teaching the Chinese language and culture to Africans. However, this sector of cooperation based on these educational centres brings the idea that for this sector, we only have an approach from China to Africa. However, it would be interesting if there were an initiative on the part of African countries to also instal or create in China, centres for teaching a language and culture mostly predominant in Africa. The centres for Asian and African Studies or Chinese and African Studies are mostly dedicated to the study of research or studies of African civilizations and not necessarily interested in studying African language and culture. However, according to Alden and Large (2019), in 2006, the Institute of West Asia and African Studies (IWAAS) of CASS, Chinese Society of African Historical Studies (CSAHS), and Peking University's Center for African Studies decided to carry out a project on the bibliography of African studies in China between 1997 and 2005.

On the other hand, the example that we are referring to, about the absence of studies dealing with African language and cultures, can be found in the book Lu Ting-en, which compiled his articles into a volume of four sections covering African history in the colonial period, history of African parties and politics, African economic history and history of China-Africa relations.

In the history of China-Africa relations, the role of capital made available by China to Africa played a very important role for the continent. There are several mechanisms for accessing the Chinese fund, such as the China-Africa Development Fund which, according to Brautigam (2009), was created in 2007 to operate in Africa in agriculture, manufacturing, electricity, transportation, telecommunications, urban infrastructure projects, and resource exploration. In terms of regional cooperation, the countries of the Community of Portuguese Language Countries—CPLP, also have their own financing instrument called the China-Portuguese-Speaking Countries Cooperation and Development Fund (CPD-Fund). China's engagement in Africa is across sectors and also privileges some instruments and/or particular programmes different from the entire African Union body. There are Chinese intervention goals for each cooperation, whether bilateral, regional, or continental. This cooperation model may also suggest the idea that mutual but unequal gains exist for this cooperation, taking into account that any cooperation instrument is designed by China, while recognizing that the plans integrate concerns of joint interest. This is what dependency theory suggests in its approach to the relationship between states. The objective is mutual, but each cooperation party tries to take maximum advantage of the negotiation forums.

Currently, it can be assumed that both China and the African continent are on an equal footing in their relationship because Africa needs infrastructure such as roads, bridges, capital, know-how and, China needs to have privileged access to African raw materials to supply their domestic industries. The cooperation instruments that will interest Africa will undoubtedly be those that go directly to the creation of infrastructure, allowing for the attraction of foreign direct investment, job creation, and the empowerment of micro, small and medium-sized enterprises-MSME in the continent. The African continent needs, on the one hand, to be autonomous in the choice of priority development projects for the continent. On the other, it is necessary that the continent has an approach of internationalization of its projects from scratch in its approach with China. Instead of having programmes, strategies, and development plans under the name China-Africa, it is urgent in the near future to have a different approach that suggests an Africa-China name, which makes it clear that the approach is from Africa to China. In the history of this cooperation, there is no knowledge of a thriving presence of African ventures or ideas in that Asian country. The instruments or mechanisms of cooperation need to be improved so that in fact they mean exclusively bilateral cooperation from A to B and from B to A. So, when the levels of cooperation reach this point, the continent can start talking about mutual gains and egalitarian.

6 Conclusion

China has recently become a major cooperation actor for Africa in all sectors. The current dynamics of cooperation suggest a stronger relationship in the economic domains, which is why there are several instruments designed by China with the aim of solidifying its position as a creditor partner of Africa, making clear the top condition and preference for the continent. Thus, the continuation of China's strategic and privileged position in Africa is subject to the financial criteria that the Asian country has, in the sense of always having a capitalist approach in its relationship with Africa. It is this approach that the continent wants to hear from its partners, especially China, which seems to be the partner solving the problems of lack of basic infrastructure and capital.

The various mechanisms or cooperation instruments designed by China already address this issue of financial availability, as China has already identified the problems that greatly affect the continent. These are urgent problems that make Africa's economic growth and development dependent. This dependence increases Africa's thirst for infrastructure, forcing the continent to give up its natural resources at any available price. Their price, which seems to be adjusted to the goals of achieving Africa's development, is related to the so-called Angolan model, which is characterized as being, one that provides infrastructure for Africa, in exchange for access to the continent's raw materials. This Angolan model has sharpened the rivalry between Japan and China, since any approach that Japan takes in relation to Africa, it has been referred almost always that its intention in Africa is not just to exploit African resources, making it clear that its rival China, only engages with Africa with the aim of extracting its resources and supplying its industry that is facing problems of raw material scarcity.

China gradually impresses African leaders with its declarations aimed at financing African projects. FOCAC has been the most reporting mechanism for funding Africa. An example of this is the Johannesburg declaration announcing the financial package for Africa, and later, the Beijing Summit of 2018, also includes a $5 billion special fund for financing Chinese imports from Africa. With these data, there is no doubt that China wants to "help" Africa in solving its problems, but it also seems true that ensuring access to African products through trade fund and infrastructure initiatives is what China has strived to invest. The sectors of cooperation between China-Africa are increasingly expanding. An example of this is the Johannesburg Declaration, in which Xi Jinping pledged to improve China-Africa relations in 10 sectors, namely: Industrialization, modernization of agriculture, infrastructure, financing, green development, trade and investment, poverty reduction, public health, culture, peace, and security. With the exception of the culture sector, most African countries face serious problems in the nine sectors that are the driving force for achieving economic growth and development. Culture is excluded for the simple fact that Africa is a multicultural continent, with different ethnic groups that place it in a leading position in relation to its Chinese partner, although, China is not left behind in the millenary record of its culture. From this understanding, it is concluded that the cultural sector, both cooperation partners, can have mutual and equal gains in this domain.

Still in the economic domain, it is evident that the financial criterion is the one that will prevail in the long term in this relationship between the two actors, not meaning therefore, to declassify the other sectors that also add positive value to cooperation. This financial criterion will favour the expansion of the Angolan model in other African countries, as most of them face problems of return on invested capital, having only two traditional factors of economic production, namely land and labour, making capital scarce as the third traditional factor of economic production. Therefore, the continent can only dispose of the raw material, the earth naturally has in cooperation with China, offering what China seeks in Africa, especially, but not exclusively, oil and gas, which are commodities that have great value for the manufacturing industry, characteristic of China.

Bibliographic References

Aiqin, C., & Jianhong, C. (2017). *China and Africa: A new paradigm of global business, China's energy diplomacy towards Africa from the perspective of politics* (p. 105). Asian Business Series. Palgrave Macmillan.

Alden, C., & Large, D. (2019). *New directions in China-Africa Studies.* Routledge.

Alves, A., & Chichava, S. (2019). *New directions in Africa China studies.* Routledge.

Alden, C., Alao, A., Zhang, C., & Barber, L. (2018). *China and Africa building peace and security cooperation on the continent.* Palgrave Macmillan.

Barber, L., & Alden, C. (2018). *Introduction: Seeking security: China's expanding involvement in security cooperation in Africa, China and Africa: Building peace and security cooperation on the continent.* Palgrave Macmillan.

Blanchard, J.-M. F. (2021). *China's maritime Silk Road Initiative, Africa and the Middle East: Feats, freezes and failures, studies in Asia-Pacific political economy.* Palgrave Macmillan.

Brautigam, D. (2009). *The Dragon's gift: The real story of China in Africa.* Oxford University Press.

Brautigam, D. (2015). *Will Africa feed China?* (p. 50). Oxford University Press.

Brautigam, D., (2019). Misdiagnosing the Chinese infrastructure push. *The American Interest.* https://www.the-american-interest.com/2019/04/04/misdiagnosing-the-chinese-infrastructure-push/. Accessed in December 2019.

Brautigam, et al. (2018). *The path ahead: The 7th forum on China-Africa cooperation.* China Africa research initiative, briefing paper, n. 01.

Dambisa, M. (2009). *Dead aid: Why aid is not working and how there is a better way for Africa* (p. 102). Farrar, Straus and Giroux.

Duggan, N. (2020). *Competition and compromise among Chinese actors in Africa, governing China in the 21st century.* Palgrave Macmillan.

Enuka, C. (2010, December). The forum on China-Africa cooperation (FOCAC): A framework for China's re engagement with Africa in the 21st Century. *Pakistan Journal of Social Science, 30*(2), 209–218.

Foster, V., Butterfield, W., Chen, C., & Pushak, N. (2009). *Building bridges China growing role as infrastructure financier for Sub-Saharan Africa.* The International Bank for Reconstruction and Development/The World Bank.

Jenkins, R. (2019). *How China is reshaping the global economy.* University Press.

Hodzi, O. (2019). *The end of China's non-intervention policy in Africa* (p. 109). Palgrave Macmillan.

International Energy Agency. (2016). *Boosting the power sector in Sub-Saharan China's involvement* (p. 10). OECD.
International Energy Agency. (2021). *Overview of Chinese power projects in sub-Saharan Africa, 2010–2020*. World Energy Outlook.
Lahtinen, A. (2018). *China's diplomacy and economic activity in Africa relations on the move* (p. 87). Palgrave Macmillan.
Lin, J. Y., & Oqubay, A. (2019). *China Africa and economic transformation*. Oxford University Press.
Li, A., Liu, H., Pan, H., Zeng, A., & He, W. (2012). *FOCAC twelve years later, achievements, challenges and the way forward* (Discussion Paper 74). Peking University, School of International Studies.
Li, S. (2017). *Mediatized China-Africa relations how media discourses negotiate the shifting of global order*. Palgrave Series in Asia and Pacific Studies. Palgrave Macmillan.
Manyeruke, C., & Abegunrin, O. (2020). *China's power in Africa a new global order*. Palgrave Macmillan.
Montenegro, R. H., & Alves, J. R. C. S. (2016). China e África além da economia: qual o impacto do FOCAC na arena multilateral (1971–2014)? [China and Africa beyond economy: what is the impact of FOCAC in the multilateral arena]. *Conjuntura Internacional, Belo Horizonte, 13*(3), 153–162.
Moyo, D. (2009). *Dead Aid: Why aid is not working and how there is a better way for Africa*. Farrar, Straus and Giroux.
Power, M. G., & Tan-Mullins, M. (2012). *China's resource diplomacy in Africa*. Palgrave Macmillan.
Skjerdal, T., & Gusu, F. (2016). *Positive portrayal of Sino-Africa relations in the Ethiopia press*. Series in Asia and Pacific Studies, chapter 11, book series. Palgrave Macmillan.
Tembe, P. E. (2021). *Impacto da Cooperação Sino - África à luz do FOCAC no crescimento e desenvolvimento económicos*. Embaixada da China em Moçambique.
Ziso, E. (2018). *A post state centric analysis of China-Africa relations: Internationalization of Chinese capital and state-society relations in Ethiopia, critical studies of the Asia Pacific*. Palgrave Macmillan.

Chapter 46
Why Is China Going Polar? Understanding Engagement and Implications for the Arctic and Antarctica

Laura C. Ferreira-Pereira⬤, Paulo Afonso B. Duarte⬤, and Natacha Santos

1 Introduction

In recent years, Chinese engagement in Polar Regions has captured unprecedented academic attention. Before the official release of China's Arctic White Paper, in 2018, a distinctive Arctic-related research agenda, much taken by the opportunities raised by the fast melting of polar ice (Bennett et al., 2020; Kossa, 2020), has developed itself. Several studies have investigated the relationship between China and the Arctic countries from a bilateral point of view (Gåsemyr, 2019; Gunnarsson & Níelsson, 2019; Kosonen, 2019; Vargö, 2019), while others have assessed China's relations with the Arctic region as a whole (Liu, 2019a; Ushakova, 2021). Scholars have stressed the logistical benefits stemming from a shorter connection between East and West, offered seasonally by the so-called Northern Sea Route (Wang et al., 2020; Kobzeva, 2021). At the same time, some works have underlined the post-2018 Artic White Paper emergence of a Polar Silk Road (Tillman et al., 2018; Woon, 2020) as an extension and byproduct of the 21st Century Maritime Silk Road, which has hitherto focused on conventional sea lanes, leaving aside the Polar Regions. Such a literature gap has stimulated studies on the geoeconomic and geostrategic relevance of Greenland and Iceland within the Chinese Polar Silk Road (Grydehøj et al., 2020; Xie et al., 2020).

When it comes to Beijing's interests and strategies in the South Pole, notably with a focus on geopolitics, there is a dearth of works with the exception of those provided

---

L. C. Ferreira-Pereira
Research Center in Political Science (CICP-UMinho), University of Minho, Braga, Portugal
e-mail: lpereira@eeg.uminho.pt

P. A. B. Duarte (✉)
Universidade do Minho & Universidade Lusófona, Braga & Porto, Portugal
e-mail: pauloduarte@eeg.uminho.pt

N. Santos
Porto, Portugal

© The Author(s), under exclusive license to Springer Nature Singapore Pte Ltd. 2023, corrected publication 2023
P. A. B. Duarte et al. (eds.), *The Palgrave Handbook of Globalization with Chinese Characteristics*, https://doi.org/10.1007/978-981-19-6700-9_46

by Brady (2010, 2017a, 2019), Duarte (2015) and Liu (2017, 2018, 2019b, 2019c). This chapter will contribute to the literature on China in Polar Regions by offering an analysis of Chinese engagement in the Artic and Antarctica in a comparative perspective. It argues that China's stance in the Arctic has been largely conditioned by the regional governance dynamics structured around the Arctic Council, while in Antarctica it has attempted to explore the absence of a more regulated interstate relations, carving for itself an advantageous position in preparation of the expiration of the Antarctic Treaty System in 2048.

The appraisal of Chinese presence in and strategy for both the Arctic and Antarctica provided by the present chapter will range from 2013 until 2021. The year 2013 represents a milestone, as it marks the formal launching of One Belt One Road (later renamed Belt and Road Initiative—BRI) and the acceptance of China's observer membership status in the Arctic Council. The importance of the year 2021 is justified largely by the launching of the 14th Five-Year Plan (2021–2025) which called for the advancement of Chinese engagement in the South Pole. The former will be made on the basis of qualitative analysis of secondary, notably scientific articles and book chapters. As for primary sources, this study relies on official sources originated from the State Council Information Office and the Ministry of Foreign Affairs of People's Republic of China, and news agencies (such as Xinhua and Reuters).

This chapter begins with a contextualization section, outlining the major general and specific drivers for China's interests and presence in Polar Regions. It then focuses on the Artic to explore the transformation of China's traditional stance in this region which resulted in the assertion of its self-assigned condition as "near Artic state." The last section is devoted to Antarctica where, metaphorically speaking, China has been strategically preparing a "nest" in anticipation of shifting trends in South Pole governance expected to unfold after the expiration of the Antarctic Treaty System in 2048. The conclusion underlines the main differences between China's interests and approaches in the Arctic and Antarctica, against the backdrop of its unprecedentedly active engagement in polar politics generated by geopolitical competition for vital resources.

2 China in the Poles: Motivations and Rationale for Growing Engagement

Chinese engagement in the Poles can only be accurately understood in connection with the country's domestic needs and foreign policy. Interestingly, this interplay between domestic and external factors has been at the origins of the BRI, a predominantly domestically driven strategy that has been at the service of an increasingly assertive stance at the foreign policy level. As part of the BRI, the Chinese government has devised a Polar Silk Road (Tillman et al., 2018; Woon, 2020), a development which will be outlined in a later section.

Among the main domestic factors that have led China to reconsider its traditional international low-profile founded on the principle of non-interference, one should stress those related to concerns with energy, food, environment, economic growth, overcapacity, and overproduction, as well as the rise of labour wage. Taken as mutually interdependent aspects, they have pushed Chinese authorities and non-state actors to embark on a so-called *Going Out Policy* as of the 2000s. Under the latter, national state and private companies have been encouraged to go abroad in search of raw materials, investment opportunities, and competitiveness skills, by learning in the process with other foreign companies (Shen & Mantzopoulos, 2013). As far as energy is concerned, in particular, China has shifted as of 1993 from a position of outstanding oil exporter to a condition of important oil importer. As a latecomer to the international oil market—when compared to the US and other Western powers that got access to the most well-placed oil fields—Beijing started to establish oil exploration contracts in exchange for the construction of infrastructure with the so-called (by the West) rogue states. As a consequence, China managed to diversify its energy sources across the world, something that helped the country to bypass or mitigate the so-called Malacca dilemma[1] (see Duarte, 2018; Butt et al., 2020), which is omnipresent in China's Foreign Policy.

The end of the One Child Policy (1st January 2016), in addition to the fast expansion of the Chinese middle class, whose diet has considerably diversified thus creating a new type of market demand(s), has impelled China to seek producing abroad what its polluted land (only 7% of its land is arable) and waters do not allow to produce domestically. Incidentally, there is clear evidence that China's status as the world's second largest economy and its international recognition as the world's factory, were accompanied by little concern with the environmental sustainability. This explains the disappearance of almost 28,000 rivers in the last two decades (Zhang, 2014). Also, a quarter of the Chinese population drinks contaminated water on a daily basis, while the air is of very poor quality in many parts of China as a result of, among other factors, a substantial dependence on charcoal (Greenstone et al., 2021).

Among the political factors underlining the shifting stance of Chinese foreign policy from a low-profile to a more assertive and pragmatic posture is the role played by the Chinese Communist Party (CCP). The party cadres have realized that, unless the Party reinvents itself and adds another layer to the cement which historically united peasants and elites around a common ideal, the country risked experiencing a tragic collapse that hit other major actors as the former Soviet Union (Shambaugh, 2008). This relates to the fear of the abrupt fall of the talented tightrope walker who strives to keep the populace united around the Chinese Dream, which is omnipresent among Chinese political elites much like the fear of a blockage in the Malacca straits (Duarte & Leandro, 2020). Such fear has been aggravated since 2019 by the successive Hong Kong protests and the controversial Huawei issue. Interestingly, as reported

---

[1] This refers to China's fear of a maritime blockade at the Straits of Malacca, although there is no historic memory of such an experience as this has never occurred in the past. Given that most of China's oil imports pass through the Straits of Malacca, a maritime blockade in this area would paralyze China's economy (Duarte, 2018).

by Harvard University's Ash Center (2020), the Chinese people's satisfaction with and support for Xi Jinping-led government and the CCP have increased significantly as a result of improvements achieved in the three key areas, notably social security, anti-corruption, and environment. Equally important, the consolidation of political legitimacy brought with it the rise of trust and optimism among the population about the future of their country, according to The Edelman Trust Barometer's data for the past years (2022).

Another major factor which has contributed to China's move towards a more assertive posture in the global arena, which also helps to explain the "Going Polar" strategy, is the negative perception of encirclement. This perception has not only derived from the US pressure on the Chinese East flank, where China has been actively building up artificial islands while claiming almost the whole of the South China Sea (Hu & Meng, 2020). It is more encompassing as it has also been fostered by the lack of proportional representation and acknowledgement within Western-based multilateral institutions and intergovernmental structures, which have downplayed China and other BRICS at both organizational and functional levels (Callahan, 2008). This applies particularly to the architecture of the Bretton Wood System, which has failed to give China—the most populous country in the world and the second largest word economy—a higher recognition within such relevant institutions, like the World Trade Organization and the International Monetary Fund.

Furthermore, China has cultivated its own alternative view of the world order based on a Community of Common Destiny, inspired in the millennial *Tianxia* model, according to which China is an important world power deemed to play an outstanding role abroad. In such a Community, all paths used to lead to the Middle Kingdom, whose emperor ruled the world in a peaceful way (Cha, 2018). Although the Middle Kingdom and its emperor (whose mandate was assigned by heaven) disappeared long ago, Xi Jinping has been attempting to emulate some of these multisecular aspects in the formulation and implementation of both domestic and foreign policies. Indeed, not only has he been governing China with exceptional power, but he also seems to endorse a vision for the rest of the world, as revealed in his book *The Governance of China* (2014, 2017). Thus, the *Tianxia* model has been implicitly alive in mid-2010s (Duarte & Ferreira-Pereira, 2021) as an alternative to the Western-based order, to the extent that according to Chinese thinking: "The problem in international politics today [...] is not "failed states" like Afghanistan, but a "failed world," a disordered world of chaos (Callahan, 2008, p. 751).

No longer feeling fully either recognized or represented within the Western-based order, China has endeavoured to meet both domestic and external role expectations, while struggling to adapt to an ever demanding role performance, which requires flexibility within its role conception (Duarte & Ferreira-Pereira, 2021). So, China has been identified by Buzan as a "reformist revisionist," since it "accepts some of the institutions of international society for a mixture of calculated and instrumental reasons. But it resists, and wants to reform others, and possibly also wants to change its status" (2010, p. 18). A clear evidence of this revisionist leaning, designed to restore Chinese millennial greatness, was the launching of the BRI and the creation of the Asian Infrastructure Investment Bank (AIIB). Despite Washington's warnings and urges against, many Western countries have become members of AIIB and showed various forms of receptiveness and participation in BRI-related initiatives. At the same time, the new Chinese multilateralism "à la carte" has also borne fruit in the foundation of successful formats of cooperation, such as the 17 + 1 in Central and Eastern Europe (Ferreira-Pereira & Duarte, 2021).

The backdrop outlined above is necessary to understand two interesting developments. On the one hand, there was a review that China made in 2015 of its security law to foresee the necessity of protecting national interests with regard to international seabed (Martinson, 2019, p. 27). On the other hand, there was the release in 2018 of China's Arctic Policy Paper, in which Beijing detaches itself from a more traditional bystander stance, admitting its interest in the Arctic seabed. Importantly, this Paper depicts China as "a near-Arctic state," even though the country's northernmost territory—Heilongjiang—is more than 900 miles away from the Arctic (Lanteigne, 2014; State Council Information Office, 2018a; Koh, 2019). Such self-recognition draws upon the idea put forward by the Chinese Rear Admiral, Yin Zhuo, who, in March 2010, observed that "The Arctic belongs to all the people around the world as no nation has sovereignty over it" (*The Diplomat*, 2010, para. 1). He also affirmed that "China must play an indispensable role in Arctic exploration as [it has] one-fifth of the world's population" (ibid., para. 3). Moreover, China's claim to be a "near-Arctic state" seems to be inspired by the endorsement of a strategic frontier that expand or contract "in accordance with the projection of the power of a nation," as Ikegami argues (2011, p. 93). Ultimately, according to this "strategic frontier doctrine," there are no fixed borders or rigid territorial boundaries.

Along these lines, one can say that although currently the Arctic is not a foreign policy priority for China when compared to South China Sea and Taiwan (The 2019 Defense White Paper; Kossa, 2020, p. 36), it serves Chinese medium to long-term goals of ensuring access to energy, minerals, and food. The same reasoning applies to Antarctica, where, since 1978, China has been building an increasingly dynamic presence, which results from a combination between more human resources and logistical infrastructures, but also more experience and sophisticated technology. Nonetheless, before addressing Chinese Antarctic activities in detail, the following section assesses how China's traditional stance towards the Arctic has developed under the impetus of China's Arctic Policy Paper, and finally analyzes whether the region may become a new hub for the Polar Silk Road.

3 China's Move from a Bystander to a "Near-Arctic" State

According to the majority of scientists, the Arctic corresponds to a geographical area encompassing "the Arctic Ocean basin and the northern parts of Scandinavia, Russia, Canada, Greenland, and the U.S. state of Alaska" (Evers, 2016, p. 1). Its singularity rests on the fact that it holds up to four million inhabitants (indigenous populations)—who are extremely dependent on the region's ecosystem and equilibrium (ibid.; Long,

2018). The Arctic has been under the threat of global warming with all the damaging consequences it entails; and observers note that it might only be a matter of time until the region becomes ice-free (Albert & Vasilache, 2017; Carrington, 2020).

The Arctic has been the object of increasing international attention due to the climate change agenda and the possibility of exploring a sort of hidden treasure. In this regard, the 2008 United States Geological Survey (USGS) published an article which estimated the undiscovered oil and gas potentially lying in the Arctic Circle (Urban, 2015; USGS, 2008). This region is also rich in several mineral resources (Turunen, 2019). Given the unprecedented pace of ice melting, new commercial maritime routes have gradually emerged (Aksenov et al., 2017; Duarte, 2017; Farré et al., 2014).

In this context, China, which has been looking for energy sources worldwide, became more interested in the Artic (geo) politics, and trade logistics. Despite being only a seasonal route, the Northern Sea Route provides China with a shorter journey (less 40% of the distance, or 15 days less) compared to the conventional sea lanes of communication between Asia and Europe (Duarte, 2017). The Arctic's governance has also become appealing to China. Since 2013, China has been an observer member of the Arctic Council—the main governmental forum to promote cooperation in the Arctic.[2] Such status provides the country with a limited influence on the Arctic issues, meaning that Beijing can only participate in working groups (Brady, 2017b; Moe & Stokke, 2019). At the same time, China has acknowledged the Arctic Circle states' exclusive voting power, territorial sovereignty, and authority to promote and defend their interests in the region (Wegge, 2014; Willis & Depledge, 2013).

The roots of Chinese engagement in the Arctic go back to 1882, when the Chinese scientists participated in the First International Polar Year (Clingendael Report, 2020). By then, however, its budget for polar expeditions was quite limited. Indeed, China only became more active in the Arctic's expeditions in the 1990s (Brady, 2012, 2017a, 2017b; Dams et al., 2020) when China began to invest in its presence in the region. To this end, the country started to purchase icebreakers, acquiring its first vessel, *Xue Long*, in 1993 from Ukraine. Later in 2004, China built its first research station in the Arctic more precisely in NyAlesung, Svalbard, Norway, called Yellow River. This contributed to a gradual consolidation of China as an emerging polar state.

China's official rhetoric to justify its presence in the Arctic encompasses two phases. The first period, spanning from 1990 to 2017, is characterized by China's concern with global warming. On this matter, Beijing argued that air currents from the Arctic were jeopardizing China in economic, social, and climate terms (Wegge, 2014). The second period of China's rhetoric has begun in 2018, when Beijing published the Arctic Policy; and has been designed to justify Chinese presence in the Arctic. In this key document, Chinese authorities acknowledged their interest in exploring the Arctic's natural resources, including shipping routes, tourism, living

---

[2] It is worth noting that this observer status is also afforded to a few more Asian states, namely India, Japan, Singapore, and South Korea.

and non-living resources, in a "lawful and rational manner" (State Council Information Office, 2018a, p. 3). Furthermore, China showed its willingness to participate in the region's governance, through international cooperation, while promoting peace and stability (ibid.). In so doing, China endeavoured to address climate change while benefiting from the economic potential of the region.

Lim (2018) considers that the 2018 Artic White Paper embodies the assertion of China's interests—rather a fundamental novelty. Incidentally, what is stated in the Arctic White Paper was foreshadowed by many attentive observers (Brady, 2012, 2017a, 2017b; Duarte, 2017; Lanteigne, 2014; Wegge, 2014). According to Wright (2011), China always struggled to engage in the Arctic. Yet, while doing this, Beijing has always been extremely cautious. Such cautiousness remained after the release of the Arctic White Paper, with China framing and justifying its polar engagement in the realm of science diplomacy, while advocating the respect for international law (State Council Information Office, 2018b; Su & Mayer, 2018). China has been developing and consolidating ties with the Arctic region in order to achieve three main benefits: gaining Nordic expertise[3]; exploring the extension of the Belt and Road Initiative (BRI) to Northern Europe[4]; and strengthening its presence in the Arctic by fostering diplomatic relations (Sverdrup-Thygeson & Hellström, 2016).

In the Arctic region, Greenland has become a case study for having developed itself as an important hub of China's Polar Silk Road. The former achieved autonomy from Denmark, in 1979, except for foreign policy and defence, and the 2009 Act has introduced the possibility of this territory's independence (Act on Greenland Self-Government, 2009). Despite Greenland's will to declare its total independence from Denmark, Nuuk relies, nonetheless, on yearly subsidies from Copenhagen. Consequently, in order to pursue independence, Greenland needs, firstly, to replace its economic dependence vis-à-vis Denmark by a new foreign investor. This fits well into China's increasingly active strategy in the Arctic. As a matter of fact, from 2008 to 2019, China was involved in five different projects. Four of them are mining projects (i.e. oil, iron, ore, rare earth metals,[5] and uranium); and the fifth aims to build airports in Nuuk, Ilulissat, and Qaqortoq (Lanteigne, 2014; Lanteigne & Shi, 2019). Worried with the geo-strategical implications stemming from Chinese dynamism in Greenland—to which one could add Beijing's will to build a satellite station that could be used for the Beidou navigational system—then US President Donald Trump made a declaration in August 2019, on the possibility of "buying Greenland" (*The New York*

---

[3] For instance, the second Chinese icebreaker—*Xue Long 2*—was designed by the Finnish enterprise Aker Arctic, which developed a unique feature called "dual-acting ice breaker". In addition, Nordic advances and know-how on the use of geothermal energy have also been applied in Chinese territory. Illustrative of this, it is worth mentioning that "[…] geothermal cooperation has led to reduction of over 5 million tons of CO_2 emissions in Chinese cities with 328 heat centrals across 40 cities/counties in China and over 500 wells drilled" (Gunnarsson & Niélsson, 2019, p. 88).

[4] China had already shown interest in including the Arctic into the BRI, namely by creating a Polar Silk Road (Spears, 2018; Sverdrup-Thygeson & Hellström, 2016; Xinhua, 2017, para. 10).

[5] Since 2018, the Chinese enterprise Shengue Resources, has been responsible for extracting, buying and selling rare earth metals. China even ships the rare earth metals to the Chinese mainland—an activity that encountered opposition from the Inuit Ataqatigiit party (Lanteigne & Shi, 2019).

Times, 2019). Although this episode was seen as controversial and even anecdotal, it was full of symbolism and political realism, as Trump and his advisers realized that Greenland's strategic location, resources, and key role in China's Arctic initiatives, could do harm to US geostrategic interests. On the other hand, its geostrategic underpinning cannot be separated from the overall context of the Sino-American rivalry, entailing a bearing of the triangular influence of China-Denmark-US relations upon the economic interactions between China and Greenland (Shi & Lanteigne, 2020).

Another case worth noting is that of Iceland. Besides exhibiting several commonalities with Greenland, it also provides useful insights given its geopolitical and geostrategic importance in China's Arctic moves. This Nordic state has hydrocarbons, minerals, and fish, which are of interest to China (Duarte, 2017). As Greenland, it matters to China's Polar Silk Road, as it further serves as "leading hub[s] for container traffic in a transarctic shipping," at a time when "a new race for the Arctic is already evident in the form of competition over shipping routes and hubs, natural resources, and political influence" (Thorhallsson & Grimsdottir, 2021, p. 7). What is more, Iceland, which saw in China a key supporter in the context of its economic collapse in October 2008, has taken advantage of Chinese interests in the Arctic in order to strengthen the national economy. Iceland's relationship with China during hard economic times helps to explain the fact that, despite US opposition, it was the first European country and NATO member to sign a Free Trade Agreement with China, in 2013 (ibid., p. 17). Thus, this Nordic state has been capitalizing on its leeway (greater than that of Greenland) to engage more with China, thereby benefiting from external players competition for its natural resources, as well as geostrategic position. Although Iceland has not formally joined China's Polar Silk Road, there have been hitherto several initiatives at the bilateral level. For example, China has explored oil and gas in Dreki, between Iceland and Norway (Lanteigne, 2016; Dams et al., 2020). Another example of Sino-Icelandic cooperation links to the implementation of a Sino-Icelandic Geothermal Research and Development Center, following the cooperation agreement, signed in 2015, between Arctic Green Energy Corporation, Sinopec Star Petroleum, and the National Energy Authority of Iceland (Thorhallsson & Grimsdottir, 2021). These initiatives have the potential to foster the eventual future inclusion of the Nordic states in the Polar Silk Road (Gunnarsson & Niélsson, 2019; Kosonen, 2019; Ministry for Foreign Affairs of Finland, 2019). This is so considering that such inclusion might represent an open door to the vast Chinese market (Askaryet al., 2019).

At this point of discussion, it is worth referring, even if briefly, to Russia: considering that 53% of Russia's coastline is located in the Arctic Ocean, and around two millions Russians live in the Russian Arctic. Moreover, against the backdrop of the EU's and the US's economic sanctions in the aftermath of the annexation of Crimea, in 2014, and the need for an economically viable partner to explore the Arctic's hydrocarbons, this country has drawn closer to China and developed a comprehensive energy cooperation at the bilateral level. In turn, China has explored this favourable juncture to strengthen its Arctic strategy (Erkan & Ates, 2019), amidst Trump Administration's criticism against Chinese activities in the high North. China and Russia have launched two relevant joint projects. One is the Power of Siberia,[6] sponsored by Gazprom. Another is Yamal LNG, one of the biggest and most complex pipelines in the world, ensuring an uninterrupted gas supply to China (Rosen, 2019). This project, coordinated by Novatek, has been included in the BRI (Shah, 2020; Tillman et al., 2018). The next section will be devoted to China's polar initiatives in the South Pole.[7] This analysis will allow one to undertake a concluding comparative exercise regarding Chinese engagement in the Artic and Antarctica.

4 China in Antarctica: Preparing the "Nest"?

Antarctica is the fifth largest continent in the world, with around 14,2 million squared kilometres in size. Most of the region (around 95%) is covered by a thick layer of ice (Harrington, 2016). Unlike the Arctic, in Antarctica there are no permanent inhabitants, only scientists originating from various corners of the world. While remote and inhospitable, Antarctica has been the subject of evolving international regulation. The Antarctic Treaty, signed in 1959 by 12 countries,[8] was the first document regulating activities in the region. Eventually, further agreements were established in 1982 and 1998, and all of these were merged into what is now known as the Antarctic Treaty System (ATS) (Antarctic Treaty, 1959; Wehrmann, 2019). The latter encompasses, among others, the Madrid Protocol (1998), which focuses on the environmental protection of Antarctica. It establishes a period of 50 years (1998–2048) during which no state can exploit the existing resources in the South Pole. The ATS's main purpose is to bring peace to the continent by prohibiting military activity, which has contributed to freezing territorial claims over the region. The ATS encourages, nonetheless, all signatory members to expand their presence in Antarctica for science purposes (Antarctic Treaty, 1959). After the expiration of the Madrid Protocol, in 2048, there is overall uncertainty about when, how, and whether states or private actors might find their own ways and strategies to explore mineral, energy and food resources in a context of global scarcity (Medeiros & Mattos, 2019; Teller, 2014).

Chinese dynamism in the South Pole has been framed by Beijing under the so-called "science diplomacy" (Su & Mayer, 2018). In its turn, the latter is part of the developing debate linked to the so-called "soft power internationalism," which argues that emerging states may resort to a broad set of tools to achieve their goals, as an alternative to war (Baykurt & de Grazia, 2021). To be sure, science diplomacy

---

[6] The Power of Siberia project is a 4,000 km-long gas pipeline which transfers natural gas from Eastern Russia to the Far East and China.

[7] While space limitations have determined the exclusive focus ascribed to the Chinese Antarctica's strategy, authors do not ignore the weight of Brazil's politics and strategy towards this area derived from its major role in South Atlantic, as a gateway to Antarctica. For a detailed study on the matter, see *The Antarctic Politics of Brazil: Where the Tropic Meets the Pole* by Ignacio Cardone (Palgrave Macmillan, 2022).

[8] These were Argentina, Australia, Belgium, Chile, France, Japan, New Zealand, Norway, South Africa, the UK, the United States of America and the former Soviet Union.

presents itself as a means through which states like China have relied on science (and also on technology) contributions to steer and justify their growing presence in the polar regions. But while in the case of the Arctic, Chinese science diplomacy has comprised mostly cooperation with the Arctic Council states to best justify its activities in this region, in Antarctica the lack of coastal states does not necessarily demand such a cooperative stance. Interestingly, in both cases (the Arctic and Antarctica), science diplomacy has been used by China to claim that its polar initiatives are mainly connected to studying issues related to climate change.

There are four different phases in the evolution of China's presence in Antarctica. During the first one, spanning from 1978 to 1984, China began to learn from the US and other established polar powers' expertise in order to develop its own polar capacities. This was a phase of exploratory activities in Antarctica, with China opting for an "opening up" posture by trying to learn more about the extreme weather polar conditions. Thus, it developed several scientific research partnerships revolving around fisheries, oceanography, and geology. In 1983, China joined the ATS, a development which enabled it to have a say in Antarctica's governance (Brady, 2017a, 2017b; Liu, 2019b). In the second period, which ranges from 1985 to 1989, China founded its first research stations in Antarctica and started to launch scientific expeditions in the region. A third phase, covering the period between 1990 and 2004, was characterized by a focus on the development of Chinese scientific research. The fourth phase, which began in 2004, and is still in progress, has been seeing a more proactive China given its attempts to consolidate itself as a great polar power (Keynuan *apud* Brady, 2010). For instance, on 18th January 2005, a group of Chinese scientists reached the Dome Argus (Dome A), the highest geographical point in Antarctica's extreme conditions, which became a motive of great pride for the Chinese (Brady, 2010). After this, China has continued to develop its know-how on Antarctica. In 2007, it became a member of the Commission for the Conservation of Antarctic Marine Living Resources (CCAMLR); and two years later, China officially began fishing krill with the support of two Chinese vessels, *Fu Rong Hai* and *Long Teng* (Liu, 2019a). Importantly, since 2016 China has been operating its first air squadron in the region (Tiezzi, 2016), while aiming to build its first airport in Antarctica (Airport Pham, 2019; Technology, 2019). It is also worth mentioning that much of China's success in its polar expeditions is due to its two icebreakers: *Xue Long* and *Xue Long 2* (Humpert, 2018) which started to be deployed since 1994 and 2018, respectively.

China has four research stations in Antarctica, which evinces the dynamism inherent to Chinese activities and presence in Antarctica. The Great Wall, located in King George, and *Zhongshan* built in Larsemann Hill, have been operating all-around the year since the 1980s. In 2009, China built its third station Kunlun, in the Dome A, only for the purpose of seasonal operations. The fourth station, Taishan, was built in 2014, in Princess Elizabeth Land, also for seasonal use only. China is currently building its fifth research station, which is expected to be concluded by 2022 (Liu, 2018; Xinhua, 2018). Its location in the Inexpressible Island, in the Ross Sea, is particularly important, given the close proximity to the US research station McMurdo Ross Sea MPA (Brady, 2017a, 2017b). Approximately 18 km from the *Zhongshan* station, China plans to build its first permanent airport at the South Pole.

According to Zhang Xia, based at Polar Research Institute of China, the new airport will allow medium and large transport aircraft, like Boeing planes, which take off and land in the South Pole, decreasing transport time and improving their efficiency (in Silk Road Briefing, 2018, para. 3).

Although there is evidence that China has endeavoured to consolidate its presence in Antarctica, no White Paper for the South Pole has been published yet. That being said, a quasi-White Paper was presented by Chinese representatives at the Antarctic Treaty Consultative Meeting, held in 2017 (Pham, 2019). This document (not available for consultation) was issued by the State Oceanic Administration and outlines relevant aspects, like the goal of increasing the budget for scientific research in Antarctica, as well as the legislation on the regulation of commercial activities; the objective of cooperating with the international community while maintaining the respect for the ATS; and the aim of enhancing krill fisheries (Tiantian, 2017). Regarding the latter issue, China considers that given that it holds one fifth of the world's population, it should be entitled to fish proportionally in the South Pole (ibid.). Furthermore, based on Xi Jinping's speech in 2014, in Hobart, Australia, the Chinese official slogan regarding Antarctica is: "Understand, protect and use" (Ministry of Foreign Affairs of PRC, 2017, para. 3). Additional guidelines for China's engagement in the South Pole were conveyed in the 13th Five-Year Plan, 2016–2020, released on 15th March 2016, which points to China's willingness to consolidate its polar capabilities (13th Five-Year Plan, 2016–2020; Liu & Brooks, 2018). By the same token, the 14th Five-Year Plan issued in March 2021 for the 2021–2025 has called for a further engagement in the South Pole, by means of "enhancing [China's] ability to participate in the Antarctic conservation and utilization" (Part IX, Chapter 33).

Besides the domain of science, Chinese interests in Antarctica have also been motivated by military purposes. In this regard, the location of Dome A is of particular relevance as this is one of the best geographical points on the planet to observe and study Space (Chinese Academy of Sciences Headquarters, 2020; Gothe-Snape, 2019). Also, China is the only polar state actor to have a research station in this privileged location. For the Chinese authorities, the relevance of Dome A stems from two main aspects. On the one hand, it fits within the national Space programme. On the other hand, it is critical for the development of the BeiDou navigation system[9]—a valuable tool which enables China to be independent from the American GPS. This is an advantage in the event of war (Brady, 2012, 2017a, 2017b, 2019; Duarte, 2017). In an ATS meeting held in 2013, the Chinese representatives suggested this area to be considered as a protected sanctuary. Yet, this proposal was rejected by the other ATS members, as they do not want to see China having overall control over such an important location (Fishman, 2019; Gothe-Snape, 2019).

---

[9] There are only four satellite navigation systems in the world. These are managed by Russia (Glonass), the USA (GPS), the European Union (Galileo) and China (BeiDou).

5 Conclusion

Drawing on a comparative perspective, this chapter has examined the interests, strategies and implications of Chinese activities in the North and South Poles. Its analysis points to China's rising engagement in polar politics in the light of geopolitical competition for natural resources and geostrategic influence. It also stressed Beijing's conception of borders as flexible, in that they can expand to reflect a state's economic growth. Hence China's claim as a "near-Arctic state"; although its borders are considerably far away from the North Pole. This study has attempted to demonstrate that China's stance in the Arctic has been largely conditioned by the regional governance structured around the Arctic Council, while, in Antarctica, this country has endeavoured to explore the absence of both coastal states and more regulated interstate relations, to carve for itself an advantageous position with the expiration of the Antarctic Treaty System in view. Indeed, in the Arctic China has been coping with less room for manoeuvre due to the active governance exerted by the Arctic Council members. But, in Antarctica, it has endeavoured to gradually fill in some prevailing institutional and governance voids.

In the South Pole, since 2016, China has been operating its first air squadron and its second icebreaker in the region, while it is currently building its fifth Antarctic research station. The country is the only state with a research station located in Antarctica's Dome A, something which endows Beijing with a sort of advantage in the study of Outer Space. Therefore, science diplomacy has been instrumental in the strategy skilfully used by China to geopolitically consolidate its presence in Antarctica, making it easier to claim its part of the South Pole in the post-2048 landscape. By then, China might have already gained an unprecedented capacity to carry out scientific missions in Antarctica, in addition to revolutionizing its toponymy by assigning names to places discovered by Chinese scientists in the region. That being said, as this work has underlined, science diplomacy is not exclusive to the South Pole. In the North Pole, moved by concerns with the climate change and global warming, China has been conducting polar expeditions and building research stations.

As the ice melts at an unprecedented speed in the Polar Regions, so does the geopolitical competition for natural resources and geostrategic influence which has been exacerbated by globalization trends. This chapter has evinced that there are new and promising prospects for China as a "near-Arctic state." At the same time, although being at a far geographical distance, Antarctica has also become near to the heart of China's global ambitions. Here, a "nest" is being prepared with decades in advance, so as to ensure the best arrangements possible after 2048. Ultimately, North and South Poles have complemented each other in China's rising engagement in polar politics, which will tend to be molded by its characteristic view of globalization dissected in this volume.

Acknowledgements The authors acknowledge that this study was conducted at the Research Center in Political Science (UIDB/CPO/00758/ 2020), University of Minho/University of Évora, and that it was supported by the Portuguese Foundation for Science and Technology and the Portuguese

Ministry of Education and Science, through national funds. The authors would like to thank Li Xing, Sabrina Evangelista Medeiros, and Sérgio Ribeiro for their valuable comments on earlier drafts.

Disclosure Statement No potential conflict of interest was reported by the author(s).

Bibliographic References

Act on Greenland Self-Government. (2009). *International relations and security network: Primary Resources in International Affairs (PRIA)* (pp. 1–7). https://www.files.ethz.ch/isn/125366/3708_Greenland_Independence.pdf

Albert, M., & Vasilache, A. (2017). Governmentality of the Arctic as an international region. *SAGE Cooperation and Conflict, 53*(1), 1–20. https://doi.org/10.1177/0010836717703674

Aleem, Z. (2017). *Trump pulling out of the Paris climate agreement is great news…for China*. Vox. https://www.vox.com/world/2017/6/3/15729424/trump-paris-climate-china

Airport Technology. (2019). *Polar air: A look at China's first permanent airport in Antarctica*. Airport Technology. https://www.airport-technology.com/features/chinas-airport-in-antarctica/

Aksenov, Y., Popova, E., Yool, A., Nurser, A., Williams, T., & Bertino, L. (2017). On the future navigability of Arctic sea routes: High-resolution projections of the Arctic Ocean and sea ice. *Maritime Policy, 75*, 300–317. https://doi.org/10.1016/j.marpol.2015.12.027

Antarctic Treaty. (1959). https://documents.ats.aq/keydocs/vol_1/vol1_2_AT_Antarctic_Treaty_e.pdf

Askary, H., Sandmark, U., & Aspling, L. (2019). *The Belt and Road Initiative: Opens great opportunities for Sweden and Scandinavia*. BRIX. https://www.brixsweden.org/wp-content/uploads/2019/12/BRI-Report-Sweden-Final.pdf

Baykurt, B., & de Grazia, V. (2021). *Soft-power internationalism: Competing for cultural influence in the 21st-century global order*. Columbia University Press.

Bennett, M., et al. (2020). The opening of the Transpolar Sea Route: Logistical, geopolitical, environmental, and socioeconomic impacts. *Marine Policy, 121*. https://doi.org/10.1016/j.marpol.2020.104178

Brady, A.-M. (2010). China's rise in Antarctica? *University of California Press, 50*(4), 759–785. https://doi.org/10.1525/as.2010.50.4.759

Brady, A.-M. (2012). *Polar stakes: China's polar activities as a benchmark for intentions* (Vol. 12(14)). The Jamestown Foundation. https://jamestown.org/program/polar-stakes-chinas-polar-activities-as-a-benchmark-for-intentions/

Brady, A.-M. (2017a). *China as a polar great power*. Woodrow Wilson Central Press and Cambridge University Press.

Brady, A.-M. (2017b). *Special report: China's expanding Antarctic interests: Implications for Australia* (pp. 1–30). Australian Strategic Policy Institute. https://s3-ap-southeast-2.amazonaws.com/ad-aspi/2017-08/SR109%20Chinas%20expanding%20interests%20in%20Antarctica.pdf?L_qDGafveA4ogNHB6K08cq86VoEzKQc

Brady, A.-M. (2019). Facing up to China's military interests in the Arctic. *China Brief, 19*(21), 21–28. https://jamestown.org/wp-content/uploads/2019/12/Read-the-12-10-2019-CB-Issue-in-PDF.pdf?x76488

Butt, K., Kharl, S., & Bhatti, K. (2020). String of pearls: Politics of ports in Indian Ocean. *South Asian Studies, 35*(1), 73–86.

Buzan, B. (2010). China in international society: Is 'peaceful rise' possible? *The Chinese Journal of International Politics, 3*(1), 5–36. https://doi.org/10.1093/cjip/pop014

Callahan, W. (2008). Chinese visions of world order: Post-hegemonic or a new hegemony? *International Studies Review, 10*(4), 749–761.

Carrington, D. (2020). Ice-free Arctic summers now very likely even with climate action. *The Guardian*. https://www.theguardian.com/world/2020/apr/21/ice-free-arctic-summers-now-very-likely-even-with-climate-action

Cha, T. (2018). Competing visions of a postmodern world order: The Philadelphian system versus the Tianxia system. *Cambridge Review of International Affairs, 31*(5), 392–414. https://doi.org/10.1080/09557571.2018.1536113

China's Arctic White Paper. (2018). http://english.www.gov.cn/archive/white_paper/2018/01/26/content_281476026660336.htm

Chinese Academy of Sciences Headquarters. (2020). *Dome A in Antarctica is the best site for optical astronomical observation on Earth*. EurekAlert. https://www.eurekalert.org/pub_releases/2020-08/caos-dai080220.php

Clingendael Report. (2020). https://www.clingendael.org/pub/2020/presence-before-power/2-presence-before-power-why-china-became-a-near-arctic-state/

Cohen, A. (2019). U.S. withdraws from Paris accord, ceding leadership to China. *Forbes*. https://www.forbes.com/sites/arielcohen/2019/11/07/us-withdraws-from-paris-accord-ceding-leadership-to-china/?sh=7c7ec52f73c1

Dams, T., Schaik, L., & Stoetman, A. (2020). *Presence before power: China's Arctic strategy in Iceland and Greenland*. Netherlands Institute of International Relations. https://www.clingendael.org/sites/default/files/2020-06/presence-before-power.pdf

Duarte, P. (2015). The dragon spits fire on ice: The Arctic and Antarctica within China's New Silk Road. *Revista da Coleção Meira Mattos, 9*(35), 471–483.

Duarte, P. (2017). *Pax Sinica*. Chiado Editora.

Duarte, P. (2018). Whose Silk Road? The Chinese, US, European Union and Russian strategic projects for regional integration in Central Asia. In C. Mendes (Ed.), *China's New Silk Road: An emerging world order* (pp. 38–49). Routledge. https://doi.org/10.4324/9781351134354

Duarte, P., & Ferreira-Pereira, L. C. (2021). The soft power of China and the European Union in the context of the Belt and Road Initiative and global strategy. *Journal of Contemporary European Studies*, 593–607. https://doi.org/10.1080/14782804.2021.1916740

Duarte, P., & Leandro, F. (Eds.). (2020). *The Belt and Road Initiative: An old archetype of a new development model*. Palgrave.

Erkan, A., & Ates, A. (2019). Will Russia be a threat to China? Sino-Russian energy relations via energy weapon model. *International Journal of Eurasia Social Sciences, 10*(36), 431–445. https://doi.org/10.35826/ijoess.2499

European Parliament. (2018). *China's Arctic policy: How China aligns rights and interests* (pp. 1–8). European Parliament. https://www.europarl.europa.eu/RegData/etudes/BRIE/2018/620231/EPRS_BRI(2018)620231_EN.pdf

Evers, J. (2016). *Arctic*. Resource Library/Encyclopedic Entry, National Geographic. https://www.nationalgeographic.org/encyclopedia/arctic/

Farré, A., Stephenson, S., Chen, L., Czub, M., Dai, Y., Demchev, D., et al. (2014). Commercial Arctic shipping through the Northeast Passage: Routes, resources, governance, technology, and infrastructure. *Polar Geography, 37*(4), 298–324. https://doi.org/10.1080/1088937X.2014.965769

Ferreira-Pereira, L. C., & Duarte, P. (2021). China and the Belt and Road Initiative in Europe: The case of Portugal. In V. Ntousas & S. Minas (Eds.), *The European Union and China's Belt and Road* (pp. 218–234). Routledge.

Fishman, D. (2019). *China's advance into the Antarctic*. Lawfare. https://www.lawfareblog.com/chinas-advance-antarctic

Gåsemyr, H. (2019). A Norwegian perspective. In A. B. Forsby (Ed.), *Nordic-China cooperation: Challenges and opportunities* (pp. 95–100). NIAS Press.

Gothe-Snape, J. (2019). *Australia declares China's plan for Antarctic conduct has 'no formal standing'*. ABC News. https://www.abc.net.au/news/2019-07-30/antarctica-china-code-of-conduct-dome-a/11318646?nw=0

Greenstone, M., He, G., Li, S., & Zou, E. (2021). *China's war on pollution: Evidence from the first five years* (Working Paper No. 28467). National Bureau of Economic Research. https://www.nber.org/system/files/working_papers/w28467/w28467.pdf

Grydehøj, A., et al. (2020). Silk Road archipelagos: Islands in the Belt and Road Initiative. *Island Studies Journal, 15*(2), 3–12. https://doi.org/10.24043/isj.137

Gunnarsson, P., & Níelsson, E. (2019). An Icelandic perspective. In A. B. Forsby (Ed.), *Nordic-China cooperation: Challenges and opportunities* (pp. 87–94). NIAS Press.

Harrington, J. (2016). China, global ecopolitics and Antarctic governance: Converging paths? *Journal of Chinese Political Science/Association of Chinese Political Studies, 22*(37–56), 1–20. https://doi.org/10.1007/s11366-016-9430-2

Harvard University's Ash Center. (2020). *Taking China's pulse*. https://news.harvard.edu/gazette/story/2020/07/long-term-survey-reveals-chinese-government-satisfaction/

Humpert, M. (2018). *China launches domestically-built 'Xue Long 2' icebreaker*. High North News. https://www.highnorthnews.com/en/china-launches-domestically-built-xue-long-2-icebreaker

Hu, W., & Meng, W. (2020). The US Indo-Pacific strategy and China's response. *China Review, 20*(3), 143–176.

Ikegami, M. (2011). Neo-imperialism: China's quasi-Manchukuo policy toward North Korea, Mongolia, and Myanmar. *Tamkang Journal of International Affairs, 14*(4), 61–98.

Kobzeva, M. (2021). Cooperation between Russia and China in Arctic shipping: Current state and prospects. *Арктика и Север, 43*(43): 75–91. https://doi.org/10.37482/issn2221-2698.2021.43.89

Koh, C. (2019). *China's strategic interest in the Arctic goes beyond economics*. Defense News. https://www.defensenews.com/opinion/commentary/2020/05/11/chinas-strategic-interest-in-the-arctic-goes-beyond-economics/

Kosonen, R. (2019). A Finnish perspective. In A. B. Forsby (Ed.), *Nordic-China cooperation: Challenges and opportunities* (pp. 81–86). NIAS Press.

Kossa, M. (2020). China's Arctic engagement: Domestic actors and foreign policy. *Global Change, Peace & Security, 32*(1), 19–38. https://doi.org/10.1080/14781158.2019.1648406

Lanteigne, M. (2014). *China's emerging Arctic strategies: Economics and institutions* (pp. 1–42). Institute of International Affairs: Centre for Arctic Policy Studies.

Lanteigne, M. (2016). 'Small is beautiful': Iceland's economic diplomacy with China. In B. Sverdrup-Thygeson (Ed.), *Dragon in the north: The Nordic countries' relations with China* (pp. 34–44). Norwegian Institute of International Affairs.

Lanteigne, M., & Shi, M. (2019). China steps up its mining interests in Greenland. *The Diplomat*. https://thediplomat.com/2019/02/china-steps-up-its-mining-interests-in-greenland/

Lim, K. (2018). *China's Arctic policy & the Polar Silk Road* (pp. 1–17). Arctic Yearbook.

Liu, C. (2019a). A Chinese perspective. In A. B. Forsby (Ed.), *Nordic-China cooperation: Challenges and opportunities* (pp. 67–73). NIAS Press.

Liu, N. (2017). *China and the future of Antarctica*. China Dialogue. https://www.chinadialogue.net/blog/9858-China-and-the-future-of-Antarctica/en

Liu, N. (2018). What does China's fifth research station mean for Antarctic governance? *The Diplomat*. https://thediplomat.com/2018/06/what-does-chinas-fifth-research-station-mean-for-antarctic-governance/

Liu, N. (2019b). *Defining the "rise" of China in Antarctica*. Australian Institute of International Affairs. https://www.internationalaffairs.org.au/australianoutlook/defining-rise-china-antarctica/

Liu, N. (2019c, June 14). What are China's intentions in Antarctica? *The Diplomat*. https://thediplomat.com/2019/06/what-are-chinas-intentions-in-antarctica/

Liu, N., & Brooks, C. (2018). China's changing position towards marine protected areas in the Southern Ocean: Implications for future Antarctic governance. *Elsevier Marine Policy, 94*, 189–195. https://doi.org/10.1016/j.marpol.2018.05.011

Lobosco, K. (2018). *Trump pulled out of a massive trade deal: Now 11 countries are going ahead without the US.* CNN Politics. https://edition.cnn.com/2018/12/29/politics/tpp-trade-trump/index.html

Long, Z. (2018). *Arctic governance: Challenges and opportunities.* Council on Foreign Relations. https://www.cfr.org/report/arctic-governance

MacDonald, A. (2019). *Precarious existence or staying the course? The foundations and future of Arctic stability* (L. Heininen, Ed., pp. 1–29). Arctic Yearbook.

Martinson, R. (2019). China as an Atlantic naval power. *The RUSI Journal, 164*(7), 18–31. https://doi.org/10.1080/03071847.2019.1700684

Medeiros, S., & Mattos, L. (2019). Antarctica as a South Atlantic maritime security issue. In E. Duarte & M. de Barros (Eds.), *Maritime security* (pp.105–127). Palgrave Macmillan. https://doi.org/10.1007/978-3-030-05273-7_5

Ministry for Foreign Affairs of Finland. (2019). *Joint action plan on bilateral partnership between China and Finland.* https://um.fi/current-affairs/-/asset_publisher/gc654PySnjTX/content/suomen-ja-kiinan-kahdenvalisen-kumppanuuden-toimeenpanosuunnitelma-julkaistu

Ministry of Foreign Affairs of People's Republic of China. (2017). https://www.fmprc.gov.cn/mfa_eng/zxxx_662805/t1465158.shtml

Moe, A., & Stokke, O. S. (2019). Asian countries and Arctic shipping: Policies, interests and footprints on governance. *Arctic Review on law and Politics, 10*, 24–52. https://doi.org/10.23865/arctic.v10.1374

Pham, C. (2019). *China's activities in the polar regions cannot go unchecked.* U.S. Naval Institute. https://www.usni.org/magazines/proceedings/2019/march/chinas-activities-polar-regions-cannot-go-unchecked

Reuters. (2021). *G7 rivals China with grand infrastructure plan.* https://www.reuters.com/world/g7-counter-chinas-belt-road-with-infrastructure-project-senior-us-official-2021-06-12/

Rosen, M. (2019). Will China freeze America out of the Arctic? *The National Interest.* https://nationalinterest.org/feature/will-china-freeze-america-out-arctic-73511

Shah, A. (2020). Russia loosens its belt. *Foreign Policy.* https://foreignpolicy.com/2020/07/16/russia-china-belt-and-road-initiative/

Shambaugh, D. (2008). *China's Communist Party: Atrophy and adaptation.* Woodrow Wilson Center Press and University of California Press

Shen, R., & Mantzopoulos, V. (2013). China's going out policy: Inception, evolution, implication. *Journal of Business and Behavioral Sciences, 25*(2), 121–136.

Shi, M., & Lanteigne, M. (2020). *Greenland in the Middle: The latest front in a great power rivalry.* Polar Research and Policy Initiative. https://polarconnection.org/greenland-in-the-middle/

Silk Road Briefing. (2018). *Belt and Road and airport Antarctica.* https://www.silkroadbriefing.com/news/2018/10/31/belt-road-airport-antarctica/

Spears, K. J. (2018). China's Arctic rising. *Canadian Sailings*, pp. 24–27. https://canadiansailings.ca/chinas-arctic-rising/

State Council Information Office of People's Republic of China. (2018a). *China's Arctic policy.* http://www.xinhuanet.com/english/2018-01/26/c_136926498.htm

State Council Information Office of People's Republic of China. (2018b). *China enters 'unmanned era' in Arctic.* China.org. http://www.china.org.cn/china/2018-08/24/content_59998746.htm

Su, P., & Mayer, M. (2018). Science diplomacy and trust building: 'Science China' in the Arctic. *Global Policy*, 1–6. https://doi.org/10.1111/1758-5899.12576

Sverdrup-Thygeson, B., & Hellström, J. (2016). Introduction: Quintet out of tune? China's bilateral relations with the Nordic states. In B. Sverdrup-Thygeson (Ed.), *Dragon in the North: The Nordic countries' relations with China.* Norwegian Institute of International Affairs.

Taylor, A. (2018). A timeline of Trump's complicated relationship with the TPP. *The Washington Post.* https://www.washingtonpost.com/news/worldviews/wp/2018/04/13/a-timeline-of-trumps-complicated-relationship-with-the-tpp/

Teller, M. (2014). *Why do so many nations want a piece of Antarctica?* BBC News. https://www.bbc.com/news/magazine-27910375

The 13th Five-Year Plan. (2016). *The 13th Five-Year Plan for economic and social development of the People's Republic of China 2016–2020*. Compilation and Translation Bureau, Central Committee of the Communist Party of China, Beijing, China. https://en.ndrc.gov.cn/policies/202105/P020210527785800103339.pdf

The 14th Five-Year Plan. (2021). *Outline of the 14th Five-Year Plan (2021–2025) for national economic and social development and vision 2035 of the People's Republic of China*. https://www.fujian.gov.cn/english/news/202108/t20210809_5665713.htm

The 2019 Defence White Paper. *China's National Defense in the new era*. http://www.xinhuanet.com/english/2019-07/24/c_138253389.htm

The Diplomat. (2010). China's Arctic play. https://thediplomat.com/2010/03/chinas-arctic-play/

The Edelman Trust Barometer. (2022). *Trust in China*. https://www.edelman.com/trust/2022-trust-barometer/trust-china

The New York Times. (2019). Trump's interest in buying Greenland seemed like a joke. Then it got ugly. https://www.nytimes.com/2019/08/21/us/politics/trump-greenland-prime-minister.html

Thorhallsson, B., & Grimsdottir, S. (2021). *Lilliputian encounters with Gulliver: Sino-Icelandic Relations from 1995 to 2021*. University of Iceland.

Tiantian, B. (2017). China releases 1st Antarctic paper. *Global Times*. https://www.globaltimes.cn/content/1048187.shtml

Tiezzi, S. (2016). China to establish Antarctic air squadron in 2016. *The Diplomat*. https://thediplomat.com/2016/02/china-to-establish-antarctic-air-squadron-in-2016/

Tillman, H., Jian, Y., & Nielsson, E. (2018). The Polar Silk Road: China's new frontier of international cooperation. *China Quarterly of International Strategic Studies, 4*(3), 345–362. https://doi.org/10.1142/S2377740018500215

Turunen, E. (2019). *Resources in the Arctic 2019*. Nordregio. https://nordregio.org/maps/resources-in-the-arctic-2019/#_ftn2

Urban, O. (2015). *Future of the Arctic oil reserves*. Stanford University. http://large.stanford.edu/courses/2015/ph240/urban2/

USGS. (2008). *Circum-Arctic resource appraisal: Estimates of undiscovered oil and gas north of the Arctic circle*. USGS Fact Sheet. https://pubs.usgs.gov/fs/2008/3049/fs2008-3049.pdf

Ushakova, E. (2021). Arctic frontier: Ice Silk Road and its role in China's advance to the Arctic. *Арктика и Север, 43*(43), 109–122. https://doi.org/10.37482/issn2221-2698.2021.43.128

Vargö, L. (2019). A Swedish perspective. In A. B. Forsby (Ed.), *Nordic-China cooperation: Challenges and opportunities* (pp. 101–108). NIAS Press.

Wang, D., et al. (2020). Feasibility of the Northern Sea Route for oil shipping from the economic and environmental perspective and its influence on China's oil imports. *Marine Policy, 118*. https://doi.org/10.1016/j.marpol.2020.104006

Wegge, N. (2014). China in the Arctic: Interests, actions and challenges. *Nordlit, 32*, 83–98. https://doi.org/10.7557/13.3072

Wehrmann, D. (2019). *Critical geopolitics of the polar regions: An inter-American perspective* (pp. 1–216). Taylor & Francis.

Willis, M., & Depledge, D. (2013). *How we learned to stop worrying about China's Arctic ambitions: Understanding China's admission to the Arctic Council*. The Arctic Institute Center for Circumpolar Security Studies. https://www.thearcticinstitute.org/china-arctic-ambitions-arctic-council/

Woon, C. (2020). Framing the Polar Silk Road: Critical geopolitics, Chinese scholars and the (re)positionings of China's Arctic interests. *Political Geography, 78*. https://doi.org/10.1016/j.polgeo.2019.102141

Wright, D. (2011). A dragon eyes the top of the world: Arctic policy debate and discussion in China. *CMSI Red Books, 8*, 1–56. https://digital-commons.usnwc.edu/cgi/viewcontent.cgi?article=1007&context=cmsi-red-books

Xie, B., Zhu, X., & Grydehøj, A. (2020). Perceiving the Silk Road archipelago: Archipelagic relations within the ancient and 21st-Century Maritime Silk Road. *Island Studies Journal, 15*(2), 55–72. https://doi.org/10.24043/isj.118

Xi, J. (2014). *The governance of China* (Vol. I). Foreign Languages Press.
Xi, J. (2017). *The governance of China* (Vol. II). Foreign Languages Press.
Xinhua. (2017). *Vision for maritime cooperation under the Belt and Road Initiative.* http://www.xinhuanet.com/english/2017-06/20/c_136380414.htm
Xinhua. (2018). Norway's 2nd largest bridge built by Chinese firm opens to traffic. *Global Times.* https://www.globaltimes.cn/content/1131225.shtml
Yi, W., & Lidegaard, M. (2015). *Deepening China-Denmark comprehensive strategic partnership and building a model for China-Europe cooperation.* https://um.dk/en/about-us/the-ministers/speeches-and-articles-by-former-ministers/martin-lidegaard-speeches-and-articles/deepening-china-denmark-comprehensive-strategic-partnership/
Zhang, H. (2014). *Confronting China's water insecurity* (No. 57, pp. 1–2). RSIS Commentaries, S. Rajaratnam School of International Studies.

Correction to: The Palgrave Handbook of Globalization with Chinese Characteristics

Correction to:
P. A. B. Duarte et al. (eds.), *The Palgrave Handbook of Globalization with Chinese Characteristics*,
https://doi.org/10.1007/978-981-19-6700-9

The original version of the book was inadvertently published with an error in the author's name and affiliation in Chapters 42 and 46 and content changes in the Frontmatter, which have now been corrected. The book has been updated with the changes.

The updated version of the book can be found at
https://doi.org/10.1007/978-981-19-6700-9

Index

A
advanced economies, 6, 43, 202, 203, 214, 271, 272, 275, 276, 278, 279, 297
Africa, 4, 12, 13, 24, 25, 37, 73, 76, 78–80, 97, 114, 127, 128, 130, 132, 134, 142, 156, 157, 167, 169, 172, 173, 175, 190, 191, 218, 229, 230, 255, 259, 307, 315, 337, 343, 355, 379, 405, 438, 442, 450, 467, 468, 489, 495, 496, 499, 517, 518, 531, 550, 564, 567, 569, 575, 577, 581–585, 623, 648, 709, 711–713, 715, 716, 723–731, 735–743, 745–749, 753–762
artificial intelligence (AI), 9, 11, 12, 143, 178, 191, 240, 246, 247, 249, 340, 343, 344, 544–555
Asian economies, 11, 310, 376, 625, 627, 631–636, 661
Asian Infrastructure Investment Bank (AIIB), 18, 25, 29, 73, 75, 79, 115, 116, 125, 133, 142, 157, 190, 195, 202, 307, 309, 312, 346, 490, 498, 503, 505, 506, 530, 533, 564, 571, 595, 600, 623, 657, 671, 699, 701, 769
Asia Pacific region, 414
Association of Southeast Asian Nations (ASEAN), 12, 75, 77–79, 141, 178, 253, 355, 452, 539, 591, 592, 594–598, 603–605, 625, 673, 675–685, 693
asymmetry, 229, 278, 361, 376, 495, 500, 507, 510, 723, 753
AUKUS, 10, 83, 170, 174, 176, 182, 183, 592, 602, 605
authoritarianism, 35, 238, 239, 246, 247

B
balance, 3, 7, 23, 30, 46, 64, 82, 85, 271, 274, 279, 305, 344, 361, 367, 383, 404, 423, 442, 451, 504, 510, 544, 554, 565, 593–595, 598, 614, 675
balance of power, 25, 85, 111, 267, 279, 306, 308, 348, 349, 431, 543, 564
Balochistan, 482
bandwagon, 690
Belarus, 11, 324, 327, 433, 436, 536, 609–617, 624
Belt and Road Initiative (BRI), 1–13, 18, 25, 29, 30, 35–41, 44–47, 55, 56, 58–64, 67, 68, 71–82, 84, 85, 97, 100, 101, 104, 109, 110, 112–120, 125–134, 141–143, 153–158, 160, 162, 163, 167–170, 175–178, 180–183, 188–191, 193, 195, 197, 202, 224, 230–232, 238, 241, 247, 256, 260, 262, 285–299, 302, 307, 309, 312–317, 319, 321–326, 337, 342, 343, 345, 349, 353–361, 363, 366–368, 375–377, 392, 403, 406, 419, 432, 434–437, 441, 447–455, 459–462, 464–470, 475, 478, 481, 485–490, 495–497, 499–501, 504–506, 508–511, 516–526, 529, 531, 532, 543, 550, 554, 564–572, 575–577, 579–584, 586, 591, 592, 594, 595, 598, 603, 609–612, 616, 617, 623–627, 631–636, 639, 640, 643, 645, 647, 649–651, 657–662, 664–669, 671–673, 675–677, 685, 689–691, 693–701, 705, 706, 708–710, 716, 717, 723–726, 731, 735, 766, 771, 773
bilateral trade China, 11, 600, 635

Brazil, 9, 12, 30, 78, 161, 206, 207, 211, 213, 214, 218, 310, 495, 496, 498–500, 502–504, 507, 510, 511, 530, 706, 708, 710, 714–716, 773
BRI projects, 5, 13, 45, 46, 116, 125–127, 129, 131–133, 157, 163, 169, 180, 181, 241, 242, 309, 318, 320, 322–324, 357, 467, 485, 489, 497, 519, 576, 598, 600, 623–625, 632, 657, 658, 665, 668, 671, 673, 675–677, 683, 684, 697
Brunei, 438, 592, 623, 674, 675, 677, 678, 681–684
Build–Operate–Transfer (BOT), 127, 128

C
Cambodia, 39, 76, 80, 117, 318, 323, 326, 327, 464, 486, 519, 521, 522, 536, 623, 625, 674, 675, 678, 681–684
capitalism, 39, 71, 139, 141, 143, 148, 157, 171, 179, 243, 302, 303, 306, 518, 577, 742, 743
Central Asia, 11, 38, 73, 76, 114, 131, 167, 322–326, 337, 343, 355, 406, 432–434, 442, 481, 485, 488–490, 522, 534, 535, 537, 586, 616, 623–625, 639, 657, 658, 660–669, 672, 723, 724
challenges, 2, 6, 8, 9, 12, 22, 23, 30, 63, 71, 73, 81, 84, 86, 109–111, 116, 118–120, 128, 144, 159, 161, 163, 168, 169, 189, 204, 209, 213, 217, 224, 228, 242, 254, 265, 281, 297, 305, 307, 345, 356, 358, 368, 392, 406, 412, 422, 442, 449, 461, 466, 468, 475, 477, 482, 485, 487, 489, 490, 496, 500, 504, 515, 525, 526, 529, 530, 537, 538, 540, 547, 549, 551, 552, 554, 570, 571, 601, 602, 604, 640–642, 646, 652, 668, 694, 696, 698, 701, 707, 716, 742
Chen, Yu-Wen, 5, 13, 125, 126, 129, 131
China, 1–13, 17–31, 35–47, 55–64, 67–86, 92–97, 100, 101, 104, 109, 111–120, 125–134, 140–149, 153–163, 167, 170–172, 175, 176, 182–184, 187–193, 195–197, 202, 206, 207, 210, 211, 214, 215, 217, 218, 227–229, 231, 233, 237, 238, 240–249, 253–256, 260–268, 271, 275–281, 285–289, 292–299, 301–303, 305–315, 317–321, 324, 326, 327, 337, 338, 340–349, 353–368, 375–385, 391–401, 403–406, 411–414, 416, 418–423, 431, 432, 434, 436, 438–442, 447–456, 459–465, 467–470, 475–481, 483–490, 495–511, 515–526, 529, 530, 532–537, 539, 540, 543–547, 549–551, 553–555, 563–572, 575–586, 591–605, 609–612, 614–617, 623–627, 631, 632, 635, 636, 639–651, 657–669, 671–673, 675, 677–685, 689, 691–701, 705–717, 723–731, 736–743, 745–749, 753–762, 765–776
China-Africa relations, 731, 735, 755
China–Indochina Corridor, 73, 75, 326, 624, 671, 675
China Global Investment Tracker, 497, 506, 507, 509, 659, 664
China–Pakistan Economic Corridor (CPEC), 8, 73, 75, 76, 326, 460, 461, 469, 475–487, 490, 523, 538, 583, 624, 627
China Standards 2035, 237, 238, 240–242, 248
Chinese domination, 575
Chinese economic statecraft, 17, 18, 22, 23
Chinese foreign policy, 25, 45, 55, 59, 60, 230, 306, 569, 706, 728, 731, 737, 767
Chinese outbound tourism demand, 415, 426
climate, 30, 83, 111, 112, 143, 147, 157, 159, 163, 168, 171, 173, 177, 178, 180, 183, 188, 189, 191, 193, 194, 197, 225, 275, 317, 340, 347, 349, 367, 368, 442, 464, 664, 770, 771, 774, 776
complexity, 4, 6, 68, 129, 169, 171–173, 175, 177, 178, 217, 286, 290, 297, 361, 368, 496, 503, 572, 696
Comprehensive and Progressive Agreement for Trans-Pacific Partnership (CPTPP), 78, 84, 312, 675
connectivity discourse, 296
constructivism, 3, 5, 91, 98, 99, 102, 103, 659
contracts, 13, 127, 342, 384, 507, 521, 532, 567, 575, 579, 659, 662, 664, 710, 736, 740, 742, 743, 745, 748, 749, 756, 757, 767
convergence, 1, 62, 64, 118, 129, 130, 232, 316, 317, 321, 449, 714

Index

corruption, 9, 45, 211, 213, 359, 464, 478, 484, 518–521, 523, 535, 632, 635, 636, 640, 645, 646, 648, 649, 651, 668, 669, 754
COVID-19, 2, 6, 7, 28, 29, 64, 76, 78, 101, 144, 154, 157–163, 168, 171, 178, 180, 189, 190, 197, 231, 232, 237, 247, 271, 281, 313, 337, 338, 340–342, 346, 348, 349, 354, 362, 364, 365, 368, 377, 379, 383, 391, 394, 418, 425, 426, 447–449, 452–455, 459, 461, 462, 470, 477, 489, 555, 570, 571, 580–582, 592, 595, 601, 640, 642, 644, 647, 648, 652, 663, 748, 749
cyber sovereignty, 237, 238, 243, 245, 246, 249

D

demography, 272, 275, 281
dependence, 9, 43, 67, 76, 84, 142, 288, 341, 342, 358, 363, 399, 467, 479, 486, 488, 509, 520, 524, 568, 571, 578, 583, 643, 660, 664, 665, 696, 701, 737, 742, 761, 767, 771
development, 1–3, 5, 8, 10, 11, 20, 23, 30, 37, 40, 41, 43–46, 59–62, 69–75, 79, 82, 84–86, 93, 94, 96, 97, 99, 103, 105, 109, 111–119, 125–134, 140, 142, 144, 145, 147, 148, 153, 154, 157, 158, 167–169, 177–180, 183, 184, 188, 191–193, 195–197, 203, 206, 212, 217, 223, 224, 228–231, 239–246, 248, 249, 254–257, 259–262, 267, 273, 276, 280, 281, 289, 291, 293, 296, 302–305, 309, 312, 313, 315, 317, 344, 346, 355–358, 361, 363, 365, 367, 368, 378, 382, 391, 397, 398, 401, 403, 405, 406, 412, 414–416, 418, 419, 421, 423, 424, 426, 431–433, 441, 442, 450, 451, 461–464, 468, 469, 475–479, 481, 482, 485–487, 489, 498, 499, 505, 508, 509, 511, 516, 517, 520, 521, 525, 529–532, 534, 536, 537, 544, 546, 549, 550, 552, 554, 555, 563, 565, 568, 569, 571, 572, 575–577, 580–585, 592, 594–596, 598–601, 603–605, 611–613, 616, 623–627, 639–642, 644–646, 650–652, 659–669, 671–673, 679, 680, 682–685, 689, 692, 694–696, 700, 701, 715, 724–726, 728, 729, 731, 736, 737, 740–742, 745, 747, 749, 753–758, 760, 761, 766, 769, 774, 775
Development Assistance for Health (DAH), 229
digital, 4–6, 84, 103, 104, 143, 147, 159, 169, 178, 180, 231, 237, 240, 241, 246, 247, 249, 280, 287, 289–291, 295, 340, 343, 362, 393, 395, 422, 550, 645
Digital Silk Road (DSR), 73, 143, 157, 159, 163, 238, 241, 247, 248, 264, 286, 452, 532, 550, 555
diplomacy, 17, 20, 27, 28, 38, 72, 83, 92, 94, 98, 103, 104, 127, 130, 147, 157, 159–161, 176, 188–190, 197, 231–233, 237, 253, 254, 266, 268, 288, 308, 346–348, 364, 365, 378, 461, 463, 477, 486, 495, 499, 501, 505, 509, 511, 530, 531, 534, 565, 566, 569–571, 592, 626, 643, 644, 651, 673, 692, 696, 706, 748, 755, 771, 773, 774, 776
domestic interests, 376, 568

E

Easternization, 673
economic effect, 412, 414, 415, 426
economic governance, 7, 62, 118, 140, 349
economic inducements, 22, 23, 27
economic relationship, 30, 313, 338, 348, 392, 399, 401, 403, 404, 406, 447, 508
economics, 1, 2, 7, 17, 19, 83, 169, 176, 224, 344, 345, 348, 572, 635, 673, 696, 728, 739, 740, 742
economic sanctions, 19, 23, 553, 585, 772
emerging market banks, 6, 202, 203, 205
Engineering, Procurement, and Construction (EPC), 127
EPC plus operation model, 127
Europe, 3, 4, 7, 18, 19, 22, 23, 26–28, 37, 38, 72, 76, 79, 84, 94, 114, 128, 142, 156, 159, 160, 167, 168, 170, 175, 190, 206, 210–214, 241, 302, 303, 305, 306, 309, 311, 317, 321–326, 339, 340, 342, 343, 346, 348, 349, 353–368, 375–377, 380–382, 385, 398, 399, 403, 405, 406, 411–424, 426, 432–434, 441, 461, 467, 486, 496, 519, 535, 539, 540, 564, 566, 575, 577, 581, 582, 584, 586, 609–611, 616, 623, 657, 660, 661,

663–665, 667, 671, 707, 712, 723, 770, 771
European tourism industry, 8, 426
European Union (EU), 3, 7, 8, 27, 38, 43, 63, 76–79, 81, 100, 114, 147, 157–159, 161, 168, 170, 178, 180, 182, 187, 188, 190, 232, 244, 267, 281, 302, 316, 317, 337–349, 353–368, 375–382, 384, 385, 392, 396, 398–401, 403–406, 411, 412, 414, 421, 433, 434, 436, 438, 442, 468, 488, 500, 504, 520, 544, 548, 568, 569, 571, 609, 610, 612, 613, 616, 617, 680, 727, 772, 775

F
financial development, 631, 634, 635
folk diplomacy, 94, 95, 101
foreign aid, 20, 22, 24, 195, 233
foreign direct investment (FDI), 24, 37, 103, 111, 125, 127, 128, 155, 157, 189, 201, 312, 319, 320, 323–325, 360, 379–381, 393, 395, 401, 477, 496, 497, 502, 509, 531, 532, 550, 566, 596, 597, 600, 614, 615, 631, 632, 644, 658, 664, 666, 676, 678–683, 730, 731, 736, 743, 745, 755, 760
framework, 3, 26, 30, 45, 69, 77, 78, 99–102, 104, 105, 111, 116, 119, 129–131, 141, 210, 248, 253, 254, 259–264, 266–268, 272, 309, 311, 312, 337, 339, 346, 356, 359–361, 367, 368, 379, 385, 403, 405, 434, 448, 449, 452–454, 461, 463, 464, 466, 467, 499, 502, 507, 508, 529, 544, 567, 569, 579, 592, 626, 639, 643, 658, 660, 661, 663, 664, 666, 667, 692, 693, 695–700, 705, 735, 737, 741

G
geopolitics, 2, 68, 112, 232, 233, 279, 345, 395, 397, 584, 592, 596, 635, 765
global governance, 3–6, 9, 35, 36, 38, 40, 42, 44, 47, 68, 77–79, 85, 86, 109–113, 118, 119, 145, 148, 224, 230, 233, 242, 463, 531, 565, 583, 659, 698, 714
globalization, 1–4, 6, 7, 9, 10, 12, 13, 37, 42, 43, 56, 58, 63, 64, 82, 110, 111, 117, 126, 127, 131–134, 140, 143, 144, 146, 148, 153, 162, 224, 239, 267, 271, 272, 281, 285, 287, 297, 298, 302, 303, 305, 306, 309, 310, 337, 340, 344, 345, 347, 349, 391, 406, 442, 495, 510, 517, 529, 531, 536, 537, 539, 540, 543, 563, 570, 577, 582, 583, 658, 671–673, 676–685, 689, 691–695, 697, 699, 716, 717, 723, 731, 745, 776
global order, 5, 6, 9, 24, 71, 117, 126, 163, 307, 308, 436, 466, 531
global power, 1, 3, 6, 7, 10, 37, 80, 109, 126, 170, 267, 272, 278–281, 308, 309, 403, 550, 565, 568, 571, 731
glocalization, 5, 13, 131–133
going global policy, 74
governance, 6, 26, 35, 36, 39, 44, 46, 72, 109, 111, 112, 116, 119, 126, 128–130, 134, 141, 143, 148, 188, 189, 225, 228, 238, 244–246, 248, 249, 280, 340, 344, 349, 361, 403, 461, 464, 486, 516, 518, 521, 522, 531, 693, 695, 708, 717, 730, 754, 766, 770, 771, 774, 776
grand strategy, 5, 67–70, 84–86, 112, 142, 240, 392, 436, 481, 580, 583, 659, 709, 731
great powers, 71, 72, 82, 112, 280, 376, 382, 383, 432, 436, 449, 534, 549, 550, 568, 569, 572, 673, 690
green credit, 6, 188, 191–197
green finance, 6, 188–193, 196, 197
grouping, 26, 27, 92, 359, 684, 685
Gulf of Guinea, 707–709, 711, 712, 715

H
hard power, 157, 266, 267, 272, 279–281, 572
headquarters, 215, 216, 218, 256, 261
health diplomacy, 223–225, 232, 233, 748
health governance, 6, 224, 230–232
Health Silk Road (HSR), 4, 6, 8, 157–159, 161, 163, 224, 230–233, 363, 447–456, 462
Healthy China 2030, 224, 225, 228, 229
hedge, 84, 463
hedging, 684, 685, 690
hegemony and game changers, 302, 321
history, 1, 2, 5, 12, 18, 37, 61, 70, 99, 102, 140, 141, 143, 209, 254, 263, 273, 285, 302, 303, 310, 311, 313, 320, 321, 339, 393, 397, 455, 495, 534,

Index 787

577, 595, 648, 661, 667, 693, 695, 696, 698, 699, 701, 735, 755, 760
human rights discourse, 47

I

India, 6–8, 11, 25, 27, 28, 40, 43, 56, 78, 83, 84, 170, 171, 182, 183, 279, 310, 323, 326, 328, 365, 391, 396, 399, 402, 438, 439, 459–463, 465–470, 475, 476, 480, 481, 483, 485–490, 523, 530, 536, 538, 539, 571, 602, 624–626, 632, 635, 673, 677, 706, 726, 737, 770
Indo/Asia-Pacific, 3, 10, 28, 81, 84, 85, 307, 393, 398, 441, 464, 468, 505, 540, 565, 568, 592, 599, 602, 672, 675, 706
Indonesia, 10, 25, 27, 29, 72, 80, 159, 161, 176, 190, 323, 328, 355, 396, 438, 535, 539, 581, 582, 591, 592, 596–599, 602–604, 623, 674, 675, 677, 679, 681–683, 723–725, 737
inequalities, 13, 168, 169, 274, 277, 279, 356, 480, 604, 736, 743, 746, 748
infrastructure, 11, 13, 21, 25, 27, 36–38, 43–45, 56, 61, 67, 73, 75, 79, 80, 97, 109, 112–115, 118, 119, 142, 153–155, 157, 159, 162, 163, 172, 175, 183, 189, 191, 195, 230, 241, 244, 247, 260, 264, 285–289, 291–295, 298, 299, 302, 311, 312, 315, 326, 353–359, 362, 376, 380, 383, 404–406, 421–423, 438, 441, 447, 460, 461, 464, 467, 477, 479–481, 486, 488, 489, 495–501, 503, 505–507, 509, 510, 519–523, 526, 529, 531, 532, 534, 536–538, 566–568, 576, 579–582, 584, 595, 596, 599, 600, 604, 605, 613, 616, 617, 623–625, 627, 632, 635, 639, 640, 644–647, 650, 651, 657, 658, 661–669, 671–673, 680, 694–697, 700, 701, 705, 709, 711, 713, 715, 723–726, 729–731, 736, 739, 742, 745–749, 753–757, 760, 761, 767, 769
interculturalism, 98, 99, 103
interdependence, 111, 174, 239, 305, 340, 342, 345, 349, 397, 551, 554, 563, 564, 566–568, 684, 706
international discourse, 5, 36, 55–59, 63
international forums, 58, 245, 453, 517, 578, 729

international integration, 537, 692, 745, 747
internationalization strategy, 507
international political economy, 337, 624, 754
international relations, 2, 5, 36, 39, 41, 47, 55, 56, 59, 60, 63, 64, 74, 78, 91, 104, 139, 145, 244, 265, 272, 286, 287, 339, 348, 462, 476, 555, 570, 599, 690, 698, 754
interpretations, 36, 98, 110, 117, 701
intervention, 12, 42, 61, 144, 157, 228, 231, 480, 523, 735, 743, 745, 749, 753, 757, 760
investment(s), 8, 11, 12, 19–21, 25, 28, 30, 37, 38, 42, 43, 45, 46, 74–77, 80, 84, 94, 102, 103, 113, 115–119, 128, 130, 145–148, 153–157, 167, 170, 171, 181–183, 189–193, 195, 204, 207, 213, 225, 228, 230, 241, 244, 264, 267, 272–276, 279–281, 287, 301, 302, 307, 309, 311–313, 315, 318, 319, 321, 326, 338, 340, 344–348, 353–359, 361, 362, 366, 367, 376, 378, 380, 383, 385, 392, 393, 395–397, 399, 401, 403–406, 421–423, 432, 433, 436, 438, 441, 442, 460, 464, 467, 476, 478, 479, 484, 487, 488, 490, 495–501, 503–511, 515, 520, 522, 529–533, 537, 544, 550, 552, 566, 567, 576, 579, 581, 582, 591, 594, 596, 598–600, 603, 610–612, 614–616, 625, 639–641, 643, 645–649, 651, 652, 658, 659, 661–665, 667–669, 672–685, 692–694, 696, 697, 700, 701, 705, 708, 709, 711–713, 716, 717, 723, 724, 726, 727, 729–731, 736, 737, 741–743, 745, 747, 753–758, 761, 767
investment risks, 346, 362, 639, 645, 652
Iqbal, Badar Alam, 11, 627, 631, 632
Iran, 8–11, 30, 82, 323, 326, 328, 451, 467, 481, 488, 489, 536, 539, 543–546, 551–555, 567, 568, 570–572, 575–580, 582–586, 624, 660
Iran–China's Comprehensive Strategic Partnership, 584

J

Jinping, Xi, 25, 36, 38–43, 45, 46, 55, 58–64, 67–75, 78, 79, 81–86, 95, 96, 98, 111, 125, 139–149, 156, 157, 167, 170, 175, 180, 182, 228–233,

237, 245, 246, 289, 302, 312,
353–355, 431, 439, 442, 452, 477,
480, 499, 500, 509, 510, 516, 529,
531, 549, 564, 565, 567–569, 575,
579, 583, 586, 594–596, 600, 601,
603, 609, 611, 613, 659, 660, 662,
693, 723, 735, 743, 745, 755, 761,
768, 775
Joint Comprehensive Plan of Action
(JCPOA), 10, 546, 554, 576, 577,
584–586

K

Kazakhstan, 11, 44, 60, 72, 75, 76, 97, 115,
142, 167, 247, 324, 328, 354, 433,
436, 442, 522, 624, 640, 642, 649,
658, 660–662, 664, 665, 667–669,
693, 723
KOF Globalization index, 676–678
Kyrgyzstan, 11, 76, 114, 115, 328, 433,
538, 539, 624, 640–652, 658,
660–664, 666–669

L

language, 35–37, 40, 42, 47, 55, 94, 98,
115, 177, 207, 212, 216, 248, 255,
262, 339, 416, 421, 480, 518, 650,
671, 698, 729, 759, 760
Laos, 39, 75, 76, 161, 191, 318, 326, 328,
438, 522, 523, 623, 674, 675, 677,
678, 681–684
Latin America and the Caribbean (LAC),
495–501, 503, 506, 509–511
Latvia, 8, 10, 11, 190, 325, 328, 366, 375,
405, 422, 609–617, 624
leadership, 6–8, 10, 29, 30, 43, 46, 67,
69–71, 85, 103, 112, 118, 128, 142,
143, 158, 169, 176–181, 196, 225,
228, 245, 247, 280, 285, 288, 292,
297, 301–309, 318, 320, 344, 376,
379, 392, 431, 432, 438, 441, 442,
452, 515, 517, 520, 524, 530, 531,
533, 537, 543, 564, 565, 568, 578,
580, 586, 601, 624, 659
liability of emergingness, 6, 201–205, 207,
214–218
loans, 18, 19, 21, 22, 116, 157, 190, 195,
197, 307, 312, 315, 323, 324, 359,
365, 367, 380, 381, 425, 463, 475,
477, 484, 497, 501, 508, 519, 520,
523, 532, 600, 601, 644, 647, 648,
658, 662, 663, 666, 667, 695, 696,
700, 701, 709, 723, 727, 731, 736,
737, 739, 741–743, 745, 747, 748,
754, 755, 757, 758
local actors, 126–128, 130, 131, 133, 134,
701
local agency, 5, 13, 125–127, 129, 130, 133
localization, 125, 127, 132, 133, 649–651

M

Malaysia, 10, 129–131, 183, 288, 324, 326,
328, 464, 519, 522, 538, 581,
591–595, 599, 602, 603, 623, 674,
675, 677, 679, 681–683
Middle East and North Africa (MENA), 10,
128, 325, 450, 563, 564, 566, 571,
572, 623
monetary policy, 281
Montenegro, 157, 294, 324, 329, 359, 375,
383, 384, 416, 417, 519, 520, 624,
758
multilateralism, 1, 2, 4, 6, 40, 80–82, 99,
110, 116, 144–146, 232, 233, 248,
254, 255, 261, 264, 265, 267, 340,
346, 347, 462, 463, 571, 627, 690,
714, 737, 769
Myanmar, 39, 75, 76, 80, 82, 114, 117, 173,
318, 323, 326, 329, 438, 467, 485,
522, 538, 539, 623, 674, 675, 678,
681–684

N

natural resources, 13, 274, 398, 479, 483,
486, 497, 508, 511, 531, 564, 582,
597, 598, 624, 652, 661, 663, 666,
673, 709, 714, 716, 729, 742, 745,
747, 755–758, 761, 770, 772, 776
network externalities, 318, 319
networks, 1–3, 25, 37, 38, 72, 84, 91, 92,
99, 102–104, 110, 111, 114, 126,
128, 143, 173–175, 177, 181, 204,
206, 225, 228, 239, 241, 243, 247,
293, 295, 302, 303, 309, 315, 316,
318–321, 326, 342, 344, 354, 355,
362, 367, 383, 401, 406, 451, 479,
500, 519–522, 534, 539, 550, 551,
570, 577, 580, 582, 583, 592, 596,
603, 605, 624, 640, 661, 664, 666,
667, 694, 697, 724, 739, 747, 748,
757
New Maritime Silk Road, 10, 725
New Silk Roads, 13, 61, 72, 158, 291, 295,
297, 302, 432, 434, 529–533, 536,

Index

537, 539, 540, 554, 575, 576, 603, 604, 623, 657, 667, 723, 731, 735, 736, 743, 745, 746, 748, 749

norms, 3–5, 20, 35, 36, 42, 44, 47, 56, 59, 64, 78, 79, 92, 110–113, 116, 119, 133, 134, 140, 141, 146, 149, 178, 204, 238, 239, 242–249, 265, 347, 377, 461–464, 469, 470, 486, 517, 518, 524, 550, 577, 659, 690, 695, 697

O

Obama, Barack, 81, 500, 568, 584, 675

One Belt One Road (OBOR), 67, 296, 297, 307, 434, 459, 611, 623, 626, 627, 664, 735, 766

opportunities, 3, 8, 10–12, 23, 60, 70, 74, 79, 99, 101, 104, 105, 130, 131, 146, 147, 161, 163, 206, 208, 225, 231, 245, 263, 265, 268, 271, 273, 315, 345, 355, 357, 367, 368, 378, 381, 382, 392, 396, 399–401, 403, 405, 406, 412, 419, 421, 424, 452, 477, 478, 480, 483, 488, 495, 500, 502, 504, 511, 521, 526, 537, 546, 549, 566, 567, 570, 582, 599, 604, 611, 624, 626, 635, 644, 657, 667, 694, 695, 701, 765, 767

P

Pakistan, 8, 27, 75, 76, 80–82, 97, 114, 129, 161, 182, 288, 297, 323, 329, 460, 467, 475–488, 490, 522, 523, 536–539, 548, 581, 582, 624–626

pandemic, 7, 28, 83, 144, 145, 154, 158–163, 170, 177, 178, 231, 232, 279, 295, 301, 310, 313, 341, 349, 354, 362–368, 383, 391, 426, 447, 448, 453–455, 461, 477, 484, 499, 508, 511, 534, 540, 570, 571, 592, 596, 642, 644, 648, 652, 669, 706

panel regression, 627, 633, 634

paradiplomacy, 266

People's Liberation Army Navy, 438

people-to-people (P2P), 5, 60, 67, 73, 93, 96, 98, 100–104, 113, 167, 231, 264, 266, 355, 357, 434, 479, 480, 489, 640, 658, 662, 666, 693, 749

people-to-people exchanges (P2PEs), 5, 92–105, 230, 260, 266, 383, 482

Philippines, 10, 28, 75, 81, 323, 329, 438, 524, 525, 535, 538, 592, 599–602,
604, 623, 674, 675, 677, 679, 681–683

political stability, 244, 536, 631, 634, 635, 659, 730, 742

politics, 6, 7, 13, 37, 55, 75, 102, 110, 128, 130, 132, 145, 154, 155, 176, 183, 224, 237, 238, 281, 285, 287, 288, 298, 303, 306, 344, 349, 358, 365, 368, 383, 423, 535, 543, 544, 546, 549, 563, 569, 572, 595, 602, 660, 671, 691–693, 696, 739, 759, 760, 766, 768, 770, 773, 776

power, 2–4, 6, 7, 13, 18, 19, 21–23, 25, 27–29, 31, 35–38, 40, 41, 43–45, 47, 57–60, 64, 69–71, 74–76, 78, 80–82, 84–86, 92, 95, 102, 110–112, 114, 118, 126, 127, 129, 133, 134, 140–142, 145, 158, 162, 170, 172, 176, 178, 180, 182, 183, 191, 194, 197, 210, 215, 225, 237–240, 242–245, 247–249, 266, 272, 277–281, 285, 287, 289, 293, 301–308, 310, 313, 315, 320–323, 325, 337, 339, 340, 344–346, 349, 356, 364, 376, 377, 382, 384, 406, 414, 432, 436–438, 449, 463, 477–481, 483, 484, 501, 506, 511, 516, 517, 520, 521, 526, 530, 532, 535–537, 540, 543–545, 547, 549–554, 563–565, 568–572, 575, 577, 578, 580, 583–586, 592, 599, 602, 603, 605, 648, 652, 659, 660, 662, 663, 673, 677, 685, 689, 690, 692, 695, 698–700, 705, 706, 708–715, 717, 724, 726, 727, 730, 735, 737, 740, 742, 743, 745, 749, 755, 757, 767–770, 774

presences, 9–11, 13, 28, 35, 57, 64, 76, 101, 111, 175, 184, 289, 305, 312, 318, 357, 362, 378, 383, 384, 393, 421, 437, 438, 453, 461, 468, 484, 485, 490, 495, 496, 499–502, 504, 506, 507, 510, 511, 522, 538, 539, 552, 563, 564, 567, 569, 571, 576, 599, 642, 646, 650, 651, 705–707, 710, 712, 714, 715, 717, 724, 730, 735, 736, 738, 740, 742, 747, 748, 760, 766, 769–771, 773–776

public diplomacy, 58, 92–96, 101, 102, 267

public–private partnership (PPP), 127, 128, 233, 503

public relations, 169, 179, 182

Putin, Vladimir, 82, 431, 433, 438, 442

R

Rahman, Mohd Nayyer, 11, 627, 631–633
regional integration, 449, 511, 536, 537, 672, 725, 726
risk perception, 11, 639, 640, 651
Ritzer, George, 132
rivalry, 9, 19, 28, 302, 303, 307, 308, 337, 339, 354, 378, 383, 385, 511, 516, 517, 536, 537, 539, 569, 583, 592, 715, 737, 753, 761, 772
Robertson, Roland, 131, 132
rules-based global order, 461, 462
Russia, 7, 8, 20, 21, 73, 76, 78, 82, 100, 114, 156, 159, 167, 182, 196, 271, 279, 308, 326, 329, 366, 384, 416, 417, 420, 432, 433, 436–442, 447–456, 466, 488, 525, 530, 549, 568, 569, 571, 581, 609, 615, 616, 624, 627, 640, 641, 643, 647, 649, 665, 666, 705, 712, 769, 772, 773, 775

S

scenarios, 6, 8, 169, 172, 175–183, 438, 544, 549, 746
secular stagnation, 7, 271–276, 278, 281
security, 2, 3, 5, 9, 12, 19, 20, 23, 28, 37, 39, 41, 43, 74–76, 80, 82, 86, 94, 97, 111, 128, 141, 146, 147, 156, 173, 224, 225, 229, 231, 247, 260, 278, 286, 287, 313, 338, 340, 343, 345, 361, 362, 365, 378, 383, 384, 400, 416, 431, 432, 436, 437, 441, 442, 461, 475, 476, 478, 480–482, 484, 485, 487, 489, 490, 509, 522, 529, 530, 536–538, 540, 544–546, 549–552, 554, 555, 563, 565, 566, 568–572, 575, 576, 585, 591, 599, 642, 646, 652, 657, 659–661, 668, 673, 676, 684, 696, 698, 706–709, 711, 713, 715, 717, 726, 747, 755, 759, 761, 768, 769
17+1, 359, 367, 375–379, 381–385, 520, 610, 617, 769
Silk Road Fund (SRF), 73, 75, 79, 115–117, 120, 125, 133, 158, 312, 671
Singapore, 25, 28, 80, 81, 158, 194, 317, 325, 329, 438, 451, 523, 539, 581, 623, 674, 675, 677, 679–684, 770
Sino-localization, 13, 132, 133
socialism with Chinese characteristics, 39, 46, 59, 69, 70, 72, 85, 141, 247, 365

socialization, 6, 141, 238, 239, 244, 245, 247–249
soft power, 1, 36, 37, 57, 62, 77, 79, 93, 95, 96, 101–104, 140, 146, 148, 157–159, 170, 230–233, 266, 272, 280, 281, 285, 363, 364, 376, 468, 570, 659, 773
South Atlantic, 4, 12, 706–717, 773
South China Sea, 10, 25, 28, 73, 77, 84, 162, 355, 480, 519, 525, 538, 580, 591, 592, 595, 598–603, 605, 692, 693, 706, 711, 713, 717, 724, 725, 768, 769
standards, 3, 5, 57, 73, 103, 115–117, 119, 126, 129, 133, 134, 143, 161, 191, 215, 223, 238–244, 247–249, 273, 294, 303, 304, 316, 318, 347, 359, 360, 364, 368, 396, 398, 416, 426, 461, 486, 549–551, 645, 666, 672, 695, 697, 726, 737, 739, 748
strategic autonomy, 7, 338–343, 349, 381, 382, 463
string of pearls, 76, 157, 481, 538, 712
sustainability, 2, 61, 103, 178, 191, 231, 295, 339, 349, 357, 360, 412, 415, 418, 426, 448, 453, 531, 568, 639–641, 647, 725, 755, 767
symbolism, 7, 286, 299, 772

T

Taiwan, 25–27, 41, 78, 83–85, 160, 176, 183, 230, 432, 578, 673, 677, 680, 709, 728, 736, 738–740, 769
TFP growth, 303
Thailand, 28, 39, 80, 81, 318, 324, 326, 330, 467, 538, 539, 595, 603, 623, 674, 675, 679, 681–683
tourism, 8, 100, 103, 104, 376, 392, 397–399, 406, 411–419, 421–426, 479, 482, 509, 524, 595, 596, 612, 641, 643, 644, 662, 664, 683, 755, 770
tourism destinations, 413, 415
trade policy, 341, 577, 728
Trans-Asian Railway (TAR), 675, 677, 684
Trans-Pacific Partnership (TPP), 81, 675
Trump, Donald, 26, 27, 38, 42, 44, 82, 83, 111, 144, 147, 155, 156, 281, 337, 340, 345, 348, 354, 362, 363, 500, 501, 511, 515, 550, 551, 553, 554, 585, 675, 706, 710, 771, 772

Index

twenty-first-Century Maritime Silk Road, 355, 434, 564, 586, 591, 605, 675, 705, 709, 712, 713, 716, 723

U

United States (US), 3, 6, 7, 9–12, 18–24, 26–28, 30, 38–44, 46, 56, 64, 67, 68, 71, 80–86, 92, 101, 111, 115, 116, 118–120, 126, 129, 133, 134, 139, 141, 144–147, 155–161, 168, 170, 173, 176, 180, 182–184, 187, 188, 190, 191, 193, 197, 214, 232, 237, 239–244, 248, 256, 267, 273–275, 277–281, 301, 302, 304–307, 309–313, 315, 317–321, 338–342, 344–346, 348, 349, 354, 362, 363, 376, 377, 382–385, 393, 395, 403, 411, 418, 436, 438, 439, 441, 465, 468, 479, 480, 484, 486, 488, 490, 496, 498, 500, 501, 504–511, 515–518, 521, 522, 524–526, 529, 531, 532, 535–540, 543–555, 564–571, 576, 578–581, 583–586, 591–593, 595, 599–602, 612, 617, 624, 649, 672, 673, 675, 677, 678, 680, 684, 685, 699, 706, 707, 710, 712–714, 717, 731, 742, 758, 767, 768, 771, 772, 774

US foreign policy, 20, 535, 540, 543
US-led world order, 673

V

Vietnam, 12, 22, 28, 39, 183, 184, 239, 318, 323, 326, 330, 438, 525, 535, 539, 582, 592, 599, 623, 674, 675, 677, 679–683, 689–701
visual analysis, 286–288, 291, 298

W

World Bank, 19, 24, 44, 78, 79, 115, 116, 133, 134, 142, 147, 154, 168, 189–191, 195, 196, 227, 264, 301, 307, 310, 312, 313, 316, 325, 393, 396, 463, 465, 484, 497, 498, 507, 530, 532, 536, 571, 594, 641, 648, 667, 674, 679, 739–741
World Economic Forum (WEF), 5, 38, 39, 140, 143–145, 148, 168, 169, 262, 398, 706, 710
world order, 5, 39, 44, 47, 81, 82, 86, 110–112, 119, 142, 147, 179, 180, 233, 247, 249, 305, 432, 449, 462, 463, 522, 537, 671, 709, 768

Printed in the United States
by Baker & Taylor Publisher Services